USA TODAY SPORTS

RON SHANDLER'S **2016**

BASEBALL FORECASTER

AND ENCYCLOPEDIA OF FANALYTICS

TRIUMPH BOOKS

This book is available in quantity at special discounts for your group or organization. For further information, contact:

Triumph Books LLC
814 North Franklin Street
Chicago, Illinois 60610
(312) 337-0747
www.triumphbooks.com

Printed in U.S.A.
ISBN: 978-1-62937-138-2

Statistics provided by Baseball Info Solutions

Cover design by Brent Hershey
Front cover photograph by Mark J. Rebilas/USA TODAY Sports Images
Author photograph by Kevin Hurley

Ron Shandler's
BASEBALL FORECASTER

Editors
Ray Murphy
Brent Hershey

Associate Editor
Brandon Kruse

• • • • • •

Technical Wizard
Rob Rosenfeld

Design
Brent Hershey

Data and Charts
Matt Cederholm

Player Commentaries
Ryan Bloomfield
Rob Carroll
Matt Cederholm
Matt Dodge
Alec Dopp
Brent Hershey
Brandon Kruse
Ray Murphy
Stephen Nickrand
Greg Pyron
Kristopher Olson
Paul Sporer
Brian Rudd
Jock Thompson
Rod Truesdell

Research and Articles
Dave Adler
Matt Cederholm
Patrick Davitt
Ed DeCaria
Brandon Kruse
Stephen Nickrand
Dave Potts
Vlad Sedler
Todd Zola

Prospects
Rob Gordon
Jeremy Deloney
Tom Mulhall

Injury Chart
Rick Wilton

Acknowledgments

Producing the *Baseball Forecaster* has been a team effort for a number of years now; the list of credits to the left is where the heavy lifting gets done. On behalf of Ron, Brent, and Ray, our most sincere thanks to each of those key contributors.

We are just as grateful to the rest of the BaseballHQ.com staff, who do the yeoman's work in populating the website with 12 months of incredible content: Andy Andres, Matt Beagle, Dan Becker, Alex Beckey, Bob Berger, Chris Blessing, Brian Brickley, Doug Dennis, Greg Fishwick, Neil FitzGerald, Colby Garrapy, Matt Gelfand, Rick Green, Phil Hertz, Joe Hoffer, Ed Hubbard, Tom Kephart, Chris Lee, Glenn Lowy, Chris Mallonee, Troy Martell, David Martin, Craig Neuman, Harold Nichols, Frank Noto, Josh Paley, Nick Richards, Mike Shears, Peter Sheridan, Skip Snow, Matthew St-Germain, Jeffrey Tomich and Michael Weddell.

Thank you to our behind-the-scenes troopers: our technical dynamic duo of Mike Krebs and Rob Rosenfeld; and to Lynda Knezovich, the patient and kind voice at the other end of your email inquiries.

Thank you to all our industry colleagues, a truly impressive group. They are competitors, but they are also colleagues working to grow this industry, which is never a more evident than at our annual First Pitch Arizona gathering each November.

Thank you to Dave Morgan, Chris Pirrone, and the team at USA Today Sports Media Group.

Thank you for all the support from the folks at Triumph Books and Action Printing.

And of course, thank *you*, readers, for your interest in what we all have to say. Your kind words, support and (respectful) criticism move us forward on the fanalytic continuum more than you know. We are grateful for your readership.

From Ray Murphy I have contributed to the *Forecaster* in various capacities for over a decade now, and the opportunity to collaborate with Ron remains as much of an honor today as it was the first time he asked. Ron's imprint continues to linger over all aspects of this entity that Brent and I now co-manage. Anyone who has attempted to "co-" anything knows how perilous an undertaking it can be. Brent and I work remarkably well together; not just because Brent has off-the-charts skills and a temperament to match, but because we share an abiding reverence for this thing that Ron created and we are now entrusted with preserving and growing. Of course, I'm no stranger to exemplary "co-" relationships, as my wife Jennifer is the first and best example of a key life lesson for me: choose your partners well.

From Brent Hershey Anniversaries force us look back. I am humbled and honored to take part in this tradition of running myself crazy for seven weeks in October-November so that fantasy baseballers everywhere can begin their preseason in early December. Thank you, Ron, for the opportunity you extended in 2011 to become more involved in this project—and for a world where analyzing baseball is a year-round activity. Thank you, Ray, for your continued collaborative spirit; it has allowed us to effectively respond to some new challenges this past year. The "co-" in our titles is a true representation of reality. But most of all, thank you Lorie, Dillon and Eden, for your own passions, talents and zest for life. When I am able to stop and reflect, I couldn't be prouder of your graceful fortitude in making this earth a better place.

From Ron Shandler It awes me to realize that my 23- and 24-year-old daughters have never known a world in which there was no *Baseball Forecaster*. How does that happen? Is it about quality, value or just perseverance? I suppose every veteran writer asks that. But after three decades of surviving naysayers, nasty competitors, baseball strikes, cheap magazines, free websites, the bursting dot-com bubble, football, high stakes trolls, daily game elitists, a declining publishing industry and greed, the survival of this book has to be attributed to one thing only: good, old-fashioned American stubbornness. You can't stop me. Just try.

This past year, when life set me off on a new, unexpected course, "Shandler's Book" has remained a constant. My eternal gratitude goes out to Ray, Brent, all the editors, writers, analysts, support personnel, production workers, advertising reps, designers, industry colleagues, media personalities, postal employees, cherished wife and daughters, and the hundreds of thousands of baseball fans over the past 30 years who made that happen. Every single one of you. (Yes, I'm talking to you!) Onward…

TABLE OF CONTENTS

Segue

by Ron Shandler

Thanksgiving 1985. Houston, TX.

I am sitting at a large table in a small house located just outside the Inner Loop. I am surrounded by 3,000 in-laws of all shapes and sizes. There are old ones and young ones, large ones in both size and presence, vegetarians and carnivores. New Yorkers, and Coloradans, and Floridians, and one or two Astros fans. There are only two decibel levels—loud and louder.

I have been married for eight months.

I am invisible, mostly because I believe that communication should be thoughtful and measured, not driven with a jackhammer. I don't know what the heck all these people are talking about anyway. Who *are* these people? I think I've made a huge mistake.

So I wander off in my head, recalling the disappointing results of my first Rotisserie Baseball league. A bunch of high school teachers, a psychologist, a tech executive and I were dipping our toes in the Roto waters, drafting players out of each league's Eastern Divisions. I finished fourth, led by Dave Stieb of the Toronto Blue Jays and his league-leading 2.48 ERA. Fourth place wouldn't have been so bad had there been more than six teams.

I had to do better.

"Ron? Ron?? Did you hear me? Wouldja pass the potatoes?"

No, I didn't hear you, dammit. How can anyone hear anything?

Where's my bag? Those books I brought to read on the plane… the *Bill James Abstract, The Hidden Game of Baseball, How Life Imitates the World Series*. Would anyone miss me if I slinked away?

I am convinced that the answer to winning this Rotisserie thing is hidden somewhere inside those three books. But Bill James, Pete Palmer and Thomas Boswell all have different measures to evaluate talent. Which one is best—runs created, linear weights or total average?

It would be pretty valuable to see all the players listed with those three "new statistics" presented side-by-side-by-side. Hmm.

There is plenty of time to think; I am unemployed. I just completed the worst 15 months of my career, taking a job in a New Hampshire bank as my ticket out of New York City traffic. This is my third forced job departure in the seven years since graduating from college. There would be three more unceremonious exits before I'd finally tell Corporate America where they could put their pink slips. It took me awhile to figure out that I was not cut out to be an employee.

I figure, what the heck, I'll just write a book. How hard could it be? I had worked for publishing companies before. I had learned how to do direct marketing. I was a good writer and a magician with LOTUS 1-2-3. And I was a control freak.

Piece of cake.

• • •

As you've undoubtedly read in numerous places before, the Rotisserie game of the 1980s was a different animal from the game we play today. The standard format was 4x4 (runs and strikeouts didn't matter), which elevated the value of speedsters and closers. Drafts took place in person, mostly because the only time you were ever "online" was at 8:00 AM at Dunkin' Donuts. Standings were published once per week because that's how often the stats were printed in *USA Today*. Trades were negotiated using ancient communication—speaking into a corded telephone.

No email. No internet. No smart phones. No real-time updates. Your greatest edge? Having access to a fax machine.

The eight statistical categories were the beginning and end of baseball analysis. A .300 hitter was drafted as a .300 hitter, no matter if his contact rate was 90% or 60%. ERA was the final arbiter for pitching effectiveness, regardless of any measures of control, dominance or command.

Saves were possibly more frustrating than they are today. While MLB teams tended to stay with their closers longer, the best 9th inning pitchers could go for $30-$35, leaving much bigger roster holes when they went down.

The debut edition of this book was entitled, *Baseball SuperSTATS 1986*, was promoted via a single one-inch advertisement in *The Sporting News* and cost $9.95. I sold 67 copies. It included all three "new statistics" as well as a few of my own, including an early version of strand rate.

The purpose of the first two editions was solely to get a better handle on player analysis. It wasn't until 1988 that we started publishing Rotisserie cheat sheets. The early embryo of the player box you see today appeared in 1990; we didn't add commentaries until 1994. The first decade of *Forecasters* were self-published and sold exclusively through mail order. The 1998 edition was the first one you could buy at amazon.com or at Barnes & Noble. USA Today took over in 2009.

The Major League game—the environment in which our fantasy game and this book lives—has undergone massive changes as well. However, like most things in life, change occurs slowly and is subtle. We often don't realize that things have changed at all until we look back in the rear view mirror several miles later. But can we learn anything by taking a macro-snapshot of the time that the Forecaster has been in existence?

Let's look at a 32-year scan, a little longer than this book has been in existence but covering the entire period since the publication of *Rotisserie League Baseball* in 1984—call it the Rotisserie Era. We're not looking for revelations; just perspective.

(All data is from baseball-reference.com and my personal records. X-axis of all graphs represents time, in 5-year increments.)

Linear-Weighted Power by year

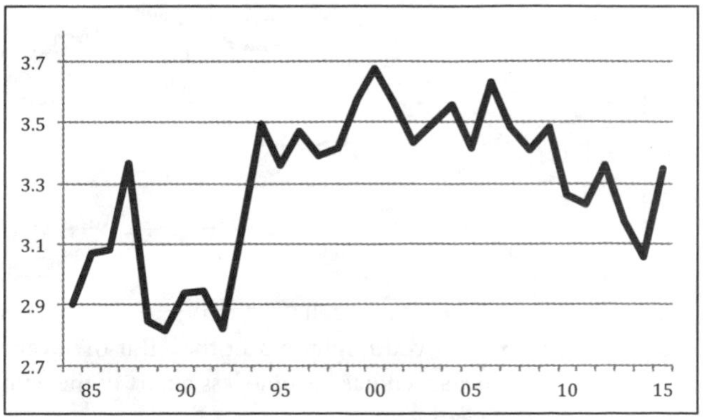

We often talk about the cyclical nature of home runs, but really, it's about power as a whole. Linear-weighted power is (HR x 1.4)+(2B x 0.8)+(3B x 0.8)/(AB-K) x100.

Note the unusual spike in 1987 (when players like Larry Sheets, Matt Nokes and Brook Jacoby each hit over 30 HRs—and 20 HRs was a stretch in any season before or after). There was a sharp correction in 1988, which was the beginning of a 5-year malaise. Power exploded in 1993 and peaked in 2000, remaining fairly stable until 2006, which was shortly after MLB implemented their strictest drug-testing program. Power tumbled for eight years after that, bottoming out in 2014. It experienced a bit of a rebound this past season.

The challenge is being able to respond to these trends by adjusting each subsequent year's projections. Periods of stability make the job easier, but then you run into a 1993, or a 2014, or even the unexpected power spike of this past season. That changes the relative value of all power hitters. A 30-HR performance in 1992 was far more valuable than a 30-HR performance in 1993, and fantasy leaguers should have paid less for HRs in '93… had they been able to predict the spike.

The takeaway: Even within short periods of time, there is volatility. That means, barring a revelation that some external variable changed in 2015, one would expect power to regress off of this year's spike.

But wait… this 2015 "correction" was the largest single-season spike since 1993. Back then it set off a whole new era in power performance. Could we be entering a new cycle?

It's possible. As you scan all the player boxes in this book, you'll see many new players being projected for 20 HRs or more, driven by nothing more than normal trends. There are players like Jonathan Schoop, whose projection is a natural step up after several years of experience. There are players like Carlos Correa, who has hit the ground running. Add these to all the established players with power returning from off-years, like Carlos Gomez. In all, I count 78 players projected for 20 or more HRs. Last year, only 64 players hit at least 20 HRs. This "correction" may have legs.

Stolen bases and times caught stealing, per game

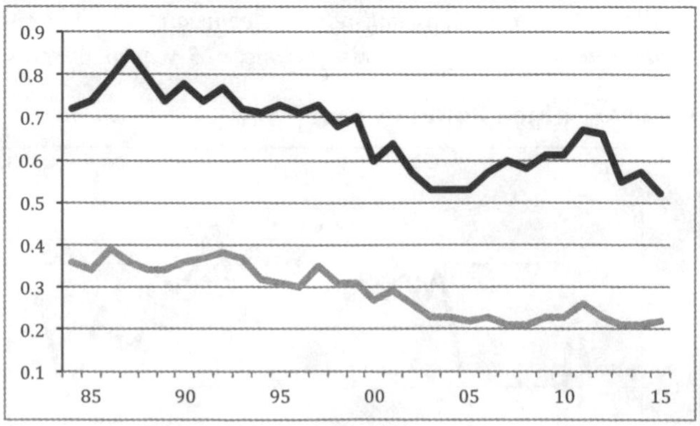

In some ways, steals have followed an inverse trend as compared to power, and you might expect that. But the overall trend is one of decline; speed has become less a part of the game today than it was 32 years ago.

Think about the players who populated our fantasy rosters in the 1980s. In the *Forecaster's* inaugural year, the top four base-stealers were Vince Coleman (107), Rickey Henderson (87), Eric Davis (80) and Tim Raines (70). Twenty-four players swiped 30 bases or more. In 2015, only seven players reached the 30-steal level.

In tandem with the declining caught-stealing trend, this graph paints an interesting picture when it comes to stolen base success. From 1984 through 2002—a period of 19 years—the stolen base success rate (SB%) reached 70 percent only four times. In the 13 years since then, it's *never fallen short of 70 percent*, hitting 74 percent twice.

The takeaway: With the trend of improving success on the basepaths, why aren't teams running more? Odds are because baserunners have become scarcer and teams are not willing to risk losing them. This is a trend that makes baseball's most dominating speedsters highly valuable.

Given that steals have always been centralized in a smaller group of elite players, it has made sense to assign a somewhat inflated value to their contribution. But these days it's even more prevalent. It makes a strong argument for drafting a Jose Altuve or Dee Gordon in the first round, or for $30-plus. I think that approach has become more reasonable to consider these days; just plan the rest of your roster around it.

Base Performance Value (Pitchers)

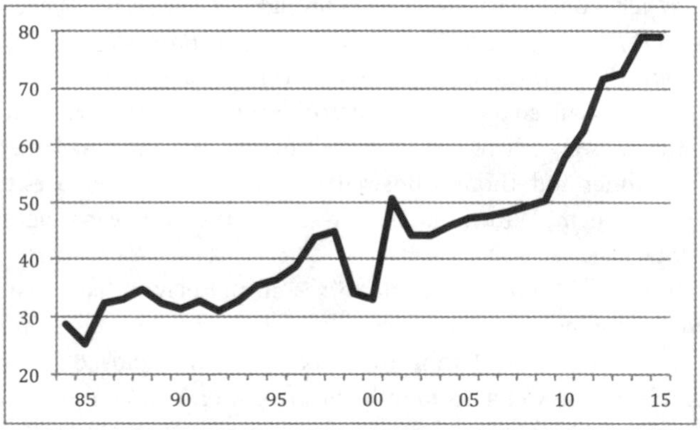

The earliest incarnation of BPV appeared in the *Forecaster's* 1993 edition. As you can tell from the above, it was during a time of stable pitching effectiveness. So when we said that "50" was the minimum level at which we'd consider rostering a pitcher, it made a bunch of sense.

Over the years, the impact of pitching evolved and the BPV formula went through several iterations. The one used for this graph is an abbreviated version of the current formula ((Dom – 5.0) x 18) + ((4.0 – Ctl) x 27) as we do not have ground ball data going back the full 32 years to use the full version. Still, this gives us a general sense of what has been going on, with little surprise.

The outlying 1999-2000 values are odd. They could have been attributed to that period's offensive explosion if the metric wasn't only looking at walk and strikeout rates. In fact, that sudden BPV drop was caused by league-wide walk rates spiking at 3.75 during that two-year period—they were 3.3 in 1998 and 3.4 in 2001. But control, dominance and command continued to rise despite the offensive surge of the early 2000s. And then they have just kept going. And going. And going.

League-wide BPV has settled in at 79 for each of the past two seasons, blowing away the old goal of "50" as being rosterable. That same relative goal in today's terms would set a rosterable BPV at about 100, a level that 188 pitchers reached this past year. (That's another reason why using BPX—the version that indexes BPV to league average—makes more sense these days.)

The takeaway: There is something big going on here, but let's set it up first.

If this graph stopped at 2009, you might conclude that BPV displayed a moderate growth trend, but nothing too extreme. Then something happened in 2010, and the ratios of strikeouts to walks went nuts. There was a nearly concurrent spike in one other metric, shown below. It's not tough to make a logical assumption that this is causal…

Number of pitchers with average FB velocity of 95+ mph (30+ IP)

Year	# pitchers
2008	20
2009	26
2010	27
2011	36
2012	32
2013	39
2014	38
2015	51

How does this happen? Is it advanced conditioning? Different development path? Lighter baseballs? New, genetically-engineered arms? How do you explain a 155% increase in extreme skill over seven years? Even a 59% increase over three years?

The stars have been slowly aligning in advance of this phenomenon, but we didn't reach the tipping point until 2010/2011. What really happened? First, a few more graphs to further set the stage.

Average closer prices in Rotisserie dollars

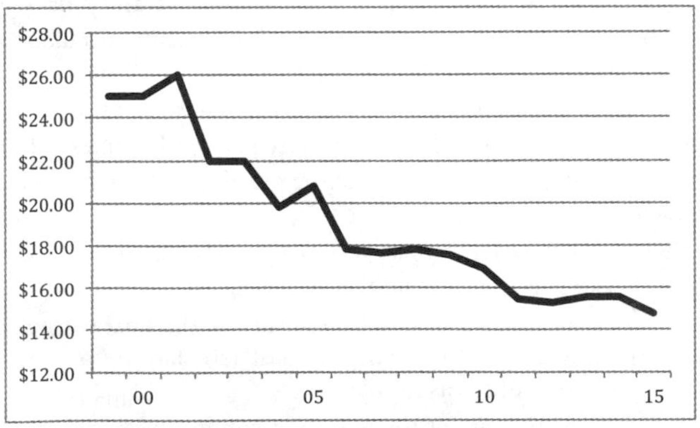

The volatility of the closer role has been the primary driver that has forced this consistent downward trend. In most all cases, a high failure rate of closers in one year has served to push the average closer price down the subsequent year. So it is no surprise that, while failure rates fluctuate annually, the underlying trend is one that has persisted over time. In the first four years of this graph, the average failure rate was 29 percent; over the most recent four years, it has been 45 percent.

Where have those lost dollars gone? In many cases, they have gone to middle relievers, a speculation on future saves. Before the LIMA Plan was introduced in 1998, you could easily roster a Ken Giles or Wade Davis-type reliever for a buck or reserve round pick. In 2015 drafts, these non-closers on Draft Day went for $6 apiece. In all, more relievers have been earning positive value.

The takeaway: Fifteen years ago, this price volatility prompted the advice to "don't draft saves," as closers were always available in-season. These days, the more appropriate advice might be, "don't pay for saves." Closers are still available in-season but there are so many candidates now that it's difficult to figure out which ones to chase.

After the average price dropped to $14.79 in 2015—the lowest level recorded—we may have reached the point where saves are cheap enough to speculate on freely at the draft. For the first time, several front-line closers went for less than $10, and with the resulting 45 percent failure rate, bargains could be plentiful. You might be able to roster two front-liners for the same cost as what you used to have to pay for a single elite arm.

That is the fallout from the ever-quickening hooks that major league managers have been employing with their bullpens. It's directly reflected here:

Number of pitchers used per game

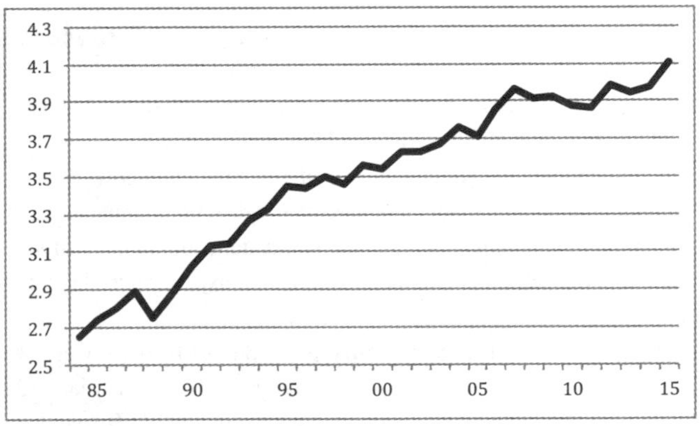

The number of pitchers used in each game has risen from 2.65 in 1984 to 4.11 this past year.

Let's return to that velocity chart, but add another piece of data:

Number of pitchers with average FB velocity of 95+ mph (30+ IP)

Year	# pitchers	# w/ fewer than 100 IP
2008	20	18 (90%)
2009	26	24 (92%)
2010	27	24 (89%)
2011	36	33 (92%)
2012	32	29 (91%)
2013	39	35 (90%)
2014	38	32 (84%)
2015	51	40 (78%)

While the number of bionic-armed pitchers has been rising, the vast majority of them are low-inning hurlers who can afford to rear back and give it all they've got. Thirty years ago, when a starting pitcher was pulled from a game, opposing batters would face one or two relievers, each throwing at 90-95 mph for 1-2 innings apiece. Today, batters are seeing 3-4 relievers, each throwing 95-100mph, often for less than an inning. Batters are at an ever-growing disadvantage.

(You also can't discount the increasing number of starting pitchers who meet the 95 mph velocity threshold. There were a record 11 starters in 2015: Nathan Eovaldi, Noah Syndegaard, Garrett Richards, Yordano Ventura, Gerrit Cole, Joe Kelly, Stephen Strasburg, Kevin Gausman, Matt Harvey, Carlos Martinez and Chris Archer. Jose Fernandez would be on this list had he pitched more innings. Jacob deGrom and Andrew Cashner just missed at 94.9 mph.)

Average number of players used per Major League roster

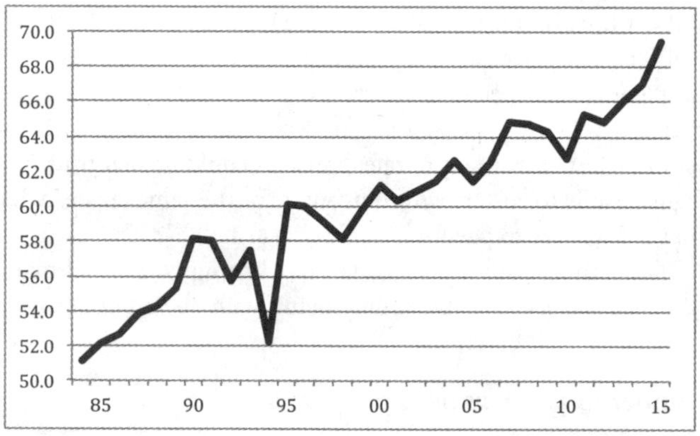

This is one of those hidden trends that is rarely talked about. In 1984, about 51 players appeared on a Major League roster during the course of a season. In 2015 that number peaked at 69.4. (That sharp drop in the middle was the 1994 strike year.)

Why has this occurred? Blame it on specialization. Blame it on escalating salaries and the rise of disabled list stays as teams attempt to protect their investments. Blame it on short hooks and better rookies and all the variables that have occurred over 30 years.

There were four fewer teams in 1984 and there were 935 batters who saw time in the Majors that year. This past year, 1,348 batters saw time. In 1984, 393 pitchers were on MLB rosters; in 2015, there were 735. In all, there are 755 more players receiving MLB paychecks today than in 1984. That's a more-than 36 percent increase in the number of players we need to analyze, value and consider rostering on our fantasy teams.

The takeaway: While the number of players seeing major league action each year is rising, the number of games has remained the same. Each team still plays 162 games, which generates a nearly fixed number of outs and innings, and a very narrow range of plate appearances. *These days, available playing time is the same but 18 more players* ***per team*** *are fighting for a piece of it.*

That is huge.

Add in the fact that the standard fantasy roster structure has held firm to 14 batters and 9 pitchers. This is a split that no longer reflects MLB reality; today's roster often has more pitchers than hitters. You can see how the environment that our game lives in has become a more challenging place for playing time prognosticators.

Playing time used to be just another element of the forecasting process. Roles were firmer and turnover was rare. There was a level of stability that gave fantasy leaguers more confidence that they could manage their roster with a sense of control. And remember, if nothing else, playing fantasy baseball has *always* been driven by the perception of control.

These days, playing time is about the most difficult element of performance to project, and these graphs show that it has been getting tougher and tougher each year. You may not have been noticing it overtly—because change can be subtle—but rest assured that your ability to make decisions that influence the fate of your team has been getting weaker each year.

Fantasy Impact

So, in summary… power is down, though cyclical. Steals are down. Pitching is way up. Our trust in saves continues to wane. Nothing very exciting here.

The biggest change over the past 30+ years is that the 23 players we draft each March now have a far lesser impact on the final standings than they did in 1984. The players rostered each spring account for a smaller percentage of each team's bottom line statistics and serve only to set a very rough foundation for contention.

When we're drafting in a standard 15-team mixed league (with six reserves), we think we are rostering 435 players out of a pool of 750-800. In reality, we are drafting from a potential pool of more than 1,300 players and growing, each year.

The upshot? In-season management now plays a larger role, and fantasy leaguers more adept at that task tend to do better.

There was once a time when you could wait out a rookie call-up for a few weeks before deciding whether to claim him out of the free agent pool. These days, any call-up with a pulse is grabbed up long before we can reasonably assess the odds of him having any staying power.

Fantasy leaguers hedge the risk of navigating this growing in-season volatility by selecting more and more speculative players at the draft. We've always searched out "sleepers," but now they have become more a part of a core drafting strategy. Back in the 1980s, Kris Bryant would have been an end-game speculation, not a nearly-full-priced $18 buy like he was in NL Tout Wars last spring. But the experts knew; the in-season churn has become so overwhelming that you have to almost play both games—draft and in-season—at the same time, before the first pitch is even thrown.

In the end, the adept fantasy tacticians win by *making successful decisions using smaller and smaller sample sizes:*

- On draft day, we hang on the results of the final spring training games to identify the last few players to win (allegedly) full-season roles.
- In the early part of the season, a handful of at-bats or innings are all we get to take a chance on a player who could have five months of impact.
- Later in the season, we might have more data but we're making decisions that will affect only a handful of at-bats or innings down the stretch.

The full-season game has become driven by the management of small sample sizes.

Segue

There is another game that is driven by the management of small sample sizes.

For many of you, "Daily," as in Daily Fantasy Sports (DFS), is a dirty word. I have spent the past two years writing about my distaste for this arrogant new format that has turned an intellectual pursuit into a get-rich-quick scheme.

Then I started playing it more regularly.

No, I haven't been drinking the DFS Kool-Aid. However, I *have* grown to appreciate the specific game types that make use of real analytical skills and take place on a level playing field.

You see, we can't use short time frames or small sample sizes as an excuse any more. Our full season game (let's call that Seasonal Fantasy Sports, or SFS) has become just a steady stream of small-sample decision points. Of course, you don't earn cash for every free agent pickup or reserve list activation, but the cash element of DFS can be compartmentalized. There are different formats; some are more skills-based, some more random. DFS games come in a variety of flavors; you just need to find your own personal Rocky Road.

For me, I stick with single-entry 50-50 games. In these, "winning" means finishing in the top half of all entries. There is no question that this is a winnable format using a skills-based approach alone. You won't necessarily get rich from these games, but you can still turn $100 into $1,000 over the course of a season. For me, that's my Cherry Garcia.

Your preference—and tolerance for riskier attacks on your gastronomic system—may vary. (There is an ice cream flavor called Wasabi Pea Dust which I would liken to entering one $3 team into a $1 million tournament. Good luck.)

The biggest advantage of DFS? That ever-growing SFS frustration—playing time—is a known commodity. Yes, your batter might get pulled for a pinch-hitter or your pitcher might get an early hook, but those are variables that you can research and plan around in the player selection process.

While the importance of the draft has been declining in the SFS game, DFS is all about the draft. The type of research is different—it's more contextual than performance-based—but you still have to assess a laundry list of variables when selecting your players.

And if you were the unlucky owner of Drew Storen, Greg Holland or Steve Cishek this past year, you'll be happy to know that most DFS games completely eliminate closers from the equation.

DFS also requires many similar skills to SFS. The variables you have to consider when deciding which SFS pitchers to activate on any given day or week are essentially the same in DFS. The budgeting challenges in a salary cap game are identical whether it's SFS or DFS.

And small-sample decision-making drives both games. When a rookie pitcher is promoted, the SFS gamer needs to make a free agent claim decision, often in advance of the first start. That decision potentially has long-term impact, but in most games, a failed pick-up is easily cut. In DFS, the risk of taking a chance on that first start is limited to that one day's game. In both cases, the decision may only affect a single outing.

Later in this book, some top DFS experts will go into more detail and share some of their insights. We're barely scratching the surface of what can be learned about this new game.

Am I about to change teams? Nah. For me, fantasy baseball will always be about the long view. The exhilaration comes with creating a successful new strategy, nailing a breakout performer that nobody else saw coming and grinding out a tough victory. Winning should provide a massive sense of great accomplishment. Picking the right players on one night just doesn't have the same pay-off for me.

But if I have an hour to kill on a Wednesday evening, I won't turn down the chance to turn $25 into $47.50.

• • •

Thanksgiving 2015. Port St. Lucie, FL.

I'm sitting at this big desk in a small house, surrounded by 3,000 books of all shapes and sizes. There are old ones and new ones, large ones in both size and presence, covering analysis, strategy and game theory. I've written some of them, in New York, New Hampshire, Virginia and Florida.

I am still married, but that first Rotisserie league ended after 10 years, a casualty of the Great Strike of 1994. I took home titles in the final three seasons.

Dave Stieb was the first player to teach me great lessons about baseball statistics. After that terrific 1985 season, I drafted him again in 1986, only to be blindsided by his 4.74 ERA follow-up. What I didn't know at the time was that his 2.48 ERA in '85 came along with a command ratio of only 1.7, down from 2.3 the previous season.

Undaunted (or more likely, stubborn), I went back to the well again in 1987. And again he disappointed, with a 4.09 ERA (and a 1.3 Cmd). After 1984, Stieb's meager strikeout rate was never high enough to drive even a 2.0 Cmd. However, he did manage a few more good seasons, which was another lesson in statistical volatility.

In some ways we're smarter; in many ways, we're not.

Bill James wrote his final *Baseball Abstract* in 1988, unsuccessfully tried his hand at fantasy-centric books in the mid-1990s and was eventually forced to take an office job with a Major League ballclub that had not won a World Series in over 80 years. Pete Palmer waited 30 years to publish a follow-up edition of *The Hidden Game*, but the only thing he changed was the Introduction. Thomas Boswell's Total Average metric never caught on.

I graduated from Dunkin' Donuts and now do "online" at Starbucks. I'm not proud.

Since 1986, I've been convinced that the answer to winning this Rotisserie thing is hidden somewhere inside *this* book. There is no question that the *Baseball Forecaster* has helped immensely—and still does. However, I'm still searching for the Holy Grail. For some unknown, unfathomable reason, I still can't predict the future with 100 percent accuracy. There must be something wrong with me.

We can put a man on the moon but I still can't tell you exactly how many home runs Carlos Correa is going to hit in 2016.

There is more work to do.

Welcome to the 30th Anniversary Edition

Yes, that's right—it's our 30th year. The subhead that appeared on the cover since 1997 (!) was "The Industry's Longest-Running Publication for Baseball Analysts & Fantasy Leaguers." Though it succumbed to Carlos Gomez's broad shoulders this edition, it remains no less true. Thirty. Years. Longest-running, indeed.

But if you are new to the *Baseball Forecaster*, the sheer volume of information in this book may seem a bit daunting. We don't recommend you assessing its contents over a single commute to work, particularly if you drive. But take your time to let it all sink in. The payoff—Yoo-Hoo or otherwise—is worth it.

But where to begin?

The best place to start is with the Encyclopedia of Fanalytics, which provides the foundation concepts for everything else that appears in these pages. It's our research archive and collective memory, just as valuable for veterans as it is for rookies. Take a cursory read-through, lingering at any section that looks interesting. You'll keep coming back here frequently.

Then just jump in. Close your eyes, flip to a random page, and put your finger down anywhere. Oh, look—J.R. Realmuto hit 7 HR with 6 SB in the second half of 2015. With favorable power and speed metrics over that span, he could be a sneaky profit center in 2016 at a thin position.

See, you've learned something already!

What's New in 2016?

Daily Fantasy: Given the explosion of the daily format over the past several years, we've put together a section of essays and tools for both the novice and the experienced player alike.

The Next Tier: We added a B-list, if you will, of players whose performance in the past two seasons didn't warrant a full treatment in our player profiles section. Presented with all the applicable stats and metrics for your own analysis.

Expanded International Prospects: Given the rise of both Cuban and Asian ballplayers, our minors team profiles more prospects from Japan, Korea and the Caribbean to keep you at the top of the talent list in your keeper league.

Answers to questions, such as: Have we figured out how to project pitcher wins? Is the "bounceback year" for real? What is a pitcher's secret weapon against Father Time? How much does a strong draft contribute to winning? And much more.

Updates

The Baseball Forecaster page at BaseballHQ.com is at www.baseballhq.com/bf2016. This is your headquarters for all information and updates regarding this book. Here you will find links to the following:

Content Updates: In a project of this magnitude, there are occasionally items that need clarification or correction. You can find them here.

Free Projections Update: As a buyer of this book, you get one free 2016 projections update. This is a set of Excel spreadsheet files that will be posted on or about March 1, 2016. Remember to keep the book handy when you visit as the access codes are hidden within these pages.

Electronic book: The complete PDF version of the *Forecaster*—plus Excel versions of most key charts—is available free to those who bought the book directly through the BaseballHQ.com website. These files will be available in January 2016 for most of you; those who have an annual standing order should have received the files just before Thanksgiving. Contact us if you do not receive information via e-mail about accessing them. Information about the e-book version can be found at the above website.

If you purchased the book through an online vendor or bookstore, or would like these files earlier, you can purchase them from us for $9.95. Contact us at support@baseballhq.com for more information.

Beyond the Forecaster

The *Baseball Forecaster* is just the beginning. The following companion products and services are described in more detail in the back of the book.

BaseballHQ.com is our home website. It provides regular updates to everything in this book, including daily updated statistics and projections. A subscription to BHQ gets you more than 1,000 articles over the course of a year updated daily from spring training through the end of the regular season, customized tools, access to data going back over a decade, plus much more. Sign up for our free BaseballHQFriday newsletter at www.baseballhq.com/friday.

First Pitch Forums are a series of conferences we run all over the country, where you can meet top industry analysts and network with fellow fantasy leaguers in your area. We'll be in cities from coast to coast in February and March. Our big annual symposium at the Arizona Fall League is the first weekend in November. See additional information at the back of this book.

The 11th edition of the *Minor League Baseball Analyst*, by Rob Gordon and Jeremy Deloney, is the minor league companion to this book, with stat boxes for 1,000-plus prospects, essays on prospects, lists upon lists, and more. It is available in January.

We still have copies available of *How to Value Players for Rotisserie Baseball*, Art McGee's ground-breaking book on valuation theory. They are still on closeout at 50% off.

RotoLab is the best draft software on the market and comes pre-loaded with our projections. Learn more at www.rotolab.com.

Even further beyond the Forecaster

Visit us on *Facebook* at www.facebook.com/baseballhq. "Like" the BaseballHQ page for updates, photos from events and links to other important stuff.

Follow us on *Twitter*. Site updates are tweeted from @BaseballHQ and many of our writers share their insights from their own personal accounts. We even have a list to follow: www.twitter.com/BaseballHQ/lists/hq-staff.

But back to baseball. Almost 300 pages await.

—Brent Hershey and Ray Murphy

CONSUMER ADVISORY

AN IMPORTANT MESSAGE FOR FANTASY LEAGUERS REGARDING PROPER USAGE OF THE *BASEBALL FORECASTER*

This document is provided in compliance with authorities to outline the prospective risks and hazards possible in the event that the Baseball Forecaster is used incorrectly. Please be aware of these potentially dangerous situations and avoid them. The publisher assumes no risk related to any financial loss or stress-induced illnesses caused by ignoring the items as described below.

1. The statistical projections in this book are intended as general guidelines, not as gospel. It is highly dangerous to use the projected statistics alone, and then live and die by them. That's like going to a ballgame, being given a choice of any seat in the park, and deliberately choosing the last row in the right field corner with an obstructed view. The projections are there, you can look at them, but there are so many better places to sit.

We have to publish those numbers, but they are stagnant, inert pieces of data. This book focuses on a live forecasting process that provides the tools so that you can understand the leading indicators and draw your own conclusions. If you at least attempt your own analyses of the data, and enhance them with the player commentaries, you can paint more robust, colorful pictures of the future.

In other words...

If you bought this book purely for the projected statistics and do not intend to spend at least some time learning about the process, then you might as well just buy an $8 magazine.

2. The player commentaries in this book are written by humans, just like you. These commentaries provide an overall evaluation of performance and likely future direction, but 60-word capsules cannot capture everything. Your greatest value will be to use these as a springboard to your own analysis of the data. Odds are, if you take the time, you'll find hidden indicators that we might have missed. Forecaster veterans say that this self-guided excursion is the best part of owning the book.

3. This book does not attempt to tackle playing time. Rather than making arbitrary decisions about how roles will shake out, the focus is on performance. The playing time projections presented here are merely to help you better evaluate each player's talent. Our online preseason projections update provides more current AB and IP expectations based on how roles are being assigned.

4. The dollar values in this book are intended solely for player-to-player comparisons. They are not driven by a finite pool of playing time—which is required for valuation systems to work properly—so they cannot be used for bid values to be used in your own draft.

There are two reasons for this:

a. The finite pool of players that will generate the finite pool of playing time will not be determined until much closer to Opening Day. And, if we are to be brutally honest, there is really no such thing as a finite pool of players.

b. Your particular league's construction will drive the values; a $10 player in a 10-team mixed league will not be the same as a $10 player in a 12-team NL-only league.

Note that book dollar values also cannot be compared to those published at BaseballHQ.com as the online values are generated by a more finite player pool.

5. Do not pass judgment on the effectiveness of this book based on the performance of a few individual players. The test, rather, is on the collective predictive value of the book's methods. Are players with better base skills more likely to produce good results than bad ones? Years of research suggest that the answer is "yes." Does that mean that every high skilled player will do well? No. But many more of them will perform well than will the average low-skilled player. You should always side with the better percentage plays, but recognize that there are factors we cannot predict. Good decisions that beget bad outcomes do not invalidate the methods.

6. If your copy of this book is not marked up and dog-eared by Draft Day, you probably did not get as much value out of it as you might have.

7. This edition of the Forecaster is not intended to provide absorbency for spills of more than 7.5 ounces.

8. This edition is not intended to provide stabilizing weight for more than 18 sheets of 20 lb. paper in winds of more than 45 mph.

9. The pages of this book are not recommended for avian waste collection. In independent laboratory studies, 87% of migratory water fowl refused to excrete on interior pages, even when coaxed.

10. This book, when rolled into a cylindrical shape, is not intended to be used as a weapon for any purpose, including but not limited to insect extermination, canine training or to influence bidding behavior at a fantasy draft.

Encyclopedia of Fanalytics

For new readers...

Everything begins here. The information in the following pages represents the foundation that powers everything we do.

You'll learn about the underlying concepts for our unique mode of analysis. You'll find answers to long-asked questions, interesting insights into what makes players tick, and innovative applications for all this newfound knowledge.

This Encyclopedia is organized into several logical sections:

1. Fundamentals
2. Batters
3. Pitchers
4. Prospects
5. Gaming

Enough talking. Jump in.

Remember to breathe.

For veteran readers...

As we do in each edition, this year's ever-expanding Encyclopedia includes relevant research results we've published over the past year. We've added some of the essays from the Research Abstracts and Gaming Abstracts sections in the 2015 *Forecaster* as well as some other essays from BaseballHQ.com.

And we continue to mold the content to best fit how fantasy leaguers use their information. Many readers consider this their fantasy information bible.

Okay, time to jump-start the analytical process for 2016. Remember to breathe—it's always good advice.

Abbreviations

Fundamentals

What is Fanalytics?

Fanalytics is the scientific approach to fantasy baseball analysis. A contraction of "fantasy" and "analytics," fanalytic gaming might be considered a mode of play that requires a more strategic and quantitative approach to player analysis and game decisions.

The three key elements of fanalytics are:

1. **Performance analysis**
2. **Performance forecasting**
3. **Gaming analysis**

For performance analysis, we tap into the vast knowledge of the sabermetric community. Founded by Bill James, this area of study provides objective and progressive new ways to assess skill. What we do in this book is called "component skills analysis." We break down performance into its component parts, then reverse-engineer it back into the traditional measures with which we are more familiar.

Our forecasting methodology is one part science and one part art. We start with a computer-generated baseline for each player. We then make subjective adjustments based on a variety of factors, such as discrepancies in skills indicators and historical guidelines gleaned from more than 20 years of research. We don't rely on a rigid model; our method forces us to get our hands dirty.

You might say that our brand of forecasting is more about finding logical journeys than blind destinations.

Gaming analysis is an integrated approach designed to help us win our fantasy leagues. It takes the knowledge gleaned from the first two elements and adds the strategic and tactical aspect of each specific fantasy game format.

Definitions

Leading Indicator: A statistical formula that can be used to project potential future performance.

Noise: Irrelevant or meaningless pieces of information that can distort the results of an analysis. In news, this is opinion or rumor that can invalidate valuable information. In forecasting, these are unimportant elements of statistical data that can artificially inflate or depress a set of numbers.

Situation Independent: Describing performance that is separate from the context of team, ballpark, or other outside variables. Strikeouts and walks, as they are unaffected by the performance of a batter's team, are often considered situation independent stats. Conversely, RBIs are situation dependent because individual performance varies greatly by the performance of other batters on the team (you can't drive in runs if there is nobody on base). Situation independent gauges are important for us to be able to isolate and judge performance on its own merits.

Soft Skills: BPIs with levels below established minimums for acceptable performance.

Surface Stats: Traditional gauges that the mainstream media uses to measure performance. Stats like batting average, wins, and ERA only touch the surface of a player's skill and often distort the truth. To uncover a player's true skill, you have to look at component skills statistics.

Component Skills Analysis

Familiar gauges like HR and ERA have long been used to measure skill. In fact, these gauges only measure the outcome of an individual event, or series of events. They represent statistical output. They are "surface stats."

Raw skill is the talent beneath the stats, the individual elements of a player's makeup. Players use these skills to create the individual events, or components, that we record using measures like HR and ERA. Our approach:

1. It's not about batting average; it's about seeing the ball and making contact. We target hitters based on elements such as their batting eye (walks to strikeouts ratio), how often they make contact and the type of contact they make. We then combine these components into an "expected batting average." By comparing each hitter's actual BA to how he should be performing, we can draw conclusions about the future.

2. It's not about home runs; it's about power. From the perspective of a round bat meeting a round ball, it may be only a fraction of an inch at the point of contact that makes the difference between a HR or a long foul ball. When a ball is hit safely, often it is only a few inches that separate a HR from a double. We tend to neglect these facts in our analyses, although the outcomes—the doubles, triples, long fly balls—may be no less a measure of that batter's raw power skill. We must incorporate all these components to paint a complete picture.

3. It's not about ERA; it's about getting the ball over the plate and keeping it in the park. Forget ERA. You want to draft pitchers who walk few batters (Control), strike out many (Dominance) and succeed at both in tandem (Command). You also want pitchers who keep the ball on the ground (because home runs are bad). All of this translates into an "expected ERA" that you can use to compare to a pitcher's actual performance.

4. It's never about wins. For pitchers, winning ballgames is less about skill than it is about offensive support. As such, projecting wins is a very high-risk exercise and valuing hurlers based on their win history is dangerous. Target skill; wins will come.

5. It's not about saves; it's about opportunity first and skills second. While the highest-skilled pitchers have the best potential to succeed as closers, they still have to be given the ball with the game on the line in the 9th inning, and that is a decision left to others. Over the past 10 years, about 40% of relievers drafted for saves failed to hold the role for the entire season. The lesson: Don't take chances on draft day. There will always be saves in the free agent pool.

Accounting for "luck"

Luck has been used as a catch-all term to describe random chance. When we use the term here, we're talking about unexplained variances that shape the statistics. While these variances may be random, they are also often measurable and projectable. To get a better read on "luck," we use formulas that capture the external variability of the data.

Through our research and the work of others, we have learned that when raw skill is separated from statistical output, what's remaining is often unexplained variance. The aggregate totals of many of these variances, for all players, is often a constant. For instance, while a pitcher's ERA might fluctuate, the rate at which his opposition's batted balls fall for hits will tend towards 30%. Large variances can be expected to regress towards 30%.

Why is all this important? Analysts complain about the lack of predictability of many traditional statistical gauges. The reason they find it difficult is that they are trying to project performance using gauges that are loaded with external noise. Raw skills gauges are more pure and follow better defined trends during a player's career. Then, as we get a better handle on the variances—explained and unexplained—we can construct a complete picture of what a player's statistics really mean.

Baseball Forecasting

Forecasting in perspective

Forecasts. Projections. Predictions. Prognostications. The crystal ball aura of this process conceals the fact it is a process. We might define it as "the systematic process of determining likely end results." At its core, it's scientific.

However, the *outcomes* of forecasted events are what is most closely scrutinized, and are used to judge the success or failure of the forecast. That said, as long as the process is sound, the forecast has done the best job it can do. *In the end, forecasting is about analysis, not prophecy.*

Baseball performance forecasting is inherently a high-risk exercise with a very modest accuracy rate. This is because the process involves not only statistics, but also unscientific elements, from random chance to human volatility. And even from within the statistical aspect there are multiple elements that need to be evaluated, from skill to playing time to a host of external variables.

Every system is comprised of the same core elements:

- Players will tend to perform within the framework of past history and/or trends.
- Skills will develop and decline according to age.
- Statistics will be shaped by a player's health, expected role and venue.

While all systems are built from these same elements, they also are constrained by the same limitations. We are all still trying to project a bunch of human beings, each one...

- with his own individual skill set
- with his own rate of growth and decline
- with his own ability to resist and recover from injury
- limited to opportunities determined by other people
- generating a group of statistics largely affected by external noise.

Research has shown that the best accuracy rate that can be attained by any system is about 70%. In fact, a simple system that uses three-year averages adjusted for age ("Marcel") can attain a success rate of 65%. This means all the advanced systems are fighting for occupation of the remaining 5%.

But there is a bigger question... *what exactly are we measuring?* When we search for accuracy, what does that mean? In fact, any quest for accuracy is going to run into a brick wall of paradoxes:

- If a slugging average projection is dead on, but the player hits 10 fewer HRs than expected (and likely, 20 more doubles), is that a success or a failure?
- If a projection of hits and walks allowed by a pitcher is on the mark, but the bullpen and defense implodes, and inflates his ERA by a run, is that a success or a failure?
- If the projection of a speedster's rate of stolen base success is perfect, but his team replaces the manager with one that doesn't run, and the player ends up with half as many SBs as expected, is that a success or a failure?
- If a batter is traded to a hitters' ballpark and all the touts project an increase in production, but he posts a statistical line exactly what would have been projected had he not been traded to that park, is that a success or a failure?
- If the projection for a bullpen closer's ERA, WHIP and peripheral numbers is perfect, but he saves 20 games instead of 40 because the GM decided to bring in a high-priced free agent at the trading deadline, is that a success or a failure?
- If a player is projected to hit .272 in 550 AB and only hits .249, is that a success or failure? Most will say "failure." But wait a minute! The real difference is only two hits per month. That shortfall of 23 points in batting average is because a fielder might have made a spectacular play, or a screaming liner might have been hit right at someone, or a long shot to the outfield might have been held up by the wind... once every 14 games. Does that constitute "failure"?

Even if we were to isolate a single statistic that measures "overall performance" and run our accuracy tests on it, the results will still be inconclusive.

According to OPS, these players are virtually identical:

BATTER	HR	RBI	SB	BA	OBA	SLG	OPS
Fowler,D	17	46	20	.250	.346	.411	.757
McCann,B	26	94	0	.232	.320	.437	.757
Walker,N	16	71	4	.269	.329	.427	.756

If I projected Fowler-caliber stats and ended up with Brian McCann's numbers, I'd hardly call that an accurate projection, especially if my fantasy team was in dire need of steals.

According to Roto dollars, these players are also dead-on:

BATTER	HR	RBI	Runs	SB	BA	R$
Rodriguez,A	33	86	83	4	.250	$17
Beltre,A	18	83	83	1	.287	$17
Burns,B	5	42	70	26	.294	$17

It's not so simple for someone to claim they have accurate projections. And so, it is best to focus on the bigger picture, especially when it comes to winning at fantasy baseball.

More on this: "The Great Myths of Projective Accuracy"

http://www.baseballhq.com/great-myths-projective-accuracy

Baseball Forecaster's forecasting process

We are all about component skills. Our approach is to assemble these evaluators in such a way that they can be used to validate our observations, analyze their relevance and project a likely future direction.

In a perfect world, if a player's raw skills improve, then so should his surface stats. If his skills decline, then his stats should follow as well. But, sometimes a player's skill indicators increase while his surface stats decline. These variances may be due to a variety of factors.

Our forecasting process is based on the expectation that events tend to move towards universal order. Surface stats will eventually approach their skill levels. Unexplained variances will regress to a mean. And from this, we can identify players whose performance may potentially change.

For most of us, this process begins with the previous year's numbers. Last season provides us with a point of reference, so it's a natural way to begin the process of looking at the future. Component skills analysis allows us to validate those numbers. A batter with few HRs but a high linear weighted power level has a good probability of improving his future HR output. A pitcher whose ERA was poor while his command ratio was solid might be a good bet for ERA improvement.

Of course, these leading indicators do not always follow the rules. There are more shades of grey than blacks and whites. When indicators are in conflict—for instance, a pitcher who is displaying both a rising strikeout rate and a rising walk rate—then we have to find ways to sort out what these indicators might be saying.

It is often helpful to look at leading indicators in a hierarchy, of sorts. In fact, a hierarchy of the most important pitching base performance indicators might look like this: Command (k/bb), Dominance (k/9), Control (bb/9) and GB/FB rate. For batters, contact rate might top the list, followed by power, walk rate and speed.

Assimilating additional research

Once we've painted the statistical picture of a player's potential, we then use additional criteria and research results to help us add some color to the analysis. These other criteria include the player's health, age, changes in role, ballpark and a variety of other factors. We also use the research results described in the following pages. This research looks at things like traditional periods of peak performance and breakout profiles.

The final element of the process is assimilating the news into the forecast. This is the element that many fantasy leaguers tend to rely on most since it is the most accessible. However, it is also the element that provides the most noise. Players, management and the media have absolute control over what we are allowed to know. Factors such as hidden injuries, messy divorces and clubhouse unrest are routinely kept from us, while we are fed red herrings and media spam. *We will never know the entire truth.*

Quite often, all you are reading is just other people's opinions... a manager who believes that a player has what it takes to be a regular or a team physician whose diagnosis is that a player is healthy enough to play. These words from experts have some element of truth, but cannot be wholly relied upon to provide an accurate expectation of future events. As such, it is often helpful to develop an appropriate cynicism for what you read.

For instance, if a player is struggling for no apparent reason and there are denials about health issues, don't dismiss the possibility that an injury does exist. There are often motives for such news to be withheld from the public.

And so, as long as we do not know all the facts, we cannot dismiss the possibility that any one fact is true, no matter how often the media assures it, deplores it, or ignores it. Don't believe everything you read; use your own judgment. If your observations conflict with what is being reported, that's powerful insight that should not be ignored.

Also remember that nothing lasts forever in major league baseball. *Reality is fluid.* One decision begets a series of events that lead to other decisions. Any reported action can easily be reversed based on subsequent events. My favorite examples are announcements of a team's new bullpen closer. Those are about the shortest realities known to man.

We need the media to provide us with context for our analyses, and the real news they provide is valuable intelligence. But separating the news from the noise is difficult. In most cases, the only thing you can trust is how that player actually performs.

Embracing imprecision

Precision in baseball prognosticating is a fool's quest. There are far too many unexpected variables and noise that can render our projections useless. The truth is, the best we can ever hope for is to accurately forecast general tendencies and percentage plays.

However, even when you follow an 80% percentage play, for instance, you will still lose 20% of the time. That 20% is what skeptics use as justification to dismiss prognosticators; they conveniently ignore the more prevalent 80%. The paradox, of course, is that fantasy league titles are often won or lost by those exceptions. Still, long-term success dictates that you always chase the 80% and accept the fact that you will be wrong 20% of the time. Or, whatever that percentage play happens to be.

For fantasy purposes, playing the percentages can take on an even less precise spin. The best projections are often the ones that are just far enough away from the field of expectation to alter decision-making. In other words, it doesn't matter if I project Player X to bat .320 and he only bats .295; it matters that I project .320 and everyone else projects .280. Those who follow my less-accurate projection will go the extra dollar to acquire him in their draft.

Or, perhaps we should evaluate the projections based upon their intrinsic value. For instance, coming into 2015, would it have been more important for me to tell you that Anthony Rizzo was going to hit 30 HRs or that Manny Machado would hit 25 HRs? By season's end, the Rizzo projection would have been more accurate, but the Machado projection—even though it was off by 10 HRs—would have been far more *valuable*. The Machado projection might have persuaded you to go an extra buck on Draft Day, yielding far more profit.

And that has to be enough. Any tout who projects a player's statistics dead-on will have just been lucky with his dart throws that day.

Perpetuity

Forecasting is not an exercise that produces a single set of numbers. It is dynamic, cyclical and ongoing. Conditions are constantly changing and we must react to those changes by adjusting our expectations. A pre-season projection is just a snapshot in time. Once the first batter steps to the plate on Opening

Day, that projection has become obsolete. Its value is merely to provide a starting point, a baseline for what is about to occur.

During the season, if a projection appears to have been invalidated by current performance, the process continues. It is then that we need to ask... What went wrong? What conditions have changed? In fact, has *anything* changed? We need to analyze the situation and revise our expectation, if necessary. This process must be ongoing.

When good projections go bad

Although we'd like to think otherwise, we cannot predict the future. All we can do is provide a sound process for constructing a "most likely expectation for future performance." If we've captured as much information as is available, used the best methodology and analyzed the results correctly, that's the best we can do.

All we can control is the process. We simply can't control outcomes.

However, one thing we *can* do is analyze the misses to see *why* they occurred. This is always a valuable exercise each year. It puts a proper focus on the variables that were out of our control as well as providing perspective on those players with whom we might have done a better job.

In general, we can organize these forecasting misses into several categories. To demonstrate, here are all the players whose 2015 Rotisserie earnings varied from projections by at least $10.

The performances that exceeded expectation

Development beyond the growth trend: These are young players for whom we knew there was skill. Some of them were prized prospects in the past who have taken their time ascending the growth curve. Others were a surprise only because their performance spike arrived sooner than anyone anticipated... Chris Archer, Nolan Arenado, Jake Arrieta, Charlie Blackmon, Xander Bogaerts, Kris Bryant, Lorenzo Cain, Gerrit Cole, Jacob deGrom, Bryce Harper, Ender Inciarte, Dallas Keuchel, Manny Machado, Carlos Martinez, David Peralta, A.J. Pollock, Danny Salazar.

Skilled players who just had big years: We knew these guys were good too; we just didn't anticipate they'd be this good... Yoenis Cespedes, Nelson Cruz, Josh Donaldson, Zack Greinke, John Lackey.

Unexpected health: We knew this player had the goods; we just didn't know whether he'd be healthy or would stay healthy all year... Jaime Garcia

Unexpected playing time: These players had the skills—and may have even displayed them at some time in the past—but had questionable playing time potential coming into this season. Some benefited from another player's injury, a rookie who didn't pan out or leveraged a short streak into a regular gig... Billy Burns, Carlos Correa, Matt Duffy, Gerardo Parra.

Unexpected return to form: These players had the skills, having displayed them at some point in the past. But those skills had been M.I.A. long enough that we began to doubt that they'd ever return; our projections model got tired of waiting. Or those previous skills displays were so inconsistent that projecting an "up year" would have been a shot in the dark; our projections model got tired of guessing. Yes, "once you display a skill, you own it" but still... Chris Davis, Kendrys Morales, Danny Valencia.

Unexpected role: This category is reserved for 2015's surprise closers. There are always some every year, relievers who are on nearly nobody's radar for front-line saves and are suddenly thrust into the role with great success (some did not clear the $10 hurdle but are worth mentioning anyway)... Santiago Casilla, Wade Davis, Jeurys Familia, Ken Giles, Jason Grilli, Andrew Miller, Roberto Osuna, A.J. Ramos, Carson Smith, Joakim Soria, Shawn Tolleson, Brad Ziegler.

Celebrate and claim we're geniuses: How these players put up the numbers they did is a mystery, but fantasy owners will likely chalk it up to their own superior scouting skills as they count their winnings. The truth is, who knows? However, the odds of a comparable follow-up for these players—particularly those with soft peripherals—will be small:

Logan Forsythe came into 2015 as a barely draftable commodity. He had shown some small signs of productivity back in 2012 (.273 BA over 315 AB) but has looked up at a .225 BA in the two years since. He got off to a good start this year and benefited from some early injuries to pick up playing time, but nobody expected a 17-HR, .281 season.

If you found yourself with 31-year-old **Chris Colabello** on your roster, congratulations. Now you can feel safe that you've bucked the odds of getting struck by lightning. This 15-HR, .321 season was a nice surprise, but with a 41% hit rate, .272 xBA and a 94 xPX, this is not something you'll ever see again.

Marco Estrada was not supposed to be this good. A flyball pitcher moving into the Rogers Centre was supposed to be a disaster waiting to happen. Instead, he posted the best numbers of his career. But beware: his 3.13 ERA belies a 4.61 xERA. He's showing declining Dom, rising Ctl (and declining FpK rate), a low 22% hit rate and the highest flyball rate of his career. He's still a disaster waiting to happen.

The performances that fell short of expectation

The DL denizens: These are players who got hurt, may not have returned fully healthy, or may have never been fully healthy (whether they'd admit it or not)... Matt Adams, Homer Bailey, Miguel Cabrera, Alex Cobb, Carl Crawford, Corey Dickerson, Sean Doolittle, Jacoby Ellsbury, Neftali Feliz, Doug Fister, Freddie Freeman, Yan Gomes, Carlos Gomez, Alex Gordon, Greg Holland, Matt Holliday, Hisashi Iwakuma, Jon Jay, Desmond Jennings, Jacob Lamb, Mat Latos, James Loney, Jed Lowrie, Jonathan Lucroy, Leonys Martin, Brandon McCarthy, Jake McGee, Devin Mesoraco, Justin Morneau, Michael Morse, Wil Myers, Steve Pearce, Dustin Pedroia, Hunter Pence, Yasiel Puig, Anthony Rendon, Alex Rios, Michael Saunders, Drew Smyly, Denard Span, George Springer, Giancarlo Stanton, Koji Uehara, Adam Wainwright, Jered Weaver, Jayson Werth, Matt Wieters, David Wright, Ryan Zimmerman.

(Some of these players seemed to be putting up sub-par numbers before they actually hit the DL. They may have been playing through the hurt before breaking down.)

Accelerated skills erosion: These are players who we knew were on the downside of their careers or had soft peripherals but we did not think they would plummet so quickly. In some cases, there were injuries involved, but all in all, 2015 might be the beginning of the end for some of these guys... Erick Aybar, Adrian Beltre, Michael Bourn, Rajai Davis, Alcides Escobar, Omar Infante, Adam LaRoche, Kyle Lohse, Yadier Molina, Brandon Moss, Mike Napoli, Aramis Ramirez, Jose Reyes, Fernando Rodney, Chase Utley.

Inflated expectations: Here are players who we really should not have expected much more than what they produced. Some had short or spotty track records, others had soft peripherals coming into 2015, and still others were inflated by media hype. Yes, for some of these, it was "What the heck was I thinking?" For others, we've almost come to expect players to ascend the growth curve faster these days. (You're 23 and you haven't broken out yet? What's the problem??) The bottom line is that player performance trends simply don't progress or regress in a straight line; still, the BPI trends were intriguing enough to take a leap of faith. We were wrong... Billy Butler, Robinson Cano, Andrew Cashner, Rusney Castillo, Starlin Castro, Lonnie Chisenhall, Michael Cuddyer, Ian Desmond, Jarrod Dyson, Scooter Gennett, Gio Gonzalez, Josh Harrison, Phil Hughes, Austin Jackson, Chris Johnson, Juan Lagares, Victor Martinez, Marcell Ozuna, Angel Pagan, Michael Pineda, Dalton Pompey, Hanley Ramirez, Wilson Ramos, Jimmy Rollins, Wilin Rosario, Pablo Sandoval, Daniel Santana, Jorge Soler, Steven Souza, Julio Teheran, Chris Tillman, Alex Wood, Eric Young, Jr.

Misplaced regression: Sometimes, we're so bullish on a player that we ignore the potential for regression within the bounds of normal random variance. Gravity is a powerful force, for... Chris Carter, Johnny Cueto, Cole Hamels, Felix Hernandez, Chris Sale, James Shields, Joe Smith, Drew Storen, Stephen Strasburg, Jordan Zimmermann.

Unexpected loss of role: This category is usually composed of closers who lost their job, sometimes through no fault of their own... Dellin Betances, Brett Cecil, Steve Cishek, Jenrry Mejia, Addison Reed, Sergio Romo, Drew Storen.

Throw our hands up and yell at the TV: These are the players for whom there is little explanation for what happened. We can speculate that they hid an injury, went off of PEDs, or just didn't have their head on right in 2015. For some, it was just the turn of an unlucky card this year:

I'm not sure what to think about **Troy Tulowitzki** anymore. He was hitting well in the first half in Colorado, but his power was M.I.A. When he got dealt to Toronto, his batting average not unexpectedly cratered. And then a shoulder injury in September mercifully ended his season. He'll end up with the most ABs since 2011. Is a sub-20 HR, .280 hitter what he's become?

All sorts of problems dogged **Anibal Sanchez** but his skills remained intact for a good part of the season. He entered June with a 5.75 ERA but his xERA was nearly two runs better. He had a solid June and came out of the first half with a 94 BPV. The wheels came off in the second half and that could be injury-related as he was eventually shut down in August. I'd be in on him again in 2016.

With the exception of 2014, **Jeff Samardzija** has always seemed to underperform his skills set. This year, the skills tumbled as well. Perhaps the most notable – and surprising – shift was his ground ball to fly ball ratio, which plummeted from 1.61 to 0.98 and led to a spike in HRs. U.S. Cellular was partially to blame, but his road numbers weren't great either.

About fantasy baseball touts

As a group, there is a strong tendency for all pundits to provide numbers that are publicly palatable, often at the expense of realism. That's because committing to either end of the range of expectation poses a high risk. Few touts will put their credibility on the line like that, even though we all know that those outliers are inevitable. Among our projections, you will find few .350 hitters and 70-steal speedsters. *Someone* is going to post a sub-2.50 ERA next year, but damned if any of us will commit to that. So we take an easier road. We'll hedge our numbers or split the difference between two equally possible outcomes.

In the world of prognosticating, this is called the *comfort zone.* This represents the outer tolerances for the public acceptability of a set of numbers. In most circumstances, even if the evidence is outstanding, prognosticators will not stray from within the comfort zone.

As for this book, occasionally we do commit to outlying numbers when we feel the data support it. But on the whole, most of the numbers here can be nearly as cowardly as everyone else's. We get around this by providing "color" to the projections in the capsule commentaries. That is where you will find the players whose projection has the best potential to stray beyond the limits of the comfort zone.

As analyst John Burnson once wrote: "The issue is not the success rate for one player, but the success rate for all players. No system is 100% reliable, and in trying to capture the outliers, you weaken the middle and thereby lose more predictive pull than you gain. At some level, everyone is an exception!"

Formula for consistent success

Anyone can win a league in any given season. Winning once proves very little, especially in redraft leagues. True success has to be defined as the ability to win consistently. It is a feat in itself to reach the mountaintop, but the battle isn't truly won unless you can stay atop that peak while others keep trying to knock you off.

What does it take to win that battle? We surveyed 12 of the most prolific fantasy champions in national experts league play. Here is how they rated six variables:

	Percent ranked			
	1-2	3-4	5-6	Score
Better in-draft strategy/tactics	77%	15%	7%	5.00
Better sense of player value	46%	46%	7%	4.15
Better luck	46%	23%	31%	3.85
Better grasp of contextual elements that affect players	31%	38%	31%	3.62
Better in-season roster management	31%	38%	31%	3.54
Better player projections	12%	31%	54%	2.62

Validating Performance

Performance validation criteria

The following is a set of support variables that helps determine whether a player's statistical output is an accurate reflection of his skills. From this we can validate or refute stats that vary from expectation, essentially asking, is this performance "fact or fluke?"

1. **Age:** Is the player at the stage of development when we might expect a change in performance?

2. **Health:** Is he coming off an injury, reconditioned and healthy for the first time in years, or a habitual resident of the disabled list?

3. **Minor league performance:** Has he shown the potential for greater things at some level of the minors? Or does his minor league history show a poor skill set that might indicate a lower ceiling?

4. **Historical trends:** Have his skill levels over time been on an upswing or downswing?

5. **Component skills indicators:** Looking beyond batting averages and ERAs, what do his support ratios look like?

6. **Ballpark, team, league:** Pitchers going to Colorado will see their ERA spike. Pitchers going to Oakland will see their ERA improve.

7. **Team performance:** Has a player's performance been affected by overall team chemistry or the environment fostered by a winning or losing club?

8. **Batting stance, pitching style/mastery:** Has a change in performance been due to a mechanical adjustment?

9. **Usage pattern, lineup position, role:** Has a change in RBI opportunities been a result of moving further up or down in the batting order? Has pitching effectiveness been impacted by moving from the bullpen to the rotation?

10. **Coaching effects:** Has the coaching staff changed the way a player approaches his conditioning, or how he approaches the game itself?

11. **Off-season activity:** Has the player spent the winter frequenting workout rooms or banquet tables?

12. **Personal factors:** Has the player undergone a family crisis? Experienced spiritual rebirth? Given up red meat? Taken up testosterone?

Skills ownership

Once a player displays a skill, he owns it. That display could occur at any time—earlier in his career, back in the minors, or even in winter ball play. And while that skill may lie dormant after its initial display, the potential is always there for him to tap back into that skill at some point, barring injury or age. That dormant skill can reappear at any time given the right set of circumstances.

Caveats:

1. The initial display of skill must have occurred over an extended period of time. An isolated 1-hit shut-out in Single-A ball amidst a 5.00 ERA season is not enough. The shorter the display of skill in the past, the more likely it can be attributed to random chance. The longer the display, the more likely that any re-emergence is for real.

2. If a player has been suspected of using performance enhancing drugs at any time, all bets are off.

Corollaries:

1. Once a player displays a vulnerability or skills deficiency, he owns that as well. That vulnerability could be an old injury problem, an inability to hit breaking pitches, or just a tendency to go into prolonged slumps.

2. The probability of a player correcting a skills deficiency declines with each year that deficiency exists.

Normal Production Variance *(Patrick Davitt)*

Even if we have a perfectly accurate understanding of a player's "normal" performance level, his actual performance can and does vary widely over any particular 150-game span—including the 150-game span we call "a season." A .300 career hitter can perform in a range of .250-.350, a 40-HR hitter from 30-50, and a 3.70/1.15 pitcher from 2.60/0.95 to 6.00/1.55. And all of these results must be considered "normal."

Contract year performance *(Tom Mullooly)*

There is a contention that players step up their game when they are playing for a contract. Research looked at contract year players and their performance during that year as compared to career levels. Of the batters and pitchers studied, 53% of the batters performed as if they were on a salary drive, while only 15% of the pitchers exhibited some level of contract year behavior.

How do players fare *after* signing a large contract (minimum $4M per year)? Research from 2005-2008 revealed that only 30% of pitchers and 22% of hitters exhibited an increase of more than 15% in BPV after signing a large deal either with their new team, or re-signing with the previous team. But nearly half of the pitchers (49%) and nearly half of the hitters (47%) saw a drop in BPV of more than 15% in the year after signing.

Risk management and reliability grades

Forecasts are constructed with the best data available, but there are factors that can impact the variability. One way we manage this risk is to assign each player Reliability Grades. The more certainty we see in a data set, the higher the reliability grades assigned to that player. The following variables are evaluated:

Health: Players with a history of staying healthy and off the DL are valuable to own. Unfortunately, while the ability to stay healthy can be considered skill, it is not very projectable. We can track the number of days spent on the disabled list and draw rough conclusions. The grades in the player boxes also include an adjustment for older players, who have a higher likelihood of getting hurt. That is the only forward-looking element of the grade.

"A" level players would have accumulated fewer than 30 days on the major league DL over the past five years. "F" grades go to those who've spent more than 120 days on the DL. Recent DL stays are given a heavier weight in the calculation.

Playing Time and Experience (PT/Exp): The greater the pool of MLB history to draw from, the greater our ability to construct a viable forecast. Length of service—and consistent service—is important. So players who bounce up and down from the majors to the minors are higher risk players. And rookies are all high risk.

For batters, we simply track plate appearances. Major league PAs have greater weight than minor league PAs. "A" level players would have averaged at least 550 major league PAs per year over the past three years. "F" graded players averaged fewer than 250 major league PA per year.

For pitchers, workload can be a double-edged sword. On one hand, small IP samples are deceptive in providing a read on a pitcher's true potential. Even a consistent 65-inning reliever can be considered higher risk since it would take just one bad outing to skew an entire season's work.

On the flipside, high workload levels also need to be monitored, especially in the formative years of a pitcher's career. Exceeding those levels elevates the risk of injury, burnout, or breakdown. So, tracking workload must be done within a range of innings. The grades capture this.

Consistency: Consistent performers are easier to project and garner higher reliability grades. Players that mix mediocrity with occasional flashes of brilliance or badness generate higher risk projections. Even those who exhibit a consistent upward or downward trend cannot be considered truly consistent as we do not know whether those trends will continue. Typically, they don't.

"A" level players are those whose runs created per game level (xERA for pitchers) has fluctuated by less than half a run during each of the past three years. "F" grades go to those whose RC/G or xERA has fluctuated by two runs or more.

Remember that these grades have nothing to do with quality of performance; they strictly refer to confidence in our expectations. So a grade of **AAA** for Kyle Lohse, for instance, only means that there is a high probability he will perform as poorly as we've projected.

Reliability and age

Peak batting reliability occurs at ages 29 and 30, followed by a minor decline for four years. So, to draft the most reliable batters, and maximize the odds of returning at least par value on your investments, you should target the age range of 28-34.

The most reliable age range for pitchers is 29-34. While we are forever looking for "sleepers" and hot prospects, it is very risky to draft any pitcher under 27 or over 35.

Evaluating Reliability *(Bill Macey)*

Fantasy baseball owners are like investors who are always looking for a good return. Calculating our expected return includes assessing the risk of our draft-day investment.

Managing risk leads to two kinds of valuation adjustments. We downgrade talented players we believe to be higher injury risks, who have a history of inconsistent performance, or whose playing time (PT) is less certain. But we upgrade players we deem more reliable with respect to health, consistency, PT, or all three.

When you head into an upcoming auction or draft, consider the following with regard to reliability:

- Reliability grades do help identify more stable investments: players with "B" grades in both Health and PT/Experience are more likely to return a higher percentage of their projected value.
- While top-end starting pitching may be more reliable than ever, the overall pool of pitchers is fraught with uncertainty and the position represents a less reliable investment than batters.
- There does not appear to be a significant market premium for reliability, at least according to the criteria measured by BaseballHQ.com.
- There are only two types of players: risky and riskier. So while it may be worth going the extra buck for a more reliable player, be warned that even the most reliable player can falter—don't go overboard bidding up a AAA-rated player simply due to his Reliability grades.

Using 3-year trends as leading indicators *(Ed DeCaria)*

It is almost irresistibly tempting to look at three numbers moving in one direction and expect that the fourth will continue that progression. However, for both hitters and pitchers riding positive trends over any consecutive three-year period, not only do most players not continue their positive trend into a fourth year, their Year 4 performance usually regresses significantly. This is true for every metric tested (whether related to playing time, batting skills, pitching skills, running skills, luck indicators, or valuation). Negative trends show similar reversals, but tend to be more "sticky," meaning that rebounds are neither as frequent nor as strong as positive trend regressions. Challenge any analysis that hints at a player's demise coming off of a negative trend or that suggests an imminent breakout following a positive trend; more often than not, such predictions do not pan out.

Health Analysis

Disabled list statistics

Year	#Players	3yr Avg	DL Days	3yr Avg
2008	422	391	28,187	26,394
2009	408	411	26,252	27,654
2010	393	408	22,911	25,783
2011	422	408	25,610	24,924
2012	409	408	30,408	27,038
2013	442	419	29,551	28,523
2014	422	424	25,839	28,599
2015	454	439	28,982	28,124

D.L. days as a leading indicator *(Bill Macey)*

Players who are injured in one year are likely to be injured in a subsequent year:

% DL batters in Year 1 who are also DL in year 2	38%
Under age 30	36%
Age 30 and older	41%
% DL batters in Year 1 and 2 who are also DL in year 3	54%
% DL pitchers in Year 1 who are also DL in year 2	43%
Under age 30	45%
Age 30 and older	41%
% DL pitchers in Yr 1 and 2 who are also DL in year 3	41%

Previously injured players also tend to spend a longer time on the DL. The average number of days on the DL was 51 days for batters and 73 days for pitchers. For the subset of these players who get hurt again the following year, the average number of days on the DL was 58 days for batters and 88 days for pitchers.

Spring training spin *(Dave Adler)*

Spring training sound bites raise expectations among fantasy leaguers, but how much of that "news" is really "noise"? Thanks to a summary listed at RotoAuthority.com, we were able to compile the stats for 2009. Verdict: Noise.

BATTERS	No.	IMPROVED	DECLINED
Weight change	30	33%	30%
Fitness program	3	0%	67%
Eye surgery	6	50%	33%
Plans more SB	6	17%	33%
PITCHERS	**No.**	**IMPROVED**	**DECLINED**
Weight change	18	44%	44%
Fitness program	4	50%	50%
Eye surgery	2	0%	50%
New pitch	5	60%	40%

In-Season Analysis

April performance as a leading indicator

We isolated all players who earned at least $10 more or $10 less than we had projected in March. Then we looked at the April stats of these players to see if we could have picked out the $10 outliers after just one month.

		Identifiable in April
Earned $10+ more than projected		
	BATTERS	39%
	PITCHERS	44%
Earned -$10 less than projected		
	BATTERS	56%
	PITCHERS	74%

Nearly three out of every four pitchers who earned at least $10 less than projected also struggled in April. For all the other surprises—batters or pitchers—April was not a strong leading indicator. Another look:

	Pct.
Batters who finished +$25	45%
Pitchers who finished +$20	44%
Batters who finished under $0	60%
Pitchers who finished under -$5	78%

April surgers are less than a 50/50 proposition to maintain that level all season. Those who finished April at the bottom of the roto rankings were more likely to continue struggling, especially pitchers. In fact, of those pitchers who finished April with a value *under -$10*, 91% finished the season in the red. Holes are tough to dig out of.

The weight of early season numbers

Early season strugglers who surge later in the year get no respect because they have to live with the weight of their early numbers all season long. Conversely, quick starters who fade late get far more accolades than they deserve.

For instance, take Pablo Sandoval's month-by-month batting average. The perception is that his .245 BA was a disappointment. Well, it was more than just a disappointment. His hot .312 start masked what was an even worse performance. From May 1 on, he batted just .232.

Month	BA	Cum BA
April	.312	.312
May	.200	.251
June	.298	.267
July	.241	.260
August	.205	.249
September	.205	.245

Seasonal trends in hitting and pitching *(Bob Berger)*

A study of monthly trends in traditional statistical categories found:

- Batting average, HR/game and RBI/game rise from April through August, then fall in September/October.
- Stolen bases decline in July and August before rebounding in September.
- ERA worsens in July/August and improves in September.
- WHIP gets worse in July/August.
- K/9 rate improves all season.

The bold statement that hitters perform better in warmer weather seems to be true broadly.

Courtship period

Any time a player is put into a new situation, he enters into what we might call a courtship period. This period might occur when a player switches leagues, or switches teams. It could be the first few games when a minor leaguer is called up. It could occur when a reliever moves into the rotation, or when a lead-off hitter is moved to another spot in the lineup. There is a team-wide courtship period when a manager is replaced. Any external situation that could affect a player's performance sets off a new decision point in evaluating that performance.

During this period, it is difficult to get a true read on how a player is going to ultimately perform. He is adjusting to the new situation. Things could be volatile during this time. For instance, a role change that doesn't work could spur other moves. A rookie hurler might buy himself a few extra starts with a solid debut, even if he has questionable skills.

It is best not to make a decision on a player who is going through a courtship period. Wait until his stats stabilize. Don't cut a struggling pitcher in his first few starts after a managerial change. Don't pick up a hitter who smacks a pair of HRs in his first game after having been traded. Unless, of course, talent and track record say otherwise.

Half-season fallacies

A popular exercise at the midpoint of each season is to analyze those players who are consistent first half to second half surgers or faders. There are several fallacies with this analytical approach.

1. Half-season consistency is rare. There are very few players who show consistent changes in performance from one half of the season to the other.

Research results from a three-year study conducted in the late-1990s: The test groups... batters with min. 300 AB full season, 150 AB first half, and pitchers with min. 100 IP full season, 50 IP first half. Of those groups (size noted):

3-year consistency in	BATTERS (98)	PITCHERS (42)
1 stat category	40%	57%
2 stat categories	18%	21%
3 stat categories	3%	5%

When the analysis was stretched to a fourth year, only 1% of all players showed consistency in even one category.

2. Analysts often use false indicators. Situational statistics provide us with tools that can be misused. Several sources offer up 3- and 5-year stats intended to paint a picture of a long-term performance. Some analysts look at a player's half-season swing over that multi-year period and conclude that he is demonstrating consistent performance.

The fallacy is that those multi-year scans may not show any consistency at all. They are not individual season performances but *aggregate* performances. A player whose 5-year batting average shows a 15-point rise in the 2nd half, for instance, may actually have experienced a BA decline in several of those years, a fact that might have been offset by a huge BA rise in one of the years.

3. It's arbitrary. The season's midpoint is an arbitrary delineator of performance swings. Some players are slow starters and might be more appropriately evaluated as pre-May 1 and post-May 1. Others bring their game up a notch with a pennant chase and might see a performance swing with August 15 as the cut-off. Each player has his own individual tendency, if, in fact, one exists at all. There's nothing magical about mid-season as the break point, and certainly not over a multi-year period.

Half-season tendencies

Despite the above, it stands to reason logically that there might be some underlying tendencies on a more global scale, first half to second half. In fact, one would think that the player population as a whole might decline in performance as the season drones on. There are many variables that might contribute to a player wearing down—workload, weather, boredom—and the longer a player is on the field, the higher the likelihood that he is going to get hurt. A recent 5-year study uncovered the following tendencies:

Batting

Overall, batting skills held up pretty well, half to half. There was a 5% erosion of playing time, likely due, in part, to September roster expansion.

Power: First half power studs (20 HRs in 1H) saw a 10% drop-off in the second half. 34% of first half 20+ HR hitters hit 15 or fewer in the second half and only 27% were able to improve on their first half output.

Speed: Second half speed waned as well. About 26% of the 20+ SB speedsters stole *at least 10 fewer bases* in the second half. Only 26% increased their second half SB output at all.

Batting average: 60% of first half .300 hitters failed to hit .300 in the second half. Only 20% showed any second half improvement at all. As for 1H strugglers, managers tended to stick with their full-timers despite poor starts. Nearly one in five of the sub-.250 1H hitters managed to hit *more than* .300 in the second half.

Pitching

Overall, there was some slight erosion in innings and ERA despite marginal improvement in some peripherals.

ERA: For those who pitched at least 100 innings in the first half, ERAs rose an average of 0.40 runs in the 2H. Of those with first half ERAs less than 4.00, only 49% were able to maintain a sub-4.00 ERA in the second half.

Wins: Pitchers who won 18 or more games in a season tended to pitch *more* innings in the 2H and had slightly better peripherals.

Saves: Of those closers who saved 20 or more games in the first half, only 39% were able to post 20 or more saves in the 2H, and 26% posted fewer than 15 saves. Aggregate ERAs of these pitchers rose from 2.45 to 3.17, half to half.

Teams

Johnson Effect *(Bryan Johnson)*: Teams whose actual won/loss record exceeds or falls short of their statistically projected record in one season will tend to revert to the level of their projection in the following season.

Law of Competitive Balance *(Bill James)*: The level at which a team (or player) will address its problems is inversely related to its current level of success. Low performers will tend to make changes to improve; high performers will not. This law explains the existence of the Plexiglass and Whirlpool Principles.

Plexiglass Principle *(Bill James)*: If a player or team improves markedly in one season, it will likely decline in the next. The opposite is true but not as often (because a poor performer gets fewer opportunities to rebound).

Whirlpool Principle *(Bill James)*: All team and player performances are forcefully drawn to the center. For teams, that center is a .500 record. For players, it represents their career average level of performance.

Other Diamonds

The Fanalytic Fundamentals

1. This is not a game of accuracy or precision. It is a game of human beings and tendencies.
2. This is not a game of projections. It is a game of market value versus real value.
3. Draft skills, not stats. Draft skills, not roles.
4. A player's ability to post acceptable stats despite lousy BPIs will eventually run out.
5. Once you display a skill, you own it.
6. Virtually every player is vulnerable to a month of aberrant performance. Or a year.
7. Exercise excruciating patience.

Aging Axioms

1. Age is the only variable for which we can project a rising trend with 100% accuracy. (Or, age never regresses.)
2. The aging process slows down for those who maintain a firm grasp on the strike zone. Plate patience and pitching command can preserve any waning skill they have left.
3. Negatives tend to snowball as you age.

Steve Avery List

Players who hang onto MLB rosters for six years searching for a skill level they only had for three.

Bylaws of Badness

1. Some players are better than an open roster spot, but not by much.

2. Some players have bad years because they are unlucky. Others have *many* bad years because they are bad... and lucky.

George Brett Path to Retirement

Get out while you're still putting up good numbers and the public perception of you is favorable. Like Mike Mussina, Billy Wagner, Chipper Jones and Mariano Rivera.

Steve Carlton Path to Retirement

Hang around the majors long enough for your numbers to become so wretched that people begin to forget your past successes.

Classic cases include Jose Mesa, Doc Gooden, Nomar Garciaparra and of course, Steve Carlton. Recent players who have taken this path include Miguel Tejada, Travis Hafner, Jason Bay, Brian Roberts and Kevin Youkilis. Current players who could be on a similar course include Jimmy Rollins, Chase Utley and Dan Uggla.

Christie Brinkley Law of Statistical Analysis

Never get married to the model.

Employment Standards

1. If you are right-brain dominant, own a catcher's mitt and are under 40, you will always be gainfully employed.
2. Some teams believe that it is better to employ a player with any experience because it has to be better than the devil they don't know.
3. It's not so good to go *pffft* in a contract year.

Laws of Prognosticating Perspective

- *Berkeley's 17th Law:* A great many problems do not have accurate answers, but do have approximate answers, from which sensible decisions can be made.
- *Ashley-Perry Statistical Axiom #4:* A complex system that works is invariably found to have evolved from a simple system that works.
- *Baseball Variation of Harvard Law:* Under the most rigorously observed conditions of skill, age, environment, statistical rules and other variables, a ballplayer will perform as he damn well pleases.

Brad Fullmer List

Players whose leading indicators indicate upside potential, year after year, but consistently fail to reach that full potential. Players like Justin Smoak, Josh Rutledge, Brett Lawrie are on the list right now.

Good Luck Truism

Good luck is rare and everyone has more of it than you do. That's the law.

The Gravity Principles

1. It is easier to be crappy than it is to be good.
2. All performance starts at zero, ends at zero and can drop to zero at any time.
3. The odds of a good performer slumping are far greater than the odds of a poor performer surging.
4. Once a player is in a slump, it takes several 3-for-5 days to get out of it. Once he is on a streak, it takes a single 0-for-4 day to begin the downward spiral. *Corollary:* Once a player is in a slump, not only does it take several 3-for-5 days to get out of it, but he also has to get his name back on the lineup card.
5. Eventually all performance comes down to earth. It may take a week, or a month, or may not happen until he's 45, but eventually it's going to happen.

Health Homilies

1. Staying healthy is a skill (and "DL Days" should be a Rotisserie category).
2. A $40 player can get hurt just as easily as a $5 player but is eight times tougher to replace.
3. Chronically injured players never suddenly get healthy.
4. There are two kinds of pitchers: those that are hurt and those that are not hurt... yet.
5. Players with back problems are always worth $10 less.
6. "Opting out of surgery" usually means it's coming anyway, just later.

The Health Hush

Players get hurt and potentially have a lot to lose, so there is an incentive for them to hide injuries. HIPAA laws restrict the disclosure of health information. Team doctors and trainers have been instructed not to talk with the media. So, when it comes to information on a player's health status, we're all pretty much in the dark.

Hidden Injury Progression

1. Player's skills implode.
2. Team and player deny injury.
3. More unexplained struggles.
4. Injury revealed; surgery follows.

The Livan Level

The point when a player's career Runs Above Replacement level has dropped so far below zero that he has effectively cancelled out any possible remaining future value. (Similarly, the Dontrelle Demarcation.)

The Momentum Maxims

1. A player will post a pattern of positive results until the day you add him to your roster.
2. Patterns of negative results are more likely to snowball than correct.
3. When an unstoppable force meets an immovable object, the wall always wins.

Paradoxes and Conundrums

1. Is a player's improvement in performance from one year to the next a point in a growth trend, an isolated outlier or a complete anomaly?
2. A player can play through an injury, post rotten numbers and put his job at risk... or... he can admit that he can't play through an injury, allow himself to be taken out of the lineup/rotation, and put his job at risk.
3. Did irregular playing time take its toll on the player's performance or did poor performance force a reduction in his playing time?
4. Is a player only in the game versus right-handers because he has a true skills deficiency versus left-handers? Or is his poor performance versus left-handers because he's never given a chance to face them?

5. The problem with stockpiling bench players in the hope that one pans out is that you end up evaluating performance using data sets that are too small to be reliable.
6. There are players who could give you 20 stolen bases if they got 400 AB. But if they got 400 AB, they would likely be on a bad team that wouldn't let them steal.

Process-Outcome Matrix *(Russo and Schoemaker)*

	Good Outcome	**Bad Outcome**
Good Process	Deserved Success	Bad Break
Bad Process	Dumb Luck	Poetic Justice

Quack!

An exclamation in response to the educated speculation that a player has used performance enhancing drugs. While it is rare to have absolute proof, there is often enough information to suggest that, "if it looks like a duck and quacks like a duck, then odds are it's a duck."

Tenets of Optimal Timing

1. If a second half fader had put up his second half stats in the first half and his first half stats in the second half, then he probably wouldn't even have had a second half.
2. Fast starters can often buy six months of playing time out of one month of productivity.
3. Poor 2nd halves don't get recognized until it's too late.
4. "Baseball is like this. Have one good year and you can fool them for five more, because for five more years they expect you to have another good one." — Frankie Frisch

The Three True Outcomes

1. Strikeouts
2. Walks
3. Home runs

The Three True Handicaps

1. Has power but can't make contact.
2. Has speed but can't hit safely.
3. Has potential but is too old.

Zombie

A player who is indestructible, continuing to get work, year-after-year, no matter how dead his skills metrics are. Like Kevin Correia, Dan Johnson, Travis Ishikawa and Dan Uggla.

Batters

Batting Eye, Contact and Batting Average

Batting average (BA, or Avg)

This is where it starts. BA is a grand old nugget that has long outgrown its usefulness. We revere .300 hitting superstars and scoff at .250 hitters, yet the difference between the two is one hit every 20 ABs. This one hit every five games is not nearly the wide variance that exists in our perceptions of what it means to be a .300 or .250 hitter. BA is a poor evaluator of performance in that it neglects the offensive value of the base on balls and assumes that all hits are created equal.

Walk rate (bb%)

(BB / (AB + BB))

A measure of a batter's plate patience. **BENCHMARKS:** The best batters will have levels more than 10%. Those with poor plate patience will have levels of 5% or less.

Walk rate and batting average *(Patrick Davitt)*

Analysts have long told us that a hitter's walk rate (bb%) is a reliable leading indicator of batting average (BA), and that changes in bb% are clues about expected improvements or declines in BA. This was probably because analysts used bb% as a proxy for a hitter's ability to "be selective" by laying off pitches outside the zone and swinging at pitches in the zone.

While the idea makes intuitive sense, a BaseballHQ.com review of several seasons' bb% and BA data showed that bb% and BA are as unconnected as they could be. In any single season, and for all seasons in the study combined, the overall correlation between the two variables was +0.01 (a score of 0.00 means two variables are completely uncorrelated).

For any given bb%, BAs always clustered around .250, with most in a range of about .240 to .260. Minimum and maximum BAs for any decile of bb% were likewise random. And even at BA extremes, the bb% was not correlated; among .300+ hitters, for example, bb% ranged from 4% to 14%).

On base average (OB)

(H + BB + HBP) / (AB + BB + HBP + Sac Flies)

Addressing a key deficiency with BA, OB gives value to events that get batters on base, but are not hits. An OB of .350 can be read as "this batter gets on base 35% of the time." When a run is scored, there is no distinction made as to how that runner reached base. So, two-thirds of the time—about how often a batter comes to the plate with the bases empty—a walk really is as good as a hit. **BENCHMARKS:** We know what a .300 hitter is, but what represents "good" for OB? That comparable level would likely be .400, with .275 representing the comparable level of futility.

Ground ball, line drive, fly ball percentages (G/L/F)

The percentage of all balls in play that are hit on the ground, as line drives and in the air. For batters, increased fly ball tendency may foretell a rise in power skills; increased line drive tendency may foretell an improvement in batting average. For a pitcher, the ability to keep the ball on the ground can contribute to his statistical output exceeding his demonstrated skill level.

*BIP Type	Total%	Out%
Ground ball	45%	72%
Line drive	20%	28%
Fly ball	35%	85%
TOTAL	*100%*	*69%*

*Data only includes fieldable balls and is net of HRs.

Line drives and luck *(Patrick Davitt)*

Given that each individual batter's hit rate sets its own baseline, and that line drives (LD) are the most productive type of batted ball, a study looked at the relationship between the two. Among the findings were that hit rates on LDs are much higher than on FBs or GBs, with individual batters consistently falling into the 72-73% range. Ninety-five percent of all batters fall between the range of 60%-86%; batters outside this range regress very quickly, often within the season.

Note that batters' BAs did not always follow their LD% up or down, because some of them enjoyed higher hit rates on other batted balls, improved their contact rates, or both. Still, it's justifiable to bet that players hitting the ball with authority but getting fewer hits than they should will correct over time.

Batting eye (Eye)

(Walks / Strikeouts)

A measure of a player's strike zone judgment. **BENCHMARKS:** The best hitters have Eye ratios more than 1.00 (indicating more walks than strikeouts) and are the most likely to be among a league's .300 hitters. Ratios less than 0.50 represent batters who likely also have lower BAs.

Batting eye as a leading indicator

There is a strong correlation between strike zone judgment and batting average. However, research shows that this is more descriptive than predictive:

	Batting Average				
Batting Eye	2011	2012	2013	2014	2015
0.00 - 0.25	.232	.243	.242	.238	.243
0.26 - 0.50	.254	.255	.253	.253	.257
0.51 - 0.75	.267	.268	.265	.268	.267
0.76 - 1.00	.276	.276	.277	.270	.280
1.01 and over	.298	.292	.284	.304	.293

We have been running the above chart for years and have always had large enough samples to make each group statistically significant. But not the past two years. The last group—1.01 and over—contained only six players in 2014 and eight players in 2015. The correlation held, but the downward pressure on batting averages continues to change the game.

We can create percentage plays for the different levels:

For Eye	Pct who bat	
Levels of	.300+	.250-
0.00 - 0.25	7%	39%
0.26 - 0.50	14%	26%
0.51 - 0.75	18%	17%
0.76 - 1.00	32%	14%
1.01 - 1.50	51%	9%
1.51 +	59%	4%

Any batter with an eye ratio more than 1.50 has about a 4% chance of hitting less than .250 over 500 at bats.

Of all .300 hitters, those with ratios of at least 1.00 have a 65% chance of repeating as .300 hitters. Those with ratios less than 1.00 have less than a 50% chance of repeating.

Only 4% of sub-.250 hitters with ratios less than 0.50 will mature into .300 hitters the following year.

In a 1995-2000 study, only 37 batters hit .300-plus with a sub-0.50 eye ratio over at least 300 AB in a season. Of this group, 30% were able to accomplish this feat on a consistent basis. For the other 70%, this was a short-term aberration.

Contact rate (ct%)

((AB - K) / AB)

Measures a batter's ability to get wood on the ball and hit it into the field of play. **BENCHMARKS:** Those batters with the best contact skill will have levels of 90% or better. The hackers of society will have levels of 75% or less.

Contact rate as a leading indicator

The more often a batter makes contact with the ball, the higher the likelihood that he will hit safely.

	Batting Average				
Contact Rate	2011	2012	2013	2014	2015
0% - 60%	.171	.197	.203	.176	.194
61% - 65%	.199	.226	.211	.217	.217
66% - 70%	.229	.231	.232	.230	.236
71% - 75%	.243	.252	.246	.243	.254
76% - 80%	.260	.255	.261	.257	.257
81% - 85%	.268	.268	.268	.266	.268
86% - 90%	.272	.278	.272	.276	.277
Over 90%	.290	.282	.270	.324	.284

Once again, the size of the highest-skilled group has dwindled, here to only 17 players in 2014 and 25 players in 2015. Last year, only four had more than 50 AB; this year only six with nearly half posting fewer than 10 AB.

Contact rate and walk rate as leading indicators

A matrix of contact rates and walk rates can provide expectation benchmarks for a player's batting average:

Contact rate (ct%)	Walk rate (bb%) 0-5	6-10	11-15	16+
65-	.179	.195	.229	.237
66-75	.190	.248	.254	.272
76-85	.265	.267	.276	.283
86+	.269	.279	.301	.309

A contact rate of 65% or lower offers virtually no chance for a player to hit even .250, no matter how high a walk rate he has. The .300 hitters most often come from the group with a minimum 86% contact and 11% walk rate.

HCt and HctX *(Patrick Davitt)*

HCt= hard hit ball rate x contact rate

HctX= Player HCt divided by league average Hct, normalized to 100

The combination of making contact and hitting the ball hard might be the most important skills for a batter. HctX correlates very strongly with BA, and at higher BA levels often does so with high accuracy. Its success with HR was somewhat limited, probably due to GB/FB differences. **BENCHMARKS:** The average major-leaguer in a given year has a HctX of 100. Elite batters have an HctX of 135 or above; weakest batters have HctX of 55 or below.

Balls in play (BIP)

(AB – K)

The total number of batted balls that are hit fair, both hits and outs. An analysis of how these balls are hit—on the ground, in the air, hits, outs, etc.—can provide analytical insight, from player skill levels to the impact of luck on statistical output.

Batting average on balls in play *(Voros McCracken)*

(H – HR) / (AB – HR – K)

Also called hit rate (h%). The percent of balls hit into the field of play that fall for hits. **BENCHMARK:** Every hitter establishes his own individual hit rate that stabilizes over time. A batter whose seasonal hit rate varies significantly from the h% he has established over the preceding three seasons (variance of at least +/- 3%) is likely to improve or regress to his individual h% mean (with over-performer declines more likely and sharper than under-performer recoveries). Three-year h% levels strongly predict a player's h% the following year.

Pitches/Plate Appearance as a leading indicator for BA *(Paul Petera)*

The art of working the count has long been considered one of the more crucial aspects of good hitting. It is common knowledge that the more pitches a hitter sees, the greater opportunity he has to reach base safely.

P/PA	OBA	BA
4.00+	.360	.264
3.75-3.99	.347	.271
3.50-3.74	.334	.274
Under 3.50	.321	.276

Generally speaking, the more pitches seen,the lower the BA, but the higher the OBA. But what about the outliers, those players that bucked the trend in year #1?

	YEAR TWO BA Improved	BA Declined
Low P/PA and Low BA	77%	23%
High P/PA and High BA	21%	79%

In these scenarios, there was a strong tendency for performance to normalize in year #2.

Expected batting average *(John Burnson)*

*xCT% * [xH1% + xH2%]*

where

xH1% = GB% x [0.0004 PX + 0.062 ln(SX)]
+ LD% x [0.93 - 0.086 ln(SX)]
+ FB% x 0.12

and

xH2% = FB% x [0.0013 PX - 0.0002 SX - 0.057]
+ GB% x [0.0006 PX]

A hitter's batting average as calculated by multiplying the percentage of balls put in play (contact rate) by the chance that a ball in play falls for a hit. The likelihood that a ball in play falls for a hit is a product of the speed of the ball and distance it is hit (PX), the speed of the batter (SX), and distribution of ground balls, fly balls, and line drives. We further split it out by non-homerun hit rate (xH1%) and homerun hit rate (xH2%). **BENCHMARKS:** In general, xBA should approximate batting average fairly closely. Those hitters who have large variances between the two gauges are candidates for further analysis. **LIMITATION:** xBA tends to understate a batter's true value if he is an extreme ground ball hitter (G/F ratio over 3.0) with a low PX. These players are not inherently weak, but choose to take safe singles rather than swing for the fences.

Expected batting average variance

xBA – BA

The variance between a batter's BA and his xBA is a measure of over- or under-achievement. A positive variance indicates the potential for a batter's BA to rise. A negative variance indicates the potential for BA to decline. **BENCHMARK:** Discount variances that are less than 20 points. Any variance more than 30 points is regarded as a strong indicator of future change.

Power

Slugging average (Slg)

(Singles + (2 x Doubles) + (3 x Triples) + (4 x HR)) / AB

A measure of the total number of bases accumulated (or the minimum number of runners' bases advanced) per at bat. It is a misnomer; it is not a true measure of a batter's slugging ability because it includes singles. Slg also assumes that each type of hit has proportionately increasing value (i.e. a double is twice as valuable as a single, etc.) which is not true. For instance, with the bases loaded, a HR always scores four runs, a triple always scores three, but a double could score two or three and a single could score one, or two, or even three. **BENCHMARKS:** Top batters will have levels over .500. The bottom batters will have levels less than .300.

Fly ball tendency and power *(Mat Olkin)*

There is a proven connection between a hitter's ground ball/fly ball tendencies and his power production.

1. *Extreme ground ball hitters generally do not hit for much power.* It's almost impossible for a hitter with a ground/fly ratio over 1.80 to hit enough fly balls to produce even 25 HRs in a season. However, this does not mean that a low G/F ratio necessarily guarantees power production. Some players have no problem getting the ball into the air, but lack the strength to reach the fences consistently.
2. *Most batters' ground/fly ratios stay pretty steady over time.* Most year-to-year changes are small and random, as they are in any other statistical category. A large, sudden change in G/F, on the other hand, can signal a conscious change in plate approach. And so...
3. *If a player posts high G/F ratios in his first few years, he probably isn't ever going to hit for all that much power.*
4. *When a batter's power suddenly jumps, his G/F ratio often drops at the same time.*
5. *Every so often, a hitter's ratio will drop significantly even as his power production remains level.* In these rare cases, impending power development is likely, since the two factors almost always follow each other.

Home runs to fly ball rate (hr/f)

The percent of fly balls that are hit for HRs.

hr/f rate as a leading indicator *(Joshua Randall)*

Each batter establishes an individual home run to fly ball rate that stabilizes over rolling three-year periods; those levels strongly predict the hr/f in the subsequent year. A batter who varies significantly from his hr/f is likely to regress toward his individual hr/f mean, with over-performance decline more likely and more severe than under-performance recovery.

Hard-hit flies as a sustainable skill *(Patrick Davitt)*

A study of data from 2009-2011 found that we should seek batters with a high Hard-Hit Fly Ball percentage (HHFB%). Among the findings:

- Avoiding pop-ups and hitting HHFBs are sustainable core power skills.
- Consistent HHFB% performance marks batters with power potential.
- When looking for candidates to regress, we should look at individual past levels of HR/HHFB, perhaps using a three-year rolling average.

Linear weighted power (LWPwr)

((Doubles x .8) + (Triples x .8) + (HR x 1.4)) / (At bats- K) x 100

A variation of the linear weights formula that considers only events that are measures of a batter's pure power. **BENCHMARKS:** Top sluggers typically top the 17 mark. Weak hitters will have a LWPwr level of less than 10.

Linear weighted power index (PX)

(Batter's LWPwr / League LWPwr) x 100

LWPwr is presented in this book in its normalized form to get a better read on a batter's accomplishment in each year. For instance, a 30-HR season today is much more of an accomplishment than 30 HRs hit in a higher offense year like 2003. **BENCHMARKS:** A level of 100 equals league average power skills. Any player with a value more than 100 has above average power skills, and those more than 150 are the Slugging Elite.

Expected LW power index (xPX) *(Bill Macey)*

*2.6 + 269*HHLD% + 724*HHFB%*

Previous research has shown that hard-hit balls are more likely to result in hits and hard-hit fly balls are more likely to end up as HRs. As such, we can use hard-hit ball data to calculate an expected skills-based power index. This metric starts with hard-hit ball data, which measures a player's fundamental skill of making solid contact, and then places it on the same scale as PX (xPX). In the above formula, HHLD% is calculated as the number of hard hit-line drives divided by the total number of balls put in play. HHFB% is similarly calculated for fly balls.

Pitches/Plate Appearance as a leading indicator for PX *(Paul Petera)*

Working the count has a positive effect on power.

P/PA	PX
4.00+	123
3.75-3.99	108
3.50-3.74	96
Under 3.50	84

As for the year #1 outliers:

	YEAR TWO	
	PX Improved	PX Declined
Low P/PA and High PX	11%	89%
High P/PA and Low PX	70%	30%

In these scenarios, there was a strong tendency for performance to normalize in year #2.

Doubles as a leading indicator for home runs *(Bill Macey)*

There is little support for the theory that hitting many doubles in year x leads to an increase in HR in year x+1. However, it was shown that batters with high doubles rates (2B/AB) also tend to hit more HR/AB than the league average; oddly, they are unable to sustain the high 2B/AB rate but do sustain their higher HR/AB rates. Batters with high 2B/AB rates and low HR/AB rates are more likely to see HR gains in the following year, but those rates will still typically trail the league average. And, batters who experience a surge in 2B/AB typically give back most of those gains in the following year without any corresponding gain in HR.

Opposite field home runs *(Ed DeCaria)*

From 2001-2008, nearly 75% of all HRs were hit to the batter's pull field, with the remaining 25% distributed roughly evenly between straight away and opposite field. Left-handers accomplished the feat slightly more often than right-handers (including switch-hitters hitting each way), and younger hitters did it significantly more often than older hitters. The trend toward pulled home runs was especially strong after age 36.

Power Quartile	AB/HR	Opp. Field	Straight Away	Pull Field
Top 25%	17.2	16%	16%	68%
2nd 25%	28.0	11%	12%	77%
3rd 25%	44.1	9%	10%	8%
Bot 25%	94.7	5%	6%	89%

Opposite field HRs serve as a strong indicator of overall home run power (AB/HR). Power hitters (smaller AB/HR rates) hit a far higher percentage of their HR to the opposite field or straight away (over 30%). Conversely, non-power hitters hit almost 90% of their home runs to their pull field.

Performance in Y2-Y4 (% of Group)

Y1 Trigger	<=30 AB/HR	5.5+ RC/G	$16+ R$
2+ OppHR	69%	46%	33%
<2 OppHR	29%	13%	12%

Players who hit just two or more OppHR in one season were 2-3 times as likely as those who hit zero or one OppHR to sustain strong AB/HR rates, RC/G levels, or R$ values over the following three seasons.

Y2-Y4 Breakout Performance
(% Breakout by Group, Age <=26 Only)

Y1 Trigger	AB/HR >35 to <=30	RC/G <4.5 to 5.5+	R$ <$8 to $16+
2+ OppHR	32%	21%	30%
<2 OppHR	23%	12%	10%

Roughly one of every 3-4 batters age 26 or younger experiences a *sustained three-year breakout* in AB/HR, RC/G or R$ after a season in which they hit 2+ OppHR, far better odds than the one in 8-10 batters who experience a breakout without the 2+ OppHR trigger.

Home runs in bunches *(Patrick Davitt)*

A study from HR data from 2010-2012 showed that batters hit HRs in a random manner, with game-gaps between HRs that correspond roughly to their average days per HR. Thus, the theory that batters hit HRs in "bunches" is a fallacy. It appears pointless to try to "time the market" by predicting the beginning or end of a drought or a bunch, or by assuming the end of one presages the beginning of the other, despite what the ex-player in the broadcast booth tells you.

Power breakout profile

It is not easy to predict which batters will experience a power spike. We can categorize power breakouts to determine the likelihood of a player taking a step up or of a surprise performer repeating his feat. Possibilities:

- Increase in playing time
- History of power skills at some time in the past
- Redistribution of already demonstrated extra base hit power
- Normal skills growth
- Situational breakouts, particularly in hitter-friendly venues
- Increased fly ball tendency
- Use of illegal performance-enhancing substances
- Miscellaneous unexplained variables

Speed

Wasted talent on the base paths

We refer to some players as having "wasted talent," a high level skill that is negated by a deficiency in another skill. Among these types are players who have blazing speed that is negated by a sub-.300 on base average.

These players can have short-term value. However, their stolen base totals are tied so tightly to their "green light" that any change in managerial strategy could completely erase that value. A higher OB mitigates that downside; the good news is that plate patience can be taught.

Players in 2015 who had at least 20 SBs with an OBP less than .300, and whose SB output could be at risk, are Billy Hamilton (57 SB, .274 OBP), Jean Segura (25, 281) and Jake Marisnick (24, .281). Note that Hamilton and Segura are returnees to this list from last year; however, that list contained six names, four of whom did not repeat.

Speed score *(Bill James)*

A measure of the various elements that comprise a runner's speed skills. Although this formula (a variation of James' original version) may be used as a leading indicator for stolen base output, SB attempts are controlled by managerial strategy which makes speed score somewhat less valuable.

Speed score is calculated as the mean value of the following four elements:

1. Stolen base efficiency = *(((SB + 3)/(SB + CS + 7)) - .4) x 20*
2. Stolen base freq. = *Square root of ((SB + CS)/(Singles + BB)) / .07*
3. Triples rating = *(3B / (AB - HR - K))* and the result assigned a value based on the following chart:

< 0.001	0	0.0105	6
0.001	1	0.013	7
0.0023	2	0.0158	8
0.0039	3	0.0189	9
0.0058	4	0.0223+	10
0.008	5		

4. Runs scored as a percentage of times on base = *(((R - HR) / (H + BB - HR)) - .1) / .04*

Speed score index (SX)

(Batter's speed score / League speed score) x 100

Normalized speed scores get a better read on a runner's accomplishment in context. A level of 100 equals league average speed skill. Values more than 100 indicate above average skill, more than 200 represent the Fleet of Feet Elite.

Statistically scouted speed (Spd) *(Ed DeCaria)*

*(104 + {[(Runs–HR+10*age_wt)/(RBI-HR+10)]/lg_av*100} / 5*
*+ {[(3B+5*age_wt)/(2B+3B+5)]/lg_av*100} / 5*
*+ {[(SoftMedGBhits+25*age_wt)/(SoftMedGB+25)]/lg_av*100} / 2*
*- {[Weight (Lbs)/Height (In)^2 * 703]/lg_av*100}*

A skills-based gauge that measures speed without relying on stolen bases. Its components are:

- *(Runs – HR) / (RBI – HR)*: This metric aims to minimize the influence of extra base hit power and team run-scoring rates on perceived speed.
- *3B / (2B + 3B)*: No one can deny that triples are a fast runner's stat; dividing them by 2B+3B instead of all balls in play dampens the power aspect of extra base hits.
- *(Soft + Medium Ground Ball Hits) / (Soft + Medium Ground Balls)*: Faster runners are more likely than slower runners to beat out routine grounders. Hard hit balls are excluded from numerator and denominator.
- *Body Mass Index (BMI)*: Calculated as *Weight (lbs) / Height (in)2 * 703*. All other factors considered, leaner players run faster than heavier ones.

In this book, the formula is scaled as an index with a midpoint of 100.

Stolen base opportunity percent (SBO)

(SB + CS) / (BB + Singles)

A rough approximation of how often a baserunner attempts a stolen base. Provides a comparative measure for players on a given team and, as a team measure, the propensity of a manager to give a "green light" to his runners.

Roto Speed (RSpd)

(Spd x (SBO + SB%))

An adjustment to the measure for raw speed that takes into account a runner's opportunities to steal and his success rate. This stat is intended to provide a more accurate predictive measure of stolen bases for the Mayberry Method.

Stolen base breakout profile *(Bob Berger)*

To find stolen base breakouts (first 30+ steal season in the majors), look for players that:

- are between 22-27 years old
- have 3-7 years of professional (minors and MLB) experience
- have previous steals at the MLB level
- have averaged 20+ SB in previous three seasons (majors and minors combined)
- have at least one professional season of 30+ SB

Overall Performance Analysis

On base plus slugging average (OPS)

A simple sum of the two gauges, it is considered one of the better evaluators of overall performance. OPS combines the two basic elements of offensive production—the ability to get on base (OB) and the ability to advance baserunners (Slg). **BENCHMARKS:** The game's top batters will have OPS levels more than .900. The worst batters will have levels less than .600.

Base Performance Value (BPV)

(Walk rate - 5) x 2)
+ ((Contact rate - 75) x 4)
+ ((Power Index - 80) x 0.8)
+ ((Spd - 80) x 0.3)

A single value that describes a player's overall raw skill level. This is more useful than traditional statistical gauges to track player performance trends and project future statistical output. The BPV formula combines and weights several BPIs.

This formula combines the individual raw skills of batting eye, contact rate, power and speed. **BENCHMARKS:** The best hitters will have a BPV of 50 or greater.

Base Performance Index (BPX)

BPV scaled to league average to account for year-to-year fluctuations in league-wide statistical performance. It's a snapshot of a player's overall skills compared to an average player. **BENCHMARK:** A level of 100 means a player had a league-average BPV in that given season.

Linear weights *(Pete Palmer)*

((Singles x .46) + (Doubles x .8) + (Triples x 1.02)
+ (Home runs x 1.4) + (Walks x .33) + (Stolen Bases x .3)
- (Caught Stealing x .6) - ((At bats - Hits) x Normalizing Factor)

(Also referred to as Batting Runs.) Formula whose premise is that all events in baseball are linear; that is, the output (runs) is directly proportional to the input (offensive events). Each of these events is then weighted according to its relative value in producing runs.

Positive events—hits, walks, stolen bases—have positive values. Negative events—outs, caught stealing—have negative values.

The normalizing factor, representing the value of an out, is an offset to the level of offense in a given year. It changes every season, growing larger in high offense years and smaller in low offense years. The value is about .26 and varies by league.

LW is not included in the player forecast boxes, but the LW concept is used with the linear weighted power gauge.

Runs above replacement (RAR)

An estimate of the number of runs a player contributes above a "replacement level" player. "Replacement" is defined as the level of performance at which another player can easily be found at little or no cost to a team. What constitutes replacement level is a topic that is hotly debated. There are a variety of formulas and rules of thumb used to determine this level for each position (replacement level for a shortstop will be very different from replacement level for an outfielder). Our estimates appear below.

One of the major values of RAR for fantasy applications is that it can be used to assemble an integrated ranking of batters and pitchers for drafting purposes.

To calculate RAR for batters:

- Start with a batter's runs created per game (RC/G).
- Subtract his position's replacement level RC/G.
- Multiply by number of games played: (AB - H + CS) / 25.5.

Replacement levels used in this book:

POS	AL	NL
C	3.18	3.28
1B	4.09	4.30
2B	3.45	3.40
3B	3.71	3.78
SS	3.41	3.18
LF	3.64	3.83
CF	3.78	3.66
RF	3.90	4.03
DH	4.28	

RAR can also be used to calculate rough projected team won-loss records. *(Roger Miller)* Total the RAR levels for all the players on a team, divide by 10 and add to 53 wins.

Runs created *(Bill James)*

(H + BB – CS) x (Total bases + (.55 x SB)) / (AB + BB)

A formula that converts all offensive events into a total of runs scored. As calculated for individual teams, the result approximates a club's actual run total with great accuracy.

Runs created per game (RC/G)

Bill James version: *Runs Created / ((AB - H + CS) / 25.5)*

RC expressed on a per-game basis might be considered the hypothetical ERA compiled against a particular batter. Another way to look at it: A batter with a RC/G of 7.00 would be expected to score 7 runs per game if he were cloned nine times and faced an average pitcher in every at bat. Cloning batters is not a practice we recommend. **BENCHMARKS:** Few players surpass the level of a 10.00 RC/G, but any level more than 7.50 can still be considered very good. At the bottom are levels less than 3.00.

Plate Appearances as a leading indicator *(Patrick Davitt)*

While targeting players "age 26 with experience" as potential breakout candidates has become a commonly accepted concept, a study has found that cumulative plate appearances, especially during the first two years of a young player's career, can also have predictive value in assessing a coming spike in production. Three main conclusions:

- When projecting players, MLB experience is more important than age.
- Players who amass 800+ PAs in their first two seasons are highly likely to have double-digit value in Year 3.
- Also target young players in the season where they attain 400 PAs, as they are twice as likely as other players to grow significantly in value.

Handedness

1. While pure southpaws account for about 27% of total ABs (RHers about 55% and switch-hitters about 18%), they hit 31% of the triples and take 30% of the walks.
2. The average lefty posts a batting average about 10 points higher than the average RHer. The on base averages of pure LHers are nearly 20 points higher than RHers, but only 10 points higher than switch-hitters.
3. LHers tend to have a better batting eye ratio than RHers, but about the same as switch-hitters.
4. Pure righties and lefties have virtually identical power skills. Switch-hitters tend to have less power, on average.
5. Switch-hitters tend to have the best speed, followed by LHers, and then RHers.
6. On an overall production basis, LHers have an 8% advantage over RHers and a 14% edge over switch-hitters.

Skill-specific aging patterns for batters *(Ed DeCaria)*

Baseball forecasters obsess over "peak age" of player performance because we must understand player ascent toward and decline from that peak to predict future value. Most published aging analyses are done using composite estimates of value such as OPS or linear weights. By contrast, fantasy GMs are typically more concerned with category-specific player value (HR, SB, AVG, etc.). We can better forecast what matters most by analyzing peak age of individual baseball skills rather than overall player value.

For batters, recognized peak age for overall batting value is a player's late 20s. But individual skills do not peak uniformly at the same time:

Contact rate (ct%): Ascends modestly by about a half point of contact per year from age 22 to 26, then holds steady within a half point of peak until age 35, after which players lose a half point of contact per year.

Walk rate (bb%): Trends the opposite way with age compared to contact rate, as batters tend to peak at age 30 and largely remain there until they turn 38.

Stolen Base Opportunity (SBO): Typically, players maintain their SBO through age 27, but then reduce their attempts steadily in each remaining year of their careers.

Stolen base success rate (SB%): Aggressive runners (>14% SBO) tend to lose about 2 points per year as they age. However, less aggressive runners (<=14% SBO) actually improve their SB% by about 2 points per year until age 28, after which they reverse course and give back 1-2 pts every year as they age.

GB%/LD%/FB%: Both GB% and LD% peak at the start of a player's career and then decline as many hitters seemingly learn to elevate the ball more. But at about age 30, hitter GB% ascends toward a second late-career peak while LD% continues to plummet and FB% continues to rise through age 38.

Hit rate (h%): Declines linearly with age. This is a natural result of a loss of speed and change in batted ball trajectory.

Isolated Power (ISO): Typically peaks from age 24-26. Similarly, home runs per fly ball, opposite field HR %, and Hard Hit % all peak by age 25 and decline somewhat linearly from that point on.

Catchers and late-career performance spikes *(Ed Spaulding)*

Many catchers—particularly second line catchers—have their best seasons late in their careers. Some possible reasons why:

1. Catchers, like shortstops, often get to the big leagues for defensive reasons and not their offensive skills. These skills take longer to develop.
2. The heavy emphasis on learning the catching/ defense/ pitching side of the game detracts from their time to learn about, and practice, hitting.
3. Injuries often curtail their ability to show offensive skills, though these injuries (typically jammed fingers, bruises on the arms, rib injuries from collisions) often don't lead to time on the disabled list.
4. The time spent behind the plate has to impact the ability to recognize, and eventually hit, all kinds of pitches.

Spring training Slg as leading indicator *(John Dewan)*

A hitter's spring training Slg .200 or more above his lifetime Slg is a leading indicator for a better than normal season.

Overall batting breakout profile *(Brandon Kruse)*

We define a breakout performance as one where a player posts a Roto value of $20+ after having never posted a value of $10. These criteria are used to validate an apparent breakout in the current season but may also be used carefully to project a potential upcoming breakout:

- Age 27 or younger
- An increase in at least two of: h%, PX or Spd
- Minimum league average PX or Spd (100)
- Minimum contact rate of 75%
- Minimum xBA of .270

In-Season Analysis

Batting order facts *(Ed DeCaria)*

Eighty-eight percent of today's leadoff hitters bat leadoff again in their next game, 78% still bat leadoff 10 games later, and 68% still bat leadoff 50 games later. Despite this level of turnover after 50 games, leadoff hitters have the best chance of retaining their role over time. After leadoff, #3 and #4 hitters are the next most likely to retain their lineup slots.

On a season-to-season basis, leadoff hitters are again the most stable, with 69% of last year's primary leadoff hitters retaining the #1 slot next year.

Plate appearances decline linearly by lineup slot. Leadoff batters receive 10-12% more PAs than when batting lower in the lineup. AL #9 batters and NL #8 batters get 9-10% fewer PAs. These results mirror play-by-play data showing a 15-20 PA drop by lineup slot over a full season.

Walk rate is largely unaffected by lineup slot in the AL. Beware strong walk rates by NL #8 hitters, as much of this "skill" will disappear if ever moved from the #8 slot.

Batting order has no discernable effect on contact rate.

Hit rate slopes gently upward as hitters are slotted deeper in the lineup.

As expected, the #3-4-5 slots are ideal for non-HR RBIs, at the expense of #6 hitters. RBIs are worst for players in the #1-2 slots. Batting atop the order sharply increases the probability of scoring runs, especially in the NL.

The leadoff slot easily has the highest stolen base attempt rate. #4-5-6 hitters attempt steals more often when batting out of those slots than they do batting elsewhere. The NL #8 hitter is a SB attempt sink hole. A change in batting order from #8 to #1 in the NL could nearly double a player's SB output due to lineup slot alone.

DOMination and DISaster rates

Week-to-week consistency is measured using a batter's BPV compiled in each week. A player earns a DOMinant week if his BPV was greater or equal to 50 for that week. A player registers a DISaster if his BPV was less than 0 for that week. The percentage of Dominant weeks, DOM%, is simply calculated as the number of DOM weeks divided by the total number of weeks played.

Is week-to-week consistency a repeatable skill? *(Bill Macey)*

To test whether consistent performance is a repeatable skill for batters, we examined how closely related a player's DOM% was from year to year.

YR1 DOM%	AVG YR2 DOM%
< 35%	37%
35%–45%	40%
46%–55%	45%
56%+	56%

Quality/consistency score (QC)

(DOM% – (2 x DIS%)) x 2)

Using the DOM/DIS percentages, this score measures both the quality of performance as well as week–to-week consistency.

Sample size reliability *(Russell Carleton)*

At what point during the season do stats become reliable indicators of skill? Measured in PA *(unlisted=did not stablize over full season)*:

100: Contact rate
150: Strikeout rate, line drive rate, pitches/PA
200: Walk rate, ground ball rate, GB/FB
250: Fly ball rate
300: HR rate, hr/f
500: OBP, Slg, OPS
550: Isolated power

Projecting RBIs *(Patrick Davitt)*

Evaluating players in-season for RBI potential is a function of the interplay among four factors:

- Teammates' ability to reach base ahead of him and to run the bases efficiently
- His own ability to drive them in by hitting, especially XBH
- Number of Games Played
- Place in the batting order

3-4-5 Hitters:
(0.69 x GP x TOB) + (0.30 x ITB) + (0.275 x HR) – (.191 x GP)

6-7-8 Hitters:
(0.63 x GP x TOB) + (0.27 x ITB) + (0.250 x HR) – (.191 x GP)

9-1-2 Hitters:
(0.57 x GP x TOB) + (0.24 x ITB) + (0.225 x HR) – (.191 x GP)

...where *GP = games played, TOB = team on-base pct.* and *ITB = individual total bases (ITB).*

Apply this pRBI formula after 70 games played or so (to reduce the variation from small sample size) to find players more than 9 RBIs over or under their projected RBI. There could be a correction coming.

You should also consider other factors, like injury or trade (involving the player or a top-of-the-order speedster) or team SB philosophy and success rate.

Remember: the player himself has an impact on his TOB. When we first did this study, we excluded the player from his TOB and got better results. The formula overestimates projected RBI for players with high OBP who skew his teams' OBP but can't benefit in RBI from that effect.

Ten-Game hitting streaks as a leading indicator *(Bob Berger)*

Research of hitting streaks from 2011 and 2012 showed that a 10-game streak can reliably predict improved longer-term BA performance during the season. A player who has put together a hitting streak of at least 10 games will improve his BA for the remainder of the season about 60% of the time. This improvement can be significant, on average as much as .020 of BA.

Other Diamonds

It's a Busy World Shortcut

For marginal utility-type players, scan their PX and Spd history to see if there's anything to mine for. If you see triple digits anywhere, stop and look further. If not, move on.

Chronology of the Classic Free-Swinger with Pop

1. Gets off to a good start.
2. Thinks he's in a groove.
3. Gets lax, careless.
4. Pitchers begin to catch on.
5. Fades down the stretch.

Errant Gust of Wind

A unit of measure used to describe the difference between your home run projection and mine.

Hannahan Concession

Players with a .218 BA rarely get 500 plate appearances, but when they do, it's usually once.

Mendoza Line

Named for Mario Mendoza, it represents the benchmark for batting futility. Usually refers to a .200 batting average, but can also be used for low levels of other statistical categories. Note that Mendoza's lifetime batting average was actually a much more robust .215.

Old Player Skills

Power, low batting average, no speed and usually good plate patience. Young players, often those with a larger frame, who possess these "old player skills" tend to decline faster than normal, often in their early 30s.

Small Sample Certitude

If players' careers were judged based what they did in a single game performance, then Tuffy Rhodes and Mark Whiten would be in the Hall of Fame.

Esix Snead List

Players with excellent speed and sub-.300 on base averages who get a lot of practice running down the line to first base, and then back to the dugout. Also used as an adjective, as in "Esix-Sneadian."

Pitchers

Strikeouts and Walks

Fundamental skills

Unreliable pitching performance is a fallacy driven by the practice of attempting to project pitching stats using gauges that are poor evaluators of skill.

How can we better evaluate pitching skill? We can start with the three statistical categories that are generally unaffected by external factors. These three stats capture the outcome of an individual pitcher versus batter match-up without regard to supporting offense, defense or bullpen:

Walks Allowed, Strikeouts and Ground Balls

Even with only these stats to observe, there is a wealth of insight that these measures can provide.

Control rate (Ctl, bb/9), or opposition walks per game

BB allowed x 9 / IP

Measures how many walks a pitcher allows per game equivalent. **BENCHMARK:** The best pitchers will have bb/9 of 2.8 or less.

Dominance rate (Dom, k/9), or opposition strikeouts/game

Strikeouts recorded x 9 / IP

Measures how many strikeouts a pitcher allows per game equivalent. **BENCHMARK:** The best pitchers will have k/9 levels of 7.0 or higher.

Command ratio (Cmd)

(Strikeouts / Walks)

A measure of a pitcher's ability to get the ball over the plate. There is no more fundamental a skill than this, and so it is used as a leading indicator to project future rises and falls in other gauges, such as ERA. **BENCHMARKS:** Baseball's best pitchers will have ratios in excess of 3.0. Pitchers with ratios less than 1.0—indicating that they walk more batters than they strike out—have virtually no potential for long-term success. If you make no other changes in your approach to drafting pitchers, limiting your focus to only pitchers with a command ratio of 2.5 or better will substantially improve your odds of success.

Command ratio as a leading indicator

The ability to get the ball over the plate—command of the strike zone—is one of the best leading indicators for future performance. Command ratio (K/BB) can be used to project potential in ERA as well as other skills gauges.

1. Research indicates that there is a high correlation between a pitcher's Cmd ratio and his ERA.

	Earned Run Average				
Command	2011	2012	2013	2014	2015
0.0 - 1.0	5.45	6.22	5.98	6.81	6.31
1.1 - 1.5	4.84	5.03	4.91	4.97	5.23
1.6 - 2.0	4.35	4.48	4.42	4.37	4.54
2.1 - 2.5	3.89	4.09	3.96	3.80	4.19
2.6 - 3.0	3.66	3.88	3.81	3.78	3.87
3.1 - 3.5	3.58	3.67	3.46	3.43	3.51
3.6 - 4.0	3.00	3.34	3.32	3.16	3.56
4.1+	2.95	3.12	2.86	2.92	3.07

On the pitching flipside, the number of arms comprising the 4.1+ group has nearly doubled since 2012. That year, 58 pitchers made up this group; in 2014 there were 93 and 90 this year.

We can create percentage plays for the different levels:

For Cmd	% with ERA of	
Levels of	3.50-	4.50+
0.0 - 1.0	0%	87%
1.1 - 1.5	7%	67%
1.6 - 2.0	7%	57%
2.1 - 2.5	19%	35%
2.6 - 3.0	26%	25%
3.1 +	53%	5%

Pitchers who maintain a Cmd over 2.5 have a high probability of long-term success. For fantasy drafting purposes, it is best to avoid pitchers with sub-2.0 ratios. Avoid bullpen closers if they have a ratio less than 2.5.

2. A pitcher's Command in tandem with Dominance (strikeout rate) provides even greater predictive abilities.

	Earned Run Average	
Command	-5.6 Dom	5.6+ Dom
0.0-0.9	5.36	5.99
1.0-1.4	4.94	5.03
1.5-1.9	4.67	4.47
2.0-2.4	4.32	4.08
2.5-2.9	4.21	3.88
3.0-3.9	4.04	3.46
4.0+	4.12	2.96

This helps to highlight the limited upside potential of soft-tossers with pinpoint control. The extra dominance makes a huge difference.

3. Research also suggests that there is a strong correlation between a pitcher's command ratio and his propensity to win ballgames. Over three quarters of those with ratios over 3.0 post winning records, and the collective W/L record of those command artists is nearly .600.

The command/winning correlation holds up in both leagues, although the effect was more pronounced in the NL. Over four times more NL hurlers than AL hurlers had Cmd over 3.0, and higher ratios were required in the NL to maintain good winning percentages. A ratio between 2.0 and 2.9 was good enough for a winning record for over 70% of AL pitchers, but that level in the NL generated an above-.500 mark slightly more than half the time.

In short, in order to have at least a 70% chance of drafting a pitcher with a winning record, you must target NL pitchers with at least a 3.0 command ratio. To achieve the same odds in the AL, a 2.0 command ratio will suffice.

Swinging strike rate as leading indicator *(Stephen Nickrand)*

An emerging indicator for predicting starting pitching performance is swinging strike rate (SwK%), which measures the percentage of total pitches against which a batter swings and misses. SwK% can help us validate and forecast a SP's Dominance (K/9) rate, which in turn allows us to identify surgers and faders with greater accuracy.

Follow these rules of thumb when targeting starting pitchers based on SwK%: SwK% baselines for SP are 8.0% in AL, 8.4% in

NL; Expected Dom (xDom) can be estimated from SwK%; and a pitcher's individual SwK% does not regress to league norms.

The few starters per year who have a 12.0% or higher SwK% are near-locks to have a 9.0 Dom or greater. In contrast, starters with a 7.0% or lower SwK% have nearly no chance at posting even an average Dom. Finally, use an 8.5% SwK% as an acceptable threshold when searching for SP based on this metric; raise it to 9.5% to begin to find SwK% difference-makers.

Fastball velocity and Dominance rate *(Stephen Nickrand)*

It is intuitive that an increase in fastball velocity for starting pitchers leads to more strikeouts. But how much? We analyzed the historical link between fastball velocity and Dominance (K/9) rate. Among the findings:

The vast majority of SP with significant fastball velocity gains

- experience a significant Dom gain during the same season.
- are likely to give back those gains during the following season.
- are likely to increase their Dom the following season, but the magnitude of the Dom increase usually is small.

The vast majority of SP with significant fastball velocity losses

- are likely to experience a significant Dom decrease during the same season.

Those SP with significant fastball velocity losses from one season to the next are just as likely to experience a fastball velocity or Dom increase as they are to experience a fastball or Dom decrease, and the amounts of the increase/decrease are nearly identical.

First-pitch strike rate as leading indicator *(Stephen Nickrand)*

The measurement of a pitcher's rate of first-pitch strikes (FpK%) can help us validate and forecast a pitcher's Control (BB/9) rate. As first-pitch strike rate increases, walks are very likely to go down, and WHIP will follow. As it goes up, walks are likely to increase, as will WHIP. So if you're wondering if a pitcher's newfound good control is likely to hold, check out his FpK%.

The FpK% baseline is 60% for starting pitchers and does not vary significantly by league. Expected Ctl (xCtl) can be estimated from FpK%, and a starting pitcher's individual FpK% does not regress to league norms. **BENCHMARKS:** Elite pitchers will have a FpK% above 68% and most of them will have a Ctl below 2.0. Avoid pitchers with a FpK% below 55%, as they are likely to have a Ctl at or above 4.0.

Power/contact rating

(BB + K) / IP

Measures the level by which a pitcher allows balls to be put into play. In general, extreme power pitchers can be successful even with poor defensive teams. Power pitchers tend to have greater longevity in the game. Contact pitchers with poor defenses behind them are high risks to have poor W-L records and ERA. **BENCHMARKS:** A level of 1.13+ describes pure throwers. A level of .93 or less describes high contact pitchers.

Balls in Play

Balls in play (BIP)

(Batters faced – (BB + HBP + SAC)) + H – K

The total number of batted balls that are hit fair, both hits and outs. An analysis of how these balls are hit—on the ground, in the air, hits, outs, etc.—can provide analytical insight, from player skill levels to the impact of luck on statistical output.

Batting average on balls in play *(Voros McCracken)*

(H – HR) / (Batters faced – (BB + HBP + SAC)) + H – K – HR

Abbreviated as BABIP; also called hit rate (H%). The percent of balls hit into the field of play that fall for hits. **BENCHMARK:** The league average is 30%, which is also the level that individual performances will regress to on a year to year basis. Any +/- variance of 3% or more can affect a pitcher's ERA.

BABIP as a leading indicator *(Voros McCracken)*

In 2000, Voros McCracken published a study that concluded that "there is little if any difference among major league pitchers in their ability to prevent hits on balls hit in the field of play." His assertion was that, while a Johan Santana would have a better ability to prevent a batter from getting wood on a ball, or perhaps keeping the ball in the park, once that ball was hit in the field of play, the probability of it falling for a hit was virtually no different than for any other pitcher.

Among the findings in his study were:

- There is little correlation between what a pitcher does one year in the stat and what he will do the next. This is not true with other significant stats (BB, K, HR).
- You can better predict a pitcher's hits per balls in play from the rate of the rest of the pitcher's team than from the pitcher's own rate.

This last point brings a team's defense into the picture. It begs the question, when a batter gets a hit, is it because the pitcher made a bad pitch, the batter took a good swing, or the defense was not positioned correctly?

Pitchers will often post hit rates per balls-in-play that are far off from the league average, but then revert to the mean the following year. As such, we can use that mean to project the direction of a pitcher's ERA.

Subsequent research has shown that ground ball or fly ball propensity has some impact on this rate.

Hit rate *(See Batting average on balls in play)*

Opposition batting average (OBA)

Hits allowed / (Batters faced – (BB + HBP + SAC))

The batting average achieved by opposing batters against a pitcher. **BENCHMARKS:** The best pitchers will have levels less than .250; the worst pitchers levels more than .300.

Opposition on base average (OOB)

(Hits allowed + BB) / ((Batters faced – (BB + HBP + SAC)) + Hits allowed + BB)

The on base average achieved by opposing batters against a pitcher. **BENCHMARK:** The best pitchers will have levels less than .300; the worst pitchers levels more than .375.

Walks plus hits divided by innings pitched (WHIP)

Essentially the same measure as opposition on base average, but used for Rotisserie purposes. **BENCHMARKS:** A WHIP of less than 1.20 is considered top level; more than 1.50 indicative of poor performance. Levels less than 1.00—allowing fewer runners than IP—represent extraordinary performance and are rarely maintained over time.

Ground ball, line drive, fly ball percentage (G/L/F)

The percentage of all balls-in-play that are hit on the ground, in the air and as line drives. For a pitcher, the ability to keep the ball on the ground can contribute to his statistical output exceeding his demonstrated skill level.

Ground ball tendency as a leading indicator *(John Burnson)*

Ground ball pitchers tend to give up fewer HRs than do fly ball pitchers. There is also evidence that GB pitchers have higher hit rates. In other words, a ground ball has a higher chance of being a hit than does a fly ball that is not out of the park.

GB pitchers have lower strikeout rates. We should be more forgiving of a low strikeout rate (under 5.5 K/9) if it belongs to an extreme ground ball pitcher.

GB pitchers have a lower ERA but a higher WHIP than do fly ball pitchers. On balance, GB pitchers come out ahead, even when considering strikeouts, because a lower ERA also leads to more wins.

Groundball and strikeout tendencies as indicators

(Mike Dranchak)

Pitchers were assembled into 9 groups based on the following profiles (minimum 23 starts in 2005):

Profile	Ground Ball Rate
Ground Ball	higher than 47%
Neutral	42% to 47%
Fly Ball	less than 42%

Profile	Strikeout Rate (k/9)
Strikeout	higher than 6.6 k/9
Average	5.4 to 6.6 k/9
Soft-Tosser	less than 5.4 k/9

Findings: Pitchers with higher strikeout rates had better ERAs and WHIPs than pitchers with lower strikeout rates, regardless of ground ball profile. However, for pitchers with similar strikeout rates, those with higher ground ball rates had better ERAs and WHIPs than those with lower ground ball rates.

Pitchers with higher strikeout rates tended to strand more baserunners than those with lower K rates. Fly ball pitchers tended to strand fewer runners than their GB or neutral counterparts within their strikeout profile.

Ground ball pitchers (especially those who lacked high-dominance) yielded more home runs per fly ball than did fly ball pitchers. However, the ERA risk was mitigated by the fact that ground ball pitchers (by definition) gave up fewer fly balls to begin with.

Extreme GB/FB pitchers *(Patrick Davitt)*

Among pitchers with normal strikeout levels, extreme GB pitchers (>3–7% of all batters faced) have ERAs about 0.4 runs lower than normal-GB% pitchers but only slight WHIP advantages. Extreme FB% pitchers (32% FB) show no ERA benefits.

Among High-K (>=24% of BF), however, extreme GBers have ERAs about 0.5 runs lower than normal-GB pitchers, and WHIPs about five points lower. Extreme FB% pitchers have ERAs about 0.2 runs lower than normal-FB pitchers, and WHIPs about 10 points lower.

Revisting Flyballs *(Jason Collette)*

The increased emphasis on defensive positioning is often associated with infield shifting, but the same data also influences how outfielders are positioned. Some managers are positioning OFs more aggressively than just the customary few steps per a right- or left-handed swinging batter. BaseballHQ.com found that five of the top 10 defensive efficiency teams in 2013 —OAK, STL, MIA, LAA and KC—also had parks among the top 10 in HR suppression.

Before dismissing flyball pitchers as toxic assets, pay more attention to park factors and OF defensive talent. In particular, be a little more willing to roster fly ball pitchers who pitch both in front of good defensive OFs and in good pitchers' parks.

Line drive percentage as a leading indicator *(Seth Samuels)*

Also beyond a pitcher's control is the percentage of balls-in-play that are line drives. Line drives do the most damage; from 1994-2003, here were the expected hit rates and number of total bases per type of BIP.

	Type of BIP		
	GB	FB	LD
H%	26%	23%	56%
Total bases	0.29	0.57	0.80

Despite the damage done by LDs, pitchers do not have any innate skill to avoid them. There is little relationship between a pitcher's LD% one year and his rate the next year. All rates tend to regress towards a mean of 22.6%.

However, GB pitchers do have a slight ability to prevent LDs (21.7%) and extreme GB hurlers even moreso (18.5%). Extreme FB pitchers have a slight ability to prevent LDs (21.1%) as well.

Home run to fly ball rate (hr/f)

HR / FB

The percent of fly balls that are hit for home runs.

hr/f as a leading indicator *(John Burnson)*

McCracken's work focused on "balls in play," omitting home runs from the study. However, pitchers also do not have much control over the percentage of fly balls that turn into HR. Research shows that there is an underlying rate of HR as a percentage of fly balls of about 10%. A pitcher's HR/FB rate will vary each year but always tends to regress to that 10%. The element that pitchers do have control over is the number of fly balls they allow. That is the underlying skill or deficiency that controls their HR rate.

Pitchers who keep the ball out of the air more often correlate well with Roto value.

Opposition home runs per game (hr/9)

(HR Allowed x 9 / IP)

Also, expected opposition HR rate = (FB x 0.10) x 9 / IP

Measures how many HR a pitcher allows per game equivalent. Since FB tend to go yard at about a 10% rate, we can also estimate this rate off of fly balls. **BENCHMARK:** The best pitchers will have hr/9 levels of less than 1.0.

Runs

Expected earned run average (xERA)

Gill and Reeve version: *(.575 x H [per 9 IP]) + (.94 x HR [per 9 IP]) + (.28 x BB [per 9 IP]) – (.01 x K [per 9 IP]) – Normalizing Factor*

John Burnson version (used in this book):

(xER x 9)/IP, where xER is defined as

xER% x (FB/10) + (1-xS%) x [0.3 x (BIP – FB/10) + BB]

where xER% = 0.96 – (0.0284 x (GB/FB))

and

xS% = (64.5 + (K/9 x 1.2) – (BB/9 x (BB/9 + 1)) / 20)

+ ((0.0012 x (GB%^2)) – (0.001 x GB%) - 2.4)

xERA represents the an equivalent of what a pitcher's real ERA might be, calculated solely with skills-based measures. It is not influenced by situation-dependent factors.

Expected ERA variance

xERA – ERA

The variance between a pitcher's ERA and his xERA is a measure of over or underachievement. A positive variance indicates the potential for a pitcher's ERA to rise. A negative variance indicates the potential for ERA improvement. **BENCHMARK:** Discount variances that are less than 0.50. Any variance more than 1.00 (one run per game) is regarded as a indicator of future change.

Projected xERA or projected ERA?

Which should we be using to forecast a pitcher's ERA? Projected xERA is more accurate for looking ahead on a purely skills basis. Projected ERA includes *situation-dependent* events—bullpen support, park factors, etc.—which are reflected better by ERA. The optimal approach is to use both gauges as *a range of expectation* for forecasting purposes.

Strand rate (S%)

(H + BB – ER) / (H + BB – HR)

Measures the percentage of allowed runners a pitcher strands (earned runs only), which incorporates both individual pitcher skill and bullpen effectiveness. **BENCHMARKS:** The most adept at stranding runners will have S% levels over 75%. Those with rates over 80% will have artificially low ERAs which will be prone to relapse. Levels below 65% will inflate ERA but have a high probability of regression.

Expected strand rate *(Michael Weddell)*

*73.935 + K/9 - 0.116 * (BB/9*(BB/9+1))*

*+ (0.0047 * GB%^2 - 0.3385 * GB%)*

+ (MAX(2,MIN(4,IP/G))/2-1)

+ (0.82 if left-handed)

This formula is based on three core skills: strikeouts per nine innings, walks per nine innings, and groundballs per balls in play, with adjustments for whether the pitcher is a starter or reliever (measured by IP/G), and his handedness.

Strand rate as a leading indicator *(Ed DeCaria)*

Strand rate often regresses/rebounds toward past rates (usually 69-74%), resulting in Year 2 ERA changes:

% of Pitchers with Year 2 Regression/Rebound

Y1 S%	RP	SP	LR
<60%	100%	94%	94%
65	81%	74%	88%
70	53%	48%	65%
75	55%	85%	100%
80	80%	100%	100%
85	100%	100%	100%

Typical ERA Regression/Rebound in Year 2

Y1 S%	RP	SP	LR
<60%	-2.54	-2.03	-2.79
65	-1.00	-0.64	-0.93
70	-0.10	-0.05	-0.44
75	0.24	0.54	0.75
80	1.15	1.36	2.29
85	1.71	2.21	n/a

Starting pitchers (SP) have a narrower range of strand rate outcomes than do relievers (RP) or swingmen/long relievers (LR). **Relief pitchers** with Y1 strand rates of <=67% or >=78% are likely to experience a +/- ERA regression in Y2. **Starters and swingmen/long relievers** with Y1 strand rates of <=65% or >=75% are likely to experience a +/- ERA regression in Y2. Pitchers with strand rates that deviate more than a few points off of their individual expected strand rates are likely to experience some degree of ERA regression in Y2. Over-performing (or "lucky") pitchers are more likely than underperforming (or "unlucky") pitchers to see such a correction.

Wins

Projecting/chasing wins

There are five events that need to occur in order for a pitcher to post a single win...

1. He must pitch well, allowing few runs.
2. The offense must score enough runs.
3. The defense must successfully field all batted balls.
4. The bullpen must hold the lead.
5. The manager must leave the pitcher in for 5 innings, and not remove him if the team is still behind.

Of these five events, only one is within the control of the pitcher. As such, projecting or chasing wins based on skills alone can be an exercise in futility.

Home field advantage *(John Burnson)*

A 2006 study found that home starting pitchers get credited with a win in 38% of their outings. Visiting team starters are credited with a win in 33% of their outings.

Usage

Batters faced per game *(Craig Wright)*

((Batters faced – (BB + HBP + SAC)) + H + BB) / G

A measure of pitcher usage and one of the leading indicators for potential pitcher burnout.

Workload

Research suggests that there is a finite number of innings in a pitcher's arm. This number varies by pitcher, by development cycle, and by pitching style and repertoire. We can measure a pitcher's potential for future arm problems and/or reduced effectiveness (burnout):

Sharp increases in usage from one year to the next. Common wisdom has suggested that pitchers who significantly increase their workload from one year to the next are candidates for burnout symptoms. This has often been called the Verducci Effect, after writer Tom Verducci. BaseballHQ.com analyst Michael Weddell tested pitchers with sharp workload increases during the period 1988-2008 and found that no such effect exists.

Starters' overuse. Consistent "batters faced per game" (BF/G) levels of 28.0 or higher, combined with consistent seasonal IP totals of 200 or more may indicate burnout potential, especially with pitchers younger than 25. Within a season, a BF/G of more than 30.0 with a projected IP total of 200 may indicate a late season fade.

Relievers' overuse. Warning flags should be up for relievers who post in excess of 100 IP in a season, while averaging fewer than 2 IP per outing.

When focusing solely on minor league pitchers, research results are striking:

Stamina: Virtually every minor league pitcher who had a BF/G of 28.5 or more in one season experienced a drop-off in BF/G the following year. Many were unable to ever duplicate that previous level of durability.

Performance: Most pitchers experienced an associated drop-off in their BPVs in the years following the 28.5 BF/G season. Some were able to salvage their effectiveness later on by moving to the bullpen.

Protecting young pitchers *(Craig Wright)*

There is a link between some degree of eventual arm trouble and a history of heavy workloads in a pitcher's formative years. Some recommendations from this research:

Teenagers (A-ball): No 200 IP seasons and no BF/G over 28.5 in any 150 IP span. No starts on three days rest.

Ages 20-22: Average no more than 105 pitches per start with a single game ceiling of 130 pitches.

Ages 23-24: Average no more than 110 pitches per start with a single game ceiling of 140 pitches.

When possible, a young starter should be introduced to the majors in long relief before he goes into the rotation.

Overall Performance Analysis

Base Performance Value (BPV)

((Dominance Rate - 5.0) x 18)
+ ((4.0 - Walk Rate) x 27))
+ (Ground ball rate as a whole number - 40%)

A single value that describes a player's overall raw skill level. This is more useful than traditional statistical gauges to track player performance trends and project future statistical output. The formula combines the individual raw skills of power, control and the ability to keep the ball down in the zone, all characteristics that are unaffected by most external factors. In tandem with a pitcher's strand rate, it provides a more complete picture of the elements that contribute to ERA, and therefore serves as an accurate tool to project likely changes in ERA. **BENCHMARKS:** A BPV of 50 is the minimum level required for long-term success. The elite of the bullpen aces will have BPVs in excess of 100 and it is rare for these stoppers to enjoy long term success with consistent levels under 75.

Base Performance Index (BPX)

BPV scaled to league average to account for year-to-year fluctuations in league-wide statistical performance. It's a snapshot of a player's overall skills compared to an average player. **BENCHMARK:** A level of 100 means a player had a league-average BPV in that given season.

Runs above replacement (RAR)

An estimate of the number of runs a player contributes above a "replacement level" player.

Batters create runs; pitchers save runs. But are batters and pitchers who have comparable RAR levels truly equal in value? Pitchers might be considered to have higher value. Saving an additional run is more important than producing an additional run. A pitcher who throws a shutout is guaranteed to win that game, whereas no matter how many runs a batter produces, his team can still lose given poor pitching support.

To calculate RAR for pitchers:

1. Start with the replacement level league ERA.
2. Subtract the pitcher's ERA. (To calculate projected RAR, use the pitcher's xERA.)
3. Multiply by number of games played, calculated as plate appearances (IP x 4.34) divided by 38.
4. Multiply the resulting RAR level by 1.08 to account for the variance between earned runs and total runs.

Handedness

1. LHers tend to peak about a year after RHers.
2. LHers post only 15% of the total saves. Typically, LHers are reserved for specialist roles so few are frontline closers.
3. RHers have slightly better command and HR rate.
4. There is no significant variance in ERA.
5. On an overall skills basis, RHers have ~6% advantage.

Skill-Specific Aging Patterns for Pitchers *(Ed DeCaria)*

Baseball forecasters obsess over "peak age" of player performance because we must understand player ascent toward and decline from that peak to predict future value. Most published aging analyses are done using composite estimates of value such as OPS or linear weights. By contrast, fantasy GMs are typically more concerned with category-specific player value (K, ERA, WHIP, etc.). We can better forecast what matters most by analyzing peak age of individual baseball skills rather than overall player value.

For pitchers, prior research has shown that pitcher value peaks somewhere in the late 20s to early 30s. But how does aging affect each demonstrable pitching skill?

Strikeout rate (k/9): Declines fairly linearly beginning at age 25.

Walk rate (bb/9): Improves until age 25 and holds somewhat steady until age 29, at which point it begins to steadily worsen. Deteriorating k/9 and bb/9 rates result in inefficiency, as it requires far more pitches to get an out. For starting pitchers, this affects the ability to pitch deep into games.

Innings Pitched per game (IP/G): Among starters, it improves slightly until age 27, then tails off considerably with age, costing pitchers nearly one full IP/G by age 33 and one more by age 39.

Hit rate (H%): Among pitchers, H% appears to increase slowly but steadily as pitchers age, to the tune of .002-.003 points per year.

Strand rate (S%): Very similar to hit rate, except strand rate decreases with age rather than increasing. GB%/LD%/FB%: Line drives increase steadily from age 24 onward, and outfield flies increase beginning at age 31. Because 70%+ of line drives fall for hits, and 10%+ of fly balls become home runs, this spells trouble for aging pitchers.

Home runs per fly ball (hr/f): As each year passes, a higher percentage of a pitcher's fly balls become home runs allowed increases with age.

Catchers' effect on pitching *(Thomas Hanrahan)*

A typical catcher handles a pitching staff better after having been with a club for a few years. Research has shown that there is an improvement in team ERA of approximately 0.37 runs from a catcher's rookie season to his prime years with a club. Expect a pitcher's ERA to be higher than expected if he is throwing to a rookie backstop.

First productive season *(Michael Weddell)*

To find those starting pitchers who are about to post their first productive season in the majors (10 wins, 150 IP, ERA of 4.00 or less), look for:

- Pitchers entering their age 23-26 seasons, especially those about to pitch their age 25 season.
- Pitchers who already have good skills, shown by an xERA in the prior year of 4.25 or less.
- Pitchers coming off of at least a partial season in the majors without a major health problem.
- To the extent that one speculates on pitchers who are one skill away, look for pitchers who only need to improve their control (bb/9).

Overall pitching breakout profile *(Brandon Kruse)*

A breakout performance is defined here as one where a player posts a Rotisserie value of $20 or higher after having never acheived $10 previously. These criteria are primarily used to validate an apparent breakout in the current season but may also be used carefully to project a potential breakout for an upcoming season.

- Age 27 or younger
- Minimum 5.6 Dom, 2.0 Cmd, 1.1 hr/9 and 50 BPV
- Maximum 30% hit rate
- Minimum 71% strand rate
- Starters should have a H% no greater than the previous year; relievers should show improved command
- Maximum xERA of 4.00

Career year drop-off *(Rick Wilton)*

Research shows that a pitcher's post-career year drop-off, on average, looks like this:

- ERA increases by 1.00
- WHIP increases by 0.14.
- Nearly 6 fewer wins

Pitchers crossing leagues *(Bob Berger)*

The AL has higher league-wide ERA and lower K/9 when compared to the NL. Fantasy owners should consider adjusting their ERA, WHIP, and K/9 expectations for pitchers moving to the "other" league. Pitchers moving to the NL may perform better than expected based on their recent career trends; pitchers moving to the AL may perform worse than expected.

Closers

Saves

There are six events that need to occur in order for a relief pitcher to post a single save:

1. The starting pitcher and middle relievers must pitch well.
2. The offense must score enough runs.
3. It must be a reasonably close game.
4. The manager must put the pitcher in for a save opportunity.
5. The pitcher must pitch well and hold the lead.
6. The manager must let him finish the game.

Of these six events, only one is within the control of the relief pitcher. As such, projecting saves for a reliever has little to do with skill and a lot to do with opportunity. However, pitchers with excellent skills may create opportunity for themselves.

Saves conversion rate (Sv%)

Saves / Save Opportunities

The percentage of save opportunities that are successfully converted. **BENCHMARK:** We look for a minimum 80% for long-term success.

Leverage index (LI) *(Tom Tango)*

Leverage index measures the amount of swing in the possible change in win probability indexed against an average value of 1.00. Thus, relievers who come into games in various situations create a composite score and if that average score is higher than 1.00, then their manager is showing enough confidence in them to try to win games with them. If the average score is below 1.00, then the manager is using them, but not showing nearly as much confidence that they can win games.

Saves chances and wins *(Patrick Davitt)*

Some fantasy owners think that good teams get more saves because they generate more wins. Other owners think that poor teams get more saves because more of their wins are by narrow margins. The "good-team" side is probably on firmer ground, though there are enough exceptions that we should be cautious about drawing broad inferences.

The 2014 study confirmed what Craig Neuman found years earlier: The argument "more wins leads to more saves" is generally correct. Over five studied seasons, the percentage of wins that were saved (Sv%W) was about 50%, and half of all team-seasons fell in the Sv%W range of 48%-56%. As a result, high-saves seasons were more common for high-win teams.

That wins-saves connection for individual team-seasons was much less solid, however, and we observed many outliers. Data for individual team-seasons showed wide ranges of both Sv%W and actual saves.

Finally, higher-win teams do indeed get more blowout wins, but while poorer teams had a higher percentage (73%) of close wins (three runs or fewer) than better teams (56%), good teams' higher number of wins meant they still had more close wins, more save opportunities and more saves, again with many outliers among individual team-seasons.

Origin of closers

History has long maintained that ace closers are not easily recognizable early on in their careers, so that every season does see its share of the unexpected. Shawn Tolleson, A.J. Ramos, Roberto Osuna, Ken Giles, Carson Smith, Wade Davis, Brad Ziegler... who would have thought it a year ago?

Accepted facts, all of which have some element of truth:

- You cannot find major league closers from pitchers who were closers in the minors.
- Closers begin their careers as starters.
- Closers are converted set-up men.
- Closers are pitchers who were unable to develop a third effective pitch.

More simply, closers are a product of circumstance.

Are the minor leagues a place to look at all?

From 1990-2004, there were 280 twenty-save seasons in Double-A and Triple-A, accomplished by 254 pitchers.

Of those 254, only 46 ever made it to the majors at all.

Of those 46, only 13 ever saved 20 games in a season.

Of those 13, only 5 ever posted more than one 20-save season in the majors: John Wetteland, Mark Wohlers, Ricky Bottalico, Braden Looper and Francisco Cordero.

Five out of 254 pitchers, over 15 years—a rate of 2%.

One of the reasons that minor league closers rarely become major league closers is because, in general, they do not get enough innings in the minors to sufficiently develop their arms into big-league caliber.

In fact, organizations do not look at minor league closing performance seriously, assigning that role to pitchers who they do not see as legitimate prospects. The average age of minor league closers over the past decade has been 27.5.

Elements of saves success

The task of finding future closing potential comes down to looking at two elements:

Talent: The raw skills to mow down hitters for short periods of time. Optimal BPVs over 100, but not under 75.

Opportunity: The more important element, yet the one that pitchers have no control over.

There are pitchers that have Talent, but not Opportunity. These pitchers are not given a chance to close for a variety of reasons (e.g. being blocked by a solid front-liner in the pen, being left-handed, etc.), but are good to own because they will not likely hurt your pitching staff. You just can't count on them for saves, at least not in the near term.

There are pitchers that have Opportunity, but not Talent. MLB managers decide who to give the ball to in the 9th inning based on their own perceptions about what skills are required to succeed, even if those perceived "skills" don't translate into acceptable metrics.

Those pitchers without the metrics may have some initial short-term success, but their long-term prognosis is poor and they are high risks to your roster. Classic examples of the short life span of these types of pitchers include Matt Karchner, Heath Slocumb, Ryan Kohlmeier, Dan Miceli, Joe Borowski and Danny Kolb. More recent examples include Tom Wilhelmsen, Kevin Gregg and Jim Johnson.

Closers' job retention *(Michael Weddell)*

Of pitchers with 20 or more saves in one year, only 67.5% of these closers earned 20 or more saves the following year. The variables that best predicted whether a closer would avoid this attrition:

- *Saves history:* Career saves was the most important factor.
- *Age:* Closers are most likely to keep their jobs at age 27. For long-time closers, their growing career saves totals more than offset the negative impact of their advanced ages. Older closers without a long history of racking up saves tend to be bad candidates for retaining their roles.
- *Performance:* Actual performance, measured by ERA+, was of only minor importance.
- *Being right-handed:* Increased the odds of retaining the closer's role by 9% over left-handers.

How well can we predict which closers will keep their jobs? Of the 10 best closers during 1989-2007, 90% saved at least 20 games during the following season. Of the 10 worst bets, only 20% saved at least 20 games the next year.

Closer volatility history

Year	Closers Drafted	Avg R$	Closers Failed	Failure %	New Sources
2008	32	$17.78	10	31%	11
2009	28	$17.56	9	32%	13
2010	28	$16.96	7	25%	13
2011	30	$15.47	11	37%	8
2012	29	$15.28	19	66%	18
2013	29	$15.55	9	31%	13
2014	28	$15.54	11	39%	15
2015	29	$14.79	13	45%	16

Drafted refers to the number of saves sources purchased in both LABR and Tout Wars experts leagues each year. These only include relievers drafted for at least $10*, specifically for saves speculation. *Avg R$* refers to the average purchase price of these pitchers in the AL-only and NL-only leagues. *Failed* is the number (and percentage) of saves sources drafted that did not return at least 50% of their value that year. The failures include those that lost their value due to ineffectiveness, injury or managerial decision. *New Sources* are arms that were drafted for less than $10 (if drafted at all) but finished with at least double-digit saves.

The failed saves investments in 2015 were Cody Allen, Joaquin Benoit, Brett Cecil, Steve Cishek, Sean Doolittle, Neftali Feliz, Greg Holland, Jenrry Mejia, Joe Nathan, Glen Perkins, Addison Reed, Fernando Rodney and Drew Storen. The new sources in 2015 were John Axford, Santiago Casilla, Wade Davis, Jeurys Famila, Ken Giles, Jason Grilli, Kevin Jepsen, Jim Johnson, Andrew Miller, Roberto Osuna, A.J. Ramos, Carson Smith, Joakim Soria, Shawn Tolleson, Tom Wilhelmsen and Brad Ziegler.

*The 2015 season represented the most justifiably risk-averse year since we began tracking closer volatility in 1999. Pre-season pricing dropped to the lowest on record and for the first time included five frontline closers whose average draft price was below $10 (Boxberger, Doolittle, Mejia, Nathan, Rodriguez). The 45% failure rate was the second highest in 12 years (behind the 66% in 2012) as was the number of new sources of saves. However, five of those 16 new sources failed to hold the job during the year (Axford, Grilli, Johnson, Soria and Wilhelmsen).

Closers and multi-year performance *(Patrick Davitt)*

A team having an "established closer"—even a successful one—in a given year does not affect how many of that team's wins are saved in the next year. However, a top closer (40-plus saves) in a given year has a significantly greater chance to retain his role in the subsequent season.

Research of saves and wins data over several seasons found that the percentage of wins that are saved is consistently 50%-54%, irrespective of whether the saves were concentrated in the hands of a "top closer" or passed around to the dreaded "committee" of lesser closers. But it also found that about two-thirds of high-save closers reprised their roles the next season, while three-quarters of low-save closers did not. Moreover, closers who held the role for two or three straight seasons averaged 34 saves per season while closers new to the role averaged 27.

BPV as a leading indicator *(Doug Dennis)*

Research has shown that base performance value (BPV) is an excellent indicator of long-term success as a closer. Here are 20-plus saves seasons, by year:

		BPV		
Year	No.	100+	75+	<75
1999	26	27%	54%	46%
2000	24	25%	54%	46%
2001	25	56%	80%	20%
2002	25	60%	72%	28%
2003	25	36%	64%	36%
2004	23	61%	61%	39%
2005	25	36%	64%	36%
2006	25	52%	72%	28%
2007	23	52%	74%	26%
MEAN	*25*	*45%*	*66%*	*34%*

Though 20-saves success with a 75+ BPV is only a 66% percentage play in any given year, the below-75 group is composed of closers who are rarely able to repeat the feat in the following season:

Year	No. with BPV < 75	No. who followed up 20+ saves <75 BPV
1999	12	2
2000	11	2
2001	5	2
2002	7	3
2003	9	3
2004	9	2
2005	9	1
2006	7	3
2007	6	0

Other Relievers

Projecting holds *(Doug Dennis)*

Here are some general rules of thumb for identifying pitchers who might be in line to accumulate holds. The percentages represent the portion of 2003's top holds leaders who fell into the category noted.

1. Left-handed set-up men with excellent BPIs. (43%)
2. A "go-to" right-handed set-up man with excellent BPIs. This is the one set-up RHer that a manager turns to with a small lead in the 7th or 8th innings. These pitchers also tend to vulture wins. (43%, but 6 of the top 9)
3. Excellent BPIs, but not a firm role as the main LHed or RHed set-up man. Roles change during the season; cream rises to the top. Relievers projected to post great BPIs often overtake lesser set-up men in-season. (14%)

Reliever efficiency percent (REff%)

(Wins + Saves + Holds) / (Wins + Losses + SaveOpps + Holds)

This is a measure of how often a reliever contributes positively to the outcome of a game. A record of consistent, positive impact on game outcomes breeds managerial confidence, and that confidence could pave the way to save opportunities. For those pitchers suddenly thrust into a closer's role, this formula helps gauge their potential to succeed based on past successes in similar roles. **BENCHMARK:** Minimum of 80%.

Vulture

A pitcher, typically a middle reliever, who accumulates an unusually high number of wins by preying on other pitchers' misfortunes. More accurately, this is a pitcher typically brought into a game after a starting pitcher has put his team behind, and then pitches well enough and long enough to allow his offense to take the lead, thereby "vulturing" a win from the starter.

In-Season Analysis

Pure Quality Starts

We've always approached performance measures on an aggregate basis. Each individual event that our statistics chronicle gets dumped into a huge pool of data. We then use our formulas to try to sort and slice and manipulate the data into more usable information.

Pure Quality Starts (PQS) take a different approach. It says that the smallest unit of measure should not be the "event" but instead be the "game." Within that game, we can accumulate all the strikeouts, hits and walks, and evaluate that outing as a whole. After all, when a pitcher takes the mound, he is either "on" or "off" his game; he is either dominant or struggling, or somewhere in between.

In PQS, we give a starting pitcher credit for exhibiting certain skills in each of his starts. Then by tracking his "PQS Score" over time, we can follow his progress. A starter earns one point for each of the following criteria:

1. *The pitcher must go a minimum of 6 innings.* This measures stamina. If he goes less than 5 innings, he automatically gets a total PQS score of zero, no matter what other stats he produces.
2. *He must allow no more than an equal number of hits to the number of innings pitched.* This measures hit prevention.
3. *His number of strikeouts must be no fewer than two less than his innings pitched.* This measures dominance.
4. *He must strike out at least twice as many batters as he walks.* This measures command.
5. *He must allow no more than one home run.* This measures his ability to keep the ball in the park.

A perfect PQS score is 5. Any pitcher who averages 3 or more over the course of the season is probably performing admirably. The nice thing about PQS is it allows you to approach each start as more than an all-or-nothing event.

Note the absence of earned runs. No matter how many runs a pitcher allows, if he scores high on the PQS scale, he has hurled a good game in terms of his base skills. The number of runs allowed—a function of not only the pitcher's ability but that of his bullpen and defense—will tend to even out over time.

It doesn't matter if a few extra balls got through the infield, or the pitcher was given the hook in the fourth or sixth inning, or the bullpen was able to strand their inherited baserunners. When we look at performance in the aggregate, those events do matter, and will affect a pitcher's peripherals and ERA. But with PQS, the minutia is less relevant than the overall performance.

In the end, a dominating performance is a dominating performance, whether Clayton Kershaw is hurling a 4-hit shutout or giving up three runs while striking out 10 in 6 IP. And a disaster is still a disaster, whether Kyle Lohse gets a 5th inning hook after giving up 5 runs on 10 hits, or "takes one for the team" and gets shelled for 8 runs in 3.1 innings.

Skill versus consistency

Two pitchers have identical 4.50 ERAs and identical 3.0 PQS averages. Their PQS logs look like this:

PITCHER A:	3	3	3	3	3
PITCHER B:	5	0	5	0	5

Which pitcher would you rather have on your team? The risk-averse manager would choose Pitcher A as he represents the perfectly known commodity. Many fantasy leaguers might opt for Pitcher B because his occasional dominating starts show that there is an upside. His Achilles Heel is inconsistency—he is unable to sustain that high level. Is there any hope for Pitcher B?

- If a pitcher's inconsistency is characterized by more poor starts than good starts, his upside is limited.
- Pitchers with extreme inconsistency rarely get a full season of starts.
- However, inconsistency is neither chronic nor fatal.

The outlook for Pitcher A is actually worse. Disaster avoidance might buy these pitchers more starts, but history shows that the lack of dominating outings is more telling of future potential. In short, consistent mediocrity is bad.

PQS DOMination and DISaster rates *(Gene McCaffrey)*

DOM% is the percentage of a starting pitcher's outings that rate as a PQS-4 or PQS-5. DIS% is the percentage that rate as a PQS-0 or PQS-1.

DOM/DIS percentages open up a new perspective, providing us with two separate scales of performance. In tandem, they measure consistency.

PQS ERA (qERA)

A pitcher's DOM/DIS split can be converted back to an equivalent ERA. By creating a grid of individual DOM% and DIS% levels, we can determine the average ERA at each cross point. The result is an ERA based purely on PQS.

Quality/consistency score (QC)

(DOM% – (2 x DIS%)) x 2)

Using PQS and DOM/DIS percentages, this score measures both the quality of performance as well as start-to-start consistency.

PQS correlation with Quality Starts *(Paul Petera)*

PQS	QS%
0	0%
1	3%
2	21%
3	51%
4	75%
5	95%

Forward-looking PQS *(John Burnson)*

PQS says whether a pitcher performed ably in a *past* start—it doesn't say anything about how he'll do in the *next* start. We built a version of PQS that attempts to do that. For each series of five starts for a pitcher, we looked at his average IP, K/9, HR/9, H/9, and K/BB, and then whether the pitcher won his next start. We catalogued the results by indicator and calculated the observed future winning percentage for each data point.

This research suggested that a forward-looking version of PQS should have these criteria:

- The pitcher must have lasted at least 6.2 innings.
- He must have recorded at least IP – 1 strikeouts.
- He must have allowed zero home runs.
- He must have allowed no more hits than IP+2.
- He must have had a Command (K/BB) of at least 2.5.

In-season ERA/xERA variance as a leading indicator

(Matt Cederholm)

Pitchers with large first-half ERA/xERA variances will see regression towards their xERA in the second half, if they are allowed (and are able) to finish out the season. Starters have a stronger regression tendency than relievers, which we would expect to see given the larger sample size. In addition, there is substantial attrition among all types of pitchers, but those who are "unlucky" have a much higher rate.

An important corollary: While a pitcher underperforming his xERA is very likely to rebound in the second half, such regression hinges on his ability to hold onto his job long enough to see that regression come to fruition. Healthy veteran pitchers with an established role are more likely to experience the second half boost than a rookie starter trying to make his mark.

Pure Quality Relief *(Patrick Davitt)*

A system for evaluating reliever outings. The scoring :

1. Two points for the first out, and one point for each subsequent out, to a maximum of four points.
2. One point for having at least one strikeout for every four full outs (one K for 1-4 outs, two Ks for 5-8 outs, etc.).
3. One point for zero baserunners, minus one point for each baserunner, though allowing the pitcher one unpenalized runner for each three full outs (one baserunner for 3-5 outs, two for 6-8 outs, three for nine outs)
4. Minus one point for each earned run, though allowing one ER for 8– or 9-out appearances.
5. An automatic PQR-0 for allowing a home run.

Avoiding relief disasters *(Ed DeCaria)*

Relief disasters (defined as ER>=3 and IP<=3), occur in 5%+ of all appearances. The chance of a disaster exceeds 13% in any 7-day period. To minimize the odds of a disaster, we created a model that produced the following list of factors, in order of influence:

1. Strength of opposing offense
2. Park factor of home stadium
3. BB/9 over latest 31 days (more walks is bad)
4. Pitch count over previous 7 days (more pitches is bad)
5. Latest 31 Days ERA>xERA (recent bad luck continues)

Daily league owners who can slot relievers by individual game should also pay attention to days of rest: pitching on less rest than one is accustomed to increases disaster risk.

Sample size reliability *(Russell Carleton)*

At what point during the season do statistics become reliable indicators of skill? Measured in batters faced:

150: K/PA, ground ball rate, line drive rate
200: Fly ball rate, GB/FB
500: K/BB
550: BB/PA

Unlisted stats did not stabilize over a full season of play. *(Note that 150 BF is roughly equivalent to six outings for a starting pitcher; 550 BF would be 22 starts, etc.)*

Pitching streaks

It is possible to find predictive value in strings of DOMinating (PQS 4/5) or DISaster (PQS 0/1) starts:

Once a pitcher enters into a DOM streak of any length, the probability is that his next start is going to be better than average. The further a player is into a DOM streak, the higher the likelihood that the subsequent performance will be high quality. In fact, once a pitcher has posted six DOM starts in a row, there is greater than a 70% probability that the streak will continue. When it does end, there is less than a 10% probability that the streak-breaker is going to be a DISaster.

Once a pitcher enters into a DIS streak of any length, the probability is that his next start is going to be below average, even if it breaks the streak. However, DIS streaks end quickly. Once a pitcher hits the skids, odds are low that he will post a good start in the short term, though the duration itself should be brief.

5-game PQS predictability *(Bill Macey)*

5-Game avg PQS	Avg PQS	DOM%	DIS%
Less than 1	2.1	27%	40%
Between 1 and 2	2.4	32%	32%
Between 2 and 3	2.6	36%	26%
Between 3 and 4	3.0	47%	19%
4 or greater	3.5	61%	12%

Pitchers with higher PQS scores in their previous 5 starts tended to pitch better in their next start. But the relative parity of subsequent DOM and DIS starts for all but the hottest of streaks warn us not to put too much effort into predicting any given start. That more than a quarter of pitchers who had been awful over their previous 5 starts still put up a dominating start next shows that anything can happen in a single game.

High pitch counts and PQS *(Patrick Davitt)*

Starting pitcher matchups are vital for both daily fantasy owners and owners in longer formats that allow "streaming" of starters. In making SP decisions, owners might be tempted to sit a starter coming off a high-pitch-count (PC) start, even a good start, believing his next-game performance is bound to suffer from fatigue.

We studied starts from 2010-12 that had both high PCs (100+, 110+ and even 120+) and high scores in the Pure Quality Start (PQS) metric. The study showed such starters had good results in starts after high-PC starts:

1st Game Pitches	Next PQS Ave
90- 99	3.0
100-109	3.1
110-119	3.3
120+	3.6

And 120+ pitch-count starters were actually better than their peers after posting high PQS scores:

1st PQS	2nd All	2nd 120+
3	3.0	3.6
4	3.1	3.6
5	3.3	3.7

Thus, we can safely ignore the conventional wisdom that a high-PC game will make a pitcher "tired" or "worn out" and therefore less likely to be effective. The opposite is true—especially if the high-PC outing was also a strong PQS performance. It appears these workhorse starters and their teams know what they're doing, and that they are highly likely to deliver a solid outing the next time out.

Days of rest as a leading indicator

Workload is only part of the equation. The other part is how often a pitcher is sent out to the mound. For instance, it's possible that a hurler might see no erosion in skill after a 120+ pitch outing if he had enough rest between starts:

PITCH COUNTS		NEXT START			
Three days rest	Pct.	PQS	DOM	DIS	qERA
< 100	72%	2.8	35%	17%	4.60
100-119	28%	2.3	44%	44%	5.21
Four Days rest					
< 100	52%	2.7	36%	27%	4.82
100-119	45%	2.9	42%	22%	4.56
120+	3%	3.0	42%	20%	4.44
Five Days rest					
< 100	54%	2.7	38%	25%	4.79
100-119	43%	3.0	44%	19%	4.44
120+	3%	3.2	48%	14%	4.28
Six Days rest					
< 100	58%	2.7	39%	30%	5.00
100-119	40%	2.8	40%	26%	4.82
120+	3%	1.8	20%	60%	7.98
20+ Days rest					
< 100	85%	1.8	20%	46%	6.12
100-119	15%	2.3	33%	33%	5.08

Managers are reluctant to put a starter on the mound with any fewer than four days rest, and the results for those who pitched deeper into games shows why. Four days rest is the most common usage pattern and even appears to mitigate the drop-off at 120+ pitches.

Perhaps most surprising is that an extra day of rest improves performance across the board and squeezes even more productivity out of the 120+ pitch outings.

Performance begins to erode at six days (and continues at 7-20 days, though those are not displayed). The 20+ Days chart represents pitchers who were primarily injury rehabs and failed call-ups, and the length of the "days rest" was occasionally well over 100 days. This chart shows the result of their performance in their first start back. The good news is that the workload was limited for 85% of these returnees. The bad news is that these are not pitchers you want active. So for those who obsess over getting your DL returnees activated in time to catch every start, the better percentage play is to avoid that first outing.

Post-DL Pitching Performance *(Bill Macey)*

One question that fantasy baseball managers frequently struggle with is whether or not to start a pitcher when he first returns from the disabled list. A 2011 study compared each pitcher's PQS score in their first post-DL start against his average PQS score for that year (limited to pitchers who had at least 15 starts during the year and whose first post-DL appearance was as a starter). The findings:

- In general, exercise caution with immediate activations. Pitchers performed worse than their yearly average in the first post-DL start, with a high rate of PQS-DIS starts.
- Avoid pitchers returning from the DL due to an arm injury, as they perform significantly worse than average.
- If there are no better options available, feel comfortable activating pitchers who spent near the minimum amount of time on the DL and/or suffered a leg injury, as they typically perform at a level consistent with their yearly average.

April ERA as a leading indicator *(Stephen Nickrand)*

A starting pitcher's April ERA can act as a leading indicator for how his ERA is likely to fare during the balance of the season. A study looked at extreme April ERA results to see what kind of in-season forecasting power they may have. From 2010-2012, 42 SP posted an ERA in April that was at least 2.00 ER better than their career ERA. The findings:

- Pitchers who come out of the gates quickly have an excellent chance at finishing the season with an ERA much better than their career ERA.
- While April ERA gems see their in-season ERA regresses towards their career ERA, their May-Sept ERA is still significantly better than their career ERA.
- Those who stumble out of the gates have a strong chance at posting an ERA worse than their career average, but their in-season ERA improves towards their career ERA.
- April ERA disasters tend to have a May-Sept ERA that closely resembles their career ERA.

Second-half ERA Reduction Drivers *(Stephen Nickrand)*

It's easy to dismiss first-half-to-second-half improvement among starting pitchers as an unpredictable event. After all, the midpoint of the season is an arbitrary cutoff. Performance swings occur throughout the season.

A study of SP who experienced significant 1H-2H ERA improvement from 2010-2012 examined what indicators drove second-half ERA improvement. Among the findings for those 79 SP with a > 1.00 ERA 1H-2H reduction:

- 97% saw their WHIP decrease, with an average decrease of 0.26
- 97% saw their strand (S%) rate improve, with an average increase of 9%
- 87% saw their BABIP (H%) improve, with an average reduction of 5%
- 75% saw their control (bb/9) rate improve, with an average reduction of 0.8
- 70% saw their HR/9 rate improve, with an average decrease of 0.5
- 68% saw their swinging strike (SwK%) rate improve, with an average increase of 1.4%
- 68% saw their BPV improve, with an average increase of 37
- 67% saw their HR per fly ball rate (hr/f) improve, with an average decrease of 4%
- 53% saw their ground ball (GB%) rate improve, with an average increase of 5%
- 52% saw their dominance (k/9) rate improve, with an average increase of 1.3

These findings highlight the power of H% and S% regression as it relates to ERA and WHIP improvement. In fact, H% and S% are more often correlated with ERA improvement than are improved skills. They also suggest that improved control has a bigger impact on ERA reduction than does increased strikeouts.

Pitcher Home/Road Splits *(Stephen Nickrand)*

One overlooked strategy in leagues that allow frequent transactions is to bench pitchers when they are on the road. Research reveals that several pitching stats and indicators are significantly and consistently worse on the road than at home.

Some home/road rules of thumb for SP:

- If you want to gain significant ground in ERA and WHIP, keep all your average or worse SP benched on the road.
- A pitcher's win percentage drops by 15% when on the road, so don't bank on road starts as a means to catch up in wins.
- Control erodes by 10% on the road, so be especially careful with keeping wild SP in your active lineups when they are away from home.
- NL pitchers at home produce significantly more strikeouts than their AL counterparts and vs. all pitchers on the road.
- hr/9, groundball rate, hit rate, strand rate, and hr/f do not show significant home vs. road variances.

Other Diamonds

The Pitching Postulates

1. Never sign a soft-tosser to a long-term contract.
2. Right-brain dominance has a very long shelf life.
3. A fly ball pitcher who gives up many HRs is expected. A GB pitcher who gives up many HRs is making mistakes.
4. Never draft a contact fly ball pitcher who plays in a hitter's park.
5. Only bad teams ever have a need for an inning-eater.
6. Never chase wins.

Dontrelle Willis List

Pitchers with BPIs so incredibly horrible that you have to wonder how they can possibly draw a major league paycheck year after year.

Chaconian

Having the ability to post many saves despite sub-Mendoza BPIs and an ERA in the stratosphere.

Vintage Eck Territory

A BPV greater than 200, a level achieved by Dennis Eckersley for four consecutive years.

ERA Benchmark

A half run of ERA over 200 innings comes out to just one earned run every four starts.

Gopheritis (also, Acute Gopheritis and Chronic Gopheritis)

The dreaded malady in which a pitcher is unable to keep the ball in the park. Pitchers with gopheritis have a FB rate of at least 40%. More severe cases have a FB% over 45%.

The Knuckleballers Rule

Knuckleballers don't follow no stinkin' rules.

Brad Lidge Lament

When a closer posts a 62% strand rate, he has nobody to blame but himself.

LOOGY (Lefty One Out GuY)

A left-handed reliever whose job it is to get one out in important situations.

Vin Mazzaro Vindication

Occasional nightmares (2.1 innings, 14 ER) are just a part of the game.

Meltdown

Any game in which a starting pitcher allows more runs than innings pitched.

The Five Saves Certainties

1. On every team, there will be save opportunities and someone will get them. At a bare minimum, there will be at least 30 saves to go around, and not unlikely more than 45.

2. Any pitcher could end up being the chief beneficiary. Bullpen management is a fickle endeavor.

3. Relief pitchers are often the ones that require the most time at the start of the season to find a groove. The weather is cold, the schedule is sparse and their usage is erratic.

4. Despite the talk about "bullpens by committee," managers prefer a go-to guy. It makes their job easier.

5. As many as 50% of the saves in any year will come from pitchers who are unselected at the end of Draft Day.

Soft-tosser

A pitcher with a strikeout rate of 5.5 or less.

Soft-tosser land

The place where feebler arms leave their fortunes in the hands of the defense, variable hit and strand rates, and park dimensions. It's a place where many live, but few survive.

Prospects

General

Minor league prospecting in perspective

In our perpetual quest to be the genius who uncovers the next Mike Trout when he's still in high school, there is an obsessive fascination with minor league prospects. That's not to say that prospecting is not important. The issue is perspective:

1. During the 10 year period of 1996 to 2005, only 8% of players selected in the first round of the Major League Baseball First Year Player Draft went on to become stars.
2. Some prospects are going to hit the ground running (Carlos Correa) and some are going to immediately struggle (Daniel Norris), no matter what level of hype follows them.
3. Some prospects are going to start fast (since the league is unfamiliar with them) and then fade (as the league figures them out). Others will start slow (since they are unfamiliar with the opposition) and then improve (as they adjust to the competition). So if you make your free agent and roster decisions based on small early samples sizes, you are just as likely to be an idiot as a genius.
4. How any individual player will perform relative to his talent is largely unknown because there is a psychological element that is vastly unexplored. Some make the transition to the majors seamlessly, some not, completely regardless of how talented they are.
5. Still, talent is the best predictor of future success, so major league equivalent base performance indicators still have a valuable role in the process. As do scouting reports, carefully filtered.
6. Follow the player's path to the majors. Did he have to repeat certain levels? Was he allowed to stay at a level long enough to learn how to adjust to the level of competition? A player with only two great months at Double-A is a good bet to struggle if promoted directly to the majors because he was never fully tested at Double-A, let alone Triple-A.
7. Younger players holding their own against older competition is a good thing. Older players reaching their physical peak, regardless of their current address, can be a good thing too. The Stephen Vogts and Justin Turners can have some very profitable years.
8. Remember team context. A prospect with superior potential often will not unseat a steady but unspectacular incumbent, especially one with a large contract.
9. Don't try to anticipate how a team is going to manage their talent, both at the major and minor league level. You might think it's time to promote J.P. Crawford and give him an everyday role. You are not running the Phillies.
10. Those who play in shallow, one-year leagues should have little cause to be looking at the minors at all. The risk versus reward is so skewed against you, and there is so much talent available with a track record, that taking a chance on an unproven commodity makes little sense.
11. Decide where your priorities really are. If your goal is to win, prospect analysis is just a *part* of the process, not the entire process.

Factors affecting minor league stats *(Terry Linhart)*

1. Often, there is an exaggerated emphasis on short-term performance in an environment that is supposed to focus on the long-term. Two poor outings don't mean a 21-year-old pitcher is washed up.
2. Ballpark dimensions and altitude create hitters parks and pitchers parks, but a factor rarely mentioned is that many parks in the lower minors are inconsistent in their field quality. Minor league clubs have limited resources to maintain field conditions, and this can artificially depress defensive statistics while inflating stats like batting average.
3. Some players' skills are so superior to the competition at their level that you can't get a true picture of what they're going to do from their stats alone.
4. Many pitchers are told to work on secondary pitches in unorthodox situations just to gain confidence in the pitch. The result is an artificially increased number of walks.
5. The #3, #4, and #5 pitchers in the lower minors are truly longshots to make the majors. They often possess only two pitches and are unable to disguise the off-speed offerings. Hitters can see inflated statistics in these leagues.

Minor league level versus age

When evaluating minor leaguers, look at the age of the prospect in relation to the median age of the league he is in:

Low level A	*Between 19-20*
Upper level A	*Around 20*
Double-A	*21*
Triple-A	*22*

These are the ideal ages for prospects at the particular level. If a prospect is younger than most and holds his own against older and more experienced players, elevate his status. If he is older than the median, reduce his status.

Triple-A experience as a leading indicator

The probability that a minor leaguer will immediately succeed in the majors can vary depending upon the level of Triple-A experience he has amassed at the time of call-up.

	BATTERS		PITCHERS	
	< 1 Yr	Full	<1 Yr	Full
Performed well	57%	56%	16%	56%
Performed poorly	21%	38%	77%	33%
2nd half drop-off	21%	7%	6%	10%

The odds of a batter achieving immediate MLB success was slightly more than 50-50. More than 80% of all pitchers promoted with less than a full year at Triple-A struggled in their first year in the majors. Those pitchers with a year in Triple-A succeeded at a level equal to that of batters.

Major League Equivalency (MLE) *(Bill James)*

A formula that converts a player's minor or foreign league statistics into a comparable performance in the major leagues. These are not projections, but conversions of current performance. MLEs contain adjustments for the level of play in individual leagues and teams. They work best with Triple-A stats, not quite as well with Double-A stats, and hardly at all with the lower levels. Foreign conversions are still a work in process. James' original formula only addressed batting. Our research has devised conversion formulas for pitchers, however, their best use comes when looking at BPIs, not traditional stats.

Adjusting to the competition

All players must "adjust to the competition" at every level of professional play. Players often get off to fast or slow starts. During their second tour at that level is when we get to see whether the slow starters have caught up or whether the league has figured out the fast starters. That second half "adjustment" period is a good baseline for projecting the subsequent season, in the majors or minors.

Premature major league call-ups often negate the ability for us to accurately evaluate a player due to the lack of this adjustment period. For instance, a hotshot Double-A player might open the season in Triple-A. After putting up solid numbers for a month, he gets a call to the bigs, and struggles. The fact is, we do not have enough evidence that the player has mastered the Triple-A level. We don't know whether the rest of the league would have caught up to him during his second tour of the league. But now he's labeled as an underperformer in the bigs when in fact he has never truly proven his skills at the lower levels.

Bull Durham prospects

There is some potential talent in older players—age 26, 27 or higher—who, for many reasons (untimely injury, circumstance, bad luck, etc.), don't reach the majors until they have already been downgraded from prospect to suspect. Equating potential with age is an economic reality for major league clubs, but not necessarily a skills reality.

Skills growth and decline is universal, whether it occurs at the major league level or in the minors. So a high-skills journeyman in Triple-A is just as likely to peak at age 27 as a major leaguer of the same age. The question becomes one of opportunity—will the parent club see fit to reap the benefits of that peak performance?

Prospecting these players for your fantasy team is, admittedly, a high risk endeavor, though there are some criteria you can use. Look for a player who is/has:

- Optimally, age 27-28 for overall peak skills, age 30-31 for power skills, or age 28-31 for pitchers.
- At least two seasons of experience at Triple-A. Career Double-A players are generally not good picks.
- Solid base skills levels.
- Shallow organizational depth at their position.
- Notable winter league or spring training performance.

Players who meet these conditions are not typically draftable players, but worthwhile reserve or FAAB picks.

Batters

MLE PX as a leading indicator *(Bill Macey)*

Looking at minor league performance (as MLE) in one year and the corresponding MLB performance the subsequent year:

	Year 1 MLE	Year 2 MLB
Observations	496	496
Median PX	95	96
Percent PX > 100	43%	46%

In addition, 53% of the players had a MLB PX in year 2 that exceeded their MLE PX in year 1. A slight bias towards improved performance in year 2 is consistent with general career trajectories.

Year 1 MLE PX	Year 2 MLB PX	Pct. Incr	Pct. MLB PX > 100
<= 50	61	70.3%	5.4%
51-75	85	69.6%	29.4%
76-100	93	55.2%	39.9%
101-125	111	47.4%	62.0%
126-150	119	32.1%	66.1%
> 150	142	28.6%	76.2%

Slicing the numbers by performance level, there is a good amount of regression to the mean.

Players rarely suddenly develop power at the MLB level if they didn't previously display that skill at the minor league level. However, the relatively large gap between the median MLE PX and MLB PX for these players, 125 to 110, confirms the notion that the best players continue to improve once they reach the major leagues.

MLE contact rate as a leading indicator *(Bill Macey)*

There is a strong positive correlation (0.63) between a player's MLE ct% in Year 1 and his actual ct% at the MLB level in Year 2.

MLE ct%	Year 1 MLE ct%	Year 2 MLB ct%
< 70%	69%	68%
70% - 74%	73%	72%
75% - 79%	77%	75%
80% - 84%	82%	77%
85% - 89%	87%	82%
90% +	91%	86%
TOTAL	**84%**	**79%**

There is very little difference between the median MLE BA in Year 1 and the median MLB BA in Year 2:

MLE ct%	Year 1 MLE BA	Year 2 MLB BA
< 70%	.230	.270
70% - 74%	.257	.248
75% - 79%	.248	.255
80% - 84%	.257	.255
85% - 89%	.266	.270
90% +	.282	.273
TOTAL	.261	.262

Excluding the <70% cohort (which was a tiny sample size), there is a positive relationship between MLE ct% and MLB BA.

Pitchers

BPIs as a leading indicator for pitching success

The percentage of hurlers that were good investments in the year that they were called up varied by the level of their historical minor league BPIs prior to that year.

Pitchers who had:	Fared well	Fared poorly
Good indicators	79%	21%
Marginal or poor indicators	18%	82%

The data used here were MLE levels from the previous two years, not the season in which they were called up. The significance? Solid current performance is what merits a call-up, but this is not a good indicator of short-term MLB success, because a) the performance data set is too small, typically just a few month's worth of statistics, and b) for those putting up good numbers at a new minor league level, there has typically not been enough time for the scouting reports to make their rounds.

Minor league BPV as a leading indicator *(Al Melchior)*

There is a link between minor league skill and how a pitching prospect will fare in his first 5 starts upon call-up.

	MLE BPV		
PQS Avg	< 50	50-99	100+
0.0-1.9	60%	28%	19%
2.0-2.9	32%	40%	29%
3.0-5.0	8%	33%	52%

Pitchers who demonstrate sub-par skills in the minors (sub-50 BPV) tend to fare poorly in their first big league starts. Three-fifths of these pitchers register a PQS average below 2.0, while only 8% average over 3.0.

Fewer than 1 out of 5 minor leaguers with a 100+ MLE BPV go on to post a sub-2.0 PQS average in their initial major league starts, but more than half average 3.0 or better.

Late season performance of rookie starting pitchers *(Ray Murphy)*

Given that a rookie's second tour of the league provides insight as to future success, do rookie pitchers typically run out of gas? We studied 2002-2005, identified 56 rookies who threw at least 75 IP and analyzed their PQS logs. The group:

All rookies	#	#GS/P	DOM%	DIS%	qERA
before 7/31	56	13.3	42%	21%	4.56
after 7/31	56	9.3	37%	29%	4.82

There is some erosion, but a 0.26 run rise in qERA is hardly cause for panic. If we re-focus our study class, the qERA variance increased to 4.44-5.08 for those who made at least 16 starts before July 31. The variance also was larger (3.97-4.56) for those who had a PQS-3 average prior to July 31. The pitchers who intersected these two sub-groups:

PQS>3+GS>15	#	#GS/P	DOM%	DIS%	qERA
before 7/31	8	19.1	51%	12%	4.23
after 7/31	8	9.6	34%	30%	5.08

While the sample size is small, the degree of flameout by these guys (0.85 runs) is more significant.

Japanese Baseball *(Tom Mulhall)*

Comparing MLB and Japanese Baseball

The Japanese major leagues are generally considered to be equivalent to Triple-A ball and the pitching is thought to be even better. However, statistics are difficult to convert due to differences in the way the game is played in Japan.

1. While strong on fundamentals, Japanese baseball's guiding philosophy is risk avoidance. Mistakes are not tolerated. Runners rarely take extra bases, batters focus on making contact rather than driving the ball, and managers play for one run at a time. Bunts are more common. As a result, offenses score fewer runs per number of hits, and pitching stats tend to look better than the talent behind them.
2. Stadiums in Japan usually have much shorter fences. This should mean more HRs, but given #1 above, it is the American players who make up the majority of Japan's power elite. No power hitters have made an equivalent transition to the MLB.
3. There are more artificial turf fields, which increases the number of ground ball singles. Only a small number of stadiums have infield grass and a few still use all dirt infields.
4. The quality of umpiring is questionable and even inept. Fewer errors are called, reflecting the cultural philosophy of low tolerance for mistakes and the desire to avoid publicly embarrassing a player. Moreover, umpires are routinely intimidated, even physically.
5. Teams have smaller pitching staffs and use a six-man rotation. Starters usually pitch once a week, typically on the same day since Monday is an off-day for the entire league. Many starters will also occasionally pitch in relief between starts. Moreover, managers push for complete games, no matter what the score or situation. Because of the style of offense, higher pitch counts are common. Despite superior conditioning, Japanese pitchers tend to burn out early due to overuse.
6. The ball is smaller and lighter, and the strike zone is closer to the batter. A new ball was introduced in 2011 with lower-elasticity rubber surrounding the cork, which limited offense and inflated pitching stats. A more hitter-friendly ball was used in 2013 and home runs increased. But continue to exercise some skepticism when analyzing pitching stats and look for possible signs of optimism in hitting stats other than the power categories.
7. Tie games are allowed. If the score remains even after 12 innings, the game goes into the books as a tie.
8. There are 18 fewer games in the Japanese schedule.

Japanese players as fantasy farm selections

Many fantasy leagues have large reserve or farm teams with rules allowing them to draft foreign players before they sign with a MLB team. With increased coverage by fantasy experts, the internet, and exposure from the World Baseball Classic, anyone willing to do a modicum of research can compile an adequate list of good players.

However, the key is not to just identify the best Japanese players—the key is to identify impact players who have the desire and opportunity to sign with a MLB team. With the success of Darvish and Tanaka, it is easy to overestimate the value of drafting these players. But since 1995, less than four dozen Japanese players have made a big league roster, and about half of them were middle relievers. Still, for owners who are allowed to carry a large reserve or farm team at reduced salaries, these players could be a real windfall, especially if your competitors do not do their homework.

A list of Japanese League players who could jump to the majors appears in the Prospects section.

Other Diamonds

Age 26 Paradox

Age 26 is when a player begins to reach his peak skill, no matter what his address is. If circumstances have him celebrating that birthday in the majors, he is a breakout candidate. If circumstances have him celebrating that birthday in the minors, he is washed up.

A-Rod 10-Step Path to Stardom

Not all well-hyped prospects hit the ground running. More often they follow an alternative path:

1. Prospect puts up phenomenal minor league numbers.
2. The media machine gets oiled up.
3. Prospect gets called up, but struggles, Year 1.
4. Prospect gets demoted.
5. Prospect tears it up in the minors, Year 2.
6. Prospect gets called up, but struggles, Year 2.
7. Prospect gets demoted.
8. The media turns their backs. Fantasy leaguers reduce their expectations.
9. Prospect tears it up in the minors, Year 3. The public shrugs its collective shoulders.
10. Prospect is promoted in Year 3 and explodes. Some lucky fantasy leaguer lands a franchise player for under $5.

Some players that are currently stuck at one of the interim steps, and may or may not ever reach Step 10, include Jesus Montero, Jonathan Singleton and Dalton Pompey.

Developmental Dogmata

1. Defense is what gets a minor league prospect to the majors; offense is what keeps him there. *(Deric McKamey)*
2. The reason why rapidly promoted minor leaguers often fail is that they are never given the opportunity to master the skill of "adjusting to the competition."
3. Rookies who are promoted in-season often perform better than those that make the club out of spring training. Inferior March competition can inflate the latter group's perceived talent level.
4. Young players rarely lose their inherent skills. Pitchers may uncover weaknesses and the players may have difficulty adjusting. These are bumps along the growth curve, but they do not reflect a loss of skill.
5. Late bloomers have smaller windows of opportunity and much less chance for forgiveness.
6. The greatest risk in this game is to pay for performance that a player has never achieved.
7. Some outwardly talented prospects simply have a ceiling that's spelled "A-A-A."

Rule 5 Reminder

Don't ignore the Rule 5 draft lest you ignore the possibility of players like Jose Bautista, Josh Hamilton, Johan Santana, Joakim Soria, Dan Uggla, Shane Victorino and Jayson Werth. All were Rule 5 draftees.

Trout Inflation

The tendency for rookies to go for exorbitant draft prices following a year when there was a very good rookie crop.

Gaming

Standard Rules and Variations

Rotisserie Baseball was invented as an elegant confluence of baseball and economics. Whether by design or accident, the result has lasted for more than three decades. But what would Rotisserie and fantasy have been like if the Founding Fathers knew then what we know now about statistical analysis and game design? You can be sure things would be different.

The world has changed since the original game was introduced yet many leagues use the same rules today. New technologies have opened up opportunities to improve elements of the game that might have been limited by the capabilities of the 1980s. New analytical approaches have revealed areas where the original game falls short.

As such, there are good reasons to tinker and experiment; to find ways to enhance the experience.

Following are the basic elements of fantasy competition, those that provide opportunities for alternative rules and experimentation. This is by no means an exhaustive list, but at minimum provides some interesting food-for-thought.

Player pool

Standard: American League-only, National League-only or Mixed League.

AL/NL-only typically drafts 8-12 teams (pool penetration of 49% to 74%). Mixed leagues draft 10-18 teams (31% to 55% penetration), though 15 teams (46%) is a common number.

Drafting of reserve players will increase the penetration percentages. A 12-team AL/NL-only league adding six reserves onto 23-man rosters would draft 93% of the available pool of players on all teams' 25-man rosters.

The draft penetration level determines which fantasy management skills are most important to your league. The higher the penetration, the more important it is to draft a good team. The lower the penetration, the greater the availability of free agents and the more important in-season roster management becomes.

There is no generally-accepted optimal penetration level, but we have often suggested that 75% (including reserves) provides a good balance between the skills required for both draft prep and in-season management.

Alternative pools: There is a wide variety of options here. Certain leagues draft from within a small group of major league divisions or teams. Some competitions, like home run leagues, only draft batters.

Bottom-tier pool: Drafting from the entire major league population, the only players available are those who posted a Rotisserie dollar value of $5 or less in the previous season. Intended as a test of an owner's ability to identify talent with upside. Best used as a pick-a-player contest with any number of teams participating.

Positional structure

Standard: 23 players. One at each defensive position (though three outfielders may be from any of LF, CF or RF), plus one additional catcher, one middle infielder (2B or SS), one corner infielder (1B or 3B), two additional outfielders and a utility player/designated hitter (which often can be a batter who qualifies anywhere). Nine pitchers, typically holding any starting or relief role.

Open: 25 players. One at each defensive position (plus DH), 5-man starting rotation and two relief pitchers. Nine additional players at any position, which may be a part of the active roster or constitute a reserve list.

40-man: Standard 23 plus 17 reserves. Used in many keeper and dynasty leagues.

Reapportioned: In recent years, new obstacles are being faced by 12-team AL/NL-only leagues thanks to changes in the real game. The 14/9 split between batters and pitchers no longer reflects how MLB teams structure their rosters. Of the 30 teams, each with 25-man rosters, not one contains 14 batters for any length of time. In fact, many spend a good part of the season with only 12 batters, which means teams often have more pitchers than hitters.

For fantasy purposes in AL/NL-only leagues, that leaves a disproportionate draft penetration into the batter and pitcher pools:

	BATTERS	PITCHERS
On all MLB rosters	195	180
Players drafted	168	108
Pct.	86%	60%

These drafts are depleting 26% more batters out of the pool than pitchers. Add in those leagues with reserve lists—perhaps an additional six players per team removing another 72 players —and post-draft free agent pools are very thin, especially on the batting side.

The impact is less in 15-team mixed leagues, though the FA pitching pool is still disproportionately deep.

	BATTERS	PITCHERS
On all rosters	381	369
Drafted	210	135
Pct.	55%	37%

One solution is to reapportion the number of batters and pitchers that are rostered. Adding one pitcher slot and eliminating one batter slot may be enough to provide better balance. The batting slot most often removed is the second catcher, since it is the position with the least depth.

Beginning in the 2012 season, the Tout Wars AL/NL-only experts leagues opted to eliminate one of the outfield slots and replace it with a "swingman" position. This position could be any batter or pitcher, depending upon the owner's needs at any given time during the season.

Selecting players

Standard: The three most prevalent methods for stocking fantasy rosters are:

Snake/Straight/Serpentine draft: Players are selected in order with seeds reversed in alternating rounds. This method has become the most popular due to its speed, ease of implementation and ease of automation.

In these drafts, the underlying assumption is that value can be ranked relative to a linear baseline. Pick #1 is better than pick #2, which is better than pick #3, and the difference between each pick is assumed to be somewhat equivalent. While a faulty assumption, we must believe in it to assume a level playing field.

Auction: Players are sold to the highest bidder from a fixed budget, typically $260. Auctions provide the team owner with more control over which players will be on his team, but can take twice as long as snake drafts.

The baseline is $0 at the beginning of each player put up for bid. The final purchase price for each player is shaped by many wildly variable factors, from roster need to geographic location of the draft. A $30 player can mean different things to different drafters.

One option that can help reduce the time commitment of auctions is to force minimum bids at each hour mark. You could mandate $15 openers in hour #1; $10 openers in hour #2, etc.

Pick-a-player / Salary cap: Players are assigned fixed dollar values and owners assemble their roster within a fixed cap. This type of roster-stocking is an individual exercise which results in teams typically having some of the same players.

In these leagues, the "value" decision is taken out of the hands of the owners. Each player has a fixed value, pre-assigned based on past season performance and/or future expectation.

Hybrid snake-auction: Each draft begins as an auction. Each team has to fill its first seven roster slots from a budget of $154. Opening bid for any player is $15. After each team has filled seven slots, it becomes a snake draft.

This method is intended to reduce draft time while still providing an economic component for selecting players.

Stat categories

Standard: The standard statistical categories for Rotisserie leagues are:

4x4: HR, RBI, SB, BA, W, Sv, ERA, WHIP

5x5: HR, R, RBI, SB, BA, W, Sv, K, ERA, WHIP

6x6: Categories typically added are Holds and OPS.

7x7, etc.: Any number of categories may be added.

In general, the more categories you add, the more complicated it is to isolate individual performance and manage the categorical impact on your roster. There is also the danger of redundancy; with multiple categories measuring like stats, certain skills can get over-valued. For instance, home runs are double-counted when using the categories of both HR and slugging average. (Though note that HRs are actually already triple-counted in standard 5x5—HRs, runs, and RBIs)

If the goal is to have categories that create a more encompassing picture of player performance, it is actually possible to accomplish more with less:

Modified 4x4: HR, (R+RBI-HR), SB, OBA, (W+QS), (Sv+Hld), K, ERA

This provides a better balance between batting and pitching in that each has three counting categories and one ratio category. In fact, the balance is shown to be even more notable here:

	BATTING	PITCHING
Pure skill counting stat	HR	K
Ratio category	OBA	ERA
Dependent upon managerial decision	SB	(Sv+Hold)
Dependent upon team support	(R+RBI-HR)	(W+QS)

Replacing saves: The problem with the Saves statistic is that we have a scarce commodity that is centered on a small group of players, thereby creating inflated demand for those players. With the rising failure rate for closers these days, the incentive to pay full value for the commodity decreases. The higher the risk, the lower the prices.

We can increase the value of the commodity by reducing the risk. We might do this by increasing the number of players that contribute to that category, thereby spreading the risk around. One way we can accomplish this is by changing the category to Saves + Holds.

Holds are not perfect, but the typical argument about them being random and arbitrary can apply to saves these days as well. In fact, many of the pitchers who record holds are far more skilled and valuable than closers; they are often called to the mound in much higher leverage situations (a fact backed up by a scan of each pitcher's Leverage Index).

Neither stat is perfect, but together they form a reasonable proxy for overall bullpen performance.

In tandem, they effectively double the player pool of draftable relievers while also flattening the values allotted to those pitchers. The more players around which we spread the risk, the more control we have in managing our pitching staffs.

Replacing wins: Using reasons similar to replacing Saves with Saves + Holds, some have argued for replacing the Wins statistic with W + QS (quality starts). This method of scoring gives value to a starting pitcher who pitches well, but fails to receive the win due to his team's poor offense or poor luck.

Keeping score

Standard: These are the most common scoring methods:

Rotisserie: Players are evaluated in several statistical categories. Totals of these statistics are ranked by team. The winner is the team with the highest cumulative ranking.

Points: Players receive points for events that they contribute to in each game. Points are totaled for each team and teams are then ranked.

Head-to-Head (H2H): Using Rotisserie or points scoring, teams are scheduled in daily or weekly matchups. The winner of each matchup is the team that finishes higher in more categories (Rotisserie) or scores the most points.

Hybrid H2H-Rotisserie: Rotisserie's category ranking system can be converted into a weekly won-loss record. Depending upon where your team finishes for that week's statistics determines how many games you win for that week. Each week, your team will play seven games.

*Place	Record	*Place	Record
1st	7-0	7th	3-4
2nd	6-1	8th	2-5
3rd	6-1	9th	2-5
4th	5-2	10th	1-6
5th	5-2	11th	1-6
6th	4-3	12th	0-7

** Based on overall Rotisserie category ranking for the week.*

At the end of each week, all the statistics revert to zero and you start over. You never dig a hole in any category that you can't climb out of, because all categories themselves are incidental to the standings.

The regular season lasts for 23 weeks, which equals 161 games. Weeks 24, 25 and 26 are for play-offs.

Free agent acquisition

Standard: Three methods are the most common for acquiring free agent players during the season.

First to the phone: Free agents are awarded to the first owner who claims them.

Reverse order of standings: Access to the free agent pool is typically in a snake draft fashion with the last place team getting the first pick, and each successive team higher in the standings picking afterwards.

Free agent acquisition budget (FAAB): Teams are given a set budget at the beginning of the season (typically, $100 or $1000) from which they bid on free agents in a closed auction process.

Vickrey FAAB: Research has shown that more than 50% of FAAB dollars are lost via overbid on an annual basis. Given that this is a scarce commodity, one would think that a system to better manage these dollars might be desirable. The Vickrey system conducts a closed auction in the same way as standard FAAB, but the price of the winning bid is set at the amount of the second highest bid, plus $1. In some cases, gross overbids (at least $10 over) are reduced to the second highest bid plus $5.

This method was designed by William Vickrey, a Professor of Economics at Columbia University. His theory was that this process reveals the true value of the commodity. For his work, Vickrey was awarded the Nobel Prize for Economics (and $1.2 million) in 1996.

Double-Bid FAAB: One of the inherent difficulties in the current FAAB system is that we have so many options for setting a bid amount. You can bid $47, or $51, or $23. You might agonize over whether to go $38 or $39. With a $100 budget, there are 100 decision points. And while you may come up with a rough guesstimate of the range in which your opponents might bid, the results for any individual player bidding are typically random within that range.

The first part of this process reduces the number of decision points. Owners must categorize their interest by bidding a fixed number of pre-set dollar amounts for each player. In a $100 FAAB league, for instance, those levels might be $1, $5, $10, $15, $20, $30, $40 or $50. All owners would set the general market value for free agents in these eight levels of interest. (This system sets a $50 maximum, but that is not absolutely necessary.)

The initial stage of the bidding process serves to screen out those who are not interested in a player at the appropriate market level. That leaves a high potential for tied owners, those who share the same level of interest.

The tied owners must then submit a second bid of equal or greater value than their first bid. These bids can be in $1 increments. The winning owner gets the player; if there is still a tie, then the player would go to the owner lower in the standings.

An advantage of this second bid is that it gives owners an opportunity to see who they are going up against, and adjust. If you are bidding against an owner close to you in the standings, you may need to be more aggressive in that second bid. If you see that the tied owner(s) wouldn't hurt you by acquiring that player, then maybe you resubmit the original bid and be content to potentially lose out on the player. If you're ahead in the standings, it's actually a way to potentially opt out on that player completely by resubmitting your original bid and forcing another owner to spend his FAAB.

Some leagues will balk at adding another layer to the weekly deadline process; it's a trade-off to having more control over managing your FAAB.

The season

Standard: Leagues are played out during the course of the entire Major League Baseball season.

Split-season: Leagues are conducted from Opening Day through the All-Star break, then re-drafted to play from the All-Star break through the end of the season.

50-game split-season: Leagues are divided into three 50-game seasons with one-week break in between.

Monthly: Leagues are divided into six seasons or rolling four-week seasons.

The advantages of these shorter time frames:

- Shorter time frames can help to maintain interest. There would be fewer abandoned teams.
- There would be more shots at a title each year.
- Given that drafting is considered the most fun aspect of the game, these splits multiply the opportunities to participate in some type of draft. Leagues may choose to do complete re-drafts and treat the year as distinct mini-seasons. Or, leagues might allow teams to drop their five worst players and conduct a restocking draft at each break.

Daily games: Participants select a roster of players from one day's MLB schedule. Scoring is based on an aggregate points-based system rather than categories, with cash prizes awarded based on the day's results. The structure and distribution of that prize pool varies across different types of events, and those differences can affect roster construction strategies. Although scoring and prizes are based on one day's play, the season-long element of bankroll management provides a proxy for overall standings.

In terms of projecting outcomes, daily games are drastically different than full-season leagues. Playing time is one key element of any projection, and daily games offer near-100% accuracy in projecting playing time: you can check pre-game lineups to see exactly which players are in the lineup that night. The other key component of any projection is performance, but that is plagued by variance in daily competitions. Even if you roster a team full of the most advantageous matchups (for instance, Mike Trout facing Franklin Morales at Coors Field), Trout will sometimes go 0-for-4 on that one night.

Single game (Quint-Inning): A game that drafts from the active rosters of two major league teams in a single game. The rules:

1. Start with five owners.

2. Prior to first pitch, conduct a simple snake draft where each owner selects five players. If you're ambitious, auction off the 25 players giving each owner a budget of $50 of real or fake money.

3. Scoring is simple. For batters, singles, walks, hit-by-pitches and stolen bases are one point each. Doubles are 2 points. Triples are 3 points. Home runs are 4 points. Pitchers get one point for each complete inning pitched but lose one point for every run they allow.

4. At the beginning of the 5th inning, each owner has the option of doubling any future points for one player on his roster. We call that player the Quint. Points for all batters are doubled beginning in the 9th inning. That means the Quint's points would be quadrupled.

5. At the end of each inning, you can cut players, claim players from the free agent pool or trade players. You must maintain five players at all times, so all adds, drops and trades must keep your roster square. Free agent claims are done in reverse order of the standings. If two teams are tied and both want the same player, it can be helpful to have a deck of cards handy - the owner who draws high card would get the player.

6. Quint-Inning is a betting game (which makes it technically illegal). Owners need to ante up to play, typically $5, though if you're using a $50 auction budget, that works fine. It then costs $1 per inning to stay in the game for the second through fourth innings. Beginning in the 5th inning, the stakes increase to $2 per inning to stay in the game. You can use higher or lower stakes if you prefer.

7. Owners can fold at any time, forfeiting any monies they contributed to the pot. Their players are released into the free agent pool and are available to the remaining owners in reverse order of the standings.

8. The owner with the most points at the end of the game wins the pot.

Post-season league: Some leagues re-draft teams from among the MLB post-season contenders and play out a separate competition. It is possible, however, to make a post-season competition that is an extension of the regular season.

Start by designating a set number of regular season finishers as qualifying for the post-season. The top four teams in a league is a good number.

These four teams would designate a fixed 23-man roster for all post-season games. First, they would freeze all of their currently-owned players who are on MLB post-season teams.

In order to fill the roster holes that will likely exist, these four teams would then pick players from their league's non-playoff teams (for the sake of the post-season only). This would be in the form of a snake draft done on the day following the end of the regular season. Draft order would be regular season finish, so the play-off team with the most regular season points would get first pick. Picks would continue until all four rosters are filled with 23 men.

Regular scoring would be used for all games during October. The team with the best play-off stats at the end of the World Series is the overall champ.

Snake Drafting

Snake draft first round history

The following tables record the comparison between pre-season projected player rankings (using Average Draft Position data from Mock Draft Central and National Fantasy Baseball Championship) and actual end-of-season results. The 12-year success rate of identifying each season's top talent is only 34%, and getting worse. During the first six years of this period, our success rate was 38%; in the six years since, it has dropped to 31%.

2008	ADP		ACTUAL = 7
1	Alex Rodriguez	1	Albert Pujols (10)
2	Hanley Ramirez	2	Jose Reyes (4)
3	David Wright	3	Hanley Ramirez (2)
4	Jose Reyes	4	Manny Ramirez
5	Matt Holliday	5	Matt Holliday (5)
6	Jimmy Rollins	6	David Wright (3)
7	Miguel Cabrera	7	Lance Berkman
8	Chase Utley	8	Dustin Pedroia
9	Ryan Howard	9	Roy Halladay
10	Albert Pujols	10	Josh Hamilton
11	Prince Fielder	11	Alex Rodriguez (1)
12	Ryan Braun	12	C.C. Sabathia
13	Johan Santana	13	Carlos Beltran
14	Carl Crawford	14	Grady Sizemore
15	Alfonso Soriano	15	Chase Utley (8)

2009	ADP		ACTUAL = 5
1	Hanley Ramirez	1	Albert Pujols (2)
2	Albert Pujols	2	Hanley Ramirez (1)
3	Jose Reyes	3	Tim Lincecum
4	David Wright	4	Dan Haren
5	Grady Sizemore	5	Carl Crawford
6	Miguel Cabrera	6	Matt Kemp
7	Ryan Braun	7	Joe Mauer
8	Jimmy Rollins	8	Derek Jeter
9	Ian Kinsler	9	Zach Greinke
10	Josh Hamilton	10	Ryan Braun (7)
11	Ryan Howard	11	Jacoby Ellsbury
12	Mark Teixeira	12	Mark Reynolds
13	Alex Rodriguez	13	Prince Fielder
14	Matt Holliday	14	Chase Utley (15)
15	Chase Utley	15	Miguel Cabrera (6)

2010	ADP		ACTUAL = 5
1	Albert Pujols	1	Carlos Gonzalez
2	Hanley Ramirez	2	Albert Pujols (1)
3	Alex Rodriguez	3	Joey Votto
4	Chase Utley	4	Roy Halladay
5	Ryan Braun	5	Carl Crawford (15)
6	Mark Teixeira	6	Miguel Cabrera (9)
7	Matt Kemp	7	Josh Hamilton
8	Prince Fielder	8	Adam Wainwright
9	Miguel Cabrera	9	Felix Hernandez
10	Ryan Howard	10	Robinson Cano
11	Evan Longoria	11	Jose Bautista
12	Tom Lincecum	12	Paul Konerko
13	Joe Mauer	13	Matt Holliday
14	David Wright	14	Ryan Braun (5)
15	Carl Crawford	15	Hanley Ramirez (2)

2011	ADP		ACTUAL = 6
1	Albert Pujols	1	Matt Kemp
2	Hanley Ramirez	2	Jacoby Ellsbury
3	Miguel Cabrera	3	Ryan Braun (10)
4	Troy Tulowitzki	4	Justin Verlander
5	Evan Longoria	5	Clayton Kershaw
6	Carlos Gonzalez	6	Curtis Granderson
7	Joey Votto	7	Adrian Gonzalez (8)
8	Adrian Gonzalez	8	Miguel Cabrera (3)
9	Robinson Cano	9	Roy Halladay (15)
10	Ryan Braun	10	Cliff Lee
11	David Wright	11	Jose Bautista
12	Mark Teixeira	12	Dustin Pedroia
13	Carl Crawford	13	Jered Weaver
14	Josh Hamilton	14	Albert Pujols (1)
15	Roy Halladay	15	Robinson Cano (9)

2012	ADP	ACTUAL = 4	
1	Matt Kemp	1	Mike Trout
2	Ryan Braun	2	Ryan Braun (2)
3	Albert Pujols	3	Miguel Cabrera (4)
4	Miguel Cabrera	4	Andrew McCutchen
5	Troy Tulowitzki	5	R.A. Dickey
6	Jose Bautista	6	Clayton Kershaw
7	Jacoby Ellsbury	7	Justin Verlander (8)
8	Justin Verlander	8	Josh Hamilton
9	Adrian Gonzalez	9	Fernando Rodney
10	Justin Upton	10	Adrian Beltre
11	Robinson Cano	11	Alex Rios
12	Joey Votto	12	David Price
13	Evan Longoria	13	Chase Headley
14	Carlos Gonzalez	14	Robinson Cano (11)
15	Prince Fielder	15	Edwin Encarnacion

2013	ADP	ACTUAL = 5	
1	Ryan Braun	1	Miguel Cabrera (2)
2	Miguel Cabrera	2	Mike Trout (3)
3	Mike Trout	3	Clayton Kershaw (15)
4	Matt Kemp	4	Chris Davis
5	Andrew McCutchen	5	Paul Goldschmidt
6	Albert Pujols	6	Andrew McCutchen (5)
7	Robinson Cano	7	Adam Jones
8	Jose Bautista	8	Jacoby Ellsbury
9	Joey Votto	9	Max Scherzer
10	Carlos Gonzalez	10	Carlos Gomez
11	Buster Posey	11	Hunter Pence
12	Justin Upton	12	Robinson Cano (7)
13	Giancarlo Stanton	13	Alex Rios
14	Prince Fielder	14	Adrian Beltre
15	Clayton Kershaw	15	Matt Harvey

2014	ADP	ACTUAL = 4	
1	Mike Trout	1	Jose Altuve
2	Miguel Cabrera	2	Clayton Kershaw (6)
3	Paul Goldschmidt	3	Michael Brantley
4	Andrew McCutchen	4	Mike Trout (1)
5	Carlos Gonzalez	5	Johnny Cueto
6	Clayton Kershaw	6	Felix Hernandez
7	Chris Davis	7	Victor Martinez
8	Ryan Braun	8	Jose Abreu
9	Adam Jones	9	Giancarlo Stanton
10	Bryce Harper	10	Andrew McCutchen (4)
11	Robinson Cano	11	Miguel Cabrera (2)
12	Hanley Ramirez	12	Carlos Gomez
13	Jacoby Ellsbury	13	Jose Bautista
14	Prince Fielder	14	Dee Gordon
15	Troy Tulowitzki	15	Anthony Rendon

2015	ADP	ACTUAL = 4	
1	Mike Trout	1	Jake Arrieta
2	Andrew McCutchen	2	Zack Greinke
3	Clayton Kershaw	3	Clayton Kershaw (3)
4	Giancarlo Stanton	4	Paul Goldschmidt (5)
5	Paul Goldschmidt	5	A.J. Pollock
6	Miguel Cabrera	6	Dee Gordon
7	Jose Abreu	7	Bryce Harper
8	Carlos Gomez	8	Josh Donaldson
9	Jose Batista	9	Jose Altuve (12)
10	Edwin Encarnacion	10	Mike Trout (1)
11	Felix Hernandez	11	Nolan Arenado
12	Jose Altuve	12	Manny Machado
13	Anthony Rizzo	13	Dallas Keuchel
14	Adam Jones	14	Max Scherzer
15	Troy Tulowitzki	15	Nelson Cruz

This is the first time since we've been keeping ADP records (2004) that a pitcher has finished ranked #1. It is also the first time that pitchers have occupied the top three spots in the rankings. It is the third time that five pitchers made it into the Top 15.

ADP attrition

Why is our success rate so low in identifying what should be the most easy-to-project players each year? We rank and draft players based on the expectation that those ranked higher will return greater value in terms of productivity and playing time, as well as being the safest investments. However, there are many variables affecting where players finish.

Earlier, it was shown that players spend an inordinate number of days on the disabled list. In fact, of the players projected to finish in the top 300, the number who lost playing time due to injuries, demotions and suspensions has been extreme:

Year	Pct. of top-ranked 300 players who lost PT
2009	51%
2010	44%
2011	49%
2012	45%
2013	51%
2014	53%
2015	47%

When you consider that about half of each season's very best players had fewer at-bats or innings pitched than we projected, it shows how tough it is to rank players each year.

The fallout? Consider: It is nearly a foregone conclusion that players like A.J. Pollock and Manny Machado—players who finished in the top 15 for the first time last year—will rank as first round picks in 2016. The above data provide a strong argument against them returning first-round value.

Yes, they are excellent players, two of the best in the game, in 2015 anyway. But the issue is not their skills profile. The issue is the profile of what makes a worthy first rounder.

Since 2004:

- Two-thirds of players finishing in the Top 15 were not in the Top 15 the previous year. There is a great deal of turnover in the first round, year-to-year.
- Of those who were first-timers, only 14% repeated in the first round the following year.
- Established superstars who finished in the Top 15 were no guarantee to repeat.

As such, the odds are against Pollock and Machado repeating in the first round, as counter-intuitive as it may seem. In past years, sudden stars like Hunter Pence, Curtis Granderson and Dustin Pedroia have failed to repeat. As talented as these players are, it's not just about skill; it's also about skill relative to the rest of a volatile player pool.

Importance of the Early Rounds *(Bill Macey)*

It's long been said that you can't win your league in the first round, but you can lose it there. An analysis of data from actual drafts reveals that this holds true—those who spend an early round pick on a player that severely under-performs expectations rarely win their league and seldom even finish in the top 3.

At the same time, drafting a player in the first round that actually returns first-round value is no guarantee of success. In fact, those that draft some of the best values still only win their league about a quarter of the time and finish in the top 3 less than half the time. Research also shows that drafting pitchers in the first round is a risky proposition. Even if the pitchers deliver first-round value, the opportunity cost of passing up on an elite batter makes you less likely to win your league.

What is the best seed to draft from?

Most drafters like mid-round so they never have to wait too long for their next player. Some like the swing pick, suggesting that getting two players at 15 and 16 is better than a 1 and a 30. Many drafters assume that the swing pick means you'd be getting something like two $30 players instead of a $40 and $20.

Equivalent auction dollar values reveal the following facts about the first two snake draft rounds:

In an AL/NL-only league, the top seed would get a $44 player (at #1) and a $24 player (at #24) for a total of $68; the 12th seed would get two $29s (at #12 and #13) for $58.

In a mixed league, the top seed would get a $47 and a $24 ($71); the 15th seed would get two $28s ($56).

Since the talent level flattens out after the 2nd round, low seeds never get a chance to catch up:

Dollar value difference between first player selected and last player selected

Round	12-team	15-team
1	$15	$19
2	$7	$8
3	$5	$4
4	$3	$3
5	$2	$2
6	$2	$1
7-17	$1	$1
18-23	$0	$0

The total value each seed accumulates at the end of the draft is hardly equitable:

Seed	Mixed	AL/NL-only
1	$266	$273
2	$264	$269
3	$263	$261
4	$262	$262
5	$259	$260
6	$261	$260
7	$260	$260
8	$261	$260
9	$261	$258
10	$257	$260
11	$257	$257
12	$258	$257
13	$254	
14	$255	
15	$256	

Of course, the draft is just the starting point for managing your roster and player values are variable. Still, it's tough to imagine a scenario where the top seed wouldn't have an advantage over the bottom seed.

Using ADPs to determine when to select players *(Bill Macey)*

Although average draft position (ADP) data provides a good idea of where in the draft each player is selected, it can be misleading when trying to determine how early to target a player. This chart summarizes the percentage of players drafted within 15 picks of his ADP as well as the average standard deviation by grouping of players.

ADP Rank	% within 15 picks	Standard Deviation
1-25	100%	2.5
26-50	97%	6.1
51-100	87%	9.6
100-150	72%	14.0
150-200	61%	17.4
200-250	53%	20.9

As the draft progresses, the picks for each player become more widely dispersed and less clustered around the average. Most top 100 players will go within one round of their ADP-converted round. However, as you reach the mid-to-late rounds, there is much more uncertainty as to when a player will be selected. Pitchers have slightly smaller standard deviations than do batters (i.e. they tend to be drafted in a narrower range). This suggests that drafters may be more likely to reach for a batter than for a pitcher.

Using the ADP and corresponding standard deviation, we can to estimate the likelihood that a given player will be available at a certain draft pick. We estimate the predicted standard deviation for each player as follows:

Stdev = -0.42 + 0.42*(ADP - Earliest Pick)

(That the figure 0.42 appears twice is pure coincidence; the numbers are not equal past two decimal points.)

If we assume that the picks are normally distributed, we can use a player's ADP and estimated standard deviation to estimate the likelihood that the player is available with a certain pick (MS Excel formula):

=1-normdist(x,ADP,Standard Deviation,True)
where «x» represents the pick number to be evaluated.

We can use this information to prepare for a snake draft by determining how early we may need to reach in order to roster a player. Suppose you have the 8th pick in a 15-team league draft and your target is 2009 sleeper candidate Nelson Cruz. His ADP is 128.9 and his earliest selection was with the 94th pick. This yields an estimated standard deviation of 14.2. You can then enter these values into the formula above to estimate the likelihood that he is still available at each of the following picks:

Pick	Likelihood Available
83	100%
98	99%
113	87%
128	53%
143	16%
158	2%

ADPs and scarcity *(Bill Macey)*

Most players are selected within a round or two of their ADP with tight clustering around the average. But every draft is unique and every pick in the draft seemingly affects the ordering of subsequent picks. In fact, deviations from "expected" sequences can sometimes start a chain reaction at that position. This is most often seen in runs at scarce positions such as the closer; once the first one goes, the next seems sure to closely follow.

Research also suggests that within each position, there is a correlation within tiers of players. The sooner players within a generally accepted tier are selected, the sooner other players within the same tier will be taken. However, once that tier is exhausted, draft order reverts to normal.

How can we use this information? If you notice a reach pick, you can expect that other drafters may follow suit. If your draft plan is to get a similar player within that tier, you'll need to adjust your picks accordingly.

Mapping ADPs to auction value *(Bill Macey)*

Reliable average auction values (AAV) are often tougher to come by than ADP data for snake drafts. However, we can estimate predicted auction prices as a function of ADP, arriving at the following equation:

$$y = -9.8\ln(x) + 57.8$$

where ln(x) is the natural log function, x represents the actual ADP, and y represents the predicted AAV.

This equation does an excellent job estimating auction prices ($r2=0.93$), though deviations are unavoidable. The asymptotic nature of the logarithmic function, however, causes the model to predict overly high prices for the top players. So be aware of that, and adjust.

The value of mock drafts *(Todd Zola)*

Most assume the purpose of a mock draft is to get to know the market value of the player pool. But even more important, mock drafting is general preparation for the environment and process, thereby allowing the drafter to completely focus on the draft when it counts. Mock drafting is more about fine-tuning your strategy than player value. Here are some tips to maximize your mock drafting experience.

1. Make sure you can seamlessly use an on-line drafting room, draft software or your own lists to track your draft or auction. The less time you spend looking, adding and adjusting names, the more time you can spend on thinking about what player is best for your team. This also gives you the opportunity to make sure your draft lists are complete, and assures all the players are listed at the correct position(s).

2. Alter the positions from which you mock. The flow of each mock will be different, but if you do a few mocks with an early initial pick, a few in the middle and a few with a late first pick, you may learn you prefer one of the spots more than the others. If you're in a league where you can choose your draft spot, this helps you decide where to select. Once you know your spot, a few mocks from that spot will help you decide how to deal with positional runs.

3. Use non-typical strategies and consider players you rarely target. We all have our favorite players. Intentionally passing on those players not only gives you an idea when others may draft them but it also forces you to research players you normally don't consider. The more players you have researched, the more prepared you'll be for any series of events that occurs during your real draft.

Auction Value Analysis

Auction values (R$) in perspective

R$ is the dollar value placed on a player's statistical performance in a Rotisserie league, and designed to measure the impact that player has on the standings.

There are several methods to calculate a player's value from his projected (or actual) statistics.

One method is Standings Gain Points, described in the book, *How to Value Players for Rotisserie Baseball*, by Art McGee (2nd edition available at BaseballHQ.com). SGP converts a player's statistics in each Rotisserie category into the number of points those stats will allow you to gain in the standings. These are then converted back into dollars.

Another popular method is the Percentage Valuation Method. In PVM, a least valuable, or replacement performance level is set for each category (in a given league size) and then values are calculated representing the incremental improvement from that base. A player is then awarded value in direct proportion to the level he contributes to each category.

As much as these methods serve to attach a firm number to projected performance, the winning bid for any player is still highly variable depending upon many factors:

- the salary cap limit
- the number of teams in the league
- each team's roster size
- the impact of any protected players
- each team's positional demands at the time of bidding
- the statistical category demands at the time of bidding
- external factors, e.g. media inflation or deflation of value

In other words, a $30 player is only a $30 player if someone in your draft pays $30 for him.

Roster slot valuation *(John Burnson)*

When you draft a player, what have you bought?

"You have bought the stats generated by this player."

No. You have bought the stats generated by his slot. Initially, the drafted player fills the slot, but he need not fill the slot for the season, and he need not contribute from Day One. If you trade the player during the season, then your bid on Draft Day paid for the stats of the original player plus the stats of the new player. If the player misses time due to injury or demotion, then you bought the stats of whoever fills the time while the drafted player is missing. At season's end, there will be more players providing positive value than there are roster slots.

Before the season, the number of players projected for positive value has to equal the total number of roster slots—after all, we can't order owners to draft more players than can fit on their rosters. However, the projected productivity should be adjusted by the potential to capture extra value in the slot. This is especially important for injury-rehab cases and late-season call-ups. For example, if we think that a player will miss half the season, then we would augment his projected stats with a half-year of stats from a replacement-level player at his position. Only then would we calculate prices. Essentially, we want to apportion $260 per team among the slots, not the players.

Average player value by draft round

Rd	AL/NL	Mxd
1	$34	$34
2	$26	$26
3	$23	$23
4	$20	$20
5	$18	$18
6	$17	$16
7	$16	$15
8	$15	$13
9	$13	$12
10	$12	$11
11	$11	$10
12	$10	$9
13	$9	$8
14	$8	$8
15	$7	$7
16	$6	$6
17	$5	$5
18	$4	$4
19	$3	$3
20	$2	$2
21	$1	$2
22	$1	$1
23	$1	$1

Benchmarks for auction players:

- All $30 players will go in the first round.
- All $20-plus players will go in the first four rounds.
- Double-digit value ends pretty much after Round 11.
- The $1 end game starts at about Round 21.

Dollar values by lineup position *(Michael Roy)*

How much value is derived from batting order position?

Pos	PA	R	RBI	R$
#1	747	107	72	$18.75
#2	728	102	84	$19.00
#3	715	95	100	$19.45
#4	698	93	104	$19.36
#5	682	86	94	$18.18
#6	665	85	82	$17.19
#7	645	81	80	$16.60
#8	623	78	80	$16.19
#9	600	78	73	$15.50

So, a batter moving from the bottom of the order to the clean-up spot, with no change in performance, would gain nearly $4 in value from runs and RBIs alone.

Dollar values: expected projective accuracy

There is a 65% chance that a player projected for a certain dollar value will finish the season with a final value within plus-or-minus $5 of that projection. That means, if you value a player at $25, you only have about a 2-in-3 shot of him finishing between $20 and $30.

If you want to get your odds up to 80%, the range now becomes +/- $9. You have an 80% shot that your $25 player will finish somewhere between $16 and $34.

How likely is it that a $30 player will repeat? *(Matt Cederholm)*

From 2003-2008, there were 205 players who earned $30 or more (using single-league 5x5 values). Only 70 of them (34%) earned $30 or more in the next season.

In fact, the odds of repeating a $30 season aren't good. As seen below, the best odds during that period were 42%. And as we would expect, pitchers fare far worse than hitters.

	Total>$30	# Repeat	% Repeat
Hitters	167	64	38%
Pitchers	38	6	16%
Total	205	70	34%
*High-Reliability**			
Hitters	42	16	38%
Pitchers	7	0	0%
Total	49	16	33%
100+ BPV			
Hitters	60	25	42%
Pitchers	31	6	19%
Total	91	31	19%
*High-Reliability and 100+ BPV**			
Hitters	12	5	42%
Pitchers	6	0	0%
Total	18	5	28%

**Reliability figures are from 2006-2008*

For players with multiple seasons of $30 or more, the numbers get better. Players with consecutive $30 seasons, 2003-2008:

	Total>$30	# Repeat	% Repeat
Two Years	62	29	55%
Three+ Years	29	19	66%

Still, a player with two consecutive seasons at $30 in value is barely a 50/50 proposition. And three consecutive seasons is only a 2/3 shot. Small sample sizes aside, this does illustrate the nature of the beast. Even the most consistent, reliable players fail 1/3 of the time. Of course, this is true whether they are kept or drafted anew, so this alone shouldn't prevent you from keeping a player.

How well do elite pitchers retain their value? *(Michael Weddell)*

An elite pitcher (one who earns at least $24 in a season) on average keeps 80% of his R$ value from year 1 to year 2. This compares to the baseline case of only 52%.

Historically, 36% of elite pitchers improve, returning a greater R$ in the second year than they did the first year. That is an impressive performance considering they already were at an elite level. 17% collapse, returning less than a third of their R$ in the second year. The remaining 47% experience a middling outcome, keeping more than a third but less than all of their R$ from one year to the next.

Valuing closers

Given the high risk associated with the closer's role, it is difficult to determine a fair draft value. Typically, those who have successfully held the role for several seasons will earn the highest draft price, but valuing less stable commodities is troublesome.

A rough rule of thumb is to start by paying $10 for the role alone. Any pitcher tagged the closer on draft day should merit at least $10. Then add anywhere from $0 to $15 for support skills.

In this way, the top level talents will draw upwards of $20-$25. Those with moderate skill will draw $15-$20, and those with more questionable skill in the $10-$15 range.

Profiling the end game

What types of players are typically the most profitable in the end-game? First, our overall track record on $1 picks:

Avg Return	%Profitable	Avg Prof	Avg. Loss
$1.89	51%	$10.37	($7.17)

On aggregate, the hundreds of players drafted in the end-game earned $1.89 on our $1 investments. While they were profitable overall, only 51% of them actually turned a profit. Those that did cleared more than $10 on average. Those that didn't—the other 49%—lost about $7 apiece.

Pos	Pct.of tot	Avg Val	%Profit	Avg Prof	Avg Loss
CA	12%	($1.68)	41%	$7.11	($7.77)
CO	9%	$6.12	71%	$10.97	($3.80)
MI	9%	$3.59	53%	$10.33	($4.84)
OF	22%	$2.61	46%	$12.06	($5.90)
SP	29%	$1.96	52%	$8.19	($7.06)
RP	19%	$0.35	50%	$11.33	($10.10)

These results bear out the danger of leaving catchers to the end; only catchers returned negative value. Corner infielder returns say leaving a 1B or 3B open until late.

Age	Pct.of tot	Avg Val	%Profit	Avg Prof	Avg Loss
< 25	15%	($0.88)	33%	$8.25	($8.71)
25-29	48%	$2.59	56%	$11.10	($8.38)
30-35	28%	$2.06	44%	$10.39	($5.04)
35+	9%	$2.15	41%	$8.86	($5.67)

The practice of speculating on younger players—mostly rookies—in the end game was a washout. Part of the reason was that those that even made it to the end game were often the long-term or fringe type. Better prospects were typically drafted earlier.

	Pct.of tot	Avg Val	%Profit	Avg Prof	Avg Loss
Injury rehabs	20%	$3.63	36%	$15.07	($5.65)

One in five end-gamers were players coming back from injury. While only 36% of them were profitable, the healthy ones returned a healthy profit. The group's losses were small, likely because they weren't healthy enough to play.

Realistic expectations of $1 endgamers *(Patrick Davitt)*

Many fantasy articles insist leagues are won or lost with $1 batters, because "that's where the profits are." But are they?

A 2011 analysis showed that when considering $1 players in deep leagues, managing $1 endgamers should be more about minimizing losses than fishing for profit. In the cohort of batters projected $0 to -$5, 82% returned losses, based on a $1 bid. Two-thirds of the projected $1 cohort returned losses. In addition, when considering $1 players, speculate on speed.

Advanced Draft Strategies

Stars & Scrubs v. Spread the Risk

Stars & Scrubs (S&S): A Rotisserie auction strategy in which a roster is anchored by a core of high priced stars and the remaining positions filled with low-cost players.

Spread the Risk (STR): An auction strategy in which available dollars are spread evenly among all roster slots.

Both approaches have benefits and risks. An experiment was conducted in 2004 whereby a league was stocked with four teams assembled as S&S, four as STR and four as a control group. Rosters were then frozen for the season.

The Stars & Scrubs teams won all three ratio categories. Those deep investments ensured stability in the categories that are typically most difficult to manage. On the batting side, however, S&S teams amassed the least amount of playing time, which in turn led to bottom-rung finishes in HRs, RBIs and Runs.

One of the arguments for the S&S approach is that it is easier to replace end-game losers (which, in turn, may help resolve the playing time issues). Not only is this true, but the results of this experiment show that replacing those bottom players is critical to success.

The Spread the Risk teams stockpiled playing time, which led to strong finishes in many counting stats, including clear victories in RBIs, wins and strikeouts. This is a key tenet in drafting philosophy; we often say that the team that compiles the most ABs will be among the top teams in RBI and Runs.

The danger is on the pitching side. More innings did yield more wins and Ks, but also destroyed ERA/WHIP.

So, what approach makes the most sense? **The optimal strategy might be to STR on offense and go S&S with your pitching staff.** STR buys more ABs, so you immediately position yourself well in four of the five batting categories. On pitching, it might be more advisable to roster a few core arms, though that immediately elevates your risk exposure. Admittedly, it's a balancing act, which is why we need to pay more attention to risk analysis and look closer at strategies like the Portfolio3 Plan.

The LIMA Plan

The LIMA Plan is a strategy for Rotisserie leagues (though the underlying concept can be used in other formats) that allows you to target high skills pitchers at very low cost, thereby freeing up dollars for offense. LIMA is an acronym for Low Investment Mound Aces, and also pays tribute to Jose Lima, a $1 pitcher in 1998 who exemplified the power of the strategy. In a $260 league:

1. Budget a maximum of $60 for your pitching staff.
2. Allot no more than $30 of that budget for acquiring saves. In 5x5 leagues, it is reasonable to forego saves at the draft (and acquire them during the season) and re-allocate this $30 to starters ($20) and offense ($10).
3. Ignore ERA. Draft only pitchers with:
   - Command ratio (K/BB) of 2.5 or better.
   - Strikeout rate of 7.0 or better.
   - Expected home run rate of 1.0 or less.
4. Draft as few innings as your league rules will allow. This is intended to manage risk. For some game formats, this should be a secondary consideration.
5. Maximize your batting slots. Target batters with:
   - Contact rate of at least 80%
   - Walk rate of at least 10%
   - PX or Spd level of at least 100

Spend no more than $29 for any player and try to keep the $1 picks to a minimum.

The goal is to ace the batting categories and carefully pick your pitching staff so that it will finish in the upper third in ERA, WHIP and saves (and Ks in 5x5), and an upside of perhaps 9th in wins. In a competitive league, that should be enough to win, and definitely enough to finish in the money. Worst case, you should have an excess of offense available that you can deal for pitching.

The strategy works because it better allocates resources. Fantasy leaguers who spend a lot for pitching are not only paying for expected performance, they are also paying for better defined roles—#1 and #2 rotation starters, ace closers, etc.—which are expected to translate into more IP, wins and saves. But roles are highly variable. A pitcher's role will usually come down to his skill and performance; if he doesn't perform, he'll lose the role.

The LIMA Plan says, let's invest in skill and let the roles fall where they may. In the long run, better skills should translate into more innings, wins and saves. And as it turns out, pitching skill costs less than pitching roles do.

In *snake draft leagues,* don't start drafting starting pitchers until Round 10. In *shallow mixed leagues,* the LIMA Plan may not be necessary; just focus on the peripheral metrics. In *simulation leagues,* build your staff around those metrics.

Variations on the LIMA Plan

LIMA Extrema: Limit your total pitching budget to only $30, or less. This can be particularly effective in shallow leagues where LIMA-caliber starting pitcher free agents are plentiful during the season.

SANTANA Plan: Instead of spending $30 on saves, you spend it on a starting pitcher anchor. In 5x5 leagues where you can reasonably punt saves at the draft table, allocating those dollars to a high-end LIMA-caliber starting pitcher can work well as long as you pick the right anchor.

Total Control Drafting (TCD)

On Draft Day, we make every effort to control as many elements as possible. In reality, the players that end up on our teams are largely controlled by the other owners. Their bidding affects your ability to roster the players you want. In a snake draft, the other owners control your roster even more. We are really only able to get the players we want within the limitations set by others.

However, an optimal roster can be constructed from a fanalytic assessment of skill and risk combined with more assertive draft day demeanor.

Why this makes sense

1. Our obsession with projected player values is holding us back. If a player on your draft list is valued at $20 and you agonize when the bidding hits $23, odds are about two chances in three that he could really earn anywhere from $15 to $25. What this means is, in some cases, and within reason, you should just pay what it takes to get the players you want.

2. There is no such thing as a bargain. Most of us *don't* just pay what it takes because we are always on the lookout for players who go under value. But we really don't know which players will cost less than they will earn because prices are still driven by the draft table. The concept of "bargain" assumes that we even know what a player's true value is.

3. "Control" is there for the taking. Most owners are so focused on their own team that they really don't pay much attention to what you're doing. There are some exceptions, and bidding wars do happen, but in general, other owners will not provide that much resistance.

How it's done

1. Create your optimal draft pool.

2. Get those players.

Start by identifying which players will be draftable based on the LIMA or Portfolio3 criteria. Then, at the draft, focus solely on your roster. When it's your bid opener, toss a player you need at about 50%-75% of your projected value. Bid aggressively and just pay what you need to pay. Of course, don't spend $40 for a player with $25 market value, but it's okay to exceed your projected value within reason.

From a tactical perspective, mix up the caliber of openers. Drop out early on some bids to prevent other owners from catching on to you.

In the end, it's okay to pay a slight premium to make sure you get the players with the highest potential to provide a good return on your investment. It's no different than the premium you might pay for a player with position flexbility or to get the last valuable shortstop. With TCD, you're just spending those extra dollars up front to ensure you are rostering your targets. As a side benefit, TCD almost asssures that you don't leave money on the table.

Mayberry Method

The foundation of the Mayberry Method (MM) is the assertion that we really can't project player performance with the level of precision that advanced metrics and modeling systems would like us to believe.

MM is named after the fictional TV village where life was simpler. MM evaluates skill by embracing the imprecision of the forecasting process and projecting performance in broad strokes rather than with hard statistics.

MM reduces every player to a 7-character code. The format of the code is 5555 AAA, where the first four characters describe elements of a player's skill on a scale of 0 to 5. These skills are indexed to the league average so that players are evaluated within the context of the level of offense or pitching in a given year.

The three alpha characters are our reliability grades (Health, Experience and Consistency) on the standard A-to-F scale. The skills numerics are forward-looking; the alpha characters grade reliability based on past history.

Batting

The first character in the MM code measures a batter's power skills. It is assigned using the following table:

Power Index	MM
0 - 49	0
50 - 79	1
80 - 99	2
100 - 119	3
120 - 159	4
160+	5

The second character measures a batter's speed skills. RSpd takes our Statistically Scouted Speed metric (Spd) and adds the elements of opportunity and success rate, to construct the formula of RSpd = Spd x (SBO + SB%).

RSpd	MM
0 - 39	0
40 - 59	1
60 - 79	2
80 - 99	3
100 - 119	4
120+	5

The third character measures expected batting average.

xBA Index	MM
0-87	0
88-92	1
93-97	2
98-102	3
103-107	4
108+	5

The fourth character measures playing time.

Role	PA	MM
Potential full-timers	450+	5
Mid-timers	250-449	3
Fringe/bench	100-249	1
Non-factors	0-99	0

Pitching

The first character in the pitching MM code measures xERA, which captures a pitcher's overall ability and is a proxy for ERA, and even WHIP.

xERA Index	MM
0-80	0
81-90	1
91-100	2
101-110	3
111-120	4
121+	5

The second character measures strikeout ability.

K/9 Index	MM
0-76	0
77-88	1
89-100	2
101-112	3
113-124	4
125+	5

The third character measures saves potential.

Description	Saves est.	MM
No hope for saves; starting pitchers	0	0
Speculative closer	1-9	1
Closer in a pen with alternatives	10-24	2
Frontline closer with firm bullpen role	25+	3

The fourth character measures **playing time.**

Role	IP	MM
Potential #1-2 starters	180+	5
Potential #3-4 starters	130-179	3
#5 starters/swingmen	70-129	1
Relievers	0-69	0

Overall Mayberry Scores

The real value of Mayberry is to provide a skills profile on a player-by-player basis. I want to be able to see this…

Player A	4455 AAB
Player B	5245 BBD
Player C	5255 BAB
Player D	5155 BAF

…and make an objective, unbiased determination about these four players without being swayed by preconceived notions and baggage. But there is a calculation that provides a single, overall value for each player.

This is the calculation for the overall MM batting score:

MM Score =
(PX score + Spd score + xBA score + PA score)
x PA score

An overall MM pitching score is calculated as:

MM Score =
((xERA score x 2) + K/9 score + Saves score + IP score)
x (IP score + Saves score)

The highest score you can get for either is 100. That makes the result of the formula easy to assess.

BaseballHQ.com analyst Patrick Davitt did some great research about using Reliability Grades to adjust the Mayberry scores. His research showed that "higher-reliability players met their Mayberry targets more often than their lower-reliability counterparts, and players with all "D" or "F" reliability scores underperform Mayberry projections far more often. Those results can be reflected by multiplying a player's MM Score by each of three reliability bonuses or penalties:"

I've taken his work a minor step further and applied slightly different multipliers to each Reliability element.

	Health	Experience	Consistency
A	x 1.10	x 1.10	x 1.10
B	x 1.05	x 1.05	x 1.05
C	x 1.00	x 1.00	x 1.00
D	x 0.90	x 0.95	x 0.95
F	x 0.80	x 0.90	x 0.90

So, let's perform the overall calculations for Player A above, using these Reliability adjustments.

Player A: 4455 AAB
= (4+4+5+5) x 5
= 90 x 1.10 x 1.10 x 1.05
= 114.3

The Portfolio3 Plan (P3)

When it comes to profitability, all players are not created equal. Every player has a different role on your team by virtue of his skill set, dollar value/draft round, position and risk profile. When it comes to a strategy for how to approach a specific player, one size does not fit all.

We need some players to return fair value more than others. A $40/first round player going belly-up is going to hurt you far more than a $1/23rd round bust. End-gamers are easily replaceable.

We rely on some players for profit more than others. First-rounders do not provide the most profit potential; that comes from players further down the value rankings.

We can afford to weather more risk with some players than with others. Since high-priced early-rounders need to return at least fair value, we cannot afford to take on excessive risk. Our risk tolerance opens up with later-round/lower cost picks.

Players have different risk profiles based solely on what roster spot they are going to fill. Catchers are more injury prone. A closer's value is highly dependent on managerial decision. These types of players are high risk even if they have great skills. That needs to affect their draft price or draft round.

For some players, the promise of providing a scarce skill, or productivity at a scarce position, may trump risk. Not always, but sometimes. The determining factor is usually price.

In the end, we need a way to integrate all these different types of players, roles and needs. We need to put some structure to the concept of a diversified draft approach. Thus:

The Portfolio3 Plan provides a three-tiered structure to the draft. Just like most folks prefer to diversify their stock portfolio, P3 advises to diversify your roster with three different types of players. Depending upon the stage of the draft (and budget constraints in auction leagues), P3 uses a different set of rules for each tier that you'll draft from. The three tiers are:

1. Core Players
2. Mid-Game Players
3. End-Game Players

Mayberry scores can be used as proxies for the skills filters. When planning your draft, pretty much all you need to remember is the number "3". That essentially represents "just over league average" and makes it easy to set your targets.

TIER 1: CORE PLAYERS

General Roster Goals

Auction target: Budget a maximum of $160. Any player purchased for $20 or more should meet the Tier 1 skills criteria

Snake draft target: 5-8 players, with an emphasis on those drafted in the earlier rounds

Reliability grades: No worse than "B" for each variable (Health, Experience and Consistency)

Playing time: No restrictions, however, pricier early round players should have more guaranteed playing time

Batter skills: Minimum MM scores of 3 in xBA *plus* either PX or RSpd

Pitcher skills: Minimum MM scores of 3 in xERA *and* K/9

Tier 1 players provide the foundation to your roster. These are your prime contributors and where you will invest the largest percentage of your budget or early round picks. There is no room for risk here, so the majority of these players should be batters.

TIER 2: MID-GAME PLAYERS

General Roster Goals

Auction target: Budget between $50 and $100; players should be under $20

Snake draft target: 7-13 players

Reliability grades: No worse than "B" for Health, no worse than "C" for Experience and Consistency

Playing time: Must have a MM score of 5 for batters (meaning full-time batters) and minimum 3 for pitchers (meaning at least mid-rotation starting pitchers)

Batter skills: Minimum MM scores of 3 in xBA or PX or RSpd

Pitcher skills: Minimum MM score of 3 in xERA or K/9

Tier 1 players are all about skill. Tier 2 is all about accumulating playing time, particularly on the batting side, with lesser regard to skill. This is where you can beef up on runs and RBI. If a player is getting 500 AB, he is likely going to provide positive value in those categories just from opportunity alone. And given that his team is seeing fit to give him those AB, he is probably also contributing somewhere else.

For pitchers, we use Tier 2 to accumulate arms whose innings provide some level of positive support, either by stockpiling strikeouts or by building your ERA foundation.

TIER 3: END-GAME PLAYERS

General Roster Goals

Auction target: Budget up to $50; players should be under $10

Snake draft target: 5-10 players

Reliability grades: No restrictions, except no "F" Health grades.

Playing time: No restrictions

Batter skills: Minimum MM scores of 3 in xBA plus either PX or RSpd (same as Tier 1)

Pitcher skills: Minimum MM score of 3 in xERA

Tier 3 players are your gambling chips, but every end-gamer must provide the promise of upside. For that reason, the focus must remain on skill and conditional opportunity. MP3 drafters should fill the majority of their pitching slots from this group.

By definition, end-gamers are typically high risk players, but risk is something you'll want to embrace here. If a a Tier 3 player does not pan out, he can be easily replaced.

As such, the best Tier 3 options should possess the MM skill levels noted above, and at least one of the following:

- playing time upside as a back-up to a risky front-liner
- an injury history that has depressed his value (but not chronically injured players)
- solid skills demonstrated at some point in the past
- minor league potential even if he has been more recently a major league bust

A complete list of players in each tier appears in the back of the book starting on page 269. One of the major benefits of the MP3 process is that any player failing to find a home in one of the tiers can be safely ignored. Either his skills are not draft-worthy or his risk-profile too dangerous, regardless of skill. By shrinking the draftable player pool, it makes the roster planning and construction process easier.

Category Targets

The the final task is to set MM targets for each category.

If you are in a league with good trading activity, this may not be important—you can always deal away excesses to beef up weak categories. But for those in leagues with little or no trading, drafting a balanced team is critical.

For skills budgeting purposes, here are targets for several standard leagues:

BATTING	PX	RSpd	xBA	PA
12-team mixed	41	28	40	66
15-team mixed	41	26	39	64
12-team AL/NL	37	23	32	54
PITCHING	**xERA***	**K/9***	**Sv**	**IP**
12-team mixed	23	33	7	29
15-team mixed	20	30	6	30
12-team AL/NL	17	27	5	25

** Make sure the majority of these points come from starting pitchers.*

As you draft, track each MM score and keep a running total of all the categories. With the above goals will allow you to shift your in-draft targets if you see you are falling behind in any area.

Building a Homogeneous Head-to-Head Team *(David Martin)*
Though variety is the spice of life, it has no place in the type of players rostered on head-to-head teams. Teams in head-to-head leagues need players cut from the same cloth—players that are completely homogenous.

Focusing on certain metrics helps build a homogenous team; Drafting a homogenous team inherently builds consistency into your roster. Our filters for such success are:

- Contact rate = minimum 80%
- xBA = minimum .280
- PX (or Spd) = minimum 120
- RC/G = minimum 5.00

Research shows that a homogeneous team based on these metrics is more likely to be a consistent team, which is the roster holy grail for head-to-head players.

Ratio Insulation in Head-to-Head Leagues *(David Martin)*
On a week-to-week basis, inequities are inherent in the head-to-head game. One way to eliminate your competitor's advantage in the pure numbers game is to build your team's foundation around the ratio categories.

One should normally insulate at the end of a draft, once your hitters are in place. To obtain several ratio insulators, target players that have:

- Cmd greater than 3.0
- Dom greater than 7.5
- xERA less than 3.30

While adopting this strategy may compromise wins, research has shown that wins come at a cost to ERA and WHIP. Roster space permitting, adding two to four insulators to your team will improve your team's weekly ERA and WHIP.

In-Season Analyses

The efficacy of streaming *(John Burnson)*
In leagues that allow weekly or daily transactions, many owners flit from hot player to hot player. But published dollar values don't capture this traffic—they assume that players are owned from April to October. For many leagues, this may be unrealistic.

We decided to calculate these "investor returns." For each week, we identified the top players by one statistic—BA for hitters, ERA for pitchers—and took the top 100 hitters and top 50 pitchers. We then said that, at the end of the week, the #1 player was picked up (or already owned) by 100% of teams, the #2 player was picked up or owned by 99% of teams, and so on, down to the 100th player, who was on 1% of teams. (For pitchers, we stepped by 2%.) Last, we tracked each player's performance in the next week, when ownership matters.

We ran this process anew for every week of the season, tabulating each player's "investor returns" along the way. If a player was owned by 100% of teams, then we awarded him 100% of his performance. If the player was owned by half the teams, we gave him half his performance. If he was owned by no one (that is, he was not among the top players in the prior week), his performance was ignored. A player's cumulative stats over the season was his investor return.

The results...

- 60% of pitchers had poorer investor returns, with an aggregate ERA 0.40 higher than their true ERA.
- 55% of batters had poorer investor returns, but with an aggregate batting average virtually identical to the true BA.

Sitting stars and starting scrubs *(Ed DeCaria)*
In setting your pitching rotation, conventional wisdom suggests sticking with trusted stars despite difficult matchups. But does this hold up? And can you carefully start inferior pitchers against weaker opponents? Here are the ERAs posted by varying skilled pitchers facing a range of different strength offenses:

	OPPOSING OFFENSE (RC/G)				
Pitcher (ERA)	5.25+	5.00	4.25	4.00	<4.00
3.00-	3.46	3.04	3.04	2.50	2.20
3.50	3.98	3.94	3.44	3.17	2.87
4.00	4.72	4.57	3.96	3.66	3.24
4.50	5.37	4.92	4.47	4.07	3.66
5.00+	6.02	5.41	5.15	4.94	4.42

Recommendations:

1. Never start below replacement-level pitchers.
2. Always start elite pitchers.
3. Other than that, never say never or always.

Playing matchups can pay off when the difference in opposing offense is severe.

Two-start pitcher weeks *(Ed DeCaria)*
A two-start pitcher is a prized possession. But those starts can mean two DOMinant outings, two DISasters, or anything else in between, as shown by these results:

PQS Pair	% Weeks	ERA	WHIP	Win/Wk	K/Wk
DOM-DOM	20%	2.53	1.02	1.1	12.0
DOM-AVG	28%	3.60	1.25	0.8	9.2
AVG-AVG	14%	4.44	1.45	0.7	6.8
DOM-DIS	15%	5.24	1.48	0.6	7.9
AVG-DIS	17%	6.58	1.74	0.5	5.7
DIS-DIS	6%	8.85	2.07	0.3	5.0

Weeks that include even one DISaster start produce terrible results. Unfortunately, avoiding such disasters is much easier in hindsight. But what is the actual impact of this decision on the stat categories?

ERA and WHIP: When the difference between opponents is extreme, inferior pitchers can be a better percentage play. This is true both for 1-start pitchers and 2-start pitchers, and for choosing inferior one-start pitchers over superior two-start pitchers.

Strikeouts per Week: Unlike the two rate stats, there is a massive shift in the balance of power between one-start and two-start pitchers in the strikeout category. Even stars with easy one-start matchups can only barely keep pace with two-start replacement-level arms in strikeouts per week.

Wins per week are also dominated by the two-start pitchers. Even the very worst two-start pitchers will earn a half of a win on average, which is the same rate as the very best one-start pitchers.

The bottom line: If strikeouts and wins are the strategic priority, use as many two-start weeks as the rules allow, even if it means using a replacement-level pitcher with two tough starts instead of a mid-level arm with a single easy start. But if ERA and/or WHIP management are the priority, two-start pitchers can be very powerful, as a single week might impact the standings by over 1.5 points in ERA/WHIP, positively or negatively.

Six Tips on Category Management *(Todd Zola)*

1. Disregard whether you are near the top or the bottom of a category; focus instead on the gaps directly above and below your squad.
2. Prorate the difference in stats between teams.
3. ERA tends to move towards WHIP.
4. As the season progresses, the number of AB/IF do not preclude a gain/loss in the ratio categories.
5. An opponent's point lost is your point gained.
6. *Most important!* Come crunch time, forget value, forget names, and forget reputation. It's all about stats and where you are situated within each category.

Consistency *(Dylan Hedges)*

Few things are as valuable to H2H league success as filling your roster with players who can produce a solid baseline of stats, week in and week out. In traditional leagues, while consistency is not as important—all we care about are aggregate numbers—filling your team with consistent players can make roster management easier.

Consistent batters have good plate discipline, walk rates and on base percentages. These are foundation skills. Those who add power to the mix are obviously more valuable, however, the ability to hit home runs consistently is rare.

Consistent pitchers demonstrate similar skills in each outing; if they also produce similar results, they are even more valuable.

We can track consistency but predicting it is difficult. Many fantasy leaguers try to predict a batter's hot or cold streaks, or individual pitcher starts, but that is typically a fool's errand. The best we can do is find players who demonstrate seasonal consistency; in-season, we must manage players and consistency tactically.

Consistency in points leagues *(Bill Macey)*

Previous research has demonstrated that week-to-week statistical consistency is important for Rotisserie-based head-to-head play. But one can use the same foundation in points-based games. A study showed that not only do players with better skills post more overall points in this format, but that the format caters to consistent performances on a week-to-week basis, even after accounting for differences in total points scored and playing-time.

Therefore, when drafting your batters in points-based head-to-head leagues, ct% and bb% make excellent tiebreakers if you are having trouble deciding between two players with similarly projected point totals. Likewise, when rostering pitchers, favor those who tend not to give up home runs.

Other Diamonds

Cellar value
The dollar value at which a player cannot help but earn more than he costs. Always profit here.

Crickets
The sound heard when someone's opening draft bid on a player is also the only bid.

Scott Elarton List
Players you drop out on when the bidding reaches $1.

End-game wasteland
Home for players undraftable in the deepest of leagues, who stay in the free agent pool all year. It's the place where even crickets keep quiet when a name is called at the draft.

FAAB Forewarnings

1. Spend early and often.
2. Emptying your budget for one prime league-crosser is a tactic that should be reserved for the desperate.
3. If you chase two rabbits, you will lose them both.

Fantasy Economics 101
The market value for a player is based on the aura of past performance, not the promise of future potential. Your greatest advantage is to leverage the space between market value and real value.

Fantasy Economics 102
The variance between market value and real value is far more important than the absolute accuracy of any individual player projection.

Hope
A commodity that routinely goes for $5 over value at the draft table.

Professional Free Agent (PFA)
Player whose name will never come up on draft day but will always end up on a roster at some point during the season as an injury replacement.

Mike Timlin List
Players who you are unable to resist drafting even though they have burned you multiple times in the past.

Seasonal Assessment Standard
If you still have reason to be reading the boxscores during the last weekend of the season, then your year has to be considered a success.

The Three Cardinal Rules for Winners
If you cherish this hobby, you will live by them or die by them...

1. Revel in your success; fame is fleeting.
2. Exercise excruciating humility.
3. 100% of winnings must be spent on significant others.

Expected Wins

by Matt Cederholm

Pity poor Shelby Miller. In 2015, he won a mere 6 games in 33 starts, with a 3.02 ERA (24% better than the league average). Perhaps he needed to study Bartolo Colon, who won 18 games in 2004 with a 5.01 ERA—in a pitcher's park. These win totals bother us, as they are at odds with how well these guys pitched. There has to be a way to figure out how many games a starter should win.

We've tackled the subject before. In 2015, Patrick Davitt took a look at unlucky pitchers. He found that lucky wins were rather rare, but unlucky losses (or no decisions) were somewhat common. Ed DeCaria also weighed in a few years ago with a ranked list of factors that explained a pitcher's Win %, but ultimately wasn't able to produce a usable forward-looking projection with then-available data.

Background and Methodology

Let's specify that we are looking strictly at starter wins; reliever wins are too situational to generate reliable models. To that end, we examined only pitchers with no bullpen appearances. In a quest for reasonable sample sizes and to capture the current environment, we only looked at pitchers with 15+ starts from 2010-2014. That yielded 531 pitcher-seasons encompassing over 15,000 starts, so that's a good place to, er, start.

Factors Affecting Wins

We hypothesized that wins would be affected by:

- Pitcher ERA
- Team offense
- Team defense
- Bullpen quality
- Innings pitched per start

In order to properly compare pitchers with more playing time, we checked each of these against wins per game started (W/GS) rather than total wins. We found that none of these factors had a particularly strong correlation:

ERA	-0.59
Innings per Start	0.53
Team Offense (R/G)	0.35
Bullpen (RA)	-0.33
Def-Defensive Runs Saved	0.13
Def-Unearned Run Average	-0.11

Not the breakthrough we had hoped for. ERA and innings per start are the closest, though they are themselves more correlated to each other (-0.67 correlation) than to wins. So a multifactor model, such as xBA or xERA, isn't likely to yield meaningful results. Of course, in a multifactor regression, some of the terms might become more significant, but without a strong starting point, it's probably wasted effort.

Is There an Alternative?

There is an alternative—and it's a wonderfully simple one. So simple, in fact, that we had our doubts going in: the Pythagorean Theorem of Baseball. Developed by Bill James, it's a fairly robust method of checking a team's "true" winning percentage, based on runs scored and runs allowed. Teams that outperform or underperform their Pythagorean estimated wins typically show strong regression in the following season. Would it work for individual pitchers?

As a reminder, here is the Pythagorean Theorem:

$$\text{Winning Percentage} = \frac{\text{Runs Scored}^{2/}}{\text{Runs allowed}^{2} + \text{Runs Scored}^{2}}$$

We tried it. And the results didn't look right. For example, Clayton Kershaw had 27 expected wins (xW) for his 2013 season. Errors were high, insults were thrown, and we were tempted to give ourselves the Hook.

Okay, not so much. There were actually two flaws in our first attempt. First, research has shown that the correct exponent for the theorem is closer to 1.80 than to 2. Various researchers have pegged it at 1.83 or 1.81, and a few have even derived a formula for deriving the exponent. In looking at all teams from 2010-2014, the lowest mean squared error (MSE) resulted from using 1.80 as the exponent, so that's what we used.

Second, while a team either wins or loses every game, starting pitchers have a third option: the no decision. So before we can apply the Pythagorean factor, we have to project how many no-decisions a starter should be expected to have. (If you want to skip the next section, you can).

No Decisions

We'll keep this simple, though we'll include a chart:

- The average no-decision percentage in our sample was 28%. In other words, 28% of starts resulted in a no-decision.
- There was no correlation in no-decision percentage between pairs of pitcher-seasons (we had 260 such pairs).
- Nearly 70% of pitchers who were above average in one season saw their no-decision percentage move towards (or past) the average in the subsequent season.
- While there are outliers, no-decision percentage is roughly normally distributed and clustered in the center:

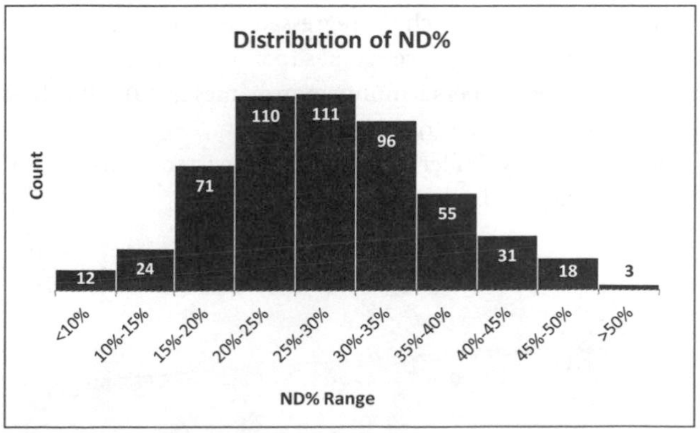

Based on the research, we concluded that individual pitchers have little control over their no-decision percentage, allowing us to use the league average (28%) for all pitchers.

The Final Formula

Putting it altogether, we have the following formula:

$$xWins = \frac{Team\ Runs\ per\ Game^{1.80}}{Pitcher\ ERA^{1.80} + Team\ Runs\ per\ Game^{1.80}} \times 0.72 \times GS$$

Of course, a model is only as good as its accuracy. Here are the results:

Correlation to Wins	0.83
R-Squared Adjusted	69%
Mean Squared Error	2.30

According to this, our expected wins formula explains nearly 70% of the variation in pitcher wins. Funny how that number matches up with our rule of thumb that the best projections are no better than 70% accurate. Coincidence, for sure, but an interesting one.

Furthermore, 70% of pitchers whose expected wins varied from actual wins from 2010-2013 showed regression in wins per start in the following year.

Statistically, a 70% R-squared is a pretty darned good fit. These are the kinds of results we hope for.

Looking at 2015

Does this work in practice? Let's look at some pitchers (not a scientific sample) whose Expected Wins in 2014 varied significantly from actual wins, and see how they did in 2015.

Overperformers

	2014				2015		
Pitcher	xW	W	Diff	W/30	W	W/30	Change
C. Kershaw	16	21	5	23	16	15	-9
B. Colon	11	15	4	15	14	13	-2
W. Peralta	13	17	4	16	5	8	-8
H. Iwakuma	11	15	4	16	9	14	-3
M. Tanaka	9	13	4	20	12	15	-5

Underperformers

	2014				2015		
Pitcher	xW	W	Diff	W/30	W	W/30	Change
Jeff Samardzija	16	7	-9	6	11	10	4
Francisco Liriano	12	7	-5	7	12	12	5
Yovani Gallardo	13	8	-5	7	13	12	5
Jose Quintana	14	9	-5	8	9	8	0
Charlie Morton	10	6	-4	7	9	12	5

**Pitchers who did not have a relief appearance in 2014 and started at least 15 games.*

While there are surely other factors affecting their 2015 win totals, each of these pitchers regressed as expected, with the outperformers winning fewer games (per 30 starts) than in 2014, and the underperformers winning more games in 2015. It's always nice when a plan comes together.

Oh, and Shelby Miller? He had 13 Expected Wins in 2015. Boom! There's your first draft target for 2016.

Predictive Power of PQS Hot Streaks

by Patrick Davitt

Back in 2010, BaseballHQ.com published a research essay on how well five-game sequences predicted the sixth game in that same sequence.

This update revisits the five-game sequence question while also assessing results after three- and four-game "hot streaks," using BaseballHQ's Pure Quality Start (PQS) method for rating starts.

Terms

PQS scoring is described in the "In-Season" section of the *Forecaster's* Encyclopedia of Fanalytics, so let's clarify four other terms this study uses:

- A "sequence" is any string of starts by a pitcher, with no more than seven days between any two starts in the sequence. To qualify for the study, a sequence also required a "next start."
- "Next start" means the start immediately after the third or fourth game that established a hot streak or a five-game sequence. A "next start" must have occurred within seven days of the last start in the streak or sequence.
- A "hot streak" is a three- or four game sequence in which all games are PQS-DOM (PQS-4 or -5), with a qualifying "next start" after the third or fourth game in the streak.
- A "Long-Term PQS score" is the PQS average of the pitcher's full run in the study period (some or all of 2010-2014).

Method

First, we assembled PQS lists for all starting pitchers from 2010-2014. We examined each streak or sequence to determine the result in that pitcher's next start, and aggregated the resulting data to get broad general results.

As well, we compared next-game results with individual pitcher PQS averages, including Long-Term, YTD and in-sequence.

Results 1: Overall

We found 25,350 starts by 567 pitchers. Within those starts, we found:

- 2,741 three-game hot streaks (STRK3) among 16,377 three-game sequences
- 1,497 were four-game hot streaks (STRK4) among 14,370 four-game sequences
- And 18,319 five game sequences (SEQ5)

First, to set PQS expectations, the overall results of all games, taken individually without regard to sequences or streaks:

PQS	n	% All*
0	4131	16.3%
1	1066	4.2%
2	2589	10.2%
3	5353	21.1%
4	5976	23.6%
5	6235	24.6%

* Percentages might not sum to 100% because of rounding

We watched throughout this research for PQS results out of alignment with these overall results.

Results 2: Actual PQS vs Expected (YTD and SEQ5)

The 2010 study wanted to look at how much actual PQS results varied from expected results, based on the pitchers' PQS averages within their YTD and SEQ5s.

That earlier study found the pitcher's YTD PQS average to be a useful predictor of PQS score in a particular start. In this study, the Standard Deviation (SD) of the differences between YTD PQS average and actual was 1.8, while the SD of differences between SEQ5 average and actual was 1.4. While this suggests that SEQ5 PQS average may be a better predictor than YTD PQS average, the truth is that in either case, the predictive value is rather limited. We also checked the outcome of a game based on the previous start, and the SD of differences was even worse, at 2.3.

Separating out the various YTD PQS cohorts, we see a pattern emerge we might have expected:

		NEXT-START PQS					
YTD	n	0	1	2	3	4	5
0.0-0.9	532	32%	5%	9%	23%	19%	13%
1.0-1.9	1156	23%	6%	12%	24%	19%	17%
2.0-2.9	6863	20%	5%	12%	22%	22%	19%
3.0-3.9	11449	13%	4%	10%	21%	25%	27%
4.0-5.0	3745	10%	3%	8%	18%	26%	35%

Not a huge surprise: The higher the YTD PQS going into a start, the higher the percentage of higher PQS scores coming out of that start. Note, however, that the highest YTD cohort (4.0-5.0) easily outpaces the overall average noted above in earning PQS-DOM scores, while the lowest YTD cohort (0.0-0.9) is way ahead of the pace of PQS-DIS outcomes.

Now, what about next-start PQS by the pitchers' SEQ5 PQS Averages?

		NEXT-START PQS					
SEQ5 PQS	n	0	1	2	3	4	5
0.0-0.9	167	66%	11%	9%	11%	2%	0%
1.0-1.9	1327	43%	10%	14%	18%	10%	6%
2.0-2.9	4915	22%	7%	15%	24%	20%	13%
3.0-3.9	7105	8%	3%	10%	24%	29%	26%
4.0-4.9	3621	0%	0%	3%	14%	29%	53%

We see a sample-size issue right away—pitchers with SEQ5 PQS averages under 1.0 don't get many sixth chances!

But pitchers with SEQ5 PQS over 3.0 beat the overall next-start averages for PQS scores of 3 and 4, while SEQ5 pitchers with SEQ5 scores of 4.0 and up notched PQS-DOMs in their next starts more than eight next starts out of 10.

As well, the SD for actual-expected differences in the SEQ5 cohort was down to 0.85, indicating reduced variability and therefore better predictive value.

Results 3: Starts After Hot Streaks

We next moved on to the question of starters who had thrown three or four excellent games in a row, focusing particularly on how likely were they to follow up with another good start.

The answer: very likely. Here's the big picture (STRK3 n = 2,741, STRK4 n = 1,497):

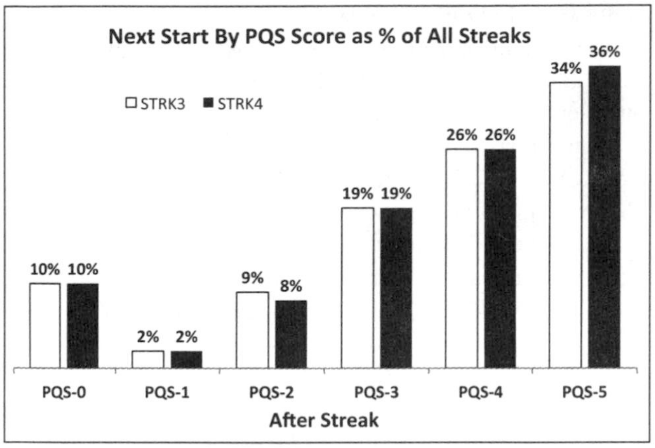

Clearly the pattern shows that hot streaks beget good next starts, with 60% of both STRK3 and STRK4 followed by PQS-DOM starts, and only 12% of such streaks followed by PQS-DIS starts.

These outcomes, though they show marked departures from the general overall PQS results shown at the start, nonetheless meet intuitive expectations. We would expect that 3- or 4-game hot streaks are more likely to be pitched by the better starters, and that better starters are more likely to throw additional PQS-DOM starts.

We also checked those expectations against our data. First, we grouped all starters (minimum five starts) into the same longer-term PQS cohorts as in the SEQ% portion, then saw how the 3- and 4-game streaks were distributed among the resulting 458 individual pitchers.

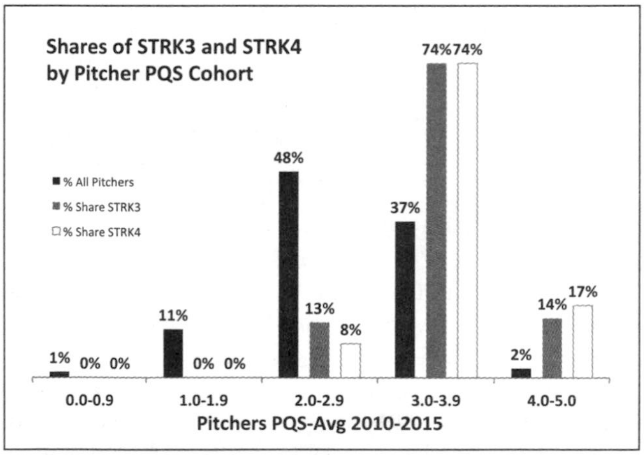

Our expectation was confirmed. Of all the STRK-3 and -4 performances, more than 88% belonged to the 39% of the pitchers whose PQS averages were 3.0 or higher. And the disproportion is even more pronounced in the pitcher cohort at or above PQS-4, who were just 2% of the pitchers but had 14% of STRK-3 and 17% of STRK-4. (Keep in mind that a pitcher's STRK-4 includes two STRK-3s.)

Meanwhile, the pitchers in the 2.0-2.9 cohort account for half the pitchers in the study, but just 13% of STRK3s and 8% of STRK4s. And the PQS-1.9 averages or lower, accounting for about 12% of pitchers, had no hot streaks at all.

Results 4: Medium pitcher results

So better pitchers have more PQS-DOM starts, more hot streaks, and more followup PQS-DOM starts. But there isn't much fantasy leverage in this. What we need to know, for streaming and daily-game purposes, is whether these streaks confer a percentage advantage on lesser pitchers.

Since we know pitchers with long-term PQS-1.9 or lower don't get the streaks, we looked at the distribution of average next-start PQS scores among pitchers by cohorts, by both career PQS average and by YTD PQS average. Again, we want to see if there is some betting advantage to be gained.

The next four tables lay out these data for:

- Long-term PQS Average (LT-PQS), STRK3s
- Long-term PQS Average, STRK4s
- YTD PQS Average, STRK3s
- YTD PQS Average, STRK4s

STRK3	NEXT-START PQS					
LT-PQS	0	1	2	3	4	5
2.0-2.9	19%	5%	15%	22%	24%	16%
3.0-3.9	10%	2%	8%	20%	26%	34%
4.0-4.9	4%	1%	5%	15%	25%	50%

STRK4	NEXT-START PQS					
LT-PQS	0	1	2	3	4	5
2.0-2.9	21%	3%	17%	22%	21%	16%
3.0-3.9	11%	2%	8%	19%	26%	35%
4.0-4.9	3%	1%	5%	13%	27%	50%

STRK3	NEXT-START PQS					
YTD-PQS	0	1	2	3	4	5
2.0-2.9	24%	0%	17%	21%	14%	24%
3.0-3.9	11%	3%	11%	22%	25%	28%
4.0-4.9	10%	2%	8%	18%	25%	37%

STRK4	NEXT-START PQS					
YTD-PQS	0	1	2	3	4	5
2.0-2.9	0%	0%	0%	0%	0%	0%
3.0-3.9	10%	4%	12%	19%	25%	30%
4.0-4.9	10%	2%	8%	19%	25%	37%

Looking first at YTD PQS, we see first that streaks by pitchers with YTD or LT PQS under 3.0 have PQS-DOM next starts 40% or less of the time. It's a bad bet if you can't beat a coin flip.

Otherwise, hardly anything has budged from the SEQ-5 results. A STRK3 or STRK4 hot run by a 3.0-3.9 pitcher gets a PQS-DOM next start between 53% and 55% of the time, and next starts after streaks by pitchers of YTD PQS averages over 4.0 turn in PQS-DOMs 62% of the time.

The exception is defining the cohorts using Long-Term PQS. A pitcher with a longer-term PQS average of 3.0-3.9 and a hot streak underway fires a PQS-DOM next start about 61% of the time, a seven or eight percentage-point gain over pitchers whose 3.0-3.9 PQS averages are in-sequence only.

This could be a useful bit of info in allowing fantasy owners to identify potentially underpriced pitchers—typically number-three or good number-four starters—for streaming and, especially, for daily games, where PQS matches up very well with Daily Fantasy Sports (DFS) points scoring:

PQS	n	DFS* Pts Ave
0	4131	1.6
1	1066	4.0
2	2589	6.2
3	5353	8.8
4	5976	11.6
5	6235	15.0

** USA Today Fantasy Score method: W=4, IP=1, K=1, ER -1*

Conclusion

Mostly, this research confirms what we knew or suspected: that pitchers with high average PQS scores (especially YTD or longer-term) are more likely than lower-PQS pitchers to throw PQS-DOMs in their next starts.

Some other learnings:

- A PQS score in one game is a poor predictor of the PQS score in the next.
- Overall, the next start after a three- or four-game hot streak is another PQS-DOM about 60% of the time, and this effect is stronger for pitchers with higher long-term PQS averages
- After a three- or four-game hot streak by a starter whose YTD or long-term PQS average is over 4.0, the next start is another PQS-DOM more than 70% of the time.
- Pitchers with long-term PQS averages under 2.0 didn't have any hot streaks.
- Middling starters—those with a long-run PQS average from 3.0-3.9—and on hot streaks get another PQS-DOM in their next start more than 60% of the time, a rate about eight percentage points higher than the same level of starters with 3.0-3.9 PQS in shorter-run averages.

How we might apply these data: In DFS tournament play, when an owner is looking to find a pitching zag to other players' zigs. When a middling (LT-PQS 3.0-3.9) starters strings together three PQS-DOM, his odds of a next-start PQS-DOM climb past 60%, within 10 percentage points of much better (and much costlier) starters.

In full-season play, the tactical edge is not so clear-cut. In deeper leagues with starting-pitcher "streaming," we might be able to choose among similar mid-grade starters.

The Bounceback Fallacy

by Patrick Davitt

A common trope found at fantasy baseball sites and in fantasy baseball expert commentary is the idea that we should target the kind of quality starting pitcher who had bad results last season.

The idea is that a good pitcher is highly likely to "bounce back" with a premium campaign, recovering at least some of value lost in the disaster season and maybe even recover all the way back to or even beyond past levels. And the canny drafter or auction bidder can grab a really high-potential pitcher at a price that is discounted because of the recency bias associated with the immediate bad season.

We at BaseballHQ.com like to challenge "common knowledge" like this, with an eye towards giving you an edge in being able to exploit instances where the "common knowledge" is perhaps not accurate.

That's what we found when we looked into this particular trope. We sifted through thousands of pitcher-seasons over more than a decade, looking for examples of starting pitchers who had a quality season, then a bad season. We wanted to see what happened to these pitchers in the next season, after the disaster.

Mostly, they got even worse.

Method

We began by assembling a database of starting pitchers (SP)—pitchers who averaged at least 17 Batters Faced per Game (BF/G) in any season from 2003 through 2013. This gave us a starting point of about 3,000 pitchers, and more than 19,000 pitcher-seasons.

We then defined a "quality" pitcher-season as one in which a SP had a rotisserie value of $10 or more. There were 451 such pitcher-seasons in the study.

We first looked for general patterns of loss and collapse in seasons after all $10 seasons.

Next, we found all the quality seasons that were followed by what we called "collapse" years, in which the pitcher lost half or more of his previous season value. So a $21 season followed by a $10 season was considered a collapse, even though the pitcher returned positive value, because the collapse year represented such a significant falloff that the pitcher would likely be considered a "bounceback candidate." There were 229 such occurrences.

Finally, we counted how many times the collapse year was followed by:

- Full bounceback (FBB): To or beyond the level of the first "quality" season
- Partial bounceback (PBB): To a positive season value higher than the collapse but not back to the pre-collapse level
- Decline (Dec): Collapse year followed by an even worse year
- No-help recovery (NHR): Value of the season after collapse was higher than the collapse year but still negative. NHR also includes pitchers who did not pitch the subsequent year.

Results 1: Proneness to Loss or Collapse

We wanted to know whether results varied with pitcher value in the pre-collapse season. Were some value tiers more prone to collapse? Were collapses after very-high-value seasons ($30+) more or less prone to recovery than middle ($20-$29) or normal ($10-$19) value seasons?

First, we looked at general proneness to loss of any kind and collapse (remembering that a collapse is a next season whose value was less than half the previous season):

Season		Next Season			
Value	n	Loss	%	Coll	%
$30+	31	29	94%	15	48%
$20-$29	99	78	79%	52	53%
$10-$19	321	237	74%	162	50%

Higher value means a more likely loss. This is to be expected: A top-value year leaves little upside and lots of downside. Even so, even more normal value achievements tended to be followed by lesser seasons, though not as often. Interestingly, a collapse appears to be a coin-flip proposition across value tiers.

More importantly, there was not a big difference in the frequency of collapse based on the first year in the pair: about half the seasons in all three value tiers had collapses the next year.

Results 2: Post-collapse

First, let's look at the general results:

Collapses	FBB	PBB	Dec	NHR
229	16	46	93	74
	7%	20%	41%	32%

Clearly, the vaunted bounceback season tends not to happen. Almost three-quarters of collapse seasons were followed by still further declines or NHRs. Full bouncebacks were extremely rare, at just 7% of the total. There might be some opportunity in the partial bouncebacks, if bidding allows pitchers to be grabbed well under pre-collapse value.

Results 3: Recovery Years by Value Tier

Finally, let's look at the recovery years, that is, the seasons that immediately followed collapse seasons.

Season Value	n	FBB	%	PBB	%	DEC	%	NHR	%
$30+	15	0	0%	8	53%	6	40%	1	7%
$20-$29	52	1	2%	13	25%	22	42%	16	31%
$10-$19	162	15	9%	25	15%	65	40%	57	35%
Overall	229	16	7%	46	20%	93	41%	74	32%

Some results jibe with expectations. Declines are around 40% in all value tiers, as in the overall results. We see only one FBB in the top two value tiers, with 9% FBBs in the lowest tier, but that makes sense in that a recovering pitcher does not need to have an enormous rebound to get to a $10 season of even a $15 season.

There are a couple of interesting anomalies: The PBB rate of 53% for the top-tier pitchers is well outside of the overall results, and might indicate that these pitchers have so much talent that they are likelier to recover to positive values, even if they can't get back to top value.

Summary and Analysis

So... How do we apply these findings?

The lesson appears to be in the nature of what not to do rather than what to do. And that is: Don't bid aggressively on pitchers who suffered a collapse in the previous season.

Common wisdom is that these pitchers will have big rebounds, but the results show the reverse is true—you are extremely unlikely to get a full bounceback, and equally likely to suffer a further decline or uselessly small recovery as to get even a partial bounceback. Proceed with caution.

Ball and Strike Rates of Starting Pitchers

by Stephen Nickrand

Our prior research on swinging strike rate and first-pitch strike rate confirmed that both have usefulness as predictive tools for a pitcher's strikeout and walk rates. In addition, our detailed research on the stats and skills posted by starting pitchers by ball-strike counts confirmed that the frequency a pitcher falls into certain ball-strike counts greatly impacts the likelihood that the at-bat ends in a walk or strikeout, and even impacts the likelihood that a batted ball falls as a hit. Here, we'll expand this line of research by showing that the percentage of pitches thrown by starting pitchers as balls or strikes have predictive value when validating and forecasting changes in the pitcher's walk (BB/9) rate.

Method

We'll begin by taking an updated five-year look at the relationship between a pitcher's control (BB/9) and dominance (K/9) rates with other stats and skills. Then we'll look closely at ball percentages to see how closely they correlate with strikeouts and walks, whether they have predictive value, and whether they are more likely to regress to a SP's own ball% or the MLB norm.

As a reminder, correlations can range from -1.0 to +1.0. The strongest correlations are at the extremes; they get weaker as they get closer to zero:

+0.70 to +1.00	Strong positive relationship
+0.40 to +0.69	Moderate positive relationship
+0.20 to +0.39	Weak positive relationship
+0.19 to -0.19	No or negligible relationship
-0.20 to -0.39	Weak negative relationship
-0.40 to -0.69	Moderate negative relationship
-0.70 to -1.00	Strong negative relationship

Results

First, let's examine a large sample of stats and skills to see how they may be correlated with a pitcher's rate of walks and strikeouts.

Control Rate Correlations

Indicator	Indicator	Correlation
As walks go up, indicator goes up—and vice-versa:		
Ctl	**Ball%**	**+0.70**
Ctl	WHIP	+0.68
Ctl	ERA	+0.57
Ctl	H%	+0.21
Ctl	HR/9	+0.15
Ctl	hr/f	+0.12
Ctl	S%	+0.05
Ctl	O-Contact%	+0.03
Ctl	FAv	+0.02
As walks go down, indicator goes up—and vice-versa:		
Ctl	**Strike%**	**-0.70**
Ctl	Swing%	-0.53
Ctl	O-Swing%	-0.49
Ctl	FpK%	-0.35
Ctl	Zone%	-0.29
Ctl	Win Pct	-0.28
Ctl	SwK%	-0.14
Ctl	Z-Contact%	-0.12
Ctl	Age	-0.10
Ctl	GB%	-0.07
Ctl	Z-Swing%	-0.04
Ctl	Contact%	-0.00

It does not come as a surprise to see that WHIP and ERA have strong negative correlations with a SP's Ctl, since walks directly impact WHIP and make the risk of ERA blowups greater. Nor is it revealing that strike% declines significantly as walks go up.

The above chart does show that ball% and strike% have the strongest correlation to a SP's control rate out of all indicators listed.

Now let's take a look at the indicators most closely correlated with a SP's dominance (K/9) rate.

Dominance Rate Correlations

Indicator	Indicator	Correlation
As strikeouts go up, indicator goes up—and vice-versa:		
Dom	SwK%	+0.70
Dom	FAv	+0.29
Dom	H%	+0.27
Dom	O-Swing%	+0.18
Dom	**Strike%**	**+0.15**
Dom	Win Pct	+0.15
Dom	FpK%	+0.08
Dom	S%	+0.06
Dom	Swing%	+0.06
Dom	hr/f	+0.02
Dom	Zone%	+0.01
As strikeouts go down, indicator goes up—and vice-versa:		
Dom	Age	-0.05
Dom	HR/9	-0.08
Dom	GB%	-0.12
Dom	Z-Swing%	-0.13
Dom	**Ball%**	**-0.15**
Dom	ERA	-0.18
Dom	WHIP	-0.21
Dom	Z-Contact%	-0.55
Dom	O-Contact%	-0.56
Dom	Contact%	-0.72

As we already know, there is a consistently strong positive correlation between swinging strike rate (SwK%) and strikeouts (Dom). There is also a moderate-to-strong negative correlation between strikeouts and the level of contact made by batters—both inside and outside the strike zone.

Unlike with a SP's control rate, strong correlations do not exist between ball/strike% and dominance rate.

Let's establish some ball% and strike% baselines so that we know the marks typically shown by starting pitchers.

From 2010 to 2015, the ball and strike percentages of starting pitchers have stayed extremely steady, both from season-to-season and by league:

Historical Ball and Strike Percentages—Starting Pitchers

Season	League	Ball%	Strike%
2010	MLB	37%	63%
2011	MLB	37%	63%
2012	MLB	36%	64%
2013	MLB	36%	64%
2014	MLB	36%	64%
2015	MLB	36%	64%

Just under two-thirds of pitches thrown by starting pitchers are strikes. A little more than one-third are balls. There are no significant differences by league.

Sixty percent of SP produce a ball% between 34% and 37%:

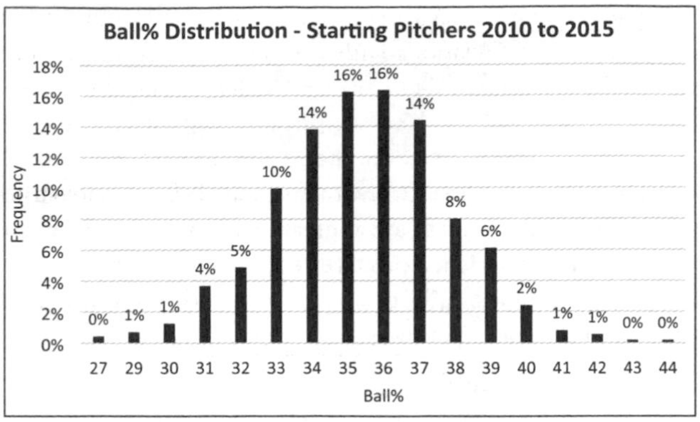

Ball% Stability

Does ball% regress to league norms or do players set their own baselines?

The average ball% vs. MLB ball% variance of SP with at least 40 IP during the last five seasons was +/-1.91%. By comparison, the average variance between a SP's ball% and their own career ball% was smaller—+/-1.71%.

This indicates that SP tend to set their own ball% baselines more often than regressing to an overall norm. This make sense, as we typically view balls, strikes, and walks as areas that are mostly under a SP's control.

Predicting Control Rate from Ball% and Strike%

We can establish a SP's expected control rate (xCtl) using their ball%. This table confirms the strong correlation between ball% and Ctl.

Expected Control Rate by Percentile

Ball%	10th	25th	50th	75th	90th
<30%	0.8	0.8	1.1	1.3	1.4
31%	1.3	1.4	1.5	2.0	2.1
32%	1.2	1.5	1.7	2.0	2.3
33%	1.5	1.6	1.9	2.2	2.5
34%	1.7	2.0	2.3	2.6	2.9
35%	1.8	2.1	2.3	2.6	2.9
36%	2.0	2.3	2.7	3.1	3.4
37%	2.3	2.7	3.0	3.3	3.7
38%	2.6	2.8	3.2	3.6	4.1
39%	2.9	3.2	3.5	4.0	4.5
40%	3.1	3.5	3.9	4.5	4.9
41%	3.5	3.9	4.6	5.1	5.5
>42%	4.2	4.7	5.1	5.6	6.6

If you flip the above data and use strike% instead of ball%, the same ranges of values apply:

Expected Control Rate by Percentile

Strike%	10th	25th	50th	75th	90th
>70%	0.8	0.8	1.1	1.3	1.4
69%	1.3	1.4	1.5	2.0	2.1
68%	1.2	1.5	1.7	2.0	2.3
67%	1.5	1.6	1.9	2.2	2.5
66%	1.7	2.0	2.3	2.6	2.9
65%	1.8	2.1	2.3	2.6	2.9
64%	2.0	2.3	2.7	3.0	3.4
63%	2.3	2.7	3.0	3.3	3.6
62%	2.6	2.8	3.2	3.6	4.1
61%	2.9	3.2	3.5	4.0	4.5
60%	3.1	3.5	3.9	4.5	4.9
59%	3.5	3.9	4.6	5.1	5.5
<58%	4.2	4.7	5.1	5.6	6.6

Ball% Outliers

From 2010 to 2014, 83 SP posted a control rate that was +/- 1.0 of their expected control rate (xCtl) based on their ball%, using the 50th percentile of the above table as xCtl.

Of those, 35 SP had at least 40 IP as a SP during the following season.

In 29 of these 35 cases (83%), the SP's control rate in year two moved in the direction of his year one xCtl.

This indicates that SP with wide variances between Ctl and xCtl will overwhelmingly experience a correction in the direction of xCtl—as calculated by using ball%—the following season.

Conclusions

- There are strong correlations between a SP's ball% and strike% and the amount of walks he allows.
- Ball% provides the closest link to a pitcher's Ctl than any other indicator.
- SwK% provides the closest link to a pitcher's Dom than any other indicator.
- There are weak correlations between a SP's ball% and strike% and the amount of strikeouts he gets.
- Ball% more often regresses to a SP's career norm than it regresses to an MLB norm.
- SP with wide variances between Ctl and xCtl will overwhelmingly experience a correction in the direction of xCtl—as calculated by using ball%—during the following season.

Estimating HR Output for Young Hitters

by Matt Cederholm

We've done a lot of research into developing various metrics, and each has its value in evaluating a hitter. But while it's great to have a bunch of ways to break down player performance, the real meat of fantasy baseball analysis is in using what we know to guide us in making decisions about future performance. In other words, what do all of our various hitting metrics— FB%, PX, xPX, HH%, hr/f, and HctX—tell us about future performance?

We'll start with home runs. Let's consider what skills produce home runs once the batter has made contact:

- **Bat speed/strength:** Specifically, the ability to hit the ball hard. Do we have something that measures this? Yes! We have hard-hit ball rate (HH%) and expected power index (xPX). Since xPX combines HH% and medium-hit balls into a metric that is correlated to actual power, this is our preferred skill.
- **Batted ball trajectory:** While a handful of homers are the result of line drives, most home runs are from fly balls. We'll use FB% as our primary indicator of potential home run trajectory.

So we need xPX and FB% to understand home run output. But what about PX? Recall that PX is based on linear-weighted power, which includes home runs as an input. Because hits and hit types are outcomes, they aren't ideal to use as skills. We want to compare outcomes to skills to see where the outliers are.

And what about hr/f? Interestingly, hr/f is a sort of intermediate measure in that it is an outcome (home runs) normalized for a skill (FB%). So it actually can be useful because it allows us to understand, for a given level of fly ball trajectory, what was a player's home run output.

So what happens when we plot xPX (our first home run-related skill: strength) with hr/f (our outcome of interest, normalized for our second home run-related skill: trajectory)?

		hr/f percentiles*				
xPX	#	10	25	50	75	90
<=70	204	0.9%	2.0%	3.8%	5.5%	7.4%
71-80	104	3.3%	5.1%	6.4%	8.1%	10.0%
81-90	111	3.8%	5.4%	7.4%	9.0%	11.0%
91-100	125	4.7%	6.6%	8.9%	11.3%	13.0%
101-110	133	6.6%	8.3%	10.9%	13.0%	16.2%
111-120	138	7.4%	9.8%	11.9%	14.7%	17.1%
121-130	118	8.5%	10.9%	12.8%	15.5%	17.4%
131-140	119	9.7%	11.9%	14.6%	17.1%	20.4%
141-160	116	11.3%	13.1%	16.5%	19.2%	21.5%
161+	55	14.4%	16.5%	19.4%	22.0%	25.8%

**Reflects all hitter seasons from 2010-2014 with 300+ AB.*

This is what we'd expect overall, as the hr/f increases at each level of power. We can now use this to validate past performance and better predict future performance, as players who stray too far from the center can be expected to regress given their xPX, as players in the more extreme percentiles should see regression.

Here's the average change in hr/f in the following season, which does show regression to the mean:

%-ile	Avg. Change
10th	2.1
25th	0.4
75th	-1.2
90th	-4.1

Note that there's some survivor bias in the bottom percentiles. Players who underperform are at greater risk of losing their jobs, and those who experience positive regression are more likely to hold on to their jobs. Still, the results are fairly robust, making them useful for finding outliers.

Application of Results

For established players, we already know that they tend to regress toward their three-year average hr/f rate. So where this newly understood relationship between xPX and hr/f may really come in handy is where we need to evaluate hitters with short major league track records who aren't as easy to pin down.

It's pretty simple, really. Look at a player and project his HR as if his hr/f was at the median for his xPX level. For example, if a player with a 125 xPX exceeds a 12.8% hr/f, we would expect a decline in the following season. The greater the deviation from the mean, the greater the probability of a decline.

Let's take a look at some younger players whose 2014 hr/f was in the highest or lowest percentiles and compare their actual performance to what it might have been if their hr/f landed in the middle of the pack (the 50th percentile would be our expectation short of additional evidence) based on their xPX level, and compare that to how they actually performed (2015 HR numbers are adjusted to match 2014 PT):

Possible Faders

	2014					2015	
Hitter	xPX	%-ile	HR	xHR	Diff	HR*	Change
Jose Abreu	132	90	36	19	-17	27	-9
Tyler Flowers	88	90	15	5	-10	11	-4
Corey Dickerson	135	75	24	18	-6	19	-5
Kole Calhoun	94	90	17	11	-6	20	+3
Rougned Odor	68	90	9	4	-5	14	+5
Kevin Kiermaier	82	90	10	6	-4	7	-3
Kolten Wong	82	75	12	8	-4	8	-4
Daniel Santana	63	90	7	3	-4	0	-7

**Adjusted to 2014 playing time.*

Possible Surgers

	2014					2015	
Hitter	xPX	%-ile	HR	xHR	Diff	HR*	Change
Anthony Rendon	146	10	21	34	13	10	-11
Nick Castellanos	135	10	11	21	10	15	+4
Xander Bogaerts	111	10	12	19	7	6	-6
Conor Gillaspie	95	10	7	13	6	8	+1
Travis D'Arnaud	136	10	13	18	5	19	+6
Nolan Arenado	134	10	18	23	5	29	+11
Eduardo Escobar	93	10	6	11	5	13	+7

**Adjusted to 2014 playing time.*

Not perfect, but what is? However, only two players in each group went in the opposite direction of what was predicted. This definitely has promise as a predictive tool.

Pitchers' Secret Weapon Against Aging

by Ed DeCaria

Pitching skills deteriorate with age. By a typical pitcher's mid-20s, strikeout rate drops, walk rate increases, fly ball and line drive rates increase, hr/f increases, and more. While not all pitchers age the same way, the general equation is clear: Birthdays + 1 = Bad.

You have to draft *someone*, though, which leaves you with only a few options: 1) Buy last year's stars and hope they hold on to most of what they had, 2) Get into bidding wars for "sleepers" whose underlying skills have not yet manifested in surface-level stats, or 3) Find pitchers who will reverse the aging process and improve their base skills next year.

As I see it, #1 is kinda boring and #2 is well-covered by the rest of this book, so let's go with #3. But, is it even possible? Do pitchers really have a secret weapon for delaying the adverse effects of aging?

Let's zero in on one specific skill: strikeouts. The following charts ("aging curves") depict the change in strikeout-related skills of MLB pitchers as they age. The highest point on each chart represents a typical peak age for that skill (though some pitchers peak earlier or later than others). The points surrounding illustrate the typical path toward and away from that peak. Each specific point along the path is calculated as the weighted average rate change in skill for all pitchers who played at that age compared to the skill level that those same pitchers exhibited the previous season. These are chained together to visually form the curve.

Here is the aging curve for strikeout rate overall:

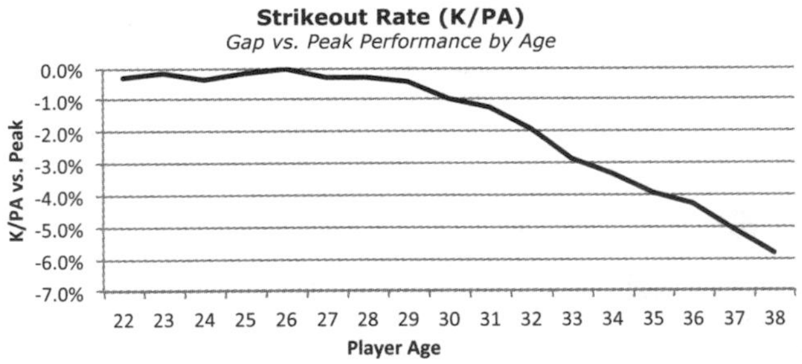

Strikeout rates remain relatively flat through a pitchers mid-20s and then fade. Even in an era where the leaguewide strikeout rate has increased by roughly 0.3% K/PA per year, the year-over-year rate change of individual pitchers and their individual strikeout rates are on average declining by about 0.4% per year.

If we're going to find pitchers who can avoid this gravitational pull on strikeout rate, we need to look deeper at the raw skills that drive strikeout rate itself. First, let's check fastball velocity, which is often cited as a cause of performance decline or improvement:

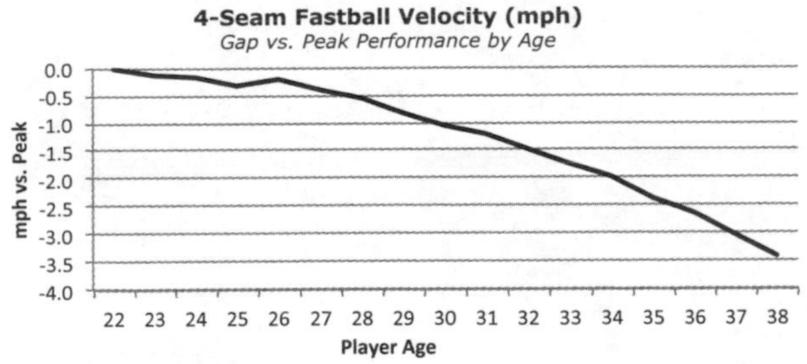

Lots of decline. Not so much improvement. Individual pitchers tend to lose about 0.2 mph per season off of their respective fastballs. What about swinging strike rate? Do pitchers learn to create better movement or better locate or sequence their pitches to fool batters into more swings-and-misses as they gain more experience?

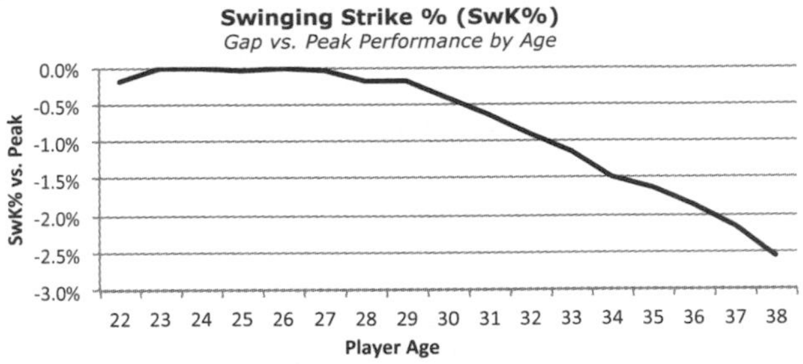

No. Individual pitchers' swinging strike rates tend to drop about 0.2% per year, and even more so later in their careers. That leaves just one stone left to turn: first pitch strikes. Do pitchers learn to get ahead in the count as they gain more experience?

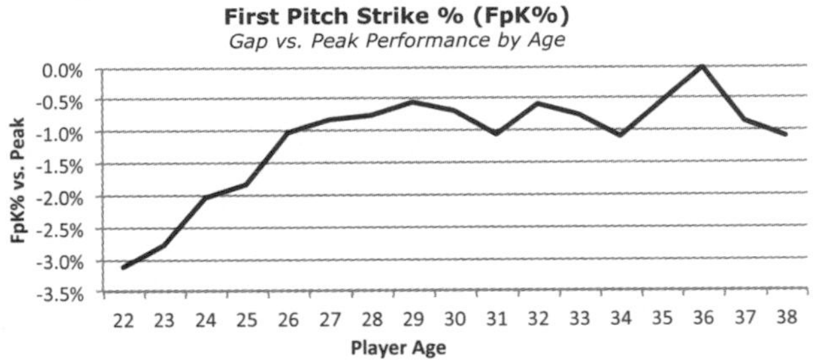

Yes! Unlike overall strikeout rate, fastball velocity, and swinging strike rate, which all saw individual pitchers exhibit a pattern of deterioration with age, first pitch strike rates for individual pitchers do seem to increase with age until about age 29, and then level out. This implies that younger pitchers may in fact be steadily "learning how to pitch" (or simply harnessing their control) early in their careers, which enables them to hold or even slightly increase their strikeout rates until their mid-to-late 20s before giving way to the physical effects of aging that result in their eventual strikeout rate decline.

To take advantage of this discovery, let's identify players who are best positioned to capitalize on a bump up in first pitch strike rate. The following players were <26 years old in 2015, faced at least 150 batters, and had above average swinging strikeout rates but below average first pitch strike rates:

Starters: Adam Conley, Brandon Finnegan, Kevin Gausman, Zachary Godley, Jonathan Gray, Sonny Gray, John Lamb, Lance McCullers, Henry Owens, Carlos Rodon, Joe Ross, Danny Salazar, Julio Teheran, Yordano Ventura.

Relievers: Elvis Araujo, J.R. Graham, Tommy Kahnle, Keone Kela, Corey Knebel, Hansel Robles, Trevor Rosenthal, Chasen Shreve, Carson Smith.

For these pitchers, maybe 2016 will be the year that Birthday + 1 = Good.

2015 Trends, 2016 Responses

by Patrick Davitt

One of the most dangerous things fantasy players can do is assume that past benchmarks and baselines are unchanging and apply just as well the next season as they did the previous year. In fact, these benchmarks and baselines change constantly, and keeping up with changes and trends can put you ahead of your league in assessing the players you want for your 2016 roster.

In this article, we'll discuss some important skills trends for you to watch. You'll want to know how we categorize players:

- Elite = Top 15% in a category
- Individual SP= >=10 GS, 90% GP as SP, >=100 IP
- Individual RP= <=2 GS, 90% GP as RP, >=20 IP
- Batters= Non-pitchers, minimum 100 PA in a season

PITCHER FUNDAMENTALS

Dominance (Dom, k/9)

The Trend

Year	K/9	SP	RP	Elite SP	Elite RP
2007	6.7	6.3	7.4	8.2	9.5
2011	7.1	6.8	7.9	8.6	9.9
2015	7.7	7.3	8.4	9.1	10.7

Dom has stayed stable since 2012, bouncing around between 7.6-7.7 K/9. Dom had increased about 15% from 2007 to 2012, from 6.7 to 7.6. The story is the same if we look separately at starters and relievers, though relievers are about 1.0 K/9 higher.

How to Play It: Raise your Dom expectations if you haven't already. A Dom of 7.0 K/9 ain't what it used to be. Raise expectations of "elite" strikeout levels for starters to the low nines, and for relievers to the high-10s.

2016 Player Targets: Lance McCullers (RHP, HOU) will finish 2015 either in the Dom elite or close to it. Carson Smith (RHP, SEA) is solidly elite already and has a path to closing.

Control (Ctl, bb/9)

The Trend

Year	bb/9	SP	RP	Elite SP	Elite RP
2007	3.3	3.1	3.7	2.1	2.5
2011	3.1	2.9	3.6	2.0	2.3
2015	2.8	2.6	3.2	1.8	2.0

The gamewide Ctl rate was stable from 2007-10, around 3.3 bb/9. Then Ctl started falling in 2011, and was down to 2.8 bb/9 in 2015, contributing to lower WHIPs. The best explanation of the decline in walks is pressure on umps through pitch-tracking software used in their evaluation (with a nod to conspiracy theorists who say MLB is pushing umps to call more strikes to shorten games).

How to Play It: Again, be aware that the environment has stabilized, but at a lower rate than even a few years ago, especially at elite levels.

2016 Player Targets: Michael Pineda (RHP, NYY) struggled with injury again in 2015, but when he was able to pitch, he notched a Ctl of 1.3 bb/9, fourth best among qualified starters. Roberto Osuna (RHP, TOR) had a 2015 Ctl of 1.9 bb/9 and was a K short of elite Dom. Because of his youth, he might be discounted at draft next year, which could be a buying opportunity. And as he matures, his Dom could rise. Is it too early to say Mariano v.2?

Command Rate (Cmd, k/bb)

The Trend

Year	k/bb	SP	RP	Elite SP	Elite RP
2007	2.0	2.0	2.0	3.4	3.2
2011	2.3	2.4	2.2	3.5	3.6
2015	2.7	2.8	2.6	4.6	4.3

We're seeing loads of new data and metrics flooding into the game, but Command Ratio remains perhaps the most critical single measure to quickly assess a pitcher's core ability. (GB% is also really important.) Cmd in 2015 was up 35% since 2007, pretty much across our splits. This year's 2.7 Cmd is the sixth-highest in baseball history, and the five higher seasons were 130 years ago or more.

How to Play It: Cmd is where the environment has really shifted. It was only a few years ago when BaseballHQ.com set a 2.0 Cmd as considered acceptable. But in 2015, a 2.0 Cmd was only 141st-best among starters. As late as 2007, an elite starter Cmd was just over 3.0, but now that will barely sneak him into the top 50. And to get into the top 15% elite, a 2015 pitcher needs a 4.6 or better—a Cmd that would have been top-four overall in 2007.

To put it into perspective, here are some big names whose 2015 Cmd left them outside the top quarter of all starters: Felix Hernandez, Justin Verlander, Cole Hamels, Jeff Samardzija, and Sonny Gray.

2016 Targets: Top names in starter Cmd look like the Cy Young ballots: Scherzer, Kershaw, Sale, Bumgarner, Greinke, Price, Kluber. But Pineda's 7.2 Cmd was second behind Scherzer (and ahead of Kershaw) among fulltime (20+ GS) starters. We should be looking at Mets rookies Jacob deGrom (5.5) and Noah Syndergaard (5.2), and longtime analyst darling Carlos Carrasco (RHP, CLE), a top pick at First Pitch Arizona, continued to intrigue with a 5.0 Cmd.

Among relievers, Darren O'Day (5.6) and Zach Britton (5.5) showed elite Cmd in the BAL pen, but they were joined by latecomer RHP Mychal Givens (5.5). Givens was a Double-A closer whose 5.0 Cmd there improved in MLB. His GB rate in the minors fell at BAL, but if he recovers even part of it, he's a future closer.

BATTER FUNDAMENTALS

Contact Rate (ct%, (AB-K)/AB

The Trend

Year	ct%	Elite
2007	82%	88%
2011	80%	86%
2015	78%	84%

As Dom rates have increased, batter contact rates (ct%) are falling across the game. Looking at qualified batters, the rate has declined steadily, and in 2015 was well under the 80% mark that used to be a BaseballHQ.com floor for rosterable batters. The mark for elite batters in this metric also fell at about the same rate.

How to Play It: Though ct% correlates well with BA and OBP, it isn't a dealbreaker, especially if a low ct% is offset by other advantages. You might think you don't want batters whose ct% marks this year were 79%, 74%, 73% and 72%, until you learn they were Josh Donaldson, Bryce Harper, Paul Goldschmidt and Mike Trout. Look for ct%, but don't obsess. Do be wary of young stars like Miguel Sano (55%), Kris Bryant (64%) and Kyle Schwarber (66%), who clearly will be challenged to maintain their decent BAs.

2016 Player Targets: The highest 2015 ct% was Nori Aoki (OF, SF) at 93%. Aoki's surface stats took a hit because spent a chunk of time on the DL, and at 33, he's past the full bloom of youth. But he has been full value for a .290-ish BA and with a full 600-PA season would have threatened 10/20 with 65 runs. Mookie Betts (OF, BOS), was comfortably in the ct% elite at 87%. Betts will be a five-cat player worthy of first-round pick in 2016 as he adds power with physical maturity—he might not be the most valuable hitter for dynasty formats, but he should be in the discussion.

Hard-hit Rate (HH%, Hard-hit balls/batted balls)

The Trend

Year	HH%	Elite
2007	33%	38%
2011	25%	31%
2015	29%	36%

Perhaps even more than making contact, the core ability for batter success is hitting the ball hard. A ball hit with authority is more likely to scoot through the infield for a hit, more likely to split the OFs for an extra-base hit, and more likely to clear the fences. Just above, we noted the pedestrian (or worse) ct% marks of some of the game's most potent offensive players, and HH% is why. Donaldson was at 38%, Harper at 42%, Goldschmidt at 40% and Trout at 41%. Confusingly, Gallo, Sano, Schwarber and Bryant, against whom we warned you just a paragraph or two back, are all likewise in the HH% elite. Caveat emptor!

How to Play It: If we take the metric at face value, big-league hitters are pasting the ball with renewed vigor after a sag in the middle of the study period. But the odd "U"-shaped pattern of the trend might reflect changes in how the stat is gathered. In the early days, whether a ball was "hard- (or medium- or soft-) hit" was subjectively determined. New technology measuring the actual speed of the ball off the bat will add objectivity.

The HH% data become more widespread and available, and several years ago BaseballHQ invented a highly useful Hard-Contact (Hct) metric that combines HH% and ct%. HH% and Hct should be a cornerstone in your planning. (The top 10 batters in 2015 Hct: David Ortiz, Conforto, Giancarlo Stanton, Cabrera, Posey, Harper, Jed Lowrie, Matt Kemp, Ryan Raburn and Adam Lind).

2016 Player Targets: The young super-sluggers mentioned earlier are obvious choices, with appropriate caution relating to whiffs. But take a hard look at rookie Michael Conforto (OF, NYM), who paired his top-10 42% HH% with an acceptable 79% ct%. Miguel Cabrera might fall off the age and injury cliff, and will be discounted in 2016, but he's top-20 in HH% at 41% and sported an 81% ct%. And if you need a justification for going the extra buck on Buster Posey (C/1B, SF), point to an elite 36% HH% and a super-elite 90% ct%.

FANTASY STATS

Finally, here without added comment are the trends in eight of the 10 standard Roto categories. We exclude wins and saves—they don't vary a lot—wins can't, and saves are always right around 50% of wins. Overall per-player levels presented (strikeouts for starters only), with elite levels in (parentheses):

Year	ERA	WHIP	K
2007	4.26 (3.48)	1.36 (1.21)	129 (179)
2011	3.83 (3.00)	1.27 (1.14)	142 (194)
2015	3.76 (3.35)	1.23 (1.18)	166 (193)

Year	HR	RBI	SB	Runs	BA	OBP
2007	11 (21)	49 (83)	7 (13)	51 (86)	.274 (.300)	.342 (.374)
2011	10 (20)	42 (75)	7 (16)	44 (76)	.261 (.290)	.327 (.356)
2015	10 (19)	38 (74)	5 (12)	40 (74)	.255 (.290)	.317 (.358)

Rotisserie Strategies in Era of the Pitchers

Compiled by Dave Adler

As Colonel John "Hannibal" Smith, leader of the A-Team, once said, "I love it when a plan comes together." Fantasy baseball players also love a good plan heading into their drafts and auctions. Over the years, numerous unorthodox strategies have been cooked up; many of these can be found in previous editions of this book. In the days of monstrous offensive output, they made sense. But now that pitchers rule the roost, do the plans still work? In the spring of 2015, BaseballHQ.com writers took a look at the plans and determined whether they were still viable.

A summary of our updated findings:

The Sweeney Plan (analysis by Patrick Davitt)

Unorthodox Strategy: Punt HR and RBI, which tend to be associated with the most expensive offensive players. Focus on high-BA base stealers, and bid heavily on pitching with the goal of winning all those categories in 4x4 leagues. A top score in the four pitching categories, along with SB, and BA in a 12-team league, turns into 72 points. Add in the single point in HR and RBI, and 74 points is often enough to win the overall crown.

Strengths: Easy to manage during the draft: target a few key batters with high BA/SB, then fill in with cheaper one-category guys. By focusing on the Denard Span/Ben Revere/Rajai Davis's of the world, there's plenty of money left over to compile a monster pitching staff. Easier in-season management, since the owner doesn't spend FAAB on the thumpers.

Weaknesses: Little margin of error—adopters only notch one point in two categories, so the other six categories must be wins. Also, high-SB players will still be expensive at auction, even as owners chase high-power guys.

Does it work in 2016: Not in auctions; high-BA burners don't exist in the same numbers as in the past. In 2007, there were 21 hitters with more than 10 SB, BA at least 10 points above league median, and less than 10 HR. In 2014, there were only six. Also, it's not going to work well in the standard 5x5 leagues of today; eliminating power hitters and playing a lot of part-timers will impact the runs category negatively. It also doesn't work well in leagues with high AB minimums. However, if executed properly, it could work in a snake draft.

The Labadini Plan (Doug Dennis)

Unorthodox Strategy: One LABR experts league season, Larry Labadini drafted a team consisting of nine $1 pitchers, spending $251 on offense—and almost won the league. The general consensus holds that hitters are more stable and make better draft-day investments. Secure a top-notch offense, make some in-season trades for pitchers, and ride to the championship.

Strengths: In deep leagues, it's rare for offensive studs to enter the free agent pool mid-season – but decent free agent pitchers can usually be had. Research shows that two-thirds of the offensive stats get rostered on draft day in standard-sized AL- or NL-only leagues, but only about one-third of pitching stats. Dominating the draft on offense means other teams will be starved for hitters, enabling trades. Buying highly-skilled middle relievers for $1 helps in ERA and WHIP; other owners will chase 4th/5th starters to supplement Wins and Ks, but risk ERA/WHIP blowups in the process.

Weaknesses: Obviously, finding the right $1 pitchers to roster. Sorting through pre-season projections looking for them leaves a motley crew of middle relievers and fledgling starters. Leagues with high minimum IP limits could also be an issue. To register saves, one has to target backup closers and hope. Pouncing on good pitchers as they enter the free agent pool requires vigilance. In shallow leagues, there will be too many decent free agent hitters available, watering down the strategy of hoarding the best hitters.

Does it work in 2016: Yes, in deep leagues. But it requires steely nerves at the auction table, the vigilance to constantly cut pitchers looking for better options on the waiver wire, and the ability to make mid-season trades for stud starters.

The Over-30 Plan (Kris Olson)

Unorthodox Strategy: Draft players age 30 and over, resulting in a stable and more predictable roster.

Strengths: Avoid paying a premium price for "the next big thing." The guy who scorched Triple-A the previous year, but never actually achieved anything in MLB will undoubtedly illicit a bidding war; this strategy keeps you out of the fray. Instead, buy guys at peak, or just into their decline, who have produced consistent.y for years. Or the "grizzled veteran" whose skills have remained strong despite the general perception of decline.

Weaknesses: Back in the 1980s and 1990s, rumor has it that there were "career-extenders" and "bat-speed-picker-uppers" available to most hitters; supposedly, there's a lack of availability these days. If so, older players can generally be expected to have a much more natural age-related decline. Plus, it's tough to gather enough SBs, since "speed is a skill of the young."

Does it work in 2016: Yes, but it takes work. While it was tough to put together a competitive starting rotation in AL-only leagues in 2015, it was possible in the NL. Saves were not a problem in either league. It's difficult to execute the plan in drafts, since young players generally populate the first round; but it can be done. It's easier to implement in auctions, where the money can be spread around on reliable oldsters. That being said, it's questionable whether one should lop off the large value that younger players generate.

The All-Lefties Plan (Ray Murphy)

Unorthodox Strategy: In 2000, Ron Shandler put together a team made up completely of left-handers. He noticed that southpaws had slightly better xERA and BPV; lefty hitters had the advantage in Batting Eye, PX, SX, and BPV, along with OPS.

Strengths: Since most pitchers are right-handed, left-handed hitters get the platoon advantage. Being on the right side of the plate, they have a better chance of beating out hits by getting to first base more quickly.

Weaknesses: No statistical differences existed in 2014; righties and lefties registered roughly the same OPS. Defensive shifts and a shrinking strike zone have helped negate the LH hitter advantage. New stadiums have taken away the edge that lefties once enjoyed.

Does it work in 2016: Not really. Taking a look at three-year park factor charts give an idea of which teams to target for left-handed power hitters, but it's better to ignore lefty/righty splits and just take hitters from power-enhancing parks (Colorado, Cincinnati, etc.) and pitchers from power-reducing parks (Oakland, San Francisco).

The Stars & Scrubs (Pitching) and Spread-the-Risk (Hitting) (Matt Cederholm)

Unorthodox Strategy: Acquire 3-4 stud/expensive pitchers, and fill in the rest with a lot of cheap $1-5 middle relievers with good ERA and WHIP or risky starters with upside. Get 7-8 solid—but unspectacular—hitters who will see regular playing time.

Strengths: With 3-4 stud pitchers (plus a closer), there's a solid foundation for all categories. Concentrating the $1-5 bids on upside players could result in a surprising contributor, but it also makes it less painful to cut pitchers to pick up free agents. By spreading the risk on consistent offensive contributors, there's no need to dip into a shallow free agent hitter pool.

Weaknesses: With pitchers being injury prone, it's risky to spend on expensive starters. Spreading the risk on offense could result in a lack of dominance in any given category.

Does it work in 2016: Yes. There are now more pitchers that have an ERA greater than one standard deviation below the mean (60) than in 1999 (40). This makes it more likely that there will be decent pitchers in the free agent pool. Thus, it's a reasonable strategy to spend on 3-4 quality pitchers and churn lesser staff members in favor of emerging free agents. Deeper hitter penetration means fewer quality free agents, so spreading the risk to consistent contributors who will see regular playing time makes sense.

The Bernhard Plan (Patrick Davitt)

Unorthodox Strategy: "So ugly, it's beautiful." Buy hitters who will get between 300-500 AB to 1) ensure a large number of ABs, and 2) help enforce a Spread-the-Risk approach. Use any approach on pitching.

Strengths: By accumulating plenty of ABs, the team should be towards the top of the counting stats by sheer force of numbers. By avoiding the expensive hitters, the owner will be in command of the mid-game in auctions.

Weaknesses: It requires ALL other owners to bid aggressively on—and win—top hitters. Losing a few players to injury erodes the advantage of high AB totals. No specific approach to pitching.

Does it work in 2016: It could work in single-league auctions, assuming other owners "cooperate." But it's unlikely to work in drafts (need to draft stud hitters early to be competitive), mixed leagues (all owners will be loading up on high-AB guys), or keeper leagues (inflation messes up bargains).

Predicting Player Value From Year-1 Performance

by Patrick Davitt

In 2008, Carlos Gonzalez produced about -$4 of fantasy value. Two seasons later, he was third in MVP voting and led all hitters with $42 in fantasy value. Every fantasy owner dreams about finding the next first-year bust who comes roaring back. But that just doesn't happen often enough to be reliable. BaseballHQ has found Year-1 results predict some subsequent-year performance, but not all—and often not in the way you'd expect.

Method

We designated each batter's first season >100AB as his "Year 1" (Y1). We looked at the 341 MLB batters whose Y1 happened from 2007 to 2013, then looked up their fantasy values (R$) over the seasons, asking how likely batters at various Y1 value levels are in subsequent seasons to 1) play again; 2) have positive values; 3) beat their own Y1 levels; and 4) produce value over $25 in subsequent seasons. A subsequent season under 100 AB is classed as "Did Not Play" (DNP).

Results 1: Overall

Not many first-year batters arrive with a fantasy bang. Overall, 183 batters (54%) had some positive value, but only five had Y1 value of R$21 or higher, and only 13 more had R$16-R$20. Meanwhile, 13% checked in at or below –R$11.

As we'd expect, the lower the Y1 value, the less likely the batter was to play in Y2 or subsequent seasons:

Yr1R$	Y2	All
>=$21	100%	100%
$16 to $20	92%	79%
$11 to $15	94%	88%
$6 to $10	96%	85%
$1 to $5	80%	63%
$0 to -$5	75%	62%
-$6 to -$10	77%	65%
<=-$11	62%	58%

Results 2: Y2 Value

Our first check was Y2 value after given Y1 value:

	Y2 R$ Value				
Y1 R$	>R$0	<=R$0	Ave	Max	Min
>=$21	100%	0%	$14	$23	$ 3
$16 to $20	77%	15%	$10	$23	-$ 7
$11 to $15	66%	28%	$ 8	$28	-$12
$6 to $10	56%	40%	$ 4	$31	-$13
$1 to $5	39%	41%	$ 1	$19	-$16
$0 to -$5	38%	38%	$ 0	$26	-$15
-$6 to -$10	56%	21%	$ 7	$31	-$13
<=-$11	40%	22%	$ 5	$38	-$ 6

This included the CarGo question: How many batters with negative Y1 value had positive Y2 value? About 45%, as it turned out. Curiously, though, the largest percentage of these was not in the "borderline" $0 to -$5 batters (38%), but in the -$6 to -$10 Y1 value tier (56%).

Why would this be? One likely answer is that a batter who gets Y2 playing time after a poor Y1 season must have his organization's faith. Borderliners hold jobs because their poor production is offset by marginal usefulness—as defensive replacements, utilitymen, rah-rah guys and so on.

Indeed those -$6 to -$10 tier players reward their teams—they matched the plus $6 to $10 tier in producing positive Y2 value and had higher average Y2 value!

Results 3: All Subsequent Seasons

Finally, we wondered about how longer-term performance might reflect Y1 value. We found that every batter in the study returned positive value at least once in any subsequent seasons he played, keeping in mind that many of them didn't play, or had few subsequent seasons.

But it's a different story when we look at batters' ability to deliver value in all seasons after Y1:

			RVal			
Yr 1 R$	All+	>Yr1%	>R$25%	Avg	Max	Min
>=$21	100%	52%	48%	$26	$54	$3
$16-$20	85%	22%	11%	$13	$35	-$7
$11-$15	50%	41%	13%	$10	$38	-$17
$6-$10	46%	41%	6%	$7	$55	-$18
$1-$5	46%	55%	8%	$6	$48	-$17
$0 to -$5	55%	67%	4%	$4	$36	-$17
-$6 to -$10	51%	92%	6%	$6	$31	-$15
<=-$11	42%	93%	5%	$4	$42	-$20
TOTAL	**50%**	**62%**	**9%**	**$7**		

This table shows batters with Yr-1 value of R$16 or more are excellent bets to at least provide positive value in subsequent seasons. Below that, a coin flip.

(The huge percentages of batters in the bottom tiers who outdo Y1 performance is explained by the "nowhere to go but up" postulate, amplified by the unwillingness of teams to keep playing batters who can't produce.)

As well, it seems clear that $25+ seasons are much more likely to come from batters who had Y1 value over $20. And average per-season value shows a sharp decline through the top three value tiers, leveling out after that, again suggesting that from Y1 R$10 down, there isn't a lot to pick.

Conclusions

The main conclusion is that batter Y1 value is only loosely tied to subsequent seasons, especially Y2. The highest likelihood of getting value in Y2 and afterwards, especially seasons over R$25, comes from the highest-value Y1 batters, to be sure. But even a R$21 batter is only a 50-50 bet to do better in Y2.

Remember that a top Y1 value batter is unlikely to be a bust, but is also unlikely to match Y1 performance. Be circumspect when thinking about bidding in 2016 on Carlos Correa, Randal Grichuk, and their ilk.

As for finding the next CarGo "big score"? These doesn't appear predictable from Y1. Instead, they look a lot like "Black Swan" events. The study showed that, say, a-$11 batter is much likelier to follow up with a DNP than with a monster year.

Batters in the –R$6 to –R$10 tier were much more likely to play again and return positive value than batters in tiers well above them. Watch for players who get PT despite low Y1 R$ value.

In sum, the best advice is to consider the batter's status (high draft pick? Big contract?) and the alternatives his club has to letting him keep swinging. And be wary of borderline-value batters, and look a little harder instead at –R$6 to –R$10 batters whose organizations show faith in them.

Change the Wins Category Now!

by Patrick Davitt

Getting a win is not a fair measure of pitching skill. And it's time we changed it as a fantasy stat.

It's true that wins provide an element of unpredictability, and unpredictability forces us to respond to the unpredictable, the inexplicable, and the bizarre. Pitcher wins are all three.

But that's also why some owners and leagues have discussed replacing the wins category with something better. And we found it: The Ryan Quality Start.

We wanted a new counting stat (not a rate) about as frequent as fantasy wins, and simple.

We've heard arguments for BaseballHQ.com's "Pure Quality Start" (PQS) and Bill James' "Game Score" (GS). Both are very comprehensive measures and highly useful. But they're just not simple enough, requiring a lot of calculations. And so, despite their merit, neither PQS nor GS is the solution for replacing Wins as a category.

So we are left with the Quality Start. Or a variation of it.

The common objection to QS is that its minimum standard—three earned runs in six innings—is a 4.50 ERA, and that's not "quality." In fact, barely 5% of 2014 QS were the minimum, and the ERA in all QS was under 1.90, and roughly equal to the ERA in all wins.

The QS easily meets two of our requirements: It's a counting stat (a QS or not). And it's simple. Innings and runs allowed are usually mentioned on the crawl and in recaps. Pitchers' QS counts are also commonly seen in most online stat packages.

The remaining issue is frequency—that the replacement stat be roughly as frequent as Wins. In a 15-team league, a typical yearly wins total is 1,350. But there are usually around 2,500 QS in a season. That's nearly double the target.

Our solution comes from Nolan Ryan, who said a QS should be three runs or less, but in a minimum seven innings. Besides addressing the "4.50 ERA" canard (3 ER in 7 IP is a 3.85), the Ryan QS total is usually around 1,400, close enough to the 1,350 requirement.

OnRoto.com has leagues that use the Ryan variation, as well as leagues using eight other QS variants that exclude Wins. We checked them all, and none was better than the Ryan at matching the Wins total target. We did figure out two other innings/ER combinations that were slightly better, but they either required a one-run maximum (too soon lost) or partial innings (too cumbersome).

So it's settled: The Ryan QS—at least seven innings, no more than three ER— should replace Wins as a scoring category in fantasy baseball.

Leagues would have to consider simultaneously instituting a category for all relief pitchers, such as Saves + Holds, to address the loss of value for middle relievers and setup men who could no longer provide value by vulturing wins. A more comprehensive relief-pitcher category would re-establish the value of setup guys while decreasing the artificially high value of "closers." But that's another topic.

How a Strong Draft Contributes to Winning

by Todd Zola

You can't win a league at the draft but you can lose it. We've all read this cliché; it's classic writer-speak. But have you ever wondered about how much a strong draft or auction contributes to winning? What follows are a series of observations derived from comparing actual drafts to the season-endings standings.

AL-only, NL-only and Mixed League Tout Wars teams from 2010-14 served as our data pool. The AL- and NL-only auctions were 12 teams, except the 2010-12 National League (13 teams). In 2013 the Mixed League adopted on base percentage (OBP) instead of batting average (BA) with all three formats converting to OBP in 2014. OnRoto, the commissioner service hosting Tout Wars, has a feature that generates final standings based on each opening day roster being active all season. These results are compared to the actual standings.

General Observations

The correlation of standings based on the draft to final standings ranges from .42 to 94 with the average around .73. So indeed, the draft can set you up but there's still a lot of work to be done.

The top hitting counting stat drafted is hitting, with stolen bases being the fewest. Perhaps surprisingly, the top pitching counting stat drafted is saves with wins being the fewest.

Managing pitching is essential but poses a challenge since in the aggregate, pitchers added to the pool after the draft/auction are a detriment to ERA and WHIP. The common game theory mistake is assuming a deficient staff can be easily fixed. The better approach is a good staff can be managed into a better one.

More hitting is acquired at the draft or auction than pitching. This speaks as much towards the construct of MLB rosters and better pitching emanating from the free agent ranks than pitching.

American and National League only

Nearly all winners improved in BA/OBP. While this by no means belies the mantra of patience, it strongly suggests seeking an offensive upgrade early. Spending FAAB and not anticipating an impact crossover deal at the MLB trade deadline is the best avenue to effect this.

A majority of champions improved their pitching ratios with in-season moves, which is quite impressive, since final pitching ratios were worse than drafted. This indicates that moves on the aggregate were detrimental.

Eight of 10 champions finished top-three in saves, with another fourth. Five did so by acquiring more saves in season than drafted, while four did so by (likely) trading away excess, suggesting either isn't more efficient than the other.

Mixed Leagues

Influx of stats is greatest in Mixed Leagues. The prescient owner should strategize using fungible roster spots (middle and corner infield, utility and a couple of outfield and pitching) along with multiple-position eligible players.

Four of five champions finished in the top three in saves, with the fifth punting. The four all drafted more saves than they ultimately totaled, suggesting owners should not rely on in-season management and instead funnel draft-day assets to the category.

The Fallacy of In-Season Player "Value"

by Patrick Davitt

In trading, many fantasy owners in category-based formats like Rotisserie misunderstand the nature of in-season "value." They calculate the "fairness" of trades by comparing current dollar values of the players involved, and insisting those values are relatively equal—"If I'm giving $24 in value, I need to get at least $24 back."

But once the auction is over, a player has no dollar value. He only has value in how much he can move your team (and other teams) in the categories.

Look at a trade in a 2015 experts' auction league.

"Tom" wanted to activate Austin Jackson from reserve for SBs and Runs, and trade an OF from his active roster. The trade candidates were Jarrod Dyson and Nelson Cruz.

Cruz was by far the more "valuable" of the two by auction price, current production and projected value. But for Tom's team, at that moment, dollar values were, well, valueless. Cruz's power couldn't move Tom in HR, which he knew he would win, nor RBI, where he was locked into second. But Tom was at the low end of a clump of teams in a very tight SB category, so Dyson's projected 20 SB could mean 6-7 points.

So even though Dyson was "worth" quite a bit less than Cruz in abstract valuation, he was worth hugely more in his potential effect on the standings. Cruz's only value—to Tom, not in general—was as a trade chip. Tom could offer Cruz to quite a few teams in the league could use his HRs and RBI to make good gains in those categories, with some of those gains at the expense of Tom's main overall competitors.

So Tom offered Cruz to a few teams with SB surpluses, but got no takers because other owners also saw the SB points up for grabs. One owner, though, had potential for a deal, because his situation was the opposite of Tom's: He couldn't gain points with SBs, but could with power.

Unfortunately, he had paid $30 at auction for his speed guy, who was projected to be worth in the high $20s for the balance of the year. And since he "valued" Cruz at $20, he insisted Tom had to give another $7 worth of "value," in the form of an extra player Tom couldn't spare—it would have cost Tom points elsewhere.

And a deal that should have been made wasn't made.

Fortunately, the strikeouts category was also tightly bunched, and Tom saw a chance to get points there. Tom found an owner who needed pop and had strikeouts to spare, and swapped Cruz one-for-one for James Shields after an exchange of one e-mail.

Using the standard thinking, Tom should have demanded more. Shields was "worth" $4-$6 less than Cruz, but Tom's projections said Shields' strikeouts could move him up in the category. And the owner getting Cruz would go past the two guys Tom was chasing in the overall standings.

That was worth $6, wasn't it?

The following section contains player boxes for every batter who had significant playing time in 2015 and/or is expected to get fantasy roster-worthy plate appearances in 2016. In most cases, high-end prospects who have yet to make their major league debuts will not appear here; you can find scouting reports for them in the Prospects section.

Snapshot Section

The top band of each player box contains the following information:

Age as of Opening Day 2016.

Bats shows which side of the plate he bats from—(L)eft, (R)ight or (B)oth.

Positions: Up to three defensive positions are listed and represent those for which he appeared a minimum of 20 games in 2015.

Ht/Wt: Each batter's height and weight.

Reliability Grades analyze each batter's forecast risk, on an A-F scale. High grades go to those who have accumulated few disabled list days (Health), have a history of substantial and regular major league playing time (PT/Exp) and have displayed consistent performance over the past three years, using RC/G (Consist).

LIMA Plan Grade evaluates how well a batter would fit into a team using the LIMA Plan draft strategy. Best grades go to batters who have excellent base skills, are expected to see regular playing time, and are in the $10-$30 Rotisserie dollar range. Lowest grades will go to poor skills, few AB and values less than $5 or more than $30.

Random Variance Score (Rand Var) measures the impact random variance had on the batter's 2015 stats and the probability that his 2016 performance will exceed or fall short of 2015. The variables tracked are those prone to regression—h%, hr/f and xBA to BA variance. Players are rated on a scale of −5 to +5 with positive scores indicating rebounds and negative scores indicating corrections. Note that this score is computer-generated and the projections will override it on occasion.

Mayberry Method (MM) acknowledges the imprecision of the forecasting process by projecting player performance in broad strokes. The four digits of MM each represent a fantasy-relevant skill—power, speed, batting average and playing time (PA)—and are all on a scale of 0 to 5.

Commentaries for each batter provide a brief analysis of BPIs and the potential impact on performance in 2016. MLB statistics are listed first for those who played only a portion of 2015 at the major league level. Note that these commentaries generally look at performance related issues only. Role and playing time expectations may impact these analyses, so you will have to adjust accordingly. Upside (UP) and downside (DN) statistical potential appears for some players; these are less grounded in hard data and more speculative of skills potential.

Player Stat Section

The past five years' statistics represent the total accumulated in the majors as well as in Triple-A, Double-A ball and various foreign leagues during each year. All non-major league stats have been converted to a major league equivalent (MLE) performance level. Minor league levels below Double-A are not included.

Nearly all baseball publications separate a player's statistical experiences in the major leagues from the minor leagues and outside leagues. While this may be appropriate for official record-keeping purposes, it is not an easy-to-analyze snapshot of a player's complete performance for a given year.

Bill James has proven that minor league statistics (converted to MLEs), at Double-A level or above, provide as accurate a record of a player's performance as major league statistics. Other researchers have also devised conversion factors for foreign leagues. Since these are adequate barometers, we include them in the pool of historical data for each year.

Team designations: An asterisk (*) appearing with a team name means that Triple-A and/or Double-A numbers are included in that year's stat line. Any stints of less than 20 AB are not included (to screen out most rehab appearances). A designation of "a/a" means the stats were accumulated at both AA and AAA levels that year. "for" represents a foreign or independent league. The designation "2TM" appears whenever a player was on more than one major league team, crossing leagues, in a season. "2AL" and "2NL" represent more than one team in the same league. Players who were cut during the season and finished 2015 as a free agent are designated as FAA (Free agent, AL) and FAN (Free agent, NL).

Stats: Descriptions of all the categories appear in the Encyclopedia.

- The leading decimal point has been suppressed on some categories to conserve space.
- Data for platoons (vL, vR), balls-in-play (G/L/F) and consistency (Wk#, DOM, DIS) are for major league performance only.
- Formulas that use BIP data, like xBA and xPX, only appear for years in which G/L/F data is available.

Batting average is presented alongside xBA. On base average and slugging average appear next, and the combined On Base Plus Slugging (OPS). OPS splits vs. left-handed and right-handed pitchers appear after the overall OPS column.

Batting eye and contact skill are measured with walk rate (bb%), contact rate (ct%). Eye is the ratio of walks to strikeouts.

Once the ball leaves the bat, it will either be a (G)round ball, (L)ine drive or (F)ly ball. Hit rate (h%), the also referred to as batting average on balls-in-play (BABIP), measures how often a ball put into play results in a base hit. Hard contact index (HctX) measures the frequency of hard contact, compared to overall league levels. Looking at the ratio of fly balls is a good springboard to the Power gauges. Linear weighted power index (PX) measures a batter's skill at hitting extra base hits as compared to overall league levels. xPX measures power by assessing how hard the ball is being hit (rather than the outcomes of those hits). And the ratio of home runs to fly balls shows the results of those hits.

To assess speed, first look at on base average (does he get on base?), then Spd (is he fast enough to steal bases?), then SBO (how often is he attempting to steal bases?) and finally, SB% (when he attempts, what is his rate of success?).

In looking at consistency, we use weekly Base Performance Value (BPV) levels. Starting with the total number of weeks the batter accumulated stats (#Wk), the percentage of DOMinating weeks (BPV over 50) and DISaster weeks (BPV under 0) is shown. The larger the variance between DOM and DIS, the greater the consistency.

The final section includes several overall performance measures: runs created per game (RC/G), runs above replacement (RAR), Base performance value (BPV), Base performance index (BPX, which is BPV indexed to each year's league average) and the Rotisserie value (R$).

2016 Projections

Forecasts are computed from a player's trends over the past five years. Adjustments were made for leading indicators and variances between skill and statistical output. After reviewing the leading indicators, you might opt to make further adjustments.

Although each year's numbers include all playing time at the Double-A level or above, the 2016 forecast only represents potential playing time at the major league level, and again is highly preliminary.

Note that the projected Rotisserie values in this book will not necessarily align with each player's historical actuals. Since we currently have no idea who is going to play second base for the Mets, or whether Corey Seager is going to break camp with the Dodgers, it is impossible to create a finite pool of playing time, something which is required for valuation. So the projections are roughly based on a 12-team AL/NL league, and include an inflated number of plate appearances, league-wide. This serves to flatten the spread of values and depress individual player dollar projections. In truth, a $25 player in this book might actually be worth $21, or $28. This level of precision is irrelevant in a process that is driven by market forces anyway. So, don't obsess over it.

Be aware of other sources that publish perfectly calibrated Rotisserie values over the winter. They are likely making arbitrary decisions as to where free agents are going to sign and who is going to land jobs in the spring. We do not make those leaps of faith here.

Bottom line… It is far too early to be making definitive projections for 2016, especially on playing time. Focus on the skill levels and trends, then consult BaseballHQ.com for playing time revisions as players change teams and roles become more defined. A free projections update will be available online in March.

Do-it-yourself analysis

Here are some data points you can look at in doing your own player analysis:

- Variance between vLH and vRH OPS
- Growth or decline in walk rate (bb%)
- Growth or decline in contact rate (ct%)
- Growth or decline in G/L/F individually, or concurrent shifts
- Variance in 2015 hit rate (h%) to 2012-2014 three-year average
- Variance between Avg and xBA each year
- Growth or decline in HctX level
- Growth or decline in power index (PX) rate
- Variance between PX and xPX each year
- Variance in 2015 hr/f rate to 2012-2014 three-year average
- Growth or decline in statistically scouted speed (Spd) score
- Concurrent growth/decline of gauges like ct%, FB, PX, xPX, hr/f
- Concurrent growth/decline of gauges like OB, Spd, SBO, SB%
- Trends in DOM/DIS splits

Abreu,Jose

Age: 29 Bats: R Pos: 1B DH	Health A	LIMA Plan B+	
Ht: 6' 3" Wt: 255	PT/Exp B	Rand Var 0	
	Consist D	MM 4145	

Hard to argue with two straight 30 HR/100 RBI seasons, but consider: low FB% hinders further HR growth, PX/xPX fell from true slugger status, and half-year xBA spiral (.324, .292, .285, .265) hints at BA downside. Consistency makes him an early-round anchor; that said, we may have already seen his ceiling.

Yr	Tm	AB	R	HR	RBI	SB	BA	xBA	OBP	SLG	OPS	vL	vR	bb%	ct%	Eye	G	L	F	h%	HctX	PX	xPX	hr/f	Spd	SBO	SB%	#Wk	DOM	DIS	RC/G	RAR	BPV	BPX	R$
11	for	252	91	18	87	2	385		484	655	1138			16	85	1.28				40		161			85	3%	62%				13.01	43.2	128	284	$27
12	for	297	72	18	91	1	339		447	582	1029			16	85	1.28				35		138			90	1%	100%				10.06	36.2	111	278	$22
13	for	285	59	10	54	2	320		406	480	886			13	84	0.90				35		103			86	8%	21%				6.76	17.0	72	180	$16
14	CHW	556	80	36	107	3	317	307	383	581	964	1098	919	8	76	0.39	45	23	31	36	120	185	132	27%	71	3%	75%	24	71%	17%	8.09	59.0	94	254	$35
15	CHW	613	88	30	101	0	290	276	347	502	850	658	908	6	77	0.28	47	21	32	33	117	136	116	20%	79	0%	0%	26	54%	31%	6.01	18.2	55	149	$26
1st Half		297	47	14	44	0	293	285	342	502	843	819	849	5	78	0.23	48	23	29	33	119	128	100	21%	109	0%	0%	14	50%	21%	5.91	6.3	61	165	$25
2nd Half		316	41	16	57	0	288	265	352	503	856	553	969	7	76	0.32	46	19	35	33	115	144	132	19%	52	0%	0%	12	58%	42%	6.10	8.3	51	138	$27
16	**Proj**	**602**	**89**	**32**	**104**	**1**	**295**	**284**	**360**	**519**	**879**	**816**	**899**	**7**	**77**	**0.36**	**46**	**22**	**32**	**34**	**118**	**144**	**124**	**22%**	**75**	**1%**	**56%**				**6.51**	**22.6**	**57**	**154**	**$29**

Ackley,Dustin

Age: 28 Bats: L Pos: LF CF	Health A	LIMA Plan D+	
Ht: 6' 1" Wt: 195	PT/Exp C	Rand Var +3	
	Consist A	MM 3333	

Had sub-Mendoza BA, herniated disk by August, then surged in Sept. (.310 BA, 4 HR) with NYY. Career-low h% torpedoed BA while xBA, plate skills held firm. FB%, PX growth came with xPX support, so while issues vs. LHP persist, power upside hints at potential late-round profit.

Yr	Tm	AB	R	HR	RBI	SB	BA	xBA	OBP	SLG	OPS	vL	vR	bb%	ct%	Eye	G	L	F	h%	HctX	PX	xPX	hr/f	Spd	SBO	SB%	#Wk	DOM	DIS	RC/G	RAR	BPV	BPX	R$
11	SEA *	604	75	11	58	10	256	249	339	389	727	652	804	11	79	0.60	40	22	38	31	115	92	110	6%	147	8%	75%	16	50%	38%	4.51	-7.3	59	131	$13
12	SEA	607	84	12	50	13	226	234	294	328	622	675	593	9	80	0.48	45	19	35	27	97	67	74	7%	122	10%	81%	28	29%	36%	3.22	-24.9	28	70	$8
13	SEA *	488	54	5	41	2	262	254	330	354	685	664	659	9	82	0.55	51	22	27	31	106	69	62	5%	109	3%	40%	24	38%	42%	3.97	0.0	35	88	$8
14	SEA	502	64	14	65	8	245	265	293	398	692	553	749	6	82	0.36	45	18	36	27	108	106	105	9%	103	11%	67%	27	44%	33%	3.85	2.3	58	157	$13
15	2 AL	238	28	10	30	2	231	263	284	429	712	422	742	7	81	0.40	44	16	40	25	120	118	144	13%	103	8%	50%	23	48%	26%	3.94	-3.2	66	178	$3
1st Half		155	18	5	14	1	206	223	269	342	611	425	621	8	79	0.39	46	13	41	23	98	87	123	10%	82	9%	33%	14	43%	36%	2.80	-8.6	27	73	$2
2nd Half		83	10	5	16	1	277	325	311	590	901	414	1000	6	86	0.42	41	21	38	27	160	170	180	18%	123	7%	100%	9	56%	11%	6.70	5.0	128	346	$6
16	**Proj**	**292**	**35**	**10**	**38**	**3**	**252**	**269**	**306**	**432**	**737**	**560**	**784**	**7**	**82**	**0.44**	**45**	**19**	**37**	**28**	**121**	**108**	**123**	**11%**	**111**	**8%**	**65%**				**4.47**	**-0.8**	**62**	**167**	**$9**

Adames,Cristhian

Age: 24 Bats: B Pos: SS	Health A	LIMA Plan D	
Ht: 6' 0" Wt: 180	PT/Exp C	Rand Var 0	
	Consist B	MM 1221	

0-3-.245 in 53 AB at COL. Glove-first prospect posted career year at Triple-A, but MLB cup of coffee didn't taste very good. Growing ct% a positive, but power skills are skeptical he can shake the "slap hitter" label. SB% history leaves him without a plus roto skill, making an empty BA the best-case scenario.

Yr	Tm	AB	R	HR	RBI	SB	BA	xBA	OBP	SLG	OPS	vL	vR	bb%	ct%	Eye	G	L	F	h%	HctX	PX	xPX	hr/f	Spd	SBO	SB%	#Wk	DOM	DIS	RC/G	RAR	BPV	BPX	R$
11																																			
12																																			
13	aa	389	36	3	29	10	257		305	337	642			7	80	0.35				31		62			103	17%	58%				3.38		16	40	$7
14	COL *	490	43	2	36	8	254	267	295	322	617	1000	0	6	81	0.31	70	20	10	31	35	53	-14	0%	111	15%	43%	3	0%	67%	3.01	-4.2	13	35	$7
15	COL *	516	45	8	37	7	268	259	304	367	671	729	515	5	86	0.37	58	18	25	30	115	59	72	0%	118	12%	45%	6	17%	50%	3.67	-1.4	38	103	$10
1st Half		274	23	5	23	4	280	254	316	392	707			5	86	0.38				31		71			104	14%	41%				4.07		44	119	$13
2nd Half		242	22	3	14	3	256	252	291	339	630	729	515	5	86	0.36	58	18	25	29	115	46	72	0%	141	10%	50%	6	17%	50%	3.24	-6.0	35	95	$8
16	**Proj**	**166**	**15**	**2**	**12**	**3**	**260**	**249**	**311**	**344**	**656**	**748**	**594**	**5**	**83**	**0.35**	**58**	**18**	**25**	**30**	**104**	**54**	**65**	**5%**	**118**	**13%**	**46%**				**3.36**	**-3.6**	**13**	**36**	**$4**

Adams,Matt

Age: 27 Bats: L Pos: 1B	Health F	LIMA Plan B	
Ht: 6' 3" Wt: 260	PT/Exp C	Rand Var +2	
	Consist C	MM 4023	

A season to forget, as torn quad in May cost him over three months. PRO: Still owns '13-'14 power skills; HctX offers hope for BA recovery. CON: Poor plate approach, xBA shake those recovery odds; health grade, struggles vs. LHP cap AB total. Still, there is a history of bigger power skill; discount 2015 and, UP: 25 HR

Yr	Tm	AB	R	HR	RBI	SB	BA	xBA	OBP	SLG	OPS	vL	vR	bb%	ct%	Eye	G	L	F	h%	HctX	PX	xPX	hr/f	Spd	SBO	SB%	#Wk	DOM	DIS	RC/G	RAR	BPV	BPX	R$
11	aa	463	51	18	64	0	234		276	398	674			5	78	0.26				26		109			86	1%	0%				3.61		36	80	$8
12	STL *	344	38	14	50	2	267	255	300	465	765	440	739	5	74	0.18	44	18	39	32	99	142	126	8%	60	5%	66%	5	20%	60%	4.81	-6.0	38	95	$9
13	STL	296	46	17	51	0	284	262	335	503	839	654	876	7	73	0.29	44	19	36	34	121	153	145	22%	70	1%	0%	26	54%	42%	5.93	11.2	52	130	$12
14	STL	527	55	15	68	3	288	265	321	457	779	528	854	5	78	0.23	35	24	41	34	109	124	130	9%	79	4%	60%	26	54%	23%	5.22	15.3	48	130	$19
15	STL	175	14	5	24	1	240	237	280	377	657	499	683	5	77	0.24	41	20	39	29	125	95	119	10%	50	3%	100%	13	38%	31%	3.59	-9.2	10	27	$1
1st Half		144	12	4	20	1	243	230	281	375	656	519	683	5	76	0.23	40	19	40	30	121	93	120	9%	53	3%	100%	8	38%	38%	3.61	-6.6	6	16	$2
2nd Half		31	2	1	4	0	226	267	273	387	660	0	681	6	81	0.33	44	24	32	25	142	108	115	13%	69	0%	0%	5	40%	20%	3.48	-1.6	44	119	-$4
16	**Proj**	**424**	**48**	**17**	**62**	**2**	**265**	**254**	**305**	**447**	**752**	**524**	**792**	**5**	**75**	**0.24**	**40**	**21**	**39**	**31**	**122**	**122**	**125**	**14%**	**57**	**3%**	**64%**				**4.71**	**-5.5**	**28**	**76**	**$15**

Ahmed,Nick

Age: 26 Bats: R Pos: SS	Health A	LIMA Plan C	
Ht: 6' 3" Wt: 205	PT/Exp C	Rand Var +1	
	Consist A	MM 1215	

Elite glove netted full-time AB, but bat was polar opposite. xBA offers scant hope for BA uptick thanks to feeble LD% and HctX, while xPX history suggests this is his HR ceiling. SB% is oddly low given excellent Spd, which may have caused 2nd half red light. Without success on basepaths, there's little room for growth.

Yr	Tm	AB	R	HR	RBI	SB	BA	xBA	OBP	SLG	OPS	vL	vR	bb%	ct%	Eye	G	L	F	h%	HctX	PX	xPX	hr/f	Spd	SBO	SB%	#Wk	DOM	DIS	RC/G	RAR	BPV	BPX	R$
11																																			
12																																			
13	aa	487	49	4	39	22	223		265	309	574			5	84	0.36				26		59			121	28%	74%				2.69		33	83	$9
14	ARI *	477	45	4	34	9	247	236	286	334	620	428	577	5	84	0.35	42	18	40	29	88	66	85	4%	126	15%	53%	9	22%	56%	3.08	-3.1	41	111	$7
15	ARI	421	49	9	34	4	226	242	275	359	634	803	575	6	81	0.36	46	17	37	26	77	82	79	7%	144	10%	44%	25	24%	28%	3.12	-8.3	47	127	$3
1st Half		233	30	6	20	4	245	242	310	365	675	948	581	8	79	0.43	47	20	34	29	80	76	78	10%	127	14%	44%	14	29%	43%	3.53	-3.9	33	89	$8
2nd Half		188	19	3	14	0	202	241	231	351	582	625	567	4	83	0.25	45	14	42	23	73	89	80	5%	141	0%	0%	11	18%	9%	2.63	-8.5	56	151	-$3
16	**Proj**	**444**	**46**	**8**	**34**	**4**	**239**	**243**	**279**	**366**	**645**	**648**	**643**	**5**	**83**	**0.33**	**44**	**17**	**39**	**27**	**81**	**79**	**82**	**6%**	**145**	**10%**	**44%**				**3.28**	**-10.8**	**35**	**94**	**$7**

Alberto,Hanser

Age: 23 Bats: R Pos: 2B	Health A	LIMA Plan D	
Ht: 5' 11" Wt: 175	PT/Exp D	Rand Var -3	
	Consist B	MM 1411	

0-4-.222 in 99 AB at TEX. Awful Eye, .216 MLB xBA say he was overmatched, and while he makes good contact, HctX, PX say it's far too weak to make an impact. Spd offers some upside, though it's threatened by SB% trend. Gold Glove in minors indicates the defense is there, but these skills are hardly award-winning.

Yr	Tm	AB	R	HR	RBI	SB	BA	xBA	OBP	SLG	OPS	vL	vR	bb%	ct%	Eye	G	L	F	h%	HctX	PX	xPX	hr/f	Spd	SBO	SB%	#Wk	DOM	DIS	RC/G	RAR	BPV	BPX	R$
11																																			
12																																			
13	aa	356	32	4	34	11	205		236	274	510			4	88	0.33				22		39			139	22%	68%				2.03		35	88	$2
14	aa	178	19	2	12	6	251		271	319	590			3	90	0.27				27		45			108	24%	57%				2.74		35	95	$3
15	TEX *	409	46	3	30	5	265	249	281	356	638	303	598	2	87	0.17	51	16	33	30	59	58	39	0%	147	12%	47%	12	8%	58%	3.31	-12.9	45	122	$7
1st Half		225	24	2	13	4	265	250	279	351	630	370	682	2	88	0.16	55	15	30	30	60	50	31	0%	163	12%	65%	6	17%	33%	3.33	-5.0	46	124	$7
2nd Half		184	21	2	16	1	265	246	284	363	647	0	400	3	86	0.19	37	21	42	30	57	69	64	0%	114	10%	19%	6	0%	83%	3.30	-4.3	40	108	$6
16	**Proj**	**136**	**14**	**2**	**10**	**3**	**245**	**241**	**266**	**346**	**613**	**328**	**725**	**3**	**84**	**0.18**	**44**	**19**	**37**	**28**	**58**	**62**	**51**	**5%**	**140**	**18%**	**57%**				**2.96**	**-5.2**	**26**	**70**	**$3**

Almonte,Abraham

Age: 27 Bats: B Pos: CF	Health A	LIMA Plan B	
Ht: 5' 9" Wt: 205	PT/Exp C	Rand Var +1	
	Consist D	MM 2325	

5-24-.250 with 7 SB in 232 AB at SD/CLE. Rode AAA-MLB shuttle through July, then quietly took off with CLE. Cut down on Ks, which boosted xBA/BA, while PX/Spd gains drove versatile production. BPV history suggests a breakout is unlikely, but at his age, 2nd half gains are worth an end-game dice roll.

Yr	Tm	AB	R	HR	RBI	SB	BA	xBA	OBP	SLG	OPS	vL	vR	bb%	ct%	Eye	G	L	F	h%	HctX	PX	xPX	hr/f	Spd	SBO	SB%	#Wk	DOM	DIS	RC/G	RAR	BPV	BPX	R$
11																																			
12	aa	319	38	4	20	24	245		310	344	654			9	80	0.46				30		69			114	34%	81%				3.74		27	68	$9
13	SEA *	512	73	13	62	21	259	248	332	398	731	475	872	10	74	0.43	50	20	30	33	67	102	29	14%	94	21%	70%	6	50%	50%	4.48	2.9	29	73	$20
14	2 TM *	481	47	7	35	9	218	223	263	309	572	670	573	6	71	0.21	50	21	28	29	85	75	108	8%	91	15%	53%	13	31%	62%	2.52	-20.6	-15	-41	$4
15	2 TM *	484	74	8	53	16	244	257	313	383	696	548	779	9	77	0.44	49	21	31	30	90	95	73	10%	94	18%	74%	18	50%	39%	4.03	-10.7	34	92	$13
1st Half		241	35	3	28	7	244	273	309	357	666	481	491	9	77	0.41	50	29	21	30	47	84	6	0%	85	19%	59%	6	17%	50%	3.57	-9.1	20	54	$11
2nd Half		243	38	5	25	9	244	262	317	408	725	568	837	10	78	0.48	49	19	32	30	99	106	84	11%	107	17%	90%	12	67%	33%	4.51	-2.2	50	135	$15
16	**Proj**	**480**	**64**	**8**	**46**	**17**	**240**	**252**	**304**	**366**	**670**	**587**	**710**	**9**	**75**	**0.38**	**50**	**22**	**28**	**30**	**79**	**89**	**69**	**8%**	**95**	**19%**	**72%**				**3.71**	**-10.1**	**32**	**88**	**$14**

RYAN BLOOMFIELD

Alonso,Yonder

Age: 29	Bats: L	Pos: 1B	Health D	LIMA Plan D+	
Ht: 6' 1"	Wt: 230		PT/Exp D	Rand Var -2	
			Consist B	MM 2133	

You'd expect more from that steady ct% and line-drive stroke, bolstered by career-best Eye and walk rate. But GB swelled as 2014's power gains were sapped by back and shoulder injuries, and season ended early. Has most of the skill ingredients for some BA upside, but power remains a liability for the position.

Yr	Tm	AB	R	HR	RBI	SB	BA	xBA	OBP	SLG	OPS	vL	vR	bb%	ct%	Eye	G	L	F	h%	HctX	PX	xPX	hr/f	Spd	SBO	SB%	#Wk	DOM	DIS	RC/G	RAR	BPV	BPX	R$
11	CIN *	446	43	15	56	4	268	268	334	435	768	651	995	9	80	0.48	42	22	36	31	90	113	98	21%	83	8%	44%	10	40%	50%	4.85	-18.2	53	118	$12
12	SD	549	47	9	62	3	273	264	348	393	741	693	760	10	82	0.61	45	24	31	32	107	88	106	6%	57	2%	100%	27	48%	22%	4.83	-9.3	36	90	$11
13	SD	334	34	6	45	6	281	247	341	368	710	637	736	9	86	0.68	46	21	33	31	107	57	84	6%	63	6%	100%	19	26%	32%	4.62	0.3	28	70	$10
14	SD	267	27	7	27	6	240	279	285	397	682	607	699	6	87	0.47	43	19	38	25	120	110	121	8%	68	13%	86%	16	44%	13%	3.85	-2.6	68	184	$5
15	SD	354	50	5	31	2	282	269	361	381	742	669	762	11	86	0.88	49	23	28	32	108	65	74	6%	85	6%	29%	19	37%	11%	4.64	-7.4	46	124	$9
1st Half		196	22	2	20	2	301	275	387	388	774	868	747	11	86	0.89	56	24	21	34	110	58	69	6%	83	8%	33%	11	27%	9%	5.05	-0.6	39	105	$10
2nd Half		158	28	3	11	0	259	264	328	373	701	369	779	10	87	0.85	41	22	36	28	107	74	81	6%	91	2%	0%	8	50%	13%	4.15	-4.6	57	154	$7
16	Proj	382	48	9	38	3	267	270	333	396	729	612	761	9	86	0.70	45	21	33	29	110	82	91	8%	76	6%	53%				4.51	-7.2	48	129	$9

Altherr,Aaron

Age: 25	Bats: R	Pos: LF	Health A	LIMA Plan C+	
Ht: 6' 5"	Wt: 220		PT/Exp D	Rand Var 0	
			Consist F	MM 4423	

5-22-.241 with 6 SB in 137 AB at PHI. Athletic OF became lineup fixture upon mid-August call-up while flashing broad range of skills at the plate and in the field. Iffy ct% and PX/xPX gap forewarn of BA struggles, but audition points to substantial role in 2016, with upside potential in HR and SB.

Yr	Tm	AB	R	HR	RBI	SB	BA	xBA	OBP	SLG	OPS	vL	vR	bb%	ct%	Eye	G	L	F	h%	HctX	PX	xPX	hr/f	Spd	SBO	SB%	#Wk	DOM	DIS	RC/G	RAR	BPV	BPX	R$
11																																			
12																																			
13																																			
14	PHI *	454	41	12	43	9	201	172	235	337	572	0	0	4	71	0.16	33	0	67	25	103	110	235	0%	95	21%	58%	2	0%	50%	2.40	-20.0	13	35	$3
15	PHI *	570	75	17	74	18	250	260	316	435	750	636	936	9	75	0.39	40	22	38	30	97	128	97	14%	127	19%	74%	8	50%	0%	4.62	-1.6	61	165	$19
1st Half		278	31	7	30	8	257	264	325	425	750			9	78	0.46				31		116			106	16%	69%				4.66		57	154	$13
2nd Half		292	44	10	44	11	243	258	307	444	751	636	936	8	73	0.34	40	22	38	30	94	141	97	14%	133	21%	77%	8	50%	0%	4.58	0.2	62	168	$24
16	Proj	392	46	13	46	11	230	254	300	411	711	512	825	7	73	0.27	40	22	38	28	85	127	87	12%	130	21%	69%				3.76	-9.6	47	126	$11

Altuve,Jose

Age: 26	Bats: R	Pos: 2B	Health A	LIMA Plan D+	
Ht: 5' 6"	Wt: 175		PT/Exp A	Rand Var -3	
			Consist D	MM 2545	

Unrealistic to expect repeat of 2014, and he didn't. BA/OBP, SB% regression made SB total merely excellent. On the other hand, struck the ball harder, hit more FB, and turned doubles into HR. And he owns LHP. Mind the BA/xBA gap, but as he enters prime, this looks like a level he can sustain.

Yr	Tm	AB	R	HR	RBI	SB	BA	xBA	OBP	SLG	OPS	vL	vR	bb%	ct%	Eye	G	L	F	h%	HctX	PX	xPX	hr/f	Spd	SBO	SB%	#Wk	DOM	DIS	RC/G	RAR	BPV	BPX	R$
11	HOU *	365	42	6	31	11	297	278	316	415	731	766	618	3	88	0.23	50	20	30	33	65	77	54	4%	121	21%	56%	11	36%	27%	4.45	-1.5	56	124	$12
12	HOU	576	80	7	37	33	290	277	340	399	740	911	676	6	87	0.54	53	20	27	32	87	72	73	5%	140	27%	75%	27	44%	7%	4.79	10.3	63	158	$24
13	HOU	626	64	5	52	35	283	264	316	363	678	733	656	5	86	0.38	49	23	28	32	94	58	78	3%	100	28%	73%	27	30%	15%	4.05	5.8	34	85	$27
14	HOU	660	85	7	59	56	341	296	377	453	830	1013	775	5	92	0.68	48	23	30	36	95	81	77	4%	124	32%	86%	27	78%	7%	6.86	60.3	82	222	$50
15	HOU	638	86	15	66	38	313	281	353	459	812	973	743	5	89	0.49	47	18	35	33	103	89	92	7%	126	29%	75%	27	67%	19%	5.82	27.2	79	214	$40
1st Half		306	42	7	35	24	301	268	344	418	763	828	729	6	89	0.58	48	18	34	32	96	72	85	8%	106	35%	77%	14	64%	21%	5.21	8.6	60	162	$39
2nd Half		332	44	8	31	14	325	291	361	497	858	1139	755	4	90	0.41	45	18	36	34	109	104	98	7%	134	24%	70%	13	69%	15%	6.42	19.8	93	251	$40
16	Proj	646	85	12	60	35	315	284	352	447	799	959	738	5	90	0.50	48	20	32	34	97	82	84	7%	128	26%	76%				5.74	27.0	73	196	$39

Alvarez,Pedro

Age: 29	Bats: L	Pos: 1B	Health A	LIMA Plan B	
Ht: 6' 3"	Wt: 235		PT/Exp B	Rand Var 0	
			Consist B	MM 4125	

He's all about the Big Fly, as low ct%, BA/xBA history say bat-on-ball skills are merely passable. But 2015's hr/f will be difficult to repeat, and gap between PX and xPX (also in decline) are red flags. Add to that perennial infirmity vs. LHP and league-worst leather. 30 HR return remains attainable, but so does... DN: 300 AB, 15 HR

Yr	Tm	AB	R	HR	RBI	SB	BA	xBA	OBP	SLG	OPS	vL	vR	bb%	ct%	Eye	G	L	F	h%	HctX	PX	xPX	hr/f	Spd	SBO	SB%	#Wk	DOM	DIS	RC/G	RAR	BPV	BPX	R$
11	PIT *	360	30	8	33	1	201	214	281	311	592	545	565	10	65	0.32	55	19	25	28	95	92	89	10%	74	2%	47%	16	19%	63%	2.76	-39.5	-20	-44	-$2
12	PIT	525	64	30	85	1	244	244	317	467	784	648	833	10	66	0.32	47	19	34	31	97	164	144	25%	72	1%	100%	27	44%	37%	5.01	-6.4	37	93	$14
13	PIT	558	70	36	100	2	233	256	296	473	770	537	842	8	67	0.26	43	20	36	28	115	176	168	26%	77	2%	100%	27	48%	30%	4.64	0.8	48	120	$17
14	PIT	398	46	18	56	8	231	235	312	405	717	504	770	10	72	0.40	45	16	39	28	118	125	138	16%	74	10%	73%	23	39%	39%	4.13	-0.6	31	84	$11
15	PIT	437	60	27	77	2	243	265	318	469	787	712	799	10	70	0.37	53	20	27	28	116	154	115	33%	54	2%	100%	27	52%	30%	5.04	-4.2	41	111	$13
1st Half		236	34	12	37	1	242	274	314	453	768	377	815	10	74	0.40	54	20	26	28	122	145	114	26%	59	2%	100%	14	43%	29%	4.81	-2.4	50	135	$13
2nd Half		201	26	15	40	1	244	252	322	488	809	952	779	10	66	0.33	51	21	28	29	110	165	116	41%	63	2%	100%	13	62%	31%	5.31	0.9	36	97	$14
16	Proj	411	52	23	68	3	236	251	312	447	759	639	786	10	69	0.35	49	19	32	28	114	144	129	26%	65	4%	80%				4.64	-6.3	30	82	$14

Amarista,Alexi

Age: 27	Bats: L	Pos: SS	Health A	LIMA Plan D	
Ht: 5' 6"	Wt: 150		PT/Exp C	Rand Var +4	
			Consist A	MM 1411	

Sometimes followed the pitcher in the batting order—no shock, given that he hits like one. Well, he makes better contact, but that's about his only plus skill with the stick. Frankly, his 2015 mound work (one up, one down) was more impressive than his bat. Maybe we could see more of that.

Yr	Tm	AB	R	HR	RBI	SB	BA	xBA	OBP	SLG	OPS	vL	vR	bb%	ct%	Eye	G	L	F	h%	HctX	PX	xPX	hr/f	Spd	SBO	SB%	#Wk	DOM	DIS	RC/G	RAR	BPV	BPX	R$
11	LAA *	415	35	3	39	10	227	223	258	318	576	0	491	4	83	0.24	43	14	43	27	27	68	53	0%	108	23%	53%	10	30%	20%	2.52	-25.7	28	62	$3
12	2 TM *	401	48	6	44	11	235	271	271	362	633	705	657	5	86	0.35	50	19	30	26	87	78	78	7%	134	18%	73%	22	55%	23%	3.25	-10.4	58	145	$6
13	SD	368	35	5	32	4	236	252	282	337	619	557	627	6	85	0.39	43	23	34	27	83	65	72	5%	120	7%	67%	27	52%	22%	3.12	-4.2	39	98	$3
14	SD	423	39	5	40	12	239	252	286	314	600	446	651	6	84	0.42	49	23	28	28	76	53	55	5%	110	12%	92%	27	30%	48%	3.15	-1.8	25	68	$7
15	SD	324	28	3	30	5	204	244	257	287	544	507	549	7	83	0.44	48	21	31	24	71	52	49	4%	124	8%	83%	26	19%	54%	2.41	-13.7	27	73	-$1
1st Half		187	16	2	18	3	214	248	285	299	584	598	583	9	83	0.56	48	22	30	25	69	53	35	4%	125	8%	75%	14	21%	50%	2.76	-7.7	31	84	$0
2nd Half		137	12	1	12	2	190	237	218	270	488	375	502	4	83	0.26	49	19	32	22	74	49	67	3%	119	8%	100%	12	17%	58%	1.96	-9.3	18	49	-$2
16	Proj	198	18	2	18	4	218	246	262	305	567	473	584	6	84	0.38	48	21	32	25	73	54	58	4%	116	10%	82%				2.66	-8.7	21	57	$2

Anderson,Tim

Age: 23	Bats: R	Pos: DH	Health A	LIMA Plan D	
Ht: 6' 1"	Wt: 180		PT/Exp F	Rand Var 0	
			Consist A	MM 1501	

2013 first rounder filled up the stat sheet during first full season in Double-A. Led the Southern League in hits while blazing around the bags (12 triples and 49 SB). Improving 4% bb% and SS footwork top the to-do list for 2016, but he's not far off. Solid growth stock.

Yr	Tm	AB	R	HR	RBI	SB	BA	xBA	OBP	SLG	OPS	vL	vR	bb%	ct%	Eye	G	L	F	h%	HctX	PX	xPX	hr/f	Spd	SBO	SB%	#Wk	DOM	DIS	RC/G	RAR	BPV	BPX	R$
11																																			
12																																			
13																																			
14	aa	44	5	1	5	0	326		326	445	771			0	77	0.00				41		97			94	10%	0%				4.88		15	41	$0
15	aa	513	70	5	41	43	292		322	396	718			4	75	0.18				38		70			144	41%	75%				4.54		11	30	$30
1st Half		305	39	1	26	24	285		308	372	680			3	76	0.14				37		63			141	39%	79%				4.13		7	19	$31
2nd Half		208	31	4	14	19	303		342	432	773			6	74	0.23				39		80			175	44%	72%				5.16		26	70	$29
16	Proj	167	23	1	12	8	266	233	301	364	665	665	665	5	75	0.20	48	22	30	35		66		3%	172	27%	73%				3.75	-8.4	11	29	$6

Andrus,Elvis

Age: 27	Bats: R	Pos: SS	Health A	LIMA Plan B	
Ht: 6' 0"	Wt: 200		PT/Exp A	Rand Var +1	
			Consist A	MM 1435	

Incremental three-year drop in on-base skills have sired similar leakage in overall SB prowess. But he drilled the ball and ran with greater aplomb as team surged in the 2H, so maybe the tide is turning. Just entering his prime years, his xPX surge and GB%/FB% shift are intriguing. If you believe, then... UP: 10 HR, 35 SB

Yr	Tm	AB	R	HR	RBI	SB	BA	xBA	OBP	SLG	OPS	vL	vR	bb%	ct%	Eye	G	L	F	h%	HctX	PX	xPX	hr/f	Spd	SBO	SB%	#Wk	DOM	DIS	RC/G	RAR	BPV	BPX	R$
11	TEX	587	96	5	60	37	279	284	347	361	708	714	706	9	87	0.76	56	23	21	31	76	57	51	5%	113	26%	76%	27	48%	15%	4.41	3.9	48	107	$26
12	TEX	629	85	3	62	21	286	275	349	378	727	687	742	8	85	0.59	57	22	21	33	101	61	76	3%	141	16%	68%	27	48%	22%	4.59	12.2	49	123	$21
13	TEX	620	91	4	67	42	271	257	328	331	659	698	644	8	84	0.54	56	21	22	32	95	40	54	3%	139	26%	84%	27	30%	37%	3.99	10.1	29	73	$30
14	TEX	619	72	2	41	27	263	268	314	333	647	760	607	7	84	0.48	59	20	21	31	75	59	36	2%	106	25%	64%	27	37%	19%	3.49	5.7	33	89	$19
15	TEX	596	69	7	62	25	258	266	309	357	667	760	616	7	87	0.59	47	21	32	29	102	67	71	4%	105	22%	74%	27	59%	15%	3.81	-10.3	49	132	$19
1st Half		308	30	3	28	9	237	249	290	315	605	695	556	8	85	0.53	48	21	31	27	88	53	63	4%	109	16%	69%	14	43%	21%	3.07	-9.5	31	84	$11
2nd Half		288	39	4	34	16	281	282	330	403	733	831	680	7	88	0.68	46	21	33	30	118	81	79	5%	98	28%	76%	13	77%	8%	4.71	5.2	67	181	$28
16	Proj	616	78	5	59	30	267	268	321	352	673	755	637	7	86	0.58	52	21	27	30	95	60	60	4%	112	23%	73%				3.92	-2.9	43	117	$24

ROB CARROLL

Aoki,Norichika

Age: 34 Bats: L Pos: LF	Health C	LIMA Plan B+	
Ht: 5' 9" Wt: 180	PT/Exp B	Rand Var 0	
	Consist A	MM 1455	

Was hitting .317 with 12 SB when felled by June leg injury. Struggled upon return, then lost most of Sept to concussion. Little power, but plate skills, Spd holding steady. Another year of helpful BA, handful of SBs likely. But at 34, injuries may continue to be part of the package, too.

Yr Tm	AB	R	HR	RBI	SB	BA	xBA	OBP	SLG	OPS	vL	vR	bb%	ct%	Eye	G	L	F	h%	HctX	PX	xPX	hr/f	Spd	SBO	SB%	#Wk	DOM	DIS	RC/G	RAR	BPV	BPX	R$
11 for	583	71	2	43	7	272		320	342	661			7	91	0.79				30		43			136	6%	68%				3.80	-21.7	55	122	$11
12 MIL	520	81	10	50	30	288	294	355	433	787	711	828	8	89	0.78	55	17	28	31	98	91	81	8%	129	27%	79%	27	59%	19%	5.35	9.2	87	218	$24
13 MIL	597	80	8	37	20	286	282	356	370	726	781	703	8	93	1.38	60	18	22	30	102	50	69	7%	141	16%	63%	27	56%	4%	4.43	6.4	74	185	$22
14 KC	491	63	1	43	17	285	292	349	360	710	863	658	8	90	0.88	62	21	17	32	73	53	40	1%	134	16%	68%	25	48%	4%	4.34	7.7	61	165	$17
15 SF	355	42	5	26	14	287	294	353	380	733	774	717	8	93	1.20	61	19	20	30	63	52	36	8%	129	17%	74%	17	53%	6%	4.65	-0.6	70	189	$13
1st Half	262	33	2	19	12	317	296	383	385	768	789	760	8	94	1.35	62	21	17	33	69	40	36	5%	129	18%	71%	11	55%	9%	5.28	5.2	63	170	$19
2nd Half	93	9	3	7	2	204	290	267	366	633	734	588	7	91	0.88	57	14	29	20	47	87	35	13%	108	11%	100%	6	50%	0%	3.14	-4.1	84	227	-$3
16 Proj	**465**	**58**	**7**	**38**	**15**	**282**	**289**	**346**	**384**	**729**	**809**	**697**	**8**	**92**	**1.00**	**60**	**18**	**22**	**30**	**71**	**59**	**46**	**7%**	**129**	**15%**	**73%**				**4.58**	**0.2**	**65**	**176**	**$16**

Arcia,Orlando

Age: 21 Bats: R Pos: SS	Health A	LIMA Plan D+	
Ht: 6' 0" Wt: 165	PT/Exp F	Rand Var 0	
	Consist F	MM 2521	

For a player with his speed, would like to see more than 30 BB in 552 PA. Still, top MIL SS prospect on steady rise towards majors. Power to gaps for now, but many observers feel that should grow with time. SB% (25-for-33 at AA-Biloxi) gradually improving. For now, that's where his value lies.

Yr Tm	AB	R	HR	RBI	SB	BA	xBA	OBP	SLG	OPS	vL	vR	bb%	ct%	Eye	G	L	F	h%	HctX	PX	xPX	hr/f	Spd	SBO	SB%	#Wk	DOM	DIS	RC/G	RAR	BPV	BPX	R$
11																																		
12																																		
13																																		
14																																		
15 aa	512	67	9	63	23	297		334	440	774			5	85	0.36				34		94			105	24%	73%				5.23		58	157	$25
1st Half	300	46	4	38	9	303		338	439	778			5	85	0.36				34		90			126	18%	63%				5.23		63	170	$28
2nd Half	212	22	4	25	14	288		327	441	768			5	84	0.36				33		99			122	32%	81%				5.22		64	173	$22
16 Proj	**166**	**21**	**2**	**20**	**9**	**294**	**258**	**329**	**417**	**746**	**746**	**746**	**5**	**84**	**0.33**	**46**	**18**	**36**	**34**		**83**		**3%**	**135**	**26%**	**77%**				**4.95**	**4.1**	**56**	**151**	**$9**

Arcia,Oswaldo

Age: 25 Bats: L Pos: LF	Health B	LIMA Plan D+	
Ht: 6' 0" Wt: 220	PT/Exp D	Rand Var +5	
	Consist C	MM 4003	

2-8-.276 in 58 AB at MIN. Derailed by early May hip injury, could never get on track in minors. Hard to give up on after power display in 2013-14, but ct% struggles persist. Out of options, which may be blessing in disguise: With others ahead of him on MIN depth chart, change of scenery could be career lifeline.

Yr Tm	AB	R	HR	RBI	SB	BA	xBA	OBP	SLG	OPS	vL	vR	bb%	ct%	Eye	G	L	F	h%	HctX	PX	xPX	hr/f	Spd	SBO	SB%	#Wk	DOM	DIS	RC/G	RAR	BPV	BPX	R$
11																																		
12 aa	262	45	8	56	2	305		362	500	862			8	75	0.36				38		136			105	6%	53%				6.49		57	143	$12
13 MIN *	479	54	21	67	3	257	231	315	446	761	659	769	8	67	0.25	42	17	41	34	93	145	131	15%	94	5%	45%	19	42%	37%	4.72	10.4	30	75	$14
14 MIN *	449	59	24	72	2	240	254	295	464	759	574	848	7	68	0.24	37	22	42	30	94	175	144	19%	86	4%	48%	20	45%	50%	4.52	11.2	53	143	$14
15 MIN *	340	32	12	43	0	195	222	238	335	573	624	779	5	70	0.18	36	23	41	24	70	100	64	11%	80	2%	0%	5	20%	40%	2.48	-20.5	-4	-11	-$1
1st Half	180	15	5	24	0	250	222	283	380	663	624	779	4	71	0.16	36	23	41	33	71	95	64	11%	82	0%	0%	5	20%	40%	3.66	-4.8	-6	-16	$2
2nd Half	160	17	7	19	0	134	222	189	285	474			6	68	0.22				14		106			79	5%	0%				1.52		-3	-8	-$4
16 Proj	**301**	**35**	**12**	**44**	**1**	**252**	**233**	**311**	**430**	**741**	**629**	**803**	**6**	**69**	**0.22**	**39**	**20**	**41**	**32**	**86**	**128**	**111**	**15%**	**90**	**3%**	**38%**				**4.31**	**-2.2**	**10**	**27**	**$9**

Arenado,Nolan

Age: 25 Bats: R Pos: 3B	Health B	LIMA Plan C	
Ht: 6' 2" Wt: 205	PT/Exp B	Rand Var 0	
	Consist B	MM 4155	

Last year, we set "UP" bar at 25 HR; he cleared it by Aug. 1. Good news is this is NOT a Coors creation (22 road HR). Yeah, he could walk more. And 2-for-7 SB? (OK, we're reaching.) No reason to think struggles vs. LHP linger (see 2014). Only 2H drops in xPX, FB%, ct% temper enthusiasm. UP: Full power repeat, plus a .300 BA

Yr Tm	AB	R	HR	RBI	SB	BA	xBA	OBP	SLG	OPS	vL	vR	bb%	ct%	Eye	G	L	F	h%	HctX	PX	xPX	hr/f	Spd	SBO	SB%	#Wk	DOM	DIS	RC/G	RAR	BPV	BPX	R$
11																																		
12 aa	516	48	13	49	0	289		333	440	773			6	89	0.59				31		95			82	2%	0%				5.16		71	178	$13
13 COL *	552	58	12	65	2	273	284	306	424	730	846	652	5	85	0.32	43	24	34	30	101	103	103	7%	104	3%	47%	23	48%	17%	4.50	7.9	66	165	$14
14 COL	432	58	18	61	2	287	300	328	500	828	973	776	5	87	0.43	38	21	42	30	127	142	134	11%	96	3%	67%	20	80%	10%	5.80	25.3	102	276	$18
15 COL	616	97	42	130	2	287	307	323	575	898	778	931	5	82	0.31	34	22	44	29	130	172	149	19%	95	6%	29%	27	70%	15%	6.46	31.1	107	289	$32
1st Half	304	49	24	68	0	283	313	314	599	913	781	945	4	86	0.30	37	17	47	26	131	175	157	19%	102	6%	0%	14	86%	7%	6.36	15.0	123	332	$34
2nd Half	312	48	18	62	2	292	301	332	551	884	775	917	6	79	0.32	32	27	41	32	128	168	141	17%	90	6%	50%	13	54%	23%	6.54	16.7	91	246	$31
16 Proj	**610**	**91**	**37**	**110**	**2**	**294**	**308**	**331**	**561**	**892**	**908**	**886**	**5**	**84**	**0.35**	**35**	**22**	**42**	**30**	**124**	**159**	**136**	**17%**	**97**	**4%**	**40%**				**6.58**	**33.3**	**95**	**258**	**$33**

Arencibia,J.P.

Age: 30 Bats: R Pos: CA	Health A	LIMA Plan D	
Ht: 6' 0" Wt: 205	PT/Exp C	Rand Var -1	
	Consist A	MM 4101	

6-17-.310 in 71 AB at TAM. You caught that, right? .310! Thank you, 37% hit rate! But even with that 71 AB stretch, he still could not pull his seasonal equivalent BA over .200. And this 5-year scan yields an aggregate BA of .205. Those HRs are nice, but if he's your #2 catcher, you'll need a bunch of .300 hitters to offset damage.

Yr Tm	AB	R	HR	RBI	SB	BA	xBA	OBP	SLG	OPS	vL	vR	bb%	ct%	Eye	G	L	F	h%	HctX	PX	xPX	hr/f	Spd	SBO	SB%	#Wk	DOM	DIS	RC/G	RAR	BPV	BPX	R$
11 TOR	443	47	23	78	1	219	240	282	438	720	838	682	8	70	0.27	35	16	50	26	110	158	153	15%	102	2%	50%	27	44%	26%	3.94	-3.6	54	120	$8
12 TOR	347	45	18	56	1	233	233	275	435	710	774	688	5	69	0.17	37	18	45	29	98	144	128	17%	72	2%	100%	22	45%	45%	3.94	-2.0	24	60	$7
13 TOR	474	45	21	55	0	194	225	227	365	592	588	594	4	69	0.12	37	20	44	23	92	127	133	15%	73	3%	0%	27	33%	48%	2.52	-18.0	8	20	$1
14 TEX *	393	39	19	60	1	193	218	225	373	598	840	492	4	67	0.13	34	16	50	23	108	141	164	14%	67	1%	100%	18	39%	33%	2.66	-8.2	12	32	$4
15 TAM *	455	47	21	65	0	194	209	215	367	582	757	1023	3	60	0.07	36	22	42	27	100	140	154	29%	77	0%	0%	6	33%	50%	2.50	-17.8	-18	-49	$2
1st Half	237	23	10	27	0	177	197	197	330	527			2	57	0.06				26		129			75	0%	0%				2.01		-37	-100	-$2
2nd Half	218	24	11	38	0	212	223	234	408	642	757	1023	3	62	0.07	36	22	42	28	104	151	154	29%	78	0%	0%	6	33%	50%	3.09	-4.6	0	0	$6
16 Proj	**101**	**10**	**6**	**15**	**0**	**199**	**224**	**232**	**403**	**635**	**655**	**626**	**3**	**64**	**0.10**	**36**	**19**	**45**	**24**	**102**	**151**	**147**	**19%**	**82**	**1%**	**54%**				**2.90**	**-2.8**	**-4**	**-10**	**$2**

Asche,Cody

Age: 26 Bats: L Pos: LF 3B	Health A	LIMA Plan D+	
Ht: 6' 1" Wt: 200	PT/Exp C	Rand Var 0	
	Consist A	MM 3113	

12-39-.245 in 425 AB at PHI. Overall, not much sign of growth, but 2H did feature most of his HR, rise in OPS, HctX, PX/xPX. Mediocre ct%, xBA suggests he'll never be BA boon, but could provide handful of HR with AB. Keep expectations modest.

Yr Tm	AB	R	HR	RBI	SB	BA	xBA	OBP	SLG	OPS	vL	vR	bb%	ct%	Eye	G	L	F	h%	HctX	PX	xPX	hr/f	Spd	SBO	SB%	#Wk	DOM	DIS	RC/G	RAR	BPV	BPX	R$
11																																		
12 aa	263	33	8	37	1	269		315	450	765			6	76	0.28				32		127			93	3%	42%				4.87		49	123	$6
13 PHI *	566	58	17	75	10	252	246	304	411	715	608	710	7	73	0.28	44	21	35	32	91	116	109	12%	110	10%	74%	10	40%	40%	4.24	3.1	35	88	$16
14 PHI	397	43	10	46	0	252	249	309	390	699	733	690	8	74	0.32	41	24	35	32	95	113	102	10%	92	1%	0%	24	54%	25%	4.07	3.3	33	89	$7
15 PHI *	486	46	13	41	1	245	241	290	388	678	585	713	6	75	0.25	38	23	39	30	99	99	113	10%	101	3%	33%	26	27%	35%	3.74	-14.0	23	62	$6
1st Half	283	21	5	13	0	248	234	288	348	636	656	628	5	76	0.24	41	24	35	31	93	70	94	7%	103	1%	0%	13	15%	46%	3.34	-10.2	5	14	$3
2nd Half	203	25	8	28	1	241	253	306	443	750	519	808	7	73	0.27	34	22	43	29	104	141	135	13%	103	5%	50%	13	38%	23%	4.31	-1.5	51	138	$10
16 Proj	**392**	**42**	**11**	**44**	**2**	**250**	**248**	**304**	**406**	**709**	**643**	**726**	**7**	**74**	**0.28**	**39**	**23**	**38**	**31**	**97**	**111**	**111**	**10%**	**99**	**4%**	**53%**				**4.09**	**-5.5**	**20**	**55**	**$9**

Avila,Alex

Age: 29 Bats: L Pos: CA 1B	Health C	LIMA Plan D	
Ht: 5' 11" Wt: 210	PT/Exp D	Rand Var +3	
	Consist A	MM 3001	

Knee injury cost him nearly two months. Time away did not help him find his ct% or stroke vs. LHP. xPX holds out faint hope for power, but not enough loft for that to matter. Can take a walk, which keeps OBP reasonable. Promise of 2011 now distant memory. Find him in the $1 bin.

Yr Tm	AB	R	HR	RBI	SB	BA	xBA	OBP	SLG	OPS	vL	vR	bb%	ct%	Eye	G	L	F	h%	HctX	PX	xPX	hr/f	Spd	SBO	SB%	#Wk	DOM	DIS	RC/G	RAR	BPV	BPX	R$
11 DET	464	63	19	82	3	295	264	389	506	895	779	939	14	72	0.56	38	22	40	38	115	160	154	14%	90	3%	75%	27	44%	26%	7.16	38.0	71	158	$20
12 DET	367	42	9	48	2	243	245	352	384	736	539	796	14	72	0.59	46	24	30	31	105	106	130	11%	79	2%	100%	26	35%	38%	4.57	4.7	26	65	$5
13 DET *	374	43	12	51	0	225	238	316	369	685	455	767	12	66	0.39	42	28	30	31	99	116	138	17%	71	0%	0%	24	25%	42%	3.84	1.4	5	13	$4
14 DET	390	44	11	47	0	218	222	327	359	686	589	720	14	61	0.40	45	25	30	32	105	136	147	15%	62	3%	0%	27	37%	44%	3.68	4.2	2	5	$3
15 DET	178	21	4	13	0	191	207	339	287	626	424	666	18	63	0.61	41	28	32	28	86	77	124	11%	82	2%	0%	19	26%	53%	3.00	-4.1	-22	-59	-$3
1st Half	68	11	2	8	0	206	211	357	309	666	180	803	19	66	0.70	33	29	38	28	76	72	129	12%	73	0%	0%	7	29%	43%	3.54	-0.5	-16	-43	-$2
2nd Half	110	10	2	5	0	182	203	328	273	601	675	590	18	61	0.56	45	27	27	28	92	81	121	11%	96	3%	0%	12	25%	58%	2.70	-3.9	-25	-68	-$3
16 Proj	**206**	**24**	**5**	**21**	**0**	**211**	**219**	**335**	**334**	**669**	**506**	**713**	**16**	**64**	**0.52**	**42**	**27**	**31**	**30**	**95**	**100**	**134**	**13%**	**76**	**2%**	**11%**				**3.55**	**-1.5**	**-21**	**-57**	**$2**

KRISTOPHER OLSON

Aviles,Mike

Age: 35 Bats: R Pos: LF 3B SS	Health A	LIMA Plan D
Ht: 5' 10" Wt: 205	PT/Exp D	Rand Var +1
	Consist A	MM 1211

Had already proven he can't hit RHP; now appears to have lost advantage vs. LHP, too. Power is long gone, and xBA, ABs are both trending downward. Factor in his age, and odds are stacked against return to double-digit SB, which is his only path to fantasy relevance.

Yr	Tm	AB	R	HR	RBI	SB	BA	xBA	OBP	SLG	OPS	vL	vR	bb%	ct%	Eye	G	L	F	h%	HctX	PX	xPX	hr/f	Spd	SBO	SB%	#Wk	DOM	DIS	RC/G	RAR	BPV	BPX	R$
11	2 AL *	426	44	12	55	18	247	260	276	408	683	924	601	4	85	0.26	42	16	43	27	98	103	93	7%	110	33%	66%	22	55%	36%	3.61	-15.4	64	142	$12
12	BOS	512	57	13	60	14	250	254	282	381	663	753	626	4	85	0.30	41	19	40	27	100	84	90	7%	69	18%	70%	26	31%	19%	3.59	-14.6	38	95	$13
13	CLE	361	54	9	46	8	252	260	282	368	650	605	689	4	89	0.37	43	20	37	26	94	72	73	7%	61	16%	62%	27	44%	26%	3.42	-5.6	40	100	$10
14	CLE	344	38	5	39	14	247	255	273	343	616	645	596	4	86	0.27	44	21	35	28	61	69	45	5%	78	25%	74%	26	38%	31%	3.16	-5.2	31	84	$9
15	CLE	290	37	5	17	3	231	240	282	317	599	650	542	6	87	0.53	49	16	35	25	88	54	71	6%	90	6%	75%	25	32%	40%	2.96	-14.1	33	89	$2
1st Half		158	21	4	9	1	253	254	308	361	669	698	630	7	88	0.63	50	18	32	27	98	62	72	9%	89	2%	100%	13	38%	38%	3.80	-3.8	44	119	$3
2nd Half		132	16	1	8	2	205	220	250	265	515	581	453	6	86	0.42	48	14	38	23	75	43	69	2%	84	10%	67%	12	25%	42%	2.11	-10.5	15	41	$0
16	Proj	199	25	3	18	5	236	246	276	332	607	644	576	5	86	0.40	46	18	36	26	81	60	66	6%	82	14%	70%				3.02	-9.3	33	88	$2

Aybar,Erick

Age: 32 Bats: B Pos: SS	Health A	LIMA Plan B+
Ht: 5' 10" Wt: 180	PT/Exp A	Rand Var 0
	Consist A	MM 1345

Another season of steady, unexciting production, fueled by high AB totals, solid BA, and decent speed. But low OBP and declining defensive metrics could soon put a dent in playing time and counting stats, and RC/G, BPV trends suggest he's not as safe an investment as R$ history indicates.

Yr	Tm	AB	R	HR	RBI	SB	BA	xBA	OBP	SLG	OPS	vL	vR	bb%	ct%	Eye	G	L	F	h%	HctX	PX	xPX	hr/f	Spd	SBO	SB%	#Wk	DOM	DIS	RC/G	RAR	BPV	BPX	R$
11	LAA	556	71	10	59	30	279	287	322	421	743	607	807	5	88	0.46	48	21	31	30	85	91	66	7%	123	27%	83%	25	64%	12%	4.81	10.1	73	162	$23
12	LAA	517	67	8	45	20	290	279	324	416	740	879	690	4	88	0.36	52	19	29	32	91	79	63	6%	116	19%	83%	25	52%	20%	4.84	13.6	61	153	$19
13	LAA	550	68	6	54	12	271	287	301	382	683	723	666	4	89	0.39	50	23	27	29	93	75	63	5%	109	15%	63%	25	52%	16%	3.90	7.5	60	150	$16
14	LAA	589	77	7	68	16	278	282	321	379	700	622	727	6	89	0.58	49	23	28	30	88	69	54	5%	102	16%	64%	27	44%	15%	4.16	16.7	57	154	$21
15	LAA	597	74	3	44	15	270	265	301	338	639	597	657	4	88	0.34	53	21	26	30	88	50	59	2%	104	14%	71%	27	33%	33%	3.51	-15.3	32	86	$15
1st Half		300	42	2	27	6	280	262	319	350	669	705	658	5	86	0.38	53	21	26	32	84	52	56	3%	111	11%	67%	14	29%	43%	3.87	-1.8	31	84	$17
2nd Half		297	32	1	17	9	259	268	283	327	610	524	655	3	90	0.29	52	21	27	29	93	48	61	1%	95	17%	75%	13	38%	23%	3.16	-8.1	33	89	$13
16	Proj	575	72	5	51	14	267	275	302	357	659	617	676	4	89	0.41	51	22	27	29	89	60	59	4%	105	15%	68%				3.66	-7.1	45	122	$17

Baez,Javier

Age: 23 Bats: R Pos: 2B	Health A	LIMA Plan C+
Ht: 6' 0" Wt: 190	PT/Exp D	Rand Var -3
	Consist F	MM 3305

1-4-.289 in 76 AB at CHC. Improved ct%, but there were still too many swings and misses, and significant drop in FB% suggests altered approach may have cost HR. The power/speed combo should at least yield moderate short-term value, even with looming BA correction, but odds are against major breakout in 2016.

Yr	Tm	AB	R	HR	RBI	SB	BA	xBA	OBP	SLG	OPS	vL	vR	bb%	ct%	Eye	G	L	F	h%	HctX	PX	xPX	hr/f	Spd	SBO	SB%	#Wk	DOM	DIS	RC/G	RAR	BPV	BPX	R$
11																																			
12																																			
13	aa	218	31	16	43	6	268		317	557	874			7	66	0.21				33		224			78	20%	75%				6.07		81	203	$11
14	CHC *	601	74	26	81	17	209	213	260	393	654	569	546	6	60	0.17	41	14	45	30	82	166	120	17%	96	24%	64%	9	33%	67%	3.17	-4.2	17	46	$15
15	CHC *	357	41	11	51	14	286	248	325	439	764	1082	617	5	69	0.18	37	31	31	39	99	116	117	6%	114	21%	72%	6	33%	67%	5.01	8.6	15	41	$16
1st Half		140	15	6	22	5	276	234	318	453	771			6	67	0.19				37		131			86	19%	83%				5.13		13	35	$9
2nd Half		217	27	5	28	9	293	246	330	430	760	1082	617	5	70	0.18	37	31	31	40	101	106	117	6%	122	23%	67%	6	33%	67%	4.94	4.4	13	35	$21
16	Proj	494	61	13	73	17	247	218	294	379	672	894	601	6	65	0.18	39	24	37	35	93	108	118	11%	109	21%	70%				3.69	-8.0	-9	-23	$18

Barnhart,Tucker

Age: 25 Bats: B Pos: CA	Health A	LIMA Plan D
Ht: 5' 11" Wt: 195	PT/Exp D	Rand Var -2
	Consist C	MM 1001

Hit 2 HR in first four games, only 1 in the 77 games after. FB% and PX/xPX cratered in 2H, matching similar punchless ineptitude from throughout minor league career. Defense is highly regarded, but he offers no plus offensive skills, so even an expanded role won't likely lead to fantasy value.

Yr	Tm	AB	R	HR	RBI	SB	BA	xBA	OBP	SLG	OPS	vL	vR	bb%	ct%	Eye	G	L	F	h%	HctX	PX	xPX	hr/f	Spd	SBO	SB%	#Wk	DOM	DIS	RC/G	RAR	BPV	BPX	R$
11																																			
12	aa	130	9	2	11	1	190		247	280	527			7	82	0.41				22		56			104	7%	46%				2.12		19	48	-$3
13	aa	339	28	3	40	1	245		326	331	656			11	81	0.64				29		66			86	1%	100%				3.65		28	70	$2
14	CIN *	310	16	2	21	0	202	189	259	258	517	167	568	7	84	0.48	60	7	33	24	79	39	38	7%	104	1%	0%	9	22%	44%	2.10	-13.2	14	38	-$4
15	CIN	242	23	3	18	0	252	245	324	326	650	433	700	9	81	0.56	47	25	28	30	62	52	43	5%	84	1%	0%	24	42%	33%	3.52	-2.0	13	35	$1
1st Half		90	10	3	7	0	267	252	316	400	716	321	795	7	81	0.41	36	25	40	30	77	81	70	10%	93	0%	0%	12	50%	33%	4.45	1.7	33	89	$1
2nd Half		152	13	0	11	0	243	243	328	283	610	486	641	11	82	0.64	54	25	21	30	53	35	27	0%	86	2%	0%	12	33%	33%	3.00	-3.5	3	8	$1
16	Proj	160	13	2	13	0	233	229	302	315	616	341	684	9	82	0.54	52	18	30	27	69	54	42	5%	92	2%	25%				3.10	-3.3	2	5	$1

Bautista,Jose

Age: 35 Bats: R Pos: RF DH	Health C	LIMA Plan A
Ht: 6' 0" Wt: 205	PT/Exp A	Rand Var +3
	Consist B	MM 4245

Shoulder injury may have contributed to slow start; shook that off, and posted best power numbers in years. Batting eye, xBA remain strong, but dip in LD% brought h% and BA back down to 2012-13 levels. Most players are declining at his age, but his career arc has been anything but typical. Keep riding him.

Yr	Tm	AB	R	HR	RBI	SB	BA	xBA	OBP	SLG	OPS	vL	vR	bb%	ct%	Eye	G	L	F	h%	HctX	PX	xPX	hr/f	Spd	SBO	SB%	#Wk	DOM	DIS	RC/G	RAR	BPV	BPX	R$
11	TOR	513	105	43	103	9	302	297	447	608	1056	1156	1025	20	78	1.19	37	16	47	31	155	191	158	23%	105	6%	64%	27	74%	7%	9.73	65.0	141	313	$35
12	TOR	332	64	27	65	5	241	280	358	527	886	718	942	15	81	0.94	37	14	49	22	130	165	145	20%	77	7%	71%	17	76%	12%	6.25	13.9	111	278	$14
13	TOR	452	82	28	73	7	259	281	358	498	856	910	842	13	81	0.82	41	16	43	26	129	150	138	18%	84	7%	78%	21	67%	5%	6.12	24.2	99	248	$20
14	TOR	553	101	35	103	6	286	290	403	524	928	1079	888	16	83	1.08	40	18	42	29	124	152	121	18%	89	4%	75%	27	81%	7%	7.46	55.4	113	305	$32
15	TOR	543	108	40	114	8	250	285	377	536	913	834	932	17	80	1.04	37	14	49	24	124	168	151	18%	96	6%	80%	27	81%	7%	6.88	33.9	121	327	$26
1st Half		256	54	17	57	3	246	285	397	520	917	1020	890	20	80	1.30	36	17	48	24	124	164	148	17%	98	5%	60%	14	86%	7%	6.91	16.0	125	338	$23
2nd Half		287	54	23	57	5	254	285	357	551	908	643	967	14	80	0.80	39	12	50	24	125	172	154	20%	90	6%	100%	13	77%	8%	6.81	16.7	116	314	$29
16	Proj	530	101	37	103	5	253	282	374	519	893	887	895	16	81	1.00	39	15	46	25	127	156	142	19%	94	4%	69%				6.57	27.3	104	281	$27

Beckham,Gordon

Age: 29 Bats: R Pos: 3B	Health B	LIMA Plan D
Ht: 6' 0" Wt: 185	PT/Exp D	Rand Var +3
	Consist B	MM 2211

Another season of futility, as career lows in FB%, xPX, and HctX finally cost him some playing time. Not even worthy of short half of platoon, as he's overmatched by both LHP (career .679 OPS) and RHP (.675). It's been years since he hit ball with authority or got on base at acceptable level, and time is running out.

Yr	Tm	AB	R	HR	RBI	SB	BA	xBA	OBP	SLG	OPS	vL	vR	bb%	ct%	Eye	G	L	F	h%	HctX	PX	xPX	hr/f	Spd	SBO	SB%	#Wk	DOM	DIS	RC/G	RAR	BPV	BPX	R$
11	CHW	499	60	10	44	5	230	230	296	337	633	541	663	7	78	0.32	39	20	40	28	76	79	66	6%	110	7%	63%	27	33%	26%	3.10	-25.9	22	49	$5
12	CHW	525	62	16	60	5	234	245	296	371	668	689	659	7	83	0.45	38	20	42	25	92	86	90	9%	94	7%	56%	27	37%	33%	3.50	-16.7	45	113	$8
13	CHW*	407	51	5	28	5	267	247	317	367	684	510	745	7	84	0.47	35	23	41	31	96	73	105	4%	116	6%	83%	20	40%	30%	4.08	1.6	46	115	$8
14	2 AL *	489	56	10	48	4	217	242	255	335	590	780	560	5	82	0.28	45	16	39	25	98	89	85	6%	79	4%	100%	24	46%	29%	2.82	-12.7	34	92	$4
15	CHW	211	24	6	20	0	209	237	275	332	607	626	593	8	80	0.44	45	19	35	23	73	79	56	10%	86	2%	0%	26	31%	46%	2.86	-11.1	26	70	-$1
1st Half		145	13	4	16	0	207	248	276	331	607	444	696	9	82	0.58	43	21	35	23	71	79	48	9%	82	3%	0%	14	43%	36%	2.90	-7.8	37	100	-$1
2nd Half		66	11	2	4	0	212	216	274	333	607	881	262	6	74	0.24	50	14	36	26	77	81	75	11%	102	0%	0%	12	17%	58%	2.77	-3.8	6	16	-$2
16	Proj	164	21	4	14	1	223	235	281	342	623	721	568	7	80	0.34	44	18	38	26	85	80	77	8%	94	3%	67%				3.06	-7.8	15	42	$2

Beckham,Tim

Age: 26 Bats: R Pos: 2B SS	Health F	LIMA Plan D
Ht: 6' 0" Wt: 195	PT/Exp F	Rand Var -1
	Consist D	MM 3413

9-36-.225 in 200 AB at TAM. Former top prospect missed most of '14 with torn ACL, then finally got a shot in majors. High hr/f led to better than expected power numbers, though xPX, minor league history say pace will be hard to maintain. Versatility, pedigree could lead to more chances, but holes in swing are major obstacle.

Yr	Tm	AB	R	HR	RBI	SB	BA	xBA	OBP	SLG	OPS	vL	vR	bb%	ct%	Eye	G	L	F	h%	HctX	PX	xPX	hr/f	Spd	SBO	SB%	#Wk	DOM	DIS	RC/G	RAR	BPV	BPX	R$
11	a/a	524	75	9	56	14	239		285	353	637			6	75	0.25				30		86			105	16%	71%				3.33		12	27	$11
12	aaa	285	33	5	23	5	225		284	311	595			8	72	0.30				30		62			101	7%	100%				3.00		-13	-33	$2
13	TAM *	467	59	3	43	14	247	231	300	341	641	900	667	7	74	0.29	63	13	25	33	38	74	-15	0%	142	18%	64%	2	0%	0%	3.37	-0.7	13	33	$10
14	aaa	62	7	0	3	0	225		245	252	498			3	74	0.10				30		30			100	16%	0%				1.66		-42	-114	-$2
15	TAM *	242	28	9	40	5	228	246	279	422	701	725	676	7	67	0.21	50	19	31	30	83	142	88	21%	102	14%	68%	21	48%	38%	3.82	-4.2	26	70	$5
1st Half		116	15	5	17	4	231	244	284	440	725	790	590	7	69	0.24	46	15	38	29	102	144	127	20%	101	26%	64%	8	38%	38%	3.96	-0.4	38	103	$5
2nd Half		126	13	4	23	1	225	247	274	406	680	672	755	6	64	0.19	54	23	24	32	67	141	52	24%	104	3%	100%	13	54%	38%	3.69	-1.5	15	41	$4
16	Proj	261	31	7	34	8	232	239	289	380	669	674	662	7	70	0.24	51	20	30	31	81	107	82	12%	112	17%	77%				3.59	-5.1	18	49	$7

BRIAN RUDD

Bell,Josh

Age: 23 Bats: B Pos: DH | Ht: 6' 3" Wt: 213
Health A | PT/Exp F | Consist F
LIMA Plan D | Rand Var 0 | MM 1311

Has developed an excellent plate approach in climb through the minors, but not yet the power one would anticipate given his size/position/pedigree. Still has time, but big platoon split in 2015 (.920 OPS vR; .632 OPS vL in AA/AAA) tempers short-term expectations. May find some AB in PIT, but impact several years out.

Yr	Tm	AB	R	HR	RBI	SB	BA	xBA	OBP	SLG	OPS	vL	vR	bb%	ct%	Eye	G	L	F	h%	HctX	PX	xPX	hr/f	Spd	SBO	SB%	#Wk	DOM	DIS	RC/G	RAR	BPV	BPX	R$
11																																			
12																																			
13																																			
14	aa	94	10	0	5	3	249		292	268	559			6	86	0.44				29		17			102	15%	73%				2.67		3	8	$0
15	a/a	489	57	5	66	8	285		354	389	744			10	86	0.75				32		65			114	8%	63%				4.85		51	138	$16
1st Half		296	29	2	37	4	275		338	359	697			9	87	0.70				31		50			123	9%	48%				4.09		42	114	$16
2nd Half		193	26	3	27	3	294		370	424	794			11	84	0.78				34		86			107	5%	100%				5.80		62	168	$15
16	**Proj**	**148**	**17**	**2**	**15**	**4**	**270**	**239**	**332**	**372**	**704**	**704**	**704**	**8**	**86**	**0.64**	**46**	**16**	**38**	**30**		**62**		**5%**	**108**	**12%**	**79%**				**4.35**	**-4.7**	**40**	**107**	**$3**

Belt,Brandon

Age: 28 Bats: L Pos: 1B | Ht: 6' 5" Wt: 220
Health C | PT/Exp C | Consist C
LIMA Plan B | Rand Var -3 | MM 4325

Skills, results closely resemble 2013, and recent LD/HctX/h% figures confirm his plus-BA profile even as ct% languishes. Plus, year-long xPX bump points to potential HR upside. But three concussions in two years, along with several other bumps/scrapes, muddy the confidence level and widen his range of outcomes.

Yr	Tm	AB	R	HR	RBI	SB	BA	xBA	OBP	SLG	OPS	vL	vR	bb%	ct%	Eye	G	L	F	h%	HctX	PX	xPX	hr/f	Spd	SBO	SB%	#Wk	DOM	DIS	RC/G	RAR	BPV	BPX	R$
11	SF *	352	42	14	39	6	236	220	325	405	730	934	648	12	68	0.42	42	14	44	31	87	130	111	16%	101	12%	46%	15	47%	47%	4.16	-22.6	32	71	$7
12	SF	411	47	7	56	12	275	247	360	421	781	768	786	12	74	0.51	38	26	37	36	95	107	112	6%	110	11%	86%	27	41%	37%	5.42	-0.1	41	103	$13
13	SF	509	76	17	67	5	289	266	360	481	841	755	867	9	75	0.42	34	24	41	35	115	143	130	11%	104	5%	71%	27	56%	22%	6.09	21.5	68	170	$21
14	SF	214	30	12	27	3	243	244	306	449	755	715	772	8	70	0.28	38	18	44	29	90	152	119	18%	108	8%	75%	14	71%	21%	4.54	2.3	52	141	$6
15	SF	492	73	18	68	9	280	257	356	478	834	802	845	10	70	0.38	33	29	38	37	122	145	156	14%	96	9%	75%	24	50%	33%	5.97	8.5	48	130	$20
1st Half		263	35	9	36	4	270	269	342	475	818	413	901	10	69	0.35	34	33	33	36	129	157	161	15%	88	9%	67%	14	50%	36%	5.57	3.2	50	135	$18
2nd Half		229	38	9	32	5	293	242	372	480	852	1011	760	11	71	0.42	32	24	43	38	114	131	151	13%	109	8%	83%	10	50%	30%	6.45	8.3	46	124	$22
16	**Proj**	**505**	**74**	**21**	**67**	**9**	**271**	**250**	**346**	**465**	**811**	**814**	**811**	**10**	**71**	**0.38**	**35**	**24**	**41**	**34**	**109**	**138**	**138**	**14%**	**104**	**8%**	**74%**				**5.56**	**5.9**	**46**	**124**	**$22**

Beltran,Carlos

Age: 39 Bats: B Pos: RF | Ht: 6' 1" Wt: 210
Health B | PT/Exp B | Consist D
LIMA Plan B+ | Rand Var 0 | MM 3035

Started slow, but then rode a vintage-era 2H to temporarily put to bed the "veteran fade" narrative. Elbow surgery last off-season puts 2014 and 1H into perspective. Continues to pound the ball, and the in-season uptick in ct%, Eye was unexpected. No longer a foundation piece, but aging incredibly well.

Yr	Tm	AB	R	HR	RBI	SB	BA	xBA	OBP	SLG	OPS	vL	vR	bb%	ct%	Eye	G	L	F	h%	HctX	PX	xPX	hr/f	Spd	SBO	SB%	#Wk	DOM	DIS	RC/G	RAR	BPV	BPX	R$
11	2 NL	520	78	22	84	4	300	298	385	525	910	923	903	12	83	0.81	40	21	39	33	154	147	147	13%	98	4%	67%	26	73%	12%	7.30	30.6	105	233	$24
12	STL	547	83	32	97	13	269	274	346	495	842	867	832	11	77	0.52	42	20	38	29	115	142	124	20%	75	12%	68%	27	56%	22%	5.88	16.2	69	173	$25
13	STL	554	79	24	84	2	296	282	339	491	830	729	871	6	84	0.42	35	24	41	32	129	122	127	13%	94	2%	67%	27	63%	11%	6.05	27.0	76	190	$25
14	NYY	403	46	15	49	3	233	258	301	402	703	564	777	8	80	0.46	44	16	39	26	105	120	101	12%	76	4%	75%	23	43%	35%	3.98	1.0	58	157	$8
15	NYY	478	57	19	67	0	276	275	337	471	808	752	831	9	82	0.53	36	22	43	30	120	125	132	11%	79	0%	0%	25	60%	16%	5.61	11.4	72	195	$15
1st Half		242	21	7	30	0	260	265	309	430	739	710	750	6	80	0.33	37	22	41	30	106	117	112	9%	79	0%	0%	13	54%	31%	4.54	-2.0	51	138	$9
2nd Half		236	36	12	37	0	292	286	364	513	877	790	914	11	85	0.81	34	21	45	30	134	133	152	13%	80	0%	0%	12	67%	0%	6.83	13.2	93	251	$21
16	**Proj**	**460**	**59**	**17**	**65**	**0**	**271**	**268**	**334**	**453**	**786**	**701**	**823**	**9**	**82**	**0.53**	**38**	**21**	**41**	**30**	**120**	**116**	**126**	**11%**	**81**	**1%**	**30%**				**5.26**	**5.9**	**53**	**142**	**$16**

Beltre,Adrian

Age: 37 Bats: R Pos: 3B | Ht: 5' 11" Wt: 220
Health B | PT/Exp A | Consist B
LIMA Plan B+ | Rand Var +2 | MM 3245

Superstars roll by their own rules; they just do. How else does one explain his lethargic Apr/May (.702 OPS), followed up by a blistering 2H, in which he played with a torn thumb ligament? Sure SEEMS like .300/30/100 has come and gone, but with full health, to doubt might be dangerous. Just like touching his head.

Yr	Tm	AB	R	HR	RBI	SB	BA	xBA	OBP	SLG	OPS	vL	vR	bb%	ct%	Eye	G	L	F	h%	HctX	PX	xPX	hr/f	Spd	SBO	SB%	#Wk	DOM	DIS	RC/G	RAR	BPV	BPX	R$
11	TEX	487	82	32	105	1	296	315	331	561	892	1075	836	5	89	0.47	38	18	44	28	156	156	160	16%	63	2%	50%	22	73%	5%	6.65	24.9	112	249	$27
12	TEX	604	95	36	102	1	321	299	359	561	921	737	985	6	86	0.44	39	21	40	33	135	136	139	17%	79	1%	100%	27	74%	7%	7.59	48.9	92	230	$33
13	TEX	631	88	30	92	1	315	287	371	509	880	948	857	7	88	0.64	38	22	40	32	129	115	127	14%	65	1%	100%	27	63%	7%	6.94	50.6	79	198	$32
14	TEX	549	79	19	77	1	324	286	388	492	879	984	845	9	87	0.77	42	22	36	35	125	111	122	11%	85	1%	50%	26	73%	12%	7.16	50.9	81	219	$28
15	TEX	567	83	18	83	1	287	288	334	453	788	939	709	7	89	0.63	42	23	36	30	131	97	110	10%	95	1%	100%	25	60%	16%	5.45	14.0	76	205	$21
1st Half		258	32	6	21	1	248	260	283	376	659	755	611	4	89	0.41	45	18	37	26	114	74	100	7%	106	2%	100%	12	50%	25%	3.61	-7.7	57	154	$6
2nd Half		309	51	12	62	0	320	310	376	518	894	1082	793	9	88	0.81	38	27	35	33	145	116	117	13%	87	0%	0%	13	69%	8%	7.36	22.5	91	246	$33
16	**Proj**	**551**	**81**	**19**	**84**	**1**	**296**	**285**	**349**	**468**	**817**	**927**	**771**	**7**	**88**	**0.66**	**40**	**22**	**38**	**31**	**131**	**101**	**120**	**11%**	**89**	**1%**	**75%**				**5.90**	**19.4**	**67**	**182**	**$25**

Bethancourt,Christian

Age: 24 Bats: R Pos: CA | Ht: 6' 2" Wt: 205
Health A | PT/Exp D | Consist B
LIMA Plan D | Rand Var -1 | MM 1213

2-12-.200 in 155 AB at ATL. Had some success at the plate (.840 OPS in 2015) during a two-month minors stint, but poor patience, lots of weak GBs continued to persist in the majors. Reputation as a stellar defender also took a hit and eroded team confidence. Pro tip: You kinda need one or the other at this level.

Yr	Tm	AB	R	HR	RBI	SB	BA	xBA	OBP	SLG	OPS	vL	vR	bb%	ct%	Eye	G	L	F	h%	HctX	PX	xPX	hr/f	Spd	SBO	SB%	#Wk	DOM	DIS	RC/G	RAR	BPV	BPX	R$
11																																			
12	aa	268	26	2	23	7	227		254	270	524			3	82	0.19				27		28			103	21%	52%				2.10		-11	-28	$1
13	ATL *	359	37	10	40	10	256	260	284	397	681	0	0	4	82	0.22	44	20	36	29	0	97	-15	0%	85	23%	56%	1	0%	100%	3.62	-0.8	41	103	$10
14	ATL *	456	31	6	44	6	243	222	263	323	586	889	465	3	78	0.13	54	15	31	30	86	63	54	0%	89	8%	74%	8	0%	75%	2.86	-8.0	-1	-3	$6
15	ATL *	357	38	5	39	5	254	254	284	370	655	433	551	4	80	0.22	51	18	31	30	76	87	58	5%	93	8%	84%	17	29%	53%	3.63	-1.9	30	81	$6
1st Half		166	18	2	15	4	229	245	250	315	566	352	560	3	83	0.17	52	17	31	26	66	62	45	4%	92	14%	100%	11	27%	45%	2.73	-5.2	19	51	$2
2nd Half		191	20	4	24	1	275	262	313	418	731	523	531	5	78	0.25	49	21	31	34	97	111	87	8%	99	4%	46%	6	33%	67%	4.53	4.1	43	116	$10
16	**Proj**	**270**	**26**	**3**	**28**	**4**	**251**	**239**	**281**	**340**	**621**	**694**	**591**	**4**	**80**	**0.19**	**52**	**17**	**31**	**30**	**85**	**68**	**63**	**4%**	**95**	**11%**	**67%**				**3.18**	**-4.8**	**6**	**16**	**$6**

Betts,Mookie

Age: 23 Bats: R Pos: CF | Ht: 5' 9" Wt: 155
Health A | PT/Exp C | Consist C
LIMA Plan C | Rand Var -1 | MM 3545

Well, that didn't take long. A rough April, but you'd never know it from full-season line. Very good plate skills, consistently hits the ball hard, and sufficent swing loft/strength for 20 HR. Plus short-term upside in his running game: Elite Spd, willingness to run, solid success rate, history of better bb%. He's just getting started.

Yr	Tm	AB	R	HR	RBI	SB	BA	xBA	OBP	SLG	OPS	vL	vR	bb%	ct%	Eye	G	L	F	h%	HctX	PX	xPX	hr/f	Spd	SBO	SB%	#Wk	DOM	DIS	RC/G	RAR	BPV	BPX	R$
11																																			
12																																			
13																																			
14	BOS *	588	106	14	72	34	318	281	392	479	871	843	798	11	86	0.85	41	21	39	35	133	114	117	8%	135	23%	76%	12	67%	8%	7.00	50.0	98	265	$40
15	BOS	597	92	18	77	21	291	277	341	479	820	843	813	7	86	0.56	38	19	42	31	119	114	115	8%	148	18%	78%	26	69%	12%	5.89	18.8	97	262	$30
1st Half		322	43	9	41	13	283	270	336	463	799	739	816	8	88	0.69	36	19	45	30	121	106	122	7%	150	20%	76%	14	71%	0%	5.53	6.6	99	268	$30
2nd Half		275	49	9	36	8	302	285	347	498	845	941	809	6	84	0.44	41	21	39	33	118	123	105	10%	138	14%	80%	12	67%	25%	6.32	11.5	92	249	$30
16	**Proj**	**609**	**102**	**20**	**77**	**26**	**303**	**283**	**364**	**497**	**861**	**899**	**847**	**8**	**86**	**0.65**	**39**	**20**	**40**	**33**	**125**	**119**	**114**	**9%**	**150**	**20%**	**77%**				**6.56**	**36.4**	**98**	**265**	**$38**

Bird,Gregory

Age: 23 Bats: L Pos: 1B | Ht: 6' 3" Wt: 215
Health A | PT/Exp F | Consist A
LIMA Plan D+ | Rand Var 0 | MM 4123

11-31-.261 in 157 AB at NYY. Put away your HR extrapolators: Had 12 in 318 AB before callup; previous seasonal career high was 20. Yes, he bailed out the team down the stretch and small sample size xPX confirms his punch. But 66% MLB ct% means that you have reason to let the Yankees fans bid into double digits.

Yr	Tm	AB	R	HR	RBI	SB	BA	xBA	OBP	SLG	OPS	vL	vR	bb%	ct%	Eye	G	L	F	h%	HctX	PX	xPX	hr/f	Spd	SBO	SB%	#Wk	DOM	DIS	RC/G	RAR	BPV	BPX	R$
11																																			
12																																			
13																																			
14	aa	95	13	6	9	0	230		334	504	838			13	69	0.50				26		218			94	0%	0%				5.58		106	286	$1
15	NYY *	475	65	23	77	1	258	256	330	469	798	752	915	10	75	0.43	27	22	51	30	149	142	203	20%	96	2%	45%	9	78%	22%	5.27	4.6	65	176	$15
1st Half		194	26	6	26	1	233	269	313	400	713			10	81	0.61				26		114			85	4%	45%				4.09		64	173	$3
2nd Half		281	39	17	51	0	276	258	341	516	857	752	915	9	72	0.35	27	22	51	33	141	164	203	20%	100	0%	0%	9	78%	22%	6.20	8.3	68	184	$23
16	**Proj**	**249**	**34**	**12**	**34**	**0**	**247**	**249**	**331**	**461**	**793**	**694**	**828**	**11**	**70**	**0.41**	**35**	**20**	**45**	**30**	**127**	**157**	**183**	**15%**	**101**	**1%**	**50%**				**5.13**	**-0.2**	**41**	**111**	**$8**

BRENT HERSHEY

Blackmon,Charlie

Age: 30	Bats: L	Pos: CF	Health C	LIMA Plan B+	
Ht: 6' 3"	Wt: 210		PT/Exp A	Rand Var -2	
			Consist B	MM 3535	

Surge to stardom complete for bat who didn't become MLB full-timer until age 27. Trick was bringing back '13 wheels and getting stronger green light. Still at age where legs should be solid, and steady Eye gains support OBP surge. Consistent uptick in HctX, xPX make 20 HR a logical next step. A legit $30 player now.

Yr	Tm	AB	R	HR	RBI	SB	BA	xBA	OBP	SLG	OPS	vL	vR	bb%	ct%	Eye	G	L	F	h%	HctX	PX	xPX	hr/f	Spd	SBO	SB%	#Wk	DOM	DIS	RC/G	RAR	BPV	BPX	R$
11	COL *	341	34	7	33	11	260	256	286	380	666	905	484	4	86	0.27	47	16	37	28	72	79	53	3%	101	24%	61%	5	20%	20%	3.54	-12.6	48	107	$8
12	COL *	341	47	6	29	7	260	266	302	392	694	853	701	6	81	0.32	49	21	30	31	88	93	86	7%	110	11%	77%	8	63%	25%	4.09	-5.9	45	113	$7
13	COL *	503	66	8	44	11	266	268	302	395	697	752	824	5	81	0.27	42	27	31	32	90	90	67	10%	134	15%	64%	16	31%	25%	4.04	-0.8	48	120	$14
14	COL	593	82	19	72	28	288	269	335	440	775	697	801	5	84	0.32	41	22	37	32	103	100	94	10%	102	25%	74%	27	52%	19%	5.02	20.1	58	157	$32
15	COL	614	93	17	58	43	287	266	347	450	797	709	828	7	82	0.41	38	25	37	33	118	100	120	9%	135	34%	77%	27	59%	22%	5.37	18.7	64	173	$36
1st Half		310	48	11	36	21	274	269	347	448	795	514	892	8	80	0.43	40	25	35	31	124	109	139	13%	107	34%	75%	14	64%	21%	5.16	6.8	56	151	$36
2nd Half		304	45	6	22	22	299	263	348	451	798	899	760	6	84	0.39	36	25	39	34	111	92	101	6%	156	34%	79%	13	54%	23%	5.59	10.1	70	189	$37
16	**Proj**	**560**	**89**	**19**	**55**	**35**	**277**	**272**	**329**	**452**	**782**	**749**	**793**	**6**	**83**	**0.36**	**39**	**24**	**37**	**31**	**105**	**106**	**99**	**11%**	**130**	**34%**	**76%**				**5.03**	**10.1**	**74**	**201**	**$30**

Blanco,Andres

Age: 32	Bats: B	Pos: 3B 2B	Health A	LIMA Plan D	
Ht: 5' 10"	Wt: 190		PT/Exp F	Rand Var -3	
			Consist F	MM 3031	

These utility types can have utility to you if they have latent power or speed, or perhaps a decent BA floor. This one's power flash seems to fit bill, but as we haven't seen it before and xPX murky, side with pessimism. And that h% came out of blue too; BA will take the ride back down with it. Heed F Consistency.

Yr	Tm	AB	R	HR	RBI	SB	BA	xBA	OBP	SLG	OPS	vL	vR	bb%	ct%	Eye	G	L	F	h%	HctX	PX	xPX	hr/f	Spd	SBO	SB%	#Wk	DOM	DIS	RC/G	RAR	BPV	BPX	R$
11	TEX *	98	11	2	6	0	213	270	257	329	586	561	621	6	82	0.33	48	24	27	24	52	84	58	12%	93	5%	0%	20	20%	60%	2.60	-7.6	37	82	-$2
12	aaa	413	36	8	31	5	190		245	280	526			7	77	0.32				23		60			90	12%	43%				2.05		-1	-3	-$3
13																																			
14	PHI *	184	15	1	10	2	202	249	246	271	517	731	781	6	78	0.27	46	27	27	25	91	61	83	9%	81	23%	23%	11	55%	36%	1.81	-11.4	0	0	-$3
15	PHI	233	32	7	25	1	292	294	360	502	863	974	798	8	81	0.48	46	20	34	34	88	142	102	11%	100	4%	50%	26	50%	31%	6.26	10.3	87	235	$7
1st Half		72	7	2	9	0	278	313	350	514	864	1009	752	9	88	0.78	51	13	37	30	89	154	112	9%	89	7%	0%	14	57%	29%	5.86	2.6	120	324	-$2
2nd Half		161	25	5	16	1	298	285	365	497	862	953	815	8	78	0.40	43	24	33	36	87	136	97	12%	106	2%	100%	12	42%	33%	6.44	8.0	72	195	$11
16	**Proj**	**130**	**14**	**3**	**11**	**1**	**245**	**272**	**306**	**401**	**707**	**782**	**668**	**7**	**80**	**0.39**	**47**	**21**	**32**	**29**	**74**	**107**	**85**	**9%**	**95**	**9%**	**31%**				**3.84**	**-3.1**	**45**	**122**	**$3**

Blanco,Gregor

Age: 32	Bats: L	Pos: CF LF RF	Health A	LIMA Plan C+	
Ht: 5' 11"	Wt: 175		PT/Exp C	Rand Var -3	
			Consist B	MM 1523	

You used to stash a guy like this as your 4th or 5th OF and build your offense around others. Today, 10-15 SB consistency with decent average is scarce. Only chink here is BA, which will revert back to prior so-so levels as h% comes down. Impactful wheels intact even as he motors towards mid-30s, so put SB in stone.

Yr	Tm	AB	R	HR	RBI	SB	BA	xBA	OBP	SLG	OPS	vL	vR	bb%	ct%	Eye	G	L	F	h%	HctX	PX	xPX	hr/f	Spd	SBO	SB%	#Wk	DOM	DIS	RC/G	RAR	BPV	BPX	R$
11	aaa	199	29	2	10	17	159		268	254	522			13	70	0.50				22		81			117	40%	87%				2.32		8	18	$0
12	SF	393	56	5	34	26	244	227	333	344	676	694	667	11	74	0.49	44	24	32	32	73	69	73	6%	144	26%	81%	27	19%	59%	3.99	-8.7	18	45	$12
13	SF	452	50	3	41	14	265	250	341	350	690	650	696	10	79	0.55	44	28	28	33	87	60	69	3%	158	16%	61%	27	22%	30%	4.01	-0.6	34	85	$12
14	SF	393	51	5	38	16	260	241	333	374	707	730	697	9	80	0.53	40	21	39	31	93	81	93	4%	139	18%	76%	27	37%	37%	4.27	5.6	49	132	$13
15	SF	327	59	5	26	13	291	268	368	413	781	741	792	11	82	0.68	45	24	30	34	84	83	76	6%	136	17%	72%	23	39%	30%	5.42	6.5	59	159	$14
1st Half		167	27	2	17	4	311	273	378	443	821	616	856	10	80	0.55	47	25	29	38	70	94	69	5%	121	15%	50%	14	29%	43%	5.83	5.9	54	146	$13
2nd Half		160	32	3	9	9	269	261	359	381	740	807	713	12	84	0.85	44	24	32	31	98	71	83	7%	140	19%	90%	9	56%	11%	5.01	2.1	60	162	$15
16	**Proj**	**312**	**49**	**4**	**26**	**12**	**268**	**253**	**348**	**380**	**728**	**725**	**729**	**11**	**80**	**0.61**	**44**	**24**	**32**	**32**	**87**	**75**	**80**	**5%**	**138**	**16%**	**73%**				**4.57**	**1.5**	**43**	**116**	**$12**

Blanks,Kyle

Age: 29	Bats: R	Pos: 1B	Health F	LIMA Plan F	
Ht: 6' 6"	Wt: 265		PT/Exp F	Rand Var -5	
			Consist B	MM 4201	

3-16-.313 in 67 AB at TEX. Hulking slugger can't stay on field. Power is real, but is an oft-injured lefty-only masher with big holes in swing, with no signs it will manifest into impactful results. BA elevated by fluky h%; it won't repeat. And to top it off, had Sept. surgery on both Achilles'. Deserves an F-minus Health grade.

Yr	Tm	AB	R	HR	RBI	SB	BA	xBA	OBP	SLG	OPS	vL	vR	bb%	ct%	Eye	G	L	F	h%	HctX	PX	xPX	hr/f	Spd	SBO	SB%	#Wk	DOM	DIS	RC/G	RAR	BPV	BPX	R$
11	SD *	481	65	16	65	4	231	229	288	404	692	528	789	7	69	0.25	40	16	45	30	109	137	115	13%	99	5%	76%	11	36%	45%	3.85	-20.5	30	67	$9
12	SD	5	0	0	0	0	200	25	333	200	533	833	0	17	60	0.50	33	0	67	33	0	0	-11	0%	91	0%	0%	2	0%	100%	2.13	-0.3	-96	-240	-$2
13	SD *	318	36	9	37	1	234	231	289	366	655	829	596	7	69	0.25	46	22	32	31	93	107	115	13%	85	3%	50%	18	22%	67%	3.49	-5.3	4	10	$3
14	2 TM *	159	22	8	21	0	249	241	325	429	754	889	793	10	69	0.36	53	20	28	31	97	137	104	18%	96	0%	0%	8	25%	50%	4.73	4.9	35	95	$3
15	TEX *	125	16	5	14	1	274	231	319	480	799	1111	714	6	64	0.18	38	15	47	39	96	175	160	14%	82	4%	100%	6	50%	33%	5.42	3.6	34	92	$2
1st Half		119	16	5	14	1	288	241	331	505	836	1111	714	6	66	0.19	38	15	47	40	99	178	160	14%	83	4%	100%	6	50%	33%	6.04	4.9	46	124	$3
2nd Half		6	0	0	0	0	0	0	102	0	102			10	19	0.14				0		0			81	0%	0%				0.00		-276	-746	-$8
16	**Proj**	**97**	**12**	**3**	**12**	**0**	**221**	**233**	**287**	**391**	**678**	**787**	**603**	**7**	**68**	**0.25**	**44**	**19**	**37**	**29**	**98**	**130**	**126**	**14%**	**86**	**3%**	**78%**				**3.58**	**-4.7**	**10**	**28**	**$2**

Bogaerts,Xander

Age: 23	Bats: R	Pos: SS	Health A	LIMA Plan B	
Ht: 6' 1"	Wt: 210		PT/Exp B	Rand Var -4	
			Consist D	MM 1425	

Top prospect lived up to billing in sophomore campaign...or did he? PRO: Good wheels + SB%, so needs only green light; steep contact gains; nice pop vs. LH. CON: Tons of GBs, gloomy xPX make double-digit HR a stretch; BA headed way down as h% corrects. A gem in keeper leagues, but for now expect regression.

Yr	Tm	AB	R	HR	RBI	SB	BA	xBA	OBP	SLG	OPS	vL	vR	bb%	ct%	Eye	G	L	F	h%	HctX	PX	xPX	hr/f	Spd	SBO	SB%	#Wk	DOM	DIS	RC/G	RAR	BPV	BPX	R$
11																																			
12	aa	92	10	4	15	1	326		332	581	913			1	77	0.04				39		187			80	12%	46%				7.00		84	210	$3
13	BOS *	488	64	12	58	7	277	291	349	427	777	1089	463	10	77	0.48	47	34	19	34	138	107	87	17%	114	7%	67%	7	43%	57%	5.22	25.0	48	120	$16
14	BOS	538	60	12	46	2	240	230	297	362	660	755	621	7	74	0.28	38	21	41	30	110	98	111	7%	98	4%	40%	26	38%	46%	3.47	4.7	21	57	$7
15	BOS	613	84	7	81	10	320	269	355	421	776	892	735	5	84	0.32	53	21	26	37	100	71	60	5%	115	7%	83%	27	33%	22%	5.62	20.0	37	100	$28
1st Half		295	37	3	37	4	302	264	339	414	752	846	721	5	85	0.36	50	19	31	35	97	76	74	4%	119	6%	80%	14	29%	21%	5.12	8.4	48	130	$22
2nd Half		318	47	4	44	6	336	271	370	428	797	932	747	5	82	0.29	55	24	21	40	103	66	48	7%	106	7%	86%	13	38%	23%	6.12	16.9	26	70	$34
16	**Proj**	**623**	**78**	**10**	**69**	**12**	**280**	**250**	**329**	**391**	**720**	**826**	**680**	**6**	**79**	**0.33**	**47**	**21**	**32**	**34**	**104**	**79**	**80**	**6%**	**115**	**9%**	**82%**				**4.56**	**8.3**	**24**	**64**	**$23**

Bour,Justin

Age: 28	Bats: L	Pos: 1B	Health A	LIMA Plan B	
Ht: 6' 4"	Wt: 250		PT/Exp C	Rand Var -1	
			Consist C	MM 3015	

23-73-.262 in 409 AB at MIA. Nudged his way into regular role and didn't let go. But that GB stroke, xPX temper power optimism; those HR were hr/f-driven. Mediocre batted ball distance (110th in MLB) makes regression certain. Marginal plate control, struggles vL will fuel inconsistency. Bank on big step back.

Yr	Tm	AB	R	HR	RBI	SB	BA	xBA	OBP	SLG	OPS	vL	vR	bb%	ct%	Eye	G	L	F	h%	HctX	PX	xPX	hr/f	Spd	SBO	SB%	#Wk	DOM	DIS	RC/G	RAR	BPV	BPX	R$
11																																			
12	aa	506	50	13	86	3	245		313	387	700			9	74	0.38				31		106			70	3%	73%				4.09		21	53	$10
13	aa	317	36	14	47	0	200		263	374	638			8	77	0.38				22		119			78	4%	0%				3.03		45	113	$2
14	MIA *	459	48	11	58	2	246	249	298	372	670	600	734	7	81	0.39	53	16	31	28	128	93	126	6%	69	3%	61%	12	33%	58%	3.73	-6.1	35	95	$9
15	MIA *	460	48	24	77	1	258	254	321	458	778	573	845	8	77	0.39	48	17	35	29	113	128	111	21%	54	1%	100%	25	48%	28%	5.05	-4.1	43	116	$14
1st Half		196	21	11	25	1	253	259	340	446	786	421	889	12	79	0.61	45	20	35	27	132	115	135	26%	63	1%	100%	12	50%	42%	5.20	0.3	50	135	$8
2nd Half		264	27	13	52	0	261	245	307	466	773	609	817	6	75	0.26	50	16	35	30	103	137	98	19%	57	0%	0%	13	46%	15%	4.92	-1.8	41	111	$18
16	**Proj**	**483**	**47**	**17**	**63**	**1**	**245**	**243**	**307**	**403**	**710**	**540**	**734**	**8**	**77**	**0.39**	**49**	**17**	**34**	**28**	**120**	**105**	**118**	**14%**	**59**	**2%**	**62%**				**4.15**	**-14.4**	**21**	**57**	**$12**

Bourjos,Peter

Age: 29	Bats: R	Pos: CF	Health C	LIMA Plan D	
Ht: 6' 1"	Wt: 185		PT/Exp F	Rand Var +3	
			Consist B	MM 2401	

Just as skills and results started to appear (see 1H), couldn't find even a semi-regular role late (see 2H), and both tanked. Lack of pop and contact clear, but so is consisently elite wheels, and surging bb% gives hope for more, especially after h% normalizes. With even semi-steady work... UP: 20 SB

Yr	Tm	AB	R	HR	RBI	SB	BA	xBA	OBP	SLG	OPS	vL	vR	bb%	ct%	Eye	G	L	F	h%	HctX	PX	xPX	hr/f	Spd	SBO	SB%	#Wk	DOM	DIS	RC/G	RAR	BPV	BPX	R$
11	LAA	502	72	12	43	22	271	252	327	438	765	840	725	6	75	0.26	47	17	36	34	87	117	88	9%	191	26%	71%	26	38%	31%	4.70	-1.2	66	147	$18
12	LAA *	197	30	3	21	3	223	214	285	325	610	606	607	8	74	0.33	52	13	35	29	58	73	64	7%	137	8%	75%	25	8%	64%	3.04	-9.8	13	33	$1
13	LAA *	223	34	4	16	6	247	222	287	356	643	608	740	5	70	0.19	59	14	27	33	78	77	65	9%	182	11%	100%	12	17%	50%	3.60	-3.2	10	25	$4
14	STL	264	32	4	24	9	231	234	294	348	643	582	680	7	70	0.26	53	20	28	31	89	89	81	9%	184	19%	75%	27	30%	56%	3.30	-4.2	24	65	$5
15	STL	195	32	4	13	5	200	222	290	333	623	651	609	9	70	0.32	49	16	35	27	70	95	57	9%	150	30%	38%	27	41%	56%	2.46	-11.8	20	54	$0
1st Half		127	23	2	8	5	236	243	324	378	702	663	720	11	73	0.44	49	20	32	31	75	97	53	7%	162	32%	45%	14	50%	43%	3.45	-3.9	42	114	$3
2nd Half		68	9	2	5	0	132	182	224	250	474	620	406	6	63	0.16	49	9	42	17	61	92	66	11%	96	22%	0%	13	31%	69%	1.09	-8.0	-31	-84	-$5
16	**Proj**	**162**	**23**	**3**	**13**	**4**	**231**	**217**	**306**	**355**	**661**	**670**	**656**	**7**	**69**	**0.25**	**51**	**15**	**33**	**31**	**75**	**88**	**68**	**9%**	**152**	**19%**	**51%**				**3.15**	**-6.3**	**3**	**7**	**$4**

STEPHEN NICKRAND

Bourn,Michael

Age: 33 Bats: L Pos: CF LF — Health: C — LIMA Plan: D+
Ht: 5' 10" Wt: 180 — PT/Exp: B — Rand Var: 0
Consist: A — MM: 1503

Bourn's identity was carved by his wheels, but his once-blazing speed has dropped to barely above average. With no power and middling contact, only a decent walk rate netted him even this many chances to run. Speed is a skill of the young; he's now 33. With playing time continuing to dwindle... DN: 200 AB, single-digit SB.

Yr	Tm	AB	R	HR	RBI	SB	BA	xBA	OBP	SLG	OPS	vL	vR	bb%	ct%	Eye	G	L	F	h%	HctX	PX	xPX	hr/f	Spd	SBO	SB%	#Wk	DOM	DIS	RC/G	RAR	BPV	BPX	R$
11	2 NL	656	94	2	50	61	294	265	349	386	734	645	772	7	79	0.38	51	27	23	37	77	70	56	2%	147	38%	81%	27	33%	44%	5.01	4.2	32	71	$35
12	ATL	624	96	9	57	42	274	251	348	391	739	728	745	10	75	0.45	54	22	25	35	100	80	86	8%	145	28%	76%	26	38%	42%	4.80	2.0	30	75	$28
13	CLE	525	75	6	50	23	263	243	316	360	676	655	685	7	75	0.30	57	20	24	34	71	72	61	7%	154	24%	66%	25	28%	56%	3.79	-4.9	19	48	$19
14	CLE *	487	58	3	29	11	242	239	294	338	632	569	724	7	73	0.28	50	24	25	32	69	73	71	4%	158	14%	64%	19	26%	63%	3.27	-8.1	14	38	$7
15	2 TM	425	39	0	30	17	238	223	310	282	592	599	590	10	75	0.43	47	25	28	32	70	39	61	0%	111	18%	71%	27	15%	67%	2.96	-17.4	-14	-38	$7
1st Half		226	22	0	18	7	235	227	304	283	587	591	586	9	74	0.39	50	25	25	32	75	43	64	0%	104	17%	64%	14	14%	71%	2.83	-11.0	-18	-49	$5
2nd Half		199	17	0	12	10	241	216	317	281	598	611	595	10	76	0.48	44	25	31	32	65	33	58	0%	114	20%	77%	13	15%	62%	3.12	-7.8	-13	-35	$8
16	Proj	352	39	2	25	15	248	233	311	321	632	604	641	8	75	0.37	50	24	27	33	71	54	64	2%	132	20%	71%				3.37	-11.0	-2	-6	$7

Bradley,Jackie

Age: 26 Bats: L Pos: RF CF — Health: A — LIMA Plan: B
Ht: 5' 10" Wt: 195 — PT/Exp: C — Rand Var: -2
Consist: F — MM: 4225

10-43-.254 with 3 SB in 209 AB at BOS. PRO: Found old power swing and then some, with a 200+ PX in Aug./Sept; solid walk rate. CON: Aberrant August (46% h%) propped BA, barely cleared .200 otherwise; late GB spike, shaky ct% put PX gains at risk; rarely runs. Power looks mostly legit, but so does a .250ish BA.

Yr	Tm	AB	R	HR	RBI	SB	BA	xBA	OBP	SLG	OPS	vL	vR	bb%	ct%	Eye	G	L	F	h%	HctX	PX	xPX	hr/f	Spd	SBO	SB%	#Wk	DOM	DIS	RC/G	RAR	BPV	BPX	R$
11																																			
12	aa	229	31	5	24	7	262		346	414	760			11	77	0.56				32		110			97	15%	68%				4.86		52	130	$5
13	BOS *	415	62	10	37	7	239	268	307	401	708	327	722	9	73	0.36	63	16	22	30	94	130	79	21%	108	16%	49%	11	36%	45%	3.90	-4.2	48	120	$8
14	BOS *	450	50	2	34	8	197	197	252	262	514	640	473	7	69	0.24	46	18	36	28	104	64	119	1%	90	9%	88%	25	16%	64%	2.15	-24.7	-30	-81	-$1
15	BOS *	503	75	17	68	6	268	265	337	461	799	918	791	9	77	0.45	48	16	36	32	108	133	134	18%	99	8%	59%	15	53%	47%	5.30	11.6	63	170	$17
1st Half		240	25	4	16	3	282	249	342	413	755	500	457	8	80	0.45	40	20	40	34	84	99	60	13%	91	10%	50%	4	25%	75%	4.82	2.8	44	119	$7
2nd Half		263	50	13	52	3	255	279	333	505	838	942	863	10	74	0.45	49	15	36	30	108	166	145	19%	111	7%	73%	11	64%	36%	5.74	10.2	84	227	$25
16	Proj	479	68	14	55	8	250	253	321	422	742	813	713	9	74	0.37	48	17	35	31	100	123	109	12%	96	10%	66%				4.47	-5.0	44	120	$15

Brantley,Michael

Age: 29 Bats: L Pos: LF CF — Health: A — LIMA Plan: C
Ht: 6' 2" Wt: 200 — PT/Exp: A — Rand Var: 0
Consist: D — MM: 3355

The main difference between this season and last year's breakout is quantity. Sure, he didn't show quite the power/speed skills, but nagging injuries likely contributed—as they did to the PT dip. PX did rebound (along with BA) in 2nd half. We'll likely look back on '14 as his best year, but he's still top-drawer.

Yr	Tm	AB	R	HR	RBI	SB	BA	xBA	OBP	SLG	OPS	vL	vR	bb%	ct%	Eye	G	L	F	h%	HctX	PX	xPX	hr/f	Spd	SBO	SB%	#Wk	DOM	DIS	RC/G	RAR	BPV	BPX	R$
11	CLE	451	63	7	46	13	266	264	318	384	702	525	782	7	83	0.45	49	20	31	31	111	82	82	6%	110	15%	72%	22	45%	9%	4.20	-9.5	47	104	$13
12	CLE	552	63	6	60	12	288	286	348	402	750	680	785	9	90	0.95	49	23	29	31	100	75	76	4%	108	13%	57%	27	59%	0%	4.87	4.7	71	178	$17
13	CLE	556	66	10	73	17	284	277	332	396	728	664	757	7	88	0.60	47	23	30	31	91	72	76	7%	108	13%	81%	27	56%	19%	4.74	11.9	57	143	$23
14	CLE	611	94	20	97	23	327	324	385	506	890	826	923	8	91	0.93	46	26	28	34	133	116	105	13%	94	13%	96%	26	85%	4%	7.54	62.1	102	276	$42
15	CLE	529	68	15	84	15	310	308	379	480	859	785	908	10	90	1.18	46	23	32	32	122	107	88	10%	76	10%	94%	26	77%	0%	6.92	36.1	92	249	$28
1st Half		280	29	4	42	9	289	294	362	414	776	755	791	11	91	1.42	50	21	29	31	115	84	74	5%	75	11%	90%	14	79%	0%	5.60	8.1	79	214	$23
2nd Half		249	39	11	42	6	333	322	399	554	953	826	1026	9	89	0.96	41	25	34	34	130	134	105	14%	84	8%	100%	12	75%	0%	8.60	26.3	110	297	$34
16	Proj	582	80	18	88	18	307	307	368	477	845	766	889	9	90	0.91	46	24	31	32	119	105	92	11%	88	11%	89%				6.57	31.9	91	245	$33

Braun,Ryan

Age: 32 Bats: R Pos: RF — Health: B — LIMA Plan: D+
Ht: 6' 2" Wt: 200 — PT/Exp: B — Rand Var: 0
Consist: C — MM: 4445

Hitting far more GB than he used to, which will cap power numbers. He's also lost some durability, as many players do moving into their 30s. Some perspective, though: If we didn't have 2011-12 to compare this to, everyone would be plenty happy. Assuming this is his "new level," we must admit, it's a pretty good level.

Yr	Tm	AB	R	HR	RBI	SB	BA	xBA	OBP	SLG	OPS	vL	vR	bb%	ct%	Eye	G	L	F	h%	HctX	PX	xPX	hr/f	Spd	SBO	SB%	#Wk	DOM	DIS	RC/G	RAR	BPV	BPX	R$
11	MIL	563	109	33	111	33	332	314	397	597	994	1049	979	9	83	0.62	42	21	37	35	154	165	154	19%	121	23%	85%	26	81%	4%	9.10	59.2	123	273	$47
12	MIL	598	108	41	112	30	319	296	391	595	987	1209	915	10	79	0.49	44	18	38	35	127	170	153	23%	113	21%	81%	27	74%	11%	8.57	55.6	105	263	$45
13	MIL	225	30	9	38	4	298	268	372	498	869	1053	777	11	75	0.48	52	16	32	36	120	142	150	16%	125	13%	44%	14	43%	14%	6.31	10.8	75	188	$10
14	MIL	530	68	19	81	11	266	277	324	453	777	823	760	7	79	0.36	47	20	33	31	115	130	125	14%	120	13%	69%	25	56%	24%	4.94	12.9	71	192	$21
15	MIL	506	87	25	84	24	285	282	356	498	854	957	821	10	77	0.47	50	19	31	33	123	136	140	20%	111	20%	86%	25	52%	24%	6.40	22.1	72	195	$31
1st Half		293	48	15	55	12	276	279	344	495	838	825	841	9	77	0.44	48	19	33	31	137	137	153	20%	106	17%	92%	14	50%	29%	6.14	11.1	71	192	$34
2nd Half		213	39	10	29	12	296	285	373	502	876	1082	791	11	77	0.51	52	20	28	34	103	134	122	22%	113	23%	80%	11	55%	18%	6.76	11.7	72	195	$26
16	Proj	532	84	24	86	17	288	280	358	497	856	981	810	9	78	0.47	49	19	32	33	119	134	136	18%	120	16%	74%				6.25	21.7	74	200	$31

Brown,Domonic

Age: 28 Bats: L Pos: RF — Health: B — LIMA Plan: D+
Ht: 6' 5" Wt: 230 — PT/Exp: B — Rand Var: +1
Consist: C — MM: 2213

5-25-.228 with 3 SB in 189 AB at PHI. At an age when many hitters are peaking, his skills have slid into the abyss. But some perspective here: Aside from one 15-game stretch (May 25-June 8, 2013) in which he hit 11 HRs, drove in 22 and batted .404 over 57 AB... he's done pretty much nuthin'.

Yr	Tm	AB	R	HR	RBI	SB	BA	xBA	OBP	SLG	OPS	vL	vR	bb%	ct%	Eye	G	L	F	h%	HctX	PX	xPX	hr/f	Spd	SBO	SB%	#Wk	DOM	DIS	RC/G	RAR	BPV	BPX	R$
11	PHI *	322	46	7	31	13	238	242	336	362	698	705	729	13	77	0.66	47	18	35	29	107	90	90	9%	104	18%	70%	13	46%	38%	4.03	-10.9	41	91	$7
12	PHI *	407	48	9	49	3	243	257	303	384	687	621	746	8	80	0.42	46	21	33	28	103	95	90	10%	81	10%	32%	10	50%	30%	3.68	-18.0	37	93	$6
13	PHI	496	65	27	83	8	272	288	324	494	818	724	857	7	80	0.40	42	23	35	29	111	137	112	19%	101	9%	73%	26	50%	15%	5.58	13.9	78	195	$22
14	PHI	473	47	10	63	7	235	247	285	349	634	536	662	7	81	0.37	50	17	33	27	93	83	79	8%	78	7%	88%	27	26%	30%	3.37	-10.3	28	76	$9
15	PHI *	399	35	7	44	10	214	220	260	312	572	622	637	6	79	0.29	45	16	39	26	89	66	97	8%	84	17%	69%	12	25%	50%	2.59	-28.2	8	22	$4
1st Half		274	22	2	24	8	199	183	247	268	515	321	543	6	79	0.30	41	9	50	25	97	54	123	0%	84	21%	69%	4	25%	50%	2.09	-23.9	-2	-5	$3
2nd Half		125	13	5	20	2	248	254	293	408	701	744	688	5	79	0.27	47	19	33	28	85	93	83	15%	98	10%	67%	8	25%	50%	3.92	-3.3	33	89	$6
16	Proj	294	31	9	40	6	238	244	289	380	669	616	685	7	80	0.34	46	17	37	27	95	89	95	10%	88	12%	69%				3.62	-10.7	30	82	$8

Bruce,Jay

Age: 29 Bats: L Pos: RF — Health: A — LIMA Plan: B+
Ht: 6' 3" Wt: 215 — PT/Exp: A — Rand Var: +4
Consist: C — MM: 4225

A decent rebound—not quite to pre-'14 levels, but solid. xBA shows that even BA would've returned with some h% normalcy. Ct% even improved a bit; that coupled with xPX, FB% return gives hope for a bit more power, and he's still on right side of 30. Bet on more of same (with higher BA), and know there's still some upside.

Yr	Tm	AB	R	HR	RBI	SB	BA	xBA	OBP	SLG	OPS	vL	vR	bb%	ct%	Eye	G	L	F	h%	HctX	PX	xPX	hr/f	Spd	SBO	SB%	#Wk	DOM	DIS	RC/G	RAR	BPV	BPX	R$
11	CIN	585	84	32	97	8	256	251	341	474	814	804	818	11	73	0.45	36	17	47	30	124	151	150	16%	95	9%	53%	27	52%	26%	5.30	2.5	65	144	$22
12	CIN	560	89	34	99	9	252	270	327	514	841	754	879	10	72	0.40	35	20	44	29	118	178	162	19%	94	9%	75%	27	59%	26%	5.69	9.0	82	205	$22
13	CIN	626	89	30	109	7	262	264	329	478	807	734	841	9	70	0.34	37	24	39	33	101	165	132	17%	86	7%	70%	27	52%	30%	5.40	14.3	60	150	$25
14	CIN	493	71	18	66	12	217	240	281	373	654	556	685	8	70	0.30	45	21	34	27	99	122	109	15%	92	14%	80%	26	35%	46%	3.44	-9.9	23	62	$12
15	CIN	580	72	26	87	9	226	256	294	434	729	666	754	9	75	0.40	37	19	44	26	117	140	144	13%	80	11%	64%	27	48%	22%	4.16	-12.3	56	151	$14
1st Half		277	33	12	40	6	238	254	332	440	773	884	730	13	75	0.57	36	20	44	28	121	136	158	13%	89	13%	60%	14	57%	14%	4.78	-0.3	62	168	$14
2nd Half		303	39	14	47	3	215	258	258	429	687	475	775	6	75	0.24	38	18	44	24	113	144	132	13%	76	8%	75%	13	38%	31%	3.59	-11.5	52	141	$14
16	Proj	574	77	28	87	8	243	257	309	456	765	683	797	9	73	0.36	39	20	41	29	110	145	134	16%	85	9%	65%				4.69	-2.1	53	142	$20

Bryant,Kris

Age: 24 Bats: R Pos: 3B — Health: A — LIMA Plan: B
Ht: 6' 5" Wt: 215 — PT/Exp: C — Rand Var: -3
Consist: C — MM: 4405

26-99-.275 with 13 SB in 559 AB at CHC. Best part: Maintained skills (even improving in some) in 2H, which is often an issue for rookies. Before we can go all-in though, that ct% MUST improve; xBA shows it could've been worse than it was, and power could even be at risk. Superstar potential, but 40 HR isn't happening—yet.

Yr	Tm	AB	R	HR	RBI	SB	BA	xBA	OBP	SLG	OPS	vL	vR	bb%	ct%	Eye	G	L	F	h%	HctX	PX	xPX	hr/f	Spd	SBO	SB%	#Wk	DOM	DIS	RC/G	RAR	BPV	BPX	R$
11																																			
12																																			
13																																			
14	a/a	492	91	33	85	12	290		377	559	935			12	63	0.37				40		229			85	11%	72%				7.48		86	232	$32
15	CHC *	587	92	28	107	15	276	233	361	492	853	797	875	12	64	0.38	34	21	45	38	106	165	147	16%	133	11%	78%	26	54%	35%	6.26	26.7	55	149	$29
1st Half		290	49	14	57	10	279	226	373	492	865	1087	825	13	64	0.42	33	18	49	39	107	162	157	14%	134	12%	83%	13	38%	46%	6.56	16.0	55	149	$32
2nd Half		297	43	14	50	5	273	240	357	492	849	651	926	11	64	0.33	35	23	42	38	106	168	139	17%	123	9%	71%	13	69%	23%	5.97	11.5	52	141	$26
16	Proj	585	86	25	98	14	261	228	356	461	817	736	842	12	64	0.37	34	21	45	37	106	159	146	15%	130	11%	77%				5.56	16.0	39	105	$27

ROD TRUESDELL

Burns,Billy

Age: 26 Bats: B Pos: CF | Ht: 5' 9" Wt: 180

Health A | PT/Exp D | Consist F | LIMA Plan B+ | Rand Var -4 | MM 1525

5-42-.294 with 26 SB in 520 AB at OAK. Speed and 1H h% drove R$. But he's not yet close to duplicating his minor league patience, and ct%+HctX combo isn't a plus. As a defensively suspect OF without power, future value will depend on "small-ball" skill growth. Use 2H as your baseline, but with SBO cooperation... UP: 50 SB.

Yr Tm	AB	R	HR	RBI	SB	BA	xBA	OBP	SLG	OPS	vL	vR	bb%	ct%	Eye	G	L	F	h%	HctX	PX	xPX	hr/f	Spd	SBO	SB%	#Wk	DOM	DIS	RC/G	RAR	BPV	BPX	R$
11																																		
12																																		
13 aa	114	21	0	6	16	288		373	320	692			12	84	0.82				34		29			110	41%	88%				4.91		16	40	$7
14 OAK *	479	55	1	19	40	189	323	248	240	488	333	0	7	80	0.39	50	50	0	23	0	44	-14	0%	119	45%	83%	6	0%	67%	2.05	-28.6	7	19	$8
15 OAK *	611	84	5	44	30	290	257	326	384	711	768	707	5	84	0.33	50	22	28	34	50	57	29	4%	175	23%	74%	23	30%	35%	4.48	-0.5	45	122	$27
1st Half	336	50	2	18	21	304	265	339	402	741	825	761	5	84	0.33	50	24	26	36	56	58	30	4%	182	27%	80%	11	27%	27%	5.06	6.1	48	130	$32
2nd Half	275	34	3	26	9	273	248	314	364	678	719	658	5	83	0.33	51	19	30	32	44	54	28	4%	152	19%	64%	12	33%	42%	3.83	-4.7	34	92	$21
16 Proj	**541**	**73**	**5**	**33**	**34**	**261**	**250**	**317**	**346**	**663**	**706**	**642**	**7**	**82**	**0.41**	**50**	**21**	**28**	**31**	**49**	**54**	**29**	**4%**	**157**	**29%**	**79%**				**3.79**	**-9.9**	**32**	**87**	**$20**

Butler,Billy

Age: 30 Bats: R Pos: DH | Ht: 6' 1" Wt: 240

Health A | PT/Exp A | Consist B | LIMA Plan B+ | Rand Var +2 | MM 2025

HR, hr/f returned to 2013 level, but h% struggles torpedoed his BA. Bottom line is that new contract, team and venue didn't change the basics. BA should rebound some along with success vL, but power remains hostage to that 50-ish GB%. Now three years off his career season, but it seems longer.

Yr Tm	AB	R	HR	RBI	SB	BA	xBA	OBP	SLG	OPS	vL	vR	bb%	ct%	Eye	G	L	F	h%	HctX	PX	xPX	hr/f	Spd	SBO	SB%	#Wk	DOM	DIS	RC/G	RAR	BPV	BPX	R$
11 KC	597	74	19	95	2	291	277	361	461	822	917	790	10	84	0.69	46	19	36	32	132	117	131	10%	56	2%	67%	27	63%	11%	5.99	2.4	69	153	$23
12 KC	614	72	29	107	2	313	288	373	510	882	1042	827	8	82	0.49	47	24	29	34	132	120	118	20%	57	2%	67%	27	52%	26%	6.94	34.1	59	148	$29
13 KC	582	62	15	82	0	289	251	374	412	787	797	783	12	82	0.77	53	20	26	33	111	84	92	12%	48	0%	0%	27	37%	37%	5.52	16.6	37	93	$19
14 KC	549	57	9	66	0	271	258	323	379	702	847	653	7	83	0.43	49	22	28	32	132	83	111	7%	54	0%	0%	27	37%	33%	4.27	3.4	29	78	$13
15 OAK	538	63	15	65	0	251	251	323	390	713	687	722	9	81	0.51	51	18	32	28	108	91	105	11%	65	0%	0%	27	44%	37%	4.21	-19.5	37	100	$10
1st Half	296	34	6	36	0	250	246	316	365	681	699	673	8	82	0.51	54	17	29	29	110	76	87	8%	77	0%	0%	14	43%	43%	3.88	-13.7	31	84	$10
2nd Half	242	29	9	29	0	252	257	331	421	752	674	785	9	80	0.52	46	19	35	28	105	110	127	13%	54	0%	0%	13	46%	31%	4.63	-5.8	46	124	$9
16 Proj	**543**	**61**	**16**	**70**	**0**	**269**	**258**	**337**	**412**	**749**	**776**	**739**	**9**	**82**	**0.52**	**50**	**20**	**31**	**30**	**116**	**94**	**110**	**12%**	**58**	**0%**	**67%**				**4.78**	**-10.4**	**29**	**79**	**$16**

Butler,Joey

Age: 30 Bats: R Pos: DH LF | Ht: 6' 2" Wt: 220

Health A | PT/Exp F | Consist A | LIMA Plan D | Rand Var -5 | MM 2101

8-30-.276 with 5 SB in 257 AB at TAM. A winning lottery ticket if you owned him in May/ June when 42% h% drove all his production. Career .295/.380/.451 minor league line with 11% bb% isn't bad. But opportunity and skills growth for soon-to-be-30-year-old will be difficult to come by.

Yr Tm	AB	R	HR	RBI	SB	BA	xBA	OBP	SLG	OPS	vL	vR	bb%	ct%	Eye	G	L	F	h%	HctX	PX	xPX	hr/f	Spd	SBO	SB%	#Wk	DOM	DIS	RC/G	RAR	BPV	BPX	R$
11 a/a	470	57	11	41	10	264		314	401	715			7	63	0.20				40		120			108	13%	63%				4.25		-2	-4	$12
12 aaa	493	62	15	52	4	241		313	384	697			10	70	0.35				31		107			88	7%	46%				3.92		13	33	$8
13 TEX *	438	53	9	37	1	242	331	322	358	681	1100	333	11	66	0.35	33	67	0	34	46	103	27	0%	89	2%	22%	4	25%	50%	3.81	-9.1	-1	-3	$5
14 STL *	91	10	3	13	0	262	334	356	381	737	250	0	13	75	0.57	50	50	0	33	0	88	-14	0%	79	0%	0%	3	0%	100%	4.69	1.7	20	54	$1
15 TAM *	377	46	12	48	5	271	246	319	422	741	699	773	7	68	0.22	58	21	21	37	66	116	63	22%	89	7%	71%	22	14%	59%	4.68	-8.2	5	14	$11
1st Half	266	32	7	32	5	283	253	327	427	755	842	774	6	68	0.20	60	23	17	39	71	114	59	29%	98	10%	71%	10	20%	40%	4.94	-3.9	5	14	$16
2nd Half	111	14	5	16	0	242	222	299	410	710	531	763	8	67	0.25	54	16	30	32	53	122	75	13%	70	0%	0%	12	8%	75%	4.13	-4.4	5	14	$1
16 Proj	**203**	**24**	**6**	**25**	**1**	**257**	**230**	**329**	**387**	**716**	**637**	**804**	**9**	**69**	**0.33**	**56**	**19**	**25**	**35**	**60**	**98**	**69**	**16%**	**83**	**3%**	**63%**				**4.29**	**-6.9**	**-10**	**-28**	**$6**

Buxton,Byron

Age: 22 Bats: R Pos: CF | Ht: 6' 2" Wt: 190

Health B | PT/Exp F | Consist F | LIMA Plan B | Rand Var -3 | MM 3505

2-9-.209 with 2 SBs in 129 AB at MIN. Rushed up from Double-A in mid-June, struggled, was injured, demoted, and ultimately benched during MIN stretch drive. Through it all, phenom flashed power+speed combo, and made better contact in Sept. Health still elusive, still worth waiting on. UP: .280, 15 HR, 25 SBs.

Yr Tm	AB	R	HR	RBI	SB	BA	xBA	OBP	SLG	OPS	vL	vR	bb%	ct%	Eye	G	L	F	h%	HctX	PX	xPX	hr/f	Spd	SBO	SB%	#Wk	DOM	DIS	RC/G	RAR	BPV	BPX	R$
11																																		
12																																		
13																																		
14																																		
15 MIN *	421	61	7	43	20	265	223	314	422	736	318	704	7	74	0.28	43	14	43	34	90	100	105	6%	194	24%	79%	10	20%	70%	4.62	1.4	49	132	$16
1st Half	274	38	4	28	16	251	247	306	413	719	348	567	7	75	0.31	62	10	29	32	60	95	32	0%	210	30%	79%	2	0%	100%	4.34	-0.6	55	149	$20
2nd Half	147	20	3	13	3	276	210	311	408	718	308	763	5	72	0.17	36	16	48	37	97	101	131	7%	126	11%	71%	8	25%	63%	4.42	0.0	16	43	$8
16 Proj	**481**	**66**	**10**	**55**	**17**	**268**	**226**	**315**	**418**	**733**	**397**	**896**	**6**	**73**	**0.23**	**47**	**13**	**40**	**35**	**82**	**102**	**91**	**7%**	**183**	**19%**	**78%**				**4.53**	**1.7**	**32**	**86**	**$20**

Byrd,Marlon

Age: 38 Bats: R Pos: LF RF | Ht: 6' 0" Wt: 245

Health B | PT/Exp A | Consist B | LIMA Plan B | Rand Var 0 | MM 4125

Late-30s power held firm, though xPX is more skeptical about his future. Depressed h% held 1st half BA down; rising GB% and falling HctX capped its recovery. At his age, these skills could recede gently—or crumble overnight. There's still value here, but also this... DN: .235 BA, 15 HR.

Yr Tm	AB	R	HR	RBI	SB	BA	xBA	OBP	SLG	OPS	vL	vR	bb%	ct%	Eye	G	L	F	h%	HctX	PX	xPX	hr/f	Spd	SBO	SB%	#Wk	DOM	DIS	RC/G	RAR	BPV	BPX	R$
11 CHC	446	51	9	35	3	276	266	324	395	719	649	740	5	83	0.32	50	22	28	32	78	82	68	9%	90	4%	60%	22	41%	32%	4.32	-12.0	35	78	$10
12 2 TM	143	10	1	9	0	210	224	243	245	488	761	348	3	78	0.16	50	26	25	26	86	24	57	4%	76	9%	0%	10	0%	80%	1.66	-13.8	-35	-88	-$3
13 2 NL	532	75	24	88	2	291	272	336	511	847	959	797	6	73	0.22	39	24	37	36	124	159	153	16%	113	5%	33%	26	65%	19%	5.91	27.6	66	165	$24
14 PHI	591	71	25	85	3	264	243	312	445	757	773	751	6	69	0.19	37	23	40	34	108	143	145	15%	74	4%	60%	27	30%	30%	4.66	15.0	25	68	$20
15 2 NL	506	58	23	73	2	247	255	290	453	743	820	717	5	71	0.20	43	21	36	30	96	140	116	17%	86	3%	67%	26	42%	23%	4.39	-4.8	36	97	$12
1st Half	225	29	14	32	1	244	253	301	467	767	911	723	7	75	0.30	38	19	43	27	105	135	121	19%	82	2%	100%	13	54%	31%	4.71	1.0	47	127	$12
2nd Half	281	29	9	41	1	249	257	282	441	723	755	711	4	69	0.14	47	22	31	33	90	145	111	15%	82	4%	50%	13	31%	15%	4.14	-3.5	26	70	$12
16 Proj	**464**	**54**	**18**	**65**	**2**	**258**	**250**	**301**	**441**	**743**	**812**	**717**	**5**	**72**	**0.20**	**42**	**22**	**36**	**32**	**102**	**128**	**123**	**15%**	**92**	**4%**	**49%**				**4.43**	**-1.8**	**24**	**64**	**$15**

Cabrera,Asdrubal

Age: 30 Bats: B Pos: SS | Ht: 6' 0" Wt: 205

Health A | PT/Exp A | Consist A | LIMA Plan A | Rand Var -2 | MM 3325

2nd half h% and power surge overcame putrid 1st half to produce value in line with recent efforts. Ran less, but h% bump compensated, adding BA sheen to an otherwise stable skill set. The xBA says he'll give back something, but pop, counting stats and AAA Reliabilty from a scarce position are worth buying.

Yr Tm	AB	R	HR	RBI	SB	BA	xBA	OBP	SLG	OPS	vL	vR	bb%	ct%	Eye	G	L	F	h%	HctX	PX	xPX	hr/f	Spd	SBO	SB%	#Wk	DOM	DIS	RC/G	RAR	BPV	BPX	R$
11 CLE	604	87	25	92	17	273	269	332	460	792	777	799	7	80	0.37	44	17	39	30	109	123	115	13%	96	15%	77%	27	56%	26%	5.20	17.7	64	142	$26
12 CLE	555	70	16	68	9	270	269	338	423	762	796	745	9	82	0.53	41	23	36	30	117	101	105	10%	67	9%	69%	27	48%	30%	4.88	15.6	49	123	$17
13 CLE	508	66	14	64	9	242	256	299	402	700	639	730	6	78	0.31	36	23	41	29	108	118	139	9%	93	11%	75%	25	32%	20%	3.92	7.5	47	118	$13
14 2 TM	553	74	14	61	10	241	250	307	387	694	689	696	8	80	0.45	38	19	42	28	118	105	127	8%	107	9%	83%	27	48%	30%	3.97	13.0	56	151	$13
15 TAM	505	66	15	58	6	265	248	315	430	744	725	752	7	79	0.34	36	21	44	31	92	107	107	9%	100	7%	67%	25	48%	28%	4.64	3.5	46	124	$14
1st Half	283	26	5	22	3	226	223	281	353	634	609	642	7	76	0.30	37	19	44	28	80	86	90	5%	112	10%	50%	14	36%	36%	3.12	-8.4	23	62	$5
2nd Half	222	40	10	36	3	315	280	357	527	884	809	932	7	82	0.40	34	23	43	35	106	133	127	13%	86	5%	100%	11	64%	18%	7.19	18.5	75	203	$26
16 Proj	**519**	**72**	**16**	**65**	**8**	**256**	**255**	**313**	**422**	**734**	**709**	**746**	**7**	**80**	**0.39**	**37**	**21**	**42**	**29**	**105**	**109**	**120**	**9%**	**95**	**9%**	**77%**				**4.48**	**6.0**	**54**	**146**	**$17**

Cabrera,Everth

Age: 29 Bats: B Pos: SS | Ht: 5' 10" Wt: 190

Health C | PT/Exp D | Consist D | LIMA Plan D | Rand Var +5 | MM 0411

0-4-.208 with 2 SBs in 96 AB at BAL. Struggled prior to May foot injury and June release. Still owns 81 SBs from 2012-13, but maybe not. In the 453 AB prior to his Biogenesis suspension, he hit .285 with 52 SBs. In the 453 AB since returning from suspension: .227 with 20 SBs. Draw your own conclusions.

Yr Tm	AB	R	HR	RBI	SB	BA	xBA	OBP	SLG	OPS	vL	vR	bb%	ct%	Eye	G	L	F	h%	HctX	PX	xPX	hr/f	Spd	SBO	SB%	#Wk	DOM	DIS	RC/G	RAR	BPV	BPX	R$
11 SD *	254	31	1	9	19	209	264	264	274	538	1000	143	7	78	0.34	100	0	0	26	0	48	2	0%	151	48%	65%	1	0%	100%	2.20	-19.0	13	29	$2
12 SD *	542	67	2	34	54	249	237	313	321	635	523	698	9	73	0.35	61	19	20	34	63	61	47	4%	122	37%	93%	21	10%	62%	3.88	-3.7	-2	-5	$21
13 SD	381	54	4	31	37	283	273	355	381	736	934	651	10	82	0.59	60	21	19	34	88	65	49	7%	146	39%	76%	18	39%	33%	4.80	14.9	45	113	$23
14 SD	357	36	3	20	18	232	254	272	300	572	642	551	5	76	0.23	67	21	12	30	60	56	31	9%	109	30%	69%	16	19%	56%	2.66	-6.3	-5	-14	$7
15 BAL *	228	18	0	9	7	185	231	225	207	432	342	535	5	77	0.23	67	19	14	24	58	20	13	0%	94	19%	72%	7	0%	86%	1.47	-16.9	-34	-92	-$3
1st Half	120	9	0	5	2	197	218	234	220	454	342	535	5	74	0.18	67	19	14	27	55	22	13	0%	94	8%	100%	7	0%	86%	1.70	-9.0	-46	-124	-$5
2nd Half	108	9	0	5	5	171	204	215	192	408			5	81	0.30				21		19			97	32%	64%				1.25		-19	-51	-$1
16 Proj	**132**	**13**	**1**	**7**	**7**	**214**	**246**	**263**	**268**	**532**	**557**	**522**	**6**	**78**	**0.29**	**64**	**20**	**16**	**27**	**69**	**40**	**34**	**5%**	**108**	**31%**	**72%**				**2.27**	**-7.6**	**-10**	**-27**	**$2**

JOCK THOMPSON

Cabrera,Melky

Age: 31	Bats: B	Pos: LF	Health: C	LIMA Plan: A	
Ht: 5' 10"	Wt: 210		PT/Exp: B	Rand Var: +2	
			Consist: D	MM: 2245	

Avoided injury and notched 600+ AB for the second time in his career, but overall productivity dipped a bit—mostly due to lousy 1H from which he recovered reasonably. Combination of plus contact and plenty of line drives should continue to drive some value via BA, but power is flat and speed is gone for good.

Yr	Tm	AB	R	HR	RBI	SB	BA	xBA	OBP	SLG	OPS	vL	vR	bb%	ct%	Eye	G	L	F	h%	HctX	PX	xPX	hr/f	Spd	SBO	SB%	#Wk	DOM	DIS	RC/G	RAR	BPV	BPX	R$
11	KC	658	102	18	87	20	305	289	339	470	809	788	818	5	86	0.37	47	20	33	34	101	108	88	10%	109	18%	67%	27	59%	22%	5.70	14.1	74	164	$33
12	SF	459	84	11	60	13	346	298	390	516	906	1111	826	7	86	0.57	52	22	26	38	105	99	80	11%	143	12%	72%	20	65%	10%	7.84	39.1	84	210	$28
13	TOR	344	39	3	30	2	279	255	322	360	682	595	717	6	86	0.49	46	22	31	32	119	57	85	3%	99	4%	50%	15	27%	20%	4.07	0.9	35	88	$7
14	TOR	568	81	16	73	6	301	297	351	458	808	785	817	7	88	0.64	49	21	30	32	117	104	90	11%	93	5%	75%	23	61%	9%	5.84	33.6	80	216	$25
15	CHW	629	70	12	77	3	273	278	314	394	709	600	748	6	86	0.45	46	24	30	30	103	79	67	7%	70	2%	100%	26	35%	19%	4.41	0.3	42	114	$16
1st Half		309	31	3	30	0	259	251	299	330	629	491	672	6	88	0.49	47	22	31	29	89	46	57	4%	84	0%	0%	14	29%	29%	3.40	-10.4	27	73	$8
2nd Half		320	39	9	47	3	288	299	329	456	785	682	829	6	84	0.43	45	26	29	32	116	112	78	11%	61	4%	100%	12	42%	8%	5.50	8.4	59	159	$24
16	Proj	**577**	**73**	**12**	**70**	**5**	**283**	**282**	**326**	**416**	**742**	**680**	**765**	**6**	**86**	**0.50**	**47**	**23**	**30**	**31**	**110**	**85**	**78**	**8%**	**85**	**5%**	**75%**				**4.84**	**4.6**	**53**	**144**	**$18**

Cabrera,Miguel

Age: 33	Bats: R	Pos: 1B	Health: B	LIMA Plan: C	
Ht: 6' 4"	Wt: 240		PT/Exp: A	Rand Var: -4	
			Consist: F	MM: 4155	

Vintage 1st half before first ever DL stint in July (Grade 3 calf strain) cost him about 6 weeks. Fortunate h% artificially inflated his BA, masking continued xBA slippage. The days of .340 BA/40 HR aren't coming back, but .300 BA/30 HR is still in range. Health may be only variable questioning his continued 1st round status.

Yr	Tm	AB	R	HR	RBI	SB	BA	xBA	OBP	SLG	OPS	vL	vR	bb%	ct%	Eye	G	L	F	h%	HctX	PX	xPX	hr/f	Spd	SBO	SB%	#Wk	DOM	DIS	RC/G	RAR	BPV	BPX	R$
11	DET	572	111	30	105	2	344	317	448	586	1033	990	1047	16	84	1.21	44	22	34	37	157	158	140	18%	75	1%	67%	27	85%	0%	10.19	67.1	120	267	$39
12	DET	622	109	44	139	4	330	315	393	606	999	913	1027	10	84	0.67	42	22	36	34	159	161	161	23%	75	3%	80%	27	81%	7%	9.08	62.1	109	273	$42
13	DET	555	103	44	137	3	348	317	442	636	1078	1210	1038	14	83	0.96	39	24	37	36	155	170	165	25%	74	1%	100%	26	69%	19%	10.96	90.2	120	300	$46
14	DET	611	101	25	109	1	313	302	371	524	895	900	894	9	81	0.51	40	25	35	35	157	154	163	14%	80	1%	50%	27	70%	15%	7.23	51.0	90	243	$33
15	DET	429	64	18	76	1	338	290	440	534	974	1016	964	15	81	0.94	42	25	33	39	142	126	124	16%	81	1%	50%	21	57%	19%	8.97	45.0	81	219	$25
1st Half		277	43	15	54	1	350	290	456	578	1034	1089	1020	16	80	0.96	42	23	35	40	146	140	140	19%	90	2%	50%	13	69%	15%	10.21	35.9	94	254	$35
2nd Half		152	21	3	22	0	316	291	410	454	864	869	863	14	82	0.89	42	29	29	37	135	99	94	8%	68	0%	0%	8	38%	25%	6.92	7.2	58	157	$6
16	Proj	**579**	**93**	**28**	**107**	**1**	**317**	**301**	**406**	**536**	**942**	**977**	**932**	**13**	**82**	**0.82**	**41**	**25**	**33**	**35**	**148**	**139**	**137**	**18%**	**77**	**1%**	**65%**				**8.10**	**45.7**	**79**	**213**	**$34**

Cain,Lorenzo

Age: 30	Bats: R	Pos: CF	Health: C	LIMA Plan: B+	
Ht: 6' 2"	Wt: 205		PT/Exp: B	Rand Var: -3	
			Consist: C	MM: 2535	

Formula for a career year: more AB, more contact, more hard-hit balls, more flyballs. xPX backs the power gains, so the power/speed combo should be repeatable. But all in the context of AB. Given health grade and AB history, another 500+ AB season is no sure thing. But with the ABs, 15ish HRs and 25ish SBs should be a lock.

Yr	Tm	AB	R	HR	RBI	SB	BA	xBA	OBP	SLG	OPS	vL	vR	bb%	ct%	Eye	G	L	F	h%	HctX	PX	xPX	hr/f	Spd	SBO	SB%	#Wk	DOM	DIS	RC/G	RAR	BPV	BPX	R$
11	KC *	509	62	10	57	11	262	260	301	393	695	167	765	5	77	0.24	50	22	28	32	65	95	57	0%	147	15%	61%	2	50%	50%	3.96	-16.9	39	87	$13
12	KC *	274	33	8	36	10	256	252	298	407	705	844	681	6	75	0.24	47	22	31	31	85	101	92	13%	118	16%	100%	12	42%	33%	4.37	-3.8	31	78	$8
13	KC	399	54	4	46	14	251	247	310	348	658	617	676	8	77	0.37	49	22	29	31	80	76	69	4%	125	19%	70%	24	38%	46%	3.61	-7.5	25	63	$11
14	KC	471	55	5	53	28	301	260	339	412	751	827	720	5	77	0.22	51	23	26	38	72	90	68	5%	129	26%	85%	25	28%	28%	5.20	17.1	31	84	$25
15	KC	551	101	16	72	28	307	283	361	477	838	959	777	6	82	0.38	46	23	31	35	116	108	110	11%	136	23%	82%	26	50%	31%	6.22	26.1	71	192	$35
1st Half		275	48	6	36	16	305	279	364	462	826	971	752	7	80	0.41	48	24	28	36	108	103	104	10%	133	24%	84%	14	43%	29%	6.19	13.5	60	162	$33
2nd Half		276	53	10	36	12	308	287	358	493	851	943	803	5	84	0.34	43	23	34	34	124	113	115	13%	131	21%	80%	12	58%	33%	6.25	14.0	78	211	$37
16	Proj	**513**	**85**	**12**	**65**	**24**	**296**	**271**	**345**	**445**	**790**	**879**	**749**	**6**	**80**	**0.32**	**47**	**23**	**30**	**35**	**97**	**99**	**92**	**10%**	**138**	**22%**	**81%**				**5.51**	**15.9**	**56**	**150**	**$30**

Calhoun,Kole

Age: 28	Bats: L	Pos: RF	Health: A	LIMA Plan: B+	
Ht: 5' 10"	Wt: 200		PT/Exp: B	Rand Var: -1	
			Consist: A	MM: 3225	

1st half was in line with what we've seen before, then a power spike in 2nd half. Can he hold these gains? PRO: xPX has visited those levels before. CON: sacrificed a lot of contact to generate that power; became hopeless vLHP. Don't count on a full power repeat; the BA losses may stick as well.

Yr	Tm	AB	R	HR	RBI	SB	BA	xBA	OBP	SLG	OPS	vL	vR	bb%	ct%	Eye	G	L	F	h%	HctX	PX	xPX	hr/f	Spd	SBO	SB%	#Wk	DOM	DIS	RC/G	RAR	BPV	BPX	R$
11																																			
12	LAA *	433	53	8	48	9	224	253	274	354	628	0	578	6	74	0.26	41	29	29	29	95	95	150	0%	93	14%	71%	9	0%	33%	3.16	-22.6	13	33	$5
13	LAA *	435	58	15	62	8	274	267	335	443	777	889	782	8	81	0.49	41	23	36	31	130	106	131	14%	97	10%	64%	10	70%	20%	5.10	10.2	58	145	$16
14	LAA *	515	94	18	61	5	276	281	326	456	782	710	793	7	79	0.35	44	24	32	32	99	129	94	13%	99	7%	53%	23	39%	13%	5.11	17.9	65	176	$20
15	LAA	630	78	26	83	4	256	248	308	422	731	663	763	7	74	0.27	42	23	35	31	91	109	117	16%	82	3%	80%	27	30%	30%	4.42	-6.4	23	62	$17
1st Half		305	33	9	46	4	266	249	320	403	724	768	707	8	78	0.37	40	24	36	32	91	90	107	10%	79	6%	80%	14	36%	29%	4.51	-2.6	24	65	$17
2nd Half		325	45	17	37	0	246	246	297	440	737	590	823	6	70	0.21	44	21	34	30	92	128	126	22%	92	0%	0%	13	23%	31%	4.31	-4.8	25	68	$18
16	Proj	**586**	**83**	**23**	**74**	**6**	**251**	**260**	**305**	**424**	**730**	**671**	**752**	**7**	**75**	**0.31**	**44**	**23**	**33**	**30**	**100**	**114**	**112**	**15%**	**91**	**6%**	**65%**				**4.34**	**-8.3**	**37**	**100**	**$19**

Canha,Mark

Age: 27	Bats: R	Pos: 1B LF	Health: A	LIMA Plan: B	
Ht: 6' 2"	Wt: 195		PT/Exp: B	Rand Var: 0	
			Consist: B	MM: 3315	

Rule 5 selection surpassed his MLEs in first taste of the majors. Still, this is essentially a collection of average skills. With more AB, he could possibly reach 20 HR in a year where the stars and playing time align, but 2015 may also be as good as it gets.

Yr	Tm	AB	R	HR	RBI	SB	BA	xBA	OBP	SLG	OPS	vL	vR	bb%	ct%	Eye	G	L	F	h%	HctX	PX	xPX	hr/f	Spd	SBO	SB%	#Wk	DOM	DIS	RC/G	RAR	BPV	BPX	R$
11																																			
12																																			
13	aa	425	52	9	48	5	241		314	382	696			10	73	0.40				31		114			92	6%	81%				4.05		33	83	$7
14	aaa	465	55	11	54	2	240		297	373	671			7	72	0.29				31		107			94	3%	62%				3.71		18	49	$8
15	OAK	441	61	16	70	7	254	251	315	426	742	587	821	7	78	0.34	42	18	40	29	108	111	114	11%	114	9%	78%	27	59%	33%	4.46	-6.1	52	141	$14
1st Half		194	28	8	31	5	242	246	304	412	716	360	908	7	78	0.36	44	16	40	27	105	104	108	13%	109	13%	83%	14	57%	43%	4.16	-5.8	46	124	$11
2nd Half		247	33	8	39	2	263	255	325	437	762	778	754	7	78	0.33	40	19	41	31	110	116	119	10%	115	5%	67%	13	62%	23%	4.70	-3.2	55	149	$16
16	Proj	**421**	**54**	**14**	**58**	**5**	**248**	**243**	**314**	**415**	**729**	**590**	**800**	**8**	**75**	**0.33**	**42**	**18**	**40**	**30**	**108**	**114**	**115**	**11%**	**118**	**6%**	**76%**				**4.28**	**-10.9**	**35**	**94**	**$13**

Cano,Robinson

Age: 33	Bats: L	Pos: 2B	Health: A	LIMA Plan: B+	
Ht: 6' 0"	Wt: 210		PT/Exp: A	Rand Var: 0	
			Consist: C	MM: 3155	

Slow start may have been caused by a stomach parasite issue that originated late in 2014. Skills-wise, the tale of the two halves is rooted in h% and hr/f. The strength of that 2H recovery means he's still an elite 2B option, and may even be undervalued if bidders remember the first three months rather than the last three.

Yr	Tm	AB	R	HR	RBI	SB	BA	xBA	OBP	SLG	OPS	vL	vR	bb%	ct%	Eye	G	L	F	h%	HctX	PX	xPX	hr/f	Spd	SBO	SB%	#Wk	DOM	DIS	RC/G	RAR	BPV	BPX	R$
11	NYY	623	104	28	118	8	302	318	349	533	882	879	884	6	85	0.40	47	22	31	32	131	147	116	17%	90	7%	80%	27	67%	11%	6.65	35.2	97	216	$33
12	NYY	627	105	33	94	3	313	324	379	550	929	646	1108	9	85	0.64	49	26	26	33	141	145	115	24%	80	3%	60%	27	70%	7%	7.57	57.7	99	248	$32
13	NYY	605	81	27	107	7	314	312	383	516	899	788	969	10	86	0.76	44	26	30	33	137	128	115	17%	76	4%	88%	26	65%	19%	7.34	58.9	91	228	$34
14	SEA	595	77	14	82	10	314	301	382	454	836	746	891	9	89	0.90	53	23	25	34	109	95	82	11%	80	7%	77%	27	59%	11%	6.38	48.2	75	203	$29
15	SEA	624	82	21	79	2	287	286	334	446	779	715	815	6	83	0.40	50	24	25	32	118	100	107	16%	72	5%	25%	27	52%	11%	5.11	14.7	48	130	$22
1st Half		314	34	5	27	2	248	269	289	363	652	516	699	5	81	0.29	53	23	24	29	123	84	108	8%	72	9%	33%	14	43%	21%	3.36	-8.1	26	70	$9
2nd Half		310	48	16	52	0	326	303	379	529	908	828	977	8	85	0.54	48	25	26	35	113	115	106	23%	78	2%	0%	13	62%	0%	7.37	26.1	71	192	$34
16	Proj	**600**	**82**	**23**	**87**	**5**	**304**	**300**	**361**	**481**	**842**	**756**	**895**	**8**	**85**	**0.58**	**50**	**24**	**26**	**33**	**120**	**108**	**103**	**17%**	**76**	**5%**	**56%**				**6.22**	**32.9**	**63**	**170**	**$30**

Carpenter,Matt

Age: 30	Bats: L	Pos: 3B	Health: A	LIMA Plan: B+	
Ht: 6' 3"	Wt: 215		PT/Exp: A	Rand Var: 0	
			Consist: D	MM: 4235	

Nearly tripled career high in HR thanks to altered approach: Hit the ball less often (ct%) but harder (stable HctX despite lower ct%), and in the air more (LD%+FB%). That huge LD% propped up BA, and xPX supports the power, but ct% reached danger levels in 2H, and hr/f is ripe for regression. Expect some pullback.

Yr	Tm	AB	R	HR	RBI	SB	BA	xBA	OBP	SLG	OPS	vL	vR	bb%	ct%	Eye	G	L	F	h%	HctX	PX	xPX	hr/f	Spd	SBO	SB%	#Wk	DOM	DIS	RC/G	RAR	BPV	BPX	R$
11	STL *	449	41	7	48	3	228	178	323	338	661	500	378	12	81	0.74	45	0	55	27	0	80	2	0%	82	6%	41%	3	33%	67%	3.49	-22.1	39	87	$2
12	STL	296	44	6	46	1	294	268	365	463	828	784	846	10	79	0.54	40	24	36	36	118	116	114	7%	103	2%	50%	24	58%	21%	6.07	12.1	61	153	$9
13	STL	626	126	11	78	3	318	293	392	481	873	820	897	10	84	0.73	39	27	34	36	116	116	103	6%	124	3%	50%	27	63%	11%	6.89	48.8	90	225	$30
14	STL	595	99	8	59	5	272	253	375	375	750	722	762	14	81	0.86	41	24	35	32	117	80	98	5%	109	4%	63%	26	50%	27%	4.86	19.6	52	141	$17
15	STL	574	101	28	84	4	272	278	365	505	871	752	926	12	74	0.54	30	29	42	32	119	164	165	16%	92	4%	57%	27	59%	26%	6.32	27.1	80	216	$23
1st Half		277	45	8	39	1	274	275	374	444	818	630	898	13	78	0.69	30	30	39	33	116	121	141	9%	83	3%	33%	14	57%	36%	5.67	8.4	61	165	$17
2nd Half		297	56	20	45	3	269	284	357	562	919	854	952	11	70	0.43	29	27	44	32	123	208	190	22%	103	5%	75%	13	62%	15%	6.89	19.4	102	276	$29
16	Proj	**579**	**100**	**19**	**75**	**4**	**277**	**272**	**367**	**460**	**827**	**755**	**861**	**12**	**77**	**0.61**	**36**	**26**	**38**	**33**	**119**	**126**	**137**	**11%**	**103**	**4%**	**58%**				**5.85**	**20.2**	**62**	**169**	**$24**

GREG PYRON

Carrera,Ezequiel

Age: 29 Bats: L Pos: LF RF | Ht: 5' 10" Wt: 185
Health A | PT/Exp D | Consist B | LIMA Plan F | Rand Var -4 | MM 1410

3-26-.273 with 2 SB in 170 AB at TOR. Another year, another team, same mediocre results, EXCEPT ... while Spd has generated modest value in the past, 2015 calls even that into question. Too many whiffs, too many ground balls, and far too many negatives just for the chance for a handful of steals.

Yr Tm	AB	R	HR	RBI	SB	BA	xBA	OBP	SLG	OPS	vL	vR	bb%	ct%	Eye	G	L	F	h%	HctX	PX	xPX	hr/f	Spd	SBO	SB%	#Wk	DOM	DIS	RC/G	RAR	BPV	BPX	R$
11 CLE *	530	75	1	33	37	244	242	304	299	603	482	680	8	82	0.48	55	19	26	30	79	40	72	0%	138	30%	79%	14	14%	43%	3.19	-31.7	19	42	$14
12 CLE *	541	69	6	42	27	251	258	290	353	643	810	660	5	80	0.28	47	26	28	30	86	67	89	7%	114	28%	75%	9	22%	44%	3.47	-22.4	22	55	$15
13 2 TM *	433	49	4	26	35	207	198	260	282	542	0	533	7	75	0.28	42	17	42	27	71	56	131	0%	137	49%	71%	5	0%	100%	2.31	-27.5	0	0	$11
14 DET *	443	62	4	32	38	257	239	316	350	666	866	590	8	80	0.44	60	12	29	31	101	66	77	0%	153	44%	70%	10	20%	50%	3.66	-3.2	37	100	$20
15 TOR *	288	42	4	34	7	259	241	309	344	653	782	675	7	77	0.32	61	17	23	32	79	63	74	11%	95	13%	67%	22	18%	59%	3.60	-9.8	4	11	$7
1st Half	189	28	2	23	7	283	242	339	354	694	838	678	8	80	0.42	59	18	23	35	76	53	62	6%	101	17%	67%	11	0%	73%	4.19	-3.4	9	24	$12
2nd Half	99	14	2	12	0	214	232	249	324	574	714	669	4	73	0.17	64	14	21	27	84	83	98	22%	90	0%	0%	11	36%	45%	2.62	-6.7	-3	-8	-$1
16 Proj	65	9	1	6	3	240	245	293	343	636	717	612	6	77	0.30	59	17	25	29	86	71	82	9%	105	27%	71%				3.27	-2.6	15	41	$0

Carter,Chris

Age: 29 Bats: R Pos: 1B | Ht: 6' 4" Wt: 250
Health A | PT/Exp B | Consist B | LIMA Plan B | Rand Var +4 | MM 5015

For the first time in three seasons, low BA sabotaged his big-time power by cutting into playing time. 2nd half xBA offers faint hope, though it was built on upper-tier ct%, PX levels. He offered up the exact same tease in 2014 (.272 xBA, 230 PX in the 2nd half). The big risk now is this... DN: 250 AB.

Yr Tm	AB	R	HR	RBI	SB	BA	xBA	OBP	SLG	OPS	vL	vR	bb%	ct%	Eye	G	L	F	h%	HctX	PX	xPX	hr/f	Spd	SBO	SB%	#Wk	DOM	DIS	RC/G	RAR	BPV	BPX	R$
11 OAK *	340	39	11	48	3	204	224	269	352	621	145	448	8	64	0.25	17	38	46	28	40	123	33	0%	81	6%	74%	6	0%	83%	3.03	-27.7	-3	-7	$2
12 OAK *	494	70	23	75	3	225	228	316	423	739	898	837	12	65	0.38	34	20	46	30	97	154	126	25%	66	4%	73%	15	47%	27%	4.39	-13.4	28	70	$10
13 HOU	506	64	29	82	2	223	226	320	451	770	782	765	12	58	0.33	31	22	47	32	94	197	171	21%	78	2%	100%	27	44%	33%	4.72	1.8	40	100	$12
14 HOU	507	68	37	88	5	227	252	308	491	799	869	772	10	64	0.31	27	22	51	27	106	210	171	22%	73	6%	71%	26	50%	31%	4.89	11.5	68	184	$18
15 HOU	391	50	24	64	1	199	223	307	427	734	736	733	13	61	0.38	30	18	52	25	99	177	175	19%	62	3%	33%	27	44%	30%	4.03	-11.2	33	89	$5
1st Half	272	34	15	40	1	195	209	311	401	711	713	710	13	60	0.38	31	17	52	26	87	166	163	17%	64	3%	50%	14	36%	36%	3.80	-11.7	19	51	$7
2nd Half	119	16	9	24	0	210	258	299	487	787	777	793	11	66	0.37	28	21	51	23	126	201	200	22%	69	4%	0%	13	54%	23%	4.53	-2.3	68	184	$0
16 Proj	404	53	27	70	2	214	238	305	462	767	779	758	11	63	0.34	29	21	50	26	106	188	174	21%	69	4%	50%				4.46	-8.7	40	109	$12

Casali,Curtis

Age: 27 Bats: R Pos: CA | Ht: 6' 2" Wt: 225
Health B | PT/Exp F | Consist F | LIMA Plan D | Rand Var +5 | MM 3203

10-18-.238 in 101 AB at TAM. Intriguing power outburst, but MLB PX (256), hr/f (32%) are simply unrepeatable. Hamstring injury that ended season early eliminated pitchers' opportunity to adjust to his poor ct% and Eye. FB%, xPX indicate some power potential, just not at 2015's crazy HR pace.

Yr Tm	AB	R	HR	RBI	SB	BA	xBA	OBP	SLG	OPS	vL	vR	bb%	ct%	Eye	G	L	F	h%	HctX	PX	xPX	hr/f	Spd	SBO	SB%	#Wk	DOM	DIS	RC/G	RAR	BPV	BPX	R$
11																																		
12																																		
13 aa	120	20	4	25	0	324		406	497	903			12	82	0.75				37		123			83	0%	0%				7.61		77	193	$5
14 TAM *	298	24	3	25	0	202	201	303	282	585	521	460	13	65	0.42	44	23	33	30	50	82	69	0%	72	0%	0%	11	9%	73%	2.73	-5.5	-23	-62	-$3
15 TAM *	213	24	13	28	1	199	228	271	423	694	864	911	9	67	0.30	43	12	46	23	95	159	117	32%	73	2%	100%	12	75%	25%	3.66	-0.4	38	103	$1
1st Half	137	13	4	13	1	185	208	266	314	580	250	924	10	68	0.35	44	17	39	24	100	100	123	14%	78	3%	100%	5	60%	40%	2.64	-5.0	-2	-5	-$2
2nd Half	76	11	9	15	0	224	277	298	618	916	937	906	7	66	0.23	42	10	48	20	91	270	115	38%	78	0%	0%	7	86%	14%	5.70	4.4	119	322	$6
16 Proj	251	24	7	27	0	223	209	313	360	673	647	680	10	68	0.37	43	17	40	30	77	106	99	11%	75	1%	100%				3.59	-1.5	-11	-29	$3

Castellanos,Nick

Age: 24 Bats: R Pos: 3B | Ht: 6' 4" Wt: 210
Health A | PT/Exp B | Consist A | LIMA Plan B+ | Rand Var -2 | MM 4025

Sure, inconsistency is frustrating, but he's still only 24. Big platoon split caused by 44% hit rate vLHP. Rediscovered LD skill, power in 2H, and result was best three months of career. (To be fair, 1H was also worst three months.) The ingredients are here for, at minimum, some growth, but at best, a breakout... UP: 25 HR.

Yr Tm	AB	R	HR	RBI	SB	BA	xBA	OBP	SLG	OPS	vL	vR	bb%	ct%	Eye	G	L	F	h%	HctX	PX	xPX	hr/f	Spd	SBO	SB%	#Wk	DOM	DIS	RC/G	RAR	BPV	BPX	R$
11																																		
12 aa	322	29	6	21	4	245		270	345	616			3	76	0.15				30		71			98	12%	50%				3.02		0	0	$3
13 DET *	551	70	15	65	3	258	242	315	408	723	545	571	8	81	0.44	59	6	35	29	59	106	-15	0%	100	3%	76%	5	0%	20%	4.41	7.4	57	143	$13
14 DET	533	50	11	66	2	259	252	306	394	700	693	702	6	74	0.26	35	29	37	33	109	108	135	8%	104	3%	50%	27	37%	37%	4.10	6.6	27	73	$11
15 DET	549	42	15	73	0	255	243	303	419	721	970	656	7	72	0.26	36	23	40	33	104	118	119	9%	95	2%	0%	27	33%	37%	4.26	-4.9	27	73	$9
1st Half	277	15	4	30	0	235	217	281	347	628	751	596	6	74	0.25	38	21	41	30	99	77	107	5%	113	2%	0%	14	21%	43%	3.19	-11.9	6	16	$2
2nd Half	272	27	11	43	0	276	268	324	493	817	1175	718	7	71	0.26	34	26	39	35	108	162	131	14%	86	3%	0%	13	46%	31%	5.51	6.9	54	146	$17
16 Proj	557	51	18	79	2	267	257	312	438	750	900	705	6	74	0.26	36	26	39	33	106	121	127	11%	97	4%	36%				4.68	0.9	25	68	$17

Castillo,Rusney

Age: 28 Bats: R Pos: RF LF | Ht: 5' 8" Wt: 186
Health A | PT/Exp F | Consist F | LIMA Plan C+ | Rand Var 0 | MM 1435

5-29-.253 with 4 SB in 289 AB at BOS. Even with slight 2H gains, this was disappointing. GB%, xPX put damper on power hopes. While Spd and SBO seem like ticket to relevance, xBA and bb% leave little room for OBP growth. OPS vLHP offers hope, but it was only 88 AB. Be glad you're not the one paying him $72M.

Yr Tm	AB	R	HR	RBI	SB	BA	xBA	OBP	SLG	OPS	vL	vR	bb%	ct%	Eye	G	L	F	h%	HctX	PX	xPX	hr/f	Spd	SBO	SB%	#Wk	DOM	DIS	RC/G	RAR	BPV	BPX	R$
11 for	441	89	13	93	29	298		324	484	808			4	89	0.34				31		112			114	36%	79%				5.66	6.9	88	196	$29
12 for	448	98	13	82	24	318		365	498	863			7	90	0.71				33		111			94	26%	76%				6.72	25.4	91	228	$31
13 for	234	40	4	28	14	255		327	353	680			10	88	0.91				28		56			141	33%	57%				3.59	-3.0	61	153	$9
14 BOS	36	6	2	6	3	333	286	400	528	928	500	1045	8	83	0.50	67	10	23	36	96	118	69	29%	94	25%	100%	3	33%	67%	8.44	4.5	73	197	$1
15 BOS *	429	49	7	43	12	250	247	290	349	639	817	566	5	80	0.28	63	13	23	30	81	67	67	10%	107	18%	62%	17	35%	47%	3.31	-14.0	17	46	$10
1st Half	186	18	3	16	7	240	230	283	330	613	565	534	6	78	0.28	66	10	24	29	82	62	67	7%	85	21%	75%	6	17%	67%	3.14	-8.0	2	5	$5
2nd Half	243	31	4	27	5	257	253	295	364	658	903	578	5	81	0.28	63	14	23	30	81	70	67	11%	118	16%	48%	11	45%	36%	3.44	-8.2	26	70	$13
16 Proj	478	70	10	59	18	267	268	315	388	703	865	627	7	84	0.44	60	15	25	30	81	75	67	9%	127	23%	61%				4.02	-11.2	48	129	$20

Castillo,Welington

Age: 29 Bats: R Pos: CA | Ht: 5' 10" Wt: 210
Health B | PT/Exp C | Consist B | LIMA Plan C+ | Rand Var +2 | MM 4215

Recipe for a power breakout: Take 2014 FB% growth, add increased HctX, and simmer over peak age season. Hit 12 of his HR on the road, so this wasn't just about Chase Field. Added bonus: Didn't sacrifice already borderline ct%, and xBA suggests room for a little more BA. With full-season AB, 25 HR could be next step.

Yr Tm	AB	R	HR	RBI	SB	BA	xBA	OBP	SLG	OPS	vL	vR	bb%	ct%	Eye	G	L	F	h%	HctX	PX	xPX	hr/f	Spd	SBO	SB%	#Wk	DOM	DIS	RC/G	RAR	BPV	BPX	R$
11 CHC *	240	24	10	22	0	224	205	263	373	636	0	400	5	71	0.18	50	13	38	28	40	107	2	0%	81	0%	0%	3	0%	100%	3.22	-8.4	4	9	$1
12 CHC *	327	34	11	43	0	245	225	324	394	717	1199	604	10	70	0.39	46	20	34	32	92	111	99	12%	69	0%	0%	16	38%	38%	4.30	0.1	12	30	$5
13 CHC	380	41	8	32	2	274	240	349	397	746	707	758	8	74	0.35	44	22	34	35	113	99	110	8%	71	2%	100%	25	32%	40%	4.68	10.7	17	43	$8
14 CHC	380	28	13	46	0	237	228	296	389	686	855	631	6	73	0.25	41	19	40	29	103	118	121	12%	62	0%	0%	24	42%	33%	3.72	2.9	20	54	$5
15 3 TM	342	42	19	57	0	237	253	296	453	750	778	739	7	73	0.27	42	18	40	27	121	142	149	19%	65	0%	0%	27	37%	37%	4.37	5.7	41	111	$8
1st Half	133	19	6	19	0	211	246	282	398	680	807	621	8	73	0.33	35	21	43	24	133	130	166	14%	59	0%	0%	14	36%	43%	3.55	-0.9	32	86	$0
2nd Half	209	23	13	38	0	254	257	306	488	794	753	807	6	73	0.23	46	17	37	29	114	150	138	22%	75	0%	0%	13	38%	31%	4.96	7.2	49	132	$13
16 Proj	488	52	20	67	0	242	241	304	417	722	816	690	7	73	0.28	42	19	39	29	113	120	131	15%	65	0%	100%				4.15	5.3	14	39	$12

Castro,Daniel

Age: 23 Bats: R Pos: 2B | Ht: 5' 11" Wt: 170
Health A | PT/Exp F | Consist A | LIMA Plan D | Rand Var -2 | MM 1221

2-5-.240 in 96 AB at ATL. Skills suggest future as utility infielder who's more glove than bat, and while Spd stands out, he's never been a big SB guy before. Unless he somehow graced your DFS roster on Oct. 2 (3-for-5, 3B, HR), you've probably already missed your shot at value.

Yr Tm	AB	R	HR	RBI	SB	BA	xBA	OBP	SLG	OPS	vL	vR	bb%	ct%	Eye	G	L	F	h%	HctX	PX	xPX	hr/f	Spd	SBO	SB%	#Wk	DOM	DIS	RC/G	RAR	BPV	BPX	R$
11																																		
12																																		
13																																		
14 aa	173	19	3	16	2	250		268	363	630			2	88	0.20				27		76			98	8%	60%				3.24		49	132	$2
15 ATL *	496	45	2	45	4	264	233	301	311	611	749	500	5	88	0.42	62	14	25	30	71	32	34	10%	106	6%	57%	9	22%	33%	3.19	-14.0	20	54	$7
1st Half	271	24	0	23	4	288	232	327	323	650	0	2000	5	89	0.52	100	0	0	32	0	28	-15	0%	105	9%	57%	1	0%	0%	3.68	-4.2	22	59	$10
2nd Half	225	21	2	22	0	236	228	268	297	565	749	473	4	86	0.32	61	14	25	27	70	38	35	10%	114	0%	0%	8	25%	38%	2.66	-10.6	20	54	$4
16 Proj	169	17	3	16	1	254	257	280	357	637	828	492	4	88	0.30	61	14	25	27	63	61	32	9%	117	6%	62%				3.38	-4.2	28	76	$4

BRANDON KRUSE

Castro,Jason

Age: 29	Bats: L	Pos: CA	Health C	LIMA Plan D+
Ht: 6' 3"	Wt: 215		PT/Exp B	Rand Var +3
			Consist C	MM 4203

Value-wrecking ct% slide now into its third year. Still, it's not hopeless: Shows pop from the CA slot, still owns those 2013 skills, and is also just 29, which is squarely in the figuring-it-out stage for many catchers. So while '13 now feels like a long time ago, any ct% spike could signal a potential return to that level.

Yr	Tm	AB	R	HR	RBI	SB	BA	xBA	OBP	SLG	OPS	vL	vR	bb%	ct%	Eye	G	L	F	h%	HctX	PX	xPX	hr/f	Spd	SBO	SB%	#Wk	DOM	DIS	RC/G	RAR	BPV	BPX	R$
11																																			
12	HOU	257	29	6	29	0	257	264	334	401	735	361	831	11	76	0.51	43	28	30	32	93	101	107	10%	90	0%	0%	22	55%	32%	4.63	3.7	36	90	$3
13	HOU	435	63	18	56	2	276	270	350	485	835	738	864	10	70	0.38	39	25	35	36	109	167	140	17%	85	3%	67%	23	61%	22%	5.96	27.8	62	155	$15
14	HOU	465	43	14	56	1	222	225	286	366	651	619	662	7	68	0.23	45	20	36	30	87	119	110	12%	98	1%	100%	26	38%	46%	3.30	-0.3	10	27	$5
15	HOU	337	38	11	31	0	211	229	283	365	648	512	707	9	66	0.29	37	24	38	28	92	124	121	13%	76	0%	0%	25	32%	44%	3.31	-4.3	5	14	$0
1st Half		199	24	7	19	0	211	242	283	372	654	558	700	9	69	0.31	35	26	39	27	102	122	136	13%	84	0%	0%	14	43%	36%	3.36	-2.6	17	46	$2
2nd Half		138	14	4	12	0	210	209	283	355	638	438	717	9	62	0.26	41	21	38	31	77	127	96	13%	76	0%	0%	11	18%	55%	3.24	-2.3	-9	-24	-$2
16	**Proj**	**396**	**44**	**12**	**42**	**0**	**233**	**233**	**303**	**389**	**693**	**550**	**744**	**9**	**67**	**0.30**	**41**	**23**	**36**	**31**	**91**	**123**	**115**	**13%**	**82**	**1%**	**78%**				**3.89**	**1.3**	**0**	**1**	**$4**

Castro,Starlin

Age: 26	Bats: R	Pos: SS 2B	Health A	LIMA Plan B
Ht: 6' 0"	Wt: 190		PT/Exp A	Rand Var 0
			Consist D	MM 2225

Pulled it out of the ditch late, notably with a 5-20-.426 Sept (.339 xBA). By then, though, he'd lost some PT; that could be an issue going forward. Career-high GB% despite reversing trend (39%) in Sept/Oct—he MUST keep it off the ground to tap into power. 2H surge gives hope, and he's still at pre-peak age. UP: 20 HR.

Yr	Tm	AB	R	HR	RBI	SB	BA	xBA	OBP	SLG	OPS	vL	vR	bb%	ct%	Eye	G	L	F	h%	HctX	PX	xPX	hr/f	Spd	SBO	SB%	#Wk	DOM	DIS	RC/G	RAR	BPV	BPX	R$
11	CHC	674	91	10	66	22	307	273	341	432	773	847	751	5	86	0.36	49	20	31	35	100	82	79	5%	149	17%	71%	27	63%	15%	5.34	11.5	65	144	$29
12	CHC	646	78	14	78	25	283	271	323	430	753	775	746	5	85	0.36	47	21	32	32	99	87	100	8%	158	23%	66%	27	63%	19%	4.72	6.9	68	170	$26
13	CHC	666	59	10	44	9	245	249	284	347	631	619	635	4	81	0.23	51	20	29	29	105	75	99	6%	116	10%	60%	27	33%	41%	3.18	-9.6	28	70	$9
14	CHC	528	58	14	65	4	292	271	339	438	777	788	773	6	81	0.35	45	22	32	34	102	107	105	10%	94	6%	50%	23	52%	17%	5.17	26.3	53	143	$19
15	CHC	547	52	11	69	5	265	251	296	375	671	643	679	4	83	0.23	54	17	29	30	87	70	75	8%	110	8%	50%	27	30%	33%	3.69	-7.6	32	86	$13
1st Half		315	26	5	36	4	257	230	293	333	627	631	626	4	84	0.27	57	15	28	29	85	46	70	7%	119	9%	57%	14	7%	36%	3.23	-9.3	18	49	$12
2nd Half		232	26	6	33	1	276	275	300	431	731	649	770	3	83	0.18	51	20	30	31	90	103	83	10%	101	6%	33%	13	54%	31%	4.35	0.9	51	138	$13
16	**Proj**	**468**	**49**	**10**	**55**	**5**	**273**	**261**	**309**	**400**	**709**	**690**	**715**	**4**	**82**	**0.26**	**50**	**19**	**30**	**31**	**95**	**83**	**89**	**9%**	**112**	**9%**	**55%**				**4.17**	**1.1**	**28**	**76**	**$15**

Cervelli,Francisco

Age: 30	Bats: R	Pos: CA	Health F	LIMA Plan D+
Ht: 6' 1"	Wt: 205		PT/Exp F	Rand Var -5
			Consist C	MM 1213

PRO: Got 451 AB and hit .295!! CON: He's Francisco Cervelli. Okay, that's not fair. Owns decent LD% and bb% rate. But xBA belies BA, and he's NEVER been able to stay healthy. So AB/BA/OB are keys to his value; all are almost certain to regress. Let someone else overbid (think about that... overbid on Francisco Cervelli?!?).

Yr	Tm	AB	R	HR	RBI	SB	BA	xBA	OBP	SLG	OPS	vL	vR	bb%	ct%	Eye	G	L	F	h%	HctX	PX	xPX	hr/f	Spd	SBO	SB%	#Wk	DOM	DIS	RC/G	RAR	BPV	BPX	R$
11	NYY	124	17	4	22	4	266	243	324	395	719	743	711	7	77	0.31	47	20	33	32	108	88	105	13%	91	15%	80%	19	32%	58%	4.37	0.0	20	44	$3
12	NYY *	355	34	2	30	5	205	75	268	262	531	1000	0	8	73	0.32	0	0	100	28	320	47	737	0%	98	5%	100%	2	50%	50%	2.32	-21.7	-22	-55	-$1
13	NYY	52	12	3	8	0	269	300	377	500	877	684	1017	13	83	0.89	30	28	42	28	143	145	148	17%	89	0%	0%	4	100%	0%	6.40	4.0	102	255	$0
14	NYY *	172	19	2	13	1	274	247	328	384	712	735	830	7	73	0.30	44	26	30	36	112	97	126	6%	98	2%	100%	17	47%	35%	4.46	4.9	17	46	$2
15	PIT	451	56	7	43	1	295	249	370	401	771	856	747	9	79	0.49	52	21	27	36	107	69	100	7%	129	1%	50%	27	22%	37%	5.20	17.2	31	84	$13
1st Half		219	26	4	28	1	301	249	376	406	782	1007	732	9	78	0.44	57	20	23	37	105	72	97	10%	106	3%	50%	14	14%	43%	5.31	9.3	21	57	$14
2nd Half		232	30	3	15	0	289	247	364	397	761	757	762	10	80	0.54	47	22	31	35	109	67	103	5%	141	0%	0%	13	31%	31%	5.09	8.5	38	103	$11
16	**Proj**	**384**	**45**	**7**	**36**	**1**	**265**	**240**	**340**	**375**	**715**	**697**	**722**	**9**	**77**	**0.40**	**46**	**22**	**32**	**33**	**114**	**76**	**115**	**7%**	**119**	**1%**	**59%**				**4.25**	**5.2**	**8**	**21**	**$9**

Cespedes,Yoenis

Age: 30	Bats: R	Pos: LF CF	Health A	LIMA Plan B+
Ht: 5' 10"	Wt: 210		PT/Exp A	Rand Var -2
			Consist C	MM 4235

Epic 2nd half HR barrage (actually started a month before move to NYM). Of course, inquiring minds want to know: Can he do it again? Smart money says no. PX/xPX look like outliers. FB% down, bb% continues slide. But some peripherals not too unlike 2012. This is a huge talent; there could be profit with a 2nd rd/$30 pick.

Yr	Tm	AB	R	HR	RBI	SB	BA	xBA	OBP	SLG	OPS	vL	vR	bb%	ct%	Eye	G	L	F	h%	HctX	PX	xPX	hr/f	Spd	SBO	SB%	#Wk	DOM	DIS	RC/G	RAR	BPV	BPX	R$
11	for	354	87	20	97	10	311		380	536	915			10	89	1.04				30		128			92	12%	75%				7.47	24.5	109	242	$26
12	OAK	487	70	23	82	16	292	269	356	505	861	853	864	8	79	0.42	40	20	40	33	114	132	114	15%	112	15%	80%	26	58%	19%	6.36	22.8	74	185	$25
13	OAK	529	74	26	80	7	240	244	294	442	737	880	672	7	74	0.27	38	17	46	28	97	136	127	14%	118	12%	50%	24	46%	29%	4.11	0.2	56	140	$17
14	2 AL	600	89	22	100	7	260	255	301	450	751	666	777	6	79	0.27	34	18	48	30	106	134	127	10%	113	7%	78%	27	56%	11%	4.66	14.5	69	186	$23
15	2 TM	633	101	35	105	7	291	289	328	542	870	736	909	5	78	0.23	42	20	38	33	123	160	131	19%	99	9%	58%	27	56%	22%	6.20	33.7	80	216	$32
1st Half		315	46	10	44	3	292	269	320	479	800	616	846	4	77	0.19	45	20	36	35	113	132	110	11%	101	10%	43%	14	50%	21%	5.32	8.1	54	146	$24
2nd Half		318	55	25	61	4	289	308	336	604	940	832	974	6	79	0.28	39	21	40	30	133	187	152	25%	94	8%	80%	13	62%	23%	7.12	24.1	105	284	$39
16	**Proj**	**593**	**94**	**28**	**102**	**7**	**276**	**271**	**322**	**495**	**817**	**760**	**836**	**6**	**78**	**0.29**	**39**	**20**	**41**	**31**	**115**	**139**	**130**	**15%**	**110**	**9%**	**63%**				**5.47**	**15.4**	**69**	**185**	**$29**

Chirinos,Robinson

Age: 32	Bats: R	Pos: CA	Health D	LIMA Plan D+
Ht: 6' 1"	Wt: 205		PT/Exp D	Rand Var 0
			Consist B	MM 4123

Shoulder injury cost most of last two months, and surely a career power year. That skill is peaking at age 32, as PX, FB% show. Becoming more selective, and while that also bumps K rate, it's a net positive for value. Health grade suggests this is a longshot, but if he ever gets 400 AB... UP: 20 HR

Yr	Tm	AB	R	HR	RBI	SB	BA	xBA	OBP	SLG	OPS	vL	vR	bb%	ct%	Eye	G	L	F	h%	HctX	PX	xPX	hr/f	Spd	SBO	SB%	#Wk	DOM	DIS	RC/G	RAR	BPV	BPX	R$
11	TAM *	337	22	5	25	1	208	174	265	296	561	833	576	7	71	0.26	54	7	39	28	43	71	44	6%	102	3%	38%	5	40%	60%	2.49	-18.0	-12	-27	-$3
12																																			
13	TEX *	293	26	6	27	1	199	194	269	305	574	445	583	9	75	0.37	24	19	57	25	98	77	175	0%	97	2%	100%	8	38%	38%	2.63	-9.9	9	23	-$2
14	TEX	306	36	13	40	0	239	259	290	415	705	759	682	5	77	0.24	42	21	37	27	100	126	130	15%	75	2%	0%	26	35%	35%	3.81	4.5	43	116	$6
15	TEX	233	33	10	34	0	232	253	325	438	762	845	717	11	73	0.45	35	19	45	27	91	145	134	13%	88	0%	0%	19	53%	26%	4.57	5.8	59	159	$3
1st Half		177	23	8	27	0	203	251	299	412	711	762	687	11	75	0.47	35	18	47	23	91	142	144	13%	79	0%	0%	14	57%	21%	3.80	0.1	59	159	$4
2nd Half		56	10	2	7	0	321	259	406	518	924	1027	837	11	70	0.41	38	23	38	43	90	157	100	13%	106	0%	0%	5	40%	40%	7.72	5.9	60	162	$0
16	**Proj**	**285**	**37**	**12**	**35**	**0**	**247**	**252**	**327**	**439**	**767**	**898**	**705**	**9**	**74**	**0.40**	**38**	**20**	**42**	**29**	**93**	**133**	**111**	**14%**	**96**	**1%**	**42%**				**4.72**	**7.9**	**36**	**99**	**$8**

Chisenhall,Lonnie

Age: 27	Bats: L	Pos: RF 3B	Health A	LIMA Plan B
Ht: 6' 2"	Wt: 190		PT/Exp C	Rand Var 0
			Consist B	MM 3315

7-44-.246 in 333 AB at CLE. Disappointing. Surged briefly after July recall, but crazy August h% (>50%) shows it wasn't real; xBA paints dimmer 2H picture. If we construct a Frankenstein hitter, plucking best skills from different years, he's a solid contributor. Still at an age when those skills could consolidate, but let's see it first.

Yr	Tm	AB	R	HR	RBI	SB	BA	xBA	OBP	SLG	OPS	vL	vR	bb%	ct%	Eye	G	L	F	h%	HctX	PX	xPX	hr/f	Spd	SBO	SB%	#Wk	DOM	DIS	RC/G	RAR	BPV	BPX	R$
11	CLE *	467	62	12	57	1	242	246	287	388	675	888	640	6	78	0.29	38	20	42	29	103	106	117	10%	107	2%	47%	14	50%	21%	3.72	-20.1	44	98	$8
12	CLE *	260	28	8	29	2	267	275	297	431	729	442	848	4	80	0.21	43	25	32	31	82	110	67	14%	95	5%	67%	9	44%	22%	4.43	-3.2	46	115	$5
13	CLE *	394	48	16	58	3	256	262	302	445	747	408	705	6	79	0.31	38	20	42	29	83	130	93	11%	107	3%	100%	22	68%	23%	4.64	4.1	64	160	$11
14	CLE	478	62	13	59	3	280	261	343	427	770	729	782	8	79	0.39	38	24	38	33	83	109	93	9%	100	3%	75%	27	56%	22%	5.06	15.7	51	138	$16
15	CLE *	490	53	9	61	5	243	237	289	367	657	624	676	6	77	0.28	41	20	40	30	80	91	74	7%	92	5%	83%	21	38%	43%	3.60	-17.0	23	62	$8
1st Half		263	26	6	31	1	234	249	269	377	646	584	584	5	78	0.22	41	21	38	28	88	99	82	7%	87	4%	45%	10	50%	40%	3.34	-11.7	30	81	$6
2nd Half		227	27	3	30	4	254	221	312	356	668	732	759	8	76	0.35	40	18	42	32	69	82	64	6%	104	7%	100%	11	27%	45%	3.90	-6.1	17	46	$10
16	**Proj**	**444**	**52**	**11**	**57**	**4**	**258**	**247**	**310**	**401**	**711**	**648**	**725**	**7**	**78**	**0.33**	**39**	**21**	**40**	**31**	**81**	**100**	**82**	**8%**	**98**	**5%**	**85%**				**4.26**	**-7.2**	**29**	**79**	**$13**

Choo,Shin-Soo

Age: 33	Bats: L	Pos: RF	Health B	LIMA Plan B
Ht: 5' 11"	Wt: 205		PT/Exp A	Rand Var -1
			Consist F	MM 4135

Credited an All-Star break chat with his wife, in which she told him, "just be you," for his turnaround. Good advice, indeed, as 2H was a return to his '13 form in most skills (with some h% fortune thrown in). With his mojo restored, injury years (see '11, '14) appear to be biggest risk going forward. Now 33, that risk is real.

Yr	Tm	AB	R	HR	RBI	SB	BA	xBA	OBP	SLG	OPS	vL	vR	bb%	ct%	Eye	G	L	F	h%	HctX	PX	xPX	hr/f	Spd	SBO	SB%	#Wk	DOM	DIS	RC/G	RAR	BPV	BPX	R$
11	CLE	313	37	8	36	12	259	245	344	390	733	688	757	10	75	0.46	45	22	32	32	116	91	128	10%	96	18%	71%	17	35%	41%	4.44	-6.7	24	53	$9
12	CLE	598	88	16	67	21	283	268	373	441	815	605	926	11	75	0.49	50	23	27	35	99	118	107	13%	82	15%	75%	27	48%	33%	5.64	13.4	42	105	$24
13	CIN	569	107	21	54	20	285	273	423	462	885	612	1011	16	77	0.84	49	21	29	34	96	126	99	16%	113	14%	65%	27	59%	15%	6.46	35.6	76	190	$29
14	TEX	455	58	13	40	3	242	236	340	374	714	673	732	11	71	0.44	50	20	30	31	113	104	110	13%	91	5%	43%	21	33%	43%	4.01	1.5	20	54	$8
15	TEX	555	94	22	82	4	276	267	375	463	838	708	917	12	74	0.52	51	21	28	34	105	130	123	19%	86	3%	67%	27	52%	33%	5.89	17.7	50	135	$21
1st Half		290	38	11	35	0	231	254	315	400	715	481	854	9	73	0.38	52	21	27	28	101	117	118	19%	73	1%	0%	14	36%	43%	3.96	-7.5	27	73	$11
2nd Half		265	56	11	47	4	325	278	435	532	967	938	985	15	74	0.68	50	21	30	40	108	144	127	19%	99	5%	80%	13	69%	23%	8.55	26.3	74	200	$32
16	**Proj**	**520**	**85**	**20**	**75**	**5**	**283**	**262**	**387**	**463**	**850**	**733**	**913**	**13**	**74**	**0.55**	**50**	**21**	**29**	**35**	**106**	**124**	**116**	**18%**	**88**	**5%**	**53%**				**6.04**	**18.1**	**44**	**118**	**$24**

ROD TRUESDELL

Clevenger,Steve

Age: 30	Bats: L	Pos: DH	Health	D	LIMA Plan	D
Ht: 6' 0"	Wt: 195		PT/Exp	F	Rand Var	-4
			Consist	C	MM	1011

2-15-.287 in 101 AB at BAL. Rode Aug hot streak, driven by 39% hit rate, to a PT burst, but predictably cooled. These are far from the worst skills for a backup CA, but he doesn't offer the single-category boost we look for at that spot. Perhaps can help with a few HR, but low FB% caps that. Limited value.

Yr Tm	AB	R	HR	RBI	SB	BA	xBA	OBP	SLG	OPS	vL	vR	bb%	ct%	Eye	G	L	F	h%	HctX	PX	xPX	hr/f	Spd	SBO	SB%	#Wk	DOM	DIS	RC/G	RAR	BPV	BPX	R$
11 CHC *	402	34	5	35	1	258	253	308	374	683	3000	0	7	86	0.53	25	25	50	29	0	82	2	0%	95	1%	100%				3.98	-21.6	55	122	$4
12 CHC	199	16	1	16	0	201	253	260	276	537	138	606	7	80	0.41	52	25	23	25	84	62	76	3%	65	2%	0%	21	33%	43%	2.24	-16.5	8	20	-$3
13 2 TM *	146	21	4	18	0	263	260	332	395	727	667	488	9	83	0.63	61	17	22	29	115	87	96	0%	87	0%	0%	6	33%	50%	4.54	0.2	50	125	$2
14 BAL *	315	26	1	28	1	232	237	285	310	595	429	641	7	82	0.41	49	19	32	28	102	65	88	0%	83	1%	100%	15	33%	40%	2.94	-10.4	21	57	$0
15 BAL *	363	35	6	42	0	267	242	325	362	687	750	739	8	84	0.54	49	19	32	30	114	60	124	7%	108	1%	0%	11	45%	27%	4.03	-14.8	34	92	$6
1st Half	174	15	3	20	0	297	295	369	385	754	2000	900	10	83	0.66	56	33	11	35	0	59	-15	0%	92	2%	0%	2	50%	50%	5.01	-2.1	28	76	$7
2nd Half	189	20	3	22	0	239	242	283	340	624	571	721	6	85	0.42	48	18	34	27	128	60	140	7%	119	0%	0%	9	44%	22%	3.23	-12.5	38	103	$5
16 Proj	194	19	2	21	0	251	247	308	332	641	323	676	8	84	0.50	50	21	29	29	104	56	101	4%	85	1%	40%				3.47	-11.3	11	30	$1

Coghlan,Chris

Age: 31	Bats: L	Pos: LF RF	Health	C	LIMA Plan	B+
Ht: 6' 0"	Wt: 195		PT/Exp	B	Rand Var	+1
			Consist	B	MM	3435

Welcome back, Coghlan. Got us hoping after '14 2H, and followed up well. Most interesting tidbit is the power surge, and it's well-supported by FB% and HctX trends. Spd better than ever at 30, too, and the potential of in-season positional flexiblity (15 games at 2B in '15) a plus. Good bet to sustain.

Yr Tm	AB	R	HR	RBI	SB	BA	xBA	OBP	SLG	OPS	vL	vR	bb%	ct%	Eye	G	L	F	h%	HctX	PX	xPX	hr/f	Spd	SBO	SB%	#Wk	DOM	DIS	RC/G	RAR	BPV	BPX	R$
11 FLA *	341	42	6	27	9	220	269	284	345	628	307	801	8	84	0.54	49	20	32	25	85	92	78	7%	84	22%	55%	12	50%	33%	3.02	-24.0	51	113	$3
12 MIA *	410	40	6	32	7	209	250	287	307	594	186	451	10	83	0.64	63	13	23	24	52	65	28	5%	93	11%	62%	9	11%	33%	2.79	-25.0	34	85	$0
13 MIA	195	10	1	10	2	256	242	318	354	672	861	641	8	78	0.40	50	21	29	32	84	73	65	2%	117	4%	100%	15	33%	53%	3.90	-0.8	23	58	$0
14 CHC *	455	56	9	45	11	268	271	338	420	757	709	832	10	77	0.46	43	26	31	33	99	118	80	9%	111	13%	67%	22	45%	41%	4.86	14.2	57	154	$14
15 CHC	440	64	16	41	11	250	273	341	443	784	348	831	12	79	0.62	46	20	34	28	114	123	126	14%	128	11%	85%	27	48%	19%	5.15	5.6	77	208	$13
1st Half	236	32	8	19	7	254	268	355	428	783	451	818	13	80	0.73	43	21	36	29	100	115	123	12%	116	11%	88%	14	50%	14%	5.24	4.7	73	197	$13
2nd Half	204	32	8	22	4	245	279	323	461	784	232	846	10	77	0.50	49	19	31	28	129	132	129	16%	130	10%	80%	13	46%	23%	5.02	2.8	77	208	$13
16 Proj	441	58	12	41	10	263	268	339	427	766	546	806	10	78	0.52	47	21	32	31	103	108	98	10%	118	10%	77%				4.98	5.4	58	156	$15

Colabello,Chris

Age: 32	Bats: R	Pos: 1B LF	Health	A	LIMA Plan	D+
Ht: 6' 4"	Wt: 220		PT/Exp	C	Rand Var	-5
			Consist	F	MM	4113

15-54-.321 in 333 AB at TOR. Another late-career surger, but there are a lot of signs this won't repeat. For one, once-in-a-lifetime h% means BA will tumble. Plus, xPX doesn't fully buy the power spike; he's still fanning a ton. Would be useful as late-game power source, but probably won't last that long. Let him go.

Yr Tm	AB	R	HR	RBI	SB	BA	xBA	OBP	SLG	OPS	vL	vR	bb%	ct%	Eye	G	L	F	h%	HctX	PX	xPX	hr/f	Spd	SBO	SB%	#Wk	DOM	DIS	RC/G	RAR	BPV	BPX	R$
11																																		
12 aa	496	55	12	69	0	221		271	359	629			6	76	0.29				27		99			76	0%	0%				3.18		21	53	$4
13 MIN *	498	53	22	68	1	243	225	311	421	731	573	655	9	65	0.28	64	14	23	33	71	141	71	30%	79	3%	37%	15	13%	67%	4.33	-4.0	18	45	$11
14 MIN *	418	37	13	66	0	219	213	269	368	637	583	705	6	68	0.22	53	14	34	29	100	127	133	13%	79	2%	0%	14	36%	50%	3.16	-12.5	12	32	$5
15 TOR *	416	66	19	68	2	314	268	361	510	871	935	868	7	71	0.25	48	25	27	40	97	138	94	23%	94	2%	100%	23	61%	30%	6.88	21.7	38	103	$21
1st Half	277	45	11	45	2	319	268	365	496	860	1078	823	7	72	0.25	48	27	25	41	97	126	81	20%	88	2%	100%	10	40%	40%	6.82	12.3	29	78	$27
2nd Half	139	21	8	23	0	302	271	357	540	897	812	942	7	70	0.26	48	22	30	38	97	163	112	28%	103	0%	0%	13	77%	23%	6.97	6.9	57	154	$9
16 Proj	293	37	11	46	1	268	245	323	443	767	720	788	7	70	0.25	52	19	29	35	94	128	107	19%	92	1%	49%				4.91	-2.1	12	32	$11

Collins,Tyler

Age: 26	Bats: L	Pos: LF	Health	A	LIMA Plan	D+
Ht: 5' 11"	Wt: 215		PT/Exp	C	Rand Var	+1
			Consist	A	MM	2213

4-25-.266 in 192 AB at DET. With marginal ct% and thus a low BA ceiling, any value lies in power/speed numbers. He's shown flashes of both at times, reaching both 20 HR and SB in the minors. But profile shows subpar Spd, and hasn't brought hard contact to MLB. Given weak plate skills, he's a shaky bet for more.

Yr Tm	AB	R	HR	RBI	SB	BA	xBA	OBP	SLG	OPS	vL	vR	bb%	ct%	Eye	G	L	F	h%	HctX	PX	xPX	hr/f	Spd	SBO	SB%	#Wk	DOM	DIS	RC/G	RAR	BPV	BPX	R$
11																																		
12																																		
13 aa	466	53	17	62	3	212		274	374	649			8	72	0.31				26		123			78	9%	36%				3.18		28	70	$6
14 DET *	492	52	15	52	9	231	233	289	363	651	400	721	7	74	0.31	35	25	40	28	96	94	148	13%	89	11%	67%	7	14%	57%	3.42	-3.9	14	38	$10
15 DET *	382	34	6	40	9	237	235	292	346	638	643	739	7	77	0.34	40	22	38	29	86	78	108	7%	93	13%	72%	16	38%	44%	3.36	-11.9	16	43	$5
1st Half	186	20	4	18	7	233	225	294	344	638	0	854	8	75	0.34	42	21	37	29	76	73	83	14%	102	17%	86%	5	60%	40%	3.46	-6.2	7	19	$7
2nd Half	196	14	2	22	2	240	244	290	348	638	818	697	7	79	0.34	39	23	38	29	91	83	116	5%	86	9%	45%	11	27%	45%	3.26	-7.7	24	65	$4
16 Proj	356	35	9	39	6	231	236	292	359	651	472	664	8	75	0.33	40	22	38	28	85	88	103	9%	90	12%	65%				3.38	-12.8	14	37	$7

Colon,Christian

Age: 27	Bats: R	Pos: SS	Health	A	LIMA Plan	D
Ht: 5' 10"	Wt: 190		PT/Exp	C	Rand Var	0
			Consist	B	MM	0351

0-6-.290 with 3 SB in 107 AB at KC. Any skills momentum he had entering '15 ground to a halt. Riding the bench in the first half didn't help, but 2H wasn't great, either. Elite ct% still gives hope for this high draft pick, but HctX shows it's all soft stuff, and the pop isn't developing. Looks like UT will remain his position.

Yr Tm	AB	R	HR	RBI	SB	BA	xBA	OBP	SLG	OPS	vL	vR	bb%	ct%	Eye	G	L	F	h%	HctX	PX	xPX	hr/f	Spd	SBO	SB%	#Wk	DOM	DIS	RC/G	RAR	BPV	BPX	R$
11 aa	491	51	5	45	13	226		276	291	567			6	89	0.63				24		41			103	16%	62%				2.57		35	78	$5
12 a/a	290	28	4	24	9	258		315	344	659			8	89	0.80				28		50			107	19%	57%				3.53		47	118	$5
13 aaa	512	57	9	46	12	242		287	326	613			6	88	0.52				26		49			121	12%	72%				3.14		41	103	$10
14 KC *	397	49	6	40	14	268	308	312	369	681	882	851	6	90	0.65	51	28	21	29	74	71	37	0%	106	18%	74%	9	56%	33%	4.00	7.0	63	170	$13
15 KC *	299	23	1	19	9	257	262	318	307	626	746	666	8	88	0.72	44	27	29	29	59	39	32	0%	95	15%	68%	18	17%	44%	3.33	-8.4	28	76	$5
1st Half	87	6	0	4	2	258	249	313	324	638	761	500	7	85	0.53	44	23	33	30	56	56	26	0%	88	13%	67%	12	8%	50%	3.46	-2.0	28	76	-$4
2nd Half	212	17	1	15	7	257	307	321	300	621	667	997	9	89	0.82	46	38	17	29	65	32	47	0%	104	16%	68%	6	33%	33%	3.28	-6.0	30	81	$8
16 Proj	195	19	1	15	6	254	288	308	320	628	577	647	7	88	0.66	45	32	23	28	61	46	39	3%	103	15%	69%				3.34	-4.3	30	80	$5

Conforto,Michael

Age: 23	Bats: L	Pos: LF	Health	A	LIMA Plan	B+
Ht: 6' 1"	Wt: 211		PT/Exp	F	Rand Var	0
			Consist	F	MM	4145

9-26-.270 in 174 AB at NYM. Fast-tracked, and more than held his own given lack of high-minors experience. Outstanding PX well supported by HctX and low GB rate, and while it's more gap power now, there's room for HR growth. A future blue-chipper —and given his current solid level, that's saying something.

Yr Tm	AB	R	HR	RBI	SB	BA	xBA	OBP	SLG	OPS	vL	vR	bb%	ct%	Eye	G	L	F	h%	HctX	PX	xPX	hr/f	Spd	SBO	SB%	#Wk	DOM	DIS	RC/G	RAR	BPV	BPX	R$
11																																		
12																																		
13																																		
14																																		
15 NYM *	347	48	14	48	1	276	273	345	477	822	481	872	10	77	0.47	39	23	39	32	142	136	158	17%	91	2%	46%	12	83%	17%	5.75	10.2	67	181	$11
1st Half	123	15	3	16	1	294	252	373	457	830			11	74	0.49				38		120			99	2%	100%				6.20		47	127	$3
2nd Half	224	33	11	32	0	266	284	330	488	818	481	872	9	79	0.45	39	23	39	29	145	144	158	17%	87	2%	0%	12	83%	17%	5.49	6.0	77	208	$16
16 Proj	442	61	20	61	1	278	279	348	498	847	572	870	10	77	0.47	39	23	39	32	131	148	142	15%	90	2%	55%				6.09	19.2	67	182	$18

Conger,Hank

Age: 28	Bats: B	Pos: CA	Health	A	LIMA Plan	D
Ht: 6' 2"	Wt: 220		PT/Exp	F	Rand Var	0
			Consist	C	MM	3001

A case in point why defense IS important in fantasy. His throwing is so poor (42 of 43 SB attempts were successful), he lost playing time to a clearly inferior hitter. Destroyed RHers all year, and if he could throw out even a modicum of base thieves, could find the strong side of a platoon. But 1 of 43? Not like that.

Yr Tm	AB	R	HR	RBI	SB	BA	xBA	OBP	SLG	OPS	vL	vR	bb%	ct%	Eye	G	L	F	h%	HctX	PX	xPX	hr/f	Spd	SBO	SB%	#Wk	DOM	DIS	RC/G	RAR	BPV	BPX	R$
11 LAA *	277	23	9	36	0	221	230	285	361	646	539	644	8	79	0.43	39	18	44	25	76	95	92	10%	70	0%	0%	21	43%	33%	3.37	-7.0	32	71	$1
12 LAA *	282	32	6	29	1	226	189	260	336	597	0	405	4	79	0.22	58	0	42	27	52	77	28	0%	89	2%	100%	4	25%	0%	2.91	-10.4	15	38	$1
13 LAA	233	23	7	21	0	249	237	310	403	713	629	724	7	74	0.28	39	20	41	31	116	115	135	10%	86	2%	0%	27	44%	41%	4.03	2.1	29	73	$2
14 LAA	231	24	4	25	0	221	210	293	325	618	622	614	9	75	0.39	37	17	47	28	84	86	80	5%	62	4%	0%	27	37%	52%	2.95	-2.6	8	22	$0
15 HOU	201	25	11	33	0	229	249	311	448	759	618	892	10	69	0.37	35	22	44	28	75	158	110	18%	65	2%	0%	26	46%	38%	4.47	4.4	43	116	$3
1st Half	90	10	4	11	0	233	261	330	422	752	575	999	13	70	0.48	31	29	40	29	87	137	114	16%	69	0%	0%	14	50%	50%	4.64	2.3	38	103	-$1
2nd Half	111	15	7	22	0	225	244	296	468	764	669	828	8	68	0.28	38	16	47	26	66	175	108	19%	76	5%	0%	12	42%	25%	4.28	1.7	51	138	$6
16 Proj	223	25	8	30	0	229	232	302	396	698	616	730	9	72	0.35	36	19	44	28	83	119	105	12%	67	2%	3%				3.80	0.2	12	33	$4

ROD TRUESDELL

Correa,Carlos

Age: 21 Bats: R Pos: SS
Ht: 6' 4" Wt: 210

Health	A	LIMA Plan	B+
PT/Exp	F	Rand Var	+1
Consist	F	MM	4255

22-68-.279 with 14 SB in 387 AB at HOU. Monstrous debut from game's youngest hitter. Plate skills, xBA say BA is real; outlook is cloudier for SB, as 2H speed skills fell flat. GB stroke, 2H xPX hint that HR repeat is unlikely as well. Career path looks scary good, though short track record presents first-round risk for 2016.

Yr	Tm	AB	R	HR	RBI	SB	BA	xBA	OBP	SLG	OPS	vL	vR	bb%	ct%	Eye	G	L	F	h%	HctX	PX	xPX	hr/f	Spd	SBO	SB%	#Wk	DOM	DIS	RC/G	RAR	BPV	BPX	R$
11																																			
12																																			
13																																			
14																																			
15	HOU *	602	86	30	102	28	286	301	351	514	866	899	836	9	80	0.50	49	22	29	32	116	145	104	24%	90	21%	84%	18	67%	6%	6.54	36.5	82	222	$36
1st Half		323	50	15	53	19	303	303	353	544	897	1027	856	7	79	0.37	44	24	33	34	127	159	137	25%	102	26%	94%	5	80%	0%	7.34	28.8	91	246	$43
2nd Half		279	36	15	49	9	265	293	347	480	827	820	830	11	80	0.65	50	22	28	28	112	129	91	24%	85	16%	69%	13	62%	8%	5.70	13.3	75	203	$28
16	Proj	**602**	**76**	**26**	**95**	**17**	**285**	**290**	**351**	**488**	**839**	**879**	**818**	**9**	**80**	**0.52**	**48**	**23**	**30**	**32**	**118**	**129**	**109**	**18%**	**91**	**14%**	**74%**				**6.09**	**34.3**	**72**	**194**	**$29**

Cowart,Kaleb

Age: 24 Bats: B Pos: 3B
Ht: 6' 3" Wt: 195

Health	A	LIMA Plan	D
PT/Exp	C	Rand Var	-5
Consist	B	MM	2301

1-4-.174 in 46 AB at LAA. Sputtering minor league career took an upturn at AAA (.323/.395/.491), though h%, hitter-friendly PCL didn't hurt. Suspect ct% was quickly exposed in majors (59%), while xPX and power baseline question HR upside. This is not the skill profile to seek from your future 3B.

Yr	Tm	AB	R	HR	RBI	SB	BA	xBA	OBP	SLG	OPS	vL	vR	bb%	ct%	Eye	G	L	F	h%	HctX	PX	xPX	hr/f	Spd	SBO	SB%	#Wk	DOM	DIS	RC/G	RAR	BPV	BPX	R$
11																																			
12																																			
13	aa	498	42	5	37	12	201		249	270	520			6	73	0.24				27		57			92	16%	69%				2.14		-20	-50	$0
14	aa	435	42	5	48	23	205		266	293	559			8	75	0.33				26		69			103	30%	75%				2.53		4	11	$7
15	LAA *	266	32	5	35	2	250	205	312	367	679	340	685	8	64	0.25	59	11	30	37	41	97	40	13%	100	6%	52%	7	0%	71%	3.81	-5.9	-15	-41	$4
1st Half		79	5	1	12	1	228	203	297	349	646			9	63	0.27				34		98			121	9%	37%				3.26		-13	-35	-$6
2nd Half		187	27	4	23	2	260	205	319	375	693	340	685	8	65	0.25	59	11	30	38	41	97	40	13%	95	5%	63%	7	0%	71%	4.07	-3.0	-15	-41	$8
16	Proj	**161**	**17**	**3**	**19**	**4**	**226**	**219**	**286**	**339**	**626**	**436**	**768**	**8**	**69**	**0.28**	**55**	**15**	**30**	**31**	**37**	**86**	**36**	**9%**	**101**	**17%**	**70%**				**3.17**	**-7.3**	**-7**	**-19**	**$3**

Cozart,Zack

Age: 30 Bats: R Pos: SS
Ht: 6' 0" Wt: 195

Health	F	LIMA Plan	B
PT/Exp	C	Rand Var	+1
Consist	D	MM	2325

Knee injury in June derailed potential career year. Eye continued its ascent as BA gains came with full xBA support. Ditto for power spike, as he hit more FB and PX took off in lockstep with xPX. Recovery could leak into spring, and mediocre BPV history trumps two good months, but late flyer could yield profit.

Yr	Tm	AB	R	HR	RBI	SB	BA	xBA	OBP	SLG	OPS	vL	vR	bb%	ct%	Eye	G	L	F	h%	HctX	PX	xPX	hr/f	Spd	SBO	SB%	#Wk	DOM	DIS	RC/G	RAR	BPV	BPX	R$
11	CIN *	360	47	8	26	6	260	248	292	389	681	667	880	4	81	0.24	58	10	32	30	115	92	163	20%	126	11%	73%	3	33%	67%	3.89	-6.4	46	102	$7
12	CIN	561	72	15	35	4	246	254	288	399	687	699	683	5	80	0.27	42	20	38	28	83	102	86	9%	134	3%	100%	26	35%	19%	3.89	-3.5	54	135	$8
13	CIN	567	74	12	63	0	254	255	284	381	665	686	658	4	82	0.25	50	18	32	29	83	88	63	8%	115	0%	0%	27	48%	19%	3.73	3.8	44	110	$11
14	CIN	506	48	4	38	7	221	231	268	300	568	702	532	5	84	0.32	45	18	38	26	84	55	77	3%	138	6%	100%	27	33%	33%	2.60	-10.6	34	92	$2
15	CIN	194	28	9	28	3	258	276	310	459	769	931	718	7	85	0.48	39	19	42	26	95	117	119	13%	101	14%	50%	10	60%	10%	4.61	4.9	79	214	$5
1st Half		194	28	9	28	3	258	276	310	459	769	931	718	7	85	0.48	39	19	42	26	95	117	119	13%	101	14%	50%	10	60%	10%	4.61	3.0	79	214	$5
2nd Half																																			
16	Proj	**497**	**63**	**13**	**51**	**5**	**252**	**256**	**294**	**393**	**687**	**771**	**661**	**5**	**83**	**0.33**	**44**	**19**	**37**	**28**	**87**	**89**	**86**	**8%**	**118**	**7%**	**66%**				**3.88**	**-3.0**	**42**	**114**	**$13**

Crawford,Brandon

Age: 29 Bats: L Pos: SS
Ht: 6' 2" Wt: 215

Health	A	LIMA Plan	A
PT/Exp	B	Rand Var	0
Consist	B	MM	4135

Posted career highs in every 5x5 category, and repeat odds are decent: HctX soared to new levels, while xBA hints at even more BA upside; 2014's xPX predicted power spike, and 2015's says he can sustain it. Still under 30, and stable skills growth, consistency net him a seat among NL's top shortstops.

Yr	Tm	AB	R	HR	RBI	SB	BA	xBA	OBP	SLG	OPS	vL	vR	bb%	ct%	Eye	G	L	F	h%	HctX	PX	xPX	hr/f	Spd	SBO	SB%	#Wk	DOM	DIS	RC/G	RAR	BPV	BPX	R$
11	SF *	303	30	4	27	4	197	224	266	279	545	445	608	9	82	0.52	51	14	35	23	75	55	79	5%	108	13%	44%	14	36%	43%	2.22	-22.2	24	53	-$2
12	SF	435	44	4	45	1	248	246	304	349	653	631	661	7	78	0.35	47	23	30	31	98	77	85	4%	87	5%	20%	27	26%	41%	3.44	-8.6	17	43	$4
13	SF	499	52	9	43	1	248	246	311	363	674	546	727	8	81	0.44	49	19	33	29	83	80	78	7%	105	2%	33%	27	41%	41%	3.72	3.2	36	90	$6
14	SF	491	54	10	69	5	246	229	324	389	713	879	637	11	74	0.46	38	20	42	32	91	103	126	6%	127	6%	63%	27	48%	37%	4.26	14.1	39	105	$11
15	SF	507	65	21	84	6	256	274	321	462	782	716	808	7	77	0.33	48	19	34	30	111	137	137	16%	83	9%	60%	27	48%	15%	4.80	15.4	57	154	$16
1st Half		283	39	12	49	4	265	278	339	473	812	977	768	8	78	0.40	47	20	33	30	115	134	132	16%	92	9%	67%	14	57%	7%	5.26	9.7	64	173	$21
2nd Half		224	26	9	35	2	246	267	298	446	744	523	871	6	75	0.25	49	17	34	29	106	140	142	16%	76	9%	50%	13	38%	23%	4.24	1.1	48	130	$10
16	Proj	**528**	**64**	**20**	**76**	**5**	**261**	**263**	**325**	**452**	**777**	**734**	**795**	**8**	**77**	**0.37**	**46**	**19**	**35**	**31**	**99**	**125**	**120**	**14%**	**95**	**7%**	**55%**				**4.90**	**12.5**	**50**	**136**	**$18**

Crawford,Carl

Age: 34 Bats: L Pos: LF
Ht: 6' 2" Wt: 225

Health	F	LIMA Plan	C+
PT/Exp	D	Rand Var	0
Consist	B	MM	2433

4-16-.265 with 10 SB in 181 AB at LA. Torn oblique puts DL streak at five years. BPV continued to fall thanks to more Ks, while xBA puts BA recovery in doubt. Still runs enough to provide SB value, and xPX hints there's some life left in his bat, but erosion of skills (and body) make this $20M man a major risk.

Yr	Tm	AB	R	HR	RBI	SB	BA	xBA	OBP	SLG	OPS	vL	vR	bb%	ct%	Eye	G	L	F	h%	HctX	PX	xPX	hr/f	Spd	SBO	SB%	#Wk	DOM	DIS	RC/G	RAR	BPV	BPX	R$
11	BOS	506	65	11	56	18	255	261	289	405	694	566	757	4	79	0.22	48	18	34	30	102	104	112	8%	111	23%	75%	23	30%	26%	3.95	-19.7	45	100	$14
12	BOS *	139	26	3	20	6	285	291	310	460	771	856	750	4	82	0.21	54	19	27	33	103	113	95	12%	113	22%	100%	6	50%	33%	5.38	2.5	63	158	$5
13	LA	435	62	6	31	15	283	278	329	407	736	551	796	6	85	0.42	47	23	30	32	104	89	90	5%	120	17%	79%	23	43%	22%	4.75	8.5	60	150	$16
14	LA	343	56	8	46	23	300	286	339	429	767	881	745	4	84	0.29	46	28	26	34	96	85	79	11%	114	31%	79%	22	41%	36%	5.21	13.7	49	132	$22
15	LA *	211	24	5	20	10	267	259	302	408	710	678	712	5	79	0.24	43	24	33	32	106	93	108	9%	99	24%	83%	16	31%	31%	4.37	-2.1	30	81	$7
1st Half		53	4	1	3	0	272	280	286	439	725	333	715	2	81	0.10	46	23	31	32	110	110	94	8%	98	0%	0%	4	50%	25%	4.39	-0.3	48	130	-$8
2nd Half		158	20	4	17	10	266	252	308	398	706	772	710	6	78	0.28	42	25	34	32	105	87	113	9%	96	30%	83%	12	25%	33%	4.38	-0.9	23	62	$12
16	Proj	**267**	**35**	**6**	**27**	**12**	**266**	**272**	**303**	**408**	**710**	**669**	**720**	**5**	**81**	**0.26**	**45**	**24**	**30**	**31**	**103**	**92**	**96**	**9%**	**105**	**24%**	**82%**				**4.30**	**-2.0**	**52**	**140**	**$11**

Crawford,J.P.

Age: 21 Bats: L Pos: DH
Ht: 6' 2" Wt: 180

Health	A	LIMA Plan	D+
PT/Exp	F	Rand Var	0
Consist	F	MM	2421

Fast-rising prospect destroyed High-A (.392/.489/.443) before spending rest of year at Double-A. Fine plate approach bodes well for ability to hit at MLB level, though power will need time to develop. Don't let success of 2015's rookies drive unrealistic expectations for 2016, but long-term future appears bright.

Yr	Tm	AB	R	HR	RBI	SB	BA	xBA	OBP	SLG	OPS	vL	vR	bb%	ct%	Eye	G	L	F	h%	HctX	PX	xPX	hr/f	Spd	SBO	SB%	#Wk	DOM	DIS	RC/G	RAR	BPV	BPX	R$
11																																			
12																																			
13																																			
14																																			
15	aa	351	43	4	27	6	241		319	364	683			10	86	0.81				27		78			123	8%	73%				3.89		65	176	$4
1st Half		144	17	2	10	2	246		340	362	702			13	88	1.16				27		74			127	8%	43%				3.99		75	203	$0
2nd Half		207	26	3	17	4	237		303	366	669			9	84	0.61				27		80			141	8%	100%				3.82		64	173	$7
16	Proj	**191**	**23**	**3**	**15**	**3**	**244**	**253**	**314**	**372**	**686**	**686**	**686**	**9**	**84**	**0.64**	**41**	**20**	**39**	**28**		**81**		**4%**	**138**	**9%**	**76%**				**3.95**	**-8.5**	**56**	**150**	**$4**

Crisp,Coco

Age: 36 Bats: B Pos: LF
Ht: 5' 10" Wt: 185

Health	F	LIMA Plan	D+
PT/Exp	C	Rand Var	+5
Consist	D	MM	1313

Started year on DL (elbow), then lingering neck issue returned for second straight season. Previously stable BPV, plate skills offer hope for rebound, but declining SBO caps his best skill, and 2013's HR total sticks out as an outlier. This profile doesn't age well, and injury risk adds to the pessimism.

Yr	Tm	AB	R	HR	RBI	SB	BA	xBA	OBP	SLG	OPS	vL	vR	bb%	ct%	Eye	G	L	F	h%	HctX	PX	xPX	hr/f	Spd	SBO	SB%	#Wk	DOM	DIS	RC/G	RAR	BPV	BPX	R$
11	OAK	531	69	8	54	49	264	273	314	379	693	593	741	7	88	0.63	42	24	34	29	108	75	83	5%	108	41%	84%	26	62%	15%	4.37	-8.7	60	133	$25
12	OAK	455	68	11	46	39	259	274	325	418	742	682	774	9	86	0.70	44	20	36	28	88	95	76	8%	125	36%	91%	26	38%	27%	5.03	6.1	77	193	$22
13	OAK	513	93	22	66	21	261	278	335	444	779	645	857	11	87	0.94	41	20	40	26	91	107	85	12%	108	18%	81%	25	56%	16%	5.27	19.4	91	228	$25
14	OAK	463	68	9	47	19	246	252	336	363	699	640	726	12	86	1.00	39	20	40	27	88	79	76	6%	103	16%	79%	26	54%	23%	4.25	7.8	64	173	$15
15	OAK	126	11	0	6	2	175	209	252	222	474	531	448	9	80	0.52	44	18	39	22	56	43	49	0%	91	7%	100%	13	8%	46%	1.80	-10.5	3	8	-$4
1st Half		45	4	0	0	1	44	159	173	67	240	410	147	13	78	0.70	51	6	43	6	59	21	63	0%	84	13%	100%	3	0%	67%	0.36	-7.1	-18	-49	-$9
2nd Half		81	7	0	6	1	247	238	299	309	607	613	605	7	81	0.40	39	24	36	30	54	55	42	0%	98	5%	100%	10	10%	40%	3.19	-3.3	15	41	-$1
16	Proj	**280**	**34**	**4**	**22**	**9**	**235**	**237**	**319**	**327**	**646**	**635**	**650**	**11**	**84**	**0.80**	**42**	**19**	**39**	**27**	**73**	**62**	**65**	**4%**	**98**	**13%**	**86%**				**3.61**	**-8.1**	**41**	**110**	**$6**

RYAN BLOOMFIELD

Cron,C.J.

Age: 26 Bats: R Pos: 1B DH | Ht: 6' 4" Wt: 235
Health A | PT/Exp C | Consist B | LIMA Plan B+ | Rand Var 0 | MM 4135

16-51-.262 in 378 AB at LAA. Found his stroke in 2H, though we've seen this before—hit .290 w/174 PX in 1H of 2014, only to falter after that (.216, 94 PX). Poor eye could leave him susceptible to continued inconsistency. Should deliver HR/RBI value, but average HctX, low LD% suggest BA won't be part of package.

Yr Tm	AB	R	HR	RBI	SB	BA	xBA	OBP	SLG	OPS	vL	vR	bb%	ct%	Eye	G	L	F	h%	HctX	PX	xPX	hr/f	Spd	SBO	SB%	#Wk	DOM	DIS	RC/G	RAR	BPV	BPX	R$
11																																		
12																																		
13 aa	519	48	11	71	7	242		269	372	641			4	82	0.20				28		93			78	11%	60%				3.29		35	88	$10
14 LAA *	432	46	15	57	1	250	255	283	413	697	751	731	4	75	0.18	35	25	40	30	111	123	122	15%	80	3%	50%	20	45%	45%	3.94	-1.3	32	86	$10
15 LAA *	471	47	20	66	3	260	263	290	448	738	672	774	4	79	0.20	44	18	37	29	95	119	107	14%	78	4%	75%	25	44%	32%	4.47	-13.4	44	119	$13
1st Half	223	21	7	30	0	245	250	260	408	668	714	557	2	79	0.10	40	19	41	28	95	110	97	7%	85	0%	0%	12	25%	50%	3.58	-12.3	35	95	$7
2nd Half	248	26	13	36	3	274	272	320	484	803	644	875	6	79	0.29	47	18	35	30	95	128	111	19%	77	7%	75%	13	62%	15%	5.34	-0.8	55	149	$19
16 Proj	536	54	23	74	3	256	265	293	448	741	719	753	4	78	0.20	40	21	38	29	101	124	112	14%	80	5%	67%				4.38	-12.2	40	107	$15

Cruz,Nelson

Age: 36 Bats: R Pos: RF DH | Ht: 6' 2" Wt: 230
Health A | PT/Exp A | Consist B | LIMA Plan B+ | Rand Var -5 | MM 4135

Continues to defy our projections while accumulating risk factors: 1) 2nd year of big PX/xPX gap, 2) falling FB%, 3) lowest ct% since 2007, 4) lowest HctX since 2008, 5) and now he's 36. Sky-high hr/f made the difference in 2015, and THAT was 9 points higher than prior career best. Don't confuse elite with indestructible.

Yr Tm	AB	R	HR	RBI	SB	BA	xBA	OBP	SLG	OPS	vL	vR	bb%	ct%	Eye	G	L	F	h%	HctX	PX	xPX	hr/f	Spd	SBO	SB%	#Wk	DOM	DIS	RC/G	RAR	BPV	BPX	R$
11 TEX *	497	66	31	90	9	262	278	311	512	823	1096	747	7	76	0.30	41	16	43	28	120	168	144	19%	75	13%	64%	24	71%	17%	5.36	-6.8	78	173	$21
12 TEX	585	86	24	90	8	260	262	319	460	779	944	727	8	76	0.34	41	18	41	30	129	141	151	13%	84	9%	67%	27	48%	19%	4.94	0.9	60	150	$20
13 TEX	413	49	27	76	5	266	264	327	506	833	821	837	8	74	0.32	42	17	41	30	120	162	154	21%	64	6%	83%	20	70%	25%	5.71	14.4	61	153	$18
14 BAL	613	87	40	108	4	271	285	333	525	859	977	823	8	77	0.39	42	17	41	29	119	173	131	20%	89	6%	44%	27	63%	15%	5.91	33.0	92	249	$30
15 SEA	590	90	44	93	3	302	277	369	566	936	1107	866	9	72	0.36	46	20	34	35	113	169	138	30%	86	3%	60%	26	50%	31%	7.49	33.1	70	189	$33
1st Half	303	41	21	50	1	304	270	364	554	919	1321	830	8	74	0.36	42	20	38	35	106	156	136	24%	95	3%	33%	14	43%	29%	7.19	14.6	69	186	$32
2nd Half	287	49	23	43	2	300	283	375	578	953	1005	919	10	70	0.36	50	21	29	35	121	184	140	39%	75	2%	100%	12	58%	33%	7.80	18.5	71	192	$33
16 Proj	551	80	34	92	4	273	267	339	506	845	969	798	9	74	0.36	44	19	37	31	118	150	140	22%	82	5%	63%				5.90	17.1	53	144	$27

Cuddyer,Michael

Age: 37 Bats: R Pos: LF | Ht: 6' 2" Wt: 220
Health F | PT/Exp C | Consist F | LIMA Plan C+ | Rand Var +1 | MM 3343

Retained F health grade with injuries to hand, neck, knee, wrist... one more punch and his next injury is free! This batch of boo-boos plus the expected Coors withdrawal extended the damage to his peripherals, with career lows in bb%, Eye, xBA, and OPS. Age raises the odds against a full rebound. Buy low or bow out.

Yr Tm	AB	R	HR	RBI	SB	BA	xBA	OBP	SLG	OPS	vL	vR	bb%	ct%	Eye	G	L	F	h%	HctX	PX	xPX	hr/f	Spd	SBO	SB%	#Wk	DOM	DIS	RC/G	RAR	BPV	BPX	R$
11 MIN	529	70	20	70	11	284	277	346	459	805	993	728	8	82	0.51	49	18	34	31	105	116	108	14%	99	8%	92%	26	54%	19%	5.71	-8.2	69	153	$21
12 COL	358	53	16	58	8	260	296	317	489	806	929	760	8	78	0.41	49	20	31	29	118	155	125	18%	91	14%	73%	19	58%	21%	5.34	-0.8	83	208	$13
13 COL	489	74	20	84	10	331	287	389	530	919	815	954	9	80	0.46	50	20	30	38	100	134	101	17%	118	8%	77%	26	65%	23%	7.83	42.0	80	200	$31
14 COL	190	32	10	31	3	332	332	376	579	955	1287	830	7	84	0.47	48	24	27	35	111	165	106	23%	106	6%	100%	10	70%	10%	8.46	21.3	116	314	$12
15 NYM	379	44	10	41	2	259	252	309	391	699	701	698	6	77	0.27	49	22	29	31	102	90	98	12%	92	2%	100%	24	25%	50%	4.10	-13.9	21	57	$7
1st Half	271	31	6	28	1	236	239	289	354	643	614	650	6	74	0.25	52	21	28	30	107	85	100	11%	98	2%	100%	14	21%	43%	3.37	-14.5	7	19	$8
2nd Half	108	13	4	13	1	315	286	359	481	840	814	856	5	84	0.35	42	25	33	34	89	103	93	13%	77	3%	100%	10	30%	60%	6.35	3.5	55	149	$5
16 Proj	360	50	11	50	3	276	278	327	439	766	836	736	7	81	0.37	47	23	30	31	102	107	101	13%	98	3%	83%				5.03	4.8	47	128	$14

Cuthbert,Cheslor

Age: 23 Bats: R Pos: 3B | Ht: 6' 1" Wt: 190
Health A | PT/Exp C | Consist B | LIMA Plan D | Rand Var 0 | MM 1321

1-8-.217 in 46 AB at KC. Forgettable debut, but wasn't given much of a look. Encouraging trends in ct%, Eye, and maybe even some stealth speed. At his age, would like to see more signs of power that scouts have been promising. Not so much banging on door as politely knocking, but 2H OPS, ct% are reasons to keep the faith.

Yr Tm	AB	R	HR	RBI	SB	BA	xBA	OBP	SLG	OPS	vL	vR	bb%	ct%	Eye	G	L	F	h%	HctX	PX	xPX	hr/f	Spd	SBO	SB%	#Wk	DOM	DIS	RC/G	RAR	BPV	BPX	R$
11																																		
12																																		
13 aa	237	20	4	23	4	196		247	315	563			6	78	0.31				23		93			83	14%	65%				2.43		26	65	-$2
14 a/a	446	36	9	49	8	243		297	355	652			7	81	0.41				28		83			82	11%	64%				3.49		33	89	$8
15 KC *	443	51	10	50	4	247	263	300	371	671	636	660	7	84	0.47	46	22	32	28	50	80	39	8%	107	6%	65%	8	25%	25%	3.74	-10.8	47	127	$8
1st Half	285	25	6	27	2	230	244	283	342	625			7	83	0.42				26		73			90	7%	53%	1	0%	0%	3.13		31	84	$6
2nd Half	158	26	3	23	2	277	279	331	425	756	636	660	8	86	0.57	46	22	32	31	51	92	39	8%	122	4%	100%	7	29%	29%	5.03	1.8	69	186	$9
16 Proj	195	21	3	23	3	254	257	308	368	676	736	631	7	82	0.44	46	22	32	29	46	77	35	6%	112	8%	71%				3.86	-4.4	29	79	$5

D Arnaud,Travis

Age: 27 Bats: R Pos: CA | Ht: 6' 2" Wt: 210
Health D | PT/Exp F | Consist B | LIMA Plan B | Rand Var 0 | MM 3235

12-41-.268 in 239 AB at NYM. Injuries were the story again, as wrist, elbow problems cost him more than half the season. Growth in FB%, hr/f was encouraging, though xPX suggests the power wasn't quite as good as it looked. Health grade means you can't pay full price for it, but ... UP: 20 HR, .285 BA (still)

Yr Tm	AB	R	HR	RBI	SB	BA	xBA	OBP	SLG	OPS	vL	vR	bb%	ct%	Eye	G	L	F	h%	HctX	PX	xPX	hr/f	Spd	SBO	SB%	#Wk	DOM	DIS	RC/G	RAR	BPV	BPX	R$
11 aa	424	61	19	66	3	290		334	504	838			6	74	0.25				35		160			83	6%	61%				5.97		63	140	$18
12 aaa	279	31	12	36	1	287		318	492	810			4	76	0.19				34		139			89	3%	38%				5.51		52	130	$8
13 NYM *	182	18	3	15	0	208	225	315	325	639	298	630	13	74	0.61	47	18	35	26	70	93	74	4%	89	0%	0%	7	29%	43%	3.29	-2.2	28	70	-$2
14 NYM *	448	58	18	53	1	252	286	305	447	752	707	722	7	84	0.49	42	20	39	26	122	130	136	10%	85	1%	100%	23	57%	17%	4.66	15.8	83	224	$12
15 NYM *	267	33	12	42	0	260	270	319	461	780	1112	758	8	80	0.43	37	21	42	29	101	127	107	15%	79	0%	0%	16	56%	19%	5.07	9.7	62	168	$6
1st Half	79	11	4	17	0	275	276	301	499	801	400	908	4	83	0.22	36	20	44	29	102	129	128	15%	88	0%	0%	5	40%	0%	5.30	3.4	71	192	$1
2nd Half	188	22	8	25	0	254	266	326	444	770	1197	681	10	78	0.49	37	22	40	29	100	126	97	15%	82	0%	0%	11	64%	27%	4.95	6.4	60	162	$9
16 Proj	424	52	16	59	0	260	265	325	444	769	805	760	8	80	0.44	40	20	40	29	104	119	113	12%	83	1%	72%				4.90	13.8	50	134	$13

Davis,Chris

Age: 30 Bats: L Pos: 1B RF DH | Ht: 6' 3" Wt: 230
Health A | PT/Exp A | Consist F | LIMA Plan B+ | Rand Var 0 | MM 5035

Okay, so maybe 2014 was more about the oblique injury than we thought. HctX, xPX, hr/f bounced all the way back, and xBA came close enough. 2016 home address will be important—since 2012, 10.9 AB/HR at Camden Yards, 16.7 on the road. Could be a dozen HRs hanging in the balance.

Yr Tm	AB	R	HR	RBI	SB	BA	xBA	OBP	SLG	OPS	vL	vR	bb%	ct%	Eye	G	L	F	h%	HctX	PX	xPX	hr/f	Spd	SBO	SB%	#Wk	DOM	DIS	RC/G	RAR	BPV	BPX	R$
11 2 AL *	398	58	26	71	2	299	278	333	559	892	906	657	5	67	0.16	38	25	37	39	105	202	137	10%	85	2%	100%	16	31%	56%	6.80	12.7	67	149	$20
12 BAL	515	75	33	85	2	270	252	326	501	827	792	836	7	67	0.22	39	23	38	34	102	162	150	25%	74	4%	40%	27	41%	37%	5.46	2.6	36	90	$20
13 BAL	584	103	53	138	4	286	297	370	634	1004	763	1142	11	66	0.36	32	22	46	34	112	266	199	30%	66	3%	80%	27	78%	11%	8.24	59.5	120	300	$38
14 BAL	450	65	26	72	2	196	235	300	404	704	677	716	12	62	0.35	35	25	41	25	96	174	154	23%	65	3%	67%	22	36%	36%	3.71	-6.1	31	84	$8
15 BAL	573	100	47	117	2	262	271	361	562	923	799	984	13	64	0.40	32	25	43	32	116	224	196	29%	60	3%	40%	27	56%	22%	6.80	31.1	80	216	$28
1st Half	287	43	18	51	0	237	249	325	474	799	844	783	12	64	0.37	32	25	43	30	111	178	194	22%	63	0%	0%	14	43%	21%	5.16	0.1	43	116	$18
2nd Half	286	57	29	66	2	287	293	396	650	1047	767	1220	14	63	0.44	31	25	44	35	122	270	198	37%	66	6%	40%	13	69%	23%	8.68	28.6	119	322	$38
16 Proj	556	93	41	110	3	254	262	348	529	877	762	933	12	64	0.37	33	24	43	32	110	206	181	27%	64	3%	52%				6.10	15.5	59	161	$27

Davis,Ike

Age: 29 Bats: L Pos: 1B | Ht: 6' 4" Wt: 220
Health F | PT/Exp D | Consist B | LIMA Plan D+ | Rand Var +2 | MM 3013

3-20-.229 in 214 AB at OAK. Torn labrum in hip ended season early, though May quad injury may have done the job first—122 xPX and .286 xBA before quad injury, 87 and .200 after. Last couple seasons have been ugly, but career 132 PX vs. RHP suggests he still has value as platoon player. Good chance he's available cheap.

Yr Tm	AB	R	HR	RBI	SB	BA	xBA	OBP	SLG	OPS	vL	vR	bb%	ct%	Eye	G	L	F	h%	HctX	PX	xPX	hr/f	Spd	SBO	SB%	#Wk	DOM	DIS	RC/G	RAR	BPV	BPX	R$
11 NYM	129	20	7	25	0	302	277	383	543	925	493	1142	12	76	0.55	42	17	41	35	119	165	126	17%	107	0%	0%	7	71%	29%	7.61	6.9	93	207	$5
12 NYM	519	66	32	90	0	227	262	308	462	771	560	868	11	73	0.43	39	21	40	25	124	157	166	21%	60	2%	0%	27	48%	30%	4.63	-10.3	58	145	$12
13 NYM *	392	49	13	41	4	207	229	323	358	680	406	727	15	68	0.54	45	20	35	27	77	119	99	12%	79	3%	100%	20	35%	50%	3.77	-9.9	23	58	$3
14 2 NL	360	43	11	51	0	233	255	344	378	722	265	765	15	78	0.81	40	23	37	27	110	107	121	10%	81	3%	0%	27	48%	26%	4.19	0.5	55	149	$6
15 OAK *	235	20	3	24	0	226	246	295	340	634	579	658	9	79	0.46	52	20	28	27	97	90	105	6%	74	0%	0%	16	50%	31%	3.29	-11.6	29	78	-$1
1st Half	161	18	3	20	0	255	266	318	390	708	417	775	9	81	0.50	50	21	29	30	112	99	126	9%	82	0%	0%	10	60%	30%	4.25	-4.3	48	130	$3
2nd Half	74	2	0	4	0	162	178	244	230	474	857	434	10	73	0.40	57	17	26	22	66	67	59	0%	75	0%	0%	6	33%	33%	1.71	-8.4	-10	-27	-$8
16 Proj	339	32	9	38	1	242	240	330	383	713	506	743	12	75	0.55	46	20	34	30	93	103	103	10%	73	2%	34%				4.23	-9.4	17	45	$6

BRANDON KRUSE

Davis,Khristopher

Age: 28	Bats: R	Pos: LF	Health B	LIMA Plan A
Ht: 5' 11"	Wt: 190		PT/Exp C	Rand Var +1
			Consist B	MM 5235

Was slow to find power stroke, then May knee injury sidelined him for 5 weeks. Came back and tore through final 183 AB with 20 HR, and a .612 SLG. Power explosion came with some 2H ct% erosion, but xBA eases concerns. Gains in bb% and vR encouraging, and full-time role should no longer be in question, so... UP: 40 HR

Yr	Tm	AB	R	HR	RBI	SB	BA	xBA	OBP	SLG	OPS	vL	vR	bb%	ct%	Eye	G	L	F	h%	HctX	PX	xPX	hr/f	Spd	SBO	SB%	#Wk	DOM	DIS	RC/G	RAR	BPV	BPX	R$
11	aa	124	8	2	12	0	180		228	281	509			6	78	0.29				22		77			94	0%	0%				2.00		17	38	-$4
12	a/a	241	36	11	37	2	305		387	516	903			12	70	0.45				40		160			80	6%	50%				7.13		58	145	$10
13	MIL *	379	51	21	52	7	233	265	294	455	749	1009	918	8	72	0.31	43	20	37	27	141	158	162	29%	95	15%	60%	16	63%	25%	4.30	2.8	61	153	$11
14	MIL	501	70	22	69	4	244	278	299	457	756	777	749	6	76	0.26	39	21	40	28	132	161	158	14%	89	5%	80%	26	54%	23%	4.45	9.9	72	195	$15
15	MIL	392	54	27	66	6	247	260	323	505	828	729	864	10	69	0.36	42	17	40	29	105	174	168	25%	92	8%	75%	22	64%	18%	5.51	9.2	64	173	$15
1st Half		148	16	5	16	0	250	246	337	446	783	509	875	11	72	0.46	37	19	44	31	109	140	165	10%	101	0%	0%	9	56%	33%	5.08	2.3	56	151	-$3
2nd Half		244	38	22	50	6	246	267	314	541	855	853	855	9	67	0.31	46	16	38	27	102	197	171	35%	81	14%	75%	13	69%	8%	5.72	8.5	70	189	$25
16	Proj	**525**	**70**	**33**	**83**	**7**	**251**	**269**	**321**	**502**	**823**	**795**	**833**	**8**	**72**	**0.33**	**41**	**19**	**40**	**29**	**120**	**169**	**164**	**22%**	**92**	**8%**	**70%**				**5.33**	**11.9**	**65**	**175**	**$20**

Davis,Rajai

Age: 35	Bats: R	Pos: CF LF	Health B	LIMA Plan C+
Ht: 5' 9"	Wt: 195		PT/Exp C	Rand Var 0
			Consist A	MM 2523

Aggressive approach in 2H led to decent power numbers, but had negative effect on rest of his game, including massive drop in production vs LHP. Spd spiked thanks to career high 11 triples, but loss of PT, further deterioration of SBO, SB% left him well short on steals. Not at an age where a full rebound is likely.

Yr	Tm	AB	R	HR	RBI	SB	BA	xBA	OBP	SLG	OPS	vL	vR	bb%	ct%	Eye	G	L	F	h%	HctX	PX	xPX	hr/f	Spd	SBO	SB%	#Wk	DOM	DIS	RC/G	RAR	BPV	BPX	R$
11	TOR	320	44	1	29	34	238	238	273	350	623	829	551	4	80	0.24	44	16	40	29	66	85	50	1%	151	71%	76%	20	35%	45%	3.12	-18.0	45	100	$11
12	TOR	447	64	8	43	46	257	248	309	378	687	783	638	6	77	0.28	45	23	32	32	80	86	75	7%	120	54%	78%	27	26%	44%	3.95	-8.3	28	70	$22
13	TOR	331	49	6	24	45	260	241	312	375	687	857	594	6	80	0.31	39	23	38	31	90	81	84	6%	129	61%	88%	23	26%	30%	4.34	3.5	36	90	$23
14	DET	461	64	8	51	36	282	269	320	401	721	939	617	5	84	0.29	50	19	31	32	73	88	57	7%	105	41%	77%	26	46%	23%	4.46	10.2	48	130	$26
15	DET	341	55	8	30	18	258	265	306	440	746	758	738	6	78	0.29	44	22	33	31	97	111	78	9%	178	35%	69%	26	50%	38%	4.39	0.0	67	181	$13
1st Half		177	29	2	12	14	277	290	338	441	779	885	716	8	82	0.52	52	24	24	33	101	96	58	6%	171	36%	82%	14	57%	29%	5.36	4.1	77	208	$15
2nd Half		164	26	6	18	4	238	240	270	439	709	642	764	4	73	0.13	35	21	44	29	92	130	101	11%	153	32%	44%	12	42%	50%	3.42	-5.8	49	132	$11
16	Proj	**298**	**45**	**6**	**28**	**18**	**261**	**256**	**305**	**412**	**717**	**798**	**669**	**5**	**79**	**0.27**	**44**	**21**	**35**	**31**	**87**	**97**	**75**	**8%**	**156**	**37%**	**71%**				**4.12**	**-2.6**	**56**	**152**	**$14**

De Aza,Alejandro

Age: 32	Bats: L	Pos: LF RF	Health A	LIMA Plan D+
Ht: 6' 0"	Wt: 195		PT/Exp B	Rand Var -1
			Consist B	MM 2411

Posted career high FB%, but by year's end, power metrics weren't much different than recent history. Speed still intact, but SB% has fallen, and now that he can't touch LHP, locking down regular AB has become a challenge. Double digit SB are no longer a given.

Yr	Tm	AB	R	HR	RBI	SB	BA	xBA	OBP	SLG	OPS	vL	vR	bb%	ct%	Eye	G	L	F	h%	HctX	PX	xPX	hr/f	Spd	SBO	SB%	#Wk	DOM	DIS	RC/G	RAR	BPV	BPX	R$
11	CHW *	537	78	12	51	29	285	266	340	440	780	702	951	8	77	0.36	49	20	31	35	98	115	81	11%	139	33%	61%	10	60%	20%	4.92	-3.5	58	129	$24
12	CHW	524	81	9	50	26	281	259	349	410	760	700	779	8	79	0.43	42	26	32	34	99	88	96	7%	123	25%	68%	24	42%	29%	4.79	-5.4	42	105	$22
13	CHW	607	84	17	62	20	264	250	323	405	728	816	702	8	76	0.34	41	25	35	32	74	100	81	11%	116	17%	71%	27	37%	44%	4.43	-3.2	35	88	$23
14	2 AL	477	56	8	41	17	252	254	314	386	700	400	766	8	75	0.33	42	27	32	32	83	101	84	7%	119	23%	63%	27	33%	44%	3.88	-3.1	34	92	$13
15	3 TM	325	51	7	35	7	262	245	333	422	755	470	800	9	74	0.37	39	23	38	33	85	108	104	8%	146	14%	58%	27	37%	48%	4.57	-2.7	46	124	$9
1st Half		185	27	6	25	3	259	258	315	470	785	464	850	6	73	0.24	41	22	37	33	86	136	122	13%	149	15%	50%	14	36%	50%	4.67	-0.8	60	162	$11
2nd Half		140	24	1	10	4	264	229	356	357	713	481	737	12	76	0.56	37	25	38	34	85	73	81	3%	121	13%	67%	13	38%	46%	4.31	-2.1	24	65	$6
16	Proj	**224**	**33**	**5**	**21**	**7**	**262**	**247**	**331**	**405**	**736**	**548**	**772**	**9**	**75**	**0.38**	**40**	**25**	**35**	**33**	**84**	**98**	**91**	**8%**	**126**	**18%**	**64%**				**4.40**	**-1.0**	**37**	**101**	**$8**

De Jesus,Ivan

Age: 29	Bats: R	Pos: 2B	Health A	LIMA Plan D
Ht: 5' 11"	Wt: 200		PT/Exp C	Rand Var -2
			Consist A	MM 2111

4-28-.244 in 201 AB at CIN. Mediocre minor league skills led to mediocre major league numbers. Offers very little power or speed, and high LD% offset by low ct%, so he's not going to hit for average, either. Versatility could help him stick around, but has virtually nothing to offer with the bat.

Yr	Tm	AB	R	HR	RBI	SB	BA	xBA	OBP	SLG	OPS	vL	vR	bb%	ct%	Eye	G	L	F	h%	HctX	PX	xPX	hr/f	Spd	SBO	SB%	#Wk	DOM	DIS	RC/G	RAR	BPV	BPX	R$
11	LA *	419	37	5	35	2	230	227	277	301	578	730	320	6	78	0.29	52	19	29	29	89	55	37	0%	82	3%	66%	7	14%	71%	2.75	-25.0	-5	-11	$1
12	2 TM *	291	35	2	31	3	270	254	307	365	672	360	768	5	74	0.21	52	28	21	36	100	76	66	0%	100	6%	55%	11	18%	45%	3.84	-4.2	0	0	$5
13	aaa	304	27	2	24	4	266		314	375	689			7	76	0.29				34		94			97	8%	61%				4.02		22	55	$4
14	aaa	417	40	3	42	1	239		304	325	628			8	76	0.38				31		69			101	2%	55%				3.28		8	22	$3
15	CIN *	386	32	4	40	2	246	232	311	345	655	728	667	9	71	0.33	50	24	27	34	73	75	78	10%	104	5%	32%	19	26%	53%	3.52	-7.4	-3	-8	$3
1st Half		247	24	3	21	2	251	230	313	348	661	476	903	8	71	0.32	45	26	30	34	80	73	75	21%	107	7%	32%	6	33%	50%	3.54	-5.1	-5	-14	$5
2nd Half		139	8	1	19	0	237	233	310	338	648	862	572	9	71	0.35	52	23	25	33	69	78	80	4%	98	0%	0%	13	23%	54%	3.47	-3.1	-3	-8	-$1
16	Proj	**193**	**16**	**3**	**20**	**1**	**246**	**247**	**308**	**368**	**675**	**661**	**681**	**8**	**74**	**0.33**	**49**	**24**	**27**	**32**	**73**	**88**	**78**	**9%**	**102**	**4%**	**52%**				**3.76**	**-2.7**	**2**	**6**	**$3**

Den Dekker,Matthew

Age: 28	Bats: L	Pos: LF	Health A	LIMA Plan D
Ht: 6' 1"	Wt: 210		PT/Exp D	Rand Var 0
			Consist A	MM 2211

5-12-.253 in 99 AB at WAS. Held on to previous year's ct% gains, and put up solid power numbers in 2H. But still looks like a BA risk, has a history of league average power, and Spd is trending downward. No reason to think he's on verge of breakout, or even consistent AB.

Yr	Tm	AB	R	HR	RBI	SB	BA	xBA	OBP	SLG	OPS	vL	vR	bb%	ct%	Eye	G	L	F	h%	HctX	PX	xPX	hr/f	Spd	SBO	SB%	#Wk	DOM	DIS	RC/G	RAR	BPV	BPX	R$
11	aa	272	35	8	23	9	179		232	314	546			6	62	0.18				25		113			114	30%	59%				2.12		-11	-24	$0
12	a/a	533	63	13	57	16	223		258	361	619			5	65	0.14				32		109			105	26%	60%				2.89		-9	-23	$9
13	NYM *	237	27	5	29	9	213	205	263	319	582	200	572	6	65	0.19	34	29	37	31	92	83	135	8%	102	21%	80%	6	0%	83%	2.76	-9.5	-27	-68	$3
14	NYM *	487	62	5	33	12	241	260	303	351	654	600	673	8	75	0.36	47	27	26	31	116	95	104	0%	98	19%	53%	12	33%	42%	3.38	-6.0	25	68	$9
15	WAS *	368	39	11	37	6	219	235	273	362	635	522	841	7	74	0.29	45	18	37	27	73	98	106	17%	89	11%	74%	17	41%	41%	3.22	-17.0	18	49	$4
1st Half		190	19	2	18	6	196	176	244	265	509	0	600	6	73	0.24	45	9	45	25	146	53	257	20%	78	15%	100%	7	29%	57%	2.19	-14.2	-28	-76	$1
2nd Half		178	20	8	18	0	244	272	303	467	770	522	890	8	76	0.35	45	19	36	28	62	145	82	17%	101	6%	0%	10	50%	30%	4.51	-0.3	67	181	$7
16	Proj	**130**	**15**	**3**	**12**	**3**	**224**	**238**	**285**	**352**	**637**	**422**	**663**	**7**	**72**	**0.28**	**41**	**25**	**34**	**29**	**88**	**93**	**109**	**9%**	**94**	**15%**	**64%**				**3.16**	**-5.6**	**9**	**24**	**$2**

Deshields Jr.,Delino

Age: 23	Bats: R	Pos: CF LF	Health A	LIMA Plan B
Ht: 5' 9"	Wt: 210		PT/Exp D	Rand Var -2
			Consist D	MM 1505

2-37-.261 with 25 SB in 425 AB at TEX. Rule 5 pickup locked down starting job in early May and never looked back. Added improved ct% to already strong bb%, but xBA warrants caution. Still too many Ks for a speedster. Should again be strong SB source, but lacks other skills necessary to be true difference maker.

Yr	Tm	AB	R	HR	RBI	SB	BA	xBA	OBP	SLG	OPS	vL	vR	bb%	ct%	Eye	G	L	F	h%	HctX	PX	xPX	hr/f	Spd	SBO	SB%	#Wk	DOM	DIS	RC/G	RAR	BPV	BPX	R$
11																																			
12																																			
13																																			
14	aa	411	58	9	44	41	206		288	309	598			10	69	0.38				28		81			105	51%	73%				2.85		-3	-8	$17
15	TEX *	451	85	2	39	25	262	237	341	374	715	765	693	11	76	0.50	47	19	34	34	71	80	56	2%	158	24%	76%	25	32%	48%	4.43	-0.9	39	105	$18
1st Half		175	36	0	14	13	275	241	355	399	754	819	740	11	74	0.48	56	13	31	37	89	93	82	0%	168	28%	87%	12	33%	58%	5.25	4.2	45	122	$13
2nd Half		276	49	2	25	12	254	235	333	359	692	737	667	10	78	0.52	43	22	35	32	62	72	44	3%	134	22%	67%	13	31%	38%	3.96	-3.7	31	84	$21
16	Proj	**502**	**85**	**3**	**47**	**31**	**248**	**222**	**327**	**344**	**671**	**724**	**643**	**10**	**73**	**0.43**	**48**	**18**	**33**	**33**	**73**	**71**	**59**	**3%**	**161**	**28%**	**75%**				**3.83**	**-8.9**	**21**	**58**	**$20**

Desmond,Ian

Age: 30	Bats: R	Pos: SS	Health A	LIMA Plan B
Ht: 6' 3"	Wt: 215		PT/Exp A	Rand Var 0
			Consist B	MM 3415

Got off to terrible start, and contact woes persisted. But 2nd half was a near clone of 2014 productivity rates, so it's probably safe to consider that his new baseline. Power/speed combo remains, as does high GB%, which could save his BA with any rebound in HctX. Still a valuable piece, but both his ceiling and floor appear lower now.

Yr	Tm	AB	R	HR	RBI	SB	BA	xBA	OBP	SLG	OPS	vL	vR	bb%	ct%	Eye	G	L	F	h%	HctX	PX	xPX	hr/f	Spd	SBO	SB%	#Wk	DOM	DIS	RC/G	RAR	BPV	BPX	R$
11	WAS	584	65	8	49	25	253	239	298	358	656	642	659	6	76	0.25	52	18	31	32	84	79	75	6%	132	24%	71%	27	30%	52%	3.56	-16.5	21	47	$15
12	WAS	513	72	25	73	21	292	279	335	511	845	902	828	6	78	0.27	48	18	35	33	112	142	115	18%	116	23%	78%	21	24%	33%	6.06	28.2	73	183	$27
13	WAS	600	77	20	80	21	280	265	331	453	784	766	789	7	76	0.30	43	22	34	34	101	126	100	13%	99	18%	78%	26	50%	31%	5.26	30.2	49	123	$28
14	WAS	593	73	24	91	24	255	247	313	430	743	771	734	7	69	0.25	50	18	32	33	97	136	107	18%	106	20%	83%	27	41%	33%	4.60	22.8	34	92	$26
15	WAS	583	69	19	62	13	233	230	290	384	674	757	653	7	68	0.24	53	16	31	31	84	113	92	15%	112	14%	72%	27	26%	48%	3.65	-1.9	12	32	$13
1st Half		307	35	7	24	2	212	219	254	336	589	621	581	5	69	0.16	52	15	32	28	81	99	91	10%	99	7%	50%	14	14%	50%	2.64	-13.9	-4	-11	$3
2nd Half		276	34	12	38	11	257	238	328	438	766	899	732	10	67	0.33	55	16	29	34	87	129	92	22%	125	18%	79%	13	38%	46%	4.99	7.4	29	78	$23
16	Proj	**577**	**71**	**21**	**73**	**19**	**252**	**243**	**310**	**419**	**729**	**783**	**714**	**7**	**70**	**0.27**	**51**	**17**	**32**	**32**	**92**	**120**	**97**	**16%**	**115**	**17%**	**77%**				**4.40**	**5.4**	**25**	**68**	**$22**

BRIAN RUDD

Dickerson,Corey

Age: 27 Bats: L Pos: LF | Ht: 6' 1" Wt: 205

Health D | PT/Exp C | Consist D | LIMA Plan A | Rand Var -1 | MM 4255

10-31-.304 in 224 AB at COL. Presumed growth year thwarted by injury, thrice. Plate discipline suffered and bad foot immobilized him, but PX/xPX skipped nary a beat. Three-year BA/xBA history establishes solid floor, and he's an LD monster. With health ... UP: .310 BA, 35 HR.

Yr	Tm	AB	R	HR	RBI	SB	BA	xBA	OBP	SLG	OPS	vL	vR	bb%	ct%	Eye	G	L	F	h%	HctX	PX	xPX	hr/f	Spd	SBO	SB%	#Wk	DOM	DIS	RC/G	RAR	BPV	BPX	R$
11																																			
12	aa	266	34	13	32	6	274		313	508	821			5	81	0.29				30		143			105	16%	65%				5.42		82	205	$9
13	COL *	509	68	12	47	6	296	287	337	492	829	581	819	6	81	0.33	40	26	34	34	108	124	107	10%	157	16%	29%	14	64%	21%	5.42	19.8	86	215	$19
14	COL	436	74	24	76	8	312	298	364	567	931	724	985	8	77	0.37	37	27	36	36	123	176	135	20%	119	13%	53%	25	60%	24%	7.33	42.6	102	276	$28
15	COL *	252	32	11	33	0	296	293	325	514	839	662	938	4	76	0.18	38	30	32	35	128	149	141	19%	115	2%	0%	16	44%	25%	5.95	8.6	68	184	$9
1st Half		127	15	5	16	0	299	288	331	512	843	787	857	5	75	0.19	42	29	28	37	135	142	145	19%	115	3%	0%	9	33%	33%	5.95	4.9	58	157	$7
2nd Half		125	17	6	17	0	293	301	318	517	835	544	1057	4	77	0.16	33	30	37	34	116	156	135	19%	111	0%	0%	7	57%	14%	5.94	4.8	76	205	$10
16	**Proj**	**529**	**74**	**26**	**82**	**5**	**299**	**297**	**337**	**542**	**879**	**639**	**952**	**6**	**78**	**0.26**	**37**	**28**	**35**	**34**	**121**	**157**	**133**	**19%**	**120**	**9%**	**44%**				**6.41**	**27.3**	**76**	**207**	**$25**

Dietrich,Derek

Age: 26 Bats: L Pos: LF 3B | Ht: 6' 0" Wt: 205

Health B | PT/Exp D | Consist A | LIMA Plan D+ | Rand Var 0 | MM 4113

10-24-.256 in 250 AB at MIA. June call-up was reasonably productive for three months before hitting the skids (one RBI in last 79 AB). Modest hit tool, platoon splits, erratic glove will likely keep him from full-time work, but if power and FB% are new baselines, he could inflict some damage from multiple positions.

Yr	Tm	AB	R	HR	RBI	SB	BA	xBA	OBP	SLG	OPS	vL	vR	bb%	ct%	Eye	G	L	F	h%	HctX	PX	xPX	hr/f	Spd	SBO	SB%	#Wk	DOM	DIS	RC/G	RAR	BPV	BPX	R$
11																																			
12	aa	133	18	3	14	0	233		263	358	622			4	69	0.13				31		95			103	4%	0%				3.01		-6	-15	$0
13	MIA *	433	61	17	54	3	226	256	285	414	699	786	644	8	72	0.29	40	25	35	28	89	136	114	16%	114	4%	100%	12	42%	25%	3.93	-1.6	46	115	$8
14	MIA *	240	41	9	28	2	235	246	281	399	680	372	762	6	75	0.26	43	19	38	28	99	114	100	11%	105	3%	100%	12	42%	42%	3.78	0.0	38	103	$5
15	MIA *	442	58	15	46	0	241	243	297	422	719	519	864	7	74	0.30	37	20	43	30	110	125	158	12%	111	5%	0%	18	44%	39%	4.03	-9.1	44	119	$7
1st Half		241	27	8	27	0	222	249	271	396	667	1089	726	6	73	0.25	33	25	42	27	125	123	172	20%	83	5%	0%	5	20%	40%	3.36	-9.0	30	81	$5
2nd Half		201	31	7	19	0	264	245	355	453	807	414	898	9	74	0.37	38	19	44	32	107	127	155	11%	130	4%	0%	13	54%	38%	4.92	2.1	56	151	$9
16	**Proj**	**358**	**52**	**13**	**39**	**1**	**245**	**246**	**329**	**426**	**755**	**603**	**785**	**7**	**73**	**0.28**	**39**	**21**	**40**	**30**	**105**	**123**	**133**	**12%**	**110**	**4%**	**37%**				**4.20**	**-3.8**	**34**	**92**	**$9**

Donaldson,Josh

Age: 30 Bats: R Pos: 3B | Ht: 6' 0" Wt: 220

Health A | PT/Exp A | Consist D | LIMA Plan C | Rand Var -2 | MM 4345

Monster 2015 wasn't a surprise as mash metrics (HctX, PX, hr/f) climbed for third straight season. Pounded RHP like never before, and home HR total increased by 12 in friendlier park. Sure, xPX warns of regression, but if 2016 is a little less monstrous, who couldn't live with that?

Yr	Tm	AB	R	HR	RBI	SB	BA	xBA	OBP	SLG	OPS	vL	vR	bb%	ct%	Eye	G	L	F	h%	HctX	PX	xPX	hr/f	Spd	SBO	SB%	#Wk	DOM	DIS	RC/G	RAR	BPV	BPX	R$
11	aaa	444	52	10	46	8	199		256	317	573			7	72	0.27				25		94			84	15%	64%				2.52		5	11	$1
12	OAK *	483	59	17	62	7	247	257	291	410	701	703	680	6	79	0.29	40	23	38	28	90	107	107	11%	67	10%	68%	17	35%	47%	3.98	-8.1	33	83	$11
13	OAK	579	89	24	93	5	301	282	384	499	883	1042	813	12	81	0.69	44	21	36	34	107	132	97	14%	101	4%	71%	27	48%	19%	6.92	47.4	85	213	$29
14	OAK	608	93	29	98	8	255	264	342	456	798	1007	727	11	81	0.58	45	13	41	28	118	138	126	15%	89	5%	100%	27	56%	30%	5.35	29.8	76	205	$24
15	TOR	620	122	41	123	6	297	297	371	568	939	1024	919	11	79	0.55	45	17	38	32	128	170	139	22%	82	3%	100%	27	74%	19%	7.71	53.6	98	265	$37
1st Half		334	62	19	56	3	296	276	352	527	879	960	860	8	78	0.38	44	17	38	33	135	147	131	18%	84	3%	100%	14	71%	21%	6.76	19.7	73	197	$36
2nd Half		286	60	22	67	3	297	319	391	615	1007	1097	985	14	79	0.75	46	18	37	31	121	196	148	26%	79	4%	100%	13	77%	15%	8.85	33.3	126	341	$38
16	**Proj**	**598**	**104**	**35**	**110**	**7**	**279**	**285**	**361**	**523**	**884**	**997**	**849**	**11**	**79**	**0.58**	**44**	**17**	**38**	**30**	**118**	**153**	**127**	**19%**	**87**	**5%**	**88%**				**6.67**	**34.7**	**88**	**237**	**$32**

Dozier,Brian

Age: 29 Bats: R Pos: 2B | Ht: 5' 11" Wt: 190

Health A | PT/Exp A | Consist A | LIMA Plan B+ | Rand Var -2 | MM 4325

Those 2,000+ PA since 2013 may have caught up with him in 2nd half (38 BPV). BA/xBA history reveal modest batting skills; average HctX could be why BA has flattened as LD%, PX inch forward. Was also late talk of hip concerns. Assuming they're addressed, help yourselves to more taters and bags.

Yr	Tm	AB	R	HR	RBI	SB	BA	xBA	OBP	SLG	OPS	vL	vR	bb%	ct%	Eye	G	L	F	h%	HctX	PX	xPX	hr/f	Spd	SBO	SB%	#Wk	DOM	DIS	RC/G	RAR	BPV	BPX	R$
11	aa	311	43	4	25	8	269		314	407	721			6	83	0.39				31		94			124	21%	49%				4.11		59	131	$7
12	MIN *	497	45	7	47	11	223	232	264	318	581	775	547	5	81	0.29	42	21	38	26	77	65	80	6%	108	15%	73%	15	20%	27%	2.74	-21.8	19	48	$4
13	MIN	558	72	18	66	14	244	256	312	414	726	978	649	8	78	0.43	38	21	41	28	89	118	99	10%	124	16%	67%	27	52%	33%	4.19	7.8	64	160	$16
14	MIN	598	112	23	71	21	242	257	345	416	762	804	743	13	78	0.69	37	20	43	27	95	124	97	11%	106	16%	75%	27	44%	19%	4.77	24.9	73	197	$24
15	MIN	628	101	28	77	12	236	261	307	444	751	762	746	9	76	0.41	33	23	44	27	98	138	129	13%	106	12%	75%	26	58%	19%	4.48	3.7	68	184	$18
1st Half		319	62	16	40	7	260	280	331	511	842	872	830	9	77	0.43	29	25	46	29	109	166	141	14%	108	14%	70%	14	71%	7%	5.65	13.3	95	257	$26
2nd Half		309	39	12	37	5	210	240	281	375	657	642	662	9	75	0.39	38	20	42	24	86	108	116	12%	99	9%	83%	12	42%	33%	3.43	-7.7	38	103	$10
16	**Proj**	**576**	**95**	**24**	**67**	**14**	**240**	**258**	**316**	**431**	**747**	**813**	**722**	**10**	**78**	**0.47**	**36**	**21**	**43**	**27**	**92**	**124**	**110**	**12%**	**115**	**14%**	**72%**				**4.49**	**4.6**	**65**	**175**	**$21**

Drew,Stephen

Age: 33 Bats: L Pos: 2B | Ht: 6' 0" Wt: 190

Health C | PT/Exp C | Consist F | LIMA Plan D+ | Rand Var +5 | MM 3113

In a season with a paucity of MI talent, his name was the one that always seemed to languish in the free agent pool. Nobody wanted him but everyone stopped to look. After all, he had some nice pop, and two straight seasons of miniscule H% had to turn around eventually, right? By time it did in the 2nd half, nobody noticed.

Yr	Tm	AB	R	HR	RBI	SB	BA	xBA	OBP	SLG	OPS	vL	vR	bb%	ct%	Eye	G	L	F	h%	HctX	PX	xPX	hr/f	Spd	SBO	SB%	#Wk	DOM	DIS	RC/G	RAR	BPV	BPX	R$
11	ARI	321	44	5	45	4	252	247	317	396	713	671	728	9	77	0.41	39	21	40	31	97	107	109	5%	113	10%	50%	16	31%	19%	4.12	-4.5	46	102	$6
12	2 TM *	328	42	8	31	1	218	237	306	346	653	563	697	11	74	0.49	32	28	40	27	102	89	122	8%	109	3%	33%	15	33%	40%	3.39	-9.6	25	63	$1
13	BOS	442	57	13	67	6	253	251	333	443	777	585	876	11	72	0.44	33	25	42	32	114	142	156	10%	117	5%	100%	23	52%	26%	5.15	18.4	60	150	$13
14	2 AL	271	18	7	26	1	162	214	237	299	536	371	584	9	72	0.36	31	17	51	20	73	109	98	7%	69	4%	50%	18	33%	50%	2.14	-11.1	17	46	-$5
15	NYY	383	43	17	44	0	201	244	271	381	652	690	642	9	81	0.52	38	16	47	20	77	108	95	12%	90	3%	0%	25	44%	36%	3.22	-12.7	59	159	$1
1st Half		236	23	11	24	0	178	236	251	364	615	617	615	9	81	0.55	35	13	52	17	73	114	99	12%	77	5%	0%	14	43%	29%	2.75	-11.3	60	162	$0
2nd Half		147	20	6	20	0	238	256	304	408	713	868	681	8	82	0.48	42	19	39	25	83	99	88	13%	111	0%	0%	11	45%	45%	4.10	-0.6	57	154	$3
16	**Proj**	**350**	**38**	**12**	**42**	**1**	**226**	**240**	**297**	**392**	**688**	**636**	**704**	**9**	**77**	**0.44**	**36**	**19**	**45**	**26**	**85**	**107**	**106**	**10%**	**95**	**3%**	**51%**				**3.79**	**-4.6**	**34**	**92**	**$6**

Drury,Brandon

Age: 23 Bats: R Pos: 3B | Ht: 6' 2" Wt: 190

Health A | PT/Exp F | Consist C | LIMA Plan D+ | Rand Var 0 | MM 3043

2-8-.214 in 56 AB at ARI. Latest model off organization's infield assembly line slashed .303/.344/.412 at AA/AAA while playing 3B and 2B. Low HR total disappointed, but HctX, xPX, and solid approach suggest more power will develop. May be another year before impact is felt.

Yr	Tm	AB	R	HR	RBI	SB	BA	xBA	OBP	SLG	OPS	vL	vR	bb%	ct%	Eye	G	L	F	h%	HctX	PX	xPX	hr/f	Spd	SBO	SB%	#Wk	DOM	DIS	RC/G	RAR	BPV	BPX	R$
11																																			
12																																			
13																																			
14	aa	105	10	3	11	0	272		309	435	744			5	80	0.27				31		119			87	0%	0%				4.71		55	149	$1
15	ARI *	580	51	6	53	3	260	267	291	362	652	913	434	4	84	0.27	56	21	23	30	108	75	110	18%	79	9%	25%	5	20%	40%	3.39	-13.3	29	78	$8
1st Half		322	21	2	30	3	257	238	286	341	627			4	83	0.23				30		63			95	16%	25%				2.97		20	54	$8
2nd Half		258	29	4	23	0	264	279	296	387	684	913	434	4	85	0.31	56	21	23	30	109	90	110	18%	82	0%	0%	5	20%	40%	3.98	-1.9	48	130	$9
16	**Proj**	**335**	**31**	**10**	**32**	**1**	**267**	**281**	**310**	**431**	**741**	**1043**	**535**	**4**	**83**	**0.26**	**56**	**21**	**23**	**30**	**98**	**108**	**99**	**16%**	**80**	**4%**	**25%**				**4.36**	**-2.6**	**36**	**98**	**$9**

Duda,Lucas

Age: 30 Bats: L Pos: 1B | Ht: 6' 4" Wt: 255

Health B | PT/Exp B | Consist B | LIMA Plan B+ | Rand Var +1 | MM 5025

Nearly identical follow-up to 2014 season with one big difference - major improvement vs LHP. This cements reliabilty as power source, legitimized by towering PX/xPX, and could buy him more playing time. Rest of game is pedestrian, but he's paid to hit HR, and as FB% and hr/f continue to climb, maybe... UP: 40 HR.

Yr	Tm	AB	R	HR	RBI	SB	BA	xBA	OBP	SLG	OPS	vL	vR	bb%	ct%	Eye	G	L	F	h%	HctX	PX	xPX	hr/f	Spd	SBO	SB%	#Wk	DOM	DIS	RC/G	RAR	BPV	BPX	R$
11	NYM *	430	55	18	68	1	276	274	352	476	828	705	888	10	79	0.57	34	22	43	31	111	136	116	9%	89	1%	100%	20	60%	30%	5.92	-4.1	76	169	$15
12	NYM *	497	52	17	63	1	233	222	313	374	687	662	745	10	71	0.40	35	23	42	30	118	99	134	13%	49	1%	100%	23	22%	57%	3.90	-22.7	0	0	$7
13	NYM *	380	50	15	38	1	222	221	333	388	721	610	831	14	68	0.52	32	20	48	29	117	130	181	14%	67	3%	16%	18	39%	33%	4.12	-5.4	26	65	$4
14	NYM	514	74	30	92	3	253	263	349	481	830	516	915	12	74	0.51	31	20	49	29	132	165	181	16%	46	4%	60%	27	56%	15%	5.55	20.6	67	181	$20
15	NYM	471	67	27	73	0	244	263	352	486	838	878	823	12	71	0.48	27	22	51	29	121	174	167	16%	57	2%	0%	25	52%	32%	5.44	0.9	66	178	$13
1st Half		290	39	10	34	0	248	255	351	428	779	926	727	11	71	0.43	28	27	45	32	120	138	159	11%	62	0%	0%	14	43%	29%	4.81	-3.0	37	100	$12
2nd Half		181	28	17	39	0	238	280	353	580	934	797	977	14	70	0.56	27	14	59	24	123	231	182	22%	60	4%	0%	11	64%	36%	6.44	7.0	114	308	$14
16	**Proj**	**539**	**76**	**33**	**97**	**1**	**256**	**258**	**360**	**500**	**860**	**742**	**899**	**13**	**71**	**0.50**	**29**	**20**	**51**	**30**	**123**	**169**	**171**	**17%**	**53**	**3%**	**27%**				**5.87**	**11.4**	**55**	**150**	**$22**

ROB CARROLL

Duffy,Matt

Age: 25 Bats: R Pos: 3B | Ht: 6' 2" Wt: 170
Health A | PT/Exp D | Consist A
LIMA Plan B+ | Rand Var -1 | MM 1535

2014 AA batting title says he didn't exactly come out of nowhere. Power has never impressed, and minor league patience (11% bb%) has yet to show up. But season-long HctX, speed metrics and historical SB% keep our interest. Solid defender will regress a tad at the plate, but should remain valuable.

Yr	Tm	AB	R	HR	RBI	SB	BA	xBA	OBP	SLG	OPS	vL	vR	bb%	ct%	Eye	G	L	F	h%	HctX	PX	xPX	hr/f	Spd	SBO	SB%	#Wk	DOM	DIS	RC/G	RAR	BPV	BPX	R$
11																																			
12																																			
13																																			
14	SF *	427	48	2	59	16	291	267	347	379	726	888	300	8	79	0.41	41	33	26	36	80	72	56	0%	123	17%	75%	11	18%	55%	4.74	12.4	29	78	$17
15	SF	573	77	12	77	12	295	276	334	428	762	642	803	5	83	0.31	53	21	27	34	104	83	91	9%	136	8%	100%	27	44%	26%	5.24	8.9	52	141	$24
1st Half		240	31	8	37	3	292	281	335	467	801	601	870	5	80	0.24	54	20	26	34	105	109	99	16%	132	5%	100%	14	50%	29%	5.55	6.1	57	154	$18
2nd Half		333	46	4	40	9	297	271	334	399	734	671	755	5	86	0.38	52	21	27	34	103	65	85	5%	135	10%	100%	13	38%	23%	5.01	3.5	48	130	$28
16	Proj	**591**	**70**	**9**	**76**	**12**	**280**	**272**	**335**	**396**	**731**	**804**	**689**	**6**	**82**	**0.36**	**48**	**26**	**26**	**33**	**94**	**77**	**77**	**7%**	**139**	**9%**	**82%**				**4.57**	**-0.8**	**36**	**98**	**$20**

Duvall,Adam

Age: 27 Bats: R Pos: LF | Ht: 6' 1" Wt: 205
Health A | PT/Exp C | Consist B
LIMA Plan D+ | Rand Var +1 | MM 4221

5-9-.219 in 64 AB at CIN. Now with 8 HR in 137 MLB AB, his power is unquestionable, but the other tools are sub-par across the board. Whether he can keep an MLB BA above water is an open question until he gets an extended opportunity. And he isn't getting any younger. But with 400 AB... UP: 25 HR.

Yr	Tm	AB	R	HR	RBI	SB	BA	xBA	OBP	SLG	OPS	vL	vR	bb%	ct%	Eye	G	L	F	h%	HctX	PX	xPX	hr/f	Spd	SBO	SB%	#Wk	DOM	DIS	RC/G	RAR	BPV	BPX	R$
11																																			
12																																			
13	aa	385	43	11	41	1	203		251	350	601			6	78	0.29				23		102			105	4%	55%				2.78		39	98	$0
14	SF *	432	51	18	63	1	219	243	258	395	653	525	629	5	72	0.19	38	21	42	26	106	132	155	14%	86	2%	100%	11	27%	45%	3.34	-5.8	30	81	$7
15	CIN *	561	61	33	77	4	226	252	266	457	723	498	895	5	70	0.18	29	24	47	26	106	158	123	28%	81	5%	77%	6	50%	50%	3.99	-12.3	43	116	$12
1st Half		319	34	15	41	2	228	253	268	433	701			5	70	0.18				28		144			92	3%	100%				3.86		36	97	$12
2nd Half		242	27	18	36	2	223	264	263	488	751	498	895	5	70	0.18	29	24	47	24	105	176	123	28%	75	9%	66%	6	50%	50%	4.16	-3.0	55	149	$12
16	Proj	**232**	**26**	**14**	**32**	**1**	**224**	**255**	**280**	**451**	**732**	**548**	**839**	**5**	**72**	**0.19**	**32**	**23**	**45**	**25**	**105**	**151**	**136**	**18%**	**90**	**4%**	**75%**				**3.90**	**-4.7**	**39**	**106**	**$6**

Dyson,Jarrod

Age: 31 Bats: L Pos: CF LF | Ht: 5' 10" Wt: 160
Health A | PT/Exp F | Consist A
LIMA Plan C | Rand Var +2 | MM 1521

Speed-only offensive profile is a limitation that finally resulted in AB decline. But 90% SB% kept him valuable despite h%-fueled 2H BA plunge. Defense and ability to survive at the plate vR also keep him relevant in the real game. This is likely all there is; bid for more of the same.

Yr	Tm	AB	R	HR	RBI	SB	BA	xBA	OBP	SLG	OPS	vL	vR	bb%	ct%	Eye	G	L	F	h%	HctX	PX	xPX	hr/f	Spd	SBO	SB%	#Wk	DOM	DIS	RC/G	RAR	BPV	BPX	R$
11	KC *	363	54	2	20	36	221	256	280	275	555	333	544	8	81	0.44	68	16	16	27	64	38	12	0%	159	41%	91%	11	9%	82%	2.89	-22.8	19	42	$10
12	KC *	355	60	0	12	34	261	250	323	332	655	510	689	8	83	0.52	57	19	24	32	89	44	56	0%	203	38%	85%	25	20%	40%	3.99	-6.0	45	113	$14
13	KC *	265	36	2	18	37	231	248	293	324	617	531	741	8	78	0.39	58	17	25	29	74	66	68	5%	154	64%	86%	21	33%	29%	3.52	-3.7	27	68	$14
14	KC	260	33	1	24	36	269	233	324	327	651	604	663	8	80	0.42	63	14	23	33	56	37	39	2%	172	52%	84%	27	19%	48%	4.09	3.1	19	51	$17
15	KC	200	31	2	18	26	250	278	311	380	691	578	715	7	82	0.38	54	23	23	30	70	77	29	6%	170	60%	90%	26	42%	35%	4.29	-0.6	54	146	$12
1st Half		94	12	0	7	9	266	287	303	404	707	770	690	4	82	0.24	50	28	22	32	76	84	16	0%	158	50%	90%	13	46%	31%	4.47	-0.2	52	141	$5
2nd Half		106	19	2	11	17	236	270	317	358	675	377	734	9	81	0.50	57	20	23	27	64	71	40	11%	154	68%	89%	13	38%	38%	4.14	-1.4	47	127	$17
16	Proj	**227**	**33**	**2**	**19**	**29**	**250**	**260**	**311**	**351**	**662**	**544**	**691**	**7**	**81**	**0.41**	**57**	**19**	**23**	**30**	**68**	**61**	**41**	**5%**	**165**	**55%**	**87%**				**4.02**	**-2.7**	**45**	**122**	**$14**

Eaton,Adam

Age: 27 Bats: L Pos: CF | Ht: 5' 8" Wt: 185
Health C | PT/Exp B | Consist C
LIMA Plan B | Rand Var -2 | MM 2435

Opened up swing successfully for 2H HR spike, but it was the 2H h% and more SBO that really salvaged his season. xPX isn't optimistic about his power going forward. Age and SB% say the running game may have reached a ceiling. There's counting stat value here (plus OBP for sim gamers), but don't get carried away.

Yr	Tm	AB	R	HR	RBI	SB	BA	xBA	OBP	SLG	OPS	vL	vR	bb%	ct%	Eye	G	L	F	h%	HctX	PX	xPX	hr/f	Spd	SBO	SB%	#Wk	DOM	DIS	RC/G	RAR	BPV	BPX	R$
11	aa	212	22	3	20	7	268		333	375	709			9	82	0.54				32		68			130	22%	52%				4.00		40	89	$4
12	ARI *	613	108	7	38	32	312	274	367	440	807	890	737	8	83	0.51	64	12	24	37	108	90	91	13%	140	26%	67%	4	50%	25%	5.76	18.3	64	160	$31
13	ARI *	285	43	4	25	5	235	261	282	341	623	708	665	6	81	0.35	57	19	25	28	89	71	63	6%	130	11%	71%	13	31%	23%	3.19	-7.8	36	90	$4
14	CHW	486	76	1	35	15	300	278	362	401	763	724	778	8	83	0.52	60	20	20	36	87	74	44	1%	155	16%	63%	23	43%	30%	5.05	15.9	56	151	$19
15	CHW	610	98	14	56	18	287	267	361	431	792	648	847	9	79	0.44	51	22	27	35	89	93	68	11%	140	14%	69%	26	38%	38%	5.29	13.6	50	135	$26
1st Half		300	41	5	15	5	243	268	308	373	681	488	745	7	81	0.39	54	20	26	28	89	79	55	8%	155	11%	63%	14	36%	36%	3.63	-7.0	51	138	$10
2nd Half		310	57	9	41	13	329	265	410	487	897	773	949	10	76	0.48	47	24	29	41	89	107	82	13%	123	16%	72%	12	42%	42%	7.28	24.0	49	132	$41
16	Proj	**553**	**87**	**9**	**49**	**17**	**287**	**268**	**357**	**415**	**772**	**717**	**793**	**8**	**80**	**0.45**	**55**	**20**	**25**	**34**	**90**	**83**	**65**	**8%**	**140**	**16%**	**66%**				**5.00**	**9.4**	**46**	**125**	**$24**

Ellis,A.J.

Age: 35 Bats: R Pos: CA | Ht: 6' 3" Wt: 220
Health C | PT/Exp D | Consist D
LIMA Plan D+ | Rand Var +1 | MM 2011

Back-up work seems to suit him. Stayed (mostly) healthy all year, and 2H productivity surged with playing time, LD% and HctX. Maintained trademark patience while posting best-ever power metrics. History and age say it's not sustainable, but OBP-leaguers should file away for #2 catcher consideration.

Yr	Tm	AB	R	HR	RBI	SB	BA	xBA	OBP	SLG	OPS	vL	vR	bb%	ct%	Eye	G	L	F	h%	HctX	PX	xPX	hr/f	Spd	SBO	SB%	#Wk	DOM	DIS	RC/G	RAR	BPV	BPX	R$
11	LA *	269	26	3	25	0	224	224	322	307	628	1069	645	13	82	0.82	49	16	35	26	119	60	99	8%	86	3%	0%	13	46%	31%	3.13	-10.3	31	69	-$1
12	LA	423	44	13	52	0	270	243	373	414	786	702	815	13	75	0.61	45	23	33	33	92	100	102	13%	102	0%	0%	27	48%	37%	5.30	12.2	38	95	$9
13	LA	390	43	10	52	0	238	238	318	364	682	671	684	10	80	0.58	44	19	37	27	120	86	138	9%	90	2%	0%	26	42%	27%	3.79	1.0	39	98	$5
14	LA	283	21	3	25	0	191	197	323	254	577	711	535	16	80	0.93	44	17	39	23	94	50	81	3%	64	0%	0%	21	33%	43%	2.55	-8.0	12	32	-$4
15	LA	181	24	7	21	0	238	257	355	403	758	913	642	15	79	0.84	44	21	35	26	103	107	108	14%	84	0%	0%	26	46%	35%	4.75	5.0	59	159	$2
1st Half		75	6	0	3	0	187	204	315	240	555	642	493	16	80	0.93	47	17	36	23	57	48	61	0%	88	0%	0%	14	43%	36%	2.37	-3.4	18	49	-$8
2nd Half		106	18	7	18	0	274	291	384	519	903	1095	753	15	78	0.78	41	24	35	29	136	150	141	24%	83	0%	0%	12	50%	33%	6.90	9.4	89	241	$8
16	Proj	**204**	**23**	**6**	**23**	**0**	**237**	**239**	**352**	**372**	**724**	**879**	**646**	**14**	**79**	**0.82**	**44**	**20**	**36**	**27**	**104**	**88**	**106**	**10%**	**82**	**0%**	**0%**				**4.31**	**3.2**	**25**	**67**	**$4**

Ellsbury,Jacoby

Age: 32 Bats: L Pos: CF | Ht: 6' 1" Wt: 195
Health D | PT/Exp A | Consist C
LIMA Plan B | Rand Var 0 | MM 1525

Wasn't the same following May knee injury. Power was already mediocre but plate skills plunged and running game never recovered following July return. Young enough to rebound, and both his BA and SBs should, if he's healthy. But lower body injuries make this skill set riskier than ever. DN: 2015 repeat.

Yr	Tm	AB	R	HR	RBI	SB	BA	xBA	OBP	SLG	OPS	vL	vR	bb%	ct%	Eye	G	L	F	h%	HctX	PX	xPX	hr/f	Spd	SBO	SB%	#Wk	DOM	DIS	RC/G	RAR	BPV	BPX	R$
11	BOS	660	119	32	105	39	321	313	376	552	928	841	965	7	85	0.53	43	23	34	34	114	145	115	17%	108	30%	72%	27	74%	4%	7.42	42.4	106	236	$49
12	BOS	303	43	4	26	14	271	259	313	370	682	648	701	6	86	0.44	47	20	33	30	85	70	91	5%	102	22%	82%	15	53%	20%	4.15	-6.2	44	110	$9
13	BOS	577	92	9	53	52	298	276	355	426	781	641	863	8	84	0.51	51	21	28	34	107	85	78	7%	136	33%	93%	25	56%	20%	5.90	26.6	62	155	$39
14	NYY	575	71	16	70	39	271	276	328	419	747	828	711	8	84	0.53	42	25	34	30	103	98	87	10%	108	28%	89%	25	60%	16%	5.06	19.4	64	173	$31
15	NYY	452	66	7	33	21	257	248	318	345	663	652	669	7	81	0.41	45	24	31	30	75	58	55	6%	129	24%	70%	21	19%	43%	3.61	-12.1	25	68	$15
1st Half		148	29	1	6	14	324	247	412	372	783	733	806	11	84	0.83	47	25	28	38	83	33	31	3%	134	31%	74%	8	25%	50%	5.65	5.1	29	78	$15
2nd Half		304	37	6	27	7	224	247	269	332	601	615	594	5	79	0.25	44	24	32	26	71	70	68	8%	119	17%	64%	13	15%	38%	2.79	-15.3	21	57	$15
16	Proj	**505**	**74**	**10**	**46**	**31**	**274**	**261**	**333**	**387**	**720**	**702**	**729**	**7**	**83**	**0.47**	**45**	**24**	**31**	**32**	**90**	**72**	**70**	**7%**	**122**	**27%**	**80%**				**4.54**	**1.9**	**46**	**125**	**$26**

Elmore,Jake

Age: 29 Bats: R Pos: 1B | Ht: 5' 9" Wt: 185
Health B | PT/Exp D | Consist B
LIMA Plan D | Rand Var +3 | MM 0201

2-16-.206 in 141 AB at TAM. Had an opportunity to turn decent plate skills and positional versatility into more AB before Logan Forsythe outplayed him. Having next to nothing in the way of power and speed is never a good thing. And the ability to hang on for an MLB pension isn't the same as being fantasy rosterable.

Yr	Tm	AB	R	HR	RBI	SB	BA	xBA	OBP	SLG	OPS	vL	vR	bb%	ct%	Eye	G	L	F	h%	HctX	PX	xPX	hr/f	Spd	SBO	SB%	#Wk	DOM	DIS	RC/G	RAR	BPV	BPX	R$
11	aa	381	41	2	29	10	231		299	298	596			9	81	0.50				28		54			95	22%	46%				2.67		14	31	$3
12	ARI *	487	58	1	51	19	264	250	330	354	684	449	515	9	85	0.67	56	14	31	31	90	64	48	0%	104	21%	66%	9	44%	11%	3.95	-21.3	44	110	$13
13	HOU *	388	46	6	28	13	244	258	308	342	650	699	597	8	83	0.54	41	27	32	28	86	65	70	6%	136	24%	49%	16	44%	38%	3.22	-16.6	44	110	$8
14	CIN *	278	29	0	16	8	213	222	288	260	548	500	400	9	79	0.51	29	29	43	27	0	46	-14	0%	89	17%	61%	2	0%	100%	2.37	-15.8	2	5	$0
15	TAM *	339	25	2	25	4	200	230	286	242	528	824	407	11	81	0.65	42	26	32	24	65	30	64	5%	73	10%	40%	13	31%	38%	2.09	-30.8	-4	-11	-$3
1st Half		204	14	2	21	3	236	256	321	302	622	860	451	11	83	0.73	40	29	31	28	69	46	73	7%	71	9%	42%	10	30%	30%	3.08	-13.0	14	38	$1
2nd Half		135	11	0	4	1	146	167	234	152	386	650	216	10	79	0.56	50	13	38	18	56	5	26	0%	94	11%	38%	3	33%	67%	1.01	-19.2	-28	-76	-$9
16	Proj	**190**	**18**	**2**	**12**	**4**	**222**	**228**	**293**	**287**	**580**	**760**	**481**	**10**	**81**	**0.57**	**46**	**21**	**33**	**26**	**74**	**45**	**54**	**4%**	**95**	**14%**	**51%**				**2.67**	**-14.8**	**2**	**4**	**$2**

JOCK THOMPSON

Encarnacion,Edwin

Age: 33 Bats: R Pos: DH 1B | Health B | LIMA Plan A
Ht: 6' 1" Wt: 230 | PT/Exp A | Rand Var 0
Consist A | MM 5055

Power unquestionably drives his value, but it's the rest of the package that keeps him in the elite tier of the player pool. Good contact for a slugger sets a nice BA floor, near-perfect Reliability and weekly consistency complete the package. Elite right-on-right platoon productivity (33 of 39 HR vs. RHP) aids his DFS utility too.

Yr	Tm	AB	R	HR	RBI	SB	BA	xBA	OBP	SLG	OPS	vL	vR	bb%	ct%	Eye	G	L	F	h%	HctX	PX	xPX	hr/f	Spd	SBO	SB%	#Wk	DOM	DIS	RC/G	RAR	BPV	BPX	R$
11	TOR	481	70	17	55	8	272	275	334	453	787	845	767	8	84	0.56	36	19	44	29	129	124	124	9%	72	8%	80%	27	63%	19%	5.29	-7.5	75	167	$16
12	TOR	542	93	42	110	13	280	285	384	557	941	1086	892	13	83	0.89	33	18	49	27	131	157	153	19%	76	9%	81%	27	81%	7%	7.47	39.7	108	270	$31
13	TOR	530	90	36	104	7	272	311	370	534	904	859	916	13	88	1.32	35	22	43	25	137	150	152	18%	66	5%	88%	25	84%	8%	6.95	37.1	122	305	$28
14	TOR	477	75	34	98	2	268	300	354	547	901	870	909	12	83	0.76	36	16	47	26	137	176	153	18%	74	2%	100%	22	68%	14%	6.75	36.9	119	322	$24
15	TOR	528	94	39	111	3	277	297	372	557	929	836	950	13	81	0.79	36	19	45	27	127	166	142	20%	51	3%	60%	27	81%	4%	7.17	25.9	101	273	$28
1st Half		283	45	17	50	1	233	265	325	459	785	804	780	12	78	0.64	40	17	43	24	93	139	110	17%	49	1%	100%	14	79%	0%	5.00	-3.8	66	178	$20
2nd Half		245	49	22	61	2	327	334	424	669	1093	869	1146	13	85	1.03	32	22	46	31	167	196	176	22%	61	5%	50%	13	85%	8%	10.33	32.0	143	386	$37
16	Proj	522	90	37	108	2	284	298	375	560	935	870	951	12	83	0.84	35	19	45	28	137	160	150	19%	62	3%	58%				7.35	28.0	103	279	$28

Escobar,Alcides

Age: 29 Bats: R Pos: SS | Health A | LIMA Plan B+
Ht: 6' 1" Wt: 185 | PT/Exp A | Rand Var +1
Consist A | MM 0525

xBA has been sitting in a narrow band for five years running, but BA ping-pongs all over the place. Combo of strong ct% plus flimsy HctX shows how rarely he actually stings the ball. Value-wise, he's a one-trick speedster, and SBO% is as errratic as BA. UP: 30 SB again, but don't pay for more than 20.

Yr	Tm	AB	R	HR	RBI	SB	BA	xBA	OBP	SLG	OPS	vL	vR	bb%	ct%	Eye	G	L	F	h%	HctX	PX	xPX	hr/f	Spd	SBO	SB%	#Wk	DOM	DIS	RC/G	RAR	BPV	BPX	R$
11	KC	548	69	4	46	26	254	262	290	343	633	576	651	4	87	0.34	53	18	29	29	65	58	46	3%	171	27%	74%	27	41%	22%	3.34	-13.7	55	122	$14
12	KC	605	68	5	52	35	293	271	331	390	721	676	739	4	83	0.27	53	23	24	34	76	65	51	4%	142	25%	88%	27	33%	26%	4.73	14.0	39	98	$25
13	KC	607	57	4	52	22	234	250	259	300	559	620	532	3	86	0.23	46	23	31	27	77	45	60	3%	140	17%	100%	26	23%	27%	2.74	-12.5	31	78	$11
14	KC	579	74	3	50	31	285	265	317	377	694	784	663	4	86	0.28	44	24	32	33	83	70	62	2%	138	25%	84%	27	41%	22%	4.31	18.7	50	135	$25
15	KC	612	76	3	47	17	257	255	293	320	614	653	598	4	88	0.35	48	22	30	29	79	41	52	2%	136	14%	77%	27	37%	22%	3.18	-22.0	35	95	$14
1st Half		286	38	2	28	5	276	262	314	357	670	600	699	4	88	0.34	44	24	32	31	76	53	56	2%	115	9%	71%	14	50%	14%	3.82	-2.2	38	103	$14
2nd Half		326	38	1	19	12	239	249	275	288	564	699	509	4	88	0.35	51	21	28	27	82	30	49	1%	152	19%	80%	13	23%	31%	2.68	-13.9	31	84	$13
16	Proj	606	72	3	48	21	261	257	294	334	628	679	609	4	87	0.30	47	23	30	30	79	48	55	2%	145	18%	79%				3.37	-12.8	33	89	$18

Escobar,Eduardo

Age: 27 Bats: B Pos: SS LF | Health A | LIMA Plan B
Ht: 5' 10" Wt: 175 | PT/Exp C | Rand Var 0
Consist A | MM 3225

Took over as regular SS in 2nd half and delivered some sneaky value with a power spike. But don't get caught extrapolating that 2H: A hot streak vs LHP drove much of it; he's still mediocre vRHP. Poor SB% precludes more SB; xBA doesn't support BA growth. That leaves an MI with a touch of pop, not an emerging star.

Yr	Tm	AB	R	HR	RBI	SB	BA	xBA	OBP	SLG	OPS	vL	vR	bb%	ct%	Eye	G	L	F	h%	HctX	PX	xPX	hr/f	Spd	SBO	SB%	#Wk	DOM	DIS	RC/G	RAR	BPV	BPX	R$
11	CHW *	496	46	4	41	11	243	296	279	321	601	667	500	5	76	0.21	67	33	0	31	0	62	2	0%	112	17%	56%	5	0%	40%	2.88	-19.4	0	0	$6
12	2AL *	269	34	1	17	6	207	227	257	270	526	844	419	6	78	0.30	51	21	28	26	80	41	42	0%	148	11%	84%	19	26%	68%	2.28	-13.6	4	10	-$1
13	MIN *	331	39	6	30	4	251	244	300	383	683	655	619	7	77	0.31	42	21	37	31	81	97	94	6%	135	11%	51%	18	33%	39%	3.76	3.3	42	105	$5
14	MIN	433	52	6	37	1	275	264	315	406	721	877	654	5	79	0.26	41	24	35	34	99	110	93	5%	113	2%	50%	27	41%	26%	4.44	15.6	49	132	$10
15	MIN	409	48	12	58	2	262	267	309	445	754	789	737	6	79	0.33	42	19	39	31	99	125	116	10%	107	6%	40%	27	44%	30%	4.62	2.7	63	170	$10
1st Half		197	17	4	29	2	254	244	286	406	692	588	741	4	77	0.17	43	18	39	31	97	105	129	7%	121	13%	40%	14	29%	36%	3.70	-2.3	37	100	$6
2nd Half		212	31	8	29	0	269	287	329	481	810	979	733	9	81	0.50	41	20	38	30	101	142	105	12%	97	0%	0%	13	62%	23%	5.57	9.0	86	232	$13
16	Proj	459	55	9	52	3	260	258	307	410	718	822	673	6	79	0.32	43	21	36	31	95	106	99	7%	111	6%	50%				4.26	2.4	39	106	$12

Escobar,Yunel

Age: 33 Bats: R Pos: 3B | Health A | LIMA Plan B+
Ht: 6' 2" Wt: 215 | PT/Exp A | Rand Var -5
Consist C | MM 1135

Forecaster usage lesson: When looking at a box of someone who performed wildly differently than expectations, check RandVar first. Here, it tells the whole story: Nothing new except a massive h% spike, which earned him a lineup position bump that offered more Runs/RBI. He will never see $20 or .300 again.

Yr	Tm	AB	R	HR	RBI	SB	BA	xBA	OBP	SLG	OPS	vL	vR	bb%	ct%	Eye	G	L	F	h%	HctX	PX	xPX	hr/f	Spd	SBO	SB%	#Wk	DOM	DIS	RC/G	RAR	BPV	BPX	R$
11	TOR	513	77	11	48	3	290	276	369	413	782	929	740	11	86	0.87	57	18	25	32	91	79	79	10%	129	3%	50%	24	54%	13%	5.35	3.6	71	158	$16
12	TOR	558	58	9	51	5	253	261	300	344	644	644	643	6	87	0.50	56	19	25	28	89	57	69	7%	91	4%	83%	27	44%	22%	3.51	-18.0	37	93	$8
13	TAM	508	61	9	56	4	256	266	332	366	698	750	674	10	86	0.78	53	19	27	28	117	76	98	8%	89	5%	50%	27	52%	19%	4.07	1.1	52	130	$10
14	TAM	476	33	7	39	1	258	244	324	340	664	689	656	8	87	0.72	49	20	31	28	105	57	75	6%	72	1%	50%	25	56%	20%	3.72	0.1	35	95	$6
15	WAS	535	75	9	56	2	314	275	375	415	790	760	800	8	87	0.64	55	22	23	35	106	65	73	8%	101	2%	50%	26	46%	23%	5.61	13.4	47	127	$20
1st Half		287	40	4	27	1	314	273	364	404	768	639	808	6	86	0.48	57	22	21	35	99	58	63	8%	107	3%	33%	14	36%	29%	5.22	4.7	37	100	$21
2nd Half		248	35	5	29	1	315	278	386	427	814	909	791	9	88	0.87	51	22	26	34	115	72	83	9%	92	1%	100%	12	58%	17%	6.07	9.6	58	157	$20
16	Proj	501	49	9	42	2	267	266	334	368	701	717	696	8	87	0.70	53	21	26	29	107	64	78	8%	94	3%	56%				4.16	-6.7	31	83	$12

Espinosa,Danny

Age: 29 Bats: B Pos: 2B | Health A | LIMA Plan D+
Ht: 6' 0" Wt: 205 | PT/Exp C | Rand Var 0
Consist C | MM 4303

Injuries afforded him an everyday job for most of 1H, and he took full advantage—ct% rebounded to tolerable levels and brought back memories of 2011-12. Regular PT dried up in 2H, and ct% deteriorated in part-time work. But 1H is enough to rekindle our interest (we're suckers like that). With 450 AB ... UP: 20 HR/10 SB.

Yr	Tm	AB	R	HR	RBI	SB	BA	xBA	OBP	SLG	OPS	vL	vR	bb%	ct%	Eye	G	L	F	h%	HctX	PX	xPX	hr/f	Spd	SBO	SB%	#Wk	DOM	DIS	RC/G	RAR	BPV	BPX	R$
11	WAS	573	72	21	66	17	236	241	323	414	737	857	703	9	71	0.34	44	16	40	30	105	132	130	14%	114	17%	74%	27	44%	41%	4.18	-5.7	44	98	$14
12	WAS	594	82	17	56	20	247	234	315	402	717	775	694	7	68	0.24	47	19	34	34	93	123	109	13%	106	19%	77%	27	33%	44%	4.11	0.0	19	48	$16
13	WAS *	441	33	4	27	6	169	173	199	245	444	529	448	4	63	0.10	51	10	39	26	71	74	95	7%	76	11%	83%	10	40%	50%	1.52	-28.6	-55	-138	-$7
14	WAS	333	31	8	27	8	219	215	283	351	634	859	532	5	63	0.15	44	22	34	32	100	115	134	12%	106	14%	89%	26	27%	54%	3.04	-2.5	-9	-24	$4
15	WAS	367	59	13	37	5	240	242	311	409	719	753	709	8	71	0.31	45	18	37	30	87	124	114	14%	100	8%	71%	24	33%	42%	4.12	3.9	32	86	$8
1st Half		240	38	8	24	3	258	247	341	425	766	845	742	10	74	0.41	42	20	38	32	99	118	130	12%	99	8%	60%	14	43%	21%	4.75	4.7	41	111	$12
2nd Half		127	21	5	13	2	205	232	250	378	628	590	640	5	66	0.16	50	15	35	27	64	135	78	19%	98	10%	100%	10	20%	70%	3.05	-4.1	14	38	$1
16	Proj	394	51	13	36	6	230	225	290	386	675	767	643	6	67	0.20	47	17	36	31	85	120	109	13%	101	11%	72%				3.52	-8.5	7	20	$9

Ethier,Andre

Age: 34 Bats: L Pos: RF LF | Health A | LIMA Plan B+
Ht: 6' 2" Wt: 200 | PT/Exp B | Rand Var -1
Consist D | MM 3145

Fixed whatever caused 2014's GB% spike, and that one adjustment allowed everything else to snap right back to historical levels. If you treat 2014 as an outlier, everything else here is remarkably stable. Don't get drawn in by that 2H BA—but otherwise, he can keep doing this for a while.

Yr	Tm	AB	R	HR	RBI	SB	BA	xBA	OBP	SLG	OPS	vL	vR	bb%	ct%	Eye	G	L	F	h%	HctX	PX	xPX	hr/f	Spd	SBO	SB%	#Wk	DOM	DIS	RC/G	RAR	BPV	BPX	R$
11	LA	487	67	11	62	0	292	265	368	421	789	563	878	11	79	0.56	44	25	31	35	102	97	80	9%	93	1%	0%	24	46%	29%	5.52	3.3	44	98	$16
12	LA	556	79	20	89	2	284	271	351	460	812	606	945	8	78	0.40	43	24	33	33	109	120	106	14%	93	3%	50%	26	54%	27%	5.57	13.2	53	133	$20
13	LA	482	54	12	52	4	272	268	360	423	783	613	854	11	80	0.60	39	24	37	32	120	109	124	8%	106	5%	57%	25	60%	16%	5.17	15.4	65	163	$13
14	LA	341	29	4	42	2	249	259	322	370	691	567	710	8	78	0.42	52	22	26	31	84	88	63	6%	121	4%	50%	27	44%	30%	3.85	0.6	39	105	$5
15	LA	395	54	14	53	2	294	281	366	486	852	474	900	10	81	0.57	38	26	35	33	116	116	122	12%	124	4%	40%	27	63%	19%	6.22	16.6	76	205	$15
1st Half		222	31	10	28	1	270	271	353	473	826	632	851	11	82	0.69	40	21	39	29	113	112	116	14%	129	3%	50%	14	71%	14%	5.70	7.3	82	222	$15
2nd Half		173	23	4	25	1	324	293	383	503	886	255	962	8	79	0.44	37	33	30	39	121	121	130	10%	116	6%	33%	13	54%	23%	6.95	11.1	67	181	$14
16	Proj	413	49	12	54	2	276	278	349	450	799	526	853	9	80	0.51	42	26	32	32	108	112	106	11%	116	5%	44%				5.32	6.0	53	143	$14

Featherston,Taylor

Age: 26 Bats: R Pos: 3B 2B SS | Health A | LIMA Plan D
Ht: 6' 1" Wt: 185 | PT/Exp F | Rand Var +3
Consist F | MM 1401

2-9-.162 with 4 SB in 154 AB. Rule 5 selection came to LAA with a power/speed profile and BA/contact questions. Spent most of season rotting on bench. Got a decent look in Sept (62 AB), where ct% ticked up (79%) but neither power nor speed showed. Likely headed back to minors for more seasoning.

Yr	Tm	AB	R	HR	RBI	SB	BA	xBA	OBP	SLG	OPS	vL	vR	bb%	ct%	Eye	G	L	F	h%	HctX	PX	xPX	hr/f	Spd	SBO	SB%	#Wk	DOM	DIS	RC/G	RAR	BPV	BPX	R$
11																																			
12																																			
13																																			
14	aa	497	51	13	42	10	234		274	390	665			5	75	0.22				29		120			102	18%	60%				3.43		39	105	$9
15	LAA *	183	25	2	10	4	157	203	193	239	432	584	401	4	70	0.15	48	18	34	21	73	61	82	6%	132	22%	67%	23	35%	61%	1.37	-17.7	-22	-59	-$4
1st Half		58	9	1	4	2	121	168	161	207	368	422	346	5	60	0.13	46	11	43	18	65	77	134	7%	103	43%	67%	13	38%	54%	0.95	-6.7	-54	-146	-$6
2nd Half		125	16	1	6	2	174	223	207	254	461	665	437	4	74	0.16	49	21	30	23	77	55	56	5%	139	15%	67%	10	30%	70%	1.60	-10.7	-9	-24	-$2
16	Proj	167	21	2	11	4	209	214	258	311	570	727	498	5	71	0.17	47	17	35	28	72	77	87	6%	127	18%	64%				2.41	-11.6	-7	-19	$2

RAY MURPHY

Fielder,Prince

Age: 32	Bats: L	Pos: DH	Health	D	LIMA Plan	B+
Ht: 5' 11"	Wt: 275		PT/Exp	B	Rand Var	-4
			Consist	D	MM	2025

An impressive, fully skills-supported comeback from 2014 neck surgery... for a half. Subsequent 2H collapse lowlighted by troubling plunges of HctX and xPX. We may not know if neck started bothering him again, but recovery gets less likely as he gets deeper into 30s. xBA says even a repeat may be too much to ask.

Yr	Tm	AB	R	HR	RBI	SB	BA	xBA	OBP	SLG	OPS	vL	vR	bb%	ct%	Eye	G	L	F	h%	HctX	PX	xPX	hr/f	Spd	SBO	SB%	#Wk	DOM	DIS	RC/G	RAR	BPV	BPX	R$
11	MIL	569	95	38	120	1	299	306	415	566	981	822	1046	16	81	1.01	43	20	37	31	140	170	145	22%	45	1%	50%	27	74%	15%	8.40	40.1	109	242	$32
12	DET	581	83	30	108	1	313	304	412	528	940	808	1017	13	86	1.01	41	25	33	33	132	126	128	18%	45	0%	100%	27	70%	11%	7.88	46.8	84	210	$30
13	DET	624	82	25	106	1	279	275	362	457	819	819	819	11	81	0.64	41	23	36	31	116	119	128	14%	37	1%	50%	27	56%	11%	5.73	21.6	55	138	$24
14	TEX	150	19	3	16	0	247	251	360	360	720	688	733	14	84	1.04	50	19	31	28	95	83	68	8%	44	0%	0%	7	29%	14%	4.32	1.2	46	124	$1
15	TEX	613	78	23	98	0	305	259	378	463	841	724	923	9	86	0.73	46	18	35	33	121	94	107	12%	26	0%	0%	27	52%	22%	6.30	14.2	46	124	$26
1st Half		317	41	13	50	0	347	282	413	530	943	824	1022	9	88	0.77	44	20	35	37	144	108	124	13%	30	0%	0%	14	64%	7%	8.35	23.5	65	176	$34
2nd Half		296	37	10	48	0	260	235	341	392	733	623	814	10	83	0.69	48	16	36	28	97	77	89	11%	29	0%	0%	13	38%	38%	4.54	-7.8	27	73	$18
16	Proj	**589**	**77**	**20**	**90**	**0**	**275**	**261**	**364**	**428**	**792**	**710**	**843**	**11**	**84**	**0.81**	**46**	**19**	**34**	**30**	**113**	**94**	**101**	**12%**	**33**	**0%**	**56%**				**5.37**	**-1.3**	**45**	**121**	**$19**

Flaherty,Ryan

Age: 29	Bats: L	Pos: 2B	Health	B	LIMA Plan	D
Ht: 6' 3"	Wt: 210		PT/Exp	D	Rand Var	+1
			Consist	A	MM	3201

Already a risk in terms of BA, when ct% dipped, BA followed with a dive to the brink of the Mendoza line. He's been teasing us for years as a LH-hitting MI with some pop in a good ballpark for those skills. But as R$ history shows, this amount of pop doesn't begin to make up for that BA. No reason to be teased any longer.

Yr	Tm	AB	R	HR	RBI	SB	BA	xBA	OBP	SLG	OPS	vL	vR	bb%	ct%	Eye	G	L	F	h%	HctX	PX	xPX	hr/f	Spd	SBO	SB%	#Wk	DOM	DIS	RC/G	RAR	BPV	BPX	R$
11	a/a	475	48	13	57	3	224		275	365	640			7	75	0.28				27		104			89	10%	31%				3.10		26	58	$5
12	BAL *	191	19	8	21	1	224	208	254	380	634	667	613	4	72	0.14	43	13	44	27	80	96	107	13%	121	3%	100%	24	25%	63%	3.20	-4.0	11	28	$1
13	BAL *	280	31	12	31	2	223	240	274	390	665	641	687	7	74	0.28	49	16	36	26	108	116	115	15%	90	3%	100%	24	38%	38%	3.55	1.1	33	83	$3
14	BAL	281	33	7	32	1	221	244	288	356	644	616	649	7	76	0.32	47	19	34	27	94	104	101	10%	80	2%	100%	26	42%	42%	3.25	0.6	27	73	$3
15	BAL	267	34	9	31	0	202	219	281	356	637	546	661	9	70	0.32	50	14	36	25	89	104	97	13%	117	0%	0%	24	29%	50%	3.11	-10.7	17	46	$0
1st Half		153	22	3	20	0	248	224	328	386	713	731	708	9	69	0.31	52	17	31	34	92	98	100	9%	126	0%	0%	12	25%	50%	4.13	0.2	10	27	$3
2nd Half		114	12	6	11	0	140	203	216	316	532	158	603	9	71	0.33	47	10	43	13	85	111	92	18%	89	0%	0%	12	33%	50%	2.02	-7.9	19	51	-$4
16	Proj	**226**	**26**	**8**	**25**	**1**	**221**	**226**	**290**	**375**	**665**	**551**	**687**	**8**	**73**	**0.31**	**48**	**15**	**37**	**27**	**92**	**103**	**101**	**13%**	**97**	**1%**	**78%**				**3.46**	**-5.3**	**11**	**29**	**$4**

Flores,Wilmer

Age: 24	Bats: R	Pos: SS 2B	Health	A	LIMA Plan	B+
Ht: 6' 3"	Wt: 205		PT/Exp	C	Rand Var	0
			Consist	A	MM	2035

Notwithstanding some late-July tears, there was plenty to be happy about in first full big-league season. Nudged his already-strong ct% to borderline-elite levels, which maximized value of his average power skills. Big platoon split not yet cast in stone; gains vRHP - and defense - may be key to unlocking full-time role and... UP: 25 HR.

Yr	Tm	AB	R	HR	RBI	SB	BA	xBA	OBP	SLG	OPS	vL	vR	bb%	ct%	Eye	G	L	F	h%	HctX	PX	xPX	hr/f	Spd	SBO	SB%	#Wk	DOM	DIS	RC/G	RAR	BPV	BPX	R$
11																																			
12	aa	251	30	7	27	0	274		318	428	746			6	86	0.48				29		95			94	0%	0%				4.78		64	160	$5
13	NYM *	519	53	11	69	1	246	269	276	384	660	447	591	4	81	0.22	51	22	27	28	69	98	47	5%	80	4%	16%	8	50%	50%	3.48	-0.4	36	90	$9
14	NYM *	479	54	14	64	1	248	257	281	391	672	382	739	4	84	0.28	40	20	40	27	101	95	103	7%	110	3%	30%	20	40%	35%	3.65	5.0	54	146	$10
15	NYM	483	55	16	59	0	263	267	295	408	703	955	637	4	87	0.30	42	21	37	27	109	86	95	10%	90	1%	0%	26	46%	23%	4.06	4.1	53	143	$11
1st Half		279	31	10	38	0	254	270	286	409	694	880	658	3	86	0.26	40	22	38	26	118	91	111	11%	94	0%	0%	14	50%	29%	3.92	-1.4	55	149	$13
2nd Half		204	24	6	21	0	275	261	308	407	715	1017	604	4	88	0.36	45	20	35	29	97	78	73	10%	93	2%	0%	12	42%	17%	4.27	1.1	52	141	$8
16	Proj	**504**	**57**	**17**	**62**	**0**	**260**	**265**	**292**	**412**	**704**	**713**	**701**	**4**	**85**	**0.29**	**41**	**21**	**38**	**28**	**98**	**92**	**87**	**10%**	**98**	**2%**	**19%**				**4.05**	**-0.5**	**38**	**102**	**$14**

Flowers,Tyler

Age: 30	Bats: R	Pos: CA	Health	A	LIMA Plan	D
Ht: 6' 4"	Wt: 245		PT/Exp	C	Rand Var	-2
			Consist	B	MM	3003

Bad news: A surge vRHP in 2H of 2014 suggested that maybe he was turning into more than a bad-side platoon 2nd C, but those gains proved to be a mirage. Worse news: There's only one year in this box where he did any damage to LHPs. Worst news of all: There's no third option for handedness of opposing pitchers.

Yr	Tm	AB	R	HR	RBI	SB	BA	xBA	OBP	SLG	OPS	vL	vR	bb%	ct%	Eye	G	L	F	h%	HctX	PX	xPX	hr/f	Spd	SBO	SB%	#Wk	DOM	DIS	RC/G	RAR	BPV	BPX	R$
11	CHW *	332	41	19	41	2	223	210	320	432	752	431	863	13	58	0.34	32	16	51	32	91	179	180	13%	86	3%	61%	10	40%	50%	4.50	3.0	28	62	$6
12	CHW	136	19	7	13	2	213	225	296	412	708	905	586	8	59	0.21	53	18	29	30	64	165	87	30%	77	11%	67%	26	27%	62%	3.64	-2.0	9	23	$1
13	CHW	256	24	10	24	0	195	208	247	355	603	455	661	5	63	0.15	42	17	41	26	86	133	106	15%	71	2%	0%	22	32%	59%	2.62	-8.9	-6	-15	-$1
14	CHW	407	42	15	50	0	241	222	297	396	693	732	679	6	61	0.16	48	24	29	36	82	137	88	21%	73	1%	0%	26	31%	58%	3.74	5.0	-10	-27	$7
15	CHW	331	21	9	39	0	239	194	295	356	652	751	627	6	69	0.20	47	17	36	32	93	88	84	11%	71	1%	0%	26	27%	54%	3.34	-3.8	-19	-51	$2
1st Half		167	13	7	19	0	222	202	270	383	653	646	654	5	67	0.16	42	16	42	29	84	117	90	15%	78	0%	0%	14	43%	50%	3.28	-2.5	-3	-8	$2
2nd Half		164	8	2	20	0	256	187	320	329	650	817	596	7	70	0.24	52	18	30	35	102	60	79	6%	70	2%	0%	12	8%	58%	3.37	-2.0	-35	-95	$2
16	Proj	**315**	**26**	**10**	**36**	**0**	**232**	**207**	**293**	**370**	**663**	**696**	**653**	**6**	**65**	**0.19**	**46**	**19**	**35**	**32**	**89**	**107**	**93**	**14%**	**73**	**2%**	**23%**				**3.41**	**-3.6**	**-32**	**-86**	**$5**

Forsythe,Logan

Age: 29	Bats: R	Pos: 2B 1B	Health	C	LIMA Plan	B
Ht: 6' 1"	Wt: 195		PT/Exp	C	Rand Var	-4
			Consist	C	MM	2315

This breakout was actually just a consolidation of skills previously displayed: xPX says the power was there all along, h% just recovered back to 2011-12 levels. xBA points out that about half of the BA gain was flimsy, and poor SBO% threatens an SB repeat. RandVar highlights regression risk, but it should be gentle.

Yr	Tm	AB	R	HR	RBI	SB	BA	xBA	OBP	SLG	OPS	vL	vR	bb%	ct%	Eye	G	L	F	h%	HctX	PX	xPX	hr/f	Spd	SBO	SB%	#Wk	DOM	DIS	RC/G	RAR	BPV	BPX	R$
11	SD *	328	36	4	32	8	226	217	297	326	623	548	577	9	70	0.34	43	20	37	31	91	87	98	0%	97	16%	57%	15	33%	53%	3.06	-16.8	0	0	$3
12	SD *	373	53	7	32	10	263	249	329	383	712	1010	603	9	79	0.46	36	29	35	32	112	77	107	7%	159	11%	83%	18	28%	28%	4.42	0.8	44	110	$9
13	SD *	245	26	7	22	6	221	253	291	360	651	651	593	9	74	0.38	42	28	29	27	98	94	105	13%	112	11%	86%	17	12%	35%	3.49	-1.2	26	65	$2
14	TAM	301	32	6	26	2	223	224	287	329	616	708	536	8	76	0.35	41	19	40	27	83	80	100	6%	107	3%	100%	27	30%	59%	3.08	-2.8	19	51	$2
15	TAM	540	69	17	68	9	281	255	359	444	804	972	728	9	79	0.50	40	20	41	33	108	109	106	10%	112	8%	69%	26	46%	23%	5.44	17.8	59	159	$20
1st Half		285	32	8	34	7	281	254	365	425	790	894	748	9	81	0.54	39	22	39	32	97	94	96	9%	110	11%	78%	14	43%	21%	5.24	8.2	53	143	$20
2nd Half		255	37	9	34	2	282	256	353	467	820	1045	704	9	78	0.46	40	18	42	33	120	126	117	11%	111	6%	50%	12	50%	25%	5.66	10.4	65	176	$20
16	Proj	**479**	**59**	**12**	**53**	**6**	**260**	**243**	**332**	**398**	**731**	**849**	**665**	**9**	**77**	**0.42**	**40**	**21**	**38**	**31**	**101**	**94**	**105**	**9%**	**112**	**7%**	**70%**				**4.43**	**2.9**	**29**	**78**	**$14**

Fowler,Dexter

Age: 30	Bats: B	Pos: CF	Health	B	LIMA Plan	B
Ht: 6' 4"	Wt: 190		PT/Exp	A	Rand Var	+1
			Consist	A	MM	3515

Skill set has achieved stability; the biggest unknown year-to-year is playing time. This was his career-high in playing time by 127 PA. Health grade shows that injuries aren't the problem; instead his relative struggles vRH confine him to the bench periodically. Set expectations for 500 AB and leave some room for profit.

Yr	Tm	AB	R	HR	RBI	SB	BA	xBA	OBP	SLG	OPS	vL	vR	bb%	ct%	Eye	G	L	F	h%	HctX	PX	xPX	hr/f	Spd	SBO	SB%	#Wk	DOM	DIS	RC/G	RAR	BPV	BPX	R$
11	COL *	578	92	6	49	13	251	250	338	406	743	762	807	12	73	0.48	43	21	35	34	103	119	102	4%	160	15%	56%	22	45%	18%	4.48	-5.2	60	133	$12
12	COL	454	72	13	53	12	300	249	389	474	863	857	866	13	72	0.53	39	27	34	39	97	115	125	12%	175	10%	71%	27	33%	33%	6.67	25.1	60	150	$20
13	COL	415	71	12	42	19	263	246	369	407	776	860	741	14	75	0.62	42	23	34	33	80	102	102	11%	135	20%	68%	23	48%	35%	4.99	11.0	50	125	$18
14	HOU	434	61	8	35	11	276	240	375	399	774	887	737	13	75	0.61	44	21	35	35	95	94	107	7%	144	10%	73%	20	45%	35%	5.23	17.4	47	127	$15
15	CHC	596	102	17	46	20	250	245	346	411	757	865	726	12	74	0.55	43	20	36	31	91	109	98	11%	162	15%	74%	26	50%	27%	4.78	8.3	59	159	$19
1st Half		302	51	8	23	11	228	231	305	374	679	833	650	10	75	0.42	40	20	41	28	80	96	77	9%	142	19%	73%	14	36%	36%	3.72	-6.4	40	108	$16
2nd Half		294	51	9	23	9	272	259	386	449	835	883	815	15	73	0.67	47	21	32	34	101	123	119	13%	166	12%	75%	12	67%	17%	6.00	13.5	74	200	$23
16	Proj	**517**	**84**	**13**	**44**	**17**	**263**	**246**	**363**	**416**	**779**	**865**	**750**	**13**	**74**	**0.58**	**43**	**21**	**35**	**33**	**92**	**104**	**105**	**10%**	**154**	**14%**	**72%**				**5.14**	**11.1**	**47**	**126**	**$20**

Franco,Maikel

Age: 23	Bats: R	Pos: 3B	Health	B	LIMA Plan	A
Ht: 6' 1"	Wt: 180		PT/Exp	C	Rand Var	-2
			Consist	F	MM	3235

14-50-.280 in 304 AB at PHI. 3B prospect hit the ground running after May callup: 10 HR in 170 1st half AB. Much to like here: nice contact foundation for a slugger, now starting to mix in some patience (see bb%), no platoon split. 2H interrupted by wrist fracture, but he returned in season's final weekend. A building block.

Yr	Tm	AB	R	HR	RBI	SB	BA	xBA	OBP	SLG	OPS	vL	vR	bb%	ct%	Eye	G	L	F	h%	HctX	PX	xPX	hr/f	Spd	SBO	SB%	#Wk	DOM	DIS	RC/G	RAR	BPV	BPX	R$
11																																			
12																																			
13	aa	277	36	12	39	1	305		324	492	816			3	87	0.22				31		109			100	4%	26%				5.67		74	185	$11
14	PHI *	577	55	14	65	2	222	240	253	358	611	277	573	4	82	0.23	49	12	40	25	32	97	26	0%	120	3%	68%	5	0%	40%	2.96	-13.3	51	138	$6
15	PHI *	445	57	18	70	3	291	283	340	492	832	825	844	7	82	0.40	47	18	35	32	103	130	119	16%	106	2%	100%	16	69%	25%	6.06	17.1	78	211	$18
1st Half		333	39	14	54	3	305	286	342	511	853	969	854	5	82	0.31	50	17	33	34	94	131	103	19%	122	3%	100%	9	56%	33%	6.47	16.7	82	222	$25
2nd Half		112	18	4	16	0	250	274	341	438	779	684	821	11	81	0.67	42	20	38	28	117	127	148	11%	83	0%	0%	7	86%	14%	4.96	1.1	76	205	-$4
16	Proj	**558**	**70**	**21**	**76**	**2**	**267**	**268**	**314**	**449**	**763**	**556**	**892**	**6**	**83**	**0.37**	**45**	**17**	**38**	**29**	**77**	**116**	**88**	**12%**	**98**	**2%**	**68%**				**4.85**	**3.6**	**56**	**150**	**$19**

RAY MURPHY

Francoeur,Jeff

Age: 32	Bats: R	Pos: RF LF	Health	A	LIMA Plan	D
Ht: 6' 4"	Wt: 220		PT/Exp	D	Rand Var	-2
			Consist	C	MM	2113

Received more PT than expected and responded with his best season since 2012. But that is faint praise for this underwhelming skill set. Plate control deteriorated in 2nd half, subpar xPX doesn't support the HR output, and hr/f is primed for regression. Even if he finds the AB again, don't expect a repeat.

Yr	Tm	AB	R	HR	RBI	SB	BA	xBA	OBP	SLG	OPS	vL	vR	bb%	ct%	Eye	G	L	F	h%	HctX	PX	xPX	hr/f	Spd	SBO	SB%	#Wk	DOM	DIS	RC/G	RAR	BPV	BPX	R$
11	KC	601	77	20	87	22	285	276	329	476	805	934	762	6	80	0.30	40	20	40	33	113	137	113	10%	102	23%	69%	26	62%	12%	5.36	3.7	72	160	$27
12	KC	561	58	16	49	4	235	252	287	378	665	695	652	6	79	0.29	45	21	34	27	100	93	106	11%	96	9%	36%	27	44%	37%	3.35	-30.7	32	80	$7
13	2 TM	245	20	3	17	3	204	219	238	298	536	539	534	4	75	0.15	47	17	36	26	81	71	86	5%	115	7%	100%	19	16%	58%	2.27	-17.8	1	3	-$2
14	SD *	480	31	8	38	6	187	223	211	272	483	393	83	3	71	0.10	39	28	33	25	51	68	83	0%	89	11%	69%	4	0%	75%	1.78	-35.6	-26	-70	-$3
15	PHI	326	34	13	45	0	258	260	286	433	718	645	769	4	76	0.17	40	24	37	30	84	115	82	14%	78	3%	0%	27	48%	33%	4.13	-6.9	30	81	$7
1st Half		167	15	5	23	0	257	264	292	413	705	602	768	5	81	0.26	43	22	35	29	78	99	72	10%	87	3%	0%	14	50%	21%	4.02	-3.9	42	114	$5
2nd Half		159	19	8	22	0	258	256	279	453	732	684	769	3	71	0.11	35	26	39	31	91	134	94	18%	72	3%	0%	13	46%	46%	4.23	-2.7	21	57	$9
16	Proj	270	25	8	30	2	232	240	264	377	641	614	656	4	75	0.15	42	22	37	28	89	98	91	11%	90	7%	54%				3.20	-13.2	5	14	$3

Franklin,Nick

Age: 25	Bats: B	Pos: 2B	Health	B	LIMA Plan	D
Ht: 6' 1"	Wt: 195		PT/Exp	C	Rand Var	+3
			Consist	B	MM	3301

3-7-.158 in 101 AB at TAM. Still strikes out far too often, but xPX/Spd combo and bb% remain intriguing. The problem is that without improvement in ct% and BA, playing time could prove elusive. DOM/DIS inconsistency is damning; at 25, he needs to start making serious strides. Time is running out.

Yr	Tm	AB	R	HR	RBI	SB	BA	xBA	OBP	SLG	OPS	vL	vR	bb%	ct%	Eye	G	L	F	h%	HctX	PX	xPX	hr/f	Spd	SBO	SB%	#Wk	DOM	DIS	RC/G	RAR	BPV	BPX	R$
11	aa	83	11	2	5	4	296		338	422	760			6	75	0.26				38		85			128	31%	57%				4.66		22	49	$2
12	a/a	472	53	8	45	10	239		300	373	673			8	74	0.33				31		98			109	13%	69%				3.71		25	63	$7
13	SEA *	511	58	15	59	11	240	239	323	385	709	599	727	11	73	0.46	35	24	41	30	103	111	140	11%	84	9%	92%	19	37%	37%	4.27	8.3	31	78	$12
14	2 AL *	460	52	10	54	11	227	208	310	337	647	369	492	11	70	0.40	41	18	41	30	71	90	103	5%	102	13%	67%	7	14%	71%	3.41	0.2	6	16	$9
15	TAM *	293	32	11	32	4	204	226	277	377	653	592	490	9	68	0.32	32	23	45	26	70	124	110	11%	114	12%	56%	11	18%	55%	3.23	-9.6	27	73	$2
1st Half		120	11	3	8	3	169	215	229	281	510	628	374	7	69	0.25	36	26	38	22	57	80	64	6%	124	17%	70%	6	17%	50%	1.96	-9.0	-5	-14	-$7
2nd Half		173	21	9	24	2	228	210	309	443	752	452	739	10	68	0.36	20	13	67	28	105	155	251	20%	104	10%	42%	5	20%	60%	4.33	0.5	49	132	$7
16	Proj	158	18	5	18	3	219	226	294	378	672	626	686	10	70	0.35	39	19	42	28	83	114	145	11%	107	12%	67%				3.58	-3.2	18	49	$3

Frazier,Todd

Age: 30	Bats: R	Pos: 3B	Health	A	LIMA Plan	B+
Ht: 6' 3"	Wt: 220		PT/Exp	A	Rand Var	+2
			Consist	B	MM	4225

A worthy followup to 2014 breakout, even reaching new highs in FB%, xPX and HctX. xBA shows he didn't deserve the BA decline. However, he again had a huge 1H followed by 2H collapse—partially due to hr/f regression. Decline in Spd/SB% cast doubt on double-digit SB going forward. Still, good value here.

Yr	Tm	AB	R	HR	RBI	SB	BA	xBA	OBP	SLG	OPS	vL	vR	bb%	ct%	Eye	G	L	F	h%	HctX	PX	xPX	hr/f	Spd	SBO	SB%	#Wk	DOM	DIS	RC/G	RAR	BPV	BPX	R$
11	CIN *	427	51	18	48	13	221	255	275	396	671	985	654	7	71	0.25	48	21	31	27	105	130	138	23%	91	20%	74%	12	42%	42%	3.53	-20.7	31	69	$8
12	CIN *	461	58	20	72	5	265	258	321	480	801	858	817	8	75	0.32	33	22	45	32	99	143	127	13%	124	7%	72%	25	60%	24%	5.32	9.5	68	170	$15
13	CIN	531	63	19	73	6	234	251	314	407	721	782	696	9	76	0.40	42	18	40	27	102	121	121	12%	97	9%	55%	27	41%	22%	3.95	-0.7	51	128	$12
14	CIN	597	88	29	80	20	273	263	336	459	795	750	807	8	77	0.37	41	22	37	31	114	127	124	17%	92	17%	71%	27	48%	19%	5.24	26.5	54	146	$30
15	CIN	619	82	35	89	13	255	273	309	498	806	908	773	7	78	0.32	33	19	48	28	127	157	156	15%	79	17%	62%	27	63%	30%	5.01	6.1	76	205	$24
1st Half		319	54	25	54	8	285	308	344	602	946	993	929	7	81	0.39	32	20	48	28	144	192	178	20%	82	18%	67%	14	79%	21%	6.99	21.5	118	319	$38
2nd Half		300	28	10	35	5	223	235	271	387	658	809	612	6	75	0.26	34	19	47	27	108	117	131	9%	77	16%	56%	13	46%	38%	3.31	-12.2	30	81	$9
16	Proj	617	80	30	86	11	260	260	319	466	784	854	761	7	77	0.33	37	20	43	30	115	135	137	15%	89	11%	66%				4.93	5.5	54	146	$25

Freeman,Freddie

Age: 26	Bats: L	Pos: 1B	Health	B	LIMA Plan	B
Ht: 6' 5"	Wt: 225		PT/Exp	A	Rand Var	0
			Consist	B	MM	4135

Strong 1H before injuries (bone spur right wrist, oblique) hit in mid-June and plagued him throughout 2H. When healthy, displayed his typical elite HctX, xPX and LD% while also boosting his FB%. Monitor wrist this spring, but with health, a few more FB and better ct%... UP: .320, 30 HR, MVP candidate.

Yr	Tm	AB	R	HR	RBI	SB	BA	xBA	OBP	SLG	OPS	vL	vR	bb%	ct%	Eye	G	L	F	h%	HctX	PX	xPX	hr/f	Spd	SBO	SB%	#Wk	DOM	DIS	RC/G	RAR	BPV	BPX	R$
11	ATL	571	67	21	76	4	282	260	346	448	795	707	837	8	75	0.37	42	23	35	34	123	122	138	14%	79	5%	50%	27	37%	33%	5.35	-14.6	41	91	$20
12	ATL	540	91	23	94	2	259	271	340	456	796	714	855	11	76	0.50	37	26	37	30	129	132	137	15%	88	1%	100%	27	52%	30%	5.32	-1.6	60	150	$18
13	ATL	551	89	23	109	1	319	274	396	501	897	764	958	11	78	0.55	38	27	35	38	120	121	151	15%	96	1%	100%	25	60%	16%	7.38	41.0	61	153	$31
14	ATL	607	93	18	78	3	288	283	386	461	847	756	885	13	76	0.62	37	31	32	35	131	134	159	12%	96	4%	43%	27	56%	22%	6.17	33.8	68	184	$24
15	ATL	416	62	18	66	3	276	279	370	471	841	656	912	12	76	0.57	37	28	36	32	129	133	151	16%	81	3%	75%	22	45%	23%	6.01	7.6	62	168	$16
1st Half		254	43	12	41	3	299	285	367	520	887	769	927	9	75	0.41	33	29	38	36	145	155	173	16%	87	6%	75%	11	55%	27%	6.87	12.0	72	195	$24
2nd Half		162	19	6	25	0	241	267	374	395	769	513	885	16	78	0.86	41	27	32	27	105	99	117	15%	82	0%	0%	11	36%	18%	4.77	-1.9	51	138	$3
16	Proj	552	81	21	86	2	283	274	379	460	839	684	907	12	77	0.61	38	28	34	34	124	120	146	14%	85	2%	61%				6.05	13.9	47	126	$24

Freese,David

Age: 33	Bats: R	Pos: 3B	Health	C	LIMA Plan	C+
Ht: 6' 2"	Wt: 225		PT/Exp	B	Rand Var	0
			Consist	A	MM	3025

14-56-.257 in 424 AB at LAA. Broken right index finger cost him several weeks in 2nd half. Above-average HctX and xPX are intact, but extreme GB% impedes any further HR output. Reversal of platoon split was largely a h% quirk, so continue to treat him as a short-side platoon option only.

Yr	Tm	AB	R	HR	RBI	SB	BA	xBA	OBP	SLG	OPS	vL	vR	bb%	ct%	Eye	G	L	F	h%	HctX	PX	xPX	hr/f	Spd	SBO	SB%	#Wk	DOM	DIS	RC/G	RAR	BPV	BPX	R$
11	STL	333	41	10	55	1	297	273	350	441	791	900	759	7	77	0.32	52	25	23	36	104	102	121	17%	75	1%	100%	20	30%	55%	5.54	6.7	29	64	$12
12	STL	501	70	20	79	3	293	265	372	467	839	886	824	10	76	0.47	52	22	26	35	119	116	119	20%	92	4%	50%	27	56%	26%	6.06	21.2	45	113	$20
13	STL	462	53	9	60	1	262	253	340	381	721	811	689	9	77	0.44	55	21	24	32	116	91	97	10%	73	2%	33%	25	24%	28%	4.28	4.4	23	58	$10
14	LAA	462	53	10	55	1	260	253	321	383	704	876	656	8	73	0.31	49	26	26	34	124	101	117	11%	75	3%	25%	25	28%	48%	4.07	5.4	13	35	$10
15	LAA *	445	54	15	60	1	254	250	305	413	719	719	752	7	75	0.29	54	18	28	31	111	114	109	16%	69	2%	50%	22	50%	32%	4.29	-3.6	27	73	$10
1st Half		281	33	10	36	1	242	250	310	402	712	735	705	8	75	0.33	53	18	29	29	116	110	116	16%	68	3%	50%	14	43%	36%	4.01	-5.2	27	73	$12
2nd Half		164	21	5	24	0	276	246	316	432	748	698	854	6	74	0.22	58	16	26	35	102	119	94	15%	75	0%	0%	8	63%	25%	4.81	0.9	25	68	$6
16	Proj	434	50	12	57	1	258	252	327	400	727	755	717	8	75	0.32	54	20	26	32	113	104	107	14%	74	2%	38%				4.26	-4.6	12	32	$12

Fuld,Sam

Age: 34	Bats: L	Pos: LF CF	Health	C	LIMA Plan	D
Ht: 5' 10"	Wt: 175		PT/Exp	D	Rand Var	+5
			Consist	C	MM	1421

Non-existent pop prevents decent plate control from translating into a palatable BA and limits SB potential. In fairness, xBA suggests some BA upside, thanks to league average (though declining) ct%. Strong defense may keep him employed, but playing time and any fantasy value are going be difficult to find going forward.

Yr	Tm	AB	R	HR	RBI	SB	BA	xBA	OBP	SLG	OPS	vL	vR	bb%	ct%	Eye	G	L	F	h%	HctX	PX	xPX	hr/f	Spd	SBO	SB%	#Wk	DOM	DIS	RC/G	RAR	BPV	BPX	R$
11	TAM	308	41	3	27	20	240	264	313	360	673	554	710	9	84	0.65	48	19	33	28	87	83	70	4%	128	35%	71%	27	37%	37%	3.71	-13.8	62	138	$8
12	TAM	98	14	0	5	7	255	268	318	327	644	623	656	8	86	0.57	51	26	23	30	67	43	44	0%	142	32%	78%	11	27%	36%	3.56	-3.7	37	93	$1
13	TAM	176	25	2	17	8	199	248	270	267	537	734	417	9	84	0.61	52	23	25	23	65	33	30	5%	168	21%	80%	27	19%	44%	2.37	-10.6	33	83	$1
14	2 AL	351	40	4	36	21	239	256	321	342	663	683	655	11	82	0.68	50	20	30	28	66	74	50	5%	118	24%	84%	22	41%	36%	3.86	-0.3	47	127	$11
15	OAK	290	34	2	22	9	197	263	276	293	569	414	599	9	81	0.55	59	18	22	24	72	69	47	4%	115	18%	75%	27	30%	44%	2.55	-20.4	34	92	$0
1st Half		179	23	1	14	6	212	280	294	324	618	569	624	10	83	0.65	59	20	21	25	70	77	46	3%	122	19%	75%	14	29%	43%	3.08	-9.8	51	138	$2
2nd Half		111	11	1	8	3	171	230	246	243	489	268	553	8	78	0.42	61	14	25	21	75	56	49	5%	93	17%	75%	13	31%	46%	1.82	-10.9	5	14	-$3
16	Proj	190	23	2	16	8	229	254	303	319	622	599	629	9	82	0.56	55	19	26	27	70	60	47	4%	115	20%	79%				3.24	-7.7	33	89	$5

Gallo,Joey

Age: 22	Bats: L	Pos: LF	Health	A	LIMA Plan	D
Ht: 6' 5"	Wt: 205		PT/Exp	F	Rand Var	0
			Consist	A	MM	5303

6-14-.204 in 108 AB at TEX. Once again showed immense power, but there will be no future so long as he continues to strike out in nearly half of his at-bats. Absent progress on that front, he will continue to be a major BA drain, though bb% buoys his OBP. May need additional seasoning in the minors. Remain patient.

Yr	Tm	AB	R	HR	RBI	SB	BA	xBA	OBP	SLG	OPS	vL	vR	bb%	ct%	Eye	G	L	F	h%	HctX	PX	xPX	hr/f	Spd	SBO	SB%	#Wk	DOM	DIS	RC/G	RAR	BPV	BPX	R$
11																																			
12																																			
13																																			
14	aa	250	36	17	46	2	211		295	456	750			11	51	0.24				32		242			81	3%	100%				4.38		46	124	$6
15	TEX *	429	49	25	64	5	212	218	303	438	741	477	836	12	52	0.27	35	27	37	34	112	209	180	32%	92	5%	100%	10	40%	50%	4.36	-0.5	27	73	$8
1st Half		228	31	13	39	3	246	238	341	494	835	477	950	13	56	0.33	41	23	36	37	129	217	189	31%	99	5%	100%	5	60%	20%	5.77	8.2	54	146	$14
2nd Half		201	17	11	25	2	174	222	260	376	635	0	566	10	47	0.22	0	57	43	28	59	198	127	33%	94	4%	100%	5	20%	80%	3.05	-9.8	-2	-5	$1
16	Proj	249	30	13	40	2	215	205	301	416	718	457	901	11	51	0.25	41	23	36	36	116	189	170	28%	91	4%	100%				4.13	-3.3	-1	-2	$6

GREG PYRON

Galvis,Freddy

Age: 26	Bats: B	Pos: SS	Health	B	LIMA Plan C
Ht: 5' 10"	Wt: 185		PT/Exp	C	Rand Var -4
			Consist	B	MM 1405

Traded some power and FB for contact and LD, with overall positive results. Between 1st half h% spike and 2nd half xPX and hr/f recovery, 2nd half is the better baseline for future performance: a smattering of power and speed, but not enough of either to offset a sub-.250 BA.

Yr Tm	AB	R	HR	RBI	SB	BA	xBA	OBP	SLG	OPS	vL	vR	bb%	ct%	Eye	G	L	F	h%	HctX	PX	xPX	hr/f	Spd	SBO	SB%	#Wk	DOM	DIS	RC/G	RAR	BPV	BPX	R$
11 a/a	543	63	7	35	19	250		283	347	630			4	82	0.26				29		70			113	26%	57%				3.10		31	69	$11
12 PHI	190	14	3	24	0	226	265	254	363	617	735	562	4	85	0.24	41	21	38	25	106	95	116	5%	75	0%	0%	10	40%	30%	3.04	-6.1	46	115	-$1
13 PHI *	446	33	8	38	3	221	218	256	340	596	688	662	5	77	0.21	36	19	46	27	95	83	115	8%	125	5%	74%	18	39%	39%	2.85	-8.9	22	55	$1
14 PHI *	254	30	6	23	2	200	217	248	347	595	496	573	6	76	0.27	41	8	51	24	84	112	117	9%	106	7%	60%	12	25%	42%	2.70	-4.7	40	108	$0
15 PHI	559	63	7	50	10	263	229	302	343	645	602	662	5	82	0.29	41	22	37	31	89	49	91	4%	138	7%	91%	27	22%	41%	3.64	-1.9	19	51	$13
1st Half	278	29	2	19	6	277	227	323	331	654	750	627	6	82	0.35	42	23	35	33	77	36	71	3%	137	7%	100%	14	14%	36%	3.85	-1.8	13	35	$11
2nd Half	281	34	5	31	4	249	233	281	356	637	503	703	4	81	0.24	40	22	39	29	101	63	110	6%	126	7%	80%	13	31%	46%	3.43	-5.5	22	59	$14
16 Proj	**532**	**57**	**9**	**49**	**7**	**241**	**231**	**279**	**349**	**629**	**597**	**642**	**5**	**80**	**0.26**	**40**	**20**	**40**	**29**	**92**	**71**	**105**	**5%**	**117**	**7%**	**78%**				**3.28**	**-12.8**	**18**	**50**	**$8**

Garcia,Adonis

Age: 31	Bats: R	Pos: 3B	Health	A	LIMA Plan D+
Ht: 5' 9"	Wt: 190		PT/Exp	D	Rand Var 0
			Consist	B	MM 2133

10-26-.277 in 191 AB at ATL. Free-swinger with puny bb% managed decent ct% with some pop. Unsustainable 29% hr/f and 5 HR in 58 AB vLHP was key to unexpected power display. Sketchy Eye highlights the BA risk, and low FB% caps the ability to offset that with power. At 31, tough to find path to value here.

Yr Tm	AB	R	HR	RBI	SB	BA	xBA	OBP	SLG	OPS	vL	vR	bb%	ct%	Eye	G	L	F	h%	HctX	PX	xPX	hr/f	Spd	SBO	SB%	#Wk	DOM	DIS	RC/G	RAR	BPV	BPX	R$
11																																		
12 aa	118	13	3	10	1	237		260	406	666			3	82	0.17				26		118			85	15%	55%				3.40		55	138	$0
13 aaa	199	13	3	8	3	211		244	294	538			4	87	0.34				23		54			102	20%	39%				2.09		33	83	-$2
14 aaa	342	38	7	30	7	243		268	354	622			3	80	0.17				28		81			97	16%	65%				3.12		24	65	$6
15 ATL *	522	53	12	62	4	245	265	268	368	636	982	706	3	83	0.18	49	22	29	28	113	80	108	22%	60	5%	75%	13	54%	23%	3.33	-21.5	21	57	$9
1st Half	289	28	2	30	3	226	235	251	302	553	0	500	3	83	0.19	44	20	36	27	0	55	-15	0%	82	7%	71%	1	0%	100%	2.49	-18.3	9	24	$4
2nd Half	233	25	10	31	1	269	281	290	449	739	982	706	3	83	0.17	49	22	29	29	113	111	108	22%	56	2%	100%	12	58%	17%	4.56	0.0	44	119	$14
16 Proj	**305**	**31**	**10**	**30**	**4**	**242**	**267**	**264**	**395**	**659**	**810**	**592**	**3**	**83**	**0.19**	**50**	**19**	**31**	**26**	**102**	**95**	**97**	**13%**	**71**	**10%**	**58%**				**3.45**	**-10.7**	**35**	**96**	**$7**

Garcia,Avisail

Age: 25	Bats: R	Pos: RF	Health	F	LIMA Plan B
Ht: 6' 4"	Wt: 240		PT/Exp	C	Rand Var 0
			Consist	B	MM 2215

Possesses raw power, at least according to hr/f, but chronically low FB% keeps that power from manifesting into PX/xPX. Dismal production vs. RHP remains a concern, with no sign of improvement. Still a work in progress, and at 25, there's time. If Aug/Sept. FB% gains prove sustainable, then... UP: 20 HR.

Yr Tm	AB	R	HR	RBI	SB	BA	xBA	OBP	SLG	OPS	vL	vR	bb%	ct%	Eye	G	L	F	h%	HctX	PX	xPX	hr/f	Spd	SBO	SB%	#Wk	DOM	DIS	RC/G	RAR	BPV	BPX	R$
11																																		
12 DET *	262	33	5	21	7	296	292	318	407	725	745	588	3	81	0.17	62	27	11	35	135	67	63	0%	133	20%	54%	6	0%	100%	4.36	-3.6	27	68	$8
13 2 AL *	418	55	13	58	6	309	254	340	453	793	640	770	5	76	0.20	56	18	26	38	107	95	92	15%	140	10%	55%	17	29%	53%	5.49	13.9	34	85	$19
14 CHW*	222	25	8	31	4	253	242	300	405	705	992	620	6	72	0.23	56	15	28	32	81	119	89	19%	76	9%	80%	10	50%	30%	4.17	1.7	19	51	$6
15 CHW	553	66	13	59	7	257	243	309	365	675	759	650	6	75	0.26	49	25	27	32	95	73	90	12%	96	10%	50%	27	33%	48%	3.65	-18.3	0	0	$13
1st Half	263	30	7	30	4	278	248	327	392	719	844	688	5	73	0.21	49	27	24	36	95	80	96	15%	79	13%	44%	14	21%	57%	4.11	-5.4	-7	-19	$15
2nd Half	290	36	6	29	3	238	237	293	341	635	697	613	7	76	0.30	48	22	29	29	94	67	84	9%	110	7%	60%	13	46%	38%	3.26	-13.6	6	16	$11
16 Proj	**515**	**62**	**15**	**60**	**8**	**266**	**247**	**312**	**400**	**713**	**838**	**670**	**6**	**75**	**0.24**	**52**	**20**	**27**	**33**	**92**	**89**	**89**	**15%**	**103**	**10%**	**58%**				**4.16**	**-9.9**	**9**	**24**	**$18**

Garcia,Greg

Age: 26	Bats: L	Pos: SS	Health	A	LIMA Plan D
Ht: 6' 0"	Wt: 190		PT/Exp	C	Rand Var 0
			Consist	B	MM 1211

2-4-.240 in 75 AB at STL. PRO: Will take a walk, and uses his average speed aggressively on the bases. CON: No power whatsoever. The wheels keeps him from being useless, but seems destined for a bench/utility role... at best.

Yr Tm	AB	R	HR	RBI	SB	BA	xBA	OBP	SLG	OPS	vL	vR	bb%	ct%	Eye	G	L	F	h%	HctX	PX	xPX	hr/f	Spd	SBO	SB%	#Wk	DOM	DIS	RC/G	RAR	BPV	BPX	R$
11																																		
12 aa	412	62	7	39	8	243		342	347	690			13	78	0.67				30		72			105	10%	57%				3.91		27	68	$7
13 aaa	354	37	2	26	10	228		301	315	616			9	78	0.47				29		71			108	14%	82%				3.20		20	50	$3
14 STL *	411	46	6	30	6	222	229	276	304	580	1167	377	7	71	0.25	100	0	0	30	115	67	-14	0%	109	11%	49%	8	0%	50%	2.63	-9.6	-13	-35	$3
15 STL *	405	40	2	30	11	240	247	313	314	627	1171	688	10	81	0.57	57	18	25	29	101	57	72	13%	92	13%	76%	12	58%	17%	3.34	-10.1	19	51	$5
1st Half	230	21	1	19	6	264	273	331	330	662	1667	1067	9	80	0.50	57	29	14	33	132	50	92		113	12%	73%	3	33%	33%	3.80	-2.9	14	38	$7
2nd Half	175	19	1	11	5	209	252	290	292	583	500	632	10	83	0.66	57	17	26	25	98	66	70	7%	86	14%	81%	9	67%	11%	2.80	-7.8	32	86	$2
16 Proj	**159**	**17**	**2**	**12**	**4**	**230**	**242**	**311**	**328**	**638**	**538**	**640**	**9**	**78**	**0.46**	**57**	**17**	**26**	**28**	**88**	**71**	**63**	**6%**	**95**	**12%**	**72%**				**3.27**	**-4.0**	**14**	**38**	**$3**

Gardner,Brett

Age: 32	Bats: L	Pos: LF CF	Health	C	LIMA Plan B
Ht: 5' 10"	Wt: 185		PT/Exp	A	Rand Var 0
			Consist	A	MM 2525

Maintained 2014's dramatic shift in approach, though power and speed metrics were off just a tad. 1st half was aided by h% and hr/f; regression in those areas contributed to a poor 2nd half. Assuming 2nd half Spd/SBO% is just a blip, expect similar numbers from this stable skill set.

Yr Tm	AB	R	HR	RBI	SB	BA	xBA	OBP	SLG	OPS	vL	vR	bb%	ct%	Eye	G	L	F	h%	HctX	PX	xPX	hr/f	Spd	SBO	SB%	#Wk	DOM	DIS	RC/G	RAR	BPV	BPX	R$
11 NYY	510	87	7	36	49	259	260	345	369	713	616	738	11	82	0.65	52	19	28	30	66	72	48	6%	166	39%	79%	27	44%	30%	4.40	-8.0	57	127	$24
12 NYY	31	7	0	3	2	323	266	417	387	804	2032	426	14	77	0.71	38	38	25	42	122	60	51	0%	96	31%	50%	5	20%	60%	5.24	0.6	16	40	$0
13 NYY	539	81	8	52	24	273	251	344	416	759	744	767	9	76	0.41	41	23	35	34	81	104	70	6%	143	22%	75%	24	42%	29%	4.89	14.3	51	128	$22
14 NYY	555	87	17	58	21	256	254	327	422	749	687	775	9	76	0.42	42	22	37	31	95	117	91	11%	141	18%	81%	27	48%	30%	4.73	17.0	60	162	$22
15 NYY	571	94	16	66	20	259	247	343	399	742	761	734	11	76	0.50	45	21	34	31	88	94	87	11%	115	15%	80%	27	37%	48%	4.70	5.1	39	105	$22
1st Half	293	60	9	39	15	297	275	373	481	854	867	849	10	76	0.48	46	22	32	36	95	128	86	13%	131	21%	83%	14	57%	21%	6.54	16.2	70	189	$34
2nd Half	278	34	7	27	5	219	216	311	313	624	673	599	11	76	0.53	44	19	36	26	81	59	89	9%	86	8%	71%	13	15%	77%	3.14	-12.2	3	8	$9
16 Proj	**567**	**89**	**16**	**59**	**22**	**256**	**250**	**335**	**404**	**739**	**724**	**746**	**10**	**77**	**0.48**	**44**	**21**	**35**	**31**	**86**	**97**	**82**	**11%**	**129**	**17%**	**81%**				**4.64**	**1.3**	**48**	**128**	**$23**

Gattis,Evan

Age: 29	Bats: R	Pos: DH	Health	B	LIMA Plan A
Ht: 6' 4"	Wt: 260		PT/Exp	C	Rand Var +1
			Consist	B	MM 4035

Move to AL/primary DH role suited him well as he posted career bests in AB, HR and RBI. Corresponding BA sink prevented any gain in R$, but xBA points to recovery. Newfound struggles vLHP are likely a sample size quirk. With rebound vL, and a blend of 2015 ct% gains with prior FB%/xPX, then... UP: 35 HR, .270 BA.

Yr Tm	AB	R	HR	RBI	SB	BA	xBA	OBP	SLG	OPS	vL	vR	bb%	ct%	Eye	G	L	F	h%	HctX	PX	xPX	hr/f	Spd	SBO	SB%	#Wk	DOM	DIS	RC/G	RAR	BPV	BPX	R$
11																																		
12 aa	182	19	7	29	1	221		283	430	714			8	81	0.45				24		130			102	6%	40%				3.90		76	190	$1
13 ATL *	375	45	22	66	0	244	264	285	483	768	808	757	5	77	0.24	41	14	45	26	115	163	136	17%	47	0%	0%	24	54%	21%	4.64	1.5	65	163	$11
14 ATL	369	41	22	52	0	263	259	317	493	810	970	773	6	74	0.23	39	17	45	30	124	163	165	18%	72	0%	0%	24	50%	25%	5.19	12.2	60	162	$13
15 HOU	566	66	27	88	0	246	267	285	463	748	698	775	5	79	0.25	46	17	37	27	109	126	116	16%	117	1%	0%	27	48%	30%	4.40	-17.5	64	173	$14
1st Half	297	35	14	50	0	242	267	272	455	726	648	771	4	77	0.17	44	19	36	27	103	131	110	17%	100	0%	0%	14	36%	36%	4.16	-11.4	52	141	$15
2nd Half	269	31	13	38	0	249	267	299	472	771	758	777	6	81	0.36	47	14	38	26	117	121	123	15%	127	2%	0%	13	62%	23%	4.67	-6.2	75	203	$12
16 Proj	**529**	**62**	**28**	**83**	**0**	**253**	**266**	**301**	**484**	**785**	**797**	**780**	**6**	**78**	**0.27**	**43**	**16**	**41**	**28**	**116**	**139**	**137**	**17%**	**104**	**1%**	**25%**				**4.84**	**-9.4**	**57**	**153**	**$18**

Gennett,Scooter

Age: 26	Bats: L	Pos: 2B	Health	A	LIMA Plan B
Ht: 5' 10"	Wt: 170		PT/Exp	C	Rand Var +1
			Consist	C	MM 2233

6-29-.264 in 375 AB at MIL. Slow start earned him a stint at AAA. Returned in mid-June with outwardly solid results, but notable skill slippage: bb% and ct% dipped, xPX decline continued, stopped running altogether. This isn't a skill set that can absorb that kind of erosion. Return of his sneaky double-digit value not a given.

Yr Tm	AB	R	HR	RBI	SB	BA	xBA	OBP	SLG	OPS	vL	vR	bb%	ct%	Eye	G	L	F	h%	HctX	PX	xPX	hr/f	Spd	SBO	SB%	#Wk	DOM	DIS	RC/G	RAR	BPV	BPX	R$
11																																		
12 aa	533	54	5	36	9	267		299	353	652			4	85	0.30				31		61			96	11%	62%				3.59		28	70	$10
13 MIL *	534	61	8	37	9	275	240	308	381	689	329	946	5	79	0.23	39	24	37	33	115	72	115	10%	151	11%	58%	14	43%	29%	3.99	5.1	32	80	$14
14 MIL	440	55	9	54	6	289	285	320	434	754	253	802	5	85	0.33	41	25	34	32	105	105	92	7%	100	8%	67%	27	52%	15%	4.95	19.3	65	176	$16
15 MIL *	450	50	8	37	1	262	263	286	386	672	310	713	3	82	0.19	49	22	30	30	80	81	78	7%	130	5%	19%	24	38%	21%	3.66	-6.7	41	111	$7
1st Half	217	19	6	24	0	244	269	274	400	673	361	723	4	80	0.21	45	24	32	28	80	100	91	11%	110	5%	0%	11	36%	36%	3.51	-4.6	44	119	$5
2nd Half	233	31	2	13	1	279	258	303	373	676	250	707	3	84	0.16	51	20	29	32	81	64	71	4%	143	5%	33%	13	38%	8%	3.79	-2.9	37	100	$9
16 Proj	**403**	**47**	**8**	**35**	**4**	**273**	**268**	**305**	**405**	**710**	**292**	**759**	**4**	**83**	**0.24**	**44**	**23**	**32**	**31**	**94**	**86**	**89**	**7%**	**122**	**8%**	**50%**				**4.16**	**-0.7**	**36**	**98**	**$12**

GREG PYRON

Giavotella,Johnny

Age: 28	Bats: R	Pos: 2B	Health B	LIMA Plan D+	
Ht: 5' 8"	Wt: 185		PT/Exp C	Rand Var -1	
			Consist B	MM 1333	

Finally got a full season in the bigs. PRO: Good ct%, solid Eye, decent speed. CON: Paltry xPX and HctX, miniscule SBO%. Ability to make contact earned him a shot at regular PT, but poor defense could push him to bench. If he can combine this BA with 2014 SBO%, then... UP: 15 SB.

Yr	Tm	AB	R	HR	RBI	SB	BA	xBA	OBP	SLG	OPS	vL	vR	bb%	ct%	Eye	G	L	F	h%	HctX	PX	xPX	hr/f	Spd	SBO	SB%	#Wk	DOM	DIS	RC/G	RAR	BPV	BPX	R$
11	KC *	631	68	8	72	11	277	262	314	393	708	740	621	5	85	0.36	43	21	36	32	81	82	66	4%	111	12%	59%	9	33%	22%	4.23	-6.6	51	113	$17
12	KC *	543	67	7	64	8	256	260	306	351	657	547	591	7	85	0.49	47	23	30	29	89	62	50	2%	102	6%	87%	14	14%	36%	3.73	-7.0	36	90	$11
13	KC *	411	40	5	39	6	240	238	313	334	647	498	713	10	83	0.62	57	14	30	28	120	72	127	0%	82	9%	56%	6	50%	17%	3.42	-3.7	35	88	$5
14	KC *	478	51	5	45	13	241	278	288	339	627	347	661	6	90	0.66	55	18	27	26	95	70	76	11%	84	17%	69%	6	33%	33%	3.23	-2.3	56	151	$9
15	LAA	453	51	4	49	2	272	272	318	375	694	674	700	7	87	0.54	46	24	30	31	71	68	48	3%	109	2%	67%	23	39%	22%	4.19	-1.1	50	135	$9
1st Half		266	29	3	31	1	271	264	320	361	681	730	667	7	85	0.53	48	24	28	31	85	61	59	5%	93	3%	50%	14	43%	29%	4.05	-1.4	33	89	$11
2nd Half		187	22	1	18	1	273	280	317	396	712	618	755	6	90	0.58	43	23	34	30	51	76	33	2%	120	2%	100%	9	33%	11%	4.38	0.8	69	186	$6
16	Proj	326	36	3	33	6	268	269	318	366	684	658	696	7	87	0.58	46	23	32	30	76	66	49	3%	109	11%	67%				4.00	-2.1	46	124	$7

Gillaspie,Conor

Age: 28	Bats: L	Pos: 3B	Health A	LIMA Plan D	
Ht: 6' 1"	Wt: 195		PT/Exp C	Rand Var +2	
			Consist C	MM 2020	

Once flashed triple-digit HctX, xPX and Spd, but now all are gone. Gave back 2014's BA gains, but note that xBA was nearly identical. Inability to hit LHP (.516 OPS in 190 career AB) relegates him to a platoon option at best... but unfortunate h% contributed to down year vR. Uninspiring skills with minimal upside.

Yr	Tm	AB	R	HR	RBI	SB	BA	xBA	OBP	SLG	OPS	vL	vR	bb%	ct%	Eye	G	L	F	h%	HctX	PX	xPX	hr/f	Spd	SBO	SB%	#Wk	DOM	DIS	RC/G	RAR	BPV	BPX	R$
11	SF *	447	42	7	41	6	236	201	303	344	647	667	771	9	79	0.45	39	11	50	29	44	75	57	11%	117	14%	35%	6	33%	17%	3.20	-26.2	30	67	$4
12	SF *	433	42	8	35	0	216	284	262	315	577	0	467	6	84	0.40	39	33	28	24	62	62	17	0%	95	0%	0%	2	50%	50%	2.69	-25.5	30	75	$0
13	CHW	408	46	13	40	0	245	243	305	390	695	451	738	8	81	0.47	37	20	42	28	109	91	110	9%	122	1%	0%	27	48%	26%	4.01	0.7	51	128	$6
14	CHW	464	50	7	57	0	282	262	336	416	752	565	805	7	83	0.46	39	22	39	33	105	98	95	5%	116	3%	0%	25	44%	24%	4.76	14.4	62	168	$12
15	2 AL	237	14	4	24	0	228	254	269	359	627	583	630	5	80	0.28	45	21	35	27	75	91	87	6%	79	2%	0%	20	35%	40%	3.11	-10.4	30	81	-$1
1st Half		168	10	3	15	0	244	252	283	375	658	619	660	5	80	0.26	45	21	34	29	80	93	96	7%	85	3%	0%	14	36%	50%	3.47	-5.8	31	84	$0
2nd Half		69	4	1	9	0	188	254	233	319	552	556	551	5	81	0.31	43	21	36	22	64	87	65	5%	85	0%	0%	6	33%	17%	2.33	-5.0	33	89	-$3
16	Proj	66	5	1	7	0	235	252	284	365	649	534	669	6	81	0.36	41	21	37	27	88	86	88	6%	98	3%	12%				3.37	-2.5	27	73	$1

Gillespie,Cole

Age: 32	Bats: R	Pos: CF	Health A	LIMA Plan D	
Ht: 6' 1"	Wt: 215		PT/Exp F	Rand Var -1	
			Consist F	MM 1311	

2-16-.290 with 4 SB in 145 AB at MIA. Makes a decent amount of contact, but nothing much happens when he does. Too many GB and little power. In multiple brief stints in majors over five seasons, he has amassed a meager .675 OPS in 388 lifetime AB. At this age, he's simply not draft-worthy.

Yr	Tm	AB	R	HR	RBI	SB	BA	xBA	OBP	SLG	OPS	vL	vR	bb%	ct%	Eye	G	L	F	h%	HctX	PX	xPX	hr/f	Spd	SBO	SB%	#Wk	DOM	DIS	RC/G	RAR	BPV	BPX	R$
11	ARI *	490	54	7	45	12	225	171	285	344	630	0	1850	8	77	0.37	40	0	60	28	78	78	151	33%	175	16%	66%	2	50%	0%	3.17	-29.9	39	87	$5
12	aaa	441	47	8	37	6	228		280	353	634			7	77	0.33				28		91			96	17%	37%				3.00		24	60	$4
13	2 NL *	294	27	5	23	4	200	218	266	292	558	481	625	8	73	0.33	40	23	36	26	106	70	92	0%	92	6%	100%	10	30%	60%	2.54	-19.0	-7	-18	-$1
14	2 AL *	214	30	7	27	6	273	275	342	424	767	665	478	9	80	0.52	52	21	26	32	84	104	67	6%	120	12%	74%	12	25%	42%	5.07	6.0	59	159	$8
15	MIA *	392	39	2	33	9	253	248	306	340	646	852	728	7	83	0.46	54	16	30	30	92	63	70	6%	104	12%	72%	16	38%	44%	3.55	-15.1	31	84	$6
1st Half		262	23	0	17	6	234	201	293	299	592	750	839	8	84	0.52	45	9	45	28	134	53	212	0%	87	13%	71%	3	67%	33%	2.91	-15.2	21	57	$5
2nd Half		130	16	2	16	3	292	265	331	423	754	862	714	6	82	0.35	55	17	28	34	87	84	55	7%	114	11%	75%	13	31%	46%	5.07	0.9	44	119	$9
16	Proj	194	22	2	20	4	256	245	315	351	666	637	699	8	80	0.42	48	21	31	31	94	67	73	4%	111	11%	72%				3.76	-3.7	21	57	$5

Gimenez,Chris

Age: 33	Bats: R	Pos: CA	Health A	LIMA Plan D	
Ht: 6' 2"	Wt: 220		PT/Exp F	Rand Var -1	
			Consist B	MM 1101	

5-14-.255 in 98 AB at TEX. Journeyman promoted from AAA on July 31 provided surprising power, thanks to an out-of-nowhere hr/f. Shaky plate control/subpar HctX makes him a BA liability. Mid-October right shoulder surgery repaired AC joint, but expected ready by spring training. Unlikely to have fantasy relevance.

Yr	Tm	AB	R	HR	RBI	SB	BA	xBA	OBP	SLG	OPS	vL	vR	bb%	ct%	Eye	G	L	F	h%	HctX	PX	xPX	hr/f	Spd	SBO	SB%	#Wk	DOM	DIS	RC/G	RAR	BPV	BPX	R$
11	SEA *	108	10	2	8	0	192	174	284	250	534	921	461	11	71	0.45	53	13	34	25	92	43	92	6%	81	7%	0%	14	29%	64%	2.04	-7.5	-30	-67	-$3
12	TAM *	361	38	8	44	0	240	217	299	346	646	838	396	8	72	0.30	43	21	36	31	95	79	72	4%	78	4%	0%	12	25%	50%	3.32	-8.9	-5	-13	$4
13	TAM *	311	30	2	16	1	170	195	266	232	498	1000	1000	12	73	0.49	100	0	0	22	0	55	-15	0%	93	3%	36%	3	33%	33%	1.87	-18.7	-9	-23	-$7
14	2 AL *	250	24	4	24	0	223	234	290	328	618	549	679	9	73	0.34	46	23	31	29	87	88	72	0%	84	4%	0%	15	27%	53%	2.99	-2.5	6	16	$0
15	TEX *	345	38	9	37	3	206	216	263	331	595	1095	711	7	72	0.27	42	18	41	26	76	89	86	16%	74	5%	100%	11	55%	27%	2.85	-9.4	-2	-5	$1
1st Half		199	14	4	16	1	186	202	232	276	507			6	70	0.20				24		65			74	4%	100%				2.03		-32	-86	-$4
2nd Half		146	25	5	21	2	234	243	305	407	713	1095	711	9	74	0.39	42	18	41	28	79	120	86	16%	81	6%	100%	11	55%	27%	4.22	1.9	37	100	$7
16	Proj	128	15	2	13	1	210	218	281	315	595	745	503	9	73	0.35	45	19	36	27	88	78	79	7%	83	4%	59%				2.82	-3.8	-8	-22	$1

Goins,Ryan

Age: 28	Bats: L	Pos: 2B SS	Health A	LIMA Plan D+	
Ht: 5' 10"	Wt: 185		PT/Exp C	Rand Var -1	
			Consist B	MM 1213	

Mid-season mechanical adjustments—position of hands, letting the ball travel deeper—resulted in 2H boon (vastly improved bb%, OBP). However, h% artificially boosted BA (xBA), and while HctX and xPX inched upward, both remained subpar. Bottom line: Improved, but needs to show it over a full season.

Yr	Tm	AB	R	HR	RBI	SB	BA	xBA	OBP	SLG	OPS	vL	vR	bb%	ct%	Eye	G	L	F	h%	HctX	PX	xPX	hr/f	Spd	SBO	SB%	#Wk	DOM	DIS	RC/G	RAR	BPV	BPX	R$
11																																			
12	aa	546	53	6	49	12	260		306	362	668			6	84	0.41				30		70			96	16%	54%				3.63		35	88	$11
13	TOR *	496	43	7	43	2	229	231	264	324	588	576	628	5	74	0.19	56	19	25	30	81	78	53	9%	86	8%	28%	7	14%	43%	2.69	-15.7	-3	-8	$2
14	TOR *	544	42	1	38	3	226	232	263	296	559	395	501	5	78	0.22	55	18	26	29	76	59	51	3%	102	7%	35%	13	23%	62%	2.46	-15.5	1	3	$0
15	TOR	376	52	5	45	2	250	242	318	354	672	586	697	9	78	0.47	54	18	28	31	84	71	76	6%	124	3%	67%	26	23%	38%	3.84	-4.7	26	70	$6
1st Half		188	20	2	24	0	223	228	267	319	586	696	559	6	80	0.30	51	15	34	27	78	64	65	4%	111	0%	0%	13	31%	38%	2.79	-8.2	19	51	$1
2nd Half		188	32	3	21	2	277	254	365	388	754	498	837	13	76	0.61	58	21	21	35	91	77	87	10%	130	4%	67%	13	15%	38%	5.04	4.4	31	84	$11
16	Proj	356	41	4	35	3	244	244	300	345	645	545	676	8	78	0.37	55	19	26	30	82	71	65	6%	114	6%	48%				3.43	-8.5	10	27	$6

Goldschmidt,Paul

Age: 28	Bats: R	Pos: 1B	Health B	LIMA Plan C	
Ht: 6' 3"	Wt: 245		PT/Exp A	Rand Var -5	
			Consist B	MM 5245	

Another stellar campaign. Continues to work around suspect ct% by making boatloads of hard contact (41% HH%, elite HctX). Outpaced xBA thanks to h%, but that wasn't out of line with his career h% (36%). Expect a little pullback in BA and SB, but with more FB, we could yet see... UP: 40 HR

Yr	Tm	AB	R	HR	RBI	SB	BA	xBA	OBP	SLG	OPS	vL	vR	bb%	ct%	Eye	G	L	F	h%	HctX	PX	xPX	hr/f	Spd	SBO	SB%	#Wk	DOM	DIS	RC/G	RAR	BPV	BPX	R$
11	ARI *	522	87	30	92	10	260	270	354	498	852	657	855	13	70	0.48	42	21	37	32	126	174	155	21%	90	9%	74%	9	44%	44%	6.04	-3.2	73	162	$23
12	ARI	514	82	20	82	18	286	274	359	490	850	1068	739	10	75	0.46	40	24	36	35	127	149	160	14%	78	15%	86%	27	56%	19%	6.41	14.3	64	160	$25
13	ARI	602	103	36	125	15	302	290	401	551	952	986	941	14	76	0.68	44	21	35	35	131	168	164	23%	92	11%	68%	27	67%	19%	7.94	56.1	96	240	$40
14	ARI	406	75	19	69	9	300	297	396	542	938	1115	894	14	73	0.58	45	22	33	37	139	194	173	19%	96	9%	75%	19	58%	16%	7.78	40.4	105	284	$24
15	ARI	567	103	33	110	21	321	284	435	570	1005	1081	984	17	73	0.78	42	23	35	39	132	169	152	22%	85	11%	81%	27	70%	7%	9.42	61.9	91	246	$42
1st Half		296	58	20	67	15	348	300	466	622	1087	1115	1079	18	77	0.96	42	23	36	40	145	175	172	25%	92	15%	79%	14	71%	7%	11.34	47.8	113	305	$55
2nd Half		271	45	13	43	6	292	268	402	513	915	1037	886	16	70	0.63	42	24	34	38	118	163	128	19%	76	7%	86%	13	69%	8%	7.57	18.3	66	178	$29
16	Proj	577	102	32	106	17	305	285	408	550	958	1052	932	15	73	0.66	43	23	34	37	131	171	156	22%	89	10%	78%				8.27	49.5	89	241	$39

Gomes,Yan

Age: 28	Bats: R	Pos: CA	Health B	LIMA Plan B	
Ht: 6' 2"	Wt: 215		PT/Exp C	Rand Var +3	
			Consist C	MM 4325	

Suffered mid-April MCL sprain in right knee and missed six weeks. BA plummetted as ct% worsened and HctX drifted to below average. xBA provides hope for modest recovery. Good bet to rebound to 20 HR plateau, but BA recovery may prove more difficult.

Yr	Tm	AB	R	HR	RBI	SB	BA	xBA	OBP	SLG	OPS	vL	vR	bb%	ct%	Eye	G	L	F	h%	HctX	PX	xPX	hr/f	Spd	SBO	SB%	#Wk	DOM	DIS	RC/G	RAR	BPV	BPX	R$
11	a/a	290	24	10	36	0	206		252	366	618			6	68	0.19				27		130			83	0%	0%				2.96		15	33	$0
12	TOR *	403	38	13	51	3	254	237	292	427	719	701	567	5	71	0.19	48	15	37	33	93	133	127	16%	72	3%	100%	15	27%	47%	4.30	1.9	24	60	$8
13	CLE	293	45	11	38	2	294	261	345	481	826	934	766	6	77	0.27	43	18	39	35	104	131	126	12%	116	3%	100%	26	54%	38%	5.85	17.3	62	155	$11
14	CLE	485	61	21	74	0	278	266	313	472	785	879	745	5	75	0.20	37	24	39	33	101	139	128	14%	101	0%	0%	26	54%	23%	5.21	25.9	54	146	$18
15	CLE	363	38	12	45	0	231	248	267	391	659	545	702	3	71	0.13	34	26	40	29	87	120	102	11%	62	0%	0%	20	40%	40%	3.35	-4.2	9	24	$4
1st Half		125	11	3	9	0	216	229	229	320	549	484	582	2	71	0.08	30	29	40	28	99	75	101	8%	92	0%	0%	8	25%	50%	2.44	-5.2	-21	-57	-$7
2nd Half		238	27	9	36	0	239	259	287	429	715	588	758	4	71	0.15	35	25	40	30	80	143	102	13%	55	0%	0%	12	50%	33%	3.88	0.7	27	73	$9
16	Proj	570	66	21	71	0	260	249	298	432	730	733	729	4	73	0.16	37	24	39	32	94	122	114	13%	83	0%	100%				4.35	9.3	15	40	$17

GREG PYRON

Gomez,Carlos

Age: 30 Bats: R Pos: CF		Health	B	LIMA Plan	B+
Ht: 6' 3" Wt: 220		PT/Exp	A	Rand Var	+1
		Consist	B	MM	4425

A disappointment, but was never fully healthy, as a bevy of nickel-and-dime injuries—hamstring, hip, wrist, knee, back, oblique—limited him to 115 G. While hard contact, power and speed metrics all suffered, plate skills plus batted-ball profile did not. Given his age and track record, he's a prime rebound candidate.

Yr Tm	AB	R	HR	RBI	SB	BA	xBA	OBP	SLG	OPS	vL	vR	bb%	ct%	Eye	G	L	F	h%	HctX	PX	xPX	hr/f	Spd	SBO	SB%	#Wk	DOM	DIS	RC/G	RAR	BPV	BPX	R$
11 MIL	231	37	8	24	16	225	235	276	403	679	857	566	6	72	0.23	44	12	44	28	107	127	122	11%	142	40%	89%	22	45%	32%	3.79	-9.1	48	107	$7
12 MIL	415	72	19	51	37	260	250	305	463	768	778	762	5	76	0.20	40	17	43	30	108	128	124	14%	127	50%	86%	25	40%	40%	4.85	0.0	57	143	$24
13 MIL	536	80	24	73	40	284	263	338	506	843	993	797	6	73	0.25	40	21	38	35	114	153	137	16%	152	37%	85%	27	48%	30%	6.07	28.1	74	185	$36
14 MIL	574	95	23	73	34	284	262	356	477	833	828	835	8	75	0.33	38	22	41	34	117	142	133	13%	121	31%	74%	26	54%	27%	5.63	28.8	69	186	$36
15 2 TM	435	61	12	56	17	255	251	314	409	724	646	745	7	77	0.31	43	19	38	31	101	110	100	10%	88	26%	65%	23	22%	35%	4.09	-5.3	37	100	$16
1st Half	227	36	6	31	7	269	257	314	423	737	612	769	4	78	0.20	44	20	36	32	103	108	99	10%	105	24%	58%	13	31%	23%	4.15	-1.8	38	103	$17
2nd Half	208	25	6	25	10	240	245	315	394	709	679	718	9	76	0.42	41	19	41	29	99	112	101	10%	69	27%	71%	10	10%	50%	4.03	-2.4	35	95	$14
16 Proj	**521**	**77**	**20**	**66**	**28**	**269**	**257**	**330**	**459**	**789**	**796**	**787**	**7**	**76**	**0.30**	**40**	**21**	**40**	**32**	**110**	**129**	**116**	**13%**	**109**	**31%**	**75%**				**5.04**	**9.6**	**60**	**162**	**$26**

Gonzalez,Adrian

Age: 34 Bats: L Pos: 1B		Health	A	LIMA Plan	B+
Ht: 6' 2" Wt: 225		PT/Exp	A	Rand Var	+1
		Consist	A	MM	4045

On the surface, looks like Mid-30s Sluggerville: As HRs have peaked, hit tool has suffered. Underneath, nothing could be further from the truth; LD, HctX, xBA history say his BA has been shortchanged recently. Pay for his 2014-15 floor, and you just might walk away with his 2011 ceiling. A friggin' line-drive machine.

Yr Tm	AB	R	HR	RBI	SB	BA	xBA	OBP	SLG	OPS	vL	vR	bb%	ct%	Eye	G	L	F	h%	HctX	PX	xPX	hr/f	Spd	SBO	SB%	#Wk	DOM	DIS	RC/G	RAR	BPV	BPX	R$
11 BOS	630	108	27	117	1	338	296	410	548	957	787	1046	11	81	0.62	47	21	32	38	129	142	128	16%	79	0%	100%	27	59%	15%	8.61	38.5	85	189	$39
12 2 TM	629	75	18	108	2	299	279	344	463	806	846	783	6	83	0.38	40	24	36	34	121	111	134	10%	61	1%	100%	27	56%	30%	5.79	6.2	52	130	$24
13 LA	583	69	22	100	1	293	272	342	461	803	747	829	7	83	0.48	38	23	39	32	123	110	138	11%	71	1%	100%	27	63%	15%	5.77	19.1	59	148	$24
14 LA	591	83	27	116	1	276	292	335	482	817	588	901	9	81	0.50	38	24	38	30	136	145	145	15%	51	1%	50%	28	68%	11%	5.72	25.7	75	203	$26
15 LA	571	76	28	90	0	275	290	350	480	830	782	850	10	81	0.58	37	26	37	30	129	127	153	16%	52	1%	0%	27	48%	22%	5.80	7.0	64	173	$20
1st Half	299	44	15	50	0	291	305	366	518	884	748	923	10	83	0.63	35	26	38	31	134	143	166	16%	56	1%	0%	14	64%	14%	6.62	12.2	84	227	$26
2nd Half	272	32	13	40	0	257	272	333	438	771	805	753	10	79	0.54	39	26	35	28	124	109	139	17%	57	0%	0%	13	31%	31%	4.97	-1.4	44	119	$15
16 Proj	**592**	**78**	**26**	**101**	**1**	**289**	**283**	**354**	**483**	**837**	**756**	**871**	**9**	**81**	**0.54**	**39**	**25**	**37**	**32**	**129**	**122**	**145**	**15%**	**56**	**1%**	**46%**				**6.10**	**15.6**	**52**	**141**	**$27**

Gonzalez,Carlos

Age: 30 Bats: L Pos: RF		Health	C	LIMA Plan	B
Ht: 6' 1" Wt: 220		PT/Exp	C	Rand Var	+1
		Consist	F	MM	4235

Splits actually undersell the length of his streak; had 4 HR as of 6/1. Overall made better contact and maintained solid HctX, but batted-ball profile, xPX, and problems with LHP are skeptical of a repeat. Spd looks gone for good, and has a career .752 OPS on the road. Those '15 HR will make it difficult to turn a '16 profit.

Yr Tm	AB	R	HR	RBI	SB	BA	xBA	OBP	SLG	OPS	vL	vR	bb%	ct%	Eye	G	L	F	h%	HctX	PX	xPX	hr/f	Spd	SBO	SB%	#Wk	DOM	DIS	RC/G	RAR	BPV	BPX	R$
11 COL	481	92	26	92	20	295	291	363	526	889	779	943	9	78	0.46	48	18	34	33	119	153	123	21%	100	19%	80%	24	63%	17%	6.84	22.9	85	189	$30
12 COL	518	89	22	85	20	303	285	371	510	881	742	961	10	78	0.49	49	22	29	35	116	134	116	19%	92	16%	80%	26	50%	23%	6.94	25.7	68	170	$30
13 COL	391	72	26	70	21	302	281	367	591	958	875	1004	9	70	0.35	38	22	41	37	112	206	171	24%	122	23%	88%	22	50%	45%	8.09	37.7	102	255	$30
14 COL	260	35	11	38	3	238	256	292	431	723	635	766	7	73	0.27	47	15	38	28	109	146	119	15%	79	6%	100%	15	40%	40%	4.25	1.2	49	132	$6
15 COL	554	87	40	97	2	271	284	325	540	864	530	997	8	76	0.35	47	16	36	29	114	166	127	26%	79	2%	100%	27	63%	19%	6.19	21.0	78	211	$25
1st Half	270	34	11	30	2	244	264	303	419	722	422	812	8	79	0.41	48	20	32	27	103	110	95	16%	82	3%	100%	14	50%	21%	4.37	-3.6	45	122	$10
2nd Half	284	53	29	67	0	296	303	345	655	1000	600	1198	7	74	0.29	46	13	41	31	125	223	159	34%	82	0%	0%	13	77%	15%	8.22	26.7	114	308	$39
16 Proj	**497**	**80**	**29**	**87**	**5**	**272**	**270**	**328**	**508**	**837**	**636**	**930**	**8**	**74**	**0.33**	**46**	**17**	**37**	**31**	**114**	**153**	**134**	**21%**	**87**	**5%**	**83%**				**5.87**	**15.1**	**67**	**180**	**$25**

Gonzalez,Marwin

Age: 27 Bats: B Pos: 1B SS 3B		Health	A	LIMA Plan	C+
Ht: 6' 1" Wt: 205		PT/Exp	D	Rand Var	-3
		Consist	C	MM	2133

Always helpful to find the elusive multi-positioner with more than a noodle bat. G/L/F, HctX, and power metrics confirm his value bump; age and good contact rates give reason to think it could continue. Still just for deep leagues only, but a step up from an end-game dart throw.

Yr Tm	AB	R	HR	RBI	SB	BA	xBA	OBP	SLG	OPS	vL	vR	bb%	ct%	Eye	G	L	F	h%	HctX	PX	xPX	hr/f	Spd	SBO	SB%	#Wk	DOM	DIS	RC/G	RAR	BPV	BPX	R$
11 a/a	413	37	3	27	5	246		286	335	621			5	87	0.43				28		67			95	9%	59%				3.18		43	96	$3
12 HOU *	244	22	3	19	3	241	262	286	342	628	296	713	6	85	0.41	54	20	27	28	90	74	67	4%	83	11%	50%	20	35%	30%	3.17	-5.4	37	93	$1
13 HOU *	376	34	5	25	9	221	240	251	307	559	575	570	4	83	0.24	54	15	30	26	99	62	84	8%	98	16%	74%	20	25%	35%	2.53	-10.4	21	53	$2
14 HOU	285	33	6	23	2	277	253	327	400	727	776	719	6	80	0.29	52	18	30	33	93	92	68	9%	90	8%	33%	26	46%	38%	4.26	8.9	33	89	$7
15 HOU	344	44	12	34	4	279	265	317	442	759	843	701	4	78	0.22	44	23	33	33	110	107	101	14%	93	11%	44%	27	48%	44%	4.62	2.2	38	103	$11
1st Half	175	21	5	18	3	246	255	271	400	671	773	612	3	78	0.15	42	20	38	29	97	110	101	10%	86	16%	60%	14	57%	36%	3.54	-2.9	33	89	$7
2nd Half	169	23	7	16	1	314	276	363	485	848	901	804	6	79	0.29	47	25	28	36	123	104	101	19%	107	8%	25%	13	38%	54%	5.93	8.6	46	124	$14
16 Proj	**333**	**39**	**9**	**29**	**4**	**270**	**262**	**312**	**412**	**724**	**782**	**699**	**5**	**80**	**0.26**	**49**	**20**	**31**	**31**	**103**	**93**	**87**	**12%**	**93**	**10%**	**47%**				**4.21**	**-9.1**	**28**	**76**	**$10**

Gordon,Alex

Age: 32 Bats: L Pos: LF		Health	C	LIMA Plan	B+
Ht: 6' 1" Wt: 220		PT/Exp	B	Rand Var	-3
		Consist	A	MM	3125

13-48-.271 in 354 AB at KC. Didn't seem to mind either off-season wrist surgery, or the groin injury that wiped out most of Jul/Aug. Patient approach, ample pop, stable BPIs. With age brings a slight injury risk increase, but with A-grade Consistency, you know what you're getting.

Yr Tm	AB	R	HR	RBI	SB	BA	xBA	OBP	SLG	OPS	vL	vR	bb%	ct%	Eye	G	L	F	h%	HctX	PX	xPX	hr/f	Spd	SBO	SB%	#Wk	DOM	DIS	RC/G	RAR	BPV	BPX	R$
11 KC	611	101	23	87	17	303	276	376	502	879	829	901	10	77	0.48	40	22	38	36	104	144	117	13%	84	14%	68%	26	65%	27%	6.69	29.9	71	158	$32
12 KC	642	93	14	72	10	294	272	368	455	822	668	908	10	78	0.52	42	25	33	36	96	116	103	8%	85	8%	67%	27	56%	15%	5.95	24.9	54	135	$24
13 KC	633	90	20	81	11	265	247	327	422	749	877	683	8	78	0.37	40	20	39	31	111	104	125	10%	121	8%	79%	26	42%	38%	4.71	13.5	47	118	$22
14 KC	563	87	19	74	12	266	260	351	432	783	787	782	10	78	0.52	43	19	38	31	108	123	118	11%	70	9%	80%	27	48%	26%	5.16	24.0	52	141	$22
15 KC *	382	44	14	52	2	276	250	367	435	802	817	805	13	74	0.55	38	25	38	34	109	111	126	13%	75	6%	29%	20	45%	35%	5.39	10.9	34	92	$12
1st Half	248	30	10	33	1	262	253	380	431	811	748	847	13	75	0.60	34	25	41	31	110	115	141	13%	74	6%	20%	14	50%	29%	5.08	3.8	41	111	$14
2nd Half	134	14	4	19	1	303	247	380	442	822	998	708	11	73	0.46	46	24	30	39	106	104	89	13%	81	4%	50%	6	33%	50%	6.03	5.4	23	62	$7
16 Proj	**500**	**66**	**17**	**67**	**7**	**272**	**253**	**360**	**434**	**794**	**848**	**768**	**11**	**76**	**0.49**	**40**	**22**	**37**	**33**	**107**	**112**	**114**	**12%**	**81**	**7%**	**61%**				**5.23**	**9.7**	**35**	**96**	**$19**

Gordon,Dee

Age: 28 Bats: L Pos: 2B		Health	B	LIMA Plan	D+
Ht: 5' 11" Wt: 170		PT/Exp	A	Rand Var	-5
		Consist	C	MM	1535

Thumbs up? Head-first slide resulted in a dislocated L thumb in July; deja-vu of his R thumb injury 2012. Improved ct% and GB% repeat led to surprising BA title; though 1H h% largely responsible. Also led league in CS, so baserunning technique is a weak spot. But chances of another 60 bags? A-OK.

Yr Tm	AB	R	HR	RBI	SB	BA	xBA	OBP	SLG	OPS	vL	vR	bb%	ct%	Eye	G	L	F	h%	HctX	PX	xPX	hr/f	Spd	SBO	SB%	#Wk	DOM	DIS	RC/G	RAR	BPV	BPX	R$
11 LA *	512	64	0	25	42	277	266	301	329	630	595	727	3	85	0.23	56	23	21	32	37	38	14	0%	160	39%	78%	11	45%	18%	3.56	-17.2	29	64	$20
12 LA *	333	40	1	18	33	226	246	272	276	548	415	632	6	80	0.32	59	21	21	28	52	36	20	2%	141	53%	75%	18	17%	56%	2.51	-19.3	6	15	$9
13 LA *	468	53	1	28	43	234	224	299	295	594	577	623	8	77	0.41	49	21	30	30	52	45	33	5%	163	44%	74%	12	33%	33%	2.98	-10.0	14	35	$18
14 LA	609	92	2	34	64	289	274	326	378	704	719	699	5	82	0.29	60	21	19	35	62	62	27	2%	189	49%	77%	27	37%	19%	4.39	17.7	48	130	$38
15 MIA	615	88	4	46	58	333	280	359	418	776	823	760	4	85	0.27	60	22	19	39	66	54	40	4%	169	40%	74%	25	44%	24%	5.62	24.5	44	119	$47
1st Half	342	43	1	21	29	339	284	360	418	778	836	755	3	84	0.20	59	24	16	40	66	55	33	2%	158	38%	73%	14	43%	36%	5.62	13.0	35	95	$45
2nd Half	273	45	3	25	29	326	275	357	418	775	806	765	5	87	0.39	60	18	22	37	66	52	47	6%	170	43%	76%	11	45%	9%	5.62	10.6	52	141	$49
16 Proj	**605**	**86**	**4**	**41**	**59**	**297**	**269**	**334**	**381**	**715**	**719**	**713**	**5**	**83**	**0.32**	**58**	**21**	**21**	**35**	**61**	**53**	**34**	**4%**	**173**	**44%**	**76%**				**4.56**	**5.8**	**37**	**99**	**$39**

Gose,Anthony

Age: 25 Bats: L Pos: CF		Health	A	LIMA Plan	C+
Ht: 6' 1" Wt: 190		PT/Exp	C	Rand Var	-2
		Consist	B	MM	1505

PRO: Slow growth in Eye; keeps ball on the ground; elite wheels; runs often. CON: Contact poor in frequency and quality; useless against LHP; low SB%; painful DOM/DIS numbers. VERDICT: These SBs have value, and youth is on his side, but risk factors are larger than they might appear.

Yr Tm	AB	R	HR	RBI	SB	BA	xBA	OBP	SLG	OPS	vL	vR	bb%	ct%	Eye	G	L	F	h%	HctX	PX	xPX	hr/f	Spd	SBO	SB%	#Wk	DOM	DIS	RC/G	RAR	BPV	BPX	R$
11 aa	509	74	15	50	59	239		309	389	698			9	67	0.31				33		115			129	57%	79%				4.09		20	44	$25
12 TOR *	586	85	5	41	39	243	241	302	349	651	710	601	8	71	0.29	60	19	21	33	67	79	51	5%	166	36%	70%	11	18%	73%	3.46	-25.2	14	35	$18
13 TOR *	540	65	5	33	21	227	225	273	330	603	425	788	6	68	0.20	52	22	26	33	83	82	100	7%	172	32%	55%	11	45%	36%	2.71	-26.0	3	8	$9
14 TOR *	444	55	6	33	32	223	220	285	301	586	461	641	8	66	0.26	62	19	19	32	64	67	56	7%	131	39%	70%	21	29%	48%	2.75	-15.9	-23	-62	$13
15 DET	485	73	5	26	23	254	237	321	367	688	546	713	8	70	0.31	54	21	25	35	77	86	54	6%	160	26%	68%	27	26%	52%	3.86	-9.4	16	43	$15
1st Half	237	35	2	13	13	274	250	317	371	689	359	726	6	74	0.24	55	24	21	36	78	72	35	6%	145	30%	68%	14	21%	50%	4.00	-2.8	10	27	$16
2nd Half	248	38	3	13	10	234	225	324	363	687	636	699	11	67	0.36	53	18	29	34	76	102	75	7%	155	22%	67%	13	31%	54%	3.73	-5.2	18	49	$14
16 Proj	**417**	**58**	**4**	**26**	**23**	**239**	**230**	**308**	**342**	**650**	**512**	**682**	**8**	**68**	**0.28**	**56**	**20**	**24**	**34**	**74**	**80**	**64**	**6%**	**151**	**32%**	**68%**				**3.34**	**-13.8**	**1**	**3**	**$13**

BRENT HERSHEY

Gosselin,Phil

Age: 27	Bats: R	Pos: 2B	Health	D	LIMA Plan	D
Ht: 6' 1"	Wt: 200		PT/Exp	D	Rand Var	-3
			Consist	D	MM	1221

3-15-.311 in 106 AB at ATL/ARI. Broken thumb in May, traded while on DL, activated in Sept. Passed the post-trade audition, with some HR help in the new ballpark. Improved bb%, ct% could indicate BA/OBP growth is supportable, but sample sizes all small. Reserve pick at best.

Yr Tm	AB	R	HR	RBI	SB	BA	xBA	OBP	SLG	OPS	vL	vR	bb%	ct%	Eye	G	L	F	h%	HctX	PX	xPX	hr/f	Spd	SBO	SB%	#Wk	DOM	DIS	RC/G	RAR	BPV	BPX	R$
11																																		
12 aa	484	45	2	38	10	216		273	284	556			7	79	0.36				27		52			96	12%	69%				2.50		1	3	$1
13 ATL *	431	37	2	30	5	220	183	255	271	526	1100	0	4	81	0.24	67	0	33	27	83	39	-15	0%	111	6%	80%	2	0%	100%	2.28	-18.2	-1	-3	$0
14 ATL *	506	58	4	25	6	276	250	301	371	672	653	603	3	79	0.17	58	17	25	34	91	77	61	4%	142	8%	66%	11	9%	36%	3.88	7.1	29	78	$11
15 2 NL *	127	21	3	18	2	302	309	351	485	836	857	875	7	85	0.52	56	19	26	34	99	123	68	13%	106	9%	67%	13	54%	31%	6.14	6.9	88	238	$4
1st Half	40	2	0	2	2	325	291	357	425	782	708	833	5	88	0.40	68	18	15	37	110	82	44	0%	95	18%	100%	7	43%	29%	6.11	2.0	56	151	-$3
2nd Half	87	19	3	16	0	292	310	349	513	862	1029	895	8	84	0.56	48	20	32	32	93	142	83	17%	111	5%	0%	6	67%	33%	6.15	4.7	103	278	$7
16 Proj	**132**	**17**	**2**	**13**	**1**	**251**	**261**	**304**	**365**	**669**	**659**	**671**	**6**	**81**	**0.32**	**57**	**18**	**25**	**30**	**96**	**79**	**64**	**8%**	**118**	**7%**	**59%**				**3.60**	**-2.5**	**27**	**74**	**$1**

Grandal,Yasmani

Age: 27	Bats: B	Pos: CA	Health	C	LIMA Plan	D+
Ht: 6' 2"	Wt: 225		PT/Exp	D	Rand Var	0
			Consist	B	MM	3005

A tale of two halves. Promising ct% rebound in 1st half delivered BA results. Left shoulder woes in 2nd half sapped h%, HctX, PX; October surgery the result. Plate approach remained strong throughout, which bodes well for 2016 comeback. With post-surgery health... UP: 25 HR, .260 BA

Yr Tm	AB	R	HR	RBI	SB	BA	xBA	OBP	SLG	OPS	vL	vR	bb%	ct%	Eye	G	L	F	h%	HctX	PX	xPX	hr/f	Spd	SBO	SB%	#Wk	DOM	DIS	RC/G	RAR	BPV	BPX	R$
11 a/a	168	16	3	20	0	267		319	409	728			7	72	0.28				35		124			81	3%	0%				4.41		29	64	$2
12 SD *	386	55	12	60	0	281	248	374	432	806	971	821	13	79	0.69	53	17	30	33	116	102	87	17%	100	0%	0%	15	53%	33%	5.73	15.6	54	135	$12
13 SD *	124	15	1	10	0	221	255	326	327	653	752	635	13	77	0.69	48	24	28	28	117	94	112	5%	86	0%	0%	6	50%	0%	3.49	-0.7	39	98	-$2
14 SD	377	47	15	49	3	225	242	327	401	728	512	781	13	69	0.50	43	19	38	28	108	139	132	15%	74	3%	100%	27	44%	44%	4.38	10.6	40	108	$7
15 LA	355	43	16	47	0	234	229	353	403	756	794	749	15	74	0.71	46	17	37	27	98	110	118	16%	68	1%	0%	27	37%	48%	4.68	9.2	38	103	$6
1st Half	199	30	12	31	0	271	261	384	497	881	651	917	16	76	0.77	47	18	35	30	110	143	145	23%	73	0%	0%	14	64%	29%	6.71	16.7	73	197	$13
2nd Half	156	13	4	16	0	186	187	314	282	596	947	529	15	72	0.64	44	16	40	23	83	64	81	9%	77	2%	0%	13	8%	69%	2.67	-5.6	-6	-16	-$4
16 Proj	**391**	**45**	**14**	**47**	**1**	**244**	**233**	**351**	**397**	**748**	**782**	**739**	**14**	**73**	**0.61**	**46**	**19**	**36**	**30**	**103**	**107**	**112**	**13%**	**72**	**1%**	**47%**				**4.67**	**10.4**	**18**	**49**	**$9**

Granderson,Curtis

Age: 35	Bats: L	Pos: RF	Health	C	LIMA Plan	A
Ht: 6' 1"	Wt: 200		PT/Exp	B	Rand Var	0
			Consist	B	MM	4325

A mini-renaissance at age 35, as harder contact and a balanced jump in LD lifted (almost) all results. Notably, .280 BA vs RHP (best since 2008) covered .183 BA vs LHP (worst since 2007). SB% also hints at reduced opportunities. Overall batting skills remain intact, but platoon possibility puts AB at risk.

Yr Tm	AB	R	HR	RBI	SB	BA	xBA	OBP	SLG	OPS	vL	vR	bb%	ct%	Eye	G	L	F	h%	HctX	PX	xPX	hr/f	Spd	SBO	SB%	#Wk	DOM	DIS	RC/G	RAR	BPV	BPX	R$
11 NYY	583	136	41	119	25	262	272	364	552	916	944	902	13	71	0.50	34	18	48	30	125	198	161	21%	122	22%	71%	27	67%	11%	6.64	25.7	106	236	$36
12 NYY	596	102	43	106	10	232	251	319	492	811	762	839	11	67	0.38	33	23	44	27	91	175	132	24%	98	9%	77%	27	52%	19%	5.17	0.3	63	158	$22
13 NYY *	240	33	8	17	8	238	231	322	411	734	792	695	11	69	0.40	34	23	44	31	95	134	135	11%	143	16%	80%	12	42%	33%	4.48	-0.9	49	123	$5
14 NYM	564	73	20	66	8	227	236	326	388	714	742	703	12	75	0.56	34	19	47	27	106	119	132	10%	92	6%	80%	27	56%	26%	4.15	0.8	49	132	$12
15 NYM	580	98	26	70	11	259	260	364	457	821	558	892	14	74	0.60	31	27	42	31	120	135	155	14%	100	9%	65%	27	44%	15%	5.55	11.8	63	170	$21
1st Half	300	43	13	29	5	253	254	349	430	779	354	876	12	74	0.53	31	28	41	30	125	120	151	14%	99	8%	71%	14	29%	21%	5.04	2.0	47	127	$17
2nd Half	280	55	13	41	6	264	267	379	486	865	721	911	15	74	0.68	30	26	43	31	115	152	159	14%	97	11%	60%	13	62%	8%	6.12	10.7	80	216	$26
16 Proj	**519**	**83**	**23**	**63**	**11**	**247**	**249**	**348**	**444**	**791**	**705**	**821**	**13**	**73**	**0.55**	**32**	**24**	**44**	**30**	**111**	**134**	**146**	**14%**	**106**	**10%**	**71%**				**5.12**	**4.8**	**58**	**157**	**$19**

Gregorius,Didi

Age: 26	Bats: L	Pos: SS	Health	A	LIMA Plan	B+
Ht: 6' 2"	Wt: 205		PT/Exp	C	Rand Var	-2
			Consist	A	MM	1225

Icon replacement is tough, especially when weak contact meets FB-to-GB shift. PX dropped as FB didn't reach the seats in new HR-friendly home, and GB didn't generate hits. Spd also dropped with limited SBO and poor SB%. Some HctX and FB recovery in 2H offer cautious hope of improvement in age-26 season.

Yr Tm	AB	R	HR	RBI	SB	BA	xBA	OBP	SLG	OPS	vL	vR	bb%	ct%	Eye	G	L	F	h%	HctX	PX	xPX	hr/f	Spd	SBO	SB%	#Wk	DOM	DIS	RC/G	RAR	BPV	BPX	R$
11 aa	148	12	2	11	2	230		261	322	583			4	81	0.22				27		61			119	13%	48%				2.64		18	40	-$1
12 CIN *	521	60	7	47	3	247	256	293	357	650	1000	556	6	82	0.36	67	13	20	29	0	67	-11	0%	157	7%	28%	4	0%	50%	3.37	-11.4	43	108	$6
13 ARI *	388	51	8	29	1	258	245	324	384	708	512	789	9	83	0.58	37	21	42	29	79	83	87	6%	137	2%	24%	23	52%	30%	4.19	7.8	59	148	$6
14 ARI *	496	62	8	43	5	239	241	292	362	654	424	706	7	83	0.45	37	20	43	27	101	82	106	6%	132	4%	100%	19	42%	26%	3.59	4.4	54	146	$7
15 NYY	525	57	9	56	5	265	252	318	370	688	626	712	6	84	0.39	45	21	34	30	83	68	65	6%	99	6%	63%	27	33%	30%	3.91	-7.4	33	89	$11
1st Half	252	25	4	17	4	242	243	296	329	625	457	676	6	83	0.37	48	20	32	28	71	59	52	6%	102	10%	67%	14	21%	43%	3.15	-7.1	24	65	$5
2nd Half	273	32	5	39	1	286	260	339	407	745	737	750	6	85	0.40	42	22	36	32	94	77	77	6%	99	3%	50%	13	46%	15%	4.70	4.8	44	119	$17
16 Proj	**549**	**64**	**11**	**54**	**4**	**256**	**249**	**314**	**377**	**690**	**570**	**732**	**7**	**83**	**0.43**	**41**	**21**	**38**	**29**	**90**	**76**	**84**	**6%**	**116**	**5%**	**63%**				**3.91**	**-2.9**	**36**	**97**	**$13**

Grichuk,Randal

Age: 24	Bats: R	Pos: LF CF	Health	B	LIMA Plan	A
Ht: 6' 1"	Wt: 195		PT/Exp	C	Rand Var	-5
			Consist	D	MM	4325

Young RH power is a precious commodity, but this one needs more polish. HctX, FB, hr/f exactly what to look for, but horrific ct% combined with inflated h% predicts BA correction. Lost time with back, groin and elbow injuries in first "full" MLB season is worrisome. Remember, patience is a virtue.

Yr Tm	AB	R	HR	RBI	SB	BA	xBA	OBP	SLG	OPS	vL	vR	bb%	ct%	Eye	G	L	F	h%	HctX	PX	xPX	hr/f	Spd	SBO	SB%	#Wk	DOM	DIS	RC/G	RAR	BPV	BPX	R$
11																																		
12																																		
13 aa	500	74	18	55	8	231		266	412	678			4	80	0.24				26		117			124	15%	59%				3.51		62	155	$12
14 STL *	546	63	20	59	6	224	231	257	392	649	689	662	4	72	0.16	39	15	46	27	141	127	162	8%	108	14%	43%	11	36%	45%	3.13	-11.8	35	95	$10
15 STL	323	49	17	47	4	276	265	329	548	877	819	907	6	66	0.20	38	21	42	37	107	202	140	19%	141	9%	67%	22	55%	14%	6.12	16.7	82	222	$13
1st Half	164	23	7	21	3	256	261	297	518	815	781	829	5	68	0.17	39	17	44	34	117	190	136	14%	153	11%	100%	11	55%	9%	5.34	4.4	81	219	$10
2nd Half	159	26	10	26	1	296	269	360	579	939	845	1002	8	64	0.23	36	25	39	40	97	215	144	25%	115	8%	33%	11	55%	18%	6.98	11.5	80	216	$16
16 Proj	**529**	**74**	**25**	**68**	**6**	**253**	**253**	**300**	**479**	**779**	**737**	**810**	**6**	**70**	**0.20**	**38**	**19**	**43**	**31**	**120**	**159**	**149**	**16%**	**140**	**12%**	**53%**				**4.66**	**1.6**	**55**	**148**	**$19**

Guerrero,Alexander

Age: 29	Bats: R	Pos: LF 3B	Health	A	LIMA Plan	D
Ht: 5' 10"	Wt: 205		PT/Exp	F	Rand Var	+1
			Consist	B	MM	2201

Plate approach keeps him from becoming an everyday player, but legitimate power ensures he will have a job. HR/AB in 1H consistent with best seasons in Cuba. Played sparingly in 2H due to minor back issues, when HctX and GB exposed BA downside. Deep league end-game target.

Yr Tm	AB	R	HR	RBI	SB	BA	xBA	OBP	SLG	OPS	vL	vR	bb%	ct%	Eye	G	L	F	h%	HctX	PX	xPX	hr/f	Spd	SBO	SB%	#Wk	DOM	DIS	RC/G	RAR	BPV	BPX	R$
11																																		
12																																		
13																																		
14 LA *	256	21	9	27	2	226	287	242	386	628	0	286	2	75	0.08	57	29	14	27	0	114	-14	0%	95	5%	100%	6	0%	83%	3.12	-5.1	25	68	$3
15 LA	219	25	11	36	1	233	253	261	434	695	649	721	3	74	0.12	41	20	39	26	109	130	152	17%	75	3%	100%	27	30%	41%	3.72	-6.5	31	84	$4
1st Half	150	18	10	30	0	253	276	278	513	792	663	849	3	75	0.13	38	21	41	27	127	164	169	21%	68	0%	0%	14	43%	43%	4.86	1.3	59	159	$8
2nd Half	69	7	1	6	1	188	201	222	261	483	631	338	3	72	0.11	50	16	34	24	70	54	115	6%	88	8%	100%	13	15%	38%	1.78	-6.1	-33	-89	-$6
16 Proj	**239**	**23**	**8**	**29**	**2**	**258**	**232**	**283**	**403**	**687**	**724**	**660**	**3**	**74**	**0.10**	**45**	**18**	**37**	**32**	**93**	**97**	**137**	**12%**	**92**	**6%**	**66%**				**3.80**	**-5.3**	**1**	**4**	**$7**

Gutierrez,Franklin

Age: 33	Bats: R	Pos: LF	Health	F	LIMA Plan	D+
Ht: 6' 2"	Wt: 195		PT/Exp	F	Rand Var	-5
			Consist	F	MM	4223

15-35-.292 in 171 AB at SEA. Late June comeback from chronic spinal disease defied expectations. HctX with friendly G/L/F profile boosted PX, while h%, bb% conspired to produce BA/OBP magic from low ct%. The nature of his disease, age and FFF Reliability score make 2016 pure speculation.

Yr Tm	AB	R	HR	RBI	SB	BA	xBA	OBP	SLG	OPS	vL	vR	bb%	ct%	Eye	G	L	F	h%	HctX	PX	xPX	hr/f	Spd	SBO	SB%	#Wk	DOM	DIS	RC/G	RAR	BPV	BPX	R$
11 SEA *	362	30	1	22	13	220	220	260	273	533	561	529	5	82	0.30	48	17	36	27	86	44	76	1%	113	18%	87%	17	18%	53%	2.42	-27.9	9	20	$1
12 SEA *	212	25	5	22	3	236	250	284	382	666	1160	397	6	77	0.29	43	21	36	28	117	104	125	9%	101	12%	57%	9	44%	33%	3.52	-6.7	36	90	$2
13 SEA *	339	34	12	39	5	193	210	225	353	578	664	846	4	64	0.11	44	13	43	26	89	138	122	23%	97	19%	60%	11	45%	27%	2.42	-16.8	4	10	$1
14																																		
15 SEA *	351	48	19	54	1	259	258	313	479	792	973	978	7	68	0.24	41	24	36	33	119	161	160	36%	74	2%	100%	16	63%	25%	5.18	7.9	39	105	$11
1st Half	195	22	4	20	1	230	246	280	344	624	956	0	6	68	0.22	42	33	25	32	75	93	27	0%	90	3%	100%	3	33%	67%	3.23	-7.9	-13	-35	$4
2nd Half	156	26	15	34	0	295	303	364	647	1012	974	1069	8	68	0.28	41	23	37	34	124	246	175	38%	71	0%	0%	13	69%	15%	8.26	16.0	108	292	$20
16 Proj	**263**	**33**	**13**	**36**	**3**	**241**	**252**	**293**	**452**	**745**	**893**	**629**	**6**	**70**	**0.21**	**43**	**19**	**38**	**29**	**109**	**152**	**132**	**19%**	**87**	**8%**	**68%**				**4.31**	**-2.0**	**33**	**88**	**$8**

MATT DODGE

Guyer,Brandon

Age: 30	Bats: R	Pos: LF RF CF	Health D	LIMA Plan D+	
Ht: 6' 2"	Wt: 195		PT/Exp D	Rand Var +5	
			Consist A	MM 2423	

Short-side platooner got unexpected 144 AB vs RHP due to injuries, and improved Eye led to uptick in OBP. Harder contact, more FB led to 2H power surge vs LHP; also showed that 30 year-old legs can still contribute. Limited upside, but double digit HR/SB potential.

Yr	Tm	AB	R	HR	RBI	SB	BA	xBA	OBP	SLG	OPS	vL	vR	bb%	ct%	Eye	G	L	F	h%	HctX	PX	xPX	hr/f	Spd	SBO	SB%	#Wk	DOM	DIS	RC/G	RAR	BPV	BPX	R$
11	TAM *	429	67	13	50	12	256	263	301	421	722	655	397	6	76	0.27	53	16	31	31	116	120	142	20%	119	20%	64%	7	29%	29%	4.18	-9.5	49	109	$13
12	TAM *	92	9	3	11	2	233	243	274	379	654	714	0	5	79	0.27	83	0	17	26	115	87	114	100%	116	8%	100%	1	100%	0%	3.54	-2.7	33	83	$0
13	aaa	356	55	5	31	17	244		288	368	656			6	78	0.28				30		88			129	25%	82%				3.65		36	90	$11
14	TAM	259	37	3	26	6	266	253	334	367	701	762	656	6	80	0.31	50	20	30	32	98	81	80	5%	124	11%	86%	25	48%	44%	4.01	2.4	35	95	$7
15	TAM	332	51	8	28	10	265	266	359	413	771	844	673	7	82	0.41	44	21	35	30	103	98	90	9%	114	17%	71%	27	48%	30%	4.47	0.7	55	149	$10
1st Half		163	20	2	16	9	264	256	360	368	728	713	746	8	80	0.44	48	22	30	32	100	74	74	5%	112	24%	82%	14	36%	36%	4.22	-1.6	32	86	$10
2nd Half		169	31	6	12	1	266	278	358	456	813	962	588	6	83	0.38	40	20	39	29	106	121	105	11%	112	8%	33%	13	62%	23%	4.71	0.7	76	205	$11
16	Proj	**328**	**51**	**6**	**30**	**9**	**262**	**259**	**345**	**394**	**739**	**821**	**650**	**6**	**80**	**0.34**	**46**	**21**	**33**	**31**	**101**	**91**	**87**	**7%**	**127**	**16%**	**74%**				**4.17**	**-3.8**	**45**	**122**	**$9**

Gyorko,Jedd

Age: 27	Bats: R	Pos: 2B SS	Health C	LIMA Plan B	
Ht: 5' 10"	Wt: 210		PT/Exp C	Rand Var -1	
			Consist C	MM 2015	

16-57-.247 in 421 AB at SD. Demoted to minors in June after slow start. Returned in July and demonstrated significant improvement, particularly vs RHP. xPX says 2013 HR levels still in reach. Dual eligibility in MI is a nice addition, but substandard bb% and Eye ensure a BA drag.

Yr	Tm	AB	R	HR	RBI	SB	BA	xBA	OBP	SLG	OPS	vL	vR	bb%	ct%	Eye	G	L	F	h%	HctX	PX	xPX	hr/f	Spd	SBO	SB%	#Wk	DOM	DIS	RC/G	RAR	BPV	BPX	R$
11	aa	236	30	5	29	1	231		291	330	622			8	74	0.33				29		77			86	1%	100%				3.21		3	7	$1
12	a/a	499	58	19	72	4	249		302	409	712			7	77	0.33				29		106			75	7%	43%				4.07		30	75	$12
13	SD	486	62	23	63	1	249	261	301	444	745	829	715	6	75	0.27	38	23	40	29	114	138	140	16%	85	2%	50%	24	54%	29%	4.45	13.5	49	123	$13
14	SD *	424	41	11	54	3	210	239	275	333	608	669	594	8	75	0.36	44	22	35	25	95	93	115	10%	66	5%	60%	20	30%	40%	2.93	-4.8	14	38	$3
15	SD *	482	39	18	63	0	242	231	288	389	677	803	654	6	75	0.26	42	21	37	29	115	96	130	14%	60	2%	0%	25	24%	56%	3.69	-1.1	9	24	$7
1st Half		202	15	5	19	0	220	204	276	339	614	840	541	7	73	0.28	45	16	40	27	112	84	123	8%	82	3%	0%	12	17%	67%	2.96	-7.0	1	3	-$3
2nd Half		280	24	13	44	0	257	249	299	425	724	779	707	5	76	0.24	41	23	35	30	117	104	132	17%	54	1%	0%	13	31%	46%	4.27	1.5	16	43	$14
16	Proj	**523**	**50**	**19**	**68**	**1**	**244**	**239**	**299**	**394**	**693**	**790**	**659**	**7**	**75**	**0.29**	**42**	**21**	**37**	**29**	**108**	**100**	**125**	**13%**	**65**	**3%**	**40%**				**3.86**	**-5.7**	**4**	**11**	**$12**

Hamilton,Billy

Age: 25	Bats: B	Pos: CF	Health B	LIMA Plan C+	
Ht: 6' 0"	Wt: 160		PT/Exp B	Rand Var +1	
			Consist A	MM 1505	

Lost 2H AB due to shoulder injury, but better success rate still netted more SB. The problem going forward: too many weakly hit FB and below-average bb% means that those SB will continue to come with significant collateral damage to BA and OBP. Needs an Esix Snead voodoo doll.

Yr	Tm	AB	R	HR	RBI	SB	BA	xBA	OBP	SLG	OPS	vL	vR	bb%	ct%	Eye	G	L	F	h%	HctX	PX	xPX	hr/f	Spd	SBO	SB%	#Wk	DOM	DIS	RC/G	RAR	BPV	BPX	R$
11																																			
12	aa	175	29	1	13	45	271		383	360	744			15	73	0.67				37		56			157	89%	73%				4.66		17	43	$16
13	CIN *	523	72	6	36	76	238	276	285	319	604	0	950	6	77	0.29	50	36	14	30	40	59	-15	0%	163	71%	81%	5	20%	40%	3.25	-13.8	19	48	$34
14	CIN	563	72	6	48	56	250	237	292	355	648	669	641	6	79	0.29	42	21	37	31	70	77	55	4%	167	58%	71%	26	46%	38%	3.37	-8.0	42	114	$28
15	CIN	412	56	4	28	57	226	216	274	289	563	641	532	6	82	0.37	43	20	38	27	70	38	58	3%	164	61%	88%	22	23%	55%	3.01	-16.6	21	57	$23
1st Half		268	39	3	19	41	224	220	275	291	566	637	536	7	83	0.41	39	23	38	26	63	37	52	4%	176	67%	87%	14	21%	43%	3.05	-11.4	29	78	$29
2nd Half		144	17	1	9	16	229	207	273	285	557	651	527	6	80	0.31	50	13	37	28	84	42	70	3%	134	50%	89%	8	25%	75%	2.94	-6.5	7	19	$12
16	Proj	**455**	**61**	**5**	**33**	**57**	**239**	**220**	**292**	**318**	**610**	**669**	**589**	**7**	**79**	**0.37**	**44**	**19**	**37**	**29**	**73**	**53**	**60**	**3%**	**164**	**59%**	**80%**				**3.29**	**-15.9**	**25**	**67**	**$26**

Hamilton,Josh

Age: 35	Bats: L	Pos: LF	Health F	LIMA Plan C+	
Ht: 6' 4"	Wt: 240		PT/Exp C	Rand Var -1	
			Consist A	MM 4123	

8-25-.253 in 170 AB at TEX. Loss of plate patience, FB-to-GB shift, and declining HctX may be attributed to multiple 2015 DL trips for lower body injuries. While PX/xPX and SLG remain strong for now, health history and age will continue their erosion. Father Time has already defeated Spd; other skills will succumb too.

Yr	Tm	AB	R	HR	RBI	SB	BA	xBA	OBP	SLG	OPS	vL	vR	bb%	ct%	Eye	G	L	F	h%	HctX	PX	xPX	hr/f	Spd	SBO	SB%	#Wk	DOM	DIS	RC/G	RAR	BPV	BPX	R$
11	TEX	487	80	25	94	8	298	297	346	536	882	825	904	7	81	0.42	41	21	38	33	119	154	126	16%	97	7%	89%	22	73%	9%	6.86	26.0	93	207	$26
12	TEX	562	103	43	128	7	285	282	354	577	930	853	965	10	71	0.37	38	21	41	33	115	196	166	26%	77	8%	64%	27	59%	33%	7.15	41.1	86	215	$33
13	LAA	576	73	21	79	4	250	251	307	432	739	596	802	8	73	0.30	39	22	39	31	99	133	128	13%	105	3%	100%	27	48%	30%	4.55	9.6	45	113	$15
14	LAA	338	43	10	44	3	263	238	331	414	745	884	695	9	68	0.30	37	25	39	36	97	132	136	11%	71	7%	50%	17	35%	35%	4.57	8.7	18	49	$10
15	TEX *	226	30	9	31	0	259	247	296	430	726	726	736	5	70	0.18	46	23	32	33	93	126	122	21%	66	0%	0%	14	29%	50%	4.38	-0.1	13	35	$4
1st Half		89	14	3	11	0	286	270	331	462	793	750	1027	6	69	0.22	33	33	33	39	116	144	175	29%	79	0%	0%	4	50%	25%	5.46	2.3	30	81	$2
2nd Half		137	16	6	20	0	241	237	269	409	678	712	659	4	71	0.15	48	20	31	30	88	115	111	19%	64	0%	0%	10	20%	60%	3.74	-3.3	5	14	$6
16	Proj	**360**	**48**	**15**	**51**	**2**	**261**	**258**	**309**	**450**	**759**	**735**	**769**	**7**	**71**	**0.24**	**40**	**25**	**34**	**33**	**100**	**137**	**136**	**17%**	**74**	**3%**	**64%**				**4.77**	**2.2**	**26**	**69**	**$13**

Hanigan,Ryan

Age: 35	Bats: R	Pos: CA	Health F	LIMA Plan D	
Ht: 6' 0"	Wt: 210		PT/Exp F	Rand Var -2	
			Consist B	MM 1111	

2nd half GB/LD shift suggests that the broken finger in May was not fully healed upon his return. xBAs have been consistent for 5 years, but fading Eye, ct% in 2015 may indicate a downturn is coming (not that .240 xBAs are paticularly appealing). At age 35, there are better $1 second catchers to choose from.

Yr	Tm	AB	R	HR	RBI	SB	BA	xBA	OBP	SLG	OPS	vL	vR	bb%	ct%	Eye	G	L	F	h%	HctX	PX	xPX	hr/f	Spd	SBO	SB%	#Wk	DOM	DIS	RC/G	RAR	BPV	BPX	R$
11	CIN	266	27	6	31	0	267	249	356	357	714	871	685	12	88	1.09	48	22	30	29	89	54	69	9%	77	0%	0%	25	32%	40%	4.37	1.3	43	96	$4
12	CIN	317	25	2	24	0	274	241	365	338	703	840	661	12	88	1.19	53	21	26	31	84	45	48	3%	77	0%	0%	27	44%	22%	4.30	1.5	39	98	$3
13	CIN	222	17	2	21	0	198	243	306	261	567	608	555	12	88	1.07	49	22	29	22	84	44	55	4%	76	2%	0%	22	32%	36%	2.37	-9.4	34	85	-$4
14	TAM	225	18	5	34	1	218	242	318	324	642	602	654	12	83	0.79	38	22	40	24	79	75	86	7%	70	2%	100%	19	53%	32%	3.33	0.0	38	103	$1
15	BOS	174	28	2	16	0	247	246	337	328	664	895	587	10	78	0.51	52	24	24	31	82	61	47	6%	88	0%	0%	17	24%	47%	3.60	-0.6	8	22	$1
1st Half		66	12	1	7	0	242	271	367	318	685	883	640	14	80	0.85	42	34	25	29	92	51	46	8%	89	0%	0%	6	17%	17%	3.76	0.0	19	51	-$1
2nd Half		108	16	1	9	0	250	233	317	333	650	897	547	8	76	0.35	59	18	23	32	77	68	48	5%	85	0%	0%	11	27%	64%	3.49	-0.9	1	3	$2
16	Proj	**218**	**26**	**3**	**23**	**0**	**235**	**246**	**330**	**318**	**648**	**777**	**608**	**11**	**81**	**0.68**	**48**	**23**	**29**	**28**	**83**	**58**	**59**	**6%**	**80**	**1%**	**62%**				**3.39**	**-2.6**	**8**	**21**	**$3**

Hardy,J.J.

Age: 33	Bats: R	Pos: SS	Health C	LIMA Plan D+	
Ht: 6' 1"	Wt: 190		PT/Exp B	Rand Var +1	
			Consist B	MM 1205	

Hard to imagine that injuries didn't play a part in 2015: 1) hit DL for right shoulder and oblique strains 2) played all season with torn labrum in left shoulder. Off-season plan to rehab the latter may only delay the inevitable, and his power skills have been fading for years. DN: sub-Mendoza BA, 150 AB, surgeon's table.

Yr	Tm	AB	R	HR	RBI	SB	BA	xBA	OBP	SLG	OPS	vL	vR	bb%	ct%	Eye	G	L	F	h%	HctX	PX	xPX	hr/f	Spd	SBO	SB%	#Wk	DOM	DIS	RC/G	RAR	BPV	BPX	R$
11	BAL	527	76	30	80	0	269	274	310	491	801	794	803	6	83	0.34	40	16	43	28	123	139	130	16%	83	0%	0%	23	70%	4%	5.32	17.2	79	176	$19
12	BAL	663	85	22	68	0	238	249	282	389	671	767	639	5	84	0.36	43	17	40	25	114	91	109	10%	103	0%	0%	27	52%	19%	3.64	-5.2	53	133	$10
13	BAL	601	66	25	76	2	263	267	306	433	738	783	720	6	88	0.52	45	17	38	26	107	101	99	12%	95	2%	67%	27	63%	19%	4.58	20.0	75	188	$17
14	BAL	529	56	9	52	0	268	234	309	372	682	621	702	5	80	0.28	43	19	38	32	104	81	96	6%	100	0%	0%	27	30%	37%	3.98	12.1	29	78	$11
15	BAL	411	45	8	37	0	219	221	253	311	564	494	593	5	79	0.23	49	17	33	26	82	62	69	7%	95	0%	0%	22	23%	50%	2.60	-22.6	4	11	$0
1st Half		190	23	4	20	0	237	219	269	332	600	473	650	5	79	0.23	50	16	34	28	89	62	64	8%	93	0%	0%	10	30%	40%	3.01	-6.1	4	11	$2
2nd Half		221	22	4	17	0	204	222	239	294	533	512	543	5	78	0.23	49	18	33	24	76	62	74	7%	97	0%	0%	12	17%	58%	2.27	-12.5	3	8	-$1
16	Proj	**431**	**48**	**10**	**43**	**0**	**240**	**234**	**280**	**354**	**634**	**595**	**648**	**5**	**81**	**0.29**	**46**	**18**	**36**	**28**	**95**	**75**	**86**	**8%**	**97**	**0%**	**67%**				**3.33**	**-9.7**	**7**	**18**	**$7**

Harper,Bryce

Age: 23	Bats: L	Pos: RF	Health C	LIMA Plan C	
Ht: 6' 3"	Wt: 225		PT/Exp B	Rand Var -5	
			Consist F	MM 5255	

Finally! Consolidated skills with remarkable consistency. Doubled bb%, improved ct% and HctX, pushed pitches/PA into elite territory (4.09) to deliver his first four-figure OPS. This may well be the dawn of an epic career, but regression is a powerful force (see h%, hr/f, health), so don't canonize him just yet.

Yr	Tm	AB	R	HR	RBI	SB	BA	xBA	OBP	SLG	OPS	vL	vR	bb%	ct%	Eye	G	L	F	h%	HctX	PX	xPX	hr/f	Spd	SBO	SB%	#Wk	DOM	DIS	RC/G	RAR	BPV	BPX	R$
11	aa	129	12	3	10	6	245		311	372	684			9	80	0.48				29		91			101	24%	75%				3.91		42	93	$1
12	WAS *	607	105	23	61	19	265	272	334	459	793	715	869	9	78	0.47	45	23	33	31	103	122	107	16%	139	16%	73%	24	54%	8%	5.27	2.1	72	180	$23
13	WAS	424	71	20	58	11	274	281	368	486	854	648	947	13	78	0.65	47	20	33	31	114	142	118	18%	95	12%	73%	22	64%	27%	6.18	19.2	81	203	$20
14	WAS	352	41	13	32	2	273	234	344	423	768	765	769	10	70	0.37	44	22	35	35	92	110	115	15%	125	4%	50%	18	44%	39%	5.02	9.3	29	78	$10
15	WAS	521	118	42	99	6	330	309	460	649	1109	986	1160	19	75	0.95	39	22	39	37	135	208	161	27%	93	5%	60%	27	85%	7%	11.16	87.2	134	362	$40
1st Half		259	58	25	60	4	347	327	474	722	1196	1120	1230	19	75	0.95	32	24	43	38	137	239	183	30%	83	8%	50%	14	86%	14%	12.81	54.2	157	424	$47
2nd Half		262	60	17	39	2	313	288	447	576	1023	839	1095	19	74	0.94	44	20	35	37	133	176	140	24%	104	2%	100%	13	85%	0%	9.61	33.9	110	297	$32
16	Proj	**529**	**104**	**37**	**101**	**5**	**300**	**291**	**414**	**578**	**991**	**864**	**1044**	**16**	**75**	**0.75**	**41**	**22**	**37**	**34**	**118**	**179**	**136**	**25%**	**98**	**4%**	**62%**				**8.59**	**55.2**	**97**	**263**	**$35**

MATT DODGE

Harrison,Josh

Age: 28	Bats: R	Pos: 3B 2B	
Ht: 5' 8"	Wt: 200		
Health	B	LIMA Plan	B+
PT/Exp	C	Rand Var	-3
Consist	F	MM	2335

Power disappointed as FB and HctX declined. Lost seven weeks in 2nd half to left thumb ligament surgery. Results post-return were mixed: tentative approach at plate (bb%); LD/FB shift helped BA beat xBA; HctX suffered. Batted ball profile, hard contact, and SB% are keys for restoring value but '14 was likely career year..

Yr Tm	AB	R	HR	RBI	SB	BA	xBA	OBP	SLG	OPS	vL	vR	bb%	ct%	Eye	G	L	F	h%	HctX	PX	xPX	hr/f	Spd	SBO	SB%	#Wk	DOM	DIS	RC/G	RAR	BPV	BPX	R$
11 PIT *	421	48	5	34	14	269	257	293	381	674	593	685	3	87	0.26	45	17	38	30	82	78	88	2%	112	22%	67%	16	31%	38%	3.78	-16.1	53	118	$11
12 PIT	249	34	3	16	7	233	241	279	345	624	580	647	4	85	0.27	37	22	41	26	101	66	111	3%	153	20%	70%	27	33%	41%	2.96	-12.4	49	123	$2
13 PIT *	356	48	6	40	16	261	276	294	412	705	981	466	4	85	0.31	47	19	35	29	122	103	122	12%	99	34%	66%	18	33%	28%	3.96	-0.3	62	155	$13
14 PIT	520	77	13	52	18	315	284	347	490	837	856	832	4	84	0.27	37	24	39	35	116	121	117	8%	122	20%	72%	27	52%	15%	6.15	34.6	81	219	$29
15 PIT	418	57	4	28	10	287	263	327	390	717	761	702	4	83	0.27	42	25	34	34	105	77	97	3%	106	17%	56%	22	32%	27%	4.21	-5.5	36	97	$13
1st Half	305	39	4	22	9	279	261	313	384	696	803	670	3	84	0.23	42	23	35	32	109	76	97	4%	100	18%	69%	14	36%	29%	4.04	-5.1	37	100	$17
2nd Half	113	18	0	6	1	310	268	366	407	773	708	820	7	80	0.35	40	30	29	39	94	80	94	0%	102	15%	20%	8	25%	25%	4.67	0.1	28	76	$2
16 Proj	467	67	6	37	13	292	270	335	423	758	794	742	5	83	0.30	41	25	35	34	106	91	105	5%	117	20%	56%				4.67	0.6	51	139	$17

Hart,Corey

Age: 34	Bats: R	Pos: 1B	
Ht: 6' 6"	Wt: 230		
Health	F	LIMA Plan	D
PT/Exp	F	Rand Var	0
Consist	B	MM	2201

2-9-.222 in 54 AB at PIT. Anagramming: Cry, O Heart! Which is what must be keeping him going after surgery on both knees and injuries to hamstring, hip, shoulder over the last three years. The quintessential lottery ticket if he makes it to 2016 spring training and you have a dollar left in the draft.

Yr Tm	AB	R	HR	RBI	SB	BA	xBA	OBP	SLG	OPS	vL	vR	bb%	ct%	Eye	G	L	F	h%	HctX	PX	xPX	hr/f	Spd	SBO	SB%	#Wk	DOM	DIS	RC/G	RAR	BPV	BPX	R$
11 MIL	492	80	26	63	7	285	283	356	510	866	1057	814	9	77	0.45	45	21	35	32	134	150	156	20%	122	10%	54%	23	83%	13%	6.18	-1.0	85	189	$22
12 MIL	562	91	30	83	5	270	267	334	507	841	893	825	7	73	0.29	40	19	41	32	122	161	162	18%	106	4%	100%	27	59%	26%	5.79	5.8	70	175	$22
13																																		
14 SEA *	302	22	8	26	2	202	220	252	331	583	568	603	6	75	0.26	40	17	43	24	98	96	138	8%	92	3%	100%	17	29%	41%	2.70	-14.0	17	46	-$1
15 PIT *	96	6	3	14	0	180	196	195	302	497	417	795	2	61	0.05	53	22	25	25	60	93	68	22%	76	0%	0%	12	25%	58%	1.83	-10.8	-51	-138	-$3
1st Half	66	5	3	12	0	215	210	235	382	617	417	795	3	62	0.07	53	22	25	29	61	120	68	22%	77	0%	0%	12	25%	58%	2.92	-4.5	-26	-70	-$1
2nd Half	30	1	0	2	0	105	153	105	131	236			0	60	0.00				17		32			83	0%	0%				0.39		-108	-292	-$5
16 Proj	131	16	4	19	1	241	228	298	376	674	581	724	6	71	0.22	46	20	34	31	101	97	128	12%	97	4%	78%				3.64	-5.9	-4	-10	$3

Headley,Chase

Age: 32	Bats: B	Pos: 3B	
Ht: 6' 2"	Wt: 220		
Health	B	LIMA Plan	B
PT/Exp	A	Rand Var	0
Consist	A	MM	2125

"The Usual" when ordering at the 2016 bar. Blandly average 3B who doesn't hit enough fly balls no matter where his home ballpark is, and didn't run in 2015. A metronome of consistency, whose best fantasy contributions are healthy accumulation of AB, and scoring runs when part of a prolific offense.

Yr Tm	AB	R	HR	RBI	SB	BA	xBA	OBP	SLG	OPS	vL	vR	bb%	ct%	Eye	G	L	F	h%	HctX	PX	xPX	hr/f	Spd	SBO	SB%	#Wk	DOM	DIS	RC/G	RAR	BPV	BPX	R$
11 SD	381	43	4	44	13	289	249	374	399	773	891	729	12	76	0.57	46	22	32	37	92	95	101	4%	77	12%	87%	21	43%	19%	5.49	7.3	29	64	$13
12 SD	604	95	31	115	17	286	268	376	498	875	801	906	12	74	0.55	48	19	32	34	117	141	134	21%	83	12%	74%	27	56%	37%	6.64	35.8	61	153	$32
13 SD	520	59	13	50	8	250	253	347	400	747	764	740	11	73	0.47	46	23	31	32	104	119	107	11%	85	8%	67%	25	48%	28%	4.52	8.8	36	90	$11
14 2 TM	470	55	13	49	7	243	251	328	372	700	721	693	10	74	0.42	41	27	32	30	114	99	120	12%	70	8%	70%	26	35%	42%	3.95	3.9	18	49	$10
15 NYY	580	74	11	62	0	259	252	324	369	693	743	670	8	77	0.38	43	27	30	32	94	80	91	8%	86	1%	0%	27	26%	44%	3.98	-9.8	15	41	$11
1st Half	311	40	8	29	0	254	258	307	373	680	605	711	7	77	0.31	46	27	27	31	105	78	94	13%	95	1%	0%	14	29%	57%	3.81	-7.4	13	35	$12
2nd Half	269	34	3	33	0	264	245	343	364	708	885	621	10	77	0.46	40	26	35	33	82	81	88	4%	82	1%	0%	13	23%	31%	4.17	-3.5	17	46	$9
16 Proj	568	70	13	63	2	257	251	337	384	721	774	699	10	75	0.44	43	25	32	32	100	92	103	10%	81	2%	69%				4.33	-4.9	13	36	$14

Hechavarria,Adeiny

Age: 27	Bats: R	Pos: SS	
Ht: 5' 11"	Wt: 185		
Health	A	LIMA Plan	B
PT/Exp	B	Rand Var	-3
Consist	B	MM	1525

Improved SB% turned on green light more frequently in 2H, but weak on-base skills relegated him to the bottom third of lineup. There, his 6% career SBO (vs 22% SBO batting elsewhere) nets few bags. Spd is strong, and GB, ct% fit the profile, but improving bb%, HctX key to unlocking... UP: 20 SB.

Yr Tm	AB	R	HR	RBI	SB	BA	xBA	OBP	SLG	OPS	vL	vR	bb%	ct%	Eye	G	L	F	h%	HctX	PX	xPX	hr/f	Spd	SBO	SB%	#Wk	DOM	DIS	RC/G	RAR	BPV	BPX	R$
11 a/a	572	53	6	41	14	229		259	327	586			4	81	0.21				27		70			117	26%	46%				2.51		23	51	$5
12 TOR *	569	64	6	58	5	264	236	300	360	660	590	677	5	77	0.23	48	21	31	33	81	68	98	7%	126	5%	71%	10	30%	50%	3.72	-6.3	13	33	$11
13 MIA	543	30	3	42	11	227	240	267	298	565	589	555	5	82	0.31	52	20	28	27	77	46	55	2%	158	16%	52%	26	31%	50%	2.49	-17.1	26	65	$3
14 MIA	536	53	1	34	7	276	262	308	356	664	742	645	5	84	0.30	54	22	24	33	100	55	73	1%	175	8%	58%	25	40%	44%	3.80	7.8	43	116	$11
15 MIA	470	54	5	48	7	281	253	315	374	689	912	637	5	83	0.29	51	20	29	33	91	58	84	5%	137	7%	78%	22	32%	32%	4.19	5.5	33	89	$13
1st Half	292	36	4	33	3	288	263	325	390	715	942	655	5	83	0.30	50	23	27	34	91	65	79	6%	123	5%	75%	14	21%	29%	4.50	3.4	32	86	$17
2nd Half	178	18	1	15	4	270	236	298	348	646	848	607	4	84	0.29	53	15	31	32	90	47	90	2%	146	11%	80%	8	50%	38%	3.70	-2.0	29	78	$6
16 Proj	554	54	4	47	9	266	250	299	353	652	749	625	5	83	0.28	52	20	28	31	90	54	79	3%	161	10%	65%				3.61	-7.6	19	52	$13

Hedges,Austin

Age: 23	Bats: R	Pos: CA	
Ht: 6' 1"	Wt: 190		
Health	A	LIMA Plan	D
PT/Exp	F	Rand Var	+2
Consist	A	MM	1101

3-11-.168 in 137 AB at SD. Glove-first prospect rushed to SD in May to serve as backup CA. MLEs indicated his offense wasn't ready for the majors, and sporadic playing time made sure that the prophecy was fulfilled. Needs more time in Triple-A than his 71 AB to date.

Yr Tm	AB	R	HR	RBI	SB	BA	xBA	OBP	SLG	OPS	vL	vR	bb%	ct%	Eye	G	L	F	h%	HctX	PX	xPX	hr/f	Spd	SBO	SB%	#Wk	DOM	DIS	RC/G	RAR	BPV	BPX	R$
11																																		
12																																		
13 aa	67	3	0	7	3	198		255	235	490			7	85	0.51				23		34			94	23%	70%				1.92		11	28	-$2
14 aa	427	26	5	36	1	196		231	276	507			4	77	0.19				25		63			91	5%	20%				1.95		-4	-11	-$4
15 SD *	208	21	4	21	1	199	224	248	301	550	420	483	6	77	0.29	45	19	36	24	68	71	56	8%	83	2%	100%	23	17%	74%	2.40	-9.2	4	11	-$2
1st Half	116	10	2	14	1	202	248	245	325	570	833	146	5	79	0.27	48	19	32	24	74	90	49	10%	81	3%	100%	10	10%	80%	2.56	-4.4	24	65	-$2
2nd Half	92	11	2	7	0	196	198	255	272	527	268	663	7	75	0.30	44	18	38	24	64	47	59	7%	103	0%	0%	13	23%	69%	2.18	-4.7	-15	-41	-$2
16 Proj	165	15	4	15	1	209	224	251	316	567	610	547	5	76	0.24	46	19	36	25	68	72	55	8%	97	3%	52%				2.54	-6.4	-9	-25	$1

Hernandez,Cesar

Age: 26	Bats: B	Pos: 2B	
Ht: 5' 10"	Wt: 166		
Health	A	LIMA Plan	C
PT/Exp	C	Rand Var	-1
Consist	C	MM	1523

Dislocated left thumb ended 2015 three weeks early, but established SB prowess in first full MLB season. Became less patient in 2H, as LD morphed into GB and drove BA and OBP under water. HctX growth is encouraging, but must recapture the 1H success to continue to show off the wheels.

Yr Tm	AB	R	HR	RBI	SB	BA	xBA	OBP	SLG	OPS	vL	vR	bb%	ct%	Eye	G	L	F	h%	HctX	PX	xPX	hr/f	Spd	SBO	SB%	#Wk	DOM	DIS	RC/G	RAR	BPV	BPX	R$
11																																		
12 a/a	532	53	2	48	18	264		299	361	660			5	84	0.30				31		65			117	27%	53%				3.41		34	85	$12
13 PHI *	522	64	2	38	25	278	246	331	344	674	581	722	7	77	0.34	52	26	22	36	73	49	48	0%	164	23%	68%	7	14%	57%	3.92	3.9	13	33	$19
14 PHI *	373	40	4	22	7	242	246	299	314	613	626	551	8	76	0.34	53	26	21	31	64	54	50	6%	132	15%	44%	16	19%	56%	2.92	-5.3	4	11	$5
15 PHI	405	57	1	35	19	272	257	339	348	687	769	653	9	79	0.47	54	24	22	34	82	58	68	2%	144	19%	79%	24	38%	42%	4.19	0.3	25	68	$14
1st Half	174	30	1	19	11	299	276	385	385	770	947	708	12	82	0.72	48	30	23	36	84	65	76	3%	128	22%	79%	14	50%	36%	5.45	6.0	42	114	$17
2nd Half	231	27	0	16	8	251	243	302	320	623	659	605	7	77	0.31	59	19	21	33	81	53	63	0%	151	16%	80%	10	20%	50%	3.36	-5.9	10	27	$12
16 Proj	354	44	2	27	14	264	256	323	341	664	707	646	8	78	0.40	54	25	21	33	74	56	59	3%	143	19%	67%				3.73	-5.2	13	34	$11

Hernandez,Enrique

Age: 24	Bats: R	Pos: 2B OF	
Ht: 5' 11"	Wt: 170		
Health	B	LIMA Plan	C+
PT/Exp	C	Rand Var	-3
Consist	B	MM	3133

7-22-.307 in 202 AB at LA. Cuckoo for Kiki? Games played at six positions provide in-season roster flexibility, but collapsed ct%, FB-to-GB shift raise red flags. Lost most of Sept. to hamstring strain, so 1H/2H, vL/vR splits are small samples driven by large h% fluctuations. More AB will tell a truer tale.

Yr Tm	AB	R	HR	RBI	SB	BA	xBA	OBP	SLG	OPS	vL	vR	bb%	ct%	Eye	G	L	F	h%	HctX	PX	xPX	hr/f	Spd	SBO	SB%	#Wk	DOM	DIS	RC/G	RAR	BPV	BPX	R$
11																																		
12 aa	81	5	1	2	2	216		245	268	513			4	88	0.31				24		33			100	21%	41%				1.92		16	40	-$2
13 aa	437	42	11	36	4	210		256	328	584			6	82	0.35				23		77			101	8%	55%				2.65		34	85	$1
14 2 TM *	497	55	10	45	4	266	264	313	401	714	581	796	6	87	0.52	38	21	41	29	94	92	115	7%	127	9%	39%	9	56%	22%	4.16	4.8	73	197	$12
15 LA *	261	28	8	29	1	269	261	306	427	733	1215	592	5	76	0.22	46	23	30	33	110	106	99	15%	131	5%	27%	20	45%	35%	4.42	0.9	41	111	$5
1st Half	156	19	4	16	1	220	267	257	374	632	1088	573	5	76	0.21	43	27	30	27	118	105	111	13%	120	6%	43%	11	55%	27%	3.07	-6.4	36	97	$4
2nd Half	105	9	4	13	0	343	243	381	505	885	1340	609	5	76	0.24	49	20	31	42	102	108	86	16%	127	3%	0%	9	33%	44%	7.13	7.5	42	114	$8
16 Proj	330	34	11	34	2	271	267	316	434	751	971	640	6	81	0.31	43	22	35	31	103	103	104	12%	141	6%	35%				4.57	3.3	37	100	$10

MATT DODGE

Herrera,Dilson

Age: 22	Bats: R	Pos: 2B	
Ht: 5' 10"	Wt: 150		
Health	A	LIMA Plan	D+
PT/Exp	F	Rand Var	-2
Consist	C	MM	3411

3-6-.211 with 2 SB in 90 AB at NYM. Broken finger interrupted 1H audition; all other results from Triple-A debut. Growth signs in ct% and HctX, with FB trajectory already in place to support xPX increase. Spd still strong, but poor SB% may curtail SBO in the near term. A growth stock with power/speed potential.

Yr	Tm	AB	R	HR	RBI	SB	BA	xBA	OBP	SLG	OPS	vL	vR	bb%	ct%	Eye	G	L	F	h%	HctX	PX	xPX	hr/f	Spd	SBO	SB%	#Wk	DOM	DIS	RC/G	RAR	BPV	BPX	R$
11																																			
12																																			
13																																			
14	NYM *	300	44	11	48	7	284	244	347	463	811	539	747	9	75	0.39	36	19	45	35	54	130	81	16%	143	13%	61%	4	50%	50%	5.55	18.5	66	178	$14
15	NYM *	417	57	11	42	11	263	237	315	410	725	725	663	7	78	0.34	33	21	46	31	87	99	108	10%	128	21%	53%	9	33%	44%	4.17	0.0	46	124	$13
1st Half		190	20	4	15	4	255	227	301	372	673	732	569	6	79	0.31	35	20	45	31	87	81	105	7%	129	19%	48%	6	33%	50%	3.55	-3.9	33	89	$5
2nd Half		227	36	8	27	7	271	235	326	442	768	500	1500	8	78	0.37	14	29	57	32	98	113	127	25%	120	22%	56%	3	33%	33%	4.72	3.3	54	146	$20
16	Proj	**226**	**29**	**8**	**25**	**6**	**254**	**241**	**322**	**422**	**745**	**923**	**695**	**8**	**77**	**0.36**	**35**	**20**	**45**	**30**	**74**	**112**	**95**	**10%**	**137**	**19%**	**55%**				**4.26**	**0.2**	**42**	**114**	**$6**

Herrera,Elian

Age: 31	Bats: B	Pos: 3B 2B	
Ht: 5' 10"	Wt: 195		
Health	A	LIMA Plan	D
PT/Exp	D	Rand Var	-2
Consist	B	MM	1313

7-33-.242 in 256 AB at MIL. On the Triple-A shuttle for 4 years, his pedigree when he first hit the majors at 27 was "defense-first utility guy." Check. One-time speed would have been an asset in this, his career year, but those skills have waned and he's swapped them out for a bit of power. Just a bit. At 31, this is it.

Yr	Tm	AB	R	HR	RBI	SB	BA	xBA	OBP	SLG	OPS	vL	vR	bb%	ct%	Eye	G	L	F	h%	HctX	PX	xPX	hr/f	Spd	SBO	SB%	#Wk	DOM	DIS	RC/G	RAR	BPV	BPX	R$
11	aa	378	47	2	24	22	218		290	286	576			9	67	0.31				32		61			121	34%	62%				2.56		-25	-56	$5
12	LA *	460	55	3	40	10	249	255	300	344	644	754	624	7	76	0.30	56	23	20	32	62	72	34	4%	115	19%	49%	14	14%	57%	3.25	-18.8	11	28	$7
13	LA *	416	43	4	27	10	210	230	261	267	528	667	400	7	76	0.29	67	17	17	27	52	42	-15	0%	101	14%	72%	3	0%	67%	2.26	-22.6	-16	-40	$1
14	MIL *	250	28	0	11	7	256	226	281	330	611	484	671	3	76	0.14	45	21	34	34	81	67	65	0%	129	17%	76%	23	13%	61%	3.19	-3.8	4	11	$3
15	MIL *	466	50	9	50	5	254	246	300	380	681	626	711	6	76	0.28	37	25	38	32	108	94	128	10%	77	7%	70%	15	40%	60%	3.88	-10.9	17	46	$9
1st Half		233	22	5	25	3	265	238	309	388	697	806	568	6	78	0.29	36	22	42	32	100	86	116	13%	66	7%	74%	7	29%	71%	4.15	-3.2	15	41	$9
2nd Half		233	27	4	25	3	243	251	292	374	666	537	812	6	74	0.27	39	27	35	31	112	103	136	8%	90	8%	67%	8	50%	50%	3.64	-6.9	21	57	$9
16	Proj	**264**	**29**	**4**	**22**	**6**	**245**	**237**	**287**	**350**	**637**	**587**	**657**	**6**	**75**	**0.24**	**43**	**23**	**34**	**31**	**91**	**79**	**92**	**5%**	**98**	**13%**	**71%**				**3.38**	**-9.9**	**5**	**13**	**$6**

Herrera,Odubel

Age: 24	Bats: L	Pos: CF	
Ht: 5' 11"	Wt: 165		
Health	A	LIMA Plan	B
PT/Exp	C	Rand Var	-5
Consist	B	MM	2525

Rule 5 draftee spent most of the season at the top of the lineup and showed enough to stay there. Much still to work on at the plate (bb%, ct%) but GB/LD stroke combined with plus speed provides multiple paths to additional value. A small HctX gain could pay off with more XBH, and better SB% could mean... UP: 30 SB.

Yr	Tm	AB	R	HR	RBI	SB	BA	xBA	OBP	SLG	OPS	vL	vR	bb%	ct%	Eye	G	L	F	h%	HctX	PX	xPX	hr/f	Spd	SBO	SB%	#Wk	DOM	DIS	RC/G	RAR	BPV	BPX	R$
11																																			
12																																			
13	aa	389	32	2	26	13	246		274	323	596			4	82	0.21				30		50			145	20%	71%				2.95		21	53	$6
14	aa	368	37	2	37	10	289		331	359	690			6	79	0.30				36		55			110	16%	55%				4.04		7	19	$12
15	PHI	495	64	8	41	16	297	249	344	418	762	720	776	5	74	0.22	47	23	29	39	86	93	83	8%	148	18%	67%	27	48%	30%	4.94	8.7	27	73	$20
1st Half		246	25	3	22	8	264	246	292	386	678	617	694	4	75	0.15	46	21	32	34	87	95	88	5%	129	23%	67%	14	50%	36%	3.76	-4.7	23	62	$13
2nd Half		249	39	5	19	8	329	251	393	450	843	790	864	7	73	0.28	48	26	26	44	85	90	78	11%	160	15%	67%	13	46%	23%	6.28	12.6	28	76	$27
16	Proj	**529**	**61**	**10**	**45**	**20**	**289**	**254**	**340**	**410**	**749**	**708**	**764**	**6**	**77**	**0.25**	**47**	**24**	**29**	**36**	**86**	**83**	**82**	**9%**	**156**	**21%**	**66%**				**4.67**	**3.9**	**21**	**56**	**$23**

Heyward,Jason

Age: 26	Bats: L	Pos: RF	
Ht: 6' 5"	Wt: 245		
Health	B	LIMA Plan	B+
PT/Exp	A	Rand Var	-1
Consist	B	MM	2435

2010's #1 rookie profiled as a future power stud, but 6 years later seems to have taken the path to least resistance as a SB source. ct%, GB%, SB% all show nice growth to support that new direction, but league average Spd makes us wonder how this all will play after he passes 30. Enjoy it while you can.

Yr	Tm	AB	R	HR	RBI	SB	BA	xBA	OBP	SLG	OPS	vL	vR	bb%	ct%	Eye	G	L	F	h%	HctX	PX	xPX	hr/f	Spd	SBO	SB%	#Wk	DOM	DIS	RC/G	RAR	BPV	BPX	R$
11	ATL	396	50	14	42	9	227	251	319	389	708	577	754	11	77	0.55	54	13	33	26	109	112	106	14%	91	10%	82%	24	42%	21%	4.09	-12.7	48	107	$7
12	ATL	587	93	27	82	21	269	261	335	479	814	635	934	9	74	0.38	44	19	37	32	112	138	132	17%	110	19%	72%	27	56%	19%	5.51	6.1	60	150	$26
13	ATL	382	67	14	38	2	254	272	349	427	776	801	766	11	81	0.66	44	21	35	28	99	116	95	13%	102	6%	33%	20	65%	20%	4.75	1.5	71	178	$10
14	ATL	573	74	11	58	20	271	251	351	384	735	477	820	10	83	0.68	45	19	36	31	95	80	80	6%	113	13%	83%	26	50%	12%	4.75	10.8	52	141	$21
15	STL	547	79	13	60	23	293	289	359	439	797	709	835	9	84	0.62	57	19	23	33	106	94	74	12%	109	16%	88%	27	48%	19%	5.84	14.9	63	170	$27
1st Half		278	38	9	29	8	281	280	331	439	770	891	733	7	81	0.40	56	19	25	32	105	105	66	16%	91	14%	80%	14	43%	21%	5.18	2.9	51	138	$23
2nd Half		269	41	4	31	15	305	295	386	439	824	590	957	12	86	0.95	59	19	22	34	108	84	81	8%	122	17%	94%	13	54%	15%	6.53	12.7	74	200	$31
16	Proj	**565**	**82**	**14**	**61**	**20**	**278**	**273**	**356**	**424**	**779**	**648**	**834**	**10**	**82**	**0.66**	**52**	**19**	**29**	**32**	**103**	**93**	**84**	**11%**	**109**	**14%**	**84%**				**5.37**	**8.9**	**62**	**168**	**$26**

Hicks,Aaron

Age: 26	Bats: B	Pos: CF	
Ht: 6' 2"	Wt: 190		
Health	C	LIMA Plan	B+
PT/Exp	C	Rand Var	-2
Consist	C	MM	2425

11-33-.256 with 13 SB in 352 AB at MIN. Came up for good in May, but DLed for forearm and hamstring strains. Serious steps forward: solid plate approach with 2H growth in HctX and LD/FB point to developing power. Ct% trend shows good adjustment to MLB; with any gains at all vs. RHP... UP: 20 HR, 20 SB

Yr	Tm	AB	R	HR	RBI	SB	BA	xBA	OBP	SLG	OPS	vL	vR	bb%	ct%	Eye	G	L	F	h%	HctX	PX	xPX	hr/f	Spd	SBO	SB%	#Wk	DOM	DIS	RC/G	RAR	BPV	BPX	R$
11																																			
12	aa	472	80	10	49	26	258		347	401	748			12	73	0.51				33		96			141	26%	68%				4.63		37	93	$18
13	MIN *	353	42	8	31	10	192	219	258	328	586	713	566	8	70	0.29	45	17	38	25	89	102	104	11%	146	18%	76%	16	44%	44%	2.68	-17.5	22	55	$2
14	MIN *	406	52	5	41	6	235	241	340	330	670	792	512	14	75	0.64	54	20	26	30	78	81	46	3%	111	11%	45%	16	38%	56%	3.57	-4.0	28	76	$6
15	MIN *	501	69	13	49	15	269	259	332	422	754	870	661	9	80	0.48	42	23	35	31	87	95	91	11%	134	13%	78%	18	44%	22%	4.90	5.6	56	151	$18
1st Half		234	29	4	18	8	267	278	326	397	723	692	557	8	79	0.43	50	27	23	32	65	86	62	11%	137	15%	78%	7	57%	43%	4.53	0.8	45	122	$12
2nd Half		267	40	10	31	7	270	256	337	443	781	942	703	9	81	0.53	38	21	41	30	97	103	103	11%	126	12%	78%	11	36%	9%	5.23	6.3	64	173	$23
16	Proj	**503**	**69**	**14**	**50**	**17**	**252**	**256**	**328**	**402**	**730**	**893**	**658**	**10**	**77**	**0.48**	**47**	**21**	**31**	**30**	**83**	**99**	**75**	**11%**	**131**	**17%**	**73%**				**4.46**	**0.7**	**45**	**121**	**$18**

Hill,Aaron

Age: 34	Bats: R	Pos: 2B 3B	
Ht: 5' 11"	Wt: 205		
Health	B	LIMA Plan	D
PT/Exp	C	Rand Var	+3
Consist	B	MM	2221

Bid farewell to the ranks of everyday players in 2015, but maintained very respectable bb%, ct%, HctX and Eye with reduced AB. Unfortunately, more GB and less Spd have dragged the BA so low that the bb% can't rescue OBP. Above average xPX should preserve MLB bench slot.

Yr	Tm	AB	R	HR	RBI	SB	BA	xBA	OBP	SLG	OPS	vL	vR	bb%	ct%	Eye	G	L	F	h%	HctX	PX	xPX	hr/f	Spd	SBO	SB%	#Wk	DOM	DIS	RC/G	RAR	BPV	BPX	R$
11	2 TM	520	61	8	61	21	246	250	299	356	655	678	648	6	86	0.49	37	21	42	27	104	75	85	4%	94	22%	75%	25	44%	28%	3.53	-24.5	48	107	$13
12	ARI	609	93	26	85	14	302	286	360	522	882	839	901	8	86	0.60	34	21	45	32	129	132	145	11%	113	12%	74%	27	63%	7%	6.75	36.1	101	253	$30
13	ARI *	351	49	11	44	1	290	275	345	455	800	911	789	8	85	0.57	39	22	40	31	108	108	120	10%	94	5%	20%	18	61%	22%	5.39	13.9	73	183	$12
14	ARI	501	52	10	60	4	244	252	287	367	654	680	645	5	82	0.30	34	25	41	28	114	89	116	6%	86	6%	57%	27	41%	30%	3.45	-3.8	36	97	$9
15	ARI	313	32	6	39	7	230	248	295	345	640	595	663	9	83	0.57	42	20	38	26	115	79	121	6%	63	11%	78%	26	46%	31%	3.45	-11.7	33	89	$4
1st Half		173	19	4	22	4	220	229	285	329	614	578	635	8	82	0.50	45	15	40	25	112	72	127	7%	68	12%	80%	14	29%	43%	3.11	-8.1	23	62	$5
2nd Half		140	13	2	17	3	243	272	306	364	671	618	697	10	84	0.68	38	25	37	28	118	89	115	4%	64	11%	75%	12	67%	17%	3.89	-3.1	49	132	$4
16	Proj	**161**	**18**	**3**	**20**	**3**	**249**	**257**	**306**	**379**	**685**	**668**	**692**	**8**	**83**	**0.51**	**38**	**22**	**39**	**28**	**114**	**87**	**118**	**6%**	**80**	**10%**	**69%**				**3.91**	**-1.5**	**42**	**112**	**$4**

Holliday,Matt

Age: 36	Bats: R	Pos: LF	
Ht: 6' 4"	Wt: 250		
Health	D	LIMA Plan	B+
PT/Exp	B	Rand Var	-1
Consist	B	MM	3135

Two right quad strains derailed the last 4 months of the season, but the year-end averages appear normal. However, look closely at the fortuitous h% along with the HctX and FB declines in the 1H with a healthy right leg. Double digit Eye and solid ct% will continue to provide value, but PX starting its decline.

Yr	Tm	AB	R	HR	RBI	SB	BA	xBA	OBP	SLG	OPS	vL	vR	bb%	ct%	Eye	G	L	F	h%	HctX	PX	xPX	hr/f	Spd	SBO	SB%	#Wk	DOM	DIS	RC/G	RAR	BPV	BPX	R$
11	STL	446	83	22	75	2	296	298	388	525	912	883	918	12	79	0.65	46	21	34	33	131	160	128	18%	72	2%	67%	25	64%	12%	7.18	23.6	92	204	$22
12	STL	599	95	27	102	4	295	270	379	497	877	1021	827	11	78	0.57	46	19	35	34	135	132	145	16%	90	4%	50%	27	52%	22%	6.61	31.4	69	173	$27
13	STL	519	103	22	94	6	299	286	388	487	875	799	898	12	83	0.80	46	21	34	32	133	121	126	15%	83	4%	86%	25	68%	0%	6.79	39.1	81	203	$28
14	STL	574	83	20	90	4	272	268	370	441	811	1004	751	11	83	0.74	46	17	38	30	140	119	142	11%	65	3%	80%	26	73%	12%	5.49	27.9	70	189	$22
15	STL	229	24	4	35	2	279	263	394	410	804	796	807	15	79	0.80	48	23	29	34	115	96	79	8%	74	4%	67%	17	47%	29%	5.56	5.5	45	122	$6
1st Half		178	20	3	26	2	303	259	417	421	839	827	841	16	78	0.85	49	24	27	38	111	84	76	8%	82	4%	67%	10	40%	30%	6.33	8.7	37	100	$9
2nd Half		51	4	1	9	0	196	274	305	373	678	707	660	11	80	0.60	44	20	37	23	130	136	88	7%	60	0%	0%	7	57%	29%	3.32	-2.0	71	192	-$5
16	Proj	**491**	**63**	**13**	**81**	**3**	**266**	**273**	**369**	**428**	**797**	**826**	**786**	**12**	**80**	**0.70**	**47**	**21**	**32**	**31**	**124**	**114**	**110**	**10%**	**69**	**3%**	**73%**				**5.28**	**10.2**	**55**	**147**	**$17**

MATT DODGE

Holt,Brock

Age: 28	Bats: L	Pos: 2B 3B RF	Health	A	LIMA Plan	D+
Ht: 5' 10"	Wt: 185		PT/Exp	C	Rand Var	-2
			Consist	C	MM	1423

Inflated h% and outlier bb% improvement powered 1H production, but regression hit hard en route to subpar 2H. If you're drafting for BA/SB value, xBA and SBO aren't optimistic. Steady LD% and multi-position eligibilty are plusses, but with power-capping GB% profile and likely PT slide, upside here is limited.

Yr Tm	AB	R	HR	RBI	SB	BA	xBA	OBP	SLG	OPS	vL	vR	bb%	ct%	Eye	G	L	F	h%	HctX	PX	xPX	hr/f	Spd	SBO	SB%	#Wk	DOM	DIS	RC/G	RAR	BPV	BPX	R$
11 aa	511	50	1	32	14	257		310	341	651			7	83	0.44				31		64			118	19%	57%				3.44		33	73	$8
12 PIT *	542	60	2	44	13	305	275	356	396	751	517	732	7	85	0.54	62	19	19	35	48	64	22	0%	139	17%	47%	6	17%	67%	4.77	6.4	51	128	$18
13 BOS *	350	35	2	29	7	220	221	279	261	540	384	536	8	81	0.44	57	17	26	26	82	31	33	0%	80	11%	67%	8	13%	50%	2.37	-14.7	-8	-20	$1
14 BOS *	557	84	5	34	17	280	272	327	384	711	763	682	7	80	0.35	50	26	23	34	97	80	66	5%	141	13%	84%	19	42%	26%	4.53	18.1	41	111	$19
15 BOS	454	56	2	45	8	280	263	349	379	727	807	701	9	79	0.47	53	24	24	35	91	74	62	2%	122	7%	89%	26	31%	35%	4.72	5.6	31	84	$12
1st Half	224	30	2	21	5	295	269	383	424	807	797	809	12	77	0.58	47	27	26	38	97	94	82	5%	126	8%	83%	14	36%	29%	5.86	10.2	46	124	$14
2nd Half	230	26	0	24	3	265	254	313	335	648	814	584	7	80	0.36	58	21	22	33	84	55	44	0%	112	5%	100%	12	25%	42%	3.71	-3.4	14	38	$10
16 Proj	322	40	1	27	7	270	258	327	354	680	731	662	8	80	0.44	54	23	23	33	86	62	53	2%	119	9%	78%				4.08	-1.3	20	55	$7

Hosmer,Eric

Age: 26	Bats: L	Pos: 1B	Health	A	LIMA Plan	B+
Ht: 6' 4"	Wt: 225		PT/Exp	A	Rand Var	-2
			Consist	C	MM	3245

Sizzling '14 postseason translated to '15 rebound, tabbing career-best OBP thanks to Eye/bb% recovery and improvement vs. LHP. xPX and steady GB% don't point to a power surge yet, but at 26, could add some loft to his swing entering his prime. With durability and 2H upticks in HctX/ct%... UP: 25 HR

Yr Tm	AB	R	HR	RBI	SB	BA	xBA	OBP	SLG	OPS	vL	vR	bb%	ct%	Eye	G	L	F	h%	HctX	PX	xPX	hr/f	Spd	SBO	SB%	#Wk	DOM	DIS	RC/G	RAR	BPV	BPX	R$
11 KC *	621	82	21	89	13	309	279	359	471	830	585	886	7	84	0.49	50	19	32	34	115	104	106	13%	88	10%	73%	22	59%	23%	6.18	9.2	62	138	$30
12 KC	535	65	14	60	16	232	262	304	359	663	591	700	9	82	0.59	54	18	28	26	121	80	95	11%	87	12%	94%	26	54%	27%	3.76	-24.6	40	100	$11
13 KC	623	86	17	79	11	302	287	353	448	801	797	803	8	84	0.51	53	22	25	34	128	96	105	13%	102	8%	73%	26	50%	8%	5.77	20.1	60	150	$28
14 KC	503	54	9	58	4	270	259	318	398	716	676	732	7	82	0.38	51	17	32	32	117	99	100	7%	82	5%	67%	23	35%	26%	4.39	3.6	45	122	$13
15 KC	599	98	18	93	7	297	289	363	459	822	730	885	9	82	0.56	52	23	24	34	116	102	94	15%	106	5%	70%	27	48%	19%	6.00	17.6	62	168	$27
1st Half	286	40	8	41	4	287	279	354	437	791	718	838	9	80	0.54	52	23	25	33	111	97	102	14%	99	7%	67%	14	43%	21%	5.48	2.6	50	135	$21
2nd Half	313	58	10	52	3	307	298	372	479	851	740	931	9	83	0.60	53	23	24	34	121	106	87	16%	113	4%	75%	13	54%	15%	6.50	11.5	72	195	$32
16 Proj	579	83	19	81	7	289	285	347	456	803	727	845	8	82	0.50	52	21	27	32	119	105	97	15%	97	6%	73%				5.65	8.0	59	159	$26

Howard,Ryan

Age: 36	Bats: L	Pos: 1B	Health	D	LIMA Plan	C+
Ht: 6' 4"	Wt: 250		PT/Exp	B	Rand Var	+5
			Consist	B	MM	4023

PRO: xPX says the power is still there, while rebounds in HctX and LD% each vouch for a revival to that career-worst h%. CON: Futility vs. LHP ate away at PT late in '15; safe to assume AB will begin to suffer. With health and age working against him, there's even more risk investing in those HR.

Yr Tm	AB	R	HR	RBI	SB	BA	xBA	OBP	SLG	OPS	vL	vR	bb%	ct%	Eye	G	L	F	h%	HctX	PX	xPX	hr/f	Spd	SBO	SB%	#Wk	DOM	DIS	RC/G	RAR	BPV	BPX	R$
11 PHI	557	81	33	116	1	253	264	346	488	835	634	921	12	69	0.44	40	21	39	31	126	175	175	22%	48	1%	100%	27	48%	41%	5.71	-8.9	57	127	$21
12 PHI	260	28	14	56	0	219	237	295	423	718	604	784	9	62	0.25	43	26	31	29	98	159	143	27%	49	0%	0%	13	38%	54%	3.98	-11.5	9	23	$4
13 PHI	286	34	11	43	0	266	251	319	465	784	539	878	7	67	0.24	39	24	38	36	120	163	160	15%	82	0%	0%	14	36%	43%	5.17	4.8	39	98	$7
14 PHI	569	65	23	95	0	223	225	310	380	690	770	658	11	67	0.35	41	22	37	29	97	123	154	16%	56	0%	0%	27	33%	44%	3.80	-6.6	5	14	$11
15 PHI	467	53	23	77	0	229	269	277	443	720	418	802	5	70	0.20	36	28	37	27	116	154	152	19%	37	0%	0%	24	54%	38%	3.98	-19.6	29	78	$9
1st Half	281	27	13	38	0	217	263	262	427	690	437	761	5	70	0.18	36	26	38	26	121	153	164	17%	44	0%	0%	14	57%	36%	3.57	-13.7	28	76	$8
2nd Half	186	26	10	39	0	247	279	299	468	766	386	863	6	71	0.22	35	31	35	30	108	156	133	22%	41	0%	0%	10	50%	40%	4.64	-2.8	35	95	$10
16 Proj	408	49	19	71	0	237	254	299	435	734	560	793	8	69	0.26	38	26	36	30	110	145	151	19%	50	2%	2%				4.19	-11.8	18	49	$12

Hundley,Nick

Age: 32	Bats: R	Pos: CA	Health	C	LIMA Plan	B
Ht: 6' 1"	Wt: 200		PT/Exp	D	Rand Var	-5
			Consist	C	MM	3215

Durability concerns abound after season-ending neck injury in late Sept., but there are reasons for optimism. Spike in ct%, 2H uptick in HctX, consistent LD stroke bode well for h% and future BA. Solid xPX should allow power to play up in Coors, too, so if healthy... UP: 25 HR. Nah, just kidding. Maybe 15.

Yr Tm	AB	R	HR	RBI	SB	BA	xBA	OBP	SLG	OPS	vL	vR	bb%	ct%	Eye	G	L	F	h%	HctX	PX	xPX	hr/f	Spd	SBO	SB%	#Wk	DOM	DIS	RC/G	RAR	BPV	BPX	R$
11 SD *	315	36	10	32	1	272	249	329	449	779	768	839	8	71	0.30	41	21	38	35	99	132	107	12%	144	2%	50%	19	47%	32%	5.14	6.8	52	116	$7
12 SD *	246	16	3	26	0	153	193	209	235	444	306	568	7	72	0.26	39	18	43	20	98	59	100	5%	103	10%	0%	14	14%	79%	1.34	-24.5	-16	-40	-$7
13 SD	373	35	13	44	1	233	240	290	389	679	553	721	7	74	0.27	43	20	37	28	86	115	99	13%	90	1%	100%	27	37%	48%	3.68	-0.2	29	73	$5
14 2 TM	218	18	6	22	1	243	219	273	358	631	570	641	4	71	0.16	37	23	40	32	98	89	109	10%	80	2%	100%	27	22%	52%	3.35	-0.6	-9	-24	$2
15 COL	366	45	10	43	5	301	267	339	467	807	727	832	5	79	0.28	43	23	34	36	97	108	107	10%	130	12%	45%	23	57%	26%	5.46	16.9	55	149	$14
1st Half	216	28	6	27	2	296	266	341	458	799	575	864	6	78	0.29	43	24	33	36	85	109	98	11%	114	12%	29%	14	50%	36%	5.16	8.5	47	127	$16
2nd Half	150	17	4	16	3	307	267	338	480	818	915	783	4	81	0.25	43	21	36	36	115	106	119	9%	138	11%	75%	9	67%	11%	5.92	8.8	63	170	$11
16 Proj	498	52	14	55	5	268	246	307	419	726	670	743	5	76	0.23	41	22	37	33	99	101	108	10%	125	7%	56%				4.38	8.7	21	58	$15

Hunter,Torii

Age: 40	Bats: R	Pos: RF	Health	A	LIMA Plan	D+
Ht: 6' 2"	Wt: 225		PT/Exp	A	Rand Var	+4
			Consist	B	MM	2123

If adrenaline rush in return to MIN fueled 1H upticks in xPX and Slg, 2H served as a bit of a reality check. GB% rise, HctX drop, ct% dip confirmed baseline regressions were due. Difficult to forecast improvement in those skills at age 40, and once PT/AB inevitably declines, don't bank on 15 HR.

Yr Tm	AB	R	HR	RBI	SB	BA	xBA	OBP	SLG	OPS	vL	vR	bb%	ct%	Eye	G	L	F	h%	HctX	PX	xPX	hr/f	Spd	SBO	SB%	#Wk	DOM	DIS	RC/G	RAR	BPV	BPX	R$
11 LAA	580	80	23	82	5	262	264	336	429	765	886	715	10	78	0.50	46	21	33	30	128	111	136	15%	91	7%	42%	27	41%	19%	4.76	-6.9	51	113	$18
12 LAA	534	81	16	92	9	313	257	365	451	817	868	798	7	75	0.29	52	23	25	39	108	96	88	16%	84	6%	90%	25	36%	52%	6.08	17.6	18	45	$26
13 DET	606	90	17	84	3	304	276	334	465	800	829	788	4	81	0.23	49	20	31	35	104	110	99	11%	107	3%	60%	26	50%	19%	5.61	22.1	56	140	$26
14 DET	549	71	17	83	4	286	284	319	446	765	799	753	4	84	0.26	48	21	31	32	115	111	97	12%	78	5%	57%	27	44%	15%	4.94	16.1	57	154	$22
15 MIN	521	67	22	81	2	240	254	293	409	702	722	693	6	80	0.33	48	17	34	26	101	105	102	15%	74	6%	29%	26	50%	35%	3.80	-15.2	40	108	$12
1st Half	282	40	12	45	1	262	265	315	443	758	682	793	7	83	0.43	47	17	36	28	108	111	116	14%	79	6%	25%	14	64%	21%	4.61	-1.7	59	159	$17
2nd Half	239	27	10	36	1	213	241	266	368	635	772	577	6	77	0.25	50	18	32	24	93	96	85	17%	70	6%	33%	12	33%	50%	2.96	-13.8	17	46	$6
16 Proj	343	41	11	47	2	254	257	301	400	701	741	685	6	80	0.30	49	19	32	29	106	94	99	12%	83	6%	45%				3.94	-8.9	28	75	$10

Iannetta,Chris

Age: 33	Bats: R	Pos: CA	Health	B	LIMA Plan	D
Ht: 6' 0"	Wt: 230		PT/Exp	C	Rand Var	+4
			Consist	C	MM	3001

Veteran catcher's days of fantasy relevance have all but extinguished. Stable bb% allows for some value as a #2 target in OBP leagues, but palpable HctX recession and LD% decay don't look favorable for h% or BA rebounds, nor his ability to stay in the lineup. Once the latter happens, what are you drafting for?

Yr Tm	AB	R	HR	RBI	SB	BA	xBA	OBP	SLG	OPS	vL	vR	bb%	ct%	Eye	G	L	F	h%	HctX	PX	xPX	hr/f	Spd	SBO	SB%	#Wk	DOM	DIS	RC/G	RAR	BPV	BPX	R$
11 COL	345	51	14	55	6	238	245	370	414	785	990	718	17	74	0.79	35	20	44	28	96	126	104	12%	71	8%	67%	27	48%	30%	5.04	8.6	55	122	$9
12 LAA *	243	29	9	27	1	235	228	321	385	706	636	756	11	71	0.44	44	20	36	29	98	100	115	16%	83	6%	25%	16	25%	44%	3.94	-1.4	15	38	$3
13 LAA	325	40	11	39	0	225	218	358	372	731	835	663	17	69	0.68	37	19	43	29	95	115	126	11%	69	1%	0%	27	41%	56%	4.34	6.2	26	65	$3
14 LAA	306	41	7	43	3	252	233	373	392	765	880	697	15	70	0.59	38	20	41	34	93	125	100	8%	72	3%	100%	26	46%	35%	4.93	14.4	35	95	$7
15 LAA	272	28	10	34	0	188	196	293	335	628	764	575	13	69	0.49	39	13	48	23	77	105	104	11%	70	1%	0%	26	31%	54%	3.04	-6.0	11	30	-$2
1st Half	158	15	3	15	0	190	175	309	272	581	892	487	15	70	0.60	45	14	41	25	68	60	67	7%	76	0%	0%	14	21%	71%	2.67	-5.6	-16	-43	-$4
2nd Half	114	13	7	19	0	184	228	271	421	692	642	718	10	68	0.36	30	11	58	20	88	169	158	15%	64	5%	0%	12	42%	33%	3.38	-1.5	51	138	$2
16 Proj	121	14	4	16	0	222	214	332	378	709	802	664	14	70	0.53	37	16	46	28	87	115	116	11%	71	3%	46%				4.02	0.9	11	29	$2

Iglesias,Jose

Age: 26	Bats: R	Pos: SS	Health	F	LIMA Plan	B
Ht: 5' 11"	Wt: 185		PT/Exp	D	Rand Var	-3
			Consist	B	MM	0425

Contusion on right finger ended '15 campaign, but not before enjoying several career-best marks. Can we expect a repeat? Upticks in ct% and Eye bode well for OBP, but poor SB% track record will likely limit SBO. Add in non-existent power, F Health grade and expected h% decline, his value becomes limited.

Yr Tm	AB	R	HR	RBI	SB	BA	xBA	OBP	SLG	OPS	vL	vR	bb%	ct%	Eye	G	L	F	h%	HctX	PX	xPX	hr/f	Spd	SBO	SB%	#Wk	DOM	DIS	RC/G	RAR	BPV	BPX	R$
11 BOS *	363	33	1	27	10	228	285	264	262	526	2000	400	5	83	0.28	75	25	0	27	105	28	2	0%	91	16%	71%	4	0%	50%	2.29	-21.0	-7	-16	$2
12 BOS *	421	44	2	22	11	235	233	281	279	560	536	284	6	85	0.42	59	16	25	27	55	32	23	8%	109	13%	78%	7	0%	43%	2.65	-15.9	11	28	$3
13 2 AL *	469	52	6	41	9	272	250	304	357	661	769	716	4	83	0.27	56	18	26	32	68	59	37	4%	135	11%	63%	22	23%	32%	3.71	3.9	31	78	$12
14																																		
15 DET	416	44	2	23	11	300	273	347	370	717	889	663	6	89	0.57	56	21	23	33	63	46	29	2%	140	15%	58%	22	36%	14%	4.40	0.0	50	135	$13
1st Half	232	19	1	12	9	323	274	374	384	758	1029	672	7	89	0.68	57	23	20	36	63	37	23	2%	145	17%	64%	14	29%	14%	5.17	6.9	46	124	$16
2nd Half	184	25	1	11	2	272	270	311	353	664	717	651	4	90	0.42	54	19	27	30	64	56	37	2%	123	11%	40%	8	50%	13%	3.52	-3.0	51	138	$10
16 Proj	498	55	4	33	11	272	258	323	345	668	751	631	5	86	0.39	56	19	25	31	64	48	32	4%	137	13%	62%				3.63	-6.6	23	62	$14

ALEC DOPP

Inciarte,Ender

Age: 25	Bats: L	Pos: RF LF CF	Health B	LIMA Plan C+	
			PT/Exp B	Rand Var -2	
Ht: 5' 10"	Wt: 165		Consist B	MM 1545	

First full season in the bigs started with some growing pains, but impressive 2H flashed signs of future impact. Surges in Eye/OBP helped above-average Spd play up on the basepaths, while LD% rise aided BA/SLG to further solidify his BPV gain. If OBP stays put and he shows some life vs. LHP... UP: 35 SB.

Yr	Tm	AB	R	HR	RBI	SB	BA	xBA	OBP	SLG	OPS	vL	vR	bb%	ct%	Eye	G	L	F	h%	HctX	PX	xPX	hr/f	Spd	SBO	SB%	#Wk	DOM	DIS	RC/G	RAR	BPV	BPX	R$
11																																			
12																																			
13	aa	473	59	4	21	37	264		298	341	639			5	89	0.45				29		50			136	37%	81%				3.64		49	123	$20
14	ARI *	527	68	5	35	23	273	271	314	358	671	646	691	6	85	0.40	52	24	25	31	87	60	51	5%	135	20%	81%	23	43%	22%	4.02	3.5	43	116	$19
15	ARI	524	73	6	45	21	303	284	338	408	747	534	824	5	89	0.45	52	22	26	33	102	66	73	5%	140	21%	68%	23	57%	9%	4.88	2.4	62	168	$24
1st Half		251	39	2	21	9	287	272	316	371	686	539	745	3	88	0.27	56	19	25	32	105	54	74	4%	133	22%	64%	11	36%	9%	3.93	-4.5	44	119	$19
2nd Half		273	34	4	24	12	319	295	358	443	802	527	893	6	90	0.64	49	24	27	34	99	76	72	6%	140	21%	71%	12	75%	8%	5.85	9.7	76	205	$29
16	**Proj**	**499**	**66**	**6**	**36**	**24**	**288**	**279**	**325**	**384**	**709**	**572**	**763**	**5**	**88**	**0.43**	**52**	**23**	**25**	**32**	**96**	**60**	**64**	**5%**	**140**	**23%**	**75%**				**4.45**	**-5.2**	**49**	**133**	**$20**

Infante,Omar

Age: 34	Bats: R	Pos: 2B	Health B	LIMA Plan D+	
			PT/Exp B	Rand Var +4	
Ht: 5' 11"	Wt: 195		Consist D	MM 1323	

Lowest BPV since '07 wasn't a fluke. Drew zero walks in April and ended 1H with worst Eye, 2nd-worst OBP and bb% among qualified batters; HctX dip only made matters worse. PT took a big hit in 2H with nagging injuries. Sans LD% stroke, Spd decline and that age thing, ABs have potential to bottom out soon.

Yr	Tm	AB	R	HR	RBI	SB	BA	xBA	OBP	SLG	OPS	vL	vR	bb%	ct%	Eye	G	L	F	h%	HctX	PX	xPX	hr/f	Spd	SBO	SB%	#Wk	DOM	DIS	RC/G	RAR	BPV	BPX	R$
11	FLA	579	55	7	49	4	276	263	315	382	696	729	685	6	88	0.51	42	22	36	30	97	66	64	4%	144	4%	67%	26	46%	12%	4.23	-5.9	63	140	$12
12	2 TM	554	69	12	53	17	274	267	300	419	719	872	656	4	88	0.32	41	20	39	29	98	86	97	6%	129	16%	85%	27	52%	22%	4.49	5.1	70	175	$18
13	DET	453	54	10	51	5	318	278	345	450	795	831	778	4	90	0.45	38	24	38	34	100	82	76	6%	119	6%	71%	22	59%	9%	5.81	25.3	73	183	$19
14	KC	528	50	6	66	9	252	247	295	337	632	584	649	6	87	0.49	38	23	39	28	94	59	76	3%	108	9%	75%	25	24%	20%	3.41	0.2	42	114	$11
15	KC	440	39	2	44	2	220	245	234	318	552	561	548	2	84	0.13	41	21	38	26	87	65	72	1%	116	5%	50%	24	33%	38%	2.42	-25.1	30	81	-$1
1st Half		264	25	0	23	1	231	244	240	307	547	625	519	1	84	0.09	39	23	37	28	79	59	61	0%	102	4%	50%	14	36%	43%	2.43	-14.3	18	49	$0
2nd Half		176	14	2	21	1	205	248	225	335	561	483	597	3	85	0.19	44	18	39	23	99	74	89	4%	127	7%	50%	10	30%	30%	2.38	-10.2	46	124	-$2
16	**Proj**	**371**	**35**	**4**	**41**	**4**	**246**	**252**	**272**	**353**	**625**	**619**	**628**	**4**	**86**	**0.28**	**40**	**21**	**38**	**27**	**94**	**67**	**77**	**3%**	**128**	**7%**	**67%**				**3.24**	**-10.9**	**39**	**106**	**$7**

Jackson,Austin

Age: 29	Bats: R	Pos: CF RF	Health B	LIMA Plan B	
			PT/Exp A	Rand Var -1	
Ht: 6' 1"	Wt: 185		Consist B	MM 2425	

9-48-.267 with 17 SB in 491 AB at SEA/CHC. First season below 500 MLB AB thanks to ankle injury in May, but results weren't hampered after return. In fact, things improved. Career-high SBO and still above-average Spd pushed him toward 20 SB, while 2H jumps in HctX/xPX say he might have 15 HR-juice left in his peak years.

Yr	Tm	AB	R	HR	RBI	SB	BA	xBA	OBP	SLG	OPS	vL	vR	bb%	ct%	Eye	G	L	F	h%	HctX	PX	xPX	hr/f	Spd	SBO	SB%	#Wk	DOM	DIS	RC/G	RAR	BPV	BPX	R$
11	DET	591	90	10	45	22	249	218	317	374	690	732	672	9	69	0.31	47	17	36	34	75	94	96	7%	203	17%	81%	27	26%	52%	4.05	-12.9	33	73	$15
12	DET	543	103	16	66	12	300	260	377	479	856	856	856	11	75	0.50	42	24	34	37	112	118	117	11%	178	12%	57%	25	48%	20%	6.33	25.0	73	183	$25
13	DET	552	99	12	49	8	272	263	337	417	754	681	784	9	77	0.40	42	28	31	34	103	103	101	9%	157	8%	67%	22	45%	23%	4.83	11.5	55	138	$18
14	2 AL	597	71	4	47	20	256	238	308	347	655	735	622	7	76	0.33	42	26	33	33	86	75	87	3%	143	16%	77%	27	30%	44%	3.72	-1.8	23	62	$16
15	2 TM *	529	58	9	49	18	262	248	303	373	675	770	657	6	73	0.22	51	24	25	34	98	83	78	10%	110	21%	64%	25	32%	56%	3.75	-8.7	6	16	$16
1st Half		270	25	3	16	8	246	235	286	334	620	805	603	5	75	0.23	51	22	27	32	89	64	63	6%	117	22%	52%	12	25%	50%	2.99	-11.7	-1	-3	$8
2nd Half		259	33	6	33	10	278	259	325	413	738	754	725	6	71	0.22	51	27	22	37	106	103	93	15%	105	20%	77%	13	38%	62%	4.67	1.9	13	35	$23
16	**Proj**	**489**	**64**	**10**	**45**	**15**	**265**	**252**	**317**	**394**	**711**	**762**	**686**	**7**	**74**	**0.29**	**47**	**25**	**28**	**34**	**96**	**92**	**88**	**10%**	**135**	**17%**	**70%**				**4.23**	**-2.5**	**21**	**58**	**$17**

Jankowski,Travis

Age: 25	Bats: L	Pos: CF	Health A	LIMA Plan C+	
			PT/Exp F	Rand Var -2	
Ht: 6' 2"	Wt: 190		Consist C	MM 1523	

2-12-.211 with 2 SB in 90 AB at SD. Former 1st-round draftee flaunted 0.98 Eye in 379 AB between AA/AAA before late-Aug callup, but 0.17 with SD voiced some concern. If he can right that ship and lift OBP, SBO and elite Spd give him massive SB value. Key will be whether BA/Slg will earn him enough AB.

Yr	Tm	AB	R	HR	RBI	SB	BA	xBA	OBP	SLG	OPS	vL	vR	bb%	ct%	Eye	G	L	F	h%	HctX	PX	xPX	hr/f	Spd	SBO	SB%	#Wk	DOM	DIS	RC/G	RAR	BPV	BPX	R$
11																																			
12																																			
13																																			
14	aa	100	11	0	8	8	207		256	257	513			6	84	0.41				25		39			111	45%	78%				2.22		14	38	$1
15	SD *	469	60	3	30	25	265	237	323	346	669	650	572	8	82	0.48	63	10	27	32	48	52	13	12%	176	28%	65%	8	38%	50%	3.71	-8.4	40	108	$16
1st Half		278	39	1	10	18	268	229	339	333	672			10	83	0.64				32		43			157	29%	70%				3.87		36	97	$17
2nd Half		191	24	2	21	9	275	245	324	387	712	650	572	7	80	0.37	63	10	27	33	47	69	13	12%	168	27%	60%	8	38%	50%	4.13	-1.6	43	116	$14
16	**Proj**	**259**	**32**	**6**	**21**	**17**	**249**	**259**	**304**	**380**	**685**	**748**	**666**	**7**	**83**	**0.46**	**63**	**9.5**	**27**	**28**	**42**	**77**	**12**	**11%**	**165**	**35%**	**71%**				**3.82**	**-4.7**	**51**	**138**	**$11**

Jaso,John

Age: 32	Bats: L	Pos: DH	Health F	LIMA Plan B	
			PT/Exp D	Rand Var -2	
Ht: 6' 2"	Wt: 205		Consist B	MM 3133	

Wrist injury placed him on DL thru June, but posted best BPV since '12 after returning. Steady Eye/bb% gives value to OBP-league owners; career-best HctX/PX skills bode quite well for BA/Slg production. Still, that .911 OPS vs. LHP is deceptive—44% h% in just 13 AB—and his 'F' health grade is, um, risky.

Yr	Tm	AB	R	HR	RBI	SB	BA	xBA	OBP	SLG	OPS	vL	vR	bb%	ct%	Eye	G	L	F	h%	HctX	PX	xPX	hr/f	Spd	SBO	SB%	#Wk	DOM	DIS	RC/G	RAR	BPV	BPX	R$
11	TAM	246	26	5	27	1	224	256	298	354	651	574	662	9	85	0.69	43	18	39	24	98	90	89	6%	79	5%	33%	22	50%	23%	3.33	-18.9	58	129	$0
12	SEA	294	41	10	50	5	276	294	394	456	850	393	927	16	83	1.10	46	25	28	30	108	115	86	14%	91	5%	100%	26	73%	15%	6.41	12.7	84	210	$10
13	OAK	207	31	3	21	2	271	247	387	372	759	442	802	16	78	0.84	40	25	35	33	75	80	58	5%	93	4%	67%	17	35%	35%	4.97	2.8	38	95	$4
14	OAK	307	42	9	40	2	264	273	337	430	767	468	793	8	80	0.47	37	26	38	30	105	117	120	10%	99	3%	100%	21	57%	14%	4.89	7.4	64	173	$8
15	TAM	185	23	5	22	1	286	282	380	459	839	911	831	13	79	0.72	53	22	26	34	125	127	115	13%	83	5%	33%	14	64%	29%	6.04	3.1	71	192	$4
1st Half		0	0	0	0	0	0	0	1000	0	1000			100	0	0.00				0		0		0%	96	0%	0%	2	50%	50%	0.00	0.0	-169	-457	-$15
2nd Half		185	23	5	22	1	286	282	377	459	836	911	827	13	79	0.69	53	22	26	34	125	127	115	13%	83	5%	33%	12	67%	25%	5.99	2.8	70	189	$4
16	**Proj**	**305**	**41**	**8**	**38**	**3**	**270**	**273**	**367**	**423**	**790**	**502**	**823**	**13**	**80**	**0.74**	**44**	**24**	**32**	**31**	**103**	**106**	**95**	**10%**	**88**	**4%**	**61%**				**5.32**	**-1.1**	**52**	**141**	**$10**

Jay,Jon

Age: 31	Bats: L	Pos: CF	Health D	LIMA Plan D	
			PT/Exp C	Rand Var +5	
Ht: 5' 11"	Wt: 195		Consist C	MM 0231	

Nagging left wrist tweak played a role in his regression, but warning signs of injury were evident early on. Posted 34 xPX and 61% GB% in presumably healthy April; eventually set career-worsts in both. And with poor health, HctX and likely PT decline, no guarantees that BA will rise back to normal levels again.

Yr	Tm	AB	R	HR	RBI	SB	BA	xBA	OBP	SLG	OPS	vL	vR	bb%	ct%	Eye	G	L	F	h%	HctX	PX	xPX	hr/f	Spd	SBO	SB%	#Wk	DOM	DIS	RC/G	RAR	BPV	BPX	R$
11	STL	455	56	10	37	6	297	278	344	424	768	727	779	6	82	0.35	54	23	23	34	85	88	69	11%	104	10%	46%	27	48%	30%	4.94	2.0	44	98	$15
12	STL	443	70	4	40	19	305	278	373	400	773	697	804	7	84	0.48	59	22	19	36	95	64	53	6%	126	19%	73%	23	39%	22%	5.15	5.7	41	103	$19
13	STL	548	75	7	67	10	276	270	351	370	721	620	749	9	81	0.50	50	27	23	33	86	70	57	7%	97	9%	67%	27	37%	30%	4.36	4.1	29	73	$18
14	STL	413	52	3	46	6	303	269	372	378	750	859	721	6	81	0.36	52	28	20	37	95	57	64	4%	115	7%	67%	26	19%	50%	4.75	10.5	19	51	$15
15	STL	210	25	1	10	0	210	248	306	257	563	414	596	8	83	0.53	60	22	18	25	80	32	46	3%	110	4%	0%	18	17%	56%	2.18	-13.9	9	24	-$3
1st Half		166	19	1	10	0	223	247	311	265	576	485	597	8	84	0.58	58	23	20	26	86	24	52	4%	112	4%	0%	12	8%	58%	2.37	-10.5	9	24	-$2
2nd Half		44	6	0	0	0	159	252	288	227	516	0	589	8	77	0.40	71	18	12	21	57	64	22	0%	100	0%	0%	6	33%	50%	1.58	-4.1	9	24	-$6
16	**Proj**	**162**	**21**	**1**	**15**	**2**	**265**	**264**	**351**	**331**	**681**	**582**	**704**	**7**	**83**	**0.47**	**59**	**23**	**18**	**32**	**80**	**45**	**48**	**4%**	**104**	**9%**	**57%**				**3.59**	**-3.9**	**10**	**26**	**$4**

Jennings,Desmond

Age: 29	Bats: R	Pos: LF	Health F	LIMA Plan D+	
			PT/Exp C	Rand Var +1	
Ht: 6' 2"	Wt: 200		Consist B	MM 2423	

1-7-.268 with 5 SB in 97 AB at TAM. Late April knee surgery shelved him until mid-August. Baseline results were subpar throughout. PRO: Plate skills have weathered the storm; still in peak years. CON: Spd tumbling; 3-year OPS dip; still can't hit RHPs. The risk here is undeniable, but it's not too late for... UP: see 2013

Yr	Tm	AB	R	HR	RBI	SB	BA	xBA	OBP	SLG	OPS	vL	vR	bb%	ct%	Eye	G	L	F	h%	HctX	PX	xPX	hr/f	Spd	SBO	SB%	#Wk	DOM	DIS	RC/G	RAR	BPV	BPX	R$
11	TAM *	585	96	19	55	33	242	248	318	404	722	791	811	10	74	0.43	47	18	35	30	86	113	100	16%	158	26%	82%	11	64%	18%	4.42	-8.9	56	124	$21
12	TAM	505	85	13	47	31	246	236	314	388	702	735	691	8	76	0.38	42	20	38	30	102	92	99	9%	163	25%	94%	24	54%	33%	4.32	-3.6	46	115	$19
13	TAM	527	82	14	54	20	252	258	334	414	748	857	697	11	78	0.56	47	17	36	30	117	113	110	10%	134	19%	71%	25	72%	20%	4.65	10.5	67	168	$19
14	TAM	479	64	10	36	15	244	252	319	378	697	833	653	9	77	0.44	49	18	34	30	104	105	103	8%	125	17%	71%	22	45%	32%	3.94	3.5	51	138	$12
15	TAM *	118	10	1	7	5	239	241	304	312	616	717	646	8	80	0.47	57	18	24	29	82	48	70	5%	112	24%	63%	6	0%	50%	3.05	-4.8	12	32	$0
1st Half		63	7	0	2	5	222	232	306	238	544	775	473	10	86	0.78	58	18	24	26	96	13	66	0%	99	35%	71%	3	0%	67%	2.41	-4.3	5	14	$0
2nd Half		55	3	1	5	0	259	245	309	396	704	633	1000	7	74	0.27	56	19	26	33	60	93	77	14%	115	7%	0%	3	0%	33%	3.88	-1.1	20	54	$1
16	**Proj**	**351**	**39**	**7**	**27**	**12**	**244**	**252**	**313**	**374**	**687**	**706**	**679**	**9**	**78**	**0.45**	**52**	**18**	**30**	**29**	**90**	**87**	**89**	**9%**	**130**	**20%**	**66%**				**3.82**	**-7.9**	**34**	**93**	**$10**

ALEC DOPP

Johnson,Chris

Age: 31 Bats: R Pos: 1B 3B	Health B	LIMA Plan D	
Ht: 6' 3" Wt: 225	PT/Exp B	Rand Var -2	
	Consist C	MM 1103	

Disappearance of LD stroke and fractured hand resulted in loss of playing time and poor 1H. Average rebounded following trade to CLE. Even with optimistic h% history and xPX, his poor plate skills, plummeting power and two straight sub-.240 BAs vR suggest that another 500 AB season is a longshot.

Yr	Tm	AB	R	HR	RBI	SB	BA	xBA	OBP	SLG	OPS	vL	vR	bb%	ct%	Eye	G	L	F	h%	HctX	PX	xPX	hr/f	Spd	SBO	SB%	#Wk	DOM	DIS	RC/G	RAR	BPV	BPX	R$
11	HOU *	459	45	10	53	3	246	248	282	382	664	635	681	5	72	0.18	46	23	31	32	106	108	110	8%	95	6%	46%	23	26%	48%	3.55	-31.2	15	33	$7
12	2 NL	488	48	15	76	5	281	254	326	451	777	672	819	6	73	0.23	39	26	35	36	98	120	112	12%	106	5%	83%	27	33%	44%	5.19	4.2	33	83	$16
13	ATL	514	54	12	68	0	321	268	358	457	816	939	772	5	77	0.25	46	27	28	40	97	104	101	11%	70	0%	0%	26	42%	38%	6.13	22.3	27	68	$21
14	ATL	582	43	10	58	6	263	244	292	361	653	988	570	4	73	0.14	48	27	25	35	83	83	74	9%	71	4%	100%	27	19%	67%	3.69	-6.0	-11	-30	$12
15	2 TM	243	18	3	18	2	255	210	286	337	624	745	550	4	70	0.14	48	21	31	36	94	69	107	6%	70	5%	67%	21	10%	71%	3.27	-15.5	-35	-95	$2
1st Half		99	8	1	7	2	232	195	280	313	594	883	393	6	69	0.19	54	13	33	33	83	72	82	4%	78	13%	67%	11	9%	73%	2.83	-7.9	-31	-84	-$1
2nd Half		144	10	2	11	0	271	223	291	354	645	634	650	3	70	0.09	44	27	30	37	101	68	123	7%	70	0%	0%	10	10%	70%	3.60	-7.6	-37	-100	$4
16	**Proj**	**301**	**24**	**5**	**29**	**2**	**258**	**234**	**293**	**357**	**650**	**775**	**595**	**4**	**72**	**0.16**	**47**	**25**	**28**	**34**	**92**	**79**	**98**	**8%**	**74**	**4%**	**75%**				**3.57**	**-14.0**	**-24**	**-65**	**$4**

Johnson,Kelly

Age: 34 Bats: L Pos: LF 2B 1B	Health B	LIMA Plan D	
Ht: 6' 1" Wt: 195	PT/Exp D	Rand Var -3	
	Consist C	MM 3213	

Bounce-back season included best BA, ct%, LD% and h% in five years. But it also featured another lofty GB% and a career-high hr/f—and at his age, this combination is unlikely to make an encore. Positional versatility and power keep him interesting, but as an end-game pick only.

Yr	Tm	AB	R	HR	RBI	SB	BA	xBA	OBP	SLG	OPS	vL	vR	bb%	ct%	Eye	G	L	F	h%	HctX	PX	xPX	hr/f	Spd	SBO	SB%	#Wk	DOM	DIS	RC/G	RAR	BPV	BPX	R$
11	2 TM	545	75	21	58	16	222	245	304	413	717	626	750	10	70	0.37	39	20	40	28	106	141	156	14%	116	17%	73%	27	48%	44%	4.01	-11.9	50	111	$12
12	TOR	507	61	16	55	14	225	226	313	365	678	607	705	11	69	0.39	45	21	34	30	94	102	113	14%	95	12%	88%	27	37%	48%	3.80	-8.4	8	20	$9
13	TAM	366	41	16	52	7	235	227	305	410	715	686	723	9	73	0.35	39	15	46	28	85	119	116	13%	109	12%	64%	26	50%	35%	4.03	4.1	39	98	$9
14	3 AL	265	29	7	27	2	215	252	296	362	659	708	653	10	73	0.41	49	21	30	27	81	114	77	12%	95	6%	50%	24	50%	29%	3.37	-0.1	34	92	$1
15	2 NL	310	38	14	47	2	265	253	314	435	750	678	758	7	74	0.28	44	23	33	32	110	112	123	19%	94	4%	67%	23	35%	48%	4.73	5.1	29	78	$9
1st Half		147	15	6	25	0	265	251	306	415	721	516	741	6	78	0.28	39	24	37	30	110	91	123	14%	92	3%	0%	11	55%	36%	4.30	0.3	27	73	$6
2nd Half		163	23	8	22	2	264	257	322	454	776	783	775	8	70	0.29	49	23	28	33	111	133	123	25%	99	5%	100%	12	17%	58%	5.14	4.3	34	92	$12
16	**Proj**	**256**	**31**	**9**	**34**	**3**	**244**	**243**	**309**	**400**	**708**	**676**	**714**	**8**	**73**	**0.34**	**45**	**21**	**34**	**30**	**98**	**106**	**112**	**15%**	**97**	**7%**	**67%**				**4.10**	**-3.5**	**16**	**44**	**$7**

Johnson,Micah

Age: 25 Bats: L Pos: 2B	Health A	LIMA Plan C	
Ht: 6' 0" Wt: 210	PT/Exp D	Rand Var -3	
	Consist C	MM 1313	

0-4-.230 with 3 SB in 100 AB at CHW. Defensive struggles and baserunning lapses earned him a May demotion back to Triple-A, where he once again showed better patience and a plus running game. With limited pop, upside is dependent on his legs, ability to get on—and glove. Check back in March.

Yr	Tm	AB	R	HR	RBI	SB	BA	xBA	OBP	SLG	OPS	vL	vR	bb%	ct%	Eye	G	L	F	h%	HctX	PX	xPX	hr/f	Spd	SBO	SB%	#Wk	DOM	DIS	RC/G	RAR	BPV	BPX	R$
11																																			
12																																			
13	aa	21	2	0	1	1	212		212	212	425			0	78	0.00				27		0			110	18%	100%				1.61		-51	-128	-$3
14	a/a	419	33	4	31	15	243		289	325	615			6	81	0.34				29		61			110	29%	50%				2.84		18	49	$8
15	CHW *	411	53	7	33	25	264	255	324	371	695	414	624	8	75	0.35	58	22	20	34	59	78	42	0%	108	30%	72%	9	22%	78%	4.09	-2.3	12	32	$16
1st Half		254	29	3	20	15	263	265	316	342	658	665	623	7	79	0.37	58	25	17	32	54	58	28	0%	106	30%	69%	6	17%	83%	3.65	-4.4	10	27	$17
2nd Half		157	25	4	13	10	264	230	336	419	754	91	628	10	68	0.33	62	8	31	36	85	117	100	0%	102	31%	75%	3	33%	67%	4.84	2.9	16	43	$15
16	**Proj**	**355**	**41**	**5**	**28**	**18**	**255**	**236**	**319**	**353**	**672**	**353**	**808**	**8**	**75**	**0.34**	**60**	**14**	**26**	**33**	**73**	**71**	**71**	**7%**	**103**	**29%**	**65%**				**3.61**	**-6.7**	**11**	**29**	**$13**

Jones,Adam

Age: 30 Bats: R Pos: CF	Health A	LIMA Plan B+	
Ht: 6' 2" Wt: 215	PT/Exp A	Rand Var +1	
	Consist A	MM 4335	

With the exception of age-based decline in his running game, he remains a model of consistency. 2H h% drag on BA was a blip and perhaps your buying opportunity. Age, health, ct% and power indices continue to project a plus-BA run-producer until further notice. A nearly risk-free stock in any fantasy portfolio.

Yr	Tm	AB	R	HR	RBI	SB	BA	xBA	OBP	SLG	OPS	vL	vR	bb%	ct%	Eye	G	L	F	h%	HctX	PX	xPX	hr/f	Spd	SBO	SB%	#Wk	DOM	DIS	RC/G	RAR	BPV	BPX	R$
11	BAL	567	68	25	83	12	280	273	319	466	785	665	829	5	80	0.26	49	18	33	31	106	120	106	17%	105	12%	75%	27	52%	22%	5.17	1.3	59	131	$23
12	BAL	648	103	32	82	16	287	290	334	505	839	800	852	5	81	0.27	46	21	33	31	125	136	108	19%	110	16%	70%	27	59%	19%	5.70	15.5	76	190	$30
13	BAL	653	100	33	108	14	285	284	318	493	811	732	846	4	79	0.18	48	20	32	32	125	137	127	20%	97	12%	82%	26	62%	19%	5.49	23.0	65	163	$34
14	BAL	644	88	29	96	7	281	270	311	469	780	1003	709	3	79	0.14	47	17	36	32	113	127	119	16%	104	6%	88%	27	52%	30%	5.05	21.0	58	157	$29
15	BAL	546	74	27	82	3	269	274	308	474	782	754	792	4	81	0.24	46	18	36	29	109	122	120	17%	94	3%	75%	25	44%	36%	4.96	7.0	61	165	$20
1st Half		276	39	10	38	3	286	280	334	464	798	975	754	5	84	0.36	45	22	33	31	109	104	116	13%	107	6%	75%	13	54%	31%	5.38	7.5	63	170	$20
2nd Half		270	35	17	44	0	252	261	280	485	765	596	836	3	79	0.14	47	14	39	26	109	141	124	20%	76	0%	0%	12	33%	42%	4.52	0.9	59	159	$19
16	**Proj**	**614**	**85**	**30**	**93**	**6**	**274**	**274**	**309**	**477**	**786**	**786**	**786**	**4**	**80**	**0.19**	**47**	**18**	**35**	**30**	**113**	**124**	**120**	**17%**	**99**	**6%**	**79%**				**5.04**	**11.1**	**55**	**150**	**$27**

Joseph,Caleb

Age: 30 Bats: R Pos: CA	Health A	LIMA Plan D+	
Ht: 6' 3" Wt: 180	PT/Exp C	Rand Var 0	
	Consist C	MM 3113	

Decent across-the-board sophomore effort from job-sharing catcher. HR and BA rose with increased MLB playing time. Both power metrics and ct% jumped in small-sample 2nd half. Despite age, health is a plus—and catchers have a sneaky habit of developing late. With 450 AB in HR-friendly venue... UP: 20 HR.

Yr	Tm	AB	R	HR	RBI	SB	BA	xBA	OBP	SLG	OPS	vL	vR	bb%	ct%	Eye	G	L	F	h%	HctX	PX	xPX	hr/f	Spd	SBO	SB%	#Wk	DOM	DIS	RC/G	RAR	BPV	BPX	R$
11	aa	375	34	6	34	4	227		288	316	604			8	82	0.48				26		61			90	7%	64%				2.97		22	49	$2
12	a/a	347	34	10	43	2	224		283	373	657			8	77	0.36				26		102			86	2%	100%				3.50		31	78	$3
13	aa	518	52	17	68	3	243		281	395	676			5	79	0.24				28		104			82	5%	53%				3.68		34	85	$10
14	BAL *	338	27	10	35	0	205	224	247	340	588	643	603	5	72	0.20	33	22	46	25	93	106	138	11%	86	2%	0%	21	24%	57%	2.66	-6.9	9	24	$0
15	BAL	320	38	11	49	0	234	249	299	394	693	712	683	8	78	0.38	33	23	43	27	104	105	120	10%	99	0%	0%	26	42%	42%	3.85	1.1	41	111	$4
1st Half		181	23	5	24	0	238	235	312	376	688	745	667	9	76	0.41	34	23	43	29	96	93	107	8%	115	0%	0%	14	50%	36%	3.85	0.4	32	86	$5
2nd Half		139	15	6	25	0	230	268	282	417	699	686	709	6	80	0.32	33	23	43	25	115	120	135	13%	85	0%	0%	12	33%	50%	3.83	0.2	55	149	$4
16	**Proj**	**360**	**37**	**13**	**49**	**1**	**235**	**247**	**289**	**397**	**687**	**706**	**676**	**6**	**77**	**0.30**	**33**	**23**	**44**	**27**	**101**	**108**	**129**	**11%**	**94**	**2%**	**52%**				**3.75**	**-0.3**	**19**	**51**	**$8**

Joyce,Matt

Age: 31 Bats: L Pos: LF	Health B	LIMA Plan D	
Ht: 6' 2" Wt: 200	PT/Exp C	Rand Var +5	
	Consist C	MM 2101	

5-21-.174 in 274 AB at LAA. 2014 HR plunge and 2H GB% spike sounded alarm for this debacle. Season effectively ended in late July following concussion and Triple-A rehab time. Patience held up relatively well and h% says BA will rebound somewhat. But minus return of better-than-average pop, the outlook is bleak.

Yr	Tm	AB	R	HR	RBI	SB	BA	xBA	OBP	SLG	OPS	vL	vR	bb%	ct%	Eye	G	L	F	h%	HctX	PX	xPX	hr/f	Spd	SBO	SB%	#Wk	DOM	DIS	RC/G	RAR	BPV	BPX	R$
11	TAM	462	69	19	75	13	277	269	347	478	825	657	866	10	77	0.46	36	21	42	32	117	144	128	12%	92	11%	93%	27	59%	22%	5.98	1.9	72	160	$20
12	TAM	399	55	17	59	4	241	244	341	429	769	631	810	12	74	0.54	38	19	43	28	106	124	117	13%	99	6%	57%	24	50%	29%	4.71	-2.1	53	133	$9
13	TAM	413	61	18	47	7	235	259	328	419	747	499	783	13	79	0.68	37	20	43	26	90	124	91	13%	83	9%	70%	27	44%	41%	4.58	1.0	67	168	$11
14	TAM	418	51	9	52	2	254	232	349	383	732	408	758	13	73	0.56	43	19	38	33	99	104	105	8%	107	5%	29%	26	35%	42%	4.40	4.3	37	100	$9
15	LAA *	283	19	6	25	0	182	208	267	299	566	262	592	10	72	0.41	41	18	42	23	78	86	92	7%	90	5%	0%	20	30%	50%	2.37	-28.2	6	16	-$5
1st Half		214	16	4	18	0	192	221	284	313	597	318	621	11	74	0.47	41	18	41	23	75	91	81	6%	94	6%	0%	14	36%	43%	2.59	-19.7	22	59	-$4
2nd Half		69	3	2	7	0	153	140	229	255	484	0	395	9	65	0.28	41	14	45	20	104	71	166	10%	91	0%	0%	6	17%	67%	1.76	-8.5	-37	-100	-$6
16	**Proj**	**124**	**12**	**3**	**14**	**1**	**211**	**217**	**308**	**342**	**650**	**362**	**685**	**11**	**72**	**0.45**	**41**	**18**	**41**	**26**	**96**	**94**	**118**	**9%**	**93**	**5%**	**43%**				**3.22**	**-5.2**	**3**	**9**	**$1**

Kang,Jung-ho

Age: 29 Bats: R Pos: 3B SS	Health A	LIMA Plan C+	
Ht: 6' 0" Wt: 215	PT/Exp F	Rand Var -1	
	Consist F	MM 4145	

Korean import struggled vs. RHP early in MLB debut, and plate skills still have a ways to go. But HctX and power asserted itself in 2nd half and provide building blocks for the future. Age, absence of track record and late-season knee injury add some immediate uncertainty, but there's legitimate value here.

Yr	Tm	AB	R	HR	RBI	SB	BA	xBA	OBP	SLG	OPS	vL	vR	bb%	ct%	Eye	G	L	F	h%	HctX	PX	xPX	hr/f	Spd	SBO	SB%	#Wk	DOM	DIS	RC/G	RAR	BPV	BPX	R$
11																																			
12																																			
13																																			
14																																			
15	PIT	421	60	15	58	5	287	273	355	461	816	721	840	6	76	0.28	50	23	28	35	116	117	105	17%	83	8%	56%	24	33%	33%	5.33	18.6	39	105	$16
1st Half		198	22	4	25	5	258	249	333	364	697	820	661	7	76	0.33	54	22	24	32	84	77	71	11%	77	9%	100%	14	21%	36%	4.06	-0.1	5	14	$9
2nd Half		223	38	11	33	0	314	293	376	547	923	608	990	5	77	0.24	46	23	31	37	144	152	134	21%	85	7%	0%	10	50%	30%	6.58	15.3	68	184	$23
16	**Proj**	**495**	**73**	**19**	**69**	**5**	**291**	**276**	**357**	**476**	**833**	**705**	**864**	**6**	**77**	**0.26**	**49**	**23**	**28**	**35**	**120**	**123**	**109**	**18%**	**88**	**8%**	**48%**				**5.50**	**12.2**	**43**	**115**	**$23**

JOCK THOMPSON

Kemp,Matt

Age: 31	Bats: R	Pos: RF	Health	D	LIMA Plan	B+
Ht: 6' 4"	Wt: 215		PT/Exp	B	Rand Var	+1
			Consist	C	MM	4335

Identical 2H surge to last year (17-58-3-.298), which many thought would be the springboard to a better start in 2015. But, no. 1H displayed inflated GB% and depressed power similar to 2014 as well. For 2016? Ongoing HctX and running game uptick are encouraging. Health remains a risk, but with it... UP: 30 HR.

Yr	Tm	AB	R	HR	RBI	SB	BA	xBA	OBP	SLG	OPS	vL	vR	bb%	ct%	Eye	G	L	F	h%	HctX	PX	xPX	hr/f	Spd	SBO	SB%	#Wk	DOM	DIS	RC/G	RAR	BPV	BPX	R$
11	LA	602	115	39	126	40	324	284	399	586	986	1142	940	11	74	0.47	36	23	41	39	122	181	164	21%	126	26%	78%	27	74%	19%	8.73	58.7	101	224	$51
12	LA	403	74	23	69	9	303	277	367	538	906	1105	818	9	74	0.39	43	22	35	36	122	155	158	22%	103	11%	69%	21	48%	19%	7.08	21.6	73	183	$23
13	LA	263	35	6	33	9	270	237	328	395	723	853	671	8	71	0.29	40	25	35	36	105	103	142	9%	79	13%	100%	14	29%	50%	4.72	0.8	8	20	$9
14	LA	541	77	25	89	8	287	287	346	506	852	781	879	9	73	0.36	43	26	31	35	128	168	140	20%	89	9%	62%	27	67%	15%	6.18	32.0	73	197	$27
15	SD	596	80	23	100	12	265	258	312	443	755	824	736	6	75	0.27	43	21	35	32	137	119	150	14%	91	10%	86%	26	38%	31%	4.82	-0.7	38	103	$23
1st Half		323	41	6	42	7	241	242	282	359	642	606	651	5	74	0.19	48	22	30	31	119	86	105	8%	101	11%	88%	14	21%	36%	3.41	-13.6	6	16	$16
2nd Half		273	39	17	58	5	293	280	346	542	888	1059	839	8	77	0.37	38	21	41	33	158	157	200	19%	81	9%	83%	12	58%	25%	6.83	15.3	75	203	$32
16	**Proj**	**568**	**81**	**24**	**96**	**13**	**280**	**264**	**335**	**471**	**806**	**872**	**785**	**8**	**74**	**0.33**	**42**	**23**	**35**	**34**	**131**	**131**	**153**	**16%**	**91**	**11%**	**81%**				**5.62**	**13.0**	**50**	**136**	**$26**

Kendrick,Howie

Age: 32	Bats: R	Pos: 2B	Health	C	LIMA Plan	B
Ht: 5' 10"	Wt: 210		PT/Exp	A	Rand Var	-1
			Consist	A	MM	1345

Second leg injury (hamstring) in three years tabs him as a bit of a Health risk and raises questions about future of his running game. Soaring GB% says his best HR years are behind him. But solid contact, h% and LD% metrics solidifies his status as a consistent producer at a scarce position. These days, BA alone has value.

Yr	Tm	AB	R	HR	RBI	SB	BA	xBA	OBP	SLG	OPS	vL	vR	bb%	ct%	Eye	G	L	F	h%	HctX	PX	xPX	hr/f	Spd	SBO	SB%	#Wk	DOM	DIS	RC/G	RAR	BPV	BPX	R$
11	LAA	537	86	18	63	14	285	284	338	464	802	840	782	6	78	0.28	52	22	27	34	112	123	127	17%	114	15%	70%	26	46%	27%	5.30	8.9	57	127	$23
12	LAA	550	57	8	67	14	287	265	325	400	725	797	694	5	79	0.25	59	21	21	35	109	81	87	9%	96	14%	70%	27	33%	37%	4.56	3.3	22	55	$18
13	LAA	478	55	13	54	6	297	289	335	439	775	862	745	5	81	0.26	51	27	21	34	115	93	88	16%	110	7%	67%	23	48%	26%	5.19	20.3	44	110	$18
14	LAA	617	85	7	75	14	293	272	347	397	744	834	714	7	82	0.44	60	19	21	35	133	78	88	7%	102	10%	74%	27	26%	22%	4.92	26.4	38	103	$25
15	LA	464	64	9	54	6	295	286	336	409	746	721	753	5	82	0.33	59	25	17	34	107	75	72	14%	93	6%	75%	22	27%	36%	4.94	10.0	30	81	$17
1st Half		305	38	7	36	4	292	287	342	416	759	730	766	7	81	0.40	57	26	17	34	99	82	68	17%	81	7%	67%	14	36%	36%	5.07	7.2	31	84	$21
2nd Half		159	26	2	18	2	302	284	323	396	719	710	724	2	84	0.16	61	22	16	35	121	62	80	9%	107	5%	100%	8	13%	38%	4.70	2.1	26	70	$9
16	**Proj**	**565**	**78**	**10**	**66**	**9**	**295**	**282**	**335**	**411**	**745**	**777**	**734**	**5**	**82**	**0.30**	**58**	**23**	**19**	**35**	**118**	**76**	**84**	**11%**	**106**	**8%**	**75%**				**4.91**	**10.8**	**33**	**89**	**$24**

Kiermaier,Kevin

Age: 26	Bats: L	Pos: CF	Health	A	LIMA Plan	B+
Ht: 6' 1"	Wt: 195		PT/Exp	C	Rand Var	0
			Consist	B	MM	2535

MLB's elite defensive OF, per highlight reels and most metrics. Sub-par patience and GB% keep a lid on his power, and his efforts vL look platoonish. But speed, contact and glove should give him opportunity to polish up some things. Age, athleticism and hr/f flashes are intriguing; there's sneaky value here.

Yr	Tm	AB	R	HR	RBI	SB	BA	xBA	OBP	SLG	OPS	vL	vR	bb%	ct%	Eye	G	L	F	h%	HctX	PX	xPX	hr/f	Spd	SBO	SB%	#Wk	DOM	DIS	RC/G	RAR	BPV	BPX	R$
11																																			
12																																			
13	TAM *	508	72	5	33	17	263	240	312	381	693	0	0	7	81	0.37	44	20	36	32	0	74	-15	0%	183	23%	56%	1	0%	100%	3.83	-6.1	51	128	$15
14	TAM *	459	58	12	46	14	264	270	314	436	750	507	837	7	79	0.34	53	17	31	31	92	116	82	13%	148	18%	73%	22	45%	32%	4.69	10.7	67	181	$16
15	TAM	505	62	10	40	18	263	275	298	420	718	625	754	5	81	0.25	48	23	29	31	86	96	57	8%	156	21%	78%	26	50%	31%	4.31	-2.8	59	159	$16
1st Half		267	35	4	16	9	255	279	289	419	709	606	735	4	81	0.22	48	23	29	30	95	103	62	6%	155	20%	90%	14	57%	21%	4.18	-1.8	62	168	$13
2nd Half		238	27	6	24	9	273	270	308	420	728	637	782	5	82	0.30	47	23	30	31	75	87	51	11%	146	22%	69%	12	42%	42%	4.46	0.3	52	141	$19
16	**Proj**	**495**	**62**	**11**	**43**	**16**	**265**	**269**	**308**	**424**	**732**	**586**	**786**	**6**	**80**	**0.30**	**50**	**21**	**30**	**31**	**87**	**97**	**66**	**9%**	**155**	**19%**	**70%**				**4.41**	**0.1**	**54**	**145**	**$18**

Kinsler,Ian

Age: 34	Bats: R	Pos: 2B	Health	A	LIMA Plan	B+
Ht: 6' 0"	Wt: 200		PT/Exp	A	Rand Var	-4
			Consist	A	MM	2335

Despite 2H HR spike, recent PX/xPX trends, bb% and age say big-time HR years are long gone. The good news is that neither power nor running game are crashing too dramatically in his mid-30s. And good health along with recent ct%, h% and LD% history are the real drivers here. So pay up.

Yr	Tm	AB	R	HR	RBI	SB	BA	xBA	OBP	SLG	OPS	vL	vR	bb%	ct%	Eye	G	L	F	h%	HctX	PX	xPX	hr/f	Spd	SBO	SB%	#Wk	DOM	DIS	RC/G	RAR	BPV	BPX	R$
11	TEX	620	121	32	77	30	255	286	355	477	832	880	816	13	89	1.25	35	18	47	24	129	130	125	12%	109	19%	88%	27	85%	0%	5.86	23.0	118	262	$30
12	TEX	655	105	19	72	21	256	268	326	423	749	988	671	8	86	0.67	38	20	42	27	100	103	88	8%	106	19%	70%	27	48%	19%	4.54	7.3	78	195	$22
13	TEX	545	85	13	72	15	277	275	344	413	757	814	733	9	89	0.86	37	24	39	29	124	87	109	7%	101	17%	58%	24	75%	8%	4.71	15.5	76	190	$23
14	DET	684	100	17	92	15	275	267	307	420	727	740	722	4	88	0.37	38	20	43	29	92	96	84	7%	116	12%	79%	27	59%	4%	4.50	21.7	76	205	$28
15	DET	624	94	11	73	10	296	265	342	428	770	798	763	6	87	0.54	34	25	41	33	100	81	93	5%	127	9%	63%	26	42%	15%	5.20	16.0	67	181	$25
1st Half		320	47	2	36	6	269	243	337	359	696	664	706	9	85	0.65	36	24	40	31	92	62	84	2%	116	9%	67%	14	29%	7%	4.16	-0.6	43	116	$19
2nd Half		304	47	9	37	4	326	290	348	500	848	957	821	3	90	0.35	32	27	41	34	109	100	103	8%	130	9%	57%	12	58%	25%	6.42	17.9	87	235	$31
16	**Proj**	**625**	**96**	**15**	**78**	**13**	**287**	**269**	**333**	**432**	**765**	**812**	**750**	**6**	**88**	**0.54**	**35**	**23**	**41**	**31**	**104**	**88**	**96**	**6%**	**125**	**12%**	**67%**				**5.02**	**14.1**	**70**	**189**	**$28**

Kipnis,Jason

Age: 29	Bats: L	Pos: 2B	Health	B	LIMA Plan	B
Ht: 5' 11"	Wt: 190		PT/Exp	A	Rand Var	-3
			Consist	F	MM	2335

Teased early in career with SB and power potential. Now the questions are how much—if any—will return, along with his BA stability. Ongoing shoulder woes could account for 2H struggles following h%-fueled 1H. But overall volatility remains troubling. Consistent LD% is a plus and with health... UP: .300 BA repeat.

Yr	Tm	AB	R	HR	RBI	SB	BA	xBA	OBP	SLG	OPS	vL	vR	bb%	ct%	Eye	G	L	F	h%	HctX	PX	xPX	hr/f	Spd	SBO	SB%	#Wk	DOM	DIS	RC/G	RAR	BPV	BPX	R$
11	CLE *	479	74	16	61	14	248	262	312	424	736	744	878	8	76	0.38	45	21	34	30	104	121	126	21%	107	13%	93%	8	50%	38%	4.61	0.1	51	113	$15
12	CLE	591	86	14	76	31	257	259	335	379	714	581	787	10	82	0.61	47	23	30	29	97	76	91	10%	105	21%	82%	27	48%	26%	4.44	4.7	41	103	$23
13	CLE	564	86	17	84	30	284	264	366	452	818	850	801	12	75	0.53	43	25	32	35	109	125	128	12%	99	21%	81%	27	48%	44%	6.03	37.0	54	135	$32
14	CLE	500	61	6	41	22	240	249	310	330	640	500	710	9	80	0.50	46	23	31	29	92	72	84	5%	95	18%	88%	23	30%	30%	3.58	2.8	26	70	$13
15	CLE	565	86	9	52	12	303	285	372	451	823	679	908	9	81	0.53	45	27	28	36	107	103	97	7%	120	12%	60%	24	50%	21%	5.87	25.1	63	170	$23
1st Half		320	56	6	35	10	341	307	419	506	925	774	1025	11	84	0.75	46	29	25	39	110	112	89	9%	122	14%	67%	14	64%	14%	7.88	30.9	85	230	$36
2nd Half		245	30	3	17	2	253	256	307	380	687	528	766	7	78	0.33	43	24	32	32	102	92	109	5%	111	9%	40%	10	30%	30%	3.78	-3.3	33	89	$7
16	**Proj**	**540**	**78**	**10**	**55**	**15**	**281**	**266**	**351**	**418**	**769**	**653**	**830**	**9**	**79**	**0.49**	**45**	**25**	**31**	**34**	**102**	**95**	**102**	**8%**	**108**	**13%**	**72%**				**5.12**	**13.9**	**48**	**129**	**$22**

La Stella,Tommy

Age: 27	Bats: L	Pos: 2B	Health	D	LIMA Plan	D+
Ht: 5' 11"	Wt: 185		PT/Exp	D	Rand Var	+5
			Consist	D	MM	1241

1-11-.269 in 67 AB at CHC. 19-for-51 spring training performance won an April roster spot before oblique strain essentially shelved him until late July. Fine ct%, average HctX and handedness could carve out 400 AB at some point somewhere. But sub-par power, running game project an empty BA and a limited ceiling.

Yr	Tm	AB	R	HR	RBI	SB	BA	xBA	OBP	SLG	OPS	vL	vR	bb%	ct%	Eye	G	L	F	h%	HctX	PX	xPX	hr/f	Spd	SBO	SB%	#Wk	DOM	DIS	RC/G	RAR	BPV	BPX	R$
11																																			
12																																			
13	aa	283	27	3	35	6	308		378	423	800			10	86	0.80				35		82			92	7%	84%				5.95		59	148	$10
14	ATL *	486	35	2	47	3	247	257	322	308	630	818	603	10	88	0.94	48	23	29	28	104	47	80	1%	80	3%	55%	19	42%	16%	3.34	-0.7	36	97	$4
15	CHC *	136	13	2	18	2	255	302	307	379	686	0	771	7	91	0.86	38	30	33	27	99	81	79	5%	83	6%	100%	8	63%	13%	4.07	-0.3	71	192	$1
1st Half		16	1	0	1	1	166	247	204	220	424	0	333	4	94	0.75	40	20	40	18	83	41	134	0%	102	39%	100%	1	0%	100%	1.59	-1.4	49	132	-$8
2nd Half		120	11	2	17	1	267	309	321	400	721	0	816	7	91	0.87	38	30	32	28	100	87	74	6%	85	3%	100%	7	71%	0%	4.52	1.0	76	205	$3
16	**Proj**	**217**	**19**	**3**	**27**	**3**	**278**	**280**	**346**	**390**	**736**	**653**	**747**	**9**	**89**	**0.91**	**41**	**25**	**34**	**30**	**102**	**74**	**76**	**4%**	**84**	**5%**	**84%**				**4.76**	**3.3**	**56**	**151**	**$7**

Lagares,Juan

Age: 27	Bats: R	Pos: CF	Health	B	LIMA Plan	C
Ht: 6' 1"	Wt: 215		PT/Exp	C	Rand Var	-1
			Consist	B	MM	1413

Ct% gains held but LD% plunged. Resulting BA struggles and less than otherworldly defense—the main reason he was in the lineup—cost him AB. Plus speed wasn't enough to exploit GB% spike, as marginal SB% fueled SBO dip. Glove and BA vL will keep him relevant in the real game. But his upside looks diminished.

Yr	Tm	AB	R	HR	RBI	SB	BA	xBA	OBP	SLG	OPS	vL	vR	bb%	ct%	Eye	G	L	F	h%	HctX	PX	xPX	hr/f	Spd	SBO	SB%	#Wk	DOM	DIS	RC/G	RAR	BPV	BPX	R$
11	aa	162	16	2	17	8	302		318	410	728			2	80	0.11				37		79			108	25%	77%				4.75		21	47	$5
12	aa	499	55	3	38	17	240		282	323	605			6	78	0.27				30		62			107	24%	60%				2.90		8	20	$8
13	NYM *	470	43	6	40	7	246	228	281	360	641	657	620	5	76	0.20	49	16	36	31	80	84	81	4%	135	13%	52%	24	21%	42%	3.27	-11.6	22	55	$7
14	NYM	416	46	4	47	13	281	249	321	382	703	875	658	5	79	0.23	46	22	32	35	93	81	89	4%	111	16%	76%	22	41%	36%	4.27	5.2	26	70	$14
15	NYM	441	47	6	41	7	259	236	289	358	647	771	599	4	80	0.18	55	14	31	31	107	64	71	6%	126	10%	70%	27	26%	41%	3.48	-10.7	19	51	$9
1st Half		296	32	3	23	5	257	234	284	345	628	841	582	3	81	0.18	56	14	30	31	103	55	73	4%	134	11%	63%	14	14%	50%	3.25	-10.2	16	43	$10
2nd Half		145	15	3	18	2	262	239	299	386	685	718	655	4	79	0.20	53	14	34	31	114	83	69	8%	103	6%	100%	13	38%	31%	3.97	-1.9	24	65	$5
16	**Proj**	**396**	**41**	**5**	**41**	**9**	**264**	**239**	**300**	**370**	**670**	**757**	**632**	**4**	**79**	**0.20**	**50**	**17**	**33**	**32**	**99**	**73**	**79**	**5%**	**123**	**13%**	**72%**				**3.75**	**-7.7**	**16**	**44**	**$12**

JOCK THOMPSON

Lamb,Jacob

Age: 25	Bats: L	Pos: 3B	Health	B	LIMA Plan	B
Ht: 6' 3"	Wt: 220		PT/Exp	D	Rand Var	-2
			Consist	B	MM	3215

Foot injury cut into 1H AB, may have factored into disappointing power. 2H ct% woes trumped solid HctX to produce "meh" rookie results. No single elite skill, but handedness, minor league success and defense give him opportunities. Needs health, fewer GBs, improvement vL to make the most of them. Still in growth mode.

Yr Tm	AB	R	HR	RBI	SB	BA	xBA	OBP	SLG	OPS	vL	vR	bb%	ct%	Eye	G	L	F	h%	HctX	PX	xPX	hr/f	Spd	SBO	SB%	#Wk	DOM	DIS	RC/G	RAR	BPV	BPX	R$
11																																		
12																																		
13																																		
14 ARI *	518	59	15	70	2	268	258	323	451	774	364	692	8	70	0.27	52	17	31	36	98	153	105	14%	98	3%	71%	9	33%	44%	5.07	20.2	49	132	$15
15 ARI	350	38	6	34	3	263	234	331	386	716	541	743	9	72	0.37	45	23	32	35	114	87	113	7%	120	5%	60%	21	29%	57%	4.37	-3.0	15	41	$6
1st Half	108	13	2	15	2	287	252	358	435	794	812	791	9	76	0.42	43	23	34	36	106	101	67	7%	112	9%	67%	8	38%	50%	5.42	2.4	39	105	$3
2nd Half	242	25	4	19	1	252	225	319	364	682	449	720	9	71	0.35	46	22	32	34	118	80	135	7%	121	3%	50%	13	23%	62%	3.95	-4.8	4	11	$8
16 Proj	**481**	**54**	**11**	**56**	**4**	**267**	**243**	**328**	**418**	**747**	**508**	**787**	**8**	**72**	**0.32**	**48**	**20**	**32**	**35**	**107**	**110**	**106**	**10%**	**108**	**5%**	**63%**				**4.75**	**1.7**	**21**	**56**	**$12**

LaRoche,Adam

Age: 36	Bats: L	Pos: DH 1B	Health	B	LIMA Plan	D+
Ht: 6' 3"	Wt: 205		PT/Exp	B	Rand Var	+1
			Consist	D	MM	3205

GB% spike and ct% plunge depressed HR output and wrecked his BA. Frustration was likely a factor in the 2H bb% and hr/f that helped finished off his season. That xPX says his power could rebound. But age, slim margin for BA error and chronic struggles vL suggest that his rebound potential, even from here, is limited.

Yr Tm	AB	R	HR	RBI	SB	BA	xBA	OBP	SLG	OPS	vL	vR	bb%	ct%	Eye	G	L	F	h%	HctX	PX	xPX	hr/f	Spd	SBO	SB%	#Wk	DOM	DIS	RC/G	RAR	BPV	BPX	R$
11 WAS	151	15	3	15	1	172	211	288	258	546	395	603	14	75	0.68	43	19	38	21	106	62	119	7%	76	2%	100%	8	13%	38%	2.34	-16.1	5	11	-$3
12 WAS	571	76	33	100	1	271	274	343	510	853	825	864	11	76	0.49	34	22	44	31	124	157	164	17%	76	1%	50%	27	63%	15%	6.18	14.5	75	188	$22
13 WAS	511	70	20	62	4	237	241	332	403	735	566	791	12	74	0.55	37	22	42	28	105	113	134	13%	102	3%	80%	26	50%	31%	4.47	-2.0	45	113	$11
14 WAS	494	73	26	92	3	259	266	362	455	817	620	891	14	78	0.76	37	22	41	28	126	131	162	16%	80	2%	100%	25	52%	16%	5.76	23.2	72	195	$20
15 CHW	429	41	12	44	0	207	209	293	340	634	383	697	10	69	0.37	43	18	40	27	103	102	129	10%	76	0%	0%	26	23%	46%	3.16	-23.6	3	8	$0
1st Half	251	29	9	31	0	231	219	339	390	729	528	790	13	67	0.46	44	19	37	31	108	124	142	15%	80	0%	0%	14	29%	43%	4.33	-6.2	18	49	$6
2nd Half	178	12	3	13	0	174	193	222	270	492	69	572	5	72	0.20	41	16	43	22	97	74	112	5%	78	0%	0%	12	17%	50%	1.82	-19.2	-15	-41	-$9
16 Proj	**437**	**52**	**17**	**58**	**1**	**232**	**233**	**316**	**391**	**708**	**500**	**769**	**11**	**73**	**0.45**	**40**	**19**	**41**	**28**	**109**	**109**	**137**	**13%**	**80**	**1%**	**89%**				**4.11**	**-17.7**	**17**	**47**	**$10**

Lawrie,Brett

Age: 26	Bats: R	Pos: 3B 2B	Health	F	LIMA Plan	B
Ht: 6' 0"	Wt: 210		PT/Exp	C	Rand Var	-2
			Consist	A	MM	3325

Career-high HR driven by AB hike, but better health did little for his skills. PRO: Held most of hr/f amid park change, age, 20-game qualifier at 2B. CON: Power-capping GB%, worst-ever ct%, bb% slipping, absent running game, lousy 2H vR. The CONs seem to have it, but not too late for FB hike that could yield... UP: 20 HR.

Yr Tm	AB	R	HR	RBI	SB	BA	xBA	OBP	SLG	OPS	vL	vR	bb%	ct%	Eye	G	L	F	h%	HctX	PX	xPX	hr/f	Spd	SBO	SB%	#Wk	DOM	DIS	RC/G	RAR	BPV	BPX	R$
11 TOR *	442	67	21	64	15	297	282	345	546	891	786	1022	7	79	0.35	38	17	45	33	122	162	147	17%	136	18%	82%	8	63%	38%	6.86	25.2	103	229	$23
12 TOR	494	73	11	48	13	273	265	324	405	729	813	697	6	83	0.38	50	20	30	31	94	85	78	9%	114	16%	62%	23	43%	35%	4.37	-2.5	47	118	$16
13 TOR *	422	45	12	48	10	252	254	308	393	701	613	742	7	81	0.43	49	17	34	28	105	91	89	10%	120	14%	66%	20	60%	25%	4.04	1.1	52	130	$11
14 TOR	259	27	12	38	0	247	238	301	421	722	595	760	6	81	0.33	47	14	39	26	118	112	122	14%	78	0%	0%	14	43%	29%	4.15	3.6	51	138	$6
15 OAK	562	64	16	60	5	260	244	299	407	706	825	660	5	74	0.19	49	18	33	32	96	103	105	12%	108	6%	71%	27	26%	48%	4.12	-7.3	24	65	$13
1st Half	292	26	7	36	4	291	238	329	425	754	877	707	5	73	0.18	48	20	32	38	96	99	114	10%	103	7%	80%	14	14%	50%	4.95	2.7	12	32	$17
2nd Half	270	38	9	24	1	226	251	266	389	655	770	609	5	76	0.22	50	17	33	26	95	108	97	13%	114	4%	50%	13	38%	46%	3.34	-10.6	38	103	$9
16 Proj	**495**	**58**	**17**	**58**	**5**	**254**	**250**	**303**	**412**	**715**	**732**	**709**	**6**	**78**	**0.28**	**48**	**17**	**35**	**30**	**104**	**102**	**107**	**12%**	**109**	**7%**	**69%**				**4.14**	**-7.1**	**32**	**85**	**$15**

LeMahieu,DJ

Age: 27	Bats: R	Pos: 2B	Health	A	LIMA Plan	B
Ht: 6' 4"	Wt: 205		PT/Exp	B	Rand Var	-4
			Consist	C	MM	1535

Career year fueled by confluence of bb%, h% upticks and SB% surge. Even with regression and near-zero power, his defense, health and ability to wring the most out of his small-ball skills should keep him valuable. DFS players take note: career .314 BA at Coors, .251 on the road.

Yr Tm	AB	R	HR	RBI	SB	BA	xBA	OBP	SLG	OPS	vL	vR	bb%	ct%	Eye	G	L	F	h%	HctX	PX	xPX	hr/f	Spd	SBO	SB%	#Wk	DOM	DIS	RC/G	RAR	BPV	BPX	R$
11 CHC *	474	40	4	38	6	266	260	294	341	635	667	465	4	86	0.27	65	17	19	30	71	54	38	0%	116	13%	40%	9	11%	56%	3.24	-20.6	30	67	$7
12 COL *	484	46	3	41	9	281	261	318	370	689	681	764	5	85	0.37	56	19	25	33	93	61	72	4%	145	14%	50%	17	41%	35%	3.96	-5.4	44	110	$11
13 COL *	547	59	3	41	23	285	286	316	375	692	652	682	4	84	0.28	55	27	18	34	97	64	64	3%	142	22%	71%	20	30%	30%	4.16	7.8	40	100	$20
14 COL	494	59	5	42	10	267	250	315	348	663	669	660	6	80	0.34	56	21	23	32	97	57	84	5%	147	14%	50%	26	35%	42%	3.58	2.7	26	70	$13
15 COL	564	85	6	61	23	301	272	358	388	746	757	743	8	81	0.47	54	26	19	36	94	58	74	7%	139	14%	88%	26	38%	31%	5.26	16.9	31	84	$27
1st Half	292	42	4	34	10	298	271	351	387	738	669	756	8	82	0.44	52	27	21	35	96	58	80	8%	132	14%	77%	14	50%	29%	4.97	6.0	29	78	$26
2nd Half	272	43	2	27	13	305	272	365	390	755	833	726	9	81	0.49	57	25	18	37	91	58	69	5%	138	14%	100%	12	25%	33%	5.58	10.1	29	78	$28
16 Proj	**554**	**73**	**5**	**52**	**21**	**281**	**268**	**331**	**365**	**696**	**708**	**692**	**7**	**82**	**0.41**	**56**	**24**	**20**	**34**	**94**	**56**	**73**	**5%**	**147**	**15%**	**83%**				**4.38**	**2.5**	**26**	**70**	**$22**

Lind,Adam

Age: 32	Bats: L	Pos: 1B	Health	C	LIMA Plan	B+
Ht: 6' 2"	Wt: 195		PT/Exp	B	Rand Var	0
			Consist	B	MM	4235

HR, hr/f rebounded while both BA, h% regressed with health and more playing time, as expected. GB% keeps a lid on power, with HR dependent on volatile hr/f. HctX history combined with good plate skills will prop up BA—particularly if he returns to platoon role. .221 BA, 0 HR in 104 AB vL say that less is clearly more here.

Yr Tm	AB	R	HR	RBI	SB	BA	xBA	OBP	SLG	OPS	vL	vR	bb%	ct%	Eye	G	L	F	h%	HctX	PX	xPX	hr/f	Spd	SBO	SB%	#Wk	DOM	DIS	RC/G	RAR	BPV	BPX	R$
11 TOR	499	56	26	87	1	251	263	295	439	734	639	771	6	79	0.30	40	22	38	27	132	119	135	17%	77	2%	50%	24	54%	38%	4.39	-27.5	46	102	$14
12 TOR *	457	45	17	65	1	274	250	332	445	778	553	795	8	78	0.40	48	17	35	32	98	110	101	12%	100	1%	100%	18	56%	17%	5.21	-2.8	49	123	$12
13 TOR	465	67	23	67	1	288	279	357	497	854	573	924	10	78	0.50	46	21	33	33	133	140	141	19%	92	1%	100%	27	52%	15%	6.40	23.4	73	183	$19
14 TOR	290	38	6	40	0	321	283	381	479	860	223	942	9	83	0.58	47	21	33	37	134	119	123	8%	107	0%	0%	21	62%	19%	6.85	20.5	81	219	$12
15 MIL	502	72	20	87	0	277	264	360	460	820	575	883	12	80	0.66	46	19	35	31	130	120	138	14%	81	0%	0%	27	48%	19%	5.86	6.9	66	178	$18
1st Half	272	35	14	51	0	298	269	373	518	892	604	947	11	80	0.62	48	17	35	33	138	141	152	18%	86	0%	0%	14	64%	14%	7.07	14.4	82	222	$24
2nd Half	230	37	6	36	0	252	256	345	391	736	552	798	12	80	0.71	44	21	35	29	120	95	122	9%	81	0%	0%	13	31%	23%	4.58	-3.9	48	130	$11
16 Proj	**459**	**65**	**19**	**75**	**0**	**285**	**274**	**357**	**475**	**832**	**527**	**906**	**10**	**80**	**0.58**	**46**	**20**	**34**	**32**	**129**	**123**	**131**	**15%**	**90**	**0%**	**84%**				**6.06**	**11.6**	**55**	**149**	**$20**

Lindor,Francisco

Age: 22	Bats: B	Pos: SS	Health	A	LIMA Plan	B
Ht: 5' 11"	Wt: 175		PT/Exp	C	Rand Var	-3
			Consist	C	MM	2435

12-51-.313 with 12 SB in 390 AB at CLE. Rushed, highly-regarded 21-year-old posted better MLB numbers than in previous two AA/AAA seasons. Contact history, speed and athleticism already earmarked him as a future elite, though xPX throws cold water on 2H HR outburst. Decent bet to avoid significant growing pains.

Yr Tm	AB	R	HR	RBI	SB	BA	xBA	OBP	SLG	OPS	vL	vR	bb%	ct%	Eye	G	L	F	h%	HctX	PX	xPX	hr/f	Spd	SBO	SB%	#Wk	DOM	DIS	RC/G	RAR	BPV	BPX	R$
11																																		
12																																		
13 aa	76	11	1	6	4	259		351	342	693			12	90	1.40				28		52			118	23%	65%				4.00		63	158	$1
14 a/a	507	61	9	51	23	248		301	342	643			7	79	0.36				30		67			104	29%	57%				3.20		16	43	$16
15 CLE *	619	74	14	71	20	295	273	347	439	785	890	804	7	82	0.44	51	21	29	34	91	91	75	13%	140	17%	68%	17	71%	18%	5.37	17.0	60	162	$28
1st Half	303	28	3	26	9	249	276	309	338	647	391	566	8	81	0.44	53	29	18	30	95	59	48	10%	132	20%	55%	4	50%	50%	3.34	-6.9	27	73	$13
2nd Half	316	46	11	45	11	339	294	379	535	913	1021	856	7	84	0.44	50	19	31	38	92	121	81	13%	137	14%	85%	13	77%	8%	7.99	32.3	88	238	$42
16 Proj	**584**	**71**	**12**	**65**	**20**	**278**	**262**	**327**	**404**	**731**	**737**	**728**	**7**	**81**	**0.41**	**50**	**21**	**29**	**33**	**93**	**81**	**68**	**9%**	**137**	**19%**	**65%**				**4.56**	**8.1**	**38**	**103**	**$25**

Lobaton,Jose

Age: 31	Bats: B	Pos: CA	Health	B	LIMA Plan	F
Ht: 6' 0"	Wt: 215		PT/Exp	F	Rand Var	+1
			Consist	B	MM	1001

Being as objective and fair-minded as we are, we'd be remiss not to point out the bb% rebound and five seasons of consistent and mostly elite patience. Beyond this? /crickets/ At best, he's a garden variety, GB-hitting, contact-challenged #2 catcher in the real game. And irrelevant in ours.

Yr Tm	AB	R	HR	RBI	SB	BA	xBA	OBP	SLG	OPS	vL	vR	bb%	ct%	Eye	G	L	F	h%	HctX	PX	xPX	hr/f	Spd	SBO	SB%	#Wk	DOM	DIS	RC/G	RAR	BPV	BPX	R$
11 TAM *	218	20	6	23	0	216	237	314	344	658	390	349	12	68	0.44	46	27	27	29	26	102	21	0%	69	0%	0%	7	14%	57%	3.52	-5.7	0	0	-$1
12 TAM *	195	17	2	21	0	201	200	295	291	586	751	584	12	71	0.47	48	16	36	27	80	78	100	5%	67	2%	0%	21	29%	52%	2.68	-9.8	-6	-15	-$3
13 TAM	277	38	7	32	0	249	256	320	394	714	653	745	10	77	0.46	44	23	32	30	88	104	82	10%	98	1%	0%	27	52%	26%	4.25	4.5	40	100	$4
14 WAS	214	18	2	12	0	234	217	287	304	591	483	633	7	71	0.25	49	24	27	32	93	64	95	5%	86	0%	0%	24	21%	58%	2.87	-3.7	-21	-57	-$1
15 WAS	136	11	3	20	0	199	201	279	294	573	403	598	10	71	0.38	47	19	34	26	75	69	89	9%	74	0%	0%	24	33%	58%	2.60	-5.1	-17	-46	-$2
1st Half	65	7	3	11	0	231	197	333	385	718	1000	691	13	71	0.53	50	13	37	28	80	98	104	18%	91	0%	0%	14	43%	50%	4.25	0.9	18	49	$0
2nd Half	71	4	0	9	0	169	205	228	211	439	205	496	7	70	0.24	44	25	31	24	72	43	76	0%	66	0%	0%	10	20%	70%	1.45	-5.4	-49	-132	-$3
16 Proj	**191**	**17**	**3**	**22**	**0**	**213**	**213**	**286**	**301**	**587**	**523**	**606**	**9**	**72**	**0.35**	**47**	**21**	**32**	**28**	**82**	**68**	**90**	**7%**	**76**	**0%**	**0%**				**2.77**	**-6.0**	**-30**	**-82**	**$1**

JOCK THOMPSON

Loney,James

Age: 32	Bats: L	Pos: 1B	Health	C	LIMA Plan B
Ht: 6' 3"	Wt: 235		PT/Exp	B	Rand Var 0
			Consist	B	MM 1035

Broken finger sidelined him for almost 6 weeks. But with memory of outlier-ish 2013 vL fading, he was already losing AB. Fine contact and sweet LD stroke will continue to fuel BA, though power metrics and HctX trends say it's producing less these days. Should remain roster-worthy even if it's only against RHPs.

Yr	Tm	AB	R	HR	RBI	SB	BA	xBA	OBP	SLG	OPS	vL	vR	bb%	ct%	Eye	G	L	F	h%	HctX	PX	xPX	hr/f	Spd	SBO	SB%	#Wk	DOM	DIS	RC/G	RAR	BPV	BPX	R$
11	LA	531	56	12	65	4	288	272	339	416	755	561	816	7	87	0.63	41	22	37	31	80	85	79	7%	80	3%	100%	27	48%	15%	5.12	-7.5	58	129	$16
12	2 TM	434	37	6	41	0	249	266	293	336	630	508	662	6	88	0.55	46	25	29	27	93	58	65	5%	55	3%	0%	27	33%	26%	3.26	-26.1	30	75	$4
13	TAM	549	54	13	75	3	299	297	348	430	778	729	797	7	86	0.57	42	30	28	33	102	89	77	10%	59	2%	75%	27	44%	22%	5.48	13.2	50	125	$20
14	TAM	600	59	9	69	4	290	271	336	380	716	601	762	6	87	0.51	42	27	31	32	92	65	78	6%	59	2%	100%	27	48%	26%	4.62	8.0	31	84	$19
15	TAM	361	25	4	32	2	280	265	322	357	680	568	713	6	91	0.68	43	24	33	30	75	51	40	4%	68	6%	33%	22	41%	23%	3.93	-10.4	37	100	$6
1st Half		122	13	2	14	1	279	262	318	369	687	670	692	6	90	0.67	38	24	38	30	78	56	52	5%	79	9%	33%	9	56%	22%	3.97	-4.2	43	116	$4
2nd Half		239	12	2	18	1	280	265	324	351	676	522	724	6	91	0.68	45	24	31	30	73	48	34	3%	66	4%	33%	13	31%	23%	3.90	-8.5	35	95	$8
16	Proj	498	42	7	53	3	284	272	329	377	706	606	739	6	89	0.60	42	26	32	31	84	60	59	5%	64	4%	47%				4.34	-11.5	28	74	$12

Longoria,Evan

Age: 30	Bats: R	Pos: 3B	Health	B	LIMA Plan B
Ht: 6' 2"	Wt: 210		PT/Exp	A	Rand Var 0
			Consist	C	MM 3225

Now healthy for an extended period, but BPIs haven't followed suit. One-time plus power-and-patience combo suddenly look stagnant, along with HctX. Two-year struggles vR are worrisome and xBA trend isn't positive. That xPX says the next HR move is up, so the news isn't all bad. Just don't bid for the hitter he once was.

Yr	Tm	AB	R	HR	RBI	SB	BA	xBA	OBP	SLG	OPS	vL	vR	bb%	ct%	Eye	G	L	F	h%	HctX	PX	xPX	hr/f	Spd	SBO	SB%	#Wk	DOM	DIS	RC/G	RAR	BPV	BPX	R$
11	TAM	483	78	31	99	3	244	286	355	495	850	943	819	14	81	0.86	37	18	45	24	123	158	137	18%	84	4%	60%	23	70%	17%	5.82	14.6	105	233	$18
12	TAM *	303	39	17	57	2	276	264	357	491	848	1064	842	11	76	0.53	38	22	40	31	126	137	147	20%	82	6%	40%	14	57%	21%	5.99	12.5	63	158	$11
13	TAM	614	91	32	88	1	269	264	343	498	842	950	799	10	74	0.43	37	19	45	32	126	164	173	16%	83	1%	100%	27	63%	33%	5.98	35.8	73	183	$23
14	TAM	624	83	22	91	5	253	249	320	404	724	824	691	8	79	0.43	39	20	41	29	110	105	118	11%	94	3%	100%	27	48%	19%	4.40	13.3	46	124	$19
15	TAM	604	74	21	73	3	270	254	328	435	764	960	695	8	78	0.39	39	21	40	31	105	111	122	11%	90	3%	75%	27	44%	33%	4.97	6.8	46	124	$18
1st Half		292	37	8	35	2	277	250	353	418	771	893	736	10	77	0.49	33	26	41	34	111	99	130	8%	91	3%	67%	14	36%	36%	5.15	4.3	37	100	$17
2nd Half		312	37	13	38	1	263	258	304	452	755	998	651	5	79	0.28	44	16	40	29	100	122	114	13%	90	1%	100%	13	54%	31%	4.76	1.2	54	146	$18
16	Proj	609	80	24	84	3	264	254	328	443	771	928	715	8	78	0.41	39	20	41	30	111	117	130	13%	91	3%	79%				5.00	6.7	42	114	$21

Lowrie,Jed

Age: 32	Bats: B	Pos: 3B	Health	F	LIMA Plan B
Ht: 6' 0"	Wt: 190		PT/Exp	B	Rand Var +4
			Consist	B	MM 3333

Same old, same old. Power flashes, hard contact, DL time and another disappointing season. Fractured thumb derailed terrific start, unlucky 2H h% left him unable to relaunch. Power indices, xBA say he deserved better; healthy LD% and FB% say he gets there IF he stays injury-free. If that happens... UP: .260 BA, 20 HR.

Yr	Tm	AB	R	HR	RBI	SB	BA	xBA	OBP	SLG	OPS	vL	vR	bb%	ct%	Eye	G	L	F	h%	HctX	PX	xPX	hr/f	Spd	SBO	SB%	#Wk	DOM	DIS	RC/G	RAR	BPV	BPX	R$
11	BOS	309	40	6	36	1	252	226	303	382	685	876	582	7	81	0.38	33	18	49	30	107	87	120	5%	124	3%	50%	20	35%	40%	3.92	-8.0	45	100	$5
12	HOU	340	43	16	42	2	244	253	331	438	769	623	819	11	81	0.66	29	19	51	26	125	121	162	11%	92	2%	100%	18	50%	17%	4.90	3.5	72	180	$7
13	OAK	603	80	15	75	1	290	272	344	446	791	772	800	8	85	0.55	33	23	43	32	94	108	99	7%	93	1%	100%	26	65%	12%	5.53	26.6	71	178	$21
14	OAK	502	59	6	50	0	249	250	321	355	676	598	707	9	84	0.65	31	24	44	29	107	79	112	3%	103	0%	0%	25	44%	16%	3.83	2.4	52	141	$7
15	HOU	230	35	9	30	1	222	263	312	400	712	908	641	11	81	0.65	35	21	44	24	131	115	152	11%	83	2%	100%	15	60%	27%	4.04	-3.6	66	178	$2
1st Half		60	11	4	10	1	300	293	432	567	999	1576	738	17	75	0.80	38	24	38	34	125	176	135	24%	88	5%	100%	4	100%	0%	8.74	6.8	103	278	$1
2nd Half		170	24	5	20	0	194	251	265	341	606	606	603	9	84	0.57	34	20	46	20	133	95	158	8%	85	0%	0%	11	45%	36%	2.84	-9.6	55	149	$3
16	Proj	389	55	13	48	2	251	263	334	422	756	877	707	10	82	0.65	34	22	44	28	117	110	131	10%	91	2%	96%				4.76	1.5	57	153	$11

Lucroy,Jonathan

Age: 30	Bats: R	Pos: CA	Health	C	LIMA Plan B+
Ht: 6' 0"	Wt: 195		PT/Exp	B	Rand Var +2
			Consist	C	MM 2245

Opened 2016 with a March hamstring issue, poor April and a fractured toe. LD% spike together with rock-solid HctX fueled 2nd half rebound. Encouraging 2H power offset by ct% decline and GB uptick, but a cliff-dive doesn't look imminent. Still a premier catching option if fully clear of September concussion.

Yr	Tm	AB	R	HR	RBI	SB	BA	xBA	OBP	SLG	OPS	vL	vR	bb%	ct%	Eye	G	L	F	h%	HctX	PX	xPX	hr/f	Spd	SBO	SB%	#Wk	DOM	DIS	RC/G	RAR	BPV	BPX	R$
11	MIL	430	45	12	59	2	265	248	313	391	703	869	662	6	77	0.29	42	24	34	32	79	87	82	11%	91	3%	67%	25	36%	40%	4.21	-2.0	19	42	$10
12	MIL	316	46	12	58	4	320	284	368	513	881	1169	782	7	86	0.50	41	21	37	34	131	112	129	12%	122	6%	80%	20	55%	15%	7.00	22.9	85	213	$16
13	MIL	521	59	18	82	9	280	281	340	455	795	859	775	8	87	0.67	39	23	38	29	133	104	135	10%	109	7%	90%	27	48%	7%	5.53	27.0	81	203	$21
14	MIL	585	73	13	69	4	301	298	373	465	837	838	837	10	88	0.93	42	22	36	33	132	119	128	7%	97	5%	50%	27	78%	0%	6.19	44.2	98	265	$23
15	MIL	371	51	7	43	1	264	274	326	391	717	639	743	9	83	0.56	45	26	29	30	128	83	104	8%	98	1%	100%	21	38%	29%	4.48	7.0	47	127	$8
1st Half		172	20	1	16	0	250	253	311	320	630	296	706	9	85	0.62	46	24	30	29	119	48	94	2%	94	0%	0%	9	33%	22%	3.41	-1.9	25	68	$1
2nd Half		199	31	6	27	1	276	290	339	452	792	812	783	9	81	0.53	44	27	29	32	135	114	112	13%	100	2%	100%	12	42%	33%	5.49	9.7	65	176	$13
16	Proj	574	75	14	74	4	279	280	342	428	771	769	771	9	84	0.62	43	24	33	31	128	95	115	9%	103	3%	75%				5.20	23.2	58	157	$20

Machado,Manny

Age: 23	Bats: R	Pos: 3B	Health	C	LIMA Plan D+
Ht: 6' 2"	Wt: 180		PT/Exp	A	Rand Var -1
			Consist	B	MM 4345

Reminder that elite prospects can break out when least expected. His was driven by huge bb%, HctX, FB% and SBO surges. Strong hr/f trend, ct% rebound obviously helped. PX/xPX and SBO say he's a tad out over his skis, and that some HR and SBs are at immediate risk. But at his age who cares? Dynasty league stud.

Yr	Tm	AB	R	HR	RBI	SB	BA	xBA	OBP	SLG	OPS	vL	vR	bb%	ct%	Eye	G	L	F	h%	HctX	PX	xPX	hr/f	Spd	SBO	SB%	#Wk	DOM	DIS	RC/G	RAR	BPV	BPX	R$
11																																			
12	BAL *	593	73	17	74	13	254	251	310	417	727	801	716	8	81	0.44	46	14	40	29	115	103	100	12%	133	12%	75%	9	44%	44%	4.40	-2.4	65	163	$16
13	BAL	667	88	14	71	6	283	277	314	432	746	762	738	4	83	0.26	47	21	32	32	101	107	73	8%	122	9%	46%	26	62%	12%	4.64	13.2	65	163	$22
14	BAL	327	38	12	32	2	278	262	324	431	755	642	802	6	79	0.29	49	20	31	32	100	106	101	15%	112	2%	100%	16	56%	25%	4.91	11.5	49	132	$10
15	BAL	633	102	35	86	20	286	279	359	502	861	763	894	10	82	0.63	44	18	38	30	120	127	122	18%	112	15%	71%	27	67%	4%	6.30	31.3	87	235	$35
1st Half		318	52	17	46	13	299	284	356	522	878	879	878	9	82	0.53	43	18	39	32	124	135	123	17%	119	17%	87%	14	71%	0%	6.94	20.4	91	246	$38
2nd Half		315	50	18	40	7	273	274	361	483	844	671	911	11	83	0.74	45	17	38	28	117	120	122	18%	105	14%	54%	13	62%	8%	5.72	10.1	83	224	$31
16	Proj	638	90	32	80	15	279	278	338	483	821	737	853	8	82	0.47	46	18	36	30	112	123	107	17%	116	12%	71%				5.67	19.1	69	186	$31

Mahtook,Mikie

Age: 26	Bats: R	Pos: LF	Health	A	LIMA Plan D+
Ht: 6' 1"	Wt: 200		PT/Exp	B	Rand Var 0
			Consist	C	MM 4413

9-19-.295 with 4 SB in 105 AB at TAM. Athletic youngster hit twice as many HR in MLB debut than in 385 Triple-A AB. Seized opportunity and pulverized LHP (7 HR over 68 AB) as advertised, held his own vR with h% luck in small sample. Plate skills, history point to BA risk, struggles vR. Watchable flyer with plenty to prove.

Yr	Tm	AB	R	HR	RBI	SB	BA	xBA	OBP	SLG	OPS	vL	vR	bb%	ct%	Eye	G	L	F	h%	HctX	PX	xPX	hr/f	Spd	SBO	SB%	#Wk	DOM	DIS	RC/G	RAR	BPV	BPX	R$
11																																			
12	aa	153	14	3	20	3	212		255	338	592			5	77	0.25				26		90			90	23%	49%				2.57		19	48	$0
13	aa	511	56	5	54	20	218		266	327	593			6	77	0.28				27		80			120	27%	68%				2.77		22	55	$9
14	aaa	489	46	9	56	15	251		305	386	691			7	67	0.24				36		119			100	17%	72%				3.96		9	24	$13
15	TAM *	490	49	12	54	12	225	222	261	368	629	1030	856	5	70	0.16	33	23	44	30	123	109	193	28%	121	18%	74%	12	58%	17%	3.14	-24.5	13	35	$8
1st Half		242	16	3	20	5	187	184	224	288	511	793	0	5	70	0.16	21	21	57	25	82	79	163	25%	106	21%	63%	4	50%	25%	1.95	-22.4	-15	-41	-$3
2nd Half		248	33	8	34	6	263	243	297	447	744	1109	931	5	69	0.16	36	24	41	35	133	139	200	29%	118	15%	86%	8	63%	13%	4.66	-1.1	36	97	$18
16	Proj	330	30	11	33	9	247	240	311	420	731	787	644	6	71	0.21	36	24	41	32	120	125	180	11%	134	18%	70%				4.06	-4.9	27	74	$10

Maldonado,Martin

Age: 29	Bats: R	Pos: CA	Health	A	LIMA Plan F
Ht: 6' 0"	Wt: 230		PT/Exp	F	Rand Var 0
			Consist	D	MM 2001

Most #2 MLB catchers have an in-season moment that tempts deep-league owners to ignore the overall track record, and ask themselves, "Could this be the surge? After all, he did hit those 8 HR in 2012 and posted good power metrics in 2014..." He didn't have that moment in 2015. Or else we missed it.

Yr	Tm	AB	R	HR	RBI	SB	BA	xBA	OBP	SLG	OPS	vL	vR	bb%	ct%	Eye	G	L	F	h%	HctX	PX	xPX	hr/f	Spd	SBO	SB%	#Wk	DOM	DIS	RC/G	RAR	BPV	BPX	R$
11	MIL *	343	33	8	42	1	236	225	288	353	641	0	0	7	73	0.27	44	20	36	30	0	91	2	0%	65	3%	55%	3	0%	100%	3.36	-10.4	-1	-2	$3
12	MIL *	354	30	11	40	1	233	230	281	370	651	612	766	6	72	0.24	43	23	34	29	78	97	78	14%	70	5%	23%	19	37%	53%	3.32	-10.3	0	0	$3
13	MIL	183	13	4	22	0	169	195	236	284	520	446	543	7	71	0.25	42	14	44	21	73	87	101	7%	82	0%	0%	26	27%	65%	1.96	-10.3	-5	-13	-$4
14	MIL	111	14	4	16	0	234	223	320	387	707	721	693	9	71	0.34	36	18	46	29	86	119	107	12%	84	0%	0%	26	31%	54%	3.91	1.5	25	68	$1
15	MIL	229	19	4	22	0	210	205	282	293	575	810	503	9	72	0.35	47	20	33	28	93	62	100	8%	52	2%	0%	25	12%	68%	2.61	-8.6	-27	-73	-$2
1st Half		135	14	3	12	0	193	194	262	274	536	611	509	9	72	0.34	46	18	36	24	99	54	110	9%	53	3%	0%	14	7%	71%	2.20	-6.8	-34	-92	-$2
2nd Half		94	5	1	10	0	234	219	311	319	630	1198	494	10	71	0.37	48	24	27	32	83	73	87	6%	66	0%	0%	11	18%	64%	3.27	-1.4	-16	-43	-$2
16	Proj	192	17	4	22	0	216	214	292	328	620	753	571	9	71	0.33	44	20	37	28	85	83	98	9%	68	1%	12%				3.01	-4.6	-20	-54	$2

JOCK THOMPSON

Marisnick,Jake

Age: 25	Bats: R	Pos: CF	Health	A	LIMA Plan	D+
Ht: 6' 4"	Wt: 225		PT/Exp	C	Rand Var	-3
			Consist	B	MM	3503

Excited owners with his April ct% and power before crashing back to earth in May. Impressed again from Sept on; the problem is what happened in between. Age, defense and speed keep him relevant, and the hr/f uptick is intriguing. But inconsistency and poor plate skills stamp him as a part-timer until further notice.

Yr Tm	AB	R	HR	RBI	SB	BA	xBA	OBP	SLG	OPS	vL	vR	bb%	ct%	Eye	G	L	F	h%	HctX	PX	xPX	hr/f	Spd	SBO	SB%	#Wk	DOM	DIS	RC/G	RAR	BPV	BPX	R$
11																																		
12 aa	223	21	2	12	12	221		251	319	569			4	79	0.19				27		69			118	37%	73%				2.58		14	35	$2
13 MIA *	374	43	10	45	12	245	244	285	383	668	431	498	5	73	0.21	42	25	33	31	72	98	55	4%	124	24%	62%	9	33%	67%	3.51	-6.6	21	53	$10
14 2 TM *	564	55	9	46	27	237	223	263	334	597	738	568	3	75	0.14	39	22	39	30	74	75	73	5%	126	31%	74%	12	25%	67%	2.90	-16.0	8	22	$15
15 HOU	339	46	9	36	24	236	223	281	383	665	669	662	5	69	0.17	42	20	38	32	72	107	94	10%	132	47%	73%	25	32%	48%	3.40	-11.6	13	35	$13
1st Half	188	21	5	21	11	245	237	282	388	670	570	734	5	71	0.17	46	21	33	32	77	101	98	11%	120	38%	73%	12	42%	50%	3.57	-4.8	13	35	$12
2nd Half	151	25	4	15	13	225	205	280	377	658	775	562	6	66	0.18	36	18	46	31	67	115	87	9%	132	60%	72%	13	23%	46%	3.18	-5.9	10	27	$15
16 Proj	**267**	**33**	**7**	**26**	**12**	**235**	**227**	**278**	**379**	**657**	**733**	**618**	**5**	**72**	**0.18**	**40**	**20**	**40**	**30**	**72**	**100**	**80**	**9%**	**135**	**30%**	**73%**				**3.37**	**-8.5**	**20**	**55**	**$6**

Markakis,Nick

Age: 32	Bats: L	Pos: RF	Health	A	LIMA Plan	B+
Ht: 6' 1"	Wt: 190		PT/Exp	A	Rand Var	-3
			Consist	A	MM	1235

Just when we thought his power was at rock-bottom, career-high GB% and unlucky hr/f dragged HR to the basement. Held onto most of his value via combination of plate skills and h% spike. But he's not fast enough to beat out these bushels of GB%, so as h% regressses, his remaining BA-driven value is at risk.

Yr Tm	AB	R	HR	RBI	SB	BA	xBA	OBP	SLG	OPS	vL	vR	bb%	ct%	Eye	G	L	F	h%	HctX	PX	xPX	hr/f	Spd	SBO	SB%	#Wk	DOM	DIS	RC/G	RAR	BPV	BPX	R$
11 BAL	641	72	15	73	12	284	275	351	406	756	628	809	9	88	0.83	43	23	34	30	112	78	96	8%	92	8%	80%	27	59%	15%	5.04	-1.8	63	140	$21
12 BAL	420	59	13	54	1	298	303	363	471	834	877	816	9	88	0.82	42	27	31	31	125	105	111	11%	103	2%	50%	18	78%	6%	6.15	11.6	86	215	$15
13 BAL	634	89	10	59	1	271	259	329	356	685	651	704	8	88	0.72	47	23	31	30	104	56	71	6%	100	2%	33%	27	48%	19%	4.07	-9.8	45	113	$15
14 BAL	642	81	14	50	4	276	258	342	386	729	673	751	9	87	0.74	46	20	34	30	103	74	85	7%	112	3%	67%	27	48%	7%	4.60	9.1	60	162	$18
15 ATL	612	73	3	53	2	296	261	370	376	746	635	795	10	86	0.84	52	21	27	34	98	60	56	2%	104	1%	67%	27	52%	19%	5.00	2.4	47	127	$16
1st Half	308	34	0	25	1	295	258	384	351	734	583	793	12	86	0.98	52	24	25	34	99	46	58	0%	96	1%	100%	14	43%	29%	4.87	0.5	35	95	$14
2nd Half	304	39	3	28	1	296	264	356	401	758	680	796	8	87	0.69	53	18	29	33	97	74	54	4%	110	2%	50%	13	62%	8%	5.09	2.4	59	159	$18
16 Proj	**573**	**72**	**9**	**51**	**3**	**283**	**265**	**350**	**386**	**736**	**658**	**772**	**9**	**87**	**0.77**	**49**	**21**	**30**	**31**	**102**	**68**	**70**	**6%**	**105**	**2%**	**63%**				**4.76**	**-0.8**	**39**	**104**	**$17**

Marte,Jefry

Age: 25	Bats: R	Pos: 1B	Health	A	LIMA Plan	D+
Ht: 6' 1"	Wt: 187		PT/Exp	C	Rand Var	+3
			Consist	B	MM	4231

4-11-.213 in 80 AB at DET. Late-developing prospect finally offered glimpses of his projected power, first at AAA and later in MLB debut. Plate skills need work but aren't awful. 1.173 OPS in 112 Triple-A AB vs. LHP hints at career as a lefty-masher. Defense and position are problematic. With opportunity, a deep-league flyer.

Yr Tm	AB	R	HR	RBI	SB	BA	xBA	OBP	SLG	OPS	vL	vR	bb%	ct%	Eye	G	L	F	h%	HctX	PX	xPX	hr/f	Spd	SBO	SB%	#Wk	DOM	DIS	RC/G	RAR	BPV	BPX	R$
11																																		
12 aa	462	50	8	47	7	220		274	314	588			7	82	0.41				25		62			96	12%	57%				2.73		21	53	$3
13 aa	245	26	1	22	6	243		300	329	630			8	78	0.37				31		73			95	12%	85%				3.41		16	40	$3
14 aa	405	39	7	41	7	222		285	313	598			8	81	0.48				26		67			82	10%	68%				2.90		22	59	$4
15 DET *	437	46	16	60	6	233	267	286	413	698	920	506	7	79	0.35	46	19	35	26	99	116	103	20%	95	13%	52%	11	45%	36%	3.76	-8.4	54	146	$8
1st Half	289	30	10	42	5	235	275	283	419	702	0	0	6	82	0.37	44	20	36	26	0	115	-15	0%	110	17%	54%	1	100%	0%	3.75	-7.1	66	178	$13
2nd Half	148	16	6	19	1	231	247	292	400	691	944	506	8	74	0.33	46	19	35	28	92	118	103	20%	84	6%	40%	10	40%	40%	3.76	-3.6	34	92	$1
16 Proj	**227**	**24**	**11**	**26**	**3**	**243**	**273**	**300**	**449**	**749**	**1006**	**535**	**7**	**79**	**0.38**	**46**	**19**	**35**	**26**	**83**	**128**	**93**	**18%**	**93**	**11%**	**62%**				**4.44**	**-4.9**	**54**	**146**	**$7**

Marte,Ketel

Age: 22	Bats: B	Pos: SS	Health	A	LIMA Plan	B
Ht: 6' 1"	Wt: 180		PT/Exp	D	Rand Var	-1
			Consist	C	MM	1533

2-17-.283 with 8 SB in 219 AB at SEA. Rushed to SS-needy Mariners in 2H after fine AAA season. Career .290 hitter with LD stroke, improving plate skills and running game. Held his own on both sides of the ball, though concerns remain about his arm and position. More minor league time is possible, but if he sticks... UP: 25 SB.

Yr Tm	AB	R	HR	RBI	SB	BA	xBA	OBP	SLG	OPS	vL	vR	bb%	ct%	Eye	G	L	F	h%	HctX	PX	xPX	hr/f	Spd	SBO	SB%	#Wk	DOM	DIS	RC/G	RAR	BPV	BPX	R$
11																																		
12																																		
13																																		
14 a/a	523	59	3	41	22	263		289	347	636			4	83	0.22				31		67			104	27%	66%				3.34		26	70	$16
15 SEA *	487	58	4	39	23	280	266	334	376	710	720	780	8	84	0.50	52	22	26	33	82	66	44	4%	141	23%	71%	11	55%	18%	4.38	-0.2	47	127	$18
1st Half	198	22	1	17	12	291	245	334	362	696			6	88	0.54				32		48			110	26%	78%				4.42		38	103	$15
2nd Half	289	34	3	21	10	265	264	326	376	702	720	780	8	80	0.46	52	22	26	32	79	78	44	4%	148	21%	62%	11	55%	18%	4.09	0.0	47	127	$21
16 Proj	**402**	**46**	**4**	**31**	**18**	**271**	**267**	**311**	**369**	**680**	**649**	**706**	**6**	**83**	**0.37**	**52**	**22**	**26**	**32**	**71**	**67**	**40**	**4%**	**143**	**24%**	**69%**				**3.95**	**-1.6**	**37**	**100**	**$15**

Marte,Starling

Age: 27	Bats: R	Pos: LF	Health	A	LIMA Plan	D+
Ht: 6' 1"	Wt: 185		PT/Exp	A	Rand Var	0
			Consist	A	MM	3545

What's not to like? His power was capped by GB trend reversal, and now PX/xPX along with poor patience suggests a ceiling. Yet HR still reached a career high fueled by soaring hr/f. Contact gains kept BA intact even with h% regression, as his running game held firm. Prime age and health say he'll keep the line moving.

Yr Tm	AB	R	HR	RBI	SB	BA	xBA	OBP	SLG	OPS	vL	vR	bb%	ct%	Eye	G	L	F	h%	HctX	PX	xPX	hr/f	Spd	SBO	SB%	#Wk	DOM	DIS	RC/G	RAR	BPV	BPX	R$
11 aa	536	74	9	40	19	297		319	436	755			3	80	0.16				36		100			118	26%	59%				4.71		45	100	$21
12 PIT *	555	71	14	68	29	255	262	294	430	723	1042	627	5	73	0.21	57	18	25	32	98	112	83	18%	185	40%	61%	9	33%	44%	3.94	-13.3	51	128	$20
13 PIT	510	83	12	35	41	280	259	343	441	784	1053	724	5	73	0.18	51	22	28	36	100	116	98	12%	194	47%	73%	24	29%	33%	4.73	10.0	54	135	$30
14 PIT	495	73	13	56	30	291	264	356	453	808	781	814	6	74	0.25	47	23	29	37	105	125	114	13%	167	32%	73%	26	50%	35%	5.33	21.8	59	159	$28
15 PIT	579	84	19	81	30	287	283	337	444	780	717	798	4	79	0.22	54	24	23	34	99	103	94	19%	119	28%	75%	27	48%	19%	4.98	4.3	44	119	$32
1st Half	303	44	13	48	16	281	282	329	459	788	1016	737	5	74	0.22	57	25	18	34	87	121	96	32%	114	31%	70%	14	50%	7%	4.97	3.6	39	105	$35
2nd Half	276	40	6	33	14	293	281	344	428	772	480	871	3	84	0.23	51	22	27	33	113	85	92	10%	120	25%	82%	13	46%	31%	4.98	3.3	49	132	$29
16 Proj	**568**	**84**	**20**	**66**	**33**	**285**	**280**	**338**	**462**	**800**	**802**	**799**	**5**	**77**	**0.21**	**52**	**23**	**26**	**34**	**102**	**116**	**98**	**17%**	**151**	**33%**	**73%**				**5.09**	**8.7**	**56**	**150**	**$33**

Martin,Leonys

Age: 28	Bats: L	Pos: CF	Health	A	LIMA Plan	C
Ht: 6' 2"	Wt: 190		PT/Exp	C	Rand Var	+2
			Consist	B	MM	1403

5-25-.219 with 14 SB in 288 AB at TEX. Even with speed, anemic power and plate skills aren't a winning long-term combination. LDs turned into soft FBs as h% plunge topedoed BA and depressed running game. More futility vL also factored into eventual job loss and 2H demotion. Plus defense may not be enough to regain job.

Yr Tm	AB	R	HR	RBI	SB	BA	xBA	OBP	SLG	OPS	vL	vR	bb%	ct%	Eye	G	L	F	h%	HctX	PX	xPX	hr/f	Spd	SBO	SB%	#Wk	DOM	DIS	RC/G	RAR	BPV	BPX	R$
11 TEX *	295	38	3	29	13	262	314	306	364	669	0	875	6	88	0.52	57	29	14	29	127	68	37	0%	120	33%	54%	4	25%	25%	3.45	-14.6	56	124	$8
12 TEX *	277	40	10	35	10	291	294	341	496	837	500	624	7	80	0.37	47	24	29	34	88	135	55	0%	101	30%	49%	12	42%	42%	5.39	4.3	74	185	$12
13 TEX	457	66	8	49	36	260	255	313	385	698	573	749	6	77	0.27	51	21	28	32	80	88	61	8%	139	40%	80%	27	30%	33%	4.09	-1.9	35	88	$23
14 TEX	533	68	7	40	31	274	242	325	364	689	581	725	7	79	0.34	50	22	28	34	88	60	68	6%	159	27%	72%	27	30%	44%	4.08	2.9	26	70	$23
15 TEX *	325	31	6	28	15	222	230	266	326	592	566	582	6	77	0.27	52	15	33	27	79	74	62	7%	92	31%	71%	19	21%	63%	2.79	-17.4	9	24	$6
1st Half	260	23	5	24	13	227	234	271	331	602	586	611	5	78	0.25	50	17	33	27	81	74	65	8%	89	32%	72%	14	29%	50%	2.86	-12.5	11	30	$8
2nd Half	65	8	1	4	2	200	202	265	306	571	286	360	8	74	0.34	69	0	31	25	61	75	32	0%	111	25%	67%	5	0%	100%	2.52	-3.9	8	22	-$5
16 Proj	**392**	**48**	**6**	**33**	**19**	**246**	**230**	**298**	**338**	**637**	**564**	**665**	**7**	**77**	**0.31**	**56**	**14**	**30**	**30**	**77**	**64**	**56**	**6%**	**122**	**27%**	**71%**				**3.32**	**-13.0**	**13**	**35**	**$13**

Martin,Russell

Age: 33	Bats: R	Pos: CA	Health	A	LIMA Plan	B
Ht: 5' 10"	Wt: 215		PT/Exp	B	Rand Var	+1
			Consist	C	MM	4125

Expected h% regression, ct% dip and fewer LDs brought his BA back to earth. Now a poster-boy for venue change impact on power—i.e., 3 HR at RHB/FB-crushing PNC Park in 2014, 13 HR in TOR this season. As such, xPX says he'll lose a few HR. But Health, stable G/L/F and plate skills point to a near-repeat.

Yr Tm	AB	R	HR	RBI	SB	BA	xBA	OBP	SLG	OPS	vL	vR	bb%	ct%	Eye	G	L	F	h%	HctX	PX	xPX	hr/f	Spd	SBO	SB%	#Wk	DOM	DIS	RC/G	RAR	BPV	BPX	R$
11 NYY	417	57	18	65	8	237	268	324	408	732	684	750	11	81	0.62	47	19	33	25	110	110	110	16%	60	9%	80%	27	41%	30%	4.37	2.1	52	116	$11
12 NYY	422	50	21	53	6	211	264	311	403	713	880	643	11	77	0.56	48	19	33	22	101	121	107	20%	51	7%	86%	27	52%	22%	3.93	-2.7	46	115	$6
13 PIT	438	51	15	55	9	226	244	327	377	703	610	729	12	75	0.54	51	17	33	27	107	108	104	14%	63	12%	64%	26	38%	35%	3.86	1.9	32	80	$9
14 PIT	379	45	11	67	4	290	255	402	430	832	693	865	13	79	0.76	49	19	32	34	109	102	92	11%	74	6%	50%	23	39%	39%	5.81	26.6	51	138	$16
15 TOR	441	76	23	77	4	240	272	329	458	787	937	747	11	76	0.50	51	16	33	27	97	140	113	21%	82	8%	44%	27	48%	26%	4.77	13.8	64	173	$14
1st Half	246	48	12	39	4	256	277	345	476	821	954	786	11	76	0.50	50	16	33	29	95	142	109	19%	91	11%	57%	14	43%	36%	5.29	11.0	70	189	$19
2nd Half	195	28	11	38	0	221	260	309	436	745	916	696	11	75	0.50	51	16	33	24	100	138	119	23%	66	4%	0%	13	54%	15%	4.18	2.4	56	151	$8
16 Proj	**426**	**59**	**19**	**69**	**5**	**246**	**260**	**344**	**436**	**781**	**816**	**770**	**12**	**76**	**0.56**	**50**	**17**	**33**	**28**	**103**	**124**	**107**	**18%**	**74**	**7%**	**51%**				**4.81**	**13.1**	**46**	**126**	**$15**

JOCK THOMPSON

Martinez,J.D.

Age: 28 Bats: R Pos: RF	Health B	LIMA Plan B+	
Ht: 6' 3" Wt: 220	PT/Exp B	Rand Var -3	
	Consist F	MM 4235	

Lofty 2014 h% made BA retrenchment a no-brainer. But despite pedestrian plate skills, he stunned everyone by maintaining huge power, even hiking his HR with more AB. FB spike and bb% uptick helped, but HctX is driving this and the BA-over-xBA repeat. Some ebb is likely, but it's official: Dude can mash.

Yr Tm	AB	R	HR	RBI	SB	BA	xBA	OBP	SLG	OPS	vL	vR	bb%	ct%	Eye	G	L	F	h%	HctX	PX	xPX	hr/f	Spd	SBO	SB%	#Wk	DOM	DIS	RC/G	RAR	BPV	BPX	R$
11 HOU *	525	66	16	88	1	283	277	339	444	783	1119	620	8	78	0.39	37	28	36	33	114	117	124	10%	78	1%	42%	10	50%	30%	5.31	2.1	48	107	$18
12 HOU *	485	38	11	58	0	230	224	292	349	641	690	683	8	76	0.37	52	17	32	28	87	81	79	12%	97	3%	0%	22	36%	32%	3.28	-23.2	16	40	$3
13 HOU	296	24	7	36	2	250	236	272	378	650	621	664	3	72	0.12	44	22	34	32	102	103	108	9%	84	3%	100%	18	33%	61%	3.57	-6.1	5	13	$4
14 DET *	506	69	30	92	7	308	287	349	568	917	1003	880	6	71	0.22	40	23	37	38	133	196	158	19%	110	9%	71%	24	54%	33%	7.23	46.2	89	241	$31
15 DET	596	93	38	102	3	282	265	344	535	879	915	870	8	70	0.30	34	22	43	34	131	175	182	21%	95	3%	60%	27	56%	30%	6.42	27.8	67	181	$28
1st Half	302	49	23	56	2	285	273	340	563	903	848	918	7	71	0.26	32	22	45	33	135	187	197	24%	85	4%	67%	14	57%	21%	6.68	15.9	74	200	$33
2nd Half	294	44	15	46	1	279	258	348	507	854	993	822	9	70	0.34	36	22	42	35	126	163	166	17%	102	3%	50%	13	54%	38%	6.13	11.0	60	162	$23
16 Proj	**580**	**78**	**31**	**94**	**4**	**276**	**265**	**327**	**505**	**832**	**886**	**815**	**7**	**71**	**0.26**	**39**	**22**	**39**	**34**	**123**	**159**	**155**	**19%**	**99**	**5%**	**66%**				**5.74**	**15.4**	**50**	**135**	**$24**

Martinez,Victor

Age: 37 Bats: B Pos: DH	Health D	LIMA Plan B+	
Ht: 6' 2" Wt: 210	PT/Exp A	Rand Var +4	
	Consist F	MM 2045	

Exhibit A on how injury and age can torpedo a season. Knee surgery delayed his spring training, shelved him later for 4 weeks spanning May/June, and fueled a lost season. Stable ct% and G/L/F along with 2H HctX and xPX say he'll rebound if healthy. But his expectations are lower—and the risk has grown.

Yr Tm	AB	R	HR	RBI	SB	BA	xBA	OBP	SLG	OPS	vL	vR	bb%	ct%	Eye	G	L	F	h%	HctX	PX	xPX	hr/f	Spd	SBO	SB%	#Wk	DOM	DIS	RC/G	RAR	BPV	BPX	R$
11 DET	540	76	12	103	1	330	298	380	470	850	823	861	8	91	0.90	43	24	33	35	117	95	94	7%	73	1%	100%	26	58%	8%	6.85	14.4	78	173	$27
12																																		
13 DET	605	68	14	83	0	301	275	355	430	785	735	813	8	90	0.87	42	22	35	32	142	84	126	7%	77	1%	0%	26	62%	8%	5.54	17.2	68	170	$22
14 DET	561	87	32	103	3	335	320	409	565	974	1123	923	11	93	1.67	41	21	38	32	158	135	147	16%	87	3%	60%	26	88%	4%	8.79	69.7	128	346	$38
15 DET	440	39	11	64	0	245	256	301	366	667	870	616	7	88	0.60	40	21	39	26	117	73	111	7%	61	0%	0%	23	43%	26%	3.65	-23.3	45	122	$6
1st Half	177	19	2	26	0	249	249	320	333	653	1006	543	8	90	0.94	46	19	35	27	98	56	66	4%	66	0%	0%	11	45%	27%	3.52	-10.1	45	122	$2
2nd Half	263	20	9	38	0	243	263	288	388	676	744	661	5	87	0.43	36	22	41	25	130	85	142	9%	64	0%	0%	12	42%	25%	3.71	-13.5	47	127	$9
16 Proj	**496**	**57**	**16**	**79**	**1**	**275**	**277**	**334**	**423**	**756**	**872**	**718**	**8**	**90**	**0.83**	**41**	**22**	**38**	**28**	**131**	**87**	**121**	**9%**	**71**	**1%**	**52%**				**4.91**	**-7.7**	**56**	**152**	**$17**

Mauer,Joe

Age: 33 Bats: L Pos: 1B DH	Health C	LIMA Plan B+	
Ht: 6' 5" Wt: 230	PT/Exp A	Rand Var +2	
	Consist C	MM 2245	

Plate skills have settled in at less than mint condition, but they aren't awful. Good health helped return hr/f to mediocrity. The problems are 1) a soaring GB% that caps his power and highlights those heavy legs, and 2) he's just not hitting the ball as hard any more. BA will uptick with h%. But it's not the best blend for a 1Bman.

Yr Tm	AB	R	HR	RBI	SB	BA	xBA	OBP	SLG	OPS	vL	vR	bb%	ct%	Eye	G	L	F	h%	HctX	PX	xPX	hr/f	Spd	SBO	SB%	#Wk	DOM	DIS	RC/G	RAR	BPV	BPX	R$
11 MIN	296	38	3	30	0	287	270	360	368	729	562	829	10	87	0.84	55	23	22	32	92	60	75	5%	92	0%	0%	17	47%	18%	4.70	-7.7	46	102	$6
12 MIN	545	81	10	85	8	319	286	416	446	861	754	918	14	84	1.02	53	25	22	37	137	83	113	10%	95	5%	67%	27	59%	7%	6.89	23.5	61	153	$25
13 MIN	445	62	11	47	0	324	288	404	476	880	882	879	12	80	0.69	47	28	25	39	124	115	113	12%	91	1%	0%	21	57%	29%	7.22	30.9	65	163	$18
14 MIN	455	60	4	55	3	277	269	361	371	732	654	776	12	79	0.63	51	27	22	34	96	79	70	5%	86	2%	100%	22	45%	32%	4.78	8.2	30	81	$12
15 MIN	592	69	10	66	2	265	276	338	380	718	720	718	10	81	0.60	56	24	20	31	104	80	80	10%	83	2%	67%	26	38%	27%	4.47	-7.9	36	97	$12
1st Half	298	32	5	41	1	275	273	343	389	733	777	708	10	82	0.58	52	25	23	32	112	76	85	9%	89	2%	50%	14	36%	21%	4.69	-4.0	35	95	$15
2nd Half	294	37	5	25	1	255	276	333	371	704	649	727	11	81	0.61	59	23	17	30	97	84	74	12%	82	1%	100%	12	42%	33%	4.26	-7.6	37	100	$10
16 Proj	**547**	**69**	**9**	**61**	**2**	**280**	**277**	**360**	**395**	**754**	**710**	**775**	**11**	**81**	**0.66**	**53**	**25**	**21**	**33**	**106**	**82**	**83**	**9%**	**85**	**2%**	**75%**				**5.04**	**-1.8**	**30**	**82**	**$17**

Maybin,Cameron

Age: 29 Bats: R Pos: CF	Health D	LIMA Plan C+	
Ht: 6' 3" Wt: 205	PT/Exp D	Rand Var -3	
	Consist B	MM 1425	

One-time elite prospect was an early Black Swan before falling apart in Ugly Duck 2H. Deteriorating patience and GB spike were culprits, but 1H was built on an elevated LD%, unsustainable h% and small sample hr/f missing PX/xPX support. Legs will determine any future value, though Health and BA/xBA are skeptical.

Yr Tm	AB	R	HR	RBI	SB	BA	xBA	OBP	SLG	OPS	vL	vR	bb%	ct%	Eye	G	L	F	h%	HctX	PX	xPX	hr/f	Spd	SBO	SB%	#Wk	DOM	DIS	RC/G	RAR	BPV	BPX	R$
11 SD	516	82	9	40	40	264	251	323	393	716	751	703	8	76	0.35	55	16	29	33	93	93	93	8%	174	35%	83%	25	44%	36%	4.54	-3.7	48	107	$22
12 SD	507	67	8	45	26	243	242	306	349	656	630	666	8	78	0.40	55	16	28	30	107	71	88	7%	138	25%	79%	27	37%	33%	3.62	-16.3	30	75	$14
13 SD *	97	11	4	8	5	176	252	255	304	560	435	481	10	79	0.51	55	19	26	18	76	79	45	9%	100	31%	68%	5	20%	60%	2.33	-5.6	30	75	-$1
14 SD *	304	28	2	18	5	226	242	280	319	599	575	646	7	77	0.33	57	17	26	29	97	72	60	2%	144	11%	60%	20	15%	55%	2.88	-8.8	26	70	$1
15 ATL	505	65	10	59	23	267	266	327	370	697	711	692	8	80	0.44	58	22	20	32	75	67	46	12%	104	19%	79%	26	31%	38%	4.28	-0.3	22	59	$20
1st Half	255	34	7	39	15	294	271	363	416	778	887	749	10	80	0.53	55	23	22	35	82	79	68	16%	98	22%	79%	14	36%	21%	5.50	7.9	34	92	$28
2nd Half	250	31	3	20	8	240	260	289	324	613	565	630	7	80	0.35	61	21	18	29	68	55	24	8%	111	15%	80%	12	25%	58%	3.22	-9.0	11	30	$12
16 Proj	**418**	**50**	**6**	**38**	**17**	**251**	**252**	**313**	**348**	**661**	**635**	**672**	**8**	**79**	**0.41**	**57**	**20**	**23**	**31**	**82**	**64**	**52**	**8%**	**127**	**19%**	**76%**				**3.71**	**-8.7**	**19**	**51**	**$13**

Mazara,Nomar

Age: 21 Bats: L Pos: DH	Health A	LIMA Plan D	
Ht: 6' 4" Wt: 195	PT/Exp F	Rand Var 0	
	Consist C	MM 2421	

Precocious youngster with decent but unspectacular year at AA-AAA—all as a 19/20-yo. Leapfrogged A+ a year earlier, posting 19 HR and 57/99 BB/K over 483 AB between A and AA. Projectable with raw power, a clue at the plate, plus arm and solid makeup. Will begin at Triple-A and be close by if TEX needs OF help.

Yr Tm	AB	R	HR	RBI	SB	BA	xBA	OBP	SLG	OPS	vL	vR	bb%	ct%	Eye	G	L	F	h%	HctX	PX	xPX	hr/f	Spd	SBO	SB%	#Wk	DOM	DIS	RC/G	RAR	BPV	BPX	R$
11																																		
12																																		
13																																		
14 aa	85	9	3	14	0	293		352	484	837			8	73	0.34				37		152			96	0%	0%				6.16		62	168	$2
15 a/a	490	56	12	57	2	276		335	403	738			8	78	0.40				33		87			91	1%	100%				4.78		28	76	$13
1st Half	279	30	8	34	1	265		330	408	738			9	75	0.39				33		96			112	1%	100%				4.69		30	81	$15
2nd Half	211	26	3	22	1	287		337	391	728			7	82	0.42				34		74			100	1%	100%				4.74		33	89	$10
16 Proj	**97**	**11**	**2**	**11**	**1**	**259**	**252**	**317**	**391**	**708**	**708**	**708**	**8**	**79**	**0.41**	**43**	**22**	**35**	**30**		**89**		**9%**	**109**	**6%**	**100%**				**4.35**	**-3.1**	**25**	**69**	**$3**

McCann,Brian

Age: 32 Bats: L Pos: CA	Health B	LIMA Plan B	
Ht: 6' 3" Wt: 230	PT/Exp B	Rand Var +1	
	Consist C	MM 3025	

Average and h% victimized again by shifting defenses, but ct% slide and regression vL also played a role. Stable power ticked upward, assisted by better patience, a few more FBs and Yankee Stadium's RF porch (16 HR at home). Both 20+ HR and stuck-in-the-mud BA look repeatable; you take the good with the bad.

Yr Tm	AB	R	HR	RBI	SB	BA	xBA	OBP	SLG	OPS	vL	vR	bb%	ct%	Eye	G	L	F	h%	HctX	PX	xPX	hr/f	Spd	SBO	SB%	#Wk	DOM	DIS	RC/G	RAR	BPV	BPX	R$
11 ATL	466	51	24	71	3	270	252	351	466	817	794	826	11	81	0.64	38	16	47	29	138	123	162	14%	64	4%	60%	25	52%	28%	5.64	19.2	65	144	$16
12 ATL	439	44	20	67	3	230	252	300	399	698	673	711	9	83	0.58	40	19	41	24	118	98	131	13%	57	3%	100%	27	48%	37%	4.00	-1.7	46	115	$8
13 ATL	356	43	20	57	0	256	273	336	461	796	616	869	10	81	0.59	35	22	42	26	118	125	150	16%	70	1%	0%	21	67%	29%	5.13	14.7	69	173	$11
14 NYY	495	57	23	75	0	232	266	286	406	692	850	633	6	84	0.42	33	22	45	23	114	106	127	12%	63	0%	0%	26	58%	23%	3.76	6.5	56	151	$11
15 NYY	465	68	26	94	0	232	248	320	437	756	753	757	10	79	0.54	36	17	47	24	110	120	131	15%	61	0%	0%	27	48%	30%	4.49	10.5	53	143	$12
1st Half	238	32	13	52	0	261	260	332	471	803	672	843	8	79	0.45	38	19	44	28	119	125	124	15%	76	0%	0%	14	50%	36%	5.24	10.1	59	159	$16
2nd Half	227	36	13	42	0	203	235	307	401	708	829	664	12	79	0.63	35	15	51	20	100	116	139	14%	52	0%	0%	13	46%	23%	3.79	0.1	49	132	$9
16 Proj	**470**	**62**	**25**	**83**	**0**	**234**	**253**	**313**	**428**	**741**	**761**	**733**	**9**	**81**	**0.53**	**35**	**19**	**46**	**24**	**113**	**112**	**135**	**14%**	**61**	**1%**	**51%**				**4.34**	**7.9**	**46**	**123**	**$14**

McCann,James

Age: 26 Bats: R Pos: CA	Health A	LIMA Plan D+	
Ht: 6' 2" Wt: 210	PT/Exp C	Rand Var -2	
	Consist A	MM 2225	

Decent effort as primary starter in first extended opportunity. Apart from being plus receiver with terrific catch-and-throw skills (42% CS), he does nothing particularly well. And GB% says he won't hit many HR. But LD stroke and average HctX should keep BA above water. Prototypical "do no harm" fantasy catcher.

Yr Tm	AB	R	HR	RBI	SB	BA	xBA	OBP	SLG	OPS	vL	vR	bb%	ct%	Eye	G	L	F	h%	HctX	PX	xPX	hr/f	Spd	SBO	SB%	#Wk	DOM	DIS	RC/G	RAR	BPV	BPX	R$
11																																		
12 aa	220	12	2	15	2	180		202	250	453			3	79	0.14				22		56			81	11%	43%				1.51		-4	-10	-$5
13 aa	441	40	6	43	2	246		285	355	639			5	79	0.26				30		84			86	6%	42%				3.32		23	58	$5
14 DET *	429	40	6	42	8	256	323	289	366	655	333	833	4	77	0.20	20	60	20	32	33	95	11	0%	77	11%	78%	3	33%	33%	3.64	4.0	17	46	$9
15 DET	401	32	7	41	0	264	254	297	387	683	916	609	4	78	0.18	50	23	27	33	90	82	63	8%	106	1%	0%	27	33%	44%	3.87	1.6	17	46	$6
1st Half	186	17	4	19	0	274	264	313	430	743	939	687	5	76	0.22	49	24	28	34	94	107	70	10%	100	0%	0%	14	36%	43%	4.70	4.9	31	84	$6
2nd Half	215	15	3	22	0	256	244	283	349	631	898	537	3	79	0.13	51	23	26	31	86	60	57	7%	108	2%	0%	13	31%	46%	3.23	-3.5	4	11	$5
16 Proj	**437**	**36**	**8**	**42**	**3**	**251**	**257**	**286**	**369**	**655**	**888**	**579**	**4**	**78**	**0.19**	**50**	**23**	**27**	**31**	**89**	**83**	**62**	**8%**	**95**	**5%**	**58%**				**3.49**	**-3.8**	**9**	**24**	**$8**

JOCK THOMPSON

McCutchen,Andrew

Age: 29	Bats: R	Pos: CF	Health	A	LIMA Plan	C
Ht: 5' 10"	Wt: 190		PT/Exp	A	Rand Var	0
			Consist	C	MM	4435

Three injuries (back, knee, Achilles) cost him a whopping 5 games. Real affect of injuries manifested via ugly Apr (.636 OPS) & career-low 16 SB attempts. Remarkably stable Eye, h%, HctX, PX, and xPX still scream superstar. His three .300/.400/.500 seasons in last four are an MLB-best; just missed the fourth. Pay up.

Yr	Tm	AB	R	HR	RBI	SB	BA	xBA	OBP	SLG	OPS	vL	vR	bb%	ct%	Eye	G	L	F	h%	HctX	PX	xPX	hr/f	Spd	SBO	SB%	#Wk	DOM	DIS	RC/G	RAR	BPV	BPX	R$
11	PIT	572	87	23	89	23	259	266	364	456	820	945	779	13	78	0.71	38	20	42	30	135	135	142	12%	113	19%	70%	27	63%	15%	5.52	12.5	83	184	$24
12	PIT	593	107	31	96	20	327	281	400	553	953	1144	900	11	78	0.53	44	22	34	38	126	140	147	19%	139	16%	63%	27	56%	19%	7.99	53.3	88	220	$40
13	PIT	583	97	21	84	27	317	288	404	508	911	1130	864	12	83	0.77	41	24	35	36	137	125	123	12%	129	19%	73%	26	69%	12%	7.44	53.3	95	238	$40
14	PIT	548	89	25	83	18	314	284	410	542	952	912	962	13	79	0.73	40	19	41	36	139	159	155	14%	127	11%	86%	26	65%	12%	8.27	65.9	110	297	$36
15	PIT	566	91	23	96	11	292	268	401	488	889	918	881	15	77	0.74	38	24	38	35	132	132	159	14%	105	8%	69%	27	59%	30%	6.88	41.0	75	203	$28
1st Half		286	43	10	51	5	297	276	391	493	884	794	904	12	81	0.75	36	22	42	34	140	128	171	10%	93	8%	71%	14	71%	21%	6.81	19.1	83	224	$28
2nd Half		280	48	13	45	6	286	261	412	482	894	1011	855	17	71	0.73	41	25	33	36	124	136	145	19%	114	8%	67%	13	46%	38%	6.94	20.1	65	176	$29
16	Proj	**573**	**94**	**25**	**91**	**16**	**301**	**274**	**402**	**507**	**909**	**970**	**893**	**14**	**78**	**0.72**	**40**	**22**	**38**	**35**	**134**	**135**	**149**	**15%**	**121**	**11%**	**73%**				**7.29**	**45.9**	**79**	**213**	**$32**

McKenry,Michael

Age: 31	Bats: R	Pos: CA	Health	D	LIMA Plan	D
Ht: 5' 10"	Wt: 205		PT/Exp	F	Rand Var	+3
			Consist	F	MM	4111

Offset ct% dip with bb% jump while everything else from '14 mini-breakout remained firm... oh, except for the inflated h% which predictably regressed. Impact vs. LHP is muted - he's never had more than 54 AB vs them in any season. Any draftable skills? Some pop, won't sink OBP.

Yr	Tm	AB	R	HR	RBI	SB	BA	xBA	OBP	SLG	OPS	vL	vR	bb%	ct%	Eye	G	L	F	h%	HctX	PX	xPX	hr/f	Spd	SBO	SB%	#Wk	DOM	DIS	RC/G	RAR	BPV	BPX	R$
11	PIT *	275	25	4	20	1	229	220	292	337	629	498	629	8	72	0.32	39	20	41	30	79	93	86	4%	87	3%	44%	15	27%	53%	3.22	-9.6	8	18	$0
12	PIT	240	25	12	39	0	233	222	320	442	762	815	746	11	70	0.40	35	14	51	28	97	151	147	14%	68	0%	0%	27	44%	48%	4.64	2.5	43	108	$4
13	PIT	115	9	3	14	0	217	239	262	348	610	475	655	4	79	0.21	37	21	42	25	97	93	101	8%	68	0%	0%	16	25%	56%	2.83	-3.0	22	55	-$2
14	COL *	251	31	10	29	2	290	279	356	462	818	961	891	9	77	0.45	36	29	35	34	105	126	108	18%	79	6%	36%	20	55%	30%	5.68	15.8	53	143	$9
15	COL	127	20	4	17	2	205	230	329	402	731	1026	670	15	68	0.54	38	17	45	27	99	142	177	10%	117	12%	50%	19	42%	37%	3.98	0.7	51	138	$0
1st Half		93	17	3	12	2	237	241	351	452	803	1212	714	15	68	0.53	39	19	42	32	103	152	176	11%	134	11%	67%	13	38%	38%	5.18	4.0	64	173	$2
2nd Half		34	3	1	5	0	118	199	268	265	533	333	557	15	68	0.55	35	13	52	14	91	117	180	8%	66	14%	0%	6	50%	33%	1.67	-2.6	16	43	-$5
16	Proj	**126**	**16**	**5**	**16**	**1**	**241**	**242**	**325**	**425**	**749**	**786**	**739**	**10**	**73**	**0.41**	**37**	**20**	**44**	**30**	**98**	**126**	**143**	**11%**	**93**	**6%**	**58%**				**4.45**	**2.5**	**40**	**109**	**$3**

Mercer,Jordy

Age: 29	Bats: R	Pos: SS	Health	B	LIMA Plan	B
Ht: 6' 3"	Wt: 205		PT/Exp	C	Rand Var	+1
			Consist	B	MM	2125

3-34-.244 in 394 AB at PIT. Defense earns the PT and 920 PA of league-average work from '13-14 garnered deep league interest. Ct% and bb% remained solid even as hr/f and xPX collapse wrecked his value. Month long knee injury not a factor (better OPS after), power rebound should put him back in double-digit R$.

Yr	Tm	AB	R	HR	RBI	SB	BA	xBA	OBP	SLG	OPS	vL	vR	bb%	ct%	Eye	G	L	F	h%	HctX	PX	xPX	hr/f	Spd	SBO	SB%	#Wk	DOM	DIS	RC/G	RAR	BPV	BPX	R$
11	a/a	491	60	14	52	7	214		254	355	609			5	83	0.31				23		96			91	15%	49%				2.78		47	104	$5
12	PIT *	271	29	4	27	2	236	249	287	356	643	367	690	7	76	0.30	47	22	31	30	61	91	86	7%	92	15%	26%	17	24%	53%	3.07	-8.6	21	53	$2
13	PIT *	429	41	9	41	5	282	269	330	418	748	1152	654	7	81	0.37	47	23	30	33	113	97	117	10%	113	7%	62%	23	52%	26%	4.83	16.1	51	128	$12
14	PIT	506	56	12	55	4	255	264	305	387	693	803	658	6	82	0.39	48	20	32	29	90	94	89	9%	108	4%	80%	27	41%	33%	4.03	10.9	52	141	$11
15	PIT *	419	36	4	36	3	240	238	288	317	604	738	580	6	81	0.35	49	21	31	29	89	58	88	3%	86	5%	60%	23	26%	52%	3.03	-9.2	11	30	$3
1st Half		239	20	2	18	3	247	249	297	326	624	661	614	6	84	0.42	44	23	33	29	100	59	105	3%	92	7%	75%	14	21%	50%	3.26	-5.9	26	70	$4
2nd Half		180	16	2	18	0	232	220	279	304	583	847	527	6	77	0.29	57	17	26	29	73	57	59	3%	86	2%	0%	9	33%	56%	2.74	-7.3	-6	-16	$1
16	Proj	**473**	**48**	**10**	**48**	**3**	**254**	**256**	**303**	**377**	**680**	**839**	**636**	**6**	**81**	**0.34**	**50**	**20**	**30**	**30**	**87**	**83**	**87**	**9%**	**98**	**5%**	**55%**				**3.81**	**-3.8**	**21**	**57**	**$11**

Mesoraco,Devin

Age: 28	Bats: R	Pos: CA	Health	F	LIMA Plan	B
Ht: 6' 1"	Wt: 220		PT/Exp	D	Rand Var	+5
			Consist	F	MM	3223

The '14 breakout now a sore thumb-level outlier after a hip injury washed out '15. Pedigree and his 25 HR-season—along with supporting power BPI—fuels hope, but his Reliability grades deliver a healthy dose of realism. At a good age to recover, but how he looks this spring will likely determine his price.

Yr	Tm	AB	R	HR	RBI	SB	BA	xBA	OBP	SLG	OPS	vL	vR	bb%	ct%	Eye	G	L	F	h%	HctX	PX	xPX	hr/f	Spd	SBO	SB%	#Wk	DOM	DIS	RC/G	RAR	BPV	BPX	R$
11	CIN *	486	50	15	60	1	244	245	304	409	713	625	579	8	78	0.40	40	15	45	28	79	121	83	11%	80	2%	40%	5	60%	20%	4.16	-3.1	52	116	$8
12	CIN	165	17	5	14	1	212	238	288	352	640	803	590	9	80	0.52	45	17	38	24	85	92	80	10%	73	5%	50%	22	45%	32%	3.19	-5.5	36	90	-$1
13	CIN	323	31	9	42	0	238	246	287	362	649	874	576	7	81	0.39	45	21	34	27	89	83	78	10%	62	3%	0%	27	41%	37%	3.43	-2.5	25	63	$4
14	CIN	384	54	25	80	1	273	287	359	534	893	925	883	10	73	0.40	34	23	43	31	123	192	166	20%	63	4%	25%	24	54%	25%	6.25	30.9	86	232	$18
15	CIN	45	2	0	2	1	178	192	275	244	519	481	536	10	80	0.56	42	14	44	22	69	40	68	0%	109	9%	100%	7	43%	43%	2.07	-2.4	7	19	-$3
1st Half		45	2	0	2	1	178	192	275	244	519	481	536	10	80	0.56	42	14	44	22	69	40	68	0%	109	9%	100%	7	43%	43%	2.07	-2.5	7	19	-$3
2nd Half																																			
16	Proj	**402**	**41**	**16**	**51**	**3**	**249**	**253**	**322**	**429**	**751**	**801**	**734**	**9**	**79**	**0.46**	**37**	**20**	**43**	**28**	**88**	**112**	**93**	**12%**	**88**	**5%**	**66%**				**4.56**	**9.2**	**45**	**121**	**$11**

Middlebrooks,Will

Age: 27	Bats: R	Pos: 3B	Health	D	LIMA Plan	D+
Ht: 6' 3"	Wt: 220		PT/Exp	D	Rand Var	+4
			Consist	B	MM	2103

9-29-.212 in 255 AB at SD. Curbed downward ct% trend w/career-best mark (76% at SD), but his worst h% yet stifled any gains. xPX remains the lighthouse on the choppy seas of this profile, buoyed by an age that still offers potential. But minors history of poor bb% drops his stock even lower for OBP leagues.

Yr	Tm	AB	R	HR	RBI	SB	BA	xBA	OBP	SLG	OPS	vL	vR	bb%	ct%	Eye	G	L	F	h%	HctX	PX	xPX	hr/f	Spd	SBO	SB%	#Wk	DOM	DIS	RC/G	RAR	BPV	BPX	R$
11	a/a	427	45	15	68	7	258		288	425	713			4	71	0.15				33		131			78	9%	86%				4.24		23	51	$12
12	BOS *	360	49	22	76	6	293	276	328	530	857	906	798	5	75	0.21	44	22	35	34	120	152	119	21%	78	10%	75%	15	40%	33%	6.22	16.2	57	143	$18
13	BOS *	527	60	24	75	4	228	247	272	409	682	782	656	6	73	0.22	41	20	39	27	116	128	127	17%	70	5%	79%	19	42%	37%	3.68	-4.9	30	75	$11
14	BOS *	319	24	5	25	1	192	209	239	277	516	454	543	6	67	0.19	41	25	34	27	100	74	114	4%	86	3%	50%	14	21%	71%	2.07	-16.6	-32	-86	-$3
15	SD *	408	31	11	41	3	202	218	232	325	557	655	582	4	74	0.15	37	21	42	24	120	79	139	11%	98	8%	43%	16	31%	50%	2.33	-30.3	0	0	-$1
1st Half		236	23	9	28	2	220	238	248	381	629	674	613	4	77	0.18	37	21	42	25	126	99	141	12%	100	7%	67%	14	36%	43%	3.11	-11.0	26	70	$5
2nd Half		172	8	2	13	1	177	191	205	247	452	452	154	3	71	0.12	36	21	43	23	89	49	110	0%	97	10%	20%	2	0%	100%	1.45	-17.9	-39	-105	-$8
16	Proj	**301**	**25**	**10**	**32**	**2**	**206**	**226**	**244**	**343**	**587**	**640**	**566**	**4**	**72**	**0.16**	**40**	**21**	**38**	**25**	**116**	**94**	**127**	**12%**	**94**	**7%**	**55%**				**2.61**	**-19.1**	**-8**	**-22**	**$3**

Miller,Bradley

Age: 26	Bats: L	Pos: SS CF	Health	A	LIMA Plan	B
Ht: 6' 2"	Wt: 200		PT/Exp	C	Rand Var	0
			Consist	C	MM	3325

Incremental improvements in strong base skills (bb%, ct%, HctX, PX) paired with a spike in SBO & SB%. Shown to be a clear platoon option, though vR alone he achieved the double-double (10+ HR/SB). Elements of poor man's Zobrist are all here including a second position. There are several paths here to a $20 season.

Yr	Tm	AB	R	HR	RBI	SB	BA	xBA	OBP	SLG	OPS	vL	vR	bb%	ct%	Eye	G	L	F	h%	HctX	PX	xPX	hr/f	Spd	SBO	SB%	#Wk	DOM	DIS	RC/G	RAR	BPV	BPX	R$
11																																			
12	aa	147	19	3	11	4	284		371	411	782			12	79	0.67				34		82			115	9%	76%				5.45		43	108	$3
13	SEA *	563	82	17	77	10	269	264	329	424	753	674	767	8	81	0.46	46	22	32	31	97	97	79	10%	137	11%	56%	15	53%	13%	4.70	7.6	60	150	$21
14	SEA	367	47	10	36	4	221	236	288	365	653	542	692	8	74	0.36	42	19	39	27	98	105	105	10%	124	7%	67%	27	37%	52%	3.40	-5.5	36	97	$4
15	SEA	438	44	11	46	13	258	254	329	402	730	513	803	10	77	0.47	48	20	31	31	103	97	96	10%	113	14%	76%	27	22%	37%	4.57	0.7	41	111	$12
1st Half		242	25	8	24	7	240	265	317	413	731	372	821	10	76	0.46	48	22	30	29	99	114	95	15%	113	13%	88%	14	21%	21%	4.47	0.4	50	135	$12
2nd Half		196	19	3	22	6	281	239	342	388	730	625	777	9	79	0.48	48	18	33	34	108	76	98	6%	111	15%	67%	13	23%	54%	4.68	1.5	29	78	$13
16	Proj	**445**	**52**	**13**	**47**	**10**	**263**	**252**	**331**	**418**	**749**	**596**	**806**	**9**	**77**	**0.45**	**46**	**20**	**34**	**31**	**101**	**101**	**97**	**11%**	**118**	**12%**	**71%**				**4.75**	**8.7**	**40**	**107**	**$16**

Molina,Yadier

Age: 33	Bats: R	Pos: CA	Health	B	LIMA Plan	B+
Ht: 5' 11"	Wt: 220		PT/Exp	A	Rand Var	0
			Consist	C	MM	1135

Right thumb injury in '14 sped up power decline (.345 Slg since), but vs. LHP (.264 Slg) he's primed for recovery. Injured left thumb to end '15, requiring another surgery. Sharp GB uptick and PX dip reminiscent of pre-'11 seasons; thus thumbs not necessarily behind it. At his age, big rebound far from guaranteed.

Yr	Tm	AB	R	HR	RBI	SB	BA	xBA	OBP	SLG	OPS	vL	vR	bb%	ct%	Eye	G	L	F	h%	HctX	PX	xPX	hr/f	Spd	SBO	SB%	#Wk	DOM	DIS	RC/G	RAR	BPV	BPX	R$
11	STL	475	55	14	65	4	305	291	349	465	814	842	806	6	91	0.75	45	20	35	31	115	101	101	9%	66	7%	44%	27	67%	7%	5.79	18.5	78	173	$19
12	STL	505	65	22	76	12	315	300	373	501	874	1021	833	8	89	0.82	40	25	35	32	124	107	112	14%	71	10%	80%	27	70%	4%	6.93	36.2	82	205	$26
13	STL	505	68	12	80	3	319	301	359	477	836	883	823	6	89	0.55	42	24	34	34	126	109	111	8%	67	4%	60%	26	62%	23%	6.32	35.5	77	193	$24
14	STL	404	40	7	38	1	282	271	333	386	719	795	695	6	86	0.51	51	23	27	31	115	75	95	7%	64	2%	50%	20	45%	25%	4.48	11.6	40	108	$10
15	STL	488	34	4	61	3	270	254	310	350	660	577	689	6	88	0.54	48	20	32	30	98	54	79	3%	67	3%	75%	25	32%	32%	3.87	0.6	29	78	$9
1st Half		271	21	2	27	0	292	250	333	373	706	538	752	6	87	0.50	46	22	32	33	103	60	88	3%	62	1%	0%	14	29%	43%	4.43	4.9	28	76	$10
2nd Half		217	13	2	34	3	244	251	282	323	604	609	600	6	89	0.61	49	19	32	27	92	46	69	3%	79	5%	100%	11	36%	18%	3.23	-3.5	32	86	$7
16	Proj	**525**	**48**	**8**	**68**	**4**	**277**	**269**	**320**	**383**	**703**	**696**	**706**	**6**	**88**	**0.56**	**47**	**22**	**31**	**30**	**108**	**68**	**89**	**6%**	**69**	**4%**	**72%**				**4.34**	**8.4**	**39**	**105**	**$16**

PAUL SPORER

Montero,Jesus

Age: 26 Bats: R Pos: 1B	Health	A	LIMA Plan	D+
Ht: 6' 3" Wt: 235	PT/Exp	D	Rand Var	-3
	Consist	B	MM	3123

5-19-.223 in 112 AB at SEA. The ultimate cage match between "Once you display a skill, you own it" and "Fool me twice, shame on me." .899 OPS in 3+ mos. at AAA renewed hope before he posted a .661 OPS after promotion. BUT THERE IS SOMETHING HERE! HctX, xPX, age all beg for one more chance.

Yr	Tm	AB	R	HR	RBI	SB	BA	xBA	OBP	SLG	OPS	vL	vR	bb%	ct%	Eye	G	L	F	h%	HctX	PX	xPX	hr/f	Spd	SBO	SB%	#Wk	DOM	DIS	RC/G	RAR	BPV	BPX	R$
11	NYY *	481	55	22	70	0	281	273	336	469	804	1181	877	8	75	0.33	39	27	34	33	138	130	155	27%	81	0%	0%	5	60%	40%	5.58	-0.7	45	100	$16
12	SEA	515	46	15	62	0	260	253	298	386	685	830	609	5	81	0.29	43	25	33	30	105	80	92	11%	67	2%	0%	28	36%	36%	3.92	-20.5	20	50	$10
13	SEA *	174	14	4	15	0	205	218	261	328	589	531	615	7	72	0.27	42	20	38	27	73	89	87	10%	113	3%	0%	8	25%	50%	2.67	-10.5	8	20	-$2
14	SEA *	381	37	11	51	1	224	243	270	367	637	818	333	6	74	0.24	64	14	21	28	68	111	57	33%	63	1%	100%	3	33%	33%	3.27	-10.1	16	43	$5
15	SEA *	506	57	17	75	2	266	245	297	418	715	576	821	4	76	0.18	45	20	35	32	134	99	122	18%	88	3%	62%	13	38%	46%	4.28	-9.5	19	51	$14
1st Half		327	36	9	41	1	252	228	281	373	655			4	75	0.17				31		79			91	2%	100%	1	100%	0%	3.60		1	3	$14
2nd Half		179	21	8	34	1	293	273	328	502	830	576	821	5	77	0.23	45	20	35	34	136	136	122	18%	85	5%	35%	12	33%	50%	5.79	3.2	54	146	$13
16	Proj	**265**	**27**	**10**	**38**	**1**	**253**	**258**	**295**	**431**	**726**	**758**	**702**	**5**	**75**	**0.23**	**43**	**23**	**35**	**30**	**113**	**117**	**109**	**15%**	**94**	**3%**	**52%**				**4.30**	**-6.6**	**25**	**67**	**$5**

Montero,Miguel

Age: 32 Bats: L Pos: CA	Health	B	LIMA Plan	C+
Ht: 5' 11" Wt: 210	PT/Exp	B	Rand Var	-1
	Consist	B	MM	3015

Power growth fueled by a career-best hr/f and corresponding xPX jump. Sprained thumb only cost time (.797 OPS in 40 G upon return). Drop in ct% offset by more line drives, so BA held steady. With a BBB reliability, this kind of pop behind the dish is capable of being the next late-career catcher power spike. UP: 20 HR.

Yr	Tm	AB	R	HR	RBI	SB	BA	xBA	OBP	SLG	OPS	vL	vR	bb%	ct%	Eye	G	L	F	h%	HctX	PX	xPX	hr/f	Spd	SBO	SB%	#Wk	DOM	DIS	RC/G	RAR	BPV	BPX	R$
11	ARI	493	65	18	86	1	282	281	351	469	820	534	904	9	80	0.48	42	22	36	32	118	113	136	13%	60	2%	50%	27	59%	19%	5.70	18.4	64	142	$18
12	ARI	486	65	15	88	0	286	239	391	438	829	767	859	13	73	0.56	43	21	36	36	99	108	121	12%	98	0%	0%	27	41%	41%	5.94	22.4	37	93	$17
13	ARI	413	44	11	42	0	230	224	318	344	662	492	719	11	73	0.46	47	21	31	29	102	83	106	11%	66	0%	0%	23	17%	48%	3.58	-1.3	4	10	$3
14	ARI	489	40	13	72	0	243	241	329	370	699	563	735	10	80	0.58	46	21	33	28	113	92	124	10%	59	3%	0%	27	41%	33%	3.87	6.0	35	95	$8
15	CHC	347	36	15	53	1	248	242	345	409	754	786	749	12	70	0.48	40	26	34	31	103	110	149	18%	67	2%	50%	24	29%	46%	4.69	9.0	16	43	$7
1st Half		204	18	10	29	0	235	242	339	402	741	979	713	13	72	0.52	39	26	36	28	102	106	158	19%	64	0%	0%	14	29%	50%	4.47	4.2	18	49	$7
2nd Half		143	18	5	24	1	266	241	354	420	773	622	806	12	69	0.42	43	25	31	35	104	116	136	16%	80	4%	50%	10	30%	40%	5.04	5.2	16	43	$7
16	Proj	**434**	**46**	**16**	**64**	**1**	**251**	**244**	**342**	**403**	**744**	**634**	**771**	**12**	**74**	**0.49**	**44**	**23**	**33**	**31**	**106**	**104**	**132**	**15%**	**68**	**2%**	**34%**				**4.55**	**9.9**	**10**	**26**	**$12**

Moore,Tyler

Age: 29 Bats: R Pos: 1B LF	Health	A	LIMA Plan	D
Ht: 6' 2" Wt: 220	PT/Exp	D	Rand Var	+5
	Consist	B	MM	4111

A clear sign that WAS season went sideways: 200 PA from him. Made noise back in 2011 w/10 HR in just 171 PA, but has 14 in 478 since. Spike in ct% reminiscent of minors work, but BA sunk by a nasty h%. xPX leaves tinge of hope for a Steve Pearce-type boom somewhere down the line, but don't chase that.

Yr	Tm	AB	R	HR	RBI	SB	BA	xBA	OBP	SLG	OPS	vL	vR	bb%	ct%	Eye	G	L	F	h%	HctX	PX	xPX	hr/f	Spd	SBO	SB%	#Wk	DOM	DIS	RC/G	RAR	BPV	BPX	R$
11	aa	519	56	25	72	2	237		269	453	722			4	71	0.15				29		162			88	2%	100%				4.09		49	109	$11
12	WAS *	257	31	17	49	4	264	273	323	523	846	780	929	8	71	0.30	40	22	38	31	101	178	148	24%	80	6%	100%	22	45%	41%	5.94	3.8	67	168	$10
13	WAS *	340	35	11	54	1	242	230	291	404	695	508	687	7	70	0.23	40	18	42	32	80	130	117	9%	92	1%	100%	21	19%	62%	3.97	-6.2	25	63	$6
14	WAS *	393	39	10	45	0	217	224	288	346	634	717	669	9	70	0.33	44	21	35	29	102	108	126	18%	64	3%	0%	12	33%	58%	3.16	-12.4	4	11	$2
15	WAS	187	14	6	27	0	203	234	250	364	614	732	563	6	76	0.24	40	17	43	24	98	114	121	10%	68	0%	0%	25	40%	36%	2.88	-14.4	28	76	-$1
1st Half		111	8	4	17	0	225	236	275	396	671	516	738	7	77	0.32	41	17	41	26	94	117	114	11%	72	0%	0%	14	43%	36%	3.62	-5.2	41	111	$0
2nd Half		76	6	2	10	0	171	226	213	316	528	1067	309	4	74	0.15	38	18	45	20	104	109	132	8%	74	0%	0%	11	36%	36%	1.97	-7.9	14	38	-$3
16	Proj	**164**	**15**	**6**	**23**	**0**	**212**	**240**	**270**	**387**	**656**	**761**	**598**	**6**	**72**	**0.25**	**40**	**19**	**41**	**25**	**98**	**126**	**126**	**13%**	**75**	**1%**	**53%**				**3.27**	**-9.5**	**15**	**41**	**$2**

Morales,Kendrys

Age: 33 Bats: B Pos: DH	Health	B	LIMA Plan	B
Ht: 6' 1" Wt: 225	PT/Exp	A	Rand Var	-1
	Consist	F	MM	3035

Return to 2012-13 levels would've worked, but instead recaptured 2010 feel (.833 OPS, minus the broken ankle). Improved ct% and bb% aided PX gains v. RHP; tremendous team situation jumped RBI/R totals v. all. Shift to DH-only and age could keep some owners cautious; but no reason he can't do this again.

Yr	Tm	AB	R	HR	RBI	SB	BA	xBA	OBP	SLG	OPS	vL	vR	bb%	ct%	Eye	G	L	F	h%	HctX	PX	xPX	hr/f	Spd	SBO	SB%	#Wk	DOM	DIS	RC/G	RAR	BPV	BPX	R$
11																																			
12	LAA	484	61	22	73	0	273	267	320	467	787	761	791	6	76	0.27	51	20	28	32	118	129	109	21%	66	1%	0%	27	48%	37%	5.14	3.4	41	103	$15
13	SEA	602	64	23	80	0	277	259	336	449	785	794	780	8	81	0.43	49	19	33	31	122	115	134	14%	70	0%	0%	27	56%	30%	5.25	12.7	54	135	$19
14	2 AL	367	28	8	42	0	218	238	274	338	612	661	584	7	81	0.40	49	18	33	25	106	89	102	8%	63	0%	0%	17	41%	41%	2.99	-11.8	32	86	$1
15	KC	569	81	22	106	0	290	282	362	485	847	771	901	9	82	0.56	45	20	35	32	126	126	135	13%	67	0%	0%	27	63%	11%	6.20	11.8	69	186	$23
1st Half		290	38	10	52	0	279	270	340	455	795	735	835	8	82	0.46	44	20	37	31	124	117	142	11%	59	0%	0%	14	50%	7%	5.39	-0.5	57	154	$21
2nd Half		279	43	12	54	0	301	293	383	516	899	804	973	11	82	0.67	46	21	32	33	128	136	127	16%	78	0%	0%	13	77%	15%	7.10	12.6	83	224	$26
16	Proj	**577**	**69**	**21**	**91**	**0**	**270**	**269**	**335**	**445**	**780**	**752**	**797**	**8**	**81**	**0.48**	**47**	**20**	**33**	**30**	**120**	**114**	**123**	**13%**	**68**	**0%**	**0%**				**5.13**	**-5.3**	**45**	**121**	**$20**

Moreland,Mitch

Age: 30 Bats: L Pos: 1B	Health	F	LIMA Plan	B
Ht: 6' 2" Wt: 230	PT/Exp	C	Rand Var	-3
	Consist	C	MM	4125

Late-Apr elbow injury likely caused déjà vu after '14, but turned out to be a speed bump. Explosion v. RHP finally delivered full breakout, but Health and age temper excitement; he's still chasing first 500-AB season. His 2H xBA says the '13 BA is still in play as a downside, but xPX says power is a safe bet.

Yr	Tm	AB	R	HR	RBI	SB	BA	xBA	OBP	SLG	OPS	vL	vR	bb%	ct%	Eye	G	L	F	h%	HctX	PX	xPX	hr/f	Spd	SBO	SB%	#Wk	DOM	DIS	RC/G	RAR	BPV	BPX	R$
11	TEX	464	60	16	51	2	259	250	320	414	733	577	783	8	80	0.42	42	18	40	29	109	104	105	11%	81	3%	50%	27	48%	30%	4.44	-16.2	46	102	$11
12	TEX	327	41	15	50	1	275	262	321	468	789	737	798	7	78	0.32	42	20	38	31	119	125	128	15%	76	3%	50%	22	50%	27%	5.26	-0.1	51	128	$10
13	TEX	462	60	23	60	0	232	255	299	437	736	701	752	9	75	0.38	43	17	39	26	114	143	136	17%	71	0%	0%	26	50%	27%	4.35	-3.5	54	135	$9
14	TEX	167	18	2	23	0	246	235	297	347	644	374	692	7	74	0.28	45	22	33	32	136	86	143	5%	74	0%	0%	10	30%	50%	3.48	-3.2	3	8	$1
15	TEX	471	51	23	85	1	278	265	330	482	812	681	876	6	76	0.29	46	20	35	32	121	135	131	18%	59	1%	100%	26	38%	38%	5.53	7.9	45	122	$17
1st Half		233	27	14	44	1	292	280	337	532	869	699	954	6	76	0.25	42	21	36	33	129	157	149	22%	56	2%	100%	13	54%	31%	6.39	8.0	60	162	$21
2nd Half		238	24	9	41	0	265	245	323	433	756	662	801	7	76	0.32	49	18	33	31	113	114	113	15%	70	0%	0%	13	23%	46%	4.75	-2.8	34	92	$14
16	Proj	**456**	**51**	**20**	**71**	**1**	**261**	**258**	**316**	**449**	**765**	**647**	**807**	**7**	**76**	**0.31**	**44**	**20**	**36**	**30**	**122**	**126**	**132**	**16%**	**66**	**1%**	**77%**				**4.84**	**-4.2**	**32**	**87**	**$15**

Morneau,Justin

Age: 35 Bats: L Pos: 1B	Health	F	LIMA Plan	C+
Ht: 6' 4" Wt: 220	PT/Exp	C	Rand Var	-4
	Consist	C	MM	2033

Concussion issues returned and limited him to just 49 G, though ended the season on the field. Ignore vL jump as it came in just 40 PA; skills remain firm vR and ensure at least a strong-side platoon. GB trending up, but a hr/f half his career rate hurt the power more. One DL-free year since '10, so heed Health grade.

Yr	Tm	AB	R	HR	RBI	SB	BA	xBA	OBP	SLG	OPS	vL	vR	bb%	ct%	Eye	G	L	F	h%	HctX	PX	xPX	hr/f	Spd	SBO	SB%	#Wk	DOM	DIS	RC/G	RAR	BPV	BPX	R$
11	MIN *	294	25	5	36	0	233	238	281	345	626	401	728	6	84	0.42	35	18	46	26	96	84	97	4%	69	0%	0%	15	40%	33%	3.23	-26.7	39	87	$1
12	MIN	505	63	19	77	1	267	263	333	440	773	569	902	9	80	0.48	41	22	37	30	109	110	115	13%	83	1%	100%	26	42%	23%	5.09	-4.8	52	130	$14
13	2 TM	572	62	17	77	0	259	258	323	411	734	525	819	8	81	0.45	41	21	38	29	99	107	94	10%	84	0%	0%	26	54%	15%	4.50	-1.4	52	130	$13
14	COL	502	62	17	82	0	319	300	364	496	860	665	927	6	88	0.57	44	23	33	34	120	115	109	11%	86	2%	0%	26	65%	8%	6.56	32.0	85	230	$25
15	COL	168	19	3	15	0	310	271	363	458	821	849	813	7	85	0.52	48	19	33	35	129	92	122	6%	123	0%	0%	12	42%	8%	6.08	3.2	67	181	$4
1st Half		100	10	3	9	0	290	293	317	450	767	900	735	3	90	0.30	46	22	31	30	128	98	117	11%	82	0%	0%	6	50%	0%	5.02	-0.4	71	192	$4
2nd Half		68	9	0	6	0	338	229	423	471	894	789	931	13	78	0.67	51	13	36	43	130	82	131	0%	153	0%	0%	6	33%	17%	7.67	4.4	51	138	$4
16	Proj	**322**	**38**	**7**	**38**	**0**	**297**	**266**	**356**	**449**	**805**	**680**	**849**	**8**	**84**	**0.54**	**45**	**19**	**35**	**34**	**120**	**95**	**115**	**7%**	**119**	**1%**	**6%**				**5.72**	**5.0**	**50**	**134**	**$12**

Morrison,Logan

Age: 28 Bats: L Pos: 1B	Health	D	LIMA Plan	D+
Ht: 6' 3" Wt: 245	PT/Exp	C	Rand Var	+2
	Consist	B	MM	2123

Utter ineptitude didn't stop him from getting a career-high 155 PA v. LHP. But numbers vs. RHP (10% bb%, 86% ct%, .203 ISO) indicate he has what it takes for a fine strong-side platooner. Spd says SB are suspect and BA unlikely to be a plus, but FB trend, HctX, xPX offers... UP: 20 HR

Yr	Tm	AB	R	HR	RBI	SB	BA	xBA	OBP	SLG	OPS	vL	vR	bb%	ct%	Eye	G	L	F	h%	HctX	PX	xPX	hr/f	Spd	SBO	SB%	#Wk	DOM	DIS	RC/G	RAR	BPV	BPX	R$
11	FLA *	486	56	24	75	2	241	281	318	457	776	723	827	10	79	0.53	47	18	35	26	121	143	129	18%	77	3%	67%	24	71%	13%	4.88	-20.0	75	167	$12
12	MIA	296	30	11	36	1	230	252	308	399	707	659	723	9	80	0.53	41	18	41	25	111	107	117	11%	63	1%	100%	17	47%	29%	4.01	-11.3	47	118	$3
13	MIA *	326	36	7	42	0	233	254	316	364	680	491	778	11	81	0.65	48	20	32	27	110	85	97	8%	103	0%	0%	17	41%	41%	3.82	-7.4	48	120	$3
14	SEA *	401	49	13	43	6	257	272	310	407	717	846	695	7	83	0.44	40	24	36	28	113	104	92	11%	61	8%	76%	20	35%	20%	4.33	2.2	48	130	$11
15	SEA	457	47	17	54	8	225	249	302	383	685	500	767	9	82	0.58	45	16	39	24	111	91	121	12%	84	10%	67%	27	48%	37%	3.70	-17.3	48	130	$8
1st Half		292	28	10	28	5	236	243	309	384	692	429	788	9	84	0.58	44	16	40	25	122	81	130	10%	108	8%	83%	14	50%	21%	3.92	-10.9	51	138	$10
2nd Half		165	19	7	26	3	206	258	290	382	672	587	724	10	80	0.58	45	17	37	22	92	111	104	14%	55	16%	50%	13	46%	54%	3.34	-9.5	48	130	$4
16	Proj	**381**	**43**	**13**	**48**	**3**	**240**	**258**	**313**	**399**	**712**	**621**	**751**	**9**	**82**	**0.55**	**44**	**19**	**37**	**26**	**108**	**98**	**107**	**12%**	**70**	**5%**	**61%**				**4.10**	**-12.1**	**43**	**117**	**$9**

PAUL SPORER

Morse,Michael

Age: 34	Bats: R	Pos: 1B	Health D	LIMA Plan D
Ht: 6' 5"	Wt: 245		PT/Exp D	Rand Var -2
			Consist F	MM 4011

5-19-.231 in 256 AB at MIA/PIT. Not prime destinations of last-chance power hitters, especially without the power (.105 ISO). Finger injury cut into '15, but 3 of last 4 PX totals are pedestrian for a 1B-only expected HR resource. Already-poor ct% and FB rates getting worse and DDF Reliability hamper rebound chances.

Yr	Tm	AB	R	HR	RBI	SB	BA	xBA	OBP	SLG	OPS	vL	vR	bb%	ct%	Eye	G	L	F	h%	HctX	PX	xPX	hr/f	Spd	SBO	SB%	#Wk	DOM	DIS	RC/G	RAR	BPV	BPX	R$
11	WAS	522	73	31	95	2	303	287	360	550	910	892	915	6	76	0.29	44	20	37	35	137	173	154	21%	62	4%	40%	27	59%	22%	6.85	8.5	75	167	$27
12	WAS	406	53	18	62	0	291	263	321	470	791	755	804	4	76	0.16	55	20	25	34	109	116	111	23%	87	1%	0%	19	37%	26%	5.31	-1.2	33	83	$15
13	2 AL *	336	36	14	28	0	212	234	261	374	635	667	642	6	72	0.23	45	19	36	25	109	117	115	16%	71	0%	0%	21	33%	57%	3.16	-14.7	16	40	$1
14	SF	438	48	16	61	0	279	269	336	475	811	827	803	7	72	0.26	45	22	33	35	101	156	130	15%	92	0%	0%	24	46%	38%	5.48	15.9	57	154	$14
15	2 NL *	263	17	6	22	0	228	216	295	329	625	672	639	9	63	0.26	57	25	18	34	93	80	91	19%	77	0%	0%	21	19%	62%	3.21	-17.1	-39	-105	-$1
1st Half		163	7	3	13	0	208	168	255	286	541	180	605	6	63	0.17	58	20	21	31	97	66	100	11%	64	0%	0%	8	13%	88%	2.35	-14.2	-62	-168	-$2
2nd Half		100	10	3	9	0	260	249	368	400	768	817	714	13	64	0.42	55	33	13	38	88	104	78	38%	91	0%	0%	13	23%	46%	4.91	-0.7	-6	-16	$3
16	**Proj**	**193**	**18**	**7**	**21**	**0**	**251**	**247**	**322**	**416**	**738**	**760**	**726**	**8**	**68**	**0.28**	**51**	**24**	**25**	**33**	**100**	**121**	**106**	**22%**	**86**	**0%**	**32%**				**4.41**	**-4.2**	**0**	**0**	**$2**

Moss,Brandon

Age: 32	Bats: L	Pos: RF 1B	Health A	LIMA Plan B
Ht: 6' 0"	Wt: 210		PT/Exp B	Rand Var +1
			Consist B	MM 4005

While he posted a lofty game total (148), it seems his hip surgery left him less than 100% all year. The 2H hr/f helps explain HR total, but 21 ft. dip in average FB distance says it wasn't just bad luck. Platoon role in the 2H dims scariness of vL output (just 38 PA). Low-BA is locked in, but good health could yield... UP: 30 HR

Yr	Tm	AB	R	HR	RBI	SB	BA	xBA	OBP	SLG	OPS	vL	vR	bb%	ct%	Eye	G	L	F	h%	HctX	PX	xPX	hr/f	Spd	SBO	SB%	#Wk	DOM	DIS	RC/G	RAR	BPV	BPX	R$
11	PHI *	442	49	17	60	3	219	196	293	399	693	0	0	9	64	0.29	50	0	50	30	0	154	2	0%	71	10%	29%	2	0%	50%	3.58	-36.9	21	47	$6
12	OAK *	461	68	29	73	4	254	259	314	505	819	770	1006	8	69	0.28	33	21	46	30	111	178	176	26%	71	4%	78%	18	61%	28%	5.42	-0.1	59	148	$16
13	OAK	446	73	30	87	4	256	256	337	522	859	649	904	10	69	0.36	30	18	52	30	113	194	174	19%	92	6%	67%	27	70%	19%	5.86	16.7	79	198	$20
14	OAK	500	70	25	81	1	234	242	334	438	772	792	768	12	69	0.44	30	21	49	29	100	156	137	15%	61	1%	100%	27	44%	41%	4.74	8.3	46	124	$14
15	2 TM	469	47	19	58	0	226	229	304	407	711	717	709	9	68	0.33	33	20	47	29	118	133	157	13%	84	1%	0%	27	48%	37%	3.98	-19.8	26	70	$5
1st Half		276	34	14	44	0	228	250	303	442	745	800	713	10	70	0.35	32	21	46	27	123	155	166	15%	70	0%	0%	14	57%	29%	4.41	-6.3	46	124	$12
2nd Half		193	13	5	14	0	223	198	306	358	663	538	703	9	66	0.31	33	19	48	31	112	100	144	8%	109	2%	0%	13	38%	46%	3.39	-10.4	-1	-3	-$4
16	**Proj**	**441**	**52**	**21**	**61**	**1**	**233**	**233**	**317**	**436**	**753**	**688**	**774**	**10**	**68**	**0.35**	**32**	**20**	**48**	**29**	**111**	**146**	**154**	**15%**	**82**	**2%**	**46%**				**4.45**	**-4.8**	**29**	**78**	**$11**

Moustakas,Mike

Age: 27	Bats: L	Pos: 3B	Health A	LIMA Plan A
Ht: 6' 0"	Wt: 195		PT/Exp B	Rand Var -3
			Consist C	MM 3035

Short a position change, has had an Alex Gordon-like career (mid-20s breakout after four underwhelming seasons; surge vLHP leading the way). Pulled less and made better contact for a transformative effort. Age & skills growth is believable, though track record tamps down exuberance. Yet, a look at his 2H says... UP: 30 HR

Yr	Tm	AB	R	HR	RBI	SB	BA	xBA	OBP	SLG	OPS	vL	vR	bb%	ct%	Eye	G	L	F	h%	HctX	PX	xPX	hr/f	Spd	SBO	SB%	#Wk	DOM	DIS	RC/G	RAR	BPV	BPX	R$
11	KC *	561	54	11	62	3	256	249	301	380	681	494	741	6	82	0.36	38	20	41	29	92	88	83	4%	91	3%	71%	17	35%	24%	3.92	-14.5	41	91	$10
12	KC	563	69	20	73	5	242	236	296	412	708	704	710	6	78	0.31	34	16	50	28	88	115	109	9%	82	6%	71%	27	48%	33%	4.01	-9.0	43	108	$12
13	KC	472	42	12	42	2	233	241	287	364	651	546	682	6	82	0.39	37	19	45	26	84	91	86	7%	73	6%	33%	26	46%	23%	3.30	-9.2	39	98	$4
14	KC *	488	47	16	57	1	217	258	272	365	638	554	653	7	83	0.46	39	20	41	23	115	100	120	9%	69	1%	100%	26	50%	23%	3.25	-6.2	50	135	$5
15	KC	549	73	22	82	1	284	274	348	470	817	823	814	7	86	0.57	40	19	41	30	119	112	114	11%	78	2%	33%	27	63%	19%	5.55	15.2	74	200	$20
1st Half		289	39	7	31	1	301	270	357	436	793	644	883	6	88	0.57	44	20	35	32	105	83	94	8%	99	4%	33%	14	57%	21%	5.38	6.0	62	168	$19
2nd Half		260	34	15	51	0	265	282	337	508	844	1023	738	8	84	0.56	35	17	48	26	135	146	138	14%	63	0%	0%	13	69%	15%	5.73	8.3	91	246	$22
16	**Proj**	**534**	**61**	**23**	**72**	**1**	**263**	**268**	**322**	**453**	**775**	**794**	**766**	**7**	**84**	**0.47**	**38**	**19**	**43**	**28**	**112**	**115**	**113**	**12%**	**72**	**2%**	**47%**				**4.88**	**4.0**	**56**	**151**	**$18**

Moya,Steven

Age: 24	Bats: L	Pos: RF	Health A	LIMA Plan D
Ht: 6' 6"	Wt: 230		PT/Exp D	Rand Var 0
			Consist C	MM 3201

0-0-.182 in 22 AB at DET. Struggles v. LHP are well-known, but he hasn't exactly crushed RHP (.712 OPS in MiLB). Holes in the swing (70% ct%) and an impatient approach (5% bb) have left his elite raw power under wraps more often than not in 2,508 MiLB plate appearances. Not quite ready.

Yr	Tm	AB	R	HR	RBI	SB	BA	xBA	OBP	SLG	OPS	vL	vR	bb%	ct%	Eye	G	L	F	h%	HctX	PX	xPX	hr/f	Spd	SBO	SB%	#Wk	DOM	DIS	RC/G	RAR	BPV	BPX	R$
11																																			
12																																			
13																																			
14	DET *	523	60	26	75	11	238	276	261	449	710	0	857	3	67	0.10	67	17	17	31	96	170	27	0%	97	19%	72%	3	0%	67%	3.85	-0.6	40	108	$17
15	DET *	522	41	16	56	4	204	196	239	346	585	0	634	4	65	0.13	33	17	50	28	95	114	89	0%	87	9%	46%	5	20%	80%	2.56	-36.4	-13	-35	$1
1st Half		262	26	8	33	2	206	210	246	340	585			5	64	0.15				29		109			83	5%	57%				2.65		-19	-51	$3
2nd Half		260	15	8	23	2	203	201	232	352	584	0	634	4	65	0.11	33	17	50	28	96	120	89	0%	94	14%	40%	5	20%	80%	2.46	-19.5	-6	-16	-$1
16	**Proj**	**202**	**18**	**6**	**24**	**3**	**233**	**218**	**262**	**377**	**639**	**639**	**639**	**4**	**65**	**0.12**	**43**	**20**	**37**	**33**		**115**		**12%**	**92**	**11%**	**60%**				**3.20**	**-9.9**	**-14**	**-38**	**$4**

Muncy,Max

Age: 25	Bats: L	Pos: 1B	Health A	LIMA Plan F
Ht: 6' 0"	Wt: 190		PT/Exp D	Rand Var -4
			Consist A	MM 3101

3-9-.206 in 102 AB at OAK. A 0.84 Eye in 1,672 MiLB PA offers fringe hope, but he was old for each level. Patience (4.38 P/PA) was bigger culprit in ct% dip than free-swinging (had a league average miss rate). Lost in the ugly BA is an impressive xPX which if real, offers fleeting hope, especially in OBP leagues.

Yr	Tm	AB	R	HR	RBI	SB	BA	xBA	OBP	SLG	OPS	vL	vR	bb%	ct%	Eye	G	L	F	h%	HctX	PX	xPX	hr/f	Spd	SBO	SB%	#Wk	DOM	DIS	RC/G	RAR	BPV	BPX	R$
11																																			
12																																			
13	aa	172	17	3	18	0	214		292	343	635			10	78	0.50				26		96			105	3%	0%				3.16		42	105	-$2
14	aa	435	45	5	48	5	225		331	318	648			14	76	0.66				28		74			96	5%	70%				3.46		22	59	$4
15	OAK *	314	33	6	37	0	225	196	294	359	653	500	660	9	69	0.31	32	13	55	31	110	109	210	8%	87	2%	0%	17	29%	47%	3.42	-10.9	10	27	$1
1st Half		153	21	3	15	0	217	202	302	377	680	500	639	11	66	0.36	29	13	58	31	104	138	207	6%	99	0%	0%	10	30%	60%	3.72	-4.3	27	73	$0
2nd Half		161	12	2	22	0	233	198	285	342	627	0	728	7	72	0.26	44	13	44	31	120	83	219	14%	88	3%	0%	7	29%	29%	3.14	-7.3	-2	-5	$2
16	**Proj**	**94**	**9**	**2**	**11**	**0**	**225**	**199**	**304**	**367**	**671**	**509**	**672**	**11**	**73**	**0.44**	**29**	**13**	**58**	**28**	**94**	**103**	**186**	**6%**	**101**	**3%**	**48%**				**3.66**	**-4.3**	**17**	**47**	**$1**

Murphy,Daniel

Age: 31	Bats: L	Pos: 2B 3B	Health B	LIMA Plan B+
Ht: 6' 1"	Wt: 215		PT/Exp A	Rand Var +3
			Consist A	MM 2255

Scariest part about secondary speed contributors is that an injury can wipe it out immediately: Had just 1 attempt after returning from June's quad injury. Has enough ct% to sell out for more pop to cover speed loss. Or just bottle up that 2H power surge that carried through post-season. Either way, UP: 20 HR

Yr	Tm	AB	R	HR	RBI	SB	BA	xBA	OBP	SLG	OPS	vL	vR	bb%	ct%	Eye	G	L	F	h%	HctX	PX	xPX	hr/f	Spd	SBO	SB%	#Wk	DOM	DIS	RC/G	RAR	BPV	BPX	R$
11	NYM	391	49	6	49	5	320	289	362	448	809	755	825	6	89	0.57	47	22	31	35	115	88	95	6%	89	9%	50%	20	45%	10%	5.80	11.5	68	151	$16
12	NYM	571	62	6	65	10	291	285	332	403	735	680	761	6	86	0.44	51	24	25	33	88	79	55	5%	84	8%	83%	27	44%	37%	4.86	8.2	45	113	$17
13	NYM	658	92	13	78	23	286	266	319	415	733	616	790	5	86	0.34	42	21	36	32	112	87	100	6%	100	16%	88%	27	52%	19%	4.84	21.9	53	133	$30
14	NYM	596	79	9	57	13	289	285	332	403	734	695	747	6	86	0.45	42	28	29	33	107	84	89	6%	94	11%	72%	26	50%	23%	4.77	23.1	52	141	$22
15	NYM	499	56	14	73	2	281	299	322	449	770	633	817	6	92	0.82	43	21	36	28	126	101	109	8%	63	3%	50%	24	67%	4%	5.07	12.7	83	224	$15
1st Half		223	17	4	29	1	287	297	339	413	751	513	821	7	93	1.00	41	25	33	30	118	80	84	6%	56	5%	33%	11	55%	0%	4.78	3.5	68	184	$8
2nd Half		276	39	10	44	1	275	304	307	478	786	712	813	5	92	0.68	44	18	38	27	132	118	129	10%	74	2%	100%	13	77%	8%	5.28	8.3	97	262	$21
16	**Proj**	**561**	**69**	**15**	**72**	**8**	**286**	**290**	**326**	**442**	**768**	**661**	**806**	**6**	**89**	**0.56**	**43**	**22**	**35**	**30**	**117**	**97**	**100**	**8%**	**78**	**8%**	**72%**				**5.12**	**14.2**	**73**	**197**	**$23**

Murphy,David

Age: 34	Bats: L	Pos: LF DH	Health A	LIMA Plan D+
Ht: 6' 3"	Wt: 210		PT/Exp C	Rand Var -2
			Consist B	MM 2023

Reputation as righty-masher is no longer warranted w/.714 OPS in last 3 yrs (1,106 PA). Don't be fooled by perceived improvements v. LHP, either, as they came in a whopping 26 PA. GB trends puts fringe power on thin ice, meaning ct% will be the carrying tool into his mid-30s. SBO says double-digit totals are toast, too.

Yr	Tm	AB	R	HR	RBI	SB	BA	xBA	OBP	SLG	OPS	vL	vR	bb%	ct%	Eye	G	L	F	h%	HctX	PX	xPX	hr/f	Spd	SBO	SB%	#Wk	DOM	DIS	RC/G	RAR	BPV	BPX	R$
11	TEX	404	46	11	46	11	275	264	328	401	729	507	809	8	85	0.54	54	17	29	30	88	78	82	11%	114	15%	65%	27	52%	37%	4.53	-4.6	53	118	$13
12	TEX	457	65	15	61	10	304	279	380	479	859	845	862	11	84	0.73	43	21	35	34	114	110	109	11%	104	10%	67%	27	59%	15%	6.52	24.7	77	193	$20
13	TEX	436	51	13	45	1	220	271	282	374	656	562	685	8	86	0.63	43	19	38	23	102	100	98	9%	86	5%	20%	26	62%	23%	3.31	-9.0	69	173	$4
14	CLE	416	40	8	58	2	262	259	319	385	703	604	727	8	85	0.59	46	19	35	29	90	89	73	6%	91	5%	40%	24	38%	29%	4.16	5.7	58	157	$9
15	2 AL	361	38	10	50	0	283	257	318	421	739	795	735	5	86	0.41	51	17	32	30	103	84	92	10%	93	2%	0%	26	50%	27%	4.68	2.8	53	143	$10
1st Half		167	21	5	22	0	323	268	366	479	845	1010	835	7	86	0.50	49	18	34	36	105	94	111	10%	121	2%	0%	14	57%	14%	6.50	8.7	69	186	$12
2nd Half		194	17	5	28	0	247	248	275	371	646	643	646	4	87	0.32	53	16	32	26	101	76	75	9%	69	2%	0%	12	42%	42%	3.40	-6.7	40	108	$8
16	**Proj**	**294**	**31**	**8**	**39**	**1**	**266**	**261**	**314**	**403**	**717**	**638**	**729**	**7**	**86**	**0.51**	**48**	**18**	**34**	**29**	**99**	**85**	**87**	**9%**	**90**	**4%**	**36%**				**4.30**	**-2.2**	**41**	**112**	**$9**

PAUL SPORER

Murphy,John Ryan

Age: 25	Bats: R	Pos: CA	Health A	LIMA Plan D	
Ht: 5' 11"	Wt: 195		PT/Exp F	Rand Var -5	
			Consist C	MM 2111	

Won backup gig out of camp, and while slash line wasn't half bad, skills weren't convinced: BA spike was product of elevated h%, as xBA and ct% remained flat; PX held firm, though declining FB% hurts HR outlook; Rand Var predicts strong overall correction. Path to relevance is long, even in two-catcher leagues.

Yr	Tm	AB	R	HR	RBI	SB	BA	xBA	OBP	SLG	OPS	vL	vR	bb%	ct%	Eye	G	L	F	h%	HctX	PX	xPX	hr/f	Spd	SBO	SB%	#Wk	DOM	DIS	RC/G	RAR	BPV	BPX	R$
11																																			
12	aa	147	19	4	13	0	212		277	372	649			8	77	0.39				25		116			96	0%	0%				3.33		48	120	-$1
13	NYY *	439	55	12	41	1	245	244	311	387	697	641	143	9	80	0.48	38	19	44	28	136	103	126	0%	82	2%	44%	5	0%	60%	4.03	4.0	47	118	$7
14	NYY *	260	20	6	30	0	234	240	273	348	622	686	690	5	73	0.20	36	27	37	30	54	91	53	5%	81	0%	0%	15	40%	53%	3.17	-1.1	2	5	$2
15	NYY	155	21	3	14	0	277	244	327	406	734	770	696	7	72	0.28	47	23	30	37	104	98	96	9%	113	0%	0%	26	35%	54%	4.72	4.3	18	49	$2
1st Half		71	7	0	5	0	239	213	282	324	606	613	598	7	70	0.24	44	21	35	34	105	72	110	0%	120	0%	0%	14	29%	64%	3.14	-1.3	-10	-27	-$3
2nd Half		84	14	3	9	0	310	267	366	476	842	892	786	8	74	0.32	49	25	25	39	103	119	84	19%	97	0%	0%	12	42%	42%	6.38	5.9	37	100	$6
16	Proj	162	20	3	16	0	251	246	304	376	680	715	646	7	74	0.30	43	25	32	32	84	93	78	8%	106	0%	50%				3.90	0.6	3	9	$1

Myers,Wil

Age: 25	Bats: R	Pos: CF 1B	Health F	LIMA Plan B	
Ht: 6' 3"	Wt: 205		PT/Exp D	Rand Var 0	
			Consist D	MM 3315	

Wrist tendinitis in May, surgery in June derailed second straight season. Pre-injury returns were promising as PX recovered and he cut down on Ks, but GB% stroke tempers odds of major power breakout. Assuming off-season recovery, still plenty of upside, but reliability grades suggest there's significant risk.

Yr	Tm	AB	R	HR	RBI	SB	BA	xBA	OBP	SLG	OPS	vL	vR	bb%	ct%	Eye	G	L	F	h%	HctX	PX	xPX	hr/f	Spd	SBO	SB%	#Wk	DOM	DIS	RC/G	RAR	BPV	BPX	R$
11	aa	354	37	5	37	7	225		301	334	636			10	74	0.43				29		90			88	10%	76%				3.33		18	40	$3
12	a/a	522	75	26	83	5	278		337	497	833			8	71	0.31				34		147			106	6%	58%				5.81		52	130	$21
13	TAM *	587	86	24	100	11	275	255	338	463	801	821	834	9	71	0.33	46	20	34	35	117	143	120	15%	95	9%	78%	16	50%	25%	5.50	23.5	45	113	$26
14	TAM *	349	40	8	40	9	221	216	301	329	630	532	649	10	72	0.41	48	16	36	29	99	88	96	7%	105	10%	89%	16	25%	50%	3.33	-5.3	12	32	$6
15	SD	225	40	8	29	5	253	255	336	427	763	793	751	11	76	0.49	48	17	36	30	110	119	104	14%	110	11%	71%	12	50%	33%	4.82	3.4	54	146	$7
1st Half		148	30	5	19	3	277	264	327	459	787	791	782	6	79	0.32	46	16	38	32	110	122	95	12%	125	14%	60%	7	71%	14%	5.05	2.7	66	178	$10
2nd Half		77	10	3	10	2	208	232	351	364	715	794	682	18	69	0.71	51	19	30	26	109	112	121	19%	84	7%	100%	5	20%	60%	4.27	-0.3	28	76	$0
16	Proj	434	62	15	57	10	246	236	332	402	734	721	737	11	72	0.46	47	16	36	31	107	111	107	13%	102	9%	83%				4.56	2.0	30	80	$15

Napoli,Mike

Age: 34	Bats: R	Pos: 1B	Health B	LIMA Plan C+	
Ht: 6' 0"	Wt: 220		PT/Exp B	Rand Var +3	
			Consist B	MM 4103	

Steady decline continued, as cracks in foundation are everywhere. Career-low BA was more about falling HctX, LD% than plain h% luck; failed to capitalize on FB% spike as he posted lowest xPX, hr/f since 2007; decline vs. RHP puts everyday AB at risk. A mild BA rebound won't be enough to save him.

Yr	Tm	AB	R	HR	RBI	SB	BA	xBA	OBP	SLG	OPS	vL	vR	bb%	ct%	Eye	G	L	F	h%	HctX	PX	xPX	hr/f	Spd	SBO	SB%	#Wk	DOM	DIS	RC/G	RAR	BPV	BPX	R$
11	TEX	369	72	30	75	4	320	312	414	631	1046	1049	1044	14	77	0.68	39	20	41	35	136	207	187	25%	73	5%	67%	24	67%	21%	9.66	39.9	125	278	$26
12	TEX	352	53	24	56	1	227	239	343	469	812	706	861	14	64	0.45	40	19	41	28	95	169	157	26%	101	1%	100%	23	39%	48%	5.17	-1.1	53	133	$9
13	BOS	498	79	23	92	1	259	251	360	482	842	899	816	13	62	0.39	37	24	39	37	106	195	156	19%	72	1%	50%	27	56%	41%	5.84	17.8	55	138	$18
14	BOS	415	49	17	55	3	248	235	370	419	789	923	739	16	68	0.59	45	19	36	32	107	139	138	17%	63	3%	60%	23	48%	39%	5.18	12.8	36	97	$11
15	2 AL	407	46	18	50	3	224	233	324	410	734	954	603	12	71	0.48	42	16	42	27	92	131	118	15%	89	6%	50%	26	42%	38%	4.21	-9.0	42	114	$6
1st Half		260	31	10	30	2	192	221	294	358	652	804	598	12	70	0.47	45	14	42	23	86	117	122	13%	87	5%	67%	14	29%	43%	3.29	-15.4	27	73	$5
2nd Half		147	15	8	20	1	279	256	376	503	880	1077	620	12	73	0.50	38	19	43	33	102	155	111	17%	88	7%	33%	12	58%	33%	6.22	4.5	67	181	$7
16	Proj	322	40	13	46	2	250	235	356	429	784	933	697	13	69	0.50	41	19	40	32	102	132	133	14%	82	4%	49%				5.01	-1.4	25	69	$10

Navarro,Dioner

Age: 32	Bats: B	Pos: CA	Health B	LIMA Plan D+	
Ht: 5' 9"	Wt: 205		PT/Exp D	Rand Var +2	
			Consist C	MM 2123	

Torn hamstring in April, intermittent AB resulted in mostly lost season. Solid plate skills stayed intact, and though xBA validates the BA drop, much of it was PX induced; xPX and h% dip say there's rebound potential. With hard contact still present, FB% growth further suggests skills are there for late profit.

Yr	Tm	AB	R	HR	RBI	SB	BA	xBA	OBP	SLG	OPS	vL	vR	bb%	ct%	Eye	G	L	F	h%	HctX	PX	xPX	hr/f	Spd	SBO	SB%	#Wk	DOM	DIS	RC/G	RAR	BPV	BPX	R$
11	LA	176	13	5	17	0	193	221	276	324	600	616	597	10	80	0.57	43	14	43	21	75	85	94	8%	78	0%	0%	18	44%	39%	2.82	-7.6	34	76	-$3
12	CIN *	276	23	6	35	0	262	280	307	380	687	750	754	6	85	0.42	34	31	34	29	119	74	96	10%	56	0%	0%	9	22%	33%	4.03	-1.9	29	73	$4
13	CHC	240	31	13	34	0	300	289	365	492	856	1123	764	9	85	0.64	41	25	34	31	104	110	91	19%	71	1%	0%	26	50%	31%	6.36	17.5	69	173	$9
14	TOR	481	40	12	69	3	274	263	317	395	712	725	707	6	84	0.42	40	24	36	31	97	83	94	8%	57	2%	100%	26	38%	42%	4.48	15.7	35	95	$14
15	TOR	171	17	5	20	0	246	248	307	374	682	894	625	9	83	0.59	37	22	41	27	110	80	123	8%	57	0%	0%	20	40%	50%	3.97	1.2	33	89	$1
1st Half		81	10	2	11	0	235	252	290	358	648	421	692	9	85	0.67	41	21	38	25	129	78	139	7%	70	0%	0%	9	44%	56%	3.62	-0.4	44	119	$0
2nd Half		90	7	3	9	0	256	245	323	389	712	1162	556	9	81	0.53	33	23	44	29	93	81	108	9%	57	0%	0%	11	36%	45%	4.31	1.4	27	73	$2
16	Proj	321	31	10	40	1	260	258	317	397	715	887	661	8	83	0.54	38	23	39	28	103	83	107	10%	56	1%	71%				4.39	5.7	26	71	$9

Norris,Derek

Age: 27	Bats: R	Pos: CA	Health A	LIMA Plan B	
Ht: 6' 0"	Wt: 210		PT/Exp C	Rand Var -1	
			Consist B	MM 3315	

Maintained double-digit R$, though much of it was product of AB spike. Batting eye plummeted, while xBA history says this is a more realistic BA level. Played through shoulder sprain the entire 2H, which likely zapped power. If first half PX/xPX is any indication, and FB% gains hold... UP: 20 HR

Yr	Tm	AB	R	HR	RBI	SB	BA	xBA	OBP	SLG	OPS	vL	vR	bb%	ct%	Eye	G	L	F	h%	HctX	PX	xPX	hr/f	Spd	SBO	SB%	#Wk	DOM	DIS	RC/G	RAR	BPV	BPX	R$
11	aa	334	62	17	38	11	190		314	392	706			15	63	0.49				24		164			104	17%	71%				3.85		48	107	$6
12	OAK *	427	47	13	61	9	212	235	274	359	633	618	630	8	74	0.32	40	22	39	26	94	102	93	13%	100	12%	80%	16	31%	63%	3.20	-14.4	24	60	$5
13	OAK	264	41	9	30	5	246	241	345	409	754	990	445	12	73	0.52	36	21	43	30	98	124	95	11%	86	6%	100%	26	46%	42%	4.81	8.7	44	110	$6
14	OAK	385	46	10	55	2	270	243	361	403	763	863	699	12	78	0.63	46	19	35	33	101	99	95	9%	99	3%	50%	26	46%	31%	5.00	17.1	46	124	$11
15	SD	515	65	14	62	4	250	238	305	404	709	810	678	6	75	0.27	42	17	41	31	95	112	105	9%	109	4%	80%	27	41%	41%	4.10	4.3	35	95	$11
1st Half		295	41	11	45	1	241	243	289	427	716	774	700	6	75	0.24	43	13	44	29	100	132	116	11%	99	2%	100%	14	43%	29%	4.10	2.8	47	127	$16
2nd Half		220	24	3	17	3	264	233	326	373	699	847	644	7	75	0.30	39	23	38	34	88	85	91	5%	117	7%	75%	13	38%	54%	4.09	2.0	17	46	$5
16	Proj	476	61	14	57	3	252	240	327	403	730	865	658	9	75	0.41	41	20	39	31	96	108	98	10%	107	3%	79%				4.43	9.1	26	69	$13

Nunez,Eduardo

Age: 29	Bats: R	Pos: SS	Health C	LIMA Plan D+	
Ht: 6' 0"	Wt: 195		PT/Exp F	Rand Var -1	
			Consist B	MM 2431	

Strong season despite limited role, May DL stint (oblique). BA spike unlikely to hold as tepid xPX questions PX and xBA gains, and while he makes plenty of contact, HctX says it's of the weaker variety. Value remains tied to his legs, though with low bb%, issues vs. LHP, it's hard to see any major gains as he approaches 30.

Yr	Tm	AB	R	HR	RBI	SB	BA	xBA	OBP	SLG	OPS	vL	vR	bb%	ct%	Eye	G	L	F	h%	HctX	PX	xPX	hr/f	Spd	SBO	SB%	#Wk	DOM	DIS	RC/G	RAR	BPV	BPX	R$
11	NYY	309	38	5	30	22	265	274	313	385	698	742	673	7	88	0.59	45	21	34	29	108	80	70	5%	115	35%	79%	26	54%	15%	4.25	0.6	66	147	$11
12	NYY *	252	28	3	23	23	229	216	262	299	562	860	539	4	83	0.26	44	16	39	27	89	46	90	3%	125	50%	81%	12	33%	50%	2.72	-9.2	15	38	$7
13	NYY	304	38	3	28	10	260	250	307	372	679	652	693	6	83	0.39	41	21	38	30	92	78	81	3%	138	17%	77%	20	45%	35%	3.93	4.5	51	128	$7
14	MIN *	253	32	5	28	10	251	265	274	377	651	586	716	3	83	0.19	56	16	27	29	80	78	43	9%	148	25%	78%	20	40%	40%	3.52	2.6	47	127	$7
15	MIN	188	23	4	20	8	282	284	327	431	758	649	809	6	85	0.41	57	16	27	32	93	100	67	10%	100	26%	67%	24	50%	25%	4.78	2.1	62	168	$7
1st Half		103	13	2	11	3	291	311	333	485	819	699	874	6	83	0.41	57	17	26	33	110	138	80	9%	103	27%	50%	12	58%	17%	5.36	3.8	90	243	$6
2nd Half		85	10	2	9	5	271	249	319	365	683	588	730	6	86	0.42	56	15	28	30	72	54	52	10%	93	25%	83%	12	42%	33%	4.10	0.0	28	76	$8
16	Proj	219	27	4	23	9	266	267	307	395	703	643	739	5	84	0.35	53	17	30	30	87	81	63	8%	117	22%	79%				4.22	0.8	51	138	$9

O Brien,Peter

Age: 25	Bats: R	Pos: LF	Health A	LIMA Plan D	
Ht: 6' 4"	Wt: 235		PT/Exp F	Rand Var +4	
			Consist A	MM 4011	

1-3-.400 in 10 AB at ARI. 471-foot HR in his fifth MLB at bat is a testament to his power, which PX/xPX confirms is very real. Impatient plate approach, ct% hint at serious BA risk, bumps in the road. Long-term position still unsettled, but the potential for 5 gms at CA could make him an interesting end-game speculation.

Yr	Tm	AB	R	HR	RBI	SB	BA	xBA	OBP	SLG	OPS	vL	vR	bb%	ct%	Eye	G	L	F	h%	HctX	PX	xPX	hr/f	Spd	SBO	SB%	#Wk	DOM	DIS	RC/G	RAR	BPV	BPX	R$
11																																			
12																																			
13																																			
14	aa	287	37	20	42	0	223		256	481	738			4	68	0.14				25		195			89	0%	0%				4.05		65	176	$7
15	ARI *	500	49	18	69	1	233	288	263	429	693	3333	393	4	70	0.14	40	40	20	30	61	142	134	100%	106	5%	15%	4	50%	25%	3.63	-16.4	34	92	$7
1st Half		300	27	10	38	1	224	242	248	392	640			3	71	0.11				28		122			83	4%	34%				3.14		16	43	$8
2nd Half		200	21	8	31	0	246	291	285	486	771	3333	393	5	67	0.17	40	40	20	32	59	172	134	100%	123	7%	0%	4	50%	25%	4.43	-0.8	57	154	$6
16	Proj	168	19	8	24	0	231	246	263	446	709	709	709	4	69	0.14	38	20	42	29		153		16%	108	3%	16%				3.81	-3.8	31	83	$4

RYAN BLOOMFIELD

Odor,Rougned

Age: 22	Bats: L	Pos: 2B	Health A	LIMA Plan B+	
Ht: 5' 11"	Wt: 190		PT/Exp D	Rand Var 0	
			Consist F	MM 3335	

16-61-.261 with 6 SB in 426 AB at TEX. Demoted after rough start, returned in mid-June to finish with third-highest OPS among AL 2B. Skills have quickly caught up with tools, foremost burgeoning PX (including 123 vs. LHP). Still learning art of the steal. Just a pup, but the word's out and he won't come cheap.

Yr	Tm	AB	R	HR	RBI	SB	BA	xBA	OBP	SLG	OPS	vL	vR	bb%	ct%	Eye	G	L	F	h%	HctX	PX	xPX	hr/f	Spd	SBO	SB%	#Wk	DOM	DIS	RC/G	RAR	BPV	BPX	R$
11																																			
12																																			
13	aa	134	18	6	17	4	309		349	529	878			6	82	0.34				34		139			115	19%	69%				6.61		88	220	$5
14	TEX *	515	57	14	62	9	260	249	292	404	695	626	727	4	82	0.24	49	15	36	29	90	90	68	8%	134	16%	47%	22	41%	23%	3.78	6.0	50	135	$15
15	TEX *	534	76	20	77	8	274	278	316	488	804	781	781	6	83	0.37	46	15	40	30	107	127	103	12%	132	14%	51%	22	55%	18%	5.16	13.7	88	238	$20
1st Half		261	34	8	38	7	273	281	330	462	791	665	711	8	84	0.53	51	14	35	30	78	119	59	9%	103	18%	65%	9	44%	33%	5.17	7.2	80	216	$19
2nd Half		273	42	12	39	1	275	277	316	513	829	842	822	4	82	0.23	43	15	42	30	122	134	127	13%	155	9%	20%	13	62%	8%	5.12	7.1	93	251	$21
16	**Proj**	**564**	**74**	**19**	**75**	**10**	**274**	**267**	**325**	**463**	**788**	**764**	**800**	**5**	**82**	**0.31**	**47**	**15**	**38**	**30**	**98**	**112**	**86**	**11%**	**133**	**15%**	**51%**				**4.80**	**9.4**	**67**	**181**	**$21**

Olivera,Hector

Age: 31	Bats: R	Pos: 3B	Health A	LIMA Plan B+	
Ht: 6' 2"	Wt: 220		PT/Exp F	Rand Var -5	
			Consist F	MM 2035	

2-11-.253 in 79 AB at ATL. Slashed .323/.407/.505 in 2800 AB in Cuba. U.S. debut was delayed until September due to hamstring injury. Small MLB sample submits he wasn't overmatched, but little else. Older player may be quicker to make adjustments, especially if previous Eye skill translates to majors.

Yr	Tm	AB	R	HR	RBI	SB	BA	xBA	OBP	SLG	OPS	vL	vR	bb%	ct%	Eye	G	L	F	h%	HctX	PX	xPX	hr/f	Spd	SBO	SB%	#Wk	DOM	DIS	RC/G	RAR	BPV	BPX	R$
11	for	214	81	10	41	0	318		415	508	922			14	90	1.70				32		109			104	1%	0%				7.73	16.0	110	244	$14
12																																			
13	for	228	43	4	37	0	294		378	425	803			12	90	1.29				31		79			122	0%	0%				5.80	11.5	84	210	$7
14																																			
15	ATL *	171	14	3	19	0	248	242	284	371	656	243	827	5	84	0.31	49	16	35	28	54	76	62	8%	107	0%	0%	6	83%	17%	3.58	-5.5	39	105	$0
1st Half		53	6	1	5	0	288	236	317	416	733			4	80	0.21				34		71			107	0%	0%				4.72		18	49	-$2
2nd Half		118	8	2	13	0	230	247	270	352	622	243	827	5	85	0.38	49	16	35	25	55	78	62	8%	97	0%	0%	6	83%	17%	3.14	-5.3	45	122	$1
16	**Proj**	**448**	**74**	**14**	**62**	**0**	**276**	**267**	**348**	**437**	**784**	**768**	**786**	**9**	**86**	**0.69**	**49**	**16**	**35**	**29**	**50**	**92**	**56**	**10%**	**134**	**0%**	**0%**				**5.18**	**7.0**	**62**	**167**	**$17**

Olt,Mike

Age: 27	Bats: R	Pos: 3B	Health C	LIMA Plan D	
Ht: 6' 2"	Wt: 210		PT/Exp D	Rand Var -5	
			Consist A	MM 4001	

4-5-.191 in 94 AB at CHC and CHW. Plus-plus power; we all see that. But finding much else is like the proverbial needle. There's this: Lifetime, he bats .277 when leading off an inning. Changing orgs, leagues hasn't helped. He could still get 20 knocks, but might be with... DN: Nippon Ham Fighters.

Yr	Tm	AB	R	HR	RBI	SB	BA	xBA	OBP	SLG	OPS	vL	vR	bb%	ct%	Eye	G	L	F	h%	HctX	PX	xPX	hr/f	Spd	SBO	SB%	#Wk	DOM	DIS	RC/G	RAR	BPV	BPX	R$
11																																			
12	TEX *	387	52	25	69	4	254	255	342	492	834	387	473	12	68	0.42	45	18	36	31	95	166	125	0%	108	5%	80%	8	13%	75%	5.76	13.8	64	160	$14
13	a/a	373	36	11	31	0	169		252	309	561			10	59	0.27				25		128			93	0%	0%				2.39		-10	-25	-$5
14	CHC *	331	34	17	50	1	188	207	257	389	646	681	561	9	58	0.22	38	12	49	26	88	187	162	19%	67	3%	41%	21	43%	48%	3.11	-6.3	19	51	$2
15	2 TM *	314	32	10	23	0	212	195	268	358	626	593	564	7	59	0.19	53	14	34	32	62	125	95	20%	91	3%	0%	7	0%	71%	3.00	-16.3	-18	-49	$0
1st Half		69	8	2	2	0	183	223	215	349	564	500	530	4	63	0.11	56	11	33	26	92	144	151	33%	104	0%	0%	2	0%	50%	2.35	-5.0	8	22	-$10
2nd Half		245	24	9	20	0	221	182	282	361	643	609	569	8	58	0.20	52	14	34	34	57	119	85	18%	85	4%	0%	5	0%	80%	3.19	-10.9	-28	-76	$2
16	**Proj**	**161**	**17**	**7**	**16**	**0**	**201**	**210**	**267**	**387**	**654**	**703**	**630**	**8**	**60**	**0.22**	**46**	**13**	**40**	**28**	**69**	**153**	**116**	**18%**	**95**	**3%**	**34%**				**3.24**	**-7.0**	**-2**	**-7**	**$2**

Orlando,Paulo

Age: 30	Bats: R	Pos: RF LF	Health A	LIMA Plan D+	
Ht: 6' 2"	Wt: 210		PT/Exp C	Rand Var +1	
			Consist A	MM 2421	

7-27-.249 with 3 SB in 241 AB at KC. Rookie's HR and SB totals were both surprising, as he averaged 6 HR and 21 SB over 10 minor-league seasons. Late-age debuts are delayed for a reason, so 2015 is likely as good as it will get. If there is upside, it will probably manifest itself on the basepaths.

Yr	Tm	AB	R	HR	RBI	SB	BA	xBA	OBP	SLG	OPS	vL	vR	bb%	ct%	Eye	G	L	F	h%	HctX	PX	xPX	hr/f	Spd	SBO	SB%	#Wk	DOM	DIS	RC/G	RAR	BPV	BPX	R$
11	a/a	354	36	3	34	9	224		258	344	602			4	79	0.22				28		76			148	25%	53%				2.69		32	71	$2
12	aa	420	39	4	29	15	226		263	299	562			5	84	0.32				26		48			99	23%	67%				2.53		16	40	$4
13	aaa	293	30	3	33	6	226		266	304	569			5	77	0.24				28		53			119	14%	61%				2.59		0	0	$2
14	aaa	501	38	4	39	21	228		264	307	571			5	79	0.23				28		57			119	29%	65%				2.56		8	22	$8
15	KC *	411	45	9	39	9	235	257	255	386	641	705	718	3	78	0.12	43	22	34	28	107	101	122	11%	124	18%	76%	21	52%	24%	3.26	-14.0	35	95	$7
1st Half		241	24	2	14	6	232	249	253	342	596	677	646	3	80	0.14	48	22	31	28	84	69	87	4%	146	16%	86%	9	56%	22%	2.94	-11.8	27	73	$4
2nd Half		170	21	7	25	3	240	271	257	448	705	724	792	2	74	0.09	40	23	38	29	125	149	154	17%	93	22%	61%	12	50%	25%	3.71	-4.4	50	135	$10
16	**Proj**	**236**	**24**	**6**	**24**	**6**	**232**	**252**	**264**	**379**	**643**	**645**	**641**	**4**	**78**	**0.17**	**43**	**22**	**35**	**27**	**109**	**95**	**127**	**9%**	**128**	**22%**	**65%**				**3.15**	**-12.1**	**32**	**87**	**$6**

Ortiz,David

Age: 40	Bats: L	Pos: DH	Health B	LIMA Plan A	
Ht: 6' 3"	Wt: 230		PT/Exp A	Rand Var +4	
			Consist C	MM 4055	

Of Ortiz, this author wrote in 2014 BF: "Last 3 years while living on borrowed time: mirror-image BA/xBA, hefty OBP/Slg/OPS, steady Eye and ct%. PX and hr/f confirm that he's still mashing. Age... reminds us this could go south at any time, but skills remain vintage." All ready to COPY/PASTE for 2017, 2018...

Yr	Tm	AB	R	HR	RBI	SB	BA	xBA	OBP	SLG	OPS	vL	vR	bb%	ct%	Eye	G	L	F	h%	HctX	PX	xPX	hr/f	Spd	SBO	SB%	#Wk	DOM	DIS	RC/G	RAR	BPV	BPX	R$
11	BOS	525	84	29	96	1	309	311	398	554	953	989	934	13	84	0.94	41	21	37	32	164	158	167	17%	70	1%	50%	27	67%	15%	8.10	32.2	112	249	$28
12	BOS	324	65	23	60	0	318	318	415	611	1026	985	1050	15	84	1.10	37	21	42	32	143	175	150	20%	66	1%	0%	17	82%	6%	9.46	39.8	128	320	$19
13	BOS	518	84	30	103	4	309	308	395	564	959	733	1092	13	83	0.86	39	23	39	33	154	162	173	18%	75	2%	100%	25	64%	8%	8.33	53.6	112	280	$31
14	BOS	518	59	35	104	0	263	282	355	517	873	893	863	13	82	0.79	37	18	46	26	159	164	187	18%	45	0%	0%	26	73%	8%	6.37	34.7	99	268	$22
15	BOS	528	73	37	108	0	273	308	360	553	913	703	1008	13	82	0.81	37	22	41	27	150	169	162	20%	49	1%	0%	27	85%	4%	7.03	23.9	105	284	$23
1st Half		281	29	14	41	0	228	271	321	423	744	342	912	12	82	0.80	42	21	36	23	130	117	116	16%	54	0%	0%	14	86%	7%	4.53	-7.8	66	178	$12
2nd Half		247	44	23	67	0	324	350	403	700	1104	1067	1123	13	82	0.82	30	24	46	32	173	229	214	24%	54	1%	0%	13	85%	0%	10.73	34.8	155	419	$37
16	**Proj**	**501**	**68**	**30**	**95**	**0**	**266**	**295**	**356**	**515**	**872**	**769**	**922**	**13**	**82**	**0.83**	**36**	**21**	**42**	**27**	**156**	**153**	**176**	**17%**	**55**	**1%**	**15%**				**6.41**	**13.8**	**85**	**230**	**$22**

Owings,Christopher

Age: 24	Bats: R	Pos: 2B SS	Health B	LIMA Plan B	
Ht: 5' 10"	Wt: 190		PT/Exp C	Rand Var 0	
			Consist B	MM 2515	

Outside of aptitude for SB, first full season disappointed. Already dubious ct%, Eye worsened and bore many empty AB that healthy LD% couldn't compensate for. Hit .177 with 66% contact vs. LHP, and power hasn't emerged. Plenty of time to consolidate skills, but looks less of a sure thing than a season ago.

Yr	Tm	AB	R	HR	RBI	SB	BA	xBA	OBP	SLG	OPS	vL	vR	bb%	ct%	Eye	G	L	F	h%	HctX	PX	xPX	hr/f	Spd	SBO	SB%	#Wk	DOM	DIS	RC/G	RAR	BPV	BPX	R$
11																																			
12	aa	297	28	5	23	3	246		267	350	617			3	75	0.12				31		70			116	10%	50%				3.04		0	0	$2
13	ARI *	601	72	8	57	15	282	262	305	397	701	250	932	3	80	0.16	47	24	29	34	66	83	63	0%	121	16%	65%	4	50%	25%	4.17	8.8	31	78	$20
14	ARI *	350	38	6	27	10	255	257	287	386	673	829	672	4	78	0.21	45	24	31	31	90	93	77	8%	159	14%	91%	18	33%	50%	3.89	5.1	45	122	$8
15	ARI	515	59	4	43	16	227	227	264	322	587	495	614	5	72	0.18	40	26	34	31	92	76	92	3%	117	19%	80%	27	30%	63%	2.85	-20.7	-3	-8	$7
1st Half		264	33	2	19	9	235	218	260	326	586	385	652	4	71	0.13	41	24	35	32	91	71	89	3%	126	18%	90%	14	29%	64%	2.96	-10.1	-11	-30	$8
2nd Half		251	26	2	24	7	219	236	269	319	587	634	575	6	73	0.24	38	28	34	29	93	81	96	3%	104	19%	70%	13	31%	62%	2.74	-11.6	2	5	$7
16	**Proj**	**522**	**58**	**8**	**44**	**14**	**243**	**244**	**278**	**363**	**640**	**564**	**663**	**4**	**75**	**0.19**	**42**	**25**	**32**	**31**	**88**	**85**	**83**	**6%**	**135**	**17%**	**77%**				**3.38**	**-13.1**	**17**	**47**	**$12**

Ozuna,Marcell

Age: 25	Bats: R	Pos: CF	Health B	LIMA Plan B+	
Ht: 6' 1"	Wt: 225		PT/Exp C	Rand Var 0	
			Consist B	MM 4235	

10-44-.259 in 459 AB at MIA. PRO: Improved ct%, plenty of hard-hit balls, steady BA/xBA. CON: Drops in PX/xPX, hr/f, everything related to SB, languid performance earned 30-game exile to AAA. VERDICT: Reality falls somewhere between 2014 and 2015, with 2nd half hinting at return to prominence.

Yr	Tm	AB	R	HR	RBI	SB	BA	xBA	OBP	SLG	OPS	vL	vR	bb%	ct%	Eye	G	L	F	h%	HctX	PX	xPX	hr/f	Spd	SBO	SB%	#Wk	DOM	DIS	RC/G	RAR	BPV	BPX	R$
11																																			
12																																			
13	MIA *	317	36	7	45	6	270	266	304	426	730	838	647	5	79	0.23	46	21	33	32	104	110	88	4%	119	10%	85%	13	31%	38%	4.56	4.2	51	128	$9
14	MIA	565	72	23	85	3	269	252	317	455	772	728	783	7	71	0.25	49	18	34	34	117	140	133	17%	125	3%	75%	26	42%	38%	5.05	19.7	49	132	$20
15	MIA *	579	64	13	53	3	263	255	309	402	711	888	646	6	77	0.29	48	21	31	32	116	102	107	9%	77	4%	48%	23	30%	43%	4.23	-1.2	25	68	$12
1st Half		297	27	4	26	1	249	224	301	337	638	840	586	7	75	0.28	53	19	28	32	110	68	96	6%	77	3%	50%	14	14%	50%	3.38	-9.0	-7	-19	$6
2nd Half		282	37	9	27	2	277	280	321	471	791	1004	749	6	78	0.29	39	25	37	33	125	136	127	13%	75	6%	48%	9	56%	33%	5.20	6.4	57	154	$17
16	**Proj**	**505**	**60**	**19**	**61**	**4**	**267**	**263**	**315**	**451**	**766**	**866**	**742**	**6**	**75**	**0.27**	**46**	**20**	**33**	**32**	**116**	**126**	**117**	**15%**	**101**	**5%**	**66%**				**4.87**	**6.8**	**39**	**106**	**$17**

ROB CARROLL

Pagan,Angel

Age: 34	Bats: B	Pos: CF	Health F	LIMA Plan C+	
Ht: 6' 2"	Wt: 200		PT/Exp C	Rand Var 0	
			Consist B	MM 1423	

Battled back and knee woes all season and it showed, with career lows in xBA, PX, SBO, and BPV. Hasn't been fully healthy since '12; at his age, he's unlikely to return to former skill baseline. So you're left with an inferior version of the original. This is what Wings was to the Beatles... if Pagan could ever be compared to a Beatle.

Yr	Tm	AB	R	HR	RBI	SB	BA	xBA	OBP	SLG	OPS	vL	vR	bb%	ct%	Eye	G	L	F	h%	HctX	PX	xPX	hr/f	Spd	SBO	SB%	#Wk	DOM	DIS	RC/G	RAR	BPV	BPX	R$
11	NYM	478	68	7	56	32	262	256	322	372	694	672	702	8	87	0.71	35	24	41	29	91	74	93	4%	114	29%	82%	22	50%	9%	4.30	-6.8	60	133	$19
12	SF	605	95	8	56	29	288	270	338	440	778	736	799	7	84	0.49	42	23	35	33	102	95	96	4%	151	22%	81%	27	59%	15%	5.40	12.3	74	185	$26
13	SF	280	44	5	30	9	282	277	334	414	749	807	725	8	87	0.64	43	23	34	31	86	86	77	6%	132	17%	69%	14	79%	0%	4.87	6.1	74	185	$10
14	SF	383	56	3	27	16	300	276	342	389	731	626	790	6	86	0.47	45	27	28	34	86	67	53	3%	123	19%	73%	18	39%	28%	4.82	10.7	49	132	$17
15	SF	512	55	3	37	12	262	237	303	332	635	714	604	6	82	0.34	43	23	34	31	84	50	69	2%	108	12%	75%	25	16%	48%	3.51	-11.9	14	38	$11
1st Half		298	26	0	19	5	268	240	304	322	626	818	555	5	84	0.35	48	22	30	32	77	37	53	0%	117	8%	71%	14	14%	50%	3.45	-8.3	13	35	$9
2nd Half		214	29	3	18	7	252	233	302	346	648	585	675	7	79	0.33	34	25	41	31	94	69	93	4%	95	16%	78%	11	18%	45%	3.59	-5.2	15	41	$13
16	Proj	392	52	4	32	13	274	254	320	367	687	680	690	7	84	0.43	41	24	34	32	88	64	73	3%	115	16%	75%				4.15	-3.0	34	92	$12

Panik,Joe

Age: 25	Bats: L	Pos: 2B	Health B	LIMA Plan B+	
Ht: 6' 1"	Wt: 190		PT/Exp B	Rand Var -3	
			Consist D	MM 2245	

Breakout season cut short by back injury. Sizable growth in multiple skills, with ct%, Eye nearing elite levels. xBA indicates .300+ BA was aided by luck, but discipline, HctX, and LD stroke suggest he could eventually do it again, legitimately. 1.38 Eye vs. LHP last year bodes well for full-time AB. Go ahead, hit the Panik button.

Yr	Tm	AB	R	HR	RBI	SB	BA	xBA	OBP	SLG	OPS	vL	vR	bb%	ct%	Eye	G	L	F	h%	HctX	PX	xPX	hr/f	Spd	SBO	SB%	#Wk	DOM	DIS	RC/G	RAR	BPV	BPX	R$
11																																			
12																																			
13	aa	522	47	3	42	7	217		277	289	566			8	85	0.56				25		53			103	10%	57%				2.55		32	80	$1
14	SF *	562	64	4	48	2	281	263	323	358	680	839	655	6	87	0.48	50	23	27	32	90	53	51	2%	140	3%	46%	17	24%	24%	4.04	10.3	47	127	$13
15	SF	382	59	8	37	3	312	288	378	455	833	769	852	9	89	0.90	43	23	34	33	118	91	90	7%	109	4%	60%	18	72%	11%	6.24	21.5	82	222	$15
1st Half		306	41	6	30	3	304	281	370	444	815	757	831	9	88	0.82	45	21	34	33	120	90	92	7%	111	5%	60%	14	71%	7%	5.91	14.2	76	205	$18
2nd Half		76	18	2	7	0	342	321	407	500	907	813	935	8	95	1.75	37	29	34	34	107	95	81	8%	103	0%	0%	4	75%	25%	7.71	6.8	105	284	$0
16	Proj	532	80	11	47	3	295	285	351	425	776	769	778	7	89	0.74	42	25	33	31	106	80	72	7%	115	3%	55%				5.27	15.4	61	165	$20

Paredes,Jimmy

Age: 27	Bats: B	Pos: DH	Health A	LIMA Plan D	
Ht: 6' 3"	Wt: 200		PT/Exp C	Rand Var -5	
			Consist B	MM 2301	

Stealth free-agent coup in mid-April who delivered immediately, but underlying skills had the last laugh in the end. Soaring 1st half h% drove unexpected playing time, but plate discipline cratered as its done in the past. There's some pop, used to be some speed, but we've probably witnessed his career 3 months.

Yr	Tm	AB	R	HR	RBI	SB	BA	xBA	OBP	SLG	OPS	vL	vR	bb%	ct%	Eye	G	L	F	h%	HctX	PX	xPX	hr/f	Spd	SBO	SB%	#Wk	DOM	DIS	RC/G	RAR	BPV	BPX	R$
11	HOU *	553	67	10	49	27	250	253	276	371	647	500	773	4	74	0.14	54	21	25	32	101	92	96	7%	131	38%	60%	9	22%	56%	3.19	-44.9	19	42	$16
12	HOU *	581	70	9	43	27	252	224	278	361	639	220	546	4	75	0.15	47	16	36	32	84	77	98	0%	131	31%	68%	6	0%	83%	3.29	-27.9	12	30	$16
13	HOU *	452	45	7	37	16	228	249	271	343	614	282	565	6	72	0.22	60	19	20	30	99	89	73	6%	116	29%	56%	13	0%	69%	2.84	-23.5	9	23	$8
14	2 AL *	464	45	8	48	18	240	243	262	356	618	1100	687	3	69	0.09	57	22	22	33	88	101	89	20%	93	22%	94%	10	40%	50%	3.27	-10.7	-8	-22	$11
15	BAL	363	46	10	42	4	275	241	310	416	726	651	740	5	69	0.17	49	23	28	37	104	104	101	14%	114	9%	50%	25	28%	52%	4.40	-10.8	7	19	$10
1st Half		241	36	10	38	3	311	272	341	502	843	624	884	5	74	0.19	47	25	28	39	103	128	104	20%	124	8%	60%	13	46%	38%	6.25	5.3	46	124	$20
2nd Half		122	10	0	4	1	205	177	248	246	494	702	455	5	61	0.15	53	20	27	34	105	49	93	0%	96	11%	33%	12	8%	67%	1.83	-14.1	-76	-205	-$9
16	Proj	221	23	4	19	5	243	230	275	354	630	617	633	4	68	0.15	53	21	25	34	98	88	92	10%	106	18%	64%				3.20	-15.0	-15	-40	$5

Parker,Kyle

Age: 26	Bats: R	Pos: LF	Health A	LIMA Plan D	
Ht: 6' 0"	Wt: 205		PT/Exp C	Rand Var 0	
			Consist B	MM 3111	

3-11-.179 in 106 AB at COL. Second straight year former 1st round pick went splat upon arrival in bigs. Steady declines in OPS and ct% are quickly stripping luster from prospect shine. Can't give up on power yet (see xPX), but he may prove to be a one-trick pony at best.

Yr	Tm	AB	R	HR	RBI	SB	BA	xBA	OBP	SLG	OPS	vL	vR	bb%	ct%	Eye	G	L	F	h%	HctX	PX	xPX	hr/f	Spd	SBO	SB%	#Wk	DOM	DIS	RC/G	RAR	BPV	BPX	R$
11																																			
12																																			
13	aa	480	54	20	57	5	267		311	450	761			6	79	0.30				30		120			101	10%	41%				4.63		55	138	$15
14	COL *	528	46	10	45	2	237	234	265	357	622	250	500	4	76	0.15	50	17	33	30	109	93	48	0%	93	6%	41%	7	0%	86%	3.08	-11.2	14	38	$5
15	COL *	463	43	10	48	5	222	219	255	343	598	645	477	4	67	0.14	46	22	32	31	90	92	126	14%	105	10%	50%	12	17%	58%	2.76	-27.9	-16	-43	$3
1st Half		279	26	6	27	3	228	237	258	344	602	0	2000	4	68	0.13	100	0	0	32	0	86	-15	0%	116	12%	47%	1	0%	0%	2.80	-15.1	-15	-41	$5
2nd Half		184	18	4	21	2	212	220	251	340	592	645	455	5	66	0.15	46	22	32	30	89	103	128	14%	95	8%	58%	11	18%	64%	2.72	-10.6	-15	-41	$1
16	Proj	201	19	6	20	2	232	241	267	380	647	668	636	4	72	0.16	46	22	32	30	80	105	115	12%	101	9%	47%				3.25	-8.0	5	13	$3

Parra,Gerardo

Age: 29	Bats: L	Pos: RF LF CF	Health A	LIMA Plan B+	
Ht: 5' 11"	Wt: 200		PT/Exp A	Rand Var -1	
			Consist C	MM 2345	

Bat died after trade to BAL (.625 OPS), and while overall skills featured nice gains, it was mostly just July hot streak (.341 xBA, 133 HctX, 157 PX). Four years of struggles vs. LHP suggest platoon is in his future. $20 season was pleasant surprise—"surprise" being the key word. Bet the under and hope for another windfall.

Yr	Tm	AB	R	HR	RBI	SB	BA	xBA	OBP	SLG	OPS	vL	vR	bb%	ct%	Eye	G	L	F	h%	HctX	PX	xPX	hr/f	Spd	SBO	SB%	#Wk	DOM	DIS	RC/G	RAR	BPV	BPX	R$
11	ARI	445	55	8	46	15	292	272	357	427	784	790	782	9	82	0.52	50	22	28	34	102	88	84	8%	131	12%	94%	27	44%	26%	5.64	5.8	56	124	$17
12	ARI	385	58	7	36	15	273	267	335	392	727	631	754	8	80	0.43	53	22	24	33	108	83	101	9%	102	22%	63%	27	30%	33%	4.34	-5.8	35	88	$13
13	ARI	601	79	10	48	10	268	283	323	403	726	501	820	7	83	0.48	55	20	25	31	111	97	97	8%	101	13%	50%	27	52%	19%	4.30	0.3	58	145	$16
14	2 NL	529	64	9	40	9	261	266	308	369	677	554	704	6	81	0.32	54	22	24	31	96	76	85	9%	107	12%	56%	28	25%	43%	3.72	-2.7	31	84	$13
15	2 TM	547	83	14	51	14	291	287	328	452	780	658	809	5	83	0.30	47	24	29	33	106	104	96	11%	115	14%	78%	27	44%	22%	5.27	7.7	62	168	$23
1st Half		260	38	7	25	6	308	285	345	477	822	741	838	5	82	0.31	48	22	30	36	124	113	129	11%	113	12%	75%	14	57%	21%	6.03	8.7	63	170	$22
2nd Half		287	45	7	26	8	275	289	313	429	741	603	781	4	85	0.30	46	25	29	31	89	96	67	10%	112	15%	80%	13	31%	23%	4.64	-1.4	60	162	$23
16	Proj	496	69	11	43	12	278	280	322	418	739	601	776	6	83	0.34	50	23	27	32	103	91	91	10%	110	14%	69%				4.61	-2.9	51	138	$19

Paulsen,Benjamin

Age: 28	Bats: L	Pos: 1B	Health A	LIMA Plan D+	
Ht: 6' 4"	Wt: 205		PT/Exp C	Rand Var -1	
			Consist A	MM 4123	

11-49-.277 in 325 AB at COL. 2014's xPX, hr/f came in only 63 AB, so results this year weren't so much declines as more realistic samples. Platoon splits made him discount DFS play vs. RHP at Coors. Too many holes, not enough HctX in swing to give hope for BA, so you'll have to settle for modest power production.

Yr	Tm	AB	R	HR	RBI	SB	BA	xBA	OBP	SLG	OPS	vL	vR	bb%	ct%	Eye	G	L	F	h%	HctX	PX	xPX	hr/f	Spd	SBO	SB%	#Wk	DOM	DIS	RC/G	RAR	BPV	BPX	R$
11	aa	547	46	14	53	1	212		248	351	599			5	74	0.19				26		102			94	5%	28%				2.74		19	42	$1
12	aa	436	47	13	43	1	240		288	382	670			6	73	0.25				30		97			102	5%	15%				3.53		14	35	$5
13	aaa	459	36	12	45	1	234		267	397	663			4	69	0.14				32		127			116	4%	32%				3.44		22	55	$4
14	COL *	498	52	17	54	2	246	255	296	428	725	1417	803	7	68	0.22	43	25	32	33	127	149	156	29%	104	8%	28%	10	50%	30%	4.08	-1.5	38	103	$10
15	COL *	450	53	13	58	2	257	248	306	425	731	554	815	7	71	0.24	45	22	33	34	98	122	110	14%	108	3%	44%	21	33%	33%	4.40	-12.7	28	76	$10
1st Half		252	29	7	27	1	245	254	300	414	714	700	848	7	72	0.28	48	22	30	31	111	121	112	17%	116	1%	100%	8	50%	13%	4.21	-7.1	35	95	$9
2nd Half		198	24	6	31	1	273	242	316	439	756	494	792	6	69	0.20	43	22	35	37	89	124	109	13%	100	6%	33%	13	23%	46%	4.66	-2.8	20	54	$11
16	Proj	362	39	13	43	1	250	253	301	438	739	600	761	6	70	0.21	45	22	32	32	110	135	129	16%	105	5%	34%				4.28	-9.4	25	66	$9

Pearce,Steve

Age: 33	Bats: R	Pos: LF 1B	Health D	LIMA Plan D+	
Ht: 5' 11"	Wt: 210		PT/Exp D	Rand Var +5	
			Consist F	MM 4223	

Consistent power skill undermined by poor BA, which can be traced to high FB%, mediocre ct%, low LD%. Took mammoth PX to drive 2014's BA surge; in other words, lightning in a bottle. Down year vs. LHP, but history (.824 OPS, 142 PX) says he's got value there. He's good depth (read: 5th OF), in both real life and fantasy.

Yr	Tm	AB	R	HR	RBI	SB	BA	xBA	OBP	SLG	OPS	vL	vR	bb%	ct%	Eye	G	L	F	h%	HctX	PX	xPX	hr/f	Spd	SBO	SB%	#Wk	DOM	DIS	RC/G	RAR	BPV	BPX	R$
11	PIT *	124	12	3	14	0	203	197	246	304	550	589	437	5	75	0.22	43	15	43	25	104	73	98	3%	72	0%	0%	14	21%	64%	2.39	-11.0	-8	-18	-$2
12	3 TM *	351	42	13	47	3	247	240	325	420	745	760	657	10	77	0.49	38	17	45	29	127	117	128	7%	75	7%	49%	15	40%	40%	4.51	-0.6	46	115	$7
13	BAL	119	14	4	13	1	261	243	362	420	782	802	749	11	79	0.60	39	17	44	30	118	112	129	10%	76	3%	100%	19	47%	37%	5.03	3.6	53	133	$1
14	BAL	338	51	21	49	5	293	294	373	556	930	1109	856	11	78	0.53	35	19	46	32	116	188	130	18%	71	5%	100%	26	62%	35%	7.48	35.5	105	284	$18
15	BAL	294	42	15	40	1	218	252	289	422	711	623	765	7	77	0.33	34	20	46	23	101	129	132	14%	77	3%	50%	22	50%	36%	3.73	-6.0	49	132	$4
1st Half		159	22	6	23	1	233	242	301	384	685	773	641	7	75	0.31	37	23	40	27	110	99	135	13%	73	5%	50%	14	43%	43%	3.58	-4.7	19	51	$5
2nd Half		135	20	9	17	0	200	266	275	467	742	488	939	8	78	0.37	30	16	54	19	91	163	127	16%	80	0%	0%	8	63%	25%	3.87	-2.9	83	224	$4
16	Proj	255	35	12	34	2	241	256	321	448	769	736	792	9	77	0.43	35	18	47	27	108	134	128	14%	77	4%	80%				4.66	0.7	55	148	$8

BRANDON KRUSE

Pederson,Joc

Age: 24 Bats: L Pos: CF | Ht: 6' 1" Wt: 185
Health A | PT/Exp B | Consist B | LIMA Plan B | Rand Var +4 | MM 4105

This is a three-true-outcomes, Rob Deerish, risk-reward kind of guy (BB, K, or HR in 49% of PA). 20 HR by June's end, then things came to screeching halt. 2nd half H% should rebound which will help a bit, but a sub-70% ct% is always going to be a huge BA risk. Pitchers are on to him; he needs to adjust.

Yr	Tm	AB	R	HR	RBI	SB	BA	xBA	OBP	SLG	OPS	vL	vR	bb%	ct%	Eye	G	L	F	h%	HctX	PX	xPX	hr/f	Spd	SBO	SB%	#Wk	DOM	DIS	RC/G	RAR	BPV	BPX	R$
11																																			
12																																			
13	aa	439	73	20	52	28	260		350	456	806			12	72	0.49				32		142			105	28%	76%				5.48		59	148	$24
14	LA *	473	68	22	49	19	239	217	335	416	751	167	561	13	61	0.37	35	24	41	34	73	148	103	0%	111	23%	56%	5	20%	60%	4.34	7.5	23	62	$18
15	LA	480	67	26	54	4	210	225	346	417	763	691	784	16	65	0.54	42	16	42	26	106	152	148	20%	100	7%	36%	27	41%	37%	4.34	0.5	44	119	$7
1st Half		274	45	20	38	2	234	253	372	504	876	727	914	17	64	0.57	42	17	41	28	121	196	174	28%	108	8%	29%	14	57%	36%	5.75	11.3	82	222	$17
2nd Half		206	22	6	16	2	180	186	312	301	613	655	593	15	65	0.50	41	14	45	24	86	94	113	10%	95	7%	50%	13	23%	38%	2.76	-11.1	-4	-11	-$6
16	**Proj**	**451**	**63**	**23**	**50**	**6**	**230**	**219**	**348**	**424**	**772**	**741**	**781**	**14**	**65**	**0.47**	**42**	**15**	**43**	**30**	**100**	**143**	**137**	**18%**	**101**	**11%**	**38%**				**4.46**	**0.7**	**21**	**57**	**$10**

Pedroia,Dustin

Age: 32 Bats: R Pos: 2B | Ht: 5' 8" Wt: 165
Health D | PT/Exp A | Consist C | LIMA Plan A | Rand Var -2 | MM 2335

Came back too soon from hamstring injury, but did a lot in those 381 AB. First 10+ HR season since '12, but that was more hr/f, less HctX, PX/xPX. BA floor high, thanks to robust ct%; just don't count on too many counting stats. Should come to spring training healthy, but at 32, injuries have pretty much shut down running game.

Yr	Tm	AB	R	HR	RBI	SB	BA	xBA	OBP	SLG	OPS	vL	vR	bb%	ct%	Eye	G	L	F	h%	HctX	PX	xPX	hr/f	Spd	SBO	SB%	#Wk	DOM	DIS	RC/G	RAR	BPV	BPX	R$
11	BOS	635	102	21	91	26	307	288	387	474	861	1010	800	12	87	1.01	48	19	33	33	118	106	115	11%	122	15%	76%	27	70%	15%	6.80	38.6	94	209	$36
12	BOS	563	81	15	65	20	290	288	347	449	797	848	775	8	89	0.80	46	20	35	30	123	98	108	9%	108	17%	77%	26	65%	12%	5.56	22.2	86	215	$24
13	BOS	641	91	9	84	17	301	284	372	415	787	937	722	10	88	0.97	50	22	28	33	116	80	83	6%	124	10%	77%	26	65%	19%	5.67	34.4	77	193	$29
14	BOS	551	72	7	53	6	278	276	337	376	712	727	707	8	86	0.68	48	24	28	31	112	75	89	5%	96	7%	50%	24	54%	13%	4.37	15.4	53	143	$16
15	BOS	381	46	12	42	2	291	270	356	441	797	834	785	9	87	0.75	50	18	32	31	98	90	93	11%	118	3%	50%	19	58%	16%	5.56	13.7	74	200	$12
1st Half		281	34	9	33	1	306	268	367	452	819	895	797	9	86	0.71	50	19	31	33	96	88	92	12%	110	2%	50%	12	58%	17%	6.03	13.9	69	186	$18
2nd Half		100	12	3	9	1	250	269	324	410	734	693	750	10	87	0.85	53	14	33	26	106	93	94	10%	124	7%	50%	7	57%	14%	4.40	0.5	81	219	-$3
16	**Proj**	**507**	**66**	**12**	**54**	**7**	**281**	**275**	**348**	**414**	**762**	**800**	**747**	**9**	**87**	**0.80**	**50**	**19**	**31**	**30**	**108**	**83**	**92**	**9%**	**121**	**8%**	**62%**				**5.03**	**11.6**	**58**	**158**	**$19**

Pena,Brayan

Age: 34 Bats: B Pos: CA | Ht: 5' 9" Wt: 230
Health A | PT/Exp D | Consist B | LIMA Plan D | Rand Var 0 | MM 1021

Plan hadn't been for him to log 300+ AB; at 34, may never happen again, especially given struggles vs. LHP. Beats balls into ground, which is fine; they weren't clearing the fence, anyway. When it comes to end-game catchers, "at first, do no harm." Elite ct% sets high BA floor, which pretty much assures that.

Yr	Tm	AB	R	HR	RBI	SB	BA	xBA	OBP	SLG	OPS	vL	vR	bb%	ct%	Eye	G	L	F	h%	HctX	PX	xPX	hr/f	Spd	SBO	SB%	#Wk	DOM	DIS	RC/G	RAR	BPV	BPX	R$
11	KC	222	17	3	24	0	248	262	288	338	625	600	636	5	89	0.50	44	23	33	27	78	62	60	5%	41	0%	0%	25	44%	36%	3.28	-7.1	31	69	$1
12	KC	212	16	2	25	0	236	271	262	321	583	645	554	4	89	0.38	48	25	27	26	111	56	92	4%	49	2%	0%	27	33%	44%	2.79	-9.5	24	60	$0
13	DET	229	19	4	22	0	297	257	315	397	713	608	801	3	89	0.23	52	20	28	32	86	67	38	7%	61	3%	0%	25	40%	32%	4.36	4.2	33	83	$4
14	CIN	348	23	5	26	2	253	268	291	353	645	459	696	5	88	0.48	44	23	33	28	101	71	71	5%	61	6%	40%	26	42%	31%	3.43	-0.2	40	108	$3
15	CIN	333	17	0	18	2	273	258	334	324	659	551	700	8	90	0.85	51	22	27	30	81	41	56	0%	60	2%	100%	26	38%	31%	3.81	0.0	28	76	$3
1st Half		191	11	0	11	0	298	258	366	340	707	569	766	9	92	1.19	51	25	24	33	75	33	44	0%	65	0%	0%	13	38%	23%	4.48	3.7	32	86	$4
2nd Half		142	6	0	7	2	239	246	289	303	592	520	616	7	87	0.56	51	19	30	27	90	52	73	0%	58	6%	100%	13	38%	38%	3.01	-3.2	23	62	$1
16	**Proj**	**164**	**10**	**1**	**12**	**1**	**263**	**259**	**309**	**339**	**647**	**552**	**686**	**6**	**89**	**0.57**	**49**	**22**	**29**	**29**	**90**	**53**	**62**	**3%**	**59**	**3%**	**60%**				**3.59**	**-0.9**	**22**	**59**	**$3**

Pence,Hunter

Age: 33 Bats: R Pos: RF | Ht: 6' 4" Wt: 220
Health F | PT/Exp B | Consist B | LIMA Plan B+ | Rand Var -1 | MM 4435

So much for seven-year run of 640+ PA. Year bookended by broken forearm, oblique strain. In between, most skills as strong as ever. Exception was Spd; end of double-digit SB may be drawing nigh. Age, ct% slip cause for bit of pause, but with better health, no reason not to expect rebound.

Yr	Tm	AB	R	HR	RBI	SB	BA	xBA	OBP	SLG	OPS	vL	vR	bb%	ct%	Eye	G	L	F	h%	HctX	PX	xPX	hr/f	Spd	SBO	SB%	#Wk	DOM	DIS	RC/G	RAR	BPV	BPX	R$
11	2 NL	606	84	22	97	8	314	282	370	502	871	990	836	8	80	0.45	51	18	31	37	114	129	115	15%	129	6%	80%	27	63%	15%	6.93	29.3	79	176	$31
12	2 NL	617	87	24	104	5	253	254	319	425	743	731	748	8	76	0.39	51	17	32	29	101	110	96	16%	117	4%	71%	27	44%	37%	4.55	-10.8	48	120	$18
13	SF	629	91	27	99	22	283	280	339	483	822	976	769	8	82	0.45	47	17	36	31	119	128	112	15%	118	15%	88%	27	48%	15%	5.92	23.2	82	205	$34
14	SF	650	106	20	74	13	277	264	332	445	777	770	779	7	80	0.40	52	14	34	32	97	112	88	11%	163	11%	68%	27	59%	26%	5.11	18.8	75	203	$27
15	SF	207	30	9	40	4	275	279	327	478	806	570	861	7	77	0.33	54	17	29	32	119	135	117	20%	88	10%	80%	11	73%	9%	5.52	3.9	58	157	$8
1st Half		71	13	2	13	1	282	277	329	451	780	500	846	7	80	0.36	58	16	26	33	124	107	94	13%	104	6%	100%	5	60%	0%	5.35	1.1	53	143	$1
2nd Half		136	17	7	27	3	272	277	327	493	819	607	868	7	75	0.32	52	18	30	32	117	150	129	23%	76	13%	75%	6	83%	17%	5.60	3.1	60	162	$12
16	**Proj**	**519**	**78**	**20**	**85**	**11**	**278**	**274**	**332**	**469**	**801**	**730**	**822**	**7**	**79**	**0.37**	**52**	**16**	**31**	**32**	**113**	**122**	**107**	**16%**	**116**	**10%**	**79%**				**5.49**	**9.9**	**63**	**171**	**$25**

Pennington,Cliff

Age: 32 Bats: B Pos: 2B SS | Ht: 5' 10" Wt: 195
Health C | PT/Exp F | Consist C | LIMA Plan D | Rand Var +2 | MM 1301

Falling up, personified: Need for MI stopgap sprung him from also-ran to playoff team. Hope he enjoyed the ride, as he's not exactly kicking down doors to opportunity with his play. Even 2014's Spd proved to be mirage. As it was with TOR, so shall it be for you: desperation play only.

Yr	Tm	AB	R	HR	RBI	SB	BA	xBA	OBP	SLG	OPS	vL	vR	bb%	ct%	Eye	G	L	F	h%	HctX	PX	xPX	hr/f	Spd	SBO	SB%	#Wk	DOM	DIS	RC/G	RAR	BPV	BPX	R$
11	OAK	515	57	8	58	14	264	243	319	369	687	670	695	8	80	0.40	36	25	40	32	74	78	76	5%	84	16%	61%	26	38%	42%	3.94	-9.9	24	53	$14
12	OAK	418	50	6	28	15	215	233	278	311	589	420	646	8	78	0.39	41	23	37	26	62	67	63	5%	103	21%	71%	26	27%	54%	2.77	-18.2	16	40	$4
13	ARI	269	25	1	18	2	242	229	310	309	618	637	608	9	80	0.48	42	22	36	30	85	55	68	1%	96	3%	100%	25	40%	48%	3.24	-3.8	12	30	$0
14	ARI	177	21	2	10	6	254	229	340	350	690	797	649	10	80	0.56	42	21	37	31	83	64	91	4%	148	13%	86%	19	32%	42%	4.07	3.5	37	100	$3
15	2 TM	210	24	3	21	3	210	227	298	281	578	427	618	11	77	0.55	44	24	32	26	96	50	88	6%	68	5%	100%	26	27%	58%	2.79	-9.6	-7	-19	$0
1st Half		94	10	0	8	2	234	224	321	255	576	567	574	12	83	0.81	47	23	30	28	115	18	96	0%	90	6%	100%	14	21%	64%	2.91	-3.7	0	0	-$2
2nd Half		116	14	3	13	1	190	229	278	302	580	395	667	11	72	0.42	41	25	34	24	81	80	81	11%	59	3%	100%	12	33%	50%	2.67	-5.7	-9	-24	$1
16	**Proj**	**188**	**21**	**2**	**16**	**4**	**227**	**230**	**309**	**311**	**620**	**581**	**634**	**10**	**78**	**0.52**	**42**	**23**	**35**	**28**	**88**	**57**	**83**	**5%**	**94**	**8%**	**87%**				**3.22**	**-5.7**	**6**	**17**	**$3**

Peralta,David

Age: 28 Bats: L Pos: LF | Ht: 6' 2" Wt: 215
Health A | PT/Exp D | Consist F | LIMA Plan B+ | Rand Var -2 | MM 4345

Very nice encore to 2014 debut. OK, so 2nd half hit rate won't last, but HctX, PX say it wasn't all luck. If he could reverse GB tilt, 20 HR is in reach. Probably needs platoon partner, but did rank 10th in OPS vs. RHP among hitters with 400+ PA. Spd surfaced in 2H, especially in September (4 SB). Solid investment.

Yr	Tm	AB	R	HR	RBI	SB	BA	xBA	OBP	SLG	OPS	vL	vR	bb%	ct%	Eye	G	L	F	h%	HctX	PX	xPX	hr/f	Spd	SBO	SB%	#Wk	DOM	DIS	RC/G	RAR	BPV	BPX	R$
11																																			
12																																			
13																																			
14	ARI *	531	64	13	69	7	271	282	309	430	739	510	848	5	84	0.34	48	21	31	30	110	104	90	10%	109	8%	71%	17	59%	18%	4.61	12.6	64	173	$17
15	ARI	462	61	17	78	9	312	286	371	522	893	686	936	9	77	0.41	52	21	27	38	119	133	115	18%	121	10%	69%	26	46%	15%	7.08	29.8	69	186	$24
1st Half		223	32	7	36	4	269	281	343	462	804	755	816	10	77	0.49	49	21	30	32	106	131	123	13%	92	10%	67%	14	50%	14%	5.44	5.7	63	170	$17
2nd Half		239	29	10	42	5	351	291	399	577	977	611	1047	7	77	0.34	55	22	24	43	131	136	108	23%	146	9%	71%	12	42%	17%	8.95	27.0	76	205	$31
16	**Proj**	**521**	**66**	**18**	**80**	**11**	**299**	**286**	**349**	**496**	**844**	**591**	**906**	**7**	**80**	**0.37**	**51**	**21**	**28**	**35**	**116**	**121**	**105**	**15%**	**119**	**11%**	**69%**				**6.17**	**23.4**	**67**	**182**	**$27**

Peralta,Jhonny

Age: 34 Bats: R Pos: SS | Ht: 6' 2" Wt: 215
Health A | PT/Exp A | Consist B | LIMA Plan B+ | Rand Var 0 | MM 2025

In 1H, appeared on his way to full repeat or better. 2H power outage a concern, but HctX, xPX say, "Chill." Still, he's 34 and enduring grind of near-everyday SS play. GB% creeping up, too, so bet against another 20+ HR season. Each year adds bit of risk. Bow out at $15? We won't stop you.

Yr	Tm	AB	R	HR	RBI	SB	BA	xBA	OBP	SLG	OPS	vL	vR	bb%	ct%	Eye	G	L	F	h%	HctX	PX	xPX	hr/f	Spd	SBO	SB%	#Wk	DOM	DIS	RC/G	RAR	BPV	BPX	R$
11	DET	525	68	21	86	0	299	262	345	478	824	765	848	7	82	0.42	36	20	44	33	100	114	116	11%	94	1%	0%	27	48%	30%	5.97	21.2	63	140	$22
12	DET	531	58	13	63	1	239	257	305	384	689	692	688	8	80	0.47	41	22	37	28	107	98	124	8%	82	2%	33%	27	56%	33%	3.85	-4.0	43	108	$7
13	DET	409	50	11	55	3	303	263	358	457	815	964	750	8	76	0.36	39	25	36	38	109	119	136	10%	76	5%	50%	21	52%	24%	5.87	26.7	40	100	$16
14	STL	560	61	21	75	3	263	278	336	443	779	879	751	9	80	0.52	39	23	38	30	117	131	132	12%	69	3%	60%	26	62%	15%	5.04	28.4	66	178	$17
15	STL	579	64	17	71	1	275	264	334	411	745	737	748	8	81	0.45	44	25	31	31	113	87	103	11%	81	3%	20%	27	33%	22%	4.68	15.1	35	95	$16
1st Half		303	34	11	42	1	297	282	350	469	819	831	815	8	81	0.44	43	26	31	34	117	113	100	14%	76	2%	50%	14	43%	7%	5.94	15.5	53	143	$22
2nd Half		276	30	6	29	0	250	245	317	348	665	666	664	8	81	0.46	45	23	31	29	109	60	107	8%	91	4%	0%	13	23%	38%	3.50	-4.8	18	49	$9
16	**Proj**	**546**	**61**	**15**	**69**	**2**	**272**	**260**	**335**	**411**	**747**	**779**	**734**	**8**	**80**	**0.45**	**42**	**24**	**34**	**32**	**112**	**93**	**118**	**10%**	**80**	**3%**	**34%**				**4.69**	**9.5**	**24**	**65**	**$17**

KRISTOPHER OLSON

Peraza,Jose

Age: 22 Bats: R Pos: 2B	Health A	LIMA Plan D+	
Ht: 6' 0" Wt: 165	PT/Exp F	Rand Var -2	
	Consist C	MM 0513	

0-1-.182 in 22 AB at LA. Hamstring injury ended his debut shortly after it began. Elite ct% and plenty of speed, but low HctX, PX hurt BA, and shortage of walks makes getting on base a challenge. Still an enticing SB source and exciting keeper, but low OBP caps short-term upside.

Yr	Tm	AB	R	HR	RBI	SB	BA	xBA	OBP	SLG	OPS	vL	vR	bb%	ct%	Eye	G	L	F	h%	HctX	PX	xPX	hr/f	Spd	SBO	SB%	#Wk	DOM	DIS	RC/G	RAR	BPV	BPX	R$
11																																			
12																																			
13																																			
14	aa	185	30	1	14	21	315		336	391	727			3	91	0.35				34		49			129	55%	71%				4.61		50	135	$13
15	LA *	503	54	3	35	29	257	231	278	325	603	779	125	3	90	0.29	37	21	42	28	38	39	37	0%	146	30%	79%	5	40%	20%	3.16	-15.0	41	111	$16
1st Half		308	30	3	27	18	256	237	278	318	595			3	89	0.26				28		34			148	29%	80%				3.10		34	92	$19
2nd Half		195	24	1	7	12	257	240	279	336	615	779	125	3	91	0.33	37	21	42	28	38	47	37	0%	147	34%	78%	5	40%	20%	3.25	-5.6	53	143	$12
16	**Proj**	**339**	**45**	**1**	**22**	**20**	**256**	**244**	**278**	**321**	**599**	**599**	**599**	**3**	**88**	**0.26**	**43**	**22**	**35**	**29**		**40**		**1%**	**169**	**32%**	**75%**				**3.06**	**-11.8**	**38**	**102**	**$10**

Perez,Carlos

Age: 25 Bats: R Pos: CA	Health A	LIMA Plan D+	
Ht: 6' 0" Wt: 195	PT/Exp D	Rand Var -2	
	Consist B	MM 1413	

4-21-.250 in 260 AB at LAA. Earned call-up with hot start in hitter-friendly PCL, hit walk-off HR in debut, but production was predictably modest after that. Struggles vs LHP exacerbated by 22% hit rate in MLB. Strong defense works in his favor, but lack of power, on-base skills leave little chance he'll make impact with his bat.

Yr	Tm	AB	R	HR	RBI	SB	BA	xBA	OBP	SLG	OPS	vL	vR	bb%	ct%	Eye	G	L	F	h%	HctX	PX	xPX	hr/f	Spd	SBO	SB%	#Wk	DOM	DIS	RC/G	RAR	BPV	BPX	R$
11																																			
12																																			
13	a/a	317	27	2	29	1	236		287	308	595			7	82	0.39				28		58			83	2%	41%				2.92		14	35	$0
14	aaa	301	23	4	24	2	213		263	311	574			6	79	0.32				26		74			96	3%	100%				2.68		18	49	-$1
15	LAA *	332	27	5	29	3	258	243	307	364	671	461	713	7	83	0.41	42	20	38	30	76	75	64	5%	95	3%	100%	23	26%	52%	3.89	1.4	34	92	$4
1st Half		181	10	3	21	1	258	237	287	369	656	401	664	4	83	0.24	38	20	43	30	86	77	91	5%	89	2%	100%	10	20%	60%	3.66	-0.6	30	81	$4
2nd Half		151	17	2	8	2	258	245	327	358	685	506	746	10	82	0.59	45	20	35	30	69	73	45	5%	108	5%	100%	13	31%	46%	4.13	1.5	40	108	$5
16	**Proj**	**356**	**30**	**5**	**29**	**3**	**242**	**237**	**297**	**344**	**641**	**467**	**705**	**8**	**81**	**0.43**	**42**	**20**	**38**	**29**	**76**	**71**	**63**	**5%**	**108**	**3%**	**94%**				**3.50**	**-3.0**	**16**	**43**	**$5**

Perez,Eury

Age: 26 Bats: R Pos: LF	Health B	LIMA Plan D	
Ht: 6' 0" Wt: 190	PT/Exp D	Rand Var 0	
	Consist A	MM 0431	

0-5-.269 with 3 SB in 119 AB at ATL. Ran wild in AAA, but SBO fell to 11% in majors before broken hand ended season in August. Batting in front of pitcher in about half his starts may have played role in lack of green light. Jump in bb% step in right direction, but OBP still too low to expect him to lock down regular role.

Yr	Tm	AB	R	HR	RBI	SB	BA	xBA	OBP	SLG	OPS	vL	vR	bb%	ct%	Eye	G	L	F	h%	HctX	PX	xPX	hr/f	Spd	SBO	SB%	#Wk	DOM	DIS	RC/G	RAR	BPV	BPX	R$
11																																			
12	WAS *	515	48	0	33	41	285	257	301	326	627	1000	0	2	84	0.14	100	0	0	34	73	32	-11	0%	116	41%	71%	5	0%	40%	3.40	-19.3	2	5	$21
13	WAS *	411	43	5	21	18	260	268	277	355	632	333	0	2	82	0.13	60	20	20	31	0	64	-15	0%	145	30%	67%	7	0%	86%	3.24	-10.4	30	75	$11
14	NYY *	222	24	1	8	16	268	214	298	340	638	2000	222	4	81	0.23	67	0	33	33	50	61	-14	0%	129	35%	82%	2	0%	50%	3.66	-1.0	22	59	$7
15	ATL *	355	40	2	23	27	265	256	314	319	633	687	622	7	80	0.37	62	21	17	33	79	40	10	0%	109	35%	72%	11	18%	55%	3.46	-9.0	1	3	$14
1st Half		265	30	2	18	24	265	243	318	327	645	1100	583	7	80	0.39	55	21	24	33	86	43	2	0%	122	41%	72%	4	0%	75%	3.57	-6.7	8	22	$19
2nd Half		90	10	0	5	3	263	252	302	296	598	567	642	5	81	0.29	65	22	13	32	76	30	14	0%	91	16%	75%	7	29%	43%	3.12	-3.4	-13	-35	$0
16	**Proj**	**100**	**11**	**1**	**5**	**6**	**257**	**262**	**312**	**325**	**637**	**780**	**610**	**4**	**81**	**0.25**	**61**	**21**	**18**	**31**	**80**	**48**	**9**	**5%**	**108**	**32%**	**75%**				**3.25**	**-3.9**	**8**	**21**	**$4**

Perez,Hernan

Age: 25 Bats: R Pos: 3B	Health A	LIMA Plan D	
Ht: 6' 1" Wt: 185	PT/Exp C	Rand Var +1	
	Consist A	MM 1411	

Was given opportunity for consistent AB, but free swinging approach didn't work out. Incredibly, went 198 straight PA without drawing unintentional BB. Could stick around as utility IF, but speed is all he has going for him offensively, and inability to get on base will prevent him from putting it to use.

Yr	Tm	AB	R	HR	RBI	SB	BA	xBA	OBP	SLG	OPS	vL	vR	bb%	ct%	Eye	G	L	F	h%	HctX	PX	xPX	hr/f	Spd	SBO	SB%	#Wk	DOM	DIS	RC/G	RAR	BPV	BPX	R$
11																																			
12	DET	2	1	0	0	0	500	277	500	500	1000	0	2000	0	100	0.00	100	0	0	50	0	0	-11	0%	118	0%	0%	2	0%	0%	12.75	0.3	37	93	-$2
13	DET *	495	53	3	37	25	266	254	289	356	646	501	388	3	85	0.22	47	20	33	31	72	67	54	0%	132	29%	77%	12	8%	67%	3.59	-5.8	43	108	$17
14	DET *	552	56	5	42	17	258	207	297	363	659	0	833	5	87	0.43	50	0	50	29	189	72	-14	0%	144	18%	72%	4	25%	75%	3.66	-0.8	63	170	$14
15	2 TM	263	14	1	21	5	243	233	257	327	584	635	552	2	78	0.08	43	22	34	31	104	66	99	1%	104	12%	83%	26	27%	54%	2.87	-14.1	0	0	$1
1st Half		92	6	0	2	1	250	213	274	326	600	648	574	3	75	0.13	43	19	38	33	126	63	143	0%	128	10%	50%	14	14%	64%	2.93	-4.7	-3	-8	-$4
2nd Half		171	8	1	19	4	240	244	247	327	575	629	539	1	79	0.06	44	24	33	30	91	68	77	2%	93	13%	100%	12	42%	42%	2.84	-9.1	3	8	$4
16	**Proj**	**203**	**16**	**0**	**15**	**6**	**253**	**242**	**274**	**334**	**608**	**655**	**574**	**3**	**82**	**0.18**	**45**	**21**	**34**	**31**	**92**	**60**	**84**	**1%**	**125**	**17%**	**75%**				**3.15**	**-8.9**	**16**	**44**	**$4**

Perez,Roberto

Age: 27 Bats: R Pos: CA	Health A	LIMA Plan D	
Ht: 5' 11" Wt: 225	PT/Exp D	Rand Var 0	
	Consist C	MM 3103	

PRO: Proved that 2014 power surge wasn't a fluke, and continued willingness to take a walk. CON: Too many GB to be elite power threat, HctX still well below average, and ct% remains a major problem. Almost certain to be a BA drag, but the plus power could make him useful if role ever expands, particularly in OBP leagues.

Yr	Tm	AB	R	HR	RBI	SB	BA	xBA	OBP	SLG	OPS	vL	vR	bb%	ct%	Eye	G	L	F	h%	HctX	PX	xPX	hr/f	Spd	SBO	SB%	#Wk	DOM	DIS	RC/G	RAR	BPV	BPX	R$
11																																			
12	aa	283	28	1	28	0	192		298	265	563			13	73	0.57				26		63			92	1%	0%				2.45		0	0	-$4
13	a/a	280	20	1	26	1	166		271	234	505			13	65	0.41				25		72			80	4%	25%				1.88		-31	-78	-$7
14	CLE *	259	31	7	36	1	257	217	324	397	721	397	786	9	66	0.29	45	17	38	36	85	125	123	5%	77	1%	100%	13	31%	62%	4.42	8.3	7	19	$5
15	CLE	184	30	7	21	0	228	237	348	402	751	841	715	15	65	0.52	53	20	27	31	88	134	120	21%	90	0%	0%	26	38%	50%	4.59	4.7	27	73	$1
1st Half		119	19	5	15	0	218	235	340	412	752	753	747	16	63	0.52	55	17	29	30	90	151	137	23%	95	0%	0%	14	43%	43%	4.64	3.1	36	97	$2
2nd Half		65	11	2	6	0	246	242	364	385	748	1009	657	13	69	0.50	51	24	24	33	84	104	90	18%	76	0%	0%	12	33%	58%	4.51	1.4	12	32	$0
16	**Proj**	**245**	**33**	**8**	**27**	**0**	**234**	**230**	**335**	**389**	**724**	**694**	**734**	**13**	**67**	**0.43**	**50**	**20**	**31**	**32**	**86**	**120**	**115**	**16%**	**83**	**1%**	**51%**				**4.25**	**3.5**	**6**	**16**	**$5**

Perez,Salvador

Age: 26 Bats: R Pos: CA	Health B	LIMA Plan B+	
Ht: 6' 3" Wt: 240	PT/Exp A	Rand Var +1	
	Consist B	MM 2235	

Heavy workload helped him pile up counting stats, but is he wearing down? Downward spiral vs LHP is alarming, ct% is no longer elite; both reached new lows in 2H. Most conerning is HR spike not supported by drops in HctX and xPX; it was all hr/f, which could regress. May not be as safe of an investment as he seems.

Yr	Tm	AB	R	HR	RBI	SB	BA	xBA	OBP	SLG	OPS	vL	vR	bb%	ct%	Eye	G	L	F	h%	HctX	PX	xPX	hr/f	Spd	SBO	SB%	#Wk	DOM	DIS	RC/G	RAR	BPV	BPX	R$
11	KC *	482	50	10	61	0	280	296	307	401	708	1285	711	4	88	0.33	42	29	29	30	106	79	86	8%	95	1%	0%	8	50%	38%	4.31	1.4	53	118	$12
12	KC *	339	46	11	44	0	301	291	327	450	778	1021	711	4	90	0.41	44	24	32	31	118	87	116	13%	79	0%	0%	16	69%	25%	5.37	11.5	65	163	$12
13	KC	496	48	13	79	0	292	272	323	433	757	867	714	4	87	0.33	47	21	33	31	108	88	96	9%	82	0%	0%	25	52%	28%	5.02	17.8	54	135	$17
14	KC	578	57	17	70	1	260	265	289	403	692	632	710	4	85	0.26	39	21	40	28	115	95	106	9%	70	1%	100%	27	52%	15%	3.99	11.1	48	130	$14
15	KC	531	52	21	70	1	260	268	280	426	706	560	775	2	85	0.16	42	21	37	27	89	99	88	12%	61	1%	100%	27	48%	22%	4.08	5.2	43	116	$13
1st Half		278	26	13	34	1	263	277	275	446	721	612	768	2	86	0.13	43	21	36	27	87	105	85	15%	74	2%	100%	14	50%	14%	4.27	3.9	54	146	$15
2nd Half		253	26	8	36	0	257	256	286	403	689	510	782	3	83	0.19	41	20	39	28	92	92	92	10%	55	0%	0%	13	46%	31%	3.87	0.7	32	86	$11
16	**Proj**	**515**	**52**	**17**	**69**	**1**	**267**	**269**	**293**	**419**	**712**	**656**	**735**	**3**	**85**	**0.23**	**42**	**21**	**37**	**29**	**101**	**91**	**96**	**10%**	**69**	**1%**	**92%**				**4.24**	**6.9**	**36**	**98**	**$16**

Peterson,Jace

Age: 26 Bats: L Pos: 2B	Health A	LIMA Plan D+	
Ht: 6' 0" Wt: 210	PT/Exp D	Rand Var 0	
	Consist A	MM 1215	

Has shown ability to take a walk, which, in theory, should allow him to take advantage of speed. But subpar ct%, lack of power have negated the bb% and kept BA/OBP down, and when he does get a chance to run, his success rate (SB%) is horrible. BPI are uninspiring and stagnant, so... DN: 250 AB

Yr	Tm	AB	R	HR	RBI	SB	BA	xBA	OBP	SLG	OPS	vL	vR	bb%	ct%	Eye	G	L	F	h%	HctX	PX	xPX	hr/f	Spd	SBO	SB%	#Wk	DOM	DIS	RC/G	RAR	BPV	BPX	R$
11																																			
12																																			
13																																			
14	SD *	375	40	2	32	13	227	241	298	316	614	607	168	9	76	0.42	63	14	23	29	80	73	57	0%	94	24%	55%	11	0%	82%	2.90	-5.7	11	30	$5
15	ATL	528	55	6	52	12	239	238	314	335	649	510	682	10	77	0.47	46	22	32	30	89	68	78	5%	106	15%	55%	27	22%	48%	3.35	-13.2	17	46	$8
1st Half		279	31	3	35	8	254	231	332	355	687	513	728	10	78	0.52	43	20	37	32	92	70	86	4%	110	19%	50%	14	21%	43%	3.73	-4.2	24	65	$13
2nd Half		249	24	3	17	4	221	245	292	313	605	508	629	9	76	0.41	50	24	26	28	85	65	68	6%	103	9%	67%	13	23%	54%	2.94	-9.9	8	22	$3
16	**Proj**	**444**	**46**	**3**	**40**	**10**	**232**	**236**	**309**	**317**	**626**	**543**	**649**	**9**	**77**	**0.44**	**53**	**19**	**27**	**30**	**85**	**63**	**68**	**3%**	**103**	**14%**	**60%**				**3.10**	**-15.3**	**8**	**20**	**$7**

BRIAN RUDD

Peterson,Shane

Age: 28 Bats: L Pos: LF CF | Ht: 6' 0" Wt: 210
Health A | PT/Exp C | Consist B | LIMA Plan D | Rand Var -2 | MM 1211

2-16-.259 in 201 AB at MIL. Early success at AAA (.320 BA, 7 HR) yielded prolonged shot in bigs, but he failed to take advantage. Dismal ct% looms over skill set, putting BA at risk, while MLB PX (67) only adds fuel to the fire. A quick glance down the BPV column tells you all need to know.

Yr Tm	AB	R	HR	RBI	SB	BA	xBA	OBP	SLG	OPS	vL	vR	bb%	ct%	Eye	G	L	F	h%	HctX	PX	xPX	hr/f	Spd	SBO	SB%	#Wk	DOM	DIS	RC/G	RAR	BPV	BPX	R$
11 a/a	394	45	6	41	9	226		294	334	628			9	78	0.44				28		80			102	12%	80%				3.27		26	58	$4
12 a/a	288	46	6	34	9	270		379	405	784			15	68	0.55				38		104			110	16%	57%				5.13		21	53	$9
13 OAK *	470	48	7	54	12	196	254	279	289	568	667	200	10	67	0.35	25	50	25	27	139	80	235	0%	79	12%	83%	1	0%	100%	2.61	-22.2	-19	-48	$3
14 aaa	543	64	6	57	7	238		295	346	641			7	69	0.26				33		98			97	7%	74%				3.41		1	3	$8
15 MIL *	373	39	7	34	0	257	250	315	379	693	641	686	8	71	0.30	52	27	21	34	94	86	88	6%	110	2%	0%	19	37%	47%	3.98	-3.5	5	14	$5
1st Half	241	27	5	21	0	256	266	307	383	690	1394	452	7	69	0.23	56	33	11	35	101	94	62	0%	116	4%	0%	6	33%	67%	3.86	-3.9	0	0	$7
2nd Half	132	12	2	13	0	258	250	327	371	698	228	806	10	77	0.45	51	24	25	32	96	75	100	8%	104	0%	0%	13	38%	38%	4.19	-0.8	18	49	$1
16 Proj	**191**	**21**	**2**	**19**	**2**	**242**	**245**	**309**	**330**	**640**	**664**	**634**	**9**	**71**	**0.34**	**53**	**27**	**20**	**33**	**98**	**70**	**85**	**6%**	**95**	**5%**	**68%**				**3.44**	**-6.4**	**-12**	**-33**	**$1**

Pham,Thomas

Age: 28 Bats: R Pos: CF | Ht: 6' 1" Wt: 175
Health C | PT/Exp D | Consist B | LIMA Plan D | Rand Var -1 | MM 2421

5-18-.268 with 2 SB in 153 AB at STL. Career minor leaguer emerged with big September (.322 BA, 4 HR). Batting eye, xBA gains drove improved BA, though excellent Spd hit a red light in majors. Hasn't posted BPIs like this before and comes with injury risk, so while gains are encouraging, let's see him do it again.

Yr Tm	AB	R	HR	RBI	SB	BA	xBA	OBP	SLG	OPS	vL	vR	bb%	ct%	Eye	G	L	F	h%	HctX	PX	xPX	hr/f	Spd	SBO	SB%	#Wk	DOM	DIS	RC/G	RAR	BPV	BPX	R$
11 aa	142	20	3	10	2	232		291	377	669			8	68	0.27				32		120			115	17%	35%				3.32		21	47	$0
12 aa	39	2	1	2	0	125		187	221	408			7	46	0.14				25		116			95	0%	0%				1.21		-79	-198	-$3
13 a/a	269	24	5	30	6	234		287	357	644			7	71	0.25				31		90			129	17%	55%				3.25		10	25	$3
14 STL *	348	43	7	30	14	259	225	309	376	685	0	0	7	72	0.26	44	20	36	34	0	91	-14	0%	149	18%	85%	4	0%	100%	4.10	2.7	20	54	$11
15 STL *	324	48	9	45	8	265	261	335	431	766	783	833	10	74	0.40	51	21	27	33	124	111	120	16%	128	9%	100%	12	50%	33%	5.17	8.0	44	119	$11
1st Half	91	13	4	18	5	271	264	322	507	829	0	1000	7	72	0.27	60	0	40	33	159	168	209	25%	107	27%	100%	2	100%	0%	6.06	4.3	72	195	$4
2nd Half	233	35	5	28	3	263	253	340	401	741	783	815	10	75	0.46	50	23	26	33	121	89	111	15%	142	4%	100%	10	40%	40%	4.80	2.6	35	95	$13
16 Proj	**161**	**21**	**3**	**19**	**4**	**257**	**252**	**313**	**399**	**713**	**697**	**716**	**8**	**72**	**0.31**	**50**	**23**	**26**	**33**	**109**	**100**	**100**	**11%**	**132**	**12%**	**79%**				**4.34**	**-0.3**	**25**	**68**	**$5**

Phegley,Joshua

Age: 28 Bats: R Pos: CA | Ht: 5' 10" Wt: 225
Health A | PT/Exp D | Consist B | LIMA Plan D+ | Rand Var +1 | MM 4123

A tale of two halves, as 1H BPV was studly, then plate approach collapsed down the stretch. PX/xPX, healthy FB% all suggest he's a legit power threat, but that steady ct% leak is ominous. Late-season concussion further clouds outlook, but HR upside makes him worth a late dart throw in deep leagues.

Yr Tm	AB	R	HR	RBI	SB	BA	xBA	OBP	SLG	OPS	vL	vR	bb%	ct%	Eye	G	L	F	h%	HctX	PX	xPX	hr/f	Spd	SBO	SB%	#Wk	DOM	DIS	RC/G	RAR	BPV	BPX	R$
11 a/a	443	43	9	46	1	217		263	332	595			6	80	0.31				25		84			89	3%	27%				2.78		26	58	$1
12 aaa	394	35	6	41	3	245		280	347	627			5	83	0.28				28		71			82	3%	100%				3.32		23	58	$4
13 CHW*	435	44	17	54	3	242	257	272	416	688	668	479	4	80	0.21	39	19	41	27	65	115	72	6%	68	5%	71%	14	21%	57%	3.79	0.9	43	108	$9
14 CHW*	456	48	19	55	0	214	271	249	405	654	1000	622	4	78	0.21	30	26	44	23	163	134	207	25%	67	2%	0%	5	40%	40%	3.23	-1.2	50	135	$5
15 OAK	225	27	9	34	0	249	265	300	449	749	788	709	6	77	0.27	37	21	43	28	101	136	120	12%	69	0%	0%	23	39%	48%	4.46	4.8	53	143	$4
1st Half	112	10	5	17	0	268	292	320	500	820	900	734	7	82	0.40	33	23	44	29	109	147	135	12%	75	0%	0%	13	46%	46%	5.51	5.6	84	227	$3
2nd Half	113	17	4	17	0	230	238	281	398	679	675	683	5	73	0.19	40	18	41	28	94	123	103	12%	65	0%	0%	10	30%	50%	3.55	-0.8	20	54	$4
16 Proj	**266**	**30**	**11**	**36**	**0**	**236**	**260**	**279**	**427**	**705**	**807**	**638**	**5**	**78**	**0.24**	**38**	**20**	**42**	**26**	**86**	**126**	**99**	**13%**	**73**	**1%**	**58%**				**3.90**	**0.9**	**41**	**110**	**$6**

Phillips,Brandon

Age: 35 Bats: R Pos: 2B | Ht: 6' 0" Wt: 200
Health B | PT/Exp A | Consist B | LIMA Plan B | Rand Var -2 | MM 1235

R$ decline fit well with "twilight of career" narrative… and then this. Suddenly became untouchable on basepaths, though SB spikes in mid-30s rarely stick. PX continued its descent, but BA gains have staying power given ct%, LD% gains. Reliability grades point to another strong year, but don't expect a repeat.

Yr Tm	AB	R	HR	RBI	SB	BA	xBA	OBP	SLG	OPS	vL	vR	bb%	ct%	Eye	G	L	F	h%	HctX	PX	xPX	hr/f	Spd	SBO	SB%	#Wk	DOM	DIS	RC/G	RAR	BPV	BPX	R$
11 CIN	610	94	18	82	14	300	282	353	457	810	851	798	7	86	0.52	45	20	35	33	119	104	112	10%	94	14%	61%	27	67%	11%	5.59	14.9	71	158	$28
12 CIN	580	86	18	77	15	281	277	321	429	750	741	754	5	86	0.35	47	21	32	30	99	90	79	11%	92	12%	88%	27	52%	19%	4.87	8.5	56	140	$23
13 CIN	606	80	18	103	5	261	258	310	396	706	746	689	6	84	0.40	46	19	34	29	99	85	92	10%	95	5%	63%	26	58%	23%	4.13	8.2	46	115	$19
14 CIN	462	44	8	51	2	266	258	306	372	678	594	704	5	84	0.31	44	22	34	30	104	79	79	6%	73	4%	40%	22	32%	32%	3.81	5.5	32	86	$10
15 CIN	588	69	12	70	23	294	272	328	395	723	710	727	4	88	0.40	45	25	30	32	96	58	66	8%	95	16%	88%	27	33%	37%	4.78	10.0	39	105	$27
1st Half	269	33	5	31	11	279	266	316	375	691	740	675	5	88	0.45	41	25	34	30	101	57	71	6%	98	16%	92%	14	36%	57%	4.35	1.0	41	111	$21
2nd Half	319	36	7	39	12	307	278	338	411	749	684	770	4	88	0.35	48	25	27	33	92	59	62	9%	90	15%	86%	13	31%	15%	5.17	8.2	38	103	$33
16 Proj	**559**	**66**	**12**	**71**	**14**	**277**	**267**	**316**	**390**	**706**	**686**	**713**	**5**	**86**	**0.38**	**45**	**23**	**32**	**30**	**100**	**69**	**76**	**8%**	**90**	**12%**	**76%**				**4.29**	**1.1**	**39**	**107**	**$22**

Pierzynski,A.J.

Age: 39 Bats: L Pos: CA | Ht: 6' 3" Wt: 235
Health A | PT/Exp C | Consist C | LIMA Plan D+ | Rand Var 0 | MM 1033

Vintage ct% returned, and when coupled with LD% spike, the .300 BA was well deserved. Single-digit HR total likely here to stay given concurrent FB%, xPX declines. Comes with little upside at this point, but that's okay; he remains a second catcher who won't hurt you.

Yr Tm	AB	R	HR	RBI	SB	BA	xBA	OBP	SLG	OPS	vL	vR	bb%	ct%	Eye	G	L	F	h%	HctX	PX	xPX	hr/f	Spd	SBO	SB%	#Wk	DOM	DIS	RC/G	RAR	BPV	BPX	R$
11 CHW	464	38	8	48	0	287	285	323	405	728	808	711	5	93	0.70	51	21	29	30	104	78	72	6%	64	0%	0%	25	52%	8%	4.64	3.4	65	144	$10
12 CHW	479	68	27	77	0	278	289	326	501	827	673	874	6	84	0.36	42	22	36	28	105	125	104	19%	86	0%	0%	27	56%	11%	5.62	18.0	74	185	$18
13 TEX	503	48	17	70	1	272	273	297	425	722	718	724	2	85	0.14	42	22	35	29	107	97	101	11%	63	2%	50%	26	50%	27%	4.26	8.1	42	105	$14
14 2 TM	338	25	5	37	0	251	242	288	337	625	490	677	4	84	0.26	46	21	32	29	97	60	91	5%	69	1%	0%	25	24%	44%	3.19	-2.6	15	41	$4
15 ATL	407	38	9	49	0	300	293	339	430	769	655	799	4	91	0.51	47	25	29	31	104	79	75	8%	69	2%	0%	26	46%	8%	5.07	14.1	58	157	$12
1st Half	202	24	5	27	0	267	289	304	416	720	621	740	4	90	0.45	48	21	31	28	122	90	89	9%	75	2%	0%	14	64%	14%	4.22	2.6	65	176	$11
2nd Half	205	14	4	22	0	332	302	374	444	818	678	863	5	92	0.59	45	29	26	35	86	69	62	8%	65	2%	0%	12	25%	0%	6.02	12.1	53	143	$13
16 Proj	**336**	**30**	**7**	**40**	**0**	**270**	**274**	**309**	**386**	**694**	**602**	**724**	**4**	**88**	**0.36**	**46**	**24**	**31**	**29**	**101**	**72**	**83**	**7%**	**68**	**2%**	**8%**				**3.98**	**1.9**	**30**	**82**	**$8**

Pillar,Kevin

Age: 27 Bats: R Pos: CF | Ht: 6' 0" Wt: 205
Health A | PT/Exp B | Consist B | LIMA Plan B+ | Rand Var -1 | MM 2435

Impressive breakout. Ct% growth, gains vs. RHP give him staying power, though hard-hit metrics (xPX, HctX) question HR upside. Runs frequently with success, so while AB spike suggests 2015 was his ceiling, all-around production should stick around.

Yr Tm	AB	R	HR	RBI	SB	BA	xBA	OBP	SLG	OPS	vL	vR	bb%	ct%	Eye	G	L	F	h%	HctX	PX	xPX	hr/f	Spd	SBO	SB%	#Wk	DOM	DIS	RC/G	RAR	BPV	BPX	R$
11																																		
12																																		
13 TOR *	607	67	10	56	17	259	237	291	391	682	680	534	4	82	0.25	36	17	47	30	58	96	55	9%	108	26%	52%	8	25%	50%	3.60	-11.6	47	118	$17
14 TOR *	521	64	11	54	22	285	285	312	445	757	783	631	4	84	0.24	51	16	33	32	98	122	82	7%	101	29%	72%	12	17%	42%	4.82	13.9	72	195	$23
15 TOR	586	76	12	56	25	278	261	314	399	713	684	723	5	85	0.33	41	22	37	31	93	78	72	7%	106	20%	86%	27	33%	19%	4.51	0.0	47	127	$24
1st Half	311	45	7	36	12	283	256	312	412	724	776	707	4	84	0.25	39	22	39	32	102	84	92	7%	103	18%	86%	14	36%	29%	4.66	2.2	42	114	$28
2nd Half	275	31	5	20	13	273	266	316	385	702	589	741	5	88	0.44	44	22	35	30	83	71	52	6%	108	21%	87%	13	31%	8%	4.33	-0.6	52	141	$21
16 Proj	**436**	**53**	**9**	**41**	**18**	**277**	**266**	**312**	**418**	**730**	**760**	**717**	**4**	**85**	**0.29**	**44**	**19**	**37**	**31**	**88**	**94**	**71**	**7%**	**107**	**24%**	**75%**				**4.49**	**1.0**	**57**	**154**	**$19**

Pirela,Jose

Age: 26 Bats: R Pos: 2B | Ht: 5' 10" Wt: 191
Health B | PT/Exp C | Consist A | LIMA Plan D | Rand Var 0 | MM 1321

1-5-.230 in 74 AB at NYY. Held .300+ BA each of last two seasons at AAA, but looked overwhelmed (0.13 Eye, .236 xBA) by MLB pitching. PX continues to head south, and mixed results on basepaths offer little hope for SB. Relevance hinges on ct% carrying over from minors, which hasn't happened yet.

Yr Tm	AB	R	HR	RBI	SB	BA	xBA	OBP	SLG	OPS	vL	vR	bb%	ct%	Eye	G	L	F	h%	HctX	PX	xPX	hr/f	Spd	SBO	SB%	#Wk	DOM	DIS	RC/G	RAR	BPV	BPX	R$
11 aa	468	40	7	36	7	216		249	315	564			4	80	0.22				26		70			102	16%	49%				2.41		16	36	$1
12 aa	317	44	7	26	7	263		308	398	706			6	83	0.39				30		87			107	14%	68%				4.18		49	123	$7
13 a/a	482	63	9	52	16	244		313	366	679			9	85	0.68				27		80			106	15%	82%				3.93		57	143	$13
14 NYY *	559	69	8	46	11	256	247	292	362	654	2167	488	5	83	0.31	53	16	32	30	108	68	51	0%	161	14%	57%	2	100%	0%	3.48	1.5	48	130	$13
15 NYY *	315	41	4	24	5	264	263	314	354	668	752	286	7	85	0.51	56	19	25	30	100	62	57	7%	105	9%	69%	14	14%	50%	3.83	-4.1	38	103	$6
1st Half	135	17	3	10	1	225	255	255	355	609	739	290	4	78	0.18	58	16	26	27	95	95	65	8%	97	4%	100%	9	22%	44%	3.00	-5.0	27	73	$0
2nd Half	180	24	1	15	4	293	299	357	354	710	800	0	9	91	1.09	44	33	22	32	89	40	13	0%	105	10%	64%	5	0%	60%	4.47	1.3	47	127	$11
16 Proj	**163**	**21**	**2**	**14**	**3**	**257**	**261**	**306**	**362**	**668**	**930**	**372**	**7**	**85**	**0.46**	**58**	**16**	**26**	**29**	**86**	**67**	**59**	**7%**	**120**	**11%**	**68%**				**3.76**	**-2.2**	**37**	**99**	**$4**

RYAN BLOOMFIELD

Piscotty,Stephen

Age: 25	Bats: R	Pos: LF	Health	A	LIMA Plan	A
Ht: 6' 3"	Wt: 210		PT/Exp	C	Rand Var	-1
			Consist	C	MM	3345

7-39-.305 in 233 AB at STL. Entering second AAA season, retooled swing to increase exit velocity. Results showcased at MLB level as HctX, PX/xPX produced .853 OPS. Whiffed too much, and inflated h%, .269 MLB xBA point to likely BA correction, but he's shown that making improvements is among his skills. Invest.

Yr	Tm	AB	R	HR	RBI	SB	BA	xBA	OBP	SLG	OPS	vL	vR	bb%	ct%	Eye	G	L	F	h%	HctX	PX	xPX	hr/f	Spd	SBO	SB%	#Wk	DOM	DIS	RC/G	RAR	BPV	BPX	R$
11																																			
12																																			
13	aa	184	13	4	18	5	259		314	371	684			7	89	0.70				27		71			84	17%	62%				3.86		53	133	$3
14	aaa	500	50	6	50	8	244		288	339	626			6	86	0.45				27		71			81	12%	58%				3.20		40	108	$8
15	STL *	553	69	15	69	6	262	268	327	434	760	887	841	9	77	0.42	45	21	34	32	128	120	135	12%	136	10%	42%	12	50%	33%	4.67	-0.7	66	178	$15
1st Half		289	35	7	27	4	223	264	293	378	671			9	80	0.50				26		110			94	13%	45%				3.45		56	151	$8
2nd Half		264	34	8	43	2	305	266	364	495	859	887	841	8	74	0.36	45	21	34	39	123	132	135	12%	148	7%	38%	12	50%	33%	6.34	13.0	67	181	$22
16	Proj	519	56	16	61	8	261	275	315	430	745	797	728	7	82	0.44	45	21	34	29	111	109	122	12%	141	12%	52%				4.49	-1.1	55	149	$14

Plawecki,Kevin

Age: 25	Bats: R	Pos: CA	Health	A	LIMA Plan	D
Ht: 6' 2"	Wt: 225		PT/Exp	F	Rand Var	0
			Consist	C	MM	1001

3-21-.219 in 233 AB at NYM. Was high-average hitter in low minors, but not so in AAA and MLB debut. Power lags, and ct% (74%) really fell off at big-league level, but all-fields swing bodes well for the future. More seasoning could bring him into realm of rosterable second CA, but probably not this year.

Yr	Tm	AB	R	HR	RBI	SB	BA	xBA	OBP	SLG	OPS	vL	vR	bb%	ct%	Eye	G	L	F	h%	HctX	PX	xPX	hr/f	Spd	SBO	SB%	#Wk	DOM	DIS	RC/G	RAR	BPV	BPX	R$
11																																			
12																																			
13																																			
14	a/a	376	38	8	42	0	246		283	357	641			5	85	0.34				27		80			80	0%	0%				3.42		39	105	$5
15	NYM *	318	23	4	27	0	207	218	252	286	538	411	609	6	77	0.26	46	20	34	26	95	59	87	5%	95	0%	0%	22	23%	55%	2.32	-14.7	-3	-8	-$3
1st Half		185	10	2	19	0	218	220	253	297	550	600	580	4	79	0.22	48	19	33	27	113	58	89	5%	82	0%	0%	12	33%	42%	2.45	-7.6	-4	-11	-$3
2nd Half		133	13	2	8	0	193	215	251	272	523	0	657	7	74	0.30	43	22	35	25	64	61	85	5%	112	0%	0%	10	10%	70%	2.16	-6.8	-5	-14	-$3
16	Proj	199	18	3	18	0	220	229	274	308	582	290	637	5	79	0.28	45	21	34	27	84	63	87	5%	104	0%	0%				2.64	-6.9	-10	-28	$1

Plouffe,Trevor

Age: 30	Bats: R	Pos: 3B	Health	B	LIMA Plan	B+
Ht: 6' 2"	Wt: 205		PT/Exp	A	Rand Var	+1
			Consist	A	MM	3225

Consistent BPI, annual production have put him among fantasy's safest bets. If not for BA (which xBA, h% say was a bit unlucky), 2015 could've been most profitable year. But entering his 30s, iffy ct%, declining LD%, and hr/f fluctuations loom as impediments. Still safe, but with yellow flag.

Yr	Tm	AB	R	HR	RBI	SB	BA	xBA	OBP	SLG	OPS	vL	vR	bb%	ct%	Eye	G	L	F	h%	HctX	PX	xPX	hr/f	Spd	SBO	SB%	#Wk	DOM	DIS	RC/G	RAR	BPV	BPX	R$
11	MIN *	478	72	18	56	5	248	256	307	433	741	782	665	8	76	0.35	43	17	40	29	115	132	128	10%	122	9%	56%	17	53%	24%	4.41	-5.6	63	140	$12
12	MIN	422	56	24	55	1	235	262	301	455	756	911	691	8	78	0.40	38	18	44	25	112	136	114	17%	91	4%	25%	24	58%	33%	4.36	-2.3	67	168	$9
13	MIN	477	44	14	52	2	254	249	309	392	701	826	663	7	77	0.30	39	25	37	30	103	98	113	10%	102	3%	67%	25	44%	32%	4.05	1.4	31	78	$9
14	MIN	520	69	14	80	2	258	266	328	423	751	783	738	9	79	0.49	38	21	40	30	113	127	133	8%	101	2%	67%	24	58%	17%	4.73	16.0	69	186	$15
15	MIN	573	74	22	86	2	244	260	307	435	742	780	727	8	78	0.40	41	18	41	28	116	124	129	12%	96	2%	67%	26	58%	19%	4.46	-1.8	59	159	$13
1st Half		295	37	10	43	1	254	266	315	444	759	773	752	8	80	0.47	39	19	42	29	106	123	128	10%	111	1%	100%	14	64%	7%	4.83	1.8	72	195	$14
2nd Half		278	37	12	43	1	234	254	300	424	724	790	702	8	76	0.35	43	17	40	27	126	126	130	14%	77	3%	50%	12	50%	33%	4.08	-4.5	46	124	$13
16	Proj	527	67	18	75	2	248	257	312	423	736	797	713	8	78	0.40	40	20	40	29	114	118	127	11%	99	3%	60%				4.40	-3.5	44	120	$15

Polanco,Gregory

Age: 24	Bats: L	Pos: RF	Health	A	LIMA Plan	B
Ht: 6' 4"	Wt: 220		PT/Exp	B	Rand Var	-1
			Consist	A	MM	2425

Strong sophomore campaign highlighted by SB total in 1H, and plenty of hard contact in 2H. Didn't run as often after wall encounter in June, and overall SB% says technique needs work. But if healthy 1H is used as springboard, he fits the Stolen Base Breakout Profile and... UP: 35 SB.

Yr	Tm	AB	R	HR	RBI	SB	BA	xBA	OBP	SLG	OPS	vL	vR	bb%	ct%	Eye	G	L	F	h%	HctX	PX	xPX	hr/f	Spd	SBO	SB%	#Wk	DOM	DIS	RC/G	RAR	BPV	BPX	R$
11																																			
12																																			
13	a/a	252	30	4	33	11	233		311	344	655			10	85	0.76				26		74			100	27%	60%				3.34		52	130	$6
14	PIT *	551	89	12	72	26	258	252	320	377	697	466	727	8	80	0.45	50	19	31	31	84	85	87	10%	104	25%	69%	17	35%	41%	4.05	-0.7	36	97	$24
15	PIT	593	83	9	52	27	256	250	320	381	701	528	747	8	80	0.45	45	20	35	31	105	87	95	6%	117	24%	73%	27	44%	22%	4.14	-12.6	42	114	$20
1st Half		273	37	3	19	17	231	242	300	330	630	304	687	9	78	0.45	50	19	31	29	94	72	77	5%	110	32%	74%	14	36%	29%	3.28	-13.0	23	62	$14
2nd Half		320	46	6	33	10	278	258	336	425	761	636	807	8	81	0.46	42	20	38	33	114	99	110	6%	122	16%	71%	13	54%	15%	4.99	1.6	58	157	$26
16	Proj	556	80	11	61	25	255	254	318	382	701	514	762	9	81	0.48	47	19	34	30	97	85	93	7%	109	24%	71%				4.11	-11.8	47	126	$22

Pollock,A.J.

Age: 28	Bats: R	Pos: CF	Health	C	LIMA Plan	C
Ht: 6' 1"	Wt: 195		PT/Exp	B	Rand Var	-3
			Consist	C	MM	3555

Already solid BPI advanced across the board to produce fantasy MVP-caliber season. Plate skills, batted ball outcomes, and basepath proficiencies all soared, especially in 2H. Of course, discussions begin with "Can he do it again?" Perhaps not, but without glaring weaknesses, he'll be in the vicinity.

Yr	Tm	AB	R	HR	RBI	SB	BA	xBA	OBP	SLG	OPS	vL	vR	bb%	ct%	Eye	G	L	F	h%	HctX	PX	xPX	hr/f	Spd	SBO	SB%	#Wk	DOM	DIS	RC/G	RAR	BPV	BPX	R$
11	aa	550	72	6	51	25	266		304	382	686			5	82	0.31				31		87			104	26%	76%				4.02		42	93	$17
12	ARI *	509	47	4	39	14	250	253	289	334	623	808	535	5	86	0.37	50	20	30	29	123	57	110	10%	100	20%	54%	10	40%	20%	3.07	-24.8	30	75	$8
13	ARI	443	64	8	38	12	269	262	322	409	730	811	678	7	81	0.40	48	18	34	31	126	98	112	7%	143	14%	80%	27	48%	22%	4.58	6.1	63	158	$14
14	ARI *	314	43	7	29	14	274	281	318	447	764	953	828	6	84	0.40	52	14	34	31	109	116	97	9%	175	23%	82%	15	73%	13%	5.04	11.0	94	254	$13
15	ARI	609	111	20	76	39	315	299	367	498	865	881	860	8	85	0.60	50	21	29	34	127	111	98	13%	128	26%	85%	27	70%	15%	7.02	45.0	87	235	$44
1st Half		317	54	10	38	18	303	280	346	464	810	887	787	6	83	0.40	52	19	29	34	115	100	84	13%	127	26%	78%	14	57%	29%	5.90	13.2	64	173	$40
2nd Half		292	57	10	38	21	329	318	389	534	923	874	936	10	88	0.91	48	23	29	35	139	121	112	13%	122	25%	91%	13	85%	0%	8.35	30.6	108	292	$48
16	Proj	584	93	17	63	30	294	289	344	471	815	844	804	7	85	0.51	50	19	31	32	123	109	102	11%	148	23%	83%				5.95	25.3	87	236	$34

Pompey,Dalton

Age: 23	Bats: B	Pos: CF	Health	A	LIMA Plan	B
Ht: 6' 2"	Wt: 195		PT/Exp	F	Rand Var	-4
			Consist	B	MM	2513

2-6-.223 with 5 SB in 94 AB at TOR. Sub-.200 BA dispatched him to AAA, where he hit .307 with 23 SB before returning in Sept. Extremely toolsy with top-drawer speed, he has little else to prove in minors. Profile is still under development, but third attempt to stick in bigs could be the charm.

Yr	Tm	AB	R	HR	RBI	SB	BA	xBA	OBP	SLG	OPS	vL	vR	bb%	ct%	Eye	G	L	F	h%	HctX	PX	xPX	hr/f	Spd	SBO	SB%	#Wk	DOM	DIS	RC/G	RAR	BPV	BPX	R$
11																																			
12																																			
13																																			
14	TOR *	204	34	4	18	13	285	241	343	439	782	259	1010	8	79	0.42	31	23	46	35	152	109	178	8%	147	32%	70%	5	20%	60%	5.19	7.7	65	176	$10
15	TOR *	480	79	9	41	25	278	229	343	394	737	859	611	9	80	0.50	43	17	40	33	109	72	81	8%	141	25%	68%	10	40%	40%	4.63	1.7	40	108	$22
1st Half		276	39	8	28	13	253	230	311	393	704	646	590	8	76	0.35	39	20	41	31	110	90	96	9%	120	23%	74%	4	50%	25%	4.15	-2.2	30	81	$22
2nd Half		204	40	1	13	13	311	223	385	395	780	1750	804	11	86	0.83	67	0	33	36	75	51	-15	0%	159	26%	63%	6	33%	50%	5.31	5.2	54	146	$22
16	Proj	382	56	10	32	18	254	246	335	406	740	694	752	9	81	0.52	39	20	41	29	99	93	86	8%	136	27%	63%				4.22	-2.2	59	159	$15

Posey,Buster

Age: 29	Bats: R	Pos: CA 1B	Health	A	LIMA Plan	B+
Ht: 6' 1"	Wt: 215		PT/Exp	A	Rand Var	-1
			Consist	A	MM	2145

As valuable a player at his position as anyone else in the game. Few match his combination of ct% and HctX, has .300+ lifetime BA vs. both LHP and RHP, and now added elite Eye. Power dropped in 2H, but xPX makes that look like a fluke. Durable, with 1B eligibility... heck, you get the idea. This guy's really good.

Yr	Tm	AB	R	HR	RBI	SB	BA	xBA	OBP	SLG	OPS	vL	vR	bb%	ct%	Eye	G	L	F	h%	HctX	PX	xPX	hr/f	Spd	SBO	SB%	#Wk	DOM	DIS	RC/G	RAR	BPV	BPX	R$
11	SF	162	17	4	21	3	284	243	368	389	756	681	786	10	81	0.60	53	18	29	33	96	69	84	10%	84	5%	100%	9	44%	33%	5.05	3.1	28	62	$4
12	SF	530	78	24	103	1	336	301	408	549	957	1262	822	12	82	0.72	47	25	29	38	113	137	104	19%	84	1%	50%	27	70%	15%	8.65	60.3	87	218	$30
13	SF	520	61	15	72	2	294	279	371	450	821	891	792	10	87	0.86	47	20	33	32	116	103	116	10%	82	2%	67%	27	56%	7%	5.95	32.6	76	190	$19
14	SF	547	72	22	89	0	311	298	364	490	854	875	844	8	87	0.68	42	24	34	32	131	113	121	13%	81	1%	0%	27	70%	19%	6.57	46.2	82	222	$27
15	SF	557	74	19	95	2	318	288	379	470	849	854	847	9	91	1.08	44	22	34	33	138	87	113	11%	58	1%	100%	27	67%	11%	6.71	43.1	70	189	$27
1st Half		286	44	14	57	1	304	300	377	500	877	761	907	11	90	1.17	44	22	34	30	139	108	115	16%	52	1%	100%	14	79%	7%	6.96	24.8	85	230	$32
2nd Half		271	30	5	38	1	332	274	381	439	820	930	778	8	92	0.96	44	23	34	35	138	66	111	6%	71	1%	100%	13	54%	15%	6.44	18.9	57	154	$22
16	Proj	559	71	21	89	2	313	288	376	480	857	904	838	9	88	0.88	43	22	34	33	130	97	113	12%	71	1%	80%				6.72	44.3	65	176	$29

ROB CARROLL

Prado,Martin

Age: 32	Bats: R	Pos: 3B	Health B	LIMA Plan B+	
Ht: 6' 1"	Wt: 190		PT/Exp A	Rand Var -2	
			Consist A	MM 1235	

BA consistency has been terrific, but declines in ct%, xBA give reason for pause, as do erosion of xPX, BPV, $R. Could be nearing point where platoon splits affect playing time even more. All just little things, but they might add up to... DN: Fewer than 500 AB, .265 BA

Yr	Tm	AB	R	HR	RBI	SB	BA	xBA	OBP	SLG	OPS	vL	vR	bb%	ct%	Eye	G	L	F	h%	HctX	PX	xPX	hr/f	Spd	SBO	SB%	#Wk	DOM	DIS	RC/G	RAR	BPV	BPX	R$
11	ATL *	577	69	13	59	4	255	259	299	374	673	673	692	6	90	0.62	51	15	35	27	87	75	71	8%	120	8%	33%	23	52%	4%	3.63	-25.1	69	153	$11
12	ATL	617	81	10	70	17	301	291	359	438	796	864	760	9	89	0.84	48	23	29	33	110	86	76	6%	125	11%	81%	27	63%	7%	5.82	20.7	81	203	$25
13	ARI	609	70	14	82	3	282	290	333	417	750	852	716	7	91	0.89	48	22	30	29	110	85	89	8%	90	5%	38%	27	67%	4%	4.81	14.1	77	193	$19
14	2 TM	536	62	12	58	3	282	276	321	412	733	979	668	5	85	0.33	49	22	29	31	102	88	78	9%	123	3%	75%	26	46%	27%	4.61	13.5	59	159	$16
15	MIA	500	52	9	63	1	288	267	338	394	732	856	695	7	86	0.54	47	23	30	32	104	66	70	7%	92	1%	100%	23	43%	30%	4.77	1.2	42	114	$14
1st Half		254	24	4	24	0	272	272	311	370	681	803	647	5	87	0.36	45	26	30	30	101	62	76	6%	91	0%	0%	11	36%	27%	3.95	-4.9	36	97	$9
2nd Half		246	28	5	39	1	305	262	364	419	783	900	745	9	86	0.71	49	21	30	34	107	71	65	8%	96	1%	100%	12	50%	33%	5.70	7.2	49	132	$19
16	**Proj**	**523**	**58**	**10**	**65**	**3**	**286**	**273**	**335**	**405**	**740**	**876**	**698**	**7**	**87**	**0.55**	**48**	**22**	**30**	**31**	**104**	**73**	**75**	**8%**	**105**	**3%**	**65%**				**4.81**	**2.8**	**42**	**114**	**$16**

Profar,Jurickson

Age: 23	Bats: B	Pos: DH	Health F	LIMA Plan D+	
Ht: 6' 0"	Wt: 165		PT/Exp F	Rand Var 0	
			Consist F	MM 2321	

Such a shame. Ongoing issues with right shoulder limited top prospect to 43 rehab AB in Low-A & AA last two seasons. Hope is he'll be ready to go by Opening Day 2016. Time away likely presents buy low oportunity, but one that will require patience, and probably more time in minors.

Yr	Tm	AB	R	HR	RBI	SB	BA	xBA	OBP	SLG	OPS	vL	vR	bb%	ct%	Eye	G	L	F	h%	HctX	PX	xPX	hr/f	Spd	SBO	SB%	#Wk	DOM	DIS	RC/G	RAR	BPV	BPX	R$
11																																			
12	TEX *	497	66	14	55	14	276	255	349	447	796	0	846	10	83	0.67	54	8	38	31	112	105	123	20%	129	12%	77%	4	25%	75%	5.50	18.9	78	195	$17
13	TEX *	430	52	9	41	7	244	246	313	359	671	541	696	9	80	0.49	41	23	35	29	97	79	88	8%	114	10%	57%	19	26%	26%	3.68	-0.5	36	90	$8
14																																			
15																																			
1st Half																																			
2nd Half																																			
16	**Proj**	**209**	**26**	**4**	**21**	**4**	**257**	**250**	**336**	**381**	**716**	**614**	**768**	**9**	**81**	**0.55**	**42**	**21**	**36**	**30**	**87**	**81**	**79**	**7%**	**118**	**11%**	**67%**				**4.22**	**-7.6**	**38**	**102**	**$6**

Puig,Yasiel

Age: 25	Bats: R	Pos: RF	Health C	LIMA Plan B+	
Ht: 6' 3"	Wt: 235		PT/Exp B	Rand Var +2	
			Consist C	MM 4425	

Recurring hamstring injury caused disappointing season and fed into post-hype backlash. When you stick to BPI, however, you see foundation of average to plus skills in bb%, power, and speed, along with steady FB% growth. Mind the health risk, but if you've got a draft table full of doubters, feel free to be the contrarian.

Yr	Tm	AB	R	HR	RBI	SB	BA	xBA	OBP	SLG	OPS	vL	vR	bb%	ct%	Eye	G	L	F	h%	HctX	PX	xPX	hr/f	Spd	SBO	SB%	#Wk	DOM	DIS	RC/G	RAR	BPV	BPX	R$
11																																			
12																																			
13	LA *	529	89	26	74	22	309	284	368	533	900	1001	897	8	76	0.38	50	19	31	37	117	154	106	22%	130	24%	62%	18	56%	28%	6.82	32.7	83	208	$35
14	LA	558	92	16	69	11	296	273	382	480	863	736	901	11	78	0.54	52	15	33	36	116	134	111	11%	143	11%	61%	28	54%	29%	6.29	34.3	85	230	$26
15	LA	282	30	11	38	3	255	249	322	436	758	924	704	8	77	0.39	44	17	39	30	106	114	89	13%	112	8%	50%	18	39%	22%	4.60	-2.0	50	135	$7
1st Half		133	14	3	10	0	278	264	368	444	812	973	769	11	78	0.59	44	21	35	34	116	113	78	8%	109	5%	0%	9	56%	11%	5.32	1.9	60	162	$2
2nd Half		149	16	8	28	3	235	236	277	430	706	887	636	6	75	0.24	44	13	42	26	97	116	100	17%	109	13%	75%	9	22%	33%	3.96	-3.8	40	108	$11
16	**Proj**	**510**	**69**	**20**	**69**	**12**	**276**	**261**	**349**	**469**	**818**	**874**	**800**	**9**	**77**	**0.43**	**46**	**17**	**37**	**33**	**110**	**124**	**100**	**14%**	**131**	**13%**	**63%**				**5.49**	**9.9**	**60**	**161**	**$23**

Pujols,Albert

Age: 36	Bats: R	Pos: 1B DH	Health B	LIMA Plan B+	
Ht: 6' 3"	Wt: 230		PT/Exp A	Rand Var +4	
			Consist A	MM 3145	

Subpar LD%, merely mortal bb% are signs bat speed has faded since peak and pitchers aren't as afraid of him, but power skills are very much intact. xBA suggests BA will bounce back. 2H is a concern, though late-season foot injury may have been an issue. Good reminder that even with 40 HR, this is Pujols version 2.0.

Yr	Tm	AB	R	HR	RBI	SB	BA	xBA	OBP	SLG	OPS	vL	vR	bb%	ct%	Eye	G	L	F	h%	HctX	PX	xPX	hr/f	Spd	SBO	SB%	#Wk	DOM	DIS	RC/G	RAR	BPV	BPX	R$
11	STL	579	105	37	99	9	299	311	366	541	906	946	897	10	90	1.05	45	17	38	28	139	137	140	18%	81	6%	90%	26	85%	4%	7.25	25.7	115	256	$33
12	LAA	607	85	30	105	8	285	303	343	516	859	926	836	8	87	0.68	41	19	40	29	128	140	126	14%	61	6%	89%	27	78%	11%	6.32	17.6	98	245	$27
13	LAA	391	49	17	64	1	258	270	330	437	767	690	790	9	86	0.73	38	20	42	26	128	109	135	12%	70	2%	50%	17	59%	12%	4.88	3.1	72	180	$11
14	LAA	633	89	28	105	5	272	299	324	466	790	737	807	7	89	0.68	46	19	35	27	139	122	110	14%	62	4%	83%	27	70%	0%	5.29	20.7	87	235	$26
15	LAA	602	85	40	95	5	244	286	307	480	787	753	799	8	88	0.69	42	16	42	22	128	125	131	18%	60	6%	63%	27	70%	11%	4.83	-1.8	88	238	$21
1st Half		298	50	25	53	1	265	311	337	557	894	710	946	9	89	0.88	39	18	43	23	140	152	146	22%	63	4%	33%	14	79%	0%	6.23	9.3	116	314	$29
2nd Half		304	35	15	42	4	224	260	277	405	681	785	638	6	87	0.54	44	14	42	21	117	99	117	14%	62	8%	80%	13	62%	23%	3.65	-14.0	61	165	$13
16	**Proj**	**595**	**82**	**30**	**95**	**4**	**266**	**279**	**325**	**464**	**789**	**763**	**798**	**8**	**88**	**0.68**	**43**	**17**	**40**	**26**	**130**	**111**	**125**	**14%**	**64**	**4%**	**67%**				**5.17**	**0.2**	**74**	**199**	**$25**

Raburn,Ryan

Age: 35	Bats: R	Pos: DH	Health B	LIMA Plan D	
Ht: 6' 0"	Wt: 185		PT/Exp F	Rand Var -5	
			Consist F	MM 4131	

Elite 2015 power skills built almost exclusively on work vs. LHP (186 PX over 151 AB), and not for the first time. Basically, for his career, he's Todd Frazier vs. LHP (.827 OPS, 156 PX), and Caleb Joseph (.693 OPS, 106 PX) vs. RHP. There's value to be mined from that, particularly in DFS.

Yr	Tm	AB	R	HR	RBI	SB	BA	xBA	OBP	SLG	OPS	vL	vR	bb%	ct%	Eye	G	L	F	h%	HctX	PX	xPX	hr/f	Spd	SBO	SB%	#Wk	DOM	DIS	RC/G	RAR	BPV	BPX	R$
11	DET	387	53	14	49	1	256	238	297	432	729	807	681	5	71	0.18	35	21	45	33	101	135	142	11%	123	2%	50%	27	48%	37%	4.31	-6.9	39	87	$9
12	DET *	265	20	4	20	2	176	201	224	277	500	477	482	6	73	0.23	43	14	43	23	108	82	138	2%	86	6%	63%	19	26%	47%	1.90	-22.9	-1	-3	-$5
13	CLE	243	40	16	55	0	272	282	357	543	901	1020	806	11	72	0.43	45	18	38	31	111	197	145	24%	71	0%	0%	26	62%	27%	6.64	18.5	92	230	$10
14	CLE *	223	21	4	25	0	195	219	244	280	524	596	463	6	74	0.25	41	23	35	24	98	66	103	8%	74	0%	0%	23	26%	61%	2.16	-10.7	-13	-35	-$2
15	CLE	173	22	8	29	0	301	288	393	543	936	1004	467	12	75	0.52	44	22	35	36	131	173	152	18%	96	0%	0%	25	48%	32%	7.58	15.1	91	246	$6
1st Half		111	12	4	20	0	297	299	388	532	919	964	627	12	79	0.65	43	21	36	35	153	164	161	13%	85	0%	0%	14	50%	29%	7.35	8.5	100	270	$7
2nd Half		62	10	4	9	0	306	267	403	565	967	1074	125	11	66	0.38	46	22	32	41	92	193	131	31%	108	0%	0%	11	45%	36%	8.01	5.8	76	205	$5
16	**Proj**	**197**	**25**	**9**	**30**	**0**	**262**	**262**	**340**	**470**	**810**	**912**	**561**	**9**	**72**	**0.37**	**43**	**21**	**36**	**32**	**110**	**148**	**133**	**18%**	**95**	**0%**	**61%**				**5.37**	**-0.4**	**40**	**107**	**$7**

Ramirez,Alexei

Age: 34	Bats: R	Pos: SS	Health A	LIMA Plan A	
Ht: 6' 2"	Wt: 180		PT/Exp A	Rand Var +3	
			Consist B	MM 1345	

xPX forecast power regression, but BA drop was simply bad luck with h%. Speed skills were match for 2H of 2014 (94 Spd, 16% SBO); could be signs he's slowing down with age. Mix n' match HR/SB history driving wild R$ swings, so best bet is to pay for skill baselines and hope to get lucky.

Yr	Tm	AB	R	HR	RBI	SB	BA	xBA	OBP	SLG	OPS	vL	vR	bb%	ct%	Eye	G	L	F	h%	HctX	PX	xPX	hr/f	Spd	SBO	SB%	#Wk	DOM	DIS	RC/G	RAR	BPV	BPX	R$
11	CHW	614	81	15	70	7	269	266	328	399	727	715	731	8	86	0.61	45	19	35	29	95	85	77	8%	114	7%	58%	27	56%	11%	4.43	4.5	65	144	$17
12	CHW	593	59	9	73	20	265	254	287	364	651	724	631	3	87	0.21	46	20	34	29	85	61	69	5%	129	20%	74%	27	37%	33%	3.56	-6.0	43	108	$17
13	CHW	637	68	6	48	30	284	278	313	380	693	701	691	4	89	0.38	49	22	29	31	88	68	51	4%	122	24%	77%	27	52%	15%	4.23	14.7	58	145	$25
14	CHW	622	82	15	74	21	273	278	305	408	713	744	703	4	87	0.30	47	20	33	29	88	92	64	8%	121	18%	84%	26	46%	12%	4.37	21.2	67	181	$26
15	CHW	583	54	10	62	17	249	277	285	357	642	707	623	5	88	0.46	50	21	29	27	82	71	61	7%	92	18%	71%	27	52%	11%	3.43	-16.9	50	135	$14
1st Half		289	20	2	26	9	221	250	248	291	539	606	524	4	87	0.30	50	19	31	25	89	50	73	3%	87	20%	75%	14	29%	21%	2.39	-15.2	24	65	$5
2nd Half		294	34	8	36	8	276	301	321	422	742	778	730	6	89	0.65	49	24	27	29	75	90	50	11%	99	16%	67%	13	77%	0%	4.66	4.9	74	200	$23
16	**Proj**	**574**	**63**	**11**	**62**	**16**	**265**	**277**	**300**	**383**	**682**	**726**	**669**	**5**	**88**	**0.41**	**48**	**21**	**30**	**28**	**85**	**76**	**61**	**7%**	**108**	**17%**	**72%**				**3.92**	**-2.7**	**51**	**137**	**$20**

Ramirez,Aramis

Age: 38	Bats: R	Pos: 3B	Health C	LIMA Plan F	
Ht: 6' 1"	Wt: 205		PT/Exp B	Rand Var +4	
			Consist B	MM 0000	

Stated back in spring that 2015 would be his final season, and if so, career ends where it began, in PIT. Ranks 63rd all-time in HR (386), 73rd all-time in RBI (1,417), and 10th all-time in games played at 3B (2,112). Not too shabby.

Yr	Tm	AB	R	HR	RBI	SB	BA	xBA	OBP	SLG	OPS	vL	vR	bb%	ct%	Eye	G	L	F	h%	HctX	PX	xPX	hr/f	Spd	SBO	SB%	#Wk	DOM	DIS	RC/G	RAR	BPV	BPX	R$
11	CHC	565	80	26	93	1	306	297	361	510	871	824	884	7	88	0.62	34	23	43	31	128	125	129	12%	96	1%	50%	27	74%	7%	6.62	23.4	96	213	$27
12	MIL	570	92	27	105	9	300	299	360	540	901	1049	853	7	86	0.54	39	19	42	31	148	148	164	13%	93	8%	82%	27	74%	7%	6.90	36.1	105	263	$29
13	MIL	304	43	12	49	0	283	265	370	461	831	887	811	11	82	0.65	41	19	39	31	123	118	144	12%	79	1%	0%	19	53%	16%	5.80	15.5	69	173	$10
14	MIL	494	47	15	66	3	285	266	330	427	757	1024	687	4	85	0.28	39	23	39	31	136	94	131	9%	78	2%	100%	24	42%	8%	4.83	15.5	48	130	$17
15	2 NL	475	43	17	75	1	246	268	297	423	720	699	726	6	86	0.46	38	19	43	26	116	109	118	10%	62	1%	100%	26	65%	19%	4.20	-6.7	63	170	$9
1st Half		242	21	10	39	1	244	276	286	438	724	571	760	5	85	0.32	37	20	43	25	106	121	110	11%	54	2%	100%	14	71%	21%	4.15	-3.4	63	170	$10
2nd Half		233	22	7	36	0	249	258	307	408	715	788	687	8	87	0.61	39	18	43	26	127	97	126	8%	76	0%	0%	12	58%	17%	4.23	-2.7	64	173	$8
16	**Proj**																																		

BRANDON KRUSE

Ramirez,Hanley

Age: 32 Bats: R Pos: LF	Health	D	LIMA Plan	B+
Ht: 6' 2" Wt: 225	PT/Exp	C	Rand Var	+4
	Consist	F	MM	4245

Came into spring with new body (linebacker), new position (LF). Began on fire, then flaws with plan became painfully apparent. Shoulder woes from May crash into wall lingered, so downplay 2H nose dive. New plan: Come into spring with new body (lighter), new position (1B). What could go wrong?

Yr Tm	AB	R	HR	RBI	SB	BA	xBA	OBP	SLG	OPS	vL	vR	bb%	ct%	Eye	G	L	F	h%	HctX	PX	xPX	hr/f	Spd	SBO	SB%	#Wk	DOM	DIS	RC/G	RAR	BPV	BPX	R$
11 FLA	338	55	10	45	20	243	255	333	379	712	994	633	12	80	0.67	51	16	33	27	103	94	96	11%	83	30%	67%	18	33%	22%	4.05	-16.5	47	104	$12
12 2 NL	604	79	24	92	21	257	262	322	437	759	794	745	8	78	0.41	47	18	34	29	114	115	115	15%	95	18%	75%	27	52%	33%	4.73	-9.9	52	130	$23
13 LA	304	62	20	57	10	345	326	402	638	1040	1142	1001	8	83	0.52	41	22	37	37	159	186	164	21%	100	14%	83%	18	67%	22%	9.94	42.0	129	323	$25
14 LA	449	64	13	71	14	283	281	369	448	817	869	801	11	81	0.67	45	21	34	32	115	124	115	10%	80	14%	74%	25	56%	16%	5.74	20.4	72	195	$21
15 BOS	401	59	19	53	6	249	277	291	426	717	710	720	5	82	0.30	50	20	30	26	113	101	84	19%	92	10%	67%	20	50%	25%	4.09	-10.1	49	132	$12
1st Half	271	47	18	43	3	277	292	325	502	827	1008	763	6	85	0.45	46	21	33	27	117	117	97	23%	102	9%	50%	14	64%	14%	5.49	2.6	80	216	$22
2nd Half	130	12	1	10	3	192	245	215	269	484	207	620	2	76	0.10	59	20	21	24	104	64	55	5%	80	15%	100%	6	17%	50%	1.87	-13.5	-14	-38	-$9
16 Proj	**457**	**67**	**21**	**64**	**6**	**261**	**279**	**315**	**459**	**775**	**737**	**789**	**7**	**81**	**0.37**	**44**	**21**	**33**	**28**	**118**	**124**	**100**	**17%**	**87**	**8%**	**70%**				**4.87**	**4.2**	**62**	**168**	**$16**

Ramirez,Jose

Age: 23 Bats: B Pos: SS 2B	Health	A	LIMA Plan	D+
Ht: 5' 9" Wt: 180	PT/Exp	C	Rand Var	+2
	Consist	F	MM	1431

6-27-.219 with 10 SB in 315 AB at CLE. Demoted after miserable two months. Improved upon recall (.259 BA, 91% ct%, 1.27 Eye in 162 AB from Aug. 3 on); xBA suggests it could have been better, if h% cooperated. No pop, but could be sneaky SB source if he can find AB. That's not a given, though.

Yr Tm	AB	R	HR	RBI	SB	BA	xBA	OBP	SLG	OPS	vL	vR	bb%	ct%	Eye	G	L	F	h%	HctX	PX	xPX	hr/f	Spd	SBO	SB%	#Wk	DOM	DIS	RC/G	RAR	BPV	BPX	R$
11																																		
12																																		
13 CLE *	494	65	2	29	29	240	220	285	302	587	650	1069	6	90	0.66	50	10	40	26	74	39	135	0%	153	37%	61%	4	25%	50%	2.67	-16.3	52	130	$14
14 CLE *	482	57	6	40	25	265	274	312	366	677	676	632	6	86	0.47	47	24	28	30	86	72	71	4%	110	30%	66%	15	33%	27%	3.77	5.5	48	130	$18
15 CLE *	489	76	7	38	23	237	263	303	351	654	574	655	9	90	0.95	48	16	36	25	95	70	70	6%	125	25%	74%	20	35%	25%	3.55	-10.9	73	197	$14
1st Half	241	34	2	16	18	250	243	314	334	648	496	481	9	88	0.79	51	13	36	28	82	56	64	2%	122	33%	80%	9	22%	33%	3.71	-3.8	53	143	$15
2nd Half	248	42	5	22	6	225	282	293	368	662	663	797	9	92	1.17	45	19	36	23	107	84	76	9%	119	17%	57%	11	45%	18%	3.41	-6.3	90	243	$13
16 Proj	**226**	**32**	**3**	**18**	**11**	**260**	**268**	**316**	**372**	**688**	**665**	**698**	**8**	**89**	**0.72**	**47**	**20**	**33**	**28**	**92**	**69**	**71**	**5%**	**117**	**27%**	**68%**				**3.92**	**-1.1**	**63**	**171**	**$9**

Ramos,Wilson

Age: 28 Bats: R Pos: CA	Health	F	LIMA Plan	C+
Ht: 6' 0" Wt: 235	PT/Exp	C	Rand Var	+3
	Consist	B	MM	2025

Stayed healthy for a change, maintained odd ability to generate high hr/f even with FB in short supply. Otherwise, worrisome signs: deepening struggles vs. RHP, two-year declines of ct%, HctX, PX/xPX. Young enough to fulfill 2013 promise, but few hints stars will align. More likely? Disappointment.

Yr Tm	AB	R	HR	RBI	SB	BA	xBA	OBP	SLG	OPS	vL	vR	bb%	ct%	Eye	G	L	F	h%	HctX	PX	xPX	hr/f	Spd	SBO	SB%	#Wk	DOM	DIS	RC/G	RAR	BPV	BPX	R$
11 WAS	389	48	15	52	0	267	257	334	445	779	789	776	9	80	0.50	50	15	36	30	106	120	119	13%	72	2%	0%	27	52%	22%	5.04	7.4	59	131	$10
12 WAS	83	11	3	10	0	265	224	354	398	752	762	748	13	77	0.63	66	14	20	31	114	82	96	23%	67	0%	0%	6	33%	33%	4.94	1.5	21	53	$0
13 WAS	287	29	16	59	0	272	279	307	470	777	700	803	5	85	0.36	57	20	24	27	143	114	108	28%	61	1%	0%	18	61%	17%	4.99	10.7	63	158	$10
14 WAS	341	32	11	47	0	267	263	299	399	698	820	661	5	83	0.30	55	22	23	29	99	86	88	17%	49	0%	0%	22	32%	50%	4.18	7.1	28	76	$9
15 WAS	475	41	15	68	0	229	240	258	358	616	620	615	4	79	0.21	55	20	25	26	91	81	83	16%	55	0%	0%	26	27%	42%	3.10	-10.2	7	19	$5
1st Half	248	25	8	38	0	266	265	294	411	705	682	714	4	81	0.24	57	21	22	30	88	93	77	18%	65	0%	0%	14	36%	29%	4.25	3.3	30	81	$11
2nd Half	227	16	7	30	0	189	213	219	300	519	540	513	4	76	0.18	54	18	28	22	94	68	91	14%	53	0%	0%	12	17%	58%	2.11	-12.1	-16	-43	-$1
16 Proj	**466**	**43**	**16**	**69**	**0**	**244**	**249**	**278**	**381**	**658**	**680**	**652**	**5**	**81**	**0.26**	**56**	**19**	**25**	**27**	**103**	**84**	**92**	**17%**	**53**	**0%**	**0%**				**3.59**	**-2.6**	**8**	**21**	**$11**

Rasmus,Colby

Age: 29 Bats: L Pos: LF CF RF	Health	B	LIMA Plan	C+
Ht: 6' 2" Wt: 195	PT/Exp	C	Rand Var	0
	Consist	D	MM	5213

Safe to assume ct% of 2011-12 isn't coming back. That's a shame. If he could add better ct% to legit power and sustain growth vs. LHP, more AB could produce monster HR totals. Instead, he comes as advertised in xBA column; a sub-.250 BA is what you'll get with your 20+ HR in <500 AB.

Yr Tm	AB	R	HR	RBI	SB	BA	xBA	OBP	SLG	OPS	vL	vR	bb%	ct%	Eye	G	L	F	h%	HctX	PX	xPX	hr/f	Spd	SBO	SB%	#Wk	DOM	DIS	RC/G	RAR	BPV	BPX	R$
11 2 TM	471	75	14	53	5	225	233	298	391	688	670	695	10	75	0.43	36	16	48	27	124	117	139	8%	121	6%	71%	25	44%	44%	3.84	-15.7	53	118	$7
12 TOR	565	75	23	75	4	223	237	289	400	689	554	740	8	74	0.32	38	20	42	26	114	115	123	13%	111	6%	57%	27	37%	33%	3.66	-15.7	37	93	$10
13 TOR	417	57	22	66	0	276	253	338	501	840	712	893	8	68	0.27	33	22	45	36	109	175	148	17%	101	1%	0%	22	59%	27%	5.85	22.2	59	148	$16
14 TOR *	369	45	18	41	4	218	241	276	427	703	684	752	7	63	0.22	34	23	42	29	111	180	170	19%	87	6%	100%	21	52%	43%	3.90	2.3	40	108	$7
15 HOU	432	67	25	61	2	238	235	314	475	789	835	770	10	64	0.31	28	20	52	31	97	178	149	18%	83	3%	67%	27	41%	33%	4.95	7.2	46	124	$12
1st Half	198	29	10	26	1	242	238	315	475	790	838	770	10	62	0.28	29	23	48	34	99	192	163	18%	85	5%	50%	14	43%	50%	4.96	2.4	47	127	$8
2nd Half	234	38	15	35	1	235	232	313	474	787	832	769	10	67	0.33	28	18	54	28	95	167	138	18%	91	2%	100%	13	38%	15%	4.95	2.7	49	132	$15
16 Proj	**382**	**55**	**21**	**52**	**2**	**237**	**239**	**307**	**463**	**770**	**756**	**775**	**9**	**66**	**0.29**	**31**	**21**	**48**	**30**	**104**	**168**	**152**	**17%**	**90**	**3%**	**76%**				**4.72**	**1.8**	**40**	**108**	**$12**

Realmuto,Jacob

Age: 25 Bats: R Pos: CA	Health	A	LIMA Plan	B+
Ht: 6' 1" Wt: 215	PT/Exp	C	Rand Var	0
	Consist	B	MM	2435

Weak first two months cloak how good rest of season was (.283 BA from June 5 on). Rare wheels for catcher, with improved SB% in 2H, when he started to hit the ball harder, too. Double-digit HR, SB within reach; if 2H guy sticks around, ceiling is even higher... UP: .275, 15 HR, 15 SB

Yr Tm	AB	R	HR	RBI	SB	BA	xBA	OBP	SLG	OPS	vL	vR	bb%	ct%	Eye	G	L	F	h%	HctX	PX	xPX	hr/f	Spd	SBO	SB%	#Wk	DOM	DIS	RC/G	RAR	BPV	BPX	R$
11																																		
12																																		
13 aa	368	35	4	33	8	221		282	321	603			8	80	0.43				27		75			105	10%	88%				3.03		30	75	$2
14 MIA *	404	54	5	56	14	258	291	313	386	699	2000	563	7	82	0.44	43	33	24	30	101	91	57	0%	123	19%	71%	6	17%	67%	4.10	7.7	54	146	$13
15 MIA	441	49	10	47	8	259	269	290	406	696	791	671	4	84	0.27	45	21	34	29	108	88	106	8%	121	13%	67%	25	44%	16%	3.96	1.8	53	143	$11
1st Half	223	22	3	18	2	247	263	277	368	644	898	562	4	84	0.29	46	22	32	28	97	74	86	5%	125	8%	50%	13	38%	15%	3.37	-2.7	44	119	$4
2nd Half	218	27	7	29	6	271	275	303	445	748	622	772	4	84	0.26	44	21	36	30	120	103	126	11%	110	17%	75%	12	50%	17%	4.62	5.3	61	165	$17
16 Proj	**462**	**54**	**11**	**54**	**12**	**260**	**268**	**304**	**413**	**717**	**777**	**703**	**6**	**83**	**0.35**	**45**	**21**	**34**	**29**	**111**	**95**	**110**	**8%**	**127**	**15%**	**71%**				**4.26**	**6.5**	**57**	**153**	**$16**

Reddick,Josh

Age: 29 Bats: L Pos: RF	Health	C	LIMA Plan	B+
Ht: 6' 2" Wt: 180	PT/Exp	B	Rand Var	0
	Consist	B	MM	3425

Traded power for contact, to positive effect. If approach sticks, days of 30+ HR may be gone for good, but so, too, may be days of sub-.250 BA. If he could sustain 2H success vs. LHP, BA could climb even higher. May even have bit of SB potential (see 2H SBO, SB%); a nice bonus, if so.

Yr Tm	AB	R	HR	RBI	SB	BA	xBA	OBP	SLG	OPS	vL	vR	bb%	ct%	Eye	G	L	F	h%	HctX	PX	xPX	hr/f	Spd	SBO	SB%	#Wk	DOM	DIS	RC/G	RAR	BPV	BPX	R$
11 BOS *	445	71	18	57	4	249	268	319	449	767	766	787	9	79	0.49	31	23	46	28	106	135	121	7%	121	7%	58%	16	56%	25%	4.77	-5.1	81	180	$12
12 OAK	611	85	32	85	11	242	249	305	463	768	751	778	8	75	0.36	29	21	50	27	103	141	131	14%	125	9%	92%	28	61%	21%	4.82	-0.7	70	175	$19
13 OAK	385	54	12	56	9	226	240	307	379	686	667	695	11	78	0.53	36	20	44	26	88	106	110	9%	113	11%	82%	24	58%	25%	3.90	-4.4	53	133	$9
14 OAK	363	53	12	54	1	264	250	316	446	763	533	849	7	83	0.44	33	18	50	29	103	115	118	8%	145	2%	50%	21	62%	14%	4.87	10.2	82	222	$11
15 OAK	526	67	20	77	10	272	276	333	449	781	654	826	9	88	0.75	38	21	41	28	97	100	92	11%	120	8%	83%	26	65%	8%	5.29	7.8	85	230	$20
1st Half	285	37	11	49	3	288	282	346	463	809	459	921	8	88	0.79	37	24	39	29	103	95	86	11%	128	5%	75%	13	62%	8%	5.75	7.5	87	235	$24
2nd Half	241	30	9	28	7	253	271	317	432	749	856	708	9	87	0.72	40	18	42	26	91	106	99	10%	112	13%	88%	13	69%	8%	4.78	-0.3	85	230	$15
16 Proj	**461**	**63**	**17**	**65**	**10**	**265**	**259**	**326**	**441**	**767**	**671**	**804**	**9**	**84**	**0.58**	**36**	**20**	**44**	**29**	**97**	**105**	**106**	**10%**	**124**	**9%**	**84%**				**5.06**	**3.2**	**71**	**191**	**$19**

Reed,A.J.

Age: 23 Bats: L Pos: DH	Health	A	LIMA Plan	D
Ht: 6' 4" Wt: 240	PT/Exp	F	Rand Var	0
	Consist	F	MM	4021

2014 SEC Player of Year (Kentucky) showed explosive power growth in 2015, mashing 34 HR in 532 AB across two levels. Promotion to AA-Corpus Christi barely slowed roll (.332/.405/.571 in 205 AB). Off-season buzz for HOU 1Bman only likely to escalate. By spring, hype may be deafening.

Yr Tm	AB	R	HR	RBI	SB	BA	xBA	OBP	SLG	OPS	vL	vR	bb%	ct%	Eye	G	L	F	h%	HctX	PX	xPX	hr/f	Spd	SBO	SB%	#Wk	DOM	DIS	RC/G	RAR	BPV	BPX	R$
11																																		
12																																		
13																																		
14																																		
15 aa	205	30	9	36	0	296		363	499	863			10	73	0.39				37		142			89	0%	0%				6.58		52	141	$8
1st Half																																		
2nd Half	205	30	9	36	0	296		363	499	863			10	73	0.39				37		142			82	0%	0%				6.58		50	135	$8
16 Proj	**96**	**13**	**5**	**15**	**0**	**268**	**260**	**334**	**476**	**810**	**810**	**810**	**9**	**75**	**0.40**	**38**	**20**	**42**	**31**		**138**		**15%**	**87**	**0%**	**0%**				**5.53**	**0.2**	**46**	**123**	**$4**

KRISTOPHER OLSON

Refsnyder,Rob

Age: 25	Bats: R	Pos: 2B	Health A	LIMA Plan D	
Ht: 6' 1"	Wt: 205		PT/Exp D	Rand Var +2	
			Consist B	MM 2331	

2-5-.302 with 2 SB in 43 AB at NYY. Continued to build off 2014 breakout, held his own in debut though BA, hr/f were small sample mirages. Ceiling is modest, defense still a work in progress. But already knows how to draw a walk; looks ready to contribute with respectable BA, decent power/speed combo at shallow position.

Yr	Tm	AB	R	HR	RBI	SB	BA	xBA	OBP	SLG	OPS	vL	vR	bb%	ct%	Eye	G	L	F	h%	HctX	PX	xPX	hr/f	Spd	SBO	SB%	#Wk	DOM	DIS	RC/G	RAR	BPV	BPX	R$
11																																			
12																																			
13																																			
14	a/a	515	64	12	49	7	278		334	426	760			8	77	0.36				34		115			101	12%	41%				4.71		46	124	$16
15	NYY *	493	60	11	53	12	249	280	321	376	697	667	1308	10	82	0.57	67	17	17	29	90	85	75	33%	94	11%	85%	6	33%	17%	4.16	-1.6	44	119	$12
1st Half		295	37	5	29	9	254	244	335	351	685			11	83	0.73				29		66			86	11%	88%	1	0%	0%	4.13		36	97	$15
2nd Half		198	23	6	24	4	242	292	299	413	712	667	1308	8	79	0.39	67	17	17	28	87	116	75	33%	99	11%	77%	5	40%	20%	4.16	-0.4	56	151	$8
16	Proj	**160**	**19**	**4**	**17**	**3**	**259**	**266**	**324**	**397**	**721**	**714**	**724**	**9**	**79**	**0.46**	**52**	**21**	**28**	**31**	**78**	**96**	**68**	**10%**	**104**	**11%**	**66%**				**4.36**	**0.6**	**38**	**103**	**$3**

Reimold,Nolan

Age: 32	Bats: R	Pos: LF	Health F	LIMA Plan D	
Ht: 6' 4"	Wt: 205		PT/Exp F	Rand Var 0	
			Consist C	MM 3301	

6-20-.247 in 170 AB at BAL. Finally managed to stay healthy enough to give us a reasonable sample to draw conclusions from, and results aren't very encouraging. xBA history confirms he's a BA drag, while power metrics and GB% suggest he won't make up for it elsewhere. BAL is nothing if not persistent.

Yr	Tm	AB	R	HR	RBI	SB	BA	xBA	OBP	SLG	OPS	vL	vR	bb%	ct%	Eye	G	L	F	h%	HctX	PX	xPX	hr/f	Spd	SBO	SB%	#Wk	DOM	DIS	RC/G	RAR	BPV	BPX	R$
11	BAL *	406	51	18	61	8	228	238	298	410	708	680	830	9	73	0.37	45	14	41	27	81	124	106	15%	133	12%	72%	20	50%	25%	4.01	-11.3	52	116	$9
12	BAL	67	10	5	10	1	313	333	333	627	960	1076	922	3	79	0.14	43	26	30	33	91	201	92	31%	104	8%	100%	5	60%	20%	7.86	5.9	116	290	$2
13	BAL *	174	19	6	15	0	183	194	238	305	544	595	579	7	67	0.22	48	13	38	24	93	88	140	15%	125	3%	0%	8	25%	50%	2.20	-9.9	-8	-20	-$3
14	2 TM *	123	12	4	19	2	235	220	313	402	715	758	672	10	60	0.29	50	18	33	35	92	159	110	23%	97	9%	56%	9	33%	56%	4.08	1.5	20	54	$1
15	BAL *	367	45	8	33	4	237	219	321	350	671	791	691	11	73	0.46	49	16	35	30	89	82	94	14%	108	5%	77%	17	35%	65%	3.77	-6.9	14	38	$5
1st Half		216	25	4	16	4	240	226	303	353	656	957	566	8	74	0.35	41	21	38	31	67	84	88	18%	108	10%	77%	5	60%	40%	3.60	-6.2	14	38	$5
2nd Half		151	20	4	17	0	234	201	344	345	690	714	718	14	72	0.60	51	15	34	30	94	78	96	13%	99	0%	0%	12	25%	75%	3.96	-2.7	11	30	$3
16	Proj	**220**	**26**	**9**	**25**	**2**	**227**	**229**	**306**	**394**	**700**	**747**	**660**	**10**	**69**	**0.37**	**48**	**17**	**35**	**29**	**87**	**119**	**105**	**17%**	**109**	**6%**	**68%**				**3.96**	**-4.0**	**11**	**30**	**$5**

Rendon,Anthony

Age: 26	Bats: R	Pos: 2B 3B	Health C	LIMA Plan A	
Ht: 6' 1"	Wt: 200		PT/Exp B	Rand Var -3	
			Consist C	MM 3335	

5-25-.264 in 311 AB at WAS. Variety of injuries (knee, oblique, quad) wiped out much of season. Didn't hit a HR until Aug 2. Despite plus speed, 2014 SB total stands out as fluke (1 in 373 career minor league PA). Price tag will be much lower, and power should bounce back, but ceiling isn't as high as many thought a year ago.

Yr	Tm	AB	R	HR	RBI	SB	BA	xBA	OBP	SLG	OPS	vL	vR	bb%	ct%	Eye	G	L	F	h%	HctX	PX	xPX	hr/f	Spd	SBO	SB%	#Wk	DOM	DIS	RC/G	RAR	BPV	BPX	R$
11																																			
12	aa	68	11	2	2	0	148		242	320	562			11	76	0.51				15		111			124	0%	0%				2.31		52	130	-$3
13	WAS *	478	55	12	54	2	267	272	343	421	764	830	682	10	79	0.55	41	26	34	32	120	113	115	7%	114	2%	64%	20	45%	20%	5.01	18.5	64	160	$12
14	WAS	613	111	21	83	17	287	279	351	473	824	825	824	9	83	0.56	40	20	40	32	136	126	146	10%	121	12%	85%	27	67%	11%	5.97	44.5	88	238	$32
15	WAS *	335	44	5	25	1	261	238	336	361	698	750	697	10	78	0.52	45	21	33	32	109	76	105	6%	108	3%	33%	16	19%	44%	4.11	-0.5	27	73	$5
1st Half		93	10	0	5	0	272	234	351	354	705	849	705	11	81	0.65	42	19	39	33	94	73	72	0%	95	7%	0%	4	25%	50%	4.00	-0.6	36	97	-$6
2nd Half		242	34	5	20	1	256	239	335	364	698	716	694	10	76	0.47	46	22	32	32	113	77	115	8%	111	1%	100%	12	17%	42%	4.15	-0.5	23	62	$9
16	Proj	**505**	**73**	**16**	**50**	**7**	**271**	**265**	**346**	**437**	**783**	**823**	**771**	**10**	**80**	**0.55**	**40**	**21**	**38**	**31**	**118**	**110**	**117**	**10%**	**115**	**7%**	**68%**				**5.20**	**14.2**	**56**	**150**	**$18**

Revere,Ben

Age: 28	Bats: L	Pos: LF CF	Health B	LIMA Plan D+	
Ht: 5' 9"	Wt: 165		PT/Exp B	Rand Var -1	
			Consist A	MM 0555	

Elite ct%, LD stroke, excellent speed consistently lead to elevated h%, high BA, and reasonable OBP. Hamstring issue that cropped up in early July, rather than deadline deal to TOR, was more than likely culprit for 2H declines in Spd, SBO. Considering relative youth and steady track record, expect return to form.

Yr	Tm	AB	R	HR	RBI	SB	BA	xBA	OBP	SLG	OPS	vL	vR	bb%	ct%	Eye	G	L	F	h%	HctX	PX	xPX	hr/f	Spd	SBO	SB%	#Wk	DOM	DIS	RC/G	RAR	BPV	BPX	R$
11	MIN *	582	68	1	37	40	267	291	304	311	615	609	624	5	91	0.58	69	20	12	29	52	27	18	0%	155	31%	78%	22	36%	18%	3.38	-26.5	44	98	$20
12	MIN *	605	78	0	37	45	294	278	330	337	667	676	675	5	90	0.53	67	19	15	33	73	26	23	0%	160	30%	80%	24	29%	21%	4.15	-7.1	41	103	$27
13	PHI	315	37	0	17	22	305	277	338	352	691	858	641	5	89	0.44	59	23	17	34	87	32	31	0%	153	30%	73%	15	27%	33%	4.34	3.3	38	95	$15
14	PHI	601	71	2	28	49	306	293	325	361	686	763	653	2	92	0.27	65	21	14	33	64	33	23	3%	175	33%	86%	27	22%	11%	4.51	13.5	52	141	$34
15	2 TM	592	84	2	45	31	306	291	342	377	719	638	747	5	89	0.50	55	26	19	34	71	44	34	2%	157	21%	82%	27	30%	15%	4.83	7.1	51	138	$29
1st Half		309	43	1	21	19	291	302	328	379	707	561	755	5	90	0.50	54	28	18	32	61	51	26	2%	166	28%	79%	14	43%	14%	4.51	-0.4	61	165	$28
2nd Half		283	41	1	24	12	322	278	356	375	731	708	739	5	89	0.50	55	24	20	36	81	37	44	2%	131	15%	86%	13	15%	15%	5.20	4.9	36	97	$31
16	Proj	**603**	**79**	**2**	**39**	**42**	**305**	**288**	**336**	**364**	**699**	**672**	**710**	**4**	**90**	**0.44**	**59**	**24**	**17**	**34**	**72**	**36**	**31**	**2%**	**156**	**27%**	**83%**				**4.64**	**1.3**	**42**	**113**	**$34**

Reyes,Jose

Age: 33	Bats: B	Pos: SS	Health C	LIMA Plan B+	
Ht: 6' 0"	Wt: 195		PT/Exp B	Rand Var 0	
			Consist B	MM 1435	

Rib injury cost him a month, Achilles problem plagued him down the stretch. League high infield fly ball percentage sent power numbers further south, while speed, xBA, and Eye continued their slow fade. Still has 30 SB potential, but age and recent health issues make him riskier than ever.

Yr	Tm	AB	R	HR	RBI	SB	BA	xBA	OBP	SLG	OPS	vL	vR	bb%	ct%	Eye	G	L	F	h%	HctX	PX	xPX	hr/f	Spd	SBO	SB%	#Wk	DOM	DIS	RC/G	RAR	BPV	BPX	R$
11	NYM	537	101	7	44	39	337	290	384	493	877	842	888	7	92	1.05	42	21	37	36	110	91	88	4%	179	27%	85%	23	74%	4%	7.53	43.0	113	251	$36
12	MIA	642	86	11	57	40	287	291	347	433	780	753	792	9	91	1.13	46	22	32	30	109	84	83	6%	127	27%	78%	27	74%	4%	5.46	24.8	90	225	$29
13	TOR	382	58	10	37	15	296	275	353	427	780	705	804	8	88	0.72	46	21	33	32	99	84	82	9%	98	18%	71%	17	59%	24%	5.38	20.2	66	165	$18
14	TOR	610	94	9	51	30	287	268	328	398	726	709	732	6	88	0.52	42	23	36	31	89	77	66	5%	131	19%	94%	26	42%	8%	4.93	28.0	67	181	$29
15	2 TM	481	57	7	53	24	274	257	310	378	688	700	683	5	87	0.42	44	20	36	30	74	67	59	5%	102	24%	80%	24	38%	25%	4.20	6.0	45	122	$20
1st Half		227	30	4	28	10	273	258	304	388	692	585	725	5	86	0.34	36	23	40	30	85	78	64	5%	85	20%	91%	11	45%	18%	4.35	1.7	43	116	$18
2nd Half		254	27	3	25	14	276	258	315	370	685	770	641	6	88	0.50	51	17	32	30	64	59	55	4%	115	28%	74%	13	31%	31%	4.08	0.0	48	130	$22
16	Proj	**505**	**69**	**8**	**50**	**25**	**285**	**266**	**328**	**399**	**727**	**720**	**730**	**6**	**88**	**0.56**	**44**	**21**	**35**	**31**	**84**	**72**	**67**	**5%**	**115**	**22%**	**81%**				**4.78**	**9.9**	**61**	**165**	**$25**

Reynolds,Mark

Age: 32	Bats: R	Pos: 1B 3B	Health A	LIMA Plan D+	
Ht: 6' 2"	Wt: 220		PT/Exp C	Rand Var 0	
			Consist A	MM 4103	

More GB than ever before left power numbers well below expected level. Career-best ct%, LD%, HctX in 2H are worth noting, but lengthy track record suggests whiffs will return. With PX, xPX, and average fly ball distance at all-time lows, no longer offers enough pop to compensate for the BA harm he'll do.

Yr	Tm	AB	R	HR	RBI	SB	BA	xBA	OBP	SLG	OPS	vL	vR	bb%	ct%	Eye	G	L	F	h%	HctX	PX	xPX	hr/f	Spd	SBO	SB%	#Wk	DOM	DIS	RC/G	RAR	BPV	BPX	R$
11	BAL	534	84	37	86	6	221	248	323	483	806	781	814	12	63	0.38	39	13	48	27	104	209	171	23%	73	8%	60%	27	56%	15%	4.92	-21.9	69	153	$16
12	BAL	457	65	23	69	1	221	236	335	429	763	722	778	14	65	0.46	37	20	42	28	100	161	138	18%	71	3%	25%	25	32%	44%	4.50	-12.9	41	103	$8
13	2 AL	445	55	21	67	3	220	217	306	393	699	725	684	10	65	0.33	39	18	42	29	94	132	125	17%	77	4%	75%	27	44%	48%	3.86	-9.8	13	33	$9
14	MIL	378	47	22	45	5	196	223	287	394	681	573	719	11	68	0.39	38	14	48	22	94	146	155	18%	89	7%	83%	26	46%	38%	3.58	-7.2	38	103	$6
15	STL	382	35	13	48	2	230	229	315	398	713	753	697	10	68	0.36	41	19	40	30	94	126	118	13%	87	5%	40%	27	48%	41%	3.98	-16.1	23	62	$4
1st Half		207	15	5	26	2	227	208	294	362	656	725	631	9	65	0.27	45	17	38	33	80	112	110	10%	81	6%	67%	14	36%	50%	3.50	-10.4	-7	-19	$3
2nd Half		175	20	8	22	0	234	255	338	440	778	784	776	12	73	0.50	38	21	41	28	110	142	125	15%	93	4%	0%	13	62%	31%	4.57	-3.1	58	157	$6
16	Proj	**343**	**39**	**14**	**45**	**2**	**220**	**224**	**311**	**396**	**707**	**699**	**709**	**11**	**68**	**0.39**	**40**	**18**	**43**	**28**	**97**	**128**	**132**	**14%**	**89**	**5%**	**53%**				**3.89**	**-13.4**	**15**	**40**	**$7**

Rios,Alex

Age: 35	Bats: R	Pos: RF	Health C	LIMA Plan B	
Ht: 6' 5"	Wt: 210		PT/Exp B	Rand Var +1	
			Consist B	MM 1423	

Signs of decline becoming more evident. Missed nearly 7 weeks after fracturing hand in April, and upon return, "hit" .181/.210/.202 in next 100 PA. Recent success vs. LHP came to abrupt halt, he's no longer a power threat, and SB potential capped by Spd, SBO, OBP all falling. PT could be next shoe to drop.

Yr	Tm	AB	R	HR	RBI	SB	BA	xBA	OBP	SLG	OPS	vL	vR	bb%	ct%	Eye	G	L	F	h%	HctX	PX	xPX	hr/f	Spd	SBO	SB%	#Wk	DOM	DIS	RC/G	RAR	BPV	BPX	R$
11	CHW	537	64	13	44	11	227	255	265	348	613	704	578	5	87	0.40	42	18	39	24	98	76	76	7%	108	15%	65%	27	48%	26%	2.96	-36.3	54	120	$7
12	CHW	605	93	25	91	23	304	288	334	516	850	857	848	4	85	0.28	40	22	38	33	119	125	111	13%	127	21%	79%	27	59%	19%	6.27	23.6	87	218	$34
13	2 AL	616	83	18	81	42	278	269	324	432	756	889	714	6	82	0.38	44	21	35	31	85	102	83	10%	118	31%	86%	27	52%	26%	5.09	14.3	61	153	$36
14	TEX	492	54	4	54	17	280	260	311	398	709	898	646	4	81	0.25	43	24	34	34	92	89	91	3%	143	22%	65%	23	43%	30%	4.26	5.1	49	132	$18
15	KC	385	40	4	32	9	255	245	287	353	640	570	668	4	83	0.22	40	22	38	30	98	70	90	3%	102	11%	100%	20	50%	35%	3.54	-13.8	26	70	$7
1st Half		137	13	1	12	4	219	213	243	263	506	482	516	1	81	0.08	38	23	39	26	60	31	53	2%	88	14%	100%	8	25%	50%	2.10	-11.4	-20	-54	-$2
2nd Half		248	27	3	20	5	274	263	311	403	714	622	749	5	83	0.32	41	22	37	32	119	91	110	4%	107	9%	100%	12	67%	25%	4.52	-2.1	51	138	$12
16	Proj	**402**	**45**	**5**	**40**	**10**	**264**	**250**	**298**	**371**	**669**	**697**	**659**	**4**	**82**	**0.25**	**41**	**22**	**37**	**31**	**94**	**74**	**88**	**4%**	**119**	**13%**	**76%**				**3.80**	**-11.9**	**32**	**87**	**$12**

BRIAN RUDD

Rivera,Rene

Age: 32 Bats: R Pos: CA | Ht: 5' 10" Wt: 215

Health A | LIMA Plan D | PT/Exp D | Rand Var +3 | Consist F | MM 2003

Hard to believe these skills netted 300+ PA; BPV was second-lowest in MLB with that many (thanks, Zunino). Plate skills were atrocious, though 1H h% collapse didn't help. Sliver of hope lies with xPX, which hints at notable PX, xBA recovery, and might be enough to warrant $1 bid in hopes of returning to 2014 form.

Yr Tm	AB	R	HR	RBI	SB	BA	xBA	OBP	SLG	OPS	vL	vR	bb%	ct%	Eye	G	L	F	h%	HctX	PX	xPX	hr/f	Spd	SBO	SB%	#Wk	DOM	DIS	RC/G	RAR	BPV	BPX	R$
11 MIN *	253	20	4	22	0	183	180	232	283	515	555	360	6	74	0.24	44	8	48	23	82	81	96	3%	62	0%	0%	15	20%	53%	2.05	-17.4	-5	-11	-$5
12 aaa	288	23	7	25	0	179		239	296	535			7	73	0.30				22		83			87	2%	0%				2.15		2	5	-$4
13 SD *	318	26	3	30	0	242	202	270	325	595	529	618	4	76	0.16	48	13	38	31	124	67	144	0%	76	4%	0%	10	10%	50%	2.84	-8.1	-8	-20	$1
14 SD	294	27	11	44	0	252	252	319	432	751	881	684	8	74	0.36	35	21	44	30	107	138	138	11%	67	0%	0%	27	48%	37%	4.63	11.3	46	124	$6
15 TAM	298	16	5	26	0	178	193	213	275	489	457	503	4	71	0.13	38	17	45	23	84	77	118	5%	42	0%	0%	26	12%	62%	1.77	-18.8	-31	-84	-$6
1st Half	207	11	4	19	0	169	206	205	280	486	450	503	4	73	0.14	35	18	46	21	82	86	119	6%	42	0%	0%	14	21%	50%	1.72	-13.9	-17	-46	-$6
2nd Half	91	5	1	7	0	198	165	232	264	495	474	504	3	67	0.10	44	15	41	28	89	56	116	4%	61	0%	0%	12	0%	75%	1.87	-5.5	-60	-162	-$5
16 Proj	299	23	9	32	0	224	219	267	363	630	674	611	5	73	0.19	39	18	43	28	97	100	124	9%	57	1%	0%				3.11	-6.1	-10	-27	$1

Rizzo,Anthony

Age: 26 Bats: L Pos: 1B | Ht: 6' 3" Wt: 240

Health A | LIMA Plan C | PT/Exp A | Rand Var +1 | Consist C | MM 4145

Another fine year makes it increasingly hard to find holes in his game: Eye, ct% continued to climb, while xBA remained in great shape; steady FB% growth, plus power make him a true 30-HR threat; no L/R splits; SB spike was icing on the cake. A 1st-rounder? There's lots of competition but he could well earn it.

Yr Tm	AB	R	HR	RBI	SB	BA	xBA	OBP	SLG	OPS	vL	vR	bb%	ct%	Eye	G	L	F	h%	HctX	PX	xPX	hr/f	Spd	SBO	SB%	#Wk	DOM	DIS	RC/G	RAR	BPV	BPX	R$
11 SD *	484	49	16	72	6	222	228	294	396	690	618	495	9	68	0.32	43	13	44	29	84	146	126	3%	59	14%	44%	11	27%	73%	3.61	-39.9	26	58	$7
12 CHC *	594	80	32	94	4	290	291	340	510	849	599	892	7	79	0.37	45	24	30	32	112	136	119	18%	83	6%	51%	15	60%	20%	6.09	10.9	68	170	$26
13 CHC	606	71	23	80	6	233	269	323	419	742	625	796	11	79	0.60	43	20	38	26	112	130	124	13%	68	7%	55%	27	63%	7%	4.34	-4.5	65	163	$13
14 CHC	524	89	32	78	5	286	286	386	527	913	928	907	12	78	0.63	36	22	42	31	106	164	135	19%	72	6%	56%	25	72%	4%	6.90	40.2	91	246	$28
15 CHC	586	94	31	101	17	278	285	387	512	899	881	905	12	82	0.74	35	22	44	29	120	143	130	15%	75	14%	74%	27	70%	15%	6.51	19.1	91	246	$31
1st Half	291	44	15	45	12	292	310	405	543	948	940	949	12	86	0.95	34	25	41	30	133	151	144	15%	74	20%	71%	14	79%	7%	7.21	17.0	111	300	$32
2nd Half	295	50	16	56	5	264	261	369	481	850	847	851	11	79	0.60	35	19	46	29	107	134	116	15%	80	7%	83%	13	62%	23%	5.85	5.9	71	192	$30
16 Proj	590	95	33	105	11	282	281	379	519	898	867	910	11	79	0.61	37	21	42	31	112	148	128	17%	71	9%	67%				6.57	23.9	85	231	$33

Robinson,Clint

Age: 31 Bats: L Pos: 1B LF | Ht: 6' 5" Wt: 225

Health A | LIMA Plan D+ | PT/Exp C | Rand Var -3 | Consist C | MM 2031

Extended MLB look yielded strong, skill-supported results. Batting eye gains were the highlight, while xBA agrees that the BA jump was well deserved. 2H FB% bump, xPX hint at some HR staying power as well. But he's a career minor leaguer over 30 with suspect BPV history. '15 was more likely career year than step forward.

Yr Tm	AB	R	HR	RBI	SB	BA	xBA	OBP	SLG	OPS	vL	vR	bb%	ct%	Eye	G	L	F	h%	HctX	PX	xPX	hr/f	Spd	SBO	SB%	#Wk	DOM	DIS	RC/G	RAR	BPV	BPX	R$
11 aaa	503	59	14	69	1	264		318	405	723			7	80	0.39				31		102			78	2%	53%				4.43		40	89	$12
12 KC *	491	46	8	44	1	225	181	298	337	635	0	0	9	84	0.64	50	0	50	25	0	78	-11	0%	83	1%	100%	2	0%	100%	3.32	-31.4	43	108	$2
13 a/a	397	37	10	38	1	203		277	332	609			9	74	0.39				25		97			91	3%	22%				2.87		20	50	-$1
14 LA *	438	45	10	45	0	218	291	275	348	623	0	929	7	74	0.30	50	38	13	27	40	102	-14	0%	105	0%	0%	3	0%	33%	3.12	-14.3	24	65	$2
15 WAS	309	44	10	34	0	272	273	358	424	782	985	757	11	83	0.71	41	25	34	30	105	94	111	11%	89	0%	0%	27	56%	33%	5.19	-1.5	58	157	$7
1st Half	131	22	4	15	0	267	295	342	427	770	1038	745	10	85	0.79	41	29	30	29	98	96	98	12%	95	0%	0%	14	50%	43%	5.09	-0.2	70	189	$5
2nd Half	178	22	6	19	0	275	254	369	421	790	958	766	11	81	0.67	40	22	38	31	111	92	120	11%	86	0%	0%	13	62%	23%	5.26	0.5	49	132	$9
16 Proj	222	27	7	24	0	246	262	326	395	720	899	699	9	79	0.49	41	25	35	28	106	97	111	11%	87	1%	40%				4.21	-6.2	30	80	$5

Rodriguez,Alex

Age: 40 Bats: R Pos: DH | Ht: 6' 3" Wt: 225

Health D | LIMA Plan B | PT/Exp D | Rand Var +1 | Consist B | MM 4125

Did 162-game PED ban actually help revive career? Showed no ill-effects of 2013 hip surgery after year off, as PX soared back to peak levels. Questionable ct%, especially in 2H, leaves little room for BA growth, but xPX and 2H FB% bolster power upside. Age, health are only real obstacles, as metrics support a repeat.

Yr Tm	AB	R	HR	RBI	SB	BA	xBA	OBP	SLG	OPS	vL	vR	bb%	ct%	Eye	G	L	F	h%	HctX	PX	xPX	hr/f	Spd	SBO	SB%	#Wk	DOM	DIS	RC/G	RAR	BPV	BPX	R$
11 NYY	373	67	16	62	4	276	261	362	461	823	750	848	11	79	0.59	49	14	37	31	111	127	116	15%	84	4%	80%	21	57%	33%	5.82	-0.2	65	144	$15
12 NYY	463	74	18	57	13	272	250	353	430	783	924	717	10	75	0.44	45	22	32	33	108	103	118	16%	97	10%	93%	22	45%	32%	5.33	5.8	33	83	$18
13 NYY *	177	24	9	24	4	243	247	342	442	784	585	856	13	71	0.52	40	20	40	29	132	142	166	16%	79	11%	67%	8	50%	50%	5.01	2.7	49	123	$4
14																																		
15 NYY	523	83	33	86	4	250	261	356	486	842	926	806	14	72	0.58	43	18	39	28	113	154	146	22%	79	3%	100%	27	48%	19%	5.90	7.0	66	178	$19
1st Half	271	45	16	47	1	284	271	390	513	902	868	912	14	75	0.65	43	21	36	33	130	146	152	21%	89	1%	100%	14	43%	7%	7.05	12.1	73	197	$24
2nd Half	252	38	17	39	3	214	250	320	456	776	967	671	14	69	0.52	43	15	42	23	93	164	140	23%	69	4%	100%	13	54%	31%	4.84	-4.8	59	159	$14
16 Proj	488	75	26	73	3	240	250	342	441	784	806	772	13	73	0.54	43	19	38	28	114	134	143	19%	82	4%	67%				4.98	-6.9	43	115	$17

Rodriguez,Yorman

Age: 23 Bats: R Pos: OF | Ht: 6' 3" Wt: 195

Health A | LIMA Plan D | PT/Exp D | Rand Var 0 | Consist B | MM 2401

The Call came in early July, but was sent down days later without an AB. Calf strain later that month cut season short. PX, HR gains point to continued development as he stays ahead of age/level curve, but ct% history hints at BA risk, bumps in the road vs. MLB pitching. A long-term hold, but needs more seasoning.

Yr Tm	AB	R	HR	RBI	SB	BA	xBA	OBP	SLG	OPS	vL	vR	bb%	ct%	Eye	G	L	F	h%	HctX	PX	xPX	hr/f	Spd	SBO	SB%	#Wk	DOM	DIS	RC/G	RAR	BPV	BPX	R$
11																																		
12																																		
13 aa	262	27	4	28	4	256		315	372	687			8	68	0.27				36		98			101	5%	100%				4.10		0	0	$4
14 CIN *	477	57	9	33	9	233	236	290	340	630	333	542	7	69	0.26	57	21	21	32	0	86	-14	0%	148	13%	59%	4	0%	100%	3.18	-8.8	7	19	$7
15 aaa	308	36	10	35	3	249		284	405	689			5	70	0.16				32		108			109	7%	76%				3.90		11	30	$6
1st Half	287	34	9	34	3	251		286	408	694			5	70	0.16				33		110			120	6%	70%				3.95		15	41	$7
2nd Half	21	2	1	1	1	222		253	370	623			4	73	0.15				26		85			111	19%	100%				3.25		2	5	-$13
16 Proj	228	26	5	23	3	235	225	287	357	645	645	645	7	69	0.24	48	20	32	32		92		9%	127	8%	77%				3.43	#N/A	-3	-9	$4

Rogers,Jason

Age: 28 Bats: R Pos: 1B | Ht: 6' 2" Wt: 245

Health A | LIMA Plan D+ | PT/Exp C | Rand Var -5 | Consist B | MM 2323

4-16-.296 in 152 AB at MIL. Held his own in first full MLB season. PRO: HctX, xPX confirm pop is very real; has plate approach to stick in majors. CON: G/L/F doesn't fit his profile, as low LD% hurts xBA, and FB% caps HR upside for now. Looming h% correction casts doubt on BA repeat, but power is in place for... UP: 20 HR.

Yr Tm	AB	R	HR	RBI	SB	BA	xBA	OBP	SLG	OPS	vL	vR	bb%	ct%	Eye	G	L	F	h%	HctX	PX	xPX	hr/f	Spd	SBO	SB%	#Wk	DOM	DIS	RC/G	RAR	BPV	BPX	R$
11																																		
12																																		
13 aa	481	54	19	68	5	236		305	409	714			9	79	0.47				26		114			88	7%	70%				4.14		53	133	$11
14 MIL *	502	56	15	59	4	246	226	303	404	706	500	250	8	77	0.36	38	13	50	29	42	113	17	0%	91	4%	75%	4	50%	25%	4.13	-0.8	43	116	$11
15 MIL *	274	38	10	32	0	287	253	360	458	818	754	853	10	77	0.50	54	16	30	34	124	109	129	11%	103	0%	0%	21	48%	38%	5.90	4.1	49	132	$8
1st Half	114	15	4	12	0	248	247	292	392	684	577	713	6	81	0.32	58	13	29	28	123	86	116	10%	94	0%	0%	12	50%	33%	3.88	-4.3	33	89	$1
2nd Half	160	23	7	20	0	315	264	405	505	910	1048	1008	13	74	0.59	48	22	30	39	128	128	148	14%	109	0%	0%	9	44%	44%	7.62	10.6	61	165	$13
16 Proj	255	32	7	31	1	264	252	339	410	750	748	766	9	77	0.44	52	18	30	32	126	97	135	12%	107	2%	77%				4.71	-3.3	27	74	$8

Rollins,Jimmy

Age: 37 Bats: B Pos: SS | Ht: 5' 8" Wt: 180

Health A | LIMA Plan B+ | PT/Exp A | Rand Var +2 | Consist B | MM 2425

Production suffered, but skills were nearly identical to 2014's resurgence. 1H h% torpedoed BA, though xBA and stable ct% should ease concerns. xPX held strong despite power dip, while Spd and 2H SB% hint he can still post double-digit HR/SB. Getting up there, but reliability grades hint he can eke out a rebound campaign.

Yr Tm	AB	R	HR	RBI	SB	BA	xBA	OBP	SLG	OPS	vL	vR	bb%	ct%	Eye	G	L	F	h%	HctX	PX	xPX	hr/f	Spd	SBO	SB%	#Wk	DOM	DIS	RC/G	RAR	BPV	BPX	R$
11 PHI	567	87	16	63	30	268	263	338	399	736	609	779	9	90	0.98	39	20	41	28	114	78	94	8%	101	22%	79%	26	62%	12%	4.72	3.6	72	160	$24
12 PHI	632	102	23	68	30	250	266	316	427	743	612	804	9	85	0.65	39	19	42	26	97	106	95	10%	98	22%	86%	27	67%	15%	4.73	11.6	73	183	$24
13 PHI	600	65	6	39	22	252	250	318	348	667	648	674	9	85	0.63	38	23	39	29	81	72	61	3%	94	17%	79%	27	44%	19%	3.84	5.9	44	110	$15
14 PHI	538	78	17	55	28	243	252	323	394	717	679	732	11	81	0.64	40	19	40	27	92	100	101	10%	117	22%	82%	24	50%	29%	4.41	18.0	64	173	$21
15 LA	517	71	13	41	12	224	244	285	358	643	762	610	8	83	0.51	38	19	43	25	93	83	106	7%	109	17%	60%	26	27%	19%	3.24	-8.5	50	135	$8
1st Half	289	33	7	24	6	208	244	263	322	585	687	563	7	83	0.45	43	20	37	23	88	70	101	8%	90	20%	46%	14	29%	21%	2.51	-14.6	31	84	$6
2nd Half	228	38	6	17	6	246	244	312	404	716	826	677	9	84	0.59	32	18	49	27	101	100	112	6%	123	13%	86%	12	25%	17%	4.33	1.6	72	195	$11
16 Proj	414	58	11	35	15	245	249	312	384	696	724	686	9	83	0.60	38	20	42	27	94	87	98	7%	109	18%	75%				4.05	-0.4	58	155	$13

RYAN BLOOMFIELD

Romine,Andrew

Age: 30	Bats: L	Pos: 3B SS	Health	A	LIMA Plan	D
Ht: 6' 1"	Wt: 200		PT/Exp	D	Rand Var	-5
			Consist	A	MM	0401

Try not to let the SB column distract you. That's all he's got, and he's not that good at it (with 2014 SB% clearly the outlier). Infrequent contact, too frequent GB, and that HctX and PX would be disavowed by many pitchers. The truth is in the three-year run of negative BPV. No SBs are worth that.

Yr	Tm	AB	R	HR	RBI	SB	BA	xBA	OBP	SLG	OPS	vL	vR	bb%	ct%	Eye	G	L	F	h%	HctX	PX	xPX	hr/f	Spd	SBO	SB%	#Wk	DOM	DIS	RC/G	RAR	BPV	BPX	R$
11	LAA *	397	44	2	22	15	208	153	261	248	509	0	432	7	72	0.26	60	0	40	28	33	32	2	0%	124	22%	68%	6	0%	67%	2.06	-26.6	-34	-76	$1
12	LAA *	368	37	2	25	15	219	275	253	278	532	833	929	4	83	0.28	38	38	23	26	73	37	66	0%	139	33%	55%	8	13%	75%	2.08	-21.4	15	38	$3
13	LAA *	471	44	2	32	10	216	243	264	271	535	667	566	6	76	0.27	57	25	18	28	48	43	12	0%	129	15%	55%	13	15%	62%	2.23	-17.6	-7	-18	$1
14	DET	251	30	2	12	12	227	223	279	275	554	746	502	7	76	0.30	59	18	23	29	54	39	32	5%	111	21%	86%	26	8%	54%	2.67	-3.8	-15	-41	$4
15	DET	184	25	2	15	10	255	229	307	315	622	640	613	6	75	0.24	58	20	22	33	46	44	39	7%	118	29%	67%	27	15%	70%	3.10	-7.1	-15	-41	$5
1st Half		70	15	2	6	5	314	247	355	443	798	808	796	7	73	0.26	55	20	25	41	67	92	58	15%	120	45%	50%	14	7%	71%	4.76	1.4	16	43	$6
2nd Half		114	10	0	9	5	219	218	276	237	513	553	498	5	76	0.22	60	20	20	29	34	17	28	0%	112	17%	100%	13	23%	69%	2.20	-6.6	-36	-97	$4
16	Proj	210	26	2	15	10	239	228	290	291	581	671	558	6	76	0.26	58	20	22	31	50	39	33	5%	117	25%	68%				2.74	-12.2	-22	-59	$3

Rosario,Eddie

Age: 24	Bats: L	Pos: LF RF	Health	A	LIMA Plan	B
Ht: 6' 0"	Wt: 170		PT/Exp	C	Rand Var	-2
			Consist	C	MM	3425

13-50-.267 with 11 SB in 453 AB at MIN. Re-applied some lost prospect sheen in season of double-figure 3B-HR-SB (one of only two in MLB). Note 40-pt PX/xPX jumps in 2H. Current plate skills vulnerable to pitcher adjustments, and road OBP was .249, so expect some ups and downs as he irons things out.

Yr	Tm	AB	R	HR	RBI	SB	BA	xBA	OBP	SLG	OPS	vL	vR	bb%	ct%	Eye	G	L	F	h%	HctX	PX	xPX	hr/f	Spd	SBO	SB%	#Wk	DOM	DIS	RC/G	RAR	BPV	BPX	R$
11																																			
12																																			
13	aa	289	31	3	30	5	254		294	362	656			5	75	0.22				33		87			105	15%	55%				3.49		14	35	$5
14	aa	316	32	6	28	6	213		245	347	592			4	77	0.18				26		103			103	20%	59%				2.64		31	84	$2
15	MIN *	548	69	15	60	12	259	242	284	438	723	811	727	3	75	0.14	39	20	41	32	96	110	111	10%	174	17%	62%	22	41%	27%	4.14	-4.1	49	132	$16
1st Half		264	28	6	28	7	254	236	287	384	671	668	725	4	77	0.20	46	18	35	31	99	82	85	9%	146	18%	62%	10	40%	40%	3.62	-7.4	29	78	$12
2nd Half		284	41	9	32	5	264	249	280	489	769	890	728	2	73	0.09	35	22	44	33	93	138	126	10%	179	16%	63%	12	42%	17%	4.63	0.6	64	173	$20
16	Proj	493	57	16	50	10	255	250	280	440	720	768	704	4	76	0.15	39	20	40	31	95	118	110	10%	147	17%	61%				4.09	-6.9	44	120	$15

Rosario,Wilin

Age: 27	Bats: R	Pos: 1B	Health	A	LIMA Plan	D
Ht: 5' 11"	Wt: 220		PT/Exp	C	Rand Var	0
			Consist	B	MM	3131

6-29-.268 in 231 AB at COL. Position change, demotions fed into fewest AB since 2011, but it was inexplicably placid performance vs. LHP that truly rendered him an afterthought. That, weak Eye, and three-year PX/xPX slide require reversals if he's to be more than a bench bat moving forward.

Yr	Tm	AB	R	HR	RBI	SB	BA	xBA	OBP	SLG	OPS	vL	vR	bb%	ct%	Eye	G	L	F	h%	HctX	PX	xPX	hr/f	Spd	SBO	SB%	#Wk	DOM	DIS	RC/G	RAR	BPV	BPX	R$
11	COL *	459	43	20	42	1	225	251	250	406	656	1089	546	3	75	0.14	40	20	40	26	120	121	137	21%	104	4%	24%	4	50%	25%	3.27	-41.9	38	84	$5
12	COL	396	67	28	71	4	270	278	312	530	843	1140	726	6	75	0.25	46	17	37	29	117	165	142	25%	75	11%	44%	27	67%	15%	5.55	1.4	68	170	$18
13	COL	449	63	21	79	4	292	266	315	486	801	901	760	3	76	0.14	41	23	36	34	111	133	122	17%	82	5%	80%	25	44%	28%	5.50	11.4	42	105	$21
14	COL	382	46	13	54	1	267	275	305	435	739	989	650	6	82	0.33	50	19	31	30	94	120	92	13%	57	1%	100%	23	52%	17%	4.68	5.4	53	143	$11
15	COL *	379	33	11	44	3	260	265	282	421	703	757	681	3	76	0.12	55	20	26	32	98	113	74	13%	79	7%	55%	21	33%	48%	4.01	-14.9	25	68	$8
1st Half		188	18	5	23	2	292	255	309	443	752	782	770	2	76	0.10	53	18	29	36	88	107	76	15%	87	7%	67%	12	42%	42%	4.88	-1.4	22	59	$10
2nd Half		191	15	6	21	1	229	282	255	399	654	728	436	3	76	0.14	57	24	19	27	119	119	71	9%	69	6%	35%	9	22%	56%	3.27	-11.0	28	76	$5
16	Proj	169	18	5	22	1	263	265	289	421	710	832	644	4	77	0.17	51	21	28	31	105	109	92	14%	79	5%	62%				4.18	-4.8	24	66	$5

Rua,Ryan

Age: 26	Bats: R	Pos: LF	Health	C	LIMA Plan	D
Ht: 6' 2"	Wt: 205		PT/Exp	F	Rand Var	+4
			Consist	C	MM	3201

4-7-.193 in 83 AB at TEX. After spoiling Sonny Gray's no-hit bid on Opening Day, season turned ugly. Foot issues cost him two months, and he never gained traction in AAA (.197 BA) or during return to TEX. Was considered mid-tier prospect with clean swing, but will essentially start over in 2016.

Yr	Tm	AB	R	HR	RBI	SB	BA	xBA	OBP	SLG	OPS	vL	vR	bb%	ct%	Eye	G	L	F	h%	HctX	PX	xPX	hr/f	Spd	SBO	SB%	#Wk	DOM	DIS	RC/G	RAR	BPV	BPX	R$
11																																			
12																																			
13	aa	86	16	3	8	1	218		269	356	625			6	70	0.23				28		94			132	4%	100%				3.17		11	28	-$1
14	TEX *	576	58	15	68	5	266	266	313	403	716	922	664	6	78	0.31	52	23	25	32	97	101	86	9%	94	8%	48%	6	33%	33%	4.25	9.3	35	95	$16
15	TEX *	225	24	9	24	2	176	196	234	332	566	658	556	7	63	0.20	51	8	41	23	76	123	92	19%	82	6%	100%	11	27%	55%	2.44	-14.1	-8	-22	-$2
1st Half		95	10	5	8	1	168	190	214	332	546	483	682	6	64	0.16	44	9	47	20	97	118	133	20%	98	5%	100%	5	20%	60%	2.21	-7.3	-7	-19	-$4
2nd Half		130	13	4	16	2	183	201	248	332	580	879	0	8	62	0.23	63	5	32	25	43	127	24	17%	79	6%	100%	6	33%	50%	2.61	-8.1	-7	-19	$0
16	Proj	163	17	6	18	2	244	228	300	394	695	797	580	7	73	0.27	54	13	33	30	78	105	76	14%	90	7%	73%				3.92	-3.1	6	17	$4

Ruf,Darin

Age: 29	Bats: R	Pos: 1B LF	Health	B	LIMA Plan	D+
Ht: 6' 3"	Wt: 240		PT/Exp	D	Rand Var	+3
			Consist	B	MM	4123

12-39-.235 in 268 AB at PHI. In an all-LHP world, that line would have read 22-61-.371. Still, there is hope against righties. Hit rate was 7% below norm, and 70% ct% was career-best. But production speaks, and it's hard to see beyond platoon profile even as power, position versatility keep him relevant.

Yr	Tm	AB	R	HR	RBI	SB	BA	xBA	OBP	SLG	OPS	vL	vR	bb%	ct%	Eye	G	L	F	h%	HctX	PX	xPX	hr/f	Spd	SBO	SB%	#Wk	DOM	DIS	RC/G	RAR	BPV	BPX	R$
11																																			
12	PHI *	522	72	32	86	1	267	265	331	514	844	1326	845	9	74	0.37	39	17	43	30	127	163	260	30%	70	1%	100%	4	50%	0%	5.93	7.4	67	168	$19
13	PHI *	556	67	19	63	1	228	213	302	385	687	656	863	10	64	0.29	41	19	41	32	96	133	156	21%	82	2%	23%	13	38%	46%	3.78	-13.6	8	20	$8
14	PHI *	185	17	4	15	1	221	233	269	351	620	916	386	6	71	0.23	44	19	36	29	114	115	135	12%	67	2%	100%	12	42%	42%	3.11	-6.0	12	32	$0
15	PHI *	294	32	12	43	1	235	249	286	401	688	1107	483	7	76	0.29	45	20	35	27	117	110	129	17%	50	2%	100%	26	38%	35%	3.85	-13.3	21	57	$4
1st Half		145	12	4	18	0	229	244	259	365	625	1113	433	4	78	0.19	46	21	34	27	109	94	120	13%	61	0%	0%	13	38%	46%	3.13	-8.9	16	43	$0
2nd Half		149	20	8	25	1	242	250	325	436	762	1102	527	9	73	0.38	44	20	36	28	123	126	137	20%	55	3%	100%	13	38%	23%	4.60	-2.5	30	81	$9
16	Proj	324	36	15	42	1	244	251	313	437	750	1003	549	7	72	0.29	44	20	36	29	113	134	136	18%	57	2%	88%				4.42	-7.1	25	67	$9

Ruggiano,Justin

Age: 34	Bats: R	Pos: LF	Health	C	LIMA Plan	D
Ht: 6' 1"	Wt: 210		PT/Exp	D	Rand Var	0
			Consist	B	MM	4201

6-15-.248 with 5 SB in 125 AB at SEA/LA. Fantasy legacy parallels his being desired and deposed by six orgs in five years. Peaks and valleys betray terrific PX/xPX and decent Spd. Power vs LHP is main source of value, but it requires paying close attention to the matchups... and crossing your fingers.

Yr	Tm	AB	R	HR	RBI	SB	BA	xBA	OBP	SLG	OPS	vL	vR	bb%	ct%	Eye	G	L	F	h%	HctX	PX	xPX	hr/f	Spd	SBO	SB%	#Wk	DOM	DIS	RC/G	RAR	BPV	BPX	R$
11	TAM *	273	31	9	37	9	238	233	285	392	677	576	748	6	70	0.22	53	13	35	31	66	119	108	14%	95	22%	73%	15	27%	53%	3.69	-12.0	19	42	$6
12	MIA *	405	51	16	54	17	291	261	355	499	853	1129	806	9	71	0.34	41	21	38	37	120	157	165	17%	101	27%	59%	17	59%	24%	5.90	8.8	61	153	$19
13	MIA	424	49	18	50	15	222	241	298	396	694	833	631	9	73	0.36	45	17	39	26	108	123	147	15%	83	23%	65%	27	41%	44%	3.63	-12.9	36	90	$11
14	CHC *	245	31	6	28	2	266	226	322	404	726	846	720	8	68	0.26	42	20	38	37	84	119	109	10%	95	9%	33%	17	53%	47%	4.26	1.1	14	38	$6
15	2 TM *	304	36	12	33	9	226	219	291	399	689	948	527	8	64	0.25	40	19	40	31	104	136	166	18%	108	23%	54%	15	47%	47%	3.56	-12.3	14	38	$6
1st Half		105	11	4	8	3	218	221	313	371	684	823	508	12	61	0.36	42	26	33	32	88	127	124	14%	96	22%	47%	9	33%	56%	3.46	-4.5	2	5	-$3
2nd Half		199	25	8	25	6	231	211	278	413	691	1054	582	6	65	0.19	39	12	49	31	119	140	210	20%	103	24%	59%	6	67%	33%	3.59	-7.5	17	46	$11
16	Proj	161	19	7	18	4	239	229	310	420	730	845	601	8	67	0.27	42	18	40	32	100	137	151	15%	98	20%	55%				4.00	-2.8	19	51	$5

Ruiz,Carlos

Age: 37	Bats: R	Pos: CA	Health	C	LIMA Plan	D
Ht: 5' 10"	Wt: 205		PT/Exp	C	Rand Var	+5
			Consist	B	MM	1221

Suffered worst season as HctX, xPX, and hr/f sank for third straight year. Plate skills couldn't stall the collective downturn as output vs. RHP all but vanished (.231 Slg). Piling it on, venerable CA's defensive metrics were among league's worst. That's an awful lot of erosion to deal with at age 37.

Yr	Tm	AB	R	HR	RBI	SB	BA	xBA	OBP	SLG	OPS	vL	vR	bb%	ct%	Eye	G	L	F	h%	HctX	PX	xPX	hr/f	Spd	SBO	SB%	#Wk	DOM	DIS	RC/G	RAR	BPV	BPX	R$
11	PHI	410	49	6	40	1	283	258	371	383	754	716	766	10	88	1.00	42	21	37	31	120	70	95	4%	72	1%	100%	26	65%	23%	4.89	5.9	54	120	$9
12	PHI	372	56	16	68	4	325	313	394	540	935	906	946	7	87	0.58	43	24	33	34	130	135	131	15%	59	4%	100%	22	82%	14%	7.72	33.8	88	220	$20
13	PHI	310	30	5	37	1	268	254	320	368	688	836	636	5	87	0.46	47	20	34	29	114	69	78	5%	77	1%	100%	19	32%	37%	3.96	2.3	41	103	$5
14	PHI	381	43	6	31	4	252	267	347	370	717	832	681	11	84	0.77	41	23	35	29	85	89	83	5%	86	5%	67%	24	50%	29%	4.17	8.0	57	154	$6
15	PHI	284	23	2	22	1	211	245	290	285	575	886	501	9	85	0.65	44	22	33	24	60	52	52	2%	82	3%	50%	26	31%	46%	2.58	-10.9	26	70	-$3
1st Half		179	13	1	15	0	223	247	300	279	579	876	539	9	85	0.69	40	26	34	26	51	41	37	2%	73	2%	0%	14	21%	43%	2.64	-6.3	17	46	-$2
2nd Half		105	10	1	7	1	190	250	274	295	569	891	418	9	84	0.50	52	16	32	22	74	72	78	4%	89	5%	100%	12	42%	50%	2.47	-4.4	39	105	-$3
16	Proj	198	20	3	18	1	235	257	316	338	654	860	587	9	85	0.66	45	21	34	27	83	70	75	5%	85	3%	73%				3.42	-2.1	35	93	$3

ROB CARROLL

Rupp,Cameron

Age: 27	Bats: R	Pos: CA	Health	A	LIMA Plan	D+
Ht: 6' 2"	Wt: 250		PT/Exp	D	Rand Var	-3
			Consist	D	MM	2003

Tied for 6th-highest HR total among CA after All-Star break, complete with xPX support. Simultaneous bb%, ct% growth show he wasn't just swinging for fences. Still, skills suggest he'll struggle to hit even .250. Power is enough to elevate value above interchangeable horde of glove-first, punchless backstops.

Yr	Tm	AB	R	HR	RBI	SB	BA	xBA	OBP	SLG	OPS	vL	vR	bb%	ct%	Eye	G	L	F	h%	HctX	PX	xPX	hr/f	Spd	SBO	SB%	#Wk	DOM	DIS	RC/G	RAR	BPV	BPX	R$
11																																			
12																																			
13	PHI *	338	27	11	35	1	219	199	259	358	617	650	778	5	67	0.17	56	11	33	29	92	112	152	0%	64	3%	38%	2	0%	50%	2.99	-7.3	-10	-25	$1
14	PHI *	254	17	5	19	0	144	155	204	241	444	0	546	7	56	0.17	43	13	45	23	60	104	123	0%	61	0%	0%	6	0%	67%	1.46	-16.9	-59	-159	-$7
15	PHI	270	24	9	28	0	233	224	301	374	675	915	597	8	74	0.34	43	19	38	28	89	93	95	12%	77	1%	0%	27	37%	48%	3.62	-1.5	11	30	$2
1st Half		111	6	1	6	0	243	210	303	333	637	1155	445	8	69	0.26	43	22	35	34	86	73	56	4%	84	0%	0%	14	21%	57%	3.37	-1.4	-22	-59	-$5
2nd Half		159	18	8	22	0	226	233	299	403	702	717	698	9	77	0.41	43	16	40	25	91	106	120	16%	69	3%	0%	13	54%	38%	3.78	0.0	32	86	$6
16	**Proj**	**388**	**31**	**13**	**37**	**0**	**224**	**210**	**285**	**365**	**650**	**779**	**619**	**8**	**70**	**0.28**	**43**	**16**	**41**	**28**	**77**	**100**	**105**	**12%**	**71**	**1%**	**16%**				**3.34**	**-5.2**	**-13**	**-36**	**$2**

Russell,Addison

Age: 22	Bats: R	Pos: 2B SS	Health	A	LIMA Plan	B+
Ht: 6' 0"	Wt: 195		PT/Exp	F	Rand Var	-1
			Consist	B	MM	3215

13-54-.242 with 4 SB in 475 AB at CHC. Some hitters see all skills suffer in MLB transition, so for power to survive unscathed at his age is great sign. MLEs give hope that ct%, SBO will improve, though xBA, ct% don't offer much potential for high BA. Less heralded than 2015 rookie peers at SS; don't overlook him.

Yr	Tm	AB	R	HR	RBI	SB	BA	xBA	OBP	SLG	OPS	vL	vR	bb%	ct%	Eye	G	L	F	h%	HctX	PX	xPX	hr/f	Spd	SBO	SB%	#Wk	DOM	DIS	RC/G	RAR	BPV	BPX	R$
11																																			
12																																			
13																																			
14	aa	241	31	10	35	4	277		316	466	782			5	80	0.29				31		130			88	15%	48%				4.90		64	173	$9
15	CHC *	519	66	14	61	5	246	226	304	393	696	527	746	8	70	0.27	41	18	41	33	83	115	105	10%	97	6%	61%	25	36%	40%	3.98	3.3	17	46	$11
1st Half		271	31	6	28	2	239	227	291	372	663	480	698	7	68	0.23	43	21	36	33	73	112	87	9%	83	8%	37%	12	25%	42%	3.48	-5.0	3	8	$8
2nd Half		248	35	8	33	3	254	226	318	415	733	557	795	8	71	0.32	39	16	45	33	93	118	120	10%	112	5%	100%	13	46%	38%	4.58	3.6	32	86	$14
16	**Proj**	**555**	**72**	**16**	**72**	**7**	**260**	**240**	**312**	**413**	**725**	**540**	**782**	**7**	**74**	**0.28**	**40**	**20**	**40**	**32**	**88**	**110**	**107**	**10%**	**106**	**9%**	**57%**				**4.30**	**1.3**	**24**	**65**	**$18**

Rutledge,Josh

Age: 27	Bats: R	Pos: 2B	Health	A	LIMA Plan	F
Ht: 6' 1"	Wt: 190		PT/Exp	D	Rand Var	+1
			Consist	B	MM	2311

1-10-.284 in 74 AB at BOS. MLB xBA was .185, meaning even his empty BA was empty. Leaving Coors hurt, but can't be only reason for HctX, PX/xPX collapses this big. What's the point of trading all that ct% if it's not to hit the ball harder? With skills fading as he reaches peak age, he's like a baseball Benjamin Button.

Yr	Tm	AB	R	HR	RBI	SB	BA	xBA	OBP	SLG	OPS	vL	vR	bb%	ct%	Eye	G	L	F	h%	HctX	PX	xPX	hr/f	Spd	SBO	SB%	#Wk	DOM	DIS	RC/G	RAR	BPV	BPX	R$
11																																			
12	COL *	633	86	21	67	19	291	290	313	492	805	798	766	3	81	0.17	49	20	31	33	90	131	112	12%	132	18%	82%	13	54%	23%	5.56	21.4	75	188	$27
13	COL *	428	59	10	33	13	260	252	308	385	692	533	684	6	80	0.34	49	18	32	31	91	87	91	10%	130	14%	84%	19	32%	53%	4.15	6.1	44	110	$13
14	COL *	363	48	5	36	4	270	238	316	398	714	840	688	6	73	0.25	46	20	34	36	98	99	101	5%	176	11%	37%	24	25%	42%	4.11	7.7	40	108	$9
15	BOS *	384	40	4	30	1	224	219	256	305	561	748	637	4	72	0.15	48	22	30	30	67	64	40	7%	135	3%	51%	11	0%	64%	2.54	-20.3	-11	-30	$0
1st Half		243	22	3	17	1	188	214	220	278	498			4	72	0.15				25		70			109	6%	51%				1.89		-13	-35	-$3
2nd Half		141	18	1	14	0	288	209	318	353	672	748	637	4	71	0.15	48	22	30	40	66	53	40	7%	133	0%	0%	11	0%	64%	4.03	-0.8	-24	-65	$4
16	**Proj**	**100**	**12**	**2**	**9**	**1**	**261**	**236**	**303**	**378**	**681**	**683**	**680**	**5**	**74**	**0.20**	**48**	**20**	**32**	**34**	**85**	**84**	**81**	**7%**	**135**	**8%**	**61%**				**3.80**	**-1.3**	**4**	**11**	**$3**

Saladino,Tyler

Age: 26	Bats: R	Pos: 3B	Health	A	LIMA Plan	D+
Ht: 6' 0"	Wt: 200		PT/Exp	C	Rand Var	+3
			Consist	B	MM	1523

4-20-.225 with 8 SB in 236 AB at CHW. FB%, xPX hint that even little pop he offered wasn't real; with less PX, xBA falls below .250. Walks evaporated as he climbed ladder; pitchers learned they need not fear throwing strikes. Yes, he's got speed—but other skills won't get him on base often enough to use it.

Yr	Tm	AB	R	HR	RBI	SB	BA	xBA	OBP	SLG	OPS	vL	vR	bb%	ct%	Eye	G	L	F	h%	HctX	PX	xPX	hr/f	Spd	SBO	SB%	#Wk	DOM	DIS	RC/G	RAR	BPV	BPX	R$
11																																			
12	a/a	467	66	4	37	32	214		320	285	605			13	74	0.60				28		53			115	27%	79%				3.11		2	5	$10
13	aa	424	39	5	44	23	200		277	274	552			10	76	0.45				25		56			95	29%	71%				2.43		0	0	$6
14	aaa	294	27	6	28	5	248		293	373	666			6	79	0.31				29		89			102	8%	79%				3.72		33	89	$5
15	CHW *	432	55	7	43	28	221	259	272	325	597	650	585	7	79	0.34	54	23	23	26	63	64	33	9%	127	32%	86%	14	43%	43%	3.05	-20.2	21	57	$12
1st Half		186	20	2	17	19	214	220	278	284	562			8	79	0.44				26		46			112	44%	89%	1	100%	0%	2.89		6	16	$9
2nd Half		246	35	6	25	9	226	266	267	356	623	650	585	5	79	0.26	54	23	23	27	62	77	33	9%	132	20%	81%	13	38%	46%	3.18	-10.9	29	78	$15
16	**Proj**	**357**	**37**	**5**	**30**	**18**	**225**	**249**	**286**	**320**	**606**	**656**	**589**	**7**	**78**	**0.37**	**53**	**22**	**25**	**27**	**56**	**63**	**30**	**7%**	**118**	**25%**	**83%**				**3.08**	**-17.0**	**19**	**50**	**$9**

Saltalamacchia,Jarrod

Age: 31	Bats: B	Pos: CA	Health	A	LIMA Plan	D+
Ht: 6' 4"	Wt: 235		PT/Exp	C	Rand Var	+2
			Consist	B	MM	4003

9-24-.225 in 200 AB at MIA/ARI. Early slump (.069 BA, 59% ct) got him released after 9 games, immediately upon return from paternity leave (classic Marlins!). Time in ARI helped restore power—hit 7 of 9 HR at Chase Field. Keep environment in mind with 2H line; less friendly park may undermine only valuable skill.

Yr	Tm	AB	R	HR	RBI	SB	BA	xBA	OBP	SLG	OPS	vL	vR	bb%	ct%	Eye	G	L	F	h%	HctX	PX	xPX	hr/f	Spd	SBO	SB%	#Wk	DOM	DIS	RC/G	RAR	BPV	BPX	R$
11	BOS	358	52	16	56	1	235	245	288	450	737	635	786	6	67	0.20	32	21	47	30	113	172	145	14%	84	2%	100%	27	44%	33%	4.25	-1.3	44	98	$8
12	BOS	405	55	25	59	0	222	242	288	454	742	494	779	9	66	0.27	31	23	47	27	95	168	160	20%	78	1%	0%	27	48%	33%	4.26	-0.3	40	100	$8
13	BOS	425	68	14	65	4	273	260	338	466	804	628	873	9	67	0.31	33	29	39	38	109	170	154	13%	68	5%	80%	27	52%	26%	5.56	22.6	46	115	$15
14	MIA	373	43	11	44	0	220	212	320	362	681	600	705	13	62	0.38	37	22	40	32	114	134	163	12%	72	1%	0%	25	28%	52%	3.75	3.3	3	8	$3
15	2 NL *	232	27	10	28	0	212	228	286	408	695	979	684	9	63	0.28	31	21	48	29	98	162	174	14%	56	0%	0%	21	57%	38%	3.78	-0.2	19	51	$1
1st Half		117	11	3	9	0	156	198	241	289	529	557	584	10	57	0.26	34	25	42	23	72	124	98	9%	71	0%	0%	10	40%	50%	2.10	-6.5	-27	-73	-$6
2nd Half		115	16	7	19	0	270	262	339	530	869	1278	761	9	69	0.31	29	19	52	33	121	194	225	17%	61	0%	0%	11	73%	27%	6.17	7.9	68	184	$8
16	**Proj**	**315**	**40**	**12**	**42**	**0**	**230**	**230**	**310**	**413**	**723**	**766**	**710**	**10**	**64**	**0.31**	**33**	**23**	**44**	**32**	**106**	**151**	**166**	**13%**	**62**	**1%**	**58%**				**4.20**	**4.0**	**11**	**29**	**$7**

Sanchez,Carlos

Age: 24	Bats: B	Pos: 2B	Health	A	LIMA Plan	D+
Ht: 5' 11"	Wt: 195		PT/Exp	C	Rand Var	+2
			Consist	A	MM	1225

5-31-.224 with 2 SB in 389 AB at CHW. Former top prospect has seen stock plummet thanks to middling skills, and stint in majors was no different. Pedigree will get him further opportunities, but other than mild SB potential (and declining SBO, lousy SB% cast doubt on that too), no reason for you to do the same.

Yr	Tm	AB	R	HR	RBI	SB	BA	xBA	OBP	SLG	OPS	vL	vR	bb%	ct%	Eye	G	L	F	h%	HctX	PX	xPX	hr/f	Spd	SBO	SB%	#Wk	DOM	DIS	RC/G	RAR	BPV	BPX	R$
11																																			
12	a/a	158	18	0	12	6	328		368	407	775			6	81	0.32				41		66			97	23%	54%				5.21		18	45	$5
13	aaa	432	41	0	23	13	218		264	267	531			6	81	0.31				27		43			105	21%	64%				2.24		1	3	$2
14	CHW *	537	48	5	45	12	248	240	288	331	619	867	423	5	77	0.25	42	26	32	31	84	64	87	0%	117	13%	69%	8	25%	75%	3.20	-3.1	9	24	$9
15	CHW *	520	54	7	45	6	246	262	277	351	628	606	591	4	78	0.20	54	23	23	30	77	80	49	7%	82	9%	59%	23	22%	61%	3.22	-16.4	12	32	$7
1st Half		270	25	2	23	4	236	256	257	320	577	291	466	3	77	0.12	56	24	20	30	49	67	15	0%	77	14%	57%	10	10%	90%	2.65	-12.9	-9	-24	$5
2nd Half		250	29	5	22	2	256	270	301	384	685	746	665	6	80	0.30	53	22	25	30	93	93	68	10%	89	5%	67%	13	31%	38%	3.90	-2.4	34	92	$10
16	**Proj**	**432**	**44**	**3**	**35**	**8**	**252**	**252**	**294**	**336**	**630**	**783**	**575**	**5**	**79**	**0.26**	**49**	**24**	**26**	**31**	**78**	**65**	**62**	**4%**	**93**	**13%**	**62%**				**3.24**	**-12.6**	**6**	**15**	**$9**

Sandoval,Pablo

Age: 29	Bats: B	Pos: 3B	Health	B	LIMA Plan	B
Ht: 5' 11"	Wt: 245		PT/Exp	A	Rand Var	+2
			Consist	B	MM	2025

Career-worst Eye, sizeable drops in FB%, xPX confirm: Yeah, he really was this bad. BPV, xBA, and vL suggest it's been years in the making. Multiple injuries likely to blame for 2H collapse, but if that means 1H represents "upside," he's still in trouble. Like namesake pandas, may soon be categorized as an endangered species.

Yr	Tm	AB	R	HR	RBI	SB	BA	xBA	OBP	SLG	OPS	vL	vR	bb%	ct%	Eye	G	L	F	h%	HctX	PX	xPX	hr/f	Spd	SBO	SB%	#Wk	DOM	DIS	RC/G	RAR	BPV	BPX	R$
11	SF	426	55	23	70	2	315	301	357	552	909	723	961	7	85	0.51	42	19	39	33	131	145	125	16%	70	5%	33%	21	62%	19%	7.19	27.7	94	209	$22
12	SF	396	59	12	63	1	283	274	342	447	789	745	809	9	85	0.64	43	20	37	31	120	103	117	10%	63	2%	50%	21	48%	24%	5.45	10.1	61	153	$13
13	SF	525	52	14	79	0	278	262	341	417	758	686	786	8	85	0.59	41	21	37	31	102	90	92	8%	54	0%	0%	25	44%	20%	4.97	15.2	46	115	$15
14	SF	588	68	16	73	0	279	263	324	415	739	563	824	6	86	0.46	43	21	37	30	114	89	111	9%	76	0%	0%	27	48%	30%	4.75	17.9	51	138	$18
15	BOS	470	43	10	47	0	245	253	292	366	658	465	744	5	84	0.34	49	19	32	27	91	79	70	8%	51	0%	0%	25	36%	32%	3.49	-14.9	28	76	$5
1st Half		274	29	7	29	0	274	261	317	401	719	392	846	5	86	0.33	48	20	32	30	94	77	73	9%	56	0%	0%	14	29%	36%	4.32	-2.4	32	86	$11
2nd Half		196	14	3	18	0	204	238	256	316	572	546	587	6	83	0.35	50	17	33	23	87	81	66	6%	53	0%	0%	11	45%	27%	2.53	-12.8	25	68	-$4
16	**Proj**	**492**	**49**	**13**	**58**	**0**	**257**	**261**	**309**	**399**	**707**	**563**	**773**	**6**	**85**	**0.44**	**46**	**19**	**35**	**28**	**101**	**89**	**88**	**9%**	**58**	**0%**	**38%**				**4.16**	**-6.7**	**35**	**95**	**$12**

BRANDON KRUSE

Sano,Miguel

Age: 23	Bats: R	Pos: DH	Health: A	LIMA Plan: A+
Ht: 6' 3"	Wt: 195		PT/Exp: F	Rand Var: -4
			Consist: C	MM: 5325

18-52-.259 in 279 AB at MIN. Gargantuan power, as advertised. Extremely low ct% (57% in majors) will depress BA, but problem not selectivity (16% bb% in bigs). Perhaps that's something on which to pin hopes for BA growth. For now, enjoy HR, which should be a lock, given PX/xPX, FB tilt.

Yr	Tm	AB	R	HR	RBI	SB	BA	xBA	OBP	SLG	OPS	vL	vR	bb%	ct%	Eye	G	L	F	h%	HctX	PX	xPX	hr/f	Spd	SBO	SB%	#Wk	DOM	DIS	RC/G	RAR	BPV	BPX	R$
11																																			
12																																			
13	aa	233	28	14	44	2	213		299	477	776			11	64	0.34				26		209			102	6%	60%				4.57		77	193	$4
14																																			
15	MIN *	520	88	29	89	5	257	249	358	496	854	881	929	14	63	0.43	33	25	42	35	120	189	174	26%	115	5%	70%	15	67%	20%	6.06	22.7	68	184	$20
1st Half		256	43	11	39	4	252	286	330	461	791	733	1100	10	70	0.38	50	30	20	32	184	156	159	0%	115	8%	78%	2	50%	50%	5.19	4.2	61	165	$17
2nd Half		264	45	18	50	1	261	242	382	530	913	891	921	16	57	0.46	32	24	43	39	105	228	175	27%	110	2%	50%	13	69%	15%	6.94	17.8	78	211	$23
16	Proj	**521**	**78**	**35**	**94**	**5**	**247**	**259**	**340**	**525**	**866**	**868**	**864**	**12**	**63**	**0.38**	**32**	**24**	**43**	**32**	**101**	**214**	**158**	**25%**	**124**	**5%**	**68%**				**6.01**	**8.7**	**77**	**208**	**$20**

Santana,Carlos

Age: 30	Bats: B	Pos: 1B DH	Health: A	LIMA Plan: A
Ht: 5' 11"	Wt: 210		PT/Exp: A	Rand Var: +2
			Consist: B	MM: 3125

Dip in HR output may have disappointed some, but not xPX, which has been wondering what's been with the PX fuss for five years. With his Spd, don't count on 10+ SB again. Lack of LD hurts h%, ultimately BA. Helps in OBP leagues (see bb%), but eligibility down to 1B, making him less useful.

Yr	Tm	AB	R	HR	RBI	SB	BA	xBA	OBP	SLG	OPS	vL	vR	bb%	ct%	Eye	G	L	F	h%	HctX	PX	xPX	hr/f	Spd	SBO	SB%	#Wk	DOM	DIS	RC/G	RAR	BPV	BPX	R$
11	CLE	552	84	27	79	5	239	268	351	457	808	964	732	15	76	0.73	45	15	40	27	120	153	137	16%	66	5%	63%	27	67%	15%	5.35	-4.7	78	173	$15
12	CLE	507	72	18	76	3	252	256	365	420	785	808	772	15	80	0.90	43	19	38	28	107	108	104	12%	83	5%	38%	26	50%	27%	5.10	-2.7	64	160	$13
13	CLE	541	75	20	74	3	268	277	377	455	832	864	815	15	80	0.85	42	22	36	30	106	131	100	13%	72	2%	75%	27	67%	4%	5.95	20.8	76	190	$18
14	CLE	541	68	27	85	5	231	262	365	427	792	864	757	17	77	0.91	40	19	40	25	117	136	125	16%	66	4%	71%	27	56%	22%	5.15	16.4	74	200	$15
15	CLE	550	72	19	85	11	231	253	357	395	752	755	750	16	78	0.89	45	18	37	26	101	108	95	12%	71	8%	79%	27	59%	22%	4.71	-3.8	54	146	$14
1st Half		262	38	9	36	3	206	243	345	359	703	584	775	17	79	0.98	45	16	38	23	106	101	106	11%	69	5%	75%	14	57%	21%	3.98	-9.7	53	143	$7
2nd Half		288	34	10	49	8	253	259	369	427	796	938	730	16	77	0.80	44	20	36	30	97	115	86	13%	78	10%	80%	13	62%	23%	5.44	2.5	57	154	$20
16	Proj	**528**	**69**	**21**	**81**	**8**	**240**	**258**	**364**	**418**	**781**	**825**	**760**	**16**	**78**	**0.88**	**43**	**19**	**38**	**27**	**107**	**117**	**105**	**13%**	**71**	**6%**	**75%**				**5.10**	**-0.9**	**60**	**162**	**$17**

Santana,Daniel

Age: 25	Bats: B	Pos: SS	Health: A	LIMA Plan: D
Ht: 5' 11"	Wt: 175		PT/Exp: C	Rand Var: +2
			Consist: F	MM: 1521

0-21-.215 with 8 SB in 261 AB at MIN. Fool's-gold nature of "breakout" foretold here a year ago. Many won't believe it: Skills say he's same guy he was in 2014, just with bit less MLB ct%, power (which xPX doubted), more GB... oh, and no 40% H%. Other than some speed, really nothing here to build on. Never was.

Yr	Tm	AB	R	HR	RBI	SB	BA	xBA	OBP	SLG	OPS	vL	vR	bb%	ct%	Eye	G	L	F	h%	HctX	PX	xPX	hr/f	Spd	SBO	SB%	#Wk	DOM	DIS	RC/G	RAR	BPV	BPX	R$
11																																			
12																																			
13	aa	539	50	1	34	23	263		287	339	625			3	81	0.18				32		53			141	29%	61%				3.15		17	43	$14
14	MIN *	502	82	7	46	23	304	265	335	448	783	786	841	5	74	0.18	46	26	28	40	85	115	63	9%	152	22%	82%	20	45%	35%	5.56	33.1	46	124	$26
15	MIN *	413	50	2	33	13	244	250	265	351	616	624	494	3	77	0.12	54	20	26	31	88	74	55	0%	146	25%	64%	22	9%	50%	3.00	-17.5	18	49	$8
1st Half		269	30	0	18	7	236	242	256	338	594	679	481	3	74	0.11	52	21	26	32	91	74	63	0%	159	23%	56%	13	0%	54%	2.72	-11.2	11	30	$7
2nd Half		144	20	2	15	6	258	262	280	375	655	368	535	3	82	0.17	60	15	25	30	72	73	29	0%	109	27%	74%	9	22%	44%	3.55	-2.3	26	70	$9
16	Proj	**169**	**23**	**1**	**15**	**7**	**253**	**253**	**287**	**361**	**648**	**644**	**650**	**4**	**78**	**0.17**	**52**	**21**	**27**	**32**	**82**	**75**	**51**	**3%**	**134**	**26%**	**72%**				**3.39**	**-3.5**	**26**	**71**	**$5**

Santana,Domingo

Age: 23	Bats: R	Pos: RF CF	Health: A	LIMA Plan: C+
Ht: 6' 5"	Wt: 225		PT/Exp: C	Rand Var: -4
			Consist: B	MM: 4205

8-26-.238 with 4 SB in 160 AB at HOU/MIL. Little doubt about power, but 61% ct%, 78 HctX in bigs suggests finding his pitch remains a challenge. For would-be power hitter, also hitting too many GB. More AB may not be the best news for your BA, if you roster him.

Yr	Tm	AB	R	HR	RBI	SB	BA	xBA	OBP	SLG	OPS	vL	vR	bb%	ct%	Eye	G	L	F	h%	HctX	PX	xPX	hr/f	Spd	SBO	SB%	#Wk	DOM	DIS	RC/G	RAR	BPV	BPX	R$
11																																			
12																																			
13	aa	416	58	21	51	10	228		292	437	728			8	63	0.24				31		170			98	17%	64%				4.09		35	88	$12
14	HOU *	460	47	12	60	4	245	224	317	384	701	100	0	10	60	0.26	33	33	33	38	86	133	235	0%	92	7%	50%	3	0%	100%	4.00	2.4	-5	-14	$10
15	2 TM *	514	73	23	81	5	274	240	350	471	821	950	681	10	63	0.32	52	19	29	39	82	154	133	28%	112	8%	45%	11	55%	36%	5.56	18.6	33	89	$20
1st Half		236	36	11	35	3	275	239	365	490	856	588	960	13	59	0.35	55	18	27	42	47	179	98	33%	110	11%	33%	3	67%	33%	5.83	9.9	39	105	$17
2nd Half		278	38	12	46	3	273	243	335	455	790	1166	623	9	67	0.29	51	19	30	37	96	135	144	26%	104	5%	70%	8	50%	38%	5.32	7.3	27	73	$22
16	Proj	**410**	**53**	**15**	**59**	**5**	**233**	**230**	**324**	**406**	**730**	**795**	**693**	**10**	**62**	**0.29**	**52**	**19**	**29**	**33**	**76**	**140**	**126**	**21%**	**116**	**9%**	**53%**				**4.04**	**-9.6**	**8**	**22**	**$11**

Sardinas,Luis

Age: 23	Bats: B	Pos: 2B	Health: A	LIMA Plan: D
Ht: 6' 1"	Wt: 150		PT/Exp: D	Rand Var: 0
			Consist: A	MM: 0413

0-4-.196 in 97 AB at MIL. New organization, similar performance in PCL, aside from few more SB opps. Added 1 to career minor-league HR total (now 6 in 1,786 AB). Youth on his side, but ceiling may be do-no-harm utilityman offering good glove work, handful of SB.

Yr	Tm	AB	R	HR	RBI	SB	BA	xBA	OBP	SLG	OPS	vL	vR	bb%	ct%	Eye	G	L	F	h%	HctX	PX	xPX	hr/f	Spd	SBO	SB%	#Wk	DOM	DIS	RC/G	RAR	BPV	BPX	R$
11																																			
12																																			
13	aa	135	11	1	13	4	253		273	304	577			3	84	0.17				29		38			92	20%	68%				2.77		2	5	$1
14	TEX *	464	51	1	36	13	253	274	274	319	592	824	552	3	84	0.18	63	21	16	30	41	55	25	0%	127	18%	66%	14	29%	50%	2.91	-6.6	24	65	$9
15	MIL *	487	45	1	28	12	235	233	267	289	556	364	482	4	82	0.24	62	14	25	28	69	37	50	0%	147	14%	72%	10	10%	60%	2.57	-23.6	14	38	$4
1st Half		266	21	0	15	6	229	236	260	284	543	471	499	4	83	0.24	61	15	24	28	73	35	59	0%	156	13%	72%	5	20%	60%	2.44	-14.5	16	43	$2
2nd Half		221	24	1	13	6	242	223	275	295	571	0	443	4	82	0.25	63	11	26	29	57	40	24	0%	133	15%	72%	5	0%	60%	2.73	-9.9	9	24	$7
16	Proj	**271**	**27**	**0**	**19**	**7**	**245**	**243**	**272**	**295**	**567**	**620**	**552**	**3**	**83**	**0.21**	**63**	**16**	**22**	**30**	**55**	**38**	**33**	**0%**	**131**	**16%**	**71%**				**2.68**	**-12.5**	**2**	**6**	**$5**

Saunders,Michael

Age: 29	Bats: L	Pos: RF	Health: F	LIMA Plan: D+
Ht: 6' 4"	Wt: 225		PT/Exp: F	Rand Var: 0
			Consist: D	MM: 2303

Debut delayed due to torn meniscus. Suffered bone bruise after two weeks of action. From there, it was like waiting for Godot. Positive reports about "resuming baseball activities" never panned out (unless you include using TV remote to tune in MLB Network). Let AB trend, health grade be your guide.

Yr	Tm	AB	R	HR	RBI	SB	BA	xBA	OBP	SLG	OPS	vL	vR	bb%	ct%	Eye	G	L	F	h%	HctX	PX	xPX	hr/f	Spd	SBO	SB%	#Wk	DOM	DIS	RC/G	RAR	BPV	BPX	R$
11	SEA *	397	47	6	31	12	187	167	266	273	540	330	474	10	63	0.29	36	15	50	28	69	76	78	4%	103	18%	68%	14	7%	79%	2.27	-34.2	-34	-76	-$1
12	SEA	507	71	19	57	21	247	259	306	432	738	774	718	8	74	0.33	45	20	35	30	111	130	136	15%	104	22%	84%	28	36%	32%	4.54	-0.3	49	123	$17
13	SEA	406	59	12	46	13	236	241	323	397	720	654	751	12	71	0.46	41	22	37	30	105	123	129	11%	106	16%	72%	25	48%	44%	4.29	3.9	39	98	$11
14	SEA *	286	45	9	40	4	267	246	348	428	776	680	836	11	72	0.45	42	22	36	34	116	121	112	13%	125	10%	44%	18	39%	28%	4.92	10.4	48	130	$10
15	TOR	31	2	0	3	0	194	151	306	194	499	1417	393	14	68	0.50	75	15	10	29	57	0	60	0%	108	0%	0%	3	0%	67%	1.87	-2.4	-66	-178	-$3
1st Half		31	2	0	3	0	194	151	306	194	499	1417	393	14	68	0.50	75	15	10	29	57	0	60	0%	108	0%	0%	3	0%	67%	1.87	-2.6	-67	-181	-$3
2nd Half																																			
16	Proj	**347**	**50**	**6**	**40**	**8**	**241**	**233**	**314**	**359**	**674**	**781**	**637**	**10**	**71**	**0.38**	**51**	**19**	**30**	**32**	**90**	**90**	**101**	**8%**	**119**	**13%**	**65%**				**3.75**	**-11.2**	**12**	**33**	**$10**

Schoop,Jonathan

Age: 24	Bats: R	Pos: 2B	Health: C	LIMA Plan: B
Ht: 6' 2"	Wt: 210		PT/Exp: D	Rand Var: 0
			Consist: D	MM: 3115

15-39-.279 in 305 AB at BAL. Knee injury cost him 2+ months. BA a nice surprise from free swinger, though history warns caution of repeat. Monitor struggles vs. LHP. HctX rose each of last three months, and power looks legit. Bullish HR forecast, but we can't find any reason to discount it.

Yr	Tm	AB	R	HR	RBI	SB	BA	xBA	OBP	SLG	OPS	vL	vR	bb%	ct%	Eye	G	L	F	h%	HctX	PX	xPX	hr/f	Spd	SBO	SB%	#Wk	DOM	DIS	RC/G	RAR	BPV	BPX	R$
11																																			
12	aa	485	54	12	45	4	226		285	352	637			8	77	0.37				27		86			88	6%	55%				3.24		22	55	$4
13	BAL *	284	30	9	29	1	238	253	268	371	639	1167	750	4	79	0.19	67	17	17	27	135	88	69	50%	89	5%	27%	2	50%	0%	3.22	-4.3	21	53	$3
14	BAL	455	48	16	45	2	209	228	244	354	598	529	625	3	73	0.11	49	14	37	25	83	109	96	13%	84	3%	100%	27	33%	41%	2.65	-10.4	13	35	$4
15	BAL *	330	36	18	44	2	274	264	295	492	788	573	892	3	74	0.11	43	19	38	32	113	147	123	17%	75	3%	100%	15	53%	27%	5.14	8.1	44	119	$11
1st Half		57	6	7	14	0	237	295	261	641	901	700	1061	3	76	0.14	44	16	40	18	134	242	184	40%	85	0%	0%	3	100%	0%	5.59	2.3	132	357	-$4
2nd Half		273	30	11	30	2	282	250	308	462	769	558	872	3	74	0.11	43	20	37	35	110	126	115	14%	78	3%	100%	12	42%	33%	5.00	6.0	27	73	$14
16	Proj	**506**	**56**	**22**	**69**	**2**	**254**	**246**	**293**	**433**	**726**	**580**	**790**	**4**	**75**	**0.15**	**45**	**17**	**38**	**30**	**105**	**119**	**125**	**15%**	**78**	**3%**	**74%**				**4.15**	**-1.2**	**19**	**52**	**$16**

KRISTOPHER OLSON

Schwarber,Kyle

Age: 23 Bats: L Pos: LF CA	Health A	LIMA Plan B	
Ht: 6' 0" Wt: 235	PT/Exp F	Rand Var -2	
	Consist F	MM 4115	

16-43-.246 in 232 AB at CHC. Huge PX/xPX hints at many "Schwarbombs" to come, especially given 2H FB% gains. But dismal ct% generates plenty of BA risk, vL issues and possible fallout from NLCS errors may cut into AB total. Wide range of outcomes include... UP: 35 HR, but also DN: .220 BA, platoon

Yr	Tm	AB	R	HR	RBI	SB	BA	xBA	OBP	SLG	OPS	vL	vR	bb%	ct%	Eye	G	L	F	h%	HctX	PX	xPX	hr/f	Spd	SBO	SB%	#Wk	DOM	DIS	RC/G	RAR	BPV	BPX	R$
11																																			
12																																			
13																																			
14																																			
15	CHC *	489	88	29	82	4	270	245	368	501	870	481	953	13	68	0.48	40	17	42	34	119	162	158	24%	91	4%	56%	14	57%	21%	6.36	23.2	57	154	$21
1st Half		264	39	12	42	1	301	258	392	511	903	800	1036	13	71	0.51	57	14	29	39	89	146	92	25%	108	1%	100%	2	0%	50%	7.34	20.1	59	159	$22
2nd Half		225	49	17	39	3	234	244	341	490	831	451	944	14	64	0.46	39	18	44	28	116	183	164	24%	76	9%	50%	12	67%	17%	5.36	5.5	57	154	$21
16	Proj	423	73	24	64	4	241	242	353	466	819	461	929	14	67	0.47	41	18	42	30	104	160	148	21%	83	6%	54%				5.30	9.4	48	130	$14

Seager,Corey

Age: 22 Bats: L Pos: SS	Health A	LIMA Plan B+	
Ht: 6' 4" Wt: 215	PT/Exp F	Rand Var +1	
	Consist A	MM 4245	

4-17-.337 with 2 SB in 98 AB with LA. Elite prospect has hit at all levels and didn't blink vs. MLB pitching (.308 xBA, 97 BPV). Made impressive ct% gains, and HctX, xPX show he squared it up with ease. While our typical track record caveat applies with so few MLB AB, he's got skills to thrive right away. Invest.

Yr	Tm	AB	R	HR	RBI	SB	BA	xBA	OBP	SLG	OPS	vL	vR	bb%	ct%	Eye	G	L	F	h%	HctX	PX	xPX	hr/f	Spd	SBO	SB%	#Wk	DOM	DIS	RC/G	RAR	BPV	BPX	R$
11																																			
12																																			
13																																			
14	aa	148	21	2	21	1	304		337	457	793			5	70	0.17				42		142			97	5%	41%				5.49		36	97	$4
15	LA *	599	86	20	82	5	280	295	330	463	793	926	1028	7	83	0.43	53	20	27	31	166	117	140	19%	91	4%	83%	6	83%	17%	5.43	28.1	68	184	$22
1st Half		307	43	12	38	3	282	287	321	476	797			5	85	0.38				30		120			96	5%	70%				5.40		76	205	$22
2nd Half		292	43	9	44	3	279	286	338	450	788	926	1028	8	81	0.47	53	20	27	32	163	114	140	19%	93	4%	100%	6	83%	17%	5.44	11.2	62	168	$21
16	Proj	588	84	19	78	5	284	283	338	480	818	752	863	7	79	0.34	49	19	32	33	147	134	126	13%	97	5%	71%				5.66	26.1	66	179	$24

Seager,Kyle

Age: 28 Bats: L Pos: 3B	Health A	LIMA Plan B+	
Ht: 6' 0" Wt: 210	PT/Exp A	Rand Var +1	
	Consist A	MM 3135	

This is the kind of boring we like, as he's the only 3B with .260 BA, 20+ HR each of last three seasons. Subtle skill growth hints there's room for more, too: ct% inched up to career-high levels, taking xBA with it; suddenly hit LHP; 2H FB% hints at more HR upside. We said it last year, and we'll say it again... UP: .285 BA, 30 HR

Yr	Tm	AB	R	HR	RBI	SB	BA	xBA	OBP	SLG	OPS	vL	vR	bb%	ct%	Eye	G	L	F	h%	HctX	PX	xPX	hr/f	Spd	SBO	SB%	#Wk	DOM	DIS	RC/G	RAR	BPV	BPX	R$
11	SEA *	554	62	8	51	11	264	261	313	383	697	570	719	7	82	0.40	30	28	42	31	119	91	118	5%	87	14%	57%	12	33%	58%	4.01	-12.9	43	96	$12
12	SEA	594	62	20	86	13	259	259	316	423	738	658	783	7	81	0.42	36	22	42	29	108	106	115	10%	74	13%	72%	28	46%	18%	4.51	-0.6	49	123	$18
13	SEA	615	79	22	69	9	260	252	338	426	764	690	808	10	80	0.56	34	21	45	29	97	111	106	10%	83	7%	75%	27	56%	22%	4.90	17.0	56	140	$19
14	SEA	590	71	25	96	7	268	268	334	454	788	661	862	8	80	0.44	37	22	41	30	131	124	142	13%	84	8%	58%	27	56%	22%	5.07	23.9	63	170	$23
15	SEA	623	85	26	74	6	266	281	328	451	779	835	747	8	84	0.55	35	24	41	28	123	113	115	12%	78	8%	50%	27	70%	15%	4.95	6.9	69	186	$20
1st Half		297	32	12	38	1	256	278	312	431	743	812	719	7	85	0.55	39	23	38	27	121	105	106	13%	75	6%	25%	14	64%	7%	4.42	-1.8	64	173	$14
2nd Half		326	53	14	36	5	276	281	343	469	812	845	781	8	83	0.56	32	25	43	29	125	121	124	12%	86	9%	63%	13	77%	23%	5.46	7.8	75	203	$26
16	Proj	612	80	24	83	8	273	270	335	452	787	767	798	8	82	0.49	35	23	42	30	120	112	121	11%	78	8%	59%				5.13	9.0	57	154	$25

Segura,Jean

Age: 26 Bats: R Pos: SS	Health A	LIMA Plan B+	
Ht: 5' 10" Wt: 205	PT/Exp A	Rand Var 0	
	Consist B	MM 1525	

Needs to be reminded that four balls = walk. Meager power skills, HctX cement "slap hitter" label, except most effective slap hitters make more contact. Batted ball profile fits like a glove with his speed, but he's a one-trick pony without much upside if plate skills stay like this. 2H Eye, declining Spd hint at... DN: .240 BA, 15 SB

Yr	Tm	AB	R	HR	RBI	SB	BA	xBA	OBP	SLG	OPS	vL	vR	bb%	ct%	Eye	G	L	F	h%	HctX	PX	xPX	hr/f	Spd	SBO	SB%	#Wk	DOM	DIS	RC/G	RAR	BPV	BPX	R$
11																																			
12	2 TM *	555	66	7	50	38	274	263	318	365	683	290	756	6	84	0.39	66	15	19	32	82	54	57	0%	155	33%	71%	10	30%	40%	3.98	-2.0	38	95	$23
13	MIL	588	74	12	49	44	294	282	329	423	752	865	716	4	86	0.30	59	18	23	33	100	76	69	10%	174	37%	77%	26	46%	31%	4.91	23.6	66	165	$35
14	MIL	513	61	5	31	20	246	265	289	326	614	511	643	5	86	0.40	59	18	23	28	79	51	52	5%	159	22%	69%	27	33%	41%	3.07	-3.4	46	124	$12
15	MIL	560	57	6	50	25	257	252	281	336	616	679	594	2	83	0.14	59	17	24	30	72	49	50	5%	126	24%	81%	26	19%	38%	3.21	-9.1	17	46	$17
1st Half		265	29	3	24	11	272	257	305	351	656	746	630	3	85	0.23	59	17	24	31	76	45	55	6%	133	17%	92%	13	31%	38%	3.80	-2.2	26	70	$16
2nd Half		295	28	3	26	14	244	247	258	322	580	633	559	1	82	0.07	59	16	25	29	69	52	45	5%	111	31%	74%	13	8%	38%	2.73	-12.1	6	16	$18
16	Proj	575	64	6	47	24	260	259	290	344	635	624	638	3	84	0.23	60	17	23	30	79	51	54	5%	149	23%	74%				3.37	-12.1	27	73	$19

Semien,Marcus

Age: 25 Bats: R Pos: SS	Health A	LIMA Plan B+	
Ht: 6' 1" Wt: 195	PT/Exp B	Rand Var -2	
	Consist B	MM 3415	

Good thing errors aren't a fantasy category; his 35 were most in a season since 2008. Bat held its own in first full year, Spd points to more SB upside, and xPX hints at power growth. BA uptick is less likely given mediocre xBA, Eye decline, but seems like good bet to repeat 10+ HR/SB. As a pre-peak SS, that's not too shabby.

Yr	Tm	AB	R	HR	RBI	SB	BA	xBA	OBP	SLG	OPS	vL	vR	bb%	ct%	Eye	G	L	F	h%	HctX	PX	xPX	hr/f	Spd	SBO	SB%	#Wk	DOM	DIS	RC/G	RAR	BPV	BPX	R$
11																																			
12																																			
13	CHW*	587	97	20	61	22	256	249	354	428	782	783	643	13	79	0.71	27	25	48	30	95	118	95	9%	132	16%	74%	5	40%	60%	5.18	30.6	77	193	$24
14	CHW*	534	68	17	62	8	224	245	301	383	684	735	637	10	74	0.42	40	21	39	27	79	119	75	10%	137	8%	77%	15	33%	53%	3.79	10.0	54	146	$10
15	OAK	556	65	15	45	11	257	242	310	405	715	879	653	7	76	0.32	38	23	39	31	95	96	117	9%	139	11%	69%	27	37%	30%	4.24	-2.5	40	108	$14
1st Half		311	35	7	20	7	260	242	308	399	707	769	686	7	77	0.31	41	20	39	32	97	94	125	8%	134	12%	78%	14	36%	29%	4.26	1.6	39	105	$14
2nd Half		245	30	8	25	4	253	243	312	412	724	992	607	8	75	0.33	34	27	39	31	94	98	107	11%	139	11%	57%	13	38%	31%	4.22	1.0	37	100	$13
16	Proj	559	72	16	56	11	245	241	316	397	713	837	660	9	76	0.42	37	23	40	30	90	101	98	10%	141	11%	71%				4.19	1.8	37	99	$16

Shaffer,Richie

Age: 25 Bats: R Pos: 1B	Health A	LIMA Plan D	
Ht: 6' 3" Wt: 218	PT/Exp D	Rand Var 0	
	Consist C	MM 5201	

4-6-.189 in 74 AB at TAM. Former first-round pick's HR barrage at AAA netted late-season MLB look. PX says the power is legit, but elephant in the room is that awful contact rate (57% in MLB), which poses major BA threat. Plate patience softens the blow in OBP leagues, but unlikely to stick unless he can put bat on ball.

Yr	Tm	AB	R	HR	RBI	SB	BA	xBA	OBP	SLG	OPS	vL	vR	bb%	ct%	Eye	G	L	F	h%	HctX	PX	xPX	hr/f	Spd	SBO	SB%	#Wk	DOM	DIS	RC/G	RAR	BPV	BPX	R$
11																																			
12																																			
13																																			
14	aa	427	46	14	51	3	190		267	360	626			9	68	0.33				24		139			98	4%	100%				3.05		35	95	$1
15	TAM *	467	62	23	64	3	220	219	300	429	729	521	1099	10	62	0.31	37	14	49	30	83	167	130	19%	80	4%	74%	9	33%	11%	4.20	-5.2	30	81	$8
1st Half		267	34	14	39	2	225	236	303	440	743			10	62	0.29				31		171			88	4%	100%				4.43		31	84	$12
2nd Half		200	29	9	24	1	213	219	297	413	710	521	1099	11	64	0.33	37	14	49	28	85	161	130	19%	81	4%	41%	9	33%	11%	3.90	-4.5	31	84	$4
16	Proj	189	24	9	24	1	218	235	316	428	745	556	1171	10	65	0.32	37	19	44	28	77	162	117	17%	92	4%	79%				4.15	-5.8	31	85	$4

Shaw,Travis

Age: 26 Bats: L Pos: 1B	Health A	LIMA Plan D+	
Ht: 6' 4" Wt: 225	PT/Exp B	Rand Var -1	
	Consist B	MM 4123	

13-36-.274 in 226 AB at BOS. Fifth call-up was the charm, as late HR binge in majors made up for poor first half in AAA. The main draw is power, and 2H PX/FB% combo shows why. Maintained 2014's ct% gains, but Eye decline, xBA give BA little room to grow. If he holds gains vs. LHP, full-time gig could mean... UP: 25 HR

Yr	Tm	AB	R	HR	RBI	SB	BA	xBA	OBP	SLG	OPS	vL	vR	bb%	ct%	Eye	G	L	F	h%	HctX	PX	xPX	hr/f	Spd	SBO	SB%	#Wk	DOM	DIS	RC/G	RAR	BPV	BPX	R$
11																																			
12	aa	110	11	2	10	1	223		329	413	743			14	68	0.49				31		174			84	7%	44%				4.35		64	160	-$1
13	aa	444	44	12	38	5	200		293	341	633			12	71	0.46				25		107			107	8%	62%				3.14		28	70	$1
14	a/a	490	61	16	61	6	252		315	415	730			8	78	0.41				30		121			87	7%	62%				4.39		52	141	$14
15	BOS *	515	56	17	61	0	250	237	304	399	703	975	736	7	77	0.34	37	20	43	29	100	98	129	18%	87	2%	0%	16	31%	31%	4.05	-13.5	30	81	$9
1st Half		257	23	4	24	0	223	199	281	319	599	0	143	7	80	0.40	75	0	25	26	88	63	78	0%	94	2%	0%	4	25%	25%	2.87	-18.0	16	43	$1
2nd Half		258	33	13	38	0	277	254	328	479	807	1011	762	7	74	0.30	36	21	44	33	97	135	132	18%	82	2%	0%	12	33%	33%	5.44	2.1	47	127	$18
16	Proj	319	36	13	37	2	255	259	323	445	767	737	781	9	76	0.41	39	21	41	30	87	127	119	13%	90	4%	51%				4.79	-3.4	42	115	$10

RYAN BLOOMFIELD

Shuck,J.B.

Age: 29	Bats: L	Pos: RF	Health A	LIMA Plan D+	
Ht: 5' 11"	Wt: 195		PT/Exp D	Rand Var 0	
			Consist D	MM 1431	

When looking for end-gamers or reserve picks, one strategy is to target one-category guys with good upside in that stat. This is one place to do that. Excellent pitch recognition, good Spd profile him as a hidden speed threat. Obstacle is mediocre SB%, but that has been over small sample sizes. If that bb% holds... UP: 20 SB

Yr Tm	AB	R	HR	RBI	SB	BA	xBA	OBP	SLG	OPS	vL	vR	bb%	ct%	Eye	G	L	F	h%	HctX	PX	xPX	hr/f	Spd	SBO	SB%	#Wk	DOM	DIS	RC/G	RAR	BPV	BPX	R$
11 HOU *	435	55	0	26	17	260	264	341	317	658	909	646	11	90	1.28	47	25	29	29	80	35	60	0%	152	20%	58%	9	44%	22%	3.54	-21.3	59	131	$9
12 aaa	315	33	0	22	8	238		297	280	577			8	92	1.08				26		28			111	19%	46%				2.54		42	105	$2
13 LAA	437	60	2	39	8	293	264	331	366	697	745	682	6	88	0.50	55	20	25	33	72	52	44	2%	125	9%	67%	27	48%	26%	4.36	0.9	43	108	$14
14 2AL *	516	48	5	41	7	213	226	251	286	537	310	394	5	90	0.51	57	8	34	23	55	45	27	6%	108	13%	48%	11	9%	36%	2.21	-27.3	40	108	$1
15 CHW	143	15	0	15	7	266	273	340	350	689	661	694	10	89	1.00	57	18	25	30	62	57	32	0%	114	27%	58%	25	44%	24%	3.85	-3.9	57	154	$3
1st Half	73	5	0	6	4	288	277	354	329	682	333	714	9	93	1.40	54	24	22	31	75	32	40	0%	90	24%	67%	14	36%	29%	4.02	-1.7	45	122	$2
2nd Half	70	10	0	9	3	243	269	325	371	696	780	670	11	84	0.82	60	12	28	29	49	85	22	0%	125	32%	50%	11	55%	18%	3.67	-2.5	68	184	$4
16 Proj	**193**	**22**	**1**	**18**	**8**	**253**	**262**	**312**	**339**	**651**	**656**	**650**	**8**	**89**	**0.78**	**56**	**16**	**28**	**28**	**62**	**55**	**34**	**2%**	**119**	**25%**	**62%**				**3.45**	**-8.0**	**52**	**141**	**$4**

Simmons,Andrelton

Age: 26	Bats: R	Pos: SS	Health A	LIMA Plan B+	
Ht: 6' 2"	Wt: 195		PT/Exp A	Rand Var 0	
			Consist B	MM 1335	

At first glance, a reliable $10 option w/little upside. But Eye growth, prime age, 2nd half bb% and associated OBP surge give hope for more. Spd history muted by nagging injuries, so expect it to bounce back. If small-sample uptick in 2nd half SB% yields a green light, then... UP: 20 SB

Yr Tm	AB	R	HR	RBI	SB	BA	xBA	OBP	SLG	OPS	vL	vR	bb%	ct%	Eye	G	L	F	h%	HctX	PX	xPX	hr/f	Spd	SBO	SB%	#Wk	DOM	DIS	RC/G	RAR	BPV	BPX	R$
11																																		
12 ATL *	340	41	5	37	9	278	271	335	396	731	796	726	8	87	0.66	56	17	27	31	85	72	45	8%	127	12%	81%	11	45%	18%	4.74	6.1	62	155	$10
13 ATL	606	76	17	59	6	248	272	296	396	692	692	691	6	91	0.73	42	18	39	25	108	86	89	8%	139	8%	55%	27	59%	7%	3.85	6.3	89	223	$13
14 ATL	540	44	7	46	4	244	250	286	331	617	679	603	6	89	0.53	52	16	31	26	102	56	87	5%	130	7%	44%	26	54%	23%	3.11	-2.9	53	143	$6
15 ATL	535	60	4	44	5	265	278	321	338	660	565	683	7	91	0.81	56	21	22	29	91	47	61	4%	106	5%	63%	27	56%	22%	3.67	-1.5	49	132	$10
1st Half	301	43	3	29	1	259	288	314	349	663	330	733	6	93	0.82	52	23	25	27	95	55	76	4%	115	4%	33%	14	64%	21%	3.52	-4.9	63	170	$12
2nd Half	234	17	1	15	4	274	261	331	325	656	786	615	8	89	0.81	61	20	19	30	85	37	42	3%	93	7%	80%	13	46%	23%	3.84	-1.6	31	84	$6
16 Proj	**588**	**60**	**7**	**50**	**9**	**269**	**268**	**319**	**356**	**675**	**690**	**670**	**7**	**90**	**0.70**	**54**	**19**	**27**	**29**	**95**	**54**	**67**	**5%**	**120**	**8%**	**64%**				**3.88**	**-3.4**	**42**	**113**	**$15**

Singleton,Jonathan

Age: 24	Bats: L	Pos: 1B	Health A	LIMA Plan D	
Ht: 6' 2"	Wt: 255		PT/Exp C	Rand Var +3	
			Consist A	MM 4003	

1-6-.191 in 47 AB with HOU. PRO: Steadily elite PX, consistent uppercut in swing, contact showing steady gains, still just 24. CON: Still Ks WAY too much, poor HctX and xPX temper optimism of immediate power surge, mental makeup still in question. A high-risk, high-reward wildcard.

Yr Tm	AB	R	HR	RBI	SB	BA	xBA	OBP	SLG	OPS	vL	vR	bb%	ct%	Eye	G	L	F	h%	HctX	PX	xPX	hr/f	Spd	SBO	SB%	#Wk	DOM	DIS	RC/G	RAR	BPV	BPX	R$
11																																		
12 aa	461	72	17	61	5	252		350	428	777			13	68	0.47				34		131			100	5%	71%				5.08		35	88	$12
13 a/a	283	28	7	31	1	200		307	322	629			13	58	0.37				32		116			92	1%	100%				3.16		-16	-40	-$1
14 HOU *	505	68	24	75	3	190	212	301	375	676	805	559	14	62	0.41	40	14	46	25	78	160	105	16%	61	5%	40%	18	22%	67%	3.47	-10.9	22	59	$6
15 HOU *	425	55	17	63	2	206	228	296	384	679	844	576	11	68	0.40	23	26	52	26	78	132	106	6%	66	3%	67%	8	38%	63%	3.63	-17.3	23	62	$4
1st Half	283	42	12	48	2	226	253	310	419	729	0	561	11	70	0.41	30	30	40	28	93	137	35	0%	69	3%	100%	3	0%	100%	4.32	-7.1	35	95	$11
2nd Half	142	14	5	15	0	167	208	268	315	583	1467	583	12	65	0.39	19	24	57	22	68	121	139	8%	69	4%	0%	5	60%	40%	2.49	-12.5	2	5	-$10
16 Proj	**245**	**30**	**9**	**32**	**1**	**211**	**208**	**305**	**380**	**685**	**1234**	**545**	**13**	**64**	**0.40**	**27**	**20**	**53**	**28**	**72**	**132**	**125**	**11%**	**69**	**3%**	**50%**				**3.76**	**-10.6**	**7**	**20**	**$4**

Sizemore,Grady

Age: 33	Bats: L	Pos: RF LF	Health D	LIMA Plan D+	
Ht: 6' 2"	Wt: 200		PT/Exp F	Rand Var 0	
			Consist A	MM 2211	

Strong August (91 BPV) had some hoping for return to pre-injury days, but it ain't happening. Last 400-AB season was in '09. Sub-par hard contact and power suppress BA and make even double-digit HR a stretch, and impactful speed long gone. Sub-.700 OPS vs. RH seals fate. Speculate elsewhere.

Yr Tm	AB	R	HR	RBI	SB	BA	xBA	OBP	SLG	OPS	vL	vR	bb%	ct%	Eye	G	L	F	h%	HctX	PX	xPX	hr/f	Spd	SBO	SB%	#Wk	DOM	DIS	RC/G	RAR	BPV	BPX	R$
11 CLE *	296	35	11	36	0	229	248	280	424	703	582	751	7	69	0.23	40	18	42	29	103	160	137	13%	83	4%	0%	16	44%	31%	3.80	-10.1	45	100	$3
12																																		
13																																		
14 2 TM *	393	38	6	28	6	231	238	296	345	641	491	715	8	78	0.43	42	20	38	28	96	86	102	5%	114	7%	86%	25	40%	32%	3.43	-4.2	35	95	$4
15 2 TM	273	24	6	33	3	253	252	307	381	688	984	667	7	78	0.33	43	23	34	30	96	93	97	8%	92	9%	50%	22	41%	45%	3.82	-4.6	30	81	$4
1st Half	123	7	1	10	1	268	238	302	350	652	788	639	5	77	0.21	48	23	28	34	100	66	100	4%	103	6%	50%	10	30%	60%	3.59	-3.4	4	11	-$1
2nd Half	150	17	5	23	2	240	263	311	407	718	1178	689	9	79	0.44	39	23	39	27	93	114	94	11%	83	11%	50%	12	50%	33%	4.00	-2.6	50	135	$8
16 Proj	**226**	**22**	**5**	**24**	**2**	**241**	**245**	**303**	**375**	**678**	**609**	**691**	**8**	**77**	**0.36**	**42**	**21**	**37**	**29**	**97**	**96**	**104**	**8%**	**96**	**8%**	**59%**				**3.70**	**-7.6**	**21**	**57**	**$4**

Smith,Seth

Age: 33	Bats: L	Pos: LF RF DH	Health A	LIMA Plan B+	
Ht: 6' 3"	Wt: 210		PT/Exp B	Rand Var +1	
			Consist B	MM 4235	

There used to be a time when a 10-HR OF was left on the scrap heap, but times have changed. Continued thump vR will keep giving him value. Surging HctX, FB% suggest 15 HR not out of question again, especially if he can find hitter-friendly home park. An investment under $10 could net you $5 of profit.

Yr Tm	AB	R	HR	RBI	SB	BA	xBA	OBP	SLG	OPS	vL	vR	bb%	ct%	Eye	G	L	F	h%	HctX	PX	xPX	hr/f	Spd	SBO	SB%	#Wk	DOM	DIS	RC/G	RAR	BPV	BPX	R$
11 COL	476	67	15	59	10	284	276	347	483	830	576	891	9	80	0.49	38	22	40	33	120	133	127	10%	123	10%	83%	27	67%	19%	6.00	14.4	85	189	$18
12 OAK	383	55	14	52	2	240	258	333	420	754	521	805	12	74	0.51	41	23	36	29	107	126	130	14%	84	4%	50%	26	58%	35%	4.56	0.0	49	123	$8
13 OAK	368	49	8	40	0	253	243	329	391	721	621	748	10	74	0.41	45	20	35	32	88	113	102	8%	87	0%	0%	27	37%	41%	4.33	3.8	36	90	$6
14 SD	443	55	12	48	1	266	281	367	440	807	744	815	13	80	0.79	47	21	32	31	115	126	115	11%	98	1%	50%	27	59%	26%	5.56	23.8	81	219	$11
15 SEA	395	54	12	42	0	248	264	330	443	773	571	801	11	75	0.47	42	20	38	30	118	139	123	11%	98	0%	0%	27	52%	22%	4.93	6.2	64	173	$7
1st Half	222	25	7	22	0	257	263	327	459	786	1071	767	9	75	0.40	41	18	40	31	114	143	107	10%	104	0%	0%	14	57%	14%	5.10	3.5	66	178	$7
2nd Half	173	29	5	20	0	237	265	335	422	757	379	851	13	75	0.57	44	21	35	29	124	133	144	11%	92	0%	0%	13	46%	31%	4.70	0.7	60	162	$6
16 Proj	**403**	**56**	**13**	**51**	**1**	**258**	**265**	**346**	**450**	**796**	**594**	**833**	**12**	**76**	**0.55**	**43**	**20**	**37**	**31**	**113**	**133**	**122**	**11%**	**93**	**1%**	**64%**				**5.30**	**8.7**	**60**	**161**	**$12**

Smoak,Justin

Age: 29	Bats: B	Pos: 1B	Health B	LIMA Plan C+	
Ht: 6' 4"	Wt: 230		PT/Exp C	Rand Var +2	
			Consist C	MM 4023	

Easy to rekindle visions of 30+ HR upside with a full-season of AB after this impressive power display. Problem is, holes in swing keep getting bigger, prior flyball tilt is M.I.A., and we can't bank on that hr/f repeating. But... but... he batted .262 with 5 HRs and an .893 OPS in September!! [ED NOTE: Calm down.]

Yr Tm	AB	R	HR	RBI	SB	BA	xBA	OBP	SLG	OPS	vL	vR	bb%	ct%	Eye	G	L	F	h%	HctX	PX	xPX	hr/f	Spd	SBO	SB%	#Wk	DOM	DIS	RC/G	RAR	BPV	BPX	R$
11 SEA	427	38	15	55	0	234	222	323	396	719	720	719	11	75	0.52	44	14	43	28	106	119	129	11%	70	0%	0%	25	48%	36%	4.24	-17.9	43	96	$5
12 SEA *	549	56	19	54	2	213	224	291	352	643	703	627	10	76	0.46	40	18	42	25	96	90	116	12%	71	1%	100%	26	35%	54%	3.33	-33.1	19	48	$3
13 SEA *	475	54	20	51	0	235	234	326	405	731	548	839	12	74	0.51	35	20	46	28	111	120	152	13%	81	0%	0%	25	44%	40%	4.41	-2.7	41	103	$8
14 SEA *	453	46	11	55	0	224	223	292	349	641	618	611	9	73	0.37	42	18	39	28	116	101	146	10%	60	3%	0%	18	33%	44%	3.23	-12.6	12	32	$4
15 TOR	296	44	18	59	0	226	274	299	470	768	839	757	9	71	0.34	43	24	34	26	114	166	142	25%	67	0%	0%	27	52%	33%	4.57	-3.2	57	154	$7
1st Half	121	19	8	25	0	256	273	343	521	864	1218	825	12	68	0.41	41	24	34	31	117	185	152	29%	95	0%	0%	14	43%	43%	6.12	3.4	73	197	$6
2nd Half	175	25	10	34	0	206	275	267	434	701	667	707	7	73	0.28	43	23	33	22	112	155	136	23%	55	0%	0%	13	62%	23%	3.63	-8.3	49	132	$8
16 Proj	**361**	**46**	**18**	**61**	**0**	**240**	**255**	**316**	**444**	**759**	**715**	**774**	**10**	**72**	**0.38**	**41**	**21**	**38**	**28**	**113**	**139**	**143**	**18%**	**66**	**1%**	**8%**				**4.62**	**-5.8**	**33**	**90**	**$11**

Smolinski,Jacob

Age: 27	Bats: R	Pos: LF	Health B	LIMA Plan D+	
Ht: 5' 11"	Wt: 215		PT/Exp D	Rand Var +2	
			Consist B	MM 3231	

6-26-.193 in 166 AB with TEX and OAK. Lefty-masher can have value in small doses; reference 80+ BPV Jul-Sept. Problem is, xPX isn't buying that power surge, largely due to absence of hard contact. And big holes against RH (72% ct%) will prevent role expansion. An end-game OF, nothing more.

Yr Tm	AB	R	HR	RBI	SB	BA	xBA	OBP	SLG	OPS	vL	vR	bb%	ct%	Eye	G	L	F	h%	HctX	PX	xPX	hr/f	Spd	SBO	SB%	#Wk	DOM	DIS	RC/G	RAR	BPV	BPX	R$
11 aa	396	31	5	27	4	208		290	298	588			10	84	0.73				24		68			85	10%	45%				2.67		39	87	-$2
12 aa	408	57	5	33	7	228		337	333	669			14	78	0.76				28		76			105	9%	62%				3.65		36	90	$4
13 a/a	370	36	6	29	7	219		298	316	614			10	79	0.53				26		69			107	8%	87%				3.13		24	60	$2
14 TEX *	382	47	10	41	4	249	261	301	398	700	1357	757	7	76	0.31	40	26	34	30	122	114	106	14%	94	7%	64%	6	50%	50%	4.03	3.8	39	105	$8
15 2AL *	297	44	13	51	3	247	271	314	453	767	833	454	9	81	0.50	45	15	40	27	95	131	93	12%	87	9%	43%	22	32%	45%	4.63	2.0	73	197	$8
1st Half	149	25	5	24	3	271	277	345	458	803	604	296	10	78	0.51	40	24	36	32	106	131	74	7%	69	10%	68%	11	18%	55%	5.46	3.9	59	159	$10
2nd Half	148	19	7	26	0	224	271	282	448	730	990	526	8	83	0.49	47	11	42	22	91	130	103	14%	103	8%	0%	11	45%	36%	3.88	-3.1	85	230	$6
16 Proj	**159**	**20**	**6**	**21**	**2**	**237**	**265**	**316**	**415**	**731**	**929**	**594**	**9**	**79**	**0.47**	**43**	**20**	**37**	**27**	**107**	**115**	**97**	**12%**	**95**	**8%**	**56%**				**4.14**	**-2.0**	**54**	**145**	**$4**

STEPHEN NICKRAND

Snider,Travis

Age: 28	Bats: L	Pos: LF RF	Health	A	LIMA Plan D
Ht: 6' 0"	Wt: 235		PT/Exp	D	Rand Var +1
			Consist	D	MM 2111

4-28-.232 in 237 AB with PIT. Almost a decade after he shot up prospect lists, his time has pretty much run out. xPX gives no hope at a power spike, especially with all those GBs and subpar HctX. Long history of poor ct% cements him as BA liability. And .700-ish OPS vs. RH last 3 yrs says he's no part-timer either.

Yr	Tm	AB	R	HR	RBI	SB	BA	xBA	OBP	SLG	OPS	vL	vR	bb%	ct%	Eye	G	L	F	h%	HctX	PX	xPX	hr/f	Spd	SBO	SB%	#Wk	DOM	DIS	RC/G	RAR	BPV	BPX	R$
11	TOR *	435	52	6	56	16	247	239	290	367	658	300	708	6	75	0.24	47	17	37	32	94	102	97	6%	72	22%	80%	10	30%	50%	3.65	-20.9	17	38	$11
12	2 TM *	373	56	13	55	3	268	259	337	437	774	1110	595	10	74	0.41	56	19	26	33	79	119	74	13%	79	8%	42%	12	25%	58%	4.93	2.2	36	90	$11
13	PIT *	299	32	5	29	3	224	216	290	331	621	291	644	8	72	0.33	52	15	33	30	96	83	78	8%	81	9%	40%	22	32%	64%	3.01	-9.6	-2	-5	$1
14	PIT	322	37	13	38	1	264	268	338	438	776	1054	734	10	79	0.51	49	19	31	30	91	119	90	16%	70	2%	50%	27	48%	33%	5.03	11.6	54	146	$9
15	2 TM *	272	28	5	31	1	236	235	310	350	660	605	674	10	74	0.42	47	21	32	30	92	82	80	7%	90	1%	100%	24	17%	63%	3.64	-8.7	12	32	$2
1st Half		181	21	3	20	1	260	234	330	381	711	813	689	9	72	0.36	50	20	31	34	90	89	72	8%	102	2%	100%	14	7%	71%	4.32	-1.2	11	30	$4
2nd Half		91	7	2	11	0	189	241	277	287	564	0	626	11	79	0.57	40	25	35	22	95	69	103	7%	64	0%	0%	10	30%	50%	2.50	-6.0	12	32	-$4
16	Proj	**158**	**17**	**4**	**18**	**1**	**233**	**243**	**311**	**364**	**675**	**535**	**700**	**10**	**76**	**0.44**	**47**	**20**	**33**	**28**	**92**	**90**	**88**	**10%**	**75**	**4%**	**59%**				**3.68**	**-4.2**	**15**	**40**	**$0**

Sogard,Eric

Age: 30	Bats: L	Pos: 2B	Health	A	LIMA Plan D+
Ht: 5' 10"	Wt: 190		PT/Exp	C	Rand Var 0
			Consist	B	MM 0313

Slap-hitting middle-infielders with modest speed like this one can be attractive targets, but when they kill your BA, they're not worth it. xBA tells us his BA isn't heading north. As he enters his 30s with consistent sub-.300 OBP, what speed he does have is at risk. Too much risk, not enough upside.

Yr	Tm	AB	R	HR	RBI	SB	BA	xBA	OBP	SLG	OPS	vL	vR	bb%	ct%	Eye	G	L	F	h%	HctX	PX	xPX	hr/f	Spd	SBO	SB%	#Wk	DOM	DIS	RC/G	RAR	BPV	BPX	R$
11	OAK *	385	44	5	29	9	229	230	287	318	605	154	652	8	86	0.58	37	19	44	26	76	60	71	8%	99	13%	71%	12	42%	42%	3.01	-18.7	38	84	$3
12	OAK *	259	28	5	22	9	223	256	282	327	609	450	487	8	85	0.56	39	26	35	24	83	60	61	7%	102	20%	72%	14	29%	36%	3.01	-9.2	37	93	$3
13	OAK	368	45	2	35	10	266	256	322	364	686	640	695	7	86	0.53	35	25	40	30	64	73	44	2%	105	16%	67%	27	56%	19%	3.93	2.1	50	125	$9
14	OAK	291	38	1	22	11	223	241	298	268	567	478	581	10	87	0.84	42	24	35	25	65	36	52	1%	89	18%	73%	26	27%	38%	2.66	-6.5	26	70	$4
15	OAK	372	40	1	37	6	247	240	294	304	598	543	609	6	87	0.46	44	22	34	28	64	37	41	1%	111	7%	86%	26	19%	46%	3.05	-13.5	23	62	$5
1st Half		242	27	0	20	5	256	234	298	293	592	581	594	5	86	0.40	41	25	35	30	70	28	45	0%	100	7%	100%	14	14%	57%	3.10	-7.9	8	22	$7
2nd Half		130	13	1	17	1	231	255	286	323	609	450	636	6	88	0.60	51	18	32	25	54	55	35	3%	118	6%	50%	12	25%	33%	2.94	-5.1	48	130	$1
16	Proj	**260**	**30**	**2**	**25**	**6**	**239**	**247**	**295**	**312**	**607**	**511**	**625**	**7**	**87**	**0.58**	**43**	**22**	**35**	**27**	**64**	**48**	**46**	**2%**	**104**	**12%**	**72%**				**3.05**	**-9.3**	**33**	**89**	**$5**

Solarte,Yangervis

Age: 28	Bats: B	Pos: 3B 1B	Health	A	LIMA Plan A
Ht: 5' 11"	Wt: 195		PT/Exp	B	Rand Var 0
			Consist	B	MM 2145

Previously unheralded prospect quietly showing signs of something more. Retaining near-elite ct% while producing tons more hard contact bodes well for power spike. Multi-year BPV surge climbed to new heights in 2H, so this wasn't a one-year aberration. Another year of growth brings... UP: 25 HR, .280 BA

Yr	Tm	AB	R	HR	RBI	SB	BA	xBA	OBP	SLG	OPS	vL	vR	bb%	ct%	Eye	G	L	F	h%	HctX	PX	xPX	hr/f	Spd	SBO	SB%	#Wk	DOM	DIS	RC/G	RAR	BPV	BPX	R$
11	aa	459	46	4	35	4	278		304	385	689			4	90	0.40				30		75			95	8%	44%				3.99		60	133	$9
12	aaa	518	47	9	37	2	244		283	340	623			5	90	0.56				26		60			84	3%	64%				3.23		47	118	$4
13	aaa	526	47	9	53	2	231		270	334	604			5	85	0.35				26		72			79	2%	100%				3.01		33	83	$4
14	2 TM	469	56	10	48	0	260	254	336	369	705	760	673	10	88	0.91	45	19	35	28	99	72	71	7%	85	1%	0%	26	42%	12%	4.23	7.0	56	151	$10
15	SD	526	63	14	63	1	270	280	320	428	748	667	771	6	89	0.61	44	19	37	28	120	94	96	8%	94	1%	100%	27	59%	15%	4.71	0.4	75	203	$13
1st Half		244	21	4	30	1	250	274	302	377	679	592	703	7	89	0.61	44	21	35	27	137	83	114	5%	80	2%	100%	14	57%	7%	3.85	-5.5	60	162	$6
2nd Half		282	42	10	33	0	287	284	336	472	807	729	831	6	90	0.61	44	18	39	29	106	104	80	10%	109	0%	0%	13	62%	23%	5.53	7.1	89	241	$20
16	Proj	**521**	**60**	**16**	**56**	**1**	**272**	**275**	**326**	**428**	**754**	**738**	**760**	**7**	**88**	**0.64**	**44**	**19**	**36**	**28**	**111**	**92**	**85**	**10%**	**89**	**1%**	**63%**				**4.81**	**2.8**	**59**	**159**	**$16**

Soler,Jorge

Age: 24	Bats: R	Pos: RF	Health	B	LIMA Plan B
Ht: 6' 4"	Wt: 215		PT/Exp	F	Rand Var -2
			Consist	F	MM 4225

Top prospect still trying to figure out MLB pitchers, who in turn keep finding holes in his swing. But those 2H gains in plate control bode well for growth. Has combined elite power and decent plate control in past, so don't write off those gains, or his ceiling for a lot more... UP: .280-30-100

Yr	Tm	AB	R	HR	RBI	SB	BA	xBA	OBP	SLG	OPS	vL	vR	bb%	ct%	Eye	G	L	F	h%	HctX	PX	xPX	hr/f	Spd	SBO	SB%	#Wk	DOM	DIS	RC/G	RAR	BPV	BPX	R$
11																																			
12																																			
13																																			
14	CHC *	264	38	16	59	1	296	312	365	594	960	701	964	10	73	0.41	52	12	36	35	128	230	131	21%	97	3%	47%	6	67%	33%	7.76	26.8	128	346	$14
15	CHC	366	39	10	47	3	262	236	324	399	723	730	720	8	67	0.26	42	28	30	37	106	107	122	14%	101	4%	75%	20	30%	50%	4.43	-4.4	2	5	$8
1st Half		192	20	4	19	0	260	235	318	396	713	799	695	7	65	0.22	43	29	29	38	113	116	133	11%	102	2%	0%	10	30%	50%	4.19	-3.5	-2	-5	$5
2nd Half		174	19	6	28	3	264	238	332	402	734	688	752	9	70	0.32	42	27	31	35	98	98	110	16%	99	6%	100%	10	30%	50%	4.71	-0.5	6	16	$12
16	Proj	**479**	**58**	**18**	**82**	**4**	**261**	**257**	**325**	**451**	**777**	**696**	**800**	**9**	**70**	**0.32**	**46**	**21**	**32**	**34**	**114**	**143**	**124**	**17%**	**102**	**4%**	**73%**				**5.08**	**3.6**	**36**	**96**	**$17**

Soto,Geovany

Age: 33	Bats: R	Pos: CA	Health	F	LIMA Plan D
Ht: 6' 1"	Wt: 235		PT/Exp	F	Rand Var 0
			Consist	C	MM 4003

When looking for your second catcher, scan xPX for signs of latent pop. Voilà! Chronic injury issues have eaten into his production, but even 300 AB would bring close to 15 HR. Three-year scan shows that's a BIG if, but what's the risk? Just DL or dump him if he gets hurt again. A $1 bid could net $5 profit. Or more.

Yr	Tm	AB	R	HR	RBI	SB	BA	xBA	OBP	SLG	OPS	vL	vR	bb%	ct%	Eye	G	L	F	h%	HctX	PX	xPX	hr/f	Spd	SBO	SB%	#Wk	DOM	DIS	RC/G	RAR	BPV	BPX	R$
11	CHC	421	46	17	54	0	228	241	310	411	721	971	643	10	71	0.36	41	19	40	28	111	143	125	14%	62	0%	0%	25	36%	36%	4.11	-1.2	37	82	$6
12	2 TM	324	45	11	39	1	198	237	270	343	613	677	589	8	77	0.39	40	21	40	22	110	94	139	11%	78	1%	100%	23	30%	26%	2.91	-12.5	24	60	$1
13	TEX	163	20	9	22	1	245	240	328	466	794	656	874	11	63	0.33	32	22	46	33	113	181	201	19%	76	7%	33%	25	32%	52%	4.95	6.0	44	110	$3
14	2 AL *	131	12	2	13	0	226	218	274	332	605	677	655	6	70	0.22	44	20	36	31	107	101	161	5%	78	0%	0%	11	45%	36%	2.99	-1.2	-1	-3	-$1
15	CHW	187	20	9	21	0	219	234	301	406	708	780	676	10	66	0.33	37	23	40	28	98	138	163	18%	69	2%	0%	26	46%	50%	3.87	0.7	19	51	$1
1st Half		107	8	4	13	0	224	227	291	383	674	798	630	8	66	0.25	39	24	37	30	95	122	157	15%	71	0%	0%	14	43%	50%	3.58	-0.6	2	5	$0
2nd Half		80	12	5	8	0	213	240	315	438	753	764	745	13	66	0.44	35	21	44	25	103	160	172	22%	69	5%	0%	12	50%	50%	4.24	1.2	42	114	$2
16	Proj	**253**	**29**	**10**	**28**	**0**	**224**	**231**	**300**	**397**	**697**	**713**	**689**	**10**	**68**	**0.33**	**38**	**21**	**40**	**29**	**105**	**130**	**167**	**15%**	**73**	**3%**	**16%**				**3.80**	**0.2**	**5**	**12**	**$4**

Souza,Steven

Age: 27	Bats: R	Pos: RF	Health	C	LIMA Plan B
Ht: 6' 4"	Wt: 225		PT/Exp	D	Rand Var 0
			Consist	C	MM 4305

PRO: Even modest power/speed combos have value in today's offense-starved environment, especially when combined with plate patience. CON: Marginal HctX and lack of uppercut feed xPX skepticism, poor SB% seemed to cost him green light in 2H. Oh, and there's that abhorrent contact rate. Low ceiling, lower floor.

Yr	Tm	AB	R	HR	RBI	SB	BA	xBA	OBP	SLG	OPS	vL	vR	bb%	ct%	Eye	G	L	F	h%	HctX	PX	xPX	hr/f	Spd	SBO	SB%	#Wk	DOM	DIS	RC/G	RAR	BPV	BPX	R$
11																																			
12																																			
13	aa	273	43	12	35	16	265		341	476	817			10	69	0.38				34		168			92	32%	70%				5.43		62	155	$14
14	WAS *	369	48	14	57	19	284	254	356	465	820	2071	105	10	75	0.44	50	13	38	35	122	136	141	33%	80	25%	70%	9	22%	78%	5.72	17.3	54	146	$21
15	TAM	373	59	16	40	12	225	220	318	399	717	730	712	11	61	0.32	45	20	35	32	91	138	99	21%	104	18%	67%	21	24%	48%	3.98	-9.0	11	30	$10
1st Half		271	41	15	33	10	210	226	301	417	718	866	673	11	60	0.30	47	18	35	28	87	160	109	27%	103	23%	67%	14	36%	43%	3.83	-8.5	23	62	$15
2nd Half		102	18	1	7	2	265	209	361	353	714	530	832	12	65	0.39	42	24	33	40	102	85	76	5%	103	9%	67%	7	0%	57%	4.29	-1.6	-16	-43	-$3
16	Proj	**406**	**62**	**13**	**48**	**16**	**261**	**235**	**348**	**418**	**766**	**665**	**816**	**11**	**68**	**0.38**	**44**	**21**	**35**	**35**	**96**	**122**	**89**	**13%**	**101**	**20%**	**69%**				**4.81**	**-0.1**	**23**	**62**	**$18**

Span,Denard

Age: 32	Bats: L	Pos: CF	Health	F	LIMA Plan B
Ht: 6' 0"	Wt: 210		PT/Exp	B	Rand Var 0
			Consist	B	MM 1455

Bad back, hip cut season in half. Was on usual pace for all but HR, and GB says not to believe that spike. Consistently elite plate control, stable xBA mean he's one of few near-.300 BA locks. Given late hip surgery, we can't put return to double-digit SB in stone, so don't make him a primary speed source.

Yr	Tm	AB	R	HR	RBI	SB	BA	xBA	OBP	SLG	OPS	vL	vR	bb%	ct%	Eye	G	L	F	h%	HctX	PX	xPX	hr/f	Spd	SBO	SB%	#Wk	DOM	DIS	RC/G	RAR	BPV	BPX	R$
11	MIN *	322	40	2	17	8	253	267	311	339	650	657	698	8	87	0.64	53	21	26	29	80	55	55	3%	129	10%	89%	15	33%	27%	3.70	-10.3	48	107	$4
12	MIN	516	71	4	41	17	283	290	342	395	738	739	737	8	88	0.76	54	21	24	32	80	78	48	4%	110	16%	74%	26	58%	23%	4.81	1.7	66	165	$16
13	WAS	610	75	4	47	20	279	285	327	380	707	539	765	6	87	0.55	54	23	23	31	69	65	41	3%	152	15%	77%	26	46%	12%	4.39	5.0	62	155	$20
14	WAS	610	94	5	37	31	302	288	355	416	771	694	802	8	89	0.77	46	24	30	33	98	80	52	3%	132	21%	82%	27	56%	7%	5.49	28.2	78	211	$30
15	WAS	246	38	5	22	11	301	301	365	431	796	542	880	9	89	0.96	50	24	26	32	97	84	73	9%	101	14%	100%	13	54%	23%	6.07	11.9	76	205	$11
1st Half		236	37	5	22	11	305	297	369	432	801	542	891	9	89	0.92	49	25	26	33	96	81	73	9%	102	14%	100%	12	50%	25%	6.20	11.5	72	195	$12
2nd Half		10	1	0	0	0	200	359	273	400	673	0	673	9	100	0.00	80	10	10	20	132	144	60	0%	84	0%	0%	1	100%	0%	3.48	-0.3	161	435	-$15
16	Proj	**477**	**68**	**5**	**37**	**17**	**293**	**288**	**349**	**405**	**755**	**620**	**804**	**8**	**88**	**0.73**	**51**	**23**	**26**	**32**	**86**	**72**	**55**	**5%**	**122**	**14%**	**84%**				**5.20**	**10.6**	**66**	**179**	**$21**

STEPHEN NICKRAND

Spangenberg,Cory

Age: 25	Bats: L	Pos: 2B	Health	B	LIMA Plan	B
Ht: 6' 0"	Wt: 195		PT/Exp	D	Rand Var	+1
			Consist	B	MM	2525

4-21-.271 with 9 SB in 344 AB at SD. Finding any nuggets of offensive value can be difficult these days, which is why young MI with wheels can't be dismissed. Surging bb% bodes well for being able to put them to better use, as does overall plate control gains in 2H. So buy him for steals, and anything else is gravy.

Yr	Tm	AB	R	HR	RBI	SB	BA	xBA	OBP	SLG	OPS	vL	vR	bb%	ct%	Eye	G	L	F	h%	HctX	PX	xPX	hr/f	Spd	SBO	SB%	#Wk	DOM	DIS	RC/G	RAR	BPV	BPX	R$
11																																			
12																																			
13	aa	287	30	2	17	16	259		294	325	620			5	75	0.21				34		50			131	37%	57%				2.95		-6	-15	$8
14	SD *	343	38	4	27	15	291	250	320	415	735	667	795	4	75	0.17	45	26	30	38	86	93	113	14%	135	32%	56%	5	20%	40%	4.30	9.1	23	62	$14
15	SD *	341	42	5	24	12	260	262	321	384	706	703	738	8	76	0.38	50	25	25	33	84	86	75	8%	142	17%	75%	20	40%	45%	4.25	0.8	35	95	$9
1st Half		177	21	2	11	7	254	255	304	356	660	705	651	7	75	0.32	52	26	22	33	77	73	58	7%	128	19%	78%	12	42%	50%	3.80	-2.3	14	38	$7
2nd Half		164	21	3	13	5	266	267	334	415	749	701	877	9	78	0.46	49	23	28	33	94	99	101	8%	142	15%	71%	8	38%	38%	4.76	2.6	53	143	$11
16	**Proj**	**459**	**54**	**9**	**33**	**15**	**263**	**260**	**312**	**406**	**718**	**646**	**737**	**6**	**76**	**0.27**	**48**	**25**	**27**	**33**	**87**	**94**	**95**	**9%**	**146**	**19%**	**70%**				**4.27**	**0.6**	**33**	**90**	**$13**

Springer,George

Age: 26	Bats: R	Pos: RF	Health	F	LIMA Plan	B
Ht: 6' 3"	Wt: 205		PT/Exp	C	Rand Var	-2
			Consist	B	MM	4525

3 reasons to believe in an age-26 breakout... 1) Huge spike in ct%, especially in 2H; 2) Top-tier power skills in 1H; 3) Impact wheels returned down the stretch. Warts are low flyball rate—which will continue to cap HR upside—and checkered injury history. Still, he's not far from ... UP: 30 HR/30 SB.

Yr	Tm	AB	R	HR	RBI	SB	BA	xBA	OBP	SLG	OPS	vL	vR	bb%	ct%	Eye	G	L	F	h%	HctX	PX	xPX	hr/f	Spd	SBO	SB%	#Wk	DOM	DIS	RC/G	RAR	BPV	BPX	R$
11																																			
12	aa	73	6	2	4	3	186		233	284	518			6	61	0.16				28		86			97	37%	57%				1.89		-45	-113	-$2
13	a/a	492	81	29	82	34	262		346	501	847			11	61	0.34				36		194			101	32%	79%				5.99		56	140	$33
14	HOU *	346	57	22	57	8	239	241	328	475	802	774	811	12	62	0.34	45	15	39	32	105	191	161	28%	133	11%	80%	14	57%	36%	5.23	13.8	65	176	$14
15	HOU	388	59	16	41	16	276	261	367	459	826	936	767	11	72	0.46	45	24	30	35	105	127	111	19%	123	17%	80%	19	63%	32%	5.84	11.9	51	138	$18
1st Half		276	43	13	29	14	264	256	365	457	822	947	754	13	68	0.48	44	26	30	34	105	140	132	22%	110	19%	82%	13	62%	31%	5.83	8.2	47	127	$24
2nd Half		112	16	3	12	2	304	271	373	464	837	908	800	7	80	0.36	48	22	30	36	104	98	67	11%	134	9%	67%	6	67%	33%	5.86	3.2	55	149	$3
16	**Proj**	**501**	**78**	**24**	**68**	**21**	**267**	**249**	**359**	**469**	**828**	**884**	**802**	**10**	**69**	**0.37**	**46**	**20**	**34**	**34**	**105**	**140**	**121**	**21%**	**140**	**18%**	**81%**				**5.66**	**12.4**	**47**	**128**	**$27**

Stanton,Giancarlo

Age: 26	Bats: R	Pos: RF	Health	F	LIMA Plan	B+
Ht: 6' 6"	Wt: 240		PT/Exp	B	Rand Var	+1
			Consist	C	MM	5235

On pace for long-awaited 50-HR breakout before broken wrist. Surge to über elitedom backed by crazy good power skills, so it was no fluke. And xBA points to better BA. But before you put 40 HR in bank, note health grade; one 500 AB season in last four makes him a risky, tantalizing play.

Yr	Tm	AB	R	HR	RBI	SB	BA	xBA	OBP	SLG	OPS	vL	vR	bb%	ct%	Eye	G	L	F	h%	HctX	PX	xPX	hr/f	Spd	SBO	SB%	#Wk	DOM	DIS	RC/G	RAR	BPV	BPX	R$
11	FLA	516	79	34	87	5	262	276	356	537	893	1042	849	12	68	0.42	45	16	38	32	136	205	172	25%	109	7%	50%	27	63%	19%	6.31	17.5	94	209	$21
12	MIA	449	75	37	86	6	290	288	361	608	969	1024	950	9	68	0.32	36	22	42	35	132	226	163	29%	84	7%	75%	23	65%	17%	7.72	32.3	99	248	$25
13	MIA	425	62	24	62	1	249	253	365	480	845	1006	789	15	67	0.53	43	18	38	31	108	180	139	22%	84	1%	100%	22	45%	27%	5.90	16.1	69	173	$13
14	MIA	539	89	37	105	13	288	278	395	555	950	1075	920	15	68	0.55	41	20	39	36	120	206	146	26%	82	8%	93%	24	75%	13%	7.94	58.0	95	257	$35
15	MIA	279	47	27	67	4	265	282	346	606	952	1172	893	11	66	0.36	35	20	45	30	145	236	210	32%	91	9%	67%	12	75%	25%	7.14	18.5	104	281	$16
1st Half		279	47	27	67	4	265	282	346	606	952	1172	893	11	66	0.36	35	20	45	30	145	236	210	32%	91	9%	67%	12	75%	25%	7.14	18.9	104	281	$16
2nd Half																																			
16	**Proj**	**490**	**79**	**37**	**103**	**7**	**275**	**272**	**369**	**565**	**935**	**1086**	**890**	**13**	**67**	**0.44**	**38**	**20**	**42**	**33**	**128**	**206**	**169**	**27%**	**87**	**7%**	**78%**				**7.27**	**34.4**	**84**	**226**	**$29**

Story,Trevor

Age: 23	Bats: R	Pos: SS	Health	A	LIMA Plan	D
Ht: 6' 1"	Wt: 175		PT/Exp	D	Rand Var	0
			Consist	F	MM	4501

Former first-rounder (Rockies) showed 20/20 upside in flashes, as reflected by that PX/Spd combo. Bugaboo remains tons of Ks. It's one that will continue to prevent consistency and make him even more a BA liability, since MLB hurlers will carve him up. Still, SS with hit tools like this are well worth the stash.

Yr	Tm	AB	R	HR	RBI	SB	BA	xBA	OBP	SLG	OPS	vL	vR	bb%	ct%	Eye	G	L	F	h%	HctX	PX	xPX	hr/f	Spd	SBO	SB%	#Wk	DOM	DIS	RC/G	RAR	BPV	BPX	R$
11																																			
12																																			
13																																			
14	aa	205	23	8	16	2	192		269	356	625			10	59	0.26				28		147			108	8%	69%				3.00		8	22	$0
15	a/a	512	60	17	58	16	260		309	467	776			7	71	0.25				34		149			116	18%	83%				5.01		53	143	$17
1st Half		279	36	9	31	11	250		314	463	777			8	71	0.32				32		153			137	22%	83%				5.00		65	176	$19
2nd Half		233	25	8	27	5	271		303	472	775			4	72	0.16				35		145			127	13%	82%				5.02		51	138	$15
16	**Proj**	**130**	**15**	**5**	**13**	**3**	**233**	**229**	**289**	**425**	**714**	**714**	**714**	**7**	**66**	**0.23**	**35**	**20**	**45**	**31**		**145**		**12%**	**136**	**13%**	**80%**				**4.10**	**0.0**	**32**	**86**	**$3**

Suarez,Eugenio

Age: 24	Bats: R	Pos: SS	Health	A	LIMA Plan	B
Ht: 5' 11"	Wt: 180		PT/Exp	C	Rand Var	-2
			Consist	B	MM	3315

13-48-.280 with 4 SB in 372 AB at CIN. Prior utility prospect raised that stock with MLB power display. While that 2H xPX/Spd combo hints he has goods to be 20/10 guy, getting there will require better pitch recognition. Mediocre ct%, Eye got worse after recall, so we can't bank on it just yet.

Yr	Tm	AB	R	HR	RBI	SB	BA	xBA	OBP	SLG	OPS	vL	vR	bb%	ct%	Eye	G	L	F	h%	HctX	PX	xPX	hr/f	Spd	SBO	SB%	#Wk	DOM	DIS	RC/G	RAR	BPV	BPX	R$
11																																			
12																																			
13	aa	442	43	7	36	7	231		290	347	638			8	77	0.36				29		85			111	18%	38%				3.03		26	65	$4
14	DET *	442	57	10	50	10	246	231	306	379	685	656	650	8	74	0.33	35	22	43	31	87	107	109	5%	113	13%	70%	17	29%	59%	3.88	7.7	31	84	$11
15	CIN *	575	67	21	69	7	263	249	310	433	743	819	744	6	76	0.28	41	21	38	32	94	112	106	12%	122	9%	54%	18	39%	39%	4.52	12.6	43	116	$17
1st Half		272	29	10	32	6	251	253	317	415	732	898	749	9	77	0.41	51	18	31	29	51	105	34	13%	117	14%	55%	5	60%	20%	4.29	1.7	45	122	$14
2nd Half		303	38	11	37	1	274	249	306	449	755	798	743	4	75	0.17	39	21	40	33	102	119	122	12%	121	3%	50%	13	31%	46%	4.74	5.6	40	108	$19
16	**Proj**	**456**	**54**	**13**	**51**	**7**	**253**	**239**	**313**	**399**	**712**	**746**	**699**	**7**	**75**	**0.30**	**40**	**21**	**39**	**31**	**83**	**101**	**95**	**9%**	**125**	**11%**	**58%**				**4.04**	**-0.6**	**24**	**64**	**$13**

Susac,Andrew

Age: 26	Bats: R	Pos: CA	Health	B	LIMA Plan	D
Ht: 6' 1"	Wt: 215		PT/Exp	F	Rand Var	-1
			Consist	A	MM	4301

3-14-.218 in 133 AB with SF. On surface, a second catcher with marginal power and a BA that will kill you. But that 1H xPX and 2H PX are evidence of dormant pop, albeit for now only vs. LH (.824 OPS). It's an attribute worth speculating on for a buck, since he won't get enough AB to hurt your BA anyway.

Yr	Tm	AB	R	HR	RBI	SB	BA	xBA	OBP	SLG	OPS	vL	vR	bb%	ct%	Eye	G	L	F	h%	HctX	PX	xPX	hr/f	Spd	SBO	SB%	#Wk	DOM	DIS	RC/G	RAR	BPV	BPX	R$
11																																			
12																																			
13	aa	262	24	8	34	1	213		297	359	656			11	71	0.40				27		116			79	1%	100%				3.47		22	55	$1
14	SF *	301	36	9	40	0	227	223	298	363	661	1011	668	9	71	0.35	37	20	43	29	103	111	156	12%	84	0%	0%	12	42%	42%	3.57	1.0	18	49	$3
15	SF *	161	18	4	15	0	226	225	297	377	673	824	578	9	66	0.30	47	19	34	32	93	121	121	10%	107	0%	0%	17	29%	47%	3.68	-0.6	12	32	-$1
1st Half		116	15	2	9	0	257	232	328	399	727	925	607	10	68	0.33	42	22	36	36	100	118	137	8%	102	0%	0%	13	31%	54%	4.49	2.4	20	54	$0
2nd Half		45	3	2	7	0	145	202	215	319	534	536	505	8	59	0.22	62	10	29	20	74	130	68	17%	112	0%	0%	4	25%	25%	2.05	-2.6	-8	-22	-$3
16	**Proj**	**157**	**18**	**5**	**18**	**0**	**232**	**234**	**311**	**399**	**710**	**887**	**612**	**10**	**70**	**0.37**	**45**	**18**	**37**	**30**	**92**	**126**	**120**	**12%**	**91**	**1%**	**100%**				**4.11**	**1.5**	**16**	**44**	**$3**

Suzuki,Ichiro

Age: 42	Bats: L	Pos: RF LF	Health	A	LIMA Plan	D+
Ht: 5' 11"	Wt: 170		PT/Exp	B	Rand Var	+4
			Consist	B	MM	0521

Hanging on as he approaches 3K hits, but just barely. Spd confirmation of great shape, but as he nears mid-40s, even 20 SB days ain't coming back. Nor is prior 5-HR baseline; see xPX. BA dive result of uncharacteristic h%, but xBA has been painting gloomy picture there for a while, so be pessimistic.

Yr	Tm	AB	R	HR	RBI	SB	BA	xBA	OBP	SLG	OPS	vL	vR	bb%	ct%	Eye	G	L	F	h%	HctX	PX	xPX	hr/f	Spd	SBO	SB%	#Wk	DOM	DIS	RC/G	RAR	BPV	BPX	R$
11	SEA	677	80	5	47	40	272	275	310	335	645	648	644	5	90	0.57	60	19	21	30	55	42	29	4%	132	24%	85%	27	37%	11%	3.83	-25.8	45	100	$23
12	2 AL	629	77	9	55	29	283	292	307	390	696	649	724	3	90	0.36	51	25	24	30	70	63	40	7%	133	23%	81%	28	64%	14%	4.31	-15.0	60	150	$24
13	NYY	520	57	7	35	20	262	264	297	342	639	753	590	5	88	0.41	52	21	27	29	62	50	33	6%	140	18%	83%	26	38%	27%	3.59	-15.4	45	113	$15
14	NYY	359	42	1	22	15	284	255	324	340	664	807	632	6	81	0.31	58	22	20	35	67	45	22	2%	136	17%	83%	27	22%	44%	4.03	-0.6	14	38	$12
15	MIA	398	45	1	21	11	229	251	282	279	561	723	514	7	87	0.61	58	18	23	26	51	26	28	1%	178	15%	69%	27	22%	44%	2.61	-27.4	39	105	$3
1st Half		168	17	1	11	6	250	253	310	292	601	720	561	8	86	0.65	68	17	15	28	28	19	16	5%	167	19%	60%	14	21%	50%	2.97	-9.4	29	78	$3
2nd Half		230	28	0	10	5	213	247	261	270	531	726	481	7	88	0.57	52	20	29	24	67	32	37	0%	155	11%	83%	13	23%	38%	2.36	-17.5	38	103	$3
16	**Proj**	**230**	**26**	**1**	**14**	**8**	**252**	**258**	**297**	**313**	**610**	**739**	**571**	**6**	**86**	**0.48**	**57**	**20**	**23**	**29**	**58**	**37**	**28**	**3%**	**143**	**16%**	**77%**				**3.23**	**-10.8**	**23**	**63**	**$6**

STEPHEN NICKRAND

Suzuki,Kurt

Age: 32	Bats: R	Pos: CA	Health	A	LIMA Plan D+
Ht: 5' 11"	Wt: 205		PT/Exp	C	Rand Var 0
			Consist	C	MM 1115

Backstops like this one whose plate control gets better in 30s can be attractive targets, given often-late-blooming power. Here, sliding HctX, LD, sub-40% FB% all prove he's hitting ball with no authority. That lack of thump also makes him a BA liability, as he's peppering the field with weak contact. It's a bad combo.

Yr	Tm	AB	R	HR	RBI	SB	BA	xBA	OBP	SLG	OPS	vL	vR	bb%	ct%	Eye	G	L	F	h%	HctX	PX	xPX	hr/f	Spd	SBO	SB%	#Wk	DOM	DIS	RC/G	RAR	BPV	BPX	R$
11	OAK	460	54	14	44	2	237	262	301	385	686	617	713	8	86	0.59	36	20	44	25	89	97	80	8%	78	4%	50%	27	63%	11%	3.75	-6.3	63	140	$6
12	2 TM	408	36	6	43	2	235	223	276	328	605	628	598	5	82	0.27	41	17	42	27	112	66	102	4%	80	2%	100%	28	21%	46%	2.99	-13.9	17	43	$3
13	2 TM	285	25	5	32	2	232	255	290	337	627	653	619	7	88	0.63	37	23	40	25	104	69	100	5%	88	3%	100%	26	38%	31%	3.24	-4.0	49	123	$2
14	MIN	452	37	3	61	0	288	268	345	383	727	810	695	7	90	0.74	44	22	34	32	101	76	82	2%	70	1%	0%	27	59%	15%	4.58	15.9	57	154	$11
15	MIN	433	36	5	50	0	240	230	296	314	610	658	587	6	86	0.49	43	19	38	27	94	50	81	4%	77	0%	0%	26	38%	35%	3.03	-9.0	23	62	$3
1st Half		225	19	3	23	0	222	224	281	307	588	617	575	7	88	0.61	45	16	39	24	91	56	92	4%	73	0%	0%	14	43%	29%	2.78	-6.8	33	89	$0
2nd Half		208	17	2	27	0	260	237	313	322	635	695	602	5	85	0.39	41	23	36	30	97	43	70	3%	85	0%	0%	12	33%	42%	3.33	-2.7	13	35	$5
16	**Proj**	**426**	**36**	**4**	**51**	**1**	**239**	**242**	**295**	**315**	**609**	**659**	**589**	**6**	**87**	**0.52**	**42**	**21**	**37**	**27**	**98**	**54**	**84**	**3%**	**78**	**1%**	**66%**				**3.02**	**-9.7**	**16**	**44**	**$3**

Sweeney,Darnell

Age: 25	Bats: B	Pos: LF	Health	A	LIMA Plan D+
Ht: 6' 1"	Wt: 150		PT/Exp	D	Rand Var -1
			Consist	B	MM 3303

3-11-.176 in 85 AB with PHI. So-so prospect now on MLB radar due to above-average pop and history of impact wheels (48 SB in Hi-A at age 22). Blending both is dependent upon better pitch recognition. That 2H gives glimmer of hope, but >115 Ks three straight years on farm mean you—and he—need patience.

Yr	Tm	AB	R	HR	RBI	SB	BA	xBA	OBP	SLG	OPS	vL	vR	bb%	ct%	Eye	G	L	F	h%	HctX	PX	xPX	hr/f	Spd	SBO	SB%	#Wk	DOM	DIS	RC/G	RAR	BPV	BPX	R$
11																																			
12																																			
13																																			
14	aa	490	63	11	41	11	240		313	375	688			10	72	0.38				31		111			103	23%	37%				3.46		30	81	$11
15	PHI *	557	61	10	48	24	221	208	277	341	618	693	613	7	71	0.27	43	14	43	29	91	93	131	12%	121	33%	59%	8	63%	38%	2.86	-32.8	10	27	$11
1st Half		311	34	6	27	20	245	223	288	368	656			6	69	0.20				34		99			125	45%	63%				3.29		7	19	$18
2nd Half		246	27	5	21	5	190	208	264	307	570	693	613	9	73	0.37	43	14	43	24	94	85	131	12%	125	19%	46%	8	63%	38%	2.37	-17.6	17	46	$2
16	**Proj**	**384**	**45**	**8**	**33**	**10**	**224**	**223**	**290**	**359**	**649**	**736**	**609**	**9**	**72**	**0.33**	**45**	**16**	**39**	**29**	**85**	**101**	**118**	**8%**	**124**	**25%**	**47%**				**3.10**	**-17.8**	**16**	**42**	**$8**

Swihart,Blake

Age: 24	Bats: B	Pos: CA	Health	A	LIMA Plan C+
Ht: 6' 1"	Wt: 175		PT/Exp	F	Rand Var -2
			Consist	B	MM 2433

5-31-.274 with 4 SB in 288 AB at BOS. Impressive rookie debut puts him on fringe of everyday gig. Profit seekers will note mediocre HctX, PX, and GB tilt and temper power hope. Of interest are those wheels, especially from a C, along with decent OBP. 5-10 HR/SB combos from backstops don't grow on trees.

Yr	Tm	AB	R	HR	RBI	SB	BA	xBA	OBP	SLG	OPS	vL	vR	bb%	ct%	Eye	G	L	F	h%	HctX	PX	xPX	hr/f	Spd	SBO	SB%	#Wk	DOM	DIS	RC/G	RAR	BPV	BPX	R$
11																																			
12																																			
13																																			
14	a/a	416	44	10	53	7	279		321	433	754			6	80	0.30				33		116			92	8%	86%				4.95		52	141	$14
15	BOS *	369	54	5	40	5	281	249	323	385	708	603	754	6	74	0.25	46	27	28	37	88	81	70	9%	117	8%	61%	22	27%	36%	4.34	6.3	12	32	$11
1st Half		201	22	1	21	2	270	243	312	341	653	610	599	6	76	0.25	49	26	25	35	92	62	59	4%	105	9%	38%	10	10%	50%	3.52	-1.5	-2	-5	$7
2nd Half		168	32	4	20	3	297	256	340	440	780	595	883	6	73	0.24	42	27	30	39	84	106	80	12%	130	7%	100%	12	42%	25%	5.55	8.2	30	81	$15
16	**Proj**	**329**	**45**	**6**	**39**	**5**	**271**	**263**	**316**	**398**	**714**	**592**	**762**	**6**	**76**	**0.27**	**45**	**27**	**28**	**34**	**87**	**93**	**72**	**9%**	**120**	**8%**	**77%**				**4.37**	**5.6**	**23**	**62**	**$11**

Swisher,Nick

Age: 35	Bats: B	Pos: DH LF	Health	F	LIMA Plan D
Ht: 6' 0"	Wt: 200		PT/Exp	C	Rand Var +3
			Consist	B	MM 2101

6-25-.196 in 219 AB at ATL/CLE. Days when we could write 20 HR, 80 RBI in pen are long gone now. Easy to blame bad health and speculate on bounceback. At least until you follow those HctX and PX trends, which may make 15 HR a reach even if health suddenly cooperates. He's an end-game wildcard now.

Yr	Tm	AB	R	HR	RBI	SB	BA	xBA	OBP	SLG	OPS	vL	vR	bb%	ct%	Eye	G	L	F	h%	HctX	PX	xPX	hr/f	Spd	SBO	SB%	#Wk	DOM	DIS	RC/G	RAR	BPV	BPX	R$
11	NYY	526	81	23	85	2	260	264	374	449	822	957	763	15	76	0.76	39	22	39	30	118	133	133	14%	71	2%	50%	27	63%	26%	5.73	7.0	65	144	$17
12	NYY	537	75	24	93	2	272	261	364	473	837	769	873	13	74	0.55	39	22	39	33	114	142	127	15%	80	3%	40%	27	48%	30%	5.92	18.3	60	150	$19
13	CLE	549	74	22	63	1	246	255	341	423	763	918	680	12	75	0.56	38	23	39	29	108	124	138	14%	79	1%	100%	26	54%	23%	4.85	12.9	49	123	$13
14	CLE	360	33	8	42	0	208	228	278	331	608	481	658	9	69	0.32	38	24	38	28	98	107	130	8%	65	0%	0%	18	33%	39%	2.98	-8.9	2	5	$0
15	2 TM *	266	19	7	29	0	201	211	304	317	622	717	582	13	74	0.57	51	18	31	25	93	83	99	12%	62	0%	0%	15	33%	40%	3.08	-13.6	8	22	-$2
1st Half		125	10	3	12	0	218	228	277	330	607	620	513	8	73	0.31	50	22	28	27	91	83	94	9%	71	0%	0%	6	0%	50%	2.98	-6.0	-1	-3	-$3
2nd Half		141	10	4	17	0	186	190	325	306	632	827	624	17	74	0.80	51	16	33	22	94	83	104	13%	66	0%	0%	9	56%	33%	3.12	-6.5	19	51	-$2
16	**Proj**	**184**	**18**	**5**	**22**	**0**	**214**	**231**	**312**	**350**	**663**	**713**	**637**	**12**	**73**	**0.52**	**44**	**21**	**35**	**26**	**99**	**98**	**116**	**11%**	**70**	**0%**	**58%**				**3.52**	**-11.0**	**4**	**9**	**$2**

Taylor,Chris

Age: 25	Bats: R	Pos: SS	Health	A	LIMA Plan D
Ht: 6' 1"	Wt: 190		PT/Exp	D	Rand Var +2
			Consist	C	MM 2501

0-1-.170 with 3 SB in 94 AB at SEA. Flopped after mid-season shot at full-time SS gig. Woeful MLB line, but not so fast. Plenty of hard contact, FBs gave him near-elite xPX that was muted by a crazy *zero* flyballs leaving park. And that h% won't repeat again. All in tiny sample, but still... UP: 10 HR, 20 SB

Yr	Tm	AB	R	HR	RBI	SB	BA	xBA	OBP	SLG	OPS	vL	vR	bb%	ct%	Eye	G	L	F	h%	HctX	PX	xPX	hr/f	Spd	SBO	SB%	#Wk	DOM	DIS	RC/G	RAR	BPV	BPX	R$
11																																			
12																																			
13	aa	256	42	1	14	16	273		361	353	713			12	76	0.56				36		64			137	22%	83%				4.67		21	53	$10
14	SEA *	438	59	3	34	15	271	219	324	371	695	699	687	7	71	0.26	41	21	38	38	52	91	62	0%	156	20%	62%	11	18%	55%	4.04	11.0	18	49	$14
15	SEA *	437	46	3	22	14	222	212	285	303	588	635	358	8	76	0.36	32	24	44	29	123	61	158	0%	133	23%	54%	10	10%	70%	2.65	-24.0	10	27	$4
1st Half		259	25	1	12	11	209	198	267	279	546	896	294	7	77	0.34	31	22	47	27	117	49	146	0%	134	28%	61%	7	14%	57%	2.28	-15.0	2	5	$4
2nd Half		178	21	1	11	3	243	240	312	338	650	423	615	9	74	0.39	35	29	35	32	138	77	190	0%	124	16%	39%	3	0%	100%	3.24	-4.6	17	46	$4
16	**Proj**	**160**	**20**	**2**	**10**	**7**	**238**	**228**	**305**	**352**	**657**	**722**	**610**	**8**	**74**	**0.35**	**37**	**24**	**39**	**31**	**98**	**85**	**128**	**5%**	**139**	**25%**	**64%**				**3.42**	**-3.3**	**17**	**46**	**$4**

Taylor,Michael

Age: 25	Bats: R	Pos: CF LF	Health	A	LIMA Plan B
Ht: 6' 3"	Wt: 210		PT/Exp	D	Rand Var -1
			Consist	B	MM 3405

14-63-.229 with 16 SB in 472 AB at WAS. Injury fill-in rode power, speed package to double-digit R$ in rookie campaign. And there's more power coming; see 125+ xPX in Aug & Sept. Ability to take a walk muted by huge holes in swing, so don't bank on BA or consistency. Still, everyone can use this... UP: 25 HR, 30 SB

Yr	Tm	AB	R	HR	RBI	SB	BA	xBA	OBP	SLG	OPS	vL	vR	bb%	ct%	Eye	G	L	F	h%	HctX	PX	xPX	hr/f	Spd	SBO	SB%	#Wk	DOM	DIS	RC/G	RAR	BPV	BPX	R$
11																																			
12																																			
13																																			
14	WAS *	467	65	17	52	27	258	240	323	417	739	1095	553	9	63	0.25	55	23	23	38	49	139	65	20%	113	31%	69%	6	17%	50%	4.45	8.7	15	41	$22
15	WAS *	498	52	15	66	18	235	219	290	364	654	667	633	7	66	0.23	46	22	32	33	91	96	115	15%	107	18%	81%	26	19%	54%	3.57	-11.0	-9	-24	$14
1st Half		240	27	7	32	10	259	218	312	398	709	686	683	7	65	0.22	45	20	35	37	88	109	110	13%	104	21%	76%	13	15%	54%	4.25	-1.1	-4	-11	$15
2nd Half		258	25	8	34	8	213	220	271	333	605	651	592	7	67	0.23	47	24	29	29	93	84	119	17%	111	15%	89%	13	23%	54%	3.01	-11.2	-16	-43	$12
16	**Proj**	**517**	**61**	**16**	**64**	**22**	**232**	**220**	**292**	**368**	**660**	**689**	**652**	**8**	**65**	**0.24**	**46**	**22**	**31**	**33**	**91**	**104**	**115**	**15%**	**115**	**23%**	**74%**				**3.54**	**-13.7**	**-7**	**-18**	**$17**

Teixeira,Mark

Age: 36	Bats: B	Pos: 1B	Health	F	LIMA Plan B+
Ht: 6' 3"	Wt: 215		PT/Exp	D	Rand Var +1
			Consist	D	MM 4145

Was on way to second 40-HR campaign of career before shin sidelined him for year in Aug. That surge came with backing of plenty of hard contact and ct% recovery, so don't dismiss it. What we can dismiss is his ability to stay healthy, and it's an issue that will get worse as he nears 40. Buy 400 AB; rest gravy.

Yr	Tm	AB	R	HR	RBI	SB	BA	xBA	OBP	SLG	OPS	vL	vR	bb%	ct%	Eye	G	L	F	h%	HctX	PX	xPX	hr/f	Spd	SBO	SB%	#Wk	DOM	DIS	RC/G	RAR	BPV	BPX	R$
11	NYY	589	90	39	111	4	248	281	341	494	835	967	773	11	81	0.69	35	18	47	24	124	151	133	17%	68	3%	80%	27	63%	19%	5.60	-0.7	91	202	$23
12	NYY	451	66	24	84	2	251	281	332	475	807	865	770	11	82	0.65	41	19	39	26	122	137	120	16%	69	3%	67%	24	67%	21%	5.32	0.4	80	200	$14
13	NYY	53	5	3	12	0	151	239	270	340	609	935	432	13	64	0.42	29	29	43	16	76	139	128	20%	71	0%	0%	3	33%	67%	2.68	-3.3	17	43	-$2
14	NYY	440	56	22	62	1	216	254	313	398	711	691	718	12	75	0.53	41	21	37	24	114	125	119	18%	63	2%	50%	25	36%	40%	3.95	-2.5	45	122	$8
15	NYY	392	57	31	79	2	255	296	357	548	906	787	958	13	78	0.69	39	19	42	25	122	179	136	23%	65	2%	100%	21	67%	10%	6.65	19.6	104	281	$16
1st Half		263	37	20	59	1	243	302	356	532	889	842	906	14	81	0.88	41	19	40	23	120	173	130	23%	58	1%	100%	14	79%	0%	6.34	9.2	111	300	$22
2nd Half		129	20	11	20	1	279	281	359	581	940	695	1081	10	73	0.43	33	19	48	30	126	194	149	24%	94	3%	100%	7	43%	29%	7.34	8.0	98	265	$6
16	**Proj**	**434**	**62**	**30**	**75**	**2**	**260**	**280**	**350**	**515**	**865**	**837**	**877**	**11**	**77**	**0.57**	**37**	**21**	**42**	**27**	**114**	**157**	**132**	**21%**	**67**	**2%**	**82%**				**6.13**	**12.3**	**72**	**195**	**$20**

STEPHEN NICKRAND

Tejada,Ruben

Age: 26	Bats: R	Pos: SS	Health	B	LIMA Plan	D+
Ht: 5' 11"	Wt: 200		PT/Exp	C	Rand Var	-1
			Consist	B	MM	1125

At first glance, a middle infielder who will neither hurt nor help. But concurrent surges in HctX, LD, xPX all give legitimate hope for more power, especially if that hr/f improves. And solid plate control got much better in 2H, so he's not a BA liability anymore. Assuming a healed broken leg, a $5 bid could yield $5 of profit.

Yr	Tm	AB	R	HR	RBI	SB	BA	xBA	OBP	SLG	OPS	vL	vR	bb%	ct%	Eye	G	L	F	h%	HctX	PX	xPX	hr/f	Spd	SBO	SB%	#Wk	DOM	DIS	RC/G	RAR	BPV	BPX	R$
11	NYM *	535	52	2	53	8	252	255	316	316	632	704	692	9	85	0.61	45	26	30	29	56	47	39	0%	107	7%	72%	18	39%	44%	3.41	-17.3	27	60	$7
12	NYM	464	53	1	25	4	289	264	333	351	685	760	647	5	84	0.37	40	30	30	34	78	51	55	1%	110	6%	50%	21	33%	33%	4.03	-0.9	24	60	$9
13	NYM *	448	44	1	25	3	210	238	249	270	520	719	432	5	86	0.39	47	19	34	24	84	49	62	0%	94	5%	54%	11	45%	18%	2.15	-18.9	25	63	-$3
14	NYM	355	30	5	34	1	237	231	342	310	652	631	658	12	79	0.68	40	24	35	29	81	55	72	5%	80	3%	33%	27	44%	44%	3.37	0.7	12	32	$2
15	NYM	360	36	3	28	2	261	257	338	350	688	731	675	10	81	0.54	40	27	33	32	94	70	101	3%	91	3%	67%	27	41%	26%	4.00	2.4	26	70	$4
1st Half		164	16	1	13	1	238	248	315	335	651	708	637	8	79	0.43	36	26	38	30	101	82	120	2%	90	5%	50%	14	50%	29%	3.33	-3.7	26	70	$0
2nd Half		196	20	2	15	1	281	265	357	362	720	744	710	11	82	0.66	43	29	28	33	88	60	85	4%	92	2%	100%	13	31%	23%	4.61	2.9	27	73	$8
16	**Proj**	**412**	**40**	**6**	**32**	**2**	**257**	**254**	**334**	**350**	**684**	**740**	**664**	**9**	**82**	**0.57**	**42**	**25**	**33**	**30**	**86**	**67**	**82**	**5%**	**91**	**3%**	**58%**				**3.89**	**-2.3**	**13**	**34**	**$5**

Telis,Tomas

Age: 25	Bats: B	Pos: CA	Health	A	LIMA Plan	D
Ht: 5' 8"	Wt: 200		PT/Exp	D	Rand Var	0
			Consist	B	MM	0311

0-2-.158 in 48 AB at TEX/MIA. Blah HctX combined with deep GB stroke zaps any hope for power, as shown by dismal xPX. Only savings grace is his ct%, which will give him decent BA floor—but not if MLB pitchers can knock bat out of his hand. Please don't Telis you're going to bid on him.

Yr	Tm	AB	R	HR	RBI	SB	BA	xBA	OBP	SLG	OPS	vL	vR	bb%	ct%	Eye	G	L	F	h%	HctX	PX	xPX	hr/f	Spd	SBO	SB%	#Wk	DOM	DIS	RC/G	RAR	BPV	BPX	R$
11																																			
12																																			
13	aa	348	27	4	37	7	251		269	336	605			2	86	0.18				28		62			79	12%	76%				3.08		25	63	$5
14	TEX *	474	43	4	45	6	273	269	299	355	655	400	576	4	88	0.33	58	18	24	30	65	59	54	0%	94	7%	72%	6	17%	67%	3.72	3.5	38	103	$11
15	2 TM *	368	41	4	26	3	254	260	287	326	613	762	301	4	88	0.38	68	15	18	28	80	47	51	0%	99	5%	53%	11	0%	45%	3.14	-7.2	29	78	$4
1st Half		263	34	4	21	1	258	257	289	359	648			4	88	0.37				28		66			90	5%	27%				3.44		42	114	$7
2nd Half		105	6	0	5	2	245	216	280	245	525	762	301	5	88	0.40	68	15	18	28	80	0	51	0%	102	5%	100%	11	0%	45%	2.40	-4.3	-7	-19	-$4
16	**Proj**	**134**	**12**	**0**	**11**	**2**	**259**	**247**	**313**	**299**	**611**	**828**	**572**	**4**	**88**	**0.33**	**64**	**16**	**20**	**30**	**74**	**30**	**52**	**0%**	**96**	**7%**	**78%**				**2.98**	**-3.1**	**5**	**12**	**$2**

Thompson,Trayce

Age: 25	Bats: R	Pos: RF	Health	A	LIMA Plan	D+
Ht: 6' 3"	Wt: 195		PT/Exp	B	Rand Var	+2
			Consist	B	MM	4431

5-16-.295 in 122 AB at CHW. Toolsy prospect made 2H splash with CHW (.896 OPS, 120+ PX/Spd, 92 BPV), even cutting down Ks—his bugaboo from minors. Will it stick? Sub-par ct% history, sobering xPX say no, and he returned to earth in Sept. HR/SB profile in minors gives him 20/20 ceiling, just not in '16.

Yr	Tm	AB	R	HR	RBI	SB	BA	xBA	OBP	SLG	OPS	vL	vR	bb%	ct%	Eye	G	L	F	h%	HctX	PX	xPX	hr/f	Spd	SBO	SB%	#Wk	DOM	DIS	RC/G	RAR	BPV	BPX	R$
11																																			
12	a/a	68	9	3	5	3	238		331	435	766			12	65	0.39				32		146			113	13%	100%				5.05		35	88	$0
13	aa	507	65	14	61	21	210		288	352	640			10	70	0.36				27		108			108	24%	71%				3.23		19	48	$12
14	aa	518	63	13	43	15	203		275	349	623			9	67	0.30				28		126			108	18%	72%				3.04		20	54	$6
15	CHW *	510	60	17	48	10	246	274	292	423	715	998	811	6	77	0.28	39	29	32	29	96	116	97	16%	116	14%	64%	10	80%	10%	4.07	-6.7	50	135	$12
1st Half		314	36	9	28	7	234	251	269	389	658			5	77	0.20				28		103			122	18%	59%				3.34		38	103	$13
2nd Half		196	24	8	20	3	265	287	327	476	804	998	811	9	77	0.41	39	29	32	31	96	137	97	16%	116	10%	75%	10	80%	10%	5.39	5.6	73	197	$10
16	**Proj**	**225**	**27**	**8**	**21**	**6**	**243**	**262**	**306**	**420**	**726**	**783**	**678**	**8**	**73**	**0.33**	**39**	**29**	**32**	**30**	**86**	**124**	**87**	**15%**	**119**	**16%**	**69%**				**4.25**	**-3.8**	**40**	**108**	**$7**

Tomas,Yasmany

Age: 25	Bats: R	Pos: RF 3B	Health	A	LIMA Plan	B
Ht: 6' 2"	Wt: 255		PT/Exp	D	Rand Var	-3
			Consist	B	MM	3225

9-48-.273 in 406 AB at ARI. Prized Cuban defector's raw strength acting as tease due to lack of uppercut in swing and terrible control of home plate. Extreme hacker approach late in year gives no short-term hope for growth, and as that h% regresses, he'll become a BA killer too. Check back in a year.

Yr	Tm	AB	R	HR	RBI	SB	BA	xBA	OBP	SLG	OPS	vL	vR	bb%	ct%	Eye	G	L	F	h%	HctX	PX	xPX	hr/f	Spd	SBO	SB%	#Wk	DOM	DIS	RC/G	RAR	BPV	BPX	R$
11	for	27	4	1	3	0	173		173	357	529			0	72	0.00				22		103			140	45%	0%				1.38	-3.4	14	31	-$2
12	for	272	45	12	49	4	278		310	476	787			5	80	0.24				31		124			93	10%	62%				5.11	0.8	59	148	$10
13	for	277	44	9	59	1	269		335	465	800			9	82	0.56				30		127			113	6%	21%				5.19	6.0	85	213	$10
14	for	241	27	4	35	5	267		317	403	720			7	81	0.38				32		102			102	20%	45%				4.06	0.4	51	138	$6
15	ARI *	427	41	10	50	5	267	250	297	396	693	797	673	4	73	0.16	55	22	23	35	99	92	78	13%	86	7%	71%	25	24%	40%	4.07	-9.7	1	3	$10
1st Half		253	24	6	37	4	301	265	336	434	770	831	791	5	78	0.24	55	21	24	37	124	94	87	11%	81	9%	67%	13	31%	15%	5.24	3.0	23	62	$17
2nd Half		174	17	4	13	1	218	226	240	339	579	763	490	3	66	0.08	55	23	22	31	66	88	64	16%	98	3%	100%	12	17%	67%	2.68	-11.4	-31	-84	$0
16	**Proj**	**497**	**55**	**13**	**65**	**6**	**260**	**260**	**302**	**411**	**713**	**849**	**656**	**5**	**76**	**0.24**	**53**	**21**	**24**	**32**	**89**	**102**	**73**	**14%**	**97**	**10%**	**52%**				**4.10**	**-10.4**	**26**	**70**	**$15**

Tomlinson,Kelby

Age: 26	Bats: R	Pos: 2B	Health	A	LIMA Plan	D
Ht: 6' 2"	Wt: 180		PT/Exp	D	Rand Var	-4
			Consist	C	MM	1531

2-20-.303 with 5 SB in 178 AB at SF. Flash of average, steals puts him on '16 end-game radar. Problem is, as h% regresses and MLB pitchers exploit complete hard contact void, even a .250 BA could be a stretch. Wheels are reason to bid, but marginal pitch recognition says not so fast. Speculate elsewhere.

Yr	Tm	AB	R	HR	RBI	SB	BA	xBA	OBP	SLG	OPS	vL	vR	bb%	ct%	Eye	G	L	F	h%	HctX	PX	xPX	hr/f	Spd	SBO	SB%	#Wk	DOM	DIS	RC/G	RAR	BPV	BPX	R$
11																																			
12																																			
13	aa	96	9	0	3	2	166		256	211	467			11	69	0.39				24		49			103	14%	66%				1.65		-30	-75	-$4
14	aa	433	50	1	25	39	233		292	281	573			8	78	0.38				30		34			150	43%	74%				2.77		3	8	$15
15	SF *	567	75	4	55	22	285	276	333	370	703	913	682	7	81	0.37	56	28	17	35	54	57	26	9%	143	22%	60%	10	50%	40%	4.16	0.0	27	73	$22
1st Half		299	39	1	25	14	280	242	330	374	704			7	82	0.42				34		66			133	27%	64%				4.17		38	103	$22
2nd Half		268	35	3	30	7	291	264	336	365	701	913	682	6	79	0.32	56	28	17	36	53	47	26	9%	147	16%	54%	10	50%	40%	4.15	-0.6	12	32	$22
16	**Proj**	**162**	**19**	**2**	**12**	**6**	**250**	**266**	**310**	**333**	**643**	**761**	**580**	**8**	**78**	**0.37**	**56**	**28**	**17**	**31**	**48**	**55**	**23**	**8%**	**149**	**23%**	**61%**				**3.31**	**-4.5**	**8**	**21**	**$5**

Toscano,Dian

Age: 27	Bats: L	Pos: DH	Health	A	LIMA Plan	D+
Ht: 5' 11"	Wt: 200		PT/Exp	F	Rand Var	0
			Consist	F	MM	1231

Scouts say presumed Cuban defector's strength is bat control, consistently posting more BBs than Ks. Fanalytic impact likely blocked by total lack of power though, leaving him as a BA/SB play. Spd tempers optimism on how much upside he'll have on basepaths anyway. Longshot to make impact.

Yr	Tm	AB	R	HR	RBI	SB	BA	xBA	OBP	SLG	OPS	vL	vR	bb%	ct%	Eye	G	L	F	h%	HctX	PX	xPX	hr/f	Spd	SBO	SB%	#Wk	DOM	DIS	RC/G	RAR	BPV	BPX	R$
11	for	150	26	2	20	5	267		383	336	719			16	90	1.86				29		45			94	11%	67%				4.46	-2.7	57	127	$4
12	for	73	6	0	16	2	332		386	442	828			8	90	0.85				37		72			103	12%	62%				6.33	3.3	65	163	$2
13																																			
14																																			
15																																			
1st Half																																			
2nd Half																																			
16	**Proj**	**120**	**19**	**3**	**14**	**4**	**240**	**261**	**348**	**349**	**697**	**697**	**697**	**14**	**91**	**1.84**	**44**	**20**	**36**	**24**		**60**		**8%**	**91**	**12%**	**71%**				**4.07**	**-5.0**	**64**	**173**	**$4**

Travis,Devon

Age: 25	Bats: R	Pos: 2B	Health	D	LIMA Plan	B
Ht: 5' 9"	Wt: 195		PT/Exp	F	Rand Var	0
			Consist	C	MM	3453

8-35-.304 with 3 SB in 217 AB at TOR. Early ROY frontrunner bagged by bum shoulder, sending him under knife in Sept. GB stroke caps HR hopes at 15 for now, and xBA shows truer BA level. But .280/15 ain't bad. Also owns that '14 Spd and takes a walk, so double-digit SB within reach, too. With health, a bright future.

Yr	Tm	AB	R	HR	RBI	SB	BA	xBA	OBP	SLG	OPS	vL	vR	bb%	ct%	Eye	G	L	F	h%	HctX	PX	xPX	hr/f	Spd	SBO	SB%	#Wk	DOM	DIS	RC/G	RAR	BPV	BPX	R$
11																																			
12																																			
13																																			
14	aa	396	49	7	37	11	259		306	391	697			6	84	0.42				29		86			129	17%	67%				4.02		57	154	$11
15	TOR *	260	42	8	36	4	282	277	341	447	788	974	812	8	79	0.41	50	22	28	33	96	116	110	16%	85	7%	79%	12	58%	8%	5.42	8.4	51	138	$9
1st Half		208	34	7	32	3	271	272	326	439	765	959	812	8	79	0.38	50	20	30	32	95	116	120	17%	79	7%	74%	9	56%	11%	4.99	4.6	48	130	$12
2nd Half		52	8	1	4	1	327	294	397	481	877	1009	813	10	79	0.55	51	27	22	40	102	119	76	11%	101	6%	100%	3	67%	0%	7.38	4.3	64	173	-$4
16	**Proj**	**322**	**46**	**9**	**33**	**7**	**285**	**289**	**345**	**449**	**794**	**929**	**737**	**8**	**80**	**0.45**	**51**	**24**	**25**	**33**	**99**	**110**	**94**	**13%**	**121**	**11%**	**75%**				**5.46**	**11.3**	**60**	**161**	**$14**

STEPHEN NICKRAND

Trout,Mike

Age: 24	Bats: R	Pos: CF	Health A	LIMA Plan C	
Ht: 6' 2"	Wt: 230		PT/Exp A	Rand Var 0	
			Consist C	MM 5445	

Hit as well as ever, but value declined by 25% in the 2H when he shuttered his running game. With SB declining for 3 straight years, this doesn't look like a temporary trend. In sim and other formats in which steals are (properly?) weighted less, draft him #1 and move on. But he's NOT the most valuable Roto star anymore.

Yr	Tm	AB	R	HR	RBI	SB	BA	xBA	OBP	SLG	OPS	vL	vR	bb%	ct%	Eye	G	L	F	h%	HctX	PX	xPX	hr/f	Spd	SBO	SB%	#Wk	DOM	DIS	RC/G	RAR	BPV	BPX	R$
11	LAA *	476	93	15	50	33	282	253	349	460	808	773	605	9	77	0.44	39	21	40	34	91	119	105	14%	159	32%	76%	11	55%	36%	5.63	7.5	70	156	$26
12	LAA *	636	144	31	92	53	328	276	398	555	953	862	999	10	75	0.47	44	23	33	40	108	144	113	22%	153	28%	90%	24	63%	13%	8.75	66.1	85	213	$54
13	LAA	589	109	27	97	33	323	287	432	557	988	954	1000	16	77	0.81	41	23	36	38	123	159	133	16%	154	18%	83%	27	74%	11%	9.11	77.6	114	285	$47
14	LAA	602	115	36	111	16	287	272	377	561	939	910	948	12	69	0.45	34	19	47	36	115	209	151	18%	146	10%	89%	27	67%	11%	7.61	62.8	115	311	$38
15	LAA	575	104	41	90	11	299	289	402	590	991	1032	978	14	73	0.58	37	24	38	35	131	190	154	25%	121	10%	61%	27	70%	7%	8.27	60.4	108	292	$35
1st Half		301	60	21	45	9	299	285	393	575	968	1000	959	12	73	0.51	35	25	40	35	136	183	163	24%	106	14%	69%	14	79%	0%	7.88	29.2	96	259	$40
2nd Half		274	44	20	45	2	299	294	411	606	1017	1057	1000	15	72	0.66	40	23	37	35	125	196	144	27%	128	5%	40%	13	62%	15%	8.70	32.8	117	316	$30
16	Proj	**589**	**109**	**35**	**96**	**13**	**300**	**278**	**398**	**565**	**963**	**965**	**961**	**13**	**73**	**0.56**	**38**	**22**	**40**	**36**	**122**	**175**	**144**	**21%**	**143**	**10%**	**72%**				**8.02**	**59.0**	**96**	**259**	**$36**

Trumbo,Mark

Age: 30	Bats: R	Pos: RF DH 1B	Health C	LIMA Plan B+	
Ht: 6' 4"	Wt: 235		PT/Exp B	Rand Var -1	
			Consist B	MM 4115	

Ignore 2H BA spike; it was driven by 37% hit rate. Using xBA and PX as your guide, you can see he's pretty much the same guy. Given recent shakier health, don't expect HR totals to come close to salad days with LAA. Still, in today's game, there's value in the 20-25 HRs he's likely to provide.

Yr	Tm	AB	R	HR	RBI	SB	BA	xBA	OBP	SLG	OPS	vL	vR	bb%	ct%	Eye	G	L	F	h%	HctX	PX	xPX	hr/f	Spd	SBO	SB%	#Wk	DOM	DIS	RC/G	RAR	BPV	BPX	R$
11	LAA	539	65	29	87	9	254	276	291	477	768	748	778	4	78	0.21	46	16	38	28	116	150	135	18%	77	13%	69%	27	56%	15%	4.61	-8.8	65	144	$19
12	LAA	544	66	32	95	4	268	248	317	491	808	808	808	6	72	0.24	45	16	39	32	114	144	132	21%	91	7%	44%	27	52%	37%	5.20	5.3	45	113	$21
13	LAA	620	85	34	100	5	234	256	294	453	747	923	685	8	70	0.29	46	17	37	28	104	158	132	21%	82	5%	71%	27	52%	26%	4.43	2.8	50	125	$19
14	ARI	328	37	14	61	2	235	241	293	415	707	796	679	8	73	0.31	45	15	40	28	111	133	135	14%	84	7%	40%	18	39%	44%	3.94	0.4	41	111	$8
15	2 TM	508	62	22	64	0	262	244	310	449	759	856	709	7	74	0.27	42	18	40	31	108	124	122	14%	112	0%	0%	27	52%	30%	4.82	0.7	44	119	$13
1st Half		256	27	10	28	0	223	238	260	406	666	801	620	5	75	0.21	45	13	42	26	117	118	145	12%	113	0%	0%	14	50%	36%	3.47	-10.5	42	114	$6
2nd Half		252	35	12	36	0	302	252	359	492	851	889	822	8	73	0.33	39	23	39	37	99	130	97	17%	104	0%	0%	13	54%	23%	6.47	11.4	44	119	$21
16	Proj	**501**	**62**	**23**	**76**	**2**	**251**	**246**	**303**	**445**	**748**	**840**	**707**	**7**	**73**	**0.28**	**43**	**17**	**39**	**30**	**108**	**130**	**125**	**16%**	**99**	**3%**	**52%**				**4.56**	**-3.8**	**30**	**81**	**$16**

Tucker,Preston

Age: 25	Bats: L	Pos: LF	Health A	LIMA Plan D+	
Ht: 6' 0"	Wt: 217		PT/Exp C	Rand Var +1	
			Consist A	MM 4021	

13-33-.243 in 300 AB at HOU. PRO: Power steadily developing, with encouraging 2H HctX and FB gains. CON: Struggles vs. LHP limit AB, dwindling plate control puts the kibosh on BA. There's little here to suggest he'll solve "cons" soon—except that age is on his side. If he DOES improve Eye, and vs. lefties... UP: 25 HR.

Yr	Tm	AB	R	HR	RBI	SB	BA	xBA	OBP	SLG	OPS	vL	vR	bb%	ct%	Eye	G	L	F	h%	HctX	PX	xPX	hr/f	Spd	SBO	SB%	#Wk	DOM	DIS	RC/G	RAR	BPV	BPX	R$
11																																			
12																																			
13	aa	237	28	8	23	0	229		293	391	683			8	78	0.40				26		112			99	2%	0%				3.70		49	123	$1
14	a/a	536	57	18	68	4	235		290	392	682			7	73	0.29				29		122			76	6%	51%				3.71		31	84	$11
15	HOU *	429	49	21	57	1	242	257	288	439	727	466	807	6	77	0.29	47	18	36	27	104	128	103	16%	72	3%	25%	22	41%	32%	4.17	-4.2	46	124	$9
1st Half		254	31	11	41	1	244	266	300	436	736	513	799	7	77	0.34	48	20	32	28	98	129	91	11%	73	1%	100%	10	50%	30%	4.42	0.1	49	132	$13
2nd Half		175	18	10	16	0	238	248	272	443	715	200	813	4	77	0.20	45	16	39	25	110	126	115	20%	82	6%	0%	12	33%	33%	3.82	-3.1	46	124	$4
16	Proj	**229**	**25**	**10**	**27**	**1**	**250**	**250**	**305**	**437**	**742**	**455**	**806**	**6**	**76**	**0.28**	**46**	**17**	**36**	**29**	**105**	**123**	**105**	**16%**	**79**	**4%**	**36%**				**4.33**	**-1.6**	**27**	**74**	**$7**

Tulowitzki,Troy

Age: 31	Bats: R	Pos: SS	Health F	LIMA Plan B	
Ht: 6' 3"	Wt: 215		PT/Exp B	Rand Var -1	
			Consist F	MM 4235	

Yes, struggled massively after trade to TOR, but things were amiss even in the 1H (see xBA). Plate skills took a precipitous dive, and DOM/DIS is troubling. He's been too good to say he won't rebound, but then how confident are we that he gets 500 PA again? (Answer: not at all.) It all means he's a riskier pick than ever.

Yr	Tm	AB	R	HR	RBI	SB	BA	xBA	OBP	SLG	OPS	vL	vR	bb%	ct%	Eye	G	L	F	h%	HctX	PX	xPX	hr/f	Spd	SBO	SB%	#Wk	DOM	DIS	RC/G	RAR	BPV	BPX	R$
11	COL	537	81	30	105	9	302	307	372	544	916	1049	864	10	85	0.75	42	20	39	31	131	150	126	17%	89	8%	75%	26	81%	19%	7.33	46.7	110	244	$30
12	COL *	208	35	10	31	2	286	288	348	501	849	671	918	9	88	0.76	46	17	37	29	103	118	98	13%	123	7%	50%	9	67%	0%	6.05	11.5	101	253	$8
13	COL	446	72	25	82	1	312	288	391	540	931	906	938	11	81	0.67	42	21	38	34	123	148	147	18%	85	1%	100%	24	75%	17%	7.82	52.8	92	230	$25
14	COL	315	71	21	52	1	340	310	432	603	1035	1348	930	14	82	0.88	38	23	39	36	150	170	164	21%	101	2%	50%	16	75%	13%	9.94	55.4	123	332	$23
15	2 TM	486	77	17	70	1	280	254	337	440	777	940	735	7	77	0.33	41	22	37	34	126	110	126	12%	82	1%	100%	25	44%	36%	5.19	10.9	35	95	$17
1st Half		274	43	9	44	0	321	257	358	489	847	1092	776	6	78	0.29	40	20	40	38	143	116	139	10%	92	0%	0%	14	43%	29%	6.63	18.6	48	130	$24
2nd Half		212	34	8	26	1	226	249	311	377	689	698	686	9	74	0.38	42	25	33	27	103	101	107	15%	76	2%	100%	11	45%	45%	3.71	-2.4	20	54	$7
16	Proj	**441**	**78**	**21**	**68**	**2**	**287**	**274**	**362**	**485**	**847**	**992**	**804**	**10**	**79**	**0.53**	**41**	**22**	**37**	**32**	**127**	**126**	**134**	**16%**	**89**	**2%**	**71%**				**6.18**	**26.0**	**57**	**154**	**$22**

Turner,Justin

Age: 31	Bats: R	Pos: 3B	Health C	LIMA Plan B+	
Ht: 6' 0"	Wt: 210		PT/Exp D	Rand Var 0	
			Consist F	MM 3245	

There's so much to like in how he's developed: LD stroke better than ever without sacrificing contact, maintained fine bb%. But it's tough to talk about "development" when a player is already 31. This might be his peak, he might sustain for another year or two, but it's not likely going to get any better from here, even with more ABs.

Yr	Tm	AB	R	HR	RBI	SB	BA	xBA	OBP	SLG	OPS	vL	vR	bb%	ct%	Eye	G	L	F	h%	HctX	PX	xPX	hr/f	Spd	SBO	SB%	#Wk	DOM	DIS	RC/G	RAR	BPV	BPX	R$
11	NYM *	475	53	4	52	7	257	276	315	355	671	629	715	8	86	0.61	49	23	28	29	68	75	60	4%	86	7%	78%	24	46%	33%	3.86	-17.2	48	107	$8
12	NYM	171	20	2	19	1	269	283	319	392	711	650	768	5	86	0.38	47	24	29	30	92	86	68	5%	92	5%	50%	25	40%	20%	4.10	-2.4	52	130	$2
13	NYM	200	12	2	16	0	280	257	319	385	704	668	735	5	83	0.32	46	22	32	33	120	80	132	4%	93	2%	0%	22	45%	32%	4.24	1.4	36	90	$1
14	LA	288	46	7	43	6	340	283	404	493	897	911	890	9	80	0.48	49	23	28	41	113	117	102	11%	99	7%	86%	26	50%	31%	7.67	29.6	62	168	$17
15	LA	385	55	16	60	5	294	291	370	491	861	751	904	9	82	0.51	36	28	36	33	114	126	118	14%	77	7%	71%	25	40%	28%	6.23	16.7	69	186	$17
1st Half		199	30	11	37	1	312	316	386	558	943	414	1095	8	82	0.49	38	29	33	33	117	150	128	20%	75	4%	50%	14	43%	36%	7.44	15.3	90	243	$21
2nd Half		186	25	5	23	4	274	265	353	419	773	979	662	9	81	0.53	34	27	40	32	110	100	108	8%	83	9%	80%	11	36%	18%	5.06	2.3	48	130	$13
16	Proj	**419**	**55**	**14**	**56**	**5**	**288**	**285**	**356**	**462**	**818**	**789**	**833**	**8**	**82**	**0.47**	**42**	**25**	**33**	**33**	**115**	**114**	**110**	**12%**	**89**	**6%**	**70%**				**5.68**	**12.4**	**57**	**154**	**$18**

Turner,Trea

Age: 23	Bats: R	Pos: 2B	Health A	LIMA Plan D	
Ht: 6' 1"	Wt: 175		PT/Exp F	Rand Var 0	
			Consist F	MM 2521	

1-1-.225 with 2 SB in 40 AB at WAS. Top MI prospect wasn't overwhelmed in MLB call-up, barely a year after his pro debut. He hit at each stop in the minors (.322 BA), flashing some plus wheels (52 SB in 185 minor league games). If given a shot at a starting job, he's a rookie-of-the-year candidate, with 30-steal upside.

Yr	Tm	AB	R	HR	RBI	SB	BA	xBA	OBP	SLG	OPS	vL	vR	bb%	ct%	Eye	G	L	F	h%	HctX	PX	xPX	hr/f	Spd	SBO	SB%	#Wk	DOM	DIS	RC/G	RAR	BPV	BPX	R$
11																																			
12																																			
13																																			
14																																			
15	WAS *	494	64	7	48	27	298	250	346	411	757	819	570	7	77	0.32	50	21	29	37	36	79	12	13%	128	24%	76%	8	13%	50%	5.16	19.4	25	68	$25
1st Half		305	38	5	36	13	287	241	336	411	747			7	77	0.32				36		86			126	20%	75%				4.92		32	86	$27
2nd Half		189	26	3	11	14	314	241	362	411	773	819	570	7	76	0.32	50	21	29	40	36	68	12	13%	132	30%	77%	8	13%	50%	5.56	7.8	16	43	$21
16	Proj	**195**	**26**	**4**	**16**	**11**	**282**	**252**	**332**	**408**	**741**	**1028**	**668**	**7**	**77**	**0.32**	**48**	**22**	**30**	**35**	**32**	**86**	**11**	**9%**	**135**	**26%**	**76%**				**4.81**	**3.3**	**29**	**78**	**$10**

Upton,Justin

Age: 28	Bats: R	Pos: LF	Health A	LIMA Plan B+	
Ht: 6' 2"	Wt: 205		PT/Exp A	Rand Var 0	
			Consist A	MM 4325	

Smooth out the maddening month-to-month swings, and these are consistent skills. The one tantalizingly upsloping line is his FB rate: it finally climbed back to 2011 levels in the 2H. While that didn't translate to big HR totals this year, that trend, his peak age, and (surely!?) a rebound vs. LHP all suggest: UP: 35 HR.

Yr	Tm	AB	R	HR	RBI	SB	BA	xBA	OBP	SLG	OPS	vL	vR	bb%	ct%	Eye	G	L	F	h%	HctX	PX	xPX	hr/f	Spd	SBO	SB%	#Wk	DOM	DIS	RC/G	RAR	BPV	BPX	R$
11	ARI	592	105	31	88	21	289	280	369	529	898	929	889	9	79	0.47	37	18	45	32	130	160	142	15%	124	19%	70%	27	81%	15%	6.53	21.3	100	222	$33
12	ARI	554	107	17	67	18	280	250	355	430	785	830	766	10	78	0.52	44	21	36	33	105	96	107	11%	127	15%	69%	27	48%	22%	5.29	8.9	50	125	$24
13	ATL	558	94	27	70	8	263	254	354	464	818	994	762	12	71	0.47	41	22	38	32	88	145	110	18%	109	5%	89%	27	56%	33%	5.69	26.4	59	148	$22
14	ATL	566	77	29	102	8	270	262	342	491	833	981	794	10	70	0.35	40	20	40	34	116	173	159	18%	95	8%	67%	26	62%	19%	5.77	32.3	67	181	$26
15	SD	542	85	26	81	19	251	240	336	454	790	558	848	11	71	0.43	39	17	44	31	109	140	131	15%	126	16%	79%	26	50%	38%	5.19	7.6	57	154	$23
1st Half		301	44	14	46	16	262	228	343	442	785	536	838	11	70	0.40	39	18	43	33	110	122	125	15%	130	18%	100%	14	36%	50%	5.56	8.7	39	105	$29
2nd Half		241	41	12	35	3	237	255	327	469	796	579	861	12	72	0.47	39	16	45	28	108	162	138	15%	113	14%	38%	12	67%	25%	4.76	1.5	76	205	$15
16	Proj	**561**	**89**	**29**	**85**	**13**	**261**	**253**	**344**	**479**	**823**	**786**	**833**	**11**	**71**	**0.43**	**39**	**19**	**42**	**32**	**108**	**150**	**135**	**17%**	**116**	**12%**	**71%**				**5.57**	**16.7**	**61**	**165**	**$26**

ROD TRUESDELL

Upton,Melvin

Age: 31 Bats: R Pos: CF	Health	D	LIMA Plan	D+
Ht: 6' 3" Wt: 185	PT/Exp	C	Rand Var	-2
	Consist	B	MM	3503

5-17-.259 with 9 SB in 205 AB at SD. Baseball's version of a bad soap opera romance plot: "It's over... but wait! No, it's really over. But wait!" Latest "but wait" came in 2H... and okay, we'll tune in next season, because he looked pretty good. UP: 2H times 2, wins "Best Fantasy Investment in a Supporting Role." DN: It's over.

Yr	Tm	AB	R	HR	RBI	SB	BA	xBA	OBP	SLG	OPS	vL	vR	bb%	ct%	Eye	G	L	F	h%	HctX	PX	xPX	hr/f	Spd	SBO	SB%	#Wk	DOM	DIS	RC/G	RAR	BPV	BPX	R$
11	TAM	560	82	23	81	36	243	244	331	429	759	746	763	11	71	0.44	41	18	41	30	103	136	133	14%	132	31%	75%	27	52%	30%	4.70	-1.5	58	129	$24
12	TAM	573	79	28	78	31	246	246	298	454	752	792	737	7	71	0.27	40	19	41	30	87	145	105	17%	125	29%	84%	25	48%	28%	4.70	0.1	52	130	$24
13	ATL	391	30	9	26	12	184	191	268	289	557	449	598	10	61	0.29	45	19	36	27	82	94	112	10%	98	18%	71%	25	12%	72%	2.40	-21.5	-27	-68	$0
14	ATL	519	67	12	35	20	208	209	287	333	620	566	633	10	67	0.33	43	18	39	29	95	102	129	9%	164	21%	74%	26	31%	31%	3.08	-12.2	19	51	$8
15	SD *	255	29	6	21	11	246	236	309	395	704	792	736	8	69	0.30	41	24	34	33	99	111	111	10%	135	23%	79%	18	39%	44%	4.17	-1.0	25	68	$6
1st Half		96	12	2	6	6	174	200	240	258	498	304	686	8	70	0.30	52	15	33	23	36	54	45	9%	136	39%	76%	5	40%	60%	1.96	-7.8	-16	-43	-$1
2nd Half		159	17	4	15	5	289	254	351	478	829	993	747	9	69	0.30	38	27	35	40	117	145	132	11%	126	14%	83%	13	38%	38%	6.07	7.4	47	127	$11
16	**Proj**	**318**	**37**	**8**	**26**	**11**	**242**	**222**	**312**	**384**	**696**	**655**	**714**	**9**	**68**	**0.31**	**43**	**20**	**36**	**33**	**88**	**106**	**110**	**10%**	**143**	**19%**	**73%**				**4.01**	**-3.8**	**12**	**34**	**$7**

Uribe,Juan

Age: 37 Bats: R Pos: 3B	Health	C	LIMA Plan	D+
Ht: 6' 0" Wt: 235	PT/Exp	C	Rand Var	0
	Consist	B	MM	3113

Turned up the power after leaving LA, hitting 11 HR from May 30 on. Otherwise, scan of three-year metrics shows a consistent skill set; BA dip had been consistently presaged by xBA. At 37, he's overextended as a regular nowadays, but skills show he can help in a part-time role. Won't give '13-'14 value, but he's not done.

Yr	Tm	AB	R	HR	RBI	SB	BA	xBA	OBP	SLG	OPS	vL	vR	bb%	ct%	Eye	G	L	F	h%	HctX	PX	xPX	hr/f	Spd	SBO	SB%	#Wk	DOM	DIS	RC/G	RAR	BPV	BPX	R$
11	LA	270	21	4	28	2	204	216	264	293	557	485	582	6	78	0.28	42	17	41	25	78	69	76	5%	46	4%	100%	15	13%	47%	2.38	-22.8	-5	-11	-$2
12	LA	162	15	2	17	0	191	218	258	284	542	385	640	7	77	0.35	48	17	35	24	90	72	81	5%	53	3%	0%	20	15%	45%	2.18	-12.5	0	0	-$3
13	LA	388	47	12	50	5	278	259	331	438	769	781	765	7	79	0.37	43	20	37	33	119	111	118	11%	96	5%	100%	27	37%	41%	5.19	13.2	50	125	$13
14	LA	386	36	9	54	0	311	246	337	440	777	733	790	4	80	0.19	47	19	34	37	109	99	87	8%	72	1%	0%	21	33%	38%	5.43	17.9	31	84	$15
15	3 NL	360	40	14	43	2	253	250	320	417	737	893	685	9	78	0.43	45	19	36	29	96	107	100	14%	55	2%	100%	25	36%	28%	4.54	-1.3	32	86	$8
1st Half		194	21	7	19	2	278	253	332	423	754	953	704	7	80	0.38	47	21	33	32	90	89	81	14%	62	4%	100%	14	29%	29%	5.00	2.0	26	70	$9
2nd Half		166	19	7	24	0	223	243	306	410	716	848	660	10	75	0.46	42	17	41	25	104	128	125	14%	53	0%	0%	11	45%	27%	4.07	-2.8	42	114	$6
16	**Proj**	**260**	**28**	**8**	**33**	**1**	**262**	**247**	**317**	**412**	**728**	**775**	**712**	**7**	**78**	**0.35**	**45**	**19**	**37**	**31**	**103**	**101**	**101**	**11%**	**65**	**2%**	**82%**				**4.47**	**-1.1**	**23**	**62**	**$8**

Urrutia,Henry

Age: 29 Bats: L Pos: LF	Health	A	LIMA Plan	D
Ht: 6' 5" Wt: 200	PT/Exp	D	Rand Var	-2
	Consist	F	MM	1131

1-6-.265 in 34 AB at BAL. Was projected as a power hitter; still hasn't shown it in USA. With just-okay Eye and Spd (the latter of which, at his size and age, isn't going to improve), 11 HR (MLE) from corner OF isn't cutting it. G/F is ominous in small sample, but consistent with minors levels. No reason to speculate right now.

Yr	Tm	AB	R	HR	RBI	SB	BA	xBA	OBP	SLG	OPS	vL	vR	bb%	ct%	Eye	G	L	F	h%	HctX	PX	xPX	hr/f	Spd	SBO	SB%	#Wk	DOM	DIS	RC/G	RAR	BPV	BPX	R$
11																																			
12																																			
13	BAL *	372	41	7	39	1	290	304	333	406	739	286	627	6	81	0.33	55	34	11	34	85	81	39	0%	127	2%	38%	7	0%	57%	4.80	8.5	40	100	$10
14	aaa	204	9	0	11	1	211		223	262	485			2	70	0.06				30		54			88	7%	52%				1.85		-43	-116	-$3
15	BAL *	494	53	11	52	1	254	240	306	361	667	0	753	7	80	0.37	52	19	29	30	102	71	57	11%	96	3%	19%	3	33%	67%	3.66	-10.7	21	57	$8
1st Half		297	29	5	31	1	248	226	302	342	644			7	78	0.35				30		65			101	4%	26%				3.39		12	32	$8
2nd Half		197	24	6	21	0	262	252	312	390	702	0	753	7	82	0.41	52	19	29	29	105	80	57	11%	97	2%	0%	3	33%	67%	4.09	-2.7	37	100	$7
16	**Proj**	**231**	**20**	**5**	**20**	**1**	**246**	**265**	**290**	**356**	**646**	**412**	**672**	**6**	**80**	**0.30**	**53**	**25**	**22**	**29**	**99**	**74**	**50**	**12%**	**108**	**3%**	**36%**				**3.43**	**-7.8**	**5**	**15**	**$4**

Urshela,Giovanny

Age: 24 Bats: R Pos: 3B	Health	A	LIMA Plan	D+
Ht: 6' 0" Wt: 195	PT/Exp	C	Rand Var	+1
	Consist	B	MM	2033

6-21-.225 in 267 AB at CLE. Apparently, a bad shoulder was responsible for his anemic 2H—and it was really anemic, so let's hope so. Solid glove man showed some pop in the minors in '14 and early '15, and FB tilt shows power potential. MLEs are pedestrian overall, but could reach double-digit HR with return to health.

Yr	Tm	AB	R	HR	RBI	SB	BA	xBA	OBP	SLG	OPS	vL	vR	bb%	ct%	Eye	G	L	F	h%	HctX	PX	xPX	hr/f	Spd	SBO	SB%	#Wk	DOM	DIS	RC/G	RAR	BPV	BPX	R$
11																																			
12																																			
13	aa	445	32	6	33	1	233		251	325	576			2	88	0.19				25		62			91	2%	41%				2.68		35	88	$1
14	a/a	486	62	14	66	1	244		285	414	699			5	84	0.36				26		118			93	4%	19%				3.86		71	192	$11
15	CLE *	348	35	9	29	0	229	250	272	349	622	677	585	6	79	0.29	42	24	34	27	77	77	74	8%	104	1%	0%	17	18%	41%	3.10	-15.4	23	62	$1
1st Half		157	17	5	15	0	253	278	287	380	667	983	481	5	83	0.28	54	25	21	28	93	74	52	15%	104	0%	0%	5	20%	60%	3.73	-4.1	33	89	$3
2nd Half		191	18	4	14	0	209	234	267	325	592	495	620	6	76	0.29	36	24	40	25	69	79	84	7%	104	3%	0%	12	17%	33%	2.65	-11.8	15	41	$0
16	**Proj**	**266**	**28**	**7**	**27**	**0**	**242**	**270**	**284**	**385**	**670**	**805**	**620**	**5**	**82**	**0.29**	**43**	**25**	**32**	**27**	**79**	**91**	**71**	**10%**	**107**	**2%**	**21%**				**3.57**	**-8.4**	**30**	**80**	**$5**

Utley,Chase

Age: 37 Bats: L Pos: 2B	Health	D	LIMA Plan	C
Ht: 6' 1" Wt: 200	PT/Exp	B	Rand Var	+5
	Consist	C	MM	2333

Looked pretty good after return from ankle injury, with a near-.300 xBA and outstanding HctX. That said, he's 37, DIS trend shows where he's headed, he can't hit LHP anymore, and he's certainly not going to bring up that Health grade. UP: Stays healthy enough to meet this projection. DN: Injured; a $1 bid loses you $1.

Yr	Tm	AB	R	HR	RBI	SB	BA	xBA	OBP	SLG	OPS	vL	vR	bb%	ct%	Eye	G	L	F	h%	HctX	PX	xPX	hr/f	Spd	SBO	SB%	#Wk	DOM	DIS	RC/G	RAR	BPV	BPX	R$
11	PHI	398	54	11	44	14	259	258	344	425	769	607	829	9	88	0.83	41	13	46	27	130	100	132	7%	120	13%	100%	19	58%	5%	4.96	2.8	89	198	$12
12	PHI	301	48	11	45	11	256	278	365	429	793	679	869	13	86	1.00	42	21	36	27	129	102	110	12%	92	13%	92%	15	60%	13%	5.29	8.3	79	198	$11
13	PHI	476	73	18	69	8	284	269	348	475	823	754	855	9	83	0.57	38	20	43	31	118	119	126	11%	115	8%	73%	24	67%	21%	5.80	28.9	83	208	$21
14	PHI	589	74	11	78	10	270	276	339	407	746	682	775	8	86	0.62	39	25	36	30	113	95	106	6%	101	7%	91%	27	67%	22%	4.77	23.3	67	181	$19
15	2 NL	373	37	8	39	4	212	257	286	343	629	557	655	8	83	0.50	44	20	36	24	113	86	106	7%	87	5%	100%	22	45%	45%	3.10	-12.3	44	119	$1
1st Half		218	18	4	25	3	179	230	257	275	532	567	518	9	85	0.66	42	17	41	19	86	58	92	5%	87	6%	100%	12	42%	50%	2.20	-14.2	33	89	-$1
2nd Half		155	19	4	14	1	258	290	328	439	766	539	837	7	79	0.34	47	24	29	30	151	129	128	11%	92	3%	100%	10	50%	40%	4.67	2.0	63	170	$4
16	**Proj**	**321**	**39**	**7**	**38**	**5**	**249**	**265**	**323**	**395**	**718**	**628**	**754**	**8**	**83**	**0.55**	**43**	**21**	**36**	**28**	**121**	**94**	**114**	**7%**	**96**	**7%**	**91%**				**4.23**	**0.1**	**57**	**154**	**$9**

Valbuena,Luis

Age: 30 Bats: L Pos: 3B 1B	Health	A	LIMA Plan	B+
Ht: 5' 10" Wt: 200	PT/Exp	B	Rand Var	+2
	Consist	B	MM	4025

PRO: Continued superb power skills and plate patience, and xBA shows BA should rebound a bit. CON: Poor ct%, hopeless vs. LHP, won't repeat 1H hr/f, and something of a man without a position. In the right situation (DHing against righties?), there's a productive power bat here. Speculate on skills, hope role finds him.

Yr	Tm	AB	R	HR	RBI	SB	BA	xBA	OBP	SLG	OPS	vL	vR	bb%	ct%	Eye	G	L	F	h%	HctX	PX	xPX	hr/f	Spd	SBO	SB%	#Wk	DOM	DIS	RC/G	RAR	BPV	BPX	R$
11	CLE *	463	51	13	56	5	244	205	296	368	664	750	412	7	73	0.28	42	12	45	31	65	93	100	7%	90	8%	60%	9	22%	56%	3.61	-28.0	10	22	$8
12	CHC *	476	52	9	49	1	228	242	309	361	670	624	657	10	75	0.47	43	21	35	28	87	102	82	5%	73	3%	17%	17	35%	24%	3.59	-26.6	28	70	$3
13	CHC	331	34	12	37	1	218	239	331	378	708	647	715	14	81	0.84	40	16	45	23	108	104	131	10%	80	5%	20%	22	64%	27%	3.84	-7.9	61	153	$2
14	CHC	478	68	16	51	1	249	255	341	435	776	610	811	12	76	0.58	31	20	48	30	120	140	155	9%	93	2%	33%	27	56%	19%	4.94	11.2	71	192	$11
15	HOU	434	62	25	56	1	224	256	310	438	748	581	808	10	76	0.47	34	20	45	24	110	136	146	17%	75	1%	100%	27	41%	33%	4.38	-7.3	56	151	$8
1st Half		276	43	19	36	1	203	251	286	438	725	620	774	10	75	0.41	33	18	49	20	101	144	150	19%	79	2%	100%	14	50%	21%	3.93	-10.6	58	157	$12
2nd Half		158	19	6	20	0	259	265	352	437	788	450	856	12	77	0.58	36	24	40	30	124	121	139	12%	78	0%	0%	13	31%	46%	5.21	0.2	54	146	$1
16	**Proj**	**421**	**54**	**20**	**50**	**1**	**244**	**258**	**335**	**446**	**782**	**598**	**825**	**12**	**77**	**0.56**	**35**	**20**	**45**	**27**	**112**	**132**	**138**	**14%**	**80**	**2%**	**39%**				**4.93**	**3.8**	**50**	**136**	**$12**

Valencia,Danny

Age: 31 Bats: R Pos: 3B LF	Health	A	LIMA Plan	C+
Ht: 6' 2" Wt: 220	PT/Exp	D	Rand Var	-4
	Consist	D	MM	4133

GB, xPX don't fully buy the power burst, but big news is that career lefty masher finally broke out vRHP—and that's the key going forward. Did he learn a new skill, or does five years of futility mean more? After all, he's yo-yo'ed vR before. At 31, old dogs rarely learn new tricks.

Yr	Tm	AB	R	HR	RBI	SB	BA	xBA	OBP	SLG	OPS	vL	vR	bb%	ct%	Eye	G	L	F	h%	HctX	PX	xPX	hr/f	Spd	SBO	SB%	#Wk	DOM	DIS	RC/G	RAR	BPV	BPX	R$
11	MIN	564	63	15	72	2	246	252	294	383	677	822	626	7	82	0.39	46	18	36	28	92	93	85	9%	91	6%	25%	27	41%	26%	3.68	-19.0	45	100	$10
12	2 AL *	471	39	9	55	1	210	228	237	326	563	592	448	3	79	0.16	43	18	39	25	118	82	114	6%	76	8%	11%	13	23%	62%	2.34	-32.7	12	30	$0
13	BAL *	423	48	19	59	1	257	278	291	470	761	1031	672	5	78	0.22	38	22	40	29	120	148	142	15%	93	5%	18%	17	47%	35%	4.53	7.2	70	175	$11
14	2 AL	264	20	4	30	1	258	251	296	371	667	835	540	5	77	0.23	45	24	31	32	111	93	106	6%	86	3%	50%	22	36%	50%	3.72	0.3	18	49	$3
15	2 AL	345	59	18	66	2	290	285	345	519	864	834	881	8	77	0.36	52	17	30	33	117	151	111	22%	83	5%	50%	27	63%	26%	6.31	16.9	70	189	$16
1st Half		117	20	5	22	2	316	297	347	547	894	900	887	5	78	0.23	48	20	33	37	118	164	129	17%	78	12%	67%	14	57%	36%	7.00	7.5	77	208	$7
2nd Half		228	39	13	44	0	276	277	344	504	848	786	878	9	76	0.43	55	16	29	31	117	144	102	25%	89	2%	0%	13	69%	15%	5.98	8.8	67	181	$12
16	**Proj**	**315**	**41**	**13**	**50**	**2**	**272**	**272**	**316**	**464**	**780**	**855**	**723**	**6**	**77**	**0.29**	**47**	**20**	**33**	**32**	**115**	**129**	**114**	**16%**	**86**	**5%**	**45%**				**5.04**	**3.7**	**46**	**123**	**$12**

ROD TRUESDELL

Van Slyke,Scott

Age: 29 Bats: R Pos: LF RF 1B	Health B	LIMA Plan D+	
Ht: 6' 5" Wt: 220	PT/Exp D	Rand Var +1	
	Consist F	MM 4213	

Late-May back inflammation cost him three weeks and nagging injuries (stiff neck in late July; wrist inflammation in mid Sept) plagued 2H. Elite 1H HctX/xPX were in line with prior levels; career .707 OPS vR cautions against extrapolating these per-AB results. Will still need to fight for playing time.

Yr	Tm	AB	R	HR	RBI	SB	BA	xBA	OBP	SLG	OPS	vL	vR	bb%	ct%	Eye	G	L	F	h%	HctX	PX	xPX	hr/f	Spd	SBO	SB%	#Wk	DOM	DIS	RC/G	RAR	BPV	BPX	R$
11	aa	457	57	14	65	4	281		345	464	809			9	74	0.37				35		144			85	9%	41%				5.45		55	122	$15
12	LA *	412	45	13	47	4	234	249	285	396	681	538	483	7	77	0.31	44	18	38	27	93	115	85	13%	82	9%	51%	7	43%	14%	3.65	-13.4	40	100	$6
13	LA *	333	49	15	50	6	257	233	356	460	816	764	850	13	66	0.45	36	17	47	35	92	166	147	16%	93	10%	64%	18	44%	44%	5.52	14.3	52	130	$11
14	LA	212	32	11	29	4	297	252	386	524	910	1045	767	12	67	0.39	35	20	45	40	107	185	174	17%	113	9%	67%	28	46%	46%	7.09	19.5	73	197	$10
15	LA	222	19	6	30	3	239	228	317	383	700	784	633	9	72	0.37	39	19	42	31	105	110	127	9%	86	7%	75%	23	48%	39%	3.98	-4.8	23	62	$3
1st Half		110	12	4	18	1	245	246	320	427	747	957	646	9	74	0.38	42	17	41	30	137	133	177	12%	77	8%	50%	12	67%	33%	4.41	-0.5	44	119	$4
2nd Half		112	7	2	12	2	232	211	315	339	654	685	614	10	71	0.36	35	21	44	31	73	87	75	6%	99	7%	100%	11	27%	45%	3.55	-3.4	3	8	$2
16	Proj	**251**	**28**	**10**	**34**	**4**	**257**	**238**	**341**	**443**	**783**	**857**	**715**	**11**	**70**	**0.39**	**37**	**19**	**43**	**33**	**99**	**138**	**132**	**13%**	**97**	**8%**	**69%**				**5.04**	**3.6**	**32**	**85**	**$6**

Vargas,Kennys

Age: 25 Bats: B Pos: DH	Health A	LIMA Plan D	
Ht: 6' 5" Wt: 275	PT/Exp D	Rand Var 0	
	Consist A	MM 3011	

5-17-.240 in 175 AB at MIN. Has flashed big power at times, but poor plate discipline (70% ct%, 5% bb% in 390 AB in MLB) caps offensive upside. Has struggled thus far to bring minors pop to big league level. Reversal of platoon splits is likely just small sample size quirk. Very much a work in progress; time is now a factor.

Yr	Tm	AB	R	HR	RBI	SB	BA	xBA	OBP	SLG	OPS	vL	vR	bb%	ct%	Eye	G	L	F	h%	HctX	PX	xPX	hr/f	Spd	SBO	SB%	#Wk	DOM	DIS	RC/G	RAR	BPV	BPX	R$
11																																			
12																																			
13																																			
14	MIN *	571	65	22	87	0	256	248	311	418	729	602	899	7	76	0.33	47	19	34	30	101	117	109	17%	65	2%	0%	10	40%	50%	4.38	5.5	33	89	$16
15	MIN *	419	49	15	53	0	242	240	321	385	706	869	514	10	68	0.37	51	26	23	32	84	100	57	18%	65	0%	0%	16	13%	69%	4.17	-15.9	-4	-11	$7
1st Half		224	26	7	21	0	239	231	290	362	652	885	516	7	68	0.22	51	26	23	32	86	88	55	20%	55	0%	0%	11	18%	55%	3.52	-12.9	-27	-73	$6
2nd Half		195	23	7	31	0	246	234	354	412	766	0	494	14	69	0.54	50	20	30	32	61	113	85	0%	89	0%	0%	5	0%	100%	4.94	-3.0	23	62	$9
16	Proj	**190**	**22**	**7**	**27**	**0**	**249**	**245**	**322**	**401**	**723**	**782**	**686**	**10**	**71**	**0.37**	**50**	**23**	**27**	**31**	**92**	**104**	**77**	**19%**	**66**	**1%**	**0%**				**4.34**	**-6.2**	**3**	**9**	**$5**

Vazquez,Christian

Age: 25 Bats: R Pos: DH	Health F	LIMA Plan D	
Ht: 5' 9" Wt: 195	PT/Exp F	Rand Var 0	
	Consist A	MM 1011	

April TJ surgery cost him entire 2015 season. Outstanding defender, but remains to be seen whether he can hit. Showed tolerable ct% (81%) and good bb% (10%) in 175 AB at BOS in 2014, but is sorely lacking in power. Draftable only in the deepest of leagues.

Yr	Tm	AB	R	HR	RBI	SB	BA	xBA	OBP	SLG	OPS	vL	vR	bb%	ct%	Eye	G	L	F	h%	HctX	PX	xPX	hr/f	Spd	SBO	SB%	#Wk	DOM	DIS	RC/G	RAR	BPV	BPX	R$
11																																			
12	aa	73	9	0	4	0	199		266	257	523			8	87	0.70				23		48			97	0%	0%				2.18		34	85	-$3
13	a/a	345	37	4	37	5	262		332	355	687			10	86	0.76				30		67			89	11%	49%				3.90		46	115	$7
14	BOS *	419	42	3	36	0	249	230	308	335	643	539	638	8	78	0.39	57	17	26	31	82	77	58	3%	77	1%	0%	12	33%	42%	3.46	1.7	16	43	$4
15																																			
1st Half																																			
2nd Half																																			
16	Proj	**192**	**20**	**2**	**18**	**1**	**253**	**244**	**311**	**341**	**652**	**560**	**677**	**9**	**82**	**0.50**	**50**	**20**	**30**	**30**	**79**	**67**	**52**	**3%**	**82**	**5%**	**41%**				**3.60**	**-10.6**	**13**	**36**	**$3**

Venable,Will

Age: 33 Bats: L Pos: CF LF RF	Health A	LIMA Plan D+	
Ht: 6' 3" Wt: 205	PT/Exp C	Rand Var 0	
	Consist D	MM 1513	

PRO: Solid bb%, plus Spd, great SB%, recovery vRHP. CON: Shaky ct%, surging GB%, xPX decline. Rise in bb% and SB were only bright spots in abysmal (but small-sample) 2H that exacerbated the negatives. Overall picture here is one of stability, but given age, SB could begin to wane.

Yr	Tm	AB	R	HR	RBI	SB	BA	xBA	OBP	SLG	OPS	vL	vR	bb%	ct%	Eye	G	L	F	h%	HctX	PX	xPX	hr/f	Spd	SBO	SB%	#Wk	DOM	DIS	RC/G	RAR	BPV	BPX	R$
11	SD *	428	56	10	50	28	237	241	293	385	678	436	742	7	74	0.31	43	21	36	30	89	101	100	9%	148	30%	90%	26	35%	35%	3.99	-16.4	39	87	$14
12	SD	417	62	9	45	24	264	270	335	429	765	684	780	9	77	0.44	48	22	29	32	106	111	97	10%	133	28%	80%	27	52%	26%	4.96	4.8	58	145	$16
13	SD	481	64	22	53	22	268	277	312	484	796	833	786	6	75	0.25	47	21	32	31	103	142	107	20%	136	26%	79%	27	56%	30%	5.20	17.2	70	175	$23
14	SD	406	47	8	33	11	224	223	288	325	613	506	631	8	74	0.31	48	19	33	29	78	76	76	8%	114	17%	65%	27	22%	48%	2.95	-9.3	7	19	$6
15	2 TM	349	40	6	33	16	244	243	320	350	669	377	710	10	73	0.39	60	18	22	32	91	75	57	11%	123	17%	94%	26	23%	50%	3.95	-4.6	10	27	$9
1st Half		200	25	6	22	6	260	252	321	410	731	586	747	8	74	0.34	57	18	26	33	97	100	76	16%	115	13%	86%	14	29%	36%	4.62	0.4	27	73	$12
2nd Half		149	15	0	11	10	221	228	318	268	586	203	656	11	72	0.46	66	18	16	31	84	40	30	0%	122	22%	100%	12	17%	67%	3.10	-6.7	-17	-46	$6
16	Proj	**320**	**38**	**6**	**30**	**11**	**240**	**239**	**309**	**351**	**659**	**490**	**689**	**8**	**74**	**0.35**	**55**	**19**	**26**	**31**	**89**	**77**	**69**	**9%**	**124**	**15%**	**81%**				**3.64**	**-7.5**	**12**	**33**	**$9**

Victorino,Shane

Age: 35 Bats: B Pos: RF LF	Health F	LIMA Plan D	
Ht: 5' 9" Wt: 190	PT/Exp D	Rand Var +1	
	Consist C	MM 1411	

1-7-.230 with 7 SB in 178 AB at BOS/LAA. Appeared in only 71 games due to calf/hamstring injuries. Difficult to draw conclusions considering sample size, though xBA and deteriorating pop are bad signs. Age and history of back and leg injuries put a serious damper on SB and any conceivable fantasy value.

Yr	Tm	AB	R	HR	RBI	SB	BA	xBA	OBP	SLG	OPS	vL	vR	bb%	ct%	Eye	G	L	F	h%	HctX	PX	xPX	hr/f	Spd	SBO	SB%	#Wk	DOM	DIS	RC/G	RAR	BPV	BPX	R$
11	PHI	519	95	17	61	19	279	286	355	491	847	1032	789	10	88	0.87	42	16	42	29	98	121	91	9%	147	16%	86%	25	72%	16%	6.16	18.2	113	251	$23
12	2 NL	595	72	11	55	39	255	260	321	383	704	906	627	8	87	0.66	46	18	36	28	89	78	72	6%	126	28%	87%	27	48%	30%	4.35	-3.8	65	163	$22
13	BOS	477	82	15	61	21	294	276	351	451	801	861	769	5	84	0.33	43	22	35	32	101	102	70	11%	104	20%	88%	25	40%	24%	5.48	20.1	62	155	$27
14	BOS *	152	16	2	12	2	238	254	267	336	604	758	650	4	81	0.21	43	25	32	28	74	73	42	6%	92	6%	100%	8	25%	25%	3.07	-2.7	21	57	$0
15	2 AL *	204	20	1	8	7	226	223	282	289	570	670	495	7	82	0.43	37	24	39	27	74	41	36	2%	126	13%	100%	20	20%	40%	2.85	-9.5	15	41	$1
1st Half		88	9	1	4	3	239	228	309	317	626	1042	490	9	84	0.65	36	21	43	27	69	55	37	4%	116	12%	100%	7	29%	29%	3.48	-2.8	36	97	-$1
2nd Half		116	11	0	4	4	216	219	273	267	541	557	500	6	80	0.30	38	26	36	27	76	31	35	0%	115	14%	100%	13	15%	46%	2.42	-7.6	-7	-19	$1
16	Proj	**99**	**11**	**1**	**7**	**3**	**242**	**244**	**301**	**344**	**645**	**707**	**594**	**6**	**83**	**0.38**	**40**	**23**	**37**	**28**	**80**	**64**	**47**	**5%**	**104**	**14%**	**95%**				**3.49**	**-3.9**	**30**	**80**	**$2**

Villar,Jonathan

Age: 25 Bats: B Pos: SS	Health A	LIMA Plan D	
Ht: 6' 1" Wt: 205	PT/Exp C	Rand Var 0	
	Consist B	MM 1501	

2-11-.284 with 7 SB in 116 AB at HOU. Though it was a tiny number of MLB AB in 2015, he did make some strides in ct% (75%) while maintaining an average bb%. Spd remains his best asset. With more consistent contact to go with Spd, GB%, bb%, and a fresh opportunity... UP: 40 SB.

Yr	Tm	AB	R	HR	RBI	SB	BA	xBA	OBP	SLG	OPS	vL	vR	bb%	ct%	Eye	G	L	F	h%	HctX	PX	xPX	hr/f	Spd	SBO	SB%	#Wk	DOM	DIS	RC/G	RAR	BPV	BPX	R$
11	aa	324	40	8	20	11	210		261	341	602			7	67	0.21				29		108			114	26%	63%				2.74		2	4	$2
12	aa	326	41	9	38	30	230		289	339	628			8	70	0.28				30		73			108	45%	77%				3.30		-11	-28	$13
13	HOU *	549	63	8	40	42	246	249	308	361	669	673	627	8	68	0.28	66	20	14	35	84	91	54	6%	142	40%	73%	11	18%	64%	3.70	4.6	6	15	$22
14	HOU *	453	55	9	46	34	213	218	279	325	604	644	608	8	67	0.27	51	19	30	30	85	91	108	13%	104	41%	76%	19	21%	47%	2.96	-3.1	-10	-27	$14
15	HOU *	396	58	6	33	31	241	239	292	352	644	761	742	7	70	0.24	57	20	23	33	73	84	45	10%	139	45%	71%	15	33%	40%	3.35	-12.8	4	11	$16
1st Half		201	26	2	12	9	247	241	288	347	635	710	659	5	72	0.20	54	22	24	34	81	77	47	6%	133	33%	57%	10	30%	50%	3.09	-6.2	1	3	$8
2nd Half		195	32	4	21	22	235	236	297	357	653	968	1167	8	68	0.28	68	11	21	33	47	91	37	25%	132	57%	79%	5	40%	20%	3.62	-2.8	2	5	$24
16	Proj	**194**	**26**	**2**	**17**	**15**	**232**	**231**	**289**	**329**	**618**	**649**	**600**	**7**	**68**	**0.25**	**58**	**21**	**21**	**33**	**83**	**75**	**65**	**8%**	**119**	**43%**	**73%**				**3.13**	**-5.8**	**-3**	**-8**	**$8**

Vogt,Stephen

Age: 31 Bats: L Pos: CA 1B	Health B	LIMA Plan B	
Ht: 6' 0" Wt: 215	PT/Exp C	Rand Var -2	
	Consist B	MM 3025	

Nice boost in bb% was swamped by inability to hold 2014's ct%, HctX and xPX. Stark dropoff between halves was partially due to h% and hr/f regression, partly due to skill erosion (BPV). Injuries (tennis elbow, wrist, groin) began to pop up in June and likely contributed to the fade. Issues vLHP could lead to strict platoon.

Yr	Tm	AB	R	HR	RBI	SB	BA	xBA	OBP	SLG	OPS	vL	vR	bb%	ct%	Eye	G	L	F	h%	HctX	PX	xPX	hr/f	Spd	SBO	SB%	#Wk	DOM	DIS	RC/G	RAR	BPV	BPX	R$
11	a/a	510	48	12	75	3	236		270	381	651			4	80	0.24				27		99			96	5%	54%				3.38		40	89	$7
12	TAM *	374	35	6	31	1	197	168	261	300	561	0	80	8	79	0.40	26	9	65	23	30	68	54	0%	90	1%	100%	9	11%	33%	2.50	-19.2	14	35	-$3
13	OAK *	431	53	11	52	0	242	247	296	386	682	667	698	7	80	0.38	30	24	46	28	98	98	109	8%	102	2%	0%	13	38%	46%	3.75	0.4	44	110	$6
14	OAK *	357	37	11	46	2	275	254	315	428	744	647	770	6	86	0.42	33	20	47	30	123	97	144	8%	105	2%	100%	17	53%	35%	4.78	14.8	67	181	$11
15	OAK	445	58	18	71	0	261	259	341	443	783	631	832	11	78	0.58	38	22	40	30	93	115	107	13%	89	2%	0%	25	48%	32%	5.15	18.3	56	151	$12
1st Half		259	39	13	53	0	290	269	380	502	882	750	933	13	77	0.67	37	23	40	33	100	133	108	16%	90	1%	0%	14	50%	21%	6.83	22.1	69	186	$22
2nd Half		186	19	5	18	0	220	243	281	360	641	379	703	8	80	0.43	39	20	41	25	82	91	106	8%	90	2%	0%	11	45%	45%	3.24	-3.1	38	103	-$2
16	Proj	**425**	**49**	**15**	**56**	**1**	**251**	**253**	**310**	**415**	**725**	**590**	**756**	**8**	**81**	**0.46**	**35**	**21**	**44**	**28**	**102**	**102**	**120**	**10%**	**94**	**2%**	**36%**				**4.34**	**7.1**	**41**	**110**	**$11**

GREG PYRON

Votto,Joey

Age: 32	Bats: L	Pos: 1B	Health	D	LIMA Plan	A
Ht: 6' 2"	Wt: 220		PT/Exp	A	Rand Var	-4
			Consist	F	MM	4245

Re-established his power bona fides after hitting a total of 30 HR across previous five half-seasons (mid-2012 thru 2014). Ultra-patient approach, high OBP were never in doubt, but pair so much better with a 150 PX. Soak in that 2H line for a minute; it's downright Bonds-ian. Critics of his approach are embarrassing themselves.

Yr Tm	AB	R	HR	RBI	SB	BA	xBA	OBP	SLG	OPS	vL	vR	bb%	ct%	Eye	G	L	F	h%	HctX	PX	xPX	hr/f	Spd	SBO	SB%	#Wk	DOM	DIS	RC/G	RAR	BPV	BPX	R$
11 CIN	599	101	29	103	8	309	299	416	531	947	987	930	16	78	0.85	39	28	33	35	137	152	145	18%	81	6%	57%	27	70%	15%	7.98	28.3	93	207	$33
12 CIN	374	59	14	56	5	337	311	474	567	1041	887	1109	20	77	1.11	38	30	32	41	134	171	161	15%	73	5%	63%	21	76%	10%	10.12	46.1	110	275	$20
13 CIN	581	101	24	73	6	305	279	435	491	926	824	977	19	76	0.98	44	27	29	37	121	128	128	18%	107	4%	67%	27	67%	0%	7.80	51.2	79	198	$29
14 CIN	220	32	6	23	1	255	276	390	409	799	969	736	18	78	0.96	41	27	33	30	109	122	147	11%	66	2%	50%	11	64%	18%	5.35	7.5	66	178	$4
15 CIN	545	95	29	80	11	314	284	459	541	1000	1009	997	21	75	1.06	42	25	33	37	127	151	149	22%	79	6%	79%	27	59%	22%	9.20	56.7	89	241	$33
1st Half	289	40	14	39	5	273	277	387	478	864	831	878	15	78	0.84	44	23	33	31	118	126	131	19%	72	7%	71%	14	50%	21%	6.44	10.6	68	184	$25
2nd Half	256	55	15	41	6	359	292	530	613	1143	1190	1121	26	72	1.25	40	28	33	46	137	181	171	25%	96	5%	86%	13	69%	23%	12.96	50.5	115	311	$41
16 Proj	533	91	25	78	8	304	282	444	515	960	992	946	20	76	1.02	41	26	33	36	124	143	149	18%	78	5%	73%				8.33	46.5	80	216	$28

Walker,Neil

Age: 30	Bats: B	Pos: 2B	Health	B	LIMA Plan	A
Ht: 6' 3"	Wt: 210		PT/Exp	B	Rand Var	0
			Consist	B	MM	3235

As expected, he regressed from 2014 career year. HR fell right back in line with historical PX/xPX, while a little less ct% paired with a few more GB% produced same effect on BA/xBA. Net result is a stable skill set with an outlier career year mixed in. Now-chronic problems with LHP threatening his full-timer status, though.

Yr Tm	AB	R	HR	RBI	SB	BA	xBA	OBP	SLG	OPS	vL	vR	bb%	ct%	Eye	G	L	F	h%	HctX	PX	xPX	hr/f	Spd	SBO	SB%	#Wk	DOM	DIS	RC/G	RAR	BPV	BPX	R$
11 PIT	596	76	12	83	9	273	262	334	408	742	672	767	8	81	0.48	44	21	35	32	127	96	120	7%	96	9%	60%	27	44%	30%	4.68	-0.7	49	109	$18
12 PIT	472	62	14	69	7	280	259	342	426	768	602	824	9	78	0.45	42	24	34	33	104	101	115	11%	86	9%	58%	25	44%	28%	5.08	9.8	39	98	$16
13 PIT *	499	62	16	54	1	252	268	322	415	738	518	805	9	82	0.59	39	23	39	28	114	106	115	11%	101	2%	33%	22	50%	27%	4.50	12.3	65	163	$10
14 PIT	512	74	23	76	2	271	282	342	467	809	727	831	8	83	0.51	38	23	39	29	102	126	106	14%	80	3%	50%	26	65%	12%	5.33	28.5	74	200	$20
15 PIT	543	69	16	71	4	269	261	328	427	756	575	793	7	80	0.40	42	21	37	31	112	105	114	10%	94	4%	80%	27	44%	22%	4.83	10.3	48	130	$16
1st Half	277	34	6	32	3	278	254	345	415	760	600	790	8	79	0.40	40	22	38	33	114	100	120	7%	85	4%	100%	14	36%	29%	4.96	5.7	39	105	$15
2nd Half	266	35	10	39	1	259	268	311	440	751	553	796	7	80	0.40	44	21	35	29	109	109	107	13%	109	3%	50%	13	54%	15%	4.69	3.6	58	157	$16
16 Proj	515	68	17	69	3	267	266	332	435	768	615	803	8	81	0.46	41	22	37	30	110	106	112	11%	92	4%	62%				4.89	9.8	50	136	$18

Wallace,Brett

Age: 29	Bats: L	Pos: 1B	Health	A	LIMA Plan	D
Ht: 6' 2"	Wt: 235		PT/Exp	C	Rand Var	0
			Consist	B	MM	4111

5-16-.302 in 96 AB at SD. "Earned" mid-season recall with .840 OPS in PCL (yawn), then had a cute 2nd half in big-league bench work. PX/xPX from that 2H catch the eye, but a) sample size is tiny, b) no associated gains in ct%, c) SD wasn't impressed enough to play him more. Good case for a Matt Stairs role, but that's about it.

Yr Tm	AB	R	HR	RBI	SB	BA	xBA	OBP	SLG	OPS	vL	vR	bb%	ct%	Eye	G	L	F	h%	HctX	PX	xPX	hr/f	Spd	SBO	SB%	#Wk	DOM	DIS	RC/G	RAR	BPV	BPX	R$
11 HOU *	440	49	6	47	2	269	238	340	378	718	549	735	10	72	0.38	52	21	27	36	89	98	91	8%	70	2%	64%	23	30%	52%	4.48	-22.5	8	18	$8
12 HOU *	539	59	20	61	0	243	232	290	399	688	711	757	6	66	0.20	38	27	35	33	114	118	138	16%	70	1%	0%	12	33%	33%	3.85	-25.3	-4	-10	$9
13 HOU *	495	61	21	62	2	241	230	291	434	725	450	787	7	61	0.18	41	22	37	35	77	165	118	22%	81	3%	63%	17	47%	41%	4.23	-5.3	17	43	$11
14 aaa	472	46	14	43	0	233		283	354	636			6	65	0.19				33		102			82	1%	0%				3.29		-19	-51	$5
15 SD *	335	34	10	38	1	240	239	292	371	663	752	950	7	68	0.23	40	29	31	32	101	101	158	25%	71	1%	100%	16	44%	38%	3.64	-17.2	-9	-24	$4
1st Half	249	20	5	24	1	214	137	261	310	571	500	556	6	67	0.19	40	0	60	30	59	78	134	0%	66	1%	100%	4	25%	50%	2.63	-19.4	-34	-92	$3
2nd Half	86	14	5	14	0	314	286	385	547	932	756	1006	9	70	0.35	40	32	28	40	108	165	159	29%	81	0%	0%	12	50%	33%	7.70	5.9	56	151	$6
16 Proj	149	18	6	18	0	257	245	321	435	756	637	794	7	67	0.24	41	26	32	34	101	134	133	20%	77	1%	61%				4.63	-2.3	1	4	$4

Weeks,Rickie

Age: 33	Bats: R	Pos: LF	Health	B	LIMA Plan	D
Ht: 5' 10"	Wt: 220		PT/Exp	D	Rand Var	+3
			Consist	F	MM	3201

Brought to Seattle to hit lefties; when he didn't do that in 47 AB vL by mid-June, he was DFA'd. Nothing in his 2015 line is significant enough to change our views of him, but those views weren't all that glowing to begin with. Still owns some skills and isn't too old to display them again, but the door to opportunities is closing fast.

Yr Tm	AB	R	HR	RBI	SB	BA	xBA	OBP	SLG	OPS	vL	vR	bb%	ct%	Eye	G	L	F	h%	HctX	PX	xPX	hr/f	Spd	SBO	SB%	#Wk	DOM	DIS	RC/G	RAR	BPV	BPX	R$
11 MIL	453	77	20	49	9	269	270	350	468	818	832	814	10	76	0.47	48	17	35	31	116	138	109	16%	101	9%	82%	22	64%	32%	5.61	6.7	68	151	$17
12 MIL	588	85	21	63	16	230	236	328	400	728	740	723	11	71	0.44	45	17	38	29	105	120	114	13%	113	12%	84%	27	41%	33%	4.24	-7.2	39	98	$14
13 MIL	350	40	10	24	7	209	237	306	357	663	705	644	10	70	0.38	49	18	33	27	92	119	99	13%	92	12%	70%	19	42%	47%	3.31	-7.7	25	63	$2
14 MIL	252	36	8	29	3	274	268	357	452	809	865	746	9	71	0.34	57	18	25	36	92	149	108	18%	99	11%	43%	26	42%	42%	5.12	10.1	53	143	$8
15 SEA	84	7	2	9	0	167	145	263	250	513	691	290	10	70	0.36	52	5	43	21	52	55	67	8%	60	0%	0%	10	20%	60%	1.89	-7.2	-35	-95	-$3
1st Half	84	7	2	9	0	167	145	263	250	513	691	290	10	70	0.36	52	5	43	21	52	55	67	8%	60	0%	0%	10	20%	60%	1.89	-7.3	-36	-97	-$3
2nd Half																																		
16 Proj	189	23	6	19	3	234	226	326	382	707	790	651	10	71	0.39	51	14	35	30	84	106	94	13%	84	8%	67%				3.92	-3.7	13	34	$4

Werth,Jayson

Age: 37	Bats: R	Pos: LF	Health	F	LIMA Plan	B
Ht: 6' 5"	Wt: 240		PT/Exp	B	Rand Var	+4
			Consist	F	MM	3225

Season started late due to offseason shoulder surgery, then missed 10 weeks after fracturing wrist in May. Result was a lost year, though strong September (7 HR, 163 PX/183 xPX, 136 HctX) says he at least ended the year healthy. Give him a pass on 2015, but Health grade urges moderation in chasing a rebound.

Yr Tm	AB	R	HR	RBI	SB	BA	xBA	OBP	SLG	OPS	vL	vR	bb%	ct%	Eye	G	L	F	h%	HctX	PX	xPX	hr/f	Spd	SBO	SB%	#Wk	DOM	DIS	RC/G	RAR	BPV	BPX	R$
11 WAS	561	69	20	58	19	232	233	330	389	718	675	730	12	71	0.46	43	17	40	29	96	118	132	12%	89	14%	86%	27	44%	33%	4.25	-17.3	32	71	$13
12 WAS *	321	45	5	34	8	292	249	381	428	809	1037	755	13	80	0.73	42	19	39	35	104	96	88	5%	119	9%	80%	16	69%	13%	5.93	10.7	61	153	$11
13 WAS	462	84	25	82	10	318	281	398	532	931	1092	884	11	78	0.59	36	26	38	36	129	142	142	18%	77	7%	91%	22	64%	14%	8.01	49.0	74	185	$31
14 WAS	534	85	16	82	9	292	262	394	455	849	933	823	13	79	0.73	40	20	40	35	134	123	142	9%	87	5%	90%	26	69%	15%	6.44	39.3	69	186	$25
15 WAS *	354	52	12	46	1	227	240	303	384	687	771	658	10	76	0.45	34	22	44	27	112	107	136	11%	62	2%	43%	16	31%	44%	3.81	-9.7	28	76	$5
1st Half	101	17	2	12	0	208	211	294	287	581	503	606	11	75	0.48	35	24	41	26	99	52	103	6%	66	0%	0%	5	20%	40%	2.70	-5.8	-14	-38	-$7
2nd Half	253	35	10	34	1	235	252	308	423	731	911	680	10	76	0.44	34	21	45	27	118	128	151	13%	65	3%	43%	11	36%	45%	4.28	-2.1	46	124	$9
16 Proj	496	79	17	71	6	269	249	355	432	787	873	761	11	77	0.56	37	22	41	32	118	110	134	11%	76	5%	82%				5.34	11.1	45	121	$20

Wieters,Matt

Age: 30	Bats: B	Pos: CA	Health	F	LIMA Plan	B
Ht: 6' 5"	Wt: 240		PT/Exp	D	Rand Var	-2
			Consist	D	MM	3025

DL'd until June as he finished recovery from May 2014 Tommy John surgery, then battled hamstring and wrist issues in 2H. Combo of lost ct% and power sure looks like he was never fully healthy. Before TJ, we saw a breakout coming; it may have been deferred rather than dashed altogether. Speculate... UP: 30 HR, still

Yr Tm	AB	R	HR	RBI	SB	BA	xBA	OBP	SLG	OPS	vL	vR	bb%	ct%	Eye	G	L	F	h%	HctX	PX	xPX	hr/f	Spd	SBO	SB%	#Wk	DOM	DIS	RC/G	RAR	BPV	BPX	R$
11 BAL	500	72	22	68	1	262	273	328	450	778	1124	665	9	83	0.57	43	18	39	28	115	122	130	14%	71	1%	100%	27	44%	19%	5.09	12.8	71	158	$15
12 BAL	526	67	23	83	3	249	265	329	435	764	908	715	10	79	0.54	44	20	35	28	110	119	113	16%	64	2%	100%	27	59%	26%	4.85	11.0	52	130	$14
13 BAL	523	59	22	79	2	235	256	287	417	704	872	628	8	80	0.41	39	18	44	25	103	122	124	12%	68	2%	100%	26	62%	27%	4.10	5.9	56	140	$11
14 BAL	104	13	5	18	0	308	292	339	500	839	799	849	5	82	0.32	28	30	43	34	138	127	161	14%	80	4%	0%	6	67%	33%	6.11	8.0	66	178	$4
15 BAL	258	24	8	25	0	267	255	319	422	742	728	746	8	74	0.31	43	25	32	33	101	109	112	13%	72	0%	0%	19	53%	37%	4.74	7.4	22	59	$4
1st Half	67	9	3	10	0	224	267	250	463	713	389	827	4	72	0.16	38	20	42	27	120	169	159	14%	79	0%	0%	6	83%	17%	3.91	0.3	56	151	-$3
2nd Half	191	15	5	15	0	283	251	343	408	751	844	718	9	75	0.38	44	27	28	36	94	89	96	12%	72	0%	0%	13	38%	46%	5.00	6.6	12	32	$7
16 Proj	475	53	19	64	0	267	260	314	450	764	769	761	7	77	0.33	38	22	40	31	113	120	132	13%	68	1%	29%				4.94	15.8	34	91	$16

Wong,Kolten

Age: 25	Bats: L	Pos: 2B	Health	A	LIMA Plan	B+
Ht: 5' 9"	Wt: 185		PT/Exp	C	Rand Var	0
			Consist	A	MM	1425

Fantastic 1H looked like a breakout, with career-best skills across the board. And then it went poof. Some of that was normal regression, as full-season skills were in lock-step with historical levels. But early-July concussion (no DL stint) may have been bigger deal than disclosed. If that 1H was real... UP: 20 HR, 25 SB

Yr Tm	AB	R	HR	RBI	SB	BA	xBA	OBP	SLG	OPS	vL	vR	bb%	ct%	Eye	G	L	F	h%	HctX	PX	xPX	hr/f	Spd	SBO	SB%	#Wk	DOM	DIS	RC/G	RAR	BPV	BPX	R$
11																																		
12 aa	523	62	7	40	16	251		298	344	642			6	85	0.43				29		59			113	21%	57%				3.29		34	85	$11
13 STL *	471	58	7	35	18	247	272	299	357	656	0	410	7	83	0.44	61	17	22	28	73	72	18	0%	137	16%	94%	8	0%	75%	3.79	1.8	47	118	$12
14 STL *	477	63	14	51	24	257	262	294	395	689	790	656	5	83	0.30	47	19	34	28	93	90	82	11%	105	25%	86%	23	48%	30%	4.10	9.9	47	127	$20
15 STL	557	71	11	61	15	262	263	321	386	707	552	772	6	83	0.38	45	22	33	30	99	80	87	7%	105	17%	65%	27	30%	26%	3.99	-2.9	41	111	$17
1st Half	298	42	9	36	7	279	280	337	443	780	680	817	7	83	0.44	43	24	34	31	111	104	108	11%	97	14%	64%	14	43%	21%	4.99	6.6	61	165	$23
2nd Half	259	29	2	25	8	243	242	303	320	623	434	717	5	83	0.31	47	21	32	29	86	52	63	3%	114	19%	67%	13	15%	31%	2.98	-9.8	19	51	$11
16 Proj	528	66	10	52	19	261	257	314	375	689	599	716	6	83	0.36	46	21	32	30	92	72	72	7%	110	19%	75%				3.92	-4.8	39	106	$19

RAY MURPHY

Wright,David

Age: 33	Bats: R	Pos: 3B	Health	F	LIMA Plan B
Ht: 6' 0"	Wt: 205		PT/Exp	C	Rand Var -3
			Consist	F	MM 3225

Missed four months with hamstring/back injuries, with mixed results upon return: Late-season PX/xPX surge offers some rebound hope, but came with further ct% losses. He's another year removed from 2012-13, another year older, and has a chronic back problem (stenosis). Even Mets fans need to temper expectations.

Yr	Tm	AB	R	HR	RBI	SB	BA	xBA	OBP	SLG	OPS	vL	vR	bb%	ct%	Eye	G	L	F	h%	HctX	PX	xPX	hr/f	Spd	SBO	SB%	#Wk	DOM	DIS	RC/G	RAR	BPV	BPX	R$
11	NYM	389	60	14	61	13	254	252	345	427	771	806	761	12	75	0.54	42	18	40	31	122	126	142	12%	77	13%	87%	19	53%	21%	5.11	0.1	50	111	$14
12	NYM	581	91	21	93	15	306	278	391	492	883	917	867	12	81	0.72	42	22	35	35	116	123	134	13%	93	13%	60%	27	59%	19%	6.83	36.0	76	190	$30
13	NYM	430	63	18	58	17	307	280	390	514	904	1072	836	11	82	0.70	38	23	39	34	122	130	141	13%	145	14%	85%	21	67%	5%	7.40	40.2	99	248	$26
14	NYM	535	54	8	63	8	269	245	324	374	698	921	634	7	79	0.37	40	23	37	33	116	84	114	5%	82	9%	62%	24	38%	46%	4.13	6.4	24	65	$15
15	NYM	152	24	5	17	2	289	249	379	434	814	1023	746	13	76	0.61	36	25	39	35	113	98	129	11%	85	6%	67%	9	22%	44%	5.86	5.1	36	97	$4
1st Half		33	3	1	4	2	333	250	371	424	796	1431	588	6	85	0.40	25	32	43	37	134	45	127	8%	90	17%	100%	2	0%	50%	6.50	1.6	16	43	-$3
2nd Half		119	21	4	13	0	277	249	381	437	818	911	788	14	74	0.65	40	23	38	35	107	115	129	12%	83	2%	0%	7	29%	43%	5.70	3.7	43	116	$7
16	Proj	**427**	**61**	**13**	**52**	**9**	**269**	**257**	**354**	**425**	**779**	**1017**	**701**	**12**	**78**	**0.59**	**37**	**25**	**39**	**32**	**118**	**106**	**128**	**10%**	**102**	**10%**	**69%**				**5.18**	**6.9**	**49**	**132**	**$14**

Yelich,Christian

Age: 24	Bats: L	Pos: LF CF	Health	B	LIMA Plan B
Ht: 6' 3"	Wt: 200		PT/Exp	B	Rand Var -1
			Consist	A	MM 2445

Continues to produce with a profile that offers some value: a mix of bb%, HctX, and Spd to fuel his BA/speed combo. What's still missing is some more lift on the ball that would unlock some power output and explode him into a five-category contributor. No sign of that yet, so buy the BA/SB and hope for more.

Yr	Tm	AB	R	HR	RBI	SB	BA	xBA	OBP	SLG	OPS	vL	vR	bb%	ct%	Eye	G	L	F	h%	HctX	PX	xPX	hr/f	Spd	SBO	SB%	#Wk	DOM	DIS	RC/G	RAR	BPV	BPX	R$
11																																			
12																																			
13	MIA *	433	62	9	41	14	276	276	356	427	782	476	941	11	72	0.44	63	23	14	37	108	114	83	17%	149	15%	73%	10	20%	20%	5.31	15.6	48	120	$16
14	MIA	582	94	9	54	21	284	271	362	402	764	819	747	11	76	0.51	61	21	18	36	113	91	97	12%	133	15%	75%	25	44%	16%	5.16	22.9	42	114	$25
15	MIA	476	63	7	44	16	300	281	366	416	782	703	812	9	79	0.47	62	23	15	37	115	85	81	13%	119	14%	76%	25	48%	32%	5.52	10.6	39	105	$20
1st Half		233	28	5	16	7	258	241	335	365	699	621	728	10	73	0.42	71	12	16	33	104	75	75	18%	131	11%	88%	13	31%	46%	4.27	-2.0	15	41	$13
2nd Half		243	35	2	28	9	342	319	396	465	861	778	894	8	84	0.54	55	31	14	40	125	94	85	7%	110	16%	69%	12	67%	17%	6.95	15.4	62	168	$28
16	Proj	**524**	**76**	**8**	**50**	**19**	**294**	**280**	**366**	**416**	**781**	**702**	**813**	**10**	**77**	**0.48**	**62**	**23**	**16**	**37**	**114**	**88**	**87**	**12%**	**126**	**15%**	**76%**				**5.47**	**13.4**	**38**	**102**	**$25**

Young,Chris

Age: 32	Bats: R	Pos: RF LF	Health	B	LIMA Plan B
Ht: 6' 2"	Wt: 200		PT/Exp	D	Rand Var -1
			Consist	B	MM 4313

Rediscovered the ability to pound LHPs, which was well-timed as his struggles vs. RHP reached new depths. Career platoon split isn't nearly as wide, and is a better predictor of future split performance. But that doesn't change the fact that his (perceived) LH-bashing ways are what will keep him employed from here.

Yr	Tm	AB	R	HR	RBI	SB	BA	xBA	OBP	SLG	OPS	vL	vR	bb%	ct%	Eye	G	L	F	h%	HctX	PX	xPX	hr/f	Spd	SBO	SB%	#Wk	DOM	DIS	RC/G	RAR	BPV	BPX	R$
11	ARI	567	89	20	71	22	236	247	331	420	751	939	694	12	75	0.58	32	20	49	28	126	135	137	10%	120	20%	71%	27	63%	22%	4.57	-10.3	73	162	$18
12	ARI	325	36	14	41	8	231	259	311	434	745	810	707	10	76	0.46	31	22	47	26	106	143	136	12%	74	15%	73%	24	46%	38%	4.38	-4.6	61	153	$7
13	OAK	335	46	12	40	10	200	231	280	379	659	712	614	10	72	0.39	29	22	50	24	82	131	120	10%	114	19%	77%	26	46%	31%	3.36	-9.7	49	123	$5
14	2 TM *	352	45	13	43	9	229	244	297	403	699	561	720	9	77	0.42	29	20	52	26	94	129	109	8%	103	15%	74%	23	48%	48%	3.93	0.4	62	168	$9
15	NYY	318	53	14	42	3	252	253	320	453	773	972	585	9	77	0.41	36	17	47	29	99	134	106	12%	105	5%	75%	26	50%	35%	4.87	0.9	66	178	$9
1st Half		192	27	10	25	2	250	260	298	464	761	1088	546	5	78	0.26	38	17	45	27	101	137	100	15%	87	5%	100%	14	50%	36%	4.64	-1.0	61	165	$11
2nd Half		126	26	4	17	1	254	242	351	437	788	861	670	13	75	0.61	32	19	49	31	96	129	116	8%	120	5%	50%	12	50%	33%	5.14	1.2	69	186	$6
16	Proj	**316**	**49**	**12**	**40**	**6**	**237**	**242**	**315**	**421**	**735**	**839**	**659**	**10**	**76**	**0.44**	**32**	**19**	**49**	**28**	**96**	**126**	**114**	**10%**	**111**	**11%**	**72%**				**4.35**	**-4.5**	**54**	**147**	**$10**

Young,Delmon

Age: 30	Bats: R	Pos: RF	Health	A	LIMA Plan D
Ht: 6' 3"	Wt: 240		PT/Exp	F	Rand Var 0
			Consist	D	MM 1221

Released by BAL on July 9th, after a 1st half that was suffocated by an hr/f dip and h% correction. BPV succinctly shows what's left when you take those away. May well catch on again, but the market for free-swinging, average-power RH batters with minimal platoon utility and lousy defense isn't exactly robust.

Yr	Tm	AB	R	HR	RBI	SB	BA	xBA	OBP	SLG	OPS	vL	vR	bb%	ct%	Eye	G	L	F	h%	HctX	PX	xPX	hr/f	Spd	SBO	SB%	#Wk	DOM	DIS	RC/G	RAR	BPV	BPX	R$
11	2 AL *	504	58	13	68	1	267	251	300	397	696	759	670	5	82	0.26	47	18	35	30	97	88	88	9%	86	1%	100%	23	35%	30%	4.14	-11.3	35	78	$12
12	DET	574	54	18	74	0	267	255	296	411	707	833	649	3	80	0.18	43	22	35	30	121	93	107	11%	62	2%	0%	27	33%	33%	4.10	-9.1	24	60	$13
13	2 TM *	381	34	12	41	0	253	239	291	389	681	684	724	5	76	0.23	42	22	36	31	113	97	142	12%	75	0%	0%	20	50%	35%	3.87	-1.1	16	40	$6
14	BAL	242	27	7	30	2	302	264	337	442	779	722	809	4	79	0.20	50	21	28	36	102	100	91	13%	100	3%	100%	25	36%	52%	5.37	10.8	36	97	$9
15	BAL	174	20	2	16	0	270	241	289	339	628	644	620	2	83	0.14	43	24	33	31	88	47	91	4%	76	0%	0%	13	15%	54%	3.39	-5.7	0	0	$2
1st Half		174	20	2	16	0	270	241	289	339	628	644	620	2	83	0.14	43	24	33	31	88	47	91	4%	76	0%	0%	13	15%	54%	3.39	-5.8	0	0	$2
2nd Half																																			
16	Proj	**202**	**21**	**5**	**23**	**0**	**271**	**248**	**302**	**390**	**692**	**703**	**687**	**4**	**80**	**0.19**	**45**	**22**	**33**	**32**	**103**	**78**	**106**	**9%**	**82**	**1%**	**78%**				**4.06**	**-4.4**	**4**	**12**	**$6**

Zimmerman,Ryan

Age: 31	Bats: R	Pos: 1B	Health	F	LIMA Plan B+
Ht: 6' 3"	Wt: 220		PT/Exp	C	Rand Var +3
			Consist	A	MM 4245

Diagnosed with plantar fasciitis in April, tried to play through it with terrible results, finally DL'd in June. Aug/Sept return was much better, though boosted by inflated h% and hr/f. Coming off a pair of injury-shortened seasons, he retains skills from 2012-13 peak, but ABs are now the question mark.

Yr	Tm	AB	R	HR	RBI	SB	BA	xBA	OBP	SLG	OPS	vL	vR	bb%	ct%	Eye	G	L	F	h%	HctX	PX	xPX	hr/f	Spd	SBO	SB%	#Wk	DOM	DIS	RC/G	RAR	BPV	BPX	R$
11	WAS	395	52	12	49	3	289	261	355	443	798	919	773	9	82	0.56	50	16	34	33	114	104	114	11%	112	3%	75%	18	56%	17%	5.64	-6.7	64	142	$13
12	WAS	578	93	25	95	5	282	274	346	478	824	861	810	9	80	0.49	48	18	33	32	139	126	144	16%	91	4%	71%	25	64%	16%	5.85	6.9	68	170	$24
13	WAS	568	84	26	79	6	275	267	344	465	809	850	794	10	77	0.45	45	21	34	32	128	127	144	18%	105	4%	100%	25	48%	20%	5.69	17.8	61	153	$23
14	WAS	214	26	5	38	0	280	283	342	449	790	779	794	9	83	0.59	44	20	35	32	121	128	115	8%	78	0%	0%	13	69%	15%	5.52	8.1	77	208	$6
15	WAS	346	43	16	73	1	249	274	308	465	773	1058	672	9	77	0.42	48	17	35	28	128	146	140	16%	75	1%	100%	17	47%	35%	4.97	-3.9	67	181	$10
1st Half		211	22	5	34	1	209	255	265	346	611	715	576	7	81	0.43	53	16	31	23	106	92	94	9%	80	2%	100%	10	30%	40%	3.00	-14.1	39	105	$5
2nd Half		135	21	11	39	0	311	304	372	652	1024	1526	827	11	71	0.41	41	18	42	36	161	242	219	26%	77	0%	0%	7	71%	29%	9.27	15.0	124	335	$17
16	Proj	**444**	**60**	**19**	**78**	**1**	**275**	**277**	**337**	**487**	**824**	**1027**	**755**	**9**	**78**	**0.47**	**45**	**19**	**36**	**31**	**132**	**143**	**148**	**16%**	**84**	**1%**	**92%**				**5.89**	**9.3**	**64**	**174**	**$19**

Zobrist,Ben

Age: 35	Bats: B	Pos: 2B LF	Health	B	LIMA Plan B+
Ht: 6' 3"	Wt: 210		PT/Exp	A	Rand Var +1
			Consist	A	MM 3245

Knee surgery cost him a month in first half, ending streak of six straight 500+ AB seasons. Skill set looks equally durable: ct% continues late-career growth, which xBA loves. Power merely average(-ish), and age/knee suggest SB may be gone for good. But there's a high floor here and no glaring weakness.

Yr	Tm	AB	R	HR	RBI	SB	BA	xBA	OBP	SLG	OPS	vL	vR	bb%	ct%	Eye	G	L	F	h%	HctX	PX	xPX	hr/f	Spd	SBO	SB%	#Wk	DOM	DIS	RC/G	RAR	BPV	BPX	R$
11	TAM	588	99	20	91	19	269	284	353	469	822	907	783	12	78	0.60	45	20	35	31	117	144	120	12%	96	15%	76%	27	67%	19%	5.77	14.3	82	182	$25
12	TAM	560	88	20	74	14	270	285	377	471	848	879	835	15	82	0.94	43	22	35	30	109	128	114	13%	108	13%	61%	27	67%	19%	6.03	23.9	93	233	$21
13	TAM	612	77	12	71	11	275	260	354	402	756	643	812	11	85	0.79	43	20	37	31	106	87	98	6%	104	7%	79%	27	63%	19%	4.98	17.6	65	163	$20
14	TAM	570	83	10	52	10	272	267	354	395	749	873	703	12	85	0.89	49	18	33	30	103	88	89	6%	111	8%	67%	25	60%	16%	4.88	19.6	70	189	$18
15	2 AL	467	76	13	56	3	276	293	359	450	809	926	753	12	88	1.11	49	19	32	29	109	108	86	10%	103	5%	43%	23	61%	9%	5.58	15.8	95	257	$15
1st Half		180	34	5	31	1	267	306	354	450	804	775	818	13	90	1.44	53	16	30	27	99	115	75	10%	87	2%	100%	10	60%	10%	5.66	5.7	105	284	$11
2nd Half		287	42	8	25	2	282	286	362	449	811	1022	713	11	87	0.95	46	20	34	30	116	104	94	10%	116	7%	33%	13	62%	8%	5.53	8.0	89	241	$17
16	Proj	**494**	**76**	**12**	**57**	**5**	**274**	**280**	**358**	**431**	**789**	**864**	**755**	**12**	**86**	**0.95**	**48**	**19**	**33**	**30**	**108**	**100**	**92**	**9%**	**105**	**5%**	**59%**				**5.36**	**16.2**	**74**	**199**	**$18**

Zunino,Mike

Age: 25	Bats: R	Pos: CA	Health	A	LIMA Plan D
Ht: 6' 2"	Wt: 220		PT/Exp	C	Rand Var +1
			Consist	A	MM 4003

11-28-.174 in 350 AB at SEA. Was allowed to flail away for 350 AB, then sent to minors in late August, followed by instructional league assignment to continue working on his swing. Watch from a distance, but if the changes pair this power with better ct%, then it might be time to get interested. Maybe.

Yr	Tm	AB	R	HR	RBI	SB	BA	xBA	OBP	SLG	OPS	vL	vR	bb%	ct%	Eye	G	L	F	h%	HctX	PX	xPX	hr/f	Spd	SBO	SB%	#Wk	DOM	DIS	RC/G	RAR	BPV	BPX	R$
11																																			
12	aa	51	6	2	7	0	303		363	520	884			9	84	0.60				32		134			89	0%	0%				6.92		90	225	$0
13	SEA *	376	49	12	44	1	201	219	256	350	606	650	609	7	67	0.22	43	19	39	26	95	117	108	10%	96	1%	100%	12	33%	67%	2.87	-9.9	6	15	$2
14	SEA	438	51	22	60	0	199	226	254	404	658	722	632	4	64	0.11	34	17	49	25	86	170	143	16%	89	5%	0%	27	30%	37%	2.83	-6.8	28	76	$5
15	SEA *	391	33	13	33	0	183	187	225	315	540	522	534	5	64	0.15	33	17	50	25	80	102	121	10%	78	1%	0%	21	14%	62%	2.18	-19.5	-27	-73	-$4
1st Half		228	21	9	18	0	162	180	229	307	536	588	522	7	59	0.18	32	17	51	22	74	116	103	12%	88	3%	0%	14	14%	64%	2.01	-13.3	-28	-76	-$4
2nd Half		163	12	4	15	0	212	198	231	327	557	484	564	2	70	0.08	34	18	48	28	89	86	150	5%	74	0%	0%	7	14%	57%	2.44	-6.8	-22	-59	-$3
16	Proj	**301**	**30**	**12**	**33**	**0**	**207**	**206**	**256**	**368**	**624**	**623**	**624**	**4**	**65**	**0.13**	**35**	**17**	**48**	**27**	**86**	**122**	**132**	**12%**	**86**	**2%**	**11%**				**2.80**	**-9.2**	**-16**	**-43**	**$3**

RAY MURPHY

THE NEXT TIER — Batters

The preceding section provided player boxes and analysis for 441 batters. As we know (and as Ron Shandler illustrated in the Introduction), far more than 441 batters will play in the major leagues in 2016. Many of those additional hitters are covered in the minor league section, but that still leaves a gap: established major leaguers who don't play enough, or well enough, to merit a player box.

This section looks to fill that gap. Here, you will find "The Next Tier" of batters who are mostly past their growth years, but who are likely to see some playing time in 2016. We are including their 2014-15 MLB stats here for reference for you to do your own analysis. This way, if Emilio Bonifacio stumbles into some playing time in June, a quick check would show that his Spd skills were still an asset as recently as 2014. Or if Drew Stubbs finds an opportunity, his power/speed blend still hold a bit of intrigue.

Batter	Pos	B	Age	Yr	AB	R	HR	RBI	SB	BA	xBA	OPS	vL	vR	bb%	ct%	Eye	GLF	HctX	PX	xPX	Spd	SBO	SB%	BPV
Barmes,Clint	6	R	35	14	102	15	0	7	1	245	221	622	558	637	8	82	0.50	38/21/41	101	45	68	47	7	50	10
		R	36	15	207	24	3	16	0	232	225	633	673	596	5	73	0.18	29/24/48	88	97	90	96	3	0	11
Barnes,Brandon	O	R	28	14	292	37	8	27	5	257	241	718	639	767	5	66	0.15	47/21/32	79	137	111	93	15	56	29
		R	29	15	255	30	2	17	4	251	235	655	545	695	8	74	0.31	42/26/31	84	71	88	116	9	67	4
Boesch,Brennan	O	L	29	14	75	6	2	7	3	187	195	496	1833	437	3	75	0.11	43/10/47	78	74	67	121	25	100	-3
		L	30	15	89	4	1	5	1	146	185	394	393	393	4	66	0.13	58/17/25	59	46	31	69	7	100	-66
Bonifacio,Emilio	4	B	29	14	394	47	3	24	26	259	252	650	959	539	6	78	0.31	53/22/26	72	64	46	138	33	76	20
		B	30	15	78	5	0	4	1	167	184	390	412	372	3	65	0.07	57/20/24	39	28	-4	79	38	20	-84
Bourgeois,Jason	O	R	32	14	33	5	0	1	0	242	242	568	1300	429	3	82	0.17	41/30/30	26	28	-14	0	0		3
		R	33	15	196	28	3	14	3	240	253	625	502	672	7	83	0.42	52/20/27	54	55	36	137	8	75	33
Butera,Drew	2	R	30	14	170	16	3	14	0	188	227	555	715	511	9	76	0.41	34/24/42	82	71	73	0	0		16
		R	31	15	107	9	1	5	0	196	186	505	586	476	5	76	0.23	33/19/49	66	43	57	88	4	0	-23
Callaspo,Alberto	5	B	31	14	404	37	4	39	0	223	239	580	518	616	9	88	0.80	42/21/37	80	47	67	1	1	0	27
		B	32	15	230	20	1	15	0	235	236	594	384	636	11	85	0.82	38/25/37	68	32	67	54	0		6
Campbell,Eric	5	R	27	14	190	16	3	16	3	263	220	680	683	678	8	71	0.31	55/17/28	89	79	81	120	5	100	3
		R	28	15	173	28	3	19	5	197	255	607	588	608	13	79	0.70	46/26/28	100	71	111	87	16	63	25
Ciriaco,Pedro	5	R	28	14	47	7	0	2	4	213	228	484	200	560	0	81	0.00	44/22/33	27	39	27	162	50	100	-8
		R	29	15	142	14	1	15	4	261	226	627	517	675	1	73	0.05	43/23/35	62	75	86	121	21	67	-5
Corporan,Carlos	2	B	30	14	170	22	6	19	0	235	243	678	606	730	8	78	0.38	39/21/40	82	93	108	0	0		26
		B	31	15	107	10	3	15	0	178	200	543	604	512	5	63	0.15	35/23/42	66	100	101	49	0		-41
Cowgill,Collin	O	R	28	14	260	37	5	21	4	250	214	684	790	586	9	72	0.35	49/16/36	61	80	42	133	5	100	11
		R	29	15	69	10	1	2	2	188	203	523	594	426	5	72	0.21	46/14/40	88	69	134	123	23	67	-4
Craig,Allen	O	R	29	14	461	41	8	46	2	215	242	594	693	559	7	75	0.31	54/21/25	100	75	105	58	3	67	7
		R	30	15	79	6	1	3	0	152	181	441	670	322	8	67	0.27	55/19/26	33	38	51	94	0		-54
Cruz,Tony	2	R	27	14	135	11	1	17	0	200	223	530	422	572	9	79	0.46	56/19/25	63	47	42	6	9	0	-1
		R	28	15	142	6	2	11	0	204	219	545	580	536	4	77	0.19	53/14/32	76	76	75	81	0		5
DeJesus,David	O0	L	34	14	238	24	6	19	0	248	273	748	476	756	11	82	0.70	44/22/35	87	106	82	4	5	0	69
		L	35	15	288	27	5	30	3	233	248	626	174	644	7	82	0.40	44/24/33	93	61	82	103	7	60	23
Denorfia,Chris	O	R	33	14	330	36	3	21	9	230	252	602	587	615	7	79	0.36	57/20/23	79	61	61	125	15	75	25
		R	34	15	212	18	3	18	0	269	244	691	597	745	7	74	0.27	51/25/25	106	80	104	95	2	0	2
Descalso,Daniel	6	L	27	14	161	20	0	10	1	242	220	644	899	575	11	80	0.61	43/17/39	72	64	50	32	8	25	26
		L	28	15	185	22	5	22	1	205	223	607	468	628	10	76	0.44	44/19/36	67	71	74	122	6	33	17
Gomes,Jonny	O	R	33	14	273	28	6	37	0	234	199	657	743	510	11	68	0.40	26/24/50	84	75	100	0	0		-16
		R	34	15	225	29	7	26	1	213	197	660	783	558	12	64	0.38	38/18/44	82	107	107	78	3	50	-8
Herrera,Jonathan	4	B	29	14	90	10	0	9	1	233	217	596	595	596	7	73	0.29	56/21/24	59	34	45	58	16	25	-18
		B	30	15	126	14	2	14	3	230	231	576	743	512	2	82	0.09	46/15/38	57	67	47	109	13	100	18
Jones,Garrett	3O	L	33	14	496	59	15	53	0	246	252	720	539	749	8	77	0.40	38/20/43	124	121	148	1	1	0	52
		L	34	15	144	12	5	17	0	215	230	618	504	640	5	74	0.22	46/19/36	73	93	52	77	0		7
Kozma,Pete	6	R	26	14	23	4	0	0	0	304	340	819	775	842	12	83	0.75	37/42/21	132	118	91	0	0		86
		R	27	15	99	15	0	2	3	152	145	388	343	405	9	79	0.48	29/16/55	35	0	21	118	16	75	-28
Leon,Sandy	2	B	25	14	64	7	1	3	0	156	194	447	511	413	9	69	0.30	53/19/28	62	47	38	0	0		-42
		B	26	15	114	8	0	3	0	184	182	439	118	569	6	75	0.25	45/19/36	47	17	29	85	4	0	-45
Lough,David	O	L	28	14	174	31	4	16	8	247	243	694	250	749	8	81	0.45	34/23/42	83	85	82	133	29	62	57
		L	29	15	134	14	4	12	2	201	214	555	567	551	4	73	0.14	44/19/37	41	67	36	139	23	33	-2
Mathis,Jeff	2	R	31	14	175	12	2	12	0	200	187	537	675	492	8	63	0.23	42/22/36	73	71	101	0	0		-45
		R	32	15	93	9	2	12	0	161	227	504	676	476	7	74	0.29	41/20/39	91	89	97	84	0		9
Maxwell,Justin	O	R	30	14	40	4	0	3	0	150	140	397	241	610	5	50	0.10	62/14/24	52	38	45	13	14	0	-128
		R	31	15	249	26	7	26	2	209	224	616	609	620	7	69	0.26	45/21/34	96	93	111	119	5	67	5

THE NEXT TIER — Batters

Batter	Pos	B	Age	Yr	AB	R	HR	RBI	SB	BA	xBA	OPS	vL	vR	bb%	ct%	Eye	GLF	HctX	PX	xPX	Spd	SBO	SB%	BPV
Mayberry,John	O	R	30	14	146	15	7	23	0	212	259	734	913	569	12	76	0.57	36/18/46	85	150	93	0	0		81
		R	31	15	110	8	3	9	1	164	242	545	628	456	8	70	0.27	40/25/35	104	116	140	98	6	100	19
McGehee,Casey	35	R	31	14	616	56	4	76	4	287	236	712	596	738	10	83	0.66	50/18/31	112	54	88	58	3	67	26
		R	32	15	237	14	2	20	1	198	230	538	645	508	8	79	0.42	57/19/25	78	60	53	47	4	50	-3
Nava,Daniel	O	B	31	14	363	41	4	37	4	270	234	706	399	769	8	78	0.41	45/20/35	104	74	93	60	6	67	17
		B	32	15	139	13	1	10	1	194	194	560	597	548	13	74	0.56	45/18/37	93	41	112	90	2	100	-16
Navarro Jr,Efren	3	L	28	14	159	17	1	14	1	245	272	642	702	630	8	83	0.48	47/26/27	113	72	82	29	10	25	34
		L	29	15	83	9	0	5	0	253	216	597	364	631	6	81	0.31	57/15/28	74	43	37	96	9	0	0
Nieuwenhuis,Kirk	O	L	26	14	112	16	3	16	4	259	284	828	522	855	13	65	0.41	41/31/28	113	208	158	80	15	100	83
		L	27	15	128	21	4	14	2	195	235	645	182	680	7	62	0.20	44/21/36	110	165	164	98	20	50	25
Parmelee,Chris	3	L	26	14	250	27	7	28	0	256	228	691	859	617	6	74	0.27	36/21/43	95	94	106	3	5	0	11
		L	27	15	97	11	4	9	0	216	241	688	364	752	4	73	0.15	21/20/59	114	153	174	92	8	0	53
Peguero,Carlos	O	L	27	14	9	1	0	1	0	222	196	633	0	708	10	44	0.20	75/25/0	96	188	48	0	0		-16
		L	28	15	75	11	4	9	2	187	196	711	786	699	15	51	0.35	34/13/53	92	210	201	89	11	100	29
Recker,Anthony	2	R	30	14	174	18	7	27	1	201	209	620	282	703	5	63	0.16	28/18/54	91	145	155	37	7	50	7
		R	31	15	80	6	2	5	1	125	174	452	756	326	12	56	0.31	40/24/36	88	73	101	72	6	100	-68
Robertson,Daniel	O	R	28	14	177	23	0	21	6	271	243	667	821	478	9	84	0.61	54/16/29	55	50	26	95	18	60	35
		R	29	15	75	10	0	7	0	280	235	605	494	733	3	91	0.29	51/19/29	79	21	47	109	0		19
Robinson,Shane	O	R	29	14	60	3	0	4	0	150	217	427	425	429	9	83	0.60	52/16/32	87	30	40	10	8	0	16
		R	30	15	180	28	0	16	6	250	237	621	592	641	6	84	0.41	52/16/32	83	48	77	154	15	86	35
Rodriguez,Sean	3O	R	29	14	237	30	12	41	2	211	260	701	729	666	4	72	0.15	39/17/44	108	162	137	81	9	67	67
		R	30	15	224	25	4	17	2	246	232	642	655	634	2	72	0.08	48/20/32	82	90	109	103	9	50	-2
Ross,David	2	R	37	14	152	16	7	15	0	184	225	629	809	518	10	62	0.28	38/21/40	75	154	118	3	3	0	21
		R	38	15	159	6	1	9	1	176	171	518	440	549	11	62	0.33	32/19/49	81	80	129	62	3	100	-46
Sands,Jerry	O	R	26	14	21	1	1	4	0	190	231	561	455	664	0	71	0.00	47/27/27	62	88	69	0	0		-6
		R	27	15	123	11	4	19	0	236	231	676	838	502	7	71	0.25	45/19/35	78	109	81	113	0		20
Schafer,Jordan	O	L	27	14	210	26	1	15	30	238	250	615	400	681	9	77	0.46	53/24/23	85	54	69	180	61	81	13
		L	28	15	69	9	0	5	0	217	210	511	688	459	4	67	0.13	47/28/26	37	47	8	105	20	0	-53
Schafer,Logan	O	L	27	14	116	13	0	8	2	181	233	554	670	538	11	77	0.56	44/18/38	89	84	96	82	12	67	34
		L	28	15	122	17	1	6	1	221	226	611	414	661	9	76	0.41	50/17/33	87	68	70	137	3	100	20
Schumaker,Skip	O	L	34	14	247	22	2	22	2	235	244	595	508	614	7	80	0.36	56/20/24	63	59	47	60	5	67	9
		L	35	15	244	23	1	21	2	242	272	642	816	623	9	79	0.45	52/27/22	84	82	63	63	7	50	20
Solano,Donovan	56	R	26	14	310	26	3	28	1	252	246	623	574	638	6	80	0.31	51/24/26	96	52	62	30	4	33	3
		R	27	15	90	6	0	7	0	189	212	459	269	534	1	80	0.06	61/11/27	106	40	106	102	0		-12
Stewart,Chris	2	R	32	14	136	9	0	10	0	294	245	693	1098	555	8	80	0.44	40/30/31	65	34	36	2	2	0	-7
		R	33	15	159	9	0	15	0	289	231	659	667	657	4	82	0.21	54/22/24	64	45	29	85	0		-1
Stubbs,Drew	O	R	29	14	388	67	15	43	20	289	245	821	944	757	7	65	0.22	44/21/35	103	156	147	179	23	87	56
		R	30	15	123	20	5	10	5	195	181	665	562	750	10	51	0.23	37/13/50	73	170	154	165	22	83	13
Sucre,Jesus	2	R	26	14	61	4	0	5	0	213	205	459	409	487	0	72	0.00	43/25/32	33	34	8	0	0		-53
		R	27	15	127	9	1	7	0	157	219	424	767	268	5	83	0.29	48/16/36	70	53	54	70	0		8
Uggla,Dan	4	R	34	14	141	14	2	10	0	149	171	442	343	475	7	67	0.24	39/17/45	103	51	126	0	0		-49
		R	35	15	120	12	2	16	0	183	197	598	668	560	14	67	0.47	41/18/41	80	86	106	113	3	0	0
Wilson,Bobby	2	R	31	14	4	0	0	0	0	250	684	500	0	667	0	100	0.00	0/75/25	0	0	-14	0	0		26
		R	32	15	132	8	1	14	0	189	199	505	296	590	8	70	0.28	50/20/30	68	53	59	49	3	0	-43
Ynoa,Rafael	O	B	26	14	67	5	0	13	0	343	315	843	802	863	6	87	0.44	52/29/19	65	91	16	0	0		74
		B	27	15	127	14	0	9	1	260	235	616	635	603	2	78	0.11	49/19/31	65	66	48	116	4	100	6
Young Jr.,Eric	O	B	29	14	280	48	1	17	30	229	263	610	566	626	8	79	0.40	63/19/18	70	57	33	195	50	83	24
		B	30	15	85	16	0	5	6	153	248	464	382	476	7	79	0.33	54/18/28	76	65	83	104	62	75	14

The following section contains player boxes for every pitcher who had significant playing time in 2015 and/or is expected to get fantasy roster-worthy innings in 2016. In most cases, high-end prospects who have yet to make their major league debuts will not appear here; you can find scouting reports for them in the Prospects section.

Snapshot Section

The top band of each player box contains the following information:

Age as of Opening Day 2016.

Throws right (R) or left (L).

Role: Starters (SP) are those projected to face 20+ batters per game; the rest are relievers (RP).

Ht/Wt: Each batter's height and weight.

Type evaluates the extent to which a pitcher allows the ball to be put into play and his ground ball or fly ball tendency. CON (contact) represents pitchers who allow the ball to be put into play a great deal. PWR (power) represents those with high strikeout and/or walk totals who keep the ball out of play. GB are those who have a ground ball rate more than 50%; xGB are those who have a GB rate more than 55%. FB are those who have a fly ball rate more than 40%; xFB are those who have a FB rate more than 45%.

Reliability Grades analyze each pitcher's forecast risk, on an A-F scale. High grades go to those who have accumulated few disabled list days (Health), have a history of substantial and regular major league playing time (PT/Exp) and have displayed consistent performance over the past three years, using xERA (Consist).

LIMA Plan Grade evaluates how well that pitcher would be a good fit for a team using the LIMA Plan draft strategy. Best grades go to pitchers who have excellent base skills and had a 2015 dollar value less than $20. Lowest grades will go to poor skills and values more than $20.

Random Variance Score (Rand Var) measures the impact random variance had on the pitcher's 2015 stats and the probability that his 2016 performance will exceed or fall short of 2015. The variables tracked are those prone to regression—H%, S%, hr/f and xERA to ERA variance. Players are rated on a scale of –5 to +5 with positive scores indicating rebounds and negative scores indicating corrections. Note that this score is computer-generated and the projections will override it on occasion.

Mayberry Method (MM) acknowledges the imprecision of the forecasting process by projecting player performance in broad strokes. The four digits of MM each represent a fantasy-relevant skill—ERA, strikeout rate, saves potential and playing time (IP)—and are all on a scale of 0 to 5.

Commentaries for each pitcher provide a brief analysis of BPIs and the potential impact on performance in 2016. MLB statistics are listed first for those who played only a portion of 2015 at the major league level. Note that these commentaries generally look at performance related issues only. Role and playing time expectations may impact these analyses, so you will have to adjust accordingly. Upside (UP) and downside (DN) statistical potential appears for some players; these are less grounded in hard data and more speculative of skills potential.

Player Stat Section

The past five years' statistics represent the total accumulated in the majors as well as in Triple-A, Double-A ball and various foreign leagues during each year. All non-major league stats have been converted to a major league equivalent (MLE) performance level. Minor league levels below Double-A are not included.

Nearly all baseball publications separate a player's statistical experiences in the major leagues from the minor leagues and outside leagues. While this may be appropriate for official record-keeping purposes, it is not an easy-to-analyze snapshot of a player's complete performance for a given year.

Bill James has proven that minor league statistics (converted to MLEs), at Double-A level or above, provide as accurate a record of a player's performance as Major league statistics. Other researchers have also devised conversion factors for foreign leagues. Since these are adequate barometers, we include them in the pool of historical data for each year.

Team designations: An asterisk (*) appearing with a team name means that Triple-A and/or Double-A numbers are included in that year's stat line. Any stints of less than 10 IP are not included (to screen out most rehab appearances). A designation of "a/a" means the stats were accumulated at both AA and AAA levels that year. "for" represents a foreign or independent league. The designation "2TM" appears whenever a player was on more than one major league team, crossing leagues, in a season. "2AL" and "2NL" represent more than one team in the same league. Players who were cut during the season and finished 2015 as a free agent are designated as FAA (Free agent, AL) and FAN (Free agent, NL).

Stats: Descriptions of all the categories appear in the Encyclopedia.

- The leading decimal point has been suppressed on some categories to conserve space.
- Data for platoons (vL, vR), balls-in-play (G/L/F) and consistency (Wk#, DOM, DIS) are for major league performance only.
- Formulas that use BIP data, like xERA and BPV, are used for years in which G/L/F data is available. Where feasible, older versions of these formulas are used otherwise.

Earned run average is presented alongside skills-based xERA. WHIP appears next, followed by opponents' overall OPS (oOPS). OPS splits vs. left-handed and right-handed batters appear to the right of oOPS. Batters faced per game (BF/G) provide a quick view of a pitcher's role—starters will generally have levels over 20.

Basic pitching skills are measured with Control, or walk rate (Ctl), Dominance, or strikeout rate (Dom), and Command, or strikeout-to-walk rate (Cmd). First-pitch strike rate (FpK) and Swinging strikeout rate (SwK) are also presented with these basic skills. Our research shows that FpK serves as a useful tool for validating Ctl, and SwK serves as a similar check on Dom.

Once the ball leaves the bat, it will either be a (G)round ball, (L)ine drive or (F)ly ball.

Random variance indicators include hit rate (H%)—often referred to as batting average on balls-in-play (BABIP)—which tends to regress to 30%. Normal strand rates (S%) fall within the tolerances of 65% to 80%. The ratio of home runs to fly balls (hr/f) is another sanity check; levels far from 10% are prone to regression.

In looking at consistency for starting pitchers, we track games started (GS), average pitch counts (APC) for all outings (for starters and relievers), the percentage of DOMinating starts (PQS 4 or 5) and DISaster starts (PQS 0 or 1). The larger the variance between DOM and DIS, the greater the consistency.

For relievers, we look at their saves success rate (Sv%) and Leverage Index (LI). A Doug Dennis study showed little correlation between saves success and future opportunity. However, you can increase your odds by prospecting for pitchers who have *both* a high saves percentage (80% or better) *and* high skills. Relievers with LI levels over 1.0 are being used more often by managers to win ballgames.

The final section includes several overall performance measures: runs above replacement (RAR), Base performance value (BPV), Base performance index (BPX, which is BPV indexed to each year's league average) and the Rotisserie value (R$).

2016 Projections

Forecasts are computed from a player's trends over the past five years. Adjustments were made for leading indicators and variances between skill and statistical output. After reviewing the leading indicators, you might opt to make further adjustments.

Although each year's numbers include all playing time at the Double-A level or above, the 2016 forecast only represents potential playing time at the major league level, and again is highly preliminary.

Note that the projected Rotisserie values in this book will not necessarily align with each player's historical actuals. Since we currently have no idea who is going to close games for the Rockies, or whether Jose Berrios is going to break camp with the Twins, it is impossible to create a finite pool of playing time, something which is required for valuation. So the projections are roughly based on a 12-team AL/NL league, and include an inflated number of innings, league-wide. This serves to flatten the spread of values and depress individual player dollar projections. In truth, a $25 player in this book might actually be worth $21, or $28. This level of precision is irrelevant in a process that is driven by market forces anyway. So, don't obsess over it.

Be aware of other sources that publish perfectly calibrated Rotisserie values over the winter. They are likely making arbitrary decisions as to where free agents are going to sign and who is going to land jobs in the spring. We do not make those leaps of faith here.

Bottom line… It is far too early to be making definitive projections for 2016, especially on playing time. Focus on the skill levels and trends, then consult BaseballHQ.com for playing time revisions as players change teams and roles become more defined. A free projections update will be available online in March.

Do-it-yourself analysis

Here are some data points you can look at in doing your own player analysis:

- Variance between vLH and vRH opposition OPS
- Variance in 2015 hr/f rate from 10%
- Variance in 2015 hit rate (H%) from 30%
- Variance in 2015 strand rate (S%) to tolerances (65% - 80%)
- Variance between ERA and xERA each year
- Growth or decline in Base Performance Value (BPV)
- Spikes in innings pitched
- Trends in average pitch counts (APC)
- Trends in DOM/DIS splits
- Trends in saves success rate (Sv%)
- Variance between Dom changes and corresponding SwK levels
- Variance between Ctl changes and corresponding FpK levels

Alburquerque,Al

Age:	30	Th:	R	Role	RP	Health	D	LIMA Plan	C
Ht:	6' 0"	Wt:	195	Type	Pwr	PT/Exp	D	Rand Var	0
						Consist	B	MM	2500

Several reasons why this once-proclaimed "closer in waiting" will keep... waiting: Dom decline, especially in 2H, raises red flags, while SwK trend casts doubt on recovery; unable to hold 2014's Ctl gains; lowest LI of career suggests he lost manager support. xERA offers little hope for rebound or shot at saves.

Yr	Tm	W	L	Sv	IP	K	ERA	xERA	WHIP	oOPS	vL	vR	BF/G	Ctl	Dom	Cmd	FpK	SwK	G	L	F	H%	S%	hr/f	GS	APC	DOM%	DIS%	Sv%	LI	RAR	BPV	BPX	R$
11	DET	6	1	0	43	67	1.87	2.59	1.15	438	468	412	4.4	6.0	13.9	2.3	52%	16%	57	14	30	28%	82%	0%	0	19			0	1.08	11.1	123	185	$6
12	DET	0	0	0	13	18	0.68	2.75	1.05	420	345	484	6.6	5.4	12.2	2.3	55%	18%	63	11	26	23%	93%	0%	0	29			0	1.55	5.5	114	149	-$1
13	DET	4	3	0	49	70	4.59	3.53	1.49	674	662	683	4.2	6.2	12.9	2.1	57%	16%	40	25	34	33%	71%	13%	0	17			0	0.98	-4.4	81	105	-$3
14	DET	3	1	1	57	63	2.51	3.24	1.17	639	721	551	3.3	3.3	9.9	3.0	51%	14%	45	19	36	28%	85%	13%	0	13			100	1.06	8.7	112	133	$4
15	DET	4	1	0	62	58	4.21	4.19	1.55	731	800	688	4.0	4.8	8.4	1.8	57%	11%	48	24	28	34%	73%	8%	0	16			0	0.80	-1.9	48	57	-$4
1st Half		0	0	0	35	34	3.12	4.11	1.44	721	907	597	4.4	4.7	8.8	1.9	52%	11%	45	25	30	31%	83%	14%	0	18			0	0.58	3.6	56	66	-$4
2nd Half		4	1	0	27	24	5.60	4.29	1.68	744	660	789	3.7	4.9	7.9	1.6	63%	12%	53	23	25	37%	63%	0%	0	14			0	1.03	-5.5	39	47	-$4
16	**Proj**	**4**	**3**	**0**	**58**	**64**	**3.81**	**3.71**	**1.42**	**675**	**705**	**651**	**3.8**	**4.8**	**9.9**	**2.1**	**56%**	**13%**	**48**	**22**	**31**	**32%**	**74%**	**9%**	**0**						**1.1**	**75**	**90**	**-$1**

Allen,Cody

Age:	27	Th:	R	Role	RP	Health	A	LIMA Plan	C+
Ht:	6' 1"	Wt:	210	Type	Pwr FB	PT/Exp	B	Rand Var	0
						Consist	A	MM	4530

Recovered from awful April (9 ER in 7 IP) in first full season as stopper. Elevated H%, LD% inflated his WHIP, but skills were better than ever, as he continued to miss bats while Cmd marched further north. Three straight years of excellent, and still growing, BPV make him one of the safer closers around.

Yr	Tm	W	L	Sv	IP	K	ERA	xERA	WHIP	oOPS	vL	vR	BF/G	Ctl	Dom	Cmd	FpK	SwK	G	L	F	H%	S%	hr/f	GS	APC	DOM%	DIS%	Sv%	LI	RAR	BPV	BPX	R$
11																																		
12	CLE *	3	3	3	68	65	3.05	3.18	1.19	710	776	654	4.9	3.2	8.5	2.7	53%	10%	39	24	37	28%	78%	6%	0	20			50	0.44	8.2	91	119	$5
13	CLE	6	1	2	70	88	2.43	3.48	1.25	679	691	669	3.9	3.3	11.3	3.4	55%	12%	30	25	45	33%	85%	9%	0	16			50	1.11	12.4	121	158	$7
14	CLE	6	4	24	70	91	2.07	3.08	1.06	601	451	757	3.7	3.4	11.8	3.5	63%	14%	36	15	48	28%	87%	9%	0	15			86	1.43	14.4	135	161	$18
15	CLE	2	5	34	69	99	2.99	3.01	1.17	596	512	676	4.1	3.2	12.9	4.0	60%	14%	33	26	41	36%	73%	3%	0	16			89	1.23	8.4	155	184	$18
1st Half		1	2	16	35	57	3.34	2.84	1.23	607	453	753	4.2	4.1	14.7	3.6	58%	13%	34	20	46	38%	71%	3%	0	17			94	1.07	2.7	165	196	$16
2nd Half		1	3	18	34	42	2.62	3.17	1.11	584	571	594	4.0	2.4	11.0	4.7	61%	15%	32	31	38	34%	76%	3%	0	16			86	1.38	5.7	144	171	$20
16	**Proj**	**4**	**3**	**38**	**65**	**85**	**2.64**	**3.06**	**1.09**	**584**	**502**	**663**	**3.8**	**3.2**	**11.7**	**3.7**	**60%**	**14%**	**34**	**22**	**44**	**31%**	**78%**	**6%**	**0**						**10.6**	**137**	**163**	**$21**

Alvarez,Henderson

Age:	26	Th:	R	Role	SP	Health	F	LIMA Plan	D+
Ht:	6' 0"	Wt:	205	Type	Con xGB	PT/Exp	B	Rand Var	+5
						Consist	B	MM	1001

Two DL stints eventually gave way to shoudler surgery in late July, putting spring return in doubt. In limited sample, lost 3 mph on fastball, which took already soft-tossing Dom to miniscule levels. GB%/Ctl combo keeps rehab worth monitoring, but shoulder woes like this typically don't end well.

Yr	Tm	W	L	Sv	IP	K	ERA	xERA	WHIP	oOPS	vL	vR	BF/G	Ctl	Dom	Cmd	FpK	SwK	G	L	F	H%	S%	hr/f	GS	APC	DOM%	DIS%	Sv%	LI	RAR	BPV	BPX	R$
11	TOR *	9	7	0	152	99	3.51	3.84	1.20	717	698	738	24.4	1.5	5.9	4.0	65%	7%	53	20	26	30%	74%	15%	10	98	50%	0%			8.1	91	137	$9
12	TOR	9	14	0	187	79	4.85	4.53	1.44	812	885	725	26.0	2.6	3.8	1.5	59%	5%	57	19	24	29%	70%	18%	31	92	32%	19%			-19.4	33	43	-$9
13	MIA	5	6	0	103	57	3.59	3.79	1.14	636	753	524	24.6	2.4	5.0	2.1	61%	7%	53	22	25	27%	66%	3%	17	85	35%	18%			3.4	57	74	$4
14	MIA	12	7	0	187	111	2.65	3.58	1.24	697	678	722	25.7	1.6	5.3	3.4	62%	7%	54	22	24	31%	81%	10%	30	87	47%	13%			25.2	85	102	$13
15	MIA	0	4	0	22	9	6.45	4.81	1.57	768	909	587	25.5	2.8	3.6	1.3	59%	5%	57	23	20	33%	56%	6%	4	84	25%	50%			-6.8	24	29	-$7
1st Half		0	4	0	22	9	6.45	4.81	1.57	768	909	587	25.5	2.8	3.6	1.3	59%	5%	57	23	20	33%	56%	6%	4	84	25%	50%			-6.8	24	29	-$7
2nd Half																																		
16	**Proj**	**6**	**8**	**0**	**102**	**51**	**4.44**	**4.09**	**1.34**	**725**	**803**	**631**	**24.7**	**2.3**	**4.6**	**2.0**	**60%**	**6%**	**55**	**22**	**23**	**31%**	**66%**	**9%**	**17**						**-6.0**	**53**	**64**	**-$3**

Alvarez,Jose

Age:	27	Th:	L	Role	RP	Health	A	LIMA Plan	B+
Ht:	5' 11"	Wt:	180	Type	Pwr	PT/Exp	D	Rand Var	0
						Consist	D	MM	2200

Former starter cracked Opening Day roster and treaded water in middle relief. Chance for larger role hinges on Cmd catching up to quietly impressive SwK/FpK combination, while GB% further brightens outlook. But Dom, xERA history suggest he's more likely to be lefty specialist. Watch, but don't invest.

Yr	Tm	W	L	Sv	IP	K	ERA	xERA	WHIP	oOPS	vL	vR	BF/G	Ctl	Dom	Cmd	FpK	SwK	G	L	F	H%	S%	hr/f	GS	APC	DOM%	DIS%	Sv%	LI	RAR	BPV	BPX	R$
11	aa	2	6	0	66	39	5.57	5.68	1.62				24.3	2.9	5.3	1.8						35%	67%								-13.2	31	46	-$8
12	aa	6	9	0	136	63	5.15	4.43	1.40				23.0	1.9	4.2	2.2						32%	62%								-19.1	51	66	-$8
13	DET *	9	11	1	167	123	4.14	4.33	1.33	866	851	872	19.8	2.3	6.6	2.9	55%	11%	40	23	37	31%	72%	16%	6	50	17%	50%	100	1.22	-5.6	68	89	$1
14	LAA *	0	2	0	31	15	5.64	5.65	1.53	667	0	2000	17.0	3.5	4.3	1.2	67%	20%	50	0	50	29%	67%	0%	0	5			0	1.79	-7.3	0	0	-$7
15	LAA	4	3	0	67	59	3.49	3.74	1.21	642	570	694	4.4	3.1	7.9	2.6	69%	11%	51	19	30	29%	72%	9%	0	16			0	0.89	3.9	88	105	$2
1st Half		2	1	0	35	33	3.38	3.71	1.07	585	535	622	5.2	3.1	8.6	2.8	70%	11%	47	18	35	25%	71%	9%	0	18			0	0.59	2.5	95	113	$3
2nd Half		2	2	0	32	26	3.62	3.79	1.36	702	608	767	3.8	3.1	7.2	2.4	67%	12%	55	20	24	32%	74%	8%	0	14			0	1.11	1.4	81	96	$0
16	**Proj**	**3**	**4**	**0**	**65**	**55**	**3.94**	**3.80**	**1.28**	**718**	**652**	**758**	**6.7**	**3.0**	**7.5**	**2.5**	**63%**	**11%**	**47**	**21**	**32**	**30%**	**72%**	**12%**	**0**						**0.2**	**80**	**96**	**-$1**

Anderson,Brett

Age:	28	Th:	L	Role	SP	Health	F	LIMA Plan	B+
Ht:	6' 4"	Wt:	225	Type	xGB	PT/Exp	C	Rand Var	+2
						Consist	A	MM	3103

Nobody thought he could make it through a season, so he goes and tosses more IP than previous three years combined. Already-elite GB% reached stratospheric levels, which will keep ERA in check, but FpK doesn't believe in Ctl trend, and he continues to lack Ks. Health history, 2H decline make repeat highly unlikely.

Yr	Tm	W	L	Sv	IP	K	ERA	xERA	WHIP	oOPS	vL	vR	BF/G	Ctl	Dom	Cmd	FpK	SwK	G	L	F	H%	S%	hr/f	GS	APC	DOM%	DIS%	Sv%	LI	RAR	BPV	BPX	R$
11	OAK	3	6	0	83	61	4.00	3.50	1.33	721	761	700	27.4	2.7	6.6	2.4	58%	7%	57	18	25	31%	72%	13%	13	104	54%	31%			-0.6	81	121	-$1
12	OAK *	5	3	0	58	40	3.28	3.47	1.20	565	515	581	21.3	1.8	6.2	3.4	62%	9%	60	24	17	30%	74%	6%	6	88	83%	17%			5.3	91	118	$2
13	OAK	1	4	3	45	46	6.04	3.36	1.61	794	853	774	12.5	4.2	9.3	2.2	58%	9%	63	16	21	37%	63%	18%	5	48	40%	60%	100	0.78	-12.0	94	122	-$7
14	COL	1	3	0	43	29	2.91	3.55	1.32	688	724	675	22.5	2.7	6.0	2.2	62%	9%	61	17	22	32%	77%	3%	8	83	38%	25%			4.5	75	89	-$1
15	LA	10	9	0	180	116	3.69	3.53	1.33	726	698	737	24.2	2.3	5.8	2.5	58%	8%	66	15	19	31%	75%	17%	31	88	39%	26%			6.0	86	103	$5
1st Half		5	4	0	96	69	3.00	3.26	1.29	691	625	724	24.3	2.4	6.5	2.7	55%	8%	68	13	19	31%	79%	13%	16	91	44%	19%			11.4	97	115	$10
2nd Half		5	5	0	84	47	4.48	3.85	1.38	763	803	749	24.1	2.1	5.0	2.4	62%	8%	64	18	18	31%	70%	21%	15	84	33%	33%			-5.4	75	89	-$1
16	**Proj**	**9**	**9**	**0**	**156**	**110**	**3.94**	**3.56**	**1.37**	**710**	**729**	**703**	**24.4**	**2.7**	**6.3**	**2.4**	**60%**	**9%**	**64**	**17**	**20**	**32%**	**71%**	**9%**	**22**						**0.4**	**84**	**99**	**$1**

Anderson,Chase

Age:	28	Th:	R	Role	SP	Health	B	LIMA Plan	C
Ht:	6' 0"	Wt:	190	Type		PT/Exp	C	Rand Var	0
						Consist	C	MM	2203

Made rotation in April and pitched well enough to stick all year. ERA spiked down the stretch, but nasty trifecta of 2H luck (H%/S%, hr/f) was to blame. In-season velocity, SwK gains boosted 2H Dom and sent BPV above league average. Holds little upside, but deep league profit is there if late-season gains hold.

Yr	Tm	W	L	Sv	IP	K	ERA	xERA	WHIP	oOPS	vL	vR	BF/G	Ctl	Dom	Cmd	FpK	SwK	G	L	F	H%	S%	hr/f	GS	APC	DOM%	DIS%	Sv%	LI	RAR	BPV	BPX	R$
11																																		
12	aa	5	4	0	104	79	3.70	4.23	1.31				20.5	2.2	6.8	3.0						32%	75%								4.1	76	99	$1
13	aaa	4	7	0	88	63	5.76	5.84	1.67				15.2	3.1	6.4	2.0						36%	66%								-20.6	41	53	-$12
14	ARI *	13	9	0	153	135	3.23	3.79	1.25	779	714	831	23.1	2.7	7.9	2.9	63%	10%	40	24	36	30%	78%	14%	21	90	52%	19%			9.7	82	98	$9
15	ARI	6	6	0	153	111	4.30	4.16	1.30	754	746	761	23.7	2.4	6.5	2.8	62%	8%	42	24	34	30%	69%	11%	27	91	41%	19%			-6.4	74	88	$0
1st Half		4	2	0	97	60	3.71	4.20	1.16	701	659	733	24.7	2.1	5.6	2.6	59%	8%	43	22	34	27%	71%	10%	16	95	50%	6%			3.0	64	76	$6
2nd Half		2	4	0	56	51	5.34	4.09	1.53	840	868	811	22.3	2.7	8.2	3.0	66%	10%	40	26	34	36%	68%	14%	11	86	27%	36%			-9.4	92	109	-$10
16	**Proj**	**8**	**8**	**0**	**145**	**116**	**4.13**	**3.99**	**1.33**	**755**	**736**	**771**	**24.0**	**2.6**	**7.2**	**2.7**	**63%**	**9%**	**41**	**24**	**35**	**31%**	**72%**	**11%**	**21**						**-3.1**	**77**	**92**	**$1**

Anderson,Cody

Age:	25	Th:	R	Role	SP	Health	B	LIMA Plan	D+
Ht:	6' 4"	Wt:	220	Type	Con	PT/Exp	D	Rand Var	-1
						Consist	F	MM	1001

7-3, 3.05 ERA in 91 IP at CLE. Strong showing in AAA (1.89 ERA in 71 IP) netted late June call-up, where he continued to roll. Focus on skills, not stats, and you'll see subpar Dom that severely limits upside given equally mediocre SwK. MLB xERA (4.50) further hints that we may have already seen his best year.

Yr	Tm	W	L	Sv	IP	K	ERA	xERA	WHIP	oOPS	vL	vR	BF/G	Ctl	Dom	Cmd	FpK	SwK	G	L	F	H%	S%	hr/f	GS	APC	DOM%	DIS%	Sv%	LI	RAR	BPV	BPX	R$
11																																		
12																																		
13																																		
14	aa	4	11	0	126	68	6.34	5.97	1.63				22.4	3.1	4.9	1.6						33%	62%								-40.3	16	19	-$19
15	CLE *	11	6	0	163	89	2.85	3.28	1.18	647	715	594	23.3	2.2	4.9	2.3	61%	8%	46	21	34	28%	78%	9%	15	86	33%	27%			22.3	63	75	$14
1st Half		5	4	0	95	55	2.13	2.85	1.12	425	389	452	23.4	1.5	5.2	3.4	61%	8%	50	19	31	29%	81%	5%	3	95	####	0%			21.4	98	116	$19
2nd Half		6	2	0	68	34	3.86	4.83	1.27	717	815	638	23.4	3.1	4.5	1.5	60%	8%	45	21	35	26%	73%	11%	12	84	17%	33%			0.9	21	25	$5
16	**Proj**	**7**	**6**	**0**	**116**	**62**	**4.44**	**4.53**	**1.38**	**788**	**846**	**743**	**22.8**	**2.7**	**4.8**	**1.8**	**61%**	**8%**	**47**	**20**	**33**	**30%**	**70%**	**10%**	**21**						**-6.9**	**39**	**46**	**-$3**

RYAN BLOOMFIELD

Andriese,Matt

Andriese,Matt			Health	A	LIMA Plan	C
Age: 26	Th: R	Role SP	PT/Exp	D	Rand Var	0
Ht: 6' 3"	Wt: 210	Type	Consist	C	MM	2101

3-5, 4.11 ERA in 66 IP at TAM. Made four trips between AAA/MLB, and while progress was made, shuttle rides will likely continue. FpK is unconvinced of Ctl growth, while xERA history doesn't lend itself to much upside. Strong GB%, 2H Dom gains are worth monitoring, but he'll have trouble posting sub-4.00 ERA.

Yr Tm	W	L	Sv	IP	K	ERA	xERA	WHIP	oOPS	vL	vR	BF/G	Ctl	Dom	Cmd	FpK	SwK	G	L	F	H%	S%	hr/f	GS	APC	DOM%	DIS%	Sv%	LI	RAR	BPV	BPX	R$
11																																	
12																																	
13 a/a	11	7	0	135	91	3.36	3.52	1.28				20.4	1.8	6.1	3.4						33%	73%								8.4	97	127	$7
14 aaa	11	8	0	162	107	4.83	4.94	1.46				24.8	2.9	5.9	2.1						32%	69%								-21.8	44	53	-$7
15 TAM *	6	8	2	131	105	3.57	4.28	1.36	728	785	677	14.4	2.0	7.2	3.6	59%	9%	49	17	35	34%	75%	11%	8	44	13%	63%	100	0.77	6.3	96	115	$3
1st Half	4	2	2	67	46	3.41	3.93	1.22	693	797	583	15.9	1.7	6.2	3.7	59%	8%	50	17	33	30%	76%	13%	6	57	17%	50%	100	0.54	4.5	87	103	$7
2nd Half	2	6	0	64	59	3.74	4.65	1.50	782	754	800	13.2	2.3	8.3	3.6	59%	10%	47	16	37	39%	75%	7%	2	33	0%	100%	0	0.96	1.8	107	127	-$1
16 Proj	**6**	**6**	**0**	**102**	**76**	**4.09**	**4.03**	**1.40**	**739**	**756**	**726**	**23.3**	**2.3**	**6.7**	**3.0**	**59%**	**9%**	**48**	**16**	**36**	**34%**	**72%**	**7%**	**13**						**-1.6**	**86**	**102**	**-$2**

Araujo,Elvis

Araujo,Elvis			Health	C	LIMA Plan	D+
Age: 24	Th: L	Role RP	PT/Exp	F	Rand Var	-2
Ht: 6' 6"	Wt: 215	Type Pwr xGB	Consist	C	MM	2300

Got his shot in May and stuck as lefty specialist, until August groin injury cut season short. Mid-90s heater and slider combo created plenty of whiffs, and he held his own vs. RHP in limited sample. Next step to relevance hinges on harnessing Ctl, but FpK suggests it won't be easy. Until then, keep your distance.

Yr Tm	W	L	Sv	IP	K	ERA	xERA	WHIP	oOPS	vL	vR	BF/G	Ctl	Dom	Cmd	FpK	SwK	G	L	F	H%	S%	hr/f	GS	APC	DOM%	DIS%	Sv%	LI	RAR	BPV	BPX	R$
11																																	
12																																	
13																																	
14 aa	1	0	3	21	18	2.93	5.27	1.75				5.3	6.1	7.8	1.3						33%	86%								2.1	47	55	-$2
15 PHI	2	1	0	35	34	3.38	4.14	1.38	619	646	580	3.8	4.9	8.8	1.8	56%	12%	49	20	31	31%	74%	3%	0	15			0	0.93	2.5	53	63	-$2
1st Half	1	1	0	23	21	3.13	4.11	1.61	744	703	795	4.3	4.3	8.2	1.9	57%	11%	54	20	26	36%	81%	6%	0	17			0	0.80	2.4	63	75	-$3
2nd Half	1	0	0	12	13	3.86	4.24	0.94	337	471	214	2.9	6.2	10.0	1.6	52%	13%	36	20	44	13%	55%	0%	0	13			0	1.13	0.2	28	33	$0
16 Proj	**2**	**2**	**0**	**34**	**32**	**3.97**	**4.02**	**1.45**	**602**	**557**	**658**	**3.7**	**4.7**	**8.5**	**1.8**	**57%**	**11%**	**51**	**21**	**28**	**32%**	**72%**	**6%**	**0**						**0.0**	**54**	**65**	**-$3**

Archer,Chris

Archer,Chris			Health	A	LIMA Plan	C
Age: 27	Th: R	Role SP	PT/Exp	A	Rand Var	0
Ht: 6' 3"	Wt: 190	Type Pwr	Consist	A	MM	3405

Early breakout generated Cy whispers until ERA doubled in 2H. Several reasons to lean toward earlier version: FpK says not to worry about 2H Ctl spike, which dinged BPV; elite SwK supports K total; equally dominant vL and R; DIS% trend, reliability grades mitigate risk. If 2H luck factors normalize... UP: 2.75 ERA

Yr Tm	W	L	Sv	IP	K	ERA	xERA	WHIP	oOPS	vL	vR	BF/G	Ctl	Dom	Cmd	FpK	SwK	G	L	F	H%	S%	hr/f	GS	APC	DOM%	DIS%	Sv%	LI	RAR	BPV	BPX	R$
11 a/a	9	7	0	147	112	4.36	4.74	1.63				24.3	4.9	6.9	1.4						33%	73%								-7.7	51	76	-$6
12 TAM *	8	12	0	157	154	4.19	3.21	1.32	624	915	435	21.0	4.2	8.8	2.1	62%	10%	44	18	38	30%	68%	11%	4	82	75%	0%	0	0.99	-3.3	90	118	$3
13 TAM *	14	10	0	179	144	3.64	3.79	1.27	660	801	455	22.1	3.1	7.3	2.4	58%	9%	47	19	34	29%	75%	12%	23	91	43%	35%			5.1	66	87	$10
14 TAM	10	9	0	195	173	3.33	3.68	1.28	650	624	685	25.7	3.3	8.0	2.4	57%	10%	47	22	31	31%	75%	7%	32	99	56%	13%			9.9	79	94	$9
15 TAM	12	13	0	212	252	3.23	3.12	1.14	613	604	622	25.5	2.8	10.7	3.8	64%	13%	46	20	34	31%	74%	10%	34	101	71%	6%			19.2	141	168	$22
1st Half	9	5	0	116	141	2.18	2.71	0.95	538	558	515	25.1	2.2	11.0	5.0	65%	13%	47	21	31	28%	81%	10%	18	100	72%	6%			25.4	164	195	$39
2nd Half	3	8	0	96	111	4.48	3.64	1.36	694	656	736	26.0	3.6	10.4	2.9	63%	13%	45	19	37	34%	69%	10%	16	103	69%	6%			-6.2	114	135	$1
16 Proj	**15**	**11**	**0**	**209**	**213**	**3.15**	**3.35**	**1.19**	**639**	**644**	**632**	**25.2**	**2.9**	**9.2**	**3.2**	**61%**	**11%**	**46**	**21**	**33**	**30%**	**76%**	**10%**	**33**						**20.9**	**111**	**132**	**$19**

Armstrong,Shawn

Armstrong,Shawn			Health	A	LIMA Plan	A
Age: 25	Th: R	Role RP	PT/Exp	F	Rand Var	+3
Ht: 6' 2"	Wt: 210	Type Pwr	Consist	B	MM	5500

0-0, 2.25 ERA in 8 IP at CLE. Another dominating year at AAA, which carried over well in brief MLB stint. Racked up Ks at elite rate, while unlucky H%, hr/f suggest numbers could have been even better. Still gives up too many walks, though if 2H Ctl gains hold, he quickly becomes LIMA gem with room for more.

Yr Tm	W	L	Sv	IP	K	ERA	xERA	WHIP	oOPS	vL	vR	BF/G	Ctl	Dom	Cmd	FpK	SwK	G	L	F	H%	S%	hr/f	GS	APC	DOM%	DIS%	Sv%	LI	RAR	BPV	BPX	R$
11																																	
12 aa	1	0	3	20	19	1.16	2.31	1.31				4.9	5.4	8.5	1.6						27%	90%								7.1	99	129	$0
13 aa	2	3	0	33	37	4.29	4.43	1.63				4.9	5.3	10.1	1.9						37%	73%								-1.7	87	114	-$4
14 a/a	6	2	15	56	61	2.78	3.28	1.25				4.7	3.4	9.8	2.9						32%	80%								6.6	106	126	$9
15 CLE *	1	2	16	58	77	3.05	3.14	1.40	590	414	767	4.5	4.6	12.1	2.6	67%	14%	35	24	41	37%	77%	14%	0	16			94	0.08	6.5	130	155	$6
1st Half	1	2	10	31	40	3.53	3.54	1.57				4.7	5.8	11.5	2.0						38%	75%	0%	0						1.7	116	138	$5
2nd Half	0	0	6	27	37	2.50	2.67	1.19	591	414	767	4.3	3.2	12.7	4.0	67%	14%	35	24	41	36%	79%	14%	0	16			100	0.08	4.8	159	188	$8
16 Proj	**3**	**2**	**0**	**58**	**71**	**3.02**	**2.83**	**1.26**				**4.5**	**4.0**	**11.0**	**2.7**	**0%**	**0%**				**32%**	**76%**		**0**						**6.8**	**122**	**145**	**$2**

Arrieta,Jake

Arrieta,Jake			Health	C	LIMA Plan	D+
Age: 30	Th: R	Role SP	PT/Exp	A	Rand Var	-5
Ht: 6' 4"	Wt: 225	Type Pwr GB	Consist	B	MM	5405

Historic 2H run capped breakout year, while underlying skills remained elite. Leaned more heavily on sinker, which fueled GB% spike without sacrificing Dom. 2H FpK suggests Ctl gains are less likely to hold, but we're nitpicking. Two straight years of sub-3.00 xERA, 130+ BPV cement his status as legit rotation anchor.

Yr Tm	W	L	Sv	IP	K	ERA	xERA	WHIP	oOPS	vL	vR	BF/G	Ctl	Dom	Cmd	FpK	SwK	G	L	F	H%	S%	hr/f	GS	APC	DOM%	DIS%	Sv%	LI	RAR	BPV	BPX	R$
11 BAL	10	8	0	119	93	5.05	4.45	1.46	791	856	715	23.8	4.4	7.0	1.6	56%	8%	46	16	39	28%	70%	15%	22	95	32%	23%			-16.3	30	45	-$4
12 BAL *	8	13	0	171	151	6.13	4.74	1.47	763	846	664	21.5	3.6	8.0	2.2	56%	8%	44	24	32	33%	58%	15%	18	82	44%	50%	0	0.79	-44.6	62	81	-$15
13 2 TM *	12	9	0	155	120	5.06	4.43	1.49	718	664	775	22.2	4.4	7.0	1.6	60%	7%	40	25	34	31%	67%	12%	14	90	14%	21%			-22.8	50	65	-$7
14 CHC	10	5	0	157	167	2.53	2.79	0.99	535	553	520	24.6	2.4	9.6	4.1	59%	11%	49	22	28	28%	74%	4%	25	97	80%	16%			23.4	136	162	$20
15 CHC	22	6	0	229	236	1.77	2.62	0.86	507	449	557	26.4	1.9	9.3	4.9	60%	11%	56	21	23	25%	81%	8%	33	104	85%	0%			62.0	150	179	$51
1st Half	8	5	0	106	110	2.80	2.89	1.03	613	607	615	26.0	2.0	9.3	4.8	64%	10%	51	22	27	29%	75%	11%	16	103	75%	0%			15.2	144	171	$32
2nd Half	14	1	0	123	126	0.88	2.38	0.72	410	329	493	26.7	1.8	9.2	5.0	56%	13%	61	20	19	22%	89%	4%	17	105	94%	0%			46.8	156	185	$67
16 Proj	**18**	**8**	**0**	**218**	**221**	**2.77**	**2.91**	**1.04**	**584**	**563**	**604**	**24.1**	**2.6**	**9.2**	**3.5**	**59%**	**10%**	**53**	**21**	**26**	**28%**	**75%**	**9%**	**35**						**31.9**	**126**	**151**	**$31**

Asher,Alec

Asher,Alec			Health	A	LIMA Plan	D+
Age: 24	Th: R	Role SP	PT/Exp	D	Rand Var	+1
Ht: 6' 4"	Wt: 218	Type Con xFB	Consist	D	MM	0001

0-6, 9.31 ERA in 29 IP at PHI. Traded from TEX as part of Hamels deal; safe to say there was a noticeable dropoff. Inability to miss bats, generate Ks question his ability to stick, while BPV, Ctl erosion point to bumpy road ahead. 2H xERA is a sinister sign that you should steer clear from even a speculative bid.

Yr Tm	W	L	Sv	IP	K	ERA	xERA	WHIP	oOPS	vL	vR	BF/G	Ctl	Dom	Cmd	FpK	SwK	G	L	F	H%	S%	hr/f	GS	APC	DOM%	DIS%	Sv%	LI	RAR	BPV	BPX	R$
11																																	
12																																	
13																																	
14 aa	11	11	0	154	102	4.66	4.29	1.26				22.5	1.9	6.0	3.1						30%	66%								-17.5	66	79	-$1
15 PHI *	6	16	0	163	110	5.54	6.15	1.55	1019	1075	955	22.9	2.8	6.1	2.1	59%	8%	36	19	45	32%	70%	16%	7	72	14%	71%			-31.6	19	22	-$15
1st Half	3	8	0	89	67	5.04	5.74	1.48				23.9	3.1	6.8	2.2						31%	73%	0%	0						-11.9	26	31	-$12
2nd Half	3	8	0	74	43	6.13	6.66	1.63	1019	1075	955	21.9	2.5	5.2	2.1	59%	8%	36	19	45	34%	67%	16%	7	72	14%	71%			-19.7	10	12	-$19
16 Proj	**6**	**10**	**0**	**109**	**71**	**5.27**	**4.79**	**1.44**	**753**	**797**	**705**	**22.6**	**2.4**	**5.9**	**2.5**	**59%**	**8%**	**36**	**19**	**45**	**32%**	**68%**	**11%**	**21**						**-17.6**	**56**	**66**	**-$8**

Avilan,Luis

Avilan,Luis			Health	A	LIMA Plan	C
Age: 26	Th: L	Role RP	PT/Exp	D	Rand Var	+1
Ht: 6' 2"	Wt: 220	Type Pwr GB	Consist	B	MM	2200

Morphed into different pitcher as GB% collapsed, but made up for it with major Dom, BPV spikes. Threw more change-ups, which became his go-to weapon (25% SwK), while impressive FpK spike drove Ctl progress. Nasty S%, hr/f in 2H hid underlying strides, but new and improved skills open shot at larger role.

Yr Tm	W	L	Sv	IP	K	ERA	xERA	WHIP	oOPS	vL	vR	BF/G	Ctl	Dom	Cmd	FpK	SwK	G	L	F	H%	S%	hr/f	GS	APC	DOM%	DIS%	Sv%	LI	RAR	BPV	BPX	R$
11 aa	4	8	1	105	68	4.82	4.62	1.46				12.5	2.9	5.9	2.0						33%	67%								-11.4	51	77	-$5
12 ATL *	4	6	1	97	81	3.31	3.60	1.31	547	528	559	8.6	3.9	7.5	1.9	55%	11%	47	20	33	28%	77%	3%	0	18			100	0.91	8.5	68	89	$3
13 ATL	5	0	0	65	38	1.52	3.68	0.95	478	383	557	3.4	3.0	5.3	1.7	54%	9%	58	19	24	21%	84%	2%	0	13			0	1.07	18.8	48	63	$9
14 ATL	4	1	0	43	25	4.57	4.41	1.57	764	729	803	3.1	4.4	5.2	1.2	51%	8%	58	19	23	32%	70%	6%	0	11			0	1.16	-4.4	12	14	-$4
15 2 NL	2	5	0	53	49	4.05	3.57	1.18	665	665	666	3.0	2.5	8.3	3.3	63%	14%	48	21	31	29%	68%	13%	0	11			0	1.51	-0.6	106	127	-$1
1st Half	2	2	0	32	27	3.06	3.45	1.08	599	684	522	3.1	1.9	7.5	3.9	66%	13%	49	21	30	29%	73%	7%	0	11			0	1.42	3.6	110	131	$2
2nd Half	0	3	0	21	22	5.57	3.74	1.33	765	636	868	2.9	3.4	9.4	2.8	60%	15%	46	20	34	30%	63%	20%	0	11			0	1.63	-4.2	101	120	-$5
16 Proj	**3**	**4**	**0**	**58**	**50**	**3.59**	**3.70**	**1.29**	**663**	**621**	**700**	**3.2**	**3.3**	**7.7**	**2.3**	**57%**	**12%**	**51**	**20**	**29**	**31%**	**72%**	**7%**	**0**						**2.6**	**79**	**94**	**$0**

RYAN BLOOMFIELD

Axford,John						Health	A	LIMA Plan	B
Age:	33	Th:	R	Role	RP	PT/Exp	C	Rand Var	+2
Ht:	6' 5"	Wt:	220	Type	Pwr GB	Consist	A	MM	2510

Save opps returned due to dismal COL pen, rather than significant bump in skills. Dom, GB% combo keeps him relevant, but inability to hit water from the boat is a major obstacle. FpK was third-worst in MLB (min. 50 IP), so odds are free passes will continue, and his new team won't be as desperate for a closer.

Yr Tm	W	L	Sv	IP	K	ERA	xERA	WHIP	oOPS	vL	vR	BF/G	Ctl	Dom	Cmd	FpK	SwK	G	L	F	H%	S%	hr/f	GS	APC	DOM%	DIS%	Sv%	LI	RAR	BPV	BPX	R$
11 MIL	2	2	46	74	86	1.95	3.00	1.14	557	481	621	4.1	3.1	10.5	3.4	61%	10%	50	15	35	31%	85%	6%	0	17			96	1.15	18.1	135	202	$26
12 MIL	5	8	35	69	93	4.67	3.42	1.44	717	671	767	4.1	5.1	12.1	2.4	54%	11%	46	24	30	33%	71%	19%	0	19			80	1.22	-5.6	105	136	$12
13 2 NL	7	7	0	65	65	4.02	3.74	1.52	796	838	761	3.9	3.6	9.0	2.5	53%	10%	45	24	31	35%	79%	17%	0	16			0	1.11	-1.2	88	114	-$2
14 2 TM	2	4	10	55	63	3.95	3.77	1.45	691	630	743	3.9	5.9	10.4	1.8	57%	10%	54	14	33	29%	75%	13%	0	17			77	1.07	-1.4	59	70	$1
15 COL	4	5	25	56	62	4.20	3.84	1.58	704	671	731	4.2	5.2	10.0	1.9	51%	11%	56	17	27	35%	74%	10%	0	18			81	1.16	-1.7	75	89	$6
1st Half	1	1	14	24	22	2.28	3.63	1.23	563	573	552	3.8	3.8	8.4	2.2	51%	9%	60	13	26	29%	82%	6%	0	16			93	1.18	4.9	86	102	$10
2nd Half	3	4	11	32	40	5.63	4.00	1.84	800	764	822	4.4	6.2	11.3	1.8	52%	12%	53	20	28	40%	70%	13%	0	19			69	1.14	-6.6	66	79	$4
16 Proj	**4**	**5**	**8**	**58**	**65**	**4.07**	**3.70**	**1.52**	**711**	**679**	**738**	**3.9**	**5.0**	**10.1**	**2.0**	**54%**	**11%**	**53**	**18**	**30**	**34%**	**75%**	**12%**	**0**						**-0.7**	**77**	**92**	**$0**

Baez,Pedro						Health	C	LIMA Plan	A
Age:	28	Th:	R	Role	RP	PT/Exp	D	Rand Var	0
Ht:	6' 2"	Wt:	230	Type	Pwr FB	Consist	D	MM	4400

Some may see decent ERA in middle relief and move on, but underlying skills paint rosier picture: major SwK spike, upper-90s heat support Dom growth; threw more FpK as Ctl entered elite territory; LI shows managerial confidence. FB tilt points to HR risk, but job opening could yield... UP: 3.00 ERA, 25 Sv.

Yr Tm	W	L	Sv	IP	K	ERA	xERA	WHIP	oOPS	vL	vR	BF/G	Ctl	Dom	Cmd	FpK	SwK	G	L	F	H%	S%	hr/f	GS	APC	DOM%	DIS%	Sv%	LI	RAR	BPV	BPX	R$
11																																	
12																																	
13 aa	1	1	0	23	19	5.47	6.30	1.71				6.6	3.2	7.3	2.3						37%	71%								-4.6	41	53	-$6
14 LA *	2	1	12	66	49	3.28	3.40	1.16	537	578	501	4.4	2.2	6.7	3.0	61%	10%	37	15	49	28%	75%	9%	0	18			100	0.46	3.7	81	97	$6
15 LA	4	2	0	51	60	3.35	3.27	1.14	693	735	678	4.0	1.9	10.6	5.5	66%	16%	38	19	44	34%	72%	7%	0	16			0	1.20	3.8	154	184	$2
1st Half	1	1	0	20	28	2.66	2.90	1.03	609	768	551	4.2	2.2	12.4	5.6	65%	17%	36	19	45	34%	75%	5%	0	16			0	1.42	3.3	177	211	$1
2nd Half	3	1	0	31	32	3.82	3.53	1.21	747	713	759	3.9	1.8	9.4	5.3	66%	15%	38	19	43	34%	71%	8%	0	16			0	1.06	0.6	138	164	$3
16 Proj	**3**	**2**	**0**	**58**	**62**	**3.31**	**3.33**	**1.14**	**714**	**755**	**698**	**4.1**	**2.0**	**9.7**	**4.7**	**66%**	**16%**	**37**	**19**	**44**	**32%**	**75%**	**9%**	**0**						**4.7**	**135**	**160**	**$2**

Bailey,Homer						Health	F	LIMA Plan	C
Age:	30	Th:	R	Role	SP	PT/Exp	B	Rand Var	0
Ht:	6' 4"	Wt:	230	Type	Pwr	Consist	C	MM	2201

Started just two games before Tommy John struck in May, putting first half of 2016 in jeopardy. That would make it nearly two full years without regular action. Pre-injury skills were consistent and solid, but best bet at value lies as 2017 keeper stash. At least you didn't cough up $105 million for him.

Yr Tm	W	L	Sv	IP	K	ERA	xERA	WHIP	oOPS	vL	vR	BF/G	Ctl	Dom	Cmd	FpK	SwK	G	L	F	H%	S%	hr/f	GS	APC	DOM%	DIS%	Sv%	LI	RAR	BPV	BPX	R$
11 CIN *	11	8	0	162	124	4.26	4.38	1.32	728	777	687	24.0	2.2	6.9	3.2	62%	10%	39	22	38	32%	71%	12%	22	96	45%	18%			-6.3	76	114	$3
12 CIN	13	10	0	208	168	3.68	3.92	1.24	718	682	747	26.5	2.3	7.3	3.2	66%	10%	45	20	35	30%	75%	12%	33	101	52%	24%			8.6	93	121	$12
13 CIN	11	12	0	209	199	3.49	3.29	1.12	660	746	575	26.5	2.3	8.6	3.7	64%	11%	46	19	34	29%	72%	10%	32	103	66%	9%			9.7	115	150	$16
14 CIN	9	5	0	146	124	3.71	3.46	1.23	703	750	666	26.3	2.8	7.7	2.8	62%	11%	51	21	29	29%	73%	13%	23	99	70%	9%			0.6	92	109	$5
15 CIN	0	1	0	11	3	5.56	5.64	1.76	1009	1424	707	25.5	3.2	2.4	0.8	63%	7%	52	17	31	31%	76%	23%	2	86	0%	100%			-2.2	-13	-15	-$6
1st Half	0	1	0	11	3	5.56	5.64	1.76	1009	1424	707	25.5	3.2	2.4	0.8	63%	7%	52	17	31	31%	76%	23%	2	86	0%	100%			-2.2	-13	-15	-$6
2nd Half																																	
16 Proj	**6**	**5**	**0**	**102**	**86**	**3.74**	**3.78**	**1.28**	**715**	**742**	**691**	**25.7**	**2.9**	**7.6**	**2.6**	**64%**	**11%**	**48**	**19**	**33**	**30%**	**74%**	**12%**	**16**						**2.8**	**83**	**99**	**$2**

Banuelos,Manny						Health	C	LIMA Plan	D+
Age:	25	Th:	L	Role	RP	PT/Exp	D	Rand Var	0
Ht:	5' 10"	Wt:	155	Type	Pwr FB	Consist	B	MM	0101

1-4, 5.13 ERA in 26 IP at ATL. Former top prospect got MLB call in July, but season was cut short due to surgery in same elbow that underwent TJS in 2012. Cmd history suggests skills are heading down the wrong path, so while it's too early to completely cut bait, odds of him fulfilling potential are slim.

Yr Tm	W	L	Sv	IP	K	ERA	xERA	WHIP	oOPS	vL	vR	BF/G	Ctl	Dom	Cmd	FpK	SwK	G	L	F	H%	S%	hr/f	GS	APC	DOM%	DIS%	Sv%	LI	RAR	BPV	BPX	R$
11 a/a	6	7	0	130	110	4.59	5.19	1.69				21.7	5.0	7.6	1.5						35%	74%								-10.4	52	77	-$8
12 aaa	0	2	0	24	19	5.55	6.32	1.80				18.5	3.8	7.1	1.9						39%	70%								-4.5	43	56	-$8
13																																	
14 a/a	2	3	0	64	49	4.96	4.77	1.40				12.9	4.1	6.9	1.7						27%	70%								-9.7	33	39	-$5
15 ATL *	7	6	0	111	79	3.48	3.96	1.47	825	840	818	20.7	4.4	6.4	1.4	62%	8%	40	24	36	30%	77%	13%	6	67	17%	50%	0	0.72	6.6	57	68	$0
1st Half	6	2	0	88	67	2.85	3.20	1.36	311	650	205	23.1	4.1	6.8	1.6	65%	13%	45	36	18	30%	78%	0%	1	75	100%	0%			12.1	75	89	$4
2nd Half	1	4	0	23	12	5.96	6.95	1.91	929	872	950	15.3	5.6	4.8	0.8	62%	7%	39	22	38	33%	72%	14%	5	66	0%	60%	0	0.72	-5.6	-9	-11	-$17
16 Proj	**5**	**8**	**0**	**102**	**78**	**4.77**	**4.83**	**1.53**	**687**	**643**	**703**	**15.8**	**4.2**	**6.9**	**1.6**	**62%**	**7%**	**39**	**22**	**38**	**31%**	**72%**	**10%**	**16**						**-10.1**	**27**	**32**	**-$7**

Barraclough,Kyle						Health	A	LIMA Plan	D
Age:	26	Th:	R	Role	RP	PT/Exp	F	Rand Var	-1
Ht:	6' 3"	Wt:	225	Type	Pwr xFB	Consist	F	MM	0510

2-1, 2.59 ERA in 24 IP at MIA. Moved quickly through minors; called up in August after just 29 IP in AA. Electric stuff, SwK leads to Dom that gives him decent upside; too bad there's this thing called a Walk. 5.0 career Ctl in minors, dismal FpK in MLB will be major roadblocks in quest for late-inning role.

Yr Tm	W	L	Sv	IP	K	ERA	xERA	WHIP	oOPS	vL	vR	BF/G	Ctl	Dom	Cmd	FpK	SwK	G	L	F	H%	S%	hr/f	GS	APC	DOM%	DIS%	Sv%	LI	RAR	BPV	BPX	R$
11																																	
12																																	
13																																	
14																																	
15 MIA *	4	1	10	53	59	3.14	2.75	1.44	563	656	497	4.3	6.8	10.1	1.5	48%	15%	32	26	42	28%	77%	5%	0	19			83	1.15	5.4	102	122	$4
1st Half	1	0	5	19	18	3.70	3.19	1.57				4.8	7.2	8.8	1.2						30%	74%	0%	0						0.6	91	107	-$3
2nd Half	3	1	5	34	41	2.84	2.51	1.37	563	656	497	4.1	6.7	10.8	1.6	48%	15%	32	26	42	27%	79%	5%	0	19			83	1.15	4.8	109	130	$7
16 Proj	**4**	**1**	**2**	**58**	**64**	**4.05**	**4.84**	**1.55**	**717**	**865**	**616**	**4.5**	**6.8**	**9.9**	**1.5**	**48%**	**15%**	**32**	**26**	**42**	**29%**	**75%**	**7%**	**0**						**-0.6**	**4**	**5**	**-$2**

Barrett,Aaron						Health	F	LIMA Plan	C
Age:	28	Th:	R	Role	RP	PT/Exp	D	Rand Var	0
Ht:	6' 3"	Wt:	225	Type	Pwr	Consist	A	MM	3300

Flashed closer-worthy skills in middle relief until injuries hit. Biceps strain in June gave way to elbow woes in August, which ended with a visit to Dr. Andrews for TJS in September. 2016 return is in doubt, and while BPV history is impressive, it's not enough to hold a meaningful roster spot. Check back in 2017.

Yr Tm	W	L	Sv	IP	K	ERA	xERA	WHIP	oOPS	vL	vR	BF/G	Ctl	Dom	Cmd	FpK	SwK	G	L	F	H%	S%	hr/f	GS	APC	DOM%	DIS%	Sv%	LI	RAR	BPV	BPX	R$
11																																	
12																																	
13 aa	1	1	26	50	54	2.71	3.20	1.26				4.0	2.7	9.7	3.6						34%	79%								7.2	126	164	$11
14 WAS	3	0	0	41	49	2.66	3.24	1.30	605	750	529	3.5	4.4	10.8	2.5	54%	13%	46	25	28	33%	79%	3%	0	14			0	1.07	5.4	100	119	$1
15 WAS	3	3	0	29	35	4.60	3.01	1.19	631	549	668	3.1	2.1	10.7	5.0	68%	14%	43	24	33	36%	59%	4%	0	12			0	1.49	-2.3	156	186	-$2
1st Half	3	2	0	21	28	5.06	2.88	1.22	657	568	705	3.0	2.5	11.8	4.7	71%	14%	42	26	32	37%	56%	6%	0	12			0	1.38	-2.9	164	194	-$1
2nd Half	0	1	0	8	7	3.38	3.36	1.13	561	452	588	3.3	1.1	7.9	7.0	61%	16%	48	17	35	34%	67%	0%	0	11			0	1.85	0.6	137	163	-$4
16 Proj	**0**	**0**	**0**	**4**	**4**	**4.50**	**3.54**	**1.25**	**651**	**654**	**649**	**3.4**	**3.1**	**8.6**	**2.8**	**64%**	**13%**	**43**	**26**	**31**	**32%**	**62%**	**5%**	**0**						**-0.3**	**94**	**112**	**-$4**

Bassitt,Chris						Health	A	LIMA Plan	D+
Age:	27	Th:	R	Role	SP	PT/Exp	D	Rand Var	0
Ht:	6' 5"	Wt:	210	Type	Pwr	Consist	A	MM	1101

1-8, 3.56 ERA in 86 IP at OAK. Went from long relief to rotation, and actually posted four straight PQS-5s in late July. He's better than brutal W-L record, but mediocre Dom/Cmd and 4.20 MLB xERA suggest a very vanilla skill set. 2nd half GB% offers some hope he can stick, but mixed leaguers can safely avoid.

Yr Tm	W	L	Sv	IP	K	ERA	xERA	WHIP	oOPS	vL	vR	BF/G	Ctl	Dom	Cmd	FpK	SwK	G	L	F	H%	S%	hr/f	GS	APC	DOM%	DIS%	Sv%	LI	RAR	BPV	BPX	R$
11																																	
12																																	
13 aa	4	2	0	48	32	2.99	3.31	1.31				24.6	3.8	6.0	1.6						28%	78%								5.2	60	79	$0
14 CHW *	4	2	0	64	51	2.82	3.79	1.44	721	792	639	22.8	4.0	7.1	1.8	61%	6%	40	27	33	32%	80%	0%	5	88	40%	20%	0	0.66	7.3	73	87	$0
15 OAK *	3	15	0	155	119	4.05	3.35	1.30	684	650	732	20.6	3.0	6.9	2.3	55%	9%	44	21	34	31%	67%	6%	13	79	46%	23%	0	0.65	-1.7	83	99	$0
1st Half	2	8	0	84	64	4.29	2.95	1.26	578	530	632	18.1	3.2	6.8	2.1	58%	7%	32	19	48	30%	63%	3%	2	53	50%	0%	0	0.40	-3.4	86	102	$0
2nd Half	1	7	0	71	55	3.76	3.83	1.35	718	684	766	24.5	2.7	7.0	2.6	54%	9%	48	22	30	33%	72%	7%	11	95	45%	27%			1.7	82	97	$0
16 Proj	**5**	**8**	**0**	**116**	**89**	**3.90**	**4.30**	**1.35**	**752**	**705**	**814**	**22.4**	**3.4**	**6.9**	**2.0**	**55%**	**8%**	**42**	**21**	**37**	**30%**	**73%**	**8%**	**22**						**0.9**	**52**	**62**	**$0**

RYAN BLOOMFIELD

Bauer,Trevor

Age:	25	Th:	R	Role	SP	Health	A	LIMA Plan	B		
Ht: 6' 1"		Wt:	190	Type	Pwr FB	PT/Exp	B	Rand Var	+1		
						Consist	B	MM	1305		

No quantum leap yet for once-top prospect. Only real difference between 1st to 2nd halves: hit, strand, and home run rates. Reining in his Ctl is key but FpK not overly optimistic. Dom growth, backed by SwK, is nice, as is higher DOM%, but such signs of "breakout" are too faint to invest too heavily.

Yr	Tm	W	L	Sv	IP	K	ERA	xERA	WHIP	oOPS	vL	vR	BF/G	Ctl	Dom	Cmd	FpK	SwK	G	L	F	H%	S%	hr/f	GS	APC	DOM%	DIS%	Sv%	LI	RAR	BPV	BPX	R$
11	aa	1	1	0	17	23	8.11	5.80	1.70				18.9	3.9	12.4	3.2						44%	51%								-8.6	101	152	-$6
12	ARI *	13	4	0	147	154	2.91	3.41	1.32	795	851	729	23.4	4.1	9.4	2.3	64%	7%	45	25	30	31%	80%	15%	4	81	25%	75%			20.0	93	121	$13
13	CLE *	7	9	0	138	104	5.04	5.44	1.72	840	908	778	24.2	5.7	6.8	1.2	57%	7%	35	20	45	32%	73%	13%	4	88	25%	25%			-20.1	30	40	-$14
14	CLE *	9	9	0	199	181	3.77	3.97	1.33	737	729	744	25.0	3.3	8.2	2.5	56%	9%	35	23	41	31%	74%	9%	26	100	46%	27%			-0.7	77	91	$4
15	CLE	11	12	0	176	170	4.55	4.21	1.31	713	705	721	24.0	4.0	8.7	2.2	59%	10%	39	20	41	28%	68%	12%	30	93	60%	27%	0	0.76	-12.8	64	77	$2
1st Half		7	5	0	97	93	3.88	4.28	1.25	667	614	717	25.4	4.0	8.6	2.2	59%	10%	38	18	44	27%	72%	9%	16	99	69%	19%			0.9	63	75	$9
2nd Half		4	7	0	79	77	5.38	4.13	1.39	768	808	725	22.5	4.1	8.8	2.1	59%	9%	41	23	36	30%	64%	15%	14	86	50%	36%	0	0.73	-13.7	66	79	-$6
16	Proj	11	11	0	189	175	4.28	4.24	1.39	730	729	731	25.2	4.1	8.4	2.0	58%	9%	38	22	40	30%	71%	10%	31						-7.4	55	66	$1

Beachy,Brandon

Age:	29	Th:	R	Role	SP	Health	F	LIMA Plan	D+		
Ht: 6' 3"		Wt:	215	Type	Pwr FB	PT/Exp	F	Rand Var	0		
						Consist	B	MM	1201		

0-1, 7.88 ERA in 8 IP at LA. Made it back from second TJS... barely. Two July PQS-0s with diminished velocity got him demoted, even DFA'd at one point. Even at AAA, Cmd was lackluster (36/21 K/BB in 47 IP). Is guy from 2011 buried under scar tissue? Might be worth a cheap flyer, nothing more.

Yr	Tm	W	L	Sv	IP	K	ERA	xERA	WHIP	oOPS	vL	vR	BF/G	Ctl	Dom	Cmd	FpK	SwK	G	L	F	H%	S%	hr/f	GS	APC	DOM%	DIS%	Sv%	LI	RAR	BPV	BPX	R$
11	ATL	7	3	0	142	169	3.68	3.29	1.21	679	707	660	23.6	2.9	10.7	3.7	61%	13%	34	21	45	32%	73%	10%	25	97	60%	12%			4.5	126	190	$9
12	ATL	5	5	0	81	68	2.00	3.96	0.96	507	446	553	24.5	3.2	7.6	2.3	61%	8%	41	18	41	21%	83%	7%	13	102	69%	8%			20.1	68	89	$12
13	ATL *	4	5	0	65	47	4.47	4.44	1.37	705	736	680	20.9	3.5	6.5	1.9	63%	9%	42	17	42	28%	71%	14%	5	90	80%	20%			-4.8	41	54	-$3
14																																		
15	LA *	1	2	0	55	32	4.94	4.94	1.58	952	717	1134	20.2	4.5	5.3	1.2	56%	6%	27	31	42	30%	70%	9%	2	80	0%	100%			-6.6	28	33	-$8
1st Half		1	0	0	11	5	2.00	4.10	1.67				16.5	5.9	3.7	0.6						30%	87%	0%	0						2.7	38	45	-$4
2nd Half		0	2	0	44	28	5.67	5.15	1.56	952	717	1134	21.4	4.2	5.7	1.4	56%	6%	27	31	42	31%	65%	9%	2	80	0%	100%			-9.3	26	31	-$9
16	Proj	3	4	0	73	59	4.48	4.40	1.37	756	766	748	22.7	3.5	7.3	2.1	61%	10%	38	19	43	30%	70%	10%	13						-4.6	53	63	-$3

Bedrosian,Cam

Age:	24	Th:	R	Role	RP	Health	A	LIMA Plan	C		
Ht: 6' 0"		Wt:	205	Type	Pwr	PT/Exp	F	Rand Var	+1		
						Consist	F	MM	2400		

1-0, 5.40 ERA in 33 IP at LAA. Closer bloodlines, but don't hand him the keys to family business just yet. Main issue is poor control (5.1 BB/9 in MLB), which FpK says is no fluke. LHB also tune him up big time. Continued to ring up strikeouts, but SwK even calls sustainabiilty of that into question. A work in progress.

Yr	Tm	W	L	Sv	IP	K	ERA	xERA	WHIP	oOPS	vL	vR	BF/G	Ctl	Dom	Cmd	FpK	SwK	G	L	F	H%	S%	hr/f	GS	APC	DOM%	DIS%	Sv%	LI	RAR	BPV	BPX	R$
11																																		
12																																		
13																																		
14	LAA *	2	2	17	59	78	3.66	2.05	1.10	801	1055	531	4.2	4.0	11.9	3.0	61%	11%	41	21	38	29%	66%	9%	0	24			81	0.67	0.6	139	166	$8
15	LAA *	2	1	3	69	70	3.98	4.14	1.51	833	1047	719	5.2	4.1	9.1	2.2	55%	7%	43	23	34	36%	73%	9%	0	19			60	0.73	-0.1	90	107	-$3
1st Half		1	0	1	38	38	3.51	4.27	1.54	871	1233	641	6.1	3.6	9.0	2.5	61%	7%	46	24	30	38%	76%	7%	0	20			100	0.67	2.1	96	114	-$3
2nd Half		1	1	2	31	32	4.54	3.99	1.48	797	830	783	4.3	4.6	9.2	2.0	51%	8%	40	23	38	33%	69%	11%	0	18			50	0.77	-2.2	84	100	-$2
16	Proj	2	2	0	65	69	4.12	3.81	1.40	664	794	597	4.7	4.2	9.6	2.3	55%	7%	42	23	35	33%	70%	5%	0						-1.2	78	93	-$3

Benoit,Joaquin

Age:	38	Th:	R	Role	RP	Health	A	LIMA Plan	C+		
Ht: 6' 3"		Wt:	220	Type	Pwr FB	PT/Exp	C	Rand Var	-5		
						Consist	A	MM	3410		

Dead arm at end of April/start of May may have contributed to shaky (for him) 1H skills. 2H rebound allays concerns, for now. Couldn't sustain 63% FpK, but he's worked around lower levels in past. Low hit rate unlikely to last, so is he at the precipice of the age-related cliff? Let's say he's toeing the edge.

Yr	Tm	W	L	Sv	IP	K	ERA	xERA	WHIP	oOPS	vL	vR	BF/G	Ctl	Dom	Cmd	FpK	SwK	G	L	F	H%	S%	hr/f	GS	APC	DOM%	DIS%	Sv%	LI	RAR	BPV	BPX	R$
11	DET	4	3	2	61	63	2.95	3.26	1.05	581	639	517	3.7	2.5	9.3	3.7	58%	14%	39	18	43	28%	75%	7%	0	15			29	1.26	7.5	117	175	$6
12	DET	5	3	2	71	84	3.68	3.36	1.14	720	721	720	3.9	2.8	10.6	3.8	58%	18%	36	20	44	28%	78%	18%	0	17			33	1.05	3.0	130	170	$5
13	DET	4	1	24	67	73	2.01	3.17	1.03	575	524	645	4.0	3.0	9.8	3.3	63%	15%	42	20	38	27%	84%	8%	0	16			92	1.19	15.3	117	152	$17
14	SD	4	2	11	54	64	1.49	2.98	0.77	459	480	440	3.9	2.3	10.6	4.6	63%	19%	35	15	50	22%	85%	5%	0	15			92	1.25	15.1	141	168	$13
15	SD	6	5	2	65	63	2.34	3.48	0.90	547	612	471	3.8	3.2	8.7	2.7	54%	17%	46	17	36	19%	81%	12%	0	15			33	1.17	13.1	95	113	$10
1st Half		5	3	1	34	30	2.12	3.72	0.79	464	655	288	3.7	3.4	7.9	2.3	49%	16%	46	13	41	13%	83%	12%	0	15			25	1.24	7.7	74	88	$13
2nd Half		1	2	1	31	33	2.59	3.23	1.02	632	576	714	3.9	2.9	9.5	3.3	58%	18%	47	22	32	26%	79%	12%	0	16			50	1.10	5.3	118	140	$7
16	Proj	4	4	2	65	64	3.17	3.59	1.11	635	657	609	3.9	3.3	8.9	2.7	58%	17%	42	18	40	26%	74%	9%	0						6.4	92	109	$5

Bergman,Christian

Age:	28	Th:	R	Role	RP	Health	D	LIMA Plan	D+		
Ht: 6' 1"		Wt:	180	Type	Con	PT/Exp	D	Rand Var	0		
						Consist	B	MM	0000		

For 22 years, the Rockies have been struggling to find the secret formula for pitching success in the thin Denver air. Keeping the ball OUT of the air is a good thing, so power groundball pitchers offer the best potential. Strikeout rates over 7, ground ball rates over 50%. Yeah, nothing remotely like that here.

Yr	Tm	W	L	Sv	IP	K	ERA	xERA	WHIP	oOPS	vL	vR	BF/G	Ctl	Dom	Cmd	FpK	SwK	G	L	F	H%	S%	hr/f	GS	APC	DOM%	DIS%	Sv%	LI	RAR	BPV	BPX	R$
11																																		
12																																		
13	aa	8	7	0	171	84	4.94	5.76	1.38				26.6	1.4	4.4	3.2						30%	72%								-22.7	29	38	-$8
14	COL *	8	11	0	156	81	5.67	6.04	1.55	902	777	994	25.2	2.0	4.6	2.3	69%	7%	33	25	42	33%	66%	10%	10	89	20%	10%			-37.2	22	27	-$16
15	COL	3	1	0	68	37	4.74	4.63	1.42	827	581	990	9.5	2.0	4.9	2.5	68%	7%	40	24	36	32%	69%	10%	4	37	25%	75%	0	0.78	-6.6	52	62	-$6
1st Half		2	0	0	39	25	4.66	4.29	1.45	840	613	1005	8.6	1.9	5.8	3.1	67%	8%	43	24	33	34%	69%	9%	1	33	0%	100%	0	0.71	-3.3	76	90	-$6
2nd Half		1	1	0	30	12	4.85	5.09	1.38	808	533	970	11.2	2.1	3.6	1.7	68%	6%	36	25	39	30%	68%	10%	3	44	33%	67%	0	0.91	-3.3	22	27	-$5
16	Proj	3	2	0	58	29	5.11	4.77	1.45	857	659	992	14.5	1.9	4.6	2.4	68%	7%	37	25	39	32%	68%	11%	8						-8.2	45	53	-$6

Berrios,Jose

Age:	22	Th:	R	Role	SP	Health	A	LIMA Plan	C+		
Ht: 6' 0"		Wt:	187	Type	Pwr	PT/Exp	F	Rand Var	0		
						Consist	B	MM	3301		

Despite being surprise playoff contender, MIN resisted urge to have him join Sano, Buxton in bigs. He shouldn't have to wait much longer. ERA (2.62), WHIP (0.96), Dom (9.9), Cmd (5.9) actually improved upon promotion to AAA. Young hurlers don't always succeed immediately, but future looks bright.

Yr	Tm	W	L	Sv	IP	K	ERA	xERA	WHIP	oOPS	vL	vR	BF/G	Ctl	Dom	Cmd	FpK	SwK	G	L	F	H%	S%	hr/f	GS	APC	DOM%	DIS%	Sv%	LI	RAR	BPV	BPX	R$
11																																		
12																																		
13																																		
14	a/a	3	5	0	44	27	5.36	3.71	1.35				20.2	3.0	5.5	1.9						31%	58%								-8.7	61	73	-$4
15	a/a	14	5	0	166	148	3.44	3.15	1.15				24.5	2.0	8.0	4.0						31%	71%								10.7	117	139	$15
1st Half		8	3	0	96	81	3.92	3.53	1.25				24.5	2.3	7.6	3.3						32%	69%								0.5	100	119	$13
2nd Half		6	2	0	70	67	2.78	2.64	1.01				24.4	1.6	8.6	5.2						28%	76%								10.2	147	175	$18
16	Proj	7	6	0	87	79	3.91	3.61	1.23				22.7	2.6	8.2	3.1	61%	10%	44	22	34	31%	70%	9%	16						0.6	98	117	$3

Betances,Dellin

Age:	28	Th:	R	Role	RP	Health	A	LIMA Plan	C+		
Ht: 6' 8"		Wt:	260	Type	Pwr	PT/Exp	C	Rand Var	-5		
						Consist	B	MM	5511		

Worthy follow-up to 2014 breakout. Elsewhere, he'd close. In NYY, has rare misfortune of sharing pen with equally skilled hurler, plus manager likes to tap him for 4+ outs. Given history, slippage of FpK, Ctl a bit concerning. But rest of package so lethal, a few extra walks is a mere annoyance. We hope.

Yr	Tm	W	L	Sv	IP	K	ERA	xERA	WHIP	oOPS	vL	vR	BF/G	Ctl	Dom	Cmd	FpK	SwK	G	L	F	H%	S%	hr/f	GS	APC	DOM%	DIS%	Sv%	LI	RAR	BPV	BPX	R$
11	NYY *	4	9	0	129	121	4.81	4.43	1.57	625	611	571	21.0	5.6	8.4	1.5	6%	1%	14	29	57	31%	70%	0%	1	36	0%	100%	0	0.48	-13.8	61	92	-$7
12	a/a	6	9	0	131	102	8.28	7.13	2.11				24.0	7.1	7.0	1.0						37%	60%								-69.1	18	24	-$41
13	NYY *	6	4	5	89	98	4.16	3.25	1.40	965	1339	804	8.5	5.0	9.9	2.0	65%	9%	36	36	29	32%	69%	25%	0	20			100	0.28	-3.3	98	127	$1
14	NYY	5	0	1	90	135	1.40	2.03	0.78	442	405	482	4.9	2.4	13.5	5.6	66%	13%	47	20	33	26%	85%	7%	0	20			20	1.19	26.0	203	242	$18
15	NYY	6	4	9	84	131	1.50	2.44	1.01	510	454	558	4.5	4.3	14.0	3.3	59%	15%	48	21	32	27%	90%	12%	0	19			69	1.42	25.5	163	194	$19
1st Half		5	1	7	42	68	1.50	2.13	0.86	409	359	445	4.4	3.9	14.6	3.8	60%	15%	51	20	29	25%	83%	5%	0	19			78	1.45	12.8	187	222	$24
2nd Half		1	3	2	42	63	1.50	2.75	1.17	608	531	686	4.6	4.7	13.5	2.9	59%	16%	45	21	34	28%	95%	19%	0	18			50	1.40	12.8	139	165	$14
16	Proj	5	3	7	87	122	2.38	2.74	1.11	569	512	624	5.4	4.2	12.6	3.0	62%	15%	47	20	32	29%	81%	10%	0						17.0	139	165	$13

KRISTOPHER OLSON

Bettis,Chad

Age: 27	Th: R	Role RP	Health	C	LIMA Plan	C
Ht: 6' 1"	Wt: 200	Type Pwr	PT/Exp	D	Rand Var	0
			Consist	A	MM	1203

8-6, 4.23 ERA in 115 IP at COL. Emergency rotation member to start year. Managed to keep head above water by keeping ball out of thin air. DOM/DIS speaks to his "not horribleness." Month-long DL stint (elbow) interrupted season-ending run of 8 PQS-DOM in 9 starts. A deep-league consideration, even in COL.

Yr	Tm	W	L	Sv	IP	K	ERA	xERA	WHIP	oOPS	vL	vR	BF/G	Ctl	Dom	Cmd	FpK	SwK	G	L	F	H%	S%	hr/f	GS	APC	DOM%	DIS%	Sv%	LI	RAR	BPV	BPX	R$
11																																		
12																																		
13	COL *	4	7	0	108	82	5.46	5.75	1.54	859	812	906	16.8	2.9	6.9	2.4	61%	8%	47	21	32	34%	69%	12%	8	49	0%	50%	0	0.91	-21.2	38	49	-$11
14	COL *	3	6	3	80	56	5.37	4.87	1.58	1020	901	1138	8.6	3.5	6.3	1.8	50%	6%	46	24	30	35%	65%	14%	0	24			60	0.70	-16.1	53	64	-$8
15	COL *	11	8	0	157	126	4.32	4.84	1.47	771	737	806	24.1	3.2	7.2	2.3	58%	10%	49	22	28	33%	73%	11%	20	94	65%	10%			-6.9	58	69	-$2
1st Half		6	5	0	95	70	4.21	4.73	1.44	704	680	735	25.4	3.0	6.6	2.2	57%	11%	49	22	29	32%	73%	7%	10	100	50%	0%			-2.9	54	64	-$2
2nd Half		5	3	0	62	56	4.21	4.70	1.46	846	814	871	22.1	3.4	8.2	2.4	60%	10%	49	23	28	34%	74%	15%	10	89	80%	20%			-1.9	69	82	-$2
16	Proj	8	9	0	145	113	4.32	4.14	1.49	803	763	844	13.9	3.3	7.0	2.2	60%	9%	48	22	30	33%	73%	11%	18						-6.4	64	77	-$4

Blanton,Joe

Age: 35	Th: R	Role RP	Health	C	LIMA Plan	C+
Ht: 6' 2"	Wt: 220	Type	PT/Exp	D	Rand Var	0
			Consist	A	MM	3300

7-2, 2.84 ERA in 76 IP in KC/PIT. Don't buy into this "revival." 5.30 ERA as SP, 2.04 in pen. Pay those two saves no mind (one in extra innings; one 3 IP). Can't completely dismiss 2H skills, but LI says he took the mound in low leverage situations (i.e. when it didn't matter). ERA may balloon if not handled with such care.

Yr	Tm	W	L	Sv	IP	K	ERA	xERA	WHIP	oOPS	vL	vR	BF/G	Ctl	Dom	Cmd	FpK	SwK	G	L	F	H%	S%	hr/f	GS	APC	DOM%	DIS%	Sv%	LI	RAR	BPV	BPX	R$
11	PHI	1	2	0	41	35	5.01	3.36	1.48	839	791	873	16.4	2.0	7.6	3.9	66%	10%	55	17	28	37%	68%	14%	8	53	25%	50%	0	0.66	-5.4	117	176	-$4
12	2 NL	10	13	0	191	166	4.71	3.61	1.26	759	799	718	26.0	1.6	7.8	4.9	62%	10%	45	23	32	32%	67%	15%	30	94	63%	10%	0	0.83	-16.4	121	157	$2
13	LAA	2	14	0	133	108	6.04	4.14	1.61	904	844	976	21.8	2.3	7.3	3.2	64%	10%	44	22	33	36%	68%	19%	20	79	30%	35%	0	0.69	-35.5	92	119	-$18
14																																		
15	2 TM *	10	4	2	115	100	3.78	4.08	1.24	668	790	558	10.9	2.2	7.8	3.6	62%	13%	49	20	31	31%	74%	11%	4	32	50%	25%	100	0.52	2.7	89	106	$7
1st Half		5	4	0	73	51	4.73	5.04	1.36	758	814	694	17.0	2.3	6.3	2.7	57%	11%	48	18	35	31%	70%	11%	4	49	50%	25%	0	0.45	-6.9	47	55	$1
2nd Half		5	0	2	42	49	2.13	2.75	1.02	593	766	464	6.7	1.9	10.4	5.4	66%	15%	50	22	28	31%	83%	10%	0	25			100	0.56	9.6	163	194	$15
16	Proj	4	3	0	65	57	4.29	3.54	1.32	777	825	730	6.5	2.1	7.9	3.8	63%	11%	48	21	31	33%	72%	15%	0						-2.7	112	133	-$2

Blazek,Michael

Age: 27	Th: R	Role RP	Health	D	LIMA Plan	C+
Ht: 6' 0"	Wt: 200	Type Pwr GB	PT/Exp	D	Rand Var	-5
			Consist	F	MM	1200

In 1H, seemed to be onto something, but Dom, GB rate had already started to erode before mid-August hand fracture ended season prematurely. xERA gives better sense of potential. Cmd finally crept into acceptable rage, but hasn't been entrusted with meaningful work, and at this rate, may never be.

Yr	Tm	W	L	Sv	IP	K	ERA	xERA	WHIP	oOPS	vL	vR	BF/G	Ctl	Dom	Cmd	FpK	SwK	G	L	F	H%	S%	hr/f	GS	APC	DOM%	DIS%	Sv%	LI	RAR	BPV	BPX	R$
11	a/a	13	6	0	146	115	4.84	4.92	1.51				24.3	4.1	7.1	1.7						31%	71%								-16.1	43	65	-$4
12	a/a	5	9	0	83	70	4.73	3.85	1.29				8.2	3.8	7.6	2.0						27%	66%								-7.4	60	79	-$2
13	2 NL *	1	3	9	63	57	3.12	3.04	1.35	759	833	711	4.9	5.5	8.1	1.5	57%	11%	44	11	45	26%	78%	12%	0	19			82	0.56	5.8	76	99	$3
14	aaa	4	4	1	102	72	5.11	5.65	1.66				12.4	3.8	6.3	1.7						35%	71%								-17.2	35	42	-$11
15	MIL	5	3	0	56	47	2.43	3.75	1.04	557	551	561	4.9	2.9	7.6	2.6	62%	11%	47	19	34	25%	78%	6%	0	19			0	0.57	10.6	83	99	$5
1st Half		5	2	0	43	39	1.67	3.39	0.93	457	413	490	4.9	2.9	8.2	2.8	63%	12%	51	19	30	24%	80%	0%	0	19			0	0.53	12.1	97	115	$10
2nd Half		0	1	0	13	8	4.97	4.95	1.42	864	942	795	4.9	2.8	5.7	2.0	62%	6%	37	20	44	28%	73%	17%	0	20			0	0.67	-1.6	40	48	-$9
16	Proj	3	2	0	44	37	4.12	4.16	1.38	664	605	708	6.8	4.0	7.6	1.9	63%	12%	48	20	32	31%	71%	7%	0						-0.9	55	66	-$3

Bolsinger,Michael

Age: 28	Th: R	Role SP	Health	A	LIMA Plan	C
Ht: 6' 2"	Wt: 210	Type Pwr GB	PT/Exp	D	Rand Var	0
			Consist	B	MM	2201

6-6, 3.62 ERA in 109 IP at LA. Through 16 starts, stood at 2.83/3.40 ERA/xERA, then shunted aside in favor of deadline acquisitions. Despite staying on roll in PCL, closed with whimper after Sept recall (PQS 3-0-0-0-0). Nice GB tilt, but FpK, Ctl slip is concerning at an age when he should be consolidating skills and peaking.

Yr	Tm	W	L	Sv	IP	K	ERA	xERA	WHIP	oOPS	vL	vR	BF/G	Ctl	Dom	Cmd	FpK	SwK	G	L	F	H%	S%	hr/f	GS	APC	DOM%	DIS%	Sv%	LI	RAR	BPV	BPX	R$
11																																		
12	aa	4	3	0	78	53	4.85	5.62	1.76				23.7	4.5	6.1	1.4						36%	73%								-8.0	38	50	-$10
13	a/a	11	7	0	144	103	4.72	5.10	1.58				24.4	3.3	6.4	1.9						35%	71%								-15.2	49	64	-$8
14	ARI *	9	9	0	144	118	4.61	4.82	1.49	872	906	843	23.0	3.0	7.4	2.5	67%	9%	52	21	26	35%	70%	16%	9	85	33%	33%	0	0.83	-15.4	68	82	-$6
15	LA *	9	9	0	156	146	3.35	3.52	1.30	705	793	636	20.7	3.6	8.4	2.3	55%	9%	53	18	29	30%	76%	12%	21	85	29%	38%			11.9	84	100	$8
1st Half		6	3	0	86	85	2.77	2.91	1.23	643	739	574	21.8	3.1	8.9	2.8	53%	9%	57	18	25	32%	77%	7%	12	87	33%	25%			12.6	111	132	$15
2nd Half		3	6	0	70	61	4.05	4.27	1.37	797	868	737	19.6	4.2	7.9	1.9	58%	9%	48	17	35	28%	75%	18%	9	81	22%	56%			-0.7	53	63	$0
16	Proj	6	6	0	102	85	4.01	3.86	1.40	734	799	679	21.7	3.4	7.6	2.2	60%	9%	52	19	29	32%	73%	11%	20						-0.6	74	88	-$1

Boxberger,Brad

Age: 28	Th: R	Role RP	Health	A	LIMA Plan	C+
Ht: 6' 2"	Wt: 220	Type Pwr FB	PT/Exp	C	Rand Var	0
			Consist	D	MM	3530

Funny how things change: 2014, elite skills, 2 Sv, underrated; 2015, significant slippage, 41 Sv, overrated? Biggest issue: total unraveling of Ctl gains. Won't be long for role if 2H FpK, Cmd keep up (did June triceps tightness linger?). Was already walking high wire with FB%, hr/f. Could rebound, but feel free to sell short.

Yr	Tm	W	L	Sv	IP	K	ERA	xERA	WHIP	oOPS	vL	vR	BF/G	Ctl	Dom	Cmd	FpK	SwK	G	L	F	H%	S%	hr/f	GS	APC	DOM%	DIS%	Sv%	LI	RAR	BPV	BPX	R$
11	a/a	2	4	11	62	80	2.13	1.63	0.98				4.3	3.8	11.7	3.1						24%	81%								13.9	138	207	$12
12	SD *	2	2	5	71	86	2.43	2.98	1.31	734	820	659	4.8	4.4	11.0	2.5	45%	12%	40	13	46	33%	82%	10%	0	24			71	0.73	13.9	116	152	$6
13	SD *	2	5	6	79	100	3.24	3.28	1.27	760	495	948	5.4	3.4	11.3	3.3	62%	13%	42	17	40	35%	76%	14%	0	22			75	0.66	6.1	125	163	$4
14	TAM	5	2	2	65	104	2.37	2.08	0.84	538	402	659	3.9	2.8	14.5	5.2	67%	15%	41	17	42	24%	82%	19%	0	17			40	1.23	11.0	204	243	$11
15	TAM	4	10	41	63	74	3.71	3.98	1.37	703	657	759	3.9	4.6	10.6	2.3	56%	13%	36	21	43	30%	78%	13%	0	17			87	1.58	1.9	81	96	$17
1st Half		4	4	20	33	45	2.48	3.42	1.29	662	625	700	3.9	4.4	12.4	2.8	60%	13%	37	20	43	32%	87%	13%	0	17			91	1.55	6.0	119	142	$21
2nd Half		0	6	21	30	29	5.04	4.62	1.45	747	687	827	4.0	4.7	8.6	1.8	51%	12%	35	22	42	29%	69%	14%	0	16			84	1.60	-4.0	40	47	$12
16	Proj	3	6	33	58	70	3.32	3.43	1.21	652	582	728	4.1	3.9	10.9	2.8	59%	13%	38	19	42	29%	77%	12%	0						4.6	106	126	$15

Boyd,Matt

Age: 25	Th: L	Role SP	Health	A	LIMA Plan	C
Ht: 6' 3"	Wt: 215	Type xFB	PT/Exp	D	Rand Var	+1
			Consist	F	MM	0201

1-6, 7.53 ERA in 57 IP in TOR/DET. Excelled across two minor-league levels. MLB hitters far more wise to finesse lefty's tricks, feasting on extreme FB% (2.7 HR/9). Did string together three PQS-4s in Sept, but they were bookended by two PQS-0s (3 2/3 IP, 12 ER). No reason to wade into this minefield.

Yr	Tm	W	L	Sv	IP	K	ERA	xERA	WHIP	oOPS	vL	vR	BF/G	Ctl	Dom	Cmd	FpK	SwK	G	L	F	H%	S%	hr/f	GS	APC	DOM%	DIS%	Sv%	LI	RAR	BPV	BPX	R$
11																																		
12																																		
13																																		
14	aa	1	4	0	43	39	8.72	7.05	1.82				19.8	2.8	8.2	2.9						42%	51%								-26.2	56	67	-$13
15	2 AL *	10	8	0	172	128	3.88	3.84	1.18	979	1122	919	21.5	2.5	6.7	2.6	59%	9%	32	16	52	26%	73%	18%	12	77	33%	33%	0	0.74	1.8	61	73	$9
1st Half		7	4	0	92	72	2.53	2.93	1.03	1327	1366	1283	22.2	1.9	7.0	3.6	61%	10%	41	19	41	25%	82%	45%	2	66	0%	50%			16.4	96	113	$22
2nd Half		3	4	0	80	56	5.44	4.90	1.36	918	1033	879	20.8	3.2	6.4	2.0	58%	8%	30	16	54	28%	65%	14%	10	79	40%	30%	0	0.74	-14.6	30	36	-$7
16	Proj	5	8	0	116	94	5.21	4.69	1.38	761	870	724	20.2	2.7	7.3	2.7	58%	8%	30	16	54	31%	65%	8%	24						-17.9	66	79	-$6

Brach,Brad

Age: 30	Th: R	Role RP	Health	A	LIMA Plan	B
Ht: 6' 6"	Wt: 215	Type Pwr	PT/Exp	D	Rand Var	-2
			Consist	B	MM	2401

Frequent multi-inning use resulted in another smattering of vulture wins. On surface, 2H looks better than first, but in reality, he got away with FpK regression, Ctl struggles. Still, he's found useful niche. Should be good for another moderately helpful ERA, handful of Ws.

Yr	Tm	W	L	Sv	IP	K	ERA	xERA	WHIP	oOPS	vL	vR	BF/G	Ctl	Dom	Cmd	FpK	SwK	G	L	F	H%	S%	hr/f	GS	APC	DOM%	DIS%	Sv%	LI	RAR	BPV	BPX	R$
11	SD *	3	7	34	79	91	2.78	2.59	1.11	747	833	709	4.1	2.1	10.4	5.0	53%	13%	26	53	21	34%	75%	0%	0	17			92	1.06	11.3	165	248	$20
12	SD	2	4	0	67	75	3.78	3.97	1.25	674	718	646	4.2	4.5	10.1	2.3	55%	11%	35	20	45	26%	76%	15%	0	17			0	1.17	1.9	75	98	$1
13	SD *	5	3	3	75	67	2.95	4.72	1.52	819	647	972	5.0	3.9	8.0	2.1	54%	9%	38	23	39	34%	84%	9%	0	19			100	0.62	8.5	63	83	$1
14	BAL *	10	2	1	86	86	3.47	3.63	1.30	640	776	543	5.6	3.3	9.1	2.7	58%	13%	36	19	45	32%	75%	8%	0	23			50	0.82	2.9	95	113	$4
15	BAL	5	3	1	79	89	2.72	3.61	1.20	627	534	729	5.2	4.3	10.1	2.3	58%	14%	44	19	36	27%	81%	10%	0	21			50	0.99	12.1	87	104	$7
1st Half		3	2	1	40	46	3.35	3.42	1.09	628	548	722	5.3	3.1	10.3	3.3	62%	16%	38	19	43	28%	73%	10%	0	21			50	0.95	3.1	117	138	$7
2nd Half		2	1	0	39	43	2.08	3.82	1.31	625	515	735	5.2	5.5	9.9	1.8	55%	12%	51	20	29	26%	88%	11%	0	21			0	1.02	9.1	58	68	$6
16	Proj	6	3	0	73	77	3.31	3.75	1.28	670	623	713	5.1	4.0	9.5	2.4	57%	12%	41	20	39	30%	77%	9%	0						5.9	82	98	$3

KRISTOPHER OLSON

Bradley,Archie

Age:	23	Th:	R	Role	SP	Health	F	LIMA Plan	D+
Ht:	6' 4"	Wt:	225	Type	Pwr xGB	PT/Exp	D	Rand Var	0
						Consist	B	MM	1103

2-3, 5.80 ERA in 36 IP at ARI. PQS-4s in first two starts, then things went downhill: a stretch of four PQS-DIS in five starts, then DL by June 4 (shoulder). From there, stops, starts, trips to Dr. James Andrews. Made it back in mid-August for five AAA starts (25 IP, 6 ER, 29/10 K/BB). Time to hit reset button.

Yr	Tm	W	L	Sv	IP	K	ERA	xERA	WHIP	oOPS	vL	vR	BF/G	Ctl	Dom	Cmd	FpK	SwK	G	L	F	H%	S%	hr/f	GS	APC	DOM%	DIS%	Sv%	LI	RAR	BPV	BPX	R$
11																																		
12																																		
13	aa	12	5	0	123	103	2.60	3.41	1.38				24.7	4.4	7.5	1.7						30%	82%								19.3	74	97	$9
14	a/a	3	7	0	79	60	4.76	3.83	1.53				20.2	5.0	6.8	1.3						31%	66%								-9.9	66	78	-$6
15	ARI *	3	3	0	57	40	4.72	4.96	1.57	768	587	985	20.9	4.2	6.3	1.5	55%	6%	58	14	28	32%	71%	10%	8	81	25%	50%			-5.3	40	48	-$6
1st Half		2	3	0	40	26	5.89	4.95	1.62	768	587	985	19.6	5.0	5.8	1.2	55%	6%	58	14	28	31%	64%	10%		81	25%	50%			-9.4	32	38	-$9
2nd Half		1	0	0	17	14	2.05	4.98	1.46				24.7	2.3	7.5	3.2						35%	91%	0%							4.1	78	92	$0
16	Proj	7	7	0	131	100	4.22	4.19	1.49	692	514	906	21.8	4.0	6.9	1.7	55%	6%	58	14	28	32%	72%	8%	26						-4.1	51	61	-$4

Britton,Zach

Age:	28	Th:	L	Role	RP	Health	B	LIMA Plan	C
Ht:	6' 3"	Wt:	195	Type	Pwr xGB	PT/Exp	B	Rand Var	+1
						Consist	F	MM	5330

As good as he was in 2014, 2015 was even better. GB rate is just silly; those 3 HR allowed must have been quite a shock. Has added whiffs to arsenal; SwK says they're here to stay. FpK says same about improved Ctl. LHB in particular have no shot. Maybe he's got one last year of being slightly underappreciated. Ha!

Yr	Tm	W	L	Sv	IP	K	ERA	xERA	WHIP	oOPS	vL	vR	BF/G	Ctl	Dom	Cmd	FpK	SwK	G	L	F	H%	S%	hr/f	GS	APC	DOM%	DIS%	Sv%	LI	RAR	BPV	BPX	R$
11	BAL *	11	14	0	171	112	4.70	4.44	1.45	735	698	748	22.8	3.4	5.9	1.7	53%	7%	53	19	28	31%	68%	9%	28	90	36%	21%			-16.0	46	70	-$3
12	BAL *	10	5	0	124	92	5.34	4.77	1.53	756	714	778	23.4	4.2	6.7	1.6	51%	10%	61	16	23	32%	66%	14%	11	89	45%	45%	0	0.73	-20.2	45	59	-$9
13	BAL *	8	8	0	143	77	5.48	5.89	1.81	837	849	832	24.6	4.2	4.8	1.1	54%	7%	58	20	22	36%	69%	13%	7	83	14%	43%	0	0.75	-28.5	23	31	-$19
14	BAL	3	2	37	76	62	1.65	2.44	0.90	500	386	559	4.0	2.7	7.3	2.7	55%	13%	75	13	12	22%	85%	17%	0	15			90	1.41	19.7	111	133	$24
15	BAL	4	1	36	66	79	1.92	1.75	0.99	547	325	636	4.0	1.9	10.8	5.6	64%	17%	79	11	9	31%	82%	20%	0	14			90	1.17	16.6	200	238	$23
1st Half		0	0	23	35	41	1.82	1.92	1.01	541	284	633	4.0	1.8	10.6	5.9	59%	15%	73	16	10	32%	82%	11%	0	14			96	1.07	9.2	194	230	$24
2nd Half		4	1	13	31	38	2.03	1.55	0.97	554	366	639	3.9	2.0	11.0	5.4	68%	19%	86	6	8	30%	82%	33%	0	14			81	1.28	7.4	208	247	$23
16	Proj	4	2	43	65	63	2.29	2.41	1.03	552	433	604	5.0	2.4	8.6	3.6	59%	13%	74	13	13	28%	79%	13%	0						13.4	142	170	$24

Brooks,Aaron

Age:	26	Th:	R	Role	SP	Health	A	LIMA Plan	C
Ht:	6' 4"	Wt:	220	Type	Con	PT/Exp	D	Rand Var	+3
						Consist	A	MM	1000

3-4, 6.67 ERA in 55 IP at KC/OAK. Befitting pitch-to-contact, finesse style, some days were better than others (see DOM/DIS). Even in minors, he's been somewhat hittable. Whether he starts long-term an open question. He's at least landed in friendly home venues. But search elsewhere for upside.

Yr	Tm	W	L	Sv	IP	K	ERA	xERA	WHIP	oOPS	vL	vR	BF/G	Ctl	Dom	Cmd	FpK	SwK	G	L	F	H%	S%	hr/f	GS	APC	DOM%	DIS%	Sv%	LI	RAR	BPV	BPX	R$
11																																		
12																																		
13	aa	7	7	0	104	54	5.00	4.96	1.36				27.1	1.0	4.7	4.9						33%	65%								-14.5	91	119	-$5
14	KC *	12	4	1	142	79	4.96	5.08	1.45	1764	1657	1825	22.4	1.7	5.0	2.9	71%	10%	38	31	31	34%	67%	20%	1	44	0%	100%	100	0.44	-21.2	58	69	-$6
15	2 AL *	10	9	0	174	120	5.16	5.37	1.50	888	827	942	22.8	1.9	6.2	3.3	63%	8%	43	22	34	36%	67%	14%	9	68	44%	33%	0	0.89	-25.7	68	81	-$11
1st Half		5	4	0	87	64	4.58	5.31	1.53	1000	667	1333	23.7	1.8	6.6	3.7	72%	12%	27	20	53	38%	71%	0%	0	29			0	0.00	-6.6	86	102	-$8
2nd Half		5	5	0	87	56	5.74	5.42	1.47	878	841	911	22.0	2.0	5.8	2.9	62%	8%	45	22	33	34%	63%	16%	9	75	44%	33%	0	1.05	-19.1	51	60	-$13
16	Proj	3	2	0	44	27	4.72	4.32	1.46	749	707	786	23.1	1.7	5.5	3.3	62%	8%	45	22	33	34%	71%	11%	8						-4.1	77	91	-$4

Buchanan,David

Age:	27	Th:	R	Role	SP	Health	A	LIMA Plan	D+
Ht:	6' 3"	Wt:	200	Type	Con	PT/Exp	D	Rand Var	+3
						Consist	C	MM	0000

2-9, 6.99 ERA in 75 IP at PHI. Came off a decent rookie season (3.75 ERA, 61 BPV in MLB) by going SPLAT to start this year (8.76 ERA in 5 starts). Ended 2015 with four starts of 2 ER or less, not that anyone kept the faith that long. Bigger picture: low Dom, worsening Ctl, more LD, LHB killed him. In a word: yuck.

Yr	Tm	W	L	Sv	IP	K	ERA	xERA	WHIP	oOPS	vL	vR	BF/G	Ctl	Dom	Cmd	FpK	SwK	G	L	F	H%	S%	hr/f	GS	APC	DOM%	DIS%	Sv%	LI	RAR	BPV	BPX	R$
11																																		
12	aa	3	5	0	72	34	4.38	4.72	1.44				25.7	2.8	4.3	1.5						30%	71%								-3.2	27	35	-$5
13	a/a	10	13	0	170	91	5.07	5.06	1.51				26.2	2.8	4.8	1.7						32%	68%								-25.2	30	40	-$11
14	PHI *	12	10	0	175	110	4.03	4.59	1.44	721	592	820	23.2	2.8	5.7	2.0	57%	8%	51	19	30	32%	73%	11%	20	91	50%	20%			-6.1	51	60	-$2
15	PHI *	6	11	0	129	69	5.55	6.36	1.78	965	1043	893	23.8	3.5	4.8	1.4	62%	8%	47	24	28	36%	70%	16%	15	82	13%	47%			-25.3	16	19	-$19
1st Half		2	5	0	46	24	6.20	6.33	1.86	917	826	982	23.9	3.8	4.6	1.2	61%	7%	48	20	32	37%	66%	7%	5	88	0%	60%			-12.7	21	25	-$21
2nd Half		4	6	0	83	45	5.19	6.37	1.74	986	1125	843	23.8	3.4	4.9	1.4	62%	8%	47	26	27	35%	73%	20%	10	79	20%	40%			-12.6	13	15	-$18
16	Proj	2	3	0	44	24	5.22	4.75	1.62	847	841	852	24.2	3.2	5.0	1.6	60%	8%	49	22	29	34%	69%	10%	8						-6.7	31	37	-$7

Buchholz,Clay

Age:	31	Th:	R	Role	SP	Health	F	LIMA Plan	B
Ht:	6' 3"	Wt:	190	Type	Pwr	PT/Exp	B	Rand Var	0
						Consist	B	MM	2203

Career year, demonstrating all the assets that we've been waiting for, along with the obligatory injury (elbow this time) so his owners wouldn't enjoy it too much. You can see the evidence of skill throughout, and FpK validates Ctl gains. The checklist: draft cheap, expect little, be pleasantly surprised, backfill innings.

Yr	Tm	W	L	Sv	IP	K	ERA	xERA	WHIP	oOPS	vL	vR	BF/G	Ctl	Dom	Cmd	FpK	SwK	G	L	F	H%	S%	hr/f	GS	APC	DOM%	DIS%	Sv%	LI	RAR	BPV	BPX	R$
11	BOS	6	3	0	83	60	3.48	4.16	1.29	706	706	706	25.2	3.4	6.5	1.9	56%	9%	51	11	39	28%	77%	10%	14	97	43%	21%			4.7	55	83	$3
12	BOS	11	8	0	189	129	4.56	4.27	1.33	757	761	751	27.7	3.0	6.1	2.0	63%	9%	48	20	33	29%	69%	13%	29	100	52%	21%			-12.8	54	71	$0
13	BOS	12	1	0	108	96	1.74	3.31	1.02	546	536	560	26.0	3.0	8.0	2.7	60%	10%	48	21	32	25%	84%	5%	16	102	69%	0%			28.3	89	116	$18
14	BOS	8	11	0	170	132	5.34	3.99	1.39	751	793	696	26.3	2.9	7.0	2.4	60%	9%	47	19	34	32%	62%	9%	28	98	57%	21%			-33.5	74	88	-$9
15	BOS	7	7	0	113	107	3.26	3.36	1.21	664	610	725	26.1	1.8	8.5	4.7	65%	11%	48	21	31	34%	73%	6%	18	95	72%	22%			9.9	130	154	$7
1st Half		7	6	0	110	104	3.27	3.32	1.19	652	608	698	26.6	1.9	8.5	4.5	65%	11%	49	21	30	33%	72%	5%	17	97	76%	18%			9.4	130	154	$8
2nd Half		0	1	0	3	3	2.70	4.60	1.80	1000	643	3500	16.0	0.0	8.1	0.0	71%	8%	23	31	46	44%	100%	17%	1	59	0%	100%			0.5	147	174	-$18
16	Proj	11	6	0	160	133	3.52	3.67	1.22	669	664	676	25.9	2.7	7.5	2.8	61%	10%	48	19	33	30%	72%	8%	25						8.7	89	106	$10

Buehrle,Mark

Age:	37	Th:	L	Role	SP	Health	A	LIMA Plan	B
Ht:	6' 2"	Wt:	240	Type	Con	PT/Exp	A	Rand Var	0
						Consist	A	MM	1005

Pitched "only" 199 IP, the horror! Dom hit new low, especially in 2H, as left shoulder needed cortisone, a rare brush with fragility. Left off playoff roster, and retirement could be looming. If he goes, we'll miss his annual 13 wins, 200 IP, ERA in the high 3s for decade-plus, one of easiest projections in book.

Yr	Tm	W	L	Sv	IP	K	ERA	xERA	WHIP	oOPS	vL	vR	BF/G	Ctl	Dom	Cmd	FpK	SwK	G	L	F	H%	S%	hr/f	GS	APC	DOM%	DIS%	Sv%	LI	RAR	BPV	BPX	R$
11	CHW	13	9	0	205	109	3.59	4.22	1.30	728	683	746	27.7	2.0	4.8	2.4	56%	7%	45	20	35	30%	75%	9%	31	101	45%	10%			8.8	56	84	$8
12	MIA	13	13	0	202	125	3.74	4.19	1.17	710	645	731	26.7	1.8	5.6	3.1	61%	8%	41	22	36	28%	73%	11%	31	99	55%	13%			6.9	71	93	$13
13	TOR	12	10	0	204	139	4.15	4.11	1.35	754	724	764	26.5	2.3	6.1	2.7	59%	7%	45	21	34	31%	72%	11%	33	100	45%	18%			-7.2	73	95	$2
14	TOR	13	10	0	202	119	3.39	4.21	1.36	743	718	752	26.8	2.0	5.3	2.6	59%	6%	44	23	34	32%	76%	7%	32	96	38%	13%			8.8	62	74	$5
15	TOR	15	8	0	199	91	3.81	4.48	1.24	751	794	736	25.8	1.5	4.1	2.8	61%	5%	46	21	33	29%	72%	10%	32	88	34%	13%			3.8	58	69	$8
1st Half		9	4	0	106	57	3.64	4.23	1.19	727	823	688	27.2	1.7	4.8	2.9	63%	6%	48	20	32	28%	73%	11%	16	94	44%	6%			4.2	67	80	$14
2nd Half		6	4	0	92	34	4.00	4.76	1.30	778	753	785	24.5	1.3	3.3	2.6	60%	5%	44	22	34	30%	72%	9%	16	83	25%	19%			-0.4	47	56	$3
16	Proj	13	9	0	189	99	3.86	4.29	1.29	750	746	751	25.5	1.8	4.7	2.7	60%	6%	45	22	34	30%	73%	9%	30						2.4	60	72	$5

Bumgarner,Madison

Age:	26	Th:	L	Role	SP	Health	A	LIMA Plan	D+
Ht:	6' 5"	Wt:	235	Type	Pwr	PT/Exp	A	Rand Var	0
						Consist	A	MM	5405

Those who withheld extra buck based on 2014 workload (regular + post-season) lost that wager. 2015 was in many ways a carbon copy. OK, traded a few GB for LD, but also incremental gains in Ctl, Dom. Fun fact: Only PQS-DIS came April 11. Even got the month of October off this year. This time, go that extra dollar.

Yr	Tm	W	L	Sv	IP	K	ERA	xERA	WHIP	oOPS	vL	vR	BF/G	Ctl	Dom	Cmd	FpK	SwK	G	L	F	H%	S%	hr/f	GS	APC	DOM%	DIS%	Sv%	LI	RAR	BPV	BPX	R$
11	SF	13	13	0	205	191	3.21	3.25	1.21	670	602	685	25.6	2.0	8.4	4.2	62%	10%	46	21	33	33%	74%	6%	33	97	70%	15%			18.5	121	181	$17
12	SF	16	11	0	208	191	3.37	3.44	1.11	670	581	694	26.5	2.1	8.3	3.9	62%	10%	48	19	33	29%	74%	12%	32	102	66%	13%			16.6	117	153	$23
13	SF	13	9	0	201	199	2.77	3.25	1.03	577	487	602	25.9	2.8	8.9	3.2	60%	11%	47	18	35	26%	76%	8%	31	103	81%	6%			27.2	110	144	$26
14	SF	18	10	0	217	219	2.98	3.08	1.09	653	539	684	26.5	1.8	9.1	5.1	66%	12%	44	20	36	31%	76%	10%	33	102	67%	12%			20.4	137	163	$23
15	SF	18	9	0	218	234	2.93	3.10	1.01	612	539	627	27.2	1.6	9.6	6.0	64%	13%	42	23	36	30%	75%	10%	32	104	72%	3%			27.9	150	179	$32
1st Half		8	5	0	113	114	3.34	3.32	1.08	654	625	659	26.8	1.7	9.1	5.4	67%	13%	40	23	37	30%	73%	11%	17	101	71%	6%			8.8	136	162	$27
2nd Half		10	4	0	105	120	2.49	2.87	0.93	565	461	590	27.5	1.5	10.3	6.7	61%	13%	43	22	35	29%	77%	9%	15	107	73%	0%			19.1	165	195	$38
16	Proj	17	9	0	218	227	2.90	3.01	1.03	617	527	639	25.8	1.8	9.4	5.2	64%	12%	44	21	35	30%	75%	10%	33						28.4	142	169	$29

KRISTOPHER OLSON

Bundy,Dylan

Age: 23	Th: R	Role SP	Health F	LIMA Plan C+
Ht: 6' 1"	Wt: 195	Type Pwr	PT/Exp F	Rand Var +5
			Consist F	MM 3301

Injuries continue to delay top prospect's arrival, with TJS erasing nearly all of 2013-14, and shoulder issue ending 2015 in May. Skills were strong in small sample, long-term upside remains high, but can he stay healthy? Likely to be handled with care, so don't count on him making major impact this season.

Yr Tm	W	L	Sv	IP	K	ERA	xERA	WHIP	oOPS	vL	vR	BF/G	Ctl	Dom	Cmd	FpK	SwK	G	L	F	H%	S%	hr/f	GS	APC	DOM%	DIS%	Sv%	LI	RAR	BPV	BPX	R$
11																																	
12 BAL *	2	0	0	18	11	3.40	3.57	1.37	533	1000	250	15.4	4.3	5.6	1.3	50%	10%	20	0	80	27%	76%	0%	0	15			0	0.40	1.4	51	66	-$3
13																																	
14																																	
15 aa	0	3	0	22	21	4.86	3.72	1.39				11.6	2.2	8.6	3.9						38%	61%								-2.4	131	156	-$5
1st Half	0	3	0	22	21	4.86	3.72	1.39				11.6	2.2	8.6	3.9						38%	61%								-2.4	131	155	-$5
2nd Half																																	
16 Proj	4	4	0	87	83	3.54	3.49	1.19				22.1	2.6	8.6	3.4	62%	9%	44	20	36	31%	72%	8%	31						4.6	108	129	$3

Burgos,Enrique

Age: 25	Th: R	Role RP	Health B	LIMA Plan D+
Ht: 6' 3"	Wt: 250	Type Pwr FB	PT/Exp F	Rand Var +1
			Consist F	MM 1510

2-2, 4.67 ERA in 27 IP at ARI. Struck out 25 in just 13 2/3 IP before landing on DL with sore shoulder. Dom remained the same upon return, but so did Ctl, an issue that's plagued him throughout his career. Power arm is enticing, but until he can cut down on free passes, he'll be a ratio killer unlikely to see the 9th.

Yr Tm	W	L	Sv	IP	K	ERA	xERA	WHIP	oOPS	vL	vR	BF/G	Ctl	Dom	Cmd	FpK	SwK	G	L	F	H%	S%	hr/f	GS	APC	DOM%	DIS%	Sv%	LI	RAR	BPV	BPX	R$
11																																	
12																																	
13																																	
14																																	
15 ARI *	2	3	13	51	70	4.51	5.15	1.73	709	822	629	4.2	6.1	12.2	2.0	55%	16%	34	27	39	39%	76%	8%	0	17			76	1.00	-3.5	88	105	-$1
1st Half	1	2	8	28	42	2.54	2.90	1.40	639	937	419	4.1	5.9	13.4	2.3	58%	16%	43	23	35	35%	82%	7%	0	18			89	1.27	5.0	132	156	$4
2nd Half	1	1	5	23	28	6.94	8.08	2.17	847	564	1014	4.4	6.6	10.8	1.6	49%	14%	22	33	44	43%	71%	8%	0	15			63	0.54	-8.5	35	41	-$8
16 Proj	2	2	2	45	55	4.43	4.23	1.55	631	941	398	4.0	6.4	11.1	1.7	58%	16%	40	23	38	33%	72%	7%	0						-2.6	45	53	-$3

Butler,Eddie

Age: 25	Th: R	Role SP	Health C	LIMA Plan D
Ht: 6' 2"	Wt: 180	Type	PT/Exp D	Rand Var +3
			Consist F	MM 0001

3-10, 5.90 ERA in 79 IP at COL. Throws hard and keeps the ball down, but there is little reason for optimism right now. FWIW, Greg Maddux was 6-14 with a 5.61 ERA and 1.4 Cmd in his first season, which is just our little way to give long-suffering Rockies fans some hope. Not that there's any other real comparison.

Yr Tm	W	L	Sv	IP	K	ERA	xERA	WHIP	oOPS	vL	vR	BF/G	Ctl	Dom	Cmd	FpK	SwK	G	L	F	H%	S%	hr/f	GS	APC	DOM%	DIS%	Sv%	LI	RAR	BPV	BPX	R$
11																																	
12																																	
13 aa	1	0	0	28	20	0.90	0.70	0.80				16.7	2.1	6.5	3.2						21%	88%								10.1	127	165	$2
14 COL *	7	11	0	129	57	5.08	5.24	1.52	973	1310	760	25.5	3.0	4.0	1.3	49%	5%	52	25	23	31%	68%	13%	3	86	0%	67%			-21.4	16	19	-$11
15 COL *	5	16	0	143	73	6.28	6.39	1.78	952	1073	831	24.3	4.3	4.6	1.1	57%	7%	50	22	28	33%	66%	17%	16	85	6%	44%			-40.8	3	3	-$25
1st Half	4	8	0	81	41	5.98	6.55	1.88	915	959	867	23.9	4.7	4.5	1.0	55%	7%	51	24	26	35%	69%	15%	11	85	9%	45%			-20.2	6	7	-$27
2nd Half	1	8	0	61	33	6.68	6.18	1.65	1032	1354	757	24.9	3.7	4.8	1.3	59%	8%	48	19	33	31%	62%	21%	5	84	0%	40%			-20.6	0	0	-$23
16 Proj	3	8	0	73	40	5.27	4.93	1.65	906	1074	748	24.9	3.6	4.9	1.3	58%	8%	49	21	30	33%	71%	13%	13						-11.7	17	21	-$10

Cahill,Trevor

Age: 28	Th: R	Role RP	Health B	LIMA Plan C
Ht: 6' 4"	Wt: 220	Type Pwr xGB	PT/Exp D	Rand Var +5
			Consist A	MM 3310

1-3, 5.40 ERA in 36 IP at ATL/CHC. Though GB% returned, Dom, SwK, and FpK all tanked in disastrous 1H. With relief role on new team, flashed best velocity of career in Sept/Oct, more changeups (35% SwK), and 11.6 Dom. Sample too small to erase recent struggles from memory, but can't be written off just yet.

Yr Tm	W	L	Sv	IP	K	ERA	xERA	WHIP	oOPS	vL	vR	BF/G	Ctl	Dom	Cmd	FpK	SwK	G	L	F	H%	S%	hr/f	GS	APC	DOM%	DIS%	Sv%	LI	RAR	BPV	BPX	R$
11 OAK	12	14	0	208	147	4.16	3.88	1.43	738	754	720	26.5	3.6	6.4	1.8	57%	8%	56	19	25	31%	72%	12%	34	100	47%	26%			-5.6	53	79	$1
12 ARI	13	12	0	200	156	3.78	3.60	1.29	706	696	718	26.2	3.3	7.0	2.1	63%	10%	61	16	23	29%	72%	12%	32	99	59%	19%			5.8	75	98	$9
13 ARI *	8	12	0	163	112	4.18	4.16	1.43	745	769	719	23.9	4.0	6.2	1.5	60%	8%	56	20	24	29%	72%	12%	25	91	28%	16%	0	0.85	-6.3	47	61	-$3
14 ARI *	5	14	1	139	126	5.21	4.77	1.58	791	929	657	16.1	4.8	8.2	1.7	57%	11%	48	24	27	33%	67%	10%	17	60	18%	47%	50	0.67	-25.2	60	72	-$11
15 2 NL *	2	6	0	80	55	5.75	4.86	1.56	725	684	751	9.4	3.9	6.2	1.6	59%	10%	63	19	18	33%	63%	17%	3	26	0%	67%	0	0.63	-17.6	44	52	-$11
1st Half	0	3	0	26	14	7.52	4.62	1.78	843	855	834	8.3	3.8	4.8	1.3	55%	7%	64	20	17	36%	56%	13%	3	30	0%	67%	0	0.40	-11.6	26	31	-$18
2nd Half	2	3	0	53	41	4.87	4.31	1.44	494	255	613	10.3	4.0	6.9	1.7	67%	16%	62	18	21	30%	67%	29%	0	21			0	0.95	-6.0	53	63	-$7
16 Proj	3	3	1	53	49	3.93	3.65	1.38	713	728	700	7.3	4.1	8.4	2.0	60%	11%	56	20	24	31%	73%	13%	0						0.2	73	87	-$2

Cain,Matt

Age: 31	Th: R	Role SP	Health F	LIMA Plan C
Ht: 6' 3"	Wt: 230	Type	PT/Exp B	Rand Var +1
			Consist B	MM 1103

2-4, 5.79 ERA in 61 IP at SF. Strained flexor tendon at end of spring training wiped out 1H, and was shell of former self when he came back. Velocity reached career low, and Dom followed suit. No longer has durability and low hr/f going for him. Looks like longshot to stay healthy or productive, much less both.

Yr Tm	W	L	Sv	IP	K	ERA	xERA	WHIP	oOPS	vL	vR	BF/G	Ctl	Dom	Cmd	FpK	SwK	G	L	F	H%	S%	hr/f	GS	APC	DOM%	DIS%	Sv%	LI	RAR	BPV	BPX	R$
11 SF	12	11	0	222	179	2.88	3.71	1.08	597	523	674	27.5	2.6	7.3	2.8	61%	10%	42	19	39	27%	73%	4%	33	106	73%	3%			29.0	82	123	$24
12 SF	16	5	0	219	193	2.79	3.71	1.04	635	711	563	27.4	2.1	7.9	3.8	62%	10%	37	21	42	27%	77%	8%	32	105	63%	0%			33.1	101	132	$32
13 SF	8	10	0	184	158	4.00	3.87	1.16	678	644	704	25.3	2.7	7.7	2.9	63%	9%	38	22	40	27%	69%	11%	30	97	53%	13%			-3.1	82	107	$8
14 SF	2	7	0	90	70	4.18	3.96	1.25	725	737	713	24.9	3.2	7.0	2.2	62%	9%	45	19	36	27%	71%	14%	15	96	53%	13%			-4.9	62	74	-$2
15 SF *	3	6	0	84	59	5.45	5.42	1.48	897	960	840	19.0	2.8	6.3	2.3	59%	9%	36	24	40	32%	66%	15%	11	76	27%	45%	0	0.68	-15.4	37	44	-$9
1st Half	1	3	0	24	16	6.23	6.03	1.65	1107	1250	1000	21.7	3.6	6.0	1.6	56%	4%	47	21	32	33%	64%	33%	1	89	0%	100%			-6.8	20	23	-$13
2nd Half	2	3	0	60	43	5.13	5.17	1.41	877	935	823	18.0	2.4	6.4	2.7	59%	10%	35	24	41	32%	68%	13%	10	75	30%	40%	0	0.66	-8.6	47	56	-$7
16 Proj	5	10	0	145	109	4.73	4.30	1.34	791	809	775	24.3	2.9	6.8	2.3	61%	10%	39	22	40	30%	68%	12%	22						-13.7	61	72	-$4

Caminero,Arquimedes

Age: 29	Th: R	Role RP	Health A	LIMA Plan B+
Ht: 6' 4"	Wt: 250	Type Pwr GB	PT/Exp D	Rand Var 0
			Consist F	MM 3300

Got lots of swings and misses in 1H, but after rough July, dramatically changed approach. Introduced sinker that he used on a third of his pitches rest of way, fueling huge GB% jump. Worked at first (163 Aug BPV), but faltered down stretch. Whatever his pitch mix, he makes a somewhat intriguing end-game flyer.

Yr Tm	W	L	Sv	IP	K	ERA	xERA	WHIP	oOPS	vL	vR	BF/G	Ctl	Dom	Cmd	FpK	SwK	G	L	F	H%	S%	hr/f	GS	APC	DOM%	DIS%	Sv%	LI	RAR	BPV	BPX	R$
11																																	
12 aa	0	0	2	18	15	3.88	4.47	1.74				6.7	5.8	7.5	1.3						36%	75%								0.3	71	93	-$5
13 MIA *	6	2	5	67	66	4.30	2.93	1.18	603	841	422	4.8	3.5	8.9	2.5	54%	10%	25	17	58	27%	64%	10%	0	16			63	0.51	-3.6	93	121	$3
14 MIA *	4	2	10	70	68	5.81	5.91	1.75	943	583	1093	6.6	4.4	8.8	2.0	56%	16%	37	5	58	38%	67%	18%	0	19			83	0.97	-17.8	58	69	-$7
15 PIT	5	1	0	75	73	3.62	3.67	1.23	661	681	649	4.4	3.5	8.8	2.5	62%	13%	48	24	29	29%	73%	12%	0	15			0	0.86	3.2	90	107	$2
1st Half	0	1	0	36	40	3.96	3.66	1.24	668	689	654	4.2	3.2	9.9	3.1	60%	15%	39	23	38	31%	71%	11%	0	15			0	0.95	0.0	108	128	-$2
2nd Half	5	0	0	38	33	3.29	3.67	1.23	656	673	644	4.6	3.8	7.7	2.1	64%	11%	55	24	21	27%	75%	13%	0	16			0	0.78	3.2	71	85	$6
16 Proj	4	2	0	65	63	3.90	3.67	1.35	700	719	689	4.9	3.8	8.7	2.3	63%	13%	49	24	28	31%	72%	11%	0						0.5	80	95	-$1

Capps,Carter

Age: 25	Th: R	Role RP	Health F	LIMA Plan A+
Ht: 6' 4"	Wt: 230	Type Pwr	PT/Exp D	Rand Var -4
			Consist B	MM 5510

1-0, 1.16 ERA in 31 IP. Arsenal includes fastball that touches triple digits, filthy curve that generated 41% SwK. Made huge gains in FpK as well, which bodes well for Ctl. Elbow issues cost him significant time for second straight year, but if it holds, could be on fast track to closer role. UP: Another sub-2.00 ERA, 25 SV

Yr Tm	W	L	Sv	IP	K	ERA	xERA	WHIP	oOPS	vL	vR	BF/G	Ctl	Dom	Cmd	FpK	SwK	G	L	F	H%	S%	hr/f	GS	APC	DOM%	DIS%	Sv%	LI	RAR	BPV	BPX	R$
11																																	
12 SEA *	2	3	19	76	96	2.13	2.58	1.17	667	798	552	5.3	2.6	11.3	4.3	55%	12%	41	28	32	35%	81%	0%	0	26			90	0.50	17.7	160	209	$15
13 SEA	3	3	0	59	66	5.49	3.79	1.63	878	1029	776	5.1	3.5	10.1	2.9	60%	13%	40	24	36	38%	71%	19%	0	20			0	1.05	-11.8	104	136	-$8
14 MIA	0	0	0	20	25	3.98	3.11	1.18	610	836	434	5.1	2.2	11.1	5.0	58%	14%	36	21	43	36%	65%	4%	0	21			0	0.44	-0.6	153	183	-$2
15 MIA *	1	2	3	46	70	1.57	1.87	1.05	474	444	500	4.1	3.5	13.7	3.9	66%	26%	41	20	39	32%	87%	11%	0	15			50	1.19	13.6	170	202	$6
1st Half	1	0	0	23	44	1.57	1.51	0.78	496	470	517	4.4	2.0	17.2	8.8	67%	27%	43	20	37	35%	88%	15%	0	16			0	0.98	6.8	278	330	$9
2nd Half	0	0	0	8	14	0.00	1.97	0.88	412	368	450	3.0	2.3	15.8	7.0	61%	21%	36	21	43	37%	100%	0%	0	12			0	1.60	3.9	236	281	$3
16 Proj	2	1	2	48	69	2.58	2.43	1.02	562	582	547	4.6	2.6	13.1	5.0	64%	21%	42	21	37	33%	77%	9%	0						8.1	185	220	$5

BRIAN RUDD

Carrasco,Carlos

Age: 29	Th: R	Role SP	
Ht: 6' 3"	Wt: 210	Type Pwr GB	
Health	D	LIMA Plan	C+
PT/Exp	B	Rand Var	+2
Consist	C	MM	5505

ERA doesn't show it, but strong encore to 2014 breakout. Handled IP jump just fine; high GB%, swing-and-miss stuff are now well-established, and FpK says pinpoint Ctl is legit. Hit DL late in year with sore shoulder, but returned with 15.1 Dom in Sept. Hard to find a flaw in these metrics; so don't hesitate to bid full value.

Yr Tm	W	L	Sv	IP	K	ERA	xERA	WHIP	oOPS	vL	vR	BF/G	Ctl	Dom	Cmd	FpK	SwK	G	L	F	H%	S%	hr/f	GS	APC	DOM%	DIS%	Sv%	LI	RAR	BPV	BPX	R$
11 CLE	8	9	0	125	85	4.62	4.08	1.36	754	888	600	25.5	2.9	6.1	2.1	58%	9%	49	17	34	30%	68%	11%	21	94	52%	24%			-10.4	59	89	-$1
12																																	
13 CLE *	4	5	1	118	94	5.15	4.76	1.50	864	980	745	16.5	3.1	7.2	2.3	67%	9%	50	22	28	35%	66%	9%	7	52	14%	86%	100	0.59	-18.8	64	83	-$9
14 CLE	8	7	1	134	140	2.55	2.73	0.99	543	516	566	13.2	1.9	9.4	4.8	63%	14%	53	20	28	29%	75%	7%	14	49	71%	7%	100	0.63	19.6	148	176	$17
15 CLE	14	12	0	184	216	3.63	2.75	1.07	646	639	651	24.3	2.1	10.6	5.0	67%	14%	51	19	30	31%	69%	13%	30	93	70%	23%			7.6	163	194	$19
1st Half	10	6	0	97	110	3.88	2.95	1.14	687	592	747	24.6	1.9	10.2	5.2	67%	14%	48	20	32	33%	68%	11%	16	94	69%	19%			0.9	157	186	$20
2nd Half	4	6	0	86	106	3.34	2.52	1.00	597	680	503	24.0	2.3	11.1	4.8	67%	15%	55	18	27	29%	70%	16%	14	91	71%	29%			6.7	170	201	$18
16 Proj	15	10	0	203	224	3.25	2.81	1.08	624	664	587	24.0	2.2	9.9	4.5	65%	13%	52	19	29	30%	73%	12%	33						17.7	148	176	$23

Cashner,Andrew

Age: 29	Th: R	Role SP	
Ht: 6' 6"	Wt: 220	Type Pwr	
Health	F	LIMA Plan	C
PT/Exp	A	Rand Var	+2
Consist	A	MM	3205

Regression was expected, but not this much. PRO: Career high IP; Dom spiked; BPV remained fairly stable. CON: Ctl waned; Cmd dipped to 1.5 vs. LHB (who had their way with him); posted ugly 4.74 ERA, 1.7 Cmd in 17 road starts. Mild rebound likely, but he's nothing more than a mid-range SP at this point.

Yr Tm	W	L	Sv	IP	K	ERA	xERA	WHIP	oOPS	vL	vR	BF/G	Ctl	Dom	Cmd	FpK	SwK	G	L	F	H%	S%	hr/f	GS	APC	DOM%	DIS%	Sv%	LI	RAR	BPV	BPX	R$
11 CHC	0	0	0	11	8	1.69	3.29	0.66	351	167	440	5.6	3.4	6.8	2.0	56%	11%	59	7	33	8%	83%	11%	1	21	0%	0%	0	0.56	3.0	67	101	-$1
12 SD *	5	5	0	70	77	3.58	3.15	1.22	688	525	815	7.2	3.1	9.9	3.2	55%	13%	53	23	24	32%	72%	17%	5	24	40%	60%	0	1.25	3.7	116	151	$3
13 SD	10	9	0	175	128	3.09	3.56	1.13	639	703	578	22.8	2.4	6.6	2.7	60%	9%	53	19	29	28%	74%	8%	26	87	65%	12%	0	0.73	16.8	84	110	$14
14 SD	5	7	0	123	93	2.55	3.60	1.13	623	675	573	26.6	2.1	6.8	3.2	63%	8%	48	20	31	29%	79%	6%	19	95	63%	11%			18.1	91	108	$10
15 SD	6	16	0	185	165	4.34	3.95	1.44	772	896	669	25.9	3.2	8.0	2.5	62%	9%	47	23	30	34%	72%	12%	31	100	48%	19%			-8.5	83	99	-$4
1st Half	3	9	0	102	92	4.06	3.90	1.39	782	915	669	25.9	2.8	8.1	2.9	60%	9%	47	20	33	33%	74%	13%	17	99	53%	18%			-1.2	95	113	-$1
2nd Half	3	7	0	83	73	4.68	4.03	1.50	759	871	669	26.0	3.7	7.9	2.1	63%	8%	47	27	26	34%	69%	9%	14	102	43%	21%			-7.3	68	81	-$7
16 Proj	9	12	0	181	155	3.68	3.67	1.30	701	765	645	24.7	2.9	7.7	2.7	61%	9%	49	22	29	31%	73%	9%	30						6.3	88	104	$6

Casilla,Santiago

Age: 35	Th: R	Role RP	
Ht: 6' 0"	Wt: 210	Type Pwr GB	
Health	D	LIMA Plan	C
PT/Exp	B	Rand Var	-2
Consist	B	MM	3320

SwK had previously hinted at potential for higher Dom—it started to come around in 2H of 2014 (8.3), and continued to rise. But FpK is still a struggle, so Ctl from 2014 looks like an anomaly. Metrics solid, but not elite, and combined with age and lack of track record, make his saves far from a sure thing.

Yr Tm	W	L	Sv	IP	K	ERA	xERA	WHIP	oOPS	vL	vR	BF/G	Ctl	Dom	Cmd	FpK	SwK	G	L	F	H%	S%	hr/f	GS	APC	DOM%	DIS%	Sv%	LI	RAR	BPV	BPX	R$
11 SF	2	2	6	52	45	1.74	3.60	1.12	534	632	481	4.3	4.4	7.8	1.8	48%	12%	52	20	29	24%	84%	3%	0	17			86	0.95	14.0	54	80	$7
12 SF	7	6	25	63	55	2.84	3.78	1.22	656	727	608	3.7	3.1	7.8	2.5	53%	10%	55	15	30	28%	83%	14%	0	14			81	1.37	9.2	89	116	$15
13 SF	7	2	2	50	38	2.16	4.03	1.28	627	652	611	3.6	4.5	6.8	1.5	54%	10%	54	17	29	26%	84%	5%	0	14			67	1.66	10.5	34	44	$4
14 SF	3	3	19	58	45	1.70	3.07	0.86	493	539	461	4.0	2.3	6.9	3.0	57%	11%	56	15	29	21%	83%	7%	0	16			83	1.37	14.7	96	115	$15
15 SF	4	2	38	58	62	2.79	3.51	1.28	680	841	531	3.6	3.6	9.6	2.7	57%	11%	46	24	30	31%	82%	13%	0	14			86	1.47	8.4	101	120	$18
1st Half	4	2	20	30	30	3.03	3.87	1.35	741	1056	518	3.7	3.6	9.1	2.5	56%	11%	45	20	35	31%	83%	14%	0	14			83	1.50	3.4	88	105	$19
2nd Half	0	0	18	28	32	2.54	3.13	1.20	613	665	549	3.6	3.5	10.2	2.9	58%	11%	49	28	24	30%	81%	12%	0	14			90	1.44	5.0	115	137	$17
16 Proj	3	2	25	44	41	2.97	3.52	1.24	661	768	575	3.8	3.4	8.4	2.5	56%	11%	51	20	29	30%	78%	9%	0						5.3	88	105	$10

Cecil,Brett

Age: 29	Th: L	Role RP	
Ht: 6' 3"	Wt: 220	Type Pwr GB	
Health	B	LIMA Plan	A
PT/Exp	C	Rand Var	0
Consist	A	MM	5510

After string of rough outings in June pushed ERA up to 5.96, was removed from closer role. From that point on, didn't allow another ER, as FpK surged and Dom, SwK returned to 2014 levels. May have ruined his chances for further ninth inning work, and FpK hints at Ctl regression, but ratios should remain strong.

Yr Tm	W	L	Sv	IP	K	ERA	xERA	WHIP	oOPS	vL	vR	BF/G	Ctl	Dom	Cmd	FpK	SwK	G	L	F	H%	S%	hr/f	GS	APC	DOM%	DIS%	Sv%	LI	RAR	BPV	BPX	R$
11 TOR *	12	13	0	202	139	4.80	4.94	1.37	779	522	876	26.5	2.8	6.2	2.2	59%	9%	38	18	43	29%	70%	13%	20	96	50%	10%			-21.5	36	54	-$2
12 TOR *	6	8	0	144	104	4.50	4.78	1.46	855	603	934	17.1	2.8	6.5	2.4	52%	10%	37	22	41	33%	71%	14%	9	49	44%	22%	0	0.72	-8.5	58	76	-$5
13 TOR	5	1	1	61	70	2.82	2.96	1.10	594	458	736	4.2	3.4	10.4	3.0	58%	12%	51	20	29	28%	76%	9%	0	15			33	0.89	7.8	124	161	$5
14 TOR	2	3	5	53	76	2.70	2.68	1.37	627	714	569	3.5	4.6	12.8	2.8	54%	17%	54	25	22	37%	80%	7%	0	14			71	1.22	6.8	140	167	$3
15 TOR	5	5	5	54	70	2.48	2.50	0.96	562	539	576	3.4	2.2	11.6	5.4	60%	15%	52	19	29	30%	77%	11%	0	13			63	1.01	9.9	181	215	$9
1st Half	2	4	5	27	31	5.00	3.36	1.37	763	1072	631	3.7	3.7	10.3	2.8	56%	14%	54	14	32	33%	67%	17%	0	15			71	0.91	-3.5	119	141	$1
2nd Half	3	1	0	27	39	0.00	1.74	0.55	334	170	491	3.1	0.7	12.8	19.5	64%	17%	49	25	25	25%	100%	0%	0	11			0	1.10	13.4	240	285	$16
16 Proj	4	4	2	58	73	2.56	2.64	1.09	589	530	629	3.7	2.9	11.3	4.0	58%	15%	50	22	28	31%	78%	10%	0						10.0	155	184	$6

Cedeno,Xavier

Age: 29	Th: L	Role RP	
Ht: 6' 0"	Wt: 205	Type Pwr GB	
Health	A	LIMA Plan	A
PT/Exp	D	Rand Var	-3
Consist	B	MM	4400

Early Ctl issues could have been worse, as FpK sat at 45% thru Aug 1. But he got it up to 71% over last 20 appearances, while Dom surged. GB%, dominance over LHB are promising, and made great strides vs RHB in 2H (8.5 Cmd). Already a solid LIMA option; potential for more if he continues to throw strike one.

Yr Tm	W	L	Sv	IP	K	ERA	xERA	WHIP	oOPS	vL	vR	BF/G	Ctl	Dom	Cmd	FpK	SwK	G	L	F	H%	S%	hr/f	GS	APC	DOM%	DIS%	Sv%	LI	RAR	BPV	BPX	R$
11 HOU *	7	9	0	139	113	5.28	4.71	1.50	1818	1000	2286	15.8	3.4	7.3	2.1	64%	3%	27	45	27	34%	65%	67%	0	12			0	1.04	-22.9	62	93	-$8
12 HOU *	2	1	2	59	56	3.12	3.86	1.41	704	616	797	3.8	3.5	8.7	2.5	50%	11%	50	15	35	34%	78%	10%	0	13			29	1.05	6.5	92	120	$0
13 2 TM *	2	0	4	47	43	2.90	3.55	1.43	811	603	1039	3.6	4.7	8.3	1.8	62%	10%	60	15	25	31%	80%	0%	0	14			57	0.61	5.5	80	105	$0
14 WAS *	5	1	4	46	47	3.05	2.82	1.09	833	1067	600	4.1	2.5	9.1	3.6	47%	8%	38	33	29	28%	75%	14%	0	12			57	0.94	3.9	117	139	$4
15 2 TM	4	1	1	46	47	2.35	3.16	1.17	614	490	768	2.9	2.7	9.2	3.4	54%	15%	53	21	26	30%	84%	13%	0	11			33	1.28	9.2	123	146	$3
1st Half	1	1	0	24	20	2.96	4.31	1.52	748	545	990	2.8	4.1	7.4	1.8	47%	13%	48	25	27	32%	85%	15%	0	12			0	1.49	3.0	49	58	-$2
2nd Half	3	0	1	22	27	1.66	2.05	0.78	443	423	469	2.9	1.2	11.2	9.0	62%	19%	61	14	24	28%	81%	8%	0	11			100	1.00	6.1	207	246	$9
16 Proj	5	1	0	58	59	2.87	3.14	1.17	603	507	715	3.4	2.9	9.2	3.2	53%	14%	53	18	29	30%	78%	10%	0						7.8	119	142	$4

Chacin,Jhoulys

Age: 28	Th: R	Role SP	
Ht: 6' 3"	Wt: 215	Type	
Health	F	LIMA Plan	D+
PT/Exp	B	Rand Var	+1
Consist	B	MM	1000

2-1, 3.38 ERA in 27 IP at ARI. Stayed healthy, and eventually made it back to majors in late August. But velocity didn't return, and lack of whiffs once again left Cmd at undesirable level. A decent GB% is really all he has going for him at this point. Subpar Cmd, health history suggest a return to relevance is unlikely.

Yr Tm	W	L	Sv	IP	K	ERA	xERA	WHIP	oOPS	vL	vR	BF/G	Ctl	Dom	Cmd	FpK	SwK	G	L	F	H%	S%	hr/f	GS	APC	DOM%	DIS%	Sv%	LI	RAR	BPV	BPX	R$
11 COL	11	14	0	194	150	3.62	3.86	1.31	707	759	654	26.7	4.0	7.0	1.7	55%	9%	56	15	28	27%	75%	12%	31	101	52%	16%			7.7	50	76	$8
12 COL *	4	7	0	92	54	4.66	5.32	1.56	821	910	720	22.3	3.9	5.3	1.4	59%	8%	39	24	37	31%	73%	12%	14	83	29%	50%			-7.3	21	27	-$8
13 COL	14	10	0	197	126	3.47	4.02	1.26	685	722	650	26.3	2.8	5.7	2.1	61%	8%	47	25	29	29%	73%	6%	31	96	48%	13%			9.7	53	69	$10
14 COL	1	7	0	63	42	5.40	4.56	1.44	790	751	821	24.7	4.0	6.0	1.5	63%	9%	43	22	35	29%	64%	12%	11	93	36%	0%			-13.0	21	25	-$7
15 ARI *	9	7	0	155	89	3.44	3.89	1.36	729	982	497	26.0	3.1	5.2	1.7	55%	10%	47	19	33	30%	76%	15%	4	85	50%	25%	0	0.84	10.0	50	60	$4
1st Half	2	4	0	62	35	3.26	3.63	1.33				25.9	3.0	5.1	1.7						30%	76%	0%	0						5.4	55	66	$0
2nd Half	7	3	0	93	54	3.57	4.06	1.39	729	982	497	26.1	3.2	5.3	1.6	55%	10%	47	19	33	30%	76%	15%	4	85	50%	25%	0	0.84	4.5	47	55	$7
16 Proj	3	4	0	58	36	4.33	4.55	1.42	768	865	677	25.7	3.3	5.5	1.7	59%	9%	46	21	33	30%	71%	10%	10						-2.6	34	40	-$4

Chafin,Andrew

Age: 26	Th: L	Role RP	
Ht: 6' 2"	Wt: 220	Type Pwr xGB	
Health	A	LIMA Plan	B
PT/Exp	D	Rand Var	-3
Consist	C	MM	2201

A starter throughout his career, settled in nicely as RP, thanks to ability to keep the ball down. But low FpK shows Ctl may be ongoing issue, and wasn't as dominant vs. LHB as it appears (2.2 Cmd, 22% hit rate). Future role unclear, but track record indicates Dom may drop significantly if he starts.

Yr Tm	W	L	Sv	IP	K	ERA	xERA	WHIP	oOPS	vL	vR	BF/G	Ctl	Dom	Cmd	FpK	SwK	G	L	F	H%	S%	hr/f	GS	APC	DOM%	DIS%	Sv%	LI	RAR	BPV	BPX	R$
11																																	
12																																	
13 aa	10	7	0	126	73	3.87	4.34	1.48				25.9	3.1	5.2	1.7						33%	73%								-0.1	50	66	-$1
14 ARI *	9	8	0	162	105	4.50	5.21	1.58	685	641	701	24.5	3.5	5.8	1.6	58%	7%	54	18	28	33%	73%	0%	3	86	0%	33%			-15.1	38	45	-$10
15 ARI	5	1	2	75	58	2.76	3.70	1.15	587	524	631	4.6	3.6	7.0	1.9	54%	9%	58	19	23	26%	76%	6%	0	18			100	1.29	11.1	64	76	$6
1st Half	5	0	1	42	29	2.98	3.77	1.18	613	568	639	5.6	3.0	6.2	2.1	57%	8%	59	19	23	28%	73%	4%	0	21			100	1.35	5.1	67	80	$8
2nd Half	0	1	1	33	29	2.48	3.61	1.10	552	474	615	3.8	4.4	8.0	1.8	50%	10%	58	19	23	22%	79%	11%	0	15			100	1.23	6.0	61	73	$4
16 Proj	4	3	0	73	57	3.49	3.73	1.34	712	628	772	6.3	3.6	7.1	2.0	53%	9%	58	19	23	30%	75%	10%	0						4.2	66	78	$0

BRIAN RUDD

Chapman,Aroldis

Age: 28	Th: L	Role: RP	Health: C	LIMA Plan: C+
Ht: 6' 4"	Wt: 205	Type: Pwr	PT/Exp: A	Rand Var: -4
			Consist: B	MM: 5530

Stuff is unrivaled—induced highest SwK in majors for second consecutive year (min. 50 IP), and struck out at least half the LHB he faced for fourth straight. Even showed ability to keep ball down in 2H. Ctl remains shaky, had a slight ERA/xERA gap, but that's looking for warts; should once again be an elite option.

Yr	Tm	W	L	Sv	IP	K	ERA	xERA	WHIP	oOPS	vL	vR	BF/G	Ctl	Dom	Cmd	FpK	SwK	G	L	F	H%	S%	hr/f	GS	APC	DOM%	DIS%	Sv%	LI	RAR	BPV	BPX	R$
11	CIN	4	1	1	50	71	3.60	3.17	1.30	534	392	598	3.8	7.4	12.8	1.7	53%	14%	53	16	31	24%	71%	7%	0	16			33	1.13	2.1	62	93	$2
12	CIN	5	5	38	72	122	1.51	2.12	0.81	450	330	501	4.1	2.9	15.3	5.3	53%	18%	37	20	43	28%	85%	7%	0	18			88	1.42	22.2	213	278	$32
13	CIN	4	5	38	64	112	2.54	2.30	1.04	544	379	592	3.8	4.1	15.8	3.9	59%	17%	34	24	42	31%	81%	15%	0	16			88	1.38	10.4	186	243	$23
14	CIN	0	3	36	54	106	2.00	1.52	0.83	406	372	415	3.7	4.0	17.7	4.4	58%	21%	43	22	35	30%	75%	4%	0	17			95	1.44	11.6	231	275	$21
15	CIN	4	4	33	66	116	1.63	2.55	1.15	527	451	554	4.3	4.5	15.7	3.5	56%	20%	37	22	41	36%	88%	6%	0	18			92	1.24	19.1	177	211	$23
1st Half		3	3	16	35	61	1.78	2.95	1.19	518	617	473	4.2	4.8	15.5	3.2	56%	19%	29	22	49	36%	85%	3%	0	17			94	1.23	9.5	156	185	$23
2nd Half		1	1	17	31	55	1.45	2.08	1.10	537	183	639	4.4	4.1	16.0	3.9	55%	21%	47	22	31	36%	91%	12%	0	19			89	1.26	9.6	203	241	$23
16	**Proj**	**4**	**3**	**40**	**65**	**115**	**1.93**	**2.17**	**1.04**	**500**	**384**	**538**	**3.9**	**4.3**	**15.9**	**3.7**	**56%**	**19%**	**40**	**22**	**38**	**32%**	**83%**	**8%**	**0**						**16.4**	**188**	**224**	**$25**

Chatwood,Tyler

Age: 26	Th: R	Role: SP	Health: F	LIMA Plan: D+
Ht: 6' 0"	Wt: 185	Type: GB	PT/Exp: D	Rand Var: 0
			Consist: A	MM: 1001

Underwent second TJS in July 2014, which knocked him out for all of 2015. Previous GB% provides some level of optimism, but save for the small 2014 sample, swing-and-miss stuff has been lacking. Ctl also a concern, given less than stellar FpK history. At least for now, odds appear stacked against return to relevance.

Yr	Tm	W	L	Sv	IP	K	ERA	xERA	WHIP	oOPS	vL	vR	BF/G	Ctl	Dom	Cmd	FpK	SwK	G	L	F	H%	S%	hr/f	GS	APC	DOM%	DIS%	Sv%	LI	RAR	BPV	BPX	R$
11	LAA *	7	13	0	158	84	4.73	5.42	1.69	830	862	786	23.0	4.6	4.8	1.0	54%	5%	47	22	31	32%	73%	10%	25	90	20%	44%	0	0.77	-15.4	20	30	-$12
12	COL *	6	9	1	126	83	5.80	5.84	1.72	836	890	774	17.9	4.3	5.9	1.4	54%	6%	56	21	23	34%	67%	19%	12	61	8%	58%	100	0.62	-27.7	27	35	-$18
13	COL *	10	6	0	145	91	3.13	3.90	1.42	711	729	697	23.7	2.9	5.7	1.9	55%	7%	59	21	21	32%	77%	7%	20	89	35%	30%			13.1	64	84	$4
14	COL	1	0	0	24	20	4.50	3.56	1.21	711	472	1015	25.3	3.0	7.5	2.5	50%	10%	46	29	26	26%	68%	22%	4	89	50%	0%			-2.2	78	93	-$3
15																																		
1st Half																																		
2nd Half																																		
16	**Proj**	**4**	**5**	**0**	**73**	**43**	**4.69**	**4.39**	**1.48**	**770**	**808**	**730**	**21.0**	**3.4**	**5.4**	**1.6**	**54%**	**6%**	**53**	**21**	**25**	**31%**	**69%**	**11%**	**15**						**-6.5**	**35**	**42**	**-$5**

Chavez,Jesse

Age: 32	Th: R	Role: SP	Health: B	LIMA Plan: B+
Ht: 6' 2"	Wt: 160	Type: Pwr	PT/Exp: B	Rand Var: 0
			Consist: A	MM: 2303

Strong out of the gate, with PQS-DOM performances in six of first eight starts. But much like 2014, hit a wall in 2nd half: LHB hit him hard, and struggled with Ctl before fractured rib ended season a few weeks early. When he's good, excellent Cmd sets strong foundation. But can't be counted on to keep it going thru Sept.

Yr	Tm	W	L	Sv	IP	K	ERA	xERA	WHIP	oOPS	vL	vR	BF/G	Ctl	Dom	Cmd	FpK	SwK	G	L	F	H%	S%	hr/f	GS	APC	DOM%	DIS%	Sv%	LI	RAR	BPV	BPX	R$
11	KC *	2	4	16	65	47	5.22	6.17	1.69	1112	924	1250	6.0	3.0	6.5	2.2	44%	12%	54	19	27	37%	71%	43%	0	40			76	0.32	-10.3	38	57	-$2
12	2 AL *	9	6	2	130	101	5.37	4.97	1.44	983	1144	888	16.2	2.4	7.0	2.9	62%	11%	36	29	35	34%	64%	26%	2	36	0%	50%	100	0.66	-21.7	65	85	-$6
13	OAK *	4	6	1	87	74	3.64	3.71	1.35	620	630	605	9.1	2.6	7.6	2.9	61%	10%	43	17	39	34%	72%	5%	0	27			50	0.93	2.4	95	124	$0
14	OAK	8	8	0	146	136	3.45	3.72	1.31	692	663	729	19.4	3.0	8.4	2.8	63%	9%	42	23	35	31%	78%	11%	21	75	52%	5%	0	0.66	5.2	89	106	$5
15	OAK	7	15	1	157	136	4.18	4.04	1.35	730	825	616	22.4	2.8	7.8	2.8	61%	9%	43	23	34	32%	72%	11%	26	86	46%	15%	100	0.74	-4.3	87	104	$1
1st Half		4	8	1	96	81	3.20	3.80	1.18	652	735	559	21.7	2.2	7.6	3.5	61%	10%	42	23	35	31%	75%	7%	14	84	50%	0%	100	0.71	9.0	99	117	$10
2nd Half		3	7	0	61	55	5.72	4.41	1.61	841	939	706	23.4	3.7	8.1	2.2	60%	8%	45	23	32	35%	68%	17%	12	89	42%	33%			-13.3	69	82	-$13
16	**Proj**	**7**	**12**	**0**	**145**	**127**	**4.04**	**3.88**	**1.34**	**713**	**754**	**661**	**20.6**	**2.9**	**7.9**	**2.7**	**62%**	**9%**	**43**	**22**	**35**	**31%**	**73%**	**11%**	**24**						**-1.4**	**83**	**99**	**$1**

Chen,Wei-Yin

Age: 30	Th: L	Role: SP	Health: C	LIMA Plan: C+
Ht: 6' 0"	Wt: 195	Type:	PT/Exp: A	Rand Var: -1
			Consist: A	MM: 2105

Remains susceptible to the long ball, but HR damage minimized by pinpoint Ctl, which this time was fully supported by FpK. Consistency has its value, but xERA and mediocre Swk/Dom say 2015 was as good as it's going to get, so don't bid on full repeat.

Yr	Tm	W	L	Sv	IP	K	ERA	xERA	WHIP	oOPS	vL	vR	BF/G	Ctl	Dom	Cmd	FpK	SwK	G	L	F	H%	S%	hr/f	GS	APC	DOM%	DIS%	Sv%	LI	RAR	BPV	BPX	R$
11	for	8	10	0	165	89	3.32	3.18	1.13				26.1	2.1	4.9	2.3						26%	73%								12.7	60	90	$11
12	BAL	12	11	0	193	154	4.02	4.33	1.26	729	682	747	25.6	2.7	7.2	2.7	60%	10%	37	21	42	29%	73%	12%	32	98	56%	16%			-0.1	73	95	$8
13	BAL	7	7	0	137	104	4.07	4.19	1.32	761	689	783	24.9	2.6	6.8	2.7	59%	8%	34	25	41	31%	73%	10%	23	95	35%	17%			-3.5	66	86	$1
14	BAL	16	6	0	186	136	3.54	3.86	1.23	727	670	746	24.9	1.7	6.6	3.9	61%	8%	41	22	38	30%	76%	10%	31	96	48%	13%			4.6	92	109	$10
15	BAL	11	8	0	191	153	3.34	4.01	1.22	758	576	815	25.5	1.9	7.2	3.7	68%	9%	40	20	39	30%	79%	12%	31	97	42%	16%			14.7	95	114	$13
1st Half		4	4	0	95	78	2.84	3.94	1.11	710	668	723	25.5	2.1	7.4	3.5	64%	9%	40	18	42	26%	83%	13%	15	96	47%	13%			13.1	95	112	$17
2nd Half		7	4	0	96	75	3.83	4.09	1.33	802	490	899	25.6	1.8	7.0	3.9	72%	10%	41	22	37	33%	76%	11%	16	98	38%	19%			1.6	97	115	$9
16	**Proj**	**12**	**8**	**0**	**189**	**144**	**3.68**	**3.97**	**1.24**	**748**	**616**	**790**	**24.8**	**2.0**	**6.9**	**3.4**	**65%**	**9%**	**39**	**21**	**39**	**30%**	**75%**	**11%**	**31**						**6.7**	**87**	**103**	**$9**

Cingrani,Tony

Age: 26	Th: L	Role: RP	Health: D	LIMA Plan: D+
Ht: 6' 4"	Wt: 215	Type: Pwr FB	PT/Exp: D	Rand Var: +1
			Consist: C	MM: 1501

0-3, 5.67 ERA in 33 IP at CIN. Worked primarily out of pen before making six AAA starts late in year. Plus Dom keeps him on our radar, but shoulder woes hampered him for second straight year, Ctl is a mess, and he's still prone to long ball. A lot of obstacles to overcome in order to tap into upside.

Yr	Tm	W	L	Sv	IP	K	ERA	xERA	WHIP	oOPS	vL	vR	BF/G	Ctl	Dom	Cmd	FpK	SwK	G	L	F	H%	S%	hr/f	GS	APC	DOM%	DIS%	Sv%	LI	RAR	BPV	BPX	R$
11																																		
12	CIN *	5	3	0	94	96	2.81	3.47	1.26	623	533	700	20.3	4.1	9.2	2.2	55%	13%	64	0	36	28%	83%	25%	0	34			0	0.86	14.0	81	105	$7
13	CIN *	10	4	0	136	162	2.60	2.46	1.06	649	533	693	18.2	3.6	10.7	3.0	57%	11%	34	21	45	25%	81%	13%	18	79	61%	22%	0	0.93	21.2	113	147	$18
14	CIN	2	8	0	63	61	4.55	4.51	1.53	811	613	862	21.5	5.0	8.7	1.7	54%	9%	35	22	44	30%	76%	15%	11	86	27%	27%	0	0.85	-6.3	35	41	-$5
15	CIN *	0	4	0	58	66	4.33	4.70	1.62	811	915	751	5.9	5.8	10.2	1.8	50%	12%	38	27	35	34%	75%	10%	1	19	0%	100%	0	1.24	-2.6	73	87	-$7
1st Half		0	3	0	25	29	3.20	2.75	1.39	699	910	546	4.3	6.4	10.1	1.6	49%	11%	35	31	35	27%	77%	5%	0	18			0	1.28	2.4	100	118	-$4
2nd Half		0	1	0	33	37	5.21	6.21	1.80	1024	930	1055	7.9	5.3	10.2	1.9	54%	14%	45	21	34	39%	74%	20%	1	21	0%	100%	0	1.15	-5.0	55	65	-$8
16	**Proj**	**3**	**8**	**0**	**116**	**126**	**4.09**	**4.28**	**1.49**	**798**	**813**	**791**	**16.1**	**5.2**	**9.8**	**1.9**	**53%**	**10%**	**35**	**25**	**41**	**31%**	**76%**	**12%**	**16**						**-1.8**	**49**	**58**	**-$3**

Cishek,Steve

Age: 30	Th: R	Role: RP	Health: A	LIMA Plan: C
Ht: 6' 6"	Wt: 215	Type: Pwr	PT/Exp: B	Rand Var: -2
			Consist: B	MM: 2410

With velocity down in early going, took a beating, lost closer gig, and was briefly demoted to AA. Despite shiny 2H ERA, never really righted the ship, and had major Ctl issues down stretch (11 BB in last 12 IP). xERA shows downside, but steady SwK suggests Dom rebound, and low price could offer small profit potential.

Yr	Tm	W	L	Sv	IP	K	ERA	xERA	WHIP	oOPS	vL	vR	BF/G	Ctl	Dom	Cmd	FpK	SwK	G	L	F	H%	S%	hr/f	GS	APC	DOM%	DIS%	Sv%	LI	RAR	BPV	BPX	R$
11	FLA *	3	2	3	78	70	2.57	2.66	1.23	591	661	545	5.2	3.6	8.2	2.3	59%	9%	57	17	26	30%	78%	3%	0	20			100	0.86	13.2	100	150	$6
12	MIA	5	2	15	64	68	2.69	3.55	1.30	663	787	548	4.0	4.1	9.6	2.3	57%	10%	52	16	31	31%	80%	6%	0	16			79	1.20	10.4	92	120	$10
13	MIA	4	6	34	70	74	2.33	2.96	1.08	568	664	459	4.1	2.8	9.6	3.4	63%	10%	53	18	29	29%	79%	6%	0	16			94	1.23	13.2	126	165	$20
14	MIA	4	5	39	65	84	3.17	2.84	1.21	643	586	713	4.1	2.9	11.6	4.0	67%	10%	43	26	31	35%	74%	6%	0	17			91	1.61	4.6	151	180	$18
15	2 NL	2	6	4	55	48	3.58	4.42	1.48	720	754	696	4.1	4.4	7.8	1.8	64%	10%	46	22	32	32%	77%	8%	0	16			44	0.91	2.6	46	55	-$1
1st Half		2	5	3	28	24	5.20	4.42	1.66	812	819	805	4.5	3.9	7.8	2.0	66%	10%	49	20	30	37%	68%	7%	0	18			43	1.15	-4.2	63	74	-$5
2nd Half		0	1	1	28	24	1.95	4.43	1.30	619	648	599	3.7	4.9	7.8	1.6	63%	10%	42	24	34	26%	88%	8%	0	14			50	0.69	6.9	29	34	$2
16	**Proj**	**3**	**5**	**5**	**58**	**57**	**3.49**	**3.69**	**1.31**	**661**	**681**	**645**	**4.0**	**3.8**	**8.8**	**2.3**	**64%**	**10%**	**47**	**22**	**31**	**31%**	**74%**	**7%**	**0**						**3.3**	**81**	**97**	**$2**

Clippard,Tyler

Age: 31	Th: R	Role: RP	Health: A	LIMA Plan: C+
Ht: 6' 3"	Wt: 200	Type: Pwr xFB	PT/Exp: C	Rand Var: -5
			Consist: C	MM: 1311

Held down closer role until he was traded at deadline, and while ERA was respectable, plenty of reasons to be wary: velocity fell for third straight year; low FpK, highest Ctl since 2010; SwK and Dom dropped off; highest FB% in MLB. Add it all up, and... DN: See 2015 xERA. That's potentially scary-bad.

Yr	Tm	W	L	Sv	IP	K	ERA	xERA	WHIP	oOPS	vL	vR	BF/G	Ctl	Dom	Cmd	FpK	SwK	G	L	F	H%	S%	hr/f	GS	APC	DOM%	DIS%	Sv%	LI	RAR	BPV	BPX	R$
11	WAS	3	0	0	88	104	1.83	3.20	0.84	535	549	522	4.6	2.6	10.6	4.0	55%	17%	20	20	60	20%	89%	9%	0	19			0	1.49	23.0	117	176	$15
12	WAS	2	6	32	73	84	3.72	4.03	1.16	621	519	725	4.1	3.6	10.4	2.9	62%	12%	30	14	57	28%	70%	7%	0	17			86	1.25	2.7	98	128	$16
13	WAS	6	3	0	71	73	2.41	3.68	0.86	517	507	527	3.8	3.0	9.3	3.0	59%	15%	28	16	56	18%	81%	9%	0	16			0	1.10	12.8	90	118	$10
14	WAS	7	4	1	70	82	2.18	3.26	1.00	541	642	423	3.7	2.9	10.5	3.6	63%	15%	37	14	49	27%	82%	6%	0	15			14	1.34	13.6	124	148	$10
15	2 TM	5	4	19	71	64	2.92	4.96	1.13	599	468	745	4.4	3.9	8.1	2.1	56%	12%	21	18	61	23%	79%	7%	0	18			76	1.25	9.2	39	46	$13
1st Half		1	3	15	35	33	2.60	4.94	1.13	549	319	766	4.5	4.2	8.6	2.1	56%	12%	22	18	61	24%	81%	5%	0	19			88	1.24	5.8	42	49	$14
2nd Half		4	1	4	36	31	3.22	4.98	1.13	649	592	719	4.3	3.7	7.7	2.1	56%	13%	21	19	60	23%	78%	8%	0	17			50	1.26	3.3	37	44	$12
16	**Proj**	**5**	**5**	**5**	**73**	**70**	**3.29**	**4.21**	**1.18**	**660**	**613**	**712**	**4.0**	**3.4**	**8.7**	**2.5**	**58%**	**14%**	**26**	**17**	**57**	**27%**	**77%**	**8%**	**0**						**6.0**	**68**	**81**	**$5**

BRIAN RUDD

Cobb,Alex

Age: 28 Th: R Role SP	Health F	LIMA Plan C	
Ht: 6' 3" Wt: 200 Type Pwr GB	PT/Exp B	Rand Var 0	
	Consist A	MM 3200	

Missed a month with tendinitis, then had Tommy John surgery in May. With DL days (334) closing the gap on career IP (499), he's a tough commit. And we're talking about an arm injury this time. Amid health issues, may still be hard to lay off that nice string of skills metrics. Just don't expect a lot from them in 2016.

Yr Tm	W	L	Sv	IP	K	ERA	xERA	WHIP	oOPS	vL	vR	BF/G	Ctl	Dom	Cmd	FpK	SwK	G	L	F	H%	S%	hr/f	GS	APC	DOM%	DIS%	Sv%	LI	RAR	BPV	BPX	R$
11 TAM *	8	3	0	120	96	2.69	3.50	1.29	655	683	617	23.5	2.7	7.2	2.6	58%	8%	54	20	26	31%	80%	7%	9	94	22%	22%			18.6	86	129	$9
12 TAM *	12	13	0	178	142	4.19	3.82	1.34	690	735	633	23.8	2.9	7.2	2.5	62%	8%	59	20	21	32%	69%	13%	23	94	48%	26%			-3.8	79	103	$3
13 TAM	11	3	0	143	134	2.76	3.04	1.15	644	677	592	26.3	2.8	8.4	3.0	59%	10%	56	22	23	28%	80%	15%	22	101	59%	14%			19.5	109	142	$15
14 TAM	10	9	0	166	149	2.87	3.16	1.14	619	590	646	25.2	2.5	8.1	3.2	59%	11%	56	16	27	29%	76%	9%	27	97	59%	11%			17.9	110	132	$14
15																																	
1st Half																																	
2nd Half																																	
16 Proj	4	3	0	58	50	3.75	3.49	1.30	701	720	676	24.7	2.8	7.7	2.8	60%	9%	54	21	25	32%	72%	9%	10						1.5	95	114	$0

Cole,A.J.

Age: 24 Th: R Role SP	Health A	LIMA Plan C	
Ht: 6' 4" Wt: 180 Type	PT/Exp D	Rand Var 0	
	Consist C	MM 1101	

1 SV, 5.79 ERA in 9 IP at WAS. Logged a save during May promotion, otherwise spent the summer as SP in Syracuse honing curveball. Didn't slow Dom drop in second year at AAA (continuing a trend), but was stingier with BB in 2H. Appears poised to take next step, but it's always the biggest one.

Yr Tm	W	L	Sv	IP	K	ERA	xERA	WHIP	oOPS	vL	vR	BF/G	Ctl	Dom	Cmd	FpK	SwK	G	L	F	H%	S%	hr/f	GS	APC	DOM%	DIS%	Sv%	LI	RAR	BPV	BPX	R$
11																																	
12																																	
13 aa	4	2	0	45	41	2.57	2.21	0.97				24.6	1.9	8.2	4.4						27%	76%								7.3	135	176	$4
14 a/a	13	3	0	134	93	3.39	4.49	1.41				22.7	2.0	6.2	3.1						35%	77%								5.8	80	96	$3
15 WAS *	5	6	1	115	71	4.29	4.36	1.39	812	935	571	20.2	2.9	5.6	2.0	43%	10%	36	27	36	31%	71%	8%	1	52	0%	100%	100	0.48	-4.6	49	58	-$3
1st Half	0	4	1	56	35	5.80	6.15	1.67	812	935	571	18.1	3.3	5.6	1.7	43%	10%	36	27	36	34%	68%	8%		52	0%	100%			-12.8	20	23	-$16
2nd Half	5	2	0	59	36	2.83	2.64	1.13				23.2	2.4	5.5	2.3						27%	75%	0%							8.2	80	95	$9
16 Proj	5	3	0	73	50	4.04	4.23	1.32				21.8	2.4	6.2	2.6	61%	8%	40	23	37	31%	70%	6%	14						-0.7	65	77	-$1

Cole,Gerrit

Age: 25 Th: R Role SP	Health D	LIMA Plan C	
Ht: 6' 4" Wt: 240 Type Pwr	PT/Exp B	Rand Var -2	
	Consist A	MM 4305	

Ctl and Cmd took another step forward, but ascended to stud status in 2015 by dismissing LHB as summarily as he has RHB. (Faced 416 of each, K'd 101 of each.) "Slipped" a bit in 2H (124 BPV) as he blew by last year's IP, but if that 1st half is the new baseline, then... UP: Cy Young award.

Yr Tm	W	L	Sv	IP	K	ERA	xERA	WHIP	oOPS	vL	vR	BF/G	Ctl	Dom	Cmd	FpK	SwK	G	L	F	H%	S%	hr/f	GS	APC	DOM%	DIS%	Sv%	LI	RAR	BPV	BPX	R$
11																																	
12 a/a	4	6	0	65	55	3.58	3.68	1.39				21.0	3.1	7.6	2.4						34%	73%								3.5	90	117	-$1
13 PIT *	15	10	0	185	138	3.27	2.80	1.15	638	614	658	23.7	2.7	6.7	2.5	63%	10%	49	25	26	28%	72%	8%	19	91	63%	0%			13.7	86	112	$16
14 PIT *	14	6	0	160	151	3.44	3.33	1.21	693	729	659	24.9	2.5	8.5	3.4	62%	10%	49	19	32	31%	73%	9%	22	100	64%	9%			6.0	107	128	$10
15 PIT	19	8	0	208	202	2.60	3.16	1.09	623	597	648	26.0	1.9	8.7	4.6	62%	11%	48	22	30	31%	77%	7%	32	101	78%	6%			35.1	132	157	$30
1st Half	12	3	0	110	113	2.28	2.97	1.11	614	573	651	26.1	2.1	9.2	4.3	61%	10%	52	22	26	31%	81%	8%	17	100	82%	6%			22.8	139	165	$36
2nd Half	7	5	0	98	89	2.95	3.37	1.06	633	622	644	25.9	1.7	8.2	4.9	62%	11%	43	23	34	30%	73%	5%	15	102	73%	7%			12.2	124	147	$23
16 Proj	17	10	0	203	197	3.05	3.21	1.16	651	649	653	24.5	2.3	8.7	3.8	62%	10%	48	22	30	31%	74%	7%	33						22.9	122	145	$21

Collmenter,Josh

Age: 30 Th: R Role RP	Health A	LIMA Plan B+	
Ht: 6' 4" Wt: 235 Type Con FB	PT/Exp B	Rand Var 0	
	Consist C	MM 1001	

Enjoyed some success in swingman role, but outside of Ctl, only truly notable for annually outshining xERA. Has history of maneuvering around modest metrics with one of H%, S% or hr/f falling on the lucky side. And with Dom in free-fall, BPVs have been telling us good fortune is getting harder to come by.

Yr Tm	W	L	Sv	IP	K	ERA	xERA	WHIP	oOPS	vL	vR	BF/G	Ctl	Dom	Cmd	FpK	SwK	G	L	F	H%	S%	hr/f	GS	APC	DOM%	DIS%	Sv%	LI	RAR	BPV	BPX	R$
11 ARI	10	10	0	154	100	3.38	4.09	1.07	652	708	594	20.0	1.6	5.8	3.6	62%	8%	33	20	47	26%	72%	8%	24	79	58%	21%	0	0.71	10.7	72	108	$13
12 ARI	5	3	0	90	80	3.69	3.97	1.26	742	806	677	13.4	2.2	8.0	3.6	59%	9%	37	19	43	31%	76%	12%	11	54	36%	27%	0	0.66	3.7	99	130	$2
13 ARI	5	5	0	92	85	3.13	4.05	1.22	649	660	642	7.8	3.2	8.3	2.6	60%	11%	33	21	47	29%	77%	7%	0	32			0	1.40	8.3	74	96	$5
14 ARI	11	9	1	179	115	3.46	4.02	1.13	676	741	608	21.8	2.0	5.8	2.9	60%	8%	39	21	40	27%	72%	8%	28	82	54%	18%	100	0.84	6.2	68	81	$11
15 ARI	4	6	1	121	63	3.79	4.73	1.26	786	737	834	11.3	1.8	4.7	2.6	59%	7%	34	26	40	29%	76%	11%	12	44	25%	33%	100	0.46	2.5	48	57	$1
1st Half	3	6	0	77	36	4.89	5.04	1.38	874	856	892	19.3	1.5	4.2	2.8	57%	7%	32	26	42	31%	70%	12%	12	73	25%	33%	0	0.63	-8.8	44	53	-$4
2nd Half	1	0	1	44	27	1.85	4.16	1.05	617	480	731	6.3	2.3	5.6	2.5	61%	9%	40	25	35	24%	88%	9%	0	25			100	0.36	11.4	57	68	$9
16 Proj	3	3	0	73	47	3.97	4.35	1.30	763	753	772	10.8	2.1	5.9	2.7	60%	9%	37	23	41	30%	72%	9%	2						-0.1	63	74	-$1

Colome,Alexander

Age: 27 Th: R Role RP	Health F	LIMA Plan B+	
Ht: 6' 2" Wt: 210 Type Pwr	PT/Exp C	Rand Var 0	
	Consist A	MM 2301	

Injuries and PEDs have clouded his past, but try to find a more spectacular 2015 1H-to-2H line than this one. Coincides with role change from SP to RP in which he retooled fastball/curveball repertoire and cultivated short-stint mindset. But still, so out of the blue... we'll need to see more before we're all in.

Yr Tm	W	L	Sv	IP	K	ERA	xERA	WHIP	oOPS	vL	vR	BF/G	Ctl	Dom	Cmd	FpK	SwK	G	L	F	H%	S%	hr/f	GS	APC	DOM%	DIS%	Sv%	LI	RAR	BPV	BPX	R$
11 aa	3	4	0	52	27	4.18	3.39	1.31				23.9	4.4	4.7	1.1						24%	69%								-1.6	38	57	-$2
12 a/a	8	4	0	92	78	3.74	3.56	1.41				22.8	4.0	7.6	1.9						32%	72%								3.1	81	106	$1
13 TAM *	5	7	0	86	73	3.33	4.08	1.43	715	685	739	21.6	3.9	7.6	1.9	61%	12%	43	22	35	32%	79%	12%	3	88	33%	33%			5.7	67	87	$0
14 TAM *	9	6	0	110	73	4.36	4.12	1.49	590	566	612	23.6	3.5	6.0	1.7	67%	9%	38	22	41	33%	69%	3%	3	77	67%	0%	0	0.68	-8.4	64	76	-$4
15 TAM	8	5	0	110	88	3.94	4.06	1.30	698	736	658	10.6	2.5	7.2	2.8	62%	11%	40	25	35	32%	71%	8%	13	40	38%	15%	0	1.06	0.3	79	94	$2
1st Half	3	4	0	69	44	4.70	4.69	1.41	763	769	754	22.6	3.1	5.7	1.8	64%	8%	41	24	35	30%	69%	12%	13	84	38%	15%			-6.2	38	45	-$3
2nd Half	5	1	0	41	44	2.66	3.10	1.13	584	653	536	5.4	1.5	9.7	6.3	59%	15%	39	25	36	36%	74%	0%	0	20			0	1.19	6.6	150	178	$10
16 Proj	6	4	0	73	67	3.72	3.76	1.32	674	733	619	8.9	2.7	8.3	3.1	61%	12%	40	25	36	34%	71%	5%	-4						2.2	94	112	$1

Colon,Bartolo

Age: 43 Th: R Role SP	Health C	LIMA Plan B	
Ht: 5' 11" Wt: 285 Type Con	PT/Exp A	Rand Var 0	
	Consist A	MM 1005	

Keeps on chooglin' with laser-beam control, stellar command, and pitching ahead in the count (primo FpK). Subpar Dom, SwK provide him little room for error, but consecutive triple-digit BPV's say he doesn't make many. Shrugs off age and girth, but nobody is impervious to natural forces forever, right? Right??

Yr Tm	W	L	Sv	IP	K	ERA	xERA	WHIP	oOPS	vL	vR	BF/G	Ctl	Dom	Cmd	FpK	SwK	G	L	F	H%	S%	hr/f	GS	APC	DOM%	DIS%	Sv%	LI	RAR	BPV	BPX	R$
11 NYY	8	10	0	164	135	4.00	3.70	1.29	751	880	621	23.9	2.2	7.4	3.4	65%	6%	44	20	36	31%	73%	11%	26	88	50%	27%	0	0.77	-1.1	96	144	$5
12 OAK	10	9	0	152	91	3.43	4.23	1.21	692	782	587	26.5	1.4	5.4	4.0	67%	5%	46	18	36	30%	75%	9%	24	89	50%	25%			11.0	84	110	$9
13 OAK	18	6	0	190	117	2.65	4.00	1.17	659	681	636	25.6	1.4	5.5	4.0	65%	7%	42	21	38	30%	80%	6%	30	93	43%	13%			28.6	83	108	$21
14 NYM	15	13	0	202	151	4.09	3.82	1.23	716	681	755	27.3	1.3	6.7	5.0	66%	6%	39	22	39	32%	69%	9%	31	97	68%	16%			-8.8	102	121	$6
15 NYM	14	13	0	195	136	4.16	4.05	1.24	741	735	748	24.7	1.1	6.3	5.7	66%	7%	42	21	37	32%	70%	11%	31	82	55%	23%	0	0.76	-4.8	103	123	$7
1st Half	9	6	0	99	79	4.55	3.93	1.20	740	769	713	26.1	1.0	7.2	7.2	67%	7%	41	20	39	32%	66%	11%	16	87	63%	19%			-7.1	121	144	$9
2nd Half	5	7	0	96	57	3.76	4.18	1.28	742	705	793	23.4	1.2	5.4	4.4	65%	7%	44	22	34	32%	74%	10%	15	77	47%	27%	0	0.74	2.4	85	101	$5
16 Proj	13	11	0	181	120	4.23	4.07	1.30	760	758	762	25.1	1.5	5.9	3.9	66%	6%	42	21	37	32%	71%	11%	30						-5.9	85	102	$3

Conley,Adam

Age: 26 Th: L Role SP	Health A	LIMA Plan B	
Ht: 6' 3" Wt: 185 Type Pwr xFB	PT/Exp D	Rand Var 0	
	Consist B	MM 1203	

5-4, 3.76 ERA in 67 IP at MIA. Even while posting 2.52 ERA in 107 AAA innings, it took 'til Aug in MIA to reclaim strikeout pitch lost to tendinitis in 2014. Threw four PQS-DOMs to end the season, but earlier DISaster outings still had excellent K/BB ratios. Speculate in the end-game, but don't overvalue heading into 2016.

Yr Tm	W	L	Sv	IP	K	ERA	xERA	WHIP	oOPS	vL	vR	BF/G	Ctl	Dom	Cmd	FpK	SwK	G	L	F	H%	S%	hr/f	GS	APC	DOM%	DIS%	Sv%	LI	RAR	BPV	BPX	R$
11																																	
12																																	
13 aa	11	7	0	139	108	4.11	3.76	1.35				22.2	2.5	7.0	2.8						33%	69%								-4.2	87	114	$2
14 aaa	3	5	0	60	39	6.12	4.57	1.57				21.9	3.7	5.9	1.6						34%	58%								-17.6	55	65	-$9
15 MIA *	13	4	0	174	123	3.53	3.73	1.35	723	767	714	21.3	3.3	6.4	1.9	58%	11%	41	19	41	30%	74%	9%	11	73	45%	27%	0	0.72	9.2	65	77	$7
1st Half	8	2	0	90	49	3.09	3.69	1.39	0	0	0	22.3	3.7	4.9	1.3	67%	0%	100	0	0	29%	78%	0%	0	6			0	0.04	9.7	49	58	$9
2nd Half	5	2	0	84	74	4.01	3.77	1.31	731	767	724	20.4	2.9	7.9	2.7	58%	11%	40	19	40	32%	70%	9%	11	78	45%	27%	0	0.77	-0.5	85	101	$5
16 Proj	8	6	0	131	102	3.95	4.44	1.34	640	675	633	21.2	3.3	7.0	2.1	58%	11%	40	19	41	31%	70%	4%	26						0.1	55	66	$2

ROB CARROLL

Cooney,Tim

Age: 25	Th: L	Role: SP	Health: A	LIMA Plan: B+
Ht: 6' 3"	Wt: 195	Type: FB	PT/Exp: D	Rand Var: -1
			Consist: C	MM: 1201

1-0, 3.16 ERA in 31 IP AT STL. Had six serviceable starts after July call-up, then season was curtailed by appendicitis. Considered a pitch-to-contact type with good Cmd, showed better Dom (8.3) for STL than in two years at AAA. With little left to prove in minors, he's one to monitor closely in spring.

Yr Tm	W	L	Sv	IP	K	ERA	xERA	WHIP	oOPS	vL	vR	BF/G	Ctl	Dom	Cmd	FpK	SwK	G	L	F	H%	S%	hr/f	GS	APC	DOM%	DIS%	Sv%	LI	RAR	BPV	BPX	R$
11																																	
12																																	
13 aa	7	10	0	118	105	3.98	4.18	1.34				24.6	1.3	8.0	6.1						37%	70%								-1.7	156	203	$1
14 aaa	14	6	0	158	97	3.64	4.56	1.36				25.4	2.5	5.5	2.2						30%	77%								1.9	46	55	$3
15 STL *	7	4	0	120	79	3.12	2.76	1.03	704	764	689	23.1	1.9	5.9	3.1	58%	9%	38	23	39	25%	73%	9%	6	80	33%	17%			12.5	84	100	$11
1st Half	6	4	0	97	59	3.30	3.01	1.02	968	1400	900	23.3	1.7	5.5	3.2	45%	10%	42	15	42	24%	73%	27%	2	71	50%	50%			7.9	76	90	$14
2nd Half	1	0	0	23	20	2.35	3.83	1.04	590	585	589	23.0	2.7	7.8	2.9	63%	9%	36	26	38	27%	75%	0%	4	85	25%	0%			4.6	81	96	-$2
16 Proj	**5**	**2**	**0**	**73**	**57**	**3.24**	**4.08**	**1.21**	**704**	**785**	**681**	**24.0**	**2.4**	**7.1**	**3.0**	**63%**	**9%**	**36**	**24**	**40**	**30%**	**75%**	**6%**	**12**						**6.4**	**77**	**92**	**$3**

Corbin,Patrick

Age: 26	Th: L	Role: SP	Health: F	LIMA Plan: B
Ht: 6' 2"	Wt: 185	Type:	PT/Exp: C	Rand Var: 0
			Consist: B	MM: 3203

6-5, 3.60 ERA in 85 IP at ARI. Far exceeded just-happy-to-be-back-from-TJS story. After 21-month layoff, broad skill base remained intact while he threw a bit harder and dialed up Cmd. Post-surgery asterisk notwithstanding, could produce a reasonable facsimile of 2013 if stamina allows.

Yr Tm	W	L	Sv	IP	K	ERA	xERA	WHIP	oOPS	vL	vR	BF/G	Ctl	Dom	Cmd	FpK	SwK	G	L	F	H%	S%	hr/f	GS	APC	DOM%	DIS%	Sv%	LI	RAR	BPV	BPX	R$
11 aa	9	8	0	160	121	4.65	4.63	1.40				26.0	2.1	6.8	3.3						34%	68%								-14.1	80	120	-$2
12 ARI *	11	10	1	186	154	3.90	4.26	1.34	783	780	784	22.1	2.2	7.4	3.3	58%	9%	46	23	31	33%	73%	13%	17	73	47%	35%	100	0.77	2.6	88	114	$6
13 ARI	14	8	0	208	178	3.41	3.48	1.17	671	560	703	26.9	2.3	7.7	3.3	70%	11%	47	22	31	29%	73%	10%	32	96	72%	6%			11.6	100	131	$16
14																																	
15 ARI *	7	5	0	101	87	3.64	4.09	1.28	743	574	788	21.9	2.0	7.7	3.9	61%	11%	47	24	30	33%	74%	12%	16	78	56%	19%			4.0	100	119	$3
1st Half	2	0	0	21	12	3.80	4.37	1.41	1000	1667	882	22.6	2.3	5.0	2.1	57%	11%	53	12	35	32%	73%	0%	1	76	0%	0%			0.4	54	64	-$8
2nd Half	5	5	0	80	75	3.60	3.45	1.25	727	527	782	22.4	1.9	8.4	4.4	62%	12%	46	24	29	33%	75%	13%	15	79	60%	20%			3.6	125	148	$6
16 Proj	**11**	**7**	**0**	**160**	**129**	**3.58**	**3.62**	**1.25**	**711**	**619**	**736**	**23.1**	**2.1**	**7.3**	**3.4**	**62%**	**10%**	**46**	**23**	**30**	**31%**	**74%**	**10%**	**28**						**7.6**	**98**	**116**	**$8**

Cosart,Jarred

Age: 26	Th: R	Role: SP	Health: C	LIMA Plan: D
Ht: 6' 3"	Wt: 195	Type: Pwr GB	PT/Exp: C	Rand Var: +2
			Consist: B	MM: 1103

2-5, 4.52 ERA in 70 IP at MIA. The sum of the parts have fallen short of the whole. Ks are sparse despite mid-90s heater, and now high GB% failed to keep the ball in the park. The one constant has been shoddy Ctl, and until he reins that in, he'll continue to be enigmatic and largely unrosterable.

Yr Tm	W	L	Sv	IP	K	ERA	xERA	WHIP	oOPS	vL	vR	BF/G	Ctl	Dom	Cmd	FpK	SwK	G	L	F	H%	S%	hr/f	GS	APC	DOM%	DIS%	Sv%	LI	RAR	BPV	BPX	R$
11 aa	1	2	0	36	20	4.91	3.91	1.29				21.3	3.0	4.8	1.6						27%	63%								-4.3	38	57	-$3
12 a/a	6	7	0	115	82	3.31	3.55	1.40				23.1	3.7	6.4	1.7						31%	75%								10.0	71	93	$2
13 HOU *	8	5	0	153	114	3.00	3.32	1.39	631	489	849	23.0	4.9	6.7	1.4	52%	6%	55	21	24	27%	79%	7%	10	102	20%	10%			16.3	63	82	$6
14 2 TM	13	11	0	180	115	3.69	4.12	1.36	671	684	657	25.5	3.6	5.7	1.6	58%	7%	54	19	26	29%	73%	6%	30	98	47%	13%			1.1	37	44	$3
15 MIA *	2	6	0	91	61	5.02	4.89	1.54	762	742	781	20.9	4.8	6.0	1.3	54%	8%	55	18	27	29%	70%	18%	13	84	23%	38%	0	0.73	-11.8	29	34	-$9
1st Half	1	4	0	61	39	5.31	5.12	1.53	780	737	825	22.2	4.2	5.8	1.4	53%	8%	55	18	27	30%	68%	18%	8	82	25%	25%	0	0.70	-10.2	24	28	-$11
2nd Half	1	2	0	30	21	4.42	4.42	1.57	727	754	710	18.6	5.9	6.4	1.1	56%	8%	56	17	27	28%	73%	16%	5	86	20%	60%			-1.7	40	48	-$6
16 Proj	**6**	**9**	**0**	**145**	**98**	**4.21**	**4.47**	**1.46**	**731**	**705**	**756**	**21.6**	**4.6**	**6.1**	**1.3**	**56%**	**7%**	**55**	**19**	**26**	**29%**	**72%**	**11%**	**29**						**-4.4**	**19**	**22**	**-$4**

Cravy,Tyler

Age: 26	Th: R	Role: RP	Health: B	LIMA Plan: D+
Ht: 6' 3"	Wt: 195	Type: FB	PT/Exp: D	Rand Var: 0
			Consist: D	MM: 0103

0-8, 5.70 ERA in 43 IP at MIL. To those who pounced after first start (PQS-5 with 19 FpK) and held tight for rerun: Oops. After that, lack of Ctl (4.6) was root of undoing, a deficit made more pronounced by lack of Dom and Cmd. Certainly not the worst debut ever, but as the saying goes, fool me once, shame on you.

Yr Tm	W	L	Sv	IP	K	ERA	xERA	WHIP	oOPS	vL	vR	BF/G	Ctl	Dom	Cmd	FpK	SwK	G	L	F	H%	S%	hr/f	GS	APC	DOM%	DIS%	Sv%	LI	RAR	BPV	BPX	R$
11																																	
12																																	
13																																	
14 a/a	8	1	0	77	56	2.20	2.91	1.04				19.7	2.3	6.6	2.9						24%	87%								14.6	79	94	$9
15 MIL *	7	15	0	138	96	4.87	4.74	1.52	851	829	868	19.3	3.6	6.2	1.7	62%	8%	40	23	37	33%	68%	10%	7	54	14%	57%	0	0.74	-15.4	48	57	-$8
1st Half	7	6	0	87	59	4.15	4.04	1.36	623	536	686	22.8	3.2	6.1	1.9	75%	8%	48	30	22	30%	71%	0%	1	63	####	0%	0	0.38	-2.0	57	67	-$1
2nd Half	0	9	0	51	36	6.12	5.94	1.78	898	880	912	15.5	4.3	6.4	1.5	59%	8%	39	21	40	36%	65%	11%	6	53	0%	67%	0	0.80	-13.5	35	42	-$21
16 Proj	**8**	**11**	**0**	**131**	**93**	**4.24**	**4.65**	**1.41**	**714**	**676**	**749**	**18.6**	**3.2**	**6.4**	**2.0**	**59%**	**8%**	**39**	**21**	**40**	**31%**	**72%**	**7%**	**25**						**-4.5**	**44**	**53**	**-$2**

Cueto,Johnny

Age: 30	Th: R	Role: SP	Health: D	LIMA Plan: C+
Ht: 5' 11"	Wt: 215	Type:	PT/Exp: A	Rand Var: 0
			Consist: B	MM: 3205

Arrival in KC jibed with Aug nosedives in Dom, SwK, FpK. Theories abound: league change, subtleties with new catcher, elbow concerns (missed start in May). Although Ctl and Cmd remained vintage, doubts have been cast, and he's entering his 30s. Expectations should be more aligned with 2015 than 2014.

Yr Tm	W	L	Sv	IP	K	ERA	xERA	WHIP	oOPS	vL	vR	BF/G	Ctl	Dom	Cmd	FpK	SwK	G	L	F	H%	S%	hr/f	GS	APC	DOM%	DIS%	Sv%	LI	RAR	BPV	BPX	R$
11 CIN	9	5	0	156	104	2.31	3.64	1.09	593	588	598	26.3	2.7	6.0	2.2	56%	8%	54	16	30	26%	80%	6%	24	100	54%	13%			31.5	67	100	$18
12 CIN	19	9	0	217	170	2.78	3.59	1.17	667	708	620	26.9	2.0	7.1	3.5	63%	9%	49	22	29	30%	78%	8%	33	105	58%	12%			33.1	99	129	$26
13 CIN	5	2	0	61	51	2.82	3.27	1.05	607	561	644	22.0	2.7	7.6	2.8	61%	11%	51	25	24	25%	79%	17%	11	87	64%	27%			7.8	93	121	$5
14 CIN	20	9	0	244	242	2.25	3.07	0.96	574	561	585	28.3	2.4	8.9	3.7	63%	10%	46	19	35	25%	82%	10%	34	108	65%	0%			44.7	120	143	$38
15 2 TM	11	13	0	212	176	3.44	3.76	1.13	675	598	743	27.1	2.0	7.5	3.8	63%	10%	43	22	36	29%	73%	9%	32	102	59%	6%			13.7	103	122	$17
1st Half	5	5	0	105	100	2.84	3.30	0.92	596	505	677	27.5	1.7	8.6	5.0	66%	12%	42	21	37	25%	74%	11%	15	103	87%	0%			14.5	129	153	$27
2nd Half	6	8	0	107	76	4.02	4.24	1.34	747	684	802	26.7	2.2	6.4	2.9	60%	9%	43	23	35	32%	72%	8%	17	101	35%	12%			-0.8	76	91	$7
16 Proj	**13**	**10**	**0**	**203**	**173**	**3.10**	**3.47**	**1.10**	**644**	**599**	**683**	**25.5**	**2.2**	**7.7**	**3.4**	**62%**	**10%**	**46**	**21**	**33**	**28%**	**75%**	**10%**	**31**						**21.5**	**101**	**120**	**$21**

Danks,John

Age: 31	Th: L	Role: SP	Health: F	LIMA Plan: D+
Ht: 6' 1"	Wt: 210	Type:	PT/Exp: A	Rand Var: 0
			Consist: A	MM: 1105

Last three seasons evoke the definition of insanity: doing the same thing over and over while expecting different results. If he does, we shouldn't. Metrics are interminably... boring, and there is nothing to suggest anything but more of them. But if you want to hang your hat on that upward Dom trend, go for it.

Yr Tm	W	L	Sv	IP	K	ERA	xERA	WHIP	oOPS	vL	vR	BF/G	Ctl	Dom	Cmd	FpK	SwK	G	L	F	H%	S%	hr/f	GS	APC	DOM%	DIS%	Sv%	LI	RAR	BPV	BPX	R$
11 CHW	8	12	0	170	135	4.33	3.84	1.34	752	704	771	27.0	2.4	7.1	2.9	63%	10%	44	20	36	32%	70%	10%	27	102	59%	19%			-8.2	85	127	$1
12 CHW	3	4	0	54	30	5.70	5.22	1.49	790	831	760	26.4	3.9	5.0	1.3	56%	7%	41	22	37	29%	63%	11%	9	93	33%	33%			-11.2	5	7	-$8
13 CHW *	6	14	0	161	101	4.71	5.06	1.36	798	831	785	25.9	2.4	5.6	2.3	62%	9%	41	22	37	29%	71%	17%	22	100	55%	14%			-16.9	30	39	-$5
14 CHW	11	11	0	194	129	4.74	4.62	1.44	785	710	810	26.7	3.4	6.0	1.7	61%	8%	42	19	38	30%	70%	10%	32	103	34%	22%			-23.9	35	42	-$7
15 CHW	7	15	0	178	124	4.71	4.72	1.41	800	734	821	25.6	2.8	6.3	2.2	62%	9%	38	21	41	31%	70%	10%	30	97	40%	30%			-16.4	52	62	-$6
1st Half	4	8	0	87	60	4.95	4.75	1.44	843	650	901	25.5	2.5	6.2	2.5	64%	9%	37	21	42	32%	70%	12%	15	96	33%	40%			-10.6	60	71	-$8
2nd Half	3	7	0	90	64	4.48	4.69	1.38	758	811	739	25.7	3.2	6.4	2.0	61%	9%	39	21	40	30%	70%	9%	15	99	47%	20%			-5.8	46	55	-$4
16 Proj	**8**	**14**	**0**	**180**	**122**	**4.73**	**4.53**	**1.41**	**790**	**757**	**801**	**25.5**	**3.0**	**6.1**	**2.0**	**62%**	**9%**	**40**	**21**	**39**	**30%**	**70%**	**11%**	**30**						**-17.0**	**47**	**56**	**-$6**

Darvish,Yu

Age: 29	Th: R	Role: SP	Health: F	LIMA Plan: B
Ht: 6' 5"	Wt: 215	Type: Pwr	PT/Exp: B	Rand Var: 0
			Consist: A	MM: 4503

Had Tommy John surgery in March 2015, just as some had warned, due to his slider-heavy approach and 2014 DL stint with elbow inflammation. Skills are elite, but we can't automatically assume they will return. Health concerns obscure short-term outlook.

Yr Tm	W	L	Sv	IP	K	ERA	xERA	WHIP	oOPS	vL	vR	BF/G	Ctl	Dom	Cmd	FpK	SwK	G	L	F	H%	S%	hr/f	GS	APC	DOM%	DIS%	Sv%	LI	RAR	BPV	BPX	R$
11 for	18	6	0	232	262	1.78	1.65	0.91				30.9	1.7	10.2	5.9						29%	82%								61.8	189	283	$46
12 TEX	16	9	0	191	221	3.90	3.48	1.28	659	674	640	28.1	4.2	10.4	2.5	58%	13%	46	22	32	31%	70%	9%	29	109	72%	3%			2.6	98	128	$13
13 TEX	13	9	0	210	277	2.83	2.86	1.07	611	655	543	26.3	3.4	11.9	3.5	57%	13%	41	21	38	27%	80%	14%	32	108	84%	0%			26.7	140	183	$27
14 TEX	10	7	0	144	182	3.06	3.18	1.26	679	721	605	27.5	3.1	11.3	3.7	62%	11%	36	23	41	35%	79%	9%	22	105	64%	14%			12.2	136	162	$10
15																																	
1st Half																																	
2nd Half																																	
16 Proj	**11**	**6**	**0**	**150**	**182**	**3.48**	**3.20**	**1.20**	**651**	**683**	**602**	**27.3**	**3.3**	**10.9**	**3.3**	**59%**	**12%**	**40**	**21**	**38**	**32%**	**73%**	**10%**	**22**						**9.0**	**126**	**149**	**$12**

ROB CARROLL

Davies,Zachary

Age: 23	Th: R	Role	SP	Health	A	LIMA Plan	B+
Ht: 6' 0"	Wt: 150	Type	xGB	PT/Exp	D	Rand Var	0
				Consist	A	MM	2101

3-2, 3.71 ERA in 34 IP at MIL. Says his slight stature motivates him; witness four PQS-DOMs in his six Sept starts. Repeatable delivery, lots of GB, and even though MiLB Ctl and Dom didn't carry over to MLB, FpK and SwK suggest they could catch up. Not a high ceiling, but perhaps an elevated floor.

Yr Tm	W	L	Sv	IP	K	ERA	xERA	WHIP	oOPS	vL	vR	BF/G	Ctl	Dom	Cmd	FpK	SwK	G	L	F	H%	S%	hr/f	GS	APC	DOM%	DIS%	Sv%	LI	RAR	BPV	BPX	R$
11																																	
12																																	
13																																	
14 aa	10	7	0	110	94	3.70	3.98	1.32				21.7	2.5	7.7	3.1						33%	73%								0.6	90	107	$3
15 MIL *	9	10	0	162	114	3.55	3.80	1.38	614	434	740	22.7	3.3	6.3	1.9	60%	11%	58	21	21	31%	74%	10%	6	90	67%	33%			8.2	66	78	$4
1st Half	3	4	0	75	60	2.93	3.29	1.36				21.0	3.5	7.2	2.0						32%	77%	0%	0						9.6	86	102	$5
2nd Half	6	6	0	87	54	4.10	4.24	1.39	614	434	740	24.4	3.1	5.6	1.8	60%	11%	58	21	21	30%	72%	10%	6	90	67%	33%			-1.4	48	57	$3
16 Proj	**7**	**6**	**0**	**102**	**75**	**3.67**	**3.85**	**1.36**	**681**	**449**	**843**	**22.4**	**3.0**	**6.6**	**2.2**	**60%**	**11%**	**54**	**22**	**24**	**32%**	**74%**	**8%**	**19**						**3.7**	**71**	**85**	**$1**

Davis,Wade

Age: 30	Th: R	Role	RP	Health	A	LIMA Plan	C
Ht: 6' 5"	Wt: 220	Type	Pwr	PT/Exp	B	Rand Var	-5
				Consist	D	MM	5531

Second straight superb year. But keeping it real, Dom slipped and FB% skied, the latter creating longball issues in 2H. Stunning S% created chasm between ERA and xERA big enough to be noteworthy. Still, you can start visualizing those save totals. He's been the boss for awhile, now he finally has the title.

Yr Tm	W	L	Sv	IP	K	ERA	xERA	WHIP	oOPS	vL	vR	BF/G	Ctl	Dom	Cmd	FpK	SwK	G	L	F	H%	S%	hr/f	GS	APC	DOM%	DIS%	Sv%	LI	RAR	BPV	BPX	R$
11 TAM	11	10	0	184	105	4.45	4.78	1.38	771	779	765	27.4	3.1	5.1	1.7	59%	6%	36	21	43	29%	70%	9%	29	102	38%	21%			-11.5	23	35	-$1
12 TAM	3	0	0	70	87	2.43	3.31	1.09	570	464	654	5.3	3.7	11.1	3.0	57%	13%	39	22	40	28%	81%	8%	0	23			0	0.85	13.7	117	153	$7
13 KC	8	11	0	135	114	5.32	4.38	1.68	822	910	721	19.9	3.9	7.6	2.0	59%	8%	41	27	32	37%	69%	11%	24	80	38%	33%	0	0.85	-24.3	51	67	-$13
14 KC	9	2	3	72	109	1.00	2.08	0.85	408	513	298	3.9	2.9	13.6	4.7	61%	15%	48	22	30	29%	87%	0%	0	17			50	1.23	24.3	194	231	$17
15 KC	8	1	17	67	78	0.94	3.04	0.79	451	453	449	3.6	2.7	10.4	3.9	61%	12%	38	21	41	21%	92%	5%	0	15			94	1.22	25.1	131	157	$23
1st Half	4	1	9	36	40	0.25	3.05	0.81	410	419	396	3.8	3.0	10.0	3.3	61%	11%	42	23	35	22%	97%	0%	0	16			100	1.17	16.5	119	141	$25
2nd Half	4	0	8	31	38	1.72	3.03	0.77	499	495	505	3.5	2.3	10.9	4.8	60%	13%	34	17	49	21%	86%	9%	0	15			89	1.28	8.7	147	174	$21
16 Proj	**8**	**2**	**40**	**73**	**86**	**1.96**	**2.98**	**0.98**	**534**	**567**	**495**	**4.5**	**2.9**	**10.6**	**3.6**	**60%**	**12%**	**40**	**22**	**38**	**27%**	**82%**	**6%**	**0**						**17.9**	**131**	**156**	**$28**

De Fratus,Justin

Age: 28	Th: R	Role	RP	Health	D	LIMA Plan	C
Ht: 6' 4"	Wt: 225	Type	Pwr	PT/Exp	D	Rand Var	+4
				Consist	B	MM	1210

Whatever went right in 2014 went wrong in 2015. Wildly inconsistent month-to-month. RHB lathered him (though 41% H% played a role) and there were far fewer FpK, Swk, runners stranded. All that in career-high IP. Even at his best, he's really just a guy. Few vulture wins, zero saves make the decision even easier: Pass.

Yr Tm	W	L	Sv	IP	K	ERA	xERA	WHIP	oOPS	vL	vR	BF/G	Ctl	Dom	Cmd	FpK	SwK	G	L	F	H%	S%	hr/f	GS	APC	DOM%	DIS%	Sv%	LI	RAR	BPV	BPX	R$
11 PHI *	7	3	15	79	86	3.52	3.36	1.29	396	700	125	5.8	3.2	9.7	3.0	47%	9%	44	11	44	34%	73%	0%	0	12			88	0.69	4.1	112	168	$10
12 PHI *	0	1	3	32	26	3.32	2.55	1.04	478	646	361	4.2	2.3	7.2	3.2	61%	12%	52	13	35	26%	70%	0%	0	14			100	0.59	2.8	100	131	$0
13 PHI *	6	3	0	56	56	3.42	3.97	1.49	738	684	759	4.0	4.3	7.6	1.8	56%	12%	44	26	30	33%	77%	8%	0	14			0	1.21	3.6	73	95	-$1
14 PHI *	3	1	3	69	60	3.11	3.64	1.24	632	578	658	4.0	2.1	7.8	3.6	65%	13%	39	22	39	32%	77%	7%	0	15			50	1.02	5.3	105	125	$3
15 PHI	0	2	0	80	68	5.51	4.48	1.55	822	686	910	5.9	3.6	7.7	2.1	55%	11%	44	20	36	34%	65%	10%	0	24			0	0.54	-15.3	63	74	-$11
1st Half	0	1	0	45	45	5.04	3.81	1.37	774	579	907	5.1	3.2	9.1	2.8	59%	12%	46	20	34	33%	65%	14%	0	21			0	0.62	-5.9	100	119	-$8
2nd Half	0	1	0	35	23	6.11	5.40	1.78	878	819	913	7.3	4.1	5.9	1.4	49%	8%	42	21	37	36%	65%	7%	0	28			0	0.41	-9.4	15	18	-$14
16 Proj	**2**	**2**	**2**	**65**	**55**	**4.48**	**4.20**	**1.46**	**773**	**689**	**819**	**5.0**	**3.3**	**7.5**	**2.3**	**58%**	**11%**	**42**	**22**	**36**	**34%**	**70%**	**8%**	**0**						**-4.2**	**67**	**79**	**-$4**

de la Rosa,Jorge

Age: 35	Th: L	Role	SP	Health	F	LIMA Plan	B+
Ht: 6' 1"	Wt: 215	Type	Pwr GB	PT/Exp	A	Rand Var	+2
				Consist	A	MM	2203

Consistently the least objectionable SP, fantasy-wise, of his MLB org. Before your eyes glaze over, check out trends in Dom and GB%. Ctl, hr/f are pretty scary, and age, health grade may dissuade, but before you go, look at this three-year split: Home 23-5, 3.58 ERA, Road 16-19, 4.21 ERA. Thanks for your time.

Yr Tm	W	L	Sv	IP	K	ERA	xERA	WHIP	oOPS	vL	vR	BF/G	Ctl	Dom	Cmd	FpK	SwK	G	L	F	H%	S%	hr/f	GS	APC	DOM%	DIS%	Sv%	LI	RAR	BPV	BPX	R$
11 COL	5	2	0	59	52	3.51	3.73	1.19	627	349	684	24.5	3.4	7.9	2.4	49%	12%	43	20	38	28%	71%	7%	10	96	70%	20%			3.2	73	110	$3
12 COL	0	2	0	11	6	9.28	5.98	1.78	1065	250	1219	17.7	1.7	5.1	3.0	62%	13%	34	14	52	33%	57%	22%	3	68	0%	100%			-6.9	58	75	-$8
13 COL	16	6	0	168	112	3.49	4.14	1.38	721	510	770	23.8	3.3	6.0	1.8	60%	10%	47	25	28	31%	76%	8%	30	92	40%	17%			7.8	43	57	$7
14 COL	14	11	0	184	139	4.10	3.79	1.24	707	532	760	24.0	3.3	6.8	2.1	55%	10%	52	18	31	27%	70%	13%	32	96	44%	19%			-8.2	64	76	$6
15 COL	9	7	0	149	134	4.17	3.88	1.36	739	670	759	24.4	3.9	8.1	2.1	58%	12%	52	21	27	30%	72%	15%	26	95	50%	23%			-3.8	70	83	$2
1st Half	6	3	0	71	66	4.46	4.15	1.46	750	934	703	23.7	4.7	8.4	1.8	58%	12%	51	19	29	31%	71%	12%	13	94	46%	31%			-4.3	53	63	$0
2nd Half	3	4	0	78	68	3.91	3.64	1.26	728	471	815	25.2	3.2	7.8	2.4	59%	12%	53	22	25	29%	73%	18%	13	96	54%	15%			0.5	84	100	$3
16 Proj	**12**	**8**	**0**	**174**	**143**	**3.96**	**3.87**	**1.31**	**716**	**571**	**757**	**23.7**	**3.6**	**7.4**	**2.1**	**57%**	**11%**	**50**	**21**	**29**	**29%**	**72%**	**12%**	**30**						**0.0**	**66**	**78**	**$6**

De La Rosa,Rubby

Age: 27	Th: R	Role	SP	Health	A	LIMA Plan	B+
Ht: 6' 1"	Wt: 205	Type	Pwr	PT/Exp	C	Rand Var	+3
				Consist	A	MM	1203

Summing up 2015: Righties cowered, lefties towered, 1H glory, 2H gory. With such seismic splits, what's the takeaway? Season IP doubled his career total (which explains at least some of that 2H), and Cmd, BPV trends do show skills are congealing, so there is a case for at least some long-term optimism.

Yr Tm	W	L	Sv	IP	K	ERA	xERA	WHIP	oOPS	vL	vR	BF/G	Ctl	Dom	Cmd	FpK	SwK	G	L	F	H%	S%	hr/f	GS	APC	DOM%	DIS%	Sv%	LI	RAR	BPV	BPX	R$
11 LA *	6	7	0	101	105	3.30	3.28	1.32	722	759	678	19.8	4.3	9.4	2.2	56%	10%	48	22	30	30%	76%	13%	10	79	50%	20%	0	0.85	8.0	93	140	$5
12 LA	0	0	0	1	0	27.00	30.13	3.00	500	500	500	4.0	27.0	0.0	0.0	50%	5%	0	0	100	0%	0%	0%	0	20			0	0.14	-1.9	-751	-980	-$5
13 BOS *	3	5	0	92	68	5.33	4.80	1.56	877	646	994	11.5	5.0	6.7	1.3	64%	11%	48	14	38	30%	67%	13%	0	17			0	0.50	-16.6	36	48	-$10
14 BOS *	6	12	0	162	120	4.46	4.53	1.48	814	832	792	22.4	3.5	6.7	1.9	52%	9%	46	22	32	33%	70%	12%	18	92	22%	33%	0	0.74	-14.3	58	69	-$7
15 ARI	14	9	0	189	150	4.67	4.13	1.36	781	949	611	25.3	3.0	7.2	2.4	57%	12%	49	18	33	30%	71%	17%	32	94	41%	9%			-16.6	75	89	$0
1st Half	6	4	0	107	97	4.89	3.56	1.27	755	902	606	26.4	2.3	8.2	3.6	63%	13%	50	20	30	31%	66%	19%	17	96	53%	0%			-12.3	114	135	$1
2nd Half	8	5	0	82	53	4.39	4.95	1.48	814	1009	617	24.1	4.0	5.8	1.5	51%	10%	48	16	36	28%	76%	15%	15	92	27%	20%			-4.3	24	29	-$2
16 Proj	**11**	**10**	**0**	**174**	**135**	**4.28**	**4.12**	**1.37**	**753**	**847**	**651**	**24.3**	**3.4**	**7.0**	**2.0**	**54%**	**10%**	**48**	**20**	**33**	**30%**	**72%**	**13%**	**30**						**-6.8**	**59**	**70**	**$1**

deGrom,Jacob

Age: 28	Th: R	Role	SP	Health	A	LIMA Plan	D+
Ht: 6' 4"	Wt: 180	Type	Pwr	PT/Exp	B	Rand Var	-1
				Consist	C	MM	4405

Dynamic follow-up to ROY campaign. Improved on every significant metric, especially in 2H when change-up, sinker became force multipliers. Another force, regression, says he can't be held to this standard of improvement, but if backsliding equates to 2014, he'd still find himself among the first SP off the board.

Yr Tm	W	L	Sv	IP	K	ERA	xERA	WHIP	oOPS	vL	vR	BF/G	Ctl	Dom	Cmd	FpK	SwK	G	L	F	H%	S%	hr/f	GS	APC	DOM%	DIS%	Sv%	LI	RAR	BPV	BPX	R$
11																																	
12																																	
13 a/a	6	7	0	136	90	4.52	4.76	1.51				24.5	2.7	6.0	2.2						35%	70%								-10.9	59	77	-$7
14 NYM *	13	6	0	179	168	2.59	2.83	1.16	613	639	594	24.5	2.6	8.4	3.2	63%	12%	45	23	31	30%	79%	6%	22	102	68%	5%			25.4	113	135	$18
15 NYM	14	8	0	191	205	2.54	3.04	0.98	574	663	475	25.0	1.8	9.7	5.4	68%	13%	44	21	35	29%	78%	9%	30	99	77%	13%			33.4	148	176	$30
1st Half	8	6	0	106	102	2.30	3.27	0.97	551	629	464	25.9	1.7	8.7	5.1	66%	12%	43	22	36	27%	80%	8%	16	101	75%	13%			21.7	131	155	$35
2nd Half	6	2	0	85	103	2.85	2.76	1.00	601	706	489	24.0	1.9	10.9	5.7	70%	15%	47	20	33	30%	75%	12%	14	98	79%	14%			11.7	169	200	$25
16 Proj	**16**	**8**	**0**	**203**	**205**	**2.89**	**3.15**	**1.10**	**626**	**698**	**560**	**24.8**	**2.1**	**9.1**	**4.2**	**66%**	**13%**	**45**	**22**	**33**	**30%**	**76%**	**9%**	**32**						**26.8**	**129**	**153**	**$25**

Delgado,Randall

Age: 26	Th: R	Role	RP	Health	D	LIMA Plan	B+
Ht: 6' 3"	Wt: 200	Type	Pwr FB	PT/Exp	C	Rand Var	-2
				Consist	B	MM	2401

Two steps forward, two steps back during second season in pen. Forward: FpK fueled 1H Ctl gain, led to higher-leverage appearances in 2H. Back: Couldn't sustain that Ctl in 2H, jump in FB% could prove troublesome. Still, there's the sense this is a growth stock. Until then, take the Ks as a dividend advance.

Yr Tm	W	L	Sv	IP	K	ERA	xERA	WHIP	oOPS	vL	vR	BF/G	Ctl	Dom	Cmd	FpK	SwK	G	L	F	H%	S%	hr/f	GS	APC	DOM%	DIS%	Sv%	LI	RAR	BPV	BPX	R$
11 ATL *	8	8	0	174	139	3.98	4.33	1.40	655	683	635	23.0	3.6	7.2	2.0	52%	8%	38	20	42	31%	74%	11%	7	89	29%	14%			-0.9	58	87	$2
12 ATL *	8	12	0	137	121	4.40	4.47	1.48	727	744	711	22.6	4.1	8.0	2.0	60%	9%	50	22	28	32%	72%	11%	17	90	35%	29%	0	0.80	-6.6	63	83	-$3
13 ARI *	7	12	0	180	127	4.73	4.73	1.33	793	765	819	22.7	2.7	6.3	2.4	60%	9%	42	20	38	29%	70%	17%	19	91	47%	5%	0	0.75	-19.1	41	53	-$4
14 ARI	4	4	0	78	86	4.87	3.89	1.36	701	690	710	7.2	4.1	10.0	2.5	56%	14%	35	21	44	33%	64%	7%	4	31	0%	75%	0	0.82	-10.8	83	99	-$3
15 ARI	8	4	1	72	73	3.25	4.13	1.33	679	688	671	4.8	4.1	9.1	2.2	63%	13%	42	18	41	30%	79%	9%	1	20	0%	100%	33	1.07	6.3	73	87	$4
1st Half	3	2	1	38	34	3.32	4.08	1.37	708	558	783	4.9	3.3	8.1	2.4	63%	13%	45	19	35	31%	81%	13%	0	20			33	0.91	3.0	79	93	$2
2nd Half	5	2	0	34	39	3.18	4.20	1.29	644	810	518	4.7	5.0	10.3	2.1	62%	13%	37	15	48	29%	76%	5%	1	20	0%	100%	0	1.25	3.3	65	77	$6
16 Proj	**6**	**4**	**0**	**73**	**72**	**3.59**	**4.04**	**1.35**	**706**	**728**	**689**	**6.5**	**4.0**	**8.9**	**2.2**	**60%**	**13%**	**40**	**19**	**42**	**31%**	**76%**	**9%**	**0**						**3.3**	**71**	**84**	**$1**

ROB CARROLL

DeSclafani,Anthony

Age: 26	Th: R	Role SP	Health A	LIMA Plan B+
Ht: 6' 1"	Wt: 190	Type FB	PT/Exp C	Rand Var 0
			Consist A	MM 2205

Used curveball more as season progressed, became primary third pitch by Aug. Above average FpK, 2013 MLE support elite Ctl, and he added more GB% to mix as well. Could fly under radar thanks to elevated 2H H%, hr/f masking late growth. Final 11 GS: 9.0 Dom, 7.2 Cmd, 3.23 xERA. Huge sleeper potential.

Yr Tm	W	L	Sv	IP	K	ERA	xERA	WHIP	oOPS	vL	vR	BF/G	Ctl	Dom	Cmd	FpK	SwK	G	L	F	H%	S%	hr/f	GS	APC	DOM%	DIS%	Sv%	LI	RAR	BPV	BPX	R$
11																																	
12																																	
13 aa	5	4	0	75	52	4.25	4.42	1.36				24.1	1.8	6.2	3.5						34%	70%								-3.6	84	109	-$2
14 MIA *	8	9	0	135	104	4.63	3.86	1.31	801	893	710	16.9	2.3	6.9	3.0	66%	9%	36	24	40	32%	64%	9%	5	42	40%	40%	0	0.40	-14.8	87	103	-$2
15 CIN	9	13	0	185	151	4.05	4.04	1.35	742	783	697	25.3	2.7	7.4	2.7	63%	10%	45	21	34	32%	72%	9%	31	94	52%	10%			-1.9	83	99	$2
1st Half	5	6	0	95	68	3.68	4.55	1.35	706	705	706	25.6	3.5	6.4	1.8	63%	9%	44	21	35	30%	73%	6%	16	94	56%	13%			3.3	43	51	$4
2nd Half	4	7	0	89	83	4.43	3.53	1.34	780	865	688	25.1	1.8	8.4	4.6	63%	11%	46	21	32	35%	70%	13%	15	94	47%	7%			-5.2	126	149	$1
16 Proj	11	14	0	203	176	3.79	3.79	1.24	700	762	634	26.0	2.3	7.8	3.4	64%	10%	42	21	37	31%	72%	9%	32						4.2	98	117	$9

Despaigne,Odrisamer

Age: 29	Th: R	Role RP	Health A	LIMA Plan D+
Ht: 6' 0"	Wt: 195	Type Con GB	PT/Exp D	Rand Var +5
			Consist A	MM 1001

Drops in Dom, SwK severely damaged what little value he had to offer, S% and hr/f finished the job. August move to bullpen didn't yield any skill improvement. xERA suggests he can salvage something from the wreckage, but mid-4 ERA doesn't have the appeal it used to, in MLB or fantasy.

Yr Tm	W	L	Sv	IP	K	ERA	xERA	WHIP	oOPS	vL	vR	BF/G	Ctl	Dom	Cmd	FpK	SwK	G	L	F	H%	S%	hr/f	GS	APC	DOM%	DIS%	Sv%	LI	RAR	BPV	BPX	R$
11																																	
12																																	
13																																	
14 SD *	5	10	0	128	98	4.05	3.99	1.40	638	713	558	23.4	3.5	6.9	2.0	60%	8%	52	19	29	31%	71%	7%	16	97	44%	25%			-4.8	66	79	-$2
15 SD	5	9	0	126	69	5.80	4.39	1.38	803	789	815	16.1	2.3	4.9	2.2	58%	6%	50	22	27	30%	59%	15%	18	61	39%	28%	0	0.53	-28.5	55	66	-$11
1st Half	3	6	0	83	46	4.75	4.26	1.24	750	743	756	20.8	1.8	5.0	2.7	59%	6%	47	23	30	28%	64%	13%	13	80	46%	15%	0	0.66	-8.1	65	77	-$6
2nd Half	2	3	0	42	23	7.87	4.63	1.68	904	866	941	11.4	3.2	4.9	1.5	57%	6%	56	22	22	34%	52%	18%	5	43	20%	60%	0	0.40	-20.4	36	43	-$20
16 Proj	4	8	0	102	60	5.55	4.31	1.46	794	807	781	16.2	3.0	5.4	1.8	59%	7%	52	21	27	31%	62%	12%	17						-19.9	46	55	-$9

Diaz,Jose

Age: 32	Th: R	Role RP	Health A	LIMA Plan C+
Ht: 6' 4"	Wt: 315	Type Pwr	PT/Exp D	Rand Var +1
			Consist B	MM 3500

1 SV, 4.18 ERA in 60 IP at CIN. Late bloomer soared to new heights in Dom and Cmd, and did so primarily in bigs, where xERA was 3.28. Added more FpK to elite SwK, but struggles vs. LHP remained (career 1.7 Cmd). That'll likely be enough to keep save opps out of reach.

Yr Tm	W	L	Sv	IP	K	ERA	xERA	WHIP	oOPS	vL	vR	BF/G	Ctl	Dom	Cmd	FpK	SwK	G	L	F	H%	S%	hr/f	GS	APC	DOM%	DIS%	Sv%	LI	RAR	BPV	BPX	R$
11 a/a	0	3	23	45	37	3.59	5.47	1.72				4.2	4.7	7.4	1.6						36%	81%								1.9	48	72	$5
12 aaa	1	2	3	45	27	4.87	5.34	1.69				4.9	4.1	5.3	1.3						34%	71%								-4.7	34	44	-$7
13 aaa	3	4	13	54	46	2.44	4.01	1.34				5.1	4.1	7.6	1.8						27%	89%								9.6	54	70	$6
14 CIN *	2	3	18	68	61	2.36	3.20	1.25	668	778	589	4.2	3.3	8.1	2.4	57%	13%	40	31	30	30%	83%	11%	0	16			90	1.22	11.6	90	107	$10
15 CIN *	2	2	9	76	79	3.65	3.87	1.26	755	774	737	4.2	2.7	9.3	3.5	60%	15%	44	22	35	32%	75%	16%	0	17			64	0.97	2.9	101	120	$4
1st Half	2	2	5	36	32	5.05	4.65	1.34	833	713	956	4.2	2.2	8.1	3.7	57%	15%	48	22	31	33%	65%	25%	0	16			56	1.07	-4.8	87	103	$0
2nd Half	0	0	4	41	47	2.43	3.18	1.19	703	820	612	4.2	3.1	10.5	3.3	61%	15%	41	22	38	31%	84%	11%	0	18			80	0.89	7.7	115	137	$8
16 Proj	2	2	0	58	63	3.91	3.43	1.31	724	777	680	4.4	3.3	9.8	3.0	58%	14%	42	25	33	33%	72%	12%	0						0.4	108	128	-$1

Dickey,R.A.

Age: 41	Th: R	Role SP	Health B	LIMA Plan C+
Ht: 6' 3"	Wt: 215	Type Con	PT/Exp A	Rand Var -2
			Consist A	MM 1005

Another solid season, but red flags abound: sharp Dom drop, downward trend in SwK; decline in FpK suggests 1H Ctl more representative than 2H; worst xERA, Cmd, and BPV since 2011 breakout. He can keep the ball dancing a while longer, but he's back of the rotation material now.

Yr Tm	W	L	Sv	IP	K	ERA	xERA	WHIP	oOPS	vL	vR	BF/G	Ctl	Dom	Cmd	FpK	SwK	G	L	F	H%	S%	hr/f	GS	APC	DOM%	DIS%	Sv%	LI	RAR	BPV	BPX	R$
11 NYM	8	13	0	209	134	3.28	3.89	1.23	690	774	634	26.5	2.3	5.8	2.5	63%	8%	51	16	33	29%	76%	8%	32	95	47%	9%	0	0.79	17.1	70	105	$12
12 NYM	20	6	0	234	230	2.73	3.22	1.05	640	682	605	27.3	2.1	8.9	4.3	62%	13%	46	20	34	28%	79%	11%	33	99	70%	3%	0	0.76	36.9	127	166	$36
13 TOR	14	13	0	225	177	4.21	4.11	1.24	728	777	672	27.7	2.8	7.1	2.5	61%	10%	40	19	40	27%	71%	13%	34	103	59%	15%			-9.4	69	90	$7
14 TOR	14	13	0	216	173	3.71	4.01	1.23	705	659	740	26.9	3.1	7.2	2.3	63%	11%	42	20	38	27%	74%	11%	34	103	65%	9%			0.7	67	79	$9
15 TOR	11	11	0	214	126	3.91	4.54	1.19	708	679	736	26.8	2.6	5.3	2.1	59%	9%	42	21	37	26%	71%	10%	33	99	52%	12%			1.5	46	55	$9
1st Half	3	9	0	108	64	5.02	4.89	1.39	792	778	803	27.5	3.5	5.3	1.5	59%	9%	43	23	35	28%	67%	13%	17	103	29%	18%			-14.0	22	26	-$7
2nd Half	8	2	0	107	62	2.78	4.21	0.99	617	600	640	26.1	1.6	5.2	3.3	59%	10%	41	19	40	25%	75%	7%	16	94	75%	6%			15.5	70	83	$25
16 Proj	10	10	0	188	120	4.18	4.26	1.21	719	707	730	26.2	2.6	5.8	2.2	60%	10%	42	20	38	27%	69%	11%	29						-5.0	54	64	$5

Doolittle,Sean

Age: 29	Th: L	Role RP	Health F	LIMA Plan C+
Ht: 6' 3"	Wt: 210	Type Pwr xFB	PT/Exp C	Rand Var -1
			Consist C	MM 4530

Slight tear in rotator cuff limited him to one game until late Aug. Injury too serious, sample size too small to read anything into 2015 skills, especially since velocity didn't return until very end. Can't assume return to elite 2014 form. Extreme FB% creates risk should Ctl or Dom regress. Set price limit and stick to it.

Yr Tm	W	L	Sv	IP	K	ERA	xERA	WHIP	oOPS	vL	vR	BF/G	Ctl	Dom	Cmd	FpK	SwK	G	L	F	H%	S%	hr/f	GS	APC	DOM%	DIS%	Sv%	LI	RAR	BPV	BPX	R$
11																																	
12 OAK	2	1	1	47	60	3.04	3.17	1.08	611	794	509	4.3	2.1	11.4	5.5	66%	13%	35	15	50	33%	73%	5%	0	18			50	1.38	5.7	162	211	$3
13 OAK	5	5	2	69	60	3.13	3.55	0.96	573	516	603	3.8	1.7	7.8	4.6	65%	12%	33	20	47	27%	68%	5%	0	15			29	1.21	6.3	106	138	$7
14 OAK	2	4	22	63	89	2.73	2.61	0.73	459	276	550	3.9	1.1	12.8	11.1	72%	17%	23	18	59	27%	66%	6%	0	15			85	1.29	7.8	200	238	$17
15 OAK	1	0	4	14	15	3.95	3.96	1.24	651	1065	531	4.8	3.3	9.9	3.0	65%	10%	35	16	49	32%	69%	6%	0	21			80	0.75	0.0	102	121	-$2
1st Half	0	0	0	1	2	0.00	1.82	1.00	500	0	667	4.0	0.0	18.0	0.0	50%	21%	0	50	50	55%	0%	0%	0	14			0	0.27	0.5	302	358	-$8
2nd Half	1	0	4	13	13	4.26	4.17	1.26	664	1162	520	4.8	3.6	9.2	2.6	66%	10%	37	14	49	31%	67%	6%	0	22			80	0.79	-0.5	85	101	-$1
16 Proj	3	3	26	55	61	3.44	3.32	1.07	596	596	595	4.0	2.5	10.0	4.0	68%	14%	34	20	45	30%	69%	6%	0						3.5	126	150	$13

Doubront,Felix

Age: 28	Th: L	Role RP	Health D	LIMA Plan D+
Ht: 6' 2"	Wt: 225	Type Pwr	PT/Exp C	Rand Var +1
			Consist B	MM 1101

3-3, 5.50 ERA in 75 IP at OAK/TOR. xERA in majors last year? 4.41. xERA over 514 career MLB innings? 4.42. So basically zero skill growth after six seasons, with FpK suggesting Ctl is about to implode. Platoon splits make bullpen logical next step. Another Andrew Miller? Probably not. But at least keep that in mind.

Yr Tm	W	L	Sv	IP	K	ERA	xERA	WHIP	oOPS	vL	vR	BF/G	Ctl	Dom	Cmd	FpK	SwK	G	L	F	H%	S%	hr/f	GS	APC	DOM%	DIS%	Sv%	LI	RAR	BPV	BPX	R$
11 BOS *	3	5	1	86	63	5.22	5.03	1.50	952	1347	632	12.3	3.6	6.7	1.8	58%	6%	44	28	28	32%	68%	11%	0	16			100	0.33	-13.5	40	60	-$6
12 BOS	11	10	0	161	167	4.86	3.91	1.45	775	760	781	24.4	4.0	9.3	2.4	58%	10%	44	23	33	32%	70%	16%	29	99	45%	24%			-16.9	83	108	-$3
13 BOS	11	6	0	162	139	4.32	4.13	1.43	729	648	760	24.3	3.9	7.7	2.0	53%	8%	46	20	34	32%	70%	8%	27	98	52%	22%	0	0.75	-9.2	56	74	-$1
14 2 TM *	4	7	0	108	76	5.42	5.15	1.57	821	858	805	17.5	3.8	6.3	1.7	58%	7%	38	23	39	33%	66%	11%	14	65	29%	36%	0	0.56	-22.3	40	48	-$11
15 2 AL *	4	6	1	123	90	4.89	4.73	1.50	818	558	900	21.3	3.5	6.6	1.9	50%	10%	47	19	34	33%	68%	12%	12	79	33%	42%	100	0.75	-14.1	52	62	-$8
1st Half	1	3	0	50	35	3.93	4.06	1.50	667	0	857	21.7	3.9	6.3	1.6	67%	9%	50	38	13	33%	72%	0%	0	33			0	0.05	0.2	63	74	-$8
2nd Half	3	3	1	73	55	5.55	4.45	1.51	822	574	901	21.3	3.2	6.8	2.1	50%	10%	47	18	35	33%	65%	13%	12	82	33%	42%	100	0.80	-14.3	60	72	-$9
16 Proj	3	4	0	80	61	4.96	4.47	1.51	783	703	814	19.9	3.7	6.8	1.9	54%	9%	44	20	35	33%	68%	9%	17						-9.9	46	55	-$7

Duffey,Tyler

Age: 25	Th: R	Role SP	Health A	LIMA Plan B
Ht: 6' 3"	Wt: 230	Type GB	PT/Exp D	Rand Var 0
			Consist C	MM 2103

5-1, 3.10 in 58 IP at MIN. Unheralded rookie exceeded expectations, posted 8.6 Dom, 5.2 Cmd over final five GS. Strong FpK, Ctl history bode well, as does GB%; the only question is the strikeouts, especially since he relies on off-speed pitches to get them. If others are paying for 2015 results x 200 IP, sit this one out.

Yr Tm	W	L	Sv	IP	K	ERA	xERA	WHIP	oOPS	vL	vR	BF/G	Ctl	Dom	Cmd	FpK	SwK	G	L	F	H%	S%	hr/f	GS	APC	DOM%	DIS%	Sv%	LI	RAR	BPV	BPX	R$
11																																	
12																																	
13																																	
14 a/a	10	3	0	127	80	4.84	4.79	1.33				25.1	1.8	5.7	3.1						31%	67%								-17.2	58	69	-$3
15 MIN *	12	9	0	196	149	3.23	3.36	1.29	702	664	738	25.2	2.4	6.8	2.9	64%	10%	50	19	31	33%	74%	8%	10	91	60%	20%			17.8	96	115	$12
1st Half	5	6	0	104	74	3.22	3.43	1.33				27.0	2.1	6.4	3.1						34%	73%	0%	0						9.5	101	120	$10
2nd Half	7	3	0	92	75	3.23	3.27	1.24	702	664	738	23.3	2.7	7.4	2.7	64%	10%	50	19	31	31%	74%	8%	10	91	60%	20%			8.3	92	109	$14
16 Proj	11	6	0	160	122	3.74	3.80	1.29	691	644	737	24.9	2.2	6.9	3.2	64%	10%	50	19	31	32%	73%	9%	26						4.3	93	110	$6

BRANDON KRUSE

Duffy,Danny

Duffy,Danny			Health	F	LIMA Plan	D+
Age: 27	Th: L	Role: SP	PT/Exp	B	Rand Var	0
Ht: 6' 3"	Wt: 205	Type: Pwr FB	Consist	A	MM	1203

In 12 relief appearances over last two seasons: 2.7 Ctl, 12.4 Dom, 4.6 Cmd. Small sample, but more to hang his hat on than his work as SP. Platoon split history (including career .588 OPS, 2.7 Cmd vs. LHH) delivers same message, but employers don't seem to hear it. Until they do, he's little more than filler.

Yr	Tm	W	L	Sv	IP	K	ERA	xERA	WHIP	oOPS	vL	vR	BF/G	Ctl	Dom	Cmd	FpK	SwK	G	L	F	H%	S%	hr/f	GS	APC	DOM%	DIS%	Sv%	LI	RAR	BPV	BPX	R$
11	KC *	7	9	0	147	126	5.09	4.90	1.49	864	811	882	22.7	3.7	7.7	2.1	52%	8%	38	22	40	33%	68%	11%	20	98	20%	25%			-20.8	54	81	-$7
12	KC	2	2	0	28	28	3.90	4.80	1.59	771	491	859	20.2	5.9	9.1	1.6	52%	10%	35	21	44	32%	76%	6%	6	88	17%	50%			0.4	19	25	-$4
13	KC *	5	2	0	93	90	4.26	4.48	1.54	608	692	571	19.4	4.4	8.7	2.0	54%	11%	32	27	41	34%	73%	0%	5	94	20%	60%			-4.5	72	94	-$4
14	KC	9	12	0	149	113	2.53	4.24	1.11	605	386	670	19.5	3.2	6.8	2.1	59%	8%	36	18	46	25%	81%	6%	25	78	52%	20%	0	0.87	22.3	50	60	$14
15	KC	7	8	1	137	102	4.08	4.56	1.39	746	591	784	19.6	3.5	6.7	1.9	57%	9%	39	25	36	30%	73%	10%	24	79	38%	21%	100	0.75	-2.0	44	52	$0
1st Half		2	4	0	56	41	5.14	4.92	1.59	819	735	846	22.7	3.9	6.6	1.7	57%	7%	36	28	36	34%	69%	9%	11	90	27%	27%			-8.2	28	34	-$12
2nd Half		5	4	1	81	61	3.35	4.32	1.25	692	451	743	17.8	3.2	6.8	2.1	57%	10%	41	22	37	27%	77%	10%	13	72	46%	15%	100	0.75	6.1	54	64	$8
16	Proj	9	9	0	160	126	4.03	4.40	1.35	723	568	767	22.8	3.6	7.1	2.0	57%	8%	38	22	40	30%	72%	8%	29						-1.4	47	56	$2

Duke,Zach

Duke,Zach			Health	B	LIMA Plan	B
Age: 33	Th: L	Role: RP	PT/Exp	D	Rand Var	+1
Ht: 6' 2"	Wt: 210	Type: Pwr xGB	Consist	D	MM	4400

Well, that didn't last long. Followed up career-best Cmd with career-worst Ctl, though elite Dom was enough to keep ERA from blowing up. With no reported injury, we're left with FpK decline as confirmation of walks, an idea 2H seems to confirm. Still earning high LI, but doesn't look as roster-worthy as a year ago.

Yr	Tm	W	L	Sv	IP	K	ERA	xERA	WHIP	oOPS	vL	vR	BF/G	Ctl	Dom	Cmd	FpK	SwK	G	L	F	H%	S%	hr/f	GS	APC	DOM%	DIS%	Sv%	LI	RAR	BPV	BPX	R$
11	ARI	3	4	1	77	32	4.93	4.51	1.57	820	571	891	16.1	2.2	3.8	1.7	59%	7%	50	22	28	34%	68%	8%	9	58	11%	22%	100	0.48	-9.3	35	53	-$7
12	WAS *	16	5	0	178	76	4.42	5.82	1.61	556	646	520	23.2	2.3	3.8	1.7	54%	11%	40	28	33	34%	75%	0%	0	27			0	0.37	-8.8	18	24	-$9
13	2 NL *	3	2	2	59	44	4.11	4.41	1.38	806	728	854	4.8	2.4	6.7	2.7	56%	10%	50	21	29	32%	72%	9%	1	20	0%	100%	100	1.09	-1.8	68	89	-$2
14	MIL	5	1	0	59	74	2.45	2.32	1.13	578	569	586	3.2	2.6	11.4	4.4	63%	13%	58	22	20	33%	79%	10%	0	13			0	1.11	9.3	170	202	$5
15	CHW	3	6	1	61	66	3.41	3.39	1.30	724	611	793	3.6	4.7	9.8	2.1	55%	11%	58	17	25	27%	80%	24%	0	15			33	1.47	4.1	84	100	$1
1st Half		3	3	1	32	29	3.41	3.78	1.36	782	757	792	3.6	4.0	8.2	2.1	60%	11%	53	16	30	28%	84%	23%	0	15			100	1.36	2.2	72	86	$1
2nd Half		0	3	0	29	37	3.41	2.92	1.24	658	502	793	3.5	5.6	11.5	2.1	50%	11%	65	18	17	25%	76%	27%	0	15			0	1.58	2.0	98	117	$0
16	Proj	3	4	0	58	60	3.40	3.21	1.29	695	593	760	3.9	3.7	9.3	2.5	57%	11%	57	20	23	30%	77%	17%	0						4.0	102	122	$1

Dunn,Mike

Dunn,Mike			Health	A	LIMA Plan	C
Age: 31	Th: L	Role: RP	PT/Exp	C	Rand Var	+1
Ht: 6' 0"	Wt: 210	Type: Pwr FB	Consist	A	MM	2510

Plenty of Dom, but xERA indicates he'll be hard-pressed to reach next level without better Ctl. 2014 FpK was step in right direction—if he can bring that back with 2015 FB%, might be onto something. LI says he has the confidence of management, so speculative flyer wouldn't be out of place in deep leagues.

Yr	Tm	W	L	Sv	IP	K	ERA	xERA	WHIP	oOPS	vL	vR	BF/G	Ctl	Dom	Cmd	FpK	SwK	G	L	F	H%	S%	hr/f	GS	APC	DOM%	DIS%	Sv%	LI	RAR	BPV	BPX	R$
11	FLA	5	6	0	63	68	3.43	3.84	1.30	723	615	809	3.7	4.4	9.7	2.2	56%	12%	39	16	46	28%	79%	12%	0	16			0	1.20	4.0	72	109	$2
12	MIA *	1	4	1	62	67	5.20	5.19	1.78	806	784	828	3.9	5.4	9.8	1.8	54%	8%	34	28	38	39%	69%	6%	0	15			14	1.11	-9.0	79	103	-$10
13	MIA	3	4	2	68	72	2.66	3.73	1.20	604	549	655	3.8	3.7	9.6	2.6	60%	12%	40	18	43	29%	80%	7%	0	16			40	1.26	10.1	90	117	$5
14	MIA	10	6	1	57	67	3.16	3.57	1.21	635	598	671	3.3	3.5	10.6	3.0	64%	14%	34	20	47	31%	75%	6%	0	13			25	1.47	4.1	109	129	$5
15	MIA	2	5	0	54	65	4.50	3.92	1.39	712	655	754	3.3	4.8	10.8	2.2	59%	13%	39	22	39	31%	70%	11%	0	14			0	1.34	-3.6	82	97	-$3
1st Half		1	4	0	27	29	4.73	4.36	1.43	735	596	867	3.4	4.7	9.8	2.1	57%	12%	39	15	46	31%	69%	9%	0	13			0	1.24	-2.5	65	78	-$5
2nd Half		1	1	0	27	36	4.28	3.50	1.35	689	732	663	3.3	4.9	11.9	2.4	61%	13%	38	29	32	32%	71%	14%	0	14			0	1.44	-1.1	96	114	-$1
16	Proj	4	4	2	51	60	3.85	3.70	1.33	681	636	718	3.2	4.3	10.6	2.4	60%	13%	37	22	41	31%	73%	9%	0						0.7	88	105	$0

Dyson,Sam

Dyson,Sam			Health	A	LIMA Plan	B+
Age: 28	Th: R	Role: RP	PT/Exp	D	Rand Var	0
Ht: 6' 1"	Wt: 205	Type: Pwr xGB	Consist	B	MM	5310

Judging by tiny FB%, you'd swear he was rolling ball to home plate. Increased use of change-up helped drive Dom breakout, complete with SwK support. Finally tamed LHB. 2H Ctl would be final piece to puzzle—and springboard to saves—but lack of FpK casts some doubt. Even so, a promising skill set.

Yr	Tm	W	L	Sv	IP	K	ERA	xERA	WHIP	oOPS	vL	vR	BF/G	Ctl	Dom	Cmd	FpK	SwK	G	L	F	H%	S%	hr/f	GS	APC	DOM%	DIS%	Sv%	LI	RAR	BPV	BPX	R$
11																																		
12	TOR *	2	2	9	46	19	3.62	4.23	1.46	1750	2000	1667	5.6	3.4	3.8	1.1	63%	4%	80	20	0	30%	75%	0%	0	13			90	0.17	2.2	31	40	$0
13	MIA *	4	12	0	117	51	3.97	4.16	1.50	959	1014	919	19.5	3.3	3.9	1.2	48%	6%	69	5	26	32%	72%	18%	1	35	0%	100%	0	0.79	-1.5	39	51	-$6
14	MIA *	5	2	1	67	49	2.33	3.20	1.33	653	781	553	6.3	3.3	6.5	2.0	60%	11%	63	19	18	31%	81%	4%	0	22			33	0.68	11.7	80	96	$3
15	2 TM	5	4	2	75	71	2.63	2.74	1.14	603	557	633	4.1	2.5	8.5	3.4	60%	13%	69	17	14	30%	78%	13%	0	15			50	1.02	12.4	132	157	$7
1st Half		3	3	0	37	36	3.62	3.17	1.26	594	536	640	4.3	3.6	8.7	2.4	59%	11%	64	19	18	31%	70%	6%	0	15			0	1.03	1.6	100	119	$3
2nd Half		2	1	2	38	35	1.66	2.34	1.03	611	584	624	4.0	1.4	8.3	5.8	60%	15%	74	15	11	29%	89%	25%	0	14			100	1.02	10.8	162	193	$11
16	Proj	4	3	2	65	57	2.76	2.97	1.26	646	682	622	5.3	2.8	7.9	2.8	60%	12%	67	17	16	32%	78%	10%	0						9.7	112	133	$4

Eickhoff,Jerad

Eickhoff,Jerad			Health	A	LIMA Plan	B+
Age: 25	Th: R	Role: SP	PT/Exp	D	Rand Var	0
Ht: 6' 4"	Wt: 200	Type: Pwr FB	Consist	F	MM	1205

3-3, 2.65 ERA in 51 IP at PHI. Skill growth timed out perfectly with ascension to majors, and closed out first stint in bigs with back-to-back 10-K gems. But MLB xERA was a run higher (3.64), and OPS, 1.9 Cmd vs. LHB shows there's still work to be done. More "youngster worth watching" than "budding ace."

Yr	Tm	W	L	Sv	IP	K	ERA	xERA	WHIP	oOPS	vL	vR	BF/G	Ctl	Dom	Cmd	FpK	SwK	G	L	F	H%	S%	hr/f	GS	APC	DOM%	DIS%	Sv%	LI	RAR	BPV	BPX	R$
11																																		
12																																		
13	aa	1	1	0	29	11	10.19	8.29	1.97				23.1	4.8	3.3	0.7						32%	50%								-22.6	-53	-70	-$14
14	aa	10	9	0	154	118	5.11	4.30	1.34				23.8	3.2	6.9	2.2						30%	64%								-26.1	55	66	-$5
15	PHI *	15	8	0	184	155	4.11	4.05	1.27	621	830	458	24.3	2.6	7.6	2.9	65%	11%	38	22	40	30%	71%	9%	8	92	75%	13%			-3.3	75	89	$8
1st Half		7	3	0	87	72	4.91	4.76	1.36				24.2	3.1	7.5	2.4						30%	68%	0%	0						-10.1	52	61	$0
2nd Half		8	5	0	98	84	3.39	3.42	1.19	621	830	458	24.5	2.3	7.7	3.4	65%	11%	38	22	40	30%	74%	9%	8	92	75%	13%			6.8	99	117	$15
16	Proj	12	11	0	181	148	4.22	4.20	1.30	697	933	512	24.1	2.8	7.3	2.6	65%	11%	38	22	40	30%	71%	10%	31						-5.7	71	85	$4

Elias,Roenis

Elias,Roenis			Health	A	LIMA Plan	C
Age: 27	Th: L	Role: SP	PT/Exp	C	Rand Var	+2
Ht: 6' 1"	Wt: 190	Type: Pwr	Consist	B	MM	1203

5-8, 4.14 ERA in 115 IP at SEA. MLEs took a bite out of skills, but in majors, it was a carbon copy of 2014: 4.18 xERA, 1.30 WHIP, 7.6 Dom, 66 BPV. Given age, sure looks like this may be his peak, which makes him serviceable back-of-rotation guy in bigs. For you, depending on format, mileage may vary.

Yr	Tm	W	L	Sv	IP	K	ERA	xERA	WHIP	oOPS	vL	vR	BF/G	Ctl	Dom	Cmd	FpK	SwK	G	L	F	H%	S%	hr/f	GS	APC	DOM%	DIS%	Sv%	LI	RAR	BPV	BPX	R$
11																																		
12																																		
13	aa	6	11	0	130	101	4.51	4.57	1.51				25.6	3.7	7.0	1.9						33%	71%								-10.4	58	75	-$6
14	SEA	10	12	0	164	143	3.85	3.81	1.31	713	655	729	23.9	3.5	7.9	2.2	60%	10%	45	21	34	30%	73%	10%	29	92	48%	17%			-2.2	70	83	$3
15	SEA *	9	10	0	177	135	5.37	4.91	1.45	730	608	765	22.2	3.1	6.9	2.2	60%	10%	44	19	36	32%	65%	12%	20	84	50%	15%	0	0.73	-30.6	50	60	-$10
1st Half		6	6	0	94	74	4.96	4.55	1.36	728	678	742	24.5	3.0	7.1	2.3	60%	10%	43	21	36	30%	67%	13%	13	93	54%	15%			-11.6	53	63	-$5
2nd Half		3	4	0	83	61	5.82	5.30	1.56	735	445	811	20.2	3.2	6.6	2.1	58%	11%	48	16	36	34%	63%	10%	7	70	43%	14%	0	0.65	-19.0	47	56	-$16
16	Proj	8	10	0	145	116	4.47	4.20	1.43	787	644	827	22.8	3.4	7.2	2.2	59%	10%	45	19	35	32%	71%	10%	27						-9.0	63	75	-$3

Eovaldi,Nathan

Eovaldi,Nathan			Health	D	LIMA Plan	B+
Age: 26	Th: R	Role: SP	PT/Exp	A	Rand Var	+1
Ht: 6' 2"	Wt: 215	Type:	Consist	A	MM	2103

Added splitter to repertoire, then tweaked grip in June, increasing velocity, which led to 2H bumps in Dom, FpK, SwK, and GB%. Perhaps Ctl regression was temporary result of tinkering. Elbow inflammation that ended season hangs a cloud over 2016 outlook, but there is reason for cautious optimism... UP: 3.50 ERA.

Yr	Tm	W	L	Sv	IP	K	ERA	xERA	WHIP	oOPS	vL	vR	BF/G	Ctl	Dom	Cmd	FpK	SwK	G	L	F	H%	S%	hr/f	GS	APC	DOM%	DIS%	Sv%	LI	RAR	BPV	BPX	R$
11	LA *	7	7	0	138	109	2.84	2.53	1.21	667	735	619	18.5	3.9	7.1	1.8	54%	10%	41	26	34	27%	76%	6%	6	60	33%	17%	0	0.63	18.7	84	127	$11
12	2 NL *	6	15	0	154	104	4.11	4.40	1.46	771	845	665	21.3	3.5	6.1	1.7	58%	8%	46	23	31	32%	73%	8%	22	94	32%	36%			-1.9	52	67	-$4
13	MIA	4	6	0	106	78	3.39	4.21	1.32	681	665	691	25.1	3.4	6.6	2.0	59%	8%	44	22	34	30%	75%	6%	18	94	67%	17%			6.3	49	64	$2
14	MIA	6	14	0	200	142	4.37	3.90	1.33	732	768	688	25.9	1.9	6.4	3.3	63%	9%	45	22	33	33%	67%	7%	33	97	55%	21%			-15.5	86	102	-$3
15	NYY	14	3	0	154	121	4.20	3.98	1.45	716	781	656	24.9	2.9	7.1	2.5	60%	9%	52	22	26	34%	71%	8%	27	98	22%	22%			-4.5	80	95	$1
1st Half		8	2	0	88	63	4.52	4.21	1.54	779	902	678	24.3	2.6	6.5	2.5	57%	8%	49	24	27	36%	72%	10%	16	93	19%	38%			-6.0	74	88	-$2
2nd Half		6	1	0	67	58	3.78	3.68	1.34	629	637	621	25.9	3.2	7.8	2.4	63%	10%	57	19	25	33%	70%	4%	11	105	27%	0%			1.5	88	104	$4
16	Proj	11	7	0	174	133	3.99	3.93	1.37	699	739	659	24.1	2.8	6.9	2.4	60%	9%	49	22	29	33%	71%	7%	30						-0.5	74	88	$2

BRANDON KRUSE

Erlin,Robert

Age: 25	Th: L	Role: SP	Health: D	LIMA Plan: C	
Ht: 6' 0"	Wt: 190	Type:	PT/Exp: D	Rand Var: 0	
			Consist: A	MM: 2101	

1-2, 4.76 ERA in 17 IP at SD. Hasn't been able to turn AA Dom into MLB strikeouts; do consistently high H%, LD% suggest too much pitching to contact? What looks like reverse splits is actually 37% career hit rate vs. LHB. Solid Ctl, rising GB% offer decent foundation to build upon, but without Dom, it's not up to code.

Yr Tm	W	L	Sv	IP	K	ERA	xERA	WHIP	oOPS	vL	vR	BF/G	Ctl	Dom	Cmd	FpK	SwK	G	L	F	H%	S%	hr/f	GS	APC	DOM%	DIS%	Sv%	LI	RAR	BPV	BPX	R$
11 aa	6	2	0	93	84	3.23	3.69	1.17				21.8	1.0	8.2	8.3						34%	75%								8.1	199	300	$6
12 aa	3	1	0	52	65	2.76	3.77	1.26				19.4	2.2	11.1	5.1						37%	81%								8.1	152	198	$2
13 SD *	11	6	0	154	115	4.41	4.66	1.44	698	823	641	21.2	2.6	6.7	2.6	62%	7%	37	25	37	34%	71%	10%	9	82	33%	22%	0	0.63	-10.3	65	84	-$2
14 SD *	4	6	0	82	61	5.28	5.32	1.53	787	755	799	19.9	2.2	6.7	3.0	65%	9%	41	27	32	36%	66%	10%	11	77	45%	36%	0	0.70	-15.7	68	81	-$8
15 SD *	8	8	0	142	98	5.21	5.27	1.47	663	1000	592	22.6	2.3	6.2	2.7	65%	9%	47	25	27	34%	67%	7%	3	73	67%	33%			-21.9	52	62	-$9
1st Half	5	5	0	84	63	5.83	6.52	1.67				23.6	2.7	6.7	2.5						36%	68%	0%	0						-19.4	35	41	-$14
2nd Half	3	3	0	58	35	4.32	3.45	1.19	663	1000	592	21.1	1.8	5.4	3.1	65%	9%	47	25	27	29%	64%	7%	3	73	67%	33%			-2.5	81	96	$0
16 Proj	**4**	**4**	**0**	**73**	**53**	**4.50**	**4.05**	**1.41**	**811**	**956**	**760**	**21.2**	**2.2**	**6.6**	**3.0**	**64%**	**8%**	**42**	**26**	**32**	**34%**	**70%**	**10%**	**14**						**-4.8**	**80**	**95**	**-$4**

Estrada,Marco

Age: 32	Th: R	Role: RP	Health: D	LIMA Plan: D+	
Ht: 6' 0"	Wt: 200	Type: xFB	PT/Exp: A	Rand Var: -5	
			Consist: B	MM: 1203	

Ahh, a rare sighting of the fabled "Career-best performance with career-worst skills." H%, S% did the heavy lifting. Nearly half his metrics are in steady decline. There's a dangerous level of disconnect between 2015 R$ and xERA, and someone's gonna (over)pay the price at the draft table. Don't let it be you.

Yr Tm	W	L	Sv	IP	K	ERA	xERA	WHIP	oOPS	vL	vR	BF/G	Ctl	Dom	Cmd	FpK	SwK	G	L	F	H%	S%	hr/f	GS	APC	DOM%	DIS%	Sv%	LI	RAR	BPV	BPX	R$
11 MIL	4	8	0	93	88	4.08	3.60	1.21	700	661	733	8.9	2.8	8.5	3.0	57%	11%	40	18	43	29%	69%	10%	7	36	86%	0%	0	0.66	-1.6	96	144	$2
12 MIL	5	7	0	138	143	3.64	3.59	1.14	703	728	681	19.4	1.9	9.3	4.9	62%	11%	34	20	45	31%	73%	10%	23	77	48%	26%	0	0.71	6.3	129	168	$9
13 MIL	7	4	0	128	118	3.87	3.60	1.08	670	651	687	24.4	2.0	8.3	4.1	60%	11%	38	18	44	27%	70%	12%	21	95	62%	14%			0.0	110	144	$8
14 MIL	7	6	0	151	127	4.36	4.15	1.20	752	719	781	16.0	2.6	7.6	2.9	61%	11%	33	18	50	27%	71%	13%	18	65	56%	0%	0	0.63	-11.5	77	91	$2
15 TOR	13	8	0	181	131	3.13	4.61	1.04	633	638	626	21.3	2.7	6.5	2.4	57%	10%	32	16	52	22%	76%	9%	28	86	50%	14%	0	0.76	18.5	53	64	$20
1st Half	6	4	0	80	67	3.59	4.43	1.16	657	653	662	18.6	3.1	7.5	2.4	57%	11%	37	17	46	26%	73%	9%	12	76	58%	17%	0	0.75	3.7	65	77	$13
2nd Half	7	4	0	101	64	2.77	4.74	0.95	612	627	586	24.4	2.4	5.7	2.4	58%	10%	28	14	57	20%	79%	8%	16	97	44%	13%			14.8	44	52	$26
16 Proj	**10**	**7**	**0**	**160**	**125**	**3.94**	**4.27**	**1.20**	**727**	**713**	**742**	**18.6**	**2.5**	**7.0**	**2.8**	**59%**	**11%**	**33**	**17**	**50**	**27%**	**72%**	**10%**	**30**						**0.4**	**69**	**82**	**$7**

Familia,Jeurys

Age: 26	Th: R	Role: RP	Health: D	LIMA Plan: C	
Ht: 6' 3"	Wt: 240	Type: Pwr xGB	PT/Exp: C	Rand Var: -3	
			Consist: D	MM: 5531	

This is how you seize an opportunity. Pushed FpK into elite territory in 2H, and added splitter in August that really blew things up (12.0 Dom after 8/1). Improved Cmd vs. LHB to 2.6, bumped it up to 4.0 in 2H. GB% is icing on already loaded cake. ERA likely to regress a bit, but otherwise, he's primed for a repeat.

Yr Tm	W	L	Sv	IP	K	ERA	xERA	WHIP	oOPS	vL	vR	BF/G	Ctl	Dom	Cmd	FpK	SwK	G	L	F	H%	S%	hr/f	GS	APC	DOM%	DIS%	Sv%	LI	RAR	BPV	BPX	R$
11 aa	4	4	0	88	80	3.33	3.84	1.31				21.3	3.1	8.3	2.7						31%	77%								6.6	84	127	$3
12 NYM *	9	9	0	149	122	5.10	4.73	1.64	644	751	560	18.5	4.7	7.3	1.6	42%	9%	48	18	33	35%	68%	0%	1	26	0%	100%	0	0.13	-19.9	61	79	-$12
13 NYM	0	0	1	11	8	4.22	5.79	1.97	908	889	918	5.8	7.6	6.8	0.9	52%	7%	52	15	33	31%	84%	18%	0	22			100	0.69	-0.5	-54	-70	-$5
14 NYM	2	5	5	77	73	2.21	3.36	1.18	587	821	377	4.2	3.7	8.5	2.3	53%	13%	57	15	28	28%	82%	5%	0	16			50	1.18	14.6	87	104	$7
15 NYM	2	2	43	78	86	1.85	2.62	1.00	569	616	531	4.1	2.2	9.9	4.5	61%	16%	58	20	22	28%	86%	14%	0	15			90	1.29	20.4	155	185	$27
1st Half	2	0	22	39	40	1.16	2.69	0.91	499	464	524	4.1	2.8	9.3	3.3	59%	15%	60	21	19	22%	94%	17%	0	16			92	1.36	13.3	130	154	$30
2nd Half	0	2	21	39	46	2.52	2.55	1.09	632	745	537	4.0	1.6	10.5	6.6	64%	17%	57	19	24	34%	80%	12%	0	15			88	1.24	7.0	181	215	$24
16 Proj	**2**	**3**	**41**	**73**	**79**	**2.51**	**2.80**	**1.15**	**624**	**764**	**506**	**5.0**	**2.7**	**9.8**	**3.6**	**60%**	**15%**	**58**	**18**	**24**	**31%**	**80%**	**10%**	**0**						**13.0**	**139**	**165**	**$22**

Farmer,Buck

Age: 25	Th: R	Role: RP	Health: A	LIMA Plan: D+	
Ht: 6' 4"	Wt: 225	Type: GB	PT/Exp: D	Rand Var: +5	
			Consist: B	MM: 0001	

0-4, 7.36 ERA in 40 IP at DET. Seeded the soil with FpK, but it would not yield above-average crop of Ctl. (Sorry.) 2H erosion of Dom led to ERA/xERA degradation. (Really sorry.) Best to let him lie fallow for a season, check levels again in the future. (Okay, we're done now.)

Yr Tm	W	L	Sv	IP	K	ERA	xERA	WHIP	oOPS	vL	vR	BF/G	Ctl	Dom	Cmd	FpK	SwK	G	L	F	H%	S%	hr/f	GS	APC	DOM%	DIS%	Sv%	LI	RAR	BPV	BPX	R$
11																																	
12																																	
13																																	
14 DET *	2	2	0	29	21	8.12	6.03	1.70	1054	1189	880	16.2	4.1	6.7	1.6	70%	11%	33	15	52	35%	51%	14%	2	49	0%	50%	0	0.42	-15.5	30	35	-$8
15 DET *	7	7	0	127	84	5.80	5.38	1.54	986	1067	920	18.5	3.1	5.9	1.9	60%	8%	45	15	40	33%	64%	18%	5	50	0%	80%	0	0.58	-28.7	36	43	-$13
1st Half	7	4	0	91	65	4.94	4.56	1.43	1106	1269	879	24.1	2.8	6.4	2.3	63%	10%	43	20	37	33%	66%	23%	2	94	0%	50%			-11.0	59	70	-$8
2nd Half	0	3	0	36	19	7.92	7.45	1.82	942	955	931	12.1	3.7	4.7	1.3	59%	7%	46	13	41	34%	59%	17%	3	43	0%	100%	0	0.55	-17.7	-17	-20	-$25
16 Proj	**3**	**6**	**0**	**87**	**52**	**6.12**	**5.16**	**1.66**	**851**	**891**	**825**	**14.8**	**3.3**	**5.4**	**1.6**	**59%**	**7%**	**46**	**13**	**41**	**33%**	**66%**	**11%**	**13**						**-23.2**	**31**	**37**	**-$14**

Farquhar,Daniel

Age: 29	Th: R	Role: RP	Health: A	LIMA Plan: C+	
Ht: 5' 9"	Wt: 185	Type: Pwr	PT/Exp: D	Rand Var: +2	
			Consist: C	MM: 3400	

1-8, 5.12 ERA in 51 IP at SEA. With eight relief losses, was opposite of a vulture: a squanderer, if you will, and it cost him setup role. Dom, SwK continued to slide, and alarming FB% jump caused xERA to swell. BPV cut in half in just two years. Still young enough to get back on track, but you can't pay without proof.

Yr Tm	W	L	Sv	IP	K	ERA	xERA	WHIP	oOPS	vL	vR	BF/G	Ctl	Dom	Cmd	FpK	SwK	G	L	F	H%	S%	hr/f	GS	APC	DOM%	DIS%	Sv%	LI	RAR	BPV	BPX	R$
11 TOR *	4	5	15	62	45	4.05	4.79	1.55	1170	1750	829	4.7	3.0	6.6	2.2	73%	5%	25	50	25	36%	74%	0%	0	14			83	0.01	-0.8	65	97	$3
12 a/a	3	3	9	68	60	2.85	2.42	1.11				6.1	2.8	7.9	2.8						28%	74%								9.7	107	140	$8
13 SEA *	0	4	22	76	104	3.74	2.59	1.18	586	485	695	5.0	3.1	12.3	4.0	55%	14%	42	25	33	35%	67%	5%	0	20			81	1.18	1.2	157	205	$10
14 SEA	3	1	1	71	81	2.66	2.98	1.13	607	641	578	4.4	2.8	10.3	3.7	59%	12%	42	27	31	31%	79%	9%	0	17			33	0.85	9.5	130	154	$5
15 SEA *	2	9	4	89	80	4.34	4.80	1.41	818	676	938	5.4	2.7	8.1	3.0	58%	11%	39	22	40	34%	73%	15%	0	19			57	0.91	-4.1	74	88	-$3
1st Half	1	4	1	44	38	5.86	5.39	1.53	848	873	827	5.8	3.4	7.9	2.3	60%	10%	41	25	34	34%	64%	15%	0	21			25	0.92	-10.3	50	60	-$10
2nd Half	1	5	3	45	42	2.86	4.22	1.29	784	451	1063	5.0	2.0	8.3	4.2	57%	12%	36	17	46	34%	83%	16%	0	18			100	0.90	6.1	108	128	$4
16 Proj	**2**	**5**	**0**	**65**	**64**	**3.59**	**3.63**	**1.28**	**718**	**622**	**803**	**5.0**	**2.7**	**8.8**	**3.2**	**58%**	**12%**	**40**	**24**	**37**	**32%**	**74%**	**9%**	**0**						**3.0**	**102**	**122**	**$0**

Feldman,Scott

Age: 33	Th: R	Role: SP	Health: F	LIMA Plan: D+	
Ht: 6' 7"	Wt: 230	Type: Con	PT/Exp: A	Rand Var: 0	
			Consist: A	MM: 1003	

It's like he took a dare to see how far he could lower Dom and still keep ERA under 4.00. May knee surgery, Sept rotator cuff ills didn't help skills either. Ctl/FpK, GB% are only metrics keeping him from going up in flames. Anyone paying for another sub-4 ERA risks getting burnt. DN: 4.50 ERA, fewer than 100 IP

Yr Tm	W	L	Sv	IP	K	ERA	xERA	WHIP	oOPS	vL	vR	BF/G	Ctl	Dom	Cmd	FpK	SwK	G	L	F	H%	S%	hr/f	GS	APC	DOM%	DIS%	Sv%	LI	RAR	BPV	BPX	R$
11 TEX *	5	2	0	82	45	4.76	4.63	1.39	614	391	837	16.4	2.4	5.0	2.0	54%	8%	62	13	25	31%	68%	13%	2	46	50%	0%	0	0.39	-8.2	40	60	-$3
12 TEX	6	11	0	124	96	5.09	4.12	1.38	745	752	736	18.5	2.3	7.0	3.0	61%	8%	42	26	32	33%	64%	11%	21	73	38%	33%	0	0.71	-16.5	83	108	-$6
13 2 TM	12	12	0	182	132	3.86	3.85	1.18	671	672	670	25.3	2.8	6.5	2.4	56%	8%	50	19	32	27%	70%	11%	30	100	50%	17%			0.0	71	92	$9
14 HOU	8	12	0	180	107	3.74	4.13	1.30	725	715	737	26.4	2.5	5.3	2.1	61%	7%	47	22	31	30%	73%	9%	29	102	41%	17%			0.0	54	64	$2
15 HOU	5	5	0	108	61	3.90	4.26	1.31	739	664	824	25.1	2.2	5.1	2.3	61%	7%	49	24	28	29%	74%	13%	18	98	44%	22%			0.8	58	69	$0
1st Half	4	4	0	60	37	4.80	3.99	1.37	770	707	829	25.0	2.1	5.6	2.6	60%	7%	50	27	24	32%	67%	15%	10	99	50%	20%			-6.2	71	84	-$2
2nd Half	1	1	0	48	24	2.79	4.60	1.24	700	619	816	25.1	2.4	4.5	1.8	61%	8%	48	20	32	27%	83%	12%	8	97	38%	25%			7.0	41	49	$2
16 Proj	**7**	**8**	**0**	**160**	**95**	**4.03**	**4.16**	**1.32**	**739**	**687**	**800**	**24.0**	**2.4**	**5.4**	**2.2**	**60%**	**7%**	**49**	**22**	**30**	**30%**	**72%**	**11%**	**28**						**-1.4**	**58**	**69**	**$1**

Feliz,Michael

Age: 23	Th: R	Role: RP	Health: A	LIMA Plan: C	
Ht: 6' 4"	Wt: 225	Type:	PT/Exp: F	Rand Var: +3	
			Consist: F	MM: 2200	

0-0, 7.88 ERA in 8 IP at HOU. Three brief MLB relief stints turned ugly, but minor league skills (where he worked mostly as SP) were solid. Going back to 2013, has 3.6 Cmd, 9.3 Dom (non-MLE) over 282 IP at A/AA. Only put in one half-season at AA, so odds are he'll begin 2016 back in minors. Wait for more data.

Yr Tm	W	L	Sv	IP	K	ERA	xERA	WHIP	oOPS	vL	vR	BF/G	Ctl	Dom	Cmd	FpK	SwK	G	L	F	H%	S%	hr/f	GS	APC	DOM%	DIS%	Sv%	LI	RAR	BPV	BPX	R$
11																																	
12																																	
13																																	
14																																	
15 HOU *	6	3	1	87	69	2.93	2.51	1.03	884	868	898	16.7	2.4	7.2	3.0	66%	13%	38	31	31	25%	75%	25%	0	35			100	0.05	11.0	95	113	$9
1st Half	2	2	1	28	19	3.91	2.68	0.90	750	750	0	15.1	1.5	6.0	3.9	75%	12%	0	33	67	21%	62%	0%	0	17			100	0.01	0.2	90	107	$1
2nd Half	4	1	0	58	50	2.46	2.43	1.10	900	900	898	17.6	2.9	7.8	2.7	65%	13%	43	30	26	27%	79%	33%	0	39			0	0.05	10.8	101	120	$13
16 Proj	**3**	**2**	**0**	**44**	**34**	**4.04**	**4.01**	**1.32**				**17.8**	**2.4**	**7.0**	**2.9**	**0%**	**0%**	**42**	**21**	**37**	**32%**	**72%**	**10%**	**8**						**-0.4**	**82**	**98**	**-$2**

BRANDON KRUSE

Feliz,Neftali

Health F | LIMA Plan D+
Age: 28 Th: R Role RP | PT/Exp D | Rand Var +5
Ht: 6' 3" Wt: 225 Type Pwr FB | Consist D | MM 1210

Began year with TEX save opps, ended year with DET save opps, but never effective. Skills did pick up with velocity in Aug/Sept, but that's a small sample given his metrics have never been closer-worthy. Lack of strikeouts, Fpk and injury history make him a poor bet for any meaningful role.

Yr	Tm	W	L	Sv	IP	K	ERA	xERA	WHIP	oOPS	vL	vR	BF/G	Ctl	Dom	Cmd	FpK	SwK	G	L	F	H%	S%	hr/f	GS	APC	DOM%	DIS%	Sv%	LI	RAR	BPV	BPX	R$
11	TEX	2	3	32	62	54	2.74	4.16	1.16	598	561	644	3.9	4.3	7.8	1.8	53%	12%	37	16	46	24%	78%	5%	0	17			84	1.10	9.2	38	58	$16
12	TEX	3	1	0	43	37	3.16	4.61	1.20	623	616	631	21.9	4.9	7.8	1.6	53%	10%	37	15	48	22%	78%	9%	7	92	57%	14%	0	0.74	4.5	24	32	$1
13	TEX	0	0	0	5	4	0.00	4.72	1.50	659	629	665	3.5	3.9	7.7	2.0	38%	9%	21	29	50	35%	100%	0%	0	18			0	0.75	2.2	34	44	-$4
14	TEX *	3	2	20	60	45	2.69	3.11	1.00	586	513	663	4.3	2.8	6.8	2.4	66%	10%	27	22	51	20%	86%	11%	0	16			87	1.44	7.8	57	68	$12
15	2 AL	3	4	10	48	39	6.38	4.58	1.56	821	768	876	4.4	3.4	7.3	2.2	57%	10%	38	26	37	35%	59%	9%	0	17			59	1.23	-14.3	57	67	-$4
1st Half		1	2	6	20	16	4.58	5.17	1.68	777	879	675	5.1	4.1	7.3	1.8	54%	9%	35	24	41	36%	74%	7%	0	21			67	1.71	-1.5	33	40	-$3
2nd Half		2	2	4	28	23	7.62	4.18	1.48	854	685	1031	4.0	2.9	7.3	2.6	60%	11%	40	27	34	35%	46%	10%	0	16			50	0.95	-12.8	72	85	-$5
16	**Proj**	**3**	**3**	**4**	**58**	**47**	**4.47**	**4.52**	**1.40**	**759**	**703**	**819**	**4.9**	**3.7**	**7.3**	**2.0**	**58%**	**10%**	**35**	**22**	**43**	**30%**	**71%**	**9%**	**0**						**-3.6**	**44**	**52**	**-$2**

Fernandez,Jose

Health F | LIMA Plan B+
Age: 23 Th: R Role SP | PT/Exp C | Rand Var +1
Ht: 6' 2" Wt: 225 Type Pwr | Consist B | MM 5503

July return from TJS, then lost month to biceps injury. Skills in 11 starts were slightly off from 2013-14, but at his level they are little more than rounding errors. The only remaining concerns are health and stamina, and they are legitimate. Hedging gets us this projection. 200 IP gets us to $30+ and a 1st-rounder.

Yr	Tm	W	L	Sv	IP	K	ERA	xERA	WHIP	oOPS	vL	vR	BF/G	Ctl	Dom	Cmd	FpK	SwK	G	L	F	H%	S%	hr/f	GS	APC	DOM%	DIS%	Sv%	LI	RAR	BPV	BPX	R$
11																																		
12																																		
13	MIA	12	6	0	173	187	2.19	3.06	0.98	522	546	494	24.3	3.0	9.7	3.2	62%	11%	45	22	33	25%	80%	7%	28	93	75%	14%			35.7	117	152	$28
14	MIA	4	2	0	52	70	2.44	2.45	0.95	536	672	393	25.6	2.3	12.2	5.4	65%	15%	49	17	35	30%	78%	10%	8	98	75%	13%			8.3	185	221	$6
15	MIA	6	1	0	65	79	2.92	2.90	1.16	638	860	446	24.1	1.9	11.0	5.6	61%	14%	40	29	31	36%	76%	8%	11	90	91%	0%			8.3	163	194	$5
1st Half		1	0	0	6	6	4.50	2.56	1.17	738	1333	160	25.0	0.0	9.0	0.0	80%	12%	53	32	16	35%	67%	33%	1	89	100%	0%			-0.4	193	229	-$13
2nd Half		5	1	0	59	73	2.76	2.93	1.16	627	805	474	24.0	2.1	11.2	5.2	59%	14%	39	28	33	36%	77%	6%	10	90	90%	0%			8.7	160	190	$7
16	**Proj**	**12**	**5**	**0**	**160**	**193**	**2.45**	**2.80**	**1.03**	**563**	**665**	**462**	**23.6**	**2.5**	**10.9**	**4.3**	**61%**	**13%**	**44**	**23**	**34**	**30%**	**78%**	**8%**	**26**						**29.7**	**149**	**177**	**$24**

Fields,Joshua

Health B | LIMA Plan A
Age: 30 Th: R Role RP | PT/Exp D | Rand Var -1
Ht: 6' 0" Wt: 190 Type Pwr xFB | Consist A | MM 3500

Started season on DL (groin), rebounded for second season of triple-digit BPV. SwK shows strikeout ability legit but control is erratic and problematic. While H% and S% are driven by events mostly out of a pitcher's control, consistently poor levels like his will keep him off the mound in 9th innings.

Yr	Tm	W	L	Sv	IP	K	ERA	xERA	WHIP	oOPS	vL	vR	BF/G	Ctl	Dom	Cmd	FpK	SwK	G	L	F	H%	S%	hr/f	GS	APC	DOM%	DIS%	Sv%	LI	RAR	BPV	BPX	R$
11	a/a	4	2	4	56	50	4.81	4.16	1.63				6.6	7.1	8.0	1.1						28%	71%								-6.1	59	89	-$3
12	a/a	4	3	12	58	60	2.98	3.30	1.23				5.6	3.2	9.3	2.9						30%	79%								7.5	100	131	$8
13	HOU	1	3	5	38	40	4.97	4.11	1.29	783	884	706	3.9	4.3	9.5	2.2	51%	10%	37	11	52	26%	68%	16%	0	16			83	1.11	-5.2	70	92	-$2
14	HOU	4	6	4	55	70	4.45	3.30	1.23	637	665	613	4.3	2.8	11.5	4.1	59%	13%	31	21	48	36%	62%	3%	0	18			50	1.05	-4.7	141	168	$1
15	HOU	4	1	0	51	67	3.55	3.37	1.14	602	705	530	3.9	3.4	11.9	3.5	60%	13%	34	18	48	33%	68%	4%	0	16			0	0.76	2.6	135	161	$2
1st Half		2	1	0	26	36	2.77	3.23	1.08	546	629	479	3.9	4.2	12.5	3.0	63%	13%	40	11	49	29%	74%	4%	0	17			0	0.80	3.8	130	154	$3
2nd Half		2	0	0	25	31	4.38	3.51	1.22	656	786	574	3.9	2.6	11.3	4.4	58%	14%	29	25	46	36%	62%	3%	0	15			0	0.72	-1.3	142	168	$1
16	**Proj**	**4**	**3**	**0**	**58**	**71**	**4.11**	**3.46**	**1.21**	**672**	**755**	**609**	**4.0**	**3.5**	**11.0**	**3.2**	**58%**	**13%**	**33**	**18**	**48**	**31%**	**68%**	**9%**	**0**						**-1.1**	**117**	**139**	**$1**

Fien,Casey

Health C | LIMA Plan B+
Age: 32 Th: R Role RP | PT/Exp C | Rand Var -1
Ht: 6' 2" Wt: 205 Type xFB | Consist B | MM 2210

Outwardly acceptable surface stats belie hidden truths. While he has been honing his precision - supported by Fpk and Ctl - other trends are concerning. SwK, Dom, xERA, BPV all in a tailspin. You might say, "I'll still take a 3.55 ERA/1.09 WHIP." But his Leverage Index trend says that mgt confidence is not as optimistic.

Yr	Tm	W	L	Sv	IP	K	ERA	xERA	WHIP	oOPS	vL	vR	BF/G	Ctl	Dom	Cmd	FpK	SwK	G	L	F	H%	S%	hr/f	GS	APC	DOM%	DIS%	Sv%	LI	RAR	BPV	BPX	R$
11	aaa	2	2	3	24	19	6.01	8.36	1.78				5.3	3.2	6.9	2.1						34%	78%								-6.2	-19	-28	-$4
12	MIN *	4	6	9	81	63	4.40	3.86	1.27	578	491	638	4.9	2.9	7.0	2.4	57%	10%	25	25	51	29%	68%	6%	0	17			75	0.98	-3.8	68	88	$2
13	MIN	5	2	0	62	73	3.92	2.93	1.02	627	750	545	3.3	1.7	10.6	6.1	67%	15%	37	20	42	29%	67%	14%	0	13			0	1.25	-0.4	159	207	$3
14	MIN	5	6	1	63	51	3.98	3.99	1.17	705	694	713	3.6	1.4	7.2	5.1	68%	11%	32	19	49	31%	69%	7%	0	14			20	1.18	-1.9	102	122	$1
15	MIN	4	6	0	63	41	3.55	4.29	1.09	648	717	597	4.1	1.1	5.8	5.1	68%	9%	37	20	43	29%	70%	7%	0	16			0	1.04	3.2	89	106	$2
1st Half		2	3	0	26	14	3.86	4.52	1.05	648	775	566	4.3	0.7	4.9	7.0	59%	8%	33	22	45	27%	67%	8%	0	17			0	1.34	0.3	81	96	-$1
2nd Half		2	3	0	38	27	3.35	4.13	1.12	647	680	621	4.0	1.4	6.5	4.5	73%	10%	39	19	42	29%	72%	6%	0	15			0	0.84	2.9	94	112	$4
16	**Proj**	**4**	**5**	**2**	**58**	**45**	**3.96**	**3.86**	**1.12**	**668**	**710**	**636**	**3.8**	**1.5**	**7.0**	**4.8**	**66%**	**11%**	**34**	**20**	**45**	**29%**	**67%**	**8%**	**0**						**0.0**	**99**	**118**	**$2**

Fiers,Mike

Health A | LIMA Plan B
Age: 31 Th: R Role SP | PT/Exp C | Rand Var 0
Ht: 6' 2" Wt: 190 Type Pwr FB | Consist D | MM 2303

Regression from 2014 was expected. FpK predicted Ctl pullback. FB% to hr/f disconnect normalized. Inflated S% regressed a bit too. It all added up to an ERA spike. Still, it wasn't all bad. Held Dom gains, which SwK says should continue. No ace, but a helpful contributor.

Yr	Tm	W	L	Sv	IP	K	ERA	xERA	WHIP	oOPS	vL	vR	BF/G	Ctl	Dom	Cmd	FpK	SwK	G	L	F	H%	S%	hr/f	GS	APC	DOM%	DIS%	Sv%	LI	RAR	BPV	BPX	R$
11	MIL *	13	3	5	128	110	2.08	2.70	1.08	786	1250	533	13.9	2.8	7.7	2.7	70%	14%	40	40	20	25%	86%	0%	0	21			83	0.07	29.5	91	137	$21
12	MIL *	10	13	0	183	174	4.45	4.23	1.34	694	690	698	23.0	2.8	8.6	3.1	60%	9%	33	28	39	33%	69%	9%	22	94	59%	18%	0	0.74	-9.7	87	113	$2
13	MIL *	2	6	0	51	38	4.68	5.82	1.50	972	999	930	13.8	3.4	6.8	2.0	60%	9%	35	26	39	30%	77%	26%	3	37	0%	100%	0	1.02	-5.1	19	25	-$5
14	MIL *	14	10	0	174	174	2.90	3.07	1.08	531	517	542	21.9	1.9	9.0	4.7	58%	10%	33	20	47	29%	78%	8%	10	80	90%	0%	0	0.74	18.0	131	156	$19
15	2 TM	7	10	0	180	180	3.69	4.00	1.25	713	664	756	24.5	3.2	9.0	2.8	60%	10%	38	20	42	30%	75%	11%	30	98	47%	13%	0	0.78	6.0	91	109	$8
1st Half		4	7	0	94	95	3.83	4.09	1.41	759	798	726	24.1	3.4	9.1	2.7	60%	10%	38	22	40	34%	76%	9%	17	95	29%	24%			1.5	90	106	$4
2nd Half		3	3	0	86	85	3.54	3.90	1.08	660	507	791	25.1	3.0	8.9	2.9	61%	11%	37	19	45	24%	75%	14%	13	102	69%	0%	0	0.74	4.5	92	110	$12
16	**Proj**	**10**	**10**	**0**	**174**	**168**	**3.57**	**3.80**	**1.22**	**719**	**672**	**760**	**20.2**	**2.8**	**8.7**	**3.1**	**60%**	**10%**	**35**	**21**	**44**	**29%**	**76%**	**12%**	**35**						**8.4**	**93**	**111**	**$11**

Finnegan,Brandon

Health A | LIMA Plan C
Age: 23 Th: L Role RP | PT/Exp F | Rand Var +5
Ht: 5' 11" Wt: 185 Type Pwr GB | Consist F | MM 2401

5-2, 3.56 ERA in 48 IP at KC/CIN. Post-trade, may get to settle in as starter after KC yo-yoed use. Showed promise in role in four Sept starts. An unfinished product (32 ER in 44 AAA IP), but some seeds are there: high GB%, 2H gains in FpK, SwK. Growing pains in the near term, but keep an eye on him.

Yr	Tm	W	L	Sv	IP	K	ERA	xERA	WHIP	oOPS	vL	vR	BF/G	Ctl	Dom	Cmd	FpK	SwK	G	L	F	H%	S%	hr/f	GS	APC	DOM%	DIS%	Sv%	LI	RAR	BPV	BPX	R$
11																																		
12																																		
13																																		
14	KC	0	1	0	7	10	1.29	1.90	1.00	546	778	433	4.0	1.3	12.9	10.0	64%	14%	59	18	24	38%	86%	0%	0	17			0	0.67	2.1	234	278	-$2
15	2 TM *	5	8	1	105	101	5.51	4.91	1.55	713	765	695	11.8	5.0	8.6	1.7	58%	10%	54	17	29	31%	67%	22%	4	38	50%	0%	50	0.85	-20.2	53	63	-$10
1st Half		1	3	1	43	43	5.02	4.71	1.63	550	603	507	10.1	6.2	9.0	1.4	50%	9%	54	22	24	31%	71%	18%	0	29			50	0.75	-5.6	60	71	-$11
2nd Half		4	5	0	62	58	5.86	5.06	1.49	805	984	767	13.4	4.1	8.4	2.0	63%	11%	54	14	32	32%	63%	23%	4	46	50%	0%	0	0.94	-14.6	50	59	-$9
16	**Proj**	**5**	**8**	**0**	**102**	**101**	**4.23**	**3.73**	**1.40**	**726**	**748**	**718**	**19.0**	**4.6**	**9.0**	**2.0**	**59%**	**10%**	**54**	**17**	**29**	**30%**	**71%**	**12%**	**16**						**-3.4**	**70**	**84**	**-$1**

Fister,Doug

Health F | LIMA Plan C
Age: 32 Th: R Role RP | PT/Exp A | Rand Var 0
Ht: 6' 8" Wt: 210 Type Con | Consist B | MM 2101

Limped into free agency with more lost velocity (FB down to 86.2 mph), compounded by month-long forearm injury, lost Ctl, fewer GB, and less effectiveness vs. RHB. Did regain some Dom after move to bullpen in early Aug (15 K in 17 IP). Young enough to salvage some vintage skills, but you may want to see them first.

Yr	Tm	W	L	Sv	IP	K	ERA	xERA	WHIP	oOPS	vL	vR	BF/G	Ctl	Dom	Cmd	FpK	SwK	G	L	F	H%	S%	hr/f	GS	APC	DOM%	DIS%	Sv%	LI	RAR	BPV	BPX	R$
11	2 AL	11	13	0	216	146	2.83	3.54	1.06	617	642	586	27.3	1.5	6.1	3.9	65%	7%	48	20	32	28%	74%	5%	31	100	65%	3%	0	0.77	29.7	94	141	$23
12	DET	10	10	0	162	137	3.45	3.45	1.19	683	734	611	25.9	2.1	7.6	3.7	63%	8%	51	22	27	31%	74%	12%	26	97	50%	23%			11.2	111	144	$12
13	DET	14	9	0	209	159	3.67	3.38	1.31	710	687	738	26.7	1.9	6.9	3.6	59%	8%	54	21	24	33%	73%	9%	32	102	63%	13%	0	0.80	5.1	104	136	$8
14	WAS	16	6	0	164	98	2.41	3.75	1.08	654	690	618	26.5	1.3	5.4	4.1	65%	6%	49	17	34	27%	84%	10%	25	99	52%	16%			26.8	88	105	$19
15	WAS	5	7	1	103	63	4.19	4.49	1.40	796	738	860	18.0	2.1	5.5	2.6	62%	6%	45	21	34	32%	74%	12%	15	66	27%	27%	100	0.86	-2.9	65	78	-$3
1st Half		3	4	0	58	29	4.34	4.82	1.36	774	702	872	25.2	2.0	4.5	2.2	62%	6%	41	23	35	30%	72%	11%	10	91	30%	30%			-2.7	46	55	-$3
2nd Half		2	3	1	45	34	4.00	4.07	1.44	825	797	848	13.1	2.2	6.8	3.1	62%	5%	49	19	32	34%	76%	13%	5	50	20%	20%	100	0.91	-0.2	90	107	-$2
16	**Proj**	**6**	**5**	**0**	**87**	**58**	**3.85**	**3.91**	**1.28**	**739**	**720**	**759**	**19.4**	**1.9**	**6.0**	**3.2**	**62%**	**6%**	**48**	**20**	**32**	**31%**	**73%**	**11%**	**17**						**1.2**	**84**	**100**	**$1**

KRISTOPHER OLSON

Floyd,Gavin

Age: 33	Th: R	Role SP	Health F	LIMA Plan C	
Ht: 6' 4"	Wt: 235	Type	PT/Exp D	Rand Var -5	
			Consist A	MM 2201	

March elbow surgery (second in two years) put season in doubt, but made September cameo in pen. Dom, xERA say not to trust low ERA, but tough to glean much from 13 IP. Relevance hinges on SwK returning to double-digits with offseason of rest, but IP history at this age makes him no more than an end-game flyer.

Yr Tm	W	L	Sv	IP	K	ERA	xERA	WHIP	oOPS	vL	vR	BF/G	Ctl	Dom	Cmd	FpK	SwK	G	L	F	H%	S%	hr/f	GS	APC	DOM%	DIS%	Sv%	LI	RAR	BPV	BPX	R$
11 CHW	12	13	0	194	151	4.37	3.66	1.16	685	764	572	25.7	2.1	7.0	3.4	65%	9%	44	19	37	29%	65%	10%	30	97	57%	13%	0	0.83	-10.2	92	138	$8
12 CHW	12	11	0	168	144	4.29	4.05	1.36	755	871	633	25.0	3.4	7.7	2.3	60%	10%	47	18	35	30%	72%	13%	29	95	48%	24%			-5.6	73	95	$2
13 CHW	0	4	0	24	25	5.18	3.83	1.60	893	940	836	22.0	4.4	9.2	2.1	68%	11%	50	21	29	35%	71%	20%	5	84	40%	40%			-3.9	75	97	-$6
14 ATL *	3	4	0	78	58	3.47	4.41	1.35	702	773	629	21.8	2.8	6.7	2.4	64%	12%	49	20	31	31%	79%	12%	9	92	44%	0%			2.6	59	70	-$1
15 CLE	0	0	0	13	7	2.70	4.46	1.13	551	384	647	7.9	2.7	4.7	1.8	58%	8%	47	23	30	26%	73%	0%	0	31			0	0.12	2.1	37	44	-$3
1st Half																																	
2nd Half	0	0	0	13	7	2.70	4.46	1.13	551	384	647	7.9	2.7	4.7	1.8	58%	8%	47	23	30	26%	73%	0%	0	31			0	0.12	2.1	37	43	-$3
16 Proj	**5**	**5**	**0**	**87**	**68**	**4.03**	**3.89**	**1.28**	**720**	**806**	**619**	**23.5**	**2.6**	**7.1**	**2.7**	**63%**	**10%**	**47**	**19**	**34**	**30%**	**72%**	**11%**	**15**						**-0.7**	**80**	**96**	**$0**

Foltynewicz,Mike

Age: 24	Th: R	Role RP	Health A	LIMA Plan D+	
Ht: 6' 4"	Wt: 220	Type Pwr FB	PT/Exp D	Rand Var +2	
			Consist C	MM 1213	

4-6, 5.71 ERA in 87 IP at ATL. Missed September to costochondritis, blood clots in arm. On the field, heavy LD/FB tilt mixed with elevated H%, hr/f to wreak havoc on ERA. Raw stuff has yet to translate to plus Dom, though FpK gains offer hope for shaky Ctl. xERA further suggests he needs more seasoning.

Yr Tm	W	L	Sv	IP	K	ERA	xERA	WHIP	oOPS	vL	vR	BF/G	Ctl	Dom	Cmd	FpK	SwK	G	L	F	H%	S%	hr/f	GS	APC	DOM%	DIS%	Sv%	LI	RAR	BPV	BPX	R$
11																																	
12																																	
13 aa	5	3	3	103	85	3.22	3.19	1.29				18.4	4.4	7.4	1.7						26%	77%								8.3	68	89	$5
14 HOU *	7	8	0	121	103	5.36	4.77	1.53	864	1062	659	14.3	4.2	7.6	1.8	52%	10%	29	21	51	33%	66%	9%	0	20			0	0.38	-24.2	55	66	-$9
15 ATL *	5	12	0	143	132	5.29	6.01	1.62	896	950	843	22.7	3.6	8.3	2.3	63%	10%	33	23	44	36%	72%	14%	15	82	33%	33%	0	0.99	-23.5	45	54	-$14
1st Half	4	7	0	98	95	4.73	5.56	1.59	844	944	744	25.4	3.9	8.8	2.2	66%	10%	33	23	44	35%	74%	11%	9	95	33%	22%			-9.2	54	64	-$11
2nd Half	1	5	0	46	37	6.50	6.96	1.68	970	958	980	18.7	2.8	7.3	2.6	59%	9%	34	23	43	36%	66%	17%	6	70	33%	50%	0	1.19	-14.3	28	33	-$19
16 Proj	**6**	**10**	**2**	**131**	**112**	**4.69**	**4.54**	**1.48**	**763**	**785**	**740**	**17.4**	**3.8**	**7.7**	**2.1**	**62%**	**9%**	**33**	**23**	**43**	**32%**	**72%**	**11%**	**24**						**-11.7**	**49**	**58**	**-$5**

Freeman,Sam

Age: 29	Th: L	Role RP	Health A	LIMA Plan D+	
Ht: 5' 11"	Wt: 165	Type Pwr GB	PT/Exp D	Rand Var -3	
			Consist B	MM 2300	

Remarkably stable ERA; odds of larger role are dwindling, however, as dismal FpK pumped more air into ballooning Ctl. Odd L/R splits, as all HR since 2014 have come vs. LHB, while career 35% H% against them suggests some bad luck, too. Dom/GB% combo keeps him relevant, but xERA offers little room for growth.

Yr Tm	W	L	Sv	IP	K	ERA	xERA	WHIP	oOPS	vL	vR	BF/G	Ctl	Dom	Cmd	FpK	SwK	G	L	F	H%	S%	hr/f	GS	APC	DOM%	DIS%	Sv%	LI	RAR	BPV	BPX	R$
11 aa	2	2	3	59	43	2.68	3.37	1.32				4.7	3.9	6.5	1.7						28%	81%								9.2	65	97	$3
12 STL *	3	7	1	68	49	3.08	3.38	1.26	654	808	534	4.2	3.5	6.6	1.9	56%	11%	46	15	39	27%	78%	10%	0	14			50	0.63	7.8	64	83	$2
13 STL *	8	2	2	82	60	3.22	3.22	1.30	515	488	536	5.5	3.6	6.6	1.8	54%	11%	39	19	42	29%	75%	0%	0	16			67	0.84	6.5	72	94	$4
14 STL *	2	1	0	58	55	3.08	4.32	1.52	638	818	518	4.2	4.0	8.5	2.1	52%	12%	56	20	24	35%	80%	8%	0	15			0	1.05	4.8	81	96	-$2
15 TEX	0	0	0	38	40	3.05	4.28	1.46	683	911	488	3.2	5.9	9.4	1.6	50%	11%	49	21	30	28%	83%	13%	0	13			0	0.98	4.3	38	45	-$3
1st Half	0	0	0	17	15	4.24	3.63	1.29	673	841	513	3.2	3.2	7.9	2.5	53%	10%	52	24	24	31%	67%	8%	0	13			0	0.90	-0.6	87	103	-$5
2nd Half	0	0	0	21	25	2.11	4.89	1.59	691	972	469	3.2	8.0	10.5	1.3	47%	11%	45	19	36	25%	94%	16%	0	13			0	1.04	4.9	-3	-4	-$1
16 Proj	**1**	**1**	**0**	**51**	**48**	**3.37**	**4.01**	**1.44**	**682**	**899**	**515**	**3.6**	**4.1**	**8.5**	**1.7**	**50%**	**11%**	**51**	**21**	**28**	**30%**	**78%**	**11%**	**0**						**3.7**	**49**	**58**	**-$2**

Frias,Carlos

Age: 26	Th: R	Role RP	Health D	LIMA Plan C	
Ht: 6' 4"	Wt: 170	Type GB	PT/Exp D	Rand Var 0	
			Consist B	MM 2000	

5-5, 4.06 ERA in 78 IP at LA. Cracked rotation in May and held his own, until July back strain cost him two months. Intriguing SwK/FpK combo lurks beneath poor Cmd, while GB tilt should keep ERA, which was skewed by 10 ER outing on 5/24, in check. Dom growth the key to being any more than late-round material.

Yr Tm	W	L	Sv	IP	K	ERA	xERA	WHIP	oOPS	vL	vR	BF/G	Ctl	Dom	Cmd	FpK	SwK	G	L	F	H%	S%	hr/f	GS	APC	DOM%	DIS%	Sv%	LI	RAR	BPV	BPX	R$
11																																	
12																																	
13 aa	1	1	0	16	7	4.97	5.27	1.56				8.8	4.0	3.8	0.9						29%	71%								-2.2	2	2	-$5
14 LA *	11	6	0	156	94	4.64	4.41	1.40	677	789	582	18.3	1.9	5.4	2.9	64%	11%	52	15	33	34%	66%	12%	2	32	50%	50%	0	0.67	-17.3	73	86	-$5
15 LA *	7	5	0	99	58	3.91	4.82	1.48	761	901	650	17.0	2.8	5.3	1.9	61%	10%	55	22	23	33%	75%	12%	13	69	8%	23%	0	0.82	0.7	43	51	-$3
1st Half	7	5	0	82	52	4.22	5.36	1.56	787	934	667	21.2	2.6	5.7	2.2	61%	10%	55	23	21	35%	75%	12%	12	77	8%	17%	0	0.89	-2.6	46	54	-$2
2nd Half	0	0	0	17	6	2.39	2.14	1.06	484	425	500	8.1	3.7	3.4	0.9	55%	11%	52	9	39	20%	80%	11%	1	34	0%	100%	0	0.50	3.2	41	48	-$4
16 Proj	**3**	**2**	**0**	**58**	**36**	**3.67**	**4.01**	**1.33**	**669**	**792**	**566**	**13.3**	**2.7**	**5.7**	**2.1**	**62%**	**10%**	**54**	**20**	**26**	**30%**	**73%**	**8%**	**6**						**2.1**	**60**	**71**	**-$1**

Gallardo,Yovani

Age: 30	Th: R	Role SP	Health A	LIMA Plan B	
Ht: 6' 2"	Wt: 210	Type	PT/Exp A	Rand Var -2	
			Consist A	MM 1105	

While career-best ERA suggests he rekindled glory days, career-worst xERA quickly refutes it. Lost another mph on fastball (now -2.3 mph since 2011), while meager SwK further supports Dom's downward spiral. Repeat odds are slim to none, and if 2H BPV collapse is any indication, we could be in for... DN: 4.50+ ERA.

Yr Tm	W	L	Sv	IP	K	ERA	xERA	WHIP	oOPS	vL	vR	BF/G	Ctl	Dom	Cmd	FpK	SwK	G	L	F	H%	S%	hr/f	GS	APC	DOM%	DIS%	Sv%	LI	RAR	BPV	BPX	R$
11 MIL	17	10	0	207	207	3.52	3.34	1.22	686	710	663	26.2	2.6	9.0	3.5	63%	10%	47	17	36	31%	76%	13%	33	105	61%	15%			10.9	118	177	$17
12 MIL	16	9	0	204	204	3.66	3.66	1.30	706	759	654	26.1	3.6	9.0	2.5	56%	8%	48	21	31	30%	76%	15%	33	105	64%	9%			8.9	92	119	$13
13 MIL	12	10	0	181	144	4.18	3.85	1.36	720	729	713	24.9	3.3	7.2	2.2	56%	7%	49	23	28	31%	71%	12%	31	98	52%	19%			-7.1	67	88	$2
14 MIL	8	11	0	192	146	3.51	3.72	1.29	698	637	742	25.5	2.5	6.8	2.7	57%	7%	51	20	29	31%	76%	12%	32	101	53%	13%			5.5	84	100	$5
15 TEX	13	11	0	184	121	3.42	4.46	1.42	729	765	694	24.0	3.3	5.9	1.8	59%	7%	49	22	29	31%	78%	9%	33	98	30%	24%			12.4	44	52	$5
1st Half	7	6	0	102	72	2.56	3.95	1.14	594	613	574	24.4	2.7	6.4	2.3	61%	7%	52	18	29	27%	80%	8%	17	100	47%	12%			17.7	71	84	$18
2nd Half	6	5	0	82	49	4.48	5.13	1.76	881	937	827	23.6	4.0	5.4	1.3	56%	7%	46	26	28	35%	76%	10%	16	96	13%	38%			-5.3	11	13	-$11
16 Proj	**12**	**10**	**0**	**181**	**132**	**3.82**	**4.12**	**1.41**	**739**	**755**	**725**	**24.2**	**3.2**	**6.6**	**2.1**	**58%**	**7%**	**49**	**22**	**29**	**31%**	**75%**	**11%**	**32**						**3.2**	**59**	**70**	**$2**

Garcia,Jaime

Age: 29	Th: L	Role SP	Health F	LIMA Plan C+	
Ht: 6' 2"	Wt: 215	Type xGB	PT/Exp C	Rand Var -2	
			Consist A	MM 4203	

Shoulder finally allowed him to pitch, though still managed to check into the DL (groin) in July. Average FpK puts his pinpoint Ctl at risk, while inability to miss bats says the drop in Dom was well deserved. Elite GB% will keep him effective, just don't expect another sub-3.00 ERA, even if arm stays attached.

Yr Tm	W	L	Sv	IP	K	ERA	xERA	WHIP	oOPS	vL	vR	BF/G	Ctl	Dom	Cmd	FpK	SwK	G	L	F	H%	S%	hr/f	GS	APC	DOM%	DIS%	Sv%	LI	RAR	BPV	BPX	R$
11 STL	13	7	0	195	156	3.56	3.47	1.32	711	770	697	25.8	2.3	7.2	3.1	58%	11%	54	18	28	33%	74%	9%	32	93	47%	16%			9.2	99	149	$9
12 STL *	8	8	0	137	113	4.08	4.06	1.34	730	649	750	24.8	2.2	7.4	3.4	63%	12%	54	20	26	34%	70%	7%	20	88	55%	20%			-1.1	96	125	$2
13 STL	5	2	0	55	43	3.58	3.35	1.30	725	905	666	26.0	2.4	7.0	2.9	68%	12%	63	14	23	31%	76%	15%	9	92	44%	11%			2.0	101	132	$0
14 STL	3	1	0	44	39	4.12	2.89	1.05	696	881	631	25.3	1.4	8.0	5.6	60%	13%	55	20	25	28%	65%	19%	7	90	43%	0%			-2.1	139	165	$0
15 STL	10	6	0	130	97	2.43	3.25	1.05	574	630	557	25.5	2.1	6.7	3.2	59%	9%	61	16	22	27%	78%	7%	20	93	70%	10%			24.5	104	124	$17
1st Half	3	3	0	48	32	1.69	2.88	0.88	529	587	512	25.3	1.3	6.0	4.6	61%	8%	67	14	19	24%	85%	12%	7	92	86%	0%			13.5	118	140	$13
2nd Half	7	3	0	82	65	2.87	3.47	1.15	598	653	582	25.6	2.5	7.2	2.8	57%	10%	58	18	24	29%	75%	5%	13	93	62%	15%			11.1	96	114	$19
16 Proj	**9**	**6**	**0**	**145**	**113**	**3.15**	**3.27**	**1.17**	**664**	**778**	**630**	**25.2**	**2.2**	**7.0**	**3.2**	**61%**	**11%**	**59**	**17**	**23**	**29%**	**75%**	**12%**	**23**						**14.6**	**105**	**125**	**$11**

Garcia,Luis

Age: 29	Th: R	Role RP	Health A	LIMA Plan D+	
Ht: 6' 2"	Wt: 210	Type Pwr xGB	PT/Exp D	Rand Var +1	
			Consist A	MM 2300	

Made it through first full season in middle relief with relative success. Threw two pitches, each with promising results, as fastball induced over 70% GB, while he put up 20% SwK with slider. Solid Dom, elite GB% should stick, but FpK doubts his poor walk rate will improve. Unless that happens, watch from afar.

Yr Tm	W	L	Sv	IP	K	ERA	xERA	WHIP	oOPS	vL	vR	BF/G	Ctl	Dom	Cmd	FpK	SwK	G	L	F	H%	S%	hr/f	GS	APC	DOM%	DIS%	Sv%	LI	RAR	BPV	BPX	R$
11																																	
12																																	
13 PHI *	3	2	4	53	40	3.00	3.58	1.41	764	746	775	5.2	5.1	6.8	1.3	47%	11%	56	17	27	27%	81%	13%	0	23			80	0.71	5.7	56	73	$1
14 PHI *	3	1	22	61	54	2.39	3.51	1.43	815	628	1042	5.0	4.5	8.0	1.8	49%	12%	70	12	19	32%	83%	25%	0	22			88	0.42	10.1	82	98	$9
15 PHI	4	6	2	67	63	3.51	3.81	1.64	748	878	660	4.2	5.0	8.5	1.7	52%	12%	63	22	15	35%	79%	13%	0	16			50	1.03	3.7	59	71	-$3
1st Half	3	3	1	38	35	3.32	3.69	1.47	717	910	597	4.4	4.5	8.3	1.8	51%	14%	61	23	17	31%	81%	22%	0	17			100	0.98	3.0	66	79	$0
2nd Half	1	3	1	29	28	3.77	3.96	1.85	785	841	742	4.0	5.7	8.8	1.6	53%	10%	66	21	13	40%	77%	0%	0	15			33	1.09	0.7	50	59	-$5
16 Proj	**3**	**4**	**0**	**65**	**59**	**3.63**	**3.81**	**1.51**	**718**	**778**	**679**	**4.4**	**4.9**	**8.1**	**1.7**	**50%**	**12%**	**61**	**20**	**20**	**32%**	**76%**	**11%**	**0**						**2.7**	**52**	**62**	**-$2**

RYAN BLOOMFIELD

Garcia,Yimi

Age: 25	Th: R	Role RP	Health A	LIMA Plan A	
Ht: 6' 1"	Wt: 175	Type Pwr xFB	PT/Exp D	Rand Var 0	
			Consist A	MM 3410	

Rookie showcased uncommon Cmd in first full season while inducing empty swings and lots of FB. This has always been his MO, and while his 1.4 hr/9 in bigs is double that of his seven seasons in minors, allowing less than a baserunner an inning has limited HR damage. Has the ingredients to be impactful in any role.

Yr	Tm	W	L	Sv	IP	K	ERA	xERA	WHIP	oOPS	vL	vR	BF/G	Ctl	Dom	Cmd	FpK	SwK	G	L	F	H%	S%	hr/f	GS	APC	DOM%	DIS%	Sv%	LI	RAR	BPV	BPX	R$
11																																		
12																																		
13	aa	4	6	19	60	73	3.14	2.61	0.91				4.6	2.1	10.8	5.2						24%	76%								5.4	146	190	$13
14	LA *	4	2	5	71	67	2.48	2.98	1.10	537	220	727	5.1	2.0	8.5	4.3	58%	11%	38	12	50	30%	81%	15%	0	17			83	0.19	11.0	127	151	$7
15	LA	3	5	1	57	68	3.34	3.36	0.95	595	584	599	3.8	1.6	10.8	6.8	64%	15%	28	17	54	28%	72%	10%	1	14	0%	100%	17	1.05	4.4	158	188	$4
1st Half		3	2	1	35	51	3.82	3.16	1.05	628	498	681	3.7	2.3	13.0	5.7	63%	17%	24	18	57	31%	71%	13%	0	14			17	1.10	0.6	174	207	$6
2nd Half		0	3	0	21	17	2.53	3.67	0.80	539	720	455	4.1	0.4	7.2	17.0	65%	13%	34	16	50	24%	73%	6%	1	15	0%	100%	0	0.95	3.8	130	154	$2
16	Proj	**4**	**4**	**2**	**58**	**60**	**3.04**	**3.42**	**1.00**	**609**	**659**	**586**	**4.3**	**1.6**	**9.4**	**5.8**	**64%**	**14%**	**30**	**17**	**53**	**28%**	**75%**	**8%**	**0**						**6.6**	**133**	**158**	**$5**

Garza,Matt

Age: 32	Th: R	Role SP	Health F	LIMA Plan C	
Ht: 6' 4"	Wt: 215	Type Pwr	PT/Exp B	Rand Var +3	
			Consist A	MM 1203	

Ugh. Last year's book cited 3-year drops in key metrics as a harbinger of rough waters ahead. Make that four years and a tsunami, as he endured career worsts nearly across the board. Doesn't look to get much better as age creeps and injuries pile up. Too much downward thrust. Sometimes it's no fun being right.

Yr	Tm	W	L	Sv	IP	K	ERA	xERA	WHIP	oOPS	vL	vR	BF/G	Ctl	Dom	Cmd	FpK	SwK	G	L	F	H%	S%	hr/f	GS	APC	DOM%	DIS%	Sv%	LI	RAR	BPV	BPX	R$
11	CHC	10	10	0	198	197	3.32	3.36	1.26	654	634	672	27.1	2.9	9.0	3.1	64%	12%	46	21	33	32%	75%	8%	31	103	68%	10%			15.2	108	162	$13
12	CHC	5	7	0	104	96	3.91	3.54	1.18	693	745	643	23.6	2.8	8.3	3.0	62%	11%	47	19	33	28%	72%	16%	18	94	56%	22%			1.4	100	130	$4
13	2 TM *	11	7	0	171	144	3.63	3.76	1.23	712	733	687	24.7	2.5	7.6	3.1	64%	10%	39	23	38	30%	74%	12%	24	101	58%	21%			5.0	83	108	$9
14	MIL	8	8	0	163	126	3.64	3.90	1.18	644	634	652	25.2	2.8	6.9	2.5	64%	9%	43	21	36	28%	70%	7%	27	94	48%	22%			2.1	72	85	$7
15	MIL	6	14	0	149	104	5.63	4.73	1.57	832	862	804	25.6	3.5	6.3	1.8	61%	8%	45	22	33	33%	67%	14%	25	92	32%	16%	0	0.83	-30.6	43	51	-$15
1st Half		4	10	0	99	68	5.55	4.64	1.55	825	841	811	26.1	3.0	6.2	2.1	63%	8%	45	23	32	33%	68%	16%	16	92	25%	6%	0	0.85	-19.3	54	64	-$16
2nd Half		2	4	0	50	36	5.80	4.91	1.61	844	906	786	24.7	4.3	6.5	1.5	58%	8%	44	21	35	32%	65%	11%	9	92	44%	33%			-11.2	22	27	-$14
16	Proj	**7**	**11**	**0**	**160**	**123**	**4.66**	**4.22**	**1.39**	**754**	**780**	**730**	**24.6**	**3.2**	**6.9**	**2.1**	**62%**	**9%**	**44**	**21**	**35**	**31%**	**69%**	**11%**	**27**						**-13.8**	**59**	**70**	**-$4**

Gausman,Kevin

Age: 25	Th: R	Role RP	Health C	LIMA Plan B+	
Ht: 6' 3"	Wt: 190	Type Pwr	PT/Exp D	Rand Var 0	
			Consist A	MM 2303	

4-7, 4.25 ERA in 112 IP at BAL. Shoulder tendinitis cost him most of May and June, but by final two months, was flashing top-prospect form (4.1 Cmd, 8.6 Dom). Re-discovering prior FpK and success vs RH batters would help, but there is something good brewing here... UP: 3.40 ERA, 13 Wins

Yr	Tm	W	L	Sv	IP	K	ERA	xERA	WHIP	oOPS	vL	vR	BF/G	Ctl	Dom	Cmd	FpK	SwK	G	L	F	H%	S%	hr/f	GS	APC	DOM%	DIS%	Sv%	LI	RAR	BPV	BPX	R$
11																																		
12																																		
13	BAL *	6	11	0	130	119	4.71	4.11	1.30	792	811	772	14.8	1.9	8.3	4.4	61%	10%	42	25	33	34%	65%	19%	5	40	20%	40%	0	0.80	-13.4	115	150	-$2
14	BAL *	8	10	0	157	125	3.60	3.92	1.35	685	700	662	21.1	3.2	7.2	2.2	57%	9%	41	23	35	31%	75%	6%	20	98	35%	20%			2.8	71	85	$2
15	BAL *	4	9	0	130	118	4.28	4.41	1.25	739	640	847	18.2	2.5	8.2	3.3	55%	12%	45	17	38	30%	72%	13%	17	75	59%	12%	0	0.72	-5.1	74	88	$0
1st Half		1	1	0	30	27	4.18	3.86	1.20	638	843	453	9.9	3.1	8.1	2.6	54%	11%	45	10	45	26%	71%	7%	2	40	50%	0%	0	0.67	-0.8	67	80	-$6
2nd Half		3	8	0	100	91	4.31	4.57	1.27	765	595	959	24.1	2.3	8.2	3.6	55%	12%	45	19	36	30%	73%	15%	15	99	60%	13%			-4.3	78	92	$2
16	Proj	**8**	**8**	**0**	**145**	**127**	**3.93**	**3.78**	**1.27**	**724**	**716**	**734**	**16.8**	**2.6**	**7.9**	**3.1**	**56%**	**10%**	**43**	**20**	**37**	**31%**	**72%**	**11%**	**24**						**0.5**	**94**	**111**	**$4**

Gee,Dillon

Age: 30	Th: R	Role SP	Health F	LIMA Plan C	
Ht: 6' 1"	Wt: 205	Type Con	PT/Exp B	Rand Var +2	
			Consist B	MM 1000	

0-3, 5.90 ERA in 40 IP at NYM. In the course of three months, went from underwhelming to unemployed. Not many can survive today's game with such low Dom, and he picked the wrong year to have bad H% fortunes. With that Ctl, he'll probably resurface on a roster next year. But there is little upside here.

Yr	Tm	W	L	Sv	IP	K	ERA	xERA	WHIP	oOPS	vL	vR	BF/G	Ctl	Dom	Cmd	FpK	SwK	G	L	F	H%	S%	hr/f	GS	APC	DOM%	DIS%	Sv%	LI	RAR	BPV	BPX	R$
11	NYM	13	6	0	161	114	4.43	4.29	1.38	739	743	735	23.5	4.0	6.4	1.6	55%	10%	47	19	33	28%	70%	11%	27	87	41%	22%	0	0.77	-9.6	33	49	$1
12	NYM	6	7	0	110	97	4.10	3.54	1.25	697	770	610	27.2	2.4	8.0	3.3	59%	11%	50	20	30	31%	70%	13%	17	103	71%	0%			-1.2	107	140	$2
13	NYM	12	11	0	199	142	3.62	4.07	1.28	738	822	666	26.3	2.1	6.4	3.0	62%	10%	43	20	38	31%	76%	10%	32	93	44%	16%			6.1	79	103	$8
14	NYM	7	8	0	137	94	4.00	4.12	1.25	715	719	711	25.9	2.8	6.2	2.2	60%	8%	44	18	38	27%	72%	12%	22	96	41%	5%			-4.3	57	68	$2
15	NYM *	8	7	0	134	76	5.53	5.96	1.66	879	1058	690	26.2	2.2	5.1	2.3	67%	10%	51	20	29	37%	67%	12%	7	77	14%	29%	0	0.70	-26.0	42	50	-$15
1st Half		2	5	0	62	37	6.88	6.63	1.77	879	1058	690	23.9	2.5	5.4	2.1	67%	10%	51	20	29	38%	61%	12%		77	14%	29%			-22.5	31	37	-$25
2nd Half		6	2	0	72	39	4.37	5.38	1.56				28.7	1.9	4.9	2.6						36%	73%	0%							-3.6	52	62	-$7
16	Proj	**3**	**3**	**0**	**58**	**37**	**4.51**	**4.28**	**1.42**	**784**	**876**	**692**	**25.6**	**2.4**	**5.8**	**2.4**	**62%**	**10%**	**47**	**19**	**34**	**32%**	**70%**	**10%**	**10**						**-3.9**	**64**	**76**	**-$4**

Geltz,Steve

Age: 28	Th: R	Role RP	Health A	LIMA Plan B+	
Ht: 5' 10"	Wt: 170	Type Pwr xFB	PT/Exp D	Rand Var -3	
			Consist B	MM 1311	

Being stranded in snowstorm cost him college eligibility. PED suspension cut into 2014. Bet you wouldn't have guessed he led team in games pitched. But by July, surpassing 2014 IP, Ks tanked and FB% returned to crazy levels. Sans whiffs, he's pretty ordinary; talk up his backstory while you seek better options.

Yr	Tm	W	L	Sv	IP	K	ERA	xERA	WHIP	oOPS	vL	vR	BF/G	Ctl	Dom	Cmd	FpK	SwK	G	L	F	H%	S%	hr/f	GS	APC	DOM%	DIS%	Sv%	LI	RAR	BPV	BPX	R$
11	a/a	3	3	0	48	56	3.93	2.82	1.10				5.6	2.8	10.5	3.7						30%	66%								0.1	127	190	$2
12	LAA *	3	1	11	61	59	3.31	2.66	1.15	1026	2000	629	5.0	3.2	8.7	2.7	64%	14%	29	14	57	28%	72%	0%	0	21			92	0.02	5.3	105	137	$7
13	aaa	5	3	3	67	65	3.43	2.36	0.99				6.2	3.3	8.7	2.6						21%	71%								3.6	92	119	$6
14	TAM *	2	4	1	50	62	3.19	3.60	1.28	851	582	973	5.1	4.3	11.1	2.6	51%	16%	13	19	69	30%	80%	27%	0	14			33	1.05	3.4	96	115	$1
15	TAM	2	6	2	67	61	3.74	4.25	1.05	594	612	575	3.8	3.5	8.2	2.3	60%	10%	34	15	51	22%	68%	9%	2	16	0%	100%	40	1.17	1.8	65	77	$3
1st Half		1	4	2	38	43	3.76	3.52	1.02	569	584	551	4.1	3.5	10.1	2.9	57%	11%	37	18	45	24%	66%	10%	2	17	0%	100%	100	1.30	1.0	102	121	$4
2nd Half		1	2	0	29	18	3.72	5.25	1.10	625	661	598	3.6	3.4	5.6	1.6	64%	9%	30	13	57	21%	71%	8%	0	14			0	1.02	0.9	16	19	$1
16	Proj	**3**	**5**	**2**	**73**	**70**	**3.56**	**4.16**	**1.23**	**677**	**700**	**654**	**4.5**	**3.6**	**8.8**	**2.4**	**62%**	**10%**	**33**	**15**	**52**	**28%**	**75%**	**8%**	**0**						**3.6**	**71**	**84**	**$2**

Gibson,Kyle

Age: 28	Th: R	Role SP	Health A	LIMA Plan B	
Ht: 6' 6"	Wt: 210	Type GB	PT/Exp A	Rand Var 0	
			Consist A	MM 2105	

Just what you hope to see from a young pitcher, cultivating swing-and-miss skills to augment strong GB profile. SwK rose monthly as slider, changeup produced more whiffs as 2H progressed. Dom still only "acceptable", but if he can pair it with the 2H Cmd, you could be looking at... UP: 15 wins, 3.50 ERA

Yr	Tm	W	L	Sv	IP	K	ERA	xERA	WHIP	oOPS	vL	vR	BF/G	Ctl	Dom	Cmd	FpK	SwK	G	L	F	H%	S%	hr/f	GS	APC	DOM%	DIS%	Sv%	LI	RAR	BPV	BPX	R$
11	aaa	3	8	0	95	75	5.64	5.60	1.60				23.4	2.6	7.1	2.7						37%	65%								-20.0	62	93	-$10
12																																		
13	MIN *	9	9	0	153	97	4.50	4.44	1.46	874	875	869	24.2	3.2	5.7	1.8	52%	8%	50	21	28	32%	70%	13%	10	90	20%	30%			-12.0	49	64	-$5
14	MIN	13	12	0	179	107	4.47	4.01	1.31	679	705	650	24.4	2.9	5.4	1.9	57%	9%	54	19	27	29%	65%	8%	31	90	42%	19%			-16.0	51	61	-$1
15	MIN	11	11	0	195	145	3.84	3.94	1.29	698	702	693	25.7	3.0	6.7	2.2	61%	10%	53	20	27	29%	72%	11%	32	101	53%	19%			3.0	71	84	$7
1st Half		6	6	0	101	65	3.04	4.03	1.24	687	681	691	26.2	3.0	5.8	2.0	63%	9%	54	21	25	27%	79%	13%	16	102	50%	19%			11.5	57	68	$12
2nd Half		5	5	0	94	80	4.69	3.84	1.34	709	721	694	25.1	3.1	7.7	2.5	58%	11%	52	19	29	32%	65%	10%	16	101	56%	19%			-8.5	86	102	$1
16	Proj	**11**	**12**	**0**	**189**	**133**	**3.99**	**3.95**	**1.36**	**714**	**729**	**695**	**24.4**	**3.0**	**6.4**	**2.2**	**58%**	**10%**	**53**	**20**	**27**	**31%**	**72%**	**10%**	**32**						**-0.6**	**66**	**79**	**$2**

Giles,Ken

Age: 25	Th: R	Role RP	Health A	LIMA Plan B	
Ht: 6' 2"	Wt: 205	Type Pwr	PT/Exp D	Rand Var -5	
			Consist F	MM 5531	

Anyone paying attention would contend his ascent to closer came a year and a half too late, and who's to argue? Cmd owes debt of gratitude to stratospheric Dom, and 2nd half FpK gains further insulate against Ctl worries. 2nd half skills say he's already reached the elite closer tier. Pay up.

Yr	Tm	W	L	Sv	IP	K	ERA	xERA	WHIP	oOPS	vL	vR	BF/G	Ctl	Dom	Cmd	FpK	SwK	G	L	F	H%	S%	hr/f	GS	APC	DOM%	DIS%	Sv%	LI	RAR	BPV	BPX	R$
11																																		
12																																		
13																																		
14	PHI *	5	1	13	74	97	1.56	1.22	0.94	450	436	461	4.1	2.9	11.7	4.0	63%	16%	44	15	41	28%	83%	3%	0	16			93	1.15	20.0	170	203	$17
15	PHI	6	3	15	70	87	1.80	3.24	1.20	569	574	565	4.3	3.2	11.2	3.5	60%	15%	45	22	33	34%	85%	3%	0	17			75	1.15	18.7	138	164	$14
1st Half		3	2	0	36	44	2.00	3.82	1.31	584	406	702	4.2	4.3	11.0	2.6	56%	16%	41	17	42	34%	85%	3%	0	17			0	0.96	8.7	102	121	$8
2nd Half		3	1	15	34	43	1.59	2.65	1.09	552	724	395	4.4	2.1	11.4	5.4	64%	15%	49	27	24	35%	86%	5%	0	17			83	1.36	10.0	175	207	$21
16	Proj	**5**	**3**	**43**	**73**	**89**	**2.06**	**2.93**	**1.09**	**541**	**560**	**526**	**4.1**	**3.1**	**11.1**	**3.6**	**61%**	**16%**	**45**	**20**	**35**	**31%**	**81%**	**3%**	**0**						**17.0**	**139**	**165**	**$26**

ROB CARROLL

Gilmartin,Sean

Age: 26	Th: L	Role: RP	Health: A	LIMA Plan: B+
Ht: 6' 2"	Wt: 190	Type: Pwr	PT/Exp: D	Rand Var: -3
			Consist: C	MM: 2300

Minor league SP adapted well to short relief in MLB, although fortuitous 1H S% made it look a little better than it was. Got a year-end spot start, and if he's going to be a fanalytic asset, starting is how it'll happen. That said, given MLEs in high minors the previous 3 years... well, short relief seems to be his new calling.

Yr	Tm	W	L	Sv	IP	K	ERA	xERA	WHIP	oOPS	vL	vR	BF/G	Ctl	Dom	Cmd	FpK	SwK	G	L	F	H%	S%	hr/f	GS	APC	DOM%	DIS%	Sv%	LI	RAR	BPV	BPX	R$
11																																		
12	a/a	6	10	0	157	99	4.48	4.26	1.33				24.1	2.2	5.7	2.6						31%	68%								-8.9	61	79	-$2
13	aaa	3	8	0	91	57	6.71	6.43	1.76				24.5	3.3	5.6	1.7						36%	63%								-31.9	21	28	-$18
14	a/a	9	7	0	146	107	4.70	4.72	1.50				24.2	2.8	6.6	2.4						35%	68%								-17.2	66	79	-$7
15	NYM	3	2	0	57	54	2.67	3.73	1.19	626	661	597	4.7	2.8	8.5	3.0	62%	13%	45	18	38	31%	77%	3%	1	17	100%	0%	0	0.69	9.1	99	118	$3
1st Half		1	0	0	26	21	1.71	4.06	1.14	587	720	463	3.5	3.8	7.2	1.9	60%	12%	51	14	36	25%	86%	4%	0	13			0	0.67	7.3	56	67	$2
2nd Half		2	2	0	31	33	3.48	3.46	1.23	657	609	693	6.5	2.0	9.6	4.7	63%	13%	39	21	39	36%	70%	3%	1	24	100%	0%	0	0.71	1.8	135	160	$3
16	Proj	2	2	0	44	40	3.40	3.73	1.25	683	710	662	6.3	2.8	8.2	3.0	62%	13%	44	18	38	32%	74%	6%	0						3.0	94	112	-$1

Giolito,Lucas

Age: 21	Th: R	Role: SP	Health: A	LIMA Plan: C
Ht: 6' 6"	Wt: 255	Type: Pwr	PT/Exp: F	Rand Var: +2
			Consist: F	MM: 2300

Elite WAS prospect fanned 10 against 3 walks per 9 IP last year between Single- and Double-A, and almost never surrendered a gopherball (just 3 total in 117 IP). Keeper-league gem, but lacks the high-minors experience/results that we look for to predict early success in MLB. So don't expect much from him in '16.

Yr	Tm	W	L	Sv	IP	K	ERA	xERA	WHIP	oOPS	vL	vR	BF/G	Ctl	Dom	Cmd	FpK	SwK	G	L	F	H%	S%	hr/f	GS	APC	DOM%	DIS%	Sv%	LI	RAR	BPV	BPX	R$
11																																		
12																																		
13																																		
14																																		
15	aa	4	2	0	47	38	4.68	4.46	1.52				25.7	3.2	7.2	2.3						36%	68%								-4.2	76	90	-$5
1st Half																																		
2nd Half		4	2	0	47	38	4.68	4.46	1.52				25.7	3.2	7.2	2.3						36%	68%								-4.2	76	90	-$5
16	Proj	5	3	0	58	51	3.99	3.88	1.33				22.3	3.6	7.9	2.2	62%	10%	46	22	32	30%	72%	11%	11						-0.2	71	85	$0

Givens,Mychal

Age: 26	Th: R	Role: RP	Health: A	LIMA Plan: A
Ht: 6' 0"	Wt: 207	Type: Pwr	PT/Exp: F	Rand Var: -2
			Consist: D	MM: 5500

2-0, 1.80 ERA in 30 IP at BAL. Stock soared for this converted SS, who handled the jump to the majors with ease while flashing impressive command of a mid-90s sinking fastball. Still inexperienced on the hill, but was closing with success at AA before call-up. UP: BAL struggles, deals Britton, he gets 15 Sv.

Yr	Tm	W	L	Sv	IP	K	ERA	xERA	WHIP	oOPS	vL	vR	BF/G	Ctl	Dom	Cmd	FpK	SwK	G	L	F	H%	S%	hr/f	GS	APC	DOM%	DIS%	Sv%	LI	RAR	BPV	BPX	R$
11																																		
12																																		
13																																		
14	aa	0	0	0	25	23	4.53	3.92	1.77				6.5	8.2	8.2	1.0						31%	72%								-2.5	78	93	-$6
15	BAL *	6	2	15	87	101	2.18	2.07	1.05	538	555	527	5.9	2.5	10.5	4.3	63%	13%	39	30	31	31%	79%	5%	0	21			88	0.79	19.2	157	187	$18
1st Half		4	1	13	47	52	1.86	1.98	1.07	0	0	0	6.5	2.4	10.0	4.2	67%	9%	100	0	0	32%	81%	0%	0	11			87	0.01	12.1	159	189	$23
2nd Half		2	1	2	41	50	2.55	2.16	1.02	553	583	535	5.4	2.6	11.0	4.3	63%	13%	38	30	32	30%	77%	5%	0	22			100	0.82	7.1	154	183	$12
16	Proj	4	1	0	58	69	2.83	2.94	1.05	587	600	577	5.8	2.5	10.7	4.2	63%	13%	38	30	32	30%	75%	8%	0						8.1	139	166	$5

Glasnow,Tyler

Age: 22	Th: R	Role: SP	Health: A	LIMA Plan: C+
Ht: 6' 8"	Wt: 225	Type: Pwr	PT/Exp: F	Rand Var: 0
			Consist: F	MM: 2300

Zoomed through the PIT system in '15, and dominated at each level—as MLEs confirm. Spent most of a season in the high minors, including 41 IP at Triple-A. So he should be ready when he does get the call, though note that IP totals will be limited at first.

Yr	Tm	W	L	Sv	IP	K	ERA	xERA	WHIP	oOPS	vL	vR	BF/G	Ctl	Dom	Cmd	FpK	SwK	G	L	F	H%	S%	hr/f	GS	APC	DOM%	DIS%	Sv%	LI	RAR	BPV	BPX	R$
11																																		
12																																		
13																																		
14																																		
15	a/a	7	4	0	104	108	2.69	2.39	1.16				20.7	3.3	9.3	2.8						30%	76%								16.3	120	142	$10
1st Half		2	2	0	38	36	3.13	2.28	1.11				18.7	2.8	8.6	3.1						30%	70%								3.9	121	144	$1
2nd Half		5	2	0	66	71	2.36	2.39	1.17				21.9	3.5	9.7	2.7						30%	79%								13.1	120	143	$15
16	Proj	4	2	0	58	56	3.71	3.68	1.24				21.0	3.6	8.8	2.4	63%	11%	45	20	35	31%	68%	3%	11						1.8	84	100	$1

Godley,Zachary

Age: 26	Th: R	Role: RP	Health: A	LIMA Plan: D+
Ht: 6' 3"	Wt: 245	Type: Pwr GB	PT/Exp: F	Rand Var: +1
			Consist: F	MM: 0101

5-1, 3.19 ERA in 37 IP at ARI. A most unusual pitching prospect, he started out as a reliever, only converting to a starter in '15. Not overpowering, and when his command is off, he can be hit hard. Given lack of experience as a SP and that sometimes shaky Cmd, expect growing pains for a while.

Yr	Tm	W	L	Sv	IP	K	ERA	xERA	WHIP	oOPS	vL	vR	BF/G	Ctl	Dom	Cmd	FpK	SwK	G	L	F	H%	S%	hr/f	GS	APC	DOM%	DIS%	Sv%	LI	RAR	BPV	BPX	R$
11																																		
12																																		
13																																		
14																																		
15	ARI *	7	2	0	61	44	4.14	3.95	1.36	688	528	809	15.9	4.1	6.5	1.6	58%	12%	46	22	32	28%	72%	13%	6	64	50%	33%	0	0.74	-1.3	49	58	-$1
1st Half		1	0	0	5	2	0.00	0.34	0.72				17.7	1.9	2.9	1.5						17%	100%	0%	0						2.4	74	88	-$7
2nd Half		6	2	0	56	42	4.51	4.27	1.42	688	528	809	15.8	4.3	6.8	1.6	58%	12%	46	22	32	28%	71%	13%	6	64	50%	33%	0	0.74	-3.8	47	55	$0
16	Proj	4	6	0	87	67	4.95	4.64	1.54	783	591	928	14.8	4.5	6.9	1.5	58%	12%	46	22	32	31%	71%	13%	12						-10.6	28	33	-$7

Gomez,Jeanmar

Age: 28	Th: R	Role: RP	Health: A	LIMA Plan: B+
Ht: 6' 3"	Wt: 220	Type: Con	PT/Exp: C	Rand Var: -3
			Consist: A	MM: 1000

Skated by in 1H via aberrant strand rate, but xERA shows his true level. Basically, he's a tweener—Cmd not quite good enough to start, stuff not quite good enough for high-leverage relief. Safe to ignore, unless, you know, you have a thing for marginally skilled middle relievers. Not that there's anything wrong with that.

Yr	Tm	W	L	Sv	IP	K	ERA	xERA	WHIP	oOPS	vL	vR	BF/G	Ctl	Dom	Cmd	FpK	SwK	G	L	F	H%	S%	hr/f	GS	APC	DOM%	DIS%	Sv%	LI	RAR	BPV	BPX	R$
11	CLE *	15	10	0	196	122	3.31	4.07	1.38	804	855	756	25.7	2.8	5.6	2.0	61%	6%	53	20	27	31%	77%	10%	10	87	20%	50%	0	0.83	15.3	56	85	$9
12	CLE *	11	13	0	160	92	5.53	4.92	1.44	810	822	800	22.0	2.8	5.2	1.8	56%	8%	48	19	33	31%	63%	15%	17	73	12%	53%	0	0.68	-30.0	32	42	-$10
13	PIT	3	0	0	81	53	3.35	3.83	1.15	617	621	614	9.8	3.1	5.9	1.9	63%	9%	55	19	26	25%	72%	10%	8	36	50%	50%	0	0.69	5.2	55	72	$2
14	PIT	2	2	1	62	38	3.19	4.35	1.50	810	1065	646	6.1	3.3	5.5	1.7	65%	9%	47	25	28	32%	82%	11%	0	22			100	0.62	4.2	34	41	-$2
15	PHI	2	3	0	75	50	3.01	4.11	1.33	697	700	695	4.9	2.0	6.0	2.9	62%	9%	49	22	29	33%	78%	6%	0	18			0	0.71	8.7	80	95	$0
1st Half		0	1	0	40	28	1.59	4.22	1.21	581	500	638	4.7	2.7	6.4	2.3	62%	8%	48	17	35	30%	85%	0%	0	18			0	0.49	11.6	67	79	$3
2nd Half		2	2	0	35	22	4.63	3.99	1.46	818	920	753	5.2	1.3	5.7	4.4	62%	9%	50	27	24	35%	70%	14%	0	19			0	0.98	-2.9	95	112	-$3
16	Proj	2	2	0	58	37	3.60	4.08	1.37	736	813	682	6.1	2.5	5.8	2.3	63%	9%	50	22	28	32%	75%	9%	0						2.6	63	76	-$2

Gonzales,Marco

Age: 24	Th: L	Role: SP	Health: A	LIMA Plan: D+
Ht: 6' 1"	Wt: 195	Type: xFB	PT/Exp: D	Rand Var: +5
			Consist: F	MM: 0100

0-0, 13.50 ERA in 3 IP at STL. Lost out on 5th starter job in final cut, then shoulder started barking. It lingered the entire first half, and he never quite got things untracked. Young and talented enough to get another shot, but he'll need to show '14 skills before his MLB club gives it to him. Follow their lead here.

Yr	Tm	W	L	Sv	IP	K	ERA	xERA	WHIP	oOPS	vL	vR	BF/G	Ctl	Dom	Cmd	FpK	SwK	G	L	F	H%	S%	hr/f	GS	APC	DOM%	DIS%	Sv%	LI	RAR	BPV	BPX	R$
11																																		
12																																		
13																																		
14	STL *	11	5	0	119	103	3.36	3.78	1.27	737	397	827	19.5	2.9	7.8	2.7	61%	10%	36	23	41	30%	77%	10%	5	62	40%	40%	0	1.07	5.6	80	95	$6
15	STL *	1	5	0	79	48	5.61	6.46	1.73	1286	500	1286	21.0	2.7	5.5	2.1	75%	3%	36	36	29	37%	69%	25%	1	66	0%	100%			-16.0	29	34	-$14
1st Half		0	1	0	28	18	6.90	6.95	1.69				21.3	2.4	5.8	2.4						36%	62%	0%	0						-10.3	19	23	-$16
2nd Half		1	4	0	50	30	4.94	6.22	1.75	1286	500	1286	20.9	2.8	5.4	1.9	75%	3%	36	36	29	38%	73%	25%	1	66	0%	100%			-6.1	34	40	-$12
16	Proj	3	3	0	58	41	4.83	4.75	1.54	786	429	882	20.4	2.8	6.4	2.3	61%	10%	36	23	41	34%	71%	8%	12						-6.2	55	65	-$6

ROD TRUESDELL

Gonzalez,Alex

Age: 24	Th: R	Role SP		Health A	LIMA Plan D+
Ht: 6' 2"	Wt: 195	Type		PT/Exp D	Rand Var 0
				Consist A	MM 0001

4-6, 3.90 ERA in 67 IP at TEX. Former first-round pick was pretty solid in '14, but the decent command he showed then went missing in 2015. Gets some GB, competes well, and Ctl did look better in 2H. But he needs at least the '14 MLE Dom rate to be effective. Still owns it, but make him show it in MLB.

Yr	Tm	W	L	Sv	IP	K	ERA	xERA	WHIP	oOPS	vL	vR	BF/G	Ctl	Dom	Cmd	FpK	SwK	G	L	F	H%	S%	hr/f	GS	APC	DOM%	DIS%	Sv%	LI	RAR	BPV	BPX	R$
11																																		
12																																		
13																																		
14	aa	7	4	0	73	55	3.25	3.83	1.38				20.6	3.1	6.7	2.2						32%	76%								4.5	75	89	$1
15	TEX *	12	13	0	155	77	4.18	4.07	1.44	632	649	617	22.1	3.7	4.5	1.2	58%	7%	49	20	31	29%	71%	9%	10	75	10%	20%	0	0.77	-4.2	37	44	-$2
1st Half		5	9	0	87	37	4.43	4.14	1.47	626	651	602	24.8	4.0	3.8	1.0	56%	6%	51	22	27	29%	69%	8%	7	95	0%	29%			-5.0	28	34	-$5
2nd Half		7	4	0	69	40	3.87	3.99	1.40	644	644	646	19.3	3.3	5.3	1.6	62%	8%	44	17	39	30%	73%	11%	3	55	33%	0%	0	0.76	0.8	50	59	$3
16	**Proj**	**8**	**6**	**0**	**94**	**58**	**3.91**	**4.58**	**1.41**	**784**	**853**	**726**	**21.0**	**3.4**	**5.5**	**1.6**	**60%**	**7%**	**47**	**19**	**34**	**30%**	**73%**	**8%**	**19**						**0.6**	**32**	**38**	**$0**

Gonzalez,Gio

Age: 30	Th: L	Role SP	Health B	LIMA Plan B+
Ht: 6' 0"	Wt: 205	Type Pwr	PT/Exp A	Rand Var 0
			Consist A	MM 3405

Threw two-seamer more in 1H and was among leaders in GB%. Perhaps didn't like so many sneaking through for hits, because he reverted somewhat to four-seamer in 2H to better results. Otherwise, as consistent a skill set as you'll see. High pitch counts limit IP, so account for that in your bid.

Yr	Tm	W	L	Sv	IP	K	ERA	xERA	WHIP	oOPS	vL	vR	BF/G	Ctl	Dom	Cmd	FpK	SwK	G	L	F	H%	S%	hr/f	GS	APC	DOM%	DIS%	Sv%	LI	RAR	BPV	BPX	R$
11	OAK	16	12	0	202	197	3.12	3.68	1.32	654	713	636	27.0	4.1	8.8	2.2	53%	10%	47	18	34	30%	79%	9%	32	106	56%	13%			20.5	74	111	$16
12	WAS	21	8	0	199	207	2.89	3.40	1.13	582	659	561	25.7	3.4	9.3	2.7	59%	10%	48	22	30	28%	75%	6%	32	100	78%	13%			27.7	102	132	$28
13	WAS	11	8	0	196	192	3.36	3.60	1.25	668	568	696	25.6	3.5	8.8	2.5	61%	10%	44	23	33	30%	75%	10%	32	104	69%	22%			12.3	87	113	$12
14	WAS	10	10	0	159	162	3.57	3.41	1.20	647	628	653	24.2	3.2	9.2	2.9	58%	11%	45	19	37	30%	71%	7%	27	97	70%	19%			3.3	103	122	$9
15	WAS	11	8	0	176	169	3.79	3.66	1.42	711	641	732	24.5	3.5	8.7	2.4	60%	10%	54	20	27	35%	73%	6%	31	95	52%	19%			3.7	92	110	$4
1st Half		6	4	0	89	78	4.16	3.60	1.43	743	646	777	25.3	3.3	7.9	2.4	56%	9%	57	22	22	34%	70%	7%	15	95	53%	13%			-2.2	87	103	$1
2nd Half		5	4	0	87	91	3.41	3.73	1.41	678	635	689	23.6	3.7	9.4	2.5	64%	11%	51	17	32	35%	76%	5%	16	95	50%	25%			5.9	98	116	$6
16	**Proj**	**12**	**9**	**0**	**181**	**180**	**3.55**	**3.56**	**1.32**	**676**	**631**	**690**	**24.1**	**3.5**	**8.9**	**2.6**	**59%**	**11%**	**49**	**20**	**31**	**32%**	**73%**	**7%**	**31**						**9.1**	**94**	**112**	**$9**

Gonzalez,Miguel

Age: 32	Th: R	Role SP	Health D	LIMA Plan D+
Ht: 6' 1"	Wt: 170	Type	PT/Exp A	Rand Var +2
			Consist A	MM 1103

Missed time with groin, shoulder, and elbow woes. Meanwhile, ERA finally spiked to match (and exceed) xERA, as he bid adieu to prior hit/strand rate fortune. Take another look at that xERA line; save for 2012 (when his MLB xERA was 4.44), he's been consistently mediocre. Let others speculate on '13-'14 return.

Yr	Tm	W	L	Sv	IP	K	ERA	xERA	WHIP	oOPS	vL	vR	BF/G	Ctl	Dom	Cmd	FpK	SwK	G	L	F	H%	S%	hr/f	GS	APC	DOM%	DIS%	Sv%	LI	RAR	BPV	BPX	R$
11	a/a	0	6	0	52	38	7.70	6.47	1.84				15.0	4.0	6.7	1.7						38%	57%								-23.9	34	51	-$13
12	BAL *	12	6	1	150	117	3.03	3.02	1.13	694	701	685	18.5	2.8	7.0	2.5	66%	9%	35	22	43	26%	77%	10%	15	94	47%	20%	100	0.69	18.2	78	102	$17
13	BAL	11	8	0	171	120	3.78	4.28	1.23	713	689	736	23.7	2.8	6.3	2.3	59%	9%	39	21	40	27%	74%	11%	28	90	54%	14%	0	0.75	1.8	55	72	$7
14	BAL	10	9	0	159	111	3.23	4.36	1.30	751	772	724	24.9	2.9	6.3	2.2	61%	9%	37	21	42	28%	82%	12%	26	95	46%	19%	0	0.75	10.1	50	60	$6
15	BAL	9	12	0	145	109	4.91	4.45	1.40	795	831	761	23.9	3.2	6.8	2.1	62%	9%	40	24	36	30%	69%	15%	26	94	27%	38%			-17.0	54	65	-$4
1st Half		7	5	0	88	67	3.87	4.22	1.20	724	716	733	24.3	2.9	6.8	2.4	62%	10%	40	23	37	26%	75%	15%	15	95	40%	33%			1.0	64	75	$5
2nd Half		2	7	0	56	42	6.55	4.82	1.70	896	1020	796	23.4	3.7	6.7	1.8	63%	8%	41	25	34	35%	63%	15%	11	92	9%	45%			-18.0	41	48	-$20
16	**Proj**	**10**	**11**	**0**	**160**	**117**	**4.48**	**4.44**	**1.41**	**792**	**823**	**760**	**22.6**	**3.2**	**6.6**	**2.1**	**62%**	**9%**	**39**	**23**	**38**	**30%**	**73%**	**13%**	**30**						**-10.1**	**50**	**60**	**-$2**

Gott,Trevor

Age: 23	Th: R	Role RP	Health A	LIMA Plan B+
Ht: 6' 0"	Wt: 190	Type xGB	PT/Exp F	Rand Var -2
			Consist A	MM 2100

4-2, 3.02 ERA in 48 IP at LAA. Some will see his numbers and speculate on a bigger '16 role, but metrics don't agree. Notably, those 2H skills, all earned in majors, are decidedly not closer-worthy. High GB rate will help keep ERA from spiking, but shaky Cmd and some issues vLHB say he's no more than marginal LIMA fodder.

Yr	Tm	W	L	Sv	IP	K	ERA	xERA	WHIP	oOPS	vL	vR	BF/G	Ctl	Dom	Cmd	FpK	SwK	G	L	F	H%	S%	hr/f	GS	APC	DOM%	DIS%	Sv%	LI	RAR	BPV	BPX	R$
11																																		
12																																		
13																																		
14	aa	2	1	2	29	26	3.35	2.92	1.38				5.4	4.7	7.8	1.7						31%	73%								1.4	91	108	-$1
15	LAA *	5	2	8	76	53	2.79	3.17	1.30	625	716	547	4.3	3.2	6.3	2.0	55%	6%	57	16	26	30%	78%	5%	0	15			62	1.13	10.9	77	92	$6
1st Half		2	0	8	38	30	2.25	2.97	1.24	468	618	316	4.4	2.8	7.1	2.5	49%	9%	44	18	38	31%	82%	8%	0	14			89	0.70	8.0	94	112	$10
2nd Half		3	2	0	38	23	3.35	4.21	1.35	664	742	601	4.3	3.6	5.5	1.5	57%	6%	61	16	23	30%	74%	4%	0	15			0	1.25	2.9	41	49	$3
16	**Proj**	**4**	**2**	**0**	**58**	**40**	**3.33**	**3.85**	**1.31**	**601**	**669**	**546**	**4.2**	**3.3**	**6.1**	**1.9**	**57%**	**6%**	**61**	**16**	**23**	**30%**	**73%**	**3%**	**0**						**4.6**	**61**	**72**	**$0**

Graham,J.R.

Age: 26	Th: R	Role RP	Health B	LIMA Plan C
Ht: 6' 0"	Wt: 185	Type Pwr GB	PT/Exp D	Rand Var +4
			Consist B	MM 2200

Not sure if he broke a mirror, walked under a ladder, or opened an umbrella indoors. But must've done one of those around Independence Day, as great 1H luck turned decidedly south. Hitting mid-90s again on gun; that, SwK, and 2H BPV give hope for better down the road—as long as a black cat isn't crossing it.

Yr	Tm	W	L	Sv	IP	K	ERA	xERA	WHIP	oOPS	vL	vR	BF/G	Ctl	Dom	Cmd	FpK	SwK	G	L	F	H%	S%	hr/f	GS	APC	DOM%	DIS%	Sv%	LI	RAR	BPV	BPX	R$
11																																		
12	aa	3	1	0	45	37	3.93	3.15	1.27				20.6	3.4	7.4	2.2						30%	68%								0.5	84	110	-$1
13	aa	1	3	0	36	24	5.15	4.58	1.59				19.7	2.6	6.2	2.3						38%	64%								-5.7	78	102	-$6
14	aa	1	5	0	71	44	6.65	5.05	1.65				11.8	3.3	5.5	1.6						36%	56%								-25.6	52	62	-$14
15	MIN	1	1	0	64	53	4.95	4.11	1.48	809	782	831	7.3	3.0	7.5	2.5	57%	11%	49	20	31	33%	70%	16%	1	27	0%	100%	0	0.49	-7.7	82	97	-$7
1st Half		0	0	0	37	28	2.92	4.27	1.32	783	791	777	7.1	2.7	6.8	2.5	55%	11%	41	22	37	30%	86%	14%	1	27	0%	100%	0	0.42	4.8	69	82	-$3
2nd Half		1	1	0	27	25	7.76	3.83	1.69	842	771	903	7.5	3.4	8.4	2.5	60%	11%	60	18	22	38%	54%	20%	0	28			0	0.58	-12.5	98	117	-$11
16	**Proj**	**2**	**3**	**0**	**58**	**48**	**4.19**	**3.83**	**1.41**	**709**	**681**	**732**	**7.8**	**3.1**	**7.4**	**2.4**	**58%**	**11%**	**52**	**20**	**28**	**33%**	**71%**	**10%**	**0**						**-1.6**	**80**	**95**	**-$3**

Graveman,Kendall

Age: 25	Th: R	Role RP	Health F	LIMA Plan C
Ht: 6' 2"	Wt: 195	Type Con GB	PT/Exp D	Rand Var 0
			Consist B	MM 2001

6-9, 4.05 ERA in 116 IP at OAK. GB specialist sidelined last month+ with strained oblique. Doesn't miss a ton of bats, so like many of his ilk, relies on command and the slings and arrows of GB-location fortune (and infield defense). Showed flashes in a handful of his starts, but ultimately needs that near-3 Cmd to succeed.

Yr	Tm	W	L	Sv	IP	K	ERA	xERA	WHIP	oOPS	vL	vR	BF/G	Ctl	Dom	Cmd	FpK	SwK	G	L	F	H%	S%	hr/f	GS	APC	DOM%	DIS%	Sv%	LI	RAR	BPV	BPX	R$
11																																		
12																																		
13																																		
14	TOR *	4	2	0	49	26	2.51	3.58	1.26	556	625	500	16.7	1.3	4.9	3.6	78%	13%	64	29	7	32%	80%	0%	0	12			0	0.36	7.5	96	115	$1
15	OAK *	8	10	0	140	88	3.74	4.56	1.41	761	724	794	23.7	3.1	5.7	1.8	59%	8%	50	21	29	30%	77%	14%	21	90	29%	33%			3.8	42	50	$0
1st Half		8	5	0	101	56	2.95	4.05	1.35	717	718	714	24.8	3.0	5.0	1.7	59%	8%	48	23	29	29%	81%	11%	13	93	31%	23%			12.6	43	51	$7
2nd Half		0	5	0	39	32	5.82	4.13	1.58	842	735	949	21.9	3.3	7.4	2.3	60%	9%	54	18	28	34%	67%	20%	8	86	25%	50%			-8.9	78	93	-$16
16	**Proj**	**5**	**7**	**0**	**94**	**60**	**3.80**	**4.06**	**1.40**	**735**	**691**	**777**	**19.9**	**2.4**	**5.8**	**2.4**	**60%**	**8%**	**52**	**20**	**28**	**32%**	**75%**	**10%**	**20**						**1.9**	**68**	**81**	**-$1**

Gray,Jonathan

Age: 24	Th: R	Role SP	Health A	LIMA Plan B+
Ht: 6' 4"	Wt: 235	Type Pwr	PT/Exp D	Rand Var +2
			Consist C	MM 2201

0-2, 5.53 ERA in 41 IP at COL. Former third-overall pick tops out in mid-90s, but has struggled to turn stuff into high-level success. Ups-and-downs of youth evident in those 100% DOM or DIS starts, but he did finally ratchet up Dom in 2H. Seeds are still there for a rotation ace, but let's see him build on 2H gains.

Yr	Tm	W	L	Sv	IP	K	ERA	xERA	WHIP	oOPS	vL	vR	BF/G	Ctl	Dom	Cmd	FpK	SwK	G	L	F	H%	S%	hr/f	GS	APC	DOM%	DIS%	Sv%	LI	RAR	BPV	BPX	R$
11																																		
12																																		
13																																		
14	aa	10	5	0	124	92	5.58	4.70	1.44				22.1	3.2	6.6	2.1						32%	62%								-28.2	51	60	-$8
15	COL *	6	8	0	155	128	5.45	5.79	1.68	856	755	949	23.3	3.3	7.4	2.3	58%	10%	43	24	33	38%	68%	10%	9	76	33%	67%			-28.4	56	67	-$17
1st Half		3	5	0	90	60	6.11	6.38	1.74				25.8	3.2	6.0	1.9						37%	66%	0%	0						-23.9	30	36	-$24
2nd Half		3	3	0	65	67	4.52	4.97	1.60	856	755	949	20.4	3.4	9.3	2.8	58%	10%	43	24	33	39%	71%	10%	9	76	33%	67%			-4.5	92	109	-$8
16	**Proj**	**7**	**5**	**0**	**116**	**98**	**4.19**	**4.01**	**1.31**	**654**	**572**	**729**	**25.4**	**3.3**	**7.6**	**2.3**	**58%**	**10%**	**43**	**24**	**33**	**30%**	**70%**	**10%**	**19**						**-3.3**	**69**	**83**	**$1**

ROD TRUESDELL

Gray,Sonny

Age: 26 | Th: R | Role: SP | Ht: 5' 11" | Wt: 195 | Type: Pwr GB
Health: A | PT/Exp: A | Consist: A
LIMA Plan: D+ | Rand Var: -3 | MM: 3205

Another fine skills season. It would've been even better without 2H fade, but a combination of July salmonella poisoning, an August sore back, and a September hip injury was likely the multifaceted culprit. Still just 26; barring further health woes, he should be a rotation anchor for years to come.

Yr Tm	W	L	Sv	IP	K	ERA	xERA	WHIP	oOPS	vL	vR	BF/G	Ctl	Dom	Cmd	FpK	SwK	G	L	F	H%	S%	hr/f	GS	APC	DOM%	DIS%	Sv%	LI	RAR	BPV	BPX	R$
11 aa	1	0	0	20	16	0.44	1.87	1.05				15.5	2.5	7.1	2.9						28%	95%								8.6	115	173	$1
12 a/a	6	9	0	152	84	4.43	4.26	1.48				24.2	3.3	5.0	1.5						32%	69%								-7.8	48	62	-$7
13 OAK *	15	10	0	182	165	3.20	3.29	1.28	570	622	499	23.4	2.8	8.1	2.9	60%	10%	53	20	28	32%	75%	8%	10	83	80%	10%	0	0.66	15.1	101	132	$13
14 OAK	14	10	0	219	183	3.08	3.36	1.19	627	639	614	27.2	3.0	7.5	2.5	58%	9%	56	18	26	28%	76%	9%	33	100	55%	6%			17.8	87	104	$16
15 OAK	14	7	0	208	169	2.73	3.62	1.08	590	579	601	26.8	2.6	7.3	2.9	59%	10%	53	17	31	26%	78%	9%	31	99	71%	6%			31.7	94	112	$26
1st Half	9	3	0	108	97	2.09	3.30	0.99	533	559	504	26.5	2.2	8.1	3.7	57%	11%	54	14	32	27%	80%	5%	16	100	88%	0%			24.9	119	142	$36
2nd Half	5	4	0	100	72	3.41	3.98	1.18	650	601	697	27.1	3.0	6.5	2.2	62%	9%	51	19	29	26%	75%	14%	15	99	53%	13%			6.9	65	78	$15
16 Proj	**15**	**9**	**0**	**210**	**177**	**2.97**	**3.49**	**1.19**	**630**	**632**	**627**	**25.6**	**2.8**	**7.6**	**2.7**	**59%**	**10%**	**54**	**18**	**28**	**29%**	**77%**	**9%**	**33**						**25.9**	**92**	**109**	**$20**

Greene,Shane

Age: 27 | Th: R | Role: RP | Ht: 6' 4" | Wt: 210 | Type: Pwr
Health: C | PT/Exp: D | Consist: B
LIMA Plan: D+ | Rand Var: +5 | MM: 1101

4-8, 6.88 ERA in 84 IP at DET. Season-long arterial issues caused numbness in two fingers of his pitching hand—seemingly the overriding reason for this disaster. He's expected to recover fully; likely to receive the chance to build on promising MLB skills from '14 (3.78 ERA, 9.3 Dom, 105 BPV). Deep speculation.

Yr Tm	W	L	Sv	IP	K	ERA	xERA	WHIP	oOPS	vL	vR	BF/G	Ctl	Dom	Cmd	FpK	SwK	G	L	F	H%	S%	hr/f	GS	APC	DOM%	DIS%	Sv%	LI	RAR	BPV	BPX	R$
11																																	
12																																	
13 aa	8	4	0	79	55	4.25	6.14	1.72				25.7	2.5	6.3	2.5						39%	77%								-3.8	50	65	-$6
14 NYY *	10	6	0	145	127	4.53	5.05	1.59	715	765	661	21.3	3.5	7.9	2.3	59%	11%	50	22	28	37%	72%	13%	14	90	43%	29%	0	0.70	-14.1	69	82	-$7
15 DET *	5	9	0	119	66	6.33	5.64	1.59	897	1017	757	20.9	3.0	5.0	1.7	62%	7%	44	23	33	33%	61%	14%	16	74	31%	56%	0	0.70	-34.7	23	27	-$17
1st Half	5	7	0	91	53	5.49	5.14	1.50	830	955	680	23.2	2.5	5.2	2.1	63%	8%	44	24	31	33%	64%	13%	13	80	38%	46%			-17.2	39	46	-$15
2nd Half	0	2	0	27	13	9.16	7.32	1.90	1144	1271	1019	16.1	4.5	4.2	0.9	59%	7%	42	19	39	34%	52%	16%	3	60	0%	100%	0	0.52	-17.5	-18	-22	-$24
16 Proj	**4**	**5**	**0**	**87**	**66**	**4.53**	**4.31**	**1.50**	**794**	**885**	**697**	**19.3**	**3.4**	**6.9**	**2.0**	**60%**	**9%**	**46**	**21**	**33**	**33%**	**72%**	**12%**	**18**						**-6.1**	**56**	**67**	**-$5**

Gregerson,Luke

Age: 32 | Th: R | Role: RP | Ht: 6' 3" | Wt: 200 | Type: xGB
Health: A | PT/Exp: C | Consist: A
LIMA Plan: C+ | Rand Var: +1 | MM: 5330

Finally made the jump from "future closer" to "closer," with spectacular results. Yet, because he barely breaks 90 mph, there's still talk that he's "not a lockdown guy." Yeah, right. Just take a look at his Dom, Cmd, SwK%, and overall BPV, and let others' skepticism help you nab a dominant closer at a discount.

Yr Tm	W	L	Sv	IP	K	ERA	xERA	WHIP	oOPS	vL	vR	BF/G	Ctl	Dom	Cmd	FpK	SwK	G	L	F	H%	S%	hr/f	GS	APC	DOM%	DIS%	Sv%	LI	RAR	BPV	BPX	R$
11 SD	3	3	0	56	34	2.75	4.18	1.37	681	770	622	4.0	3.1	5.5	1.8	55%	12%	49	22	29	31%	80%	4%	0	14			0	1.15	8.2	43	65	$1
12 SD	2	0	9	72	72	2.39	3.30	1.09	612	663	578	3.8	2.6	9.0	3.4	60%	16%	50	18	32	28%	83%	11%	0	14			69	1.19	14.4	120	156	$10
13 SD	6	8	4	66	64	2.71	3.27	1.01	572	624	521	3.7	2.4	8.7	3.6	60%	14%	45	20	35	27%	73%	5%	0	13			44	1.26	9.4	113	148	$8
14 OAK	5	5	3	72	59	2.12	3.24	1.01	604	526	663	3.9	1.9	7.3	3.9	60%	14%	52	15	33	26%	84%	9%	0	14			27	1.31	14.5	112	133	$9
15 HOU	7	3	31	61	59	3.10	2.71	0.95	573	606	537	3.7	1.5	8.7	5.9	67%	16%	60	16	23	28%	70%	13%	0	14			86	1.23	6.5	155	184	$19
1st Half	3	1	18	32	32	3.34	2.82	0.93	585	618	546	3.8	1.7	8.9	5.3	68%	15%	59	13	28	25%	69%	17%	0	14			90	1.27	2.5	153	181	$20
2nd Half	4	2	13	29	27	2.83	2.60	0.98	560	592	525	3.7	1.3	8.5	6.8	66%	16%	62	21	18	30%	70%	7%	0	13			81	1.20	4.0	158	188	$19
16 Proj	**6**	**4**	**37**	**65**	**59**	**2.98**	**2.95**	**1.01**	**587**	**599**	**576**	**3.6**	**1.8**	**8.2**	**4.5**	**63%**	**15%**	**55**	**18**	**27**	**28%**	**72%**	**9%**	**0**						**7.9**	**131**	**156**	**$21**

Greinke,Zack

Age: 32 | Th: R | Role: SP | Ht: 6' 2" | Wt: 195 | Type: Pwr
Health: C | PT/Exp: A | Consist: A
LIMA Plan: D+ | Rand Var: -5 | MM: 4305

A brilliant season, to be sure. But (you knew that "but" was coming, didn't you?) take a look at xERA, and scan over to hit rate. Now, do you want a 200-IP guy with around a 3.00 ERA? Sure! But can you afford one who will probably be bid up to near-2.00 ERA expectations? Unlikely.

Yr Tm	W	L	Sv	IP	K	ERA	xERA	WHIP	oOPS	vL	vR	BF/G	Ctl	Dom	Cmd	FpK	SwK	G	L	F	H%	S%	hr/f	GS	APC	DOM%	DIS%	Sv%	LI	RAR	BPV	BPX	R$
11 MIL	16	6	0	172	201	3.83	2.82	1.20	708	738	679	25.5	2.4	10.5	4.5	60%	11%	47	22	31	33%	71%	14%	28	101	71%	11%			2.4	151	227	$14
12 2 TM	15	5	0	212	200	3.48	3.34	1.20	663	691	635	25.5	2.3	8.5	3.7	59%	9%	49	22	29	31%	73%	10%	34	100	65%	12%			14.1	118	154	$18
13 LA	15	4	0	178	148	2.63	3.43	1.11	647	733	568	25.6	2.3	7.5	3.2	58%	11%	46	24	31	28%	79%	9%	28	101	64%	11%			27.0	96	125	$21
14 LA	17	8	0	202	207	2.71	2.93	1.15	660	627	689	25.7	1.9	9.2	4.8	63%	12%	49	23	29	32%	80%	12%	32	100	75%	6%			25.6	141	168	$21
15 LA	19	3	0	223	200	1.66	3.14	0.84	507	535	482	26.3	1.6	8.1	5.0	64%	13%	48	19	33	24%	84%	7%	32	101	88%	0%			63.3	128	152	$49
1st Half	7	2	0	115	98	1.48	3.31	0.89	532	559	510	25.9	1.6	7.6	4.9	63%	11%	47	19	34	25%	88%	6%	17	100	94%	0%			35.3	120	143	$47
2nd Half	12	1	0	107	102	1.84	2.96	0.79	479	512	447	26.8	1.7	8.6	5.1	64%	14%	49	19	31	22%	81%	8%	15	103	80%	0%			28.0	136	161	$51
16 Proj	**18**	**6**	**0**	**210**	**198**	**2.80**	**3.12**	**1.06**	**629**	**654**	**607**	**25.8**	**1.9**	**8.5**	**4.5**	**62%**	**12%**	**48**	**21**	**31**	**29%**	**77%**	**10%**	**32**						**30.1**	**128**	**152**	**$28**

Griffin,A.J.

Age: 28 | Th: R | Role: SP | Ht: 6' 5" | Wt: 230 | Type: xFB
Health: F | PT/Exp: C | Consist: F
LIMA Plan: C | Rand Var: 0 | MM: 1100

Recovered from '14 TJ surgery, then just before going on a rehab stint, shoulder tendinitis struck, and he missed ANOTHER full season. Brutal. Expected to be ready for spring training, and owns those 2012 skills. But don't draft until he proves he's healthy. Even then, stash him until he shakes off two years of rust.

Yr Tm	W	L	Sv	IP	K	ERA	xERA	WHIP	oOPS	vL	vR	BF/G	Ctl	Dom	Cmd	FpK	SwK	G	L	F	H%	S%	hr/f	GS	APC	DOM%	DIS%	Sv%	LI	RAR	BPV	BPX	R$
11 a/a	2	4	0	38	24	5.91	5.70	1.56				23.8	2.9	5.7	2.0						33%	64%								-9.2	29	43	-$6
12 OAK *	14	4	0	184	139	3.03	2.92	1.07	630	629	631	22.4	1.8	6.8	3.8	62%	9%	37	24	39	27%	75%	10%	15	95	53%	27%			22.5	105	137	$22
13 OAK	14	10	0	200	171	3.83	4.10	1.13	688	666	713	25.7	2.4	7.7	3.2	60%	9%	32	18	49	26%	74%	13%	32	100	56%	3%			1.0	83	108	$14
14																																	
15																																	
1st Half																																	
2nd Half																																	
16 Proj	**4**	**4**	**0**	**58**	**43**	**4.15**	**4.33**	**1.28**	**731**	**720**	**743**	**23.7**	**2.4**	**6.7**	**2.7**	**60%**	**9%**	**34**	**20**	**45**	**29%**	**72%**	**11%**	**10**						**-1.4**	**66**	**79**	**-$1**

Grilli,Jason

Age: 39 | Th: R | Role: RP | Ht: 6' 4" | Wt: 235 | Type: Pwr FB
Health: F | PT/Exp: B | Consist: B
LIMA Plan: B | Rand Var: 0 | MM: 3520

Recaptured '12-'13 magic for half a season, then caught a spike and ruptured his Achilles', of all things. Skills clearly show that he still has the goods, but he'll be 39 years old, and while he's vowed he'll be ready by spring, that's a tough injury from which to recover for anyone. High risk/reward pick.

Yr Tm	W	L	Sv	IP	K	ERA	xERA	WHIP	oOPS	vL	vR	BF/G	Ctl	Dom	Cmd	FpK	SwK	G	L	F	H%	S%	hr/f	GS	APC	DOM%	DIS%	Sv%	LI	RAR	BPV	BPX	R$
11 PIT *	6	2	4	65	69	2.63	3.55	1.35	601	766	508	4.9	4.0	9.5	2.4	59%	13%	45	22	33	32%	83%	7%	0	19			100	1.41	10.6	94	141	$6
12 PIT	1	6	2	59	90	2.91	2.88	1.14	635	485	767	3.8	3.4	13.8	4.1	57%	15%	31	24	45	33%	80%	12%	0	16			40	1.20	8.0	166	217	$5
13 PIT	0	2	33	50	74	2.70	2.57	1.06	595	707	496	3.7	2.3	13.3	5.7	62%	15%	33	25	42	35%	78%	9%	0	16			94	1.17	7.2	188	244	$16
14 2 TM	1	5	12	54	57	4.00	3.83	1.33	702	683	711	3.8	3.5	9.5	2.7	61%	11%	32	26	42	33%	71%	6%	0	15			71	1.10	-1.7	87	103	$2
15 ATL	3	4	24	34	45	2.94	3.35	1.13	620	598	636	3.9	2.7	12.0	4.5	61%	16%	27	26	47	34%	75%	5%	0	16			92	1.56	4.2	149	178	$11
1st Half	3	3	22	32	42	2.84	3.48	1.17	639	620	652	4.0	2.8	11.9	4.2	61%	15%	25	27	48	35%	77%	5%	0	17			92	1.51	4.4	141	167	$12
2nd Half	0	1	2	2	3	4.50	1.27	0.50	286	0	400	2.3	0.0	13.5	0.0	71%	22%	75	0	25	27%	0%	0%	0	9			100	2.05	-0.1	296	351	-$9
16 Proj	**2**	**3**	**12**	**44**	**52**	**3.23**	**3.35**	**1.19**	**646**	**655**	**638**	**3.8**	**3.0**	**10.8**	**3.5**	**60%**	**14%**	**31**	**25**	**43**	**32%**	**75%**	**7%**	**0**						**3.9**	**121**	**144**	**$5**

Grimm,Justin

Age: 27 | Th: R | Role: RP | Ht: 6' 3" | Wt: 210 | Type: Pwr
Health: B | PT/Exp: C | Consist: C
LIMA Plan: B+ | Rand Var: -5 | MM: 4510

One of our pre-'15 sleeper candidates took another step up with elite SwK/Dom. Fly in ointment is Ctl spike; 1st half was a fluke (see FpK), but it lingered into 2nd half, for real this time, so is worth tracking. If Ctl reverses, though, he's again a candidate for... UP: 30 SV

Yr Tm	W	L	Sv	IP	K	ERA	xERA	WHIP	oOPS	vL	vR	BF/G	Ctl	Dom	Cmd	FpK	SwK	G	L	F	H%	S%	hr/f	GS	APC	DOM%	DIS%	Sv%	LI	RAR	BPV	BPX	R$
11																																	
12 TEX *	12	7	0	149	96	4.06	4.06	1.36	935	1006	855	20.7	2.1	5.8	2.8	61%	8%	44	29	27	33%	69%	8%	2	50	50%	50%	0	0.33	-0.8	78	102	$2
13 2 TM *	10	12	0	146	113	5.78	5.37	1.61	846	860	830	17.9	3.4	6.9	2.1	58%	8%	43	21	36	35%	64%	13%	17	61	29%	35%	0	0.80	-34.4	49	64	-$14
14 CHC	5	2	0	69	70	3.78	3.49	1.25	632	528	684	4.0	3.5	9.1	2.6	61%	11%	49	16	35	31%	70%	6%	0	16			0	0.67	-0.4	96	115	$1
15 CHC	3	5	3	50	67	1.99	3.09	1.15	575	507	608	3.3	4.7	12.1	2.6	59%	14%	45	25	30	27%	87%	12%	0	14			50	1.04	12.1	114	136	$6
1st Half	1	2	1	20	33	1.35	2.37	1.25	580	347	657	3.4	5.0	14.9	3.0	68%	15%	54	23	23	36%	92%	11%	0	15			100	1.15	6.4	165	196	$2
2nd Half	2	3	2	30	34	2.43	3.57	1.08	572	580	567	3.2	4.6	10.3	2.3	53%	13%	40	26	34	22%	83%	13%	0	13			40	0.96	5.6	81	96	$8
16 Proj	**4**	**4**	**2**	**58**	**70**	**3.06**	**3.14**	**1.19**	**611**	**573**	**632**	**4.2**	**3.9**	**10.9**	**2.8**	**60%**	**12%**	**47**	**21**	**32**	**30%**	**76%**	**10%**	**0**						**6.4**	**114**	**136**	**$4**

ROD TRUESDELL

Guthrie,Jeremy

Age: 37	Th: R	Role	SP	Health	B	LIMA Plan	D+
Ht: 6' 1"	Wt: 205	Type	Con	PT/Exp	A	Rand Var	+3
				Consist	B	MM	0001

Threw his soft stuff more, and the result was a FB spike and accompanying HR damage. Otherwise, this was not that different from past mediocrity. In short, the yo-yoishness (that's a word, you can look it up... okay, please don't look it up) of his skills oscillates around a midpoint of bleahness. (That's a word, too.)

Yr Tm	W	L	Sv	IP	K	ERA	xERA	WHIP	oOPS	vL	vR	BF/G	Ctl	Dom	Cmd	FpK	SwK	G	L	F	H%	S%	hr/f	GS	APC	DOM%	DIS%	Sv%	LI	RAR	BPV	BPX	R$
11 BAL	9	17	0	208	130	4.33	4.43	1.34	770	767	773	26.1	2.9	5.6	2.0	59%	7%	40	21	40	29%	71%	10%	32	98	38%	13%	0	0.73	-9.9	42	63	$1
12 2 TM	8	12	0	182	101	4.76	4.76	1.41	822	868	775	23.9	2.5	5.0	2.0	59%	7%	41	23	36	30%	71%	14%	29	89	34%	21%	0	0.74	-16.6	42	55	-$7
13 KC	15	12	0	212	111	4.04	4.55	1.39	784	905	623	27.4	2.5	4.7	1.9	62%	6%	43	22	35	30%	75%	12%	33	102	39%	12%			-4.5	38	50	$1
14 KC	13	11	0	203	124	4.13	4.23	1.30	728	828	601	27.0	2.2	5.5	2.5	63%	8%	44	20	37	30%	71%	9%	32	101	53%	19%			-9.7	62	74	$2
15 KC	8	8	0	148	84	5.95	5.17	1.55	878	957	781	22.1	2.7	5.1	1.9	63%	7%	34	26	40	32%	66%	14%	24	83	21%	21%	0	0.68	-36.3	32	38	-$16
1st Half	6	5	0	90	47	5.42	5.07	1.46	808	939	635	24.6	2.4	4.7	2.0	62%	7%	35	27	38	32%	65%	10%	16	92	31%	6%			-16.1	33	40	-$12
2nd Half	2	3	0	59	37	6.75	5.33	1.69	981	986	976	19.4	3.1	5.7	1.9	65%	7%	33	25	43	33%	67%	20%	8	72	0%	50%	0	0.57	-20.2	30	36	-$22
16 Proj	**6**	**6**	**0**	**116**	**68**	**5.05**	**4.74**	**1.47**	**838**	**908**	**751**	**22.9**	**2.6**	**5.3**	**2.0**	**63%**	**7%**	**38**	**23**	**39**	**31%**	**70%**	**14%**	**22**						**-15.5**	**41**	**49**	**-$8**

Hahn,Jesse

Age: 26	Th: R	Role	SP	Health	D	LIMA Plan	B+
Ht: 6' 5"	Wt: 190	Type	GB	PT/Exp	D	Rand Var	-1
				Consist	B	MM	2101

Uh-oh. Missed second half with (cue ominous music): a flexor tendon injury. This comes after missing the better part of two years after TJ surgery. Was throwing long-toss by season's end, so maybe, just maybe, this will work out okay. If healthy, seeds of a solid mid-rotation starter are firmly planted. That's a large IF.

Yr Tm	W	L	Sv	IP	K	ERA	xERA	WHIP	oOPS	vL	vR	BF/G	Ctl	Dom	Cmd	FpK	SwK	G	L	F	H%	S%	hr/f	GS	APC	DOM%	DIS%	Sv%	LI	RAR	BPV	BPX	R$
11																																	
12																																	
13																																	
14 SD *	9	5	0	116	102	2.76	2.88	1.24	623	656	583	17.4	3.7	7.9	2.1	60%	11%	50	22	27	29%	78%	8%	12	84	58%	8%	0	0.89	14.0	90	108	$8
15 OAK	6	6	0	97	64	3.35	3.83	1.17	623	735	502	25.4	2.3	6.0	2.6	61%	8%	53	25	23	28%	71%	7%	16	96	50%	6%			7.3	75	90	$5
1st Half	6	6	0	97	64	3.35	3.83	1.17	623	735	502	25.4	2.3	6.0	2.6	61%	8%	53	25	23	28%	71%	7%	16	96	50%	6%			7.3	75	89	$5
2nd Half																																	
16 Proj	**8**	**6**	**0**	**116**	**87**	**3.49**	**3.69**	**1.24**	**650**	**735**	**557**	**21.1**	**2.9**	**6.7**	**2.4**	**60%**	**9%**	**52**	**24**	**25**	**30%**	**72%**	**7%**	**22**						**6.8**	**74**	**88**	**$5**

Hale,David

Age: 28	Th: R	Role	RP	Health	D	LIMA Plan	D+
Ht: 6' 2"	Wt: 210	Type	GB	PT/Exp	C	Rand Var	+5
				Consist	C	MM	0001

5-5, 6.09 ERA in 78 IP at COL. Morphing into a FB guy, which is terrific news for opposing hitters in Coors Field; not so much for Rockies fans. Marginal Cmd, less-than-dominant stuff a volatile mix. Only bright sign is SwK rebound, so there's some K/9 upside to watch. That might help him improve all the way to marginal.

Yr Tm	W	L	Sv	IP	K	ERA	xERA	WHIP	oOPS	vL	vR	BF/G	Ctl	Dom	Cmd	FpK	SwK	G	L	F	H%	S%	hr/f	GS	APC	DOM%	DIS%	Sv%	LI	RAR	BPV	BPX	R$
11																																	
12 aa	8	4	0	146	104	4.96	4.46	1.52				23.4	4.5	6.4	1.4						31%	68%								-17.0	47	61	-$9
13 ATL *	7	9	0	126	77	3.73	5.10	1.58	572	683	480	23.1	2.8	5.5	2.0	61%	14%	63	23	13	35%	77%	0%	2	85	100%	0%			2.1	48	63	-$4
14 ATL	4	5	0	87	44	3.30	4.58	1.47	714	769	667	8.5	4.0	4.5	1.1	52%	9%	56	19	25	29%	78%	7%	6	31	67%	33%	0	0.83	4.8	7	8	-$2
15 COL *	5	8	0	128	88	7.26	6.73	1.76	861	880	846	21.0	3.1	6.2	2.0	61%	12%	47	20	33	37%	59%	16%	12	76	33%	8%	0	0.79	-52.2	26	31	-$27
1st Half	2	6	0	79	53	6.80	7.08	1.75	870	926	813	25.8	2.8	6.0	2.1	63%	11%	48	17	35	37%	64%	20%	8	95	25%	13%			-27.6	16	19	-$29
2nd Half	3	2	0	49	35	8.00	6.16	1.78	849	793	887	16.2	3.5	6.4	1.9	57%	12%	46	24	30	38%	53%	10%	4	60	50%	0%	0	0.82	-24.6	42	50	-$23
16 Proj	**4**	**4**	**0**	**73**	**46**	**5.65**	**4.62**	**1.64**	**851**	**876**	**830**	**15.0**	**3.5**	**5.7**	**1.6**	**57%**	**11%**	**50**	**20**	**29**	**35%**	**66%**	**10%**	**11**						**-15.1**	**37**	**45**	**-$10**

Hamels,Cole

Age: 32	Th: L	Role	SP	Health	C	LIMA Plan	C+
Ht: 6' 3"	Wt: 195	Type	Pwr	PT/Exp	A	Rand Var	+1
				Consist	A	MM	4405

Some will see 2H ERA spike and worry about league change, but xERA, BPV splits show there was no real difference in rock-solid skills. Only some nagging injuries the last couple of years give any pause, and even those haven't hurt IP totals much. Play up that 2H ERA, and you might score an ace for the price of a jack.

Yr Tm	W	L	Sv	IP	K	ERA	xERA	WHIP	oOPS	vL	vR	BF/G	Ctl	Dom	Cmd	FpK	SwK	G	L	F	H%	S%	hr/f	GS	APC	DOM%	DIS%	Sv%	LI	RAR	BPV	BPX	R$
11 PHI	14	9	0	216	194	2.79	3.02	0.99	596	662	577	26.6	1.8	8.1	4.4	62%	12%	52	15	33	27%	75%	10%	31	98	77%	10%	0	0.76	30.7	126	189	$29
12 PHI	17	6	0	215	216	3.05	3.32	1.12	661	629	673	28.0	2.2	9.0	4.2	63%	14%	43	22	35	30%	78%	12%	31	107	77%	0%			25.6	125	163	$27
13 PHI	8	14	0	220	202	3.60	3.46	1.16	699	712	695	27.4	2.0	8.3	4.0	63%	13%	43	21	37	31%	71%	9%	33	104	76%	3%			7.2	115	149	$13
14 PHI	9	9	0	205	198	2.46	3.20	1.15	641	636	641	27.6	2.6	8.7	3.4	61%	13%	46	22	31	30%	81%	8%	30	105	83%	3%			32.3	111	132	$20
15 2 TM	13	8	0	212	215	3.65	3.39	1.19	669	646	675	27.5	2.6	9.1	3.5	61%	14%	48	21	31	30%	72%	12%	32	104	66%	6%			8.3	119	142	$16
1st Half	5	6	0	113	119	3.02	3.28	1.13	630	481	670	27.5	2.8	9.5	3.4	61%	14%	49	21	31	29%	77%	12%	17	107	82%	0%			13.2	122	145	$21
2nd Half	8	2	0	99	96	4.36	3.51	1.25	712	822	680	27.5	2.5	8.7	3.6	60%	14%	46	21	32	32%	67%	12%	15	102	47%	13%			-4.9	115	137	$10
16 Proj	**12**	**9**	**0**	**203**	**198**	**3.36**	**3.31**	**1.17**	**668**	**677**	**665**	**26.7**	**2.4**	**8.8**	**3.6**	**61%**	**13%**	**47**	**21**	**32**	**30%**	**74%**	**11%**	**30**						**15.1**	**116**	**139**	**$16**

Hammel,Jason

Age: 33	Th: R	Role	SP	Health	D	LIMA Plan	B
Ht: 6' 6"	Wt: 225	Type	Pwr	PT/Exp	A	Rand Var	+1
				Consist	B	MM	3303

Slowed a bit by 2nd half hammy, but another solid year. The key: he's thrown his best pitch, the slider, more than ever (over 1/3 of the time in '15), and results speak for themselves. This seems tied to elbow health, as his down '13 further suggests. So there's the rub. Nice upside pick—after you grab your core guys.

Yr Tm	W	L	Sv	IP	K	ERA	xERA	WHIP	oOPS	vL	vR	BF/G	Ctl	Dom	Cmd	FpK	SwK	G	L	F	H%	S%	hr/f	GS	APC	DOM%	DIS%	Sv%	LI	RAR	BPV	BPX	R$
11 COL	7	13	1	170	94	4.76	4.66	1.43	778	808	752	23.1	3.6	5.0	1.4	59%	7%	44	21	35	29%	69%	11%	27	85	41%	26%	100	0.78	-17.1	14	22	-$5
12 BAL	8	6	0	118	113	3.43	3.48	1.24	637	586	692	24.7	3.2	8.6	2.7	57%	11%	53	19	28	30%	74%	10%	20	97	50%	15%			8.5	100	130	$7
13 BAL	7	8	1	139	96	4.97	4.52	1.46	813	881	716	23.5	3.1	6.2	2.0	56%	8%	40	22	38	31%	70%	13%	23	89	22%	17%	100	0.77	-19.0	46	60	-$7
14 2 TM	10	11	0	176	158	3.47	3.53	1.12	680	691	670	23.8	2.2	8.1	3.6	57%	10%	40	22	38	28%	74%	12%	29	93	72%	17%	0	0.75	5.9	103	122	$12
15 CHC	10	7	0	171	172	3.74	3.57	1.16	714	696	728	22.9	2.1	9.1	4.3	61%	11%	38	25	37	30%	73%	13%	31	89	55%	26%			4.6	122	146	$12
1st Half	5	4	0	103	104	2.89	3.31	0.95	616	652	588	25.4	1.6	9.1	5.8	62%	12%	38	23	39	27%	75%	10%	16	97	75%	13%			13.5	137	163	$22
2nd Half	5	3	0	68	68	5.03	3.99	1.47	847	750	933	20.2	2.9	9.0	3.1	60%	11%	39	26	35	35%	70%	17%	15	80	33%	40%			-8.9	101	119	-$5
16 Proj	**10**	**9**	**0**	**174**	**159**	**3.70**	**3.62**	**1.21**	**714**	**709**	**718**	**21.7**	**2.3**	**8.2**	**3.5**	**59%**	**10%**	**40**	**23**	**37**	**30%**	**74%**	**12%**	**32**						**5.7**	**102**	**122**	**$10**

Hand,Brad

Age: 26	Th: L	Role	RP	Health	C	LIMA Plan	D+
Ht: 6' 3"	Wt: 220	Type		PT/Exp	C	Rand Var	+3
				Consist	A	MM	1101

Reached new levels of futility against RH hitters, which threatens to turn him into a LOOGY faster than you can say Jeremy Affeldt. There's also that matter of nosediving FpK and marginal SwK: there's serious Cmd downside brewing here. Thus, only draftable in your All-Time Body Part League as Rollie Fingers' setup man.

Yr Tm	W	L	Sv	IP	K	ERA	xERA	WHIP	oOPS	vL	vR	BF/G	Ctl	Dom	Cmd	FpK	SwK	G	L	F	H%	S%	hr/f	GS	APC	DOM%	DIS%	Sv%	LI	RAR	BPV	BPX	R$
11 FLA *	12	12	0	169	100	3.75	3.92	1.37	789	812	783	22.8	4.4	5.3	1.2	54%	7%	29	17	54	25%	76%	10%	12	90	8%	33%			4.0	34	51	$5
12 MIA *	11	8	0	152	133	4.96	4.62	1.55	1169	1850	962	23.7	5.1	7.9	1.6	43%	3%	50	0	50	31%	69%	14%	1	96	0%	100%			-17.6	54	71	-$8
13 MIA *	4	6	0	102	83	4.03	3.96	1.46	553	530	564	19.9	4.9	7.3	1.5	52%	9%	42	20	37	29%	74%	9%	2	43	0%	0%	0	0.73	-2.1	58	76	-$3
14 MIA *	5	8	1	133	85	4.21	4.00	1.34	732	594	789	15.4	3.2	5.7	1.8	59%	7%	50	18	32	29%	70%	9%	16	56	31%	31%	100	0.58	-7.6	50	60	-$2
15 MIA	4	7	0	93	67	5.30	4.39	1.49	784	512	887	10.7	3.1	6.5	2.1	52%	9%	46	23	30	33%	65%	10%	12	41	8%	50%	0	0.60	-15.4	57	68	-$8
1st Half	1	2	0	40	27	5.80	4.29	1.51	757	716	777	7.7	2.5	6.0	2.5	57%	9%	46	28	26	37%	57%	0%	3	30	0%	33%	0	0.55	-9.2	66	78	-$12
2nd Half	3	5	0	53	40	4.92	4.47	1.47	806	282	964	15.5	3.6	6.8	1.9	48%	9%	46	20	34	30%	71%	16%	9	58	11%	56%	0	0.68	-6.3	50	60	-$6
16 Proj	**4**	**6**	**0**	**87**	**62**	**4.63**	**4.46**	**1.44**	**766**	**569**	**840**	**13.4**	**3.6**	**6.4**	**1.8**	**55%**	**8%**	**45**	**20**	**35**	**31%**	**70%**	**10%**	**9**						**-7.1**	**43**	**51**	**-$5**

Happ,J.A.

Age: 33	Th: L	Role	SP	Health	D	LIMA Plan	B
Ht: 6' 5"	Wt: 205	Type	Pwr	PT/Exp	A	Rand Var	0
				Consist	B	MM	2303

Sensational for two months after trade to PIT: 6.2 Cmd, nearly 10 Dom, sub-3.00 xERA. Wow. So there's a thing called "recency bias" that makes us think the most recent events will continue into the future. There's also a thing called "a career of mediocrity" that we think probably offsets those two recent months here.

Yr Tm	W	L	Sv	IP	K	ERA	xERA	WHIP	oOPS	vL	vR	BF/G	Ctl	Dom	Cmd	FpK	SwK	G	L	F	H%	S%	hr/f	GS	APC	DOM%	DIS%	Sv%	LI	RAR	BPV	BPX	R$
11 HOU *	7	15	0	174	146	5.00	4.60	1.51	806	751	819	24.4	4.8	7.5	1.6	56%	8%	33	23	44	30%	69%	10%	28	106	29%	21%			-22.7	49	74	-$8
12 2 TM	10	11	0	145	144	4.79	3.98	1.40	787	730	807	22.4	3.5	9.0	2.6	64%	10%	44	17	39	33%	68%	12%	24	91	54%	17%	0	0.73	-13.8	89	116	-$2
13 TOR	5	7	0	93	77	4.56	4.83	1.47	734	802	708	23.1	4.4	7.5	1.7	60%	8%	36	18	46	31%	71%	8%	18	96	39%	44%			-8.0	31	40	-$5
14 TOR	11	11	0	158	133	4.22	4.03	1.34	770	874	743	22.4	2.9	7.6	2.6	62%	8%	41	20	40	31%	72%	12%	26	90	50%	27%	0	0.82	-9.2	77	92	$1
15 2 TM	11	8	0	172	151	3.61	3.83	1.27	698	680	705	22.4	2.4	7.9	3.4	60%	9%	42	24	34	32%	74%	9%	31	89	39%	19%	0	0.78	7.5	99	117	$9
1st Half	4	5	0	92	72	3.93	4.04	1.33	723	720	724	24.1	2.2	7.1	3.3	61%	8%	43	24	34	33%	72%	8%	16	95	44%	13%			0.4	89	106	$4
2nd Half	7	3	0	80	79	3.25	3.60	1.20	670	632	683	20.7	2.6	8.9	3.4	59%	10%	40	25	34	31%	76%	11%	15	83	33%	27%	0	0.79	7.1	108	128	$15
16 Proj	**11**	**10**	**0**	**174**	**153**	**3.99**	**3.97**	**1.32**	**727**	**740**	**723**	**21.8**	**3.0**	**7.9**	**2.6**	**60%**	**9%**	**40**	**22**	**38**	**31%**	**73%**	**10%**	**33**						**-0.6**	**79**	**95**	**$5**

ROD TRUESDELL

Harang,Aaron

Age: 38	Th: R	Role SP	Health D	LIMA Plan D+	
Ht: 6' 7"	Wt: 260	Type FB	PT/Exp A	Rand Var 0	
			Consist A	MM 0103	

Once again outpitched middling skills for two months, then reality (and plantar fasciitis) set in, and he was awful afterward. This is a 38-year-old flyball pitcher whose ERA is driven by whichever direction strand rate blows in any given season. He owns a D health rating and his last sub-4.00 xERA was in 2007. No, just... no.

Yr	Tm	W	L	Sv	IP	K	ERA	xERA	WHIP	oOPS	vL	vR	BF/G	Ctl	Dom	Cmd	FpK	SwK	G	L	F	H%	S%	hr/f	GS	APC	DOM%	DIS%	Sv%	LI	RAR	BPV	BPX	R$
11	SD	14	7	0	171	124	3.64	4.22	1.37	758	787	732	25.7	3.1	6.5	2.1	62%	9%	41	18	41	30%	77%	9%	28	98	46%	18%			6.4	54	81	$7
12	LA	10	10	0	180	131	3.61	4.96	1.40	711	761	662	25.4	4.3	6.6	1.5	56%	8%	39	20	41	29%	76%	6%	31	100	32%	23%			9.0	20	26	$4
13	2 TM	5	12	0	143	113	5.40	4.37	1.35	795	800	789	24.1	2.5	7.1	2.8	58%	8%	36	20	44	30%	64%	13%	26	94	46%	27%			-27.1	74	96	-$8
14	ATL	12	12	0	204	161	3.57	4.18	1.40	723	747	702	26.5	3.1	7.1	2.3	59%	9%	39	23	38	33%	76%	6%	33	103	52%	9%			4.4	60	72	$3
15	PHI	6	15	0	172	108	4.86	4.96	1.39	802	827	780	25.8	2.7	5.6	2.1	62%	8%	36	20	44	30%	69%	11%	29	98	34%	21%			-19.0	44	52	-$7
1st Half		4	11	0	106	73	4.08	4.59	1.24	726	769	693	26.2	2.3	6.2	2.7	63%	8%	36	19	45	29%	70%	8%	17	99	59%	12%			-1.5	63	75	$1
2nd Half		2	4	0	66	35	6.11	5.60	1.64	915	902	925	25.3	3.3	4.7	1.5	60%	7%	37	22	41	32%	67%	14%	12	97	0%	33%			-17.5	12	15	-$20
16	**Proj**	**6**	**9**	**0**	**131**	**89**	**4.71**	**4.63**	**1.43**	**796**	**812**	**780**	**24.9**	**3.0**	**6.2**	**2.1**	**60%**	**8%**	**37**	**21**	**42**	**31%**	**70%**	**10%**	**22**						**-12.1**	**46**	**55**	**-$6**

Hardy,Blaine

Age: 29	Th: L	Role RP	Health A	LIMA Plan B+	
Ht: 6' 2"	Wt: 230	Type Pwr	PT/Exp D	Rand Var -2	
			Consist B	MM 2200	

Fine as typical LOOGY (61 IP in 70 G). However, his paths to fanalytic relevance would be: 1) returning to starting, or 2) more likely, becoming a closer. He isn't awful vs. RH hitters, so the latter isn't totally out of the question, and 2H highlights skills upside. So yes, Lloyd... er, Blaine... we're tellin' you there's a chance.

Yr	Tm	W	L	Sv	IP	K	ERA	xERA	WHIP	oOPS	vL	vR	BF/G	Ctl	Dom	Cmd	FpK	SwK	G	L	F	H%	S%	hr/f	GS	APC	DOM%	DIS%	Sv%	LI	RAR	BPV	BPX	R$
11	a/a	4	4	8	69	51	4.35	4.95	1.57				7.2	4.5	6.7	1.5						31%	75%								-3.4	40	60	-$1
12	a/a	4	3	4	75	46	3.99	6.01	1.72				8.6	3.7	5.5	1.5						35%	80%								0.3	24	31	-$6
13	a/a	8	3	1	92	60	2.21	3.31	1.21				12.3	3.3	5.9	1.8						25%	87%								18.7	54	71	$9
14	DET *	5	3	0	86	70	3.11	3.26	1.31	611	553	657	6.1	3.6	7.3	2.0	54%	8%	52	19	28	30%	76%	3%	0	17			0	1.04	6.7	82	97	$2
15	DET	5	3	0	61	55	3.08	4.22	1.35	704	631	770	3.8	3.2	8.1	2.5	68%	11%	39	24	37	33%	77%	3%	0	14			0	1.08	6.7	75	89	$1
1st Half		3	1	0	37	27	2.68	4.64	1.19	639	482	760	4.3	3.4	6.6	1.9	64%	9%	33	23	44	28%	75%	0%	0	15			0	0.87	5.9	38	45	$3
2nd Half		2	2	0	24	28	3.70	3.55	1.60	790	793	787	3.2	3.0	10.4	3.5	73%	13%	47	26	27	42%	78%	10%	0	13			0	1.30	0.8	132	156	-$2
16	**Proj**	**4**	**3**	**0**	**58**	**50**	**3.17**	**3.95**	**1.39**	**707**	**666**	**744**	**4.7**	**3.4**	**7.7**	**2.3**	**64%**	**10%**	**46**	**23**	**32**	**33%**	**78%**	**7%**	**0**						**5.7**	**72**	**86**	**$0**

Haren,Dan

Age: 35	Th: R	Role RP	Health B	LIMA Plan D+	
Ht: 6' 5"	Wt: 215	Type #### FB	PT/Exp A	Rand Var -2	
			Consist A	MM ####	

Despite what ERA says, xERA and BPV both showed the continuing decline. Unlike so many athletes, it appears he recognizes it, too, as he's announced his retirement. He finishes with at 153-131, 3.75 ERA, 3 All-Star teams and two top-10 Cy Young finishes. Nicely done, Dan.

Yr	Tm	W	L	Sv	IP	K	ERA	xERA	WHIP	oOPS	vL	vR	BF/G	Ctl	Dom	Cmd	FpK	SwK	G	L	F	H%	S%	hr/f	GS	APC	DOM%	DIS%	Sv%	LI	RAR	BPV	BPX	R$
11	LAA	16	10	0	238	192	3.17	3.39	1.02	630	617	648	27.2	1.2	7.3	5.8	64%	10%	43	20	38	28%	71%	8%	34	108	71%	9%	0	0.82	22.6	118	177	$27
12	LAA	12	13	0	177	142	4.33	4.08	1.29	775	731	825	24.9	1.9	7.2	3.7	64%	9%	40	21	40	31%	72%	13%	30	95	53%	17%			-6.9	96	125	$4
13	WAS	10	14	1	170	151	4.67	3.75	1.24	760	722	792	23.1	1.6	8.0	4.9	65%	10%	36	22	42	32%	67%	13%	30	90	40%	20%	100	0.83	-16.8	114	148	$2
14	LA	13	11	0	186	145	4.02	3.81	1.18	718	668	767	24.3	1.7	7.0	4.0	62%	8%	41	20	39	29%	71%	12%	32	97	53%	16%			-6.3	98	117	$7
15	2 NL	11	9	0	187	132	3.60	4.50	1.13	734	860	622	24.0	1.8	6.3	3.5	64%	7%	31	20	49	27%	76%	11%	32	91	53%	22%			8.3	74	88	$13
1st Half		6	5	0	99	71	3.45	4.28	1.05	690	792	593	24.8	1.6	6.5	3.9	64%	6%	32	20	48	25%	74%	10%	16	96	63%	13%			6.2	82	97	$17
2nd Half		5	4	0	88	61	3.77	4.74	1.22	780	938	651	23.3	2.0	6.2	3.1	63%	7%	29	21	50	28%	77%	11%	16	86	44%	31%			2.1	64	76	$8
16	Proj																																	

Harris,Will

Age: 31	Th: R	Role RP	Health A	LIMA Plan B	
Ht: 6' 4"	Wt: 225	Type Pwr	PT/Exp D	Rand Var -5	
			Consist A	MM 4311	

What looked like a 2H "collapse" was mostly just stats better matching the skills. Regardless, this was still more of the solid, closer-worthy skills he's posted pretty consistently for four seasons now, with a nice little FpK and GB% uptick. In short, a sizable paycheck is just an inning away—the 9th. UP: 30 Sv.

Yr	Tm	W	L	Sv	IP	K	ERA	xERA	WHIP	oOPS	vL	vR	BF/G	Ctl	Dom	Cmd	FpK	SwK	G	L	F	H%	S%	hr/f	GS	APC	DOM%	DIS%	Sv%	LI	RAR	BPV	BPX	R$
11																																		
12	COL *	5	2	1	70	66	4.34	4.17	1.36	922	724	1073	4.6	2.7	8.5	3.2	54%	12%	37	23	40	34%	69%	13%	0	17			50	0.65	-2.8	94	122	-$1
13	ARI	4	1	0	53	53	2.91	3.18	1.23	661	509	759	3.6	2.6	9.1	3.5	58%	11%	47	23	29	33%	77%	7%	0	14			0	1.01	6.2	119	155	$2
14	ARI *	3	5	1	75	67	2.37	3.58	1.30	740	721	757	4.3	3.6	8.1	2.3	55%	11%	35	25	40	30%	85%	10%	0	17			33	0.76	12.6	80	95	$3
15	HOU	5	5	2	71	68	1.90	3.24	0.90	525	455	586	4.1	2.8	8.6	3.1	60%	9%	51	19	30	20%	88%	15%	0	17			33	1.28	18.0	109	130	$12
1st Half		4	1	0	39	39	0.93	3.03	0.75	439	404	470	4.4	3.0	9.1	3.0	61%	8%	50	22	28	15%	100%	16%	0	18			0	1.16	14.5	110	130	$17
2nd Half		1	4	2	32	29	3.06	3.49	1.08	619	512	709	3.7	2.5	8.1	3.2	58%	10%	52	16	32	26%	77%	14%	0	15			67	1.40	3.6	108	128	$6
16	**Proj**	**4**	**5**	**4**	**73**	**68**	**2.58**	**3.33**	**1.12**	**621**	**506**	**709**	**3.9**	**2.9**	**8.5**	**2.9**	**59%**	**10%**	**50**	**21**	**30**	**27%**	**81%**	**12%**	**0**						**12.3**	**101**	**121**	**$8**

Harrison,Matt

Age: 30	Th: L	Role SP	Health F	LIMA Plan D	
Ht: 6' 4"	Wt: 240	Type Con	PT/Exp F	Rand Var +5	
			Consist C	MM 0000	

1-2, 6.75 ERA in 16 IP at TEX. Fought back after a year of rehab from spinal fusion surgery (despite having a guaranteed contract that paid him regardless), a gutty show of determination. That said, it's clear his skills were not there, and may never be again. We're rooting for him, but he's simply not draftable.

Yr	Tm	W	L	Sv	IP	K	ERA	xERA	WHIP	oOPS	vL	vR	BF/G	Ctl	Dom	Cmd	FpK	SwK	G	L	F	H%	S%	hr/f	GS	APC	DOM%	DIS%	Sv%	LI	RAR	BPV	BPX	R$
11	TEX	14	9	0	186	126	3.39	3.92	1.28	685	729	667	24.9	2.8	6.1	2.2	56%	8%	47	20	32	30%	75%	7%	30	97	43%	13%	0	0.75	12.6	60	91	$11
12	TEX	18	11	0	213	133	3.29	4.15	1.26	714	571	764	27.4	2.5	5.6	2.3	62%	8%	49	20	31	29%	77%	11%	32	101	50%	13%			19.1	61	79	$16
13	TEX	0	2	0	11	12	8.44	4.34	1.97	970	432	1149	25.5	5.9	10.1	1.7	57%	14%	45	23	32	40%	58%	20%	2	98	0%	50%			-6.0	46	60	-$7
14	TEX *	2	1	0	33	17	3.29	4.31	1.58	783	593	824	20.9	4.5	4.7	1.0	55%	7%	48	25	27	31%	78%	6%	4	86	25%	50%			1.8	42	50	-$3
15	TEX *	2	5	0	51	20	8.05	6.67	1.97	878	1009	840	27.0	4.2	3.6	0.9	58%	3%	40	21	39	37%	56%	14%	3	90	0%	33%			-25.6	9	11	-$17
1st Half		1	3	0	35	15	8.65	7.02	2.15				28.7	4.6	4.0	0.9						41%	55%	0%	0						-20.1	23	28	-$22
2nd Half		1	2	0	16	5	6.75	5.79	1.56	878	1009	840	23.0	3.4	2.8	0.8	58%	3%	40	21	39	29%	59%	14%	3	90	0%	33%			-5.5	-22	-26	-$7
16	**Proj**	**3**	**4**	**0**	**58**	**27**	**5.38**	**5.27**	**1.62**	**824**	**837**	**820**	**24.3**	**3.7**	**4.2**	**1.1**	**58%**	**6%**	**45**	**21**	**34**	**32%**	**67%**	**7%**	**11**						**-10.2**	**-2**	**-2**	**-$8**

Harvey,Matt

Age: 27	Th: R	Role SP	Health C	LIMA Plan C	
Ht: 6' 4"	Wt: 215	Type Pwr	PT/Exp B	Rand Var -1	
			Consist B	MM 4405	

Innings limit be damned, apparently. And with these BPIs, who can blame NYM, or him? Came back as good as ever from TJS, with a notable uptick in 2H skills—a good sign. Of course, how that affects his 2016 health is mostly unknown, and that risk is about the only reason not to go that one extra buck.

Yr	Tm	W	L	Sv	IP	K	ERA	xERA	WHIP	oOPS	vL	vR	BF/G	Ctl	Dom	Cmd	FpK	SwK	G	L	F	H%	S%	hr/f	GS	APC	DOM%	DIS%	Sv%	LI	RAR	BPV	BPX	R$
11	aa	5	3	0	60	54	4.33	3.57	1.32				20.6	2.9	8.1	2.7						33%	66%								-2.9	94	141	-$1
12	NYM *	10	10	0	169	168	3.50	3.41	1.29	631	662	592	23.2	3.8	8.9	2.4	60%	13%	38	24	37	30%	75%	10%	10	98	70%	0%			10.8	89	115	$10
13	NYM	9	5	0	178	191	2.27	2.73	0.93	530	456	603	26.5	1.6	9.6	6.2	64%	13%	48	20	33	29%	76%	5%	26	104	85%	0%			35.1	157	205	$28
14																																		
15	NYM	13	8	0	189	188	2.71	3.25	1.02	609	676	544	26.0	1.8	8.9	5.1	68%	12%	46	18	36	29%	78%	10%	29	96	76%	7%			29.3	137	164	$26
1st Half		7	6	0	104	100	3.11	3.45	1.07	662	724	607	26.3	1.9	8.6	4.5	70%	12%	43	18	38	28%	77%	12%	16	97	75%	13%			11.0	125	149	$25
2nd Half		6	2	0	85	88	2.22	3.01	0.95	545	625	454	25.8	1.6	9.3	5.9	66%	12%	49	17	33	29%	79%	7%	13	96	77%	0%			18.2	152	180	$28
16	**Proj**	**15**	**8**	**0**	**203**	**205**	**2.82**	**3.07**	**1.04**	**601**	**616**	**585**	**24.2**	**1.9**	**9.1**	**4.7**	**65%**	**13%**	**46**	**19**	**35**	**29%**	**75%**	**8%**	**32**						**28.6**	**135**	**161**	**$27**

Hatcher,Chris

Age: 31	Th: R	Role RP	Health D	LIMA Plan A	
Ht: 6' 1"	Wt: 205	Type Pwr	PT/Exp D	Rand Var 0	
			Consist D	MM 3500	

Missed two months with a strained oblique, then the erstwhile catcher reestablished himself as closer material upon return. In truth, skills weren't off that much in 1H, either. Retained '14 Dom gains, and even built on them, and again shackled both RH and LH hitters. If given a shot... UP: 35 saves.

Yr	Tm	W	L	Sv	IP	K	ERA	xERA	WHIP	oOPS	vL	vR	BF/G	Ctl	Dom	Cmd	FpK	SwK	G	L	F	H%	S%	hr/f	GS	APC	DOM%	DIS%	Sv%	LI	RAR	BPV	BPX	R$
11	FLA *	2	2	6	58	53	3.02	3.34	1.30	960	618	1237	4.5	3.8	8.3	2.2	45%	5%	53	11	36	30%	78%	15%	0	18			67	0.36	6.6	86	129	$4
12	MIA *	1	0	11	62	47	1.78	3.59	1.32	889	1134	669	5.3	3.5	6.9	2.0	53%	5%	37	22	41	30%	90%	15%	0	27			92	0.16	17.0	70	92	$7
13	MIA *	4	4	33	76	56	5.88	6.43	1.84	961	1130	876	5.3	4.3	6.6	1.5	66%	7%	35	29	35	37%	69%	9%	0	26			92	0.62	-18.9	28	36	$0
14	MIA *	1	5	5	78	78	3.07	3.27	1.18	666	641	687	4.7	2.1	9.0	4.3	66%	11%	47	20	33	32%	76%	8%	0	18			50	0.99	6.5	129	153	$4
15	LA	3	5	4	39	45	3.69	3.47	1.23	685	688	682	3.4	3.0	10.4	3.5	60%	13%	43	18	39	32%	73%	10%	0	13			67	1.18	1.3	127	151	$1
1st Half		1	4	2	18	19	6.38	4.18	1.58	765	700	795	3.2	3.4	9.3	2.7	59%	12%	43	20	38	39%	57%	5%	0	13			50	1.33	-5.5	96	114	-$6
2nd Half		2	1	2	21	26	1.31	2.88	0.92	600	675	555	3.6	2.6	11.3	4.3	61%	14%	43	15	41	24%	100%	16%	0	14			100	0.99	6.8	155	184	$7
16	**Proj**	**4**	**6**	**0**	**66**	**73**	**3.43**	**3.35**	**1.28**	**707**	**705**	**708**	**3.9**	**2.9**	**9.9**	**3.5**	**62%**	**12%**	**45**	**18**	**37**	**33%**	**76%**	**10%**	**0**						**4.3**	**124**	**148**	**$1**

ROD TRUESDELL

Heaney,Andrew

Age: 25	Th: L	Role	SP	Health	A	LIMA Plan	B
Ht: 6' 2"	Wt: 185	Type	FB	PT/Exp	D	Rand Var	0
				Consist	A	MM	1105

6-4, 3.49 ERA in 105 IP at LAA. Top prospect fit bill with strong showing in first full season in majors. PRO: PQS-4/5 in >50% of starts; 100+ BPV in two months. CON: So-so SwK%, FpK%; strong skills only vL; slider only true K pitch. Some will bet on a breakout. You'll see mixed bag and check back in a year.

Yr Tm	W	L	Sv	IP	K	ERA	xERA	WHIP	oOPS	vL	vR	BF/G	Ctl	Dom	Cmd	FpK	SwK	G	L	F	H%	S%	hr/f	GS	APC	DOM%	DIS%	Sv%	LI	RAR	BPV	BPX	R$
11																																	
12																																	
13 aa	4	1	0	34	20	3.65	3.83	1.34				23.3	2.5	5.3	2.1						31%	73%								0.9	61	79	-$2
14 MIA *	9	9	0	167	139	3.89	3.59	1.22	847	611	944	21.7	2.2	7.5	3.4	60%	10%	45	19	35	31%	70%	18%	5	68	60%	40%	0	0.66	-3.1	95	113	$5
15 LAA *	12	6	0	184	141	3.92	3.89	1.34	679	568	723	23.9	2.4	6.9	2.8	62%	9%	38	22	40	33%	71%	7%	18	91	56%	17%			1.0	85	101	$5
1st Half	7	2	0	91	75	4.05	4.00	1.41	419	286	535	24.2	2.4	7.3	3.0	60%	13%	38	25	38	36%	69%	8%	2	89	100%	0%			-1.0	98	116	$3
2nd Half	5	4	0	93	66	3.79	4.42	1.27	711	630	739	24.4	2.4	6.4	2.6	62%	8%	38	22	40	30%	72%	7%	16	92	50%	19%			2.0	66	79	$6
16 Proj	**13**	**8**	**0**	**189**	**143**	**3.87**	**4.21**	**1.29**	**656**	**586**	**681**	**23.0**	**2.4**	**6.8**	**2.9**	**62%**	**8%**	**38**	**22**	**40**	**32%**	**71%**	**5%**	**34**						**2.2**	**76**	**90**	**$7**

Hellickson,Jeremy

Age: 29	Th: R	Role	SP	Health	F	LIMA Plan	C
Ht: 6' 1"	Wt: 190	Type		PT/Exp	B	Rand Var	+1
				Consist	D	MM	1203

On surface, more mediocrity. But 4 reasons to speculate on post-hype potential: 1) surging DOM% spiked in 2H; 2) good SwK% foretells more Ks; 3) 125+ BPV in two separate months; 4) halted ominous OPS vR trend. Even with poor consistency grade, his risk is minimal as an end-gamer. Bid a buck, no more.

Yr Tm	W	L	Sv	IP	K	ERA	xERA	WHIP	oOPS	vL	vR	BF/G	Ctl	Dom	Cmd	FpK	SwK	G	L	F	H%	S%	hr/f	GS	APC	DOM%	DIS%	Sv%	LI	RAR	BPV	BPX	R$
11 TAM	13	10	0	189	117	2.95	4.58	1.15	660	726	585	26.7	3.4	5.6	1.6	60%	10%	35	20	45	23%	79%	8%	29	102	45%	7%			23.1	21	31	$17
12 TAM	10	11	0	177	124	3.10	4.39	1.25	710	703	717	23.9	3.0	6.3	2.1	60%	9%	42	21	37	27%	82%	12%	31	97	42%	23%			19.9	52	68	$12
13 TAM	12	10	0	174	135	5.17	4.16	1.35	775	785	763	23.0	2.6	7.0	2.7	60%	10%	40	20	40	31%	64%	11%	31	90	35%	26%	0	1.04	-28.0	74	96	-$4
14 TAM *	2	9	0	88	75	5.36	6.12	1.71	759	585	966	21.1	2.7	7.7	2.8	63%	10%	36	23	41	40%	69%	10%	13	91	46%	54%			-17.6	67	79	-$12
15 ARI	9	12	0	146	121	4.62	4.22	1.33	781	790	774	23.6	2.7	7.5	2.8	63%	11%	42	21	36	31%	69%	13%	27	92	48%	30%			-11.9	83	98	-$1
1st Half	6	5	0	91	76	5.06	4.20	1.35	787	869	723	24.5	2.5	7.5	3.0	64%	11%	42	20	38	32%	65%	12%	16	95	44%	25%			-12.3	89	106	-$1
2nd Half	3	7	0	55	45	3.90	4.24	1.30	771	653	852	22.2	2.9	7.3	2.5	62%	10%	43	24	34	29%	76%	16%	11	87	55%	36%			0.4	73	87	$0
16 Proj	**8**	**14**	**0**	**160**	**129**	**4.10**	**4.08**	**1.33**	**741**	**681**	**798**	**21.5**	**2.7**	**7.3**	**2.6**	**62%**	**10%**	**40**	**22**	**38**	**31%**	**72%**	**10%**	**31**						**-2.8**	**75**	**89**	**$2**

Hendricks,Kyle

Age: 26	Th: R	Role	SP	Health	A	LIMA Plan	B+
Ht: 6' 3"	Wt: 190	Type	GB	PT/Exp	C	Rand Var	+1
				Consist	A	MM	3203

Near-4 ERA and lack of sexy stuff will keep bidders away, but xERA gives legit hope for more, especially after that 2H and his results vR. That said, good-not-great SwK% and offspeed-heavy pitch mix profile him as a mid-rotation guy, not budding anchor. Nothing wrong with that—not everyone can win a Cy Young.

Yr Tm	W	L	Sv	IP	K	ERA	xERA	WHIP	oOPS	vL	vR	BF/G	Ctl	Dom	Cmd	FpK	SwK	G	L	F	H%	S%	hr/f	GS	APC	DOM%	DIS%	Sv%	LI	RAR	BPV	BPX	R$
11																																	
12																																	
13 a/a	13	4	0	166	106	2.46	3.17	1.22				24.9	1.9	5.7	2.9						31%	80%								28.9	90	117	$16
14 CHC *	17	7	0	183	127	3.45	3.42	1.23	610	584	633	24.7	1.9	6.3	3.3	64%	8%	48	19	33	31%	72%	5%	13	89	62%	15%			6.5	94	112	$11
15 CHC	8	7	0	180	167	3.95	3.28	1.16	677	797	580	23.1	2.2	8.4	3.9	63%	9%	51	22	27	30%	68%	12%	32	87	59%	16%			0.3	121	144	$9
1st Half	4	4	0	92	75	3.82	3.55	1.15	692	723	667	23.3	1.7	7.3	4.4	63%	8%	50	18	32	30%	69%	10%	16	86	50%	19%			1.7	115	136	$9
2nd Half	4	3	0	88	92	4.09	3.00	1.17	661	872	484	22.9	2.7	9.4	3.5	63%	9%	53	26	20	31%	66%	17%	16	88	69%	13%			-1.4	129	153	$9
16 Proj	**11**	**7**	**0**	**174**	**142**	**3.56**	**3.45**	**1.19**	**674**	**743**	**615**	**23.5**	**2.1**	**7.3**	**3.5**	**63%**	**9%**	**50**	**21**	**28**	**31%**	**71%**	**8%**	**30**						**8.6**	**104**	**123**	**$11**

Hendriks,Liam

Age: 27	Th: R	Role	RP	Health	A	LIMA Plan	B+
Ht: 6' 1"	Wt: 205	Type	Pwr	PT/Exp	C	Rand Var	0
				Consist	C	MM	4410

Former starter has found comfy home in pen, posting elite skills in first full year as RP as fastball surged into mid-90s. Combo of high SwK% and FpK% says he can keep elite command going, and while surface stats eroded in 2H, that was due to fluky H%. At worst, a LIMA gem. At best, a new closer. UP: 30 SV

Yr Tm	W	L	Sv	IP	K	ERA	xERA	WHIP	oOPS	vL	vR	BF/G	Ctl	Dom	Cmd	FpK	SwK	G	L	F	H%	S%	hr/f	GS	APC	DOM%	DIS%	Sv%	LI	RAR	BPV	BPX	R$
11 MIN *	12	8	0	163	111	3.98	3.57	1.25	866	842	899	22.8	1.4	6.1	4.3	62%	8%	46	24	29	33%	67%	13%	4	94	0%	0%			-0.7	114	171	$7
12 MIN *	10	11	0	192	119	4.03	4.19	1.31	890	768	1020	24.7	2.6	5.6	2.1	54%	5%	41	24	35	29%	72%	17%	16	91	19%	44%			-0.3	49	64	$4
13 MIN *	5	11	0	146	84	5.83	5.73	1.55	907	929	879	24.5	1.8	5.2	2.9	59%	9%	37	22	42	35%	63%	14%	8	89	13%	50%	0	0.64	-35.3	49	63	-$17
14 2 AL *	13	4	0	176	121	3.18	3.21	1.13	786	814	762	21.7	1.0	6.2	6.2	70%	8%	39	25	37	31%	72%	8%	6	61	33%	50%	0	0.75	12.2	153	183	$13
15 TOR	5	0	0	65	71	2.92	2.96	1.08	605	746	499	4.5	1.5	9.9	6.5	69%	12%	46	23	31	33%	73%	5%	0	18			0	0.91	8.3	161	191	$5
1st Half	2	0	0	38	36	2.58	3.08	0.99	562	748	423	5.1	1.4	8.5	6.0	67%	9%	50	22	28	29%	75%	6%	0	19			0	0.88	6.5	142	168	$6
2nd Half	3	0	0	26	35	3.42	2.78	1.22	666	742	606	3.9	1.7	12.0	7.0	72%	14%	41	24	35	40%	71%	4%	0	16			0	0.94	1.8	188	223	$4
16 Proj	**5**	**2**	**2**	**65**	**65**	**3.05**	**3.11**	**1.08**	**615**	**668**	**569**	**6.9**	**1.5**	**9.0**	**5.9**	**67%**	**10%**	**41**	**23**	**35**	**32%**	**73%**	**7%**	**0**						**7.3**	**141**	**168**	**$6**

Hernandez,Felix

Age: 30	Th: R	Role	SP	Health	A	LIMA Plan	C+
Ht: 6' 3"	Wt: 225	Type	Pwr GB	PT/Exp	A	Rand Var	+2
				Consist	A	MM	5405

First 3.50+ ERA since '07 at age *21*. While skills deteriorated some, culprit was really hr/f. Continues to get first-pitch and swinging Ks at high rates, so return of 4+ Cmd and near-3 ERA in cards. Real concern is 2K innings before age 30, and late elbow stiffness raises a red flag. A touch of risk now.

Yr Tm	W	L	Sv	IP	K	ERA	xERA	WHIP	oOPS	vL	vR	BF/G	Ctl	Dom	Cmd	FpK	SwK	G	L	F	H%	S%	hr/f	GS	APC	DOM%	DIS%	Sv%	LI	RAR	BPV	BPX	R$
11 SEA	14	14	0	234	222	3.47	3.20	1.22	660	662	656	29.2	2.6	8.6	3.3	63%	10%	50	19	31	31%	73%	10%	33	109	70%	6%			13.7	112	169	$17
12 SEA	13	9	0	232	223	3.06	3.19	1.14	629	643	608	28.5	2.2	8.7	4.0	63%	11%	49	22	29	31%	74%	8%	33	104	70%	9%			27.2	124	162	$25
13 SEA	12	10	0	204	216	3.04	2.83	1.13	643	671	610	26.5	2.0	9.5	4.7	62%	11%	51	21	27	32%	75%	10%	31	102	74%	10%			20.8	146	190	$20
14 SEA	15	6	0	236	248	2.14	2.54	0.92	546	519	584	26.8	1.8	9.5	5.4	65%	13%	56	18	26	27%	80%	10%	34	101	88%	6%			46.7	157	187	$38
15 SEA	18	9	0	202	191	3.53	3.25	1.18	682	699	665	26.6	2.6	8.5	3.3	63%	11%	56	17	27	29%	74%	15%	31	98	77%	13%			10.9	118	140	$18
1st Half	10	5	0	110	106	3.02	3.05	1.07	609	649	565	25.8	2.7	8.6	3.2	61%	12%	58	19	24	27%	75%	14%	17	96	76%	18%			12.9	119	141	$27
2nd Half	8	4	0	91	85	4.14	3.50	1.31	765	757	772	27.7	2.5	8.4	3.4	66%	11%	55	15	30	32%	73%	16%	14	100	79%	7%			-2.0	117	139	$8
16 Proj	**15**	**8**	**0**	**196**	**194**	**3.16**	**3.00**	**1.12**	**651**	**650**	**652**	**26.3**	**2.3**	**8.9**	**3.9**	**64%**	**11%**	**55**	**18**	**27**	**30%**	**75%**	**13%**	**29**						**19.4**	**132**	**157**	**$20**

Hernandez,Roberto

Age: 35	Th: R	Role	SP	Health	A	LIMA Plan	D+
Ht: 6' 4"	Wt: 230	Type	GB	PT/Exp	B	Rand Var	0
				Consist	B	MM	1000

Chronic 4+ ERA history and five clubs in four years mean his pension-earning days are mercifully nearing an end. Bad SwK% gives no hope of rebirth as SP, and skills weren't much better in relief. With last positive RAR season in '10, fanalytic impact has been nil for years anyway. Continue to avoid.

Yr Tm	W	L	Sv	IP	K	ERA	xERA	WHIP	oOPS	vL	vR	BF/G	Ctl	Dom	Cmd	FpK	SwK	G	L	F	H%	S%	hr/f	GS	APC	DOM%	DIS%	Sv%	LI	RAR	BPV	BPX	R$
11 CLE	7	15	0	189	109	5.25	4.10	1.40	776	801	748	26.0	2.9	5.2	1.8	59%	8%	55	19	27	30%	64%	13%	32	94	34%	22%			-30.4	49	74	-$9
12 CLE	0	3	0	14	2	7.53	5.33	1.40	964	1072	805	20.7	1.9	1.3	0.7	59%	3%	51	18	31	25%	50%	24%	3	77	0%	67%			-6.2	1	1	-$7
13 TAM	6	13	1	151	113	4.89	3.53	1.34	797	905	668	20.1	2.3	6.7	3.0	61%	8%	53	22	24	31%	67%	21%	24	75	46%	25%	100	0.84	-19.0	91	119	-$4
14 2 NL	8	11	0	165	105	4.10	4.45	1.39	742	745	738	22.6	4.0	5.7	1.4	56%	9%	50	20	30	28%	73%	12%	29	86	31%	34%	0	0.87	-7.3	24	28	-$2
15 HOU	3	5	0	85	42	4.36	4.58	1.37	774	732	813	17.9	2.8	4.5	1.6	64%	7%	52	19	29	29%	70%	11%	11	66	36%	18%	0	0.66	-4.1	36	43	-$4
1st Half	3	5	0	83	41	4.46	4.61	1.38	781	735	822	19.4	2.8	4.5	1.6	64%	7%	52	19	29	29%	70%	11%	11	72	36%	18%	0	0.73	-5.1	34	40	-$4
2nd Half	0	0	0	2	1	0.00	3.44	1.00	500	667	0	4.0	0.0	4.5	0.0	50%	12%	43	43	14	30%	100%	0%	0	13			0	0.04	1.0	102	121	-$6
16 Proj	**2**	**4**	**0**	**58**	**36**	**4.66**	**4.14**	**1.37**	**778**	**812**	**744**	**20.6**	**2.9**	**5.6**	**2.0**	**61%**	**8%**	**52**	**20**	**27**	**30%**	**69%**	**15%**	**12**						**-5.0**	**54**	**65**	**-$4**

Herrera,Kelvin

Age: 26	Th: R	Role	RP	Health	A	LIMA Plan	B
Ht: 5' 10"	Wt: 200	Type	Pwr	PT/Exp	D	Rand Var	-4
				Consist	A	MM	3311

Flamethrower continues to light up radar guns and miss bats, leading many to peg him as future bullpen stopper. Problem is, that upside has hidden subpar skills last two years; sub-3 ERA was product of S% in '14 and H% in '15. Big fade in 2H makes return to '11-'13 skills unlikely. Don't look for profit here.

Yr Tm	W	L	Sv	IP	K	ERA	xERA	WHIP	oOPS	vL	vR	BF/G	Ctl	Dom	Cmd	FpK	SwK	G	L	F	H%	S%	hr/f	GS	APC	DOM%	DIS%	Sv%	LI	RAR	BPV	BPX	R$
11 KC *	5	1	13	55	49	2.38	2.09	0.91	1232	2500	733	5.3	2.0	7.9	4.0	56%	0%	29	14	57	24%	79%	25%	0	16			81	1.25	10.6	122	184	$12
12 KC	4	3	3	84	77	2.35	3.16	1.19	643	742	580	4.5	2.2	8.2	3.7	59%	12%	56	20	25	32%	81%	7%	0	17			75	1.20	17.3	121	158	$9
13 KC *	5	8	4	76	96	3.23	2.90	1.09	701	738	661	4.2	3.2	11.3	3.5	56%	15%	48	18	34	28%	76%	18%	0	17			67	1.19	6.0	121	157	$8
14 KC	4	3	0	70	59	1.41	3.43	1.14	561	617	508	4.1	3.3	7.6	2.3	55%	13%	49	27	24	28%	86%	0%	0	16			0	1.14	20.1	73	87	$7
15 KC	4	3	0	70	64	2.71	3.79	1.12	578	470	677	4.0	3.4	8.3	2.5	61%	14%	45	23	33	26%	78%	8%	0	15			0	1.17	10.7	81	97	$5
1st Half	1	2	0	33	34	2.20	3.02	0.98	501	375	655	3.7	3.0	9.4	3.1	60%	15%	53	23	24	25%	80%	10%	0	14			0	0.99	7.1	118	140	$5
2nd Half	3	1	0	37	30	3.16	4.48	1.24	642	572	689	4.2	3.6	7.3	2.0	61%	12%	38	22	39	27%	77%	7%	0	16			0	1.34	3.7	49	58	$5
16 Proj	**4**	**4**	**5**	**73**	**68**	**3.21**	**3.47**	**1.16**	**611**	**588**	**631**	**4.0**	**3.2**	**8.5**	**2.6**	**59%**	**13%**	**47**	**23**	**30**	**28%**	**73%**	**8%**	**0**						**6.8**	**90**	**108**	**$6**

STEPHEN NICKRAND

Heston,Chris

Age: 28	Th: R	Role SP	Health A	LIMA Plan C+	
Ht: 6' 4"	Wt: 185	Type GB	PT/Exp C	Rand Var 0	
			Consist C	MM 1103	

It's natural to want to invest in a SP who posted a sub-4 ERA in first full MLB season. But this isn't the place to do that. So-so SwK%, poor FpK% make it very unlikely he can hold on to a 2.0+ Cmd. See 2H for what he'll produce without it. If you had him during that 1H, congrats—but don't take him for another spin.

Yr Tm	W	L	Sv	IP	K	ERA	xERA	WHIP	oOPS	vL	vR	BF/G	Ctl	Dom	Cmd	FpK	SwK	G	L	F	H%	S%	hr/f	GS	APC	DOM%	DIS%	Sv%	LI	RAR	BPV	BPX	R$
11																																	
12 aa	9	8	0	149	113	2.75	3.05	1.25				24.2	2.5	6.8	2.8						32%	76%								23.1	99	130	$12
13 aaa	7	6	0	109	79	5.64	5.45	1.65				25.5	3.5	6.5	1.9						36%	66%								-23.8	45	58	-$12
14 SF *	12	9	0	178	104	3.29	3.33	1.23	675	916	384	23.3	2.6	5.3	2.0	46%	9%	47	35	18	28%	74%	0%	1	34	0%	100%	0	0.25	9.9	62	73	$9
15 SF	12	11	0	178	141	3.95	3.82	1.31	728	818	645	24.1	3.2	7.1	2.2	56%	9%	53	21	26	30%	71%	12%	31	90	35%	32%			0.2	72	86	$6
1st Half	8	5	0	98	80	3.78	3.38	1.23	695	819	599	25.3	2.4	7.4	3.1	58%	9%	56	22	22	31%	69%	10%	16	92	50%	19%			2.2	102	121	$11
2nd Half	4	6	0	80	61	4.16	4.40	1.41	768	817	713	22.7	4.3	6.9	1.6	55%	9%	49	20	31	28%	74%	14%	15	88	20%	47%			-2.0	35	42	-$1
16 Proj	**9**	**11**	**0**	**174**	**126**	**4.15**	**4.10**	**1.37**	**747**	**820**	**677**	**23.9**	**3.4**	**6.5**	**1.9**	**56%**	**9%**	**51**	**21**	**28**	**30%**	**71%**	**9%**	**31**						**-4.0**	**54**	**65**	**$0**

Hill,Rich

Age: 36	Th: L	Role SP	Health D	LIMA Plan B+	
Ht: 6' 5"	Wt: 220	Type Pwr	PT/Exp D	Rand Var 0	
			Consist A	MM 2400	

2-1, 1.55 ERA in 29 IP at BOS. Oh, to be a lefty and blessed with infinite opportunities. After years of chronically terrible control, changed arm slot this summer and actually found something (7.2 Cmd, double-digit Dom vL and vR in four Sept starts). Easy to call it a blip, but it's just enough to hold our attention.

Yr Tm	W	L	Sv	IP	K	ERA	xERA	WHIP	oOPS	vL	vR	BF/G	Ctl	Dom	Cmd	FpK	SwK	G	L	F	H%	S%	hr/f	GS	APC	DOM%	DIS%	Sv%	LI	RAR	BPV	BPX	R$
11 BOS *	1	0	1	24	25	1.16	1.62	0.97	349	259	452	4.8	3.4	9.4	2.8	53%	15%	36	29	36	23%	92%	0%	0	14			100	0.82	8.2	120	181	$2
12 BOS	1	0	0	20	21	1.83	3.96	1.42	685	674	697	3.3	5.0	9.6	1.9	62%	7%	43	24	33	33%	86%	0%	0	14			0	1.10	5.3	58	76	-$2
13 CLE	1	2	0	39	51	6.28	4.13	1.73	719	696	749	2.9	6.8	11.9	1.8	48%	10%	42	20	38	38%	63%	8%	0	12			0	1.28	-11.5	51	67	-$8
14 2AL *	3	3	2	48	50	3.69	3.51	1.51	801	679	1125	4.6	4.9	9.3	1.9	41%	14%	38	31	31	35%	73%	0%	0	7			67	1.07	0.3	100	119	-$2
15 BOS *	7	5	0	83	80	3.53	3.59	1.36	410	358	423	10.2	4.7	8.7	1.9	61%	12%	48	16	35	29%	76%	9%	4	109	100%	0%			4.4	76	90	$2
1st Half	2	2	0	22	23	4.71	4.90	2.02				4.2	11.1	9.7	0.9						29%	77%	0%	0						-2.0	70	83	-$13
2nd Half	5	3	0	61	57	3.11	3.13	1.13	410	358	423	26.9	2.4	8.4	3.5	61%	12%	48	16	35	29%	76%	9%	4	109	100%	0%			6.4	105	124	$7
16 Proj	**5**	**4**	**0**	**58**	**61**	**3.77**	**3.70**	**1.30**	**624**	**687**	**587**	**21.7**	**4.1**	**9.5**	**2.3**	**58%**	**11%**	**46**	**18**	**36**	**31%**	**70%**	**5%**	**11**						**1.3**	**83**	**99**	**$1**

Hochevar,Luke

Age: 32	Th: R	Role RP	Health F	LIMA Plan C	
Ht: 6' 5"	Wt: 225	Type Pwr	PT/Exp D	Rand Var 0	
			Consist C	MM 2310	

Couldn't match '13 bullpen breakout in return from '14 TJ surgery, but this was far from a flop. PRO: 2H uptick in SwK, FpK% supports a better Cmd; still owns that sterling '13. CON: Even 2H SwK far from elite '13 rate, with cutter only K pitch after flashing four pre-TJS. Too many warts here to make him elite plan B.

Yr Tm	W	L	Sv	IP	K	ERA	xERA	WHIP	oOPS	vL	vR	BF/G	Ctl	Dom	Cmd	FpK	SwK	G	L	F	H%	S%	hr/f	GS	APC	DOM%	DIS%	Sv%	LI	RAR	BPV	BPX	R$
11 KC	11	11	0	198	128	4.68	4.00	1.28	742	766	714	26.9	2.8	5.8	2.1	57%	8%	50	18	32	28%	65%	12%	31	101	45%	16%			-18.1	57	85	$1
12 KC	8	16	0	185	144	5.73	4.23	1.42	818	877	749	25.0	3.0	7.0	2.4	59%	9%	43	22	35	32%	61%	14%	32	94	44%	31%			-39.2	67	87	-$13
13 KC	5	2	2	70	82	1.92	2.89	0.82	533	607	452	4.5	2.2	10.5	4.8	69%	14%	35	19	46	22%	86%	11%	0	18			40	0.92	16.9	143	187	$12
14																																	
15 KC	1	1	1	51	49	3.73	4.14	1.28	737	748	730	4.4	2.8	8.7	3.1	63%	10%	37	17	46	31%	76%	10%	0	18			50	0.87	1.5	95	113	-$1
1st Half	0	0	0	14	15	5.02	4.04	1.47	830	911	775	3.9	2.5	9.4	3.8	58%	10%	37	16	47	37%	68%	10%	0	15			0	0.51	-1.9	117	139	-$9
2nd Half	1	1	1	36	34	3.22	4.17	1.21	699	681	711	4.6	3.0	8.4	2.8	65%	11%	37	17	46	28%	79%	10%	0	19			100	1.06	3.3	86	103	$1
16 Proj	**3**	**3**	**5**	**65**	**58**	**3.64**	**3.90**	**1.28**	**750**	**792**	**708**	**7.9**	**2.8**	**7.9**	**2.9**	**62%**	**10%**	**41**	**19**	**40**	**30%**	**76%**	**11%**	**0**						**2.6**	**87**	**103**	**$2**

Holland,Derek

Age: 29	Th: L	Role SP	Health F	LIMA Plan C	
Ht: 6' 2"	Wt: 210	Type	PT/Exp C	Rand Var +3	
			Consist A	MM 2203	

After knee sidelined him in '14, bum shoulder did him in this time. When he pitched, was either great or terrible 90% of the time (via DOM/DIS%). Bad health and skill inconsistency cements risk in his profile. If healthy in spring, view only as an end-game flyer; his prior upper-rotation upside appears gone.

Yr Tm	W	L	Sv	IP	K	ERA	xERA	WHIP	oOPS	vL	vR	BF/G	Ctl	Dom	Cmd	FpK	SwK	G	L	F	H%	S%	hr/f	GS	APC	DOM%	DIS%	Sv%	LI	RAR	BPV	BPX	R$
11 TEX	16	5	0	198	162	3.95	3.80	1.35	724	601	765	26.3	3.0	7.4	2.4	58%	8%	46	20	34	31%	74%	11%	32	100	47%	22%			-0.3	74	112	$7
12 TEX	12	7	0	175	145	4.67	4.08	1.22	745	656	770	25.2	2.7	7.4	2.8	59%	8%	43	17	40	27%	68%	15%	27	95	63%	15%	0	0.81	-14.2	83	108	$4
13 TEX	10	9	0	213	189	3.42	3.78	1.29	711	671	722	27.1	2.7	8.0	3.0	63%	10%	41	23	36	32%	76%	9%	33	99	58%	15%			11.6	90	117	$10
14 TEX *	4	1	0	57	45	2.90	4.38	1.37	601	618	596	20.0	2.5	7.1	2.8	66%	10%	41	17	41	33%	82%	0%	5	95	100%	0%	0	0.66	5.9	74	89	$1
15 TEX	4	3	0	59	41	4.91	4.25	1.30	828	740	848	24.5	2.6	6.3	2.4	63%	7%	42	23	35	28%	68%	17%	10	91	50%	40%			-6.9	63	75	-$3
1st Half	0	1	0	1	0	9.00	5.63	2.00	1750	0	1750	4.0	0.0	0.0	0.0	75%	11%	50	0	50	26%	0%	50%	1	9	0%	100%			-0.6	28	33	-$12
2nd Half	4	2	0	58	41	4.84	4.22	1.28	811	740	828	26.8	2.7	6.4	2.4	63%	7%	42	23	35	28%	67%	16%	9	100	56%	33%			-6.2	63	75	-$3
16 Proj	**11**	**6**	**0**	**174**	**139**	**3.97**	**4.01**	**1.30**	**764**	**695**	**783**	**24.5**	**2.7**	**7.2**	**2.7**	**63%**	**9%**	**42**	**21**	**37**	**30%**	**74%**	**12%**	**29**						**-0.1**	**77**	**92**	**$5**

Holland,Greg

Age: 30	Th: R	Role RP	Health B	LIMA Plan D+	
Ht: 5' 10"	Wt: 205	Type ####	PT/Exp A	Rand Var -1	
			Consist B	MM ####	

Among the Hollands, this one entered year as a clear Dutch treat after back-to-back 40-save seasons. Balky elbow made his owners pay the full cost of dating him, leading to big velocity drop and loss of job in Sept, followed by TJ surgery that should keep him out for all of 2016.

Yr Tm	W	L	Sv	IP	K	ERA	xERA	WHIP	oOPS	vL	vR	BF/G	Ctl	Dom	Cmd	FpK	SwK	G	L	F	H%	S%	hr/f	GS	APC	DOM%	DIS%	Sv%	LI	RAR	BPV	BPX	R$
11 KC *	7	1	6	82	95	1.96	1.77	1.01	521	522	519	5.3	3.3	10.4	3.1	60%	17%	45	16	39	26%	82%	6%	0	21			67	1.38	20.0	133	201	$15
12 KC	7	4	16	67	91	2.96	3.31	1.37	653	577	712	4.3	4.6	12.2	2.7	50%	13%	45	18	36	36%	78%	3%	0	17			80	1.41	8.8	120	156	$10
13 KC	2	1	47	67	103	1.21	2.10	0.87	479	512	439	3.8	2.4	13.8	5.7	58%	17%	39	27	33	30%	89%	7%	0	16			94	1.34	22.0	201	262	$31
14 KC	1	3	46	62	90	1.44	2.29	0.91	472	494	444	3.7	2.9	13.0	4.5	57%	15%	48	17	35	28%	87%	7%	0	15			96	1.21	17.7	182	217	$26
15 KC	3	2	32	45	49	3.83	3.88	1.46	692	777	615	4.0	5.2	9.9	1.9	63%	15%	49	22	29	32%	73%	6%	0	15			86	1.23	0.7	63	75	$11
1st Half	2	0	16	23	24	2.74	3.61	1.04	510	589	429	3.8	4.7	9.4	2.0	62%	15%	50	19	31	21%	74%	6%	0	14			94	1.10	3.5	70	83	$14
2nd Half	1	2	16	22	25	4.98	4.17	1.89	857	961	770	4.2	5.8	10.4	1.8	64%	15%	48	25	27	42%	73%	6%	0	16			80	1.37	-2.7	56	67	$7
16 Proj																																	

Holmberg,David

Age: 24	Th: L	Role SP	Health A	LIMA Plan D	
Ht: 6' 3"	Wt: 225	Type Con FB	PT/Exp D	Rand Var +4	
			Consist C	MM 0000	

1-4, 7.62 ERA in 28 IP at CIN. Life's good when you're a lefty, v. 2. This one looks like LOOGY on surface, but he couldn't even muster 1.0+ Cmd against them in small MLB sample. Freefall in Cmd, subpar SwK, FpK give no hope for something more. Horrific DIS% seals fate. No thanks.

Yr Tm	W	L	Sv	IP	K	ERA	xERA	WHIP	oOPS	vL	vR	BF/G	Ctl	Dom	Cmd	FpK	SwK	G	L	F	H%	S%	hr/f	GS	APC	DOM%	DIS%	Sv%	LI	RAR	BPV	BPX	R$
11																																	
12 aa	5	5	0	95	58	4.34	5.03	1.47				27.2	2.1	5.5	2.6						34%	72%								-3.8	56	74	-$5
13 ARI *	5	8	0	161	99	3.74	4.29	1.40	950	1100	900	25.2	3.0	5.5	1.8	55%	5%	25	25	50	31%	75%	0%	1	80	0%	100%			2.5	47	61	-$1
14 CIN *	4	8	0	123	68	4.84	5.59	1.65	849	958	817	21.9	3.5	5.0	1.4	55%	9%	38	17	45	34%	72%	19%	5	74	40%	40%	0	0.62	-16.6	25	30	-$12
15 CIN *	8	11	0	149	77	6.11	7.26	1.82	1025	574	1173	25.5	3.7	4.6	1.3	53%	5%	40	18	42	34%	71%	24%	6	89	33%	50%			-39.4	-13	-15	-$24
1st Half	4	6	0	92	44	6.33	7.70	1.93				27.4	3.8	4.3	1.1						36%	71%	0%	0						-27.0	-16	-19	-$31
2nd Half	4	5	0	56	32	5.74	6.55	1.63	1025	574	1173	22.8	3.4	5.2	1.5	53%	5%	40	18	42	31%	71%	24%	6	89	33%	50%			-12.4	-5	-6	-$13
16 Proj	**1**	**2**	**0**	**29**	**16**	**5.20**	**5.28**	**1.64**	**879**	**638**	**955**	**24.1**	**3.3**	**5.0**	**1.5**	**54%**	**7%**	**39**	**17**	**43**	**33%**	**72%**	**10%**	**5**						**-4.4**	**18**	**22**	**-$6**

Hoover,J.J.

Age: 28	Th: R	Role RP	Health A	LIMA Plan C+	
Ht: 6' 3"	Wt: 230	Type Pwr xFB	PT/Exp C	Rand Var -5	
			Consist A	MM 1310	

Former elite bullpen prospect put rough '14 behind him...or did he? Skills reveal the real truth. Sexy surface stats product of friendly H%, S% pendulum. Steady Cmd erosion, FpK nosedive, all rolled up into ominous xERA trend. More worries if long FB history returns. It's time to ignore his closer hype.

Yr Tm	W	L	Sv	IP	K	ERA	xERA	WHIP	oOPS	vL	vR	BF/G	Ctl	Dom	Cmd	FpK	SwK	G	L	F	H%	S%	hr/f	GS	APC	DOM%	DIS%	Sv%	LI	RAR	BPV	BPX	R$
11 a/a	3	6	2	106	100	3.06	2.82	1.21				9.9	3.4	8.5	2.5						29%	75%								11.5	99	149	$7
12 CIN *	5	0	14	68	77	1.75	1.16	0.89	512	427	589	4.3	3.4	10.2	3.0	59%	11%	24	20	57	22%	83%	5%	0	19			88	0.70	18.9	135	176	$18
13 CIN	5	5	3	66	67	2.86	3.86	1.11	627	477	722	3.9	3.5	9.1	2.6	61%	10%	31	21	48	26%	78%	7%	0	17			60	1.29	8.2	78	101	$6
14 CIN	1	10	0	63	75	4.88	4.07	1.39	785	948	660	5.1	4.5	10.8	2.4	61%	11%	28	19	53	30%	72%	15%	0	21			0	0.87	-8.8	80	95	-$4
15 CIN	8	2	1	64	52	2.94	4.46	1.17	663	717	607	3.9	4.3	7.3	1.7	53%	11%	40	20	40	22%	79%	10%	0	17			14	1.10	8.1	32	38	$6
1st Half	5	0	1	36	27	1.49	4.09	0.99	476	419	530	3.9	4.0	6.7	1.7	51%	10%	48	20	32	21%	83%	0%	0	16			50	1.01	11.1	39	47	$11
2nd Half	3	2	0	28	25	4.82	4.92	1.39	883	1057	696	4.0	4.8	8.0	1.7	55%	11%	31	21	49	24%	75%	18%	0	17			0	1.21	-3.0	23	28	-$1
16 Proj	**5**	**5**	**2**	**65**	**63**	**4.05**	**4.32**	**1.36**	**776**	**852**	**708**	**4.3**	**4.2**	**8.7**	**2.1**	**57%**	**11%**	**33**	**20**	**47**	**29%**	**75%**	**11%**	**0**						**-0.7**	**54**	**65**	**$0**

STEPHEN NICKRAND

House,T.J.

Age: 26	Th: L	Role SP	Health B	LIMA Plan C	
Ht: 6' 1"	Wt: 205	Type xGB	PT/Exp D	Rand Var +5	
			Consist F	MM 3100	

Entered year as top $1 target due to strong '14 finish. Shoulder soreness shushed that talk, but his 130 BPV over 12 starts in '14 2nd half with CLE wasn't a tiny blip. Key is health. If it cooperates, swing-and-miss stuff and extreme GB tilt gives him unique combo. An intriguing stash that you'll be able to get for nothing.

Yr Tm	W	L	Sv	IP	K	ERA	xERA	WHIP	oOPS	vL	vR	BF/G	Ctl	Dom	Cmd	FpK	SwK	G	L	F	H%	S%	hr/f	GS	APC	DOM%	DIS%	Sv%	LI	RAR	BPV	BPX	R$
11																																	
12 aa	8	5	0	124	77	5.34	4.46	1.48				23.3	3.3	5.6	1.7						32%	63%								-20.4	49	64	-$9
13 a/a	9	11	0	164	116	4.82	5.19	1.61				26.0	3.1	6.4	2.1						36%	70%								-19.3	55	71	-$11
14 CLE *	6	7	0	159	115	3.74	4.29	1.36	749	608	808	22.9	2.1	6.5	3.0	61%	10%	61	21	18	33%	74%	18%	18	83	39%	28%	0	0.72	0.1	79	94	$0
15 CLE *	0	6	0	34	18	8.32	7.60	2.17	945	268	1033	21.2	6.9	4.6	0.7	63%	5%	60	31	10	35%	61%	20%	4	69	0%	100%			-18.3	-7	-9	-$15
1st Half	0	6	0	34	18	8.32	7.60	2.17	945	268	1033	21.2	6.9	4.6	0.7	63%	5%	60	31	10	35%	61%	20%	4	69	0%	100%			-18.3	-7	-9	-$15
2nd Half																																	
16 Proj	5	3	0	58	40	4.15	3.61	1.33	638	515	689	21.3	2.8	6.3	2.2	61%	10%	61	21	18	31%	69%	10%	11						-1.4	75	90	-$1

Hudson,Daniel

Age: 29	Th: R	Role RP	Health F	LIMA Plan B+	
Ht: 6' 3"	Wt: 225	Type Pwr	PT/Exp D	Rand Var 0	
			Consist A	MM 3310	

Eased back on mound from TJ surgery via pen work. Results mixed on surface, but that 2H—especially his sexy SwK—gives legit hope that he can be an impact arm in pen. Those gains were hidden by aberrant hit rate, so don't put stock in apparent late fade. Murky future role increases profit potential. UP: 30 Sv

Yr Tm	W	L	Sv	IP	K	ERA	xERA	WHIP	oOPS	vL	vR	BF/G	Ctl	Dom	Cmd	FpK	SwK	G	L	F	H%	S%	hr/f	GS	APC	DOM%	DIS%	Sv%	LI	RAR	BPV	BPX	R$
11 ARI	16	12	0	222	169	3.49	3.80	1.20	694	698	691	27.9	2.0	6.9	3.4	60%	10%	42	19	39	30%	72%	6%	33	104	67%	6%			12.5	89	133	$16
12 ARI	3	2	0	45	37	7.35	4.34	1.63	910	994	807	22.4	2.4	7.3	3.1	56%	10%	37	27	36	37%	57%	17%	9	89	22%	44%			-18.6	83	108	-$11
13																																	
14 ARI	0	1	0	3	2	13.50	4.22	1.50	769	500	1200	4.3	0.0	6.8	0.0	54%	8%	45	18	36	42%	0%	0%	0	16			0	0.68	-3.2	145	172	-$4
15 ARI	4	3	4	68	71	3.86	3.78	1.32	691	624	743	4.5	3.3	9.4	2.8	57%	13%	43	22	35	32%	73%	10%	1	18	0%	100%	67	1.11	0.9	101	121	$1
1st Half	2	3	1	37	35	3.65	3.95	1.24	654	585	711	5.0	3.6	8.5	2.3	55%	12%	45	21	34	28%	74%	11%	1	20	0%	100%	50	1.23	1.4	78	92	$1
2nd Half	2	0	3	31	36	4.11	3.58	1.40	732	670	778	4.1	2.9	10.6	3.6	60%	15%	41	23	36	37%	73%	9%	0	16			75	0.99	-0.6	130	154	$2
16 Proj	3	2	5	44	41	3.61	3.65	1.24	653	668	639	7.0	2.7	8.5	3.1	57%	12%	41	23	36	31%	73%	8%	0						1.9	97	115	$1

Hudson,Tim

Age: 40	Th: R	Role RP	Health F	LIMA Plan D	
Ht: 6' 1"	Wt: 175	Type #### GB	PT/Exp A	Rand Var	
			Consist A	MM	

Poor health, big skill dip provided writing on wall to end brilliant 17-year career. Among SP with 1,000+ IP from '99 to '15, check out how many categories he led or was near the top of: wins (1st), IP (2nd), GB% (4th), Ks (8th), ERA (23rd). Proof that you don't need overpowering stuff to be a durable rotation anchor.

Yr Tm	W	L	Sv	IP	K	ERA	xERA	WHIP	oOPS	vL	vR	BF/G	Ctl	Dom	Cmd	FpK	SwK	G	L	F	H%	S%	hr/f	GS	APC	DOM%	DIS%	Sv%	LI	RAR	BPV	BPX	R$
11 ATL	16	10	0	215	158	3.22	3.32	1.14	627	692	571	26.8	2.3	6.6	2.8	62%	10%	57	19	25	28%	73%	9%	33	97	55%	9%			19.1	91	136	$20
12 ATL	16	7	0	179	102	3.62	4.03	1.21	666	668	663	26.8	2.4	5.1	2.1	62%	8%	55	19	25	28%	71%	8%	28	94	39%	11%			8.7	60	78	$12
13 ATL	8	7	0	131	95	3.97	3.52	1.19	662	661	662	25.4	2.5	6.5	2.6	65%	10%	56	18	27	29%	67%	10%	21	96	57%	19%			-1.8	85	110	$4
14 SF	9	13	0	189	120	3.57	3.61	1.23	713	755	667	25.5	1.6	5.7	3.5	63%	9%	53	21	26	31%	72%	9%	31	90	45%	19%			4.1	90	107	$6
15 SF	8	9	0	124	64	4.44	4.26	1.38	746	836	674	21.9	2.7	4.7	1.7	63%	9%	56	21	23	30%	70%	14%	22	77	18%	27%	0	0.74	-7.3	45	54	-$3
1st Half	5	7	0	92	49	4.68	3.99	1.38	763	775	754	26.1	2.1	4.8	2.2	65%	10%	58	21	21	31%	69%	19%	15	90	20%	13%			-8.2	64	76	-$3
2nd Half	3	2	0	31	15	3.73	5.09	1.40	691	989	390	14.9	4.3	4.3	1.0	58%	8%	50	21	29	28%	72%	3%	7	55	14%	57%	0	0.64	0.9	-11	-13	-$3
16 Proj																																	

Hughes,Jared

Age: 30	Th: R	Role RP	Health C	LIMA Plan B	
Ht: 6' 7"	Wt: 245	Type Con xGB	PT/Exp D	Rand Var -5	
			Consist B	MM 2000	

With back-to-back near-2 ERAs, a future closer? Well, a check of xERA confirms he's no 2-ERA guy. Solid SwK does mean he's got K upside, but he's set the bar so low, we just can't bank on big gains. Only redeemable skill is GB, but it's not enough to expand role. He's fine as a LIMA arm, but don't mine here for saves.

Yr Tm	W	L	Sv	IP	K	ERA	xERA	WHIP	oOPS	vL	vR	BF/G	Ctl	Dom	Cmd	FpK	SwK	G	L	F	H%	S%	hr/f	GS	APC	DOM%	DIS%	Sv%	LI	RAR	BPV	BPX	R$
11 PIT *	6	6	0	115	68	4.08	4.05	1.45	630	782	546	8.2	3.2	5.3	1.7	59%	7%	66	21	14	32%	70%	25%	0	16			0	0.72	-2.0	56	85	-$2
12 PIT	2	2	2	76	50	2.85	3.73	1.15	677	734	629	4.8	2.6	5.9	2.3	53%	11%	60	17	23	26%	79%	13%	0	18			50	0.96	10.8	74	97	$5
13 PIT *	3	3	2	55	39	2.99	4.11	1.51	786	967	664	5.0	3.8	6.4	1.7	58%	12%	56	20	23	33%	80%	8%	0	18			100	0.70	5.9	63	82	-$1
14 PIT	7	5	0	64	36	1.96	3.34	1.09	609	592	622	4.1	2.7	5.0	1.9	60%	11%	65	19	17	24%	85%	13%	0	14			0	1.09	14.1	62	74	$7
15 PIT	3	1	0	67	36	2.28	3.86	1.33	720	684	741	3.7	2.6	4.8	1.9	61%	10%	64	18	19	30%	84%	8%	0	13			0	1.14	13.9	60	72	$2
1st Half	1	1	0	37	27	2.45	3.30	1.15	629	641	620	3.8	2.0	6.6	3.4	65%	12%	63	14	23	30%	78%	4%	0	13			0	1.18	6.8	107	127	$3
2nd Half	2	0	0	30	9	2.08	4.63	1.55	825	744	865	3.7	3.3	2.7	0.8	56%	8%	64	22	14	31%	89%	13%	0	13			0	1.11	7.1	2	3	$1
16 Proj	4	2	0	65	36	3.22	3.97	1.40	747	755	742	4.1	2.9	4.9	1.7	59%	10%	62	19	19	31%	77%	8%	0						6.0	51	60	-$1

Hughes,Phil

Age: 30	Th: R	Role SP	Health D	LIMA Plan A	
Ht: 6' 5"	Wt: 240	Type Con FB	PT/Exp A	Rand Var +1	
			Consist C	MM 2105	

Premium strikethrower couldn't make '14 resurgence stick. Blame SwK falling off cliff, and return of gopheritis. Solid SwK history favors rebound, but looking back reminds us of consistent 4+ ERAs, too. And big struggles vRHB—especially late—cement risk in profile. The risk-averse should side with pessimism.

Yr Tm	W	L	Sv	IP	K	ERA	xERA	WHIP	oOPS	vL	vR	BF/G	Ctl	Dom	Cmd	FpK	SwK	G	L	F	H%	S%	hr/f	GS	APC	DOM%	DIS%	Sv%	LI	RAR	BPV	BPX	R$
11 NYY	5	5	0	75	47	5.79	4.93	1.49	799	841	729	19.6	3.3	5.7	1.7	68%	7%	32	23	45	31%	62%	8%	14	76	29%	43%	0	0.86	-17.0	24	36	-$7
12 NYY	16	13	0	191	165	4.19	4.30	1.26	765	610	928	25.5	2.2	7.8	3.6	66%	9%	32	20	48	30%	74%	12%	32	101	53%	22%			-4.1	91	119	$9
13 NYY	4	14	0	146	121	5.19	4.44	1.46	832	863	793	21.4	2.6	7.5	2.9	71%	9%	31	23	46	34%	68%	11%	29	85	38%	52%	0	0.76	-23.8	74	96	-$10
14 MIN	16	10	0	210	186	3.52	3.39	1.13	674	619	733	26.7	0.7	8.0	11.6	73%	9%	36	23	40	34%	70%	6%	32	95	66%	3%			5.7	139	166	$15
15 MIN	11	9	0	155	94	4.40	4.42	1.29	812	761	869	24.1	0.9	5.4	5.9	72%	6%	35	24	40	31%	73%	13%	25	84	36%	20%	0	0.73	-8.4	86	102	$1
1st Half	7	6	0	105	64	4.27	4.35	1.22	778	771	785	27.3	0.9	5.5	6.4	73%	6%	35	25	41	30%	72%	13%	16	92	38%	13%			-4.0	88	104	$5
2nd Half	4	3	0	50	30	4.68	4.58	1.44	881	738	1025	19.5	1.1	5.4	5.0	68%	6%	37	23	40	34%	74%	14%	9	71	33%	33%	0	0.63	-4.4	83	98	-$6
16 Proj	12	11	0	180	135	4.07	3.93	1.27	780	723	844	22.1	1.1	6.8	6.3	71%	8%	35	23	42	32%	73%	12%	33						-2.3	105	125	$5

Hunter,Tommy

Age: 29	Th: R	Role RP	Health C	LIMA Plan C	
Ht: 6' 3"	Wt: 260	Type	PT/Exp C	Rand Var 0	
			Consist A	MM 2110	

Former closer dispatched to low-leverage work, and safe money suggests that's where he belongs. History of mediocre Dom, inconsistent SwK don't give hope for sustained growth or role re-expansion, leaving him as a control artist with only a modest GB tilt. It's not an attractive formula for a bullpen arm.

Yr Tm	W	L	Sv	IP	K	ERA	xERA	WHIP	oOPS	vL	vR	BF/G	Ctl	Dom	Cmd	FpK	SwK	G	L	F	H%	S%	hr/f	GS	APC	DOM%	DIS%	Sv%	LI	RAR	BPV	BPX	R$
11 2 AL *	6	6	1	115	61	5.01	5.34	1.44	782	864	686	16.9	1.5	4.8	3.2	66%	6%	41	21	38	33%	68%	11%	11	65	18%	18%	50	0.95	-15.2	52	78	-$5
12 BAL *	10	9	1	163	93	5.24	5.58	1.37	864	840	891	18.0	1.9	5.1	2.7	60%	7%	45	20	35	30%	68%	20%	20	63	25%	25%	50	0.87	-24.6	27	35	-$7
13 BAL	6	5	4	86	68	2.81	3.55	0.98	617	857	344	4.9	1.5	7.1	4.9	64%	11%	39	21	40	25%	78%	11%	0	19			67	1.09	11.2	105	137	$10
14 BAL	3	2	11	61	45	2.97	3.27	1.10	643	639	647	4.0	1.8	6.7	3.8	65%	8%	51	24	25	29%	75%	9%	0	14			65	1.16	5.8	101	120	$7
15 2 TM	4	2	1	60	47	4.18	3.93	1.24	711	754	674	4.3	2.1	7.0	3.4	66%	11%	45	21	35	30%	69%	11%	0	15			50	0.82	-1.6	93	111	-$1
1st Half	2	1	0	34	25	3.93	3.75	1.19	664	659	668	4.5	1.3	6.6	5.0	68%	11%	48	19	33	32%	67%	6%	0	15			0	0.96	0.1	109	129	-$1
2nd Half	2	1	1	26	22	4.50	4.18	1.31	774	922	680	4.0	3.1	7.6	2.4	63%	11%	40	23	36	28%	72%	18%	0	15			100	0.67	-1.7	71	85	$0
16 Proj	4	2	2	58	44	3.81	3.74	1.20	702	774	637	4.6	2.0	6.8	3.4	65%	10%	45	22	34	29%	72%	12%	0						1.1	91	108	$1

Hutchison,Drew

Age: 25	Th: R	Role SP	Health F	LIMA Plan C	
Ht: 6' 3"	Wt: 195	Type Pwr	PT/Exp B	Rand Var +5	
			Consist C	MM 2303	

Unmitigated disaster after entering season with breakout written all over him. Before you move on, note that skills weren't drastically different; a trifecta of hit-strand-hr/f trouble did him in. Triple-digit BPV in May, Aug confirm upside, and that late FpK surge supports further Ctl reduction. If healthy, a profit center.

Yr Tm	W	L	Sv	IP	K	ERA	xERA	WHIP	oOPS	vL	vR	BF/G	Ctl	Dom	Cmd	FpK	SwK	G	L	F	H%	S%	hr/f	GS	APC	DOM%	DIS%	Sv%	LI	RAR	BPV	BPX	R$
11 aa	3	0	0	15	19	1.46	1.39	0.89				18.6	1.2	11.2	9.4						33%	82%								4.6	278	418	$1
12 TOR *	7	4	0	75	59	4.18	4.31	1.33	756	750	763	22.4	2.7	7.1	2.6	54%	9%	45	25	30	31%	72%	15%	11	90	36%	27%			-1.5	65	85	$0
13 a/a	0	4	0	27	26	7.16	6.09	1.75				17.4	2.7	8.7	3.3						42%	57%								-10.8	85	111	-$9
14 TOR	11	13	0	185	184	4.48	3.84	1.26	723	811	615	24.6	2.9	9.0	3.1	59%	11%	36	19	45	31%	67%	10%	32	95	53%	28%			-16.9	96	115	$2
15 TOR	13	5	0	150	129	5.57	4.22	1.48	825	750	906	22.1	2.6	7.7	2.9	64%	10%	40	24	36	35%	65%	13%	28	84	36%	39%	0	0.73	-29.8	86	102	-$8
1st Half	8	2	0	93	85	5.23	4.08	1.47	781	684	892	24.2	2.7	8.2	3.0	62%	10%	40	25	35	36%	65%	10%	17	94	41%	35%			-14.5	93	110	-$6
2nd Half	5	3	0	57	44	6.12	4.46	1.50	896	865	928	19.5	2.5	6.9	2.8	69%	10%	39	22	39	33%	64%	16%	11	71	27%	45%	0	0.67	-15.3	74	87	-$12
16 Proj	11	8	0	145	127	4.02	3.88	1.29	724	720	728	21.3	2.6	7.9	3.0	62%	10%	39	22	39	31%	72%	10%	28						-1.1	89	106	$5

STEPHEN NICKRAND

Iglesias,Raisel

Age: 26 Th: R Role SP	Health C	LIMA Plan B	
Ht: 6' 2" Wt: 185 Type Pwr	PT/Exp F	Rand Var +2	
	Consist F	MM 3405	

3-7, 4.15 ERA in 95 IP at CIN. Don't be fooled by mediocre MLB stat line. Those 2H gains were real, and they weren't confined to one or two skills. Soaring Cmd supported by FpK and SwK upticks, so it can stick. And GB rose each of last four months. Breakout targets don't get much better. UP: 3.00 ERA, 200 Ks.

Yr	Tm	W	L	Sv	IP	K	ERA	xERA	WHIP	oOPS	vL	vR	BF/G	Ctl	Dom	Cmd	FpK	SwK	G	L	F	H%	S%	hr/f	GS	APC	DOM%	DIS%	Sv%	LI	RAR	BPV	BPX	R$
11																																		
12																																		
13																																		
14																																		
15	CIN *	4	10	0	124	122	4.26	3.78	1.21	682	753	618	20.9	2.7	8.8	3.3	62%	13%	47	21	32	30%	69%	14%	16	87	63%	19%	0	0.72	-4.6	92	109	$2
1st Half		2	4	0	54	43	4.85	4.85	1.44	750	782	708	19.1	3.0	7.2	2.4	59%	12%	34	27	38	33%	69%	4%	4	71	25%	25%	0	0.63	-5.8	57	68	-$7
2nd Half		2	6	0	71	79	3.82	2.88	1.03	655	737	590	23.7	2.4	10.1	4.2	63%	13%	53	18	29	27%	68%	20%	12	95	75%	17%			1.2	146	174	$9
16	Proj	**12**	**9**	**0**	**189**	**187**	**3.66**	**3.38**	**1.21**	**689**	**759**	**622**	**21.1**	**2.7**	**8.9**	**3.4**	**61%**	**12%**	**45**	**22**	**33**	**31%**	**71%**	**9%**	**36**						**6.9**	**112**	**133**	**$12**

Iwakuma,Hisashi

Age: 34 Th: R Role SP	Health F	LIMA Plan B	
Ht: 6' 3" Wt: 210 Type	PT/Exp A	Rand Var +2	
	Consist A	MM 4203	

Shoulder soreness sidelined him for most of 1H. That 2H shows what to expect when he's healthy: pinpoint control (supported by elite FpK), swing-and-miss stuff (supported by SwK), and a bunch of groundballs. It's a profile that makes him a low-risk mid-3s ERA target. Just heed health grade and don't expect 200 IP.

Yr	Tm	W	L	Sv	IP	K	ERA	xERA	WHIP	oOPS	vL	vR	BF/G	Ctl	Dom	Cmd	FpK	SwK	G	L	F	H%	S%	hr/f	GS	APC	DOM%	DIS%	Sv%	LI	RAR	BPV	BPX	R$
11	for	6	7	0	119	85	3.03	3.35	1.16				27.9	1.8	6.4	3.5						29%	77%								13.5	95	142	$9
12	SEA	9	5	2	125	101	3.16	3.74	1.28	718	716	720	17.3	3.1	7.3	2.3	60%	10%	52	20	27	28%	81%	17%	16	64	44%	13%	100	0.59	13.2	77	101	$9
13	SEA	14	6	0	220	185	2.66	3.29	1.01	630	599	667	26.2	1.7	7.6	4.4	63%	11%	49	18	34	26%	80%	12%	33	94	58%	3%			32.6	117	152	$29
14	SEA	15	9	0	179	154	3.52	3.00	1.05	642	702	573	25.3	1.1	7.7	7.3	66%	10%	50	21	29	30%	70%	13%	28	91	64%	18%			4.9	139	165	$16
15	SEA	9	5	0	130	111	3.54	3.34	1.06	674	703	645	25.8	1.5	7.7	5.3	68%	11%	50	18	31	28%	73%	15%	20	93	60%	10%			6.8	127	152	$11
1st Half		0	1	0	16	11	6.61	4.26	1.41	959	922	1011	23.7	1.7	6.1	3.7	65%	9%	45	23	32	30%	61%	28%	3	86	0%	33%			-5.3	87	103	-$23
2nd Half		9	4	0	113	100	3.10	3.21	1.01	630	662	599	26.2	1.4	7.9	5.6	69%	12%	51	18	31	28%	75%	13%	17	95	71%	6%			12.1	134	159	$16
16	Proj	**11**	**8**	**0**	**174**	**142**	**3.53**	**3.33**	**1.12**	**686**	**704**	**665**	**24.3**	**1.5**	**7.4**	**4.8**	**66%**	**10%**	**49**	**20**	**31**	**29%**	**73%**	**14%**	**28**						**9.3**	**119**	**141**	**$13**

Jackson,Edwin

Age: 32 Th: R Role RP	Health C	LIMA Plan B	
Ht: 6' 3" Wt: 210 Type Pwr	PT/Exp B	Rand Var -4	
	Consist A	MM 1200	

Once teased us as a SP with overpowering stuff and occassional mid-3s ERAs. Now he's struggling to even make a club in any role. SP days are gone; see horrible pre-'15 ERA trend. Concurrent and steady plummets in BPV, FpK give no hope of rebound. That near-3 ERA as RP was driven by friendly H%, S%, hr/f. Move on.

Yr	Tm	W	L	Sv	IP	K	ERA	xERA	WHIP	oOPS	vL	vR	BF/G	Ctl	Dom	Cmd	FpK	SwK	G	L	F	H%	S%	hr/f	GS	APC	DOM%	DIS%	Sv%	LI	RAR	BPV	BPX	R$
11	2 TM	12	9	0	200	148	3.79	3.96	1.44	768	800	736	26.9	2.8	6.7	2.4	58%	10%	44	25	31	33%	75%	8%	31	101	52%	10%	0	0.76	3.8	67	100	$3
12	WAS	10	11	0	190	168	4.03	3.80	1.22	719	758	677	25.5	2.8	8.0	2.9	62%	13%	47	17	36	29%	70%	12%	31	96	48%	16%			-0.4	94	123	$9
13	CHC	8	18	0	175	135	4.98	3.98	1.46	775	816	741	25.1	3.0	6.9	2.3	56%	9%	51	20	28	33%	66%	10%	31	95	42%	26%			-24.1	72	94	-$9
14	CHC	6	15	0	141	123	6.33	4.32	1.64	869	930	816	22.6	4.0	7.9	2.0	55%	11%	39	26	35	35%	62%	12%	27	89	30%	33%	0	0.77	-45.0	50	59	-$19
15	2 NL	4	3	1	56	40	3.07	4.41	1.17	622	565	657	4.9	3.4	6.5	1.9	54%	11%	41	22	37	25%	75%	7%	0	19			50	0.77	6.1	44	52	$2
1st Half		2	1	0	29	21	2.17	4.32	1.24	584	490	631	5.8	3.4	6.5	1.9	56%	10%	47	21	33	29%	81%	0%	0	22			0	0.53	6.4	50	59	$2
2nd Half		2	2	1	27	19	4.05	4.50	1.09	667	633	693	4.1	3.4	6.4	1.9	53%	12%	35	23	42	21%	68%	13%	0	16			100	0.97	-0.3	37	44	$2
16	Proj	**3**	**4**	**0**	**58**	**45**	**4.37**	**4.23**	**1.34**	**728**	**742**	**718**	**7.8**	**3.4**	**7.0**	**2.0**	**55%**	**11%**	**42**	**23**	**35**	**29%**	**69%**	**10%**	**0**						**-2.9**	**53**	**63**	**-$2**

Jansen,Kenley

Age: 28 Th: R Role RP	Health D	LIMA Plan C+	
Ht: 6' 5" Wt: 265 Type Pwr xFB	PT/Exp A	Rand Var 0	
	Consist A	MM 5530	

The curious case of an über-elite closer with a brittle body. Has combined filthy cutter/slider with pinpoint control, and soaring FpK supports it. Even halted increasing struggles vL. Besides near-flunking health, only bugaboo is all those FBs, but with his command, that risk is tiny. With full season of health... UP: 50 Sv.

Yr	Tm	W	L	Sv	IP	K	ERA	xERA	WHIP	oOPS	vL	vR	BF/G	Ctl	Dom	Cmd	FpK	SwK	G	L	F	H%	S%	hr/f	GS	APC	DOM%	DIS%	Sv%	LI	RAR	BPV	BPX	R$
11	LA	2	1	5	54	96	2.85	2.38	1.04	494	494	493	4.3	4.4	16.1	3.7	60%	17%	27	24	49	33%	74%	7%	0	19			83	0.88	7.2	177	266	$7
12	LA	5	3	25	65	99	2.35	2.63	0.85	504	518	490	3.9	3.0	13.7	4.5	61%	15%	33	19	48	24%	78%	10%	0	16			78	1.31	13.3	175	229	$22
13	LA	4	3	28	77	111	1.88	2.29	0.86	509	531	494	3.9	2.1	13.0	6.2	64%	16%	37	24	39	29%	83%	10%	0	17			88	1.33	18.8	192	251	$24
14	LA	2	3	44	65	101	2.76	2.43	1.13	610	710	521	3.9	2.6	13.9	5.3	67%	17%	35	28	37	38%	78%	9%	0	16			90	1.27	7.9	193	230	$21
15	LA	2	1	36	52	80	2.41	2.46	0.78	513	566	459	3.7	1.4	13.8	10.0	70%	18%	35	11	54	29%	77%	10%	0	15			95	1.22	10.0	223	266	$22
1st Half		2	1	13	19	32	1.93	1.92	0.54	446	549	371	3.5	0.5	15.4	32.0	69%	22%	33	9	58	25%	75%	11%	0	14			93	1.48	4.7	276	328	$17
2nd Half		0	0	23	34	48	2.67	2.79	0.92	547	573	515	3.8	1.9	12.8	6.9	70%	16%	36	12	52	30%	78%	10%	0	15			96	1.07	5.4	194	231	$24
16	Proj	**3**	**2**	**44**	**65**	**100**	**2.42**	**2.30**	**0.89**	**535**	**593**	**481**	**3.6**	**2.0**	**13.9**	**6.9**	**67%**	**17%**	**35**	**18**	**47**	**31%**	**78%**	**10%**	**0**						**12.4**	**208**	**248**	**$26**

Janssen,Casey

Age: 34 Th: R Role RP	Health F	LIMA Plan C	
Ht: 6' 4" Wt: 205 Type	PT/Exp C	Rand Var +3	
	Consist B	MM 2210	

Plain and simply, he never really fooled enough hitters to stick as a stopper. There's not much to like from him as middleman either. While that near-5 ERA was driven by fluky S%, steady BPV decline and ballooning xERA tell us all we need to know. Rising FB seals fate. There just aren't reasons to speculate here anymore.

Yr	Tm	W	L	Sv	IP	K	ERA	xERA	WHIP	oOPS	vL	vR	BF/G	Ctl	Dom	Cmd	FpK	SwK	G	L	F	H%	S%	hr/f	GS	APC	DOM%	DIS%	Sv%	LI	RAR	BPV	BPX	R$
11	TOR	6	0	2	56	53	2.26	3.08	1.10	594	539	659	4.1	2.3	8.6	3.8	64%	9%	47	21	31	30%	80%	4%	0	16			50	0.85	11.5	118	178	$7
12	TOR	1	1	22	64	67	2.54	2.92	0.86	564	467	666	3.9	1.6	9.5	6.1	62%	10%	43	21	36	25%	77%	12%	0	15			88	1.03	11.5	149	195	$17
13	TOR	4	1	34	53	50	2.56	3.10	0.99	558	619	458	3.8	2.2	8.5	3.8	64%	8%	48	23	30	27%	76%	7%	0	15			94	1.39	8.5	120	156	$18
14	TOR	3	3	25	46	28	3.94	4.32	1.18	697	733	669	3.8	1.4	5.5	4.0	68%	8%	34	22	44	29%	71%	9%	0	14			83	0.96	-1.1	74	88	$9
15	WAS	2	5	0	40	27	4.95	4.57	1.15	724	557	808	3.5	1.8	6.1	3.4	69%	7%	29	25	46	28%	59%	9%	0	13			0	1.06	-4.9	68	81	-$3
1st Half		0	1	0	14	5	3.21	4.69	1.07	638	499	730	3.8	1.3	3.9	3.0	63%	6%	30	30	39	28%	67%	0%	0	14			0	0.82	1.3	43	51	-$5
2nd Half		2	4	0	26	21	5.88	4.50	1.19	770	598	844	3.3	2.1	7.3	3.5	72%	7%	29	21	50	28%	54%	13%	0	12			0	1.17	-6.2	82	97	-$2
16	Proj	**4**	**4**	**2**	**58**	**46**	**4.27**	**3.90**	**1.20**	**712**	**657**	**759**	**3.6**	**2.1**	**7.1**	**3.4**	**67%**	**8%**	**39**	**22**	**40**	**30%**	**67%**	**10%**	**0**						**-2.2**	**88**	**105**	**$0**

Jeffress,Jeremy

Age: 28 Th: R Role RP	Health A	LIMA Plan A	
Ht: 6' 1" Wt: 205 Type Pwr xGB	PT/Exp D	Rand Var -1	
	Consist A	MM 4310	

High-octane RP with history of drug issues found home in pen of team that drafted him. Three reasons he's legit closer material now: 1) 4 years of Cmd gains; 2) coveted combo of Ks and GBs; 3) handled 2H high-leverage use with ease. Subpar FpK reminds us of prior bad Ctl, but that's his only risk now. UP: 30 Sv.

Yr	Tm	W	L	Sv	IP	K	ERA	xERA	WHIP	oOPS	vL	vR	BF/G	Ctl	Dom	Cmd	FpK	SwK	G	L	F	H%	S%	hr/f	GS	APC	DOM%	DIS%	Sv%	LI	RAR	BPV	BPX	R$
11	KC *	4	7	4	71	48	5.78	5.48	1.80	706	790	619	8.4	6.3	6.1	1.0	43%	8%	56	12	32	32%	68%	8%	0	22			67	1.11	-16.1	28	42	-$9
12	KC *	5	4	3	73	63	5.80	4.59	1.62	838	594	1029	6.3	4.8	7.9	1.6	53%	9%	48	26	26	35%	62%	0%	0	22			43	0.64	-16.0	66	87	-$9
13	TOR *	2	0	7	38	35	1.78	3.43	1.43	592	284	829	4.6	4.5	8.3	1.8	60%	12%	69	23	8	32%	88%	50%	0	19			88	0.67	9.7	86	113	$3
14	2 TM *	5	2	5	74	65	2.33	3.68	1.44	709	967	509	5.1	3.7	7.9	2.1	60%	7%	59	26	16	34%	83%	7%	0	16			63	0.85	12.9	90	107	$4
15	MIL	5	0	0	68	67	2.65	3.08	1.26	666	752	617	4.0	2.9	8.9	3.0	56%	12%	58	24	18	32%	81%	15%	0	15			0	1.15	11.0	117	139	$4
1st Half		2	0	0	37	37	2.89	3.15	1.26	662	739	616	4.0	2.9	8.9	3.1	55%	12%	58	22	20	32%	80%	14%	0	15			0	1.05	4.9	119	141	$3
2nd Half		3	0	0	31	30	2.35	2.99	1.27	671	765	618	3.9	2.9	8.8	3.0	56%	12%	58	27	16	32%	84%	15%	0	15			0	1.27	6.1	115	137	$5
16	Proj	**5**	**2**	**5**	**64**	**61**	**2.70**	**3.10**	**1.27**	**636**	**789**	**538**	**4.4**	**3.3**	**8.6**	**2.6**	**57%**	**10%**	**58**	**25**	**17**	**31%**	**80%**	**11%**	**0**						**10.0**	**102**	**121**	**$5**

Jepsen,Kevin

Age: 31 Th: R Role RP	Health D	LIMA Plan C+	
Ht: 6' 3" Wt: 235 Type Pwr	PT/Exp C	Rand Var -5	
	Consist C	MM 2310	

Injury to incumbent closer opened door and he handled it with aplomb, converting 10 of 11 tries. However, that success was product of friendly H%, S%, and hr/f rates more than skills, which were barely closer-worthy. Some will see ERA trend and bid on encore. You'll see yo-yo BPV as reason to speculate elsewhere.

Yr	Tm	W	L	Sv	IP	K	ERA	xERA	WHIP	oOPS	vL	vR	BF/G	Ctl	Dom	Cmd	FpK	SwK	G	L	F	H%	S%	hr/f	GS	APC	DOM%	DIS%	Sv%	LI	RAR	BPV	BPX	R$
11	LAA *	2	5	7	41	22	5.42	6.33	1.75	981	894	1068	4.7	3.6	4.7	1.3	54%	7%	55	16	29	35%	71%	13%	0	14			64	1.32	-7.6	10	14	-$4
12	LAA *	5	4	4	70	65	3.08	2.72	1.14	647	744	552	3.8	2.6	8.4	3.2	52%	9%	35	23	42	30%	73%	6%	0	14			67	1.16	8.0	112	146	$7
13	LAA	1	3	0	36	36	4.50	4.10	1.53	769	865	679	3.6	3.5	9.0	2.6	53%	9%	40	20	39	37%	71%	7%	0	15			0	1.12	-2.8	86	111	-$5
14	LAA	0	2	2	65	75	2.63	2.93	1.05	547	628	470	3.5	3.2	10.4	3.3	65%	13%	48	20	33	27%	77%	8%	0	14			50	1.04	8.9	127	151	$5
15	2 AL	3	6	15	70	59	2.33	4.03	1.13	560	653	449	3.8	3.5	7.6	2.2	57%	11%	46	20	35	25%	82%	7%	0	16			75	1.45	14.1	67	80	$11
1st Half		1	5	5	34	30	3.41	4.41	1.43	694	804	571	3.9	4.7	7.9	1.7	57%	10%	49	21	31	29%	80%	13%	0	16			56	1.72	2.3	41	48	$3
2nd Half		2	1	10	35	29	1.27	3.68	0.85	421	506	312	3.6	2.3	7.4	3.2	58%	12%	43	19	39	22%	86%	3%	0	15			91	1.17	11.7	92	109	$19
16	Proj	**2**	**4**	**5**	**58**	**54**	**3.29**	**3.74**	**1.24**	**653**	**754**	**545**	**3.7**	**3.3**	**8.4**	**2.6**	**58%**	**11%**	**44**	**20**	**36**	**30%**	**76%**	**9%**	**0**						**4.8**	**85**	**101**	**$2**

STEPHEN NICKRAND

Jimenez,Ubaldo

Age: 32	Th: R	Role SP	Health C	LIMA Plan B+	
Ht: 6' 5"	Wt: 210	Type Pwr	PT/Exp A	Rand Var +1	
			Consist B	MM 2305	

That 1H reminded us of why we used to speculate on him. Predictably, his 2H told us why we shouldn't. So-so SwK, FpK didn't support early Cmd, and given alternating <2.0 Cmd years, it's clearly a chronic issue. Without it, even improved GB tilt won't be panacea. Keep him relegated to the end of your end game.

Yr Tm	W	L	Sv	IP	K	ERA	xERA	WHIP	oOPS	vL	vR	BF/G	Ctl	Dom	Cmd	FpK	SwK	G	L	F	H%	S%	hr/f	GS	APC	DOM%	DIS%	Sv%	LI	RAR	BPV	BPX	R$
11 2 TM	10	13	0	188	180	4.68	3.72	1.40	752	710	791	25.7	3.7	8.6	2.3	53%	8%	47	20	33	32%	67%	9%	32	102	44%	22%			-17.2	79	119	-$1
12 CLE	9	17	0	177	143	5.40	5.03	1.61	817	854	778	26.0	4.8	7.3	1.5	52%	8%	38	23	38	32%	69%	12%	31	101	35%	19%			-30.2	16	21	-$16
13 CLE	13	9	0	183	194	3.30	3.66	1.33	684	661	708	24.3	3.9	9.6	2.4	58%	9%	44	20	36	31%	78%	9%	32	99	56%	19%			12.7	88	114	$11
14 BAL	6	9	0	125	116	4.81	4.47	1.52	737	779	683	22.1	5.5	8.3	1.5	55%	7%	41	22	37	29%	70%	11%	22	92	32%	36%	0	0.74	-16.5	20	23	-$7
15 BAL	12	10	0	184	168	4.11	3.81	1.36	728	702	756	24.7	3.3	8.2	2.5	60%	8%	49	22	29	32%	72%	13%	32	96	44%	22%			-3.3	85	101	$4
1st Half	7	4	0	94	93	2.96	3.46	1.23	650	642	660	24.6	2.8	8.9	3.2	61%	9%	46	26	28	31%	79%	11%	16	95	56%	19%			11.7	109	130	$15
2nd Half	5	6	0	90	75	5.32	4.19	1.49	807	768	846	24.8	3.9	7.5	1.9	60%	8%	52	19	30	32%	66%	15%	16	96	31%	25%			-15.0	59	71	-$8
16 Proj	**11**	**12**	**0**	**189**	**175**	**4.39**	**4.02**	**1.42**	**739**	**732**	**746**	**23.5**	**4.1**	**8.3**	**2.0**	**58%**	**8%**	**46**	**21**	**33**	**31%**	**71%**	**12%**	**34**						**-9.9**	**63**	**75**	**-$1**

Johnson,Erik

Age: 26	Th: R	Role SP	Health A	LIMA Plan D	
Ht: 6' 3"	Wt: 230	Type xFB	PT/Exp C	Rand Var 0	
			Consist F	MM 0101	

3-1, 3.34 ERA in 35 IP at CHW. Club's former top SP prospect finally showing that upside...or is he? Insanely high S% deserves credit for MLB ERA, so it's not repeating. One PQS DOM in six starts confirms wobbly skill base. Chronic subpar FpK offers no hope for the sustained Cmd he needs to succeed. For now, pass.

Yr Tm	W	L	Sv	IP	K	ERA	xERA	WHIP	oOPS	vL	vR	BF/G	Ctl	Dom	Cmd	FpK	SwK	G	L	F	H%	S%	hr/f	GS	APC	DOM%	DIS%	Sv%	LI	RAR	BPV	BPX	R$
11																																	
12																																	
13 CHW *	15	5	0	170	130	2.67	3.38	1.24	809	1012	491	23.8	3.1	6.9	2.3	52%	8%	46	19	35	28%	82%	15%	5	101	20%	20%			25.1	72	94	$16
14 CHW *	6	8	0	129	70	7.10	6.59	1.93	821	1105	599	24.6	5.0	4.9	1.0	50%	9%	43	24	32	36%	62%	4%	5	92	20%	40%			-53.6	13	15	-$28
15 CHW *	14	9	0	168	140	3.31	4.16	1.41	814	849	776	24.4	3.5	7.5	2.1	56%	9%	24	24	52	32%	79%	15%	6	106	17%	0%			13.5	68	81	$8
1st Half	7	5	0	85	78	3.98	4.14	1.46				24.3	3.4	8.2	2.4						35%	72%	0%	0						-0.2	86	102	$3
2nd Half	7	4	0	83	62	2.63	4.19	1.35	814	849	776	24.6	3.7	6.8	1.8	56%	9%	24	24	52	28%	87%	15%	6	106	17%	0%			13.6	49	58	$12
16 Proj	**5**	**7**	**0**	**102**	**72**	**4.20**	**5.26**	**1.46**	**701**	**735**	**666**	**23.9**	**3.7**	**6.4**	**1.7**	**56%**	**9%**	**24**	**24**	**52**	**31%**	**73%**	**5%**	**18**						**-3.0**	**17**	**20**	**-$3**

Johnson,Jim

Age: 33	Th: R	Role RP	Health A	LIMA Plan C	
Ht: 6' 6"	Wt: 240	Type xGB	PT/Exp B	Rand Var +3	
			Consist C	MM 3110	

Former back-to-back 50-saver got another dose of high-leverage work, but 10.17 ERA over final two months tells you how that worked. Lack of Ks validated by subpar SwK. Ballooning struggles vR suggest he'll struggle in a setup role too. Only savings grace - GBs, but that's not enough to make him roster-worthy again.

Yr Tm	W	L	Sv	IP	K	ERA	xERA	WHIP	oOPS	vL	vR	BF/G	Ctl	Dom	Cmd	FpK	SwK	G	L	F	H%	S%	hr/f	GS	APC	DOM%	DIS%	Sv%	LI	RAR	BPV	BPX	R$
11 BAL	6	5	9	91	58	2.67	3.32	1.11	628	567	690	5.3	2.1	5.7	2.8	64%	10%	61	15	24	27%	77%	8%	0	18			64	1.11	14.3	86	130	$12
12 BAL	2	1	51	69	41	2.49	3.41	1.02	556	581	526	3.8	2.0	5.4	2.7	57%	7%	62	16	21	25%	76%	7%	0	14			94	1.29	12.9	84	109	$27
13 BAL	3	8	50	70	56	2.94	3.17	1.28	699	740	653	3.9	2.3	7.2	3.1	61%	9%	58	20	21	32%	79%	11%	0	15			85	1.39	8.0	103	134	$22
14 2 AL	5	2	2	53	42	7.09	4.66	1.95	861	941	776	4.9	5.9	7.1	1.2	63%	8%	58	20	22	37%	63%	14%	0	18			67	0.60	-22.0	4	5	-$12
15 2 NL	2	6	10	67	50	4.46	3.67	1.46	743	675	793	4.0	2.7	6.8	2.5	61%	8%	62	17	21	34%	70%	11%	0	15			59	1.41	-4.1	89	106	-$1
1st Half	2	3	5	41	31	2.20	3.63	1.24	644	541	726	4.0	2.9	6.8	2.4	62%	10%	60	16	24	30%	84%	7%	0	14			63	1.46	8.9	83	99	$5
2nd Half	0	3	5	26	19	8.06	3.74	1.79	878	875	880	4.1	2.5	6.7	2.7	60%	6%	64	19	17	40%	53%	20%	0	15			56	1.34	-13.0	96	114	-$11
16 Proj	**3**	**5**	**5**	**65**	**49**	**4.09**	**3.56**	**1.34**	**673**	**677**	**671**	**3.9**	**2.9**	**6.8**	**2.3**	**61%**	**8%**	**61**	**19**	**21**	**31%**	**70%**	**11%**	**0**						**-1.0**	**82**	**97**	**$0**

Jones,Nate

Age: 30	Th: R	Role RP	Health F	LIMA Plan C+	
Ht: 6' 5"	Wt: 220	Type Pwr	PT/Exp D	Rand Var +1	
			Consist F	MM 5510	

Former Plan-B closer showed why he'll be in those discussions again after late elite skill flash in return from '14 TJ surgery. Prior to going under knife, ability to miss bats, get groundballs, and improved control all pointed to role expansion. If healthy, the only roadblock is opportunity. With it... UP: 30 Sv

Yr Tm	W	L	Sv	IP	K	ERA	xERA	WHIP	oOPS	vL	vR	BF/G	Ctl	Dom	Cmd	FpK	SwK	G	L	F	H%	S%	hr/f	GS	APC	DOM%	DIS%	Sv%	LI	RAR	BPV	BPX	R$
11 aa	2	3	12	63	57	4.33	4.83	1.63				6.7	4.6	8.0	1.8						36%	74%								-3.0	65	98	$0
12 CHW	8	0	0	72	65	2.39	4.00	1.38	686	528	774	4.6	4.0	8.2	2.0	55%	11%	46	23	32	31%	84%	6%	0	18			0	1.19	14.4	62	81	$5
13 CHW	4	5	0	78	89	4.15	2.87	1.22	659	710	621	4.5	3.0	10.3	3.4	61%	14%	51	21	28	33%	66%	9%	0	18			0	1.36	-2.8	133	173	$1
14 CHW	0	0	0	0	0	0.00	0.00	0.00		3000	2000	2.5	0.0	0.0	0.0						0%	20%	0%	0	15			0	1.50	0.0	-22	-26	-$5
15 CHW	2	2	0	19	27	3.32	2.51	0.95	695	567	770	3.8	2.8	12.8	4.5	59%	16%	46	14	41	21%	85%	33%	0	15			0	1.17	1.5	177	211	-$1
1st Half																																	
2nd Half	2	2	0	19	27	3.32	2.51	0.95	695	567	770	3.8	2.8	12.8	4.5	59%	16%	46	14	41	21%	85%	33%	0	15			0	1.17	1.5	177	211	-$1
16 Proj	**5**	**3**	**3**	**58**	**67**	**2.99**	**3.04**	**1.12**	**603**	**507**	**662**	**4.4**	**3.1**	**10.4**	**3.4**	**58%**	**13%**	**47**	**19**	**34**	**30%**	**75%**	**8%**	**0**						**7.0**	**130**	**154**	**$6**

Jungmann,Taylor

Age: 26	Th: R	Role SP	Health A	LIMA Plan D+	
Ht: 6' 6"	Wt: 210	Type Pwr	PT/Exp D	Rand Var +2	
			Consist A	MM 1205	

9-8, 3.77 ERA in 119 IP at MIL. Former 1st-rounder took small steps forward in MLB debut. PRO: Dom trend, especially in 2nd half; gets some GBs. CON: Mediocre FpK gives little hope for better control, decent-only SwK caps further strikeout growth; chronic 4.00+ xERA says he's not ready.

Yr Tm	W	L	Sv	IP	K	ERA	xERA	WHIP	oOPS	vL	vR	BF/G	Ctl	Dom	Cmd	FpK	SwK	G	L	F	H%	S%	hr/f	GS	APC	DOM%	DIS%	Sv%	LI	RAR	BPV	BPX	R$
11																																	
12																																	
13 aa	10	10	0	139	70	5.49	4.62	1.57				23.5	5.1	4.5	0.9						28%	65%								-27.9	21	27	-$12
14 a/a	12	10	0	154	122	4.45	4.74	1.52				23.8	3.9	7.1	1.8						33%	72%								-13.5	55	65	-$5
15 MIL *	11	11	0	179	151	4.97	4.04	1.43	703	719	688	23.7	3.9	7.6	1.9	57%	9%	46	21	33	32%	65%	10%	21	97	57%	24%			-22.2	69	82	-$5
1st Half	5	4	0	96	71	5.48	4.13	1.48	645	662	629	24.4	3.8	6.6	1.7	57%	8%	55	17	29	33%	61%	6%	6	99	83%	0%			-18.0	64	76	-$11
2nd Half	6	7	0	82	80	4.37	4.05	1.36	729	745	713	23.3	4.0	8.7	2.2	57%	9%	42	22	35	30%	70%	11%	15	97	47%	33%			-4.2	68	81	$2
16 Proj	**13**	**13**	**0**	**189**	**153**	**4.32**	**4.30**	**1.47**	**779**	**800**	**759**	**23.6**	**4.1**	**7.3**	**1.8**	**57%**	**9%**	**47**	**20**	**33**	**32%**	**72%**	**9%**	**34**						**-8.3**	**46**	**55**	**-$2**

Kahnle,Thomas

Age: 26	Th: R	Role RP	Health A	LIMA Plan D	
Ht: 6' 1"	Wt: 230	Type Pwr GB	PT/Exp D	Rand Var +3	
			Consist A	MM 1300	

0-1, 4.86 ERA in 33 IP at COL. Those strikeouts keep future closer label attached, and with full support from SwK, they'll keep coming. But when you can't find home plate, how much do they matter? Poor FpK, terrible 41% ball% give no hope that will change, so he'll continue to be relegated to low leverage work.

Yr Tm	W	L	Sv	IP	K	ERA	xERA	WHIP	oOPS	vL	vR	BF/G	Ctl	Dom	Cmd	FpK	SwK	G	L	F	H%	S%	hr/f	GS	APC	DOM%	DIS%	Sv%	LI	RAR	BPV	BPX	R$
11																																	
12																																	
13 aa	1	3	15	60	61	3.73	3.89	1.58				5.7	7.3	9.2	1.3						27%	78%								1.0	70	91	$2
14 COL	2	1	0	69	63	4.19	3.82	1.19	628	570	683	5.3	4.1	8.3	2.0	50%	11%	47	17	36	25%	67%	10%	0	20			0	0.83	-3.8	64	76	-$1
15 COL *	1	4	8	60	60	5.41	4.53	1.58	778	829	744	4.7	6.1	9.0	1.5	51%	14%	55	24	21	30%	67%	17%	0	18			67	0.83	-10.8	60	71	-$5
1st Half	1	2	4	38	42	4.40	3.65	1.36	679	981	479	4.9	4.6	9.8	2.1	54%	14%	60	23	17	30%	69%	17%	0	18			67	0.69	-2.1	86	102	-$2
2nd Half	0	2	4	22	19	7.17	6.07	1.97	866	697	981	4.4	8.7	7.6	0.9	49%	13%	51	24	24	30%	64%	17%	0	18			67	0.94	-8.7	25	30	-$10
16 Proj	**1**	**1**	**0**	**29**	**28**	**5.13**	**4.32**	**1.52**	**729**	**703**	**749**	**4.9**	**6.0**	**8.6**	**1.4**	**50%**	**13%**	**52**	**21**	**27**	**28%**	**67%**	**15%**	**0**						**-4.2**	**21**	**25**	**-$5**

Karns,Nathan

Age: 28	Th: R	Role SP	Health A	LIMA Plan B	
Ht: 6' 3"	Wt: 230	Type Pwr	PT/Exp C	Rand Var 0	
			Consist C	MM 2303	

While late ERA spike will keep bidders away, there are some solid reasons for optimism now... 1) Cmd uptick in 2H coupled with big FpK, SwK growth; 2) Those 2H gains hidden by aberrant hr/f; 3) DOM/DIS reflects high-floor profile. If those late gains stick, his rising ceiling will make him target for... UP: 3.25 ERA, 200 K.

Yr Tm	W	L	Sv	IP	K	ERA	xERA	WHIP	oOPS	vL	vR	BF/G	Ctl	Dom	Cmd	FpK	SwK	G	L	F	H%	S%	hr/f	GS	APC	DOM%	DIS%	Sv%	LI	RAR	BPV	BPX	R$
11																																	
12																																	
13 WAS *	10	7	0	145	130	4.48	4.73	1.43	1060	1266	845	23.6	3.5	8.1	2.3	64%	10%	36	31	33	32%	73%	36%	3	82	0%	100%			-10.9	59	77	-$2
14 TAM *	10	10	0	157	134	6.62	5.65	1.65	661	384	859	24.3	4.2	7.7	1.8	49%	10%	43	13	43	35%	60%	23%	2	103	50%	0%			-55.9	44	53	-$21
15 TAM	7	5	0	147	145	3.67	3.90	1.28	699	690	708	23.0	3.4	8.9	2.6	58%	10%	42	22	37	30%	76%	13%	26	90	46%	15%	0	0.80	5.2	87	104	$6
1st Half	4	4	0	98	94	3.21	3.88	1.24	652	661	638	24.2	3.5	8.6	2.5	56%	9%	44	21	35	29%	77%	10%	17	96	47%	12%			9.0	83	99	$10
2nd Half	3	1	0	49	51	4.59	3.93	1.35	791	757	819	21.0	3.3	9.4	2.8	60%	12%	38	22	40	30%	73%	18%	9	81	44%	22%	0	0.83	-3.8	95	113	-$3
16 Proj	**11**	**8**	**0**	**174**	**163**	**3.98**	**3.95**	**1.33**	**709**	**701**	**716**	**22.1**	**3.5**	**8.4**	**2.4**	**59%**	**10%**	**40**	**22**	**38**	**30%**	**73%**	**11%**	**33**						**-0.4**	**75**	**89**	**$5**

STEPHEN NICKRAND

Kazmir,Scott

Age: 32	Th: L	Role SP	Health	D	LIMA Plan	C+
Ht: 6' 0"	Wt: 185	Type Pwr	PT/Exp	A	Rand Var	-2
			Consist	A	MM	2203

It's amazing how helpful or hurtful the H% and S% pendulum can be. While skills eroded, was saved by friendly S%. Because we can't bet on that happening again, neither can we expect anything near a 3-ERA again. Rising xERA trend, big 2H skill erosion put even a 4.00 ERA at risk. He'll struggle to return a profit.

Yr Tm	W	L	Sv	IP	K	ERA	xERA	WHIP	oOPS	vL	vR	BF/G	Ctl	Dom	Cmd	FpK	SwK	G	L	F	H%	S%	hr/f	GS	APC	DOM%	DIS%	Sv%	LI	RAR	BPV	BPX	R$
11 LAA *	0	5	0	17	11	17.90	9.61	2.94	1643	2667	1214	16.3	11.1	5.8	0.5	36%	3%	30	10	60	43%	33%	17%	1	63	0%	100%			-29.3	9	14	-$16
12																																	
13 CLE	10	9	0	158	162	4.04	3.53	1.32	735	573	794	23.2	2.7	9.2	3.4	61%	11%	41	23	36	34%	73%	12%	29	95	52%	21%			-3.5	113	147	$4
14 OAK	15	9	0	190	164	3.55	3.60	1.16	648	673	641	24.3	2.4	7.8	3.3	62%	10%	44	19	37	29%	71%	8%	32	93	66%	19%			4.6	98	116	$13
15 2 AL	7	11	0	183	155	3.10	4.03	1.21	678	783	641	24.6	2.9	7.6	2.6	61%	11%	43	20	37	28%	79%	10%	31	95	48%	32%			19.5	80	95	$13
1st Half	5	5	0	98	92	2.56	3.62	1.12	610	574	622	25.0	3.0	8.4	2.8	65%	11%	46	21	33	27%	80%	8%	16	96	63%	19%			17.0	94	112	$21
2nd Half	2	6	0	85	63	3.72	4.50	1.31	752	1027	662	24.2	2.8	6.7	2.4	57%	10%	40	19	42	29%	78%	12%	15	93	33%	47%			2.5	64	75	$3
16 Proj	**9**	**10**	**0**	**174**	**151**	**3.84**	**3.83**	**1.24**	**689**	**745**	**670**	**23.6**	**2.8**	**7.8**	**2.8**	**61%**	**10%**	**43**	**20**	**38**	**30%**	**72%**	**10%**	**30**						**2.6**	**85**	**101**	**$7**

Kela,Keone

Age: 23	Th: R	Role RP	Health	A	LIMA Plan	B+
Ht: 6' 1"	Wt: 190	Type Pwr GB	PT/Exp	D	Rand Var	-3
			Consist	B	MM	5510

Sterling debut from top RP prospect. Only six relievers had a 10+ Dom and 50%+ GB%. This was one of them. And he's more than heat; see filthy 27% SwK with curveball. Further growth supported by huge 1H-2H skills surge. Even with S% regression, you can put a 3.00 ERA in stone. And speculate on... UP: 30 Sv

Yr Tm	W	L	Sv	IP	K	ERA	xERA	WHIP	oOPS	vL	vR	BF/G	Ctl	Dom	Cmd	FpK	SwK	G	L	F	H%	S%	hr/f	GS	APC	DOM%	DIS%	Sv%	LI	RAR	BPV	BPX	R$
11																																	
12																																	
13																																	
14 aa	2	1	5	39	47	2.22	2.45	1.34				4.5	6.3	11.1	1.8						28%	83%								7.3	114	135	$2
15 TEX	7	5	1	60	68	2.39	3.01	1.16	615	739	527	3.6	2.7	10.1	3.8	58%	14%	51	21	29	32%	82%	9%	0	15			25	1.21	11.7	139	166	$7
1st Half	5	5	1	34	33	3.18	3.67	1.29	664	755	574	3.8	2.9	8.7	3.0	63%	13%	48	19	32	32%	78%	9%	0	16			33	1.25	3.3	105	125	$6
2nd Half	2	0	0	26	35	1.37	2.22	0.99	545	702	473	3.3	2.4	12.0	5.0	50%	16%	54	23	23	31%	88%	8%	0	14			0	1.16	8.4	183	217	$8
16 Proj	**5**	**3**	**2**	**65**	**78**	**2.62**	**2.72**	**1.08**	**558**	**681**	**480**	**3.7**	**3.0**	**10.7**	**3.6**	**56%**	**15%**	**52**	**21**	**27**	**30%**	**76%**	**7%**	**0**						**10.8**	**143**	**170**	**$8**

Kelley,Shawn

Age: 32	Th: R	Role RP	Health	D	LIMA Plan	A
Ht: 6' 2"	Wt: 220	Type Pwr FB	PT/Exp	D	Rand Var	-2
			Consist	A	MM	4510

Typecast as a middleman these days, but not so fast. Prior xFB tilt now thing of past; see that FB% trend. With top-tier FpK teaming with impact SwK, 4.0+ Cmd is legit. Next step is opportunity, and he's had a manager's confidence in the past (LI). If the late forearm soreness is nothing serious... UP: 30 SV

Yr Tm	W	L	Sv	IP	K	ERA	xERA	WHIP	oOPS	vL	vR	BF/G	Ctl	Dom	Cmd	FpK	SwK	G	L	F	H%	S%	hr/f	GS	APC	DOM%	DIS%	Sv%	LI	RAR	BPV	BPX	R$
11 SEA *	1	1	0	30	25	0.92	2.69	1.08	417	683	226	4.7	2.7	7.3	2.7	62%	12%	38	6	56	26%	99%	0%	0	17			0	0.56	11.3	89	134	$2
12 SEA *	4	4	6	64	65	2.52	2.83	1.12	717	747	701	4.2	2.7	9.1	3.4	60%	12%	29	20	51	29%	81%	8%	0	16			67	1.00	11.8	115	150	$8
13 NYY	4	2	0	53	71	4.39	3.42	1.31	729	760	707	4.0	3.9	12.0	3.1	65%	12%	33	21	46	33%	71%	13%	0	17			0	1.33	-3.4	122	159	-$1
14 NYY	3	6	4	52	67	4.53	3.30	1.26	663	612	709	3.7	3.5	11.7	3.4	61%	15%	34	23	44	34%	65%	9%	0	15			57	1.33	-5.0	128	152	$0
15 SD	2	2	0	51	63	2.45	3.04	1.09	596	667	536	3.9	2.6	11.0	4.2	72%	15%	43	19	38	31%	81%	9%	0	15			0	0.88	9.5	149	177	$3
1st Half	1	2	0	30	33	3.64	3.35	1.21	692	910	512	4.5	2.1	10.0	4.7	76%	15%	42	18	41	34%	73%	9%	0	17			0	0.76	1.2	143	169	$1
2nd Half	1	0	0	22	30	0.83	2.64	0.92	446	290	569	3.2	3.3	12.5	3.8	67%	16%	44	22	33	26%	95%	7%	0	14			0	1.00	8.4	157	186	$7
16 Proj	**3**	**3**	**3**	**58**	**73**	**2.94**	**3.11**	**1.14**	**614**	**606**	**620**	**3.7**	**3.1**	**11.3**	**3.6**	**66%**	**14%**	**38**	**21**	**41**	**31%**	**77%**	**9%**	**0**						**7.3**	**134**	**160**	**$5**

Kelly,Joe

Age: 28	Th: R	Role SP	Health	D	LIMA Plan	B
Ht: 6' 1"	Wt: 175	Type	PT/Exp	C	Rand Var	+1
			Consist	A	MM	2103

10-6, 4.82 ERA in 134 IP at BOS. A true flamethrower, but still trying to turn stuff into skills and results. PRO: Cmd uptick supported by FpK rise, late SwK surge; three years of rising Dom. CON: Bad OPS and Cmd vR; ugly DOM% indication of game-to-game mediocrity. Don't draft him without a bench.

Yr Tm	W	L	Sv	IP	K	ERA	xERA	WHIP	oOPS	vL	vR	BF/G	Ctl	Dom	Cmd	FpK	SwK	G	L	F	H%	S%	hr/f	GS	APC	DOM%	DIS%	Sv%	LI	RAR	BPV	BPX	R$
11 aa	6	4	0	59	43	4.33	4.78	1.53				23.4	3.4	6.5	1.9						34%	72%								-2.9	54	81	-$2
12 STL *	7	12	0	179	112	3.35	4.17	1.40	740	917	607	21.0	2.8	5.6	2.0	60%	8%	52	21	27	32%	77%	11%	16	71	44%	6%	0	0.78	14.6	57	74	$3
13 STL	10	5	0	124	79	2.69	4.17	1.35	694	691	696	14.4	3.2	5.7	1.8	55%	8%	51	21	28	30%	83%	9%	15	53	33%	13%	0	0.87	18.1	46	60	$7
14 2 TM	6	4	0	96	66	4.20	4.00	1.35	693	689	695	24.4	3.9	6.2	1.6	57%	7%	55	21	24	28%	70%	11%	17	93	41%	24%			-5.5	38	45	-$2
15 BOS *	11	7	0	153	124	4.76	4.53	1.44	768	702	838	22.5	3.3	7.3	2.2	62%	8%	46	25	29	32%	68%	12%	25	95	28%	20%			-15.2	61	73	-$3
1st Half	2	6	0	88	68	5.45	4.51	1.48	756	668	849	23.6	3.8	7.0	1.9	62%	7%	48	23	29	32%	63%	11%	14	96	29%	21%			-16.1	57	67	-$12
2nd Half	9	1	0	66	55	3.85	4.56	1.37	783	745	825	21.2	2.6	7.6	2.9	62%	9%	43	28	29	32%	76%	13%	11	93	27%	18%			0.9	72	85	$7
16 Proj	**12**	**6**	**0**	**145**	**107**	**4.08**	**4.07**	**1.39**	**737**	**722**	**752**	**20.7**	**3.3**	**6.7**	**2.0**	**60%**	**8%**	**49**	**24**	**28**	**31%**	**72%**	**11%**	**30**						**-2.1**	**58**	**68**	**$1**

Kendrick,Kyle

Age: 31	Th: R	Role SP	Health	C	LIMA Plan	D+
Ht: 6' 3"	Wt: 210	Type Con	PT/Exp	A	Rand Var	+5
			Consist	A	MM	0001

Days when he used to produce sub-4 ERAs are long gone. That's hardly a surprise, since he has always needed a friendly H% or S% to deliver positive value. Sure, he's getting ahead of guys better than in past, but that steadily increasing LD% shows that they are feasting on him more than ever. Stay far away.

Yr Tm	W	L	Sv	IP	K	ERA	xERA	WHIP	oOPS	vL	vR	BF/G	Ctl	Dom	Cmd	FpK	SwK	G	L	F	H%	S%	hr/f	GS	APC	DOM%	DIS%	Sv%	LI	RAR	BPV	BPX	R$
11 PHI	8	6	0	115	59	3.22	4.27	1.22	734	766	708	14.1	2.4	4.6	2.0	60%	6%	45	19	36	27%	79%	11%	15	51	47%	40%	0	0.87	10.2	43	64	$6
12 PHI	11	12	0	159	116	3.90	4.21	1.27	731	701	760	18.2	2.8	6.6	2.4	63%	10%	47	18	36	29%	73%	11%	25	68	52%	28%	0	1.06	2.3	68	89	$6
13 PHI	10	13	0	182	110	4.70	4.24	1.40	751	679	812	26.7	2.3	5.4	2.3	63%	7%	49	20	31	32%	67%	10%	30	96	47%	23%			-18.7	62	81	-$5
14 PHI	10	13	0	199	121	4.61	4.35	1.36	769	826	725	27.0	2.6	5.5	2.1	63%	8%	45	21	35	30%	69%	11%	32	97	56%	16%			-21.4	52	62	-$5
15 COL	7	13	0	142	80	6.32	5.10	1.52	924	980	876	23.3	2.8	5.1	1.8	64%	7%	39	22	39	30%	64%	17%	27	82	19%	44%			-41.4	31	37	-$17
1st Half	3	10	0	102	54	6.00	5.06	1.45	893	941	851	26.4	2.6	4.8	1.9	63%	6%	39	23	39	29%	64%	17%	17	92	18%	35%			-25.6	33	40	-$18
2nd Half	4	3	0	40	26	7.14	5.21	1.71	1003	1071	940	18.1	3.6	5.8	1.6	65%	7%	39	20	41	33%	63%	19%	10	66	20%	60%			-15.8	25	30	-$15
16 Proj	**7**	**9**	**0**	**116**	**70**	**5.56**	**4.66**	**1.48**	**859**	**895**	**828**	**21.6**	**2.8**	**5.4**	**1.9**	**64%**	**7%**	**43**	**21**	**37**	**31%**	**66%**	**14%**	**23**						**-22.8**	**42**	**50**	**-$9**

Kennedy,Ian

Age: 31	Th: R	Role SP	Health	B	LIMA Plan	B+
Ht: 6' 0"	Wt: 190	Type Pwr	PT/Exp	A	Rand Var	+3
			Consist	A	MM	3405

It would be easy to view '14 as an aberration, since return of 4+ ERA gives him three in four years. But only reason it reached that threshold was fluky hr/f. Another year of BPV gains—coupled with 2nd half spike of same— makes '14 much more likely than '15. Among established SP, this one has sneaky profit potential.

Yr Tm	W	L	Sv	IP	K	ERA	xERA	WHIP	oOPS	vL	vR	BF/G	Ctl	Dom	Cmd	FpK	SwK	G	L	F	H%	S%	hr/f	GS	APC	DOM%	DIS%	Sv%	LI	RAR	BPV	BPX	R$
11 ARI	21	4	0	222	198	2.88	3.50	1.09	641	656	626	27.3	2.2	8.0	3.6	64%	9%	39	22	40	28%	77%	8%	33	104	70%	6%			29.1	101	152	$28
12 ARI	15	12	0	208	187	4.02	4.06	1.30	775	790	759	27.2	2.4	8.1	3.4	65%	11%	37	21	42	32%	73%	11%	33	102	58%	9%			-0.1	96	126	$9
13 2 NL	7	10	0	181	163	4.91	4.14	1.40	781	828	736	25.6	3.6	8.1	2.2	62%	10%	38	23	39	31%	68%	13%	31	100	48%	19%			-23.4	64	83	-$6
14 SD	13	13	0	201	207	3.63	3.56	1.29	698	689	706	25.6	3.1	9.3	3.0	64%	11%	40	23	38	32%	73%	8%	33	103	70%	3%			2.8	100	119	$9
15 SD	9	15	0	168	174	4.28	3.74	1.30	815	842	788	23.8	2.8	9.3	3.3	61%	11%	38	23	39	31%	74%	17%	30	97	60%	20%			-6.5	108	129	$4
1st Half	4	8	0	80	74	4.84	3.89	1.31	861	805	925	22.6	2.6	8.3	3.2	60%	11%	39	24	37	30%	71%	21%	15	93	53%	27%			-8.6	97	115	-$2
2nd Half	5	7	0	88	100	3.77	3.60	1.28	774	880	681	24.9	3.0	10.2	3.4	62%	11%	38	22	40	32%	76%	14%	15	101	67%	13%			2.1	120	142	$8
16 Proj	**11**	**13**	**0**	**180**	**181**	**3.69**	**3.66**	**1.26**	**725**	**746**	**705**	**24.0**	**3.0**	**9.1**	**3.1**	**63%**	**11%**	**39**	**23**	**39**	**31%**	**74%**	**10%**	**31**						**6.1**	**100**	**119**	**$10**

Kershaw,Clayton

Age: 28	Th: L	Role SP	Health	C	LIMA Plan	C
Ht: 6' 3"	Wt: 225	Type Pwr	PT/Exp	A	Rand Var	-1
			Consist	A	MM	5505

Over last five years, this ace ranks first among SP in wins, ERA, WHIP, Ks and is second in Cmd and SwK. Another uptick in SwK gives full support to double-digit Dom. Elite FpK solidifies recent pinpoint control. And rising BPV trend, additional spike in 2nd half favor return of sub-2 ERA. Wow. Just wow.

Yr Tm	W	L	Sv	IP	K	ERA	xERA	WHIP	oOPS	vL	vR	BF/G	Ctl	Dom	Cmd	FpK	SwK	G	L	F	H%	S%	hr/f	GS	APC	DOM%	DIS%	Sv%	LI	RAR	BPV	BPX	R$
11 LA	21	5	0	233	248	2.28	2.95	0.98	554	512	563	27.6	2.1	9.6	4.6	64%	12%	43	18	39	28%	79%	7%	33	105	88%	3%			48.0	137	206	$40
12 LA	14	9	0	228	229	2.53	3.23	1.02	593	570	599	27.3	2.5	9.1	3.6	65%	11%	47	19	34	27%	78%	8%	33	105	82%	6%			41.7	121	157	$36
13 LA	16	9	0	236	232	1.83	2.93	0.92	521	477	532	27.5	2.0	8.8	4.5	65%	12%	46	23	31	26%	82%	6%	33	104	88%	3%			59.2	130	169	$44
14 LA	21	3	0	198	239	1.77	2.27	0.86	521	477	531	27.7	1.4	10.8	7.7	69%	15%	52	19	29	29%	81%	7%	27	101	93%	4%			48.2	187	223	$40
15 LA	16	7	0	233	301	2.13	2.31	0.88	521	554	511	27.0	1.6	11.6	7.2	68%	16%	50	22	28	29%	79%	10%	33	103	88%	3%			52.7	194	231	$47
1st Half	5	6	0	114	147	3.08	2.45	1.04	608	610	607	26.7	2.1	11.6	5.4	64%	16%	51	23	25	31%	74%	16%	17	102	88%	0%			12.4	181	214	$31
2nd Half	11	1	0	119	154	1.21	2.18	0.73	432	493	414	27.3	1.1	11.7	10.3	72%	17%	49	20	31	27%	86%	5%	16	104	88%	6%			40.2	206	245	$62
16 Proj	**18**	**6**	**0**	**225**	**270**	**1.94**	**2.41**	**0.88**	**518**	**519**	**518**	**26.5**	**1.6**	**10.8**	**6.6**	**68%**	**15%**	**49**	**21**	**30**	**28%**	**80%**	**8%**	**31**						**56.1**	**177**	**211**	**$46**

STEPHEN NICKRAND

Keuchel,Dallas			Health	A	LIMA Plan	D+
Age: 28	Th: L	Role: SP	PT/Exp	A	Rand Var	0
Ht: 6' 3"	Wt: 210	Type: xGB	Consist	A	MM	5305

After this splendid follow-up to '14 breakout, he's firmly among the elite. Sure, touch of hit and strand rate friendship helped pushed 1H ERA down. But he's a legit 3.00-ERA guy now; see sterling DOM/DIS%. SwK-fueled elite 2H suggests it's a level he can maintain, and as an extreme GBer, his blowup risk is very low.

Yr Tm	W	L	Sv	IP	K	ERA	xERA	WHIP	oOPS	vL	vR	BF/G	Ctl	Dom	Cmd	FpK	SwK	G	L	F	H%	S%	hr/f	GS	APC	DOM%	DIS%	Sv%	LI	RAR	BPV	BPX	R$
11 a/a	10	7	0	164	79	4.53	4.37	1.36				25.3	2.1	4.3	2.1						31%	67%								-11.8	43	65	-$1
12 HOU *	9	12	0	178	81	4.56	4.48	1.40	823	750	844	23.4	2.9	4.1	1.4	55%	6%	52	17	31	29%	69%	16%	16	87	19%	38%			-12.0	25	33	-$5
13 HOU	6	10	0	154	123	5.15	3.72	1.54	812	750	832	22.0	3.0	7.2	2.4	63%	9%	56	21	23	35%	69%	17%	22	81	36%	18%	0	0.90	-24.4	81	106	-$11
14 HOU	12	9	0	200	146	2.93	3.07	1.18	655	595	674	27.9	2.2	6.6	3.0	65%	9%	64	17	19	30%	76%	10%	29	104	59%	3%			20.1	102	121	$15
15 HOU	20	8	0	232	216	2.48	2.80	1.02	575	453	608	27.6	2.0	8.4	4.2	61%	11%	62	19	20	28%	79%	14%	33	106	76%	3%			42.3	137	164	$37
1st Half	10	3	0	124	102	2.03	2.87	0.96	519	341	566	28.2	2.2	7.4	3.3	62%	10%	65	20	15	25%	81%	13%	17	106	71%	0%			29.7	115	136	$43
2nd Half	10	5	0	108	114	3.01	2.74	1.09	638	574	656	26.9	1.7	9.5	5.7	61%	12%	58	17	25	31%	76%	14%	16	106	81%	6%			12.7	163	193	$30
16 Proj	**16**	**10**	**0**	**210**	**187**	**3.01**	**2.95**	**1.12**	**621**	**545**	**643**	**25.3**	**2.1**	**8.0**	**3.9**	**62%**	**10%**	**60**	**18**	**22**	**30%**	**75%**	**11%**	**33**						**24.7**	**126**	**150**	**$23**

Kimbrel,Craig			Health	A	LIMA Plan	C+
Age: 28	Th: R	Role: RP	PT/Exp	A	Rand Var	0
Ht: 5' 11"	Wt: 220	Type: Pwr	Consist	A	MM	5530

As we watch that R$ drop closer to $20 after another ERA and xERA uptick, some will remove him from among top-tier of stoppers. Not so fast. This ERA spike was fueled by funky hr/f, not lack of skill, so it's headed back down. Strong finish cements elite status. For first time in years, there's profit potential now.

Yr Tm	W	L	Sv	IP	K	ERA	xERA	WHIP	oOPS	vL	vR	BF/G	Ctl	Dom	Cmd	FpK	SwK	G	L	F	H%	S%	hr/f	GS	APC	DOM%	DIS%	Sv%	LI	RAR	BPV	BPX	R$
11 ATL	4	3	46	77	127	2.10	2.21	1.04	499	442	549	3.9	3.7	14.8	4.0	55%	16%	45	15	40	33%	81%	5%	0	17			85	1.32	17.5	189	284	$29
12 ATL	3	1	42	63	116	1.01	1.43	0.65	358	331	387	3.7	2.0	16.7	8.3	71%	20%	49	19	32	28%	89%	10%	0	15			93	1.29	23.3	273	356	$34
13 ATL	4	3	50	67	98	1.21	2.12	0.88	487	574	393	3.8	2.7	13.2	4.9	56%	14%	47	24	29	28%	91%	10%	0	15			93	1.30	22.0	189	247	$32
14 ATL	0	3	47	62	95	1.61	2.36	0.91	430	425	436	3.9	3.8	13.9	3.7	58%	17%	41	23	35	26%	83%	5%	0	17			92	1.44	16.2	166	198	$26
15 SD	4	2	39	59	87	2.58	2.61	1.04	569	629	508	3.9	3.3	13.2	4.0	61%	16%	46	20	34	30%	80%	14%	0	17			91	1.49	10.1	171	204	$22
1st Half	1	2	21	31	44	3.19	2.96	1.29	681	757	596	3.9	4.1	12.8	3.1	63%	17%	41	26	33	35%	78%	13%	0	15			95	1.47	2.9	140	166	$18
2nd Half	3	0	18	28	43	1.91	2.26	0.78	443	470	416	4.0	2.5	13.7	5.4	59%	14%	52	12	36	23%	84%	14%	0	18			86	1.51	7.2	207	246	$27
16 Proj	**3**	**2**	**41**	**65**	**99**	**1.95**	**2.25**	**0.93**	**495**	**528**	**460**	**3.7**	**3.2**	**13.7**	**4.3**	**59%**	**16%**	**46**	**20**	**34**	**28%**	**83%**	**11%**	**0**						**16.2**	**183**	**218**	**$26**

Kluber,Corey			Health	B	LIMA Plan	C
Age: 30	Th: R	Role: SP	PT/Exp	A	Rand Var	0
Ht: 6' 4"	Wt: 215	Type: Pwr	Consist	A	MM	5405

On surface, a big step back from '14 breakout. But this was the same pitcher both years. After hit, strand, and hr/f gods were firmly on his side that year, regression in those marks and a few more FBs sent ERA above 3.00. That GB/FB is the only concern here; long history of GB tilt favors return to it. A low-risk 3-ERA target.

Yr Tm	W	L	Sv	IP	K	ERA	xERA	WHIP	oOPS	vL	vR	BF/G	Ctl	Dom	Cmd	FpK	SwK	G	L	F	H%	S%	hr/f	GS	APC	DOM%	DIS%	Sv%	LI	RAR	BPV	BPX	R$
11 CLE *	7	11	0	155	121	6.46	5.45	1.64	740	900	286	23.1	4.2	7.0	1.7	68%	12%	27	47	27	34%	61%	0%	0	30			0	0.15	-48.0	41	61	-$19
12 CLE *	13	12	0	188	157	4.53	4.91	1.52	834	860	801	24.7	3.2	7.5	2.3	57%	12%	45	22	33	35%	71%	13%	12	90	33%	25%			-12.1	64	84	-$5
13 CLE	11	5	0	147	136	3.85	3.25	1.26	729	751	704	23.4	2.0	8.3	4.1	60%	11%	46	26	29	33%	72%	12%	24	88	42%	17%	0	0.73	0.3	119	155	$6
14 CLE	18	9	0	236	269	2.44	2.74	1.09	624	687	553	28.0	1.9	10.3	5.3	64%	12%	48	21	31	33%	80%	7%	34	103	82%	9%			37.7	158	189	$30
15 CLE	9	16	0	222	245	3.49	3.07	1.05	650	740	549	27.7	1.8	9.9	5.4	63%	13%	42	22	36	30%	70%	11%	32	102	78%	6%			13.0	150	178	$22
1st Half	3	9	0	119	141	3.64	2.80	1.14	668	773	557	28.2	1.8	10.7	5.9	65%	14%	46	22	31	35%	69%	10%	17	104	76%	0%			4.7	168	199	$19
2nd Half	6	7	0	103	104	3.31	3.37	0.96	629	704	539	27.1	1.8	9.1	5.0	62%	12%	38	21	41	26%	71%	12%	15	100	80%	13%			8.3	130	154	$25
16 Proj	**15**	**11**	**0**	**218**	**227**	**3.04**	**3.02**	**1.08**	**640**	**703**	**568**	**25.4**	**1.9**	**9.4**	**5.0**	**62%**	**12%**	**45**	**21**	**34**	**31%**	**74%**	**9%**	**33**						**24.6**	**142**	**169**	**$25**

Knebel,Corey			Health	A	LIMA Plan	A
Age: 24	Th: R	Role: RP	PT/Exp	F	Rand Var	+2
Ht: 6' 3"	Wt: 195	Type: Pwr	Consist	D	MM	4510

0-0, 3.22 ERA in 50 IP at MIL. Late hr/f spike, low-leverage use hid huge 2nd half skill spike. Risk is control; history of wildness, subpar FpK both suggest caution there. But with all those Ks and a GB tilt, don't let that prevent you from investing. A premium growth stock among young RP and immediate LIMA gem.

Yr Tm	W	L	Sv	IP	K	ERA	xERA	WHIP	oOPS	vL	vR	BF/G	Ctl	Dom	Cmd	FpK	SwK	G	L	F	H%	S%	hr/f	GS	APC	DOM%	DIS%	Sv%	LI	RAR	BPV	BPX	R$
11																																	
12																																	
13																																	
14 DET *	5	1	3	54	64	3.06	2.28	1.13	776	733	826	5.1	4.1	10.6	2.6	59%	9%	48	16	36	27%	74%	0%	0	21			50	0.37	4.6	119	142	$4
15 MIL *	1	2	6	66	77	3.68	3.95	1.28	744	764	728	4.2	3.3	10.5	3.2	58%	10%	49	20	31	32%	76%	20%	0	17			75	0.49	2.3	98	117	$2
1st Half	1	2	6	37	38	3.90	3.84	1.30	721	616	801	4.3	3.5	9.2	2.7	60%	10%	50	20	30	31%	73%	17%	0	18			86	0.43	0.3	86	102	$3
2nd Half	0	0	0	29	39	3.41	2.88	1.24	759	872	676	4.2	3.1	12.1	3.9	56%	11%	49	19	32	33%	81%	22%	0	17			0	0.53	2.0	161	191	$1
16 Proj	**3**	**1**	**1**	**58**	**70**	**3.38**	**3.06**	**1.22**	**687**	**709**	**671**	**4.5**	**3.6**	**10.8**	**3.0**	**58%**	**10%**	**49**	**20**	**31**	**31%**	**76%**	**14%**	**0**						**4.2**	**125**	**148**	**$2**

Koehler,Tom			Health	A	LIMA Plan	B
Age: 30	Th: R	Role: SP	PT/Exp	A	Rand Var	0
Ht: 6' 2"	Wt: 235	Type: Pwr	Consist	A	MM	1105

Once upon a time, a near-4 ERA and 1.30ish WHIP would be of value in the middle of your rotation. In today's pitching-heavy world, not so much. Mediocre Cmd will continue due to marginal FpK, SwK, history of near-4 Ctl. Steadily rising xERA trend seals fate. There's nothing here worth speculating on.

Yr Tm	W	L	Sv	IP	K	ERA	xERA	WHIP	oOPS	vL	vR	BF/G	Ctl	Dom	Cmd	FpK	SwK	G	L	F	H%	S%	hr/f	GS	APC	DOM%	DIS%	Sv%	LI	RAR	BPV	BPX	R$
11 aaa	12	7	0	150	94	5.09	4.72	1.56				23.5	4.7	5.6	1.2						30%	68%								-21.4	33	50	-$8
12 MIA *	12	12	0	164	130	5.28	5.74	1.67	896	818	941	19.9	4.0	7.1	1.8	61%	5%	24	27	49	35%	70%	20%	1	26	0%	0%	0	0.70	-25.6	41	53	-$15
13 MIA *	5	12	0	166	106	4.31	3.99	1.37	754	706	796	21.1	3.7	5.7	1.6	59%	8%	48	22	30	28%	70%	10%	23	78	39%	30%	0	0.72	-9.2	45	59	-$4
14 MIA	10	10	0	191	153	3.81	4.06	1.30	691	649	737	25.1	3.3	7.2	2.2	59%	9%	43	18	39	29%	72%	7%	32	92	56%	9%			-1.6	60	72	$4
15 MIA	11	14	0	187	137	4.08	4.53	1.37	739	760	717	25.0	3.7	6.6	1.8	58%	8%	46	18	36	29%	73%	11%	31	93	45%	16%	0	0.77	-2.8	43	51	$2
1st Half	7	4	0	92	66	3.52	4.30	1.24	699	749	643	23.7	3.0	6.5	2.1	59%	7%	46	17	37	27%	76%	12%	15	89	53%	20%	0	0.78	5.0	58	69	$10
2nd Half	4	10	0	95	71	4.63	4.75	1.50	776	770	784	26.3	4.3	6.7	1.5	58%	8%	46	19	34	31%	71%	10%	16	97	38%	13%			-7.8	28	33	-$6
16 Proj	**10**	**13**	**0**	**181**	**133**	**4.36**	**4.45**	**1.42**	**756**	**742**	**771**	**23.9**	**3.7**	**6.6**	**1.8**	**59%**	**8%**	**45**	**19**	**36**	**30%**	**71%**	**9%**	**32**						**-8.9**	**41**	**49**	**-$2**

Kontos,George			Health	A	LIMA Plan	B
Age: 31	Th: R	Role: RP	PT/Exp	D	Rand Var	-5
Ht: 6' 3"	Wt: 215	Type:	Consist	C	MM	2100

This was the first year he didn't spend the summer riding the Frisco-Fresno shuttle, and it would seem his numbers were roster-worthy in a deep NL league. But he never made it out of the free agent pool in Tout Wars-NL, which shows that the touts recognized the weak skills support to the nice ERA/WHIP.

Yr Tm	W	L	Sv	IP	K	ERA	xERA	WHIP	oOPS	vL	vR	BF/G	Ctl	Dom	Cmd	FpK	SwK	G	L	F	H%	S%	hr/f	GS	APC	DOM%	DIS%	Sv%	LI	RAR	BPV	BPX	R$
11 NYY *	4	4	2	95	78	3.74	5.06	1.37	625	400	691	8.5	3.1	7.3	2.3	52%	18%	20	7	73	29%	82%	9%	0	13			67	0.37	2.4	40	60	$1
12 SF *	4	1	1	75	64	2.14	2.33	1.04	591	468	653	4.3	2.2	7.7	3.5	60%	13%	51	15	34	28%	81%	8%	0	15			50	0.62	17.4	116	152	$9
13 SF *	5	4	4	79	67	4.38	4.14	1.30	788	1024	689	4.6	2.4	7.6	3.2	65%	11%	38	25	37	32%	69%	11%	0	17			67	1.01	-5.0	82	106	$1
14 SF *	7	3	4	80	71	2.85	2.87	1.16	587	498	635	5.9	2.5	7.9	3.2	56%	10%	39	18	43	30%	76%	3%	0	20			67	0.56	8.8	108	128	$8
15 SF	4	4	0	73	44	2.33	3.98	0.94	595	684	544	3.9	1.5	5.4	3.7	58%	10%	43	22	35	23%	83%	11%	0	14			0	1.00	14.7	78	93	$8
1st Half	2	1	0	41	26	1.74	3.73	0.82	527	459	557	4.0	1.1	5.7	5.2	62%	11%	41	24	34	22%	87%	10%	0	14			0	0.68	11.3	92	109	$11
2nd Half	2	3	0	32	18	3.09	4.30	1.09	679	889	523	3.7	2.0	5.1	2.6	53%	10%	44	20	36	24%	80%	14%	0	15			0	1.37	3.4	60	71	$4
16 Proj	**4**	**3**	**0**	**58**	**44**	**3.55**	**3.85**	**1.20**	**713**	**776**	**677**	**4.6**	**2.1**	**6.9**	**3.3**	**58%**	**11%**	**42**	**21**	**37**	**30%**	**74%**	**10%**	**0**						**3.0**	**88**	**105**	**$1**

Lackey,John			Health	F	LIMA Plan	D+
Age: 37	Th: R	Role: SP	PT/Exp	A	Rand Var	-3
Ht: 6' 6"	Wt: 235	Type:	Consist	A	MM	2205

Best season since '07, and at age 36 nonetheless. Before you bank on a repeat, three reasons for caution: 1) Skills no better than last two years; 2) Inflated S% won't repeat—that was reason for sub-3 ERA; 3) Even with now-elite FpK, SwK is at his max, so Cmd likely has peaked. Bid using mid-3s ERA as baseline.

Yr Tm	W	L	Sv	IP	K	ERA	xERA	WHIP	oOPS	vL	vR	BF/G	Ctl	Dom	Cmd	FpK	SwK	G	L	F	H%	S%	hr/f	GS	APC	DOM%	DIS%	Sv%	LI	RAR	BPV	BPX	R$
11 BOS	12	12	0	160	108	6.41	4.63	1.62	852	915	778	26.5	3.2	6.1	1.9	61%	7%	40	22	37	35%	61%	10%	28	102	29%	32%			-48.7	42	64	-$17
12																																	
13 BOS	10	13	0	189	161	3.52	3.50	1.16	703	657	760	26.8	1.9	7.7	4.0	64%	10%	47	18	35	29%	75%	13%	29	99	66%	10%			8.1	111	145	$12
14 2 TM	14	10	0	198	164	3.82	3.67	1.28	730	719	742	26.9	2.1	7.5	3.5	68%	10%	44	22	34	32%	74%	12%	31	99	65%	13%			-1.9	99	117	$6
15 STL	13	10	0	218	175	2.77	3.81	1.21	679	749	620	27.2	2.2	7.2	3.3	71%	10%	46	21	33	30%	81%	10%	33	95	61%	9%			32.2	95	113	$21
1st Half	6	5	0	104	77	3.30	4.14	1.24	681	745	620	27.3	2.3	6.7	3.0	71%	9%	45	20	35	31%	75%	7%	16	93	50%	13%			8.5	82	97	$14
2nd Half	7	5	0	114	98	2.28	3.52	1.18	678	754	621	27.0	2.1	7.7	3.6	71%	10%	48	21	31	30%	87%	13%	17	96	71%	6%			23.7	107	127	$27
16 Proj	**13**	**11**	**0**	**203**	**164**	**3.65**	**3.74**	**1.26**	**715**	**747**	**684**	**26.3**	**2.2**	**7.3**	**3.3**	**68%**	**10%**	**45**	**21**	**34**	**31%**	**74%**	**11%**	**31**						**7.9**	**94**	**112**	**$10**

STEPHEN NICKRAND

Lamb,John

Age: 25 Th: L Role SP	Health A	LIMA Plan D+	
Ht: 6' 3" Wt: 195 Type Pwr FB	PT/Exp D	Rand Var +2	
	Consist B	MM 1203	

1-5, 5.80 ERA in 50 IP at CIN. PRO: finally regained velocity he owned prior to 2011 TJ surgery; flashed intriguing small sample skills (10.5 Dom, 3.4 Ctl in MLB). CON: impressive SwK% doesn't quite support MLB Dom; plagued by occasional wildness and gopheritis. Still work to do, but worthy of a late-round flyer.

Yr Tm	W	L	Sv	IP	K	ERA	xERA	WHIP	oOPS	vL	vR	BF/G	Ctl	Dom	Cmd	FpK	SwK	G	L	F	H%	S%	hr/f	GS	APC	DOM%	DIS%	Sv%	LI	RAR	BPV	BPX	R$
11 aa	1	2	0	35	18	3.25	3.85	1.35				18.2	3.1	4.7	1.5						29%	77%								3.0	43	65	-$2
12																																	
13 aaa	1	2	0	16	8	8.28	4.45	1.53				23.2	4.0	4.6	1.1						31%	42%								-8.7	33	43	-$7
14 aaa	8	10	0	138	104	4.30	5.14	1.56				22.5	4.2	6.8	1.6						32%	76%								-9.6	38	46	-$6
15 CIN *	11	7	0	161	158	4.29	4.69	1.45	852	1156	770	22.9	3.3	8.8	2.7	59%	11%	38	22	41	35%	73%	14%	10	91	40%	30%			-6.4	77	92	-$1
1st Half	9	1	0	79	65	3.55	4.61	1.41				23.9	3.3	7.4	2.2						31%	79%	0%	0						4.0	57	67	$7
2nd Half	2	6	0	82	93	5.00	4.76	1.50	852	1156	770	22.1	3.3	10.2	3.1	59%	11%	38	22	41	38%	67%	14%	10	91	40%	30%			-10.5	97	115	-$8
16 Proj	7	9	0	160	135	4.11	4.48	1.45	701	958	632	21.7	3.6	7.6	2.1	59%	11%	38	22	41	32%	74%	8%	31						-3.0	56	66	-$2

Latos,Mat

Age: 28 Th: R Role SP	Health D	LIMA Plan C	
Ht: 6' 6" Wt: 245 Type	PT/Exp B	Rand Var +3	
	Consist A	MM 2203	

Limited by injuries (knee) again in 2015. Unsightly ERA, but S% and hr/f played a large role (see xERA). Many of his skills (Dom, SwK%, Cmd, GB%) were in line with pre-2014 levels, and he regained roughly half of the 2 mph velocity loss from 2014. If health cooperates, RandVar confirms there is sneaky value here.

Yr Tm	W	L	Sv	IP	K	ERA	xERA	WHIP	oOPS	vL	vR	BF/G	Ctl	Dom	Cmd	FpK	SwK	G	L	F	H%	S%	hr/f	GS	APC	DOM%	DIS%	Sv%	LI	RAR	BPV	BPX	R$
11 SD	9	14	0	194	185	3.47	3.57	1.18	655	697	607	25.8	2.9	8.6	3.0	60%	11%	43	16	41	30%	72%	7%	31	102	71%	3%			11.2	98	147	$14
12 CIN	14	4	0	209	185	3.48	3.75	1.16	681	753	608	26.0	2.8	8.0	2.9	62%	11%	46	18	36	28%	74%	12%	33	99	52%	12%			13.7	93	121	$19
13 CIN	14	7	0	211	187	3.16	3.56	1.21	668	699	642	27.5	2.5	8.0	3.2	64%	11%	45	21	34	31%	75%	7%	32	101	66%	6%			18.3	100	130	$17
14 CIN *	7	5	0	126	87	3.33	3.66	1.24	652	609	691	24.3	2.5	6.2	2.4	59%	8%	38	22	40	29%	76%	7%	16	96	63%	6%			6.4	68	81	$5
15 3 TM	4	10	0	116	100	4.95	3.89	1.31	742	803	688	20.6	2.5	7.7	3.1	61%	11%	44	24	32	32%	63%	12%	21	75	38%	33%	0	0.76	-14.2	94	112	-$4
1st Half	3	6	0	75	67	4.90	4.03	1.31	721	772	673	23.0	2.9	8.0	2.8	63%	11%	41	25	34	32%	63%	9%	14	85	43%	21%			-8.7	86	102	-$3
2nd Half	1	4	0	41	33	5.05	3.64	1.29	782	866	714	17.2	1.8	7.2	4.1	58%	11%	49	23	28	32%	64%	17%	7	62	29%	57%	0	0.77	-5.5	110	131	-$6
16 Proj	7	9	0	145	119	3.71	3.78	1.26	720	754	690	21.4	2.4	7.4	3.1	60%	10%	44	22	34	31%	74%	10%	28						4.6	89	106	$5

Leake,Mike

Age: 28 Th: R Role SP	Health B	LIMA Plan C+	
Ht: 5' 10" Wt: 190 Type Con GB	PT/Exp A	Rand Var 0	
	Consist A	MM 2005	

Calling cards of Ctl/GB% remained strong, but gave back 2014 Dom gains that had unlocked a higher level. Without those additional Ks, he's at mercy of H%/S% and hr/f fluctuations. A new home park might offer some shelter on hr/f going forward, but he needs more than that to be better than average.

Yr Tm	W	L	Sv	IP	K	ERA	xERA	WHIP	oOPS	vL	vR	BF/G	Ctl	Dom	Cmd	FpK	SwK	G	L	F	H%	S%	hr/f	GS	APC	DOM%	DIS%	Sv%	LI	RAR	BPV	BPX	R$
11 CIN	12	9	0	168	118	3.86	3.64	1.17	714	743	688	23.9	2.0	6.3	3.1	58%	8%	48	21	31	28%	72%	14%	26	88	50%	12%	0	0.81	1.6	85	128	$10
12 CIN	8	9	0	179	116	4.58	4.00	1.35	805	806	803	25.2	2.1	5.8	2.8	63%	7%	49	25	27	31%	70%	17%	30	90	40%	27%			-12.4	76	100	-$3
13 CIN	14	7	0	192	122	3.37	3.93	1.25	719	717	721	25.8	2.2	5.7	2.5	59%	7%	49	21	30	29%	77%	12%	31	94	42%	10%			11.8	69	90	$11
14 CIN	11	13	0	214	164	3.70	3.45	1.25	730	801	674	27.3	2.1	6.9	3.3	60%	8%	53	20	26	31%	73%	13%	33	97	58%	3%			1.2	98	117	$7
15 2 NL	11	10	0	192	119	3.70	3.95	1.16	686	727	635	25.9	2.3	5.6	2.4	61%	7%	52	22	27	26%	72%	14%	30	92	47%	17%			6.1	68	81	$11
1st Half	5	5	0	107	69	4.39	3.98	1.29	739	792	673	26.4	2.5	5.8	2.3	60%	7%	52	24	23	29%	69%	18%	17	94	41%	18%			-5.6	67	79	$4
2nd Half	6	5	0	85	50	2.85	3.90	1.00	615	641	583	25.4	2.0	5.3	2.6	63%	7%	51	18	31	23%	75%	10%	13	89	54%	15%			11.7	70	83	$19
16 Proj	11	10	0	189	124	3.87	3.80	1.23	722	757	684	25.7	2.2	5.9	2.7	61%	7%	51	21	28	29%	71%	13%	30						2.2	77	92	$8

Lee,Cliff

Age: 37 Th: L Role SP	Health F	LIMA Plan C+	
Ht: 6' 3" Wt: 205 Type	PT/Exp B	Rand Var 0	
	Consist A	MM 4300	

Missed entire 2015 season due to a tear in the flexor tendon in his left elbow. Opted for third rehab attempt instead of surgery in March 2015, but was unable to take the mound. It appears his career could be over. If he is done, he finishes with with 143 wins, 3.52 ERA, 4 All-Star teams and 2008 AL Cy Young award.

Yr Tm	W	L	Sv	IP	K	ERA	xERA	WHIP	oOPS	vL	vR	BF/G	Ctl	Dom	Cmd	FpK	SwK	G	L	F	H%	S%	hr/f	GS	APC	DOM%	DIS%	Sv%	LI	RAR	BPV	BPX	R$
11 PHI	17	8	0	233	238	2.40	2.83	1.03	607	518	634	28.8	1.6	9.2	5.7	65%	10%	46	21	32	30%	80%	9%	32	106	81%	9%			44.3	146	219	$35
12 PHI	6	9	0	211	207	3.16	3.23	1.11	690	626	707	28.2	1.2	8.8	7.4	71%	9%	45	18	37	32%	77%	12%	30	103	80%	3%			22.3	150	195	$20
13 PHI	14	8	0	223	222	2.87	2.94	1.01	631	537	659	28.3	1.3	9.0	6.9	68%	10%	44	22	33	30%	76%	11%	31	105	77%	0%			27.4	149	194	$29
14 PHI	4	5	0	81	72	3.65	3.36	1.38	762	536	815	27.1	1.3	8.0	6.0	65%	8%	48	22	30	37%	75%	9%	13	98	46%	15%			0.9	134	159	-$1
15																																	
1st Half																																	
2nd Half																																	
16 Proj	1	1	0	29	28	3.13	3.14	1.16	689	565	723	27.2	1.3	8.7	6.6	68%	9%	46	21	33	33%	77%	10%	4						3.0	144	172	-$1

Lester,Jon

Age: 32 Th: L Role SP	Health A	LIMA Plan C+	
Ht: 6' 4" Wt: 240 Type Pwr	PT/Exp A	Rand Var 0	
	Consist A	MM 4305	

Got off to a slow start by his standards, but rebounded with superb 2H. GB% reversed a three-year decline and paired well with continued Dom rebirth (which SwK% backs), all of which peaked after July 1. If he can hang on to 2H Cmd/GB%, then... UP: his first skill supported sub-3.00 ERA.

Yr Tm	W	L	Sv	IP	K	ERA	xERA	WHIP	oOPS	vL	vR	BF/G	Ctl	Dom	Cmd	FpK	SwK	G	L	F	H%	S%	hr/f	GS	APC	DOM%	DIS%	Sv%	LI	RAR	BPV	BPX	R$
11 BOS	15	9	0	192	182	3.47	3.46	1.26	690	580	728	25.8	3.5	8.5	2.4	58%	9%	50	16	34	29%	76%	11%	31	103	61%	16%			11.1	87	130	$14
12 BOS	9	14	0	205	166	4.82	3.92	1.38	773	738	785	26.5	3.0	7.3	2.4	58%	9%	49	22	29	32%	67%	14%	33	104	52%	18%			-20.4	77	101	-$4
13 BOS	15	8	0	213	177	3.75	3.88	1.29	702	670	711	27.4	2.8	7.5	2.6	61%	9%	45	20	35	31%	73%	8%	33	108	61%	9%			2.9	81	106	$9
14 2 AL	16	11	0	220	220	2.46	3.19	1.10	635	697	617	27.7	2.0	9.0	4.6	61%	10%	42	21	37	31%	81%	7%	32	109	81%	9%			34.8	129	154	$26
15 CHC	11	12	0	205	207	3.34	3.13	1.12	661	658	662	25.9	2.1	9.1	4.4	61%	11%	49	22	29	31%	72%	10%	32	100	72%	13%			15.8	135	161	$19
1st Half	4	6	0	96	93	3.74	3.57	1.33	746	801	731	25.6	2.6	8.7	3.3	60%	10%	47	24	29	33%	75%	12%	16	98	63%	19%			2.7	111	132	$7
2nd Half	7	6	0	109	114	2.98	2.75	0.94	579	544	591	26.1	1.6	9.4	6.0	61%	11%	51	20	29	29%	69%	8%	16	101	81%	6%			13.1	156	185	$29
16 Proj	15	10	0	218	211	3.23	3.25	1.15	663	661	663	25.9	2.2	8.7	3.9	61%	10%	47	21	32	31%	74%	9%	33						19.5	122	145	$21

Lewis,Colby

Age: 36 Th: R Role SP	Health F	LIMA Plan B	
Ht: 6' 4" Wt: 240 Type FB	PT/Exp B	Rand Var 0	
	Consist F	MM 1105	

Underwent Oct. 2015 left knee surgery to repair meniscus; expected ready by spring training. PRO: Excellent Ctl; SwK% hints at league-average Dom upside. CON: Elevated FB% and HR combination is engrained; BPX shows he hasn't seen league-average since 2012. Fantasy relevance nearly non-existent.

Yr Tm	W	L	Sv	IP	K	ERA	xERA	WHIP	oOPS	vL	vR	BF/G	Ctl	Dom	Cmd	FpK	SwK	G	L	F	H%	S%	hr/f	GS	APC	DOM%	DIS%	Sv%	LI	RAR	BPV	BPX	R$
11 TEX	14	10	0	200	169	4.40	4.07	1.21	738	829	616	26.2	2.5	7.6	3.0	66%	9%	34	17	49	28%	70%	12%	32	100	59%	19%			-11.4	81	121	$8
12 TEX	6	6	0	105	93	3.43	3.77	1.08	715	771	641	26.7	1.2	8.0	6.6	69%	9%	33	21	46	29%	75%	11%	16	102	69%	6%			7.6	122	159	$9
13 a/a	0	2	0	24	14	11.14	10.50	2.30				17.5	3.7	5.1	1.4						41%	53%								-21.5	-48	-63	-$15
14 TEX	10	14	0	170	133	5.18	4.48	1.52	840	853	823	26.3	2.5	7.0	2.8	66%	8%	33	23	44	35%	69%	10%	29	97	31%	10%			-30.2	69	82	-$11
15 TEX	17	9	0	205	142	4.66	4.49	1.24	738	756	717	26.1	1.8	6.2	3.4	63%	9%	34	22	44	30%	65%	9%	33	96	52%	21%			-17.6	75	89	$5
1st Half	8	4	0	104	75	4.83	4.54	1.27	755	787	704	26.0	1.9	6.5	3.4	64%	7%	35	18	46	31%	64%	8%	17	95	53%	18%			-11.2	78	93	$3
2nd Half	9	5	0	100	67	4.49	4.44	1.20	720	712	728	26.2	1.8	6.0	3.4	62%	10%	32	26	42	28%	66%	10%	16	98	50%	25%			-6.5	70	83	$8
16 Proj	11	12	0	181	137	4.56	4.19	1.28	760	788	726	25.3	2.0	6.8	3.4	65%	9%	33	22	45	31%	68%	10%	29						-13.4	80	96	$2

Lincecum,Tim

Age: 32 Th: R Role SP	Health F	LIMA Plan C	
Ht: 5' 11" Wt: 170 Type Pwr	PT/Exp A	Rand Var -1	
	Consist B	MM 2300	

Injuries (forearm, hip, back) cost him most of the season. Sept. hip surgery to repair impingement and a torn labrum puts spring training availability in question. Skills and velocity (87 mph) continued to decline and DIS% was dreadful. Had retained some utility as a home-game spot-start play; even that appears gone now.

Yr Tm	W	L	Sv	IP	K	ERA	xERA	WHIP	oOPS	vL	vR	BF/G	Ctl	Dom	Cmd	FpK	SwK	G	L	F	H%	S%	hr/f	GS	APC	DOM%	DIS%	Sv%	LI	RAR	BPV	BPX	R$
11 SF	13	14	0	217	220	2.74	3.35	1.21	646	628	663	27.3	3.6	9.1	2.6	53%	12%	48	19	33	29%	79%	8%	33	109	73%	6%			32.3	94	141	$22
12 SF	10	15	0	186	190	5.18	3.97	1.47	767	722	813	25.0	4.4	9.2	2.1	55%	12%	46	24	30	32%	66%	15%	33	100	48%	24%			-26.7	72	94	-$8
13 SF	10	14	0	198	193	4.37	3.60	1.32	711	664	755	26.3	3.5	8.8	2.5	56%	12%	45	23	32	31%	69%	12%	32	103	56%	13%			-12.3	88	114	$2
14 SF	12	9	1	156	134	4.74	3.86	1.39	772	750	791	20.4	3.6	7.7	2.1	54%	10%	47	23	30	31%	68%	14%	26	81	54%	35%	100	0.78	-19.2	66	79	-$3
15 SF	7	4	0	76	60	4.13	4.71	1.48	736	605	858	22.2	4.5	7.1	1.6	50%	11%	44	21	35	30%	74%	9%	15	88	40%	40%			-1.5	28	34	-$2
1st Half	7	4	0	76	60	4.13	4.71	1.48	737	605	858	22.2	4.5	7.1	1.6	50%	11%	44	21	35	30%	74%	9%	15	88	40%	40%			-1.5	29	34	-$2
2nd Half																																	
16 Proj	4	4	0	58	53	4.33	3.99	1.39	733	669	794	22.9	3.9	8.2	2.1	54%	11%	46	22	32	31%	71%	11%	11						-2.6	64	76	-$2

GREG PYRON

Liriano,Francisco

Age: 32 | Th: L | Role: SP | Ht: 6' 2" | Wt: 215 | Type: Pwr GB
Health: D | PT/Exp: A | Consist: A | LIMA Plan: C | Rand Var: 0 | MM: 3403

Ultra-consistent over past 3 years (see ERA!), but skills shined brightest in this one. Still-peaking Dom, with SwK support, and elite GB% more than compensate for subpar FpK and occasionally shaky Ctl (4.9 in Aug). Not past his health woes, but can count on plenty of Ks and a plus ERA if he gets ~30 starts.

Yr Tm	W	L	Sv	IP	K	ERA	xERA	WHIP	oOPS	vL	vR	BF/G	Ctl	Dom	Cmd	FpK	SwK	G	L	F	H%	S%	hr/f	GS	APC	DOM%	DIS%	Sv%	LI	RAR	BPV	BPX	R$
11 MIN	9	10	0	134	112	5.09	4.35	1.49	726	669	744	22.7	5.0	7.5	1.5	49%	12%	49	15	36	29%	67%	10%	24	88	46%	29%	0	0.75	-19.0	26	40	-$5
12 2AL	6	12	0	157	167	5.34	4.12	1.47	741	603	784	20.4	5.0	9.6	1.9	54%	13%	44	21	35	31%	65%	13%	28	80	50%	32%	0	0.83	-25.7	60	78	-$9
13 PIT *	18	9	0	180	182	3.36	3.15	1.26	611	321	689	24.4	3.4	9.1	2.7	58%	14%	50	24	25	31%	74%	8%	26	96	65%	15%			11.1	102	133	$15
14 PIT	7	10	0	162	175	3.38	3.33	1.30	644	735	622	23.8	4.5	9.7	2.2	56%	14%	54	19	27	29%	76%	12%	29	94	62%	17%			7.2	85	102	$6
15 PIT	12	7	0	187	205	3.38	3.21	1.21	631	599	639	24.9	3.4	9.9	2.9	57%	15%	51	22	26	30%	74%	12%	31	96	65%	10%			13.5	116	138	$15
1st Half	5	6	0	102	113	2.99	2.94	1.02	552	583	543	25.3	3.0	9.9	3.3	60%	15%	54	19	27	26%	74%	13%	16	97	75%	6%			12.3	130	154	$23
2nd Half	7	1	0	84	92	3.84	3.54	1.43	719	617	747	24.5	3.8	9.8	2.6	55%	15%	48	26	26	35%	74%	10%	15	96	53%	13%			1.3	99	118	$7
16 Proj	**11**	**8**	**0**	**174**	**185**	**3.41**	**3.34**	**1.28**	**650**	**591**	**665**	**23.4**	**3.9**	**9.6**	**2.5**	**56%**	**14%**	**51**	**22**	**27**	**30%**	**75%**	**11%**	**30**						**11.8**	**97**	**115**	**$11**

Lobstein,Kyle

Age: 26 | Th: L | Role: SP | Ht: 6' 3" | Wt: 200 | Type:
Health: F | PT/Exp: D | Consist: B | LIMA Plan: D+ | Rand Var: +4 | MM: 0001

3-8, 5.94 ERA in 64 IP at DET. Late-May shoulder inflammation sidelined him for three months. Displayed GB lean, little else. It's tough to get by with an 86 mph fastball and meager Cmd, as xERA shows. SwK hints Dom could creep closer to 6.0, but that's still not enough. Unlikely to have fantasy relevance.

Yr Tm	W	L	Sv	IP	K	ERA	xERA	WHIP	oOPS	vL	vR	BF/G	Ctl	Dom	Cmd	FpK	SwK	G	L	F	H%	S%	hr/f	GS	APC	DOM%	DIS%	Sv%	LI	RAR	BPV	BPX	R$
11																																	
12 aa	8	7	0	144	111	4.40	4.48	1.51				23.1	4.1	7.0	1.7						32%	71%								-6.8	57	74	-$5
13 a/a	13	7	0	168	118	4.15	4.48	1.50				25.8	2.9	6.3	2.2						35%	72%								-5.9	65	85	-$2
14 DET *	10	13	0	185	125	5.03	5.58	1.65	665	620	686	25.1	2.9	6.1	2.1	53%	9%	45	17	38	37%	69%	7%	6	90	33%	17%	0	0.70	-29.5	50	59	-$16
15 DET *	3	10	0	81	42	6.48	6.18	1.75	829	634	915	21.9	3.6	4.6	1.3	57%	8%	52	20	28	35%	63%	11%	11	78	9%	36%	0	0.68	-25.2	14	16	-$16
1st Half	3	5	0	48	20	4.34	4.73	1.45	739	606	807	25.5	3.0	3.8	1.3	56%	8%	56	19	25	30%	70%	7%	8	89	13%	25%			-2.2	20	24	-$9
2nd Half	0	5	0	34	22	9.50	8.79	2.19	1073	753	1163	18.7	4.5	5.8	1.3	58%	7%	42	21	37	41%	57%	19%	3	60	0%	67%	0	0.54	-23.0	-9	-10	-$27
16 Proj	**3**	**7**	**0**	**73**	**46**	**5.83**	**4.92**	**1.74**	**894**	**713**	**965**	**22.5**	**3.5**	**5.7**	**1.6**	**56%**	**8%**	**47**	**19**	**34**	**36%**	**67%**	**8%**	**15**						**-16.7**	**32**	**38**	**-$12**

Locke,Jeff

Age: 28 | Th: L | Role: SP | Ht: 6' 0" | Wt: 185 | Type: GB
Health: A | PT/Exp: B | Consist: A | LIMA Plan: D+ | Rand Var: +1 | MM: 1103

Process or results? In early June, made a mechanical adjustment, altered between-start routine and intensified focus on getting ahead. 2H FpK says it was successful—though Ctl, ERA never got the memo. Some potential small Ctl gains if it continues, but subpar Dom and .274 oppBA cloud the overall outlook.

Yr Tm	W	L	Sv	IP	K	ERA	xERA	WHIP	oOPS	vL	vR	BF/G	Ctl	Dom	Cmd	FpK	SwK	G	L	F	H%	S%	hr/f	GS	APC	DOM%	DIS%	Sv%	LI	RAR	BPV	BPX	R$
11 PIT *	8	13	0	170	113	4.62	4.46	1.47	954	917	961	22.8	3.4	6.0	1.8	42%	6%	34	28	38	32%	69%	14%	4	74	0%	75%			-14.2	51	77	-$5
12 PIT *	11	8	0	176	135	3.60	4.22	1.38	749	836	716	23.1	2.8	6.9	2.5	62%	9%	49	15	36	32%	76%	17%	6	70	33%	33%	0	0.64	9.0	70	92	$5
13 PIT	10	7	0	166	125	3.52	4.11	1.38	686	748	667	23.7	4.5	6.8	1.5	58%	9%	53	21	26	28%	75%	9%	30	91	30%	23%			7.2	30	39	$4
14 PIT *	10	7	0	181	117	4.12	4.33	1.37	722	521	776	25.3	3.0	5.8	1.9	58%	10%	51	20	30	30%	72%	13%	21	93	48%	19%			-8.4	46	55	-$1
15 PIT	8	11	0	168	129	4.49	4.07	1.42	735	802	715	24.5	3.2	6.9	2.2	62%	9%	51	24	25	32%	69%	11%	30	93	33%	20%			-11.0	67	79	-$4
1st Half	5	4	0	91	70	4.15	4.00	1.41	712	673	723	24.6	3.3	6.9	2.1	60%	9%	53	23	25	32%	71%	10%	16	94	38%	25%			-2.1	67	80	-$1
2nd Half	3	7	0	77	59	4.89	4.15	1.44	762	932	705	24.4	3.1	6.9	2.2	65%	9%	49	26	25	32%	67%	13%	14	91	29%	14%			-8.8	66	78	-$7
16 Proj	**8**	**9**	**0**	**160**	**116**	**4.15**	**4.08**	**1.40**	**731**	**755**	**723**	**23.9**	**3.3**	**6.6**	**2.0**	**61%**	**9%**	**51**	**22**	**27**	**31%**	**72%**	**11%**	**28**						**-3.7**	**56**	**67**	**-$1**

Lohse,Kyle

Age: 37 | Th: R | Role: RP | Ht: 6' 2" | Wt: 210 | Type:
Health: A | PT/Exp: A | Consist: A | LIMA Plan: C | Rand Var: +5 | MM: 1101

After years of outperforming his xERA by a wide margin, ERA spiked thanks to hr/f misfortune, long overdue H% correction and 2nd half loss of control. A profile like this is prone to fall off the cliff at some point, and when you're 37, there's no guarantee that even a parachute will provide a soft landing.

Yr Tm	W	L	Sv	IP	K	ERA	xERA	WHIP	oOPS	vL	vR	BF/G	Ctl	Dom	Cmd	FpK	SwK	G	L	F	H%	S%	hr/f	GS	APC	DOM%	DIS%	Sv%	LI	RAR	BPV	BPX	R$
11 STL	14	8	0	188	111	3.39	4.09	1.17	680	696	667	25.8	2.0	5.3	2.6	67%	6%	41	22	37	28%	73%	7%	30	93	47%	10%			12.8	60	91	$14
12 STL	16	3	0	211	143	2.86	4.02	1.09	642	664	623	26.2	1.6	6.1	3.8	69%	7%	41	24	36	28%	77%	8%	33	95	67%	0%			30.1	85	111	$26
13 MIL	11	10	0	199	125	3.35	4.03	1.17	700	727	676	25.2	1.6	5.7	3.5	66%	8%	40	21	38	28%	77%	11%	32	94	53%	6%			12.6	76	99	$13
14 MIL	13	9	0	198	141	3.54	3.99	1.15	682	725	643	26.4	2.0	6.4	3.1	64%	9%	40	19	41	28%	73%	9%	31	97	52%	16%			4.9	78	93	$12
15 MIL	5	13	2	152	108	5.85	4.60	1.46	847	853	843	18.0	2.5	6.4	2.5	64%	10%	39	23	38	32%	64%	15%	22	69	41%	18%	100	0.69	-35.4	63	75	-$13
1st Half	5	9	0	98	70	6.24	4.49	1.38	818	732	886	25.0	2.0	6.4	3.2	64%	10%	37	24	39	31%	58%	15%	17	96	47%	12%			-27.6	76	90	-$13
2nd Half	0	4	2	54	38	5.13	4.81	1.62	900	1039	752	12.0	3.5	6.3	1.8	63%	10%	42	21	37	33%	73%	16%	5	46	20%	40%	100	0.61	-7.9	40	47	-$14
16 Proj	**4**	**6**	**0**	**102**	**70**	**4.40**	**4.28**	**1.34**	**770**	**818**	**726**	**18.5**	**2.4**	**6.2**	**2.6**	**65%**	**9%**	**40**	**22**	**38**	**30%**	**71%**	**11%**	**19**						**-5.5**	**65**	**78**	**-$3**

Lorenzen,Michael

Age: 24 | Th: R | Role: SP | Ht: 6' 3" | Wt: 180 | Type:
Health: A | PT/Exp: D | Consist: B | LIMA Plan: D+ | Rand Var: +1 | MM: 1003

4-9, 5.40 ERA in 113 IP at CIN. College CF/closer is still learning to mix his four pitches and getting acclimated to life as an MLB starter. The road is long, but 2nd half FpK and SwK gains are a needed first step. If the winds of fortune could push down LD% and hr/f, that would be a big help too. Very much a work in progress.

Yr Tm	W	L	Sv	IP	K	ERA	xERA	WHIP	oOPS	vL	vR	BF/G	Ctl	Dom	Cmd	FpK	SwK	G	L	F	H%	S%	hr/f	GS	APC	DOM%	DIS%	Sv%	LI	RAR	BPV	BPX	R$
11																																	
12																																	
13																																	
14 aa	4	6	0	121	76	3.50	4.16	1.38				21.1	3.2	5.7	1.8						30%	77%								3.6	48	58	-$1
15 CIN *	8	11	0	156	100	4.59	5.14	1.52	882	1007	784	20.5	3.8	5.8	1.5	57%	9%	41	28	31	30%	73%	16%	21	74	19%	33%	0	0.69	-12.1	27	32	-$8
1st Half	5	4	0	84	53	3.61	5.07	1.47	808	964	709	22.6	4.2	5.6	1.3	55%	8%	41	26	34	27%	83%	18%	11	85	27%	27%	0	0.66	3.7	17	20	-$2
2nd Half	3	7	0	72	47	5.74	5.22	1.57	970	1048	891	18.6	3.3	5.9	1.8	58%	10%	40	32	28	34%	64%	13%	10	64	10%	40%	0	0.73	-15.8	40	48	-$14
16 Proj	**6**	**10**	**0**	**145**	**95**	**4.32**	**4.55**	**1.47**	**793**	**892**	**711**	**20.5**	**3.5**	**5.9**	**1.7**	**57%**	**9%**	**40**	**29**	**30**	**31%**	**73%**	**12%**	**30**						**-6.4**	**32**	**38**	**-$5**

Loup,Aaron

Age: 28 | Th: L | Role: RP | Ht: 5' 11" | Wt: 205 | Type: xGB
Health: A | PT/Exp: C | Consist: B | LIMA Plan: C+ | Rand Var: +5 | MM: 4300

Ah, the perils of 40-inning sample sizes. Finally turned plus SwK rates into big Dom, while simultaneously spiking his FpK and Ctl. But that was all washed away by the hit/strand/HR troika turning against him. All 6 of HR allowed (and 13 of 15 career) came vR; that's an Achilles' heel that locks him into specialist role.

Yr Tm	W	L	Sv	IP	K	ERA	xERA	WHIP	oOPS	vL	vR	BF/G	Ctl	Dom	Cmd	FpK	SwK	G	L	F	H%	S%	hr/f	GS	APC	DOM%	DIS%	Sv%	LI	RAR	BPV	BPX	R$
11																																	
12 TOR *	0	5	3	76	56	3.26	3.94	1.31	547	462	638	4.5	2.0	6.6	3.4	58%	6%	55	17	27	33%	76%	0%	0	13			60	1.16	7.1	91	119	$1
13 TOR	4	6	2	69	53	2.47	3.06	1.14	670	506	777	4.4	1.7	6.9	4.1	59%	9%	60	17	23	30%	81%	11%	0	16			67	0.96	12.0	116	152	$6
14 TOR	4	4	4	69	56	3.15	3.58	1.17	647	559	695	4.0	3.9	7.3	1.9	56%	10%	54	20	26	25%	74%	9%	0	15			50	1.25	5.0	58	69	$4
15 TOR	2	5	0	42	46	4.46	2.88	1.28	776	696	831	3.1	1.5	9.8	6.6	66%	10%	55	22	23	36%	69%	21%	0	12			0	1.07	-2.6	169	201	-$3
1st Half	2	4	0	32	35	5.12	2.76	1.14	721	676	747	3.5	1.4	9.9	7.0	65%	10%	52	23	25	33%	56%	18%	0	13			0	1.01	-4.5	171	203	-$2
2nd Half	0	1	0	11	11	2.53	3.22	1.69	917	732	1087	2.5	1.7	9.3	5.5	67%	9%	62	19	19	42%	94%	29%	0	10			0	1.16	1.9	162	192	-$5
16 Proj	**2**	**4**	**0**	**44**	**38**	**3.51**	**3.16**	**1.17**	**695**	**578**	**773**	**3.9**	**2.1**	**7.9**	**3.7**	**60%**	**9%**	**56**	**20**	**25**	**30%**	**72%**	**12%**	**0**						**2.4**	**118**	**141**	**$0**

Lowe,Mark

Age: 33 | Th: R | Role: RP | Ht: 6' 3" | Wt: 210 | Type: Pwr
Health: C | PT/Exp: D | Consist: F | LIMA Plan: B+ | Rand Var: -5 | MM: 3400

This lightning strike of a season was fueled by velocity spike (avg velo > 95 for 1st time since 2011) and well-supported by skills (BPV nearly 2x his previous career high). But Health, Consistency remind us that lightning rarely strikes twice. He's an easy armchair scout, though: 95-96 mph good; 92-93 mph bad.

Yr Tm	W	L	Sv	IP	K	ERA	xERA	WHIP	oOPS	vL	vR	BF/G	Ctl	Dom	Cmd	FpK	SwK	G	L	F	H%	S%	hr/f	GS	APC	DOM%	DIS%	Sv%	LI	RAR	BPV	BPX	R$
11 TEX	2	3	1	45	42	3.80	3.75	1.44	768	802	739	3.8	3.8	8.4	2.2	58%	10%	49	19	32	32%	78%	14%	0	15			33	1.00	0.8	76	114	-$1
12 TEX	0	2	0	39	28	3.43	4.60	1.22	707	750	663	4.5	3.0	6.4	2.2	63%	8%	34	22	44	27%	77%	9%	0	18			0	0.30	2.8	47	61	-$2
13 LAA *	4	1	1	40	33	5.53	5.88	1.79	849	1026	696	5.3	4.8	7.4	1.5	41%	8%	37	17	46	36%	70%	6%	0	22			25	0.99	-8.3	41	53	-$7
14 CLE *	4	4	17	49	41	6.76	6.97	1.92	1035	900	1087	4.8	4.5	7.6	1.7	68%	14%	30	15	56	39%	66%	13%	0	21			85	0.72	-18.1	32	38	-$5
15 2AL *	1	3	1	55	61	1.96	2.97	1.05	612	724	523	3.8	2.0	10.0	5.1	67%	14%	40	27	32	31%	85%	9%	0	14			20	1.18	13.6	145	172	$5
1st Half	0	0	0	25	31	0.72	3.14	1.24	578	634	535	4.1	3.6	11.2	3.1	70%	13%	38	32	30	35%	94%	0%	0	16			0	1.13	10.0	120	142	$3
2nd Half	1	3	1	30	30	3.00	2.83	0.90	639	788	511	3.5	0.6	9.0	15.0	64%	16%	42	24	34	28%	74%	15%	0	13			25	1.22	3.6	166	196	$7
16 Proj	**2**	**3**	**0**	**44**	**44**	**3.54**	**3.57**	**1.22**	**660**	**729**	**602**	**4.0**	**3.1**	**9.1**	**2.9**	**64%**	**12%**	**39**	**24**	**36**	**30%**	**72%**	**8%**	**0**						**2.3**	**98**	**116**	**$0**

GREG PYRON

Lyles,Jordan

Age: 25	Th: R	Role SP	Health F	LIMA Plan D+
Ht: 6' 4"	Wt: 215	Type	PT/Exp C	Rand Var +1
			Consist B	MM 1003

Underwent season-ending surgery in June to repair MCL and capsule in left big toe, but expected ready for spring training. GB% is step one to a valid skill set, but there's no step two here: Cmd intolerable, lefties rake him, home ballpark is instant death. BPX has never even sniffed a third digit. Avoid.

Yr Tm	W	L	Sv	IP	K	ERA	xERA	WHIP	oOPS	vL	vR	BF/G	Ctl	Dom	Cmd	FpK	SwK	G	L	F	H%	S%	hr/f	GS	APC	DOM%	DIS%	Sv%	LI	RAR	BPV	BPX	R$
11 HOU *	5	11	0	156	104	4.79	4.66	1.39	817	795	834	20.6	2.4	6.0	2.5	62%	9%	41	21	38	32%	67%	12%	15	79	40%	13%	0	0.80	-16.4	55	82	-$5
12 HOU *	10	12	0	182	128	4.72	4.60	1.37	772	886	683	23.9	2.4	6.3	2.6	61%	7%	54	17	29	32%	68%	15%	25	95	36%	32%			-15.8	59	77	-$3
13 HOU *	9	11	1	165	103	5.64	5.11	1.53	801	751	859	21.8	3.0	5.6	1.9	56%	7%	48	21	30	33%	64%	12%	25	91	36%	28%	50	1.01	-36.2	39	50	-$14
14 COL	7	4	0	127	90	4.33	3.90	1.37	750	844	654	24.8	3.3	6.4	2.0	57%	8%	52	23	26	30%	70%	12%	22	95	55%	9%			-9.3	57	68	-$2
15 COL	2	5	0	49	30	5.14	4.45	1.49	751	797	697	21.2	3.5	5.5	1.6	58%	8%	50	26	25	32%	63%	5%	10	77	40%	40%			-7.1	33	39	-$6
1st Half	2	5	0	49	30	5.14	4.45	1.49	751	797	697	21.2	3.5	5.5	1.6	58%	8%	50	26	25	32%	63%	5%	10	77	40%	40%			-7.1	33	39	-$6
2nd Half																																	
16 Proj	**6**	**9**	**0**	**131**	**85**	**4.87**	**4.27**	**1.45**	**768**	**800**	**734**	**22.1**	**3.1**	**5.9**	**1.9**	**58%**	**8%**	**50**	**22**	**28**	**32%**	**67%**	**10%**	**25**						**-14.6**	**51**	**61**	**-$7**

Lynn,Lance

Age: 29	Th: R	Role SP	Health B	LIMA Plan C+
Ht: 6' 5"	Wt: 240	Type Pwr	PT/Exp A	Rand Var -3
			Consist A	MM 2305

Narrowly missed second straight sub-3.00 ERA, but skills are full of pessimism: eroding FpK threatens Ctl (as seen in 2H); 2014-15 ERA dip really just a function of some friendly S% and hr/f. BPX shows this skill set is merely average, and xERA screams that next ERA is likely closer to 4.00 than 3.00. TJS means 2017.

Yr Tm	W	L	Sv	IP	K	ERA	xERA	WHIP	oOPS	vL	vR	BF/G	Ctl	Dom	Cmd	FpK	SwK	G	L	F	H%	S%	hr/f	GS	APC	DOM%	DIS%	Sv%	LI	RAR	BPV	BPX	R$
11 STL *	8	4	1	110	93	3.67	3.51	1.32	591	723	504	15.1	2.9	7.6	2.6	57%	10%	57	11	32	33%	71%	12%	2	31	50%	0%	50	0.94	3.7	92	138	$4
12 STL	18	7	0	176	180	3.78	3.58	1.32	728	841	624	21.3	3.3	9.2	2.8	61%	10%	44	24	32	32%	73%	10%	29	86	59%	14%	0	0.83	5.0	99	130	$11
13 STL	15	10	0	202	198	3.97	3.63	1.31	701	765	652	25.9	3.4	8.8	2.6	63%	10%	43	23	34	32%	70%	7%	33	102	64%	15%			-2.6	88	115	$8
14 STL	15	10	0	204	181	2.74	3.81	1.26	662	697	635	26.2	3.2	8.0	2.5	60%	9%	44	20	36	30%	80%	6%	33	105	67%	9%			25.2	80	95	$16
15 STL	12	11	0	175	167	3.03	3.95	1.37	708	809	623	24.2	3.5	8.6	2.5	56%	9%	44	22	34	33%	80%	8%	31	98	55%	16%			20.2	82	98	$11
1st Half	6	4	0	92	97	2.53	3.66	1.23	638	628	647	25.7	3.0	9.5	3.1	58%	10%	41	21	37	32%	81%	5%	15	105	73%	0%			16.3	108	128	$18
2nd Half	6	7	0	83	70	3.58	4.30	1.52	784	986	594	22.8	4.0	7.6	1.9	54%	9%	47	22	31	33%	79%	11%	16	92	38%	31%			3.9	53	63	$3
16 Proj																																	

Lyons,Tyler

Age: 28	Th: L	Role SP	Health B	LIMA Plan A
Ht: 6' 4"	Wt: 200	Type	PT/Exp D	Rand Var +1
			Consist B	MM 2201

3-1, 3.75 ERA in 60 IP at STL. Used exclusively as a starter in the minors, but served as a swingman in majors. Dom spike is a great sign; some of that comes from kicking it up a notch in relief work (9.4 Dom, 1.7 Ctl in 42.1 career MLB IP). Perfect $1 staff-filler in NL-only leagues. LIMA agrees.

Yr Tm	W	L	Sv	IP	K	ERA	xERA	WHIP	oOPS	vL	vR	BF/G	Ctl	Dom	Cmd	FpK	SwK	G	L	F	H%	S%	hr/f	GS	APC	DOM%	DIS%	Sv%	LI	RAR	BPV	BPX	R$
11																																	
12 a/a	9	13	0	153	117	4.50	4.45	1.38				23.7	2.2	6.9	3.2						34%	68%								-9.2	82	107	-$2
13 STL *	9	6	0	153	112	4.08	3.21	1.18	725	630	762	21.1	2.1	6.6	3.2	59%	9%	47	19	33	30%	65%	10%	8	66	50%	25%	0	0.97	-4.0	93	121	$6
14 STL *	8	6	0	120	97	4.87	4.99	1.45	682	280	806	19.7	2.2	7.3	3.3	62%	11%	43	16	40	35%	68%	10%	4	49	75%	25%	0	0.54	-16.7	79	95	-$6
15 STL *	12	6	0	155	133	3.73	5.08	1.36	751	746	752	19.6	1.6	7.7	4.7	60%	10%	39	25	36	34%	79%	19%	8	56	38%	38%	0	0.61	4.5	99	118	$5
1st Half	7	4	0	81	79	4.07	5.63	1.50	868	1139	813	23.3	1.9	8.8	4.6	58%	9%	40	29	31	38%	78%	24%	5	86	20%	40%			-1.1	101	120	$2
2nd Half	5	2	0	74	54	3.34	4.48	1.22	669	589	701	16.5	1.4	6.6	4.9	62%	10%	39	22	39	30%	80%	17%	3	44	67%	33%	0	0.55	5.6	98	116	$8
16 Proj	**5**	**3**	**0**	**73**	**61**	**3.84**	**3.67**	**1.23**	**708**	**553**	**758**	**55.8**	**1.9**	**7.6**	**4.1**	**61%**	**10%**	**42**	**21**	**37**	**32%**	**71%**	**9%**	**5**						**1.1**	**107**	**127**	**$1**

Madson,Ryan

Age: 35	Th: R	Role RP	Health F	LIMA Plan B+
Ht: 6' 6"	Wt: 210	Type Pwr GB	PT/Exp D	Rand Var -5
			Consist F	MM 4300

BPV column makes a nice anagram: 128-<blank>-<blank>-<blank>-128. Three full years after April 2012 TJ surgery, but finally made it all the way back. FpK and GB% even suggest this version might be a bit better than the original. Of course, Health/Age are very real risks, as that blank space reminds us.

Yr Tm	W	L	Sv	IP	K	ERA	xERA	WHIP	oOPS	vL	vR	BF/G	Ctl	Dom	Cmd	FpK	SwK	G	L	F	H%	S%	hr/f	GS	APC	DOM%	DIS%	Sv%	LI	RAR	BPV	BPX	R$
11 PHI	4	2	32	61	62	2.37	3.05	1.15	593	506	660	4.0	2.4	9.2	3.9	59%	15%	49	18	34	32%	79%	4%	0	16			94	1.18	11.7	128	193	$18
12																																	
13																																	
14																																	
15 KC	1	2	3	63	58	2.13	3.18	0.96	573	547	597	3.6	2.0	8.2	4.1	66%	14%	55	13	32	26%	82%	9%	0	13			60	1.12	14.3	128	152	$7
1st Half	1	1	0	33	31	1.65	3.24	0.83	494	549	444	3.6	2.5	8.5	3.4	64%	14%	54	9	38	20%	88%	10%	0	14			0	0.91	9.3	118	141	$8
2nd Half	0	1	3	31	27	2.64	3.11	1.11	650	546	755	3.6	1.5	7.9	5.4	69%	13%	56	18	26	31%	78%	9%	0	13			100	1.32	5.0	137	163	$6
16 Proj	**2**	**2**	**0**	**58**	**55**	**2.91**	**3.09**	**1.06**	**590**	**532**	**641**	**3.7**	**2.1**	**8.6**	**4.1**	**63%**	**14%**	**53**	**15**	**32**	**29%**	**74%**	**7%**	**0**						**7.5**	**129**	**153**	**$3**

Maness,Seth

Age: 27	Th: R	Role RP	Health A	LIMA Plan C
Ht: 6' 0"	Wt: 190	Type Con xGB	PT/Exp C	Rand Var +4
			Consist B	MM 3100

There's so much noise in reliever sample sizes, it's easy to put too much weight on them. Here, you can put aside the year-to-year noise and focus on these career numbers: vs RHB: .677 OPS, 17 BB/107 K. vLHB: .814 OPS, 20 BB/29 K. He's a righty specialist with some Holds value; no more, no less.

Yr Tm	W	L	Sv	IP	K	ERA	xERA	WHIP	oOPS	vL	vR	BF/G	Ctl	Dom	Cmd	FpK	SwK	G	L	F	H%	S%	hr/f	GS	APC	DOM%	DIS%	Sv%	LI	RAR	BPV	BPX	R$
11																																	
12 aa	11	3	0	124	68	3.62	3.91	1.17				24.7	0.7	5.0	7.6						31%	72%								6.0	162	211	$7
13 STL *	7	4	1	87	49	3.05	4.34	1.37	725	726	724	5.2	1.7	5.1	3.1	67%	7%	68	19	12	33%	79%	17%	0	13			33	1.16	8.8	73	95	$2
14 STL	6	4	3	80	55	2.91	3.17	1.10	668	852	565	4.3	1.2	6.2	5.0	67%	9%	56	19	25	29%	77%	11%	0	15			100	1.14	8.2	112	133	$7
15 STL	4	2	3	63	46	4.26	3.71	1.42	788	845	759	3.6	1.8	6.5	3.5	67%	9%	56	19	25	35%	72%	14%	0	13			50	1.34	-2.3	102	121	-$2
1st Half	3	0	3	32	24	3.66	3.34	1.31	759	659	807	3.2	0.6	6.8	12.0	66%	8%	53	22	25	36%	73%	8%	0	11			75	1.26	1.2	137	163	$1
2nd Half	1	2	0	31	22	4.88	4.11	1.53	817	1010	710	3.9	3.2	6.3	2.0	67%	11%	59	17	25	33%	72%	20%	0	15			0	1.42	-3.6	65	77	-$5
16 Proj	**4**	**2**	**0**	**58**	**39**	**3.43**	**3.55**	**1.32**	**760**	**870**	**702**	**4.3**	**1.7**	**6.0**	**3.6**	**67%**	**9%**	**58**	**19**	**23**	**32%**	**77%**	**13%**	**0**						**3.8**	**99**	**118**	**$0**

Martinez,Carlos

Age: 24	Th: R	Role SP	Health A	LIMA Plan C+
Ht: 6' 0"	Wt: 185	Type Pwr GB	PT/Exp B	Rand Var -1
			Consist A	MM 4405

Shut down in late Sept. due to right shoulder strain, but is expected ready for spring training. Breakout was well-backed by skills: FpK confirms the Ctl gains, nudged Dom and GB% north at same time, significant strides vL (2.1 Cmd vs 0.6 in '14). Challenge now is to hold those gains while taking a run at 200 IP.

Yr Tm	W	L	Sv	IP	K	ERA	xERA	WHIP	oOPS	vL	vR	BF/G	Ctl	Dom	Cmd	FpK	SwK	G	L	F	H%	S%	hr/f	GS	APC	DOM%	DIS%	Sv%	LI	RAR	BPV	BPX	R$
11																																	
12 aa	4	3	0	71	50	3.05	3.32	1.21				19.2	2.6	6.3	2.4						29%	77%								8.5	74	97	$3
13 STL *	8	4	1	108	86	3.24	3.09	1.25	704	764	661	11.9	2.9	7.1	2.4	62%	10%	52	19	29	30%	74%	4%	1	23	0%	100%	100	0.75	8.3	88	115	$6
14 STL	2	4	1	89	84	4.03	3.54	1.41	713	849	609	6.8	3.6	8.5	2.3	58%	14%	51	22	27	34%	70%	6%	7	24	29%	57%	17	1.34	-3.2	83	99	-$3
15 STL	14	7	0	180	184	3.01	3.28	1.29	687	756	623	24.4	3.2	9.2	2.9	63%	11%	54	20	25	32%	78%	11%	29	92	62%	7%	0	0.82	21.2	113	134	$15
1st Half	9	3	0	100	105	2.70	3.28	1.25	666	718	618	24.4	3.7	9.5	2.6	64%	11%	56	20	25	29%	83%	15%	16	93	69%	6%	0	0.79	15.6	104	123	$21
2nd Half	5	4	0	80	79	3.39	3.29	1.33	712	803	629	24.4	2.5	8.9	3.6	62%	12%	53	21	26	36%	74%	5%	13	90	54%	8%	0	0.85	5.6	125	148	$8
16 Proj	**13**	**8**	**0**	**185**	**180**	**3.35**	**3.29**	**1.25**	**658**	**751**	**578**	**25.2**	**3.1**	**8.8**	**2.8**	**61%**	**12%**	**53**	**21**	**26**	**31%**	**73%**	**8%**	**30**						**13.8**	**105**	**126**	**$13**

Martinez,Nicholas

Age: 25	Th: R	Role SP	Health A	LIMA Plan D+
Ht: 6' 1"	Wt: 175	Type Con	PT/Exp C	Rand Var 0
			Consist F	MM 0001

7-7, 3.96 ERA in 125 IP at TEX. Had a 0.35 ERA on May 1, a 2.03 ERA on June 1 and a 5.86 ERA the rest of the way. However, his near-5 xERA was a FULL-season experience. Maintaining a sub-4.00 ERA with a sub-2.0 Cmd is quite a trick. A repeat would be even more unlikely. Watch from a safe distance.

Yr Tm	W	L	Sv	IP	K	ERA	xERA	WHIP	oOPS	vL	vR	BF/G	Ctl	Dom	Cmd	FpK	SwK	G	L	F	H%	S%	hr/f	GS	APC	DOM%	DIS%	Sv%	LI	RAR	BPV	BPX	R$
11																																	
12																																	
13 aa	2	0	0	32	19	1.54	0.32	0.66				22.3	2.2	5.4	2.5						15%	79%								9.2	102	133	$4
14 TEX	5	12	0	140	77	4.55	5.24	1.46	795	832	746	21.0	3.5	4.9	1.4	53%	7%	33	20	47	29%	72%	8%	24	83	29%	33%	0	0.84	-14.1	5	6	-$8
15 TEX *	8	8	0	156	91	3.91	4.76	1.46	799	676	904	22.2	3.1	5.3	1.7	60%	8%	42	24	34	31%	76%	11%	21	88	29%	29%	0	0.69	0.9	36	43	-$2
1st Half	5	5	0	97	57	3.43	4.77	1.37	770	642	878	26.5	3.2	5.3	1.7	60%	8%	43	23	34	29%	78%	9%	16	99	38%	19%			6.3	31	37	$2
2nd Half	3	3	0	59	34	4.71	5.63	1.60	889	780	990	18.6	3.0	5.3	1.8	63%	7%	39	27	34	34%	73%	18%	5	66	0%	60%	0	0.51	-5.4	29	34	-$10
16 Proj	**4**	**5**	**0**	**87**	**50**	**3.91**	**4.80**	**1.37**	**729**	**689**	**770**	**20.9**	**3.1**	**5.1**	**1.6**	**58%**	**7%**	**38**	**23**	**39**	**29%**	**74%**	**8%**	**17**						**0.6**	**24**	**29**	**-$2**

GREG PYRON

Masterson,Justin

Age: 31 | Th: R | Role: RP | Ht: 6' 6" | Wt: 250 | Type: Pwr GB
Health: D | PT/Exp: B | Consist: C | LIMA Plan: C | Rand Var: +3 | MM: 2201

4-2, 5.61 ERA in 59 IP at BOS. Underwent Sept. arthroscopic surgery on right shoulder; expected ready by spring training. 3 reasons for concern: 2013-14 Dom growth evaporated as velocity dipped (2013: 92 mph; 2015: 87); chronic issues vL. Likely hasn't been healthy since 2013, but still tough to muster any optimism.

Yr Tm	W	L	Sv	IP	K	ERA	xERA	WHIP	oOPS	vL	vR	BF/G	Ctl	Dom	Cmd	FpK	SwK	G	L	F	H%	S%	hr/f	GS	APC	DOM%	DIS%	Sv%	LI	RAR	BPV	BPX	R$
11 CLE	12	10	0	216	158	3.21	3.56	1.28	667	746	560	26.7	2.7	6.6	2.4	57%	8%	55	18	27	31%	75%	6%	33	102	55%	12%	0	0.75	19.6	78	118	$14
12 CLE	11	15	0	206	159	4.93	4.08	1.45	736	825	613	26.6	3.8	6.9	1.8	58%	9%	56	19	25	31%	66%	11%	34	101	47%	26%			-23.3	55	72	-$7
13 CLE	14	10	0	193	195	3.45	3.08	1.20	624	698	507	25.1	3.5	9.1	2.6	58%	10%	58	18	24	29%	72%	11%	29	94	79%	10%	0	0.72	9.9	104	136	$15
14 2 TM	7	9	0	129	116	5.88	3.83	1.63	826	910	729	21.1	4.8	8.1	1.7	55%	10%	58	20	22	34%	64%	15%	25	80	40%	48%	0	0.71	-33.9	52	62	-$14
15 BOS *	4	4	0	78	59	5.53	5.16	1.64	870	917	814	15.7	4.3	6.9	1.6	56%	7%	52	18	30	34%	66%	13%	9	56	44%	44%	0	0.80	-15.0	47	56	-$10
1st Half	3	4	0	62	42	5.88	5.23	1.70	849	919	739	21.7	4.5	6.1	1.4	54%	7%	52	20	28	35%	64%	10%	9	85	44%	44%			-14.7	43	51	-$12
2nd Half	1	0	0	15	17	4.11	3.40	1.37	935	905	941	7.4	3.5	10.0	2.8	63%	10%	53	13	35	31%	78%	21%	0	27			0	0.85	-0.3	115	136	-$2
16 Proj	**4**	**3**	**0**	**73**	**62**	**4.56**	**4.05**	**1.48**	**818**	**859**	**776**	**13.7**	**4.0**	**7.7**	**1.9**	**58%**	**9%**	**53**	**17**	**30**	**32%**	**71%**	**13%**	**8**						**-5.4**	**60**	**72**	**-$4**

Matusz,Brian

Age: 29 | Th: L | Role: RP | Ht: 6' 4" | Wt: 200 | Type: Pwr FB
Health: A | PT/Exp: D | Consist: A | LIMA Plan: A | Rand Var: -2 | MM: 2400

PRO: Strong Dom buttressed by SwK; dominance vL; Ctl slipped in opposition to FpK gains, so no worry there (see 2nd half). CON: Still has problems vR (7.1 Ctl in 2015); ERA benefitted from favorable S%. Unlikely to take the next step (or be viable as a starter, as periodically rumored) until he solves RHBs.

Yr Tm	W	L	Sv	IP	K	ERA	xERA	WHIP	oOPS	vL	vR	BF/G	Ctl	Dom	Cmd	FpK	SwK	G	L	F	H%	S%	hr/f	GS	APC	DOM%	DIS%	Sv%	LI	RAR	BPV	BPX	R$
11 BAL *	3	12	0	110	72	7.02	6.81	1.73	1121	1058	1141	22.8	3.6	5.9	1.6	58%	6%	28	22	50	34%	62%	20%	12	79	0%	75%			-41.8	4	6	-$19
12 BAL *	8	11	1	145	107	5.28	5.23	1.56	818	528	933	14.4	3.6	6.6	1.8	60%	8%	41	20	40	33%	68%	12%	16	50	19%	38%	50	1.34	-22.7	42	54	-$11
13 BAL	2	1	0	51	50	3.53	3.54	1.16	616	502	747	3.2	2.8	8.8	3.1	59%	13%	39	21	40	30%	70%	6%	0	13			0	1.04	2.1	100	130	$0
14 BAL	2	3	0	52	53	3.48	4.02	1.32	750	626	876	3.6	3.0	9.2	3.1	58%	10%	35	15	50	32%	79%	9%	0	15			0	1.42	1.6	99	118	-$1
15 BAL	1	4	0	49	56	2.94	3.80	1.18	638	565	721	3.6	3.7	10.3	2.8	61%	13%	35	20	45	29%	79%	9%	0	14			0	0.96	6.2	99	118	$1
1st Half	1	2	0	27	29	2.36	4.56	1.35	661	465	856	4.5	5.4	9.8	1.8	57%	12%	26	26	48	28%	85%	6%	0	18			0	0.74	5.3	34	40	$0
2nd Half	0	2	0	22	27	3.63	3.00	0.99	605	656	520	2.8	1.6	10.9	6.8	66%	15%	46	14	41	29%	68%	13%	0	11			0	1.15	0.9	176	209	$1
16 Proj	**2**	**4**	**0**	**58**	**61**	**3.58**	**3.69**	**1.23**	**682**	**584**	**784**	**3.5**	**3.1**	**9.5**	**3.1**	**60%**	**12%**	**37**	**18**	**45**	**30%**	**75%**	**10%**	**0**						**2.8**	**102**	**122**	**$0**

Matz,Steven

Age: 25 | Th: L | Role: SP | Ht: 6' 2" | Wt: 200 | Type: Pwr GB
Health: D | PT/Exp: D | Consist: A | LIMA Plan: B | Rand Var: -3 | MM: 3203

4-0, 2.27 ERA in 36 IP at NYM. Suffered a partially torn left lat muscle in early July and spent about two months on the shelf. Combination of GB lean, solid Dom, good Ctl and success vR propelled the much-hyped prospect to a strong, albeit brief, debut. Expect a few bumps along the way, but future is bright.

Yr Tm	W	L	Sv	IP	K	ERA	xERA	WHIP	oOPS	vL	vR	BF/G	Ctl	Dom	Cmd	FpK	SwK	G	L	F	H%	S%	hr/f	GS	APC	DOM%	DIS%	Sv%	LI	RAR	BPV	BPX	R$
11																																	
12																																	
13																																	
14 aa	6	5	0	71	60	2.25	2.97	1.15				23.6	1.6	7.6	4.7						32%	81%								13.1	137	164	$6
15 NYM *	12	4	0	137	123	2.15	2.78	1.12	650	650	644	23.5	2.7	8.0	2.9	62%	9%	46	21	34	28%	84%	12%	6	96	67%	17%			30.8	100	119	$19
1st Half	9	4	0	104	94	2.03	2.53	1.08	544	400	553	23.9	2.9	8.2	2.8	65%	11%	37	10	53	26%	85%	13%	2	106	100%	0%			24.7	101	120	$25
2nd Half	3	0	0	33	29	1.89	2.73	1.08	704	708	699	21.7	1.9	7.7	4.1	60%	7%	49	25	25	29%	85%	11%	4	91	50%	25%			8.5	124	147	$0
16 Proj	**12**	**8**	**0**	**174**	**151**	**3.33**	**3.37**	**1.15**	**483**	**516**	**465**	**23.2**	**2.4**	**7.8**	**3.2**	**60%**	**7%**	**49**	**25**	**25**	**30%**	**72%**	**8%**	**30**						**13.6**	**102**	**121**	**$14**

Matzek,Tyler

Age: 25 | Th: L | Role: SP | Ht: 6' 3" | Wt: 210 | Type: Pwr
Health: A | PT/Exp: D | Consist: D | LIMA Plan: F | Rand Var: -4 | MM: 0000

Essentially a lost year. Began the season by walking 19 in 22 IP and was sent to Triple-A to work on mechanics. There, he walked seven in one inning and was sent to Rookie League. There, problems continued and he eventually got a several week long mental break. Obviously, he has a long way to go.

Yr Tm	W	L	Sv	IP	K	ERA	xERA	WHIP	oOPS	vL	vR	BF/G	Ctl	Dom	Cmd	FpK	SwK	G	L	F	H%	S%	hr/f	GS	APC	DOM%	DIS%	Sv%	LI	RAR	BPV	BPX	R$
11																																	
12																																	
13 aa	8	9	0	142	75	5.34	6.36	1.86				25.6	5.2	4.7	0.9						33%	73%								-25.9	4	5	-$20
14 COL *	11	15	0	184	140	4.30	4.71	1.49	749	434	848	24.8	3.7	6.8	1.9	58%	9%	50	20	30	32%	73%	8%	19	88	47%	16%	0	0.86	-12.8	52	62	-$5
15 COL	2	1	0	22	15	4.09	6.28	1.82	823	710	847	20.4	7.8	6.1	0.8	46%	7%	40	22	38	29%	79%	8%	5	80	20%	40%			-0.3	-81	-97	-$5
1st Half	2	1	0	22	15	4.09	6.28	1.82	823	710	847	20.4	7.8	6.1	0.8	46%	7%	40	22	38	29%	79%	8%	5	80	20%	40%			-0.3	-82	-97	-$5
2nd Half																																	
16 Proj	**4**	**4**	**0**	**58**	**37**	**5.10**	**5.58**	**1.75**	**882**	**630**	**945**	**23.3**	**5.7**	**5.8**	**1.0**	**50%**	**8%**	**44**	**21**	**35**	**32%**	**72%**	**10%**	**11**						**-8.1**	**-29**	**-34**	**-$8**

Maurer,Brandon

Age: 25 | Th: R | Role: RP | Ht: 6' 5" | Wt: 220 | Type:
Health: D | PT/Exp: D | Consist: B | LIMA Plan: B+ | Rand Var: -3 | MM: 2200

Hit DL with right shoulder inflammation in early Aug and did not return. xERA says this wasn't as good as it looked, but still some promising trends. Elite SwK% points to Dom upside, which would pair nicely with GB tilt (granted, it's a small sample) and decent Ctl. A classic Holds/LIMA guy with upside.

Yr Tm	W	L	Sv	IP	K	ERA	xERA	WHIP	oOPS	vL	vR	BF/G	Ctl	Dom	Cmd	FpK	SwK	G	L	F	H%	S%	hr/f	GS	APC	DOM%	DIS%	Sv%	LI	RAR	BPV	BPX	R$
11																																	
12 aa	9	2	0	138	106	3.71	3.88	1.43				24.4	3.2	6.9	2.2						34%	73%								5.2	80	104	$1
13 SEA *	8	12	0	137	111	5.95	5.38	1.57	883	919	835	18.8	3.3	7.3	2.2	59%	10%	44	19	37	35%	63%	15%	14	70	29%	36%	0	0.74	-35.2	50	65	-$14
14 SEA *	2	4	3	89	75	4.23	4.06	1.34	705	631	759	7.4	2.6	7.6	2.9	63%	10%	39	18	43	33%	69%	6%	7	30	0%	86%	75	0.72	-5.4	84	100	-$2
15 SD	7	4	0	51	39	3.00	3.83	1.06	568	427	711	3.9	2.6	6.9	2.6	61%	13%	48	22	30	26%	73%	7%	0	15			0	1.15	6.1	78	93	$4
1st Half	5	1	0	42	32	1.73	3.45	0.79	444	399	493	4.1	1.9	6.9	3.6	64%	14%	48	21	31	21%	78%	3%	0	15			0	0.99	11.5	98	116	$8
2nd Half	2	3	0	9	7	8.68	5.72	2.25	985	536	1374	3.4	5.8	6.8	1.2	52%	10%	47	26	26	40%	63%	22%	0	15			0	1.61	-5.4	-10	-11	-$13
16 Proj	**4**	**3**	**0**	**58**	**47**	**3.54**	**3.91**	**1.27**	**681**	**671**	**691**	**8.2**	**2.7**	**7.3**	**2.7**	**62%**	**11%**	**44**	**19**	**36**	**31%**	**73%**	**7%**	**0**						**3.1**	**81**	**96**	**$0**

May,Trevor

Age: 26 | Th: R | Role: RP | Ht: 6' 5" | Wt: 215 | Type: Pwr FB
Health: A | PT/Exp: C | Consist: A | LIMA Plan: B+ | Rand Var: +1 | MM: 2311

Spent first three months of the season as a starter and nearly entire 2nd half in the bullpen. Showed skills growth as SP (7.9 Dom, 1.9 Ctl in 83.1 IP), but took it to another level as RP (10.6 Dom, 2.3 Ctl in 31.1 IP). Absent further strides vL, he may fit best as late-inning RP with... UP: 20 Sv

Yr Tm	W	L	Sv	IP	K	ERA	xERA	WHIP	oOPS	vL	vR	BF/G	Ctl	Dom	Cmd	FpK	SwK	G	L	F	H%	S%	hr/f	GS	APC	DOM%	DIS%	Sv%	LI	RAR	BPV	BPX	R$
11																																	
12 aa	10	13	0	150	129	5.53	5.19	1.55				23.4	4.6	7.8	1.7						31%	67%								-27.9	40	52	-$12
13 aa	9	9	0	152	129	5.18	4.74	1.55				24.6	3.9	7.7	2.0						34%	67%								-24.6	61	80	-$10
14 MIN *	11	12	0	144	118	5.06	4.42	1.49	900	892	907	22.2	4.0	7.4	1.9	62%	10%	36	23	41	33%	66%	12%	9	84	22%	44%	0	0.70	-23.4	62	74	-$7
15 MIN	8	9	0	115	110	4.00	3.86	1.33	752	759	743	10.3	2.0	8.6	4.2	63%	11%	39	21	40	35%	72%	8%	16	39	38%	25%	0	0.87	-0.6	117	140	$2
1st Half	4	7	0	80	71	4.37	4.05	1.37	753	752	755	23.1	2.0	8.0	3.9	61%	10%	40	21	39	35%	69%	7%	15	86	40%	20%			-4.0	106	126	$1
2nd Half	4	2	0	34	39	3.15	3.43	1.25	749	782	722	4.4	2.1	10.2	4.9	70%	13%	37	22	40	35%	79%	11%	1	17	0%	####	0	0.90	3.5	143	169	$4
16 Proj	**6**	**5**	**4**	**73**	**68**	**3.29**	**3.74**	**1.20**	**669**	**677**	**662**	**9.6**	**2.7**	**8.4**	**3.1**	**64%**	**11%**	**37**	**22**	**40**	**30%**	**76%**	**9%**	**0**						**6.0**	**94**	**112**	**$5**

McAllister,Zach

Age: 28 | Th: R | Role: RP | Ht: 6' 6" | Wt: 240 | Type: Pwr
Health: D | PT/Exp: C | Consist: B | LIMA Plan: A | Rand Var: 0 | MM: 3411

Skills surged in first full season as RP (velocity also up 3 mph from SP days) as he posted career bests nearly across the board (see terrific BPX). Concurrent Dom/SwK gains confirm his nastiness out of the pen, and gains vL plugged one of the remaining leaks in this skill set. A premier LIMA play.

Yr Tm	W	L	Sv	IP	K	ERA	xERA	WHIP	oOPS	vL	vR	BF/G	Ctl	Dom	Cmd	FpK	SwK	G	L	F	H%	S%	hr/f	GS	APC	DOM%	DIS%	Sv%	LI	RAR	BPV	BPX	R$
11 CLE *	12	4	0	172	120	3.99	4.31	1.38	860	1069	659	25.0	1.9	6.3	3.2	51%	7%	43	27	30	34%	71%	5%	4	85	0%	50%			-0.9	84	126	$3
12 CLE *	11	10	0	189	153	3.97	4.53	1.37	767	724	820	23.9	2.7	7.3	2.7	61%	9%	41	19	40	32%	75%	12%	22	96	50%	18%			1.1	66	86	$4
13 CLE	9	9	0	134	101	3.75	4.46	1.36	739	737	741	24.1	3.3	6.8	2.1	61%	7%	37	22	41	30%	75%	8%	24	96	38%	25%			1.9	48	63	$2
14 CLE *	11	8	0	155	121	4.04	3.95	1.34	750	789	715	19.5	2.5	7.0	2.9	62%	8%	42	21	37	33%	70%	7%	15	66	47%	47%	0	0.91	-5.6	84	100	$2
15 CLE	4	4	1	69	84	3.00	3.37	1.35	702	632	764	4.9	3.0	11.0	3.7	57%	11%	43	21	36	36%	81%	10%	1	20	0%	100%	50	0.87	8.2	137	163	$2
1st Half	2	2	0	40	49	3.15	3.23	1.38	705	623	774	5.8	2.7	11.0	4.1	55%	10%	45	23	33	39%	79%	8%	1	23	0%	100%	0	0.86	4.0	148	176	$2
2nd Half	2	2	1	29	35	2.79	3.58	1.31	698	644	749	4.1	3.4	10.9	3.2	60%	12%	42	18	40	33%	85%	13%	0	17			50	0.88	4.2	123	146	$3
16 Proj	**5**	**4**	**2**	**73**	**75**	**3.30**	**3.59**	**1.30**	**692**	**669**	**713**	**7.3**	**2.9**	**9.3**	**3.2**	**60%**	**10%**	**42**	**20**	**38**	**33%**	**78%**	**9%**	**0**						**5.9**	**108**	**129**	**$3**

GREG PYRON

McCarthy,Brandon

Age: 32	Th: R	Role SP	Health F	LIMA Plan C+
Ht: 6' 7"	Wt: 200	Type	PT/Exp B	Rand Var +5
			Consist A	MM 3201

Surprised in 2014 with both skills growth and a random stretch of good health. The latter ended early in 2015, as he underwent TJS in late April, projecting for a mid-2016 return. Not at all clear whether this early-30s skill spike is sustainable; and early post-TJS results will likely be noisy. Check back in a year.

Yr Tm	W	L	Sv	IP	K	ERA	xERA	WHIP	oOPS	vL	vR	BF/G	Ctl	Dom	Cmd	FpK	SwK	G	L	F	H%	S%	hr/f	GS	APC	DOM%	DIS%	Sv%	LI	RAR	BPV	BPX	R$
11 OAK	9	9	0	171	123	3.32	3.47	1.13	659	675	640	27.6	1.3	6.5	4.9	61%	8%	47	21	32	30%	71%	6%	25	100	64%	4%			13.1	106	160	$13
12 OAK	8	6	0	111	73	3.24	4.23	1.25	706	769	636	26.1	1.9	5.9	3.0	67%	7%	41	24	35	30%	77%	8%	18	92	39%	17%			10.6	73	95	$6
13 ARI	5	11	0	135	76	4.53	3.95	1.35	759	716	807	26.2	1.4	5.1	3.6	68%	6%	48	25	27	33%	67%	10%	22	91	32%	18%			-11.1	79	103	-$4
14 2 TM	10	15	0	200	175	4.05	3.11	1.28	746	751	741	26.1	1.5	7.9	5.3	67%	9%	53	23	25	34%	72%	16%	32	95	56%	6%			-7.6	133	158	$3
15 LA	3	0	0	23	29	5.87	2.99	1.22	898	691	1124	23.5	1.6	11.3	7.3	66%	12%	38	22	40	29%	68%	38%	4	92	50%	0%			-5.4	178	212	-$3
1st Half	3	0	0	23	29	5.87	2.99	1.22	898	691	1124	23.5	1.6	11.3	7.3	66%	12%	38	22	40	29%	68%	38%	4	92	50%	0%			-5.4	178	212	-$3
2nd Half																																	
16 Proj	**5**	**4**	**0**	**73**	**63**	**4.03**	**3.49**	**1.22**	**683**	**649**	**721**	**24.6**	**1.9**	**7.8**	**4.1**	**66%**	**9%**	**45**	**23**	**32**	**32%**	**69%**	**11%**	**12**						**-0.6**	**111**	**132**	**$1**

McCullers,Lance

Age: 22	Th: R	Role SP	Health A	LIMA Plan B
Ht: 6' 2"	Wt: 205	Type Pwr	PT/Exp D	Rand Var -1
			Consist F	MM 4405

6-7, 3.22 ERA in 126 IP at HOU. May call-up had a great nine-start run upon arrival. Got a little shaky and spent a few weeks back in Triple-A in August, then bounced back to triple-digit BPV in Sept/Oct. FpK still needs refinement, and you can expect workload restrictions. Just a pup, but has lead dog potential.

Yr Tm	W	L	Sv	IP	K	ERA	xERA	WHIP	oOPS	vL	vR	BF/G	Ctl	Dom	Cmd	FpK	SwK	G	L	F	H%	S%	hr/f	GS	APC	DOM%	DIS%	Sv%	LI	RAR	BPV	BPX	R$
11																																	
12																																	
13																																	
14																																	
15 HOU *	9	8	1	158	172	2.70	2.70	1.14	659	590	729	21.5	3.2	9.8	3.0	57%	10%	46	22	32	29%	79%	9%	22	96	59%	27%			24.6	115	137	$18
1st Half	7	3	1	87	99	1.67	1.87	1.04	574	516	635	21.1	3.3	10.2	3.1	56%	10%	48	19	34	28%	85%	4%	10	97	50%	30%			24.7	134	159	$29
2nd Half	2	5	0	70	72	3.97	3.72	1.27	729	653	804	22.1	3.2	9.3	2.9	58%	10%	46	24	30	31%	72%	14%	12	95	67%	25%			0.0	92	109	$4
16 Proj	**9**	**10**	**0**	**181**	**189**	**3.49**	**3.32**	**1.18**	**649**	**581**	**718**	**21.7**	**3.2**	**9.4**	**2.9**	**57%**	**10%**	**46**	**22**	**32**	**29%**	**72%**	**10%**	**33**						**10.6**	**105**	**126**	**$13**

McGee,Jake

Age: 29	Th: L	Role RP	Health D	LIMA Plan A+
Ht: 6' 3"	Wt: 235	Type Pwr FB	PT/Exp C	Rand Var -2
			Consist A	MM 5510

We often write about the inherent inconsistency of RPs just because of the nature of 60-IP sample sizes. This one is as stable as they come, as narrow-range xERA and BPV show. Growing FB% is a crack in the armor, as 2013 hr/f reminds us how those FBs can turn into trouble. But that's picking nits. UP: 25 Sv

Yr Tm	W	L	Sv	IP	K	ERA	xERA	WHIP	oOPS	vL	vR	BF/G	Ctl	Dom	Cmd	FpK	SwK	G	L	F	H%	S%	hr/f	GS	APC	DOM%	DIS%	Sv%	LI	RAR	BPV	BPX	R$
11 TAM *	9	4	9	61	58	3.75	4.67	1.38	801	510	1143	4.2	2.9	8.6	2.9	56%	10%	33	18	49	33%	78%	13%	0	14			90	1.10	1.5	74	111	$5
12 TAM	5	2	0	55	73	1.95	2.49	0.80	452	665	291	3.1	1.8	11.9	6.6	62%	14%	44	19	37	27%	78%	7%	0	13			0	1.39	14.1	187	244	$10
13 TAM	5	3	1	63	75	4.02	3.20	1.18	659	678	648	3.7	3.2	10.8	3.4	63%	12%	43	19	39	30%	70%	13%	0	16			20	1.16	-1.2	130	169	$2
14 TAM	5	2	19	71	90	1.89	2.68	0.90	486	572	452	3.8	2.0	11.4	5.6	65%	14%	38	19	43	29%	79%	3%	0	16			83	1.38	16.3	166	198	$18
15 TAM	1	2	6	37	48	2.41	2.95	0.94	544	607	513	3.8	1.9	11.6	6.0	62%	13%	39	16	46	30%	78%	7%	0	16			60	1.30	7.1	173	206	$5
1st Half	0	0	3	17	27	1.56	2.11	0.63	400	500	346	3.3	0.5	14.0	27.0	63%	16%	31	20	49	29%	80%	6%	0	14			75	1.26	5.1	248	294	$5
2nd Half	1	2	3	20	21	3.15	3.81	1.20	658	704	637	4.2	3.2	9.5	3.0	61%	11%	44	13	44	30%	77%	8%	0	18			50	1.35	2.0	107	127	$4
16 Proj	**3**	**3**	**5**	**58**	**72**	**2.62**	**2.84**	**0.98**	**561**	**643**	**521**	**3.6**	**2.1**	**11.1**	**5.3**	**63%**	**13%**	**40**	**17**	**43**	**30%**	**76%**	**8%**	**0**						**9.6**	**161**	**191**	**$8**

McHugh,Collin

Age: 29	Th: R	Role SP	Health A	LIMA Plan C+
Ht: 6' 2"	Wt: 195	Type	PT/Exp B	Rand Var 0
			Consist F	MM 2205

ERA slippage now casts 2014 as a career year, but four reasons why he should get back under 3.50 ERA: 1) turned LDs into GBs. 2) SwK stability and 2nd half Dom recovery suggest he can hold 8.0+ Dom tier. 3) FpK gains now confirm the Ctl, support 3.0+ Cmd. 4) 2nd half DOM%/DIS% shows a new level. Strong buy.

Yr Tm	W	L	Sv	IP	K	ERA	xERA	WHIP	oOPS	vL	vR	BF/G	Ctl	Dom	Cmd	FpK	SwK	G	L	F	H%	S%	hr/f	GS	APC	DOM%	DIS%	Sv%	LI	RAR	BPV	BPX	R$
11 aa	8	2	2	93	80	2.79	2.58	1.17				20.7	2.7	7.8	2.8						30%	75%								13.2	109	164	$9
12 NYM *	7	13	0	170	130	3.81	3.94	1.30	1044	1192	937	21.2	2.8	6.9	2.4	60%	9%	33	28	39	30%	73%	19%	4	50	25%	75%	0	1.17	4.2	68	88	$5
13 2 NL *	6	9	0	139	85	5.41	5.62	1.60	1053	1252	914	22.8	2.2	5.5	2.5	54%	9%	40	28	32	36%	67%	18%	5	62	0%	40%	0	0.56	-26.5	49	64	-$15
14 HOU *	11	9	0	174	167	2.91	2.49	1.05	588	609	556	22.4	2.4	8.7	3.5	58%	11%	42	24	34	27%	74%	9%	25	99	68%	12%			17.8	118	141	$18
15 HOU	19	7	0	204	171	3.89	3.90	1.28	705	648	755	26.8	2.3	7.6	3.2	62%	11%	45	20	35	32%	71%	9%	32	101	63%	13%			1.9	96	114	$12
1st Half	9	4	0	107	85	4.54	4.03	1.30	748	681	807	26.8	2.3	7.1	3.1	60%	11%	46	18	36	31%	67%	11%	17	101	47%	18%			-7.7	91	108	$7
2nd Half	10	3	0	97	86	3.17	3.75	1.25	656	613	696	26.9	2.4	8.0	3.3	64%	11%	45	22	33	32%	76%	6%	15	102	80%	7%			9.5	102	121	$17
16 Proj	**14**	**8**	**0**	**189**	**158**	**3.49**	**3.68**	**1.21**	**669**	**641**	**699**	**23.7**	**2.4**	**7.6**	**3.2**	**61%**	**11%**	**44**	**22**	**34**	**30%**	**73%**	**8%**	**32**						**10.9**	**93**	**111**	**$13**

Medlen,Kris

Age: 30	Th: R	Role RP	Health F	LIMA Plan B+
Ht: 5' 10"	Wt: 190	Type GB	PT/Exp C	Rand Var 0
			Consist C	MM 2103

Returned from March 2014 TJ surgery (his 2nd), flashed 8.2 Dom/6.0 Cmd in Aug. Those skills evaporated as SP in Sept/Oct (4.1 Dom, 1.3 Cmd). Maybe just ran out of steam in recovery, but all of these samples are too flimsy to interpret. Will be two years clear of TJS by Opening Day; 2011-13 BPV are worth speculation.

Yr Tm	W	L	Sv	IP	K	ERA	xERA	WHIP	oOPS	vL	vR	BF/G	Ctl	Dom	Cmd	FpK	SwK	G	L	F	H%	S%	hr/f	GS	APC	DOM%	DIS%	Sv%	LI	RAR	BPV	BPX	R$
11 ATL	0	0	0	2	2	0.00	2.87	0.43	250	0	500	4.0	0.0	7.7	0.0	75%	4%	33	17	50	18%	0%	0%	0	12			0	3.05	1.1	150	225	-$3
12 ATL	10	1	1	138	120	1.57	2.97	0.91	529	519	539	10.4	1.5	7.8	5.2	66%	10%	53	19	28	26%	85%	6%	12	38	92%	0%	50	0.81	41.7	131	171	$29
13 ATL	15	12	0	197	157	3.11	3.60	1.22	706	730	680	25.6	2.1	7.2	3.3	65%	11%	45	24	31	31%	78%	10%	31	95	71%	13%	0	0.82	18.4	94	123	$16
14																																	
15 KC *	7	3	0	89	54	4.36	4.92	1.34	705	734	671	17.6	2.4	5.5	2.3	58%	9%	50	17	33	29%	74%	10%	8	62	38%	13%	0	0.87	-4.3	32	39	-$1
1st Half	1	1	0	18	6	6.48	7.74	1.56				19.3	1.8	3.2	1.8						29%	69%	0%	0						-5.5	-47	-55	-$15
2nd Half	6	2	0	71	48	3.83	4.22	1.28	705	734	671	17.1	2.6	6.1	2.3	58%	9%	50	17	33	29%	75%	10%	8	62	38%	13%	0	0.87	1.1	52	61	$2
16 Proj	**10**	**6**	**0**	**131**	**93**	**3.79**	**3.86**	**1.29**	**777**	**773**	**779**	**18.0**	**2.3**	**6.4**	**2.8**	**63%**	**10%**	**50**	**19**	**31**	**29%**	**76%**	**16%**	**24**						**2.8**	**81**	**96**	**$4**

Mejia,Jenrry

Age: 26	Th: R	Role RP	Health F	LIMA Plan C
Ht: 6' 0"	Wt: 205	Type Pwr GB	PT/Exp C	Rand Var -5
			Consist B	MM 2300

After getting tagged with an 80-game suspension for a banned substance in April, he returned in July only to get busted again, earning a 162-game suspension. While knee-jerk reaction might be "how dumb can you be?", this really seems like a glimpse of just how much performance pressure these guys face. Sad.

Yr Tm	W	L	Sv	IP	K	ERA	xERA	WHIP	oOPS	vL	vR	BF/G	Ctl	Dom	Cmd	FpK	SwK	G	L	F	H%	S%	hr/f	GS	APC	DOM%	DIS%	Sv%	LI	RAR	BPV	BPX	R$
11 aaa	1	2	0	28	18	2.90	1.62	1.03				21.8	4.0	5.6	1.4						20%	71%								3.6	75	112	$0
12 NYM *	4	6	0	98	49	4.29	4.74	1.52	897	822	964	12.8	3.2	4.5	1.4	54%	7%	67	11	22	32%	72%	17%	3	60	33%	33%	0	0.57	-3.4	34	44	-$6
13 NYM	1	2	0	27	27	2.30	2.65	1.17	641	683	609	22.4	1.3	8.9	6.8	60%	13%	58	22	20	34%	83%	13%	5	87	80%	20%			5.3	160	209	-$1
14 NYM	6	6	28	94	98	3.65	3.59	1.48	723	647	792	6.6	3.9	9.4	2.4	59%	12%	50	20	30	35%	78%	11%	7	25	29%	43%	90	1.25	1.0	91	109	$10
15 NYM	1	0	0	7	7	0.00	3.25	0.82	481	573	414	3.9	2.5	8.6	3.5	44%	14%	47	12	41	23%	100%	0%	0	15			0	1.17	3.6	113	135	-$2
1st Half																																	
2nd Half	1	0	0	7	7	0.00	3.25	0.82	481	573	414	3.9	2.5	8.6	3.5	44%	14%	47	12	41	23%	100%	0%	0	15			0	1.17	3.6	113	135	-$2
16 Proj	**1**	**1**	**0**	**22**	**20**	**3.51**	**3.80**	**1.45**	**667**	**597**	**731**	**7.9**	**3.2**	**8.3**	**2.6**	**59%**	**12%**	**50**	**20**	**30**	**35%**	**78%**	**9%**	**0**						**1.2**	**91**	**108**	**-$3**

Melancon,Mark

Age: 31	Th: R	Role RP	Health A	LIMA Plan C
Ht: 6' 2"	Wt: 215	Type xGB	PT/Exp A	Rand Var -3
			Consist A	MM 5331

Overcame an ominous April (5.23 ERA, velocity dip) to post another rock-solid season of 9th inning work. That slow start placed a drag on full-season skills; 2nd half levels were much more in line with 2013-14 peak. Doesn't have 100-K upside of the elite closer tier, but AAA Reliability makes him a rare "safe" closer play.

Yr Tm	W	L	Sv	IP	K	ERA	xERA	WHIP	oOPS	vL	vR	BF/G	Ctl	Dom	Cmd	FpK	SwK	G	L	F	H%	S%	hr/f	GS	APC	DOM%	DIS%	Sv%	LI	RAR	BPV	BPX	R$
11 HOU	8	4	20	74	66	2.78	3.16	1.22	631	704	581	4.4	3.1	8.0	2.5	61%	10%	57	22	21	29%	79%	11%	0	16			80	1.12	10.6	94	141	$14
12 BOS *	0	2	12	67	62	4.59	3.82	1.21	754	875	655	4.3	2.1	8.3	4.0	62%	10%	50	24	26	31%	64%	22%	0	18			92	0.62	-4.7	105	137	$2
13 PIT	3	2	16	71	70	1.39	2.33	0.96	511	357	638	3.9	1.0	8.9	8.8	65%	12%	60	24	16	31%	85%	3%	0	14			76	1.31	21.6	170	222	$16
14 PIT	3	5	33	71	71	1.90	2.50	0.87	473	415	524	3.8	1.4	9.0	6.5	69%	14%	57	20	23	27%	78%	5%	0	14			89	1.37	16.1	159	190	$22
15 PIT	3	2	51	77	62	2.23	3.00	0.93	541	380	673	3.8	1.6	7.3	4.4	62%	12%	58	20	23	26%	78%	8%	0	14			96	1.35	16.4	123	146	$30
1st Half	1	1	27	40	28	1.58	3.13	0.98	532	390	651	3.8	1.8	6.3	3.5	66%	11%	65	15	21	25%	86%	8%	0	13			96	1.31	11.8	108	128	$30
2nd Half	2	1	24	37	34	2.95	2.85	0.87	551	369	697	3.7	1.5	8.3	5.7	58%	13%	48	26	25	26%	67%	8%	0	15			96	1.39	4.6	137	162	$29
16 Proj	**3**	**3**	**41**	**73**	**66**	**2.25**	**2.73**	**0.94**	**533**	**423**	**624**	**3.7**	**1.6**	**8.2**	**5.2**	**64%**	**13%**	**56**	**22**	**22**	**27%**	**77%**	**8%**	**0**						**15.3**	**139**	**166**	**$25**

RAY MURPHY

Miley,Wade

Age:	29	**Th:**	L	**Role**	SP	**Health**	A	**LIMA Plan**	C		
Ht:	6' 0"	**Wt:**	220	**Type**		**PT/Exp**	A	**Rand Var**	0		
						Consist	A	**MM**	2205		

Hideous April (-46 BPV) trashed his entire 1st half line. 2nd half skills snapped back to historical norms, though low S% kept ERA inflated. AAA Reliability is not a good thing at this level as it caps his upside. ERA may well drift back into the 3s, but without a ton of Ks or Ws, there isn't much value to be scratched out.

Yr Tm	W	L	Sv	IP	K	ERA	xERA	WHIP	oOPS	vL	vR	BF/G	Ctl	Dom	Cmd	FpK	SwK	G	L	F	H%	S%	hr/f	GS	APC	DOM%	DIS%	Sv%	LI	RAR	BPV	BPX	R$
11 ARI *	12	5	0	170	107	4.42	4.47	1.44	873	808	885	24.1	3.1	5.7	1.8	60%	9%	46	24	30	31%	70%	15%	7	82	43%	29%	0	0.73	-9.9	47	71	-$1
12 ARI	16	11	0	195	144	3.33	3.89	1.18	685	544	723	25.2	1.7	6.7	3.9	60%	9%	43	23	34	31%	73%	7%	29	94	59%	14%	0	0.82	16.5	95	123	$17
13 ARI	10	10	0	203	147	3.55	3.79	1.32	727	704	732	25.7	2.9	6.5	2.2	59%	8%	52	21	27	30%	76%	13%	33	98	52%	18%			7.8	68	89	$7
14 ARI	8	12	0	201	183	4.34	3.59	1.40	746	727	752	26.2	3.4	8.2	2.4	63%	10%	51	21	28	32%	71%	14%	33	97	48%	15%			-14.8	86	102	-$3
15 BOS	11	11	0	194	147	4.46	4.16	1.37	740	674	760	26.0	3.0	6.8	2.3	61%	9%	49	21	30	32%	68%	9%	32	100	56%	16%			-11.9	70	83	-$1
1st Half	8	7	0	89	62	4.53	4.63	1.44	750	572	803	24.3	3.5	6.2	1.8	62%	8%	48	17	34	31%	69%	8%	16	93	44%	31%			-6.3	44	52	-$1
2nd Half	3	4	0	104	85	4.40	3.78	1.30	732	766	722	27.6	2.5	7.3	2.9	60%	9%	49	24	27	32%	67%	10%	16	106	69%	0%			-5.6	92	109	$0
16 Proj	**10**	**10**	**0**	**189**	**148**	**4.04**	**3.88**	**1.36**	**730**	**684**	**742**	**25.4**	**3.0**	**7.1**	**2.4**	**61%**	**9%**	**49**	**21**	**29**	**32%**	**71%**	**10%**	**31**						**-1.8**	**75**	**89**	**$2**

Miller,Andrew

Age:	31	**Th:**	L	**Role**	RP	**Health**	F	**LIMA Plan**	C+		
Ht:	6' 7"	**Wt:**	210	**Type**	Pwr	**PT/Exp**	C	**Rand Var**	-2		
						Consist	B	**MM**	5530		

Lefty closer bias? What's that? Won closer role by starting hot and staying that way, fully repeating 2014's other-worldly skills. July scare with a strained forearm reminds us that health will be a perpetual risk, but FpK spike closes the door on any lingering Ctl concerns. He may be brittle, but he's a stud.

Yr Tm	W	L	Sv	IP	K	ERA	xERA	WHIP	oOPS	vL	vR	BF/G	Ctl	Dom	Cmd	FpK	SwK	G	L	F	H%	S%	hr/f	GS	APC	DOM%	DIS%	Sv%	LI	RAR	BPV	BPX	R$
11 BOS *	9	6	0	131	98	4.52	4.59	1.62	857	812	874	19.3	5.5	6.7	1.2	58%	8%	45	23	31	31%	72%	12%	12	72	17%	42%	0	0.61	-9.4	47	71	-$6
12 BOS	3	2	0	40	51	3.35	3.32	1.19	588	429	829	3.2	4.5	11.4	2.6	54%	10%	43	23	34	28%	73%	9%	0	13			0	1.17	3.3	105	137	$1
13 BOS	1	2	0	31	48	2.64	2.47	1.37	624	725	526	3.6	5.0	14.1	2.8	59%	14%	56	21	23	36%	85%	20%	0	15			0	0.81	4.6	153	199	-$1
14 2AL	5	5	1	62	103	2.02	1.80	0.80	456	467	446	3.3	2.5	14.9	6.1	59%	15%	47	22	31	29%	77%	9%	0	14			50	1.54	13.2	226	270	$11
15 NYY	3	2	36	62	100	1.90	2.14	0.86	475	616	442	4.1	2.9	14.6	5.0	66%	18%	48	18	33	27%	83%	13%	0	16			95	1.22	15.7	210	250	$25
1st Half	0	1	17	26	43	1.03	2.02	0.68	348	375	342	4.0	3.4	14.7	4.3	67%	17%	52	15	33	18%	88%	7%	0	16			100	1.20	9.5	202	240	$22
2nd Half	3	1	19	35	57	2.55	2.22	0.99	564	756	514	4.2	2.5	14.5	5.7	65%	19%	46	20	34	33%	81%	16%	0	16			90	1.24	6.2	217	257	$27
16 Proj	**3**	**3**	**35**	**58**	**90**	**2.27**	**2.09**	**0.95**	**497**	**561**	**466**	**3.6**	**3.0**	**14.0**	**4.7**	**62%**	**16%**	**49**	**20**	**31**	**31%**	**78%**	**10%**	**0**						**12.1**	**198**	**236**	**$22**

Miller,Shelby

Age:	25	**Th:**	R	**Role**	SP	**Health**	A	**LIMA Plan**	C+		
Ht:	6' 3"	**Wt:**	215	**Type**	Pwr	**PT/Exp**	A	**Rand Var**	-2		
						Consist	B	**MM**	2205		

Season-long storyline was the old witticism, "he should sue for non-support," per record/ERA juxtaposition. Skills say he has little to gripe about. PRO: Recovered some lost Cmd, GB growth always helpful. CON: Subpar Dom and Cmd; xERA puts to rest any argument that he was unlucky. ERA downside outweighs W/L upside.

Yr Tm	W	L	Sv	IP	K	ERA	xERA	WHIP	oOPS	vL	vR	BF/G	Ctl	Dom	Cmd	FpK	SwK	G	L	F	H%	S%	hr/f	GS	APC	DOM%	DIS%	Sv%	LI	RAR	BPV	BPX	R$
11 aa	9	3	0	87	77	2.27	2.19	1.12				21.3	3.0	8.0	2.7						29%	79%								17.9	112	168	$11
12 STL *	12	10	0	150	153	4.58	4.54	1.37	463	485	445	19.1	3.1	9.1	3.0	57%	13%	42	15	42	33%	70%	0%	1	33	100%	0%	0	0.88	-10.5	81	106	$1
13 STL	15	9	0	173	169	3.06	3.73	1.21	670	761	588	23.3	3.0	8.8	3.0	62%	10%	38	20	41	29%	79%	10%	31	96	55%	13%			17.2	94	123	$16
14 STL	10	9	0	183	127	3.74	4.44	1.27	697	707	690	23.9	3.6	6.2	1.7	60%	7%	40	19	41	26%	74%	10%	31	89	42%	13%	0	0.75	0.1	33	40	$5
15 ATL	6	17	0	205	171	3.02	4.02	1.25	663	732	594	26.1	3.2	7.5	2.3	61%	10%	48	18	34	29%	77%	6%	33	98	61%	9%			23.8	75	89	$13
1st Half	5	4	0	109	88	2.07	3.74	1.10	584	686	484	25.9	2.8	7.3	2.6	62%	9%	51	18	31	27%	82%	5%	17	97	65%	6%			25.4	84	99	$25
2nd Half	1	13	0	97	83	4.10	4.34	1.42	746	782	711	26.3	3.6	7.7	2.1	60%	10%	45	18	37	32%	72%	7%	16	100	56%	13%			-1.6	64	76	-$1
16 Proj	**9**	**14**	**0**	**196**	**163**	**3.75**	**4.03**	**1.27**	**684**	**731**	**640**	**25.3**	**3.3**	**7.5**	**2.3**	**61%**	**9%**	**43**	**19**	**38**	**29%**	**72%**	**8%**	**32**						**5.1**	**68**	**80**	**$8**

Milone,Tommy

Age:	29	**Th:**	L	**Role**	SP	**Health**	C	**LIMA Plan**	B+		
Ht:	6' 0"	**Wt:**	205	**Type**		**PT/Exp**	C	**Rand Var**	0		
						Consist	C	**MM**	1103		

9-5, 3.92 ERA in 129 IP at MIN. Tale of three seasons: Got wrecked in four April starts and sent down. Shredded Triple-A for two months (3 BB/47 K in 39 IP), returned to MIN for 2nd half with uneven results. Dom/Cmd recovery paired with 2nd half DOM% points to some spot-start utility. Hey, that's progress.

Yr Tm	W	L	Sv	IP	K	ERA	xERA	WHIP	oOPS	vL	vR	BF/G	Ctl	Dom	Cmd	FpK	SwK	G	L	F	H%	S%	hr/f	GS	APC	DOM%	DIS%	Sv%	LI	RAR	BPV	BPX	R$
11 WAS *	13	6	0	174	140	3.84	3.57	1.18	742	1164	695	24.1	1.0	7.2	7.2	71%	8%	31	20	49	33%	68%	5%	5	82	20%	40%			2.1	176	264	$11
12 OAK	13	10	0	190	137	3.74	4.10	1.28	738	749	734	25.5	1.7	6.5	3.8	68%	9%	38	25	37	31%	75%	11%	31	98	52%	16%			6.4	87	113	$9
13 OAK	12	9	0	156	126	4.14	4.22	1.27	738	790	724	23.8	2.2	7.3	3.2	67%	9%	35	20	45	30%	73%	11%	26	93	46%	23%	0	0.75	-5.4	83	108	$4
14 2AL *	7	6	0	146	90	4.75	5.43	1.51	763	729	771	23.4	3.0	5.6	1.8	63%	8%	39	21	39	32%	72%	10%	21	88	24%	24%	0	0.75	-18.2	27	32	-$9
15 MIN *	13	5	1	167	126	3.25	3.77	1.20	731	603	772	23.2	2.1	6.8	3.2	64%	8%	42	23	35	29%	78%	12%	23	86	57%	30%	100	0.86	14.6	80	95	$13
1st Half	8	1	0	98	75	2.24	3.43	1.15	698	454	812	26.1	2.2	6.8	3.2	60%	8%	40	22	38	28%	86%	11%	10	98	50%	40%			20.8	84	100	$22
2nd Half	5	4	1	69	51	4.70	4.14	1.28	759	827	744	21.0	2.1	6.7	3.2	67%	8%	43	24	33	30%	66%	12%	13	78	62%	23%	100	0.90	-6.2	84	100	$1
16 Proj	**10**	**9**	**0**	**174**	**126**	**4.05**	**4.10**	**1.27**	**721**	**667**	**736**	**24.1**	**2.3**	**6.5**	**2.8**	**65%**	**8%**	**40**	**22**	**38**	**30%**	**71%**	**10%**	**29**						**-1.9**	**73**	**87**	**$4**

Minor,Mike

Age:	28	**Th:**	L	**Role**	SP	**Health**	F	**LIMA Plan**	B+		
Ht:	6' 4"	**Wt:**	220	**Type**		**PT/Exp**	C	**Rand Var**	0		
						Consist	D	**MM**	2201		

Battled shoulder problems throughout 2014, eventually undergoing surgery in May 2015 to repair torn left labrum. He was throwing before end of season, but it's a long road back to regaining 2012-13's skills. Taking a flyer isn't unreasonable. But take a moment to identify the nearest exit, which may be behind you.

Yr Tm	W	L	Sv	IP	K	ERA	xERA	WHIP	oOPS	vL	vR	BF/G	Ctl	Dom	Cmd	FpK	SwK	G	L	F	H%	S%	hr/f	GS	APC	DOM%	DIS%	Sv%	LI	RAR	BPV	BPX	R$
11 ATL *	9	8	0	183	162	3.99	4.60	1.42	785	835	774	25.1	2.9	7.9	2.8	64%	9%	37	27	35	34%	75%	8%	15	92	27%	20%			-1.1	75	113	$2
12 ATL	11	10	0	179	145	4.12	4.18	1.15	702	724	694	24.3	2.8	7.3	2.6	59%	8%	35	21	44	26%	69%	12%	30	95	50%	17%			-2.2	68	89	$10
13 ATL	13	9	0	205	181	3.21	3.68	1.09	657	583	680	25.6	2.0	8.0	3.9	64%	10%	35	22	43	28%	75%	9%	32	98	75%	3%			16.6	102	132	$20
14 ATL *	8	14	0	163	132	5.00	5.34	1.45	798	887	774	23.9	2.6	7.3	2.8	61%	8%	41	23	36	33%	70%	13%	25	97	52%	28%			-25.3	54	64	-$8
15																																	
1st Half																																	
2nd Half																																	
16 Proj	**6**	**6**	**0**	**102**	**85**	**4.17**	**3.99**	**1.27**	**746**	**767**	**740**	**24.2**	**2.6**	**7.5**	**2.9**	**61%**	**9%**	**37**	**23**	**40**	**30%**	**71%**	**12%**	**17**						**-2.6**	**80**	**96**	**$1**

Montero,Rafael

Age:	25	**Th:**	R	**Role**	SP	**Health**	F	**LIMA Plan**	C		
Ht:	6' 0"	**Wt:**	185	**Type**	Pwr xFB	**PT/Exp**	D	**Rand Var**	+2		
						Consist	B	**MM**	1201		

Spent the spring in competition for 5th SP job, then made team as RP. After four appearances, sent to Triple-A to stretch out as SP. Made it back to NY for one start, then shoulder started barking. Essentially shelved for rest of year, though no surgery required. Still young and intriguing, now has some questions to answer.

Yr Tm	W	L	Sv	IP	K	ERA	xERA	WHIP	oOPS	vL	vR	BF/G	Ctl	Dom	Cmd	FpK	SwK	G	L	F	H%	S%	hr/f	GS	APC	DOM%	DIS%	Sv%	LI	RAR	BPV	BPX	R$
11																																	
12																																	
13 a/a	12	7	0	155	132	2.60	2.52	1.09				22.5	1.8	7.6	4.3						30%	76%								24.3	133	173	$18
14 NYM *	7	7	0	124	110	3.35	3.57	1.30	825	923	711	19.7	3.7	8.0	2.1	60%	9%	34	22	44	29%	77%	15%	8	84	25%	25%	0	0.60	6.1	76	90	$4
15 NYM	0	1	0	10	13	4.50	3.62	1.40	661	1457	471	9.2	4.5	11.7	2.6	50%	10%	48	19	33	37%	64%	0%	1	38	100%	0%	0	1.31	-0.7	115	137	-$4
1st Half	0	1	0	10	13	4.50	3.62	1.40	661	1457	471	9.2	4.5	11.7	2.6	50%	10%	48	19	33	37%	64%	0%	1	38	100%	0%	0	1.31	-0.7	115	137	-$4
2nd Half																																	
16 Proj	**6**	**5**	**0**	**87**	**76**	**3.56**	**4.29**	**1.26**	**635**	**713**	**546**	**20.9**	**3.4**	**7.8**	**2.3**	**60%**	**9%**	**34**	**22**	**44**	**29%**	**75%**	**7%**	**17**						**4.3**	**61**	**73**	**$3**

Montgomery,Michael

Age:	27	**Th:**	L	**Role**	SP	**Health**	A	**LIMA Plan**	D+		
Ht:	6' 5"	**Wt:**	180	**Type**	GB	**PT/Exp**	D	**Rand Var**	+1		
						Consist	A	**MM**	1101		

4-6, 4.60 ERA in 90 IP at SEA. Finally developed some Cmd in early-season Triple-A stint, earning a June call-up. Couldn't hold that new skill in majors, though FpK is more optimistic about Ctl issues. Long-term GB tilt gives him something to start with, but he'll need that Cmd to stick to become relevant. Watch.

Yr Tm	W	L	Sv	IP	K	ERA	xERA	WHIP	oOPS	vL	vR	BF/G	Ctl	Dom	Cmd	FpK	SwK	G	L	F	H%	S%	hr/f	GS	APC	DOM%	DIS%	Sv%	LI	RAR	BPV	BPX	R$
11 aaa	5	11	0	151	107	5.63	4.73	1.54				23.5	3.9	6.4	1.7						33%	63%								-31.4	49	73	-$13
12 a/a	5	12	0	150	91	6.70	6.33	1.73				25.2	3.7	5.5	1.5						35%	62%								-49.6	15	20	-$27
13 aaa	7	8	0	109	65	5.50	5.00	1.61				24.1	3.9	5.4	1.4						33%	65%								-21.9	35	45	-$11
14 aaa	10	5	0	126	81	5.49	4.72	1.53				21.9	3.7	5.8	1.6						33%	63%								-27.2	45	54	-$10
15 SEA *	8	9	0	155	111	4.44	4.04	1.36	754	841	725	24.1	3.2	6.5	2.0	63%	9%	51	20	29	30%	68%	13%	16	91	44%	25%			-9.2	60	71	-$2
1st Half	8	5	0	103	69	2.75	2.45	1.09	524	664	480	25.2	2.4	6.1	2.6	65%	9%	45	20	35	27%	75%	4%	7	98	71%	0%			15.3	90	107	$13
2nd Half	0	4	0	52	42	7.77	7.16	1.89	984	995	979	22.4	4.8	7.2	1.5	61%	10%	58	19	23	37%	60%	28%	9	85	22%	44%			-24.6	14	17	-$32
16 Proj	**5**	**6**	**0**	**102**	**72**	**4.36**	**4.14**	**1.44**	**747**	**821**	**721**	**22.5**	**3.4**	**6.4**	**1.9**	**62%**	**9%**	**53**	**20**	**28**	**31%**	**72%**	**12%**	**19**						**-5.0**	**55**	**66**	**-$4**

RAY MURPHY

Moore,Matt

Age: 27	Th: L	Role SP	Health F	LIMA Plan B
Ht: 6' 3"	Wt: 200	Type Pwr FB	PT/Exp C	Rand Var +1
			Consist A	MM 2403

4-3, 5.43 ERA in 63 IP at TAM. Struggled in first 6 post-TJS starts, was sent to minors for a month, then returned to much better results. Still a tick behind pre-injury velocity, but 4 PQS-DOM in last 5 starts a hopeful small sample (2.3 Ctl, 7.4 Dom) for... UP: sub-3.50 ERA

Yr Tm	W	L	Sv	IP	K	ERA	xERA	WHIP	oOPS	vL	vR	BF/G	Ctl	Dom	Cmd	FpK	SwK	G	L	F	H%	S%	hr/f	GS	APC	DOM%	DIS%	Sv%	LI	RAR	BPV	BPX	R$
11 TAM *	13	3	0	164	200	2.05	2.05	0.98	651	697	633	20.8	2.5	11.0	4.4	60%	16%	43	19	38	29%	83%	13%	1	56	100%	0%	0	0.79	38.3	155	233	$29
12 TAM	11	11	0	177	175	3.81	4.24	1.35	706	685	712	24.5	4.1	8.9	2.2	60%	12%	37	20	43	30%	74%	9%	31	98	45%	23%			4.6	64	83	$7
13 TAM	17	4	0	150	143	3.29	4.23	1.30	655	617	672	23.8	4.5	8.6	1.9	51%	10%	39	18	42	27%	77%	8%	27	97	41%	22%			10.6	48	63	$12
14 TAM	0	2	0	10	6	2.70	4.75	1.50	777	1010	703	22.0	4.5	5.4	1.2	44%	7%	45	27	27	29%	86%	11%	2	92	0%	50%			1.3	-1	-2	-$3
15 TAM *	5	7	0	103	93	5.10	5.17	1.48	839	785	866	23.4	3.1	8.1	2.6	60%	10%	39	22	39	34%	69%	11%	12	88	33%	42%			-14.5	60	72	-$7
1st Half	0	2	0	15	16	6.26	6.60	1.80	714	804	657	23.1	3.8	9.7	2.5	62%	11%	33	33	33	42%	67%	0%	1	81	0%	100%			-4.2	62	74	-$16
2nd Half	5	5	0	88	77	4.90	4.93	1.43	849	783	881	23.4	3.0	7.8	2.6	60%	10%	40	21	39	32%	69%	12%	11	89	36%	36%			-10.3	60	71	-$6
16 Proj	**11**	**8**	**0**	**160**	**156**	**3.76**	**3.95**	**1.31**	**703**	**668**	**717**	**23.1**	**3.6**	**8.8**	**2.4**	**58%**	**11%**	**39**	**20**	**41**	**30%**	**74%**	**10%**	**29**						**3.9**	**77**	**92**	**$7**

Morales,Franklin

Age: 30	Th: L	Role RP	Health D	LIMA Plan B
Ht: 6' 1"	Wt: 210	Type	PT/Exp C	Rand Var -1
			Consist B	MM 1100

Back to the pen, but now as a GB specialist, with career best Cmd. H% fluctuation explains 1H/2H ERA split, but FpK says that improved Ctl is not sustainable. 2H return to .900+ oOPS vs RHB may destine him for LOOGY usage in the near future, further reducing his value (as if that were possible).

Yr Tm	W	L	Sv	IP	K	ERA	xERA	WHIP	oOPS	vL	vR	BF/G	Ctl	Dom	Cmd	FpK	SwK	G	L	F	H%	S%	hr/f	GS	APC	DOM%	DIS%	Sv%	LI	RAR	BPV	BPX	R$
11 2 TM	1	2	0	46	42	3.69	4.22	1.27	757	789	725	3.9	3.7	8.2	2.2	60%	10%	30	16	54	28%	75%	9%	0	15			0	0.94	1.4	55	83	-$1
12 BOS	3	4	1	76	76	3.77	3.98	1.23	685	490	788	8.8	3.5	9.0	2.5	57%	11%	40	19	41	28%	75%	13%	9	36	44%	33%	100	1.14	2.3	84	109	$2
13 BOS *	3	3	0	45	36	4.48	4.28	1.42	737	446	925	6.8	4.1	7.2	1.7	57%	10%	39	24	38	29%	71%	7%	1	22	0%	0%	0	1.12	-3.4	51	66	-$3
14 COL	6	9	0	142	100	5.37	4.66	1.62	859	699	923	17.0	4.1	6.3	1.5	56%	9%	43	25	33	32%	71%	16%	22	64	36%	41%	0	0.87	-28.7	24	28	-$15
15 KC	4	2	0	62	41	3.18	3.91	1.16	687	570	768	3.9	2.0	5.9	2.9	53%	7%	49	22	28	29%	74%	7%	0	14			0	0.88	6.0	79	94	$2
1st Half	3	0	0	33	21	2.70	3.69	0.96	598	670	523	3.8	1.9	5.7	3.0	57%	8%	51	22	27	25%	71%	4%	0	14			0	0.81	5.2	80	95	$5
2nd Half	1	2	0	29	20	3.72	4.17	1.38	778	400	948	3.9	2.2	6.2	2.9	49%	7%	48	22	30	33%	76%	11%	0	14			0	0.96	0.9	79	94	-$1
16 Proj	**3**	**3**	**0**	**58**	**42**	**4.04**	**4.20**	**1.35**	**757**	**601**	**845**	**5.3**	**3.0**	**6.5**	**2.2**	**55%**	**9%**	**44**	**22**	**34**	**30%**	**73%**	**10%**	**0**						**-0.6**	**58**	**69**	**-$2**

Morgan,Adam

Age: 26	Th: L	Role SP	Health A	LIMA Plan D+
Ht: 6' 1"	Wt: 195	Type Con xFB	PT/Exp D	Rand Var 0
			Consist B	MM 0001

5-7, 4.48 ERA in 84 IP at PHI. Lost 2014 to shoulder surgery, and continued his recovery in the majors (note APC). S% shows little help from the pen, but low velocity (89 mph), low Dom, extreme FB pitchers shoulder a lot of their own blame. Avoid.

Yr Tm	W	L	Sv	IP	K	ERA	xERA	WHIP	oOPS	vL	vR	BF/G	Ctl	Dom	Cmd	FpK	SwK	G	L	F	H%	S%	hr/f	GS	APC	DOM%	DIS%	Sv%	LI	RAR	BPV	BPX	R$
11																																	
12 aa	4	1	0	36	25	3.93	3.84	1.34				24.7	2.7	6.4	2.4						32%	71%								0.4	73	95	-$2
13 aaa	2	7	0	71	42	4.66	6.24	1.69				20.1	3.3	5.3	1.6						34%	76%								-7.0	15	20	-$9
14																																	
15 PHI *	5	13	0	153	77	5.13	5.50	1.51	775	617	820	23.6	2.7	4.5	1.7	66%	10%	31	20	49	31%	69%	10%	15	83	47%	27%			-22.0	17	20	-$13
1st Half	1	7	0	81	39	5.33	6.38	1.74	800	719	818	24.6	3.7	4.3	1.2	65%	13%	34	17	49	34%	72%	18%	2	88	50%	0%			-13.7	2	2	-$21
2nd Half	4	6	0	72	38	4.90	5.02	1.26	771	587	819	23.2	1.6	4.8	2.9	67%	10%	30	21	49	29%	65%	9%	13	82	46%	31%			-8.3	50	59	-$3
16 Proj	**6**	**10**	**0**	**123**	**70**	**4.78**	**5.35**	**1.52**	**779**	**592**	**827**	**22.2**	**2.8**	**5.1**	**1.8**	**67%**	**10%**	**30**	**21**	**49**	**32%**	**72%**	**7%**	**24**						**-12.4**	**25**	**29**	**-$8**

Morin,Michael

Age: 25	Th: R	Role RP	Health D	LIMA Plan A
Ht: 6' 4"	Wt: 220	Type Pwr FB	PT/Exp D	Rand Var +5
			Consist B	MM 3400

4-2, 6.37 ERA in 35 IP at LAA. 1H woes preceded June DL trip for oblique strain, then sent to minors when still not effective. SwK and FpK support big Dom and Cmd, but was far too hittable. Positive sample in Sept, with 18 K in 11 IP, keeps hopes aflicker.

Yr Tm	W	L	Sv	IP	K	ERA	xERA	WHIP	oOPS	vL	vR	BF/G	Ctl	Dom	Cmd	FpK	SwK	G	L	F	H%	S%	hr/f	GS	APC	DOM%	DIS%	Sv%	LI	RAR	BPV	BPX	R$
11																																	
12																																	
13 aa	0	2	10	31	29	2.39	2.95	1.10				4.7	1.4	8.4	6.0						32%	81%								5.7	164	214	$3
14 LAA	4	4	0	59	54	2.90	3.67	1.19	629	737	511	4.1	2.9	8.2	2.8	63%	12%	44	17	39	30%	76%	5%	0	15			0	1.07	6.1	92	110	$3
15 LAA *	8	4	2	53	57	6.23	4.78	1.44	720	687	740	3.7	2.4	9.8	4.0	63%	16%	39	18	43	38%	56%	7%	0	12			67	0.70	-14.7	112	133	-$4
1st Half	2	1	1	19	16	7.14	5.46	1.41	688	699	680	3.3	2.4	7.5	3.1	59%	13%	40	10	50	32%	51%	13%	0	11			100	0.59	-7.3	53	63	-$8
2nd Half	6	3	1	34	42	5.73	4.40	1.46	747	678	790	3.9	2.4	11.0	4.5	67%	19%	38	26	36	42%	58%	0%	0	12			50	0.79	-7.4	144	171	-$1
16 Proj	**6**	**4**	**0**	**58**	**58**	**4.09**	**3.62**	**1.30**	**734**	**757**	**715**	**3.9**	**2.4**	**9.0**	**3.7**	**63%**	**15%**	**41**	**18**	**41**	**34%**	**70%**	**8%**	**0**						**-0.9**	**116**	**138**	**$0**

Morris,Bryan

Age: 29	Th: R	Role RP	Health B	LIMA Plan D+
Ht: 6' 3"	Wt: 225	Type xGB	PT/Exp C	Rand Var -3
			Consist B	MM 2101

An effective groundballer, and FpK and SwK suggest potential Ctl and Dom upside. However, current weak Cmd limits chances and effectiveness in the late innings. For now, only contributes to ERA and Holds, but improved Ctl would start whittling down WHIP to something more tolerable.

Yr Tm	W	L	Sv	IP	K	ERA	xERA	WHIP	oOPS	vL	vR	BF/G	Ctl	Dom	Cmd	FpK	SwK	G	L	F	H%	S%	hr/f	GS	APC	DOM%	DIS%	Sv%	LI	RAR	BPV	BPX	R$
11 aa	3	4	3	78	50	4.07	4.04	1.50				9.6	3.8	5.8	1.5						33%	71%								-1.2	59	89	-$2
12 PIT *	2	2	5	86	67	3.28	4.18	1.31	375	125	533	7.0	2.0	7.0	3.5	65%	20%	73	0	27	33%	78%	0%	0	15			83	0.16	7.8	89	116	$3
13 PIT	5	7	0	65	37	3.46	4.18	1.31	705	745	674	4.9	3.9	5.1	1.3	58%	12%	58	18	25	25%	78%	16%	0	17			0	1.18	3.2	23	29	$0
14 2 NL	8	1	0	64	50	1.82	3.47	1.27	684	726	652	4.5	3.4	7.0	2.1	64%	14%	59	19	21	28%	91%	15%	0	16			0	1.34	15.3	72	86	$6
15 MIA	5	4	0	63	47	3.14	3.99	1.48	721	796	667	4.1	3.7	6.7	1.8	64%	12%	61	18	22	33%	79%	7%	0	15			0	1.05	6.4	60	71	-$1
1st Half	3	1	0	30	25	3.56	3.87	1.68	794	736	843	4.6	3.6	7.4	2.1	66%	13%	61	20	20	38%	80%	11%	0	16			0	0.71	1.5	76	90	-$3
2nd Half	2	3	0	33	22	2.76	4.11	1.29	645	871	510	3.8	3.9	6.1	1.6	61%	11%	60	16	23	28%	78%	4%	0	14			0	1.33	4.9	43	51	$2
16 Proj	**6**	**4**	**0**	**73**	**52**	**3.37**	**3.87**	**1.38**	**705**	**778**	**655**	**4.4**	**3.6**	**6.5**	**1.8**	**63%**	**13%**	**60**	**18**	**22**	**30%**	**77%**	**10%**	**0**						**5.3**	**57**	**68**	**$1**

Morton,Charlie

Age: 32	Th: R	Role SP	Health F	LIMA Plan B+
Ht: 6' 5"	Wt: 235	Type xGB	PT/Exp C	Rand Var +2
			Consist A	MM 2103

9-9, 4.81 ERA in 129 IP at PIT. Lingering effects of 2014 hip/hernia issues caused early season DL trip. 2nd half struggles traceable to H%/S% swing, and FB% spike. DOM%/DIS% and RAR tell us that this is a middling SP that helps with counting stats but little else.

Yr Tm	W	L	Sv	IP	K	ERA	xERA	WHIP	oOPS	vL	vR	BF/G	Ctl	Dom	Cmd	FpK	SwK	G	L	F	H%	S%	hr/f	GS	APC	DOM%	DIS%	Sv%	LI	RAR	BPV	BPX	R$
11 PIT	10	10	0	172	110	3.83	4.02	1.53	737	960	567	26.5	4.0	5.8	1.4	55%	8%	59	23	19	32%	74%	6%	29	94	31%	24%			2.4	32	48	-$1
12 PIT	2	6	0	50	25	4.65	4.25	1.45	812	740	886	24.8	2.0	4.5	2.3	61%	7%	57	21	23	33%	69%	13%	9	88	33%	22%			-3.9	61	80	-$6
13 PIT *	8	6	0	154	101	3.46	3.47	1.30	683	844	552	22.6	3.1	5.9	1.9	59%	9%	63	18	19	29%	74%	9%	20	86	50%	15%			7.7	63	83	$5
14 PIT	6	12	0	157	126	3.72	3.45	1.27	682	664	698	25.6	3.3	7.2	2.2	61%	8%	56	21	23	30%	71%	9%	26	96	50%	8%			0.4	76	90	$3
15 PIT *	11	10	0	149	112	4.40	4.15	1.37	769	894	633	24.1	2.9	6.7	2.3	62%	8%	57	21	21	32%	69%	15%	23	87	39%	22%			-8.1	67	80	$0
1st Half	8	3	0	66	41	3.54	3.61	1.28	709	804	624	24.8	2.5	5.5	2.2	66%	6%	62	22	16	30%	73%	16%	8	87	50%	25%			3.5	65	77	$7
2nd Half	3	7	0	83	71	5.10	3.80	1.43	801	936	639	24.7	3.1	7.7	2.4	60%	10%	54	21	25	33%	65%	15%	15	86	33%	20%			-11.6	86	102	-$6
16 Proj	**9**	**10**	**0**	**152**	**112**	**4.11**	**3.69**	**1.35**	**730**	**820**	**640**	**24.1**	**3.0**	**6.6**	**2.2**	**61%**	**8%**	**58**	**21**	**21**	**31%**	**70%**	**11%**	**26**						**-2.7**	**73**	**87**	**$1**

Moscot,Jon

Age: 24	Th: R	Role SP	Health F	LIMA Plan D+
Ht: 6' 4"	Wt: 205	Type	PT/Exp D	Rand Var 0
			Consist C	MM 0101

1-1, 4.63 ERA in 12 IP at CIN. Left (non-throwing) shoulder fracture ended MLB debut in the 1st inning of his 3rd start. MLE BPVs indicate he is not ready yet to contribute in the majors, and he will likely add to his 71 IP total in Triple-A before returning. Only interesting with Dom improvement.

Yr Tm	W	L	Sv	IP	K	ERA	xERA	WHIP	oOPS	vL	vR	BF/G	Ctl	Dom	Cmd	FpK	SwK	G	L	F	H%	S%	hr/f	GS	APC	DOM%	DIS%	Sv%	LI	RAR	BPV	BPX	R$
11																																	
12																																	
13 aa	2	1	0	31	25	4.25	6.07	1.72				23.5	3.7	7.2	2.0						37%	79%								-1.5	40	52	-$6
14 a/a	8	11	0	167	107	3.70	4.36	1.34				24.8	2.6	5.8	2.2						30%	76%								0.8	50	60	$1
15 CIN *	8	2	0	66	36	4.25	5.03	1.48	729	741	715	23.7	3.5	4.9	1.4	62%	5%	41	15	44	29%	75%	12%	3	62	0%	33%			-2.4	19	23	-$2
1st Half	8	2	0	66	36	4.25	5.03	1.48	729	741	715	23.7	3.5	4.9	1.4	62%	5%	41	15	44	29%	75%	12%	3	62	0%	33%			-2.4	19	23	-$2
2nd Half																																	
16 Proj	**6**	**3**	**0**	**73**	**49**	**4.15**	**5.30**	**1.55**				**23.9**	**3.4**	**6.1**	**1.8**	**0%**	**0%**				**33%**	**77%**		**13**						**-1.7**	**35**	**42**	**-$4**

MATT DODGE

Motte,Jason

Age: 34	Th: R	Role: RP	Health: F	LIMA Plan: B+
Ht: 6' 0"	Wt: 205	Type: Con FB	PT/Exp: D	Rand Var: -2
			Consist: A	MM: 1100

Grabbed a share of closing duties in June, but right shoulder strain ended his season in August. Dom has not yet returned post-2013 TJS, and SwK hints that it may not ever. Ctl, velocity, FpK showed recovery and generated more soft hit balls, but don't count on him for strikeouts at this stage in his career.

Yr Tm	W	L	Sv	IP	K	ERA	xERA	WHIP	oOPS	vL	vR	BF/G	Ctl	Dom	Cmd	FpK	SwK	G	L	F	H%	S%	hr/f	GS	APC	DOM%	DIS%	Sv%	LI	RAR	BPV	BPX	R$
11 STL	5	2	9	68	63	2.25	3.21	0.96	558	738	454	3.4	2.1	8.3	3.9	61%	12%	44	18	39	27%	76%	3%	0	14			69	1.35	14.2	115	173	$12
12 STL	4	5	42	72	86	2.75	2.91	0.92	576	381	756	4.2	2.1	10.8	5.1	71%	14%	41	20	40	25%	77%	13%	0	17			86	1.43	11.2	155	202	$27
13																																	
14 STL	1	0	0	25	17	4.68	4.75	1.52	891	733	989	3.8	3.2	6.1	1.9	63%	10%	37	21	42	29%	81%	20%	0	14			0	0.49	-2.9	38	45	-$4
15 CHC	8	1	6	48	34	3.91	4.69	1.22	689	828	610	3.6	2.0	6.3	3.1	67%	7%	30	23	47	30%	69%	5%	0	14			86	1.33	0.3	67	79	$4
1st Half	6	1	4	32	22	2.84	4.69	1.04	587	704	529	3.5	2.6	6.3	2.4	68%	8%	31	18	51	24%	77%	6%	0	14			100	1.66	4.4	52	62	$8
2nd Half	2	0	2	17	12	5.94	4.71	1.56	855	987	762	3.9	1.1	6.5	6.0	66%	6%	30	30	41	40%	60%	4%	0	15			67	0.71	-4.1	95	113	-$5
16 Proj	**4**	**3**	**0**	**44**	**31**	**3.65**	**4.13**	**1.21**	**705**	**716**	**697**	**3.7**	**1.9**	**6.3**	**3.3**	**67%**	**8%**	**36**	**22**	**42**	**30%**	**71%**	**6%**	**0**						**1.7**	**77**	**91**	**$0**

Mujica,Edward

Age: 32	Th: R	Role: RP	Health: C	LIMA Plan: C
Ht: 6' 3"	Wt: 225	Type: Con	PT/Exp: C	Rand Var: +3
			Consist: A	MM: 2110

Earned some consideration as a Plan B closer with BOS and OAK, but didn't establish traction. Ctl rebounded on continued strong FpK, but big 2nd half drop in SwK for an already low Dom limits value and opportunity. Low S% suggests some ERA recovery, but now barely an average reliever.

Yr Tm	W	L	Sv	IP	K	ERA	xERA	WHIP	oOPS	vL	vR	BF/G	Ctl	Dom	Cmd	FpK	SwK	G	L	F	H%	S%	hr/f	GS	APC	DOM%	DIS%	Sv%	LI	RAR	BPV	BPX	R$
11 FLA	9	6	0	76	63	2.96	3.16	1.03	638	570	700	4.4	1.7	7.5	4.5	61%	11%	48	18	34	27%	75%	10%	0	17			0	1.12	9.2	116	174	$9
12 2 NL	0	3	2	65	47	3.03	3.62	1.04	643	669	620	3.7	1.7	6.5	3.9	70%	11%	51	16	33	26%	75%	11%	0	13			25	1.21	7.9	101	132	$4
13 STL	2	1	37	65	46	2.78	3.52	1.01	674	659	687	3.9	0.7	6.4	9.2	72%	13%	45	16	39	27%	80%	12%	0	14			90	1.29	8.6	119	156	$19
14 BOS	2	4	8	60	43	3.90	3.99	1.38	790	904	694	4.0	2.1	6.5	3.1	69%	11%	43	21	36	33%	74%	9%	0	15			89	0.95	-1.2	80	96	$0
15 2 AL	3	5	1	47	30	4.75	4.12	1.25	788	838	756	4.0	1.3	5.7	4.3	70%	12%	45	17	38	29%	69%	18%	0	14			20	1.23	-4.6	90	107	-$3
1st Half	2	2	0	24	18	3.80	3.62	1.10	744	590	889	4.2	1.5	6.8	4.5	65%	15%	45	18	37	26%	76%	20%	0	16			0	1.00	0.5	105	124	-$1
2nd Half	1	3	1	24	12	5.70	4.65	1.39	827	1185	668	3.8	1.1	4.6	4.0	75%	8%	46	16	38	31%	64%	16%	0	13			33	1.41	-5.1	75	89	-$5
16 Proj	**3**	**5**	**2**	**65**	**44**	**4.16**	**3.93**	**1.24**	**762**	**831**	**713**	**3.9**	**1.4**	**6.0**	**4.2**	**70%**	**11%**	**45**	**18**	**37**	**30%**	**72%**	**14%**	**0**						**-1.6**	**92**	**110**	**$0**

Nelson,Jimmy

Age: 27	Th: R	Role: SP	Health: A	LIMA Plan: B
Ht: 6' 6"	Wt: 245	Type: Pwr GB	PT/Exp: B	Rand Var: 0
			Consist: B	MM: 2203

PRO: Big improvement vs. RHB; GB profile; monthly velocity increase; 8-start PQS-DOM streak. CON: Greater struggles vs. LHB; weakening FpK and Ctl; LD to the head ended season two weeks early. ABB Reliability score suggests more of same (except the concussion), but underwhelming Cmd caps the upside.

Yr Tm	W	L	Sv	IP	K	ERA	xERA	WHIP	oOPS	vL	vR	BF/G	Ctl	Dom	Cmd	FpK	SwK	G	L	F	H%	S%	hr/f	GS	APC	DOM%	DIS%	Sv%	LI	RAR	BPV	BPX	R$
11																																	
12 aa	2	4	0	46	37	4.88	4.28	1.72				20.9	7.6	7.2	0.9						29%	71%								-4.9	55	72	-$8
13 MIL *	10	10	0	162	147	3.67	3.79	1.43	286	473	63	22.3	4.0	8.2	2.0	49%	11%	42	33	25	33%	74%	0%	1	36	0%	0%	0	0.28	4.0	81	105	$3
14 MIL *	12	11	0	180	151	3.01	3.14	1.21	793	804	782	23.5	2.7	7.6	2.8	63%	10%	48	20	32	30%	76%	8%	12	79	58%	17%	0	0.83	16.3	96	114	$13
15 MIL	11	13	0	177	148	4.11	3.90	1.29	704	876	568	25.1	3.3	7.5	2.3	60%	10%	51	20	29	29%	70%	12%	30	93	53%	23%			-3.2	75	89	$5
1st Half	6	8	0	102	83	4.50	3.96	1.31	741	894	631	25.3	3.2	7.3	2.3	61%	11%	49	20	31	29%	69%	14%	17	93	41%	24%			-6.8	73	87	$3
2nd Half	5	5	0	75	65	3.58	3.82	1.25	654	855	473	24.8	3.5	7.8	2.2	59%	10%	53	20	27	29%	72%	8%	13	93	69%	23%			3.5	77	91	$7
16 Proj	**11**	**12**	**0**	**174**	**147**	**3.76**	**3.78**	**1.29**	**677**	**774**	**590**	**25.5**	**3.4**	**7.6**	**2.3**	**61%**	**10%**	**50**	**20**	**30**	**30%**	**72%**	**8%**	**28**						**4.3**	**75**	**89**	**$7**

Neris,Hector

Age: 27	Th: R	Role: RP	Health: A	LIMA Plan: D+
Ht: 6' 2"	Wt: 175	Type: Pwr xFB	PT/Exp: D	Rand Var: +1
			Consist: B	MM: 1201

2-2, 3.79 ERA in 40 IP at PHI. Lots of swings and misses, but pitched behind in the count far too frequently (FpK). H% correction in 2nd half helped, but his hr/f is concerning for a flyball pitcher. Needs better Ctl and fewer HR to move into higher leverage situations.

Yr Tm	W	L	Sv	IP	K	ERA	xERA	WHIP	oOPS	vL	vR	BF/G	Ctl	Dom	Cmd	FpK	SwK	G	L	F	H%	S%	hr/f	GS	APC	DOM%	DIS%	Sv%	LI	RAR	BPV	BPX	R$
11																																	
12																																	
13 aa	6	4	0	97	79	5.12	4.80	1.43				9.0	3.6	7.3	2.0						30%	68%								-15.0	45	59	-$6
14 PHI *	7	3	2	78	60	4.16	3.92	1.30	0	0	0	6.6	3.4	6.9	2.0	100%	22%	50	0	50	28%	71%	0%	0	9			40	1.97	-4.0	57	68	$1
15 PHI *	3	5	1	78	70	4.19	4.99	1.55	772	770	772	5.8	4.2	8.1	1.9	52%	14%	39	15	46	34%	76%	15%	0	21			33	0.69	-2.2	56	67	-$5
1st Half	1	3	1	40	31	4.31	5.58	1.92	717	650	762	6.5	6.1	7.0	1.1	58%	15%	38	25	38	37%	76%	0%	0	23			33	0.70	-1.7	51	60	-$10
2nd Half	2	2	0	38	39	4.06	3.76	1.17	775	778	772	5.3	2.2	9.3	4.3	52%	14%	39	14	47	29%	75%	16%	0	21			0	0.69	-0.5	126	150	$2
16 Proj	**4**	**4**	**0**	**73**	**62**	**4.29**	**4.56**	**1.41**	**716**	**782**	**670**	**5.8**	**3.6**	**7.7**	**2.1**	**52%**	**14%**	**39**	**14**	**47**	**31%**	**73%**	**9%**	**0**						**-2.9**	**58**	**69**	**-$2**

Neshek,Pat

Age: 35	Th: R	Role: RP	Health: A	LIMA Plan: B+
Ht: 6' 3"	Wt: 210	Type: Pwr xFB	PT/Exp: D	Rand Var: 0
			Consist: C	MM: 2300

Death, taxes, and regression: all are unavoidable. Rebounds in S% and hr/f were not unexpected, and whipsawing H% explained 1H/2H ERA and WHIP gyrations. Continued FpK growth suggests Ctl will remain strong; still a useful reliever, but question is for how much longer.

Yr Tm	W	L	Sv	IP	K	ERA	xERA	WHIP	oOPS	vL	vR	BF/G	Ctl	Dom	Cmd	FpK	SwK	G	L	F	H%	S%	hr/f	GS	APC	DOM%	DIS%	Sv%	LI	RAR	BPV	BPX	R$
11 SD *	2	3	3	51	30	3.80	5.05	1.60	742	661	819	4.6	5.6	5.3	0.9	54%	9%	30	19	51	27%	81%	12%	0	19			50	0.70	0.9	15	23	-$3
12 OAK *	5	3	11	64	52	3.39	4.08	1.33	530	1108	369	4.5	2.1	7.3	3.5	63%	13%	35	17	48	34%	76%	12%	0	14			69	1.21	4.9	96	125	$5
13 OAK	2	1	0	40	29	3.35	4.90	1.36	738	922	644	3.9	3.3	6.5	1.9	54%	11%	33	19	48	29%	82%	10%	0	15			0	0.39	2.6	37	48	-$2
14 STL	7	2	6	67	68	1.87	3.21	0.79	480	541	442	3.6	1.2	9.1	7.6	67%	13%	35	11	54	25%	80%	4%	0	14			60	1.38	15.5	144	172	$14
15 HOU	3	6	1	55	51	3.62	3.88	1.12	709	768	673	3.4	2.0	8.4	4.3	69%	11%	32	22	46	28%	74%	11%	0	13			25	1.32	2.3	108	128	$2
1st Half	3	1	1	31	28	2.90	3.54	0.84	578	582	575	3.4	1.5	8.1	5.6	67%	11%	38	15	48	22%	73%	10%	0	13			50	1.30	4.1	123	146	$6
2nd Half	0	5	0	24	23	4.56	4.31	1.48	860	951	798	3.4	2.7	8.7	3.3	71%	11%	25	31	44	35%	74%	13%	0	12			0	1.35	-1.8	89	106	-$5
16 Proj	**3**	**5**	**0**	**58**	**53**	**3.59**	**3.86**	**1.16**	**692**	**779**	**638**	**3.5**	**2.3**	**8.3**	**3.6**	**66%**	**12%**	**32**	**19**	**49**	**29%**	**74%**	**9%**	**0**						**2.6**	**98**	**116**	**$1**

Nicasio,Juan

Age: 29	Th: R	Role: RP	Health: D	LIMA Plan: C
Ht: 6' 3"	Wt: 210	Type: Pwr	PT/Exp: C	Rand Var: 0
			Consist: D	MM: 2300

Power arm adapted to venue change and full time bullpen role. Big jump in Dom supported by SwK, but equivalent jump in Ctl combined with elevated H% created too many baserunners for high leverage usage. Cheap strikeouts at the end of the draft, but not worth the potential damage to ERA and WHIP.

Yr Tm	W	L	Sv	IP	K	ERA	xERA	WHIP	oOPS	vL	vR	BF/G	Ctl	Dom	Cmd	FpK	SwK	G	L	F	H%	S%	hr/f	GS	APC	DOM%	DIS%	Sv%	LI	RAR	BPV	BPX	R$
11 COL *	9	5	0	128	106	3.53	3.75	1.24	735	859	595	23.7	2.0	7.4	3.7	58%	9%	46	22	32	32%	74%	11%	13	89	38%	23%			6.5	100	151	$7
12 COL	2	3	0	58	54	5.28	4.19	1.62	861	902	825	23.4	3.4	8.4	2.5	60%	8%	40	25	36	37%	69%	11%	11	93	45%	27%			-9.0	77	100	-$8
13 COL	9	9	0	158	119	5.14	4.41	1.47	785	737	827	22.7	3.7	6.8	1.9	57%	8%	45	21	34	32%	66%	10%	31	92	29%	26%			-24.7	47	61	-$9
14 COL *	9	8	1	129	89	5.50	6.06	1.59	860	900	827	13.3	3.3	6.2	1.9	59%	8%	46	20	34	33%	70%	18%	14	49	36%	36%	100	0.76	-28.0	21	25	-$12
15 LA	1	3	1	58	65	3.86	4.04	1.56	742	969	634	4.9	4.9	10.0	2.0	62%	12%	43	25	32	37%	73%	2%	1	20	0%	100%	33	1.05	0.8	68	81	-$4
1st Half	1	2	1	34	38	2.91	3.76	1.35	631	785	558	5.3	4.5	10.1	2.2	60%	12%	44	23	33	33%	76%	0%	1	22	0%	100%	50	1.01	4.4	82	97	-$1
2nd Half	0	1	0	24	27	5.18	4.45	1.85	883	1205	730	4.5	5.5	10.0	1.8	66%	11%	42	28	30	41%	70%	5%	0	18			0	1.08	-3.6	50	59	-$9
16 Proj	**2**	**3**	**0**	**58**	**54**	**3.94**	**4.05**	**1.41**	**717**	**831**	**644**	**6.9**	**4.2**	**8.4**	**2.0**	**61%**	**10%**	**44**	**23**	**33**	**32%**	**72%**	**7%**	**0**						**0.1**	**59**	**70**	**-$3**

Nicolino,Justin

Age: 24	Th: L	Role: SP	Health: A	LIMA Plan: D+
Ht: 6' 3"	Wt: 225	Type: Con FB	PT/Exp: D	Rand Var: -1
			Consist: F	MM: 0003

5-4, 4.01 ERA in 74 IP at MIA. Strong FpK delivered excellent Ctl, but... that's about it (though he did have perfect oOPS splits). Dom this low can't sustain any SP, no matter how few the free passes; simply needs to miss more bats. Balance of 2015 IP were at AAA; gotta think he'll return there to open 2016.

Yr Tm	W	L	Sv	IP	K	ERA	xERA	WHIP	oOPS	vL	vR	BF/G	Ctl	Dom	Cmd	FpK	SwK	G	L	F	H%	S%	hr/f	GS	APC	DOM%	DIS%	Sv%	LI	RAR	BPV	BPX	R$
11																																	
12																																	
13 aa	3	2	0	45	27	6.16	6.49	1.88				23.7	2.5	5.3	2.1						41%	65%								-12.8	48	62	-$11
14 aa	14	4	0	170	67	3.29	3.48	1.18				24.4	1.0	3.5	3.4						30%	72%								9.4	80	95	$9
15 MIA *	12	11	0	189	74	4.39	5.19	1.51	758	758	758	25.6	2.4	3.5	1.5	65%	5%	44	18	38	32%	73%	9%	12	87	17%	33%			-10.0	18	22	-$7
1st Half	5	5	0	95	42	4.20	5.47	1.58	685	606	715	26.2	2.5	4.0	1.6	67%	5%	40	23	37	34%	75%	8%	2	73	0%	50%			-2.8	23	28	-$9
2nd Half	7	6	0	94	32	4.59	4.90	1.44	770	795	764	25.0	2.3	3.1	1.3	64%	5%	45	17	38	30%	70%	9%	10	90	20%	30%			-7.2	13	15	-$5
16 Proj	**6**	**9**	**0**	**131**	**54**	**4.49**	**4.93**	**1.44**	**811**	**852**	**801**	**24.8**	**1.9**	**3.8**	**2.0**	**64%**	**5%**	**45**	**17**	**38**	**32%**	**70%**	**7%**	**22**						**-8.5**	**39**	**47**	**-$6**

MATT DODGE

Niese,Jon

Age: 29	Th: L	Role SP	Health D	LIMA Plan C	
Ht: 6' 3"	Wt: 220	Type GB	PT/Exp A	Rand Var +1	
			Consist A	MM 2103	

Stayed healthy for once, but skills were ill. Dom drop mostly vL, but both sides swung less and SwK sunk. Perennially hittable, he needs great Ctl to avoid awful WHIP; FpK says that's still possible, but without a SwK return, that likely just means more hits. Was already fringe at his peak, the decline could be swift.

Yr Tm	W	L	Sv	IP	K	ERA	xERA	WHIP	oOPS	vL	vR	BF/G	Ctl	Dom	Cmd	FpK	SwK	G	L	F	H%	S%	hr/f	GS	APC	DOM%	DIS%	Sv%	LI	RAR	BPV	BPX	R$
11 NYM	11	11	0	157	138	4.40	3.49	1.41	754	664	781	25.7	2.5	7.9	3.1	59%	9%	51	21	28	35%	70%	10%	26	92	42%	15%	0	0.76	-9.0	103	155	$1
12 NYM	13	9	0	190	155	3.40	3.70	1.17	663	665	663	26.3	2.3	7.3	3.2	63%	8%	48	21	31	28%	75%	13%	30	101	70%	7%			14.3	95	124	$16
13 NYM	8	8	0	143	105	3.71	3.93	1.44	739	660	765	25.9	3.0	6.6	2.2	61%	8%	52	21	27	33%	75%	8%	24	98	50%	17%			2.7	67	88	$0
14 NYM	9	11	0	188	138	3.40	3.68	1.27	722	656	742	26.2	2.2	6.6	3.1	63%	8%	48	23	30	31%	76%	10%	30	93	57%	10%			7.8	87	103	$7
15 NYM	9	10	0	177	113	4.13	4.18	1.40	764	789	757	23.3	2.8	5.8	2.1	62%	6%	55	21	25	31%	73%	14%	29	82	55%	28%	0	0.77	-3.6	60	71	-$1
1st Half	3	8	0	90	63	3.90	4.24	1.49	791	726	810	26.9	3.1	6.3	2.0	60%	7%	53	23	24	33%	77%	14%	15	95	53%	27%			0.7	61	73	-$4
2nd Half	6	2	0	87	50	4.36	4.11	1.30	733	861	698	20.3	2.5	5.2	2.1	65%	6%	56	19	25	29%	69%	14%	14	71	57%	29%	0	0.78	-4.3	60	71	$2
16 Proj	**9**	**9**	**0**	**167**	**115**	**3.89**	**3.91**	**1.35**	**741**	**729**	**745**	**23.5**	**2.6**	**6.2**	**2.4**	**62%**	**7%**	**52**	**21**	**27**	**31%**	**73%**	**12%**	**30**						**1.5**	**72**	**85**	**$2**

Nola,Aaron

Age: 23	Th: R	Role SP	Health A	LIMA Plan B	
Ht: 6' 1"	Wt: 195	Type GB	PT/Exp D	Rand Var 0	
			Consist D	MM 2205	

6-2, 3.59 ERA in 78 IP at PHI. Short-term scouting report nailed it: Would arrive quickly with polish. '14 draftee had MLB-ready Ctl and GB, though his 7.9 Dom surpassed expectations. HR issue was mostly bad luck, but will need to improve against LHB and maintain the strikeouts before he takes the next step.

Yr Tm	W	L	Sv	IP	K	ERA	xERA	WHIP	oOPS	vL	vR	BF/G	Ctl	Dom	Cmd	FpK	SwK	G	L	F	H%	S%	hr/f	GS	APC	DOM%	DIS%	Sv%	LI	RAR	BPV	BPX	R$
11																																	
12																																	
13																																	
14 aa	2	0	0	24	14	2.86	5.09	1.32				19.9	1.8	5.1	2.8						29%	88%								2.6	38	46	-$2
15 PHI *	16	6	0	187	151	3.08	3.56	1.17	703	834	618	24.1	1.8	7.2	4.1	64%	9%	48	20	32	30%	77%	15%	13	86	54%	8%			20.3	106	126	$19
1st Half	10	3	0	100	75	2.25	2.76	1.06				24.3	1.2	6.7	5.4						29%	81%	0%	0						21.2	143	170	$29
2nd Half	6	3	0	87	76	4.05	4.48	1.30	703	834	618	23.8	2.4	7.9	3.3	64%	9%	48	20	32	31%	74%	15%	13	86	54%	8%			-0.9	77	91	$7
16 Proj	**12**	**9**	**0**	**189**	**151**	**3.52**	**3.68**	**1.23**	**647**	**776**	**564**	**24.1**	**1.9**	**7.2**	**3.7**	**64%**	**9%**	**48**	**20**	**32**	**31%**	**75%**	**11%**	**32**						**10.3**	**103**	**122**	**$11**

Nolasco,Ricky

Age: 33	Th: R	Role SP	Health F	LIMA Plan C	
Ht: 6' 2"	Wt: 225	Type	PT/Exp B	Rand Var +5	
			Consist B	MM 2205	

Biggest change since '14: Health drop from B to F. Injuries (elbow 2x, ankle) wreaked havoc on his results, going from fringe to unusable. Ignore '15 H%/S%, but career rates are also bleak. S% always a struggle as he's super-hittable (9.8 H/9). Might reach '14 xERA, but you'll get WHIPped in the process.

Yr Tm	W	L	Sv	IP	K	ERA	xERA	WHIP	oOPS	vL	vR	BF/G	Ctl	Dom	Cmd	FpK	SwK	G	L	F	H%	S%	hr/f	GS	APC	DOM%	DIS%	Sv%	LI	RAR	BPV	BPX	R$
11 FLA	10	12	0	206	148	4.67	3.82	1.40	770	835	708	27.0	1.9	6.5	3.4	65%	9%	45	24	31	34%	68%	10%	33	97	48%	15%			-18.6	87	132	-$3
12 MIA	12	13	0	191	125	4.48	4.27	1.37	755	809	696	26.8	2.2	5.9	2.7	63%	9%	47	22	32	32%	68%	9%	31	96	39%	23%			-10.9	71	93	-$1
13 2 NL	13	11	0	199	165	3.70	3.62	1.21	693	721	660	24.5	2.1	7.4	3.6	60%	11%	43	24	33	31%	71%	9%	33	94	42%	12%	0	0.75	4.0	99	129	$11
14 MIN	6	12	0	159	115	5.38	4.13	1.52	861	906	816	25.7	2.2	6.5	3.0	58%	9%	42	22	36	35%	67%	12%	27	98	41%	22%			-32.1	79	94	-$13
15 MIN	5	2	0	37	35	6.75	4.34	1.71	856	758	942	19.2	3.4	8.4	2.5	52%	10%	41	28	32	40%	59%	8%	8	74	25%	50%	0	0.71	-12.8	80	95	-$8
1st Half	5	1	0	33	28	5.51	4.34	1.65	810	693	898	21.3	2.8	7.7	2.8	51%	9%	41	26	33	40%	64%	3%	7	83	29%	43%			-6.2	83	99	-$7
2nd Half	0	1	0	5	7	15.43	4.32	2.14	1167	1027	1429	12.0	7.7	13.5	1.8	58%	13%	38	38	23	39%	25%	67%	1	44	0%	100%	0	0.38	-6.6	51	61	-$11
16 Proj	**9**	**10**	**0**	**181**	**141**	**4.54**	**4.00**	**1.43**	**781**	**780**	**782**	**23.4**	**2.3**	**7.0**	**3.0**	**57%**	**10%**	**43**	**24**	**33**	**35%**	**69%**	**9%**	**33**						**-13.0**	**85**	**101**	**-$4**

Nolin,Sean

Age: 26	Th: L	Role RP	Health C	LIMA Plan D+	
Ht: 6' 4"	Wt: 230	Type xFB	PT/Exp D	Rand Var -1	
			Consist A	MM 0101	

1-2, 5.28 ERA in 29 IP at OAK. Extreme flyballers with weak Dom are stream options by nature. Venue plays a much larger role for them than any other profile. Scouting report is littered with average grades (arsenal, command, mechanics). Best case: back-end arm could scratch out mid-rotation value in right environment.

Yr Tm	W	L	Sv	IP	K	ERA	xERA	WHIP	oOPS	vL	vR	BF/G	Ctl	Dom	Cmd	FpK	SwK	G	L	F	H%	S%	hr/f	GS	APC	DOM%	DIS%	Sv%	LI	RAR	BPV	BPX	R$
11																																	
12 aa	1	0	0	15	15	1.52	1.83	1.11				19.6	3.6	9.1	2.5						28%	85%								4.6	123	160	-$2
13 TOR *	9	5	0	112	98	3.78	4.45	1.45	1927	2333	1768	22.7	2.9	7.9	2.7	55%	0%	30	30	40	35%	75%	25%	1	35	0%	100%			1.2	80	104	$0
14 TOR *	4	6	0	88	62	4.74	4.57	1.48	1250	0	1667	21.1	3.8	6.4	1.7	0%	11%	25	50	25	31%	69%	100%	0	18			0	0.00	-10.9	46	55	-$6
15 OAK *	3	4	0	76	45	4.11	5.02	1.53	793	904	736	16.6	3.9	5.3	1.4	59%	7%	42	16	41	30%	76%	9%	6	83	17%	33%			-1.4	26	31	-$5
1st Half	2	1	0	34	20	3.42	5.05	1.65				15.0	5.0	5.4	1.1						31%	82%	0%	0						2.3	29	34	-$6
2nd Half	1	3	0	43	24	4.66	4.99	1.44	793	904	736	18.2	3.0	5.1	1.7	59%	7%	42	16	41	30%	71%	9%	6	83	17%	33%			-3.7	26	31	-$5
16 Proj	**3**	**4**	**0**	**73**	**48**	**4.33**	**4.95**	**1.50**	**655**	**741**	**610**	**18.8**	**3.7**	**6.0**	**1.6**	**59%**	**7%**	**42**	**16**	**41**	**31%**	**73%**	**7%**	**15**						**-3.3**	**28**	**34**	**-$5**

Norris,Bud

Age: 31	Th: R	Role RP	Health C	LIMA Plan C	
Ht: 6' 0"	Wt: 220	Type Pwr	PT/Exp A	Rand Var +5	
			Consist B	MM 2301	

Many believed bullpen role would allow him to shine. (1H/2H is also SP/RP demarcation.) Crazy H% as RP and S% all season tanked ERA, but he has never thrown enough strikes (3.5 career Ctl) to leverage full Dom potential, and that caps his ceiling. There is a better pitcher here; pen work and patience may reveal it again.

Yr Tm	W	L	Sv	IP	K	ERA	xERA	WHIP	oOPS	vL	vR	BF/G	Ctl	Dom	Cmd	FpK	SwK	G	L	F	H%	S%	hr/f	GS	APC	DOM%	DIS%	Sv%	LI	RAR	BPV	BPX	R$
11 HOU	6	11	0	186	176	3.77	3.81	1.33	732	811	650	25.6	3.4	8.5	2.5	59%	11%	40	21	39	31%	76%	12%	31	102	55%	13%			3.9	80	120	$6
12 HOU	7	13	0	168	165	4.65	4.10	1.37	751	782	720	25.3	3.5	8.8	2.5	58%	11%	39	21	40	31%	69%	12%	29	97	59%	21%			-13.2	81	105	-$2
13 2 AL	10	12	0	177	147	4.18	4.27	1.49	779	889	629	24.2	3.4	7.5	2.2	61%	10%	40	21	38	34%	74%	8%	30	94	47%	27%	0	0.88	-6.8	61	79	-$3
14 BAL	15	8	0	165	139	3.65	3.77	1.22	710	753	659	24.5	2.8	7.6	2.7	60%	8%	42	21	37	28%	74%	11%	28	98	46%	7%			1.9	80	95	$9
15 2 TM	3	11	0	83	71	6.72	4.42	1.58	895	894	896	9.9	3.4	7.7	2.3	58%	10%	43	23	34	34%	59%	17%	11	39	27%	27%	0	0.82	-28.3	69	82	-$14
1st Half	2	8	0	58	42	6.63	4.69	1.56	894	991	739	22.0	3.1	6.5	2.1	58%	9%	43	23	34	33%	60%	16%	11	84	27%	27%	0	0.83	-19.2	54	64	-$15
2nd Half	1	3	0	25	29	6.93	3.78	1.62	898	586	1154	4.3	4.0	10.6	2.6	59%	12%	46	22	32	38%	58%	17%	0	18			0	0.82	-9.0	106	126	-$10
16 Proj	**5**	**9**	**0**	**102**	**94**	**4.12**	**3.95**	**1.41**	**766**	**738**	**797**	**9.5**	**3.4**	**8.4**	**2.5**	**59%**	**10%**	**43**	**22**	**35**	**33%**	**73%**	**10%**	**0**						**-2.0**	**80**	**95**	**-$1**

Norris,Daniel

Age: 23	Th: L	Role RP	Health B	LIMA Plan C	
Ht: 6' 2"	Wt: 180	Type Pwr FB	PT/Exp D	Rand Var +2	
			Consist B	MM 1303	

3-2, 3.75 ERA in 60 IP at TOR/DET. Whirlwind season: Earned SP role in camp, demoted to AAA on May 1, dealt to DET on July 31, 54-pitch inning on Sept. 29, and news of cancer diagnosis on Oct. 29. Improved FpK from horrendous to not-good, but HRs a bigger issue than Ctl. Tools are there, needs time.

Yr Tm	W	L	Sv	IP	K	ERA	xERA	WHIP	oOPS	vL	vR	BF/G	Ctl	Dom	Cmd	FpK	SwK	G	L	F	H%	S%	hr/f	GS	APC	DOM%	DIS%	Sv%	LI	RAR	BPV	BPX	R$
11																																	
12																																	
13																																	
14 TOR *	6	2	0	65	83	4.98	4.14	1.35	667	594	719	15.0	4.1	11.5	2.8	43%	7%	35	20	45	32%	66%	11%	1	28	0%	100%	0	0.85	-10.0	95	113	-$2
15 2 AL *	6	12	0	151	115	5.14	5.04	1.56	732	880	680	22.7	3.8	6.9	1.8	53%	9%	40	17	43	33%	68%	11%	13	80	31%	46%			-21.9	48	58	-$12
1st Half	2	9	0	86	73	5.06	5.45	1.72	816	944	788	24.4	4.5	7.6	1.7	54%	9%	30	21	49	36%	71%	9%	5	88	20%	40%			-11.6	53	63	-$16
2nd Half	4	3	0	65	42	5.25	4.49	1.35	675	854	596	20.7	2.8	5.9	2.1	52%	10%	46	14	40	29%	63%	13%	8	75	38%	50%			-10.3	44	53	-$6
16 Proj	**9**	**8**	**0**	**145**	**130**	**4.48**	**4.30**	**1.40**	**783**	**928**	**733**	**18.5**	**3.8**	**8.1**	**2.1**	**53%**	**9%**	**40**	**17**	**43**	**31%**	**71%**	**10%**	**28**						**-9.3**	**61**	**73**	**-$1**

Nova,Ivan

Age: 29	Th: R	Role SP	Health F	LIMA Plan C	
Ht: 6' 4"	Wt: 225	Type	PT/Exp D	Rand Var +2	
			Consist A	MM 1103	

When all of your bad seasons are HR-heavy, it's not just hr/f bad luck. TJ return kept expectations light, but he still disappointed. His fastball is awful (career 5% SwK) and he lacks reliable 3rd pitch (change-up sparsely used, has career .294 ISO). Needs a better fastball or return to the slider to get back on the radar.

Yr Tm	W	L	Sv	IP	K	ERA	xERA	WHIP	oOPS	vL	vR	BF/G	Ctl	Dom	Cmd	FpK	SwK	G	L	F	H%	S%	hr/f	GS	APC	DOM%	DIS%	Sv%	LI	RAR	BPV	BPX	R$
11 NYY *	17	6	0	181	113	3.79	4.03	1.34	706	681	730	24.3	2.9	5.6	1.9	60%	7%	53	18	29	29%	74%	8%	27	92	37%	19%	0	0.82	3.5	50	75	$8
12 NYY	12	8	0	170	153	5.02	3.95	1.47	860	848	872	26.7	3.0	8.1	2.7	58%	9%	45	22	32	34%	70%	17%	28	96	46%	21%			-21.1	89	116	-$6
13 NYY *	11	6	0	157	130	3.08	3.57	1.29	678	676	680	24.8	2.8	7.4	2.7	54%	10%	54	20	26	31%	78%	8%	20	91	50%	20%	0	0.77	15.2	86	112	$10
14 NYY	2	2	0	21	12	8.27	4.53	1.84	1033	764	1444	24.0	2.6	5.2	2.0	64%	5%	49	20	31	36%	59%	26%	4	82	0%	75%			-11.6	51	60	-$7
15 NYY	6	11	0	94	63	5.07	4.50	1.40	793	899	682	24.3	3.2	6.0	1.9	55%	8%	49	19	32	30%	66%	13%	17	90	35%	18%			-12.9	50	60	-$5
1st Half	1	2	0	17	9	2.65	5.31	1.41	787	859	696	24.7	3.7	4.8	1.3	49%	10%	46	13	41	28%	86%	9%	3	86	0%	33%			2.8	10	12	-$6
2nd Half	5	9	0	77	54	5.61	4.33	1.40	794	908	679	24.2	3.0	6.3	2.1	54%	8%	50	20	30	30%	62%	15%	14	91	43%	14%			-15.7	59	70	-$5
16 Proj	**9**	**10**	**0**	**131**	**94**	**4.12**	**4.13**	**1.38**	**769**	**813**	**722**	**24.3**	**3.1**	**6.5**	**2.1**	**55%**	**9%**	**50**	**19**	**31**	**30%**	**73%**	**12%**	**23**						**-2.5**	**61**	**72**	**$0**

PAUL SPORER

Nuno,Vidal

Age: 28	Th: L	Role: RP	Health: A	LIMA Plan: B+
Ht: 5' 11"	Wt: 210	Type: FB	PT/Exp: C	Rand Var: 0
			Consist: C	MM: 2201

1-5, 3.74 ERA in 89 IP at ARI/SEA. Role matters. Has standard issues that plague wannabe SPs: big platoon split; weaker 2nd, 3rd time thru lineup; too many HRs. But all three were quelled in pen with skills support (9.3 Dom, 4.3 Cmd, 1.08 WHIP in 38 IP). Capable as a #5 SP, but has impact potential as RP.

Yr Tm	W	L	Sv	IP	K	ERA	xERA	WHIP	oOPS	vL	vR	BF/G	Ctl	Dom	Cmd	FpK	SwK	G	L	F	H%	S%	hr/f	GS	APC	DOM%	DIS%	Sv%	LI	RAR	BPV	BPX	R$
11																																	
12 aa	9	5	0	114	80	3.19	4.88	1.42				24.2	2.3	6.3	2.8						33%	82%								11.6	61	79	$3
13 NYY *	3	2	0	45	33	2.15	2.47	0.94	654	691	643	16.9	1.7	6.6	3.9	66%	4%	35	18	47	24%	85%	6%	3	63	33%	0%	0	1.03	9.5	105	137	$4
14 2 TM	2	12	0	162	129	4.56	4.08	1.26	745	582	793	21.9	2.6	7.2	2.8	67%	9%	38	19	43	29%	68%	12%	28	83	43%	25%	0	0.71	-16.4	76	91	-$3
15 2 TM *	5	8	0	146	118	3.81	4.58	1.29	772	562	836	13.6	1.9	7.3	3.8	65%	11%	42	17	41	31%	76%	14%	10	41	40%	50%	0	0.91	2.8	82	98	$3
1st Half	4	4	0	82	66	3.37	4.21	1.24	621	431	690	15.8	1.6	7.3	4.5	75%	14%	41	16	44	32%	78%	11%	0	30			0	0.75	5.9	102	121	$7
2nd Half	1	4	0	64	52	4.36	4.20	1.34	828	620	887	12.0	2.3	7.3	3.3	62%	10%	43	17	40	31%	74%	15%	10	47	40%	50%	0	0.99	-3.1	92	109	-$3
16 Proj	**4**	**6**	**0**	**102**	**80**	**3.78**	**4.00**	**1.25**	**747**	**559**	**805**	**15.8**	**2.1**	**7.1**	**3.3**	**67%**	**10%**	**40**	**17**	**42**	**30%**	**75%**	**11%**	**9**						**2.3**	**88**	**105**	**$1**

O Day,Darren

Age: 33	Th: R	Role: RP	Health: B	LIMA Plan: B
Ht: 6' 4"	Wt: 220	Type: Pwr FB	PT/Exp: C	Rand Var: -5
			Consist: A	MM: 4510

Once seen as a ROOGY, now has 3 of 4 years handling LHB while still eviscerating RHB. Rising SwK yielded best Dom yet and really brings LIMA value into full bloom. 4th-best ERA and WHIP among RP since '12 (min 200 IP). S% is high, but consistently so. It all looks "closerish;" just needs chance for... UP: 25 Saves

Yr Tm	W	L	Sv	IP	K	ERA	xERA	WHIP	oOPS	vL	vR	BF/G	Ctl	Dom	Cmd	FpK	SwK	G	L	F	H%	S%	hr/f	GS	APC	DOM%	DIS%	Sv%	LI	RAR	BPV	BPX	R$
11 TEX *	1	1	1	38	37	4.21	5.50	1.27	929	900	938	4.6	2.3	8.8	3.9	68%	11%	35	17	48	28%	82%	30%	0	17			100	0.47	-1.3	59	88	-$2
12 BAL	7	1	0	67	69	2.28	3.34	0.94	613	664	584	3.8	1.9	9.3	4.9	65%	12%	34	23	43	26%	81%	8%	0	15			0	1.10	14.3	128	167	$10
13 BAL	5	3	2	62	59	2.18	3.38	1.00	617	922	443	3.6	2.2	8.6	3.9	63%	12%	37	22	41	26%	85%	10%	0	14			33	1.22	12.9	110	144	$8
14 BAL	5	2	4	69	73	1.70	2.99	0.89	550	633	497	4.0	2.5	9.6	3.8	59%	14%	45	17	38	23%	87%	10%	0	16			50	1.33	17.3	128	152	$12
15 BAL	6	2	6	65	82	1.52	2.95	0.93	540	627	493	3.8	1.9	11.3	5.9	66%	15%	35	20	45	29%	89%	7%	0	16			55	1.21	19.7	164	196	$14
1st Half	5	0	2	32	42	1.14	2.90	0.82	507	781	366	3.8	2.3	11.9	5.3	66%	15%	37	19	44	23%	100%	13%	0	16			50	1.18	11.0	168	200	$17
2nd Half	1	2	4	34	40	1.87	2.99	1.04	571	488	617	3.7	1.6	10.7	6.7	65%	16%	33	21	46	34%	82%	3%	0	15			57	1.23	8.7	161	190	$12
16 Proj	**5**	**2**	**5**	**65**	**74**	**2.14**	**3.07**	**1.01**	**605**	**714**	**543**	**3.7**	**2.1**	**10.2**	**4.9**	**63%**	**14%**	**37**	**20**	**42**	**29%**	**84%**	**9%**	**0**						**14.6**	**142**	**169**	**$10**

Oberg,Scott

Age: 26	Th: R	Role: RP	Health: A	LIMA Plan: D
Ht: 6' 2"	Wt: 205	Type: Pwr GB	PT/Exp: D	Rand Var: +4
			Consist: B	MM: 1210

Actually did his best work at home (3.94 ERA), but a 23% H% says it's a fraud, especially with a 5.1 Dom. PRO: 95+ mph heat, four pitches, handled LHB, strong GB lean. CON: Weak SwK for RP, terrible control, HR trouble in the last place you can afford it. Needs return of minors Dom (9.5) to have a chance.

Yr Tm	W	L	Sv	IP	K	ERA	xERA	WHIP	oOPS	vL	vR	BF/G	Ctl	Dom	Cmd	FpK	SwK	G	L	F	H%	S%	hr/f	GS	APC	DOM%	DIS%	Sv%	LI	RAR	BPV	BPX	R$
11																																	
12																																	
13																																	
14 aa	0	1	15	27	17	3.84	3.62	1.27				4.1	2.2	5.5	2.5						31%	70%								-0.3	72	86	$3
15 COL	3	4	1	58	44	5.09	4.51	1.53	839	781	872	4.0	4.8	6.8	1.4	55%	9%	54	18	28	28%	71%	21%	0	16			33	1.00	-8.1	25	30	-$6
1st Half	2	1	1	31	20	6.10	4.42	1.52	937	810	1004	4.2	3.5	5.8	1.7	54%	9%	55	18	27	29%	67%	30%	0	15			50	1.00	-8.2	43	51	-$8
2nd Half	1	3	0	27	24	3.95	4.63	1.54	719	746	702	3.9	6.3	7.9	1.3	56%	8%	53	19	28	28%	75%	10%	0	16			0	1.00	0.0	5	6	-$4
16 Proj	**2**	**3**	**5**	**44**	**34**	**4.81**	**4.47**	**1.53**	**810**	**772**	**832**	**3.9**	**5.1**	**7.1**	**1.4**	**55%**	**8%**	**54**	**18**	**28**	**28%**	**72%**	**18%**	**0**						**-4.5**	**20**	**24**	**-$3**

Oberholtzer,Brett

Age: 27	Th: L	Role: SP	Health: D	LIMA Plan: C
Ht: 6' 1"	Wt: 225	Type: Con	PT/Exp: D	Rand Var: 0
			Consist: B	MM: 1001

2-2, 4.46 ERA in 38 IP at HOU. Newly-earned Health grade came via two DL stints (lat, blister) and likely explains sudden Ctl spike (4.0) as everything else was in place. Has consistently allowed too much contact to be useful. If we're going to excuse the Ctl, we can't get psyched about the GB spike yet. Blah.

Yr Tm	W	L	Sv	IP	K	ERA	xERA	WHIP	oOPS	vL	vR	BF/G	Ctl	Dom	Cmd	FpK	SwK	G	L	F	H%	S%	hr/f	GS	APC	DOM%	DIS%	Sv%	LI	RAR	BPV	BPX	R$
11 aa	11	12	0	155	107	4.22	3.69	1.32				23.8	2.8	6.2	2.2						31%	68%								-5.3	70	105	$3
12 a/a	10	10	0	167	119	4.48	5.10	1.42				25.2	2.0	6.4	3.1						33%	72%								-9.6	63	82	-$3
13 HOU *	10	11	0	152	106	3.94	3.92	1.26	654	745	617	21.4	2.3	6.3	2.8	66%	9%	36	22	42	30%	71%	7%	10	85	70%	10%	0	0.69	-1.4	69	90	$4
14 HOU *	6	15	0	175	120	4.51	4.90	1.38	752	726	760	25.3	1.6	6.2	3.9	61%	8%	37	20	43	34%	70%	6%	24	94	46%	25%			-16.7	81	96	-$6
15 HOU *	9	6	0	108	70	4.32	4.87	1.42	811	959	754	23.0	2.4	5.8	2.4	60%	7%	49	18	34	32%	73%	10%	8	82	25%	50%			-4.7	49	58	-$2
1st Half	4	3	0	52	40	4.86	5.44	1.56	791	1036	705	20.7	3.3	7.0	2.1	59%	8%	51	14	35	34%	72%	8%	7	81	29%	57%			-5.8	45	53	-$6
2nd Half	5	3	0	56	29	3.81	4.34	1.29	935	625	1121	25.7	1.6	4.7	2.9	68%	6%	33	39	28	30%	73%	20%	1	86	0%	0%			1.0	58	68	$2
16 Proj	**5**	**7**	**0**	**87**	**57**	**4.28**	**4.35**	**1.37**	**778**	**906**	**731**	**23.6**	**2.1**	**5.9**	**2.8**	**62%**	**8%**	**42**	**19**	**40**	**32%**	**71%**	**9%**	**15**						**-3.5**	**68**	**81**	**-$2**

Odorizzi,Jake

Age: 26	Th: R	Role: SP	Health: C	LIMA Plan: C+
Ht: 6' 2"	Wt: 190	Type: Pwr FB	PT/Exp: B	Rand Var: -1
			Consist: A	MM: 2305

1H: Sacrificed Dom for Ctl and GB spikes; results followed as stranding runners was easier with less traffic. Only an oblique injury could stop him. 2H: A '14 copy as Dom and Ctl both went up while H% and S% regressed to average. Some HR bad luck was behind RH jump in 2H. If '14 Dom and '15 Ctl meet, UP: 15 W

Yr Tm	W	L	Sv	IP	K	ERA	xERA	WHIP	oOPS	vL	vR	BF/G	Ctl	Dom	Cmd	FpK	SwK	G	L	F	H%	S%	hr/f	GS	APC	DOM%	DIS%	Sv%	LI	RAR	BPV	BPX	R$
11 aa	5	3	0	69	45	4.97	4.56	1.32				23.7	2.7	5.9	2.2						28%	66%								-8.7	41	61	-$2
12 KC *	15	6	0	153	117	3.36	3.89	1.32	820	899	400	22.6	3.0	6.9	2.3	56%	7%	27	27	46	30%	77%	8%	2	76	0%	50%			12.3	69	89	$10
13 TAM *	9	7	1	154	129	3.83	3.46	1.22	744	846	627	21.5	2.7	7.5	2.8	57%	8%	32	26	42	29%	71%	8%	4	76	25%	25%	100	0.80	0.7	83	108	$7
14 TAM	11	13	0	168	174	4.13	3.96	1.28	692	663	726	23.2	3.2	9.3	2.9	61%	10%	30	21	49	31%	71%	9%	31	98	52%	29%			-8.0	90	108	$4
15 TAM	9	9	0	169	150	3.35	3.99	1.15	680	630	745	25.0	2.4	8.0	3.3	60%	11%	37	22	41	29%	75%	9%	28	98	57%	18%			12.8	92	110	$13
1st Half	4	5	0	77	63	2.47	3.75	1.02	612	610	614	25.7	1.8	7.4	4.2	61%	10%	41	22	37	27%	78%	6%	12	97	50%	8%			14.2	104	124	$17
2nd Half	5	4	0	93	87	4.08	4.19	1.26	736	648	844	24.5	3.0	8.4	2.8	60%	11%	34	22	44	30%	72%	11%	16	100	63%	25%			-1.3	83	99	$9
16 Proj	**11**	**11**	**0**	**189**	**170**	**3.73**	**3.94**	**1.22**	**692**	**649**	**746**	**23.7**	**2.7**	**8.1**	**3.0**	**61%**	**11%**	**34**	**22**	**44**	**29%**	**73%**	**9%**	**32**						**5.3**	**84**	**100**	**$10**

Osuna,Roberto

Age: 20	Th: R	Role: RP	Health: A	LIMA Plan: B
Ht: 6' 2"	Wt: 230	Type: Pwr xFB	PT/Exp: D	Rand Var: -3
			Consist: F	MM: 4430

The joys of prospecting: Spent '14 at High-A logging 22 IP at age 19, only to secure RP role in '15 camp and assume closer's role by late June. Allowed 4 of his 7 total HR in Sept. for ugly finish (6.00 ERA); velocity never faltered, he was missing spots. Biggest risk is age/the unknown (return to SP?). Skills are elite.

Yr Tm	W	L	Sv	IP	K	ERA	xERA	WHIP	oOPS	vL	vR	BF/G	Ctl	Dom	Cmd	FpK	SwK	G	L	F	H%	S%	hr/f	GS	APC	DOM%	DIS%	Sv%	LI	RAR	BPV	BPX	R$
11																																	
12																																	
13																																	
14																																	
15 TOR	1	6	20	70	75	2.58	3.41	0.92	591	638	537	4.0	2.1	9.7	4.7	63%	15%	34	20	46	25%	77%	9%	0	16			87	1.36	11.8	131	156	$15
1st Half	1	2	3	38	43	2.13	3.43	0.92	521	480	555	4.3	2.4	10.2	4.3	63%	15%	31	22	47	27%	76%	2%	0	18			75	1.49	8.6	128	152	$13
2nd Half	0	4	17	32	32	3.13	3.38	0.92	675	766	505	3.7	1.7	9.1	5.3	62%	16%	39	17	45	23%	78%	16%	0	14			89	1.22	3.3	134	159	$18
16 Proj	**2**	**3**	**38**	**65**	**69**	**3.14**	**3.33**	**1.03**	**661**	**728**	**571**	**3.9**	**2.2**	**9.5**	**4.2**	**63%**	**15%**	**35**	**19**	**46**	**27%**	**75%**	**11%**	**0**						**6.6**	**124**	**148**	**$19**

Ottavino,Adam

Age: 30	Th: R	Role: RP	Health: F	LIMA Plan: A
Ht: 6' 5"	Wt: 220	Type: Pwr	PT/Exp: D	Rand Var: -5
			Consist: B	MM: 3320

Early-May TJ shut down the makings of a breakout closer; eyeing mid-'16 return. His gift is his curse: three-headed slider (velocity and release points vary) dominates, but 40%+ usage made injury almost inevitable. Unfazed by Coors (.686 career OPS). Once healthy, the 200-pt. platoon split is remaining hurdle.

Yr Tm	W	L	Sv	IP	K	ERA	xERA	WHIP	oOPS	vL	vR	BF/G	Ctl	Dom	Cmd	FpK	SwK	G	L	F	H%	S%	hr/f	GS	APC	DOM%	DIS%	Sv%	LI	RAR	BPV	BPX	R$
11 aaa	7	8	0	141	94	5.18	5.52	1.73				24.7	4.6	6.0	1.3						35%	70%								-21.5	35	52	-$13
12 COL *	5	1	0	99	99	4.43	4.60	1.46	717	745	698	6.4	3.8	9.1	2.4	59%	12%	48	26	26	34%	72%	16%	0	25			0	0.64	-5.0	74	97	-$4
13 COL	1	3	0	78	78	2.64	3.62	1.33	672	853	544	6.6	3.6	9.0	2.5	61%	12%	46	22	33	32%	82%	7%	0	25			0	1.01	11.8	89	116	$2
14 COL	1	4	1	65	70	3.60	3.09	1.28	735	943	645	3.6	2.2	9.7	4.4	61%	12%	47	19	34	35%	74%	10%	0	14			17	1.31	1.1	140	166	$0
15 COL	1	0	3	10	13	0.00	1.89	0.48	265	321	217	3.5	1.7	11.3	6.5	51%	13%	63	5	32	16%	100%	0%	0	14			100	1.05	5.1	198	236	$1
1st Half	1	0	3	10	13	0.00	1.89	0.48	265	321	217	3.5	1.7	11.3	6.5	51%	13%	63	5	32	16%	100%	0%	0	14			100	1.05	5.1	198	235	$1
2nd Half																																	
16 Proj	**1**	**1**	**12**	**36**	**35**	**3.45**	**3.45**	**1.28**	**699**	**816**	**631**	**5.6**	**2.9**	**8.8**	**3.0**	**60%**	**12%**	**47**	**23**	**30**	**32%**	**76%**	**11%**	**0**						**2.3**	**105**	**125**	**$3**

PAUL SPORER

Owens,Henry

Age: 23	Th: L	Role SP	Health A	LIMA Plan B	
Ht: 6' 6"	Wt: 220	Type Pwr xFB	PT/Exp D	Rand Var 0	
			Consist B	MM 1301	

4-4, 4.57 ERA in 63 IP at BOS. Former 1st-rounder got the call in Aug, but showed mixed bag of results. PRO: Elite SwK confirms Dom upside; consistently baffles RHB. CON: Poor FpK says walk issues aren't gone; tons of fly balls. Future potential here, but that Ctl/FB% combo is a gamble right now.

Yr Tm	W	L	Sv	IP	K	ERA	xERA	WHIP	oOPS	vL	vR	BF/G	Ctl	Dom	Cmd	FpK	SwK	G	L	F	H%	S%	hr/f	GS	APC	DOM%	DIS%	Sv%	LI	RAR	BPV	BPX	R$
11																																	
12																																	
13 aa	3	1	0	30	40	2.08	2.58	1.14				20.0	4.3	11.8	2.8						27%	87%								6.7	118	154	$1
14 a/a	17	5	0	159	145	3.63	3.23	1.26				24.9	3.4	8.2	2.4						30%	72%								2.1	90	107	$9
15 BOS *	7	12	0	185	136	4.49	3.69	1.36	726	859	699	24.2	4.2	6.6	1.6	54%	13%	35	16	49	28%	67%	8%	11	96	45%	18%			-12.0	57	68	-$2
1st Half	2	7	0	97	64	4.81	3.40	1.37				24.0	5.1	5.9	1.2						25%	64%	0%	0						-10.1	50	60	-$7
2nd Half	5	5	0	88	73	4.13	4.02	1.35	726	859	699	24.5	3.1	7.4	2.4	54%	13%	35	16	49	31%	71%	8%	11	96	45%	18%			-1.9	72	85	$3
16 Proj	**8**	**7**	**0**	**116**	**101**	**4.16**	**4.55**	**1.33**	**639**	**754**	**614**	**24.0**	**3.8**	**7.8**	**2.1**	**54%**	**13%**	**35**	**16**	**49**	**29%**	**71%**	**7%**	**20**						**-2.8**	**52**	**62**	**$1**

Papelbon,Jonathan

Age: 35	Th: R	Role RP	Health A	LIMA Plan C+	
Ht: 6' 4"	Wt: 215	Type	PT/Exp B	Rand Var -5	
			Consist A	MM 3331	

Consistency on surface, but this was a tale of two halves. Dominant 1st half propelled by Dom, SwK, FpK "revival," but once those flattened, 2nd half BPV followed suit. Which to believe? Premium fastball velocity a distant memory; only 14% SwK on slider/splitter after Aug (20% before). Proceed with caution.

Yr Tm	W	L	Sv	IP	K	ERA	xERA	WHIP	oOPS	vL	vR	BF/G	Ctl	Dom	Cmd	FpK	SwK	G	L	F	H%	S%	hr/f	GS	APC	DOM%	DIS%	Sv%	LI	RAR	BPV	BPX	R$
11 BOS	4	1	31	64	87	2.94	2.47	0.93	546	428	663	4.0	1.4	12.2	8.7	68%	18%	38	21	41	33%	68%	5%	0	16			91	1.27	8.0	197	297	$20
12 PHI	5	6	38	70	92	2.44	2.84	1.06	621	627	616	4.1	2.3	11.8	5.1	62%	13%	41	18	40	31%	83%	12%	0	16			90	1.24	13.6	169	221	$24
13 PHI	5	1	29	62	57	2.92	3.58	1.14	631	644	618	4.2	1.6	8.3	5.2	64%	11%	40	17	43	31%	78%	8%	0	16			81	1.18	7.2	124	162	$15
14 PHI	2	3	39	66	63	2.04	3.25	0.90	500	462	539	3.9	2.0	8.5	4.2	64%	13%	42	16	42	26%	78%	3%	0	15			91	1.42	14.0	119	142	$23
15 2 NL	4	3	24	63	56	2.13	3.42	1.03	640	786	495	4.4	1.7	8.0	4.7	66%	14%	50	15	35	27%	86%	11%	0	15			92	0.95	14.3	125	149	$17
1st Half	1	1	14	33	34	1.65	3.12	1.01	601	737	479	4.3	1.9	9.4	4.9	69%	16%	51	14	35	29%	87%	7%	0	15			100	0.96	9.3	145	172	$17
2nd Half	3	2	10	31	22	2.64	3.73	1.04	683	833	515	4.5	1.5	6.5	4.4	63%	11%	49	16	35	25%	85%	16%	0	15			83	0.93	5.0	104	123	$16
16 Proj	**3**	**4**	**33**	**73**	**67**	**2.84**	**3.34**	**1.05**	**621**	**684**	**558**	**4.0**	**1.9**	**8.3**	**4.4**	**65%**	**13%**	**45**	**16**	**39**	**28%**	**77%**	**9%**	**0**						**10.1**	**121**	**144**	**$19**

Parker,Jarrod

Age: 27	Th: R	Role SP	Health F	LIMA Plan D+	
Ht: 6' 1"	Wt: 195	Type	PT/Exp C	Rand Var 0	
			Consist F	MM 1100	

Former top prospect fractured his right elbow on rehab in early May, ending his season after just four starts. Concerning by itself, but particularly so after undergoing TJS twice since '10. Likely destined for a spot in the bullpen upon return; hard to forecast much of a significant role. For now, monitor his health.

Yr Tm	W	L	Sv	IP	K	ERA	xERA	WHIP	oOPS	vL	vR	BF/G	Ctl	Dom	Cmd	FpK	SwK	G	L	F	H%	S%	hr/f	GS	APC	DOM%	DIS%	Sv%	LI	RAR	BPV	BPX	R$
11 ARI *	11	8	0	136	95	4.10	3.50	1.33	513	286	641	21.0	3.5	6.3	1.8	55%	7%	35	6	59	30%	69%	0%	1	73	0%	0%			-2.6	65	98	$3
12 OAK *	14	8	0	202	157	3.35	3.43	1.28	670	685	654	25.1	3.1	7.0	2.3	55%	10%	44	26	30	30%	75%	7%	29	98	62%	10%			16.6	78	102	$13
13 OAK	12	8	0	197	134	3.97	4.28	1.22	695	725	654	25.6	2.9	6.1	2.1	60%	10%	41	19	40	27%	71%	10%	32	94	56%	16%			-2.6	51	67	$7
14																																	
15																																	
1st Half																																	
2nd Half																																	
16 Proj	**3**	**2**	**0**	**36**	**26**	**3.86**	**4.26**	**1.28**	**684**	**708**	**654**	**23.2**	**3.2**	**6.4**	**2.0**	**58%**	**10%**	**42**	**22**	**36**	**29%**	**71%**	**7%**	**6**						**0.4**	**50**	**59**	**-$2**

Parnell,Bobby

Age: 31	Th: R	Role RP	Health F	LIMA Plan D+	
Ht: 6' 3"	Wt: 205	Type Pwr xGB	PT/Exp D	Rand Var +1	
			Consist F	MM 1210	

Inherited limited role after returning from TJS mid-season, but as 2nd half BPV shows, something in that arm was clearly amiss. Tough to blame FpK/SwK for post-injury Cmd regression, as both were relatively steady. Another year removed from TJS may help, but until MLB skills rebound convincingly, don't touch him.

Yr Tm	W	L	Sv	IP	K	ERA	xERA	WHIP	oOPS	vL	vR	BF/G	Ctl	Dom	Cmd	FpK	SwK	G	L	F	H%	S%	hr/f	GS	APC	DOM%	DIS%	Sv%	LI	RAR	BPV	BPX	R$
11 NYM	4	6	6	59	64	3.64	3.57	1.47	679	685	672	4.5	4.1	9.7	2.4	57%	11%	51	17	32	35%	76%	8%	0	18			50	1.10	2.2	93	140	$2
12 NYM	5	4	7	69	61	2.49	3.23	1.24	648	626	666	3.9	2.6	8.0	3.1	59%	10%	62	17	22	32%	81%	9%	0	15			58	1.13	12.9	113	148	$8
13 NYM	5	5	22	50	44	2.16	3.09	1.00	555	606	519	4.0	2.2	7.9	3.7	65%	10%	52	22	26	28%	78%	3%	0	16			85	1.66	10.5	114	149	$14
14 NYM	0	0	0	1	1	9.00	7.71	3.00	1100	1667	667	6.0	9.0	9.0	1.0	100%	4%	25	25	50	52%	67%	0%	0	25			0	1.74	-0.6	-78	-93	-$4
15 NYM	2	4	1	24	13	6.38	5.68	1.96	794	921	731	3.7	6.4	4.9	0.8	58%	8%	55	24	21	35%	64%	0%	0	14			33	1.00	-7.1	-51	-61	-$8
1st Half	1	0	1	8	6	0.00	3.05	0.91	487	347	561	3.3	2.3	7.0	3.0	56%	13%	47	24	29	24%	100%	0%	0	13			100	1.44	3.7	88	105	$0
2nd Half	1	4	0	16	7	9.37	7.25	2.45	891	1112	783	3.9	8.3	3.9	0.5	58%	6%	57	24	19	39%	58%	0%	0	14			0	0.84	-10.9	-119	-141	-$11
16 Proj	**3**	**6**	**2**	**44**	**34**	**4.66**	**4.21**	**1.59**	**717**	**768**	**684**	**3.9**	**4.4**	**7.0**	**1.6**	**59%**	**9%**	**57**	**20**	**23**	**34%**	**69%**	**5%**	**0**						**-3.7**	**41**	**48**	**-$4**

Paxton,James

Age: 27	Th: L	Role SP	Health F	LIMA Plan C	
Ht: 6' 4"	Wt: 220	Type Pwr GB	PT/Exp C	Rand Var 0	
			Consist B	MM 2201	

Second hobbled season in a row, this time due to late-May injury on pitching hand. PRO: Frustrates RHBs with regularity; GB% profile remains above-average; still young. CON: FpK/Ctl issues not sorted out; Dom upside capped by poor SwK on every pitch. VERDICT: Upside here is limited, even with full health.

Yr Tm	W	L	Sv	IP	K	ERA	xERA	WHIP	oOPS	vL	vR	BF/G	Ctl	Dom	Cmd	FpK	SwK	G	L	F	H%	S%	hr/f	GS	APC	DOM%	DIS%	Sv%	LI	RAR	BPV	BPX	R$
11 aa	3	0	0	39	45	2.04	2.47	1.12				22.0	3.0	10.5	3.5						31%	83%								9.1	134	202	$3
12 aa	9	4	0	106	96	3.68	4.34	1.58				22.3	4.8	8.1	1.7						34%	76%								4.4	72	95	-$2
13 SEA *	11	11	0	170	131	4.25	4.35	1.48	533	790	475	22.8	3.2	6.9	2.1	54%	10%	59	17	24	34%	71%	13%	4	96	75%	0%			-8.1	67	88	-$3
14 SEA	6	4	0	74	59	3.04	3.50	1.20	612	527	629	23.3	3.5	7.2	2.0	54%	8%	55	23	23	28%	74%	6%	13	91	38%	23%			6.4	67	80	$4
15 SEA	3	4	0	67	56	3.90	4.47	1.43	704	1054	606	22.8	3.9	7.5	1.9	53%	7%	48	17	34	31%	76%	11%	13	85	38%	46%			0.6	56	67	-$3
1st Half	3	3	0	58	45	3.70	4.41	1.30	664	1082	568	25.1	3.4	6.9	2.0	54%	7%	49	15	36	28%	75%	11%	10	92	50%	30%			1.9	60	71	-$1
2nd Half	0	1	0	9	11	5.19	4.87	2.31	935	984	899	15.3	7.3	11.4	1.6	50%	10%	46	29	25	47%	79%	14%	3	62	0%	100%			-1.3	34	40	-$11
16 Proj	**7**	**6**	**0**	**116**	**97**	**3.69**	**3.91**	**1.35**	**672**	**934**	**615**	**23.0**	**3.6**	**7.5**	**2.1**	**54%**	**7%**	**51**	**18**	**31**	**31%**	**74%**	**8%**	**21**						**3.9**	**68**	**81**	**$2**

Peacock,Brad

Age: 28	Th: R	Role SP	Health F	LIMA Plan D+	
Ht: 6' 1"	Wt: 210	Type Pwr FB	PT/Exp C	Rand Var +1	
			Consist A	MM 1300	

Suffered left intercostal strain in April, which effectively ended his season. Outlook wasn't promising prior, though, given all those fly balls and little control of his offerings, which is a risky combo. Once a promising farmhand with Dom upside, but you have no business investing in that anymore.

Yr Tm	W	L	Sv	IP	K	ERA	xERA	WHIP	oOPS	vL	vR	BF/G	Ctl	Dom	Cmd	FpK	SwK	G	L	F	H%	S%	hr/f	GS	APC	DOM%	DIS%	Sv%	LI	RAR	BPV	BPX	R$
11 WAS *	17	3	0	159	149	2.68	2.35	1.07	438	355	568	22.0	2.9	8.5	2.9	60%	5%	32	8	61	27%	77%	0%	2	67	0%	0%	0	1.30	24.7	109	164	$22
12 aaa	12	9	0	135	115	6.17	5.28	1.65				21.5	4.3	7.7	1.8						35%	62%								-35.7	54	70	-$16
13 HOU *	11	8	0	162	141	4.21	4.23	1.31	779	919	594	21.0	3.3	7.8	2.4	56%	8%	37	19	45	29%	73%	14%	14	83	43%	36%	0	0.79	-7.0	60	78	$3
14 HOU	4	9	0	132	119	4.72	4.59	1.56	801	793	811	21.0	4.8	8.1	1.7	57%	9%	37	21	42	31%	74%	12%	24	85	29%	29%	0	0.81	-15.8	32	38	-$9
15 HOU	0	1	0	5	3	5.40	5.05	1.40	808	1167	422	22.0	3.6	5.4	1.5	68%	6%	31	31	38	31%	57%	0%	1	85	0%	0%			-0.9	9	11	-$5
1st Half	0	1	0	5	3	5.40	5.05	1.40	808	1167	422	22.0	3.6	5.4	1.5	68%	6%	31	31	38	31%	57%	0%	1	85	0%	0%			-0.9	9	11	-$5
2nd Half																																	
16 Proj	**4**	**3**	**0**	**58**	**51**	**4.81**	**4.48**	**1.47**	**765**	**816**	**691**	**21.2**	**4.0**	**8.0**	**2.0**	**56%**	**8%**	**37**	**20**	**43**	**32%**	**69%**	**9%**	**12**						**-6.1**	**49**	**59**	**-$4**

Peavy,Jake

Age: 35	Th: R	Role SP	Health F	LIMA Plan B+	
Ht: 6' 1"	Wt: 195	Type FB	PT/Exp B	Rand Var 0	
			Consist A	MM 1103	

8-6, 3.58 ERA in 110.2 IP at SF. April back strain shelved him for two months, but DOM%/DIS% show he finished quite strong. Is it tenable? Uptick in FpK somewhat validates 2H Ctl/Cmd impovement, but H% fortune had a lot to do with 2nd half oOPS. Combine that with middling Dom? End-gamer or spot option only.

Yr Tm	W	L	Sv	IP	K	ERA	xERA	WHIP	oOPS	vL	vR	BF/G	Ctl	Dom	Cmd	FpK	SwK	G	L	F	H%	S%	hr/f	GS	APC	DOM%	DIS%	Sv%	LI	RAR	BPV	BPX	R$
11 CHW *	8	8	0	141	118	5.12	4.32	1.31	701	669	740	23.2	1.7	7.5	4.4	63%	10%	39	23	39	34%	62%	8%	18	98	67%	17%	0	0.81	-20.4	108	163	-$2
12 CHW	11	12	0	219	194	3.37	3.82	1.10	671	714	614	27.6	2.0	8.0	4.0	63%	10%	37	19	45	28%	74%	10%	32	109	75%	0%			17.4	104	136	$22
13 2 AL	12	5	0	145	121	4.17	4.00	1.15	697	731	659	25.7	2.2	7.5	3.4	66%	9%	33	21	47	28%	68%	10%	23	103	74%	13%			-5.4	86	112	$7
14 2 TM	7	13	0	203	158	3.73	4.12	1.28	742	766	719	26.6	2.8	7.0	2.5	64%	10%	38	20	42	29%	74%	9%	32	101	56%	9%			0.3	67	80	$4
15 SF *	8	9	0	143	99	4.39	4.07	1.27	684	650	720	23.4	2.2	6.2	2.8	63%	9%	38	17	45	30%	68%	8%	19	92	58%	16%			-7.5	67	80	$1
1st Half	0	6	0	46	32	6.94	6.32	1.73	801	733	861	23.4	3.5	6.2	1.8	62%	10%	41	11	48	36%	60%	10%	3	84	0%	67%			-17.0	27	32	-$26
2nd Half	8	3	0	97	67	3.17	4.18	1.04	666	637	695	24.1	1.6	6.2	3.9	64%	8%	37	18	45	26%	74%	8%	16	93	69%	6%			9.5	85	101	$14
16 Proj	**8**	**10**	**0**	**160**	**120**	**4.33**	**4.24**	**1.28**	**749**	**756**	**741**	**24.4**	**2.4**	**6.8**	**2.8**	**64%**	**9%**	**36**	**20**	**44**	**30%**	**69%**	**9%**	**27**						**-7.2**	**72**	**85**	**$2**

ALEC DOPP

Pelfrey,Mike

Age: 32	Th: R	Role	SP	Health	F	LIMA Plan	D+
Ht: 6' 7"	Wt: 250	Type	Con	PT/Exp	B	Rand Var	0
				Consist	F	MM	1003

So bad, and so much of it. Posted 2nd-lowest SwK/Dom among qualified SPs. FpK volatility debunks that odd 2nd half Ctl swing. And two season-ending arm surgeries. Normally, bad pitchers get very little rope. This one got 30 starts' worth.

Yr	Tm	W	L	Sv	IP	K	ERA	xERA	WHIP	oOPS	vL	vR	BF/G	Ctl	Dom	Cmd	FpK	SwK	G	L	F	H%	S%	hr/f	GS	APC	DOM%	DIS%	Sv%	LI	RAR	BPV	BPX	R$
11	NYM	7	13	0	194	105	4.74	4.63	1.47	777	776	778	25.3	3.0	4.9	1.6	64%	6%	46	20	35	31%	69%	9%	33	95	30%	24%	0	0.75	-19.1	30	46	-$8
12	NYM	0	0	0	20	13	2.29	3.77	1.42	683	672	697	28.3	1.8	5.9	3.3	64%	9%	53	27	20	36%	82%	0%	3	102	33%	0%			4.2	89	116	-$3
13	MIN	5	13	0	153	101	5.19	4.59	1.55	789	762	821	23.4	3.1	6.0	1.9	55%	6%	43	21	36	34%	67%	7%	29	94	21%	34%			-24.9	44	57	-$13
14	MIN	0	3	0	24	10	7.99	6.83	1.99	924	648	1315	23.8	6.8	3.8	0.6	50%	5%	44	18	38	30%	62%	15%	5	91	0%	100%			-12.4	-94	-112	-$9
15	MIN	6	11	0	165	86	4.26	4.45	1.48	772	834	716	23.8	2.5	4.7	1.9	58%	6%	51	23	26	33%	71%	7%	30	89	30%	37%			-6.1	47	56	-$6
1st Half		5	5	0	91	45	3.94	4.54	1.49	755	777	735	24.8	3.2	4.4	1.4	60%	5%	55	21	24	32%	73%	7%	16	91	38%	38%			0.2	28	33	-$4
2nd Half		1	6	0	73	41	4.66	4.33	1.46	792	891	690	22.7	1.6	5.0	3.2	55%	7%	46	25	29	35%	68%	8%	14	86	21%	36%			-6.3	72	85	-$10
16	**Proj**	**5**	**12**	**0**	**160**	**92**	**4.71**	**4.51**	**1.50**	**781**	**806**	**756**	**23.3**	**2.7**	**5.2**	**2.0**	**57%**	**6%**	**47**	**22**	**31**	**33%**	**69%**	**8%**	**30**						**-14.8**	**47**	**56**	**-$10**

Peralta,Wily

Age: 27	Th: R	Role	SP	Health	D	LIMA Plan	D+
Ht: 6' 1"	Wt: 245	Type	GB	PT/Exp	A	Rand Var	+1
				Consist	D	MM	1103

Young ground-baller spent June-July on DL with left oblique injury, and BPV shows he wasn't the same guy upon return. Fastball velocity dip prompted Dom/SwK slide, while shaky FpK culminated in sharp 2H Ctl fall-off. First major injury in a while, yes, but even those healthy 1H BPIs netted out a below-average BPX.

Yr	Tm	W	L	Sv	IP	K	ERA	xERA	WHIP	oOPS	vL	vR	BF/G	Ctl	Dom	Cmd	FpK	SwK	G	L	F	H%	S%	hr/f	GS	APC	DOM%	DIS%	Sv%	LI	RAR	BPV	BPX	R$
11	a/a	11	7	0	151	140	3.31	3.23	1.27				23.7	3.3	8.3	2.5						31%	75%								11.8	93	140	$10
12	MIL *	9	12	0	176	146	5.34	5.17	1.71	601	639	564	23.4	4.8	7.5	1.6	61%	9%	55	21	24	36%	68%	0%	5	76	60%	20%	0	0.66	-28.7	56	72	-$18
13	MIL	11	15	0	183	129	4.37	4.17	1.42	722	753	692	25.1	3.6	6.3	1.8	58%	9%	51	21	28	30%	71%	12%	32	93	41%	22%			-11.4	46	60	-$2
14	MIL	17	11	0	199	154	3.53	3.62	1.30	714	820	606	26.2	2.8	7.0	2.5	58%	9%	54	19	28	30%	77%	14%	32	100	59%	13%			5.1	83	99	$9
15	MIL	5	10	0	109	60	4.72	4.67	1.54	844	889	796	23.9	3.1	5.0	1.6	57%	7%	52	20	28	32%	72%	13%	20	88	35%	40%			-10.2	37	44	-$8
1st Half		1	5	0	54	35	4.00	4.10	1.43	832	901	763	25.7	2.3	5.8	2.5	56%	9%	54	19	28	32%	77%	16%	9	91	56%	22%			-0.3	74	87	-$6
2nd Half		4	5	0	55	25	5.43	5.27	1.65	856	879	828	22.5	3.8	4.1	1.1	57%	5%	50	21	29	32%	68%	11%	11	85	18%	55%			-9.9	0	0	-$10
16	**Proj**	**11**	**14**	**0**	**174**	**120**	**4.14**	**4.15**	**1.45**	**780**	**842**	**716**	**23.9**	**3.1**	**6.2**	**2.0**	**57%**	**8%**	**52**	**20**	**28**	**32%**	**74%**	**12%**	**31**						**-3.8**	**58**	**69**	**-$2**

Perez,Martin

Age: 25	Th: L	Role	SP	Health	F	LIMA Plan	B
Ht: 6' 0"	Wt: 190	Type	xGB	PT/Exp	D	Rand Var	0
				Consist	B	MM	2003

3-6, 4.46 ERA in 79 IP at TEX. Returned from TJS mid-season, and while Dom/xERA were forgettable, two reasons for optimism: 1) Post-injury FpK rose to elite ranks, 2) Heavy GB% lean applied to every pitch, which is rare. SwK/health limit upside now, but elements of breakout are aligning here.

Yr	Tm	W	L	Sv	IP	K	ERA	xERA	WHIP	oOPS	vL	vR	BF/G	Ctl	Dom	Cmd	FpK	SwK	G	L	F	H%	S%	hr/f	GS	APC	DOM%	DIS%	Sv%	LI	RAR	BPV	BPX	R$
11	a/a	8	6	0	137	102	4.69	4.93	1.56				22.3	3.5	6.7	1.9						35%	70%								-12.6	55	83	-$6
12	TEX *	8	10	0	165	83	4.95	4.68	1.51	819	596	924	21.0	3.7	4.5	1.2	60%	7%	49	21	30	30%	68%	8%	6	55	0%	50%	0	0.75	-19.0	28	36	-$11
13	TEX *	15	8	0	168	109	3.77	4.27	1.35	728	759	718	25.0	2.5	5.9	2.3	61%	10%	48	21	31	31%	75%	12%	20	93	55%	25%			2.0	56	72	$5
14	TEX	4	3	0	51	35	4.38	3.73	1.34	743	707	753	25.9	3.3	6.1	1.8	60%	8%	53	23	25	30%	67%	8%	8	97	13%	38%			-4.1	52	61	-$2
15	TEX *	3	7	0	104	69	4.74	4.71	1.49	729	537	777	22.5	2.3	5.9	2.5	65%	8%	60	18	22	35%	67%	5%	14	87	29%	29%			-10.1	66	79	-$8
1st Half		0	0	0	14	12	4.86	5.12	1.52				14.8	2.1	8.1	3.9						39%	68%	0%	0						-1.5	101	120	-$10
2nd Half		3	7	0	91	56	4.73	4.65	1.48	729	537	777	24.4	2.4	5.6	2.3	65%	8%	60	18	22	34%	67%	5%	14	87	29%	29%			-8.5	62	73	-$7
16	**Proj**	**11**	**9**	**0**	**160**	**101**	**4.01**	**4.04**	**1.38**	**729**	**644**	**756**	**23.8**	**2.9**	**5.7**	**2.0**	**62%**	**9%**	**56**	**19**	**25**	**31%**	**71%**	**9%**	**28**						**-1.0**	**58**	**69**	**$1**

Perez,Williams

Age: 25	Th: R	Role	SP	Health	C	LIMA Plan	D+
Ht: 6' 1"	Wt: 230	Type	GB	PT/Exp	D	Rand Var	0
				Consist	C	MM	1003

7-6, 4.78 ERA in 116.2 IP at ATL. Stepped into rotation in mid-May and posted 1.50 ERA in first 6 GS. It didn't last. Blame 2H S% correction for some of it, but futile Cmd and allowing tons of hard contact is never a good combo. Quality GB% lean, but otherwise, no solid indicator(s) of future upside.

Yr	Tm	W	L	Sv	IP	K	ERA	xERA	WHIP	oOPS	vL	vR	BF/G	Ctl	Dom	Cmd	FpK	SwK	G	L	F	H%	S%	hr/f	GS	APC	DOM%	DIS%	Sv%	LI	RAR	BPV	BPX	R$
11																																		
12																																		
13																																		
14	aa	7	6	0	133	84	3.41	3.47	1.31				21.1	2.6	5.7	2.2						31%	73%								5.4	73	86	$3
15	ATL *	10	7	1	155	104	3.98	4.60	1.49	809	865	748	21.6	3.6	6.0	1.7	57%	7%	51	20	29	32%	75%	12%	20	81	20%	25%	100	0.72	-0.3	46	55	-$1
1st Half		6	0	1	77	56	2.49	4.15	1.45	681	781	601	20.6	3.8	6.6	1.7	56%	5%	52	20	28	32%	85%	10%	8	73	38%	13%	100	0.67	14.0	59	70	$7
2nd Half		4	7	0	78	48	5.44	5.04	1.52	899	909	885	22.7	3.3	5.5	1.7	57%	7%	50	20	29	32%	65%	13%	12	89	8%	33%			-14.3	34	40	-$10
16	**Proj**	**6**	**8**	**0**	**131**	**85**	**4.20**	**4.34**	**1.44**	**742**	**783**	**696**	**21.6**	**3.4**	**5.8**	**1.7**	**57%**	**7%**	**51**	**20**	**29**	**31%**	**71%**	**7%**	**26**						**-3.9**	**42**	**51**	**-$4**

Perkins,Glen

Age: 33	Th: L	Role	RP	Health	B	LIMA Plan	B
Ht: 6' 0"	Wt: 205	Type	Pwr FB	PT/Exp	A	Rand Var	-1
				Consist	B	MM	3430

Side, neck, back issues colored his season, esp. in the 2H. Dominant 1st half fueled by extreme H%-S%-hr/f trifecta and obscenely low oOPS vs. RHH. xERA warned of regression, and it was spot-on. FpK and Ctl still in fine shape, but SwK decline legitimizes 3-yr Dom/BPV dip. FB% profile isn't promising, either. Lots of red flags.

Yr	Tm	W	L	Sv	IP	K	ERA	xERA	WHIP	oOPS	vL	vR	BF/G	Ctl	Dom	Cmd	FpK	SwK	G	L	F	H%	S%	hr/f	GS	APC	DOM%	DIS%	Sv%	LI	RAR	BPV	BPX	R$
11	MIN	4	4	2	62	65	2.48	3.04	1.23	644	589	681	3.9	3.1	9.5	3.1	65%	12%	50	21	29	33%	80%	4%	0	14			40	1.22	11.1	116	174	$5
12	MIN	3	1	16	70	78	2.56	3.12	1.04	631	488	721	4.0	2.0	10.0	4.9	63%	14%	42	19	39	29%	82%	12%	0	15			80	0.92	12.6	144	188	$14
13	MIN	2	0	36	63	77	2.30	2.67	0.93	562	544	568	3.9	2.2	11.1	5.1	70%	14%	36	26	38	28%	79%	9%	0	15			90	1.16	12.1	155	202	$21
14	MIN	4	3	34	62	66	3.65	3.34	1.18	720	772	700	4.1	1.6	9.6	6.0	65%	12%	35	23	42	34%	73%	9%	0	15			83	1.13	0.7	143	170	$15
15	MIN	3	5	32	57	54	3.32	3.91	1.19	701	850	648	4.0	1.6	8.5	5.4	64%	11%	34	22	45	31%	80%	12%	0	14			91	1.50	4.5	123	146	$14
1st Half		0	1	27	34	32	1.31	3.54	0.90	495	766	390	3.8	1.3	8.4	6.4	63%	12%	35	21	44	27%	90%	5%	0	13			100	1.43	11.2	129	153	$24
2nd Half		3	4	5	23	22	6.35	4.45	1.63	972	980	969	4.2	2.0	8.7	4.4	64%	10%	32	22	46	37%	70%	20%	0	15			63	1.59	-6.7	113	134	$0
16	**Proj**	**4**	**4**	**33**	**58**	**60**	**3.68**	**3.38**	**1.17**	**706**	**738**	**693**	**3.8**	**1.8**	**9.3**	**5.1**	**65%**	**12%**	**35**	**23**	**42**	**31%**	**75%**	**13%**	**0**						**2.0**	**132**	**157**	**$15**

Petit,Yusmeiro

Age: 31	Th: R	Role	RP	Health	A	LIMA Plan	A
Ht: 6' 1"	Wt: 250	Type	FB	PT/Exp	C	Rand Var	0
				Consist	C	MM	3301

Filthy '14 campaign from the 'pen/rotation had us thinking full-time SP gig, but now that year seems like an outlier. Dom/SwK tumbled back to norms (even with 2H surge), and while Ctl is still elite, that FpK trend says it might not last long. He's healthy, but if Cmd dwindles further, IP will continue to suffer.

Yr	Tm	W	L	Sv	IP	K	ERA	xERA	WHIP	oOPS	vL	vR	BF/G	Ctl	Dom	Cmd	FpK	SwK	G	L	F	H%	S%	hr/f	GS	APC	DOM%	DIS%	Sv%	LI	RAR	BPV	BPX	R$
11																																		
12	SF *	7	7	0	171	118	3.48	4.47	1.42	936	885	1100	25.0	2.0	6.2	3.1	70%	2%	38	25	38	35%	76%	0%	1	94	0%	100%			11.3	80	105	$2
13	SF *	9	7	0	136	115	4.36	4.47	1.30	660	562	717	24.3	1.6	7.6	4.7	69%	13%	30	26	44	33%	70%	7%	7	91	57%	14%	0	0.73	-8.3	108	141	$1
14	SF	5	5	0	117	133	3.69	3.03	1.02	635	777	510	11.8	1.7	10.2	6.0	69%	13%	36	21	43	30%	66%	9%	12	43	50%	17%	0	0.52	0.7	152	182	$8
15	SF	1	1	1	76	59	3.67	4.34	1.18	743	828	680	7.5	1.8	7.0	3.9	63%	10%	33	21	46	29%	75%	10%	1	27	0%	0%	100	0.84	2.7	89	106	$1
1st Half		1	1	1	48	29	4.50	5.01	1.19	770	930	670	9.2	2.1	5.4	2.6	66%	10%	30	20	50	26%	69%	11%	1	31	0%	0%	100	0.63	-3.2	50	60	-$1
2nd Half		0	0	0	28	30	2.25	3.27	1.18	697	693	701	5.7	1.3	9.6	7.5	56%	11%	38	25	38	36%	84%	7%	0	22			0	1.06	5.9	154	183	$3
16	**Proj**	**2**	**2**	**0**	**73**	**67**	**3.50**	**3.63**	**1.18**	**718**	**783**	**666**	**9.3**	**1.7**	**8.3**	**5.0**	**65%**	**12%**	**34**	**23**	**43**	**32%**	**74%**	**9%**	**0**						**4.1**	**117**	**139**	**$2**

Petricka,Jacob

Age: 28	Th: R	Role	RP	Health	B	LIMA Plan	D+
Ht: 6' 5"	Wt: 205	Type	xGB	PT/Exp	C	Rand Var	-1
				Consist	A	MM	2010

Third year in the bigs was also his worst by ERA and oOPS. PRO: Proven GB% tilt validates ability to keep ball in the yard; FpK backs up 3-year Ctl improvement; 2H SwK showed some life. CON: Dom nosediving; lefties are still a major problem. This profiles as situational saves, not a full-time or long-term closer option.

Yr	Tm	W	L	Sv	IP	K	ERA	xERA	WHIP	oOPS	vL	vR	BF/G	Ctl	Dom	Cmd	FpK	SwK	G	L	F	H%	S%	hr/f	GS	APC	DOM%	DIS%	Sv%	LI	RAR	BPV	BPX	R$
11																																		
12	aa	3	3	0	58	23	6.94	7.15	2.01				27.8	6.3	3.6	0.6						32%	67%								-20.8	-19	-25	-$17
13	CHW *	6	1	1	74	58	2.63	3.92	1.56	688	775	644	6.9	4.8	7.1	1.5	51%	9%	63	21	16	33%	82%	0%	0	20			50	0.94	11.3	70	92	$1
14	CHW	1	6	14	73	55	2.96	3.57	1.37	671	830	549	4.6	4.1	6.8	1.7	61%	8%	63	17	19	30%	78%	7%	0	18			78	1.52	7.0	53	63	$5
15	CHW	4	3	2	52	33	3.63	3.77	1.42	716	851	666	3.5	3.1	5.7	1.8	65%	9%	65	18	17	32%	74%	7%	0	13			67	1.16	2.1	62	73	-$1
1st Half		2	2	2	29	19	3.10	3.45	1.38	739	783	720	3.6	2.5	5.9	2.4	65%	8%	67	18	16	32%	79%	14%	0	12			67	1.22	3.1	84	99	$0
2nd Half		2	1	0	23	14	4.30	4.20	1.48	687	958	604	3.4	3.9	5.5	1.4	64%	11%	64	18	19	32%	68%	0%	0	13			0	1.10	-1.0	34	41	-$2
16	**Proj**	**4**	**4**	**2**	**65**	**43**	**3.74**	**4.04**	**1.50**	**728**	**890**	**648**	**4.6**	**4.1**	**5.9**	**1.5**	**63%**	**9%**	**64**	**18**	**18**	**32%**	**74%**	**7%**	**0**						**1.8**	**40**	**47**	**-$2**

ALEC DOPP

Phelps,David

Age: 29	Th: R	Role: RP	Health: F	LIMA Plan: D+
Ht: 6' 2"	Wt: 200	Type: Pwr	PT/Exp: B	Rand Var: 0
			Consist: A	MM: 1201

Swing-man pressed into starting role again with similar results. Unable to hold up as 2nd half deteriorated and more arm problems shelved him in August. Once-interesting Dom has faded with SwK in tow, only 1st half Ctl saved this from being worse. Full-time relief work might help, but that's just us being optimistic.

Yr Tm	W	L	Sv	IP	K	ERA	xERA	WHIP	oOPS	vL	vR	BF/G	Ctl	Dom	Cmd	FpK	SwK	G	L	F	H%	S%	hr/f	GS	APC	DOM%	DIS%	Sv%	LI	RAR	BPV	BPX	R$
11 aaa	6	6	0	107	72	4.51	6.23	1.64				26.6	2.5	6.1	2.4						36%	77%								-7.6	36	55	-$7
12 NYY	4	4	0	100	96	3.34	3.82	1.19	682	786	597	12.5	3.4	8.7	2.5	62%	7%	43	19	38	27%	78%	14%	11	51	45%	45%	0	0.83	8.3	84	110	$6
13 NYY	6	5	0	87	79	4.98	3.97	1.42	749	756	738	17.1	3.6	8.2	2.3	59%	7%	42	22	36	33%	65%	9%	12	68	58%	17%	0	0.92	-12.0	70	91	-$4
14 NYY	5	5	1	113	92	4.38	4.21	1.42	751	699	805	15.5	3.7	7.3	2.0	62%	6%	41	24	35	31%	72%	11%	17	60	35%	12%	100	0.86	-8.9	52	62	-$4
15 MIA	4	8	0	112	77	4.50	4.48	1.36	729	758	705	21.0	2.7	6.2	2.3	65%	5%	42	23	35	31%	68%	9%	19	81	47%	32%	0	0.72	-7.4	60	71	-$4
1st Half	4	4	0	83	56	4.03	4.30	1.26	683	657	706	20.6	2.4	6.1	2.5	67%	5%	44	22	34	30%	69%	8%	13	79	54%	23%	0	0.69	-0.7	67	79	$0
2nd Half	0	4	0	29	21	5.83	4.97	1.64	854	1078	705	21.8	3.4	6.4	1.9	58%	5%	37	24	39	35%	66%	11%	6	86	33%	50%			-6.8	40	47	-$14
16 Proj	3	5	0	73	56	4.42	4.35	1.45	776	821	735	18.1	3.3	7.0	2.1	61%	6%	41	23	36	32%	72%	10%	8						-4.1	56	67	-$4

Pineda,Michael

Age: 27	Th: R	Role: SP	Health: F	LIMA Plan: B+
Ht: 6' 7"	Wt: 265	Type:	PT/Exp: C	Rand Var: +5
			Consist: B	MM: 3303

Another year removed from 2012 labrum surgery, with intriguing skills masked by mediocre ERA. Consolidated elite Ctl as Dom and GB% soared. Lost ground in 2nd half but real damage came from flukish hr/f and S%. Velocity ticked up all year despite August DL time. With health and better luck... UP: 16 wins, 3.00 ERA.

Yr Tm	W	L	Sv	IP	K	ERA	xERA	WHIP	oOPS	vL	vR	BF/G	Ctl	Dom	Cmd	FpK	SwK	G	L	F	H%	S%	hr/f	GS	APC	DOM%	DIS%	Sv%	LI	RAR	BPV	BPX	R$
11 SEA	9	10	0	171	173	3.74	3.53	1.10	621	653	587	24.9	2.9	9.1	3.1	64%	12%	36	19	45	27%	69%	9%	28	96	75%	11%			4.3	100	150	$13
12																																	
13 a/a	2	1	0	32	28	5.23	4.30	1.32				16.7	3.7	7.8	2.1						28%	64%								-5.5	52	68	-$4
14 NYY	5	5	0	76	59	1.89	3.39	0.83	526	533	518	22.3	0.8	7.0	8.4	67%	12%	39	19	42	25%	81%	5%	13	88	77%	8%			17.5	120	143	$11
15 NYY	12	10	0	161	156	4.37	3.21	1.23	752	741	762	24.7	1.2	8.7	7.4	64%	12%	48	22	30	34%	68%	15%	27	94	56%	15%			-8.1	152	180	$6
1st Half	8	5	0	100	105	3.79	3.03	1.21	734	730	737	25.8	1.2	9.5	8.1	64%	13%	50	20	30	36%	71%	10%	16	97	63%	13%			2.1	167	198	$12
2nd Half	4	5	0	61	51	5.31	3.50	1.25	782	758	809	23.2	1.2	7.5	6.4	62%	12%	46	25	29	32%	63%	22%	11	90	45%	18%			-10.2	127	151	-$5
16 Proj	11	10	0	160	141	3.82	3.41	1.13	690	684	695	21.7	1.6	8.0	4.9	64%	12%	43	21	36	30%	70%	12%	29						2.8	120	143	$11

Pomeranz,Drew

Age: 27	Th: L	Role: RP	Health: D	LIMA Plan: A
Ht: 6' 5"	Wt: 240	Type: Pwr	PT/Exp: C	Rand Var: 0
			Consist: C	MM: 3411

Control, pitch-counts plagued him as an SP; June move to the pen yielded mph spike, 2.61 ERA and 9th inning consideration. GB% fade, gopheritis impacted 2nd half results. Balky shoulder required arthroscopic surgery in October. FpK says Ctl still needs work. But if healthy, both-sides effectiveness keep him watchable.

Yr Tm	W	L	Sv	IP	K	ERA	xERA	WHIP	oOPS	vL	vR	BF/G	Ctl	Dom	Cmd	FpK	SwK	G	L	F	H%	S%	hr/f	GS	APC	DOM%	DIS%	Sv%	LI	RAR	BPV	BPX	R$
11 COL *	3	2	0	42	32	3.35	2.06	1.03	700	522	727	18.1	2.3	6.8	2.9	57%	5%	47	26	26	27%	66%	0%	4	67	25%	25%			3.1	107	160	$2
12 COL *	6	13	0	147	122	4.31	5.15	1.59	775	464	864	20.3	4.2	7.5	1.8	56%	10%	44	20	36	34%	75%	14%	22	77	18%	64%			-5.3	49	64	-$7
13 COL *	8	6	0	113	95	5.86	5.64	1.69	951	405	1150	21.2	4.3	7.6	1.8	54%	8%	51	17	32	35%	66%	19%	4	52	0%	100%	0	0.78	-27.7	43	57	-$13
14 OAK *	8	5	0	115	106	2.90	3.48	1.24	586	664	563	16.7	3.3	8.3	2.5	52%	9%	46	18	36	29%	81%	10%	10	57	50%	20%	0	0.75	12.0	82	97	$7
15 OAK	5	6	3	86	82	3.66	3.85	1.19	651	438	749	6.7	3.2	8.6	2.6	58%	12%	42	22	36	28%	71%	9%	9	27	22%	33%	50	1.27	3.2	87	103	$5
1st Half	2	3	1	57	46	3.65	4.28	1.27	648	354	775	9.9	4.0	7.3	1.8	59%	11%	45	23	32	27%	72%	8%	8	39	25%	25%	100	0.98	2.2	47	56	$3
2nd Half	3	3	2	29	36	3.68	3.12	1.02	657	586	693	4.1	1.8	11.0	6.0	57%	13%	37	18	45	30%	69%	12%	1	18	0%	100%	40	1.50	1.0	164	195	$7
16 Proj	6	5	2	80	80	3.48	3.56	1.23	684	567	727	9.6	2.9	9.0	3.1	55%	11%	43	19	38	31%	75%	10%	4						4.8	104	124	$4

Porcello,Rick

Age: 27	Th: R	Role: SP	Health: B	LIMA Plan: C+
Ht: 6' 5"	Wt: 200	Type:	PT/Exp: A	Rand Var: +4
			Consist: A	MM: 3205

2nd half DL timeout helped, whether triceps-related or not. GB% rebounded along with bottom line over final eight starts. But stubborn gopheritis hung on, as both 2014 H% and effectiveness vL now look like outliers. Dom surge a plus even without SwK endorsement, but suddenly his sinker/slider combo looks less stable.

Yr Tm	W	L	Sv	IP	K	ERA	xERA	WHIP	oOPS	vL	vR	BF/G	Ctl	Dom	Cmd	FpK	SwK	G	L	F	H%	S%	hr/f	GS	APC	DOM%	DIS%	Sv%	LI	RAR	BPV	BPX	R$
11 DET	14	9	0	182	104	4.75	4.05	1.41	774	857	650	25.3	2.3	5.1	2.3	61%	7%	51	19	30	32%	67%	10%	31	92	29%	23%			-18.1	60	90	-$2
12 DET	10	12	0	176	107	4.59	4.15	1.53	808	883	725	25.3	2.2	5.5	2.4	63%	8%	53	24	23	35%	71%	12%	31	91	32%	26%			-12.6	69	90	-$9
13 DET	13	8	0	177	142	4.32	3.32	1.28	709	808	602	23.0	2.1	7.2	3.4	60%	9%	55	21	24	32%	68%	14%	29	89	48%	17%	0	0.84	-10.0	105	137	$4
14 DET	15	13	0	205	129	3.43	3.74	1.23	712	732	686	26.3	1.8	5.7	3.1	64%	8%	49	22	29	30%	74%	9%	31	95	55%	13%	0	0.83	7.9	80	96	$10
15 BOS	9	15	0	172	149	4.92	3.77	1.36	787	815	751	26.3	2.0	7.8	3.9	60%	9%	46	22	33	34%	67%	14%	28	98	64%	14%			-20.3	111	132	-$4
1st Half	4	9	0	95	75	6.08	4.11	1.40	818	806	832	25.6	2.1	7.1	3.4	58%	9%	43	21	36	33%	59%	15%	16	94	56%	19%			-24.8	93	110	-$12
2nd Half	5	6	0	77	74	3.49	3.36	1.31	747	826	643	27.3	1.9	8.6	4.6	63%	9%	49	23	28	35%	77%	14%	12	104	75%	8%			4.5	132	156	$6
16 Proj	12	13	0	189	149	3.81	3.55	1.25	703	749	647	24.8	2.0	7.1	3.6	62%	9%	49	22	29	31%	72%	11%	31						3.6	102	122	$8

Price,David

Age: 30	Th: L	Role: SP	Health: B	LIMA Plan: D+
Ht: 6' 6"	Wt: 220	Type: Pwr	PT/Exp: A	Rand Var: -3
			Consist: A	MM: 4405

Charmed S% fueled season-long ERA excellence as outstanding 2014 WHIP remained intact. Soaring win total combined with both to drive career-best R$. All despite a mediocre GB% and Cmd that slipped from being transcendental to merely elite. Moral: It pays big-time to be both very lucky and very good.

Yr Tm	W	L	Sv	IP	K	ERA	xERA	WHIP	oOPS	vL	vR	BF/G	Ctl	Dom	Cmd	FpK	SwK	G	L	F	H%	S%	hr/f	GS	APC	DOM%	DIS%	Sv%	LI	RAR	BPV	BPX	R$
11 TAM	12	13	0	224	218	3.49	3.32	1.14	659	508	709	27.0	2.5	8.7	3.5	60%	9%	44	19	37	29%	72%	10%	34	109	62%	12%			12.5	111	167	$19
12 TAM	20	5	0	211	205	2.56	3.10	1.10	602	520	626	27.0	2.5	8.7	3.5	63%	9%	53	20	27	29%	80%	11%	31	107	74%	13%			37.9	120	157	$32
13 TAM	10	8	0	187	151	3.33	3.34	1.10	661	489	712	27.4	1.3	7.3	5.6	68%	8%	45	22	33	30%	72%	9%	27	100	78%	7%			12.4	119	155	$15
14 2 AL	15	12	0	248	271	3.26	3.00	1.08	647	657	644	29.7	1.4	9.8	7.1	70%	11%	41	21	38	32%	73%	10%	34	110	82%	3%			14.7	159	189	$23
15 2 AL	18	5	0	220	225	2.45	3.36	1.08	621	658	609	27.8	1.9	9.2	4.8	67%	12%	40	23	36	30%	80%	8%	32	106	81%	3%			41.1	132	157	$33
1st Half	8	2	0	117	107	2.54	3.62	1.13	659	657	659	28.0	1.7	8.2	4.9	68%	11%	38	25	37	31%	80%	7%	17	104	82%	6%			20.5	118	140	$31
2nd Half	10	3	0	103	118	2.35	3.07	1.02	578	660	548	27.5	2.2	10.3	4.7	66%	14%	44	21	35	29%	80%	9%	15	108	80%	0%			20.5	148	176	$36
16 Proj	16	8	0	218	221	2.83	3.12	1.08	630	621	632	27.2	1.8	9.2	5.1	67%	11%	43	22	36	31%	77%	9%	31						30.4	137	163	$27

Putnam,Zach

Age: 28	Th: R	Role: RP	Health: F	LIMA Plan: C
Ht: 6' 2"	Wt: 225	Type: Pwr	PT/Exp: D	Rand Var: +3
			Consist: C	MM: 2410

Dominance and SwK are now at closer-worthy levels, but the good news ended there. His struggles weren't confined to the expected H% regression from 2014. 1st half hr/f was brutal; GB% plunge and Ctl spike plagued him all season. His bad luck will subside, but stay away until the volatility follows suit.

Yr Tm	W	L	Sv	IP	K	ERA	xERA	WHIP	oOPS	vL	vR	BF/G	Ctl	Dom	Cmd	FpK	SwK	G	L	F	H%	S%	hr/f	GS	APC	DOM%	DIS%	Sv%	LI	RAR	BPV	BPX	R$
11 CLE *	7	4	9	76	65	4.31	3.99	1.32	915	692	1060	6.1	2.6	7.7	2.9	53%	14%	30	43	26	32%	68%	17%	0	14			64	0.58	-3.5	85	127	$4
12 COL *	3	4	12	63	37	4.69	6.41	1.84	929	500	1417	5.7	4.0	5.4	1.3	67%	17%	43	14	43	37%	76%	0%	0	15			71	0.05	-5.2	22	28	-$5
13 CHC *	1	1	4	23	21	6.33	5.85	1.77	1251	1625	1000	4.7	2.6	8.5	3.2	68%	11%	53	27	20	43%	62%	33%	0	14			80	0.18	-6.9	94	122	-$5
14 CHW	5	3	6	55	46	1.98	3.41	1.08	551	623	468	4.3	3.3	7.6	2.3	61%	14%	53	15	32	25%	82%	4%	0	18			86	1.47	11.9	78	93	$8
15 CHW	3	3	0	49	64	4.07	3.36	1.36	734	770	702	4.3	4.4	11.8	2.7	58%	17%	44	21	35	32%	75%	18%	0	17			0	0.89	-0.6	115	137	-$2
1st Half	2	3	0	27	41	4.05	2.73	1.28	713	655	757	3.9	4.1	13.8	3.4	63%	19%	47	16	36	33%	76%	25%	0	16			0	1.14	-0.3	165	196	-$1
2nd Half	1	0	0	22	23	4.09	4.20	1.45	759	885	623	4.9	4.9	9.4	1.9	51%	16%	41	25	34	32%	73%	10%	0	19			0	0.52	-0.3	55	66	-$3
16 Proj	3	3	2	51	51	3.68	3.76	1.37	731	794	668	4.6	4.0	9.0	2.3	58%	16%	47	19	34	31%	76%	11%	0						1.8	81	96	$0

Quackenbush,Kevin

Age: 27	Th: R	Role: RP	Health: A	LIMA Plan: C
Ht: 6' 4"	Wt: 220	Type: Pwr	PT/Exp: D	Rand Var: 0
			Consist: B	MM: 3400

The second time around is often tougher. Occupied a permanent seat on the AAA-to-SD shuttle during the 1st half, struggled with S% and HR on the road afterward as he tried to settle in. GB% uptick was encouraging; BPV points to some upside. But SwK limits his ceiling and keeps him fringy for now.

Yr Tm	W	L	Sv	IP	K	ERA	xERA	WHIP	oOPS	vL	vR	BF/G	Ctl	Dom	Cmd	FpK	SwK	G	L	F	H%	S%	hr/f	GS	APC	DOM%	DIS%	Sv%	LI	RAR	BPV	BPX	R$
11																																	
12																																	
13 a/a	10	2	17	65	72	1.74	2.60	1.25				4.6	3.9	9.9	2.6						32%	86%								17.0	119	155	$15
14 SD	3	3	6	54	56	2.48	3.40	1.10	568	512	633	4.0	3.0	9.3	3.1	64%	9%	37	27	36	29%	78%	4%	0	16			86	1.17	8.4	101	121	$6
15 SD	3	2	0	58	58	4.01	3.73	1.23	670	799	565	4.3	3.1	8.9	2.9	60%	9%	44	21	36	30%	70%	10%	0	18			0	0.47	-0.4	100	119	-$1
1st Half	1	1	0	27	22	3.33	4.24	1.37	658	780	580	4.8	3.3	7.3	2.2	59%	9%	41	28	31	33%	73%	0%	0	21			0	0.48	2.1	61	72	-$3
2nd Half	2	1	0	31	36	4.60	3.32	1.12	680	813	544	3.9	2.9	10.3	3.6	60%	10%	46	14	40	27%	66%	19%	0	16			0	0.47	-2.4	133	158	$1
16 Proj	4	2	0	58	58	3.65	3.55	1.18	624	669	580	4.1	3.2	9.0	2.9	61%	9%	41	22	36	30%	70%	8%	0						2.2	96	114	$1

JOCK THOMPSON

Qualls,Chad

Age: 37	Th: R	Role: RP	Health: C	LIMA Plan: A
Ht: 6' 4"	Wt: 240	Type: xGB	PT/Exp: C	Rand Var: +5
			Consist: A	MM: 5210

PRO: Rising Dom supported by SwK; elite Ctl supported by FpK; outstanding GB% supported by history; "proven closer" experience. CON: Average velocity; lofty hr/f, and he isn't getting younger. Plenty of PRO here, and S% was a culprit in his ERA woes. But always being around the plate limits his upside.

Yr Tm	W	L	Sv	IP	K	ERA	xERA	WHIP	oOPS	vL	vR	BF/G	Ctl	Dom	Cmd	FpK	SwK	G	L	F	H%	S%	hr/f	GS	APC	DOM%	DIS%	Sv%	LI	RAR	BPV	BPX	R$
11 SD	6	8	0	74	43	3.51	3.76	1.25	689	881	537	4.0	2.4	5.2	2.2	64%	9%	57	17	26	28%	74%	11%	0	14			0	1.22	4.0	63	95	$2
12 3 TM	2	1	0	52	27	5.33	4.44	1.47	809	988	679	3.9	2.4	4.6	1.9	59%	8%	55	19	26	32%	66%	15%	0	14			0	0.81	-8.5	52	67	-$7
13 MIA	5	2	0	62	49	2.61	3.14	1.23	658	600	698	3.8	2.8	7.1	2.6	65%	11%	63	17	20	30%	81%	11%	0	13			0	1.41	9.6	95	123	$3
14 HOU	1	5	19	51	43	3.33	2.97	1.15	667	828	512	3.7	0.9	7.5	8.6	66%	11%	57	18	25	33%	74%	13%	0	12			76	1.15	2.6	147	175	$7
15 HOU	3	5	4	49	46	4.38	3.00	1.11	681	614	714	3.4	1.6	8.4	5.1	65%	12%	60	15	25	30%	63%	17%	0	12			67	1.03	-2.5	145	172	$1
1st Half	1	4	4	25	23	5.11	3.17	1.26	725	586	813	3.7	2.6	8.4	3.3	63%	12%	66	12	22	30%	63%	25%	0	14			67	1.37	-3.5	126	149	-$1
2nd Half	2	1	0	25	23	3.65	2.82	0.97	633	655	621	3.1	0.7	8.4	11.5	68%	13%	54	19	28	30%	64%	11%	0	11			0	0.70	1.0	163	193	$3
16 Proj	3	5	5	58	49	3.63	3.05	1.15	677	721	648	3.4	1.6	7.6	4.8	65%	11%	59	17	25	31%	71%	14%	0						2.4	131	156	$3

Quintana,Jose

Age: 27	Th: L	Role: SP	Health: A	LIMA Plan: B
Ht: 6' 1"	Wt: 220	Type:	PT/Exp: A	Rand Var: 0
			Consist: A	MM: 3205

1H issues tied to struggles vR and team's woes. But across-the-board 2H upticks resulted in another quietly solid season from a pitcher with less-than-ideal team/venue support. Strike-thrower won't wow you with mph or SwK, but BPV trend speaks for itself. And those DOM%/DIS% splits are H2H gold.

Yr Tm	W	L	Sv	IP	K	ERA	xERA	WHIP	oOPS	vL	vR	BF/G	Ctl	Dom	Cmd	FpK	SwK	G	L	F	H%	S%	hr/f	GS	APC	DOM%	DIS%	Sv%	LI	RAR	BPV	BPX	R$
11																																	
12 CHW *	7	9	0	185	117	3.68	4.06	1.35	754	700	775	22.7	2.8	5.7	2.0	61%	8%	47	22	31	30%	74%	11%	22	87	32%	32%	0	0.73	7.6	55	72	$3
13 CHW	9	7	0	200	164	3.51	3.85	1.22	695	717	687	25.2	2.5	7.4	2.9	66%	9%	43	20	37	29%	75%	10%	33	101	55%	12%			8.8	86	112	$10
14 CHW	9	11	0	200	178	3.32	3.51	1.24	662	686	653	25.9	2.3	8.0	3.4	66%	9%	45	22	33	33%	73%	5%	32	105	66%	6%			10.3	104	124	$9
15 CHW	9	10	0	206	177	3.36	3.60	1.27	722	657	741	26.9	1.9	7.7	4.0	69%	9%	47	23	30	33%	75%	9%	32	105	66%	6%			15.4	112	134	$11
1st Half	4	7	0	99	84	3.81	3.89	1.36	759	572	814	26.4	2.4	7.6	3.2	68%	10%	44	23	32	34%	73%	8%	16	103	56%	6%			1.9	96	114	$4
2nd Half	5	3	0	107	93	2.94	3.34	1.19	688	742	673	27.4	1.5	7.8	5.2	69%	9%	50	23	27	33%	77%	9%	16	108	75%	6%			13.4	127	151	$17
16 Proj	10	8	0	203	170	3.37	3.61	1.26	702	684	708	25.5	2.2	7.5	3.5	67%	9%	46	22	32	32%	75%	8%	33						14.8	101	121	$11

Ramirez,Erasmo

Age: 26	Th: R	Role: SP	Health: B	LIMA Plan: C+
Ht: 5' 11"	Wt: 200	Type:	PT/Exp: C	Rand Var: 0
			Consist: B	MM: 2103

Scenery change helped fuel rebound year from once promising prospect. But the real keys were the return of his control to near-elite levels and his sudden ability to induce GBs. 2H Dom slippage, average velocity along with his DOM%/DIS% offer caution about his future, for now. Expect some regression.

Yr Tm	W	L	Sv	IP	K	ERA	xERA	WHIP	oOPS	vL	vR	BF/G	Ctl	Dom	Cmd	FpK	SwK	G	L	F	H%	S%	hr/f	GS	APC	DOM%	DIS%	Sv%	LI	RAR	BPV	BPX	R$
11 a/a	10	8	0	153	106	4.45	4.24	1.34				24.4	1.7	6.3	3.7						34%	67%								-9.6	93	140	$0
12 SEA *	7	6	0	136	101	3.35	3.11	1.14	616	612	622	17.4	1.8	6.6	3.6	64%	12%	40	24	36	29%	72%	10%	8	55	50%	25%	0	0.76	11.1	102	133	$10
13 SEA *	8	6	0	121	96	4.36	4.71	1.42	772	791	742	23.3	3.1	7.2	2.3	59%	9%	42	21	36	32%	73%	14%	13	91	54%	31%	0	0.74	-7.3	56	73	-$2
14 SEA *	7	11	0	162	117	4.34	4.66	1.38	815	790	848	21.2	2.5	6.5	2.6	61%	11%	38	19	43	32%	72%	13%	14	76	29%	50%	0	0.63	-12.0	59	70	-$4
15 TAM	11	6	0	163	126	3.75	3.76	1.13	655	565	756	19.6	2.2	6.9	3.2	65%	11%	48	20	32	28%	69%	10%	27	71	44%	26%	0	0.70	4.3	91	109	$11
1st Half	7	3	0	73	61	3.80	3.82	1.13	633	543	756	15.9	3.1	7.5	2.4	59%	13%	47	21	33	26%	68%	9%	12	59	50%	25%	0	0.64	1.4	76	91	$12
2nd Half	4	3	0	90	65	3.70	3.71	1.13	672	584	754	24.3	1.5	6.5	4.3	70%	10%	49	20	31	29%	71%	11%	15	86	40%	27%			2.9	103	123	$11
16 Proj	9	8	0	160	120	4.01	3.93	1.25	702	660	754	20.5	2.3	6.8	2.9	63%	11%	44	21	36	30%	70%	10%	32						-0.9	81	96	$5

Ramos,A.J.

Age: 29	Th: R	Role: RP	Health: A	LIMA Plan: D+
Ht: 5' 10"	Wt: 205	Type: Pwr FB	PT/Exp: C	Rand Var: -4
			Consist: A	MM: 3531

Seized closer job early and held on despite 2H bumps. Dom/SwK combo remained formidable all season, but eroding Ctl and GB% eventually caught up with him as hr/f luck turned and he struggled vL. Control history says he has work to do, but SwK looks closer-worthy. Health and role keep him attractive.

Yr Tm	W	L	Sv	IP	K	ERA	xERA	WHIP	oOPS	vL	vR	BF/G	Ctl	Dom	Cmd	FpK	SwK	G	L	F	H%	S%	hr/f	GS	APC	DOM%	DIS%	Sv%	LI	RAR	BPV	BPX	R$
11																																	
12 MIA *	3	3	21	78	89	2.11	2.13	1.04	754	436	1056	4.6	3.3	10.2	3.1	65%	18%	32	23	45	26%	83%	20%	0	14			81	0.94	18.3	124	162	$19
13 MIA	3	4	0	80	86	3.15	3.97	1.26	603	740	484	5.0	4.8	9.7	2.0	61%	12%	39	19	43	28%	75%	5%	0	20			0	0.98	7.1	61	79	$3
14 MIA	7	0	0	64	73	2.11	3.89	1.23	543	522	555	4.0	6.0	10.3	1.7	57%	14%	42	19	39	25%	82%	2%	0	16			0	1.36	12.9	42	49	$6
15 MIA	2	4	32	70	87	2.30	3.10	1.01	562	602	529	3.9	3.3	11.1	3.3	59%	17%	43	16	40	26%	82%	9%	0	15			84	1.27	14.4	132	157	$21
1st Half	0	1	13	38	46	1.19	2.69	0.74	413	438	389	3.8	2.4	11.0	4.6	62%	18%	47	14	40	22%	85%	3%	0	15			81	1.28	12.9	158	188	$22
2nd Half	2	3	19	33	41	3.58	3.58	1.32	718	820	652	4.1	4.4	11.3	2.6	57%	15%	40	19	41	30%	79%	16%	0	16			86	1.26	1.5	102	121	$18
16 Proj	4	3	37	73	86	3.02	3.43	1.14	587	631	554	4.0	4.4	10.6	2.4	58%	15%	42	18	40	26%	75%	7%	0						8.4	94	111	$20

Ray,Robbie

Age: 24	Th: L	Role: SP	Health: A	LIMA Plan: B
Ht: 6' 2"	Wt: 195	Type: Pwr	PT/Exp: D	Rand Var: 0
			Consist: D	MM: 1203

5-12, 3.52 ERA in 128 IP at ARI. PRO: Velocity hike and Dom rebound; FpK surge; 2H GB gains. CON: Career-long control issues; sub-par secondary pitches; overall volatility. Encouraging second MLB effort for SP with sneaky fastball and time to grow. H% history and unsettled repertoire say it won't happen overnight.

Yr Tm	W	L	Sv	IP	K	ERA	xERA	WHIP	oOPS	vL	vR	BF/G	Ctl	Dom	Cmd	FpK	SwK	G	L	F	H%	S%	hr/f	GS	APC	DOM%	DIS%	Sv%	LI	RAR	BPV	BPX	R$
11																																	
12																																	
13 aa	5	2	0	58	50	4.42	4.27	1.44				22.4	3.1	7.8	2.5						34%	69%								-4.0	79	103	-$3
14 DET *	8	10	0	129	79	5.85	5.78	1.73	993	889	1038	20.2	4.0	5.5	1.4	54%	6%	35	24	41	35%	66%	12%	6	61	33%	50%	0	0.65	-33.5	30	36	-$17
15 ARI *	7	15	0	169	166	3.57	3.88	1.43	731	723	733	22.5	3.9	8.8	2.3	61%	9%	43	22	35	34%	75%	7%	23	98	43%	22%			8.3	88	104	$3
1st Half	4	7	0	84	81	3.12	3.57	1.40	648	766	623	22.1	3.8	8.7	2.3	59%	8%	34	20	46	34%	77%	4%	7	101	43%	0%			8.7	94	112	$6
2nd Half	3	8	0	85	85	4.01	3.86	1.45	769	711	795	23.5	4.0	9.0	2.2	61%	10%	48	23	29	34%	74%	10%	16	97	44%	31%			-0.5	79	94	$0
16 Proj	10	13	0	174	145	3.98	4.27	1.42	764	765	764	24.5	3.8	7.5	2.0	61%	9%	42	22	36	32%	73%	7%	30						-0.4	52	62	$1

Rea,Colin

Age: 26	Th: R	Role: SP	Health: B	LIMA Plan: C
Ht: 6' 5"	Wt: 220	Type: GB	PT/Exp: F	Rand Var: -1
			Consist: F	MM: 2101

2-2, 4.26 ERA in 32 IP at SD. Impressive control gains and HR-prevention fueled sinkerballer's 1.08 ERA in 75 IP at AA. Just modestly effective as he advanced to AAA and SD before year-ending forearm strain. Average secondary stuff says Cmd and GB% are crucial. #4-5 SP upside, now with some health questions.

Yr Tm	W	L	Sv	IP	K	ERA	xERA	WHIP	oOPS	vL	vR	BF/G	Ctl	Dom	Cmd	FpK	SwK	G	L	F	H%	S%	hr/f	GS	APC	DOM%	DIS%	Sv%	LI	RAR	BPV	BPX	R$
11																																	
12																																	
13																																	
14																																	
15 SD *	7	6	0	133	93	2.49	2.59	1.12	700	662	759	21.9	2.3	6.3	2.8	51%	6%	46	24	30	28%	78%	7%	6	88	33%	17%			24.2	94	112	$14
1st Half	3	2	0	77	53	1.58	1.85	0.98				22.6	1.7	6.1	3.6						27%	83%	0%	0						22.8	120	143	$20
2nd Half	4	4	0	56	40	3.75	3.61	1.30	700	662	759	21.0	3.0	6.5	2.1	51%	6%	46	24	30	30%	72%	7%	6	88	33%	17%			1.5	69	82	$5
16 Proj	4	4	0	73	51	3.86	4.00	1.26	675	634	738	22.0	2.5	6.3	2.5	51%	6%	46	24	30	30%	70%	7%	13						0.9	70	83	$0

Reed,Addison

Age: 27	Th: R	Role: RP	Health: A	LIMA Plan: A
Ht: 6' 4"	Wt: 220	Type: Pwr FB	PT/Exp: B	Rand Var: -1
			Consist: A	MM: 2411

Cmd plunge and inflated H% produced wretched 1H and led to loss of closer job—and eventual June demotion. 2H Dom and Ctl rebounds were aided by overdue luck in the form of a soaring S%. Season-long GB% gains look fluky and need confirming. But 2H BPV and "proven closer" tag keep him watchable.

Yr Tm	W	L	Sv	IP	K	ERA	xERA	WHIP	oOPS	vL	vR	BF/G	Ctl	Dom	Cmd	FpK	SwK	G	L	F	H%	S%	hr/f	GS	APC	DOM%	DIS%	Sv%	LI	RAR	BPV	BPX	R$
11 CHW *	0	1	4	49	66	1.70	1.59	0.86	802	875	728	6.1	2.0	12.0	5.8	61%	18%	20	35	45	27%	85%	11%	0	23			67	0.13	13.6	193	290	$8
12 CHW	3	2	29	55	54	4.75	4.13	1.36	753	773	737	3.8	2.9	8.8	3.0	66%	10%	33	24	43	34%	67%	9%	0	15			88	1.53	-5.0	91	118	$8
13 CHW	5	4	40	71	72	3.79	3.75	1.11	603	608	597	4.3	2.9	9.1	3.1	65%	12%	33	22	45	28%	67%	7%	0	17			83	1.19	0.7	96	125	$19
14 ARI	1	7	32	59	69	4.25	3.51	1.21	740	610	863	4.1	2.3	10.5	4.6	66%	14%	29	23	48	32%	72%	14%	0	16			84	1.25	-3.7	134	160	$11
15 2 NL	3	3	4	56	51	3.38	4.15	1.38	714	699	726	4.4	3.1	8.2	2.7	57%	9%	43	18	39	34%	76%	5%	0	17			50	1.18	4.1	86	103	$1
1st Half	2	2	3	24	20	5.92	5.03	1.73	862	742	950	4.5	4.1	7.4	1.8	53%	7%	43	16	41	37%	65%	6%	0	19			60	1.26	-5.9	45	53	-$6
2nd Half	1	1	1	32	31	1.42	3.52	1.11	587	662	526	4.3	2.3	8.8	3.9	60%	11%	43	20	37	31%	88%	3%	0	16			33	1.12	9.9	118	140	$6
16 Proj	3	5	5	73	74	3.56	3.68	1.26	692	655	724	4.2	2.7	9.1	3.3	61%	11%	37	21	42	32%	74%	8%	0						3.6	105	126	$3

JOCK THOMPSON

Richards,Garrett

Age: 28	Th: R	Role SP	Health D	LIMA Plan C+	
Ht: 6' 3"	Wt: 210	Type Pwr GB	PT/Exp A	Rand Var 0	
			Consist B	MM 3205	

Instructive DOM%/DIS%: Good, not great. Returned earlier than expected from 2014 knee injury to post GB-fueled workhorse season. But Ctl wasn't as sharp, and hanging sliders became a thing. 2014 Cmd and hr/f combo now looks outlier-ish, but power arsenal sets a nice floor. Pay for the projection, hope for more.

Yr Tm	W	L	Sv	IP	K	ERA	xERA	WHIP	oOPS	vL	vR	BF/G	Ctl	Dom	Cmd	FpK	SwK	G	L	F	H%	S%	hr/f	GS	APC	DOM%	DIS%	Sv%	LI	RAR	BPV	BPX	R$
11 LAA *	12	4	0	157	96	3.94	3.89	1.30	989	1140	813	22.3	2.7	5.5	2.1	66%	9%	43	28	28	29%	71%	31%	3	36	0%	67%	0	0.64	0.1	54	81	$5
12 LAA *	11	6	1	148	102	4.23	4.65	1.54	793	900	682	14.7	3.9	6.2	1.6	55%	11%	45	22	33	33%	73%	9%	9	40	22%	22%	33	0.95	-3.9	50	65	-$4
13 LAA	7	8	1	145	101	4.16	3.70	1.34	699	751	626	13.2	2.7	6.3	2.3	54%	9%	58	19	23	31%	70%	11%	17	50	59%	18%	50	0.78	-5.2	75	98	$0
14 LAA	13	4	0	169	164	2.61	3.08	1.04	529	519	542	26.1	2.7	8.8	3.2	55%	11%	51	21	28	28%	74%	4%	26	101	81%	8%			23.4	113	135	$21
15 LAA	15	12	0	207	176	3.65	3.75	1.24	664	628	707	27.0	3.3	7.6	2.3	60%	12%	55	17	28	28%	73%	12%	32	102	63%	9%			8.1	81	97	$13
1st Half	9	5	0	94	74	3.35	3.93	1.21	626	604	651	26.2	3.3	7.1	2.2	61%	12%	55	15	30	28%	74%	8%	15	97	67%	7%			7.1	72	86	$16
2nd Half	6	7	0	113	102	3.89	3.60	1.26	697	648	755	27.8	3.3	8.1	2.4	59%	12%	55	19	26	29%	72%	15%	17	105	59%	12%			1.0	89	105	$11
16 Proj	**15**	**10**	**0**	**203**	**171**	**3.48**	**3.57**	**1.22**	**648**	**645**	**651**	**25.5**	**3.1**	**7.6**	**2.5**	**58%**	**11%**	**53**	**19**	**28**	**29%**	**73%**	**10%**	**32**						**12.0**	**85**	**101**	**$14**

Rivero,Felipe

Age: 24	Th: L	Role RP	Health B	LIMA Plan B+	
Ht: 6' 2"	Wt: 195	Type GB	PT/Exp D	Rand Var -3	
			Consist C	MM 2100	

Fine MLB debut from left-handed SP-turned-RP, called up in mid-April and never looked back. Compensated for 2H Dom plunge with nice GB spike. Mid-90s stuff was effective vR, death vL, and even earned save consideration. Limited fastball-centric repertoire suggests second time around may not be as easy.

Yr Tm	W	L	Sv	IP	K	ERA	xERA	WHIP	oOPS	vL	vR	BF/G	Ctl	Dom	Cmd	FpK	SwK	G	L	F	H%	S%	hr/f	GS	APC	DOM%	DIS%	Sv%	LI	RAR	BPV	BPX	R$
11																																	
12																																	
13																																	
14 aa	2	7	0	44	31	4.34	4.60	1.49				18.8	3.5	6.4	1.9						33%	72%								-3.2	54	65	-$4
15 WAS	2	1	2	48	43	2.79	3.41	0.95	544	486	600	3.9	2.0	8.0	3.9	63%	12%	45	21	33	26%	70%	5%	0	16			67	1.10	7.0	112	133	$4
1st Half	1	0	0	14	16	2.63	3.17	1.02	651	488	757	4.9	1.3	10.5	8.0	63%	15%	39	14	47	33%	77%	6%	0	20			0	0.71	2.2	171	203	-$2
2nd Half	1	1	2	35	27	2.86	3.52	0.92	500	485	517	3.6	2.3	7.0	3.0	63%	10%	48	24	28	24%	68%	4%	0	14			100	1.22	4.7	89	106	$6
16 Proj	**2**	**4**	**0**	**44**	**33**	**3.44**	**3.77**	**1.15**	**574**	**546**	**606**	**5.3**	**2.8**	**6.8**	**2.4**	**63%**	**10%**	**48**	**24**	**28**	**27%**	**70%**	**6%**	**0**						**2.8**	**72**	**86**	**$0**

Roark,Tanner

Age: 29	Th: R	Role SP	Health A	LIMA Plan C	
Ht: 6' 2"	Wt: 230	Type Con	PT/Exp B	Rand Var +2	
			Consist B	MM 2101	

Last year's 31-start "rock" was squeezed out of the rotation before Opening Day. Efforts as swingman eventually netted 12 starts and a 4.82 ERA. The only real surprise was soaring hr/f coinciding with that GB% rebound. Despite the fine Ctl, what's left is a mundane skill set. And 2014 was a career year.

Yr Tm	W	L	Sv	IP	K	ERA	xERA	WHIP	oOPS	vL	vR	BF/G	Ctl	Dom	Cmd	FpK	SwK	G	L	F	H%	S%	hr/f	GS	APC	DOM%	DIS%	Sv%	LI	RAR	BPV	BPX	R$
11 aa	9	9	0	117	72	5.87	5.47	1.61				24.7	3.0	5.6	1.9						35%	63%								-27.7	39	58	-$11
12 aaa	6	17	0	148	100	5.47	5.74	1.63				23.5	2.8	6.1	2.1						36%	67%								-26.5	43	57	-$17
13 WAS *	16	4	2	159	103	3.04	2.60	1.08	476	634	358	13.2	1.8	5.8	3.3	71%	7%	50	24	26	28%	72%	3%	5	54	80%	0%	100	0.95	16.3	99	129	$18
14 WAS	15	10	0	199	138	2.85	3.80	1.09	632	672	591	25.7	1.8	6.3	3.5	65%	9%	41	21	38	28%	77%	7%	31	97	71%	6%			21.7	84	100	$19
15 WAS	4	7	1	111	70	4.38	4.17	1.31	784	866	709	11.7	2.1	5.7	2.7	60%	8%	48	22	31	30%	71%	15%	12	45	25%	25%	50	0.90	-5.7	71	85	-$2
1st Half	4	3	1	60	29	4.33	4.39	1.31	775	861	700	12.1	1.6	4.3	2.6	61%	7%	50	20	30	29%	71%	15%	6	46	33%	17%	50	1.10	-2.7	62	74	-$1
2nd Half	0	4	0	51	41	4.44	3.92	1.30	794	873	721	11.2	2.7	7.3	2.7	58%	8%	44	24	32	30%	71%	17%	6	44	17%	33%	0	0.67	-3.0	81	96	-$4
16 Proj	**5**	**6**	**0**	**102**	**68**	**3.94**	**3.97**	**1.25**	**729**	**810**	**654**	**20.9**	**2.1**	**6.1**	**2.9**	**63%**	**8%**	**45**	**22**	**33**	**30%**	**72%**	**11%**	**15**						**0.3**	**75**	**89**	**$1**

Robertson,David

Age: 31	Th: R	Role RP	Health C	LIMA Plan C+	
Ht: 5' 11"	Wt: 195	Type Pwr	PT/Exp B	Rand Var +2	
			Consist A	MM 5530	

GB% plunge set stage for Sept implosion, as gopheritis and disastrous S% fueled ERA spike. But the bad news was confined to a single month. Dom remained elite as SwK reached new highs; Ctl and FpK became otherworldly. Sub-3 ERA will depend on GB% reversal, but fundamentals and big contract keep his job safe.

Yr Tm	W	L	Sv	IP	K	ERA	xERA	WHIP	oOPS	vL	vR	BF/G	Ctl	Dom	Cmd	FpK	SwK	G	L	F	H%	S%	hr/f	GS	APC	DOM%	DIS%	Sv%	LI	RAR	BPV	BPX	R$
11 NYY	4	0	1	67	100	1.08	2.57	1.13	506	466	549	3.9	4.7	13.5	2.9	61%	11%	46	22	32	31%	91%	2%	0	17			25	1.38	23.5	139	210	$11
12 NYY	2	7	2	61	81	2.67	2.84	1.17	638	575	710	3.8	2.8	12.0	4.3	65%	10%	45	20	35	34%	80%	10%	0	15			40	1.15	10.1	163	213	$5
13 NYY	5	1	3	66	77	2.04	2.66	1.04	584	484	695	3.7	2.4	10.4	4.3	59%	10%	51	20	29	29%	84%	11%	0	15			60	1.19	15.0	151	197	$9
14 NYY	4	5	39	64	96	3.08	2.38	1.06	588	437	765	4.1	3.2	13.4	4.2	61%	13%	44	23	33	31%	75%	16%	0	17			89	1.67	5.3	177	211	$20
15 CHW	6	5	34	63	86	3.41	2.60	0.93	573	462	651	4.2	1.8	12.2	6.6	68%	14%	36	30	34	30%	67%	14%	0	16			83	1.35	4.3	184	219	$21
1st Half	4	2	18	35	49	2.60	2.61	0.95	542	485	583	4.2	1.8	12.7	7.0	70%	17%	34	29	37	32%	77%	10%	0	16			82	1.30	5.8	192	228	$24
2nd Half	2	3	16	29	37	4.40	2.59	0.91	611	432	734	4.1	1.9	11.6	6.2	67%	12%	37	31	31	27%	55%	19%	0	17			84	1.41	-1.5	174	206	$17
16 Proj	**5**	**5**	**39**	**65**	**89**	**3.10**	**2.54**	**1.00**	**584**	**462**	**693**	**3.9**	**2.5**	**12.2**	**4.9**	**64%**	**13%**	**41**	**23**	**36**	**30%**	**73%**	**13%**	**0**						**6.9**	**173**	**205**	**$22**

Robles,Hansel

Age: 25	Th: R	Role RP	Health A	LIMA Plan B+	
Ht: 5' 11"	Wt: 185	Type Pwr xFB	PT/Exp D	Rand Var -1	
			Consist B	MM 2400	

Credible relief work from prospect who had lost SP cachet while ascending through the minors. No longer has same GB tilt displayed early in his career, and HR could be an ongoing issue. But Ctl and Dom took 2H leap forward, and two-pitch power stuff out of the pen is intriguing. Sophomore effort should be watched.

Yr Tm	W	L	Sv	IP	K	ERA	xERA	WHIP	oOPS	vL	vR	BF/G	Ctl	Dom	Cmd	FpK	SwK	G	L	F	H%	S%	hr/f	GS	APC	DOM%	DIS%	Sv%	LI	RAR	BPV	BPX	R$
11																																	
12																																	
13																																	
14 aa	7	6	0	111	91	4.36	4.18	1.39				15.5	3.3	7.4	2.3						32%	70%								-8.4	69	83	-$3
15 NYM	4	3	0	54	61	3.67	3.64	1.02	655	560	717	3.8	3.0	10.2	3.4	60%	13%	33	18	49	24%	70%	12%	0	16			0	1.02	2.0	113	135	$3
1st Half	2	2	0	23	19	4.37	4.52	1.19	609	516	668	3.6	3.6	7.5	2.1	60%	10%	33	23	44	27%	62%	3%	0	15			0	1.10	-1.1	51	60	-$2
2nd Half	2	1	0	31	42	3.16	3.08	0.89	690	595	753	4.0	2.6	12.1	4.7	60%	15%	32	13	54	21%	81%	19%	0	16			0	0.96	3.1	158	187	$7
16 Proj	**4**	**3**	**0**	**58**	**58**	**3.95**	**3.86**	**1.17**	**715**	**610**	**784**	**5.4**	**3.1**	**9.1**	**2.9**	**60%**	**13%**	**33**	**17**	**50**	**28%**	**70%**	**9%**	**0**						**0.1**	**90**	**107**	**$1**

Rodney,Fernando

Age: 39	Th: R	Role RP	Health B	LIMA Plan B+	
Ht: 5' 11"	Wt: 220	Type Pwr GB	PT/Exp A	Rand Var +3	
			Consist A	MM 2310	

Aging sucks. Long-time control volatility had recently been neutralized by Dom and GB%. But 1H Cmd plunge coupled with unexpected gopheritis led to loss of closer job. Dom and Ctl rebounded in 2H, but soaring hr/f hung tough. Skill set is clinging on by his fingertips, though now too combustible for 9th inning work.

Yr Tm	W	L	Sv	IP	K	ERA	xERA	WHIP	oOPS	vL	vR	BF/G	Ctl	Dom	Cmd	FpK	SwK	G	L	F	H%	S%	hr/f	GS	APC	DOM%	DIS%	Sv%	LI	RAR	BPV	BPX	R$
11 LAA	3	5	3	32	26	4.50	4.87	1.69	672	766	588	3.8	7.9	7.3	0.9	62%	9%	58	19	22	28%	72%	5%	0	16			43	1.69	-2.2	-45	-68	-$3
12 TAM	2	2	48	75	76	0.60	2.58	0.78	417	435	394	3.7	1.8	9.2	5.1	61%	13%	58	17	25	23%	95%	4%	0	15			96	1.24	31.4	152	198	$37
13 TAM	5	4	37	67	82	3.38	3.24	1.34	634	716	538	4.3	4.9	11.1	2.3	56%	13%	51	25	25	32%	74%	7%	0	18			82	1.34	4.0	97	126	$17
14 SEA	1	6	48	66	76	2.85	3.19	1.34	646	726	530	4.1	3.8	10.3	2.7	60%	11%	49	24	27	34%	79%	6%	0	16			94	1.36	7.3	110	131	$19
15 2 TM	7	5	16	63	58	4.74	4.05	1.40	776	845	721	4.1	4.2	8.3	2.0	59%	10%	51	18	31	30%	70%	16%	0	16			70	1.22	-6.0	66	79	$4
1st Half	2	3	16	33	27	5.18	4.62	1.58	824	852	798	4.4	4.6	7.4	1.6	58%	9%	51	15	34	32%	69%	12%	0	17			84	1.30	-5.0	36	43	$4
2nd Half	5	2	0	30	31	4.25	3.46	1.21	722	837	635	3.8	3.6	9.4	2.6	60%	11%	50	22	28	27%	71%	23%	0	16			0	1.14	-1.0	99	117	$5
16 Proj	**4**	**3**	**2**	**44**	**41**	**4.20**	**3.80**	**1.41**	**729**	**802**	**657**	**3.9**	**4.2**	**8.5**	**2.0**	**59%**	**11%**	**51**	**21**	**28**	**31%**	**72%**	**12%**	**0**						**-1.3**	**69**	**83**	**-$1**

Rodon,Carlos

Age: 23	Th: L	Role SP	Health A	LIMA Plan B+	
Ht: 6' 3"	Wt: 234	Type Pwr	PT/Exp D	Rand Var 0	
			Consist F	MM 2403	

Top 2014 draft pick held his own in first MLB exposure. Dom and SwK firm all season, GB% and HR avoidance were pluses. Control was a different story, FpK says he has work to do. DOM%/DIS% says you'll have to take the good with the bad for now. Could take a while, but if the light goes on quickly... UP: 15 wins, sub-3 ERA.

Yr Tm	W	L	Sv	IP	K	ERA	xERA	WHIP	oOPS	vL	vR	BF/G	Ctl	Dom	Cmd	FpK	SwK	G	L	F	H%	S%	hr/f	GS	APC	DOM%	DIS%	Sv%	LI	RAR	BPV	BPX	R$
11																																	
12																																	
13																																	
14																																	
15 CHW	9	6	0	139	139	3.75	4.00	1.44	725	524	799	23.3	4.6	9.0	2.0	53%	11%	47	23	30	32%	75%	10%	23	94	61%	22%	0	0.87	3.7	63	75	$2
1st Half	3	2	0	60	62	4.18	4.18	1.64	763	543	851	21.1	5.2	9.2	1.8	55%	11%	49	25	26	36%	75%	9%	10	87	50%	20%	0	0.98	-1.6	52	62	-$7
2nd Half	6	4	0	79	77	3.42	3.86	1.29	694	506	757	25.6	4.1	8.8	2.1	51%	11%	45	22	33	29%	76%	10%	13	101	69%	23%			5.3	70	83	$9
16 Proj	**12**	**8**	**0**	**174**	**175**	**3.62**	**3.83**	**1.40**	**717**	**514**	**791**	**26.1**	**4.4**	**9.1**	**2.0**	**53%**	**11%**	**47**	**23**	**30**	**31%**	**76%**	**10%**	**28**						**7.4**	**68**	**81**	**$6**

JOCK THOMPSON

Rodriguez,Eduardo

Age: 23	Th: L	Role SP	Health A	LIMA Plan B+	
Ht: 6' 2"	Wt: 200	Type	PT/Exp D	Rand Var 0	
			Consist A	MM 2203	

10-6, 3.85 ERA in 122 IP at BOS. Nice start for talented rookie. Maintained decent Cmd and mid-90s velocity throughout, grew 2H FpK, finished with a four-PQS-DOM kick. High pitch counts and poor SwK reflect fastball dependency and a work-in-progress slider. But keeper leagues should be buying his futures now.

Yr Tm	W	L	Sv	IP	K	ERA	xERA	WHIP	oOPS	vL	vR	BF/G	Ctl	Dom	Cmd	FpK	SwK	G	L	F	H%	S%	hr/f	GS	APC	DOM%	DIS%	Sv%	LI	RAR	BPV	BPX	R$
11																																	
12																																	
13 aa	4	3	0	60	52	4.68	3.83	1.34				22.5	3.4	7.8	2.3						31%	66%								-6.0	74	97	-$3
14 aa	6	8	0	120	93	4.42	4.35	1.46				23.3	2.8	7.0	2.5						35%	69%								-10.0	77	92	-$5
15 BOS *	14	9	0	170	136	3.92	3.96	1.30	701	820	662	24.1	2.4	7.2	3.0	57%	9%	43	24	33	32%	71%	10%	21	96	57%	14%			0.9	84	100	$7
1st Half	8	5	0	95	82	3.90	3.44	1.24	614	604	616	24.0	2.1	7.8	3.6	53%	9%	42	24	34	33%	68%	7%	8	96	63%	25%			0.7	110	130	$10
2nd Half	6	4	0	75	54	3.94	4.40	1.37	752	930	691	25.4	2.6	6.5	2.5	59%	8%	44	23	33	31%	75%	12%	13	96	54%	8%			0.2	67	79	$3
16 Proj	**12**	**10**	**0**	**174**	**141**	**4.01**	**3.97**	**1.36**	**729**	**839**	**694**	**23.5**	**2.6**	**7.3**	**2.8**	**57%**	**9%**	**43**	**23**	**34**	**33%**	**72%**	**9%**	**31**						**-0.9**	**81**	**97**	**$3**

Rodriguez,Francisco

Age: 34	Th: R	Role RP	Health A	LIMA Plan C	
Ht: 6' 0"	Wt: 195	Type Pwr	PT/Exp B	Rand Var -3	
			Consist A	MM 5530	

Fastball velocity ticked below 90 mph for the first time ever, but it didn't matter. Leads now with devastating change-up that drove career-best FpK and SwK. Cmd also peaked as ERA improved to a 5-year-low and he dominated vL and vR alike. Clearly a profile crest, and HR will bite occasionally. But he's made us believers.

Yr Tm	W	L	Sv	IP	K	ERA	xERA	WHIP	oOPS	vL	vR	BF/G	Ctl	Dom	Cmd	FpK	SwK	G	L	F	H%	S%	hr/f	GS	APC	DOM%	DIS%	Sv%	LI	RAR	BPV	BPX	R$
11 2 NL	6	2	23	72	79	2.64	3.17	1.30	663	776	515	4.2	3.3	9.9	3.0	57%	13%	52	17	31	34%	81%	6%	0	16			79	1.37	11.5	120	181	$14
12 MIL	2	7	3	72	72	4.38	3.87	1.33	708	723	684	3.9	3.9	9.0	2.3	61%	8%	42	26	33	30%	69%	12%	0	16			30	1.15	-3.2	77	101	-$1
13 2 TM	3	2	10	47	54	2.70	3.22	1.20	734	513	1003	4.0	2.7	10.4	3.9	60%	11%	36	25	39	31%	86%	15%	0	16			100	0.91	6.7	129	168	$6
14 MIL	5	5	44	68	73	3.04	2.99	0.99	648	526	772	3.9	2.4	9.7	4.1	59%	12%	44	21	35	23%	83%	23%	0	15			90	1.19	5.8	132	157	$23
15 MIL	1	3	38	57	62	2.21	2.76	0.86	547	538	558	3.6	1.7	9.8	5.6	63%	14%	46	24	30	24%	81%	14%	0	14			95	1.01	12.3	153	183	$22
1st Half	0	2	18	31	36	1.45	2.69	0.87	493	434	546	3.8	2.6	10.5	4.0	60%	15%	48	25	27	24%	88%	11%	0	15			100	1.12	9.6	143	170	$22
2nd Half	1	1	20	26	26	3.12	2.83	0.85	610	642	572	3.4	0.7	9.0	13.0	68%	13%	45	22	33	25%	72%	17%	0	12			91	0.89	2.7	166	197	$22
16 Proj	**3**	**4**	**40**	**65**	**70**	**2.74**	**2.90**	**0.99**	**625**	**569**	**686**	**3.6**	**2.1**	**9.7**	**4.7**	**62%**	**13%**	**44**	**23**	**33**	**26%**	**81%**	**17%**	**0**						**9.8**	**141**	**167**	**$22**

Rodriguez,Wandy

Age: 37	Th: L	Role SP	Health F	LIMA Plan C	
Ht: 5' 10"	Wt: 195	Type	PT/Exp D	Rand Var +1	
			Consist A	MM 1101	

6-4, 4.61 ERA in 86 IP at TEX. Spotty comeback from strike-thrower following 2014 knee surgery. First 10 starts produced 49/21 K/BB, 50% GB% and 3.03 ERA through 59 IP. Threw fewer strikes afterward as H% surged and HR became a problem. FpK is a plus; age, SwK, PQS-DIS% are red flags. Risk trumps reward.

Yr Tm	W	L	Sv	IP	K	ERA	xERA	WHIP	oOPS	vL	vR	BF/G	Ctl	Dom	Cmd	FpK	SwK	G	L	F	H%	S%	hr/f	GS	APC	DOM%	DIS%	Sv%	LI	RAR	BPV	BPX	R$
11 HOU	11	11	0	191	166	3.49	3.75	1.31	739	628	768	26.9	3.3	7.8	2.4	62%	9%	45	20	35	30%	78%	13%	30	105	57%	7%			10.7	76	114	$10
12 2 NL	12	13	0	206	139	3.76	4.19	1.27	695	689	697	25.7	2.5	6.1	2.5	66%	8%	48	20	32	29%	73%	10%	33	94	52%	15%	0	0.83	6.4	69	90	$9
13 PIT	6	4	0	63	46	3.59	3.87	1.12	707	785	681	21.7	1.7	6.6	3.8	62%	7%	42	19	39	27%	75%	13%	12	86	50%	25%			2.1	92	120	$3
14 PIT	0	2	0	27	20	6.75	4.68	1.69	1059	898	1087	20.8	2.7	6.8	2.5	62%	8%	42	15	42	33%	71%	26%	6	76	17%	50%			-9.9	69	82	-$7
15 TEX *	6	4	0	101	84	4.56	4.80	1.50	794	838	779	18.2	3.6	7.5	2.1	65%	6%	41	25	34	33%	72%	11%	15	94	40%	33%	0	0.76	-7.4	57	68	-$5
1st Half	5	4	0	79	63	4.23	4.54	1.49	759	839	732	25.1	3.5	7.2	2.0	66%	6%	43	23	34	33%	73%	9%	14	101	36%	36%			-2.6	55	65	-$3
2nd Half	1	0	0	8	9	11.74	5.28	2.35	1107	833	1188	13.3	5.9	10.6	1.8	60%	5%	20	44	36	47%	50%	22%	1	59	100%	0%	0	0.65	-7.4	30	35	-$12
16 Proj	**4**	**8**	**0**	**102**	**77**	**4.45**	**4.19**	**1.35**	**730**	**757**	**722**	**24.1**	**3.1**	**6.8**	**2.2**	**65%**	**7%**	**44**	**21**	**35**	**30%**	**69%**	**11%**	**18**						**-6.1**	**60**	**72**	**-$3**

Romo,Sergio

Age: 33	Th: R	Role RP	Health A	LIMA Plan A+	
Ht: 5' 10"	Wt: 185	Type Pwr	PT/Exp B	Rand Var +1	
			Consist A	MM 5510	

Soaring FpK and SwK obviously fueled the outstanding 2H. Year-long GB% rebound and health were also positives. Bookend 1H/2H BPVs say he's one of the best closers-in-waiting around. Newfound trouble vs. LHP may be biggest obstacle to retaking 9th inning gig, but he has handled lefties before.

Yr Tm	W	L	Sv	IP	K	ERA	xERA	WHIP	oOPS	vL	vR	BF/G	Ctl	Dom	Cmd	FpK	SwK	G	L	F	H%	S%	hr/f	GS	APC	DOM%	DIS%	Sv%	LI	RAR	BPV	BPX	R$
11 SF	3	1	1	48	70	1.50	2.03	0.71	458	599	402	2.7	0.9	13.1	14.0	72%	17%	34	24	42	29%	81%	5%	0	10			50	1.39	14.5	223	335	$10
12 SF	4	2	14	55	63	1.79	2.64	0.85	525	491	537	3.1	1.6	10.2	6.3	67%	16%	49	21	30	26%	86%	12%	0	12			93	1.43	15.2	168	219	$15
13 SF	5	8	38	60	58	2.54	3.39	1.08	614	745	511	3.8	1.8	8.7	4.8	69%	14%	41	24	36	30%	80%	8%	0	15			88	1.58	9.9	126	165	$21
14 SF	6	4	23	58	59	3.72	3.27	0.95	622	777	528	3.6	1.9	9.2	4.9	69%	15%	37	18	45	25%	67%	13%	0	14			82	1.26	0.1	130	154	$13
15 SF	0	5	2	57	71	2.98	2.70	1.06	622	929	467	3.3	1.6	11.1	7.1	70%	17%	45	23	32	35%	72%	7%	0	13			50	1.26	6.9	181	216	$3
1st Half	0	3	0	25	36	4.32	2.72	1.24	690	934	574	3.0	2.5	13.0	5.1	64%	16%	44	23	34	39%	66%	10%	0	12			0	1.29	-1.1	187	222	-$3
2nd Half	0	2	2	32	35	1.95	2.67	0.93	565	921	372	3.5	0.8	9.7	11.7	74%	19%	46	24	30	32%	79%	4%	0	13			50	1.24	8.0	177	210	$8
16 Proj	**3**	**5**	**9**	**58**	**66**	**2.92**	**2.81**	**1.00**	**606**	**825**	**484**	**3.3**	**1.6**	**10.3**	**6.4**	**70%**	**16%**	**42**	**22**	**36**	**31%**	**74%**	**9%**	**0**						**7.4**	**161**	**192**	**$8**

Rondon,Bruce

Age: 25	Th: R	Role RP	Health F	LIMA Plan C	
Ht: 6' 3"	Wt: 275	Type Pwr	PT/Exp D	Rand Var +5	
			Consist D	MM 3520	

Flame-thrower with wipeout slider and a world of late-inning potential returned in June following TJS. Showed off high-90s velocity, Dom and SwK, but little else during legit closer audition. Attitude and work habits sent him home early, putting career at a crossroads. With successful slap upside the head... UP: 30 saves.

Yr Tm	W	L	Sv	IP	K	ERA	xERA	WHIP	oOPS	vL	vR	BF/G	Ctl	Dom	Cmd	FpK	SwK	G	L	F	H%	S%	hr/f	GS	APC	DOM%	DIS%	Sv%	LI	RAR	BPV	BPX	R$
11																																	
12 a/a	1	1	14	30	26	1.45	3.03	1.28				4.1	4.6	8.0	1.7						26%	93%								9.4	77	100	$6
13 DET *	2	3	15	58	63	2.68	2.58	1.18	720	873	608	3.9	3.8	9.6	2.6	47%	15%	47	24	29	29%	78%	9%	0	15			79	0.93	8.5	110	143	$9
14																																	
15 DET	1	0	5	31	36	5.81	4.31	1.61	770	865	696	4.1	5.5	10.5	1.9	54%	12%	41	25	34	35%	64%	10%	0	17			56	1.14	-7.1	58	69	-$5
1st Half	1	0	0	3	5	10.80	4.37	1.80	840	619	1000	3.4	5.4	13.5	2.5	53%	10%	22	22	56	48%	33%	0%	0	12			0	1.45	-2.8	97	116	-$9
2nd Half	0	0	5	28	31	5.20	4.30	1.59	760	896	653	4.3	5.5	10.1	1.8	54%	13%	43	25	32	34%	68%	13%	0	17			56	1.08	-4.2	54	64	-$4
16 Proj	**3**	**2**	**16**	**58**	**65**	**4.02**	**3.61**	**1.36**	**627**	**733**	**544**	**3.9**	**4.2**	**10.1**	**2.4**	**54%**	**13%**	**43**	**25**	**32**	**32%**	**72%**	**10%**	**0**						**-0.4**	**90**	**107**	**$5**

Rondon,Hector

Age: 28	Th: R	Role RP	Health A	LIMA Plan C	
Ht: 6' 3"	Wt: 180	Type Pwr GB	PT/Exp B	Rand Var -5	
			Consist B	MM 5430	

Lost sole possession of closer role following some May hiccups, but re-seized it again in July and proceeded to flourish. Velocity rose as FpK, SwK and GB% all surged in the 2H, producing exquisite ERA and WHIP and just one blown save. Track record remains light and some regression is in store. But we like the trajectory.

Yr Tm	W	L	Sv	IP	K	ERA	xERA	WHIP	oOPS	vL	vR	BF/G	Ctl	Dom	Cmd	FpK	SwK	G	L	F	H%	S%	hr/f	GS	APC	DOM%	DIS%	Sv%	LI	RAR	BPV	BPX	R$
11																																	
12																																	
13 CHC	2	1	0	55	44	4.77	4.39	1.41	737	546	908	5.4	4.1	7.2	1.8	54%	11%	43	22	35	29%	68%	10%	0	21			0	0.65	-6.1	40	52	-$5
14 CHC	4	4	29	63	63	2.42	2.99	1.06	526	616	454	4.0	2.1	9.0	4.2	65%	12%	49	23	28	30%	77%	4%	0	16			88	1.16	10.4	131	156	$17
15 CHC	6	4	30	70	69	1.67	3.04	1.00	568	640	503	3.9	1.9	8.9	4.6	63%	11%	52	20	27	28%	86%	8%	0	15			88	1.51	19.8	138	164	$23
1st Half	3	1	12	34	29	2.10	3.42	1.02	591	473	678	3.8	2.1	7.6	3.6	61%	10%	48	23	29	27%	82%	7%	0	15			80	1.50	7.9	106	126	$18
2nd Half	3	3	18	36	40	1.26	2.68	0.98	546	769	310	4.1	1.8	10.1	5.7	65%	12%	57	18	25	30%	91%	8%	0	15			95	1.52	11.9	169	200	$27
16 Proj	**4**	**3**	**40**	**58**	**62**	**2.98**	**2.90**	**1.08**	**577**	**630**	**531**	**3.9**	**2.3**	**9.5**	**4.1**	**62%**	**11%**	**50**	**21**	**28**	**30%**	**73%**	**8%**	**0**						**7.0**	**138**	**164**	**$20**

Rosenthal,Trevor

Age: 26	Th: R	Role RP	Health A	LIMA Plan C	
Ht: 6' 2"	Wt: 220	Type Pwr	PT/Exp A	Rand Var -4	
			Consist B	MM 4531	

A closer's S% is his own doing as nobody follows him to the mound. So while improved Ctl, GB spike drove ERA down, anomalous 1H S% helped a lot. Skill-wise, the same pitcher half-to-half. But 2H S% regression, shaky FpK ensures more anxious moments. 2016 regression looks inevitable.

Yr Tm	W	L	Sv	IP	K	ERA	xERA	WHIP	oOPS	vL	vR	BF/G	Ctl	Dom	Cmd	FpK	SwK	G	L	F	H%	S%	hr/f	GS	APC	DOM%	DIS%	Sv%	LI	RAR	BPV	BPX	R$
11																																	
12 STL *	8	8	0	132	114	3.06	2.40	1.09	513	395	597	13.2	3.2	7.8	2.4	58%	13%	54	13	33	26%	73%	11%	0	19			0	0.63	15.6	94	123	$14
13 STL	2	4	3	75	108	2.63	2.47	1.10	608	586	626	4.2	2.4	12.9	5.4	63%	15%	44	19	36	36%	77%	6%	0	17			38	1.21	11.5	190	247	$7
14 STL	2	6	45	70	87	3.20	3.69	1.41	641	523	738	4.3	5.4	11.1	2.1	56%	13%	38	25	37	33%	76%	3%	0	18			88	1.42	4.7	71	85	$17
15 STL	2	4	48	69	83	2.10	3.28	1.27	619	526	686	4.2	3.3	10.9	3.3	57%	12%	46	19	35	35%	85%	5%	0	18			94	1.66	15.8	131	156	$24
1st Half	1	1	24	38	42	0.70	3.30	1.04	508	505	503	4.1	3.1	9.9	3.2	59%	13%	45	18	37	28%	95%	3%	0	17			96	1.47	15.4	118	140	$28
2nd Half	1	3	24	30	41	3.86	3.24	1.55	743	548	885	4.4	3.6	12.2	3.4	55%	12%	46	21	33	43%	76%	7%	0	18			92	1.88	0.4	147	175	$18
16 Proj	**3**	**4**	**41**	**73**	**90**	**3.05**	**3.25**	**1.30**	**639**	**530**	**724**	**4.4**	**3.7**	**11.1**	**3.0**	**57%**	**13%**	**43**	**21**	**36**	**35%**	**77%**	**5%**	**0**						**8.2**	**121**	**144**	**$19**

JOCK THOMPSON

Ross,Joe

Age: 23	Th: R	Role: RP	Health: A	LIMA Plan: C+	
Ht: 6' 4"	Wt: 205	Type: GB	PT/Exp: D	Rand Var: 0	
			Consist: C	MM: 3203	

5-5, 3.64 ERA in 77 IP at WAS. Youngster arrived quickly with fewer than 100 IP in the high minors. Didn't seem overmatched even with late-season fatigue. Held swing-and-miss gains from 2014, as sinker/slider repertoire continued to generate plenty of GB. Could see some early AAA time, but he's close. And he's good.

Yr	Tm	W	L	Sv	IP	K	ERA	xERA	WHIP	oOPS	vL	vR	BF/G	Ctl	Dom	Cmd	FpK	SwK	G	L	F	H%	S%	hr/f	GS	APC	DOM%	DIS%	Sv%	LI	RAR	BPV	BPX	R$
11																																		
12																																		
13																																		
14	aa	2	0	0	20	17	3.89	4.51	1.28				20.5	0.4	7.7	17.8						37%	72%								-0.4	388	462	-$2
15	WAS *	10	8	0	153	127	3.47	3.10	1.15	628	809	461	20.2	2.4	7.5	3.2	59%	12%	50	16	34	29%	71%	10%	13	72	62%	31%	0	0.71	9.3	96	115	$11
1st Half		5	4	0	82	72	3.45	3.49	1.22	557	1004	314	23.6	1.8	8.0	4.5	71%	14%	57	17	26	33%	72%	0%	3	100	67%	0%			5.1	126	150	$11
2nd Half		5	4	0	71	54	3.49	2.65	1.07	654	762	534	17.3	3.1	6.9	2.3	55%	12%	48	16	36	24%	70%	12%	10	66	60%	40%	0	0.69	4.1	76	90	$12
16	Proj	**10**	**8**	**0**	**145**	**117**	**3.50**	**3.56**	**1.13**	**626**	**850**	**435**	**19.4**	**2.5**	**7.3**	**2.9**	**61%**	**12%**	**51**	**17**	**32**	**27%**	**71%**	**9%**	**28**						**8.3**	**92**	**109**	**$11**

Ross,Robbie

Age: 27	Th: L	Role: RP	Health: A	LIMA Plan: C	
Ht: 5' 11"	Wt: 215	Type: Pwr GB	PT/Exp: C	Rand Var: +1	
			Consist: F	MM: 2210	

Return to fulltime bullpen work and change of scenery set stage for 2H rebound. Mid-season velocity spike reminiscent of his 2013 dominance, though 2014 HR surge hasn't abated. Where platoon splits go from here is anyone's guess. Volatility keeps him risky and caps his upside. That Consistency score speaks volumes.

Yr	Tm	W	L	Sv	IP	K	ERA	xERA	WHIP	oOPS	vL	vR	BF/G	Ctl	Dom	Cmd	FpK	SwK	G	L	F	H%	S%	hr/f	GS	APC	DOM%	DIS%	Sv%	LI	RAR	BPV	BPX	R$
11	aa	1	1	0	38	30	3.14	4.01	1.12				25.0	1.2	7.1	5.9						29%	81%								3.8	125	189	$0
12	TEX	6	0	0	65	47	2.22	3.52	1.20	624	613	632	4.6	3.2	6.5	2.0	58%	8%	62	18	20	28%	83%	8%	0	18			0	0.97	14.4	71	93	$6
13	TEX	4	2	0	62	58	3.03	3.43	1.32	684	950	523	4.1	2.7	8.4	3.1	68%	11%	45	28	26	33%	78%	8%	0	15			0	1.18	6.4	100	130	$1
14	TEX *	8	10	0	139	86	5.53	5.61	1.60	851	766	892	15.7	3.0	5.6	1.9	67%	7%	54	19	27	34%	66%	12%	12	50	17%	42%	0	0.75	-30.7	34	41	-$14
15	BOS	0	2	6	61	53	3.86	3.71	1.30	729	649	775	4.8	3.0	7.9	2.7	62%	10%	50	25	26	31%	74%	15%	0	19			75	0.90	0.8	89	106	$0
1st Half		0	0	0	27	18	4.28	4.50	1.50	820	751	855	5.8	3.6	5.9	1.6	60%	9%	50	25	25	31%	76%	18%	0	22			0	0.67	-1.1	37	44	-$7
2nd Half		0	2	6	33	35	3.51	3.12	1.14	652	578	701	4.2	2.4	9.5	3.9	64%	11%	49	24	26	31%	71%	13%	0	16			75	1.05	1.9	132	157	$5
16	Proj	**2**	**2**	**5**	**58**	**47**	**4.01**	**3.68**	**1.36**	**739**	**714**	**754**	**5.7**	**2.8**	**7.4**	**2.6**	**64%**	**9%**	**51**	**23**	**26**	**32%**	**73%**	**13%**	**0**						**-0.3**	**85**	**101**	**-$1**

Ross,Tyson

Age: 29	Th: R	Role: SP	Health: B	LIMA Plan: B	
Ht: 6' 5"	Wt: 225	Type: Pwr xGB	PT/Exp: A	Rand Var: 0	
			Consist: A	MM: 4405	

DL avoidance keyed another effective season. Dom approached double-digits as slider/fastball combination generated ultra-elite GB%. FpK says control is still his biggest obstacle to managing pitch count and taking a step forward. If he can somehow resolve this and stay healthy... UP: 16 wins, 2.50 ERA.

Yr	Tm	W	L	Sv	IP	K	ERA	xERA	WHIP	oOPS	vL	vR	BF/G	Ctl	Dom	Cmd	FpK	SwK	G	L	F	H%	S%	hr/f	GS	APC	DOM%	DIS%	Sv%	LI	RAR	BPV	BPX	R$
11	OAK *	6	5	0	73	53	5.23	5.24	1.68	617	617	616	18.2	4.2	6.5	1.6	57%	8%	48	22	30	35%	68%	3%	6	60	50%	33%	0	0.76	-11.6	47	71	-$7
12	OAK *	8	13	0	152	98	4.76	4.73	1.56	870	974	759	20.2	3.9	5.8	1.5	55%	7%	50	23	27	33%	69%	10%	13	72	23%	38%	0	0.97	-13.9	45	59	-$10
13	SD	3	8	0	125	119	3.17	3.20	1.15	627	709	548	14.4	3.2	8.6	2.7	54%	12%	55	15	30	28%	74%	8%	16	57	81%	19%	0	1.09	10.8	102	133	$7
14	SD	13	14	0	196	195	2.81	3.02	1.21	634	635	632	26.2	3.3	9.0	2.7	58%	13%	57	21	22	30%	79%	11%	31	101	68%	10%			22.6	107	127	$16
15	SD	10	12	0	196	212	3.26	3.07	1.31	652	721	584	24.9	3.9	9.7	2.5	58%	13%	62	19	19	32%	75%	9%	33	98	73%	3%			17.0	111	132	$12
1st Half		5	7	0	102	111	3.63	3.27	1.46	680	805	569	26.0	4.7	9.8	2.1	57%	13%	62	20	17	34%	74%	6%	17	102	76%	0%			4.2	90	107	$7
2nd Half		5	5	0	94	101	2.86	2.87	1.14	619	635	602	23.8	3.0	9.6	3.3	58%	12%	61	16	23	30%	76%	11%	16	94	69%	6%			12.8	132	157	$19
16	Proj	**11**	**13**	**0**	**203**	**203**	**3.26**	**3.21**	**1.27**	**654**	**701**	**607**	**21.6**	**3.5**	**9.0**	**2.5**	**57%**	**12%**	**58**	**19**	**23**	**31%**	**75%**	**9%**	**38**						**17.6**	**103**	**122**	**$13**

Rusin,Chris

Age: 29	Th: L	Role: SP	Health: A	LIMA Plan: D+	
Ht: 6' 2"	Wt: 195	Type: Con GB	PT/Exp: C	Rand Var: +3	
			Consist: C	MM: 0000	

6-10, 5.33 ERA in 132 IP at COL. Dropping a mediocre pitcher into a horrendous venue rarely works out. On the plus side, he built on an already attractive GB%, while his FpK took a huge step forward and held firm all season. But he still allows too much contact for us to consider this for too long.

Yr	Tm	W	L	Sv	IP	K	ERA	xERA	WHIP	oOPS	vL	vR	BF/G	Ctl	Dom	Cmd	FpK	SwK	G	L	F	H%	S%	hr/f	GS	APC	DOM%	DIS%	Sv%	LI	RAR	BPV	BPX	R$
11	a/a	8	4	0	139	77	4.22	4.70	1.41				22.6	1.9	5.0	2.6						33%	71%								-4.7	55	83	-$1
12	CHC *	10	12	0	173	97	5.62	5.70	1.63	881	678	955	23.3	3.6	5.1	1.4	53%	10%	45	25	30	33%	67%	14%	7	72	43%	43%			-34.2	19	24	-$19
13	CHC *	10	13	0	187	90	4.21	4.41	1.40	750	521	819	24.7	2.6	4.3	1.6	58%	8%	48	23	29	30%	71%	13%	13	79	31%	38%			-8.0	34	44	-$3
14	CHC *	8	13	0	159	83	5.54	6.05	1.67	830	458	1128	26.4	2.7	4.7	1.8	59%	8%	48	18	34	35%	68%	7%	0	49			0	0.32	-35.3	24	28	-$19
15	COL *	9	12	0	166	99	6.05	6.67	1.72	867	867	867	24.3	2.9	5.4	1.8	67%	9%	52	21	27	36%	68%	15%	22	90	36%	27%	0	0.77	-42.7	14	17	-$23
1st Half		6	5	0	81	45	6.19	7.30	1.82	843	998	792	25.0	3.0	5.0	1.7	66%	10%	52	23	26	37%	69%	15%	7	92	43%	29%	0	0.78	-22.2	2	2	-$25
2nd Half		3	7	0	85	54	5.91	4.52	1.63	880	788	906	24.1	2.8	5.7	2.0	68%	8%	52	20	28	35%	66%	16%	15	88	33%	27%	0	0.76	-20.5	56	66	-$21
16	Proj	**3**	**4**	**0**	**58**	**32**	**5.53**	**4.59**	**1.63**	**892**	**812**	**916**	**24.7**	**2.8**	**5.0**	**1.8**	**64%**	**9%**	**50**	**22**	**28**	**34%**	**68%**	**14%**	**10**						**-11.2**	**44**	**52**	**-$9**

Ryu,Hyun-Jin

Age: 29	Th: L	Role: SP	Health: F	LIMA Plan: B+	
Ht: 6' 2"	Wt: 255	Type: Pwr	PT/Exp: B	Rand Var: 0	
			Consist: A	MM: 4303	

2014 ended early due to shoulder issues. Unable to answer the bell last March, opted for season-ending surgery in late May. Already throwing in Oct., reports say he'll be ready by February. Command of a broad repertoire—not velocity—is his game. With health, that 2013-14 body of work says he'll return good value.

Yr	Tm	W	L	Sv	IP	K	ERA	xERA	WHIP	oOPS	vL	vR	BF/G	Ctl	Dom	Cmd	FpK	SwK	G	L	F	H%	S%	hr/f	GS	APC	DOM%	DIS%	Sv%	LI	RAR	BPV	BPX	R$
11	for	11	7	0	126	121	4.17	3.88	1.23				21.3	3.4	8.7	2.6						27%	72%								-3.5	72	108	$6
12	for	9	9	0	183	199	3.30	2.96	1.21				27.3	2.8	9.8	3.5						33%	72%								16.2	127	165	$15
13	LA	14	8	0	192	154	3.00	3.51	1.20	660	738	633	26.1	2.3	7.2	3.1	59%	9%	51	19	31	30%	77%	9%	30	102	60%	7%			20.5	97	126	$16
14	LA	14	7	0	152	139	3.38	3.23	1.19	658	665	656	24.3	1.7	8.2	4.8	62%	9%	47	22	30	33%	72%	6%	26	94	73%	12%			6.9	127	151	$11
15																																		
1st Half																																		
2nd Half																																		
16	Proj	**9**	**6**	**0**	**131**	**125**	**3.39**	**3.30**	**1.21**	**651**	**683**	**640**	**24.7**	**2.5**	**8.6**	**3.5**	**61%**	**9%**	**49**	**21**	**30**	**32%**	**73%**	**8%**	**21**						**9.3**	**116**	**138**	**$9**

Sabathia,CC

Age: 35	Th: L	Role: SP	Health: F	LIMA Plan: C	
Ht: 6' 7"	Wt: 285	Type: Pwr	PT/Exp: A	Rand Var: +3	
			Consist: B	MM: 2303	

Wasn't as awful as 1H ERA suggests, with all of H%, S% and hr/f working against him. Even with post-June velocity and GB upticks, he wasn't as good as 2H ERA either. Year-long Dom plunge is ominous, and HRs look here to stay. Neither reliable nor profitable for 3 years. Age, Health say that's unlikely to change.

Yr	Tm	W	L	Sv	IP	K	ERA	xERA	WHIP	oOPS	vL	vR	BF/G	Ctl	Dom	Cmd	FpK	SwK	G	L	F	H%	S%	hr/f	GS	APC	DOM%	DIS%	Sv%	LI	RAR	BPV	BPX	R$
11	NYY	19	8	0	237	230	3.00	3.17	1.23	666	554	709	29.8	2.3	8.7	3.8	63%	12%	47	23	30	33%	77%	8%	33	109	79%	0%			27.7	120	180	$23
12	NYY	15	6	0	200	197	3.38	3.29	1.14	666	667	665	29.8	2.0	8.9	4.5	63%	12%	48	21	31	31%	74%	13%	28	108	75%	4%			15.8	132	172	$21
13	NYY	14	13	0	211	175	4.78	3.89	1.37	770	662	804	28.4	2.8	7.5	2.7	65%	10%	45	22	33	32%	68%	13%	32	104	44%	6%			-23.7	83	108	-$2
14	NYY	3	4	0	46	48	5.28	3.29	1.48	875	570	921	26.1	2.0	9.4	4.8	70%	11%	48	22	30	37%	71%	23%	8	100	50%	13%			-8.7	142	169	-$5
15	NYY	6	10	0	167	137	4.73	4.08	1.42	797	519	862	25.0	2.7	7.4	2.7	62%	9%	46	22	32	32%	71%	17%	29	93	34%	24%			-15.9	84	100	-$6
1st Half		3	8	0	95	83	5.59	3.86	1.40	835	472	937	25.7	1.7	7.9	4.6	65%	10%	44	22	35	34%	65%	18%	16	93	31%	19%			-19.1	117	139	-$10
2nd Half		3	2	0	72	54	3.61	4.41	1.45	743	609	767	24.2	4.0	6.7	1.7	59%	9%	49	22	29	30%	79%	14%	13	94	38%	31%			3.2	41	48	-$1
16	Proj	**8**	**10**	**0**	**160**	**141**	**4.39**	**3.78**	**1.42**	**781**	**571**	**829**	**25.3**	**2.8**	**7.9**	**2.9**	**64%**	**10%**	**47**	**22**	**31**	**33%**	**73%**	**15%**	**27**						**-8.4**	**93**	**111**	**-$2**

Salas,Fernando

Age: 31	Th: R	Role: RP	Health: C	LIMA Plan: A	
Ht: 6' 2"	Wt: 200	Type: Pwr FB	PT/Exp: D	Rand Var: +3	
			Consist: A	MM: 4400	

Career best Dom, Ctl threw Cmd and BPV into an elite class, at least for this season. Yet despite xERA repeat, career-worst H%, S% and hr/f combo added nearly a run to his ERA. FpK and SwK remain positive. But FB tilt keeps mid-level ceiling intact—and makes him too dependent on luck for roster consideration.

Yr	Tm	W	L	Sv	IP	K	ERA	xERA	WHIP	oOPS	vL	vR	BF/G	Ctl	Dom	Cmd	FpK	SwK	G	L	F	H%	S%	hr/f	GS	APC	DOM%	DIS%	Sv%	LI	RAR	BPV	BPX	R$
11	STL	5	6	24	75	75	2.28	3.52	0.95	566	649	502	4.3	2.5	9.0	3.6	59%	11%	34	14	52	24%	81%	7%	0	17			80	1.45	15.4	106	159	$20
12	STL	1	4	0	59	60	4.30	4.13	1.41	720	681	747	3.9	4.1	9.2	2.2	67%	13%	38	24	38	33%	71%	8%	0	16			0	1.18	-2.0	70	91	-$4
13	STL *	1	5	12	52	38	3.48	2.88	1.09	715	829	645	4.1	2.0	6.6	3.3	69%	10%	32	15	53	28%	70%	7%	0	17			80	1.05	2.4	96	125	$5
14	LAA	5	0	0	59	61	3.38	3.41	1.09	637	510	771	4.2	2.1	9.4	4.4	64%	13%	29	30	42	30%	71%	8%	0	17			0	1.00	2.6	117	140	$3
15	LAA	5	2	0	64	74	4.24	3.38	1.15	716	729	707	3.7	1.7	10.5	6.2	66%	13%	35	22	43	33%	66%	11%	0	14			0	1.12	-2.2	155	185	$1
1st Half		1	1	0	33	34	4.59	3.76	1.17	699	861	589	3.8	1.9	9.2	4.9	67%	14%	33	23	44	33%	61%	7%	0	14			0	0.90	-2.6	126	149	-$2
2nd Half		4	1	0	30	40	3.86	2.98	1.12	735	603	849	3.7	1.5	11.9	8.0	65%	13%	37	21	42	35%	72%	15%	0	15			0	1.36	0.4	189	224	$5
16	Proj	**5**	**2**	**0**	**65**	**70**	**3.77**	**3.32**	**1.12**	**681**	**634**	**719**	**3.7**	**2.0**	**9.6**	**4.9**	**65%**	**13%**	**34**	**23**	**43**	**31%**	**69%**	**10%**	**0**						**1.5**	**132**	**157**	**$3**

JOCK THOMPSON

Salazar,Danny

Age:	26	Th:	R	Role	SP	Health	A	LIMA Plan	C+
						PT/Exp	B	Rand Var	0
Ht:	6' 0"	Wt:	195	Type	Pwr	Consist	C	MM	3405

Noted here last year that GB pitch could cut into DIS% and he obliged. Ctl rebound helped, as FpK steadied and Dom stayed superb. 2nd half H%, S% fueled ERA and WHIP gains, but overall this was a nice step forward. High ceiling remains intact; HR and volatility are still hurdles. Regardless, we'll take him as is.

Yr Tm	W	L	Sv	IP	K	ERA	xERA	WHIP	oOPS	vL	vR	BF/G	Ctl	Dom	Cmd	FpK	SwK	G	L	F	H%	S%	hr/f	GS	APC	DOM%	DIS%	Sv%	LI	RAR	BPV	BPX	R$
11																																	
12 aa	4	0	0	34	20	2.44	2.62	1.12				22.3	2.2	5.3	2.5						27%	78%								6.6	82	107	$1
13 CLE *	8	8	1	145	176	3.08	2.86	1.11	655	588	733	18.4	2.4	10.9	4.6	67%	15%	34	26	40	32%	75%	14%	10	82	50%	40%			14.0	150	195	$14
14 CLE *	10	14	0	171	184	4.25	4.63	1.43	751	696	786	23.4	3.3	9.7	3.0	59%	12%	34	23	42	35%	73%	10%	20	93	40%	35%			-10.7	89	106	-$2
15 CLE	14	10	0	185	195	3.45	3.44	1.13	673	724	628	25.2	2.6	9.5	3.7	59%	12%	44	19	37	29%	74%	12%	30	102	63%	20%			11.6	123	147	$18
1st Half	7	4	0	90	108	4.10	3.14	1.19	714	739	693	24.9	2.5	10.8	4.3	58%	13%	45	19	37	32%	70%	15%	15	102	53%	27%			-1.5	150	178	$14
2nd Half	7	6	0	95	87	2.84	3.74	1.07	634	710	560	25.5	2.7	8.2	3.1	60%	11%	43	19	38	26%	78%	10%	15	102	73%	13%			13.1	98	116	$22
16 Proj	**14**	**11**	**0**	**189**	**193**	**3.44**	**3.50**	**1.20**	**674**	**669**	**678**	**22.8**	**2.7**	**9.2**	**3.4**	**60%**	**12%**	**39**	**21**	**40**	**31%**	**75%**	**10%**	**33**						**12.0**	**111**	**132**	**$15**

Sale,Chris

Age:	27	Th:	L	Role	SP	Health	C	LIMA Plan	C+
						PT/Exp	A	Rand Var	+3
Ht:	6' 6"	Wt:	180	Type	Pwr	Consist	A	MM	5505

Inflated H% and return of HR proclivity fueled ERA spike, but the bad news ends there. FpK and SwK remained unshakeable, driving Ctl and Dom to career marks. DL avoidance a nice bonus. Four straight years of 70%+ DOM% and single-digit DIS% speak to his fantasy royalty. More run support would ice the package.

Yr Tm	W	L	Sv	IP	K	ERA	xERA	WHIP	oOPS	vL	vR	BF/G	Ctl	Dom	Cmd	FpK	SwK	G	L	F	H%	S%	hr/f	GS	APC	DOM%	DIS%	Sv%	LI	RAR	BPV	BPX	R$
11 CHW	2	2	8	71	79	2.79	3.00	1.11	612	558	660	5.0	3.4	10.0	2.9	60%	12%	50	18	32	28%	78%	11%	0	19			80	1.25	10.1	116	174	$9
12 CHW	17	8	0	192	192	3.05	3.27	1.14	660	601	682	25.7	2.4	9.0	3.8	57%	11%	45	23	32	30%	77%	12%	29	101	72%	7%	0	0.87	22.9	120	157	$24
13 CHW	11	14	0	214	226	3.07	2.94	1.07	636	360	699	28.9	1.9	9.5	4.9	63%	11%	47	21	32	30%	76%	13%	30	108	77%	3%			21.2	144	187	$23
14 CHW	12	4	0	174	208	2.17	2.81	0.97	567	393	608	26.3	2.0	10.8	5.3	67%	14%	41	18	41	29%	81%	8%	26	106	81%	4%			33.7	158	188	$27
15 CHW	13	11	0	209	274	3.41	2.74	1.09	649	610	657	27.5	1.8	11.8	6.5	67%	15%	43	22	35	34%	73%	13%	31	107	71%	6%			14.3	185	220	$23
1st Half	6	4	0	103	141	2.87	2.60	0.97	576	472	593	27.2	1.9	12.3	6.4	68%	17%	42	20	37	32%	73%	9%	15	108	80%	7%			13.9	190	225	$30
2nd Half	7	7	0	105	133	3.93	2.89	1.21	716	702	718	27.9	1.7	11.4	6.7	67%	14%	43	24	34	36%	72%	16%	16	106	63%	6%			0.4	179	213	$17
16 Proj	**15**	**9**	**0**	**203**	**247**	**3.05**	**2.78**	**1.07**	**633**	**526**	**659**	**21.4**	**2.0**	**10.9**	**5.5**	**66%**	**14%**	**43**	**21**	**36**	**32%**	**76%**	**12%**	**37**						**22.9**	**164**	**196**	**$25**

Samardzija,Jeff

Age:	31	Th:	R	Role	SP	Health	A	LIMA Plan	C
						PT/Exp	A	Rand Var	+2
Ht:	6' 5"	Wt:	225	Type		Consist	B	MM	2205

So much for those who like to draft players in their contract year. Old school attitude on W/L history is that he's just "not a winner" but there is plenty of skill here. Ctl still solid; Dom drop not supported by SwK and 94 mph fastball. FB spike and S% fail hurt most, but are correctable. New digs could make 2015 disappear.

Yr Tm	W	L	Sv	IP	K	ERA	xERA	WHIP	oOPS	vL	vR	BF/G	Ctl	Dom	Cmd	FpK	SwK	G	L	F	H%	S%	hr/f	GS	APC	DOM%	DIS%	Sv%	LI	RAR	BPV	BPX	R$
11 CHC	8	4	0	88	87	2.97	4.11	1.30	613	660	581	5.1	5.1	8.9	1.7	56%	11%	41	18	41	27%	78%	5%	0	20			0	0.85	10.6	41	62	$6
12 CHC	9	13	0	175	180	3.81	3.45	1.22	698	759	636	25.8	2.9	9.3	3.2	60%	13%	45	22	33	30%	72%	13%	28	99	64%	11%			4.3	112	146	$10
13 CHC	8	13	0	214	214	4.34	3.49	1.35	736	783	695	27.7	3.3	9.0	2.7	60%	11%	48	20	31	32%	70%	13%	33	105	70%	9%			-12.5	100	130	$1
14 2 TM	7	13	0	220	202	2.99	3.05	1.07	646	662	631	26.6	1.8	8.3	4.7	65%	12%	50	19	31	29%	75%	11%	33	101	73%	6%			20.3	129	154	$19
15 CHW	11	13	0	214	163	4.96	4.25	1.29	765	839	689	28.4	2.1	6.9	3.3	62%	10%	39	21	40	31%	64%	11%	32	104	47%	9%			-26.4	85	101	-$2
1st Half	5	4	0	116	97	4.33	3.90	1.27	740	797	690	28.9	1.7	7.5	4.4	65%	11%	40	23	37	33%	68%	9%	17	105	59%	0%			-5.3	107	127	$3
2nd Half	6	9	0	98	66	5.71	4.69	1.32	796	880	686	27.9	2.5	6.1	2.4	60%	9%	38	19	43	29%	60%	13%	15	104	33%	20%			-21.1	58	69	-$8
16 Proj	**10**	**13**	**0**	**218**	**185**	**3.95**	**3.75**	**1.24**	**726**	**787**	**666**	**28.0**	**2.4**	**7.7**	**3.2**	**62%**	**11%**	**43**	**20**	**36**	**30%**	**72%**	**11%**	**32**						**0.4**	**94**	**112**	**$8**

Sampson,Keyvius

Age:	25	Th:	R	Role	RP	Health	A	LIMA Plan	D+
						PT/Exp	D	Rand Var	+1
Ht:	6' 2"	Wt:	225	Type	Pwr FB	Consist	C	MM	0201

2-6, 6.54 ERA in 52 IP at CIN. MLB debut from prospect with inconsistent stuff and volatile track record to match. Dom is decent, but Ctl is a mess and a big reason why he didn't pitch past the 6th inning in any of his 12 starts. FpK, GB%, PQS-DIS% aren't exactly bright spots. He's not an option you want to linger over.

Yr Tm	W	L	Sv	IP	K	ERA	xERA	WHIP	oOPS	vL	vR	BF/G	Ctl	Dom	Cmd	FpK	SwK	G	L	F	H%	S%	hr/f	GS	APC	DOM%	DIS%	Sv%	LI	RAR	BPV	BPX	R$
11																																	
12 aa	8	11	0	122	111	4.67	3.35	1.30				19.4	3.8	8.1	2.2						30%	63%								-9.9	83	109	$0
13 a/a	12	7	0	141	122	3.51	3.34	1.26				20.6	3.6	7.8	2.2						28%	74%								6.2	77	100	$8
14 aaa	2	5	0	92	82	5.40	4.86	1.56				10.6	5.6	8.0	1.4						29%	68%								-18.7	44	52	-$10
15 CIN *	5	12	0	135	106	5.26	5.38	1.73	853	920	799	21.2	5.1	7.1	1.4	55%	9%	39	22	39	35%	70%	10%	12	80	25%	50%	0	0.73	-21.5	46	54	-$16
1st Half	2	4	0	67	57	3.73	4.63	1.68				23.1	5.4	7.6	1.4						34%	77%	0%	0						1.9	63	75	-$10
2nd Half	3	8	0	68	50	6.74	6.10	1.79	853	920	799	19.7	4.7	6.6	1.4	55%	9%	39	22	39	35%	62%	10%	12	80	25%	50%	0	0.73	-23.4	28	34	-$22
16 Proj	**4**	**7**	**0**	**87**	**73**	**4.90**	**4.87**	**1.58**	**676**	**736**	**626**	**16.7**	**4.8**	**7.5**	**1.6**	**55%**	**9%**	**39**	**22**	**39**	**32%**	**70%**	**8%**	**15**						**-10.1**	**22**	**27**	**-$7**

Sanchez,Aaron

Age:	24	Th:	R	Role	RP	Health	C	LIMA Plan	B
						PT/Exp	D	Rand Var	-2
Ht:	6' 4"	Wt:	200	Type	Pwr xGB	Consist	B	MM	2111

Began 1st half in rotation, where gilt-edged GB% and H% offset poor Cmd and hr/f spike. Strained lat shelved him in early June; returned in 2nd half as a RP with velocity rebound and better results. SP role is still his future, and sinking mid-90s stuff speaks to both high floor and ceiling. But both FpK, SwK urge patience.

Yr Tm	W	L	Sv	IP	K	ERA	xERA	WHIP	oOPS	vL	vR	BF/G	Ctl	Dom	Cmd	FpK	SwK	G	L	F	H%	S%	hr/f	GS	APC	DOM%	DIS%	Sv%	LI	RAR	BPV	BPX	R$
11																																	
12																																	
13																																	
14 TOR *	5	9	3	133	102	3.96	3.47	1.37	367	469	306	12.1	4.5	6.9	1.5	53%	7%	66	15	20	28%	71%	6%	0	19			100	1.17	-3.6	65	77	$0
15 TOR	7	6	0	92	61	3.22	4.08	1.28	666	878	435	9.3	4.3	5.9	1.4	53%	7%	61	18	22	25%	78%	16%	11	35	18%	18%	0	1.08	8.5	30	36	$4
1st Half	5	4	0	66	42	3.55	4.55	1.44	738	968	476	25.5	5.0	5.7	1.1	53%	7%	58	19	23	26%	79%	18%	11	97	18%	18%			3.4	3	3	$3
2nd Half	2	2	0	26	19	2.39	2.99	0.87	467	608	333	3.3	2.4	6.5	2.7	54%	7%	68	14	18	21%	73%	8%	0	13			0	1.19	5.1	98	116	$5
16 Proj	**6**	**7**	**2**	**102**	**73**	**3.67**	**3.77**	**1.35**	**703**	**938**	**505**	**7.2**	**3.9**	**6.5**	**1.7**	**53%**	**7%**	**65**	**16**	**20**	**29%**	**73%**	**11%**	**0**						**3.6**	**54**	**64**	**$2**

Sanchez,Anibal

Age:	32	Th:	R	Role	SP	Health	F	LIMA Plan	C
						PT/Exp	A	Rand Var	+3
Ht:	6' 0"	Wt:	205	Type	Pwr	Consist	B	MM	2303

More season-ending injuries, this time a rotator cuff strain. But poor start hints that physical woes are taking a toll. GB% dip and soaring hr/f wrecked his ERA from the get-go with help from poor S%. Problems compounded when Ctl disappeared in July. Could bounce back if healthy, but DN: 5.00 ERA, more DL time.

Yr Tm	W	L	Sv	IP	K	ERA	xERA	WHIP	oOPS	vL	vR	BF/G	Ctl	Dom	Cmd	FpK	SwK	G	L	F	H%	S%	hr/f	GS	APC	DOM%	DIS%	Sv%	LI	RAR	BPV	BPX	R$
11 FLA	8	9	0	196	202	3.67	3.38	1.28	711	671	751	25.9	2.9	9.3	3.2	63%	12%	44	20	36	32%	74%	10%	32	101	66%	16%			6.7	109	165	$10
12 2 TM	9	13	0	196	167	3.86	3.70	1.27	716	645	797	26.5	2.2	7.7	3.5	66%	10%	46	21	32	32%	72%	11%	31	99	68%	13%			3.6	103	134	$8
13 DET	14	8	0	182	202	2.57	3.08	1.15	616	673	548	25.7	2.7	10.0	3.7	62%	13%	45	22	33	32%	79%	6%	29	103	72%	7%			29.1	131	170	$22
14 DET	8	5	0	126	102	3.43	3.58	1.10	597	562	648	23.4	2.1	7.3	3.4	60%	10%	46	19	35	29%	67%	3%	21	95	48%	19%	0	0.75	4.9	97	116	$8
15 DET	10	10	0	157	138	4.99	4.11	1.28	768	681	866	26.4	2.8	7.9	2.8	65%	10%	40	21	39	29%	66%	16%	25	101	48%	12%			-19.8	85	101	-$1
1st Half	7	7	0	112	100	4.65	3.85	1.16	705	654	763	27.0	2.6	8.0	3.1	67%	10%	41	21	38	27%	64%	15%	17	103	59%	12%			-9.5	94	112	$5
2nd Half	3	3	0	45	38	5.84	4.75	1.59	912	742	1099	25.1	3.4	7.7	2.2	62%	9%	37	22	42	33%	70%	18%	8	97	25%	13%			-10.4	60	71	-$14
16 Proj	**11**	**10**	**0**	**174**	**156**	**4.30**	**3.79**	**1.28**	**733**	**660**	**820**	**24.5**	**2.7**	**8.1**	**3.0**	**63%**	**10%**	**42**	**21**	**37**	**31%**	**70%**	**12%**	**29**						**-7.3**	**91**	**109**	**$4**

Santana,Ervin

Age:	33	Th:	R	Role	SP	Health	A	LIMA Plan	B
						PT/Exp	A	Rand Var	0
Ht:	6' 2"	Wt:	185	Type		Consist	A	MM	2105

7-5, 4.00 ERA in 108 IP at MIN. Season began in July thanks to 80-game PED suspension. Started poorly, coughing up 11 HR in 55 IP. Roared down the stretch as SwK soared—8.7 Dom, 1 HR allowed, 6 PQS-DOMs over his final 7 starts. Particularly given his hiatus, this skill set looks remarkably stable. Buy the projection.

Yr Tm	W	L	Sv	IP	K	ERA	xERA	WHIP	oOPS	vL	vR	BF/G	Ctl	Dom	Cmd	FpK	SwK	G	L	F	H%	S%	hr/f	GS	APC	DOM%	DIS%	Sv%	LI	RAR	BPV	BPX	R$
11 LAA	11	12	0	229	178	3.38	3.87	1.22	693	703	681	28.8	2.8	7.0	2.5	63%	9%	44	19	38	28%	76%	10%	33	105	58%	6%			15.7	72	108	$15
12 LAA	9	13	0	178	133	5.16	4.38	1.27	774	867	664	25.5	3.1	6.7	2.2	62%	9%	43	20	37	25%	66%	19%	30	95	47%	23%			-25.1	59	77	-$2
13 KC	9	10	0	211	161	3.24	3.66	1.14	668	675	659	26.8	2.2	6.9	3.2	66%	10%	46	21	32	27%	77%	12%	32	100	66%	6%			16.2	89	116	$15
14 ATL	14	10	0	196	179	3.95	3.57	1.31	724	763	676	26.4	2.9	8.2	2.8	63%	12%	43	25	33	32%	71%	9%	31	96	68%	3%			-5.0	91	108	$5
15 MIN *	10	5	0	129	90	3.79	4.10	1.31	729	804	651	26.6	2.9	6.3	2.2	61%	10%	41	21	38	29%	74%	10%	17	99	53%	24%			2.7	56	66	$4
1st Half	3	0	0	29	16	2.59	3.85	1.21	454	594	343	28.9	2.5	5.0	2.0	69%	12%	53	0	47	26%	85%	13%	1	93	100%	0%			4.9	42	50	-$2
2nd Half	7	5	0	100	74	4.14	4.47	1.34	747	816	674	26.8	3.0	6.7	2.2	61%	10%	40	23	37	30%	72%	9%	16	99	50%	25%			-2.2	58	69	$5
16 Proj	**13**	**8**	**0**	**189**	**142**	**3.74**	**4.06**	**1.30**	**733**	**779**	**681**	**26.7**	**2.7**	**6.8**	**2.5**	**63%**	**10%**	**43**	**22**	**35**	**30%**	**75%**	**11%**	**29**						**5.2**	**69**	**82**	**$8**

JOCK THOMPSON

Santiago,Hector

Age: 28	Th: L	Role SP		Health A		LIMA Plan C+	
Ht: 6' 0"	Wt: 210	Type Pwr xFB		PT/Exp A		Rand Var -3	
				Consist A		MM 1303	

Hope you listened (and acted accordingly) on July 1, when the numbers screamed "CASH OUT!" Multi-year ERAs look acceptable, and he gets points for DISaster avoidance, but there's very little substance underneath. Stagnant BPV; uninspiring FpK and SwK; worrisome FB trend. xERA tells the truth.

Yr Tm	W	L	Sv	IP	K	ERA	xERA	WHIP	oOPS	vL	vR	BF/G	Ctl	Dom	Cmd	FpK	SwK	G	L	F	H%	S%	hr/f	GS	APC	DOM%	DIS%	Sv%	LI	RAR	BPV	BPX	R$
11 CHW *	7	5	0	89	66	4.34	4.06	1.50	170	0	311	22.5	4.7	6.7	1.4	56%	6%	60	13	27	31%	71%	0%	0	33			0	0.43	-4.4	57	86	-$2
12 CHW	4	1	4	70	79	3.33	4.11	1.34	680	592	744	7.3	5.1	10.1	2.0	56%	9%	38	20	42	27%	81%	14%	4	32	50%	50%	67	0.83	6.0	60	78	$3
13 CHW	4	9	0	149	137	3.56	4.38	1.40	739	686	762	19.3	4.3	8.3	1.9	57%	9%	36	20	44	30%	78%	9%	23	79	52%	17%	0	0.88	5.5	46	59	$1
14 LAA	6	9	0	127	108	3.75	4.53	1.36	698	606	732	18.1	3.7	7.6	2.0	56%	8%	31	19	50	29%	76%	8%	24	76	29%	25%	0	0.80	-0.1	45	54	$0
15 LAA	9	9	0	181	162	3.59	4.74	1.26	723	633	752	23.5	3.5	8.1	2.3	57%	9%	30	16	54	27%	78%	10%	32	96	47%	16%	0	0.74	8.4	58	69	$9
1st Half	5	4	0	101	91	2.40	4.38	1.10	631	425	720	24.5	3.0	8.1	2.7	58%	9%	30	18	52	25%	86%	9%	16	100	63%	0%	0	0.71	19.6	72	85	$21
2nd Half	4	5	0	79	71	5.11	5.21	1.46	831	1045	784	22.4	4.2	8.1	1.9	57%	9%	30	15	55	29%	71%	12%	16	91	31%	31%			-11.2	40	47	-$6
16 Proj	**8**	**10**	**0**	**174**	**155**	**4.07**	**4.57**	**1.40**	**756**	**698**	**777**	**23.3**	**3.9**	**8.0**	**2.0**	**57%**	**8%**	**32**	**18**	**50**	**30%**	**75%**	**10%**	**31**						**-2.4**	**48**	**57**	**$1**

Scheppers,Tanner

Age: 29	Th: R	Role RP		Health F		LIMA Plan D+	
Ht: 6' 4"	Wt: 200	Type Pwr		PT/Exp D		Rand Var 0	
				Consist B		MM 1200	

4-1, 5.63 ERA in 38 IP at TEX. Another fractured season: Count ankle, knee, finger and April among the problems. Still sits mid-90s with fastball, but FpK says he struggles to get ahead, and Ctl/Dom say that he can't finish. Batted-ball profile is trending the wrong way. Broken until proven otherwise.

Yr Tm	W	L	Sv	IP	K	ERA	xERA	WHIP	oOPS	vL	vR	BF/G	Ctl	Dom	Cmd	FpK	SwK	G	L	F	H%	S%	hr/f	GS	APC	DOM%	DIS%	Sv%	LI	RAR	BPV	BPX	R$
11 a/a	4	1	2	44	35	4.31	4.17	1.56				6.8	4.4	7.2	1.7						34%	71%								-2.0	70	106	-$2
12 TEX *	2	3	12	63	54	4.34	5.57	1.51	908	949	881	4.2	1.9	7.7	4.2	53%	9%	43	20	37	37%	75%	15%	0	14			80	0.95	-2.6	89	116	$0
13 TEX	6	2	1	77	59	1.88	3.48	1.07	605	599	610	4.0	2.8	6.9	2.5	60%	10%	50	19	31	25%	87%	9%	0	14			33	1.26	18.8	77	100	$10
14 TEX	0	1	0	23	17	9.00	4.50	1.78	922	925	916	13.9	3.9	6.7	1.7	56%	7%	56	14	31	34%	51%	24%	4	52	25%	50%	0	0.76	-14.9	48	57	-$9
15 TEX *	4	3	2	58	46	4.56	4.61	1.58	778	768	786	4.2	5.5	7.2	1.3	55%	8%	40	19	40	30%	73%	13%	0	16			40	1.08	-4.3	46	55	-$4
1st Half	3	0	0	36	29	3.00	3.00	1.24	691	830	581	4.1	5.2	7.1	1.4	57%	9%	50	15	35	21%	80%	15%	0	17			0	1.37	4.3	59	69	$0
2nd Half	1	3	2	22	18	7.10	7.26	2.14	928	661	1133	4.4	6.0	7.3	1.2	52%	8%	24	27	49	41%	66%	9%	0	16			67	0.62	-8.5	31	37	-$12
16 Proj	**3**	**2**	**0**	**44**	**35**	**4.25**	**4.49**	**1.54**	**745**	**786**	**714**	**4.3**	**4.3**	**7.3**	**1.7**	**56%**	**9%**	**47**	**18**	**35**	**32%**	**74%**	**9%**	**0**						**-1.5**	**40**	**47**	**-$4**

Scherzer,Max

Age: 31	Th: R	Role SP		Health A		LIMA Plan D+	
Ht: 6' 3"	Wt: 220	Type Pwr FB		PT/Exp A		Rand Var 0	
				Consist A		MM 5505	

Your choice of what to drool over here, but let's play the Grade Game. Mayberry? Perfection for a SP. Reliability? Likewise. RandVar? 2015 is repeatable. LIMA? Open up the wallet. Remember his performance down the stretch in THAT environment. Plus, he just threw strike one while you were reading this.

Yr Tm	W	L	Sv	IP	K	ERA	xERA	WHIP	oOPS	vL	vR	BF/G	Ctl	Dom	Cmd	FpK	SwK	G	L	F	H%	S%	hr/f	GS	APC	DOM%	DIS%	Sv%	LI	RAR	BPV	BPX	R$
11 DET	15	9	0	195	174	4.43	3.78	1.35	780	840	706	25.2	2.6	8.0	3.1	62%	10%	40	20	39	32%	71%	13%	33	101	52%	9%			-11.7	93	139	$4
12 DET	16	7	0	188	231	3.74	3.35	1.27	721	831	588	24.6	2.9	11.1	3.9	61%	13%	36	22	41	34%	75%	12%	32	102	63%	19%			6.3	136	177	$14
13 DET	21	3	0	214	240	2.90	3.16	0.97	583	645	494	26.1	2.4	10.1	4.3	64%	13%	36	19	45	27%	73%	8%	32	106	88%	3%			25.6	132	172	$33
14 DET	18	5	0	220	252	3.15	3.24	1.18	663	685	629	27.4	2.6	10.3	4.0	63%	12%	37	22	42	33%	76%	8%	33	110	82%	6%			16.2	131	156	$20
15 WAS	14	12	0	229	276	2.79	3.00	0.92	600	657	538	27.2	1.3	10.9	8.1	71%	16%	36	19	45	29%	76%	11%	33	102	82%	6%			32.9	173	207	$37
1st Half	9	6	0	119	139	1.82	2.96	0.78	489	533	446	28.3	1.1	10.5	9.9	71%	15%	35	18	48	27%	80%	5%	16	103	100%	0%			31.4	174	206	$52
2nd Half	5	6	0	110	137	3.85	3.05	1.07	714	774	643	26.3	1.6	11.2	6.9	71%	17%	37	20	43	31%	72%	17%	17	100	65%	12%			1.6	173	205	$22
16 Proj	**16**	**8**	**0**	**210**	**246**	**3.15**	**3.05**	**1.05**	**643**	**694**	**577**	**25.8**	**2.0**	**10.5**	**5.3**	**67%**	**14%**	**37**	**20**	**44**	**30%**	**75%**	**10%**	**32**						**21.1**	**151**	**179**	**$27**

Schultz,Bo

Age: 30	Th: R	Role RP		Health A		LIMA Plan D+	
Ht: 6' 3"	Wt: 220	Type		PT/Exp D		Rand Var -1	
				Consist F		MM 1000	

0-1, 3.56 ERA in 43 IP at TOR. Late bloomer worth knowing? PRO: FpK/SwK point to some Ctl/Dom upside; plenty of grounders; fastball just over 95 mph. CON: 22% H% in MLB won't repeat; trouble with HRs; won't get tons of chances as a 30something. Better bullpen options elsewhere.

Yr Tm	W	L	Sv	IP	K	ERA	xERA	WHIP	oOPS	vL	vR	BF/G	Ctl	Dom	Cmd	FpK	SwK	G	L	F	H%	S%	hr/f	GS	APC	DOM%	DIS%	Sv%	LI	RAR	BPV	BPX	R$
11																																	
12 aa	2	3	0	21	10	2.85	4.28	1.55				5.5	3.2	4.3	1.3						34%	80%								3.1	49	64	-$4
13 a/a	5	6	1	105	56	4.16	4.28	1.44				12.0	3.3	4.9	1.5						30%	72%								-3.8	39	51	-$3
14 ARI *	10	9	0	143	66	6.96	7.14	1.86	948	882	1009	21.0	3.0	4.1	1.4	61%	9%	48	24	28	37%	63%	13%	0	32			0	0.43	-56.9	2	2	-$28
15 TOR *	2	2	8	64	45	3.31	3.55	1.19	637	536	702	5.5	3.2	6.3	2.0	62%	11%	49	17	34	25%	78%	16%	0	20			62	0.82	5.2	52	61	$4
1st Half	2	1	7	40	27	2.42	3.26	1.20	527	484	560	6.1	3.1	6.1	1.9	64%	13%	47	22	31	26%	84%	12%	0	28			64	1.09	7.5	61	72	$8
2nd Half	0	1	1	25	18	4.74	4.17	1.18	720	581	797	4.7	3.3	6.6	2.0	61%	10%	50	14	36	23%	67%	19%	0	17			50	0.70	-2.4	58	68	-$2
16 Proj	**2**	**2**	**0**	**44**	**28**	**4.36**	**4.48**	**1.46**	**814**	**662**	**913**	**8.3**	**3.2**	**5.8**	**1.8**	**62%**	**11%**	**49**	**17**	**34**	**31%**	**74%**	**12%**	**0**						**-2.1**	**46**	**54**	**-$4**

Scribner,Evan

Age: 30	Th: R	Role RP		Health B		LIMA Plan A	
Ht: 6' 3"	Wt: 190	Type Pwr		PT/Exp D		Rand Var +5	
				Consist B		MM 4400	

For a while, a chic pick for saves due to killer base skills. But for second year in a row, overall numbers (and stopper chances) ruined by outlier hr/f. Although FB% dipped, opponents continued to square him up (LDs), and Sept shoulder injury clouds his future. S%, hr/f should correct, but as a RP, his chances are dwindling.

Yr Tm	W	L	Sv	IP	K	ERA	xERA	WHIP	oOPS	vL	vR	BF/G	Ctl	Dom	Cmd	FpK	SwK	G	L	F	H%	S%	hr/f	GS	APC	DOM%	DIS%	Sv%	LI	RAR	BPV	BPX	R$
11 SD *	2	3	10	43	33	4.89	3.88	1.39	810	937	692	4.7	3.1	6.9	2.2	61%	5%	39	22	39	32%	63%	5%	0	23			91	0.13	-5.0	74	111	$1
12 OAK *	5	0	9	71	60	2.93	2.98	1.16	637	834	501	5.0	2.8	7.5	2.7	60%	7%	38	25	38	28%	77%	5%	0	20			100	0.46	9.5	89	116	$9
13 OAK *	3	1	1	71	63	3.18	2.88	1.12	747	618	861	5.7	2.1	8.0	3.9	56%	7%	35	18	47	30%	73%	7%	0	27			50	0.18	6.0	117	153	$4
14 OAK *	5	1	16	59	63	3.56	3.64	1.12	777	316	1099	4.4	1.4	9.7	6.7	79%	12%	34	20	46	32%	73%	25%	0	13			80	0.12	1.3	169	201	$9
15 OAK	2	2	0	60	64	4.35	3.00	1.03	758	704	798	4.4	0.6	9.6	16.0	70%	13%	39	23	38	29%	69%	23%	0	17			0	0.91	-2.9	174	207	$0
1st Half	2	1	0	42	44	3.64	2.99	1.00	708	715	703	4.2	0.6	9.4	14.7	72%	14%	41	21	38	29%	76%	21%	0	16			0	1.06	1.7	172	204	$3
2nd Half	0	1	0	18	20	6.00	3.01	1.11	873	677	1026	4.9	0.5	10.0	20.0	66%	13%	35	27	37	31%	53%	26%	0	20			0	0.50	-4.5	180	213	-$6
16 Proj	**2**	**2**	**0**	**58**	**59**	**4.27**	**3.15**	**1.10**	**748**	**758**	**740**	**4.6**	**1.2**	**9.2**	**7.5**	**65%**	**11%**	**39**	**22**	**40**	**31%**	**68%**	**16%**	**0**						**-2.2**	**150**	**178**	**$0**

Severino,Luis

Age: 22	Th: R	Role SP		Health A		LIMA Plan C+	
Ht: 6' 0"	Wt: 195	Type Pwr xGB		PT/Exp D		Rand Var +2	
				Consist A		MM 3303	

5-3, 2.89 ERA in 62 IP. Top prospect impressed in 11-start trial with Ctl/Dom/Cmd numbers backed by ample FpK and SwK. Hard fastball/slider combination induced plenty of groundballs and whiffs, and allowed him to work deep into games. Next on the docket: proof of durability, effectiveness of third pitch.

Yr Tm	W	L	Sv	IP	K	ERA	xERA	WHIP	oOPS	vL	vR	BF/G	Ctl	Dom	Cmd	FpK	SwK	G	L	F	H%	S%	hr/f	GS	APC	DOM%	DIS%	Sv%	LI	RAR	BPV	BPX	R$
11																																	
12																																	
13																																	
14 aa	2	2	0	25	26	2.82	2.61	1.10				16.3	2.1	9.5	4.5						32%	75%								2.8	148	176	$0
15 NYY *	14	5	0	162	143	3.05	2.96	1.16	705	705	702	21.5	2.8	8.0	2.8	63%	10%	51	19	30	29%	75%	17%	11	93	55%	9%			18.1	97	115	$17
1st Half	6	2	0	79	68	3.37	2.77	1.18				21.1	2.6	7.7	2.9						30%	70%	0%	0						5.8	106	125	$13
2nd Half	8	3	0	82	76	2.75	3.14	1.15	705	705	702	21.8	3.0	8.3	2.8	63%	10%	51	19	30	27%	81%	17%	11	93	55%	9%			12.3	88	105	$20
16 Proj	**11**	**8**	**0**	**160**	**140**	**3.28**	**3.61**	**1.23**	**622**	**642**	**598**	**21.9**	**2.9**	**7.9**	**2.7**	**63%**	**10%**	**51**	**19**	**30**	**30%**	**75%**	**9%**	**29**						**13.4**	**92**	**110**	**$11**

Shaw,Bryan

Age: 28	Th: R	Role RP		Health A		LIMA Plan B+	
Ht: 6' 1"	Wt: 210	Type Pwr		PT/Exp C		Rand Var -2	
				Consist A		MM 3210	

Reliable, won't-hurt-you reliever good for about 2 saves and a couple dozen holds (47 over last two seasons), it seems. But guys with league average skills turn over quickly in these days of 95+ mph relievers (he sits 91). So if his S% regresses or Cmd wavers, he could be roto-irrelevant in a flash.

Yr Tm	W	L	Sv	IP	K	ERA	xERA	WHIP	oOPS	vL	vR	BF/G	Ctl	Dom	Cmd	FpK	SwK	G	L	F	H%	S%	hr/f	GS	APC	DOM%	DIS%	Sv%	LI	RAR	BPV	BPX	R$
11 ARI *	5	1	16	67	49	2.56	3.44	1.19	699	587	776	4.2	2.5	6.6	2.6	56%	11%	60	22	18	28%	83%	13%	0	15			94	0.58	11.3	73	110	$11
12 ARI	1	6	2	59	41	3.49	4.03	1.42	747	863	630	3.9	3.6	6.2	1.7	57%	9%	56	21	23	31%	76%	10%	0	15			50	0.78	3.8	48	62	-$2
13 CLE	7	3	1	75	73	3.24	3.58	1.17	586	678	506	4.5	3.4	8.8	2.6	57%	11%	43	25	33	29%	73%	6%	0	18			20	0.99	5.8	88	115	$5
14 CLE	5	5	2	76	64	2.59	3.62	1.09	602	776	493	3.9	2.6	7.5	2.9	59%	11%	46	18	36	27%	79%	8%	0	16			22	1.37	10.8	90	107	$9
15 CLE	3	3	2	64	54	2.95	3.81	1.22	693	673	704	3.6	2.7	7.6	2.8	62%	11%	46	24	31	29%	81%	14%	0	14			33	1.21	8.0	89	105	$3
1st Half	1	1	1	29	28	1.88	3.84	1.12	646	517	692	3.3	3.1	8.8	2.8	64%	12%	35	26	39	25%	93%	13%	0	13			50	1.13	7.4	87	103	$4
2nd Half	2	2	1	35	26	3.82	3.78	1.30	728	738	718	3.9	2.3	6.6	2.9	59%	10%	53	22	25	31%	74%	14%	0	15			25	1.28	0.6	88	105	$2
16 Proj	**4**	**3**	**2**	**65**	**55**	**3.24**	**3.65**	**1.19**	**660**	**722**	**616**	**3.7**	**2.8**	**7.6**	**2.7**	**60%**	**11%**	**46**	**22**	**31**	**28%**	**76%**	**11%**	**0**						**5.8**	**86**	**102**	**$3**

BRENT HERSHEY

Shields,James

Age: 34	Th: R	Role SP	Health A	LIMA Plan B
Ht: 6' 3"	Wt: 215	Type Pwr	PT/Exp A	Rand Var +2
			Consist A	MM 3305

A model of durability (8 straight seasons with at least 33 GS), but a few cracks are showing: doubled his walk rate; LHB beat him up; and HR followed him around all year. Still deftly avoids DIS starts and FpK/SwK point to a Cmd rebound, but if the 2nd half represents the tip of the decline, then DN: 4.00+ ERA

Yr Tm	W	L	Sv	IP	K	ERA	xERA	WHIP	oOPS	vL	vR	BF/G	Ctl	Dom	Cmd	FpK	SwK	G	L	F	H%	S%	hr/f	GS	APC	DOM%	DIS%	Sv%	LI	RAR	BPV	BPX	R$
11 TAM	16	12	0	249	225	2.82	3.21	1.04	623	602	648	29.5	2.3	8.1	3.5	63%	11%	46	18	35	26%	78%	11%	33	108	67%	9%			34.7	107	161	$32
12 TAM	15	10	0	228	223	3.52	3.23	1.17	678	706	645	28.6	2.3	8.8	3.8	61%	11%	52	19	29	30%	73%	13%	33	110	70%	6%			13.9	127	165	$21
13 KC	13	9	0	229	196	3.15	3.72	1.24	678	614	753	27.8	2.7	7.7	2.9	58%	10%	42	23	35	30%	77%	9%	34	108	71%	9%			20.2	87	113	$16
14 KC	14	8	0	227	180	3.21	3.56	1.18	702	698	706	27.6	1.7	7.1	4.1	63%	10%	45	21	34	30%	76%	10%	34	107	65%	9%			14.8	104	124	$15
15 SD	13	7	0	202	216	3.91	3.68	1.33	776	890	660	26.1	3.6	9.6	2.7	60%	13%	45	21	34	31%	77%	18%	33	101	70%	6%			1.2	99	117	$8
1st Half	7	3	0	104	123	4.14	3.31	1.32	799	932	679	26.1	3.0	10.6	3.5	63%	15%	43	22	34	33%	74%	18%	17	98	76%	6%			-2.3	131	155	$9
2nd Half	6	4	0	98	93	3.67	4.09	1.35	752	850	636	26.1	4.2	8.5	2.0	58%	11%	46	19	35	28%	79%	17%	16	105	63%	6%			3.5	64	76	$7
16 Proj	13	8	0	210	198	3.52	3.62	1.26	728	771	681	26.3	2.9	8.5	2.9	60%	11%	45	21	34	30%	77%	14%	33						11.4	96	114	$13

Shoemaker,Matthew

Age: 29	Th: R	Role SP	Health A	LIMA Plan B+
Ht: 6' 2"	Wt: 225	Type FB	PT/Exp C	Rand Var +1
			Consist B	MM 2203

A shaky 2015 confirmed that 2014 was the outlier, and included bullpen work, a short trip to the minors, and a Sept forearm strain. Ctl and Cmd regressed as an increase in fly balls led to more HR. With middling velocity and lack of a knockout skill, expect more of the same. Not the place to mine for upside.

Yr Tm	W	L	Sv	IP	K	ERA	xERA	WHIP	oOPS	vL	vR	BF/G	Ctl	Dom	Cmd	FpK	SwK	G	L	F	H%	S%	hr/f	GS	APC	DOM%	DIS%	Sv%	LI	RAR	BPV	BPX	R$
11 a/a	12	7	0	177	114	3.39	3.93	1.26				26.8	2.3	5.8	2.5						29%	77%								12.0	61	92	$10
12 aaa	11	10	0	177	100	5.43	5.79	1.59				26.9	2.0	5.1	2.5						36%	67%								-30.8	44	57	-$17
13 LAA *	11	13	0	189	131	4.25	4.70	1.35	328	490	0	26.3	1.3	6.2	4.6	53%	10%	42	25	33	34%	71%	0%	1	93	100%	0%			-9.1	99	128	$0
14 LAA *	17	4	0	162	144	3.47	3.54	1.17	658	702	610	20.2	1.8	8.0	4.5	63%	11%	41	20	39	31%	73%	9%	20	78	65%	10%	0	0.81	5.3	121	144	$12
15 LAA	7	10	0	135	116	4.46	4.13	1.26	758	727	791	22.8	2.3	7.7	3.3	60%	10%	39	18	42	29%	71%	14%	24	84	46%	25%	0	0.76	-8.2	93	111	$1
1st Half	4	7	0	84	71	4.91	4.13	1.26	781	773	789	23.7	2.0	7.6	3.7	62%	10%	39	18	43	30%	67%	15%	15	84	40%	20%			-9.8	99	117	$0
2nd Half	3	3	0	51	45	3.71	4.12	1.25	719	645	795	21.3	2.8	7.9	2.8	58%	9%	39	19	42	29%	77%	13%	9	83	56%	33%	0	0.70	1.6	84	100	$2
16 Proj	10	8	0	145	118	4.03	4.02	1.29	755	746	764	22.4	2.4	7.3	3.1	61%	10%	40	19	41	31%	73%	11%	22						-1.3	86	102	$4

Shreve,Chasen

Age: 25	Th: L	Role RP	Health A	LIMA Plan B+
Ht: 6' 3"	Wt: 190	Type Pwr	PT/Exp D	Rand Var -3
			Consist D	MM 2400

ERA is intriguing, but interest soon fades with a deeper dive. Strike one is pretty much a coin flip, and though he has a swing-and-miss splitter, it can't compensate for all the runners on base. Favorable H% (1st half) and S% (whole season) propelled 2015; pass until he can tame the walks.

Yr Tm	W	L	Sv	IP	K	ERA	xERA	WHIP	oOPS	vL	vR	BF/G	Ctl	Dom	Cmd	FpK	SwK	G	L	F	H%	S%	hr/f	GS	APC	DOM%	DIS%	Sv%	LI	RAR	BPV	BPX	R$
11																																	
12 aa	2	1	0	18	14	4.86	5.46	1.95				8.0	7.9	7.0	0.9						33%	75%								-1.9	44	58	-$6
13 aa	3	1	0	43	24	5.65	4.91	1.73				5.4	4.9	5.1	1.1						34%	65%								-9.4	41	54	-$8
14 ATL *	5	3	9	76	91	2.68	2.68	1.08	526	652	408	4.9	1.8	10.7	6.1	65%	12%	48	16	35	34%	76%	0%	0	14			90	0.47	10.0	185	220	$10
15 NYY	6	2	0	58	64	3.09	4.13	1.41	738	738	738	4.3	5.1	9.9	1.9	53%	12%	46	13	41	28%	86%	16%	0	19			0	1.05	6.3	64	77	$1
1st Half	6	1	0	34	35	1.87	3.50	0.92	524	670	441	4.4	3.2	9.4	2.9	56%	14%	41	14	46	22%	83%	6%	0	19			0	1.16	8.7	100	119	$10
2nd Half	0	1	0	25	29	4.74	5.06	2.07	973	804	1082	4.1	7.7	10.6	1.4	50%	9%	52	13	35	35%	88%	32%	0	19			0	0.94	-2.4	14	16	-$10
16 Proj	3	3	0	58	62	3.60	3.90	1.45	728	715	736	4.5	4.3	9.6	2.2	52%	11%	47	13	39	32%	80%	12%	0						2.6	82	97	-$1

Siegrist,Kevin

Age: 26	Th: L	Role RP	Health D	LIMA Plan C+
Ht: 6' 5"	Wt: 215	Type Pwr xFB	PT/Exp D	Rand Var -5
			Consist D	MM 3510

Garnered a few stray saves as primary setup man, and even flashed the skill-worthiness to handle that gig in the 1st half. But walks plagued him after July 1, lefties continued to have their way with him, and the LD+FB numbers are worrisome. Strong FpK provides hope of better Cmd, but heed the Reliability grades.

Yr Tm	W	L	Sv	IP	K	ERA	xERA	WHIP	oOPS	vL	vR	BF/G	Ctl	Dom	Cmd	FpK	SwK	G	L	F	H%	S%	hr/f	GS	APC	DOM%	DIS%	Sv%	LI	RAR	BPV	BPX	R$
11																																	
12 aa	1	2	0	32	23	3.92	3.37	1.15				16.0	2.4	6.3	2.6						26%	69%								0.4	69	90	-$2
13 STL *	5	2	1	67	86	1.14	0.74	0.84	432	388	479	3.9	3.7	11.5	3.1	61%	10%	39	24	37	20%	89%	3%	0	15			100	0.84	22.7	151	197	$14
14 STL	1	4	0	30	37	6.82	4.17	1.58	818	827	811	3.8	4.7	11.0	2.3	65%	10%	30	20	49	36%	58%	12%	0	16			0	1.32	-11.5	77	92	-$7
15 STL	7	1	6	75	90	2.17	3.83	1.17	605	811	511	3.9	4.1	10.8	2.6	63%	11%	31	21	48	29%	83%	5%	0	16			60	1.22	16.5	94	111	$11
1st Half	3	0	4	37	48	1.45	3.45	1.13	669	896	551	3.7	2.9	11.6	4.0	63%	11%	22	27	51	32%	92%	7%	0	15			67	1.13	11.6	130	154	$13
2nd Half	4	1	2	37	42	2.89	4.23	1.21	537	698	472	4.0	5.3	10.1	1.9	63%	11%	40	14	46	26%	75%	2%	0	16			50	1.31	4.9	57	68	$10
16 Proj	5	3	7	65	76	3.41	3.60	1.18	632	694	598	4.0	3.8	10.5	2.8	64%	11%	33	21	47	29%	73%	7%	0						4.4	98	116	$6

Simon,Alfredo

Age: 35	Th: R	Role RP	Health B	LIMA Plan D+
Ht: 6' 6"	Wt: 265	Type	PT/Exp A	Rand Var 0
			Consist A	MM 1003

After his last start, complained that he pitched through knee injury all season that affected both velocity and keeping the ball down. But we're just as worried about his age, affects of late-career role switch, multi-year Dom and SwK dive, BPV trend, increasing walk rate, dumpster-fire 2nd half ... you can stop us at any time.

Yr Tm	W	L	Sv	IP	K	ERA	xERA	WHIP	oOPS	vL	vR	BF/G	Ctl	Dom	Cmd	FpK	SwK	G	L	F	H%	S%	hr/f	GS	APC	DOM%	DIS%	Sv%	LI	RAR	BPV	BPX	R$
11 BAL *	5	9	0	134	97	4.85	4.86	1.47	834	808	862	21.2	3.2	6.6	2.1	57%	9%	43	20	37	32%	69%	11%	16	83	44%	38%	0	0.84	-15.0	48	72	-$6
12 CIN	3	2	1	61	52	2.66	3.77	1.43	747	745	748	7.5	3.2	7.7	2.4	63%	9%	54	21	25	34%	81%	4%	0	28			100	0.61	10.2	82	108	$1
13 CIN	6	4	1	88	63	2.87	3.90	1.07	625	729	543	5.7	2.7	6.5	2.4	58%	10%	45	18	36	25%	77%	9%	0	21			33	0.73	10.7	67	88	$8
14 CIN	15	10	0	196	127	3.44	3.93	1.21	690	715	665	25.6	2.6	5.8	2.3	62%	9%	48	21	31	27%	75%	12%	32	94	53%	16%			7.3	61	73	$11
15 DET	13	12	0	187	117	5.05	4.81	1.44	808	862	734	26.5	3.3	5.6	1.7	56%	8%	44	22	35	30%	67%	11%	31	99	39%	32%			-25.2	35	42	-$7
1st Half	7	5	0	91	70	3.94	4.34	1.36	751	842	603	26.1	3.0	6.9	2.3	56%	10%	43	23	35	31%	73%	9%	15	100	53%	20%			0.2	65	77	$3
2nd Half	6	7	0	96	47	6.11	5.29	1.52	861	883	835	26.8	3.6	4.4	1.2	55%	7%	45	21	35	29%	62%	13%	16	98	25%	44%			-25.4	6	7	-$16
16 Proj	9	11	0	160	104	4.51	4.37	1.37	775	825	718	15.5	3.0	5.8	1.9	58%	9%	46	21	34	30%	69%	11%	24						-10.9	47	56	-$2

Skaggs,Tyler

Age: 24	Th: L	Role SP	Health F	LIMA Plan B+
Ht: 6' 4"	Wt: 215	Type Pwr	PT/Exp D	Rand Var 0
			Consist B	MM 2203

Will be a full 18 months past his Tommy John surgery when spring training opens, and is expected to participate with no restrictions. Which is not the same as being risk-free, of course. Pre-injury, his Ctl, Cmd and GB% were all on the upswing. Count on an innings limit, but pieces in place for future value.

Yr Tm	W	L	Sv	IP	K	ERA	xERA	WHIP	oOPS	vL	vR	BF/G	Ctl	Dom	Cmd	FpK	SwK	G	L	F	H%	S%	hr/f	GS	APC	DOM%	DIS%	Sv%	LI	RAR	BPV	BPX	R$
11 aa	4	1	0	58	64	2.68	2.59	1.06				22.4	2.1	10.0	4.8						31%	77%								9.0	151	227	$5
12 ARI *	10	9	0	152	122	3.53	3.99	1.28	785	333	863	22.2	2.7	7.3	2.7	52%	10%	34	18	48	30%	76%	13%	6	87	33%	50%			9.0	71	93	$8
13 ARI *	8	13	0	143	127	4.48	4.16	1.40	780	710	799	23.2	3.1	8.0	2.6	62%	9%	45	20	35	34%	68%	17%	7	94	29%	43%			-10.9	82	107	-$2
14 LAA	5	5	0	113	86	4.30	3.59	1.21	674	742	655	25.8	2.4	6.8	2.9	64%	9%	50	19	31	30%	65%	9%	18	95	61%	11%			-7.8	87	103	$0
15																																	
1st Half																																	
2nd Half																																	
16 Proj	8	8	0	145	119	3.95	3.79	1.27	695	711	691	23.4	2.8	7.4	2.6	63%	9%	48	19	33	30%	71%	9%	25						0.1	83	99	$4

Smith,Carson

Age: 26	Th: R	Role RP	Health A	LIMA Plan B+
Ht: 6' 6"	Wt: 215	Type Pwr xGB	PT/Exp D	Rand Var -1
			Consist B	MM 5520

It's all timing. Got BABIP'd in Jul/Aug (38% H%), right when the closer's role was up for grabs. But make no mistake, these are the skills of a lockdown stopper: abilty to throw strikes; huge swing-and-miss numbers; elite GB%; sub-.600 oOPS. Plus youth on his side. If he takes over sooner rather than later ... UP: 40 Sv

Yr Tm	W	L	Sv	IP	K	ERA	xERA	WHIP	oOPS	vL	vR	BF/G	Ctl	Dom	Cmd	FpK	SwK	G	L	F	H%	S%	hr/f	GS	APC	DOM%	DIS%	Sv%	LI	RAR	BPV	BPX	R$
11																																	
12																																	
13 aa	1	3	15	50	61	2.50	2.48	1.18				4.6	3.2	10.9	3.4						33%	78%								8.4	140	182	$8
14 SEA *	2	3	10	51	48	2.44	2.98	1.24	249	83	369	4.3	2.6	8.4	3.2	64%	10%	81	6	13	33%	79%	0%	0	13			77	0.62	8.3	118	140	$5
15 SEA	2	5	13	70	92	2.31	2.20	1.01	542	593	502	4.1	2.8	11.8	4.2	59%	13%	65	17	18	31%	77%	7%	0	15			72	1.40	14.2	180	214	$13
1st Half	1	2	5	32	38	1.97	2.22	0.81	499	543	466	3.6	1.7	10.7	6.3	58%	11%	60	19	21	26%	79%	13%	0	14			83	1.22	7.9	185	219	$12
2nd Half	1	3	8	38	54	2.61	2.16	1.18	575	631	531	4.5	3.8	12.8	3.4	60%	14%	69	15	15	35%	76%	0%	0	17			67	1.58	6.4	175	208	$13
16 Proj	2	4	23	65	77	2.41	2.42	1.13	594	655	546	4.1	2.9	10.6	3.7	59%	13%	65	17	18	32%	78%	5%	0						12.5	156	186	$14

BRENT HERSHEY

Smith,Joe

Age: 32	Th: R	Role RP	Health A	LIMA Plan A
Ht: 6' 2"	Wt: 205	Type Pwr GB	PT/Exp C	Rand Var 0
			Consist B	MM 4210

Missed almost two weeks in Sept with sprained ankle when he slipped on hotel stairs. Fitting, as he's been picking up stray saves when others stumble. But both H%/S% were finally normal in 2015, his xERA history is tepid, and has only marginal bat-missing ability. Small plan-B value in deep leagues; nothing more.

Yr	Tm	W	L	Sv	IP	K	ERA	xERA	WHIP	oOPS	vL	vR	BF/G	Ctl	Dom	Cmd	FpK	SwK	G	L	F	H%	S%	hr/f	GS	APC	DOM%	DIS%	Sv%	LI	RAR	BPV	BPX	R$
11	CLE	3	3	0	67	45	2.01	3.44	1.09	541	460	582	3.8	2.8	6.0	2.1	59%	6%	57	20	23	26%	81%	2%	0	14			0	1.05	15.9	68	102	$6
12	CLE	7	4	0	67	53	2.96	3.68	1.16	594	585	600	3.9	3.4	7.1	2.1	57%	9%	58	17	25	26%	76%	8%	0	15			0	1.22	8.8	73	96	$5
13	CLE	6	2	3	63	54	2.29	3.59	1.22	643	698	592	3.7	3.3	7.7	2.3	59%	9%	49	21	30	28%	85%	10%	0	14			38	1.37	12.3	77	101	$6
14	LAA	7	2	15	75	68	1.81	2.67	0.80	491	584	385	3.8	1.8	8.2	4.5	66%	8%	59	15	26	22%	80%	8%	0	15			79	1.25	17.8	136	162	$18
15	LAA	5	5	5	65	57	3.58	3.49	1.27	684	786	587	3.9	2.6	7.9	3.0	63%	8%	52	23	25	32%	72%	9%	0	14			56	1.29	3.1	101	120	$3
1st Half		2	2	0	35	32	2.80	3.24	1.08	568	705	422	3.8	2.3	8.2	3.6	66%	9%	48	25	26	30%	71%	0%	0	14			0	1.29	5.1	111	132	$4
2nd Half		3	3	5	30	25	4.50	3.79	1.50	807	881	743	4.0	3.0	7.5	2.5	59%	8%	56	21	23	34%	73%	18%	0	15			83	1.28	-2.0	88	104	$2
16	Proj	**6**	**4**	**7**	**65**	**56**	**3.09**	**3.32**	**1.16**	**639**	**714**	**568**	**3.7**	**2.6**	**7.7**	**3.0**	**62%**	**8%**	**54**	**20**	**26**	**29%**	**75%**	**10%**	**0**						**7.0**	**101**	**120**	**$7**

Smith,Will

Age: 26	Th: L	Role RP	Health A	LIMA Plan B+
Ht: 6' 5"	Wt: 250	Type Pwr	PT/Exp C	Rand Var 0
			Consist A	MM 4510

Forgot to wipe the sunscreen/rosin mix off his arm on 5/21, but a six-game suspension didn't slow him down. Went from very good to elite the old-fashioned way: walked less, struck out more, induced additional GB. Not a flamethrower, and H% history notable, but at least deserves a monogrammed towel. UP: 30 Sv

Yr	Tm	W	L	Sv	IP	K	ERA	xERA	WHIP	oOPS	vL	vR	BF/G	Ctl	Dom	Cmd	FpK	SwK	G	L	F	H%	S%	hr/f	GS	APC	DOM%	DIS%	Sv%	LI	RAR	BPV	BPX	R$
11	aa	13	9	0	161	90	4.10	4.31	1.40				25.2	2.4	5.0	2.1						32%	71%								-3.1	53	80	$2
12	KC *	10	13	0	179	120	4.56	5.28	1.54	853	897	835	25.2	2.7	6.0	2.2	57%	7%	42	23	35	35%	72%	11%	16	88	50%	44%			-12.0	48	63	-$8
13	KC *	8	5	4	122	123	3.65	3.77	1.24	631	557	684	10.6	2.3	9.0	3.8	63%	16%	43	16	41	32%	74%	19%	1	26	0%	100%	44	1.72	3.3	109	142	$7
14	MIL	1	3	1	66	86	3.70	3.15	1.42	737	516	872	3.7	4.2	11.8	2.8	53%	13%	44	23	33	36%	76%	11%	0	14			17	1.48	0.3	119	142	-$1
15	MIL	7	2	0	63	91	2.84	2.88	1.20	649	786	545	3.5	3.4	12.9	3.8	60%	16%	46	15	39	35%	79%	9%	0	14			0	1.15	8.8	165	196	$6
1st Half		4	0	0	31	40	1.47	2.99	1.04	500	652	386	3.3	3.5	11.7	3.3	60%	16%	49	13	38	30%	84%	0%	0	13			0	0.89	9.4	143	170	$9
2nd Half		3	2	0	33	51	4.13	2.78	1.35	781	902	688	3.7	3.3	14.1	4.3	60%	15%	43	17	40	40%	74%	17%	0	15			0	1.42	-0.7	184	219	$3
16	Proj	**5**	**3**	**4**	**65**	**83**	**3.03**	**3.06**	**1.27**	**701**	**700**	**702**	**4.2**	**3.1**	**11.4**	**3.7**	**60%**	**14%**	**44**	**18**	**37**	**35%**	**79%**	**10%**	**0**						**7.5**	**145**	**172**	**$5**

Smyly,Drew

Age: 27	Th: L	Role RP	Health F	LIMA Plan A
Ht: 6' 3"	Wt: 190	Type Pwr FB	PT/Exp B	Rand Var -1
			Consist A	MM 3403

If-if-if. Numbers and skills to pay for, but Health concerns—a torn labrum cost him most of 2015—color everything. Very good control, great Dom; stifiles LHB; hits the DL—all are consistent parts of this profile, even with just 3+ years under his belt. Account for all that in setting your target price.

Yr	Tm	W	L	Sv	IP	K	ERA	xERA	WHIP	oOPS	vL	vR	BF/G	Ctl	Dom	Cmd	FpK	SwK	G	L	F	H%	S%	hr/f	GS	APC	DOM%	DIS%	Sv%	LI	RAR	BPV	BPX	R$
11	aa	4	3	0	46	44	1.35	2.00	1.06				22.2	2.8	8.7	3.1						28%	88%								14.6	124	187	$6
12	DET *	4	5	0	117	114	4.51	4.39	1.36	732	671	759	16.3	3.1	8.8	2.8	58%	9%	40	19	41	32%	70%	10%	18	76	56%	33%	0	0.83	-7.2	78	102	-$3
13	DET	6	0	2	76	81	2.37	3.06	1.04	601	471	699	4.8	2.0	9.6	4.8	59%	11%	43	18	39	30%	79%	5%	0	20			33	1.12	14.0	139	182	$10
14	2 AL	9	10	0	153	133	3.24	3.79	1.16	688	486	763	22.1	2.5	7.8	3.2	62%	10%	37	20	43	28%	77%	10%	25	93	56%	16%	0	0.73	9.5	89	106	$10
15	TAM	5	2	0	67	77	3.11	3.53	1.17	701	507	751	22.9	2.7	10.4	3.9	61%	12%	37	19	44	30%	82%	14%	12	95	50%	25%			7.1	129	154	$4
1st Half		0	1	0	17	21	2.70	2.73	0.78	600	583	604	21.0	1.6	11.3	7.0	64%	11%	45	11	45	19%	89%	24%	3	86	67%	33%			2.6	183	217	-$3
2nd Half		5	1	0	50	56	3.24	3.81	1.30	731	484	794	23.6	3.1	10.1	3.3	59%	12%	35	21	44	33%	81%	12%	9	98	44%	22%			4.5	111	132	$7
16	Proj	**9**	**5**	**0**	**138**	**146**	**3.10**	**3.37**	**1.11**	**670**	**514**	**726**	**14.0**	**2.5**	**9.6**	**3.9**	**61%**	**11%**	**39**	**18**	**43**	**29%**	**79%**	**12%**	**15**						**14.6**	**123**	**146**	**$13**

Snell,Blake

Age: 23	Th: L	Role SP	Health A	LIMA Plan C
Ht: 6' 4"	Wt: 180	Type Pwr	PT/Exp F	Rand Var -3
			Consist F	MM 3400

The projection all came together as he blew through three levels in 2015 and is on the cusp of heading to Tampa. Most encouraging sign was how he refined his command as the season went on. Once called upon, advanced arsenal will give him fighting chance to stick at the MLB level.

Yr	Tm	W	L	Sv	IP	K	ERA	xERA	WHIP	oOPS	vL	vR	BF/G	Ctl	Dom	Cmd	FpK	SwK	G	L	F	H%	S%	hr/f	GS	APC	DOM%	DIS%	Sv%	LI	RAR	BPV	BPX	R$
11																																		
12																																		
13																																		
14																																		
15	a/a	12	4	0	113	117	1.95	2.44	1.11				21.2	3.4	9.4	2.8						28%	85%								28.0	112	133	$18
1st Half		5	2	0	59	57	1.90	2.87	1.20				23.6	3.9	8.7	2.2						27%	88%								14.9	90	107	$15
2nd Half		7	2	0	54	60	1.93	1.85	1.00				18.9	2.7	10.0	3.8						28%	82%								13.6	144	171	$21
16	Proj	**6**	**2**	**0**	**58**	**59**	**3.79**	**3.54**	**1.26**				**23.7**	**3.5**	**9.2**	**2.6**	**60%**	**9%**	**46**	**21**	**33**	**31%**	**71%**	**8%**	**10**						**1.2**	**94**	**112**	**$1**

Soria,Joakim

Age: 32	Th: R	Role RP	Health F	LIMA Plan B
Ht: 6' 3"	Wt: 200	Type Pwr	PT/Exp C	Rand Var -3
			Consist B	MM 4410

Changed teams at the deadline for the second straight season; again went from a closer to a setup man. As expected, couldn't repeat 2014 skills, but Cmd still an asset, and FpK/SwK holding up as he hits his mid-30s. Numbers say he still is saves-worthy, though the health cloud should keep price reasonable.

Yr	Tm	W	L	Sv	IP	K	ERA	xERA	WHIP	oOPS	vL	vR	BF/G	Ctl	Dom	Cmd	FpK	SwK	G	L	F	H%	S%	hr/f	GS	APC	DOM%	DIS%	Sv%	LI	RAR	BPV	BPX	R$
11	KC	5	5	28	60	60	4.03	3.51	1.28	709	631	793	4.3	2.5	9.0	3.5	57%	10%	40	21	39	32%	71%	10%	0	17			80	1.32	-0.6	111	166	$12
12																																		
13	TEX	1	0	0	24	28	3.80	3.43	1.35	624	316	943	3.9	5.3	10.6	2.0	56%	10%	52	18	30	29%	73%	12%	0	17			0	1.04	0.2	78	102	-$3
14	2 AL	2	4	18	44	48	3.25	2.93	0.99	605	675	503	3.8	1.2	9.7	8.0	63%	10%	43	22	35	32%	67%	5%	0	14			90	1.12	2.7	164	195	$9
15	2 TM	3	1	24	68	64	2.53	3.54	1.09	628	722	536	3.8	2.5	8.5	3.4	61%	10%	42	23	35	27%	83%	13%	0	16			80	1.35	12.0	105	125	$15
1st Half		3	0	18	33	28	2.48	3.51	0.95	659	812	510	3.7	1.4	7.7	5.6	62%	9%	43	18	40	23%	92%	19%	0	15			90	1.47	6.0	123	145	$21
2nd Half		0	1	6	35	36	2.57	3.58	1.23	596	637	554	3.8	3.6	9.3	2.6	60%	11%	42	27	31	31%	79%	4%	0	17			60	1.25	6.0	89	106	$10
16	Proj	**3**	**3**	**7**	**58**	**58**	**3.01**	**3.22**	**1.10**	**630**	**683**	**569**	**3.7**	**2.2**	**9.1**	**4.2**	**61%**	**10%**	**42**	**22**	**35**	**30%**	**75%**	**9%**	**0**						**6.8**	**125**	**149**	**$6**

Storen,Drew

Age: 28	Th: R	Role RP	Health C	LIMA Plan B
Ht: 6' 1"	Wt: 195	Type Pwr	PT/Exp C	Rand Var 0
			Consist A	MM 4410

The Blame Game (pick one): A) Front office, as surface stats dove after Papelbon acquisition. B) 2H strand rate, as premium skills held firm after demotion. 3) Himself, as an awful 6-appearance Sept ended with a broken hand after punching a locker. Answer is probably a bit of each—but things sure were swell in the 1H.

Yr	Tm	W	L	Sv	IP	K	ERA	xERA	WHIP	oOPS	vL	vR	BF/G	Ctl	Dom	Cmd	FpK	SwK	G	L	F	H%	S%	hr/f	GS	APC	DOM%	DIS%	Sv%	LI	RAR	BPV	BPX	R$
11	WAS	6	3	43	75	74	2.75	3.16	1.02	599	541	643	4.2	2.4	8.8	3.7	66%	9%	47	17	35	26%	78%	11%	0	15			90	1.42	11.1	120	180	$25
12	WAS	3	1	4	30	24	2.37	3.31	0.99	496	635	418	3.1	2.4	7.1	3.0	59%	14%	54	18	28	26%	73%	0%	0	11			80	1.21	6.1	96	125	$3
13	WAS	4	2	3	62	58	4.52	3.85	1.36	729	816	668	3.9	2.8	8.5	3.1	59%	10%	41	20	39	33%	69%	10%	0	14			38	1.09	-5.0	96	126	-$2
14	WAS	2	1	11	56	46	1.12	3.23	0.98	540	592	500	3.4	1.8	7.3	4.2	63%	11%	53	15	33	27%	91%	4%	0	12			79	1.21	18.2	116	138	$11
15	WAS	2	2	29	55	67	3.44	3.17	1.11	603	706	482	3.9	2.6	11.0	4.2	62%	13%	38	24	38	32%	70%	8%	0	15			85	1.13	3.6	143	170	$13
1st Half		1	0	25	32	37	1.97	2.94	0.97	516	665	334	3.8	2.0	10.4	5.3	62%	15%	41	23	37	30%	80%	3%	0	14			93	1.26	7.9	153	181	$22
2nd Half		1	2	4	23	30	5.48	3.47	1.30	712	762	657	4.1	3.5	11.7	3.3	61%	10%	36	25	39	34%	59%	13%	0	16			57	0.94	-4.3	130	154	$2
16	Proj	**3**	**2**	**5**	**58**	**61**	**3.25**	**3.25**	**1.13**	**621**	**697**	**551**	**3.6**	**2.5**	**9.5**	**3.7**	**62%**	**11%**	**43**	**21**	**36**	**31%**	**73%**	**8%**	**0**						**5.1**	**124**	**147**	**$4**

Strasburg,Stephen

Age: 27	Th: R	Role SP	Health F	LIMA Plan B+
Ht: 6' 4"	Wt: 230	Type Pwr	PT/Exp A	Rand Var +2
			Consist A	MM 5505

It's usually oversimplified to say "Health is everything." But take a gander at skills history: start with xERA, move to Ctl/Dom/Cmd and FpK/SwK, then to BPV/BPX, and finish with the 2H. Pitched around ankle, neck, back, oblique injuries in 2015 to earn that "F." Before asking "What if?", remember: Health. Is. Everything.

Yr	Tm	W	L	Sv	IP	K	ERA	xERA	WHIP	oOPS	vL	vR	BF/G	Ctl	Dom	Cmd	FpK	SwK	G	L	F	H%	S%	hr/f	GS	APC	DOM%	DIS%	Sv%	LI	RAR	BPV	BPX	R$
11	WAS	1	1	0	24	24	1.50	2.68	0.71	398	296	489	17.6	0.8	9.0	12.0	72%	12%	38	25	38	26%	76%	0%	5	66	60%	40%			7.2	158	237	$2
12	WAS	15	6	0	159	197	3.16	2.96	1.15	649	714	578	23.3	2.7	11.1	4.1	62%	12%	44	23	33	32%	76%	11%	28	93	71%	14%			16.7	149	194	$19
13	WAS	8	9	0	183	191	3.00	2.98	1.05	587	629	550	24.4	2.8	9.4	3.4	59%	11%	52	17	31	27%	74%	11%	30	95	77%	13%			19.5	125	163	$19
14	WAS	14	11	0	215	242	3.14	2.78	1.12	672	653	687	25.5	1.8	10.1	5.6	65%	12%	46	23	31	32%	76%	13%	34	97	79%	12%			16.0	158	188	$20
15	WAS	11	7	0	127	155	3.46	2.94	1.11	653	572	737	22.7	1.8	11.0	6.0	66%	12%	42	23	34	33%	72%	12%	23	89	61%	26%			7.8	168	200	$13
1st Half		5	5	0	61	63	5.16	3.76	1.49	781	699	852	21.3	2.7	9.3	3.5	66%	8%	44	25	31	38%	67%	12%	13	83	38%	38%			-9.0	118	140	-$3
2nd Half		6	2	0	66	92	1.90	2.29	0.75	512	449	590	24.6	1.1	12.5	11.5	65%	15%	40	21	40	27%	84%	13%	10	97	90%	10%			16.9	213	253	$27
16	Proj	**14**	**9**	**0**	**189**	**223**	**3.15**	**2.79**	**1.08**	**637**	**603**	**670**	**23.0**	**2.0**	**10.7**	**5.4**	**64%**	**12%**	**44**	**22**	**34**	**32%**	**75%**	**12%**	**32**						**18.8**	**160**	**191**	**$22**

BRENT HERSHEY

Street,Huston

Age: 32	Th: R	Role: RP	Health: D	LIMA Plan: C
Ht: 6' 0"	Wt: 195	Type: Pwr FB	PT/Exp: A	Rand Var: -2
			Consist: B	MM: 2330

Early warning or 2nd half aberration? Previously reliable FpK was M.I.A. all season. Typically elite Ctl became a real 2nd half problem as both ERA/xERA, H% soared and LHBs suddenly owned him. Even with velocity now dipping under 89mph, SwK says he's still missing bats. Now owns both performance and Health risk.

Yr Tm	W	L	Sv	IP	K	ERA	xERA	WHIP	oOPS	vL	vR	BF/G	Ctl	Dom	Cmd	FpK	SwK	G	L	F	H%	S%	hr/f	GS	APC	DOM%	DIS%	Sv%	LI	RAR	BPV	BPX	R$
11 COL	1	4	29	58	55	3.86	3.38	1.22	781	811	760	3.9	1.4	8.5	6.1	67%	13%	35	24	41	32%	75%	14%	0	15			88	1.18	0.6	128	193	$11
12 SD	2	1	23	39	47	1.85	2.76	0.72	425	384	461	3.6	2.5	10.8	4.3	63%	14%	42	20	38	19%	77%	6%	0	15			96	1.19	10.4	147	191	$15
13 SD	2	5	33	57	46	2.70	3.93	1.02	691	689	693	3.8	2.2	7.3	3.3	64%	12%	30	22	48	22%	89%	16%	0	15			94	1.22	8.1	79	104	$17
14 2 TM	2	2	41	59	57	1.37	3.36	0.94	521	482	561	3.8	2.1	8.6	4.1	64%	13%	36	20	43	26%	90%	6%	0	15			93	1.45	17.4	112	134	$23
15 LAA	3	3	40	62	57	3.18	4.13	1.16	641	758	522	4.1	2.9	8.2	2.9	56%	14%	34	20	45	27%	77%	9%	0	17			89	1.56	6.0	82	98	$19
1st Half	3	2	23	35	35	2.34	3.77	0.89	508	541	473	3.9	2.3	9.1	3.9	56%	13%	26	23	51	23%	79%	7%	0	16			88	1.69	7.0	104	123	$26
2nd Half	0	1	17	28	22	4.23	4.59	1.48	793	1002	578	4.3	3.6	7.2	2.0	55%	14%	44	17	39	32%	76%	12%	0	17			89	1.41	-0.9	54	64	$10
16 Proj	2	3	33	58	53	3.08	3.80	1.14	657	721	595	3.9	2.6	8.2	3.1	60%	13%	36	20	44	28%	78%	10%	0						6.3	91	108	$15

Strickland,Hunter

Age: 27	Th: R	Role: RP	Health: A	LIMA Plan: B
Ht: 6' 5"	Wt: 200	Type:	PT/Exp: F	Rand Var: -1
			Consist: A	MM: 4321

3-3, 2.45 ERA in 51 IP at SF. Learned from 2014 post-season bombing. Mixed more breaking stuff with 97mph heat in stellar rookie season. SwK held firm despite 2nd half Dom fade, outstanding Ctl never wavered. Imposing physical presence adds to closer-in-waiting foundation. With opportunity, now ready for.. UP: 30 Sv

Yr Tm	W	L	Sv	IP	K	ERA	xERA	WHIP	oOPS	vL	vR	BF/G	Ctl	Dom	Cmd	FpK	SwK	G	L	F	H%	S%	hr/f	GS	APC	DOM%	DIS%	Sv%	LI	RAR	BPV	BPX	R$
11																																	
12 aa	2	2	1	41	25	5.53	6.19	1.71				8.1	3.0	5.5	1.8						36%	69%								-7.7	29	38	-$8
13																																	
14 SF *	2	1	12	43	48	1.98	2.10	0.90	440	500	400	3.4	0.9	10.0	11.2	84%	13%	56	25	19	30%	81%	0%	0	11			100	0.45	9.2	289	345	$9
15 SF *	4	4	5	73	70	2.27	1.62	0.87	543	509	562	3.8	1.6	8.6	5.3	65%	15%	40	20	40	25%	76%	8%	0	13			71	1.28	15.2	164	195	$12
1st Half	1	2	5	41	43	2.07	1.51	0.93	517	517	517	4.7	1.6	9.4	6.0	65%	15%	39	28	33	30%	75%	0%	0	17			83	0.96	9.6	195	231	$13
2nd Half	3	2	0	32	27	2.53	3.44	0.78	559	502	587	3.2	1.7	7.6	4.5	65%	15%	40	16	44	19%	76%	11%	0	12			0	1.44	5.6	109	130	$11
16 Proj	4	3	14	73	69	2.88	3.26	1.02	640	603	661	3.9	1.6	8.5	5.4	65%	15%	40	21	39	29%	74%	8%	0						9.6	129	154	$12

Stroman,Marcus

Age: 25	Th: R	Role: SP	Health: F	LIMA Plan: A
Ht: 5' 9"	Wt: 185	Type: xGB	PT/Exp: D	Rand Var: -5
			Consist: A	MM: 4203

Torn knee ligament derailed him in March. Scrambled back for pos-tseason drive in Sept and gave us a hint of what we missed. Top-tier Ctl/GB% combo projects to a high floor. Shows enough Dom to be a #2 or #3 now, with plenty of growth-age upside. Right now, durability is his only visible hurdle.

Yr Tm	W	L	Sv	IP	K	ERA	xERA	WHIP	oOPS	vL	vR	BF/G	Ctl	Dom	Cmd	FpK	SwK	G	L	F	H%	S%	hr/f	GS	APC	DOM%	DIS%	Sv%	LI	RAR	BPV	BPX	R$
11																																	
12																																	
13 aa	9	5	0	112	114	3.70	3.81	1.20				22.5	2.1	9.2	4.4						32%	74%								2.3	117	153	$6
14 TOR *	13	10	1	166	151	3.70	3.23	1.20	633	646	620	20.3	2.0	8.1	4.0	58%	9%	54	18	28	33%	69%	6%	20	80	65%	20%	100	0.84	0.8	124	147	$9
15 TOR	4	0	0	27	18	1.67	3.13	0.96	554	514	646	25.8	2.0	6.0	3.0	66%	8%	64	18	18	24%	88%	14%	4	93	75%	0%			7.6	96	114	$2
1st Half																																	
2nd Half	4	0	0	27	18	1.67	3.13	0.96	554	514	646	25.8	2.0	6.0	3.0	66%	8%	64	18	18	24%	88%	14%	4	93	75%	0%			7.6	96	114	$2
16 Proj	15	8	0	174	151	3.24	3.12	1.15	635	604	685	22.9	2.1	7.8	3.6	63%	8%	57	19	24	30%	73%	10%	30						15.4	118	140	$16

Strop,Pedro

Age: 31	Th: R	Role: RP	Health: C	LIMA Plan: B+
Ht: 6' 1"	Wt: 220	Type: Pwr GB	PT/Exp: C	Rand Var: -2
			Consist: A	MM: 5510

Aside from more S% volatility and FB spike—with a few more HR prodding his ERA—this effort was almost indistinguishable from 2014. Slowly improving FpK has helped Ctl settle in and complement rock-solid Dom, as top-shelf GB% remains intact. Prototypical LIMA pick; and you never know when Saves might find him.

Yr Tm	W	L	Sv	IP	K	ERA	xERA	WHIP	oOPS	vL	vR	BF/G	Ctl	Dom	Cmd	FpK	SwK	G	L	F	H%	S%	hr/f	GS	APC	DOM%	DIS%	Sv%	LI	RAR	BPV	BPX	R$
11 2 AL *	6	5	11	70	63	3.42	4.33	1.58	519	515	521	4.9	4.4	8.1	1.8	58%	10%	56	20	24	36%	78%	0%	0	16			73	1.12	4.5	77	116	$4
12 BAL	5	2	3	66	58	2.44	3.72	1.34	613	674	556	4.0	5.0	7.9	1.6	53%	11%	64	16	20	28%	82%	6%	0	16			30	1.25	12.9	48	63	$5
13 2 TM	2	5	1	57	66	4.55	3.24	1.24	663	653	671	3.8	4.1	10.4	2.5	55%	13%	49	26	26	29%	64%	14%	0	15			25	1.25	-4.9	103	135	-$2
14 CHC	2	4	2	61	71	2.21	2.65	1.07	535	621	478	3.8	3.7	10.5	2.8	56%	16%	55	24	21	27%	79%	7%	0	14			33	1.12	11.5	122	145	$6
15 CHC	2	6	3	68	81	2.91	2.98	1.00	538	641	475	3.6	3.8	10.7	2.8	58%	17%	51	20	29	23%	73%	11%	0	14			60	1.30	8.8	118	141	$7
1st Half	1	3	2	37	42	2.70	2.99	0.93	534	725	410	3.5	3.9	10.3	2.6	57%	16%	54	15	31	20%	74%	12%	0	14			67	1.27	5.7	111	132	$8
2nd Half	1	3	1	31	39	3.16	2.95	1.09	543	539	545	3.6	3.7	11.2	3.0	58%	18%	49	25	26	28%	72%	11%	0	14			50	1.35	3.1	127	151	$5
16 Proj	2	5	3	58	67	3.01	2.96	1.11	573	639	529	3.6	3.9	10.4	2.7	56%	15%	53	22	25	27%	74%	10%	0						6.8	112	134	$4

Syndergaard,Noah

Age: 23	Th: R	Role: SP	Health: A	LIMA Plan: C
Ht: 6' 6"	Wt: 240	Type: Pwr	PT/Exp: D	Rand Var: +1
			Consist: B	MM: 5405

9-7, 3.24 ERA in 150 IP at NYM. Highly anticipated debut from flame-throwing phenom who didn't disappoint. Late-season gopheritis was neutralized by dominance and GB tilt. Control, repertoire, poise and youth all point to sky-high ceiling, which could come quickly. With luck... UP: 18 wins, 2.50 ERA, 200 Ks.

Yr Tm	W	L	Sv	IP	K	ERA	xERA	WHIP	oOPS	vL	vR	BF/G	Ctl	Dom	Cmd	FpK	SwK	G	L	F	H%	S%	hr/f	GS	APC	DOM%	DIS%	Sv%	LI	RAR	BPV	BPX	R$
11																																	
12																																	
13 aa	6	1	0	54	63	3.04	3.42	1.09				19.2	1.8	10.4	5.7						31%	79%								5.5	151	197	$4
14 aaa	9	7	0	133	129	3.62	3.88	1.33				21.2	2.3	8.7	3.7						35%	73%								2.0	114	136	$3
15 NYM *	12	7	0	180	196	2.99	2.88	1.03	645	691	601	23.8	1.9	9.8	5.1	64%	13%	46	20	34	29%	76%	14%	24	99	63%	13%			21.5	145	173	$23
1st Half	6	4	0	88	89	2.83	2.84	1.08	661	614	705	23.0	2.0	9.0	4.6	65%	11%	46	21	33	30%	76%	9%	10	97	60%	20%			12.4	138	164	$21
2nd Half	6	3	0	91	107	3.15	2.84	0.97	635	740	527	25.6	1.9	10.5	5.6	64%	14%	47	19	34	27%	76%	18%	14	101	64%	7%			9.1	164	195	$25
16 Proj	15	8	0	198	211	3.06	3.04	1.12	653	697	609	22.0	2.1	9.6	4.7	64%	13%	46	20	34	31%	76%	11%	35						21.9	142	169	$22

Tanaka,Masahiro

Age: 27	Th: R	Role: SP	Health: F	LIMA Plan: C+
Ht: 6' 2"	Wt: 205	Type:	PT/Exp: A	Rand Var: 0
			Consist: A	MM: 4303

Forearm and wrist woes that shelved him for all of May looked like the beginning of the end, but elbow held up throughout 2nd half. And despite being more HR-prone, command and GB% remained near-vintage as velocity actually ticked up. Despite October surgery to remove bone spurs, skills say he's worthy of risk allocation.

Yr Tm	W	L	Sv	IP	K	ERA	xERA	WHIP	oOPS	vL	vR	BF/G	Ctl	Dom	Cmd	FpK	SwK	G	L	F	H%	S%	hr/f	GS	APC	DOM%	DIS%	Sv%	LI	RAR	BPV	BPX	R$
11 for	19	5	0	226	229	1.58	2.21	0.96				31.6	1.3	9.1	6.8						29%	87%								65.8	192	289	$44
12 for	10	4	0	173	160	2.33	2.97	1.13				31.1	1.2	8.3	6.8						34%	80%								36.0	185	242	$23
13 for	22	0	1	199	164	1.52	2.41	1.03				29.5	1.7	7.4	4.4						29%	88%								57.7	132	173	$38
14 NYY	13	5	0	136	141	2.77	2.76	1.06	657	632	687	27.1	1.4	9.3	6.7	62%	14%	47	24	29	31%	79%	14%	20	100	80%	5%			16.3	155	185	$16
15 NYY	12	7	0	154	139	3.51	3.34	0.99	674	697	654	25.4	1.6	8.1	5.1	63%	12%	47	19	34	25%	73%	17%	24	95	75%	4%			8.7	129	153	$17
1st Half	4	3	0	59	61	3.94	3.31	1.11	723	745	708	24.2	1.8	9.3	5.1	62%	13%	46	18	35	29%	71%	17%	10	90	60%	10%			0.1	142	168	$6
2nd Half	8	4	0	95	78	3.23	3.37	0.92	642	673	608	26.2	1.4	7.4	5.2	63%	11%	47	20	33	23%	74%	17%	14	99	86%	0%			8.5	120	143	$24
16 Proj	13	6	0	174	157	3.19	3.15	1.06	669	670	669	26.4	1.5	8.1	5.3	62%	13%	47	21	32	29%	75%	14%	26						16.6	130	155	$19

Tazawa,Junichi

Age: 30	Th: R	Role: RP	Health: B	LIMA Plan: C+
Ht: 5' 11"	Wt: 200	Type: Pwr	PT/Exp: C	Rand Var: +1
			Consist: A	MM: 3310

Long-time set-up man finally inherited August closing opportunity—with disastrous results. H% had already been running amok, but he began missing fewer bats and his control occasionally left the building. Fatigue was a factor, and sample size says he'll rebound at least a tad. But his LIMA star has lost some luster.

Yr Tm	W	L	Sv	IP	K	ERA	xERA	WHIP	oOPS	vL	vR	BF/G	Ctl	Dom	Cmd	FpK	SwK	G	L	F	H%	S%	hr/f	GS	APC	DOM%	DIS%	Sv%	LI	RAR	BPV	BPX	R$
11 BOS *	4	3	0	40	41	5.02	4.68	1.38	974	1500	722	8.9	2.5	9.1	3.6	46%	9%	13	0	88	35%	66%	14%	0	18			0	0.21	-5.4	93	139	-$2
12 BOS *	4	3	5	86	89	2.56	3.10	1.23	558	519	583	5.6	2.5	9.3	3.7	67%	15%	49	24	27	34%	79%	3%	0	18			63	0.82	15.5	126	165	$9
13 BOS	5	4	0	68	72	3.16	3.31	1.20	744	790	704	4.0	1.6	9.5	6.0	62%	13%	34	27	39	34%	79%	12%	0	15			0	1.09	5.9	140	182	$3
14 BOS	4	3	0	63	64	2.86	3.42	1.19	660	615	702	3.7	2.4	9.1	3.8	60%	12%	37	28	36	32%	79%	8%	0	15			0	1.34	6.9	114	136	$3
15 BOS	2	7	3	59	56	4.14	3.81	1.33	751	808	710	4.0	2.0	8.6	4.3	64%	12%	40	19	40	35%	70%	7%	0	16			30	1.17	-1.3	119	141	-$1
1st Half	0	3	0	35	38	2.55	3.10	0.99	560	572	552	3.8	1.8	9.7	5.4	66%	13%	45	18	37	29%	78%	9%	0	15			0	1.16	6.2	149	177	$2
2nd Half	2	4	3	23	18	6.56	4.94	1.84	1002	1113	922	4.5	2.3	6.9	3.0	61%	11%	35	20	45	42%	63%	5%	0	17			33	1.18	-7.5	75	89	-$7
16 Proj	4	4	1	58	56	3.59	3.55	1.24	712	739	691	4.0	2.1	8.6	4.0	62%	12%	39	23	38	33%	73%	8%	0						2.7	114	136	$1

JOCK THOMPSON

Teheran,Julio

			Health A	LIMA Plan B
Age: 25	Th: R	Role SP	PT/Exp A	Rand Var 0
Ht: 6' 2"	Wt: 200	Type Pwr	Consist A	MM 2205

FpK volatility warned of precarious Ctl and ERA despite two stellar years. Wavering 1H velocity chipped in, as Ks plunged and LD%, H%, hr/f all climbed. Dom and mph firmed up in the 2H, but Ctl and LHBs were season-long problems. Youth says he's still learning, and not yet the mainstay we once thought.

Yr Tm	W	L	Sv	IP	K	ERA	xERA	WHIP	oOPS	vL	vR	BF/G	Ctl	Dom	Cmd	FpK	SwK	G	L	F	H%	S%	hr/f	GS	APC	DOM%	DIS%	Sv%	LI	RAR	BPV	BPX	R$
11 ATL *	16	4	0	164	122	3.19	3.39	1.28	828	968	598	22.5	3.0	6.7	2.2	60%	7%	30	24	46	30%	76%	13%	3	70	0%	67%	0	0.72	15.2	76	115	$13
12 ATL *	7	9	0	137	92	5.55	5.16	1.49	467	250	579	21.1	2.7	6.0	2.2	52%	8%	22	33	44	33%	64%	0%	1	50	0%	100%	0	0.71	-26.0	44	58	-$12
13 ATL	14	8	0	186	170	3.20	3.67	1.17	700	823	580	25.8	2.2	8.2	3.8	65%	11%	38	21	41	30%	78%	10%	30	96	60%	10%			15.3	105	137	$16
14 ATL	14	13	0	221	186	2.89	3.73	1.08	639	687	587	26.8	2.1	7.6	3.6	60%	11%	35	21	44	28%	77%	8%	33	99	73%	6%			23.2	93	111	$22
15 ATL	11	8	0	201	171	4.04	4.15	1.31	737	893	583	25.5	3.3	7.7	2.3	57%	11%	40	24	36	29%	73%	13%	33	99	55%	15%			-1.8	68	81	$6
1st Half	6	4	0	102	78	4.60	4.35	1.41	793	893	709	25.5	3.2	6.9	2.2	58%	11%	39	26	34	31%	71%	13%	17	96	47%	12%			-8.0	56	66	-$1
2nd Half	5	4	0	99	93	3.45	3.95	1.20	678	894	427	25.6	3.4	8.5	2.5	56%	12%	40	21	39	27%	76%	13%	16	103	63%	19%			6.2	79	94	$12
16 Proj	**12**	**9**	**0**	**189**	**161**	**3.60**	**3.94**	**1.23**	**703**	**824**	**579**	**24.9**	**2.8**	**7.7**	**2.8**	**59%**	**11%**	**38**	**22**	**40**	**29%**	**75%**	**10%**	**31**						**8.5**	**79**	**94**	**$11**

Tepera,Ryan

			Health A	LIMA Plan D+
Age: 28	Th: R	Role RP	PT/Exp D	Rand Var -3
Ht: 6' 1"	Wt: 180	Type Pwr	Consist D	MM 1200

0-2, 3.27 ERA in 33 IP at TOR. Odd MLB debut was helped by unsustainable H%, hindered by unprecedented gopheritis. Slight GB tilt, promising FpK and mid-90s stuff are interesting in light of 1.06 ERA, 37 K in 34 IP at AAA. But minors history suggests he's not this good. The jury's out until we see more.

Yr Tm	W	L	Sv	IP	K	ERA	xERA	WHIP	oOPS	vL	vR	BF/G	Ctl	Dom	Cmd	FpK	SwK	G	L	F	H%	S%	hr/f	GS	APC	DOM%	DIS%	Sv%	LI	RAR	BPV	BPX	R$
11																																	
12 aa	7	3	0	74	46	6.40	6.13	1.88				21.8	4.7	5.6	1.2						37%	65%								-21.8	30	39	-$15
13 aa	10	8	1	116	85	5.48	5.15	1.62				15.6	4.5	6.6	1.5						33%	67%								-23.1	38	50	-$10
14 aaa	7	3	2	64	54	5.11	5.90	1.76				5.7	3.8	7.6	2.0						39%	71%								-10.8	55	66	-$6
15 TOR *	3	3	4	67	51	2.48	2.72	1.01	670	568	746	4.8	2.9	6.9	2.3	64%	10%	45	16	38	21%	85%	22%	0	15			80	0.50	12.3	68	81	$8
1st Half	1	1	0	36	29	1.42	1.64	0.85	593	620	571	5.2	2.7	7.4	2.8	69%	9%	40	29	31	19%	92%	15%	0	15			0	0.38	11.2	98	116	$9
2nd Half	2	2	4	31	22	3.69	3.95	1.18	734	535	930	4.5	3.2	6.3	1.9	60%	10%	49	7	44	23%	78%	25%	0	14			80	0.60	1.1	37	43	$6
16 Proj	**3**	**2**	**0**	**44**	**34**	**3.74**	**4.30**	**1.35**	**740**	**636**	**818**	**6.2**	**3.6**	**7.0**	**1.9**	**63%**	**10%**	**46**	**16**	**39**	**29%**	**76%**	**11%**	**0**						**1.2**	**53**	**63**	**-$2**

Thornburg,Tyler

			Health F	LIMA Plan D+
Age: 27	Th: R	Role RP	PT/Exp D	Rand Var 0
Ht: 5' 11"	Wt: 190	Type Pwr FB	Consist C	MM 1200

0-2, 3.67 ERA in 34 IP at MIL. Volatility still plagues once-promising prospect. Posted 5.28 ERA, 1.6 Cmd in 17 starts at AAA-Colorado Springs before improving to 2.8 Cmd as MLB RP. Role change and less altitude likely agreed with him. But erratic FpK and hr/f histories combined with lofty FB, LD rates are instructive.

Yr Tm	W	L	Sv	IP	K	ERA	xERA	WHIP	oOPS	vL	vR	BF/G	Ctl	Dom	Cmd	FpK	SwK	G	L	F	H%	S%	hr/f	GS	APC	DOM%	DIS%	Sv%	LI	RAR	BPV	BPX	R$
11																																	
12 MIL *	10	4	0	135	116	4.17	4.45	1.37	922	757	1071	19.5	3.1	7.8	2.5	53%	8%	42	20	38	31%	73%	32%	3	48	0%	100%	0	0.42	-2.5	66	86	$1
13 MIL *	3	10	0	141	121	4.43	4.64	1.50	575	479	684	18.5	3.6	7.7	2.2	60%	7%	36	24	39	34%	72%	1%	7	59	86%	0%	0	0.52	-9.8	64	84	-$7
14 MIL	3	1	0	30	28	4.25	4.91	1.52	670	458	808	4.9	6.4	8.5	1.3	54%	11%	36	19	45	29%	70%	3%	0	19			0	0.94	-1.9	-5	-6	-$3
15 MIL *	2	9	0	123	79	5.53	6.75	1.69	723	741	709	13.5	3.7	5.8	1.6	61%	10%	35	24	41	33%	73%	17%	0	27			0	0.73	-23.8	0	0	-$17
1st Half	1	5	0	76	41	6.18	7.77	1.93	1014	1056	991	19.0	4.1	4.8	1.2	69%	8%	33	26	41	36%	72%	19%	0	34			0	0.18	-20.8	-16	-19	-$26
2nd Half	1	4	0	47	39	4.48	5.10	1.31	575	603	552	8.8	3.2	7.4	2.3	57%	10%	37	22	41	26%	76%	15%	0	25			0	0.92	-3.0	31	37	-$3
16 Proj	**1**	**3**	**0**	**44**	**36**	**4.11**	**4.43**	**1.47**	**805**	**778**	**829**	**14.1**	**3.5**	**7.5**	**2.1**	**58%**	**9%**	**36**	**23**	**41**	**32%**	**75%**	**10%**	**5**						**-0.8**	**55**	**65**	**-$4**

Tillman,Chris

			Health A	LIMA Plan D+
Age: 28	Th: R	Role SP	PT/Exp A	Rand Var +1
Ht: 6' 5"	Wt: 210	Type	Consist A	MM 1103

A poorer 1H start than in 2014, but this time he couldn't gain much 2H traction. Remove the year-long S% woes and H% swings, and little has changed. Both FpK and SwK remain consistent and mediocre. His bottom line should improve, but if you bet on a rebound to prior profitability, you're rolling the dice.

Yr Tm	W	L	Sv	IP	K	ERA	xERA	WHIP	oOPS	vL	vR	BF/G	Ctl	Dom	Cmd	FpK	SwK	G	L	F	H%	S%	hr/f	GS	APC	DOM%	DIS%	Sv%	LI	RAR	BPV	BPX	R$
11 BAL *	6	11	0	138	91	5.94	6.08	1.65	812	797	833	22.1	4.1	5.9	1.4	53%	6%	37	18	45	32%	68%	5%	13	90	31%	54%			-34.1	12	18	-$15
12 BAL *	17	12	0	179	143	4.02	3.95	1.31	639	601	701	23.0	2.9	7.2	2.4	55%	9%	35	21	44	30%	72%	11%	15	96	60%	20%			-0.1	70	91	$8
13 BAL	16	7	0	206	179	3.71	3.87	1.22	730	744	711	25.6	3.0	7.8	2.6	57%	9%	39	22	40	27%	76%	14%	33	105	52%	15%			4.0	77	101	$13
14 BAL	13	6	0	207	150	3.34	4.21	1.23	671	670	672	25.6	2.9	6.5	2.3	58%	8%	41	20	39	28%	76%	8%	34	100	41%	15%			10.2	59	70	$11
15 BAL	11	11	0	173	120	4.99	4.58	1.39	763	698	828	23.9	3.3	6.2	1.9	58%	8%	43	21	35	30%	65%	10%	31	95	29%	32%			-22.0	43	52	-$5
1st Half	6	7	0	84	60	5.57	5.02	1.56	827	718	963	23.1	4.0	6.4	1.6	55%	8%	39	20	40	32%	65%	9%	16	92	19%	44%			-16.7	26	31	-$12
2nd Half	5	4	0	89	60	4.45	4.17	1.22	700	674	719	24.7	2.7	6.1	2.2	60%	7%	47	22	31	27%	66%	12%	15	98	40%	20%			-5.3	61	72	$1
16 Proj	**11**	**9**	**0**	**174**	**127**	**4.34**	**4.29**	**1.32**	**734**	**704**	**768**	**24.0**	**3.1**	**6.6**	**2.1**	**58%**	**8%**	**42**	**21**	**37**	**29%**	**70%**	**11%**	**30**						**-8.1**	**53**	**63**	**$2**

Tolleson,Shawn

			Health F	LIMA Plan C+
Age: 28	Th: R	Role RP	PT/Exp C	Rand Var -1
Ht: 6' 2"	Wt: 210	Type Pwr	Consist F	MM 3430

Was building on nice 2014 as 9th inning opened up, and the stars aligned. Ctl gains propelled 1st half—with fine FpK throughout—as Dom shined afterward. 2nd half HR cut into ERA, but with minimal damage. Modest GB%, MLB track record are cautions, and he's not lights-out elite. But his role and high floor are good things.

Yr Tm	W	L	Sv	IP	K	ERA	xERA	WHIP	oOPS	vL	vR	BF/G	Ctl	Dom	Cmd	FpK	SwK	G	L	F	H%	S%	hr/f	GS	APC	DOM%	DIS%	Sv%	LI	RAR	BPV	BPX	R$
11 aa	4	2	12	44	47	1.65	3.22	1.22				4.7	2.0	9.5	4.7						35%	88%								12.6	147	222	$9
12 LA *	3	2	5	60	67	3.75	3.19	1.19	698	988	485	4.1	3.7	10.1	2.7	67%	12%	38	22	40	28%	72%	10%	0	16			100	0.65	1.9	99	129	$3
13 LA	0	0	0	0	0	0.00	0.00	0.00		0	1000	2.0	0.0	0.0	0.0						0%	100%	0%	0	11			0	0.70	0.0	-22	-29	-$5
14 TEX	3	1	0	72	69	2.76	3.80	1.17	659	643	672	4.6	3.5	8.7	2.5	56%	10%	40	18	42	26%	84%	12%	0	18			0	0.75	8.6	79	94	$4
15 TEX	6	4	35	72	76	2.99	3.40	1.15	675	705	638	4.1	2.1	9.5	4.5	66%	11%	42	21	37	31%	80%	12%	0	16			95	1.24	8.7	133	159	$20
1st Half	2	1	12	35	35	2.60	3.34	1.07	634	665	592	4.1	1.8	9.1	5.0	66%	12%	41	21	37	30%	79%	9%	0	16			100	1.33	5.8	134	159	$15
2nd Half	4	3	23	38	41	3.35	3.45	1.22	711	744	674	4.1	2.4	9.8	4.1	66%	10%	43	20	37	32%	80%	16%	0	16			92	1.16	2.9	133	158	$24
16 Proj	**5**	**3**	**38**	**65**	**68**	**3.21**	**3.43**	**1.17**	**649**	**694**	**607**	**4.1**	**2.7**	**9.4**	**3.4**	**62%**	**10%**	**41**	**20**	**39**	**31%**	**75%**	**9%**	**0**						**6.0**	**114**	**136**	**$18**

Tomlin,Josh

			Health F	LIMA Plan B+
Age: 31	Th: R	Role SP	PT/Exp D	Rand Var +1
Ht: 6' 1"	Wt: 190	Type FB	Consist D	MM 2203

7-2, 3.02 ERA in 66 IP at CLE. Shoulder woes shelved him until mid-August, when 57/8 K/BB fueled down-the-stretch fantasy windfall. H% luck and LD% avoidance helped, along with unprecedented success vL—a combo unlikely to repeat. Cmd is a legit skill, but history of health and HR issues keep him an end-game speculation.

Yr Tm	W	L	Sv	IP	K	ERA	xERA	WHIP	oOPS	vL	vR	BF/G	Ctl	Dom	Cmd	FpK	SwK	G	L	F	H%	S%	hr/f	GS	APC	DOM%	DIS%	Sv%	LI	RAR	BPV	BPX	R$
11 CLE	12	7	0	165	89	4.25	4.04	1.08	712	753	666	25.5	1.1	4.8	4.2	65%	8%	38	22	40	26%	65%	11%	26	91	42%	4%			-6.2	72	109	$9
12 CLE	5	8	0	103	56	6.36	4.82	1.46	860	945	768	21.5	2.2	4.9	2.2	64%	8%	42	21	37	31%	59%	13%	16	77	25%	31%	0	0.89	-29.9	49	64	-$13
13 CLE *	2	0	0	23	11	2.52	1.91	0.92	500	0	667	14.3	0.0	4.4	0.0	67%	8%	38	0	63	28%	69%	0%	0	36			0	0.23	3.8	0	0	$0
14 CLE *	8	10	0	144	119	4.24	4.54	1.24	781	718	848	18.8	1.6	7.4	4.8	68%	10%	37	27	36	31%	71%	15%	16	69	50%	25%	0	0.94	-8.9	100	119	$2
15 CLE *	8	4	0	90	71	3.73	4.04	1.07	642	448	838	23.3	1.0	7.1	6.9	66%	10%	38	16	46	27%	75%	15%	10	95	80%	10%			2.6	140	167	$6
1st Half																																	
2nd Half	8	4	0	90	71	3.73	4.04	1.07	642	448	838	23.3	1.0	7.1	6.9	66%	10%	38	16	46	27%	75%	15%	10	95	80%	10%			2.6	140	166	$6
16 Proj	**9**	**8**	**0**	**145**	**113**	**3.96**	**3.79**	**1.17**	**726**	**696**	**757**	**23.9**	**1.5**	**7.0**	**4.5**	**66%**	**9%**	**39**	**21**	**40**	**30%**	**71%**	**11%**	**24**						**0.1**	**101**	**120**	**$6**

Treinen,Blake

			Health A	LIMA Plan C
Age: 28	Th: R	Role RP	PT/Exp D	Rand Var +2
Ht: 6' 5"	Wt: 215	Type Pwr xGB	Consist B	MM 3110

Something in the WAS water? Prototypical late-inning candidate finally showed Dom consistent with power stuff; even grew his already top-shelf GB%. But 1st half H% blocked a breakout, while control and effectiveness vL deteriorated all season. FpK is optimistic and skills keep us attentive. But he has lots to prove.

Yr Tm	W	L	Sv	IP	K	ERA	xERA	WHIP	oOPS	vL	vR	BF/G	Ctl	Dom	Cmd	FpK	SwK	G	L	F	H%	S%	hr/f	GS	APC	DOM%	DIS%	Sv%	LI	RAR	BPV	BPX	R$
11																																	
12																																	
13 aa	6	7	0	119	68	4.60	5.14	1.55				24.7	2.5	5.1	2.0						34%	71%								-10.7	43	56	-$8
14 WAS *	10	5	0	131	79	3.46	4.10	1.40	678	798	564	17.9	2.3	5.4	2.4	57%	8%	59	22	19	33%	75%	3%	7	49	43%	14%	0	0.56	4.5	69	82	$1
15 WAS	2	5	0	68	65	3.86	3.24	1.39	692	934	493	4.7	4.3	8.6	2.0	59%	11%	63	22	15	32%	72%	15%	0	17			0	0.93	0.9	82	97	-$2
1st Half	2	2	0	38	41	3.79	2.91	1.39	706	909	494	5.6	3.8	9.7	2.6	58%	12%	65	22	14	35%	73%	14%	0	20			0	0.86	0.8	115	137	-$1
2nd Half	0	3	0	30	24	3.94	3.70	1.38	673	980	491	3.8	4.9	7.3	1.5	60%	10%	60	23	17	28%	72%	15%	0	14			0	1.00	0.1	38	45	-$3
16 Proj	**3**	**4**	**2**	**65**	**49**	**3.83**	**3.64**	**1.42**	**716**	**927**	**540**	**7.4**	**3.4**	**6.8**	**2.0**	**58%**	**10%**	**61**	**22**	**17**	**32%**	**73%**	**11%**	**0**						**1.0**	**69**	**82**	**-$1**

JOCK THOMPSON

Tropeano,Nicholas

Age: 25	Th: R	Role SP	Health A	LIMA Plan B+
Ht: 6' 4"	Wt: 205	Type Pwr FB	PT/Exp D	Rand Var 0
			Consist F	MM 1201

3-2, 3.82 ERA in 38 IP at LAA. Shaky sample, but sharp improvements in Dom and Ctl at the MLB level were well-supported by SwK and FpK spikes. Solid fastball (avg. velocity, OK SwK) sets up plus secondary pitches. Components are all there for mid-rotation value, just needs MLB IP at this point.

Yr Tm	W	L	Sv	IP	K	ERA	xERA	WHIP	oOPS	vL	vR	BF/G	Ctl	Dom	Cmd	FpK	SwK	G	L	F	H%	S%	hr/f	GS	APC	DOM%	DIS%	Sv%	LI	RAR	BPV	BPX	R$
11																																	
12																																	
13 aa	7	10	5	134	113	4.69	4.95	1.46				20.4	2.6	7.6	2.9						35%	70%								-13.6	71	92	-$4
14 HOU *	10	8	0	146	115	3.46	2.72	1.09	626	648	576	21.2	2.5	7.1	2.8	54%	9%	40	13	46	26%	70%	0%	4	92	50%	25%			5.1	91	109	$10
15 LAA *	6	8	0	126	117	4.43	4.50	1.47	700	712	686	22.4	3.0	8.4	2.8	64%	12%	39	21	40	36%	70%	5%	7	81	43%	43%	0	0.68	-7.2	87	104	-$4
1st Half	3	2	0	50	41	4.39	4.10	1.38	511	665	300	23.3	2.6	7.3	2.9	58%	11%	50	11	39	34%	68%	0%	1	97	100%	0%			-2.6	86	101	-$4
2nd Half	3	6	0	76	77	4.45	4.76	1.52	734	722	746	21.9	3.3	9.1	2.8	65%	12%	36	23	41	37%	71%	5%	6	79	33%	50%	0	0.67	-4.6	89	105	-$4
16 Proj	**6**	**6**	**0**	**102**	**88**	**4.10**	**4.13**	**1.33**	**656**	**652**	**661**	**21.7**	**2.7**	**7.8**	**2.9**	**65%**	**12%**	**36**	**23**	**41**	**33%**	**70%**	**6%**	**19**						**-1.7**	**81**	**97**	**$0**

Uehara,Koji

Age: 41	Th: R	Role RP	Health F	LIMA Plan B+
Ht: 6' 2"	Wt: 195	Type Pwr xFB	PT/Exp B	Rand Var -4
			Consist B	MM 4530

Fantasy hot potato who gets tougher to project with each passing year. PRO: Rock-solid SwK; best FpK yet; no platoon split; maintained WHIP. CON: Age; Health (hamstring, wrist in '15); dwindling IP; Cmd halved; Ctl doubled; FB lean makes hr/f suspect. Music could stop at any moment, which would mean DN: 10 Sv.

Yr Tm	W	L	Sv	IP	K	ERA	xERA	WHIP	oOPS	vL	vR	BF/G	Ctl	Dom	Cmd	FpK	SwK	G	L	F	H%	S%	hr/f	GS	APC	DOM%	DIS%	Sv%	LI	RAR	BPV	BPX	R$
11 2 AL	2	3	0	65	85	2.35	2.61	0.72	535	472	597	3.7	1.2	11.8	9.4	67%	17%	32	14	53	22%	83%	14%	0	14			0	1.06	12.7	188	283	$10
12 TEX	0	0	1	36	43	1.75	2.74	0.64	466	545	369	3.5	0.8	10.8	14.3	67%	19%	33	17	51	21%	84%	10%	0	14			100	0.66	10.1	184	240	$5
13 BOS	4	1	21	74	101	1.09	2.24	0.57	400	338	466	3.6	1.1	12.2	11.2	70%	20%	40	11	48	20%	89%	7%	0	14			88	1.34	25.5	209	272	$27
14 BOS	6	5	26	64	80	2.52	2.70	0.92	629	613	650	3.9	1.1	11.2	10.0	64%	20%	32	23	45	29%	84%	14%	0	15			84	1.48	9.7	181	216	$18
15 BOS	2	4	25	40	47	2.23	3.54	0.92	562	507	614	3.7	2.0	10.5	5.2	73%	20%	27	17	56	27%	79%	5%	0	15			93	1.38	8.6	140	166	$14
1st Half	2	3	19	30	32	2.70	3.68	0.93	575	492	652	3.6	1.8	9.6	5.3	70%	19%	30	16	53	28%	73%	5%	0	14			90	1.41	4.7	133	157	$17
2nd Half	0	1	6	10	15	0.87	3.17	0.87	522	549	491	4.0	2.6	13.1	5.0	83%	21%	14	19	67	26%	100%	7%	0	17			100	1.27	3.9	157	186	$4
16 Proj	**3**	**3**	**26**	**52**	**60**	**2.78**	**3.07**	**0.95**	**599**	**557**	**645**	**3.7**	**1.8**	**10.4**	**5.8**	**68%**	**19%**	**34**	**16**	**50**	**28%**	**75%**	**8%**	**0**						**7.6**	**151**	**180**	**$15**

Urena,Jose

Age: 24	Th: R	Role RP	Health B	LIMA Plan D+
Ht: 6' 2"	Wt: 195	Type Con	PT/Exp D	Rand Var -1
			Consist B	MM 0001

1-5, 5.25 ERA in 62 IP at MIA. Minors work (6.4 Dom, 2.0 Ctl in 702 IP) said Ctl would be key; when it tanked (3.6 in MLB), the results fit. Elements of intrigue: 95+ mph, SwK says Dom was low, good slider and changeup both showed promise. Seeds of something here, needs time to sew raw materials together.

Yr Tm	W	L	Sv	IP	K	ERA	xERA	WHIP	oOPS	vL	vR	BF/G	Ctl	Dom	Cmd	FpK	SwK	G	L	F	H%	S%	hr/f	GS	APC	DOM%	DIS%	Sv%	LI	RAR	BPV	BPX	R$
11																																	
12																																	
13																																	
14 aa	13	8	0	162	100	3.78	3.82	1.24				25.3	1.6	5.6	3.5						31%	71%								-0.7	87	104	$5
15 MIA *	7	6	0	129	61	4.34	4.77	1.53	818	871	777	18.1	3.1	4.3	1.4	58%	9%	48	20	32	32%	72%	7%	9	50	33%	33%	0	0.59	-6.0	31	37	-$6
1st Half	6	4	0	89	40	2.60	3.62	1.33	750	699	798	23.0	3.1	4.1	1.3	59%	8%	53	18	28	28%	82%	10%	7	75	43%	29%	0	0.65	14.9	40	47	$3
2nd Half	1	2	0	41	21	8.13	7.25	1.96	947	1307	746	13.0	3.2	4.7	1.5	56%	9%	39	23	38	40%	57%	3%	2	29	0%	50%	0	0.55	-20.9	15	17	-$27
16 Proj	**4**	**3**	**0**	**73**	**39**	**4.79**	**4.67**	**1.51**	**814**	**980**	**703**	**18.2**	**2.5**	**4.9**	**2.0**	**57%**	**9%**	**45**	**21**	**34**	**34%**	**68%**	**7%**	**14**						**-7.4**	**43**	**51**	**-$6**

Velasquez,Vincent

Age: 24	Th: R	Role RP	Health A	LIMA Plan B+
Ht: 6' 3"	Wt: 205	Type Pwr xFB	PT/Exp F	Rand Var 0
			Consist F	MM 2501

1-1, 4.37 ERA in 56 IP at HOU. Just 77 IP in '14 limited him to swingman role. Skills held firm as SP and RP; Ctl will drive success: 3.4 w/HOU followed minors path (3.1), but FpK is promising. Arsenal points to bright future: big fastball, great changeup, strikeout curve. Could come quickly. UP: sub-3.50 ERA

Yr Tm	W	L	Sv	IP	K	ERA	xERA	WHIP	oOPS	vL	vR	BF/G	Ctl	Dom	Cmd	FpK	SwK	G	L	F	H%	S%	hr/f	GS	APC	DOM%	DIS%	Sv%	LI	RAR	BPV	BPX	R$
11																																	
12																																	
13																																	
14																																	
15 HOU *	5	1	0	89	97	3.55	3.02	1.20	720	644	808	12.7	3.4	9.9	2.9	61%	11%	31	22	47	30%	72%	7%	7	51	57%	29%	0	0.64	4.5	108	128	$4
1st Half	3	0	0	52	58	2.87	2.52	1.15	714	693	750	20.6	3.6	10.1	2.8	64%	9%	22	22	56	29%	76%	5%	5	92	40%	40%			7.0	116	138	$7
2nd Half	2	1	0	37	39	4.52	3.73	1.27	724	591	843	8.3	3.2	9.6	3.0	59%	12%	39	22	39	31%	66%	9%	2	37	100%	0%	0	0.59	-2.5	96	114	$0
16 Proj	**6**	**2**	**0**	**116**	**126**	**3.83**	**3.74**	**1.23**	**696**	**616**	**786**	**10.9**	**3.4**	**9.8**	**2.9**	**61%**	**11%**	**32**	**22**	**46**	**31%**	**71%**	**7%**	**4**						**1.9**	**95**	**113**	**$5**

Ventura,Yordano

Age: 25	Th: R	Role SP	Health B	LIMA Plan B
Ht: 6' 0"	Wt: 180	Type Pwr GB	PT/Exp B	Rand Var +1
			Consist A	MM 3305

Early-season struggles exacerbated by dust-ups with opposing teams. Officially demoted in mid-July, but returned immediately to fill injury void. Threat alone may have worked: 5.19 ERA, 7.7 Dom before, 3.10 ERA, 9.4 Dom after. It's coming along... and the electric 2nd half points toward UP: 200 Ks

Yr Tm	W	L	Sv	IP	K	ERA	xERA	WHIP	oOPS	vL	vR	BF/G	Ctl	Dom	Cmd	FpK	SwK	G	L	F	H%	S%	hr/f	GS	APC	DOM%	DIS%	Sv%	LI	RAR	BPV	BPX	R$
11																																	
12 aa	1	2	0	29	21	5.20	2.98	1.28				20.1	3.8	6.5	1.7						28%	56%								-4.3	74	97	-$4
13 KC *	8	7	0	150	140	3.71	3.76	1.37	693	687	700	21.7	3.5	8.4	2.4	53%	8%	49	15	36	33%	74%	18%	3	81	33%	33%			2.9	86	112	$3
14 KC	14	10	0	183	159	3.20	3.78	1.30	669	642	705	25.2	3.4	7.8	2.3	61%	11%	48	21	31	30%	77%	8%	30	96	60%	17%	0	0.77	12.3	75	89	$10
15 KC	13	8	0	163	156	4.08	3.56	1.30	698	734	658	24.8	3.2	8.6	2.7	60%	11%	52	21	27	31%	70%	11%	28	95	54%	21%			-2.3	98	117	$6
1st Half	3	6	0	67	54	4.68	3.70	1.26	731	832	625	23.1	2.8	7.2	2.6	58%	9%	52	20	28	30%	64%	13%	12	88	50%	33%			-5.9	84	100	-$4
2nd Half	10	2	0	96	102	3.66	3.45	1.32	676	671	681	26.0	3.5	9.6	2.8	61%	12%	52	21	27	33%	73%	10%	16	99	56%	13%			3.6	109	129	$13
16 Proj	**15**	**10**	**0**	**196**	**181**	**3.71**	**3.60**	**1.31**	**689**	**697**	**679**	**23.7**	**3.3**	**8.3**	**2.5**	**60%**	**11%**	**50**	**21**	**29**	**31%**	**73%**	**10%**	**34**						**6.1**	**88**	**105**	**$10**

Verlander,Justin

Age: 33	Th: R	Role SP	Health D	LIMA Plan B
Ht: 6' 5"	Wt: 225	Type Pwr FB	PT/Exp A	Rand Var -1
			Consist A	MM 2205

Out with triceps injury until mid-June. After '14, his first 6 starts (6.62 ERA, 1.8 Cmd) looked like the nail in the coffin. Then resurrected ace form (2.27 ERA, 4.6 Cmd thereafter) by establishing fastball up in the zone. Skills are fully believable, but once-elite Health grade now preaches caution.

Yr Tm	W	L	Sv	IP	K	ERA	xERA	WHIP	oOPS	vL	vR	BF/G	Ctl	Dom	Cmd	FpK	SwK	G	L	F	H%	S%	hr/f	GS	APC	DOM%	DIS%	Sv%	LI	RAR	BPV	BPX	R$
11 DET	24	5	0	251	250	2.40	3.14	0.92	555	504	617	28.5	2.0	9.0	4.4	61%	11%	40	18	42	25%	79%	9%	34	116	88%	0%			47.7	124	187	$45
12 DET	17	8	0	238	239	2.64	3.35	1.06	601	608	593	29.0	2.3	9.0	4.0	61%	12%	42	22	36	29%	78%	8%	33	114	79%	3%			40.3	121	158	$36
13 DET	13	12	0	218	217	3.46	3.75	1.31	691	658	739	27.2	3.1	8.9	2.9	65%	11%	38	23	39	33%	76%	8%	34	109	65%	9%			10.9	94	122	$11
14 DET	15	12	0	206	159	4.54	4.27	1.40	756	686	849	27.9	2.8	6.9	2.4	62%	9%	40	20	41	33%	68%	7%	32	107	56%	9%			-20.4	66	79	-$3
15 DET	5	8	0	133	113	3.38	4.04	1.09	634	620	650	26.8	2.2	7.6	3.5	64%	10%	35	20	46	28%	72%	7%	20	108	70%	5%			9.7	92	110	$9
1st Half	0	2	0	23	12	6.75	5.84	1.59	895	976	807	26.3	4.0	4.8	1.2	64%	7%	38	18	44	28%	63%	17%	4	100	0%	0%			-7.8	-5	-6	-$24
2nd Half	5	6	0	111	101	2.68	3.71	0.98	574	541	612	26.9	1.8	8.2	4.6	64%	11%	34	20	46	27%	75%	5%	16	109	88%	6%			17.5	111	132	$16
16 Proj	**12**	**10**	**0**	**189**	**163**	**3.78**	**3.92**	**1.23**	**703**	**682**	**728**	**26.2**	**2.5**	**7.8**	**3.1**	**63%**	**10%**	**37**	**20**	**42**	**30%**	**73%**	**9%**	**29**						**4.3**	**88**	**105**	**$10**

Villarreal,Pedro

Age: 28	Th: R	Role RP	Health A	LIMA Plan C
Ht: 6' 1"	Wt: 230	Type Con	PT/Exp D	Rand Var 0
			Consist C	MM 1000

1-3, 3.42 ERA in 50 IP at CIN. Skills are capable (Ctl, FpK say he's a strike-thrower) of knocking around as an MLB swingman or long reliever. Something to stifle lefties would really help, but the lack of a standout pitch at this age will keep him from the fantasy-relevant roles.

Yr Tm	W	L	Sv	IP	K	ERA	xERA	WHIP	oOPS	vL	vR	BF/G	Ctl	Dom	Cmd	FpK	SwK	G	L	F	H%	S%	hr/f	GS	APC	DOM%	DIS%	Sv%	LI	RAR	BPV	BPX	R$
11 aa	7	4	0	92	58	4.43	4.22	1.27				22.0	1.8	5.6	3.1						30%	68%								-5.5	66	100	$0
12 CIN *	4	14	0	150	90	5.71	5.56	1.59	0	0	0	24.4	2.4	5.4	2.2	100%	17%	0	0	100	35%	64%	0%	0	12			0	0.02	-31.2	43	55	-$18
13 CIN *	4	10	2	115	73	6.42	7.10	1.68	1397	1300	1471	14.8	2.7	5.7	2.1	56%	7%	28	24	48	34%	67%	33%	1	61	0%	100%	50	0.41	-36.4	1	2	-$18
14 CIN *	6	4	2	71	53	3.76	4.44	1.38	627	745	570	5.5	2.6	6.7	2.6	52%	10%	36	26	38	32%	75%	6%	0	18			33	1.11	-0.2	66	78	$0
15 CIN *	2	3	1	76	46	4.13	4.66	1.43	778	825	745	6.7	2.0	5.4	2.7	65%	9%	42	23	35	34%	72%	10%	0	27			100	0.68	-1.6	64	76	-$4
1st Half	2	2	1	44	23	4.72	4.92	1.54	860	745	921	6.6	2.2	4.7	2.1	60%	6%	43	29	29	35%	68%	11%	0	27			100	0.59	-4.1	52	62	-$7
2nd Half	0	1	0	32	23	3.34	4.20	1.27	732	861	632	7.2	1.7	6.4	3.8	67%	10%	42	20	38	31%	78%	10%	0	27			0	0.72	2.5	90	107	-$1
16 Proj	**2**	**3**	**0**	**58**	**38**	**4.37**	**4.29**	**1.43**	**800**	**838**	**775**	**7.5**	**2.2**	**6.0**	**2.7**	**64%**	**9%**	**42**	**23**	**34**	**33%**	**72%**	**10%**	**0**						**-2.9**	**67**	**80**	**-$4**

PAUL SPORER

Vizcaino,Arodys

Age: 25 Th: R Role RP	Health F	LIMA Plan B	Elite velocity (98 mph) sets up his unhittable curve (.250 OPS, 21 Ks in 46 PA), a combo that had him closing a month after his July 7 debut. Ctl remains his primary flaw, and low hr/f was lucky given FB lean, so don't ignore that elevated xERA. But with health, there's UP: 35 SVs.
Ht: 6' 0" Wt: 190 Type Pwr FB	PT/Exp D	Rand Var -5	
	Consist C	MM 2520	

Yr	Tm	W	L	Sv	IP	K	ERA	xERA	WHIP	oOPS	vL	vR	BF/G	Ctl	Dom	Cmd	FpK	SwK	G	L	F	H%	S%	hr/f	GS	APC	DOM%	DIS%	Sv%	LI	RAR	BPV	BPX	R$
11	ATL *	4	4	0	74	74	4.04	3.58	1.32	636	696	593	9.0	3.2	9.0	2.8	56%	9%	35	17	48	33%	69%	4%	0	19			0	1.28	-0.9	99	148	$1
12																																		
13																																		
14	CHC *	1	1	1	37	31	4.91	4.85	1.58	837	200	1318	4.5	4.2	7.6	1.8	59%	7%	40	20	40	34%	69%	17%	0	19			50	0.02	-5.3	59	70	-$5
15	ATL	3	1	9	34	37	1.60	3.67	1.19	615	583	641	3.9	3.5	9.9	2.8	58%	12%	35	28	37	31%	87%	3%	0	15			90	1.12	9.8	97	116	$6
1st Half																																		
2nd Half		3	1	9	34	37	1.60	3.67	1.19	615	583	641	3.9	3.5	9.9	2.8	58%	12%	35	28	37	31%	87%	3%	0	15			90	1.12	9.8	97	115	$6
16	**Proj**	**4**	**3**	**20**	**65**	**73**	**3.11**	**3.68**	**1.33**	**656**	**600**	**701**	**5.2**	**3.5**	**10.1**	**2.9**	**58%**	**12%**	**35**	**28**	**37**	**34%**	**77%**	**5%**	**0**						**6.9**	**99**	**118**	**$10**

Vogelsong,Ryan

Age: 38 Th: R Role SP	Health D	LIMA Plan C	Ctl took Cmd back below 2.0, eliminating his appeal everywhere. 2H xERA less meaningful when half was from the bullpen. Dom did spike to 8.7 in six 2H starts, but results didn't follow as four were PQS-0s. He lived on the margins when he was good and now at 38, he'll struggle to generate positive value again.
Ht: 6' 4" Wt: 215 Type Pwr	PT/Exp A	Rand Var 0	
	Consist B	MM 1201	

Yr	Tm	W	L	Sv	IP	K	ERA	xERA	WHIP	oOPS	vL	vR	BF/G	Ctl	Dom	Cmd	FpK	SwK	G	L	F	H%	S%	hr/f	GS	APC	DOM%	DIS%	Sv%	LI	RAR	BPV	BPX	R$
11	SF	13	7	0	180	139	2.71	3.85	1.25	671	727	626	25.1	3.1	7.0	2.3	62%	8%	46	20	34	29%	81%	8%	28	98	61%	7%	0	0.75	27.4	67	100	$16
12	SF	14	9	0	190	158	3.37	4.02	1.23	688	722	653	25.4	2.9	7.5	2.5	61%	8%	44	18	38	29%	75%	8%	31	99	61%	13%			15.1	78	101	$15
13	SF	4	6	0	104	67	5.73	4.62	1.56	840	736	928	24.6	3.3	5.8	1.8	60%	6%	41	27	32	33%	65%	13%	19	92	26%	32%			-23.8	35	45	-$12
14	SF	8	13	0	185	151	4.00	3.95	1.28	730	787	675	24.4	2.8	7.4	2.6	62%	8%	38	24	37	30%	71%	9%	32	96	50%	13%			-5.8	72	86	$3
15	SF	9	11	0	135	108	4.67	4.62	1.47	781	906	679	18.1	3.9	7.2	1.9	60%	7%	45	19	36	31%	71%	11%	22	70	50%	41%	0	0.82	-11.7	48	57	-$4
1st Half		6	6	0	90	65	4.10	4.79	1.38	738	869	640	23.1	3.9	6.5	1.7	61%	5%	44	19	37	28%	74%	12%	15	87	60%	33%	0	0.73	-1.5	33	39	$0
2nd Half		3	5	0	45	43	5.80	4.28	1.64	862	970	762	12.8	3.8	8.6	2.3	58%	9%	47	19	34	37%	65%	10%	7	52	29%	57%	0	0.92	-10.2	77	91	-$12
16	**Proj**	**5**	**7**	**0**	**87**	**71**	**4.31**	**4.21**	**1.41**	**768**	**829**	**714**	**21.5**	**3.4**	**7.3**	**2.1**	**60%**	**7%**	**43**	**22**	**35**	**31%**	**72%**	**11%**	**15**						**-3.7**	**60**	**72**	**-$3**

Volquez,Edinson

Age: 32 Th: R Role SP	Health A	LIMA Plan C+	ERA didn't regress much despite WHIP jump. Has crushed xERA twice in a row now. Common thread is elite bullpens: 5 ER on 36 inherited runners from PIT and KC. Still some positives: regained some Dom, held Ctl gains, and logged first 200-IP year. Just too much traffic on bases to trust ERA; heed xERA instead.
Ht: 6' 0" Wt: 220 Type Pwr	PT/Exp A	Rand Var -1	
	Consist A	MM 1205	

Yr	Tm	W	L	Sv	IP	K	ERA	xERA	WHIP	oOPS	vL	vR	BF/G	Ctl	Dom	Cmd	FpK	SwK	G	L	F	H%	S%	hr/f	GS	APC	DOM%	DIS%	Sv%	LI	RAR	BPV	BPX	R$
11	CIN *	9	9	0	196	168	4.49	4.64	1.49	833	862	811	25.6	4.4	7.7	1.7	54%	12%	52	18	30	31%	73%	21%	20	98	35%	20%			-13.2	51	77	-$3
12	SD	11	11	0	183	174	4.14	4.14	1.45	706	700	711	25.1	5.2	8.6	1.7	53%	11%	51	21	28	30%	72%	10%	32	101	44%	25%			-2.8	44	57	$1
13	2 NL	9	12	0	170	142	5.71	4.28	1.59	804	836	771	23.5	4.1	7.5	1.8	57%	9%	48	23	30	34%	65%	12%	32	91	25%	28%	0	0.77	-38.7	51	67	-$16
14	PIT	13	7	0	193	140	3.04	3.95	1.23	674	728	634	25.3	3.3	6.5	2.0	60%	9%	50	17	33	27%	78%	9%	31	93	61%	23%	0	0.76	16.7	56	67	$12
15	KC	13	9	0	200	155	3.55	4.22	1.31	692	692	691	25.0	3.2	7.0	2.2	58%	10%	46	21	33	30%	74%	8%	33	97	55%	15%	0	0.77	10.2	62	74	$10
1st Half		8	4	0	96	73	3.48	4.13	1.20	641	590	701	25.1	3.1	6.9	2.2	60%	11%	47	20	33	28%	72%	7%	16	95	50%	19%			5.7	65	77	$14
2nd Half		5	5	0	105	82	3.61	4.31	1.40	737	795	683	24.9	3.4	7.1	2.1	56%	9%	45	22	33	32%	76%	8%	17	99	59%	12%	0	0.76	4.5	59	70	$6
16	**Proj**	**11**	**9**	**0**	**181**	**142**	**3.98**	**4.10**	**1.35**	**715**	**738**	**693**	**24.2**	**3.5**	**7.1**	**2.0**	**58%**	**10%**	**48**	**20**	**32**	**30%**	**72%**	**9%**	**31**						**-0.3**	**57**	**68**	**$3**

Wacha,Michael

Age: 25 Th: R Role SP	Health C	LIMA Plan C	1H/2H split paints fuzzy picture. Bulk of season was great: 2.88 ERA, 1.15 WHIP, 8.7 Dom, 3.6 Cmd in 119 IP (mid-May thru Aug). Rough Sept. (7.88 ERA) smacks of classic fatigue (velocity drop, HR jump). Glimpses of greatness every year, stable Dom/Ctl, and GB lean all hint at even more. UP: sub-3.00 ERA
Ht: 6' 6" Wt: 210 Type Pwr	PT/Exp B	Rand Var 0	
	Consist B	MM 2205	

Yr	Tm	W	L	Sv	IP	K	ERA	xERA	WHIP	oOPS	vL	vR	BF/G	Ctl	Dom	Cmd	FpK	SwK	G	L	F	H%	S%	hr/f	GS	APC	DOM%	DIS%	Sv%	LI	RAR	BPV	BPX	R$
11																																		
12																																		
13	STL *	9	4	0	150	127	2.79	2.68	1.06	603	493	710	19.3	2.2	7.7	3.5	58%	12%	44	17	39	27%	77%	7%	9	69	33%	22%	0	0.66	19.9	105	137	$16
14	STL	5	6	0	107	94	3.20	3.70	1.20	636	581	687	23.5	2.8	7.9	2.8	64%	11%	42	22	36	30%	74%	5%	19	89	47%	21%			7.2	87	104	$5
15	STL	17	7	0	181	153	3.38	3.91	1.21	672	617	716	25.4	2.9	7.6	2.6	63%	10%	46	22	32	29%	76%	11%	30	98	70%	13%			13.1	83	99	$16
1st Half		10	3	0	101	80	2.66	3.68	1.09	609	593	625	25.9	2.0	7.1	3.5	64%	10%	48	22	30	28%	78%	8%	16	97	81%	0%			16.2	99	117	$25
2nd Half		7	4	0	80	73	4.28	4.22	1.38	751	656	808	24.8	3.9	8.2	2.1	63%	10%	43	22	35	29%	73%	15%	14	99	57%	29%			-3.1	63	74	$4
16	**Proj**	**13**	**8**	**0**	**189**	**163**	**3.35**	**3.74**	**1.21**	**661**	**588**	**722**	**22.8**	**2.9**	**7.8**	**2.7**	**63%**	**11%**	**44**	**21**	**35**	**29%**	**75%**	**9%**	**33**						**14.3**	**84**	**100**	**$14**

Wainwright,Adam

Age: 34 Th: R Role SP	Health F	LIMA Plan B+	Rallied from April Achilles injury to pitch out of the pen late in 2H, but too small to matter (8 IP including post-season). Pre-injury sample not instructive, either. Sinking Dom is the only major concern in the skill set—well, outside of the Health grade—but enough to remove "ace" status. Elite Ctl ensures a soft decline.
Ht: 6' 7" Wt: 235 Type	PT/Exp A	Rand Var -5	
	Consist A	MM 3205	

Yr	Tm	W	L	Sv	IP	K	ERA	xERA	WHIP	oOPS	vL	vR	BF/G	Ctl	Dom	Cmd	FpK	SwK	G	L	F	H%	S%	hr/f	GS	APC	DOM%	DIS%	Sv%	LI	RAR	BPV	BPX	R$
11																																		
12	STL	14	13	0	199	184	3.94	3.36	1.25	701	724	681	26.0	2.4	8.3	3.5	64%	9%	51	23	26	32%	69%	10%	32	97	69%	13%			1.8	115	151	$11
13	STL	19	9	0	242	219	2.94	2.94	1.07	636	631	639	28.1	1.3	8.2	6.3	65%	10%	49	23	28	31%	74%	8%	34	104	82%	6%			27.5	139	181	$29
14	STL	20	9	0	227	179	2.38	3.31	1.03	580	625	542	28.1	2.0	7.1	3.6	61%	9%	46	24	30	27%	78%	5%	32	102	72%	6%			38.1	98	117	$30
15	STL	2	1	0	28	20	1.61	3.35	1.04	590	661	540	15.9	1.3	6.4	5.0	54%	8%	51	26	23	30%	83%	0%	4	55	50%	25%	0	0.51	8.1	110	131	$1
1st Half		2	1	0	25	18	1.44	3.24	1.04	604	660	564	24.5	1.1	6.5	6.0	51%	8%	50	28	22	30%	85%	0%	4	85	50%	25%			7.8	115	137	$2
2nd Half		0	0	0	3	2	3.00	4.26	1.00	481	650	375	4.3	3.0	6.0	2.0	77%	12%	60	10	30	24%	67%	0%	0	14			0	0.13	0.4	65	77	-$5
16	**Proj**	**15**	**8**	**0**	**189**	**146**	**3.01**	**3.44**	**1.16**	**662**	**690**	**637**	**26.6**	**2.0**	**7.0**	**3.5**	**60%**	**9%**	**49**	**25**	**26**	**30%**	**75%**	**7%**	**28**						**22.2**	**99**	**118**	**$18**

Walden,Jordan

Age: 28 Th: R Role RP	Health F	LIMA Plan C+	Biceps injury ended season after April and gave him a 4th straight season with a DL stint; could face surgery. Results weren't just sample size volatility: SwK says Dom might've been light and Ctl improvement supported by FpK spike. Skills not the question, but the health always will be.
Ht: 6' 5" Wt: 250 Type Pwr	PT/Exp D	Rand Var -5	
	Consist A	MM 3500	

Yr	Tm	W	L	Sv	IP	K	ERA	xERA	WHIP	oOPS	vL	vR	BF/G	Ctl	Dom	Cmd	FpK	SwK	G	L	F	H%	S%	hr/f	GS	APC	DOM%	DIS%	Sv%	LI	RAR	BPV	BPX	R$
11	LAA	5	5	32	60	67	2.98	3.38	1.24	642	650	631	4.1	3.9	10.0	2.6	60%	13%	45	18	37	31%	76%	5%	0	18			76	1.70	7.1	98	148	$17
12	LAA	3	2	1	39	48	3.46	3.68	1.36	674	606	743	3.8	4.2	11.1	2.7	60%	14%	40	25	36	34%	76%	8%	0	16			50	0.61	2.7	105	137	-$1
13	ATL	4	3	1	47	54	3.45	3.53	1.13	620	542	690	3.9	2.7	10.3	3.9	62%	15%	31	18	51	31%	71%	6%	0	16			33	1.23	2.4	123	160	$2
14	ATL	0	2	3	50	62	2.88	3.27	1.20	541	599	488	3.5	4.9	11.2	2.3	58%	15%	45	19	36	28%	76%	5%	0	15			60	1.40	5.3	93	110	$2
15	STL	0	1	1	10	12	0.87	3.27	1.06	505	425	561	3.5	3.5	10.5	3.0	69%	22%	42	27	31	29%	91%	0%	0	13			100	1.47	3.9	114	136	-$2
1st Half		0	1	1	10	12	0.87	3.27	1.06	505	425	561	3.5	3.5	10.5	3.0	69%	22%	42	27	31	29%	91%	0%	0	13			100	1.47	3.9	114	136	-$2
2nd Half																																		
16	**Proj**	**2**	**2**	**0**	**44**	**52**	**3.01**	**3.43**	**1.25**	**621**	**599**	**642**	**3.6**	**4.0**	**10.8**	**2.7**	**60%**	**14%**	**40**	**21**	**39**	**31%**	**77%**	**7%**	**0**						**5.1**	**104**	**124**	**$1**

Walker,Taijuan

Age: 23 Th: R Role SP	Health D	LIMA Plan B	Never outran the hideous start (7.33 ERA in first 9 GS) which masked a pretty strong summer (3.62 ERA in last 20 GS). IP cap hit in mid-Sept. Threw more strikes (Ctl gains), but they weren't always quality strikes (HR spike). It's all here—stuff, skills, size, pedigree—so next step is cutting DIS% to reach UP: 3.25 ERA
Ht: 6' 4" Wt: 230 Type Pwr	PT/Exp C	Rand Var +2	
	Consist A	MM 3305	

Yr	Tm	W	L	Sv	IP	K	ERA	xERA	WHIP	oOPS	vL	vR	BF/G	Ctl	Dom	Cmd	FpK	SwK	G	L	F	H%	S%	hr/f	GS	APC	DOM%	DIS%	Sv%	LI	RAR	BPV	BPX	R$
11																																		
12	aa	7	10	0	127	110	5.27	4.37	1.45				21.6	3.5	7.8	2.3						33%	63%								-19.7	71	93	-$7
13	SEA *	10	10	0	156	156	3.33	3.04	1.22	546	536	563	22.6	3.3	9.0	2.7	57%	10%	38	21	40	30%	74%	0%	3	78	33%	0%			10.3	101	132	$11
14	SEA *	9	7	0	116	109	3.85	3.70	1.25	642	729	501	20.5	3.2	8.4	2.7	61%	10%	47	27	26	29%	73%	7%	5	78	40%	20%	0	0.57	-1.5	82	97	$4
15	SEA	11	8	0	170	157	4.56	3.78	1.20	716	714	719	24.3	2.1	8.3	3.9	63%	11%	39	22	39	30%	66%	13%	29	91	55%	24%			-12.5	110	131	$5
1st Half		7	6	0	91	90	4.34	3.87	1.28	724	689	777	24.3	2.6	8.9	3.5	62%	11%	39	20	40	32%	70%	12%	16	91	69%	31%			-4.2	108	128	$7
2nd Half		4	2	0	78	67	4.83	3.67	1.10	706	752	667	24.4	1.6	7.7	4.8	64%	10%	38	25	38	28%	59%	14%	13	91	38%	15%			-8.3	111	131	$3
16	**Proj**	**12**	**10**	**0**	**189**	**174**	**3.83**	**3.56**	**1.20**	**668**	**710**	**615**	**22.2**	**2.6**	**8.3**	**3.2**	**62%**	**10%**	**42**	**25**	**34**	**30%**	**70%**	**9%**	**34**						**3.0**	**99**	**117**	**$11**

PAUL SPORER

Warren,Adam

Age: 28	Th: R	Role	RP	Health	A	LIMA Plan	B
Ht: 6' 1"	Wt: 200	Type	Pwr	PT/Exp	C	Rand Var	-1
				Consist	B	MM	3201

He shone brightest in the pen (2.29 ERA, 4.1 Cmd in 35 IP), but held his own for 17 starts (3.66, 2.2 in 96 IP). Dom drop normal given workload distribution, but it was actually better as RP than in '14 (9.4). Best role might be multi-IP reliever: platoon-free, ample Ks, mid-90s heat, and a deep arsenal.

Yr Tm	W	L	Sv	IP	K	ERA	xERA	WHIP	oOPS	vL	vR	BF/G	Ctl	Dom	Cmd	FpK	SwK	G	L	F	H%	S%	hr/f	GS	APC	DOM%	DIS%	Sv%	LI	RAR	BPV	BPX	R$
11 aaa	6	8	0	152	91	5.00	5.36	1.58				24.8	3.5	5.4	1.5						32%	70%								-19.8	27	40	-$10
12 NYY *	7	8	0	155	87	5.19	6.13	1.71	1588	1500	1636	26.0	3.0	5.1	1.7	59%	5%	29	29	43	36%	71%	33%	1	77	0%	100%			-22.5	25	33	-$18
13 NYY	3	2	1	77	64	3.39	4.02	1.43	766	896	625	9.7	3.5	7.5	2.1	56%	11%	45	22	32	31%	81%	13%	2	38	50%	50%	100	0.58	4.5	63	82	-$1
14 NYY	3	6	3	79	76	2.97	3.31	1.11	615	525	690	4.7	2.7	8.7	3.2	58%	12%	45	24	31	29%	73%	6%	0	19			50	1.26	7.4	105	126	$6
15 NYY	7	7	1	131	104	3.29	3.84	1.16	648	603	680	12.4	2.7	7.1	2.7	60%	9%	45	23	32	28%	73%	8%	17	50	41%	29%	100	1.01	10.9	79	94	$9
1st Half	5	5	0	87	58	3.52	4.26	1.18	658	649	665	22.1	2.9	6.0	2.1	59%	8%	45	20	35	26%	73%	9%	14	87	43%	21%	0	1.29	4.8	52	62	$10
2nd Half	2	2	1	44	46	2.84	3.06	1.13	628	520	710	6.7	2.2	9.3	4.2	61%	10%	47	28	25	32%	75%	7%	3	29	33%	67%	100	0.84	6.1	132	157	$7
16 Proj	**4**	**5**	**0**	**87**	**76**	**3.32**	**3.62**	**1.23**	**682**	**641**	**716**	**7.8**	**2.8**	**7.8**	**2.8**	**59%**	**10%**	**46**	**24**	**30**	**30%**	**75%**	**9%**	**3**						**6.9**	**89**	**106**	**$3**

Watson,Tony

Age: 31	Th: L	Role	RP	Health	A	LIMA Plan	B
Ht: 6' 4"	Wt: 225	Type	Pwr	PT/Exp	C	Rand Var	-5
				Consist	B	MM	4311

SwK dip and fewer sliders explain the Dom loss, but change-up got better and raw skills still have K/IP potential. Ability vR has paid off with the largest workload of any reliever, since 2013 (224 IP). Sustained excellence + increasing LI + these skills = closer-worthy arm. "Draft skills, not roles" posterboy. UP: 20 SV

Yr Tm	W	L	Sv	IP	K	ERA	xERA	WHIP	oOPS	vL	vR	BF/G	Ctl	Dom	Cmd	FpK	SwK	G	L	F	H%	S%	hr/f	GS	APC	DOM%	DIS%	Sv%	LI	RAR	BPV	BPX	R$
11 PIT *	5	5	0	75	63	3.47	3.42	1.25	711	708	713	4.4	3.7	7.5	2.0	63%	9%	32	24	44	27%	76%	13%	0	15			0	1.28	4.4	68	102	$3
12 PIT	5	2	0	53	53	3.38	3.86	1.13	623	554	691	3.2	3.9	8.9	2.3	64%	12%	40	18	42	25%	73%	9%	0	13			0	1.21	4.2	74	97	$3
13 PIT	3	1	2	72	54	2.39	3.44	0.88	544	483	582	4.2	1.5	6.8	4.5	63%	12%	44	19	37	24%	76%	7%	0	16			50	1.14	13.1	103	135	$9
14 PIT	10	2	2	77	81	1.63	2.76	1.02	613	531	646	3.9	1.7	9.4	5.4	65%	14%	48	21	32	30%	88%	8%	0	15			22	1.34	20.1	149	177	$13
15 PIT	4	1	1	75	62	1.91	3.42	0.96	525	493	536	3.8	2.0	7.4	3.6	66%	12%	48	21	32	26%	81%	5%	0	14			33	1.38	19.1	104	124	$10
1st Half	1	1	1	39	37	2.09	3.01	0.91	528	767	456	3.9	1.9	8.6	4.6	65%	13%	49	21	30	25%	81%	10%	0	15			50	1.29	8.9	132	156	$10
2nd Half	3	0	0	37	25	1.72	3.87	1.01	522	282	628	3.7	2.2	6.1	2.8	66%	11%	46	21	33	26%	81%	0%	0	14			0	1.47	10.2	75	89	$11
16 Proj	**6**	**1**	**5**	**73**	**69**	**2.04**	**3.16**	**0.99**	**562**	**495**	**592**	**3.7**	**2.1**	**8.5**	**4.1**	**65%**	**12%**	**46**	**20**	**34**	**27%**	**81%**	**6%**	**0**						**17.2**	**121**	**144**	**$11**

Weaver,Jered

Age: 33	Th: R	Role	SP	Health	F	LIMA Plan	C
Ht: 6' 7"	Wt: 210	Type	xFB	PT/Exp	A	Rand Var	0
				Consist	A	MM	1103

xERA told us we were living on the wire with him for years and it finally snapped. With fastball velocity that resembles many changeups, batters feasted: one of only four SPs with 159+ IP, 9+ H/9, and 1.4 HR/9. An xFB arm with a growing HR issue is the new normal. Anything under 4.00 ERA is a gift.

Yr Tm	W	L	Sv	IP	K	ERA	xERA	WHIP	oOPS	vL	vR	BF/G	Ctl	Dom	Cmd	FpK	SwK	G	L	F	H%	S%	hr/f	GS	APC	DOM%	DIS%	Sv%	LI	RAR	BPV	BPX	R$
11 LAA	18	8	0	236	198	2.41	3.75	1.01	598	578	621	28.1	2.1	7.6	3.5	64%	10%	32	19	49	26%	80%	6%	33	114	79%	6%			44.7	88	133	$35
12 LAA	20	5	0	189	142	2.81	4.01	1.02	605	541	690	24.6	2.1	6.8	3.2	61%	9%	36	21	43	25%	77%	9%	30	95	60%	17%			27.9	78	102	$29
13 LAA	11	8	0	154	117	3.27	4.17	1.14	671	638	725	26.4	2.2	6.8	3.2	60%	10%	31	22	47	28%	75%	8%	24	100	63%	8%			11.4	74	96	$12
14 LAA	18	9	0	213	169	3.59	4.25	1.21	684	723	620	26.1	2.7	7.1	2.6	56%	9%	33	19	48	28%	75%	9%	34	99	47%	9%			4.1	65	78	$13
15 LAA	7	12	0	159	90	4.64	4.83	1.23	767	777	757	25.7	1.9	5.1	2.7	61%	9%	34	19	47	28%	66%	10%	26	94	31%	15%			-13.3	53	63	-$1
1st Half	4	8	0	97	49	4.75	4.85	1.24	770	781	757	26.9	1.5	4.6	3.1	60%	8%	36	19	45	28%	66%	11%	15	95	27%	20%			-9.4	56	67	-$1
2nd Half	3	4	0	62	41	4.48	4.80	1.22	762	767	755	24.2	2.5	5.9	2.4	61%	9%	31	19	50	27%	66%	8%	11	92	36%	9%			-3.9	50	59	$0
16 Proj	**10**	**11**	**0**	**160**	**110**	**4.17**	**4.36**	**1.19**	**725**	**727**	**723**	**24.7**	**2.3**	**6.2**	**2.8**	**60%**	**9%**	**33**	**20**	**47**	**27%**	**69%**	**10%**	**26**						**-4.0**	**62**	**74**	**$6**

Webster,Allen

Age: 26	Th: R	Role	SP	Health	A	LIMA Plan	D+
Ht: 6' 2"	Wt: 190	Type		PT/Exp	D	Rand Var	+5
				Consist	D	MM	0100

1-1, 5.81 ERA in 31 IP at ARI. IP counts have hr/f bouncing around, but skills remain awful regardless. Can't find plate enough to utilize solid SwK totals and he's crushed when they don't swing-and-miss: 9.5 H/9, 1.5 HR/9 in 120 MLB IP. Time to see if RP role coaxes fastball command, but as SP? Ignore entirely.

Yr Tm	W	L	Sv	IP	K	ERA	xERA	WHIP	oOPS	vL	vR	BF/G	Ctl	Dom	Cmd	FpK	SwK	G	L	F	H%	S%	hr/f	GS	APC	DOM%	DIS%	Sv%	LI	RAR	BPV	BPX	R$
11 aa	6	3	0	91	64	4.96	4.50	1.48				21.7	3.1	6.3	2.0						34%	66%								-11.4	60	90	-$4
12 aa	6	9	0	131	110	5.11	4.85	1.70				20.4	4.4	7.6	1.7						38%	67%								-17.7	72	94	-$14
13 BOS *	9	6	0	135	120	5.33	3.85	1.33	926	1253	550	19.4	4.0	8.0	2.0	62%	13%	43	21	36	28%	61%	19%	7	67	29%	57%	0	0.71	-24.5	64	83	-$4
14 BOS *	9	7	1	181	118	4.25	4.14	1.44	736	703	773	24.1	3.7	5.9	1.6	60%	12%	46	21	33	31%	71%	5%	11	87	18%	27%			-11.4	51	61	-$4
15 ARI *	5	7	0	108	67	7.66	7.27	1.88	968	1226	796	21.2	3.7	5.6	1.5	58%	10%	47	15	39	37%	60%	26%	5	57	0%	40%	0	0.48	-49.3	7	8	-$27
1st Half	3	3	0	48	35	7.83	6.60	1.82	943	890	983	22.3	4.9	6.5	1.3	55%	10%	47	15	37	35%	58%	27%	4	79	0%	50%			-22.9	15	17	-$24
2nd Half	2	4	0	60	33	7.54	7.81	1.93	1006	1882	547	20.4	2.7	4.9	1.8	62%	10%	45	14	40	39%	62%	24%	1	40	0%	0%	0	0.26	-26.5	4	5	-$29
16 Proj	**3**	**3**	**0**	**58**	**40**	**5.41**	**4.72**	**1.57**	**833**	**924**	**743**	**21.0**	**3.7**	**6.2**	**1.7**	**59%**	**12%**	**45**	**19**	**36**	**33%**	**67%**	**11%**	**12**						**-10.3**	**34**	**41**	**-$7**

Wheeler,Zack

Age: 26	Th: R	Role	SP	Health	F	LIMA Plan	B+
Ht: 6' 4"	Wt: 195	Type	Pwr	PT/Exp	C	Rand Var	0
				Consist	A	MM	2301

Entered season as key cog for NYM, lost 2015 to TJS and now eyes June 2016 return. Poor Ctl could take even longer after TJ, but big Dom, velocity, and GB lean make up a solid foundation. Wasn't yet a finished product pre-surgery; 2017 is a better breakout bet.

Yr Tm	W	L	Sv	IP	K	ERA	xERA	WHIP	oOPS	vL	vR	BF/G	Ctl	Dom	Cmd	FpK	SwK	G	L	F	H%	S%	hr/f	GS	APC	DOM%	DIS%	Sv%	LI	RAR	BPV	BPX	R$
11																																	
12 a/a	12	8	0	149	132	3.44	2.58	1.19				23.9	3.3	8.0	2.4						29%	69%								10.5	101	132	$12
13 NYM *	11	7	0	169	148	3.38	3.58	1.29	696	766	639	23.1	3.7	7.9	2.2	52%	9%	43	23	33	29%	77%	10%	17	102	59%	12%			10.2	72	94	$9
14 NYM	11	11	0	185	187	3.54	3.37	1.33	678	745	615	24.8	3.8	9.1	2.4	54%	10%	54	19	27	31%	75%	10%	32	103	59%	19%			4.5	92	109	$6
15																																	
1st Half																																	
2nd Half																																	
16 Proj	**6**	**5**	**0**	**87**	**81**	**3.67**	**3.73**	**1.30**	**649**	**712**	**593**	**24.0**	**3.9**	**8.3**	**2.1**	**53%**	**10%**	**50**	**21**	**30**	**30%**	**72%**	**8%**	**15**						**3.2**	**72**	**86**	**$2**

Wilhelmsen,Tom

Age: 32	Th: R	Role	RP	Health	C	LIMA Plan	B
Ht: 6' 6"	Wt: 220	Type	Pwr	PT/Exp	C	Rand Var	-3
				Consist	B	MM	2320

Elbow injury ate April. Saved best for last, spending final month+ as closer: 1.04 ERA, 0.98 WHIP, 17 K, 6 BB, 11 Sv in 17 IP. Ctl always an issue and Dom rarely enough to offset (3.0 Cmd in '12, just 2.1 career). Big fastball, steady SwK, RH dominance, HR suppression enough for a role, but not necessarily the 9th.

Yr Tm	W	L	Sv	IP	K	ERA	xERA	WHIP	oOPS	vL	vR	BF/G	Ctl	Dom	Cmd	FpK	SwK	G	L	F	H%	S%	hr/f	GS	APC	DOM%	DIS%	Sv%	LI	RAR	BPV	BPX	R$
11 SEA *	6	5	0	93	62	5.55	5.13	1.58	580	508	651	10.5	4.0	6.0	1.5	59%	12%	34	21	45	32%	66%	5%	0	20			0	0.59	-18.5	34	51	-$8
12 SEA	4	3	29	79	87	2.50	3.37	1.11	578	637	519	4.5	3.3	9.9	3.0	57%	12%	48	16	35	28%	80%	7%	0	17			85	1.38	14.9	115	150	$20
13 SEA	0	3	24	59	45	4.12	4.54	1.32	603	743	468	4.3	5.0	6.9	1.4	55%	11%	43	23	34	26%	67%	4%	0	17			83	1.13	-1.8	9	11	$6
14 SEA	3	2	1	79	72	2.27	3.48	1.05	542	505	573	5.6	4.1	8.2	2.0	59%	13%	52	19	29	21%	82%	10%	2	21	0%	100%	33	0.92	14.4	67	80	$8
15 SEA	2	2	13	62	60	3.19	4.19	1.37	696	874	564	5.0	4.2	8.7	2.1	53%	11%	42	20	37	32%	77%	5%	0	20			87	1.24	5.9	63	75	$5
1st Half	1	2	0	25	28	4.68	3.99	1.72	830	1110	636	5.2	4.0	10.1	2.5	52%	12%	42	25	33	42%	71%	4%	0	20			0	0.85	-2.2	95	113	-$7
2nd Half	1	0	13	37	32	2.19	4.32	1.14	593	704	505	4.9	4.4	7.8	1.8	54%	11%	42	17	41	23%	83%	5%	0	20			87	1.52	8.1	42	50	$13
16 Proj	**2**	**2**	**15**	**65**	**60**	**3.32**	**4.05**	**1.33**	**669**	**770**	**585**	**5.0**	**4.2**	**8.2**	**1.9**	**55%**	**12%**	**45**	**20**	**35**	**29%**	**75%**	**6%**	**0**						**5.2**	**56**	**66**	**$6**

Williams,Jerome

Age: 34	Th: R	Role	RP	Health	D	LIMA Plan	C
Ht: 6' 3"	Wt: 240	Type		PT/Exp	B	Rand Var	+5
				Consist	A	MM	1000

Best that can be said of 2015 is "Sure he earned -$15, but I mean, the skills suggest he's more of a -$5 guy." Rare arm who doesn't get much better in the pen, either: 4.56 ERA, 1.8 Cmd as SP (860 IP); 4.60, 2.3 at RP (153 IP). Fantasy baseball hasn't cared for years, MLB may now be ready to do the same.

Yr Tm	W	L	Sv	IP	K	ERA	xERA	WHIP	oOPS	vL	vR	BF/G	Ctl	Dom	Cmd	FpK	SwK	G	L	F	H%	S%	hr/f	GS	APC	DOM%	DIS%	Sv%	LI	RAR	BPV	BPX	R$
11 LAA *	11	2	0	118	72	3.95	4.87	1.40	769	628	911	23.7	2.3	5.5	2.4	62%	11%	50	16	34	32%	76%	13%	6	68	50%	17%	0	0.82	-0.1	45	68	$2
12 LAA	6	8	1	138	98	4.58	3.79	1.26	743	747	738	17.9	2.3	6.4	2.8	60%	10%	54	18	28	30%	66%	14%	15	64	40%	20%	100	0.67	-9.5	86	112	$0
13 LAA	9	10	0	169	107	4.57	4.30	1.39	772	818	716	19.7	2.9	5.7	1.9	58%	10%	47	21	32	30%	70%	13%	25	71	28%	32%	0	0.74	-14.7	48	63	-$4
14 3 TM	6	7	0	115	82	4.77	4.10	1.40	756	787	720	13.4	2.8	6.4	2.3	63%	8%	45	23	32	32%	67%	10%	11	50	27%	9%	0	0.67	-14.7	62	74	-$5
15 PHI	4	12	1	121	74	5.80	4.70	1.61	863	794	913	16.8	2.5	5.5	2.2	62%	9%	47	23	30	34%	68%	17%	21	60	38%	38%	50	0.98	-27.5	56	66	-$15
1st Half	3	7	0	70	41	6.43	5.01	1.70	899	772	988	23.4	2.4	5.3	2.2	61%	9%	41	26	33	35%	66%	16%	14	81	29%	43%			-21.3	48	57	-$20
2nd Half	1	5	1	51	33	4.94	4.24	1.49	810	823	798	11.9	2.6	5.8	2.2	62%	9%	56	19	26	32%	71%	18%	7	44	57%	29%	50	1.14	-6.2	67	80	-$9
16 Proj	**2**	**4**	**0**	**58**	**38**	**5.07**	**4.28**	**1.48**	**807**	**792**	**821**	**15.1**	**2.7**	**5.9**	**2.2**	**61%**	**9%**	**48**	**21**	**30**	**32%**	**69%**	**14%**	**8**						**-8.0**	**60**	**72**	**-$6**

PAUL SPORER

Wilson,Alex

Wilson,Alex			Health	D	LIMA Plan	C+
Age: 29	Th: R	Role: RP	PT/Exp	D	Rand Var	-5
Ht: 6' 0"	Wt: 215	Type:	Consist	B	MM	1010

Increased usage of sinker and cutter generated more GB, and led to surprisingly excellent Ctl as well. He even jumped into closer mix late in year, converting 2 of 3 chances. But new approach brought Dom down to dangerous level, leaving little margin for error. Wouldn't be shocking if ERA doubles in 2016.

Yr Tm	W	L	Sv	IP	K	ERA	xERA	WHIP	oOPS	vL	vR	BF/G	Ctl	Dom	Cmd	FpK	SwK	G	L	F	H%	S%	hr/f	GS	APC	DOM%	DIS%	Sv%	LI	RAR	BPV	BPX	R$
11 a/a	10	4	0	133	99	3.99	4.50	1.46				22.8	3.1	6.7	2.2						33%	74%								-0.8	61	92	$1
12 aaa	5	3	1	73	61	5.43	6.02	1.88				8.5	4.6	7.6	1.6						40%	70%								-12.7	55	72	-$12
13 BOS *	4	2	0	45	34	4.89	5.08	1.68	818	567	1108	5.0	3.9	6.9	1.8	56%	9%	31	30	39	37%	70%	0%	0	18			0	0.88	-5.7	58	76	-$6
14 BOS *	7	1	5	70	49	4.38	4.18	1.45	624	787	476	5.6	4.1	6.3	1.6	61%	8%	44	18	38	30%	70%	10%	0	23			50	0.54	-5.5	52	62	-$1
15 DET	3	3	2	70	38	2.19	3.98	1.03	609	566	645	4.6	1.4	4.9	3.5	62%	7%	50	15	35	26%	82%	7%	1	17	0%	100%	50	0.94	15.3	78	93	$7
1st Half	1	3	0	44	25	2.06	3.95	0.98	564	651	489	5.8	1.2	5.2	4.2	63%	7%	48	15	37	27%	79%	2%	1	21	0%	100%	0	0.82	10.2	85	101	$8
2nd Half	2	0	2	26	13	2.39	4.04	1.10	683	422	894	3.5	1.7	4.4	2.6	60%	7%	55	14	31	25%	88%	15%	0	14			67	1.07	5.1	67	79	$6
16 Proj	4	2	9	58	37	3.89	4.33	1.38	756	627	865	5.0	2.8	5.7	2.1	61%	7%	49	17	34	31%	74%	9%	0						0.5	55	65	$2

Wilson,C.J.

Wilson,C.J.			Health	F	LIMA Plan	B
Age: 35	Th: L	Role: SP	PT/Exp	A	Rand Var	0
Ht: 6' 1"	Wt: 210	Type: Pwr	Consist	A	MM	1203

Ctl rebound was nice, but not enough to offset some troubling signs: Lowest GB% of career; further loss of velocity, and four-seam fastball wasn't fooling anyone (.339 BA, .509 SLG against it); elbow soreness early in year, then bone spurs ended season in July. Note Health grade, and use 4.00 ERA as baseline.

Yr Tm	W	L	Sv	IP	K	ERA	xERA	WHIP	oOPS	vL	vR	BF/G	Ctl	Dom	Cmd	FpK	SwK	G	L	F	H%	S%	hr/f	GS	APC	DOM%	DIS%	Sv%	LI	RAR	BPV	BPX	R$
11 TEX	16	7	0	223	206	2.94	3.34	1.19	651	658	650	26.9	3.0	8.3	2.8	59%	9%	49	19	32	29%	77%	8%	34	106	59%	15%			27.6	96	144	$23
12 LAA	13	10	0	202	173	3.83	4.07	1.34	684	590	713	25.4	4.0	7.7	1.9	57%	8%	50	20	30	29%	74%	11%	34	101	47%	12%			4.7	57	75	$8
13 LAA	17	7	0	212	188	3.39	3.94	1.34	684	485	741	27.7	3.6	8.0	2.2	60%	9%	44	22	33	31%	76%	7%	33	111	48%	9%			12.4	68	89	$12
14 LAA	13	10	0	176	151	4.51	3.99	1.45	724	572	774	24.5	4.4	7.7	1.8	59%	8%	48	23	30	31%	70%	11%	31	100	39%	29%			-16.6	48	57	-$3
15 LAA	8	8	0	132	110	3.89	4.06	1.24	682	729	668	26.3	3.1	7.5	2.4	59%	9%	43	22	35	29%	71%	10%	21	101	62%	10%			1.2	71	85	$5
1st Half	7	6	0	108	93	3.82	3.86	1.20	681	767	655	26.4	2.8	7.7	2.7	59%	9%	44	21	34	29%	71%	10%	17	101	71%	6%			1.9	85	101	$8
2nd Half	1	2	0	24	17	4.18	5.03	1.44	685	561	727	26.3	4.6	6.5	1.4	60%	8%	38	25	38	29%	72%	7%	4	102	25%	25%			-0.6	9	10	-$11
16 Proj	9	9	0	145	119	3.99	4.14	1.36	693	600	722	25.3	3.9	7.4	1.9	59%	8%	46	22	33	30%	72%	9%	24						-0.6	51	61	$2

Wilson,Justin

Wilson,Justin			Health	A	LIMA Plan	B+
Age: 28	Th: L	Role: RP	PT/Exp	C	Rand Var	-1
Ht: 6' 2"	Wt: 205	Type: Pwr	Consist	A	MM	3400

First two months were nothing special, with 1.6 Cmd, 10% SwK thru mid-June. But then... surge in SwK took Dom to new level, and he returned to FpK-heavy approach; also had 32:1 K:BB ratio vs RHB in 2nd half. Should continue to be solid LIMA option and strong source of Holds and K's; could even sneak some Saves.

Yr Tm	W	L	Sv	IP	K	ERA	xERA	WHIP	oOPS	vL	vR	BF/G	Ctl	Dom	Cmd	FpK	SwK	G	L	F	H%	S%	hr/f	GS	APC	DOM%	DIS%	Sv%	LI	RAR	BPV	BPX	R$
11 aaa	10	8	3	124	73	4.84	5.10	1.64				18.5	4.7	5.3	1.1						31%	71%								-13.7	28	41	-$6
12 PIT *	9	6	0	140	113	4.69	3.58	1.35	1111	1053	1161	15.8	4.5	7.3	1.6	58%	10%	20	53	27	28%	66%	0%	0	13			0	0.43	-11.7	63	82	-$1
13 PIT	6	1	0	74	59	2.08	3.59	1.06	543	501	563	5.1	3.4	7.2	2.1	59%	10%	53	17	30	24%	82%	7%	0	21			0	1.11	16.3	68	89	$8
14 PIT	3	4	0	60	61	4.20	3.68	1.32	643	681	622	3.7	4.5	9.2	2.0	61%	10%	51	14	34	29%	68%	7%	0	15			0	1.05	-3.4	72	86	-$2
15 NYY	5	0	0	61	66	3.10	3.17	1.13	602	629	588	3.3	3.0	9.7	3.3	60%	13%	44	27	29	30%	73%	7%	0	14			0	1.26	6.5	118	140	$4
1st Half	2	0	0	29	28	3.07	3.35	1.09	553	601	521	3.1	4.3	8.6	2.0	50%	13%	52	28	20	24%	71%	7%	0	13			0	1.35	3.2	69	82	$2
2nd Half	3	0	0	32	38	3.13	3.02	1.17	644	664	633	3.6	1.7	10.8	6.3	68%	13%	37	27	37	36%	74%	7%	0	16			0	1.16	3.3	163	193	$6
16 Proj	4	1	0	58	58	3.39	3.48	1.21	623	645	613	3.9	3.5	9.0	2.6	61%	11%	47	21	31	29%	72%	7%	0						4.1	93	110	$2

Wilson,Tyler

Wilson,Tyler			Health	A	LIMA Plan	C
Age: 26	Th: R	Role: SP	PT/Exp	D	Rand Var	-1
Ht: 6' 2"	Wt: 185	Type: Con GB	Consist	A	MM	1000

2-2, 3.50 ERA in 36 IP at BAL. Rode AAA/MLB shuttle all year, but allowed just 1 HR in bigs, thanks to high GB% and lucky hr/f. Whiffs were way down at both levels, and SwK was one of lowest in majors. Previous Dom marks provide some level of optimism, but at least for now, far more downside than up.

Yr Tm	W	L	Sv	IP	K	ERA	xERA	WHIP	oOPS	vL	vR	BF/G	Ctl	Dom	Cmd	FpK	SwK	G	L	F	H%	S%	hr/f	GS	APC	DOM%	DIS%	Sv%	LI	RAR	BPV	BPX	R$
11																																	
12																																	
13 aa	7	5	0	89	57	4.55	4.94	1.35				23.3	2.2	5.8	2.6						30%	72%								-7.5	41	53	-$2
14 a/a	14	8	0	167	126	4.28	4.75	1.39				25.0	2.4	6.8	2.9						33%	72%								-11.0	65	78	$0
15 BAL *	7	7	0	130	63	4.76	5.44	1.54	757	722	796	21.9	2.3	4.3	1.9	58%	5%	52	18	30	34%	71%	3%	5	58	20%	40%	0	0.66	-12.9	29	35	-$9
1st Half	4	5	0	82	37	4.52	5.61	1.51	720	713	729	20.9	1.5	4.1	2.7	60%	7%	49	19	32	34%	73%	0%	1	46	0%	0%	0	0.55	-5.7	38	46	-$9
2nd Half	3	2	0	48	26	5.17	5.16	1.60	789	728	841	23.7	3.5	4.8	1.3	56%	4%	55	17	28	33%	68%	6%	4	72	25%	50%			-7.2	28	33	-$10
16 Proj	4	3	0	58	35	4.64	4.25	1.47	876	763	998	23.4	2.5	5.5	2.2	58%	6%	52	18	30	33%	71%	12%	9						-4.8	61	73	-$4

Wisler,Matthew

Wisler,Matthew			Health	A	LIMA Plan	C
Age: 23	Th: R	Role: SP	PT/Exp	D	Rand Var	0
Ht: 6' 3"	Wt: 195	Type: FB	Consist	C	MM	1103

8-8, 4.71 ERA in 109 IP at ATL. Finished strong, with 4 PQS-DOM outings in final 5 starts, but gave plenty of reasons to temper short-term expectations: Ctl suffered upon promotion to majors; high FB%; awful 0.7 Cmd vs LHB. Until he gets last one figured out, there will be plenty more bumps in the road.

Yr Tm	W	L	Sv	IP	K	ERA	xERA	WHIP	oOPS	vL	vR	BF/G	Ctl	Dom	Cmd	FpK	SwK	G	L	F	H%	S%	hr/f	GS	APC	DOM%	DIS%	Sv%	LI	RAR	BPV	BPX	R$
11																																	
12																																	
13 aa	8	5	0	105	94	3.31	2.87	1.12				20.7	2.2	8.1	3.7						30%	72%								7.2	115	150	$8
14 a/a	10	5	0	147	121	4.06	4.32	1.32				21.7	2.3	7.4	3.2						32%	72%								-5.7	82	97	$2
15 ATL *	11	12	0	174	116	5.04	4.99	1.46	819	986	664	23.3	2.8	6.0	2.2	59%	8%	34	23	43	32%	67%	10%	19	89	37%	37%	0	0.74	-23.1	44	53	-$8
1st Half	5	5	0	82	52	4.97	4.59	1.41	684	533	781	23.2	2.0	5.6	2.8	63%	9%	42	18	40	33%	65%	5%	3	82	33%	33%			-10.2	65	78	-$7
2nd Half	6	7	0	92	64	5.11	5.13	1.51	843	1050	640	23.9	3.4	6.3	1.8	59%	8%	32	24	44	31%	70%	11%	16	90	38%	38%	0	0.74	-12.9	30	36	-$8
16 Proj	9	11	0	160	121	4.43	4.33	1.36	786	876	708	22.3	2.6	6.8	2.7	60%	8%	36	22	42	32%	70%	9%	30						-9.3	67	80	-$1

Wood,Alex

Wood,Alex			Health	A	LIMA Plan	B+
Age: 25	Th: L	Role: SP	PT/Exp	B	Rand Var	0
Ht: 6' 4"	Wt: 215	Type: Pwr	Consist	B	MM	3205

Clearly a step backward after 2014 breakout. Velocity dipped for second year in row, leading to noticeable decline in Dom/SwK, and Cmd fell to 1.9 vs RHB (3.7 in 2014). But still getting GB and stifling LHB, and throw out 2 starts in COL (15 ER in 11 IP), and ERA was 3.32. Good time to buy at a discount.

Yr Tm	W	L	Sv	IP	K	ERA	xERA	WHIP	oOPS	vL	vR	BF/G	Ctl	Dom	Cmd	FpK	SwK	G	L	F	H%	S%	hr/f	GS	APC	DOM%	DIS%	Sv%	LI	RAR	BPV	BPX	R$
11																																	
12																																	
13 ATL *	8	5	0	140	132	2.43	2.83	1.22	670	622	690	13.4	2.8	8.5	3.0	62%	10%	49	24	27	32%	80%	5%	11	42	36%	45%	0	0.60	24.7	113	147	$13
14 ATL	11	11	0	172	170	2.78	3.20	1.14	651	667	645	19.8	2.4	8.9	3.8	62%	10%	46	19	35	30%	79%	10%	24	77	75%	0%	0	0.91	20.4	121	144	$16
15 2 NL	12	12	0	190	139	3.84	4.01	1.36	724	517	788	25.0	2.8	6.6	2.4	63%	8%	49	23	28	32%	73%	9%	32	91	41%	13%			2.8	70	84	$5
1st Half	6	5	0	100	74	3.34	4.10	1.41	733	580	775	26.6	2.5	6.7	2.6	65%	7%	47	23	31	34%	77%	6%	16	97	44%	6%			7.6	77	91	$6
2nd Half	6	7	0	90	65	4.40	3.92	1.29	713	461	805	23.5	3.1	6.5	2.1	60%	10%	53	23	24	29%	67%	14%	16	85	38%	19%			-4.9	64	76	$3
16 Proj	12	12	0	189	161	3.33	3.60	1.25	682	575	719	23.9	2.7	7.7	2.9	62%	9%	49	22	30	31%	75%	9%	32						14.7	92	110	$12

Wood,Travis

Wood,Travis			Health	A	LIMA Plan	B+
Age: 29	Th: L	Role: RP	PT/Exp	A	Rand Var	0
Ht: 5' 11"	Wt: 175	Type: Pwr FB	Consist	B	MM	2400

In 7 first half starts, gave up 9 HR in 37 IP. Moved to bullpen in May, and it worked out quite well. Velocity and SwK jumped substantially, and he had 11.2 Dom, just 2 HR allowed rest of way (64 IP). FB% will always leave him prone to long ball, but outlook much more promising if he stays in pen.

Yr Tm	W	L	Sv	IP	K	ERA	xERA	WHIP	oOPS	vL	vR	BF/G	Ctl	Dom	Cmd	FpK	SwK	G	L	F	H%	S%	hr/f	GS	APC	DOM%	DIS%	Sv%	LI	RAR	BPV	BPX	R$
11 CIN *	8	9	0	158	116	5.26	5.21	1.56	813	807	815	21.7	3.2	6.6	2.0	54%	7%	32	22	45	34%	67%	7%	18	81	33%	22%	0	0.79	-25.7	49	73	-$10
12 CHC *	9	16	0	197	151	4.47	4.25	1.28	745	614	779	24.5	3.0	6.9	2.3	58%	7%	34	22	44	28%	70%	13%	26	96	46%	15%			-11.2	53	69	$2
13 CHC	9	12	0	200	144	3.11	4.34	1.15	643	599	656	25.7	3.0	6.5	2.2	61%	8%	33	22	44	26%	76%	7%	32	97	66%	16%			18.8	47	62	$15
14 CHC	8	13	0	174	146	5.03	4.59	1.53	782	619	837	25.2	3.9	7.6	1.9	57%	7%	34	23	42	33%	69%	9%	31	98	39%	26%			-27.5	42	50	-$11
15 CHC	5	4	4	101	118	3.84	3.67	1.24	663	597	698	7.8	3.5	10.5	3.0	62%	11%	35	23	43	31%	72%	10%	9	32	22%	56%	100	0.79	1.5	108	128	$5
1st Half	4	3	1	57	61	4.71	4.06	1.31	737	652	772	11.1	3.5	9.6	2.8	60%	9%	31	25	44	30%	69%	14%	7	45	29%	43%	100	0.82	-5.3	88	105	$2
2nd Half	1	1	3	43	57	2.70	3.16	1.15	560	540	573	5.5	3.5	11.8	3.4	65%	13%	40	19	41	33%	76%	2%	2	23	0%	100%	100	0.76	6.7	136	161	$8
16 Proj	3	3	0	65	67	3.55	3.87	1.30	693	603	732	8.9	3.5	9.3	2.7	60%	10%	35	22	43	31%	75%	8%	0						3.4	86	102	$0

BRIAN RUDD

Worley,Vance

Worley,Vance				
Age: 28 Th: R Role SP	Health	B	LIMA Plan	C
Ht: 6' 2" Wt: 230 Type Con	PT/Exp	D	Rand Var	-1
	Consist	D	MM	1001

4-6, 4.02 ERA in 71 IP at PIT. Bumped from rotation by mid-May, roster by Aug. Just as FpK, Ctl took a positive turn in 2H, hr/f did him in. Bullpen may be best role (.639 oOPS, 6.9 Dom, 3.7 Cmd), but even there, lack of Ks limits ceiling. GB% should minimize risk, but there's no real reason to give him a whirl(y).

Yr Tm	W	L	Sv	IP	K	ERA	xERA	WHIP	oOPS	vL	vR	BF/G	Ctl	Dom	Cmd	FpK	SwK	G	L	F	H%	S%	hr/f	GS	APC	DOM%	DIS%	Sv%	LI	RAR	BPV	BPX	R$
11 PHI *	16	5	0	182	161	2.99	3.39	1.23	673	570	775	21.7	2.9	7.9	2.7	61%	6%	39	24	37	30%	79%	7%	21	87	71%	14%	0	0.80	21.5	88	133	$17
12 PHI	6	9	0	133	107	4.20	4.16	1.51	806	847	764	25.7	3.2	7.2	2.3	61%	6%	46	24	30	35%	74%	10%	23	95	39%	22%			-3.0	68	89	-$5
13 MIN *	7	8	0	107	51	5.81	6.57	1.79	1004	1013	994	25.9	2.7	4.3	1.6	59%	4%	47	22	31	37%	68%	16%	10	92	10%	40%			-25.6	15	19	-$17
14 PIT *	11	6	0	157	111	3.44	3.75	1.23	679	666	691	25.4	1.5	6.4	4.3	63%	6%	49	20	30	32%	73%	9%	17	88	59%	6%	0	0.76	5.9	109	129	$7
15 PIT *	7	7	0	106	64	3.78	4.52	1.39	761	800	736	15.9	2.2	5.5	2.4	58%	6%	46	21	33	32%	75%	8%	8	50	25%	38%	0	0.80	2.4	55	66	$0
1st Half	2	4	0	59	38	3.51	4.47	1.39	751	756	746	15.8	2.6	5.8	2.2	57%	6%	45	21	34	32%	76%	6%	7	58	29%	29%	0	0.77	3.3	58	68	-$1
2nd Half	5	3	0	47	26	4.12	4.94	1.38	804	1108	700	16.3	1.8	5.1	2.8	64%	6%	50	21	29	32%	74%	17%	1	31	0%	100%	0	0.87	-0.9	49	58	$1
16 Proj	5	4	0	73	46	4.01	4.20	1.40	771	775	767	22.4	2.1	5.7	2.7	60%	6%	46	22	32	33%	73%	9%	12						-0.4	69	82	-$2

Wright,Mike

Wright,Mike				
Age: 26 Th: R Role SP	Health	C	LIMA Plan	D+
Ht: 6' 5" Wt: 195 Type FB	PT/Exp	D	Rand Var	0
	Consist	A	MM	0001

3-5, 6.04 ERA in 45 IP at BAL. Burst onto scene with 14 scoreless IP, but then Cmd, Ctl went awry (16/15 K/BB, 30 ER in next 30 1/3 IP). Month lost to calf strain couldn't have helped. Despite imposing size, hasn't shown much Dom; FpK doesn't offer much hope that better Ctl is near, either.

Yr Tm	W	L	Sv	IP	K	ERA	xERA	WHIP	oOPS	vL	vR	BF/G	Ctl	Dom	Cmd	FpK	SwK	G	L	F	H%	S%	hr/f	GS	APC	DOM%	DIS%	Sv%	LI	RAR	BPV	BPX	R$
11																																	
12 aa	5	3	0	62	38	5.84	5.72	1.56				22.8	2.5	5.6	2.3						34%	64%								-14.1	36	47	-$9
13 a/a	11	3	0	150	116	3.75	4.67	1.47				23.9	2.4	6.9	2.9						36%	75%								2.1	78	102	$0
14 aaa	5	11	0	143	85	5.17	5.08	1.54				23.9	2.6	5.3	2.1						34%	66%								-25.1	48	57	-$13
15 BAL *	12	6	0	126	77	4.42	4.60	1.43	887	919	855	19.8	3.4	5.5	1.6	54%	8%	38	19	43	29%	72%	14%	9	65	11%	67%	0	0.83	-7.0	34	41	-$1
1st Half	6	3	0	75	51	4.72	4.42	1.39	761	913	600	20.9	3.2	6.2	1.9	53%	7%	42	19	40	30%	68%	11%	6	85	17%	50%			-7.0	47	56	-$2
2nd Half	6	3	0	51	25	3.97	4.86	1.48	1114	931	1284	18.3	3.8	4.5	1.2	58%	8%	31	21	48	29%	77%	18%	3	46	0%	100%	0	0.91	0.0	17	21	-$1
16 Proj	6	4	0	73	44	4.79	4.96	1.48	818	790	845	21.2	3.0	5.5	1.8	56%	8%	35	20	45	31%	70%	9%	15						-7.4	32	38	-$5

Wright,Steven

Wright,Steven				
Age: 31 Th: R Role SP	Health	F	LIMA Plan	D+
Ht: 6' 1" Wt: 220 Type FB	PT/Exp	D	Rand Var	0
	Consist	A	MM	0001

5-4, 4.09 ERA in 73 IP at BOS. Another late-bloomer with a knuckler? Maybe not. Held his own (see DOM/DIS), but inability to get ahead, rising Ctl (2.3, 3.9, 4.8 in June-Aug), FB tilt might've gotten him if concussion during BP hadn't. Could be "Wakefield Lite," but that's not exactly a strong selling point.

Yr Tm	W	L	Sv	IP	K	ERA	xERA	WHIP	oOPS	vL	vR	BF/G	Ctl	Dom	Cmd	FpK	SwK	G	L	F	H%	S%	hr/f	GS	APC	DOM%	DIS%	Sv%	LI	RAR	BPV	BPX	R$
11 a/a	2	4	0	49	29	7.56	6.88	1.90				25.9	5.4	5.2	1.0						33%	61%								-22.0	-3	-5	-$13
12 a/a	10	7	0	142	90	4.05	4.84	1.63				25.2	5.2	5.7	1.1						31%	76%								-0.6	35	46	-$7
13 BOS *	10	7	0	149	83	4.86	5.62	1.79	659	760	350	24.5	5.0	5.0	1.0	46%	9%	38	26	36	34%	73%	0%	1	61	0%	100%	0	0.57	-18.2	23	30	-$15
14 BOS *	6	6	0	121	74	4.55	5.06	1.46	632	667	603	23.5	2.4	5.5	2.4	56%	10%	59	21	21	33%	71%	17%	1	58	100%	0%	0	0.26	-12.1	46	55	-$6
15 BOS *	7	9	0	125	83	4.95	5.18	1.54	722	653	791	22.6	3.3	6.0	1.8	55%	9%	43	14	43	33%	70%	12%	9	74	56%	22%	0	0.76	-15.3	38	45	-$9
1st Half	5	5	0	82	49	4.49	4.96	1.52	724	728	718	21.0	3.2	5.3	1.7	60%	9%	45	12	43	32%	72%	11%	4	61	75%	0%	0	0.76	-5.3	36	43	-$7
2nd Half	2	4	0	42	34	5.86	5.60	1.58	719	546	900	26.6	3.5	7.2	2.0	48%	10%	39	17	44	34%	65%	14%	5	100	40%	40%			-9.9	41	49	-$12
16 Proj	4	5	0	73	48	4.87	5.01	1.59	817	718	920	24.1	3.6	5.9	1.6	53%	10%	42	15	43	33%	71%	8%	13						-8.1	29	35	-$7

Young,Chris

Young,Chris				
Age: 37 Th: R Role SP	Health	D	LIMA Plan	D+
Ht: 6' 10" Wt: 255 Type xFB	PT/Exp	C	Rand Var	-5
	Consist	F	MM	0001

Overpayment alert! Yes, he's outpitched ERA in past; yes, he keeps racking up double-digit wins; yes, he helped World Series run. Still, he's 37, career-low hit rate won't last, and xERA history gives an idea of what will happen if (when) the planets realign. Best use? Nominate him for $1, pray someone says, "$2."

Yr Tm	W	L	Sv	IP	K	ERA	xERA	WHIP	oOPS	vL	vR	BF/G	Ctl	Dom	Cmd	FpK	SwK	G	L	F	H%	S%	hr/f	GS	APC	DOM%	DIS%	Sv%	LI	RAR	BPV	BPX	R$
11 NYM	1	0	0	24	22	1.88	4.37	0.96	548	378	789	23.8	4.1	8.3	2.0	58%	9%	19	15	66	16%	90%	8%	4	99	50%	25%			6.1	34	51	$1
12 NYM	4	9	0	115	80	4.15	5.20	1.35	784	843	727	24.7	2.8	6.3	2.2	63%	9%	22	20	58	30%	73%	8%	20	92	50%	20%			-1.9	37	48	-$2
13 aaa	1	2	0	32	11	10.08	11.33	2.46				24.1	4.2	3.2	0.8						40%	63%								-24.5	-80	-104	-$18
14 SEA	12	9	0	165	108	3.65	5.06	1.23	733	810	632	22.9	3.3	5.9	1.8	59%	8%	22	19	59	25%	77%	9%	29	91	48%	28%	0	0.78	1.8	18	21	$7
15 KC	11	6	0	123	83	3.06	5.09	1.09	640	732	542	14.7	3.1	6.1	1.9	58%	10%	25	17	58	22%	78%	8%	18	58	39%	17%	0	0.69	13.7	27	33	$13
1st Half	7	4	0	75	47	2.64	4.95	1.01	618	688	534	17.6	2.5	5.6	2.2	59%	9%	26	17	56	23%	78%	6%	11	69	36%	9%	0	0.74	12.2	38	45	$18
2nd Half	4	2	0	48	36	3.72	5.33	1.20	674	808	552	11.8	4.1	6.7	1.6	56%	10%	24	15	61	21%	78%	11%	7	47	43%	29%	0	0.65	1.4	12	14	$4
16 Proj	6	8	0	116	73	4.49	5.26	1.38	815	918	703	20.6	3.2	5.7	1.8	59%	9%	24	18	59	28%	73%	9%	19						-7.6	17	20	-$3

Ziegler,Brad

Ziegler,Brad				
Age: 36 Th: R Role RP	Health	A	LIMA Plan	C
Ht: 6' 4" Wt: 210 Type Con xGB	PT/Exp	B	Rand Var	-5
	Consist	A	MM	4030

Unorthodox 30-Sv year featured elite GB%, worst Dom since rookie year. Hit rate (and sub-2 ERA) won't last, but he's a stable commodity, including ability to outpitch xERA. One caveat: While not reliant on fastball, velocity dipped to 84mph. How low can it go with no effect? Ride may not end yet, but be vigilant.

Yr Tm	W	L	Sv	IP	K	ERA	xERA	WHIP	oOPS	vL	vR	BF/G	Ctl	Dom	Cmd	FpK	SwK	G	L	F	H%	S%	hr/f	GS	APC	DOM%	DIS%	Sv%	LI	RAR	BPV	BPX	R$
11 2 TM	3	2	1	58	44	2.16	2.96	1.23	598	889	464	3.6	2.9	6.8	2.3	58%	8%	69	18	13	31%	81%	0%	0	13			50	0.96	12.8	90	135	$4
12 ARI	6	1	0	69	42	2.49	2.92	1.09	578	749	501	3.4	2.8	5.5	2.0	65%	10%	76	17	8	26%	77%	13%	0	12			0	0.93	12.9	79	103	$7
13 ARI	8	1	13	73	44	2.22	3.16	1.14	594	647	550	3.8	2.7	5.4	2.0	63%	10%	70	19	11	26%	81%	13%	0	13			87	1.50	14.8	72	94	$13
14 ARI	5	3	1	67	54	3.49	3.23	1.25	681	596	734	4.1	3.2	7.3	2.3	59%	11%	64	17	19	29%	73%	14%	0	14			11	1.39	2.1	86	102	$2
15 ARI	0	3	30	68	36	1.85	3.24	0.96	524	621	430	4.0	2.3	4.8	2.1	59%	9%	73	14	14	22%	82%	11%	0	14			94	1.37	17.7	76	91	$18
1st Half	0	1	12	36	19	1.25	3.28	0.86	501	651	349	3.6	2.5	4.8	1.9	57%	10%	70	15	16	19%	90%	13%	0	13			86	1.50	12.0	66	78	$18
2nd Half	0	2	18	32	17	2.53	3.20	1.06	548	589	507	4.4	2.0	4.8	2.4	60%	8%	76	13	12	26%	76%	8%	0	16			100	1.20	5.6	87	103	$19
16 Proj	3	3	29	64	40	3.15	3.20	1.09	585	630	549	3.9	2.6	5.6	2.2	60%	10%	70	16	14	26%	71%	11%	0						6.4	80	95	$14

Zimmermann,Jordan

Zimmermann,Jordan				
Age: 30 Th: R Role SP	Health	A	LIMA Plan	B
Ht: 6' 2" Wt: 220 Type	PT/Exp	A	Rand Var	0
	Consist	A	MM	3205

Another year of pinpoint Ctl, backed by FpK. Rough first month, as it took a while for fastball velocity to warm up. Could've finished strong, with spike in SwK, Dom in Aug/Sept, but hr/f refused to cooperate. May never reach top echelon, but there's something to be said for his consistency, reliability.

Yr Tm	W	L	Sv	IP	K	ERA	xERA	WHIP	oOPS	vL	vR	BF/G	Ctl	Dom	Cmd	FpK	SwK	G	L	F	H%	S%	hr/f	GS	APC	DOM%	DIS%	Sv%	LI	RAR	BPV	BPX	R$
11 WAS	8	11	0	161	124	3.18	3.75	1.15	671	703	643	25.5	1.7	6.9	4.0	63%	8%	39	19	42	30%	74%	6%	26	95	62%	8%			15.2	95	143	$13
12 WAS	12	8	0	196	153	2.94	3.78	1.17	686	650	723	25.2	2.0	7.0	3.6	69%	9%	43	23	33	30%	78%	9%	32	97	56%	6%			25.8	94	123	$20
13 WAS	19	9	0	213	161	3.25	3.50	1.09	654	702	601	27.0	1.7	6.8	4.0	67%	9%	48	21	31	28%	73%	10%	32	96	66%	6%			16.2	103	134	$22
14 WAS	14	5	0	200	182	2.66	3.22	1.07	631	655	606	25.0	1.3	8.2	6.3	71%	11%	40	24	36	31%	77%	6%	32	91	75%	9%			26.6	130	155	$22
15 WAS	13	10	0	202	164	3.66	3.82	1.20	699	776	617	25.2	1.7	7.3	4.2	67%	9%	42	22	36	31%	74%	11%	33	94	58%	9%			7.5	105	125	$13
1st Half	7	5	0	107	77	3.04	4.06	1.23	651	734	569	25.9	1.7	6.5	3.9	66%	8%	41	22	37	32%	76%	5%	17	95	65%	12%			12.2	90	107	$16
2nd Half	6	5	0	95	87	4.36	3.55	1.18	754	821	677	24.4	1.8	8.2	4.6	68%	10%	44	21	36	29%	70%	19%	16	93	50%	6%			-4.6	121	144	$9
16 Proj	14	9	0	203	174	3.42	3.49	1.16	688	739	633	24.7	1.6	7.7	4.7	68%	9%	43	22	35	31%	74%	10%	33						13.6	115	137	$16

Zito,Barry

Zito,Barry				
Age: 38 Th: L Role SP	Health	C	LIMA Plan	
Ht: 6' 2" Wt: 205 Type	PT/Exp	C	Rand Var	
	Consist	B	MM	

0-0, 10.29 ERA in 7 IP at OAK. Got Sept nostalgia start vs. Tim Hudson; after 91/60 K/BB in 138 IP in AAA "comeback," the results were predictable. They can't take the 2002 Cy Young away from him... though if he'd stuck around much longer, he'd have risked a petition drive.

Yr Tm	W	L	Sv	IP	K	ERA	xERA	WHIP	oOPS	vL	vR	BF/G	Ctl	Dom	Cmd	FpK	SwK	G	L	F	H%	S%	hr/f	GS	APC	DOM%	DIS%	Sv%	LI	RAR	BPV	BPX	R$
11 SF *	5	4	0	71	45	5.07	4.01	1.28	816	978	781	18.3	3.6	5.6	1.5	55%	7%	40	22	38	25%	64%	16%	9	67	22%	33%	0	0.54	-9.9	33	49	-$2
12 SF	15	8	0	184	114	4.15	4.92	1.39	758	559	823	25.0	3.4	5.6	1.6	55%	7%	40	20	40	29%	72%	9%	32	96	34%	28%			-3.1	26	34	$2
13 SF	5	11	0	133	86	5.74	5.00	1.70	874	938	857	20.3	3.6	5.8	1.6	57%	8%	36	26	38	35%	68%	11%	25	79	20%	52%	0	0.67	-30.8	20	26	-$18
14																																	
15 OAK *	8	7	0	145	67	5.05	5.62	1.72	1325	2000	1192	24.4	4.8	4.2	0.9	57%	8%	41	17	41	31%	72%	33%	2	50	0%	100%	0	0.53	-19.4	10	12	-$16
1st Half	5	7	0	103	53	5.08	5.39	1.68				27.3	4.4	4.7	1.1						32%	70%	0%	0						-14.1	21	25	-$17
2nd Half	3	0	0	42	14	4.97	6.20	1.82	1325	2000	1192	19.5	5.9	3.0	0.5	57%	8%	41	17	41	29%	76%	33%	2	50	0%	100%	0	0.53	-5.2	-15	-18	-$13
16 Proj																																	

KRISTOPHER OLSON

THE NEXT TIER — Pitchers

The preceding section provided player boxes and analysis for 406 pitchers. As we know (and as Ron Shandler illustrated in the Introduction), far more than 406 pitchers will play in the major leagues in 2016. Many of those additional pitchers are covered in the minor league section, but that still leaves a gap: established major leaguers who don't play enough, or well enough, to merit a player box.

This section looks to fill that gap. Here, you will find "The Next Tier" of pitchers who are mostly past their growth years, but who are likely to see some playing time in 2016. We are including their 2014-15 MLB stats here for reference for you to do your own analysis. This way, if Ryan Webb is rumored to be pushing for save opps at some point in 2016, a quick check here would confirm that his skills are nowhere near closer-worthy. Or if Shaun Marcum sneaks into a rotation in 2016, this chart shows that his 2015 skills weren't nearly as bad as his ERA looked, and he might be a viable option as an injury replacement.

Name	Age	T	Yr	W	Sv	IP	K	ERA	xERA	WHIP	vL	vR	Ctl	Dom	Cmd	FpK	SwK	GLF	H%	S%	BPV
Abad,Fernando	28	L	14	2	0	57	51	1.57	3.29	0.85	527	475	2.4	8.0	3.4	61	11	41/17/42	21	87	100
	29	L	15	2	0	48	45	4.15	4.40	1.34	859	753	3.6	8.5	2.4	52	11	39/14/47	28	79	73
Albers,Matt	31	R	14	0	0	10	8	0.90	3.31	1.30	668	686	2.7	7.2	2.7	64	12	53/27/20	33	92	88
	32	R	15	2	0	37	28	1.21	3.50	1.07	728	516	2.2	6.8	3.1	59	7	59/14/28	27	95	100
Badenhop,Burke	31	R	14	0	1	71	40	2.29	3.54	1.26	721	646	2.4	5.1	2.1	62	4	61/20/19	30	81	65
	32	R	15	2	0	66	36	3.93	4.79	1.37	750	670	2.7	4.9	1.8	59	7	47/19/34	31	71	40
Bass,Anthony	26	R	14	1	2	27	7	6.33	4.94	1.44	720	974	2.3	2.3	1.0	62	7	51/19/29	27	61	8
	27	R	15	0	0	64	45	4.50	4.16	1.34	796	725	2.8	6.3	2.3	64	9	49/23/28	31	67	65
Bastardo,Antonio	28	L	14	5	0	64	81	3.94	3.76	1.20	640	599	4.8	11.4	2.4	57	13	30/17/53	28	67	84
	29	L	15	4	1	57	64	2.98	4.07	1.13	448	626	4.1	10.0	2.5	62	15	31/18/51	26	75	80
Beimel,Joe	37	L	14	3	0	45	25	2.20	4.10	1.18	504	791	2.8	5.0	1.8	65	8	50/20/30	26	86	42
	38	L	15	2	1	47	22	3.99	5.10	1.37	825	778	3.0	4.2	1.4	69	7	42/16/42	27	77	13
Belisle,Matt	34	R	14	4	0	65	43	4.87	4.13	1.44	813	711	2.6	6.0	2.3	68	8	46/25/29	33	66	60
	35	R	15	1	0	34	25	2.67	4.38	1.46	784	639	4.0	6.7	1.7	67	9	52/19/28	32	81	42
Boyer,Blaine	32	R	14	0	0	40	29	3.57	3.69	1.04	813	508	1.8	6.5	3.6	68	11	43/21/37	27	65	89
	33	R	15	3	1	65	33	2.49	4.48	1.25	436	823	2.6	4.6	1.7	63	8	48/24/28	28	83	37
Breslow,Craig	33	L	14	2	1	54	37	5.96	5.39	1.86	838	927	4.6	6.1	1.3	52	7	37/23/40	36	70	0
	34	L	15	0	1	65	46	4.15	4.96	1.42	805	836	3.2	6.4	2.0	55	10	35/18/47	29	78	42
Broxton,Jonathan	30	R	14	4	7	59	49	2.30	3.74	1.02	564	572	2.9	7.5	2.6	61	11	46/10/44	24	80	81
	31	R	15	4	0	60	63	4.62	3.42	1.38	833	721	3.3	9.4	2.9	60	12	53/20/28	34	68	112
Carpenter,David	28	R	14	6	3	61	67	3.54	3.33	1.26	167	533	2.4	9.9	4.2	70	12	38/24/38	11	0	130
	29	R	15	0	0	25	15	4.01	4.99	1.38	706	850	3.3	5.5	1.7	58	12	38/22/40	28	77	26
Chamberlain,Joba	28	R	14	2	2	63	59	3.57	3.27	1.29	650	643	3.4	8.4	2.5	57	11	53/23/24	31	72	90
	29	R	15	0	0	28	23	4.88	4.43	1.70	1073	848	2.9	7.5	2.6	59	10	42/27/31	37	78	76
Cotts,Neal	34	L	14	2	2	67	63	4.32	3.91	1.34	775	680	3.1	8.5	2.7	66	11	35/25/40	32	69	82
	35	L	15	1	0	63	58	3.41	4.16	1.26	573	867	3.1	8.2	2.6	55	10	37/21/42	28	82	79
Cunniff,Brandon	26	R	15	2	0	35	37	4.63	4.26	1.40	877	577	5.7	9.5	1.7	62	13	44/22/34	27	69	41
Delabar,Steve	30	R	14	3	0	26	21	4.91	5.23	1.48	482	903	6.7	7.4	1.1	53	11	32/25/43	24	69	-37
	31	R	15	2	1	29	30	5.22	4.31	1.43	783	816	4.3	9.2	2.1	65	14	42/16/42	30	68	70
Detwiler,Ross	28	L	14	2	1	63	39	4.00	4.34	1.41	516	848	3.0	5.6	1.9	59	7	46/20/33	31	73	43
	29	L	15	1	0	58	41	7.25	5.72	2.02	660	1136	5.6	6.3	1.1	53	8	44/22/33	37	66	-14
Diekman,Jake	27	L	14	5	0	71	100	3.80	2.99	1.42	577	748	4.4	12.7	2.9	55	14	43/26/30	38	73	129
	28	L	15	2	0	58	69	4.01	3.54	1.44	722	664	4.8	10.6	2.2	59	12	56/15/28	33	73	96
Duensing,Brian	31	L	14	3	0	54	33	3.31	4.43	1.33	587	843	3.3	5.5	1.7	59	9	46/19/35	28	79	33
	32	L	15	4	1	49	24	4.25	4.91	1.38	776	717	3.9	4.4	1.1	60	8	51/19/30	27	71	4
Frasor,Jason	36	R	14	4	0	47	46	2.66	3.40	1.23	668	641	3.4	8.7	2.6	60	9	47/24/29	30	80	90
	37	R	15	1	0	28	22	1.29	5.04	1.61	897	550	5.8	7.1	1.2	65	8	46/23/31	31	93	-5
Friedrich,Christian	26	L	14	0	0	24	27	5.92	3.71	1.44	400	943	3.7	10.0	2.7	55	14	39/25/36	35	59	97
	27	L	15	0	0	58	45	5.25	4.67	1.71	659	965	3.9	6.9	1.8	54	11	47/23/29	37	69	46
Frieri,Ernesto	28	R	14	1	11	42	48	7.34	3.78	1.46	879	894	3.0	10.4	3.4	61	11	33/20/48	34	54	116
	29	R	15	1	2	23	19	4.63	5.20	1.33	753	836	4.2	7.3	1.7	64	9	29/13/57	23	76	24
Furbush,Charlie	28	L	14	1	1	42	51	3.61	2.99	1.16	594	701	1.9	10.8	5.7	63	14	35/25/39	34	71	157
	29	L	15	1	0	22	17	2.08	3.43	0.65	255	577	2.1	7.1	3.4	62	11	48/16/36	14	75	97
Germen,Gonzalez	26	R	14	0	0	30	31	4.75	4.14	1.45	1126	598	4.2	9.2	2.2	56	14	36/20/44	30	76	67
	27	R	15	0	1	39	33	4.42	5.13	1.73	802	855	6.1	7.7	1.3	57	13	45/21/34	33	76	-2
Gomes,Brandon	29	R	14	2	0	34	24	3.71	4.38	1.15	649	673	2.9	6.4	2.2	61	11	32/22/46	24	74	46
	30	R	15	2	1	59	44	4.27	4.49	1.19	620	836	2.3	6.7	2.9	63	12	35/16/49	27	70	72
Gorzelanny,Tom	31	L	14	0	0	21	23	0.86	3.63	1.43	792	553	3.4	9.9	2.9	61	10	44/21/35	37	97	107
	32	L	15	2	0	39	36	5.95	5.00	1.73	664	1063	5.3	8.2	1.6	59	12	39/21/40	35	66	23
Hernandez,David	30	R	15	1	0	34	33	4.28	3.94	1.31	739	803	2.9	8.8	3.0	55	11	39/19/41	30	74	96
Howell,J.P.	31	L	14	3	0	49	48	2.39	3.31	1.14	512	585	4.6	8.8	1.9	55	10	58/18/25	24	80	70
	32	L	15	6	1	44	39	1.43	3.50	1.39	518	823	2.9	8.0	2.8	59	10	60/15/24	34	93	104
Jennings,Dan	27	L	14	0	0	40	38	1.34	3.92	1.54	753	724	3.8	8.5	2.2	52	12	49/20/32	36	95	77
	28	L	15	2	0	56	46	3.99	3.68	1.40	635	687	3.8	7.3	1.9	57	9	65/16/19	32	71	72
Layne,Tom	29	L	14	2	0	19	14	0.95	3.73	1.16	411	929	3.8	6.6	1.8	57	7	47/28/25	26	91	42
	30	L	15	2	1	48	45	3.97	3.97	1.43	418	950	5.1	8.5	1.7	54	9	55/22/23	30	72	48

THE NEXT TIER — Pitchers

Name	Age	T	Yr	W	Sv	IP	K	ERA	xERA	WHIP	vL	vR	Ctl	Dom	Cmd	FpK	SwK	GLF	H%	S%	BPV
Logan,Boone	29	L	14	2	0	25	32	6.84	3.13	1.68	938	883	4.0	11.5	2.9	58	16	50/25/25	39	64	128
	30	L	15	0	0	35	44	4.33	3.90	1.61	602	909	4.3	11.2	2.6	61	16	43/19/38	40	74	106
Lopez,Javier	36	L	14	1	0	38	22	3.11	4.24	1.33	538	783	4.5	5.3	1.2	65	9	66/13/22	26	77	16
	37	L	15	1	0	39	26	1.60	3.41	0.89	323	734	3.7	5.9	1.6	60	9	67/14/18	17	82	53
Machi,Jean	32	R	14	7	2	66	51	2.58	3.18	0.95	686	551	2.4	6.9	2.8	60	13	52/20/28	23	76	89
	33	R	15	2	4	58	42	5.12	4.51	1.40	530	959	3.4	6.5	1.9	55	9	49/20/31	30	66	52
Manship,Jeff	29	R	14	1	0	23	16	6.65	5.14	1.65	609	917	5.5	6.3	1.1	58	11	43/22/35	32	57	-14
	30	R	15	1	0	39	33	0.92	3.14	0.76	644	310	2.3	7.6	3.3	62	11	50/22/28	20	90	102
Marcum,Shaun	33	R	15	3	0	35	30	5.40	4.21	1.23	1021	597	2.8	7.7	2.7	58	11	33/22/45	25	65	73
Marquis,Jason	36	R	15	3	0	47	37	6.46	4.37	1.65	766	1078	2.7	7.0	2.6	53	10	46/23/31	36	65	79
Masset,Nick	32	R	14	2	0	45	36	5.80	4.42	1.78	951	815	4.8	7.2	1.5	59	9	52/21/28	37	66	30
	33	R	15	2	0	25	18	4.68	4.54	1.56	744	858	3.2	6.5	2.0	55	8	45/25/30	34	72	52
Mattheus,Ryan	30	R	14	0	0	9	4	1.04	4.43	1.27	733	633	4.2	4.2	1.0	51	7	50/23/27	26	91	-9
	31	R	15	2	0	56	37	4.02	4.30	1.52	869	646	2.9	5.9	2.1	61	9	53/24/23	35	73	60
Morrow,Brandon	29	R	14	1	0	33	30	5.67	4.15	1.65	948	708	4.9	8.1	1.7	52	9	51/19/30	35	64	44
	30	R	15	2	0	33	23	2.73	3.65	1.09	613	761	1.9	6.3	3.3	53	11	47/21/32	27	79	86
Noesi,Hector	27	R	14	8	0	172	123	4.75	4.37	1.37	728	834	2.9	6.4	2.2	62	10	38/21/41	30	70	53
	28	R	15	0	0	33	22	6.89	5.74	1.78	792	1045	4.7	6.1	1.3	58	11	39/18/42	33	65	0
O Flaherty,Eric	29	L	14	1	1	20	15	2.25	3.21	0.95	536	658	1.8	6.8	3.8	60	9	54/18/28	22	88	105
	30	L	15	1	0	30	21	8.10	5.36	2.17	677	1162	5.4	6.3	1.2	65	10	58/23/19	41	60	4
O Sullivan,Sean	26	R	14	0	0	13	7	6.39	4.20	1.34	962	741	1.4	5.0	3.5	58	7	39/22/39	29	57	68
	27	R	15	1	0	71	35	6.08	5.35	1.61	1172	775	2.5	4.4	1.8	62	6	41/19/40	32	67	30
Ogando,Alexi	30	R	14	2	1	25	22	6.84	5.36	1.92	732	848	5.4	7.9	1.5	58	10	35/19/46	40	62	10
	31	R	15	3	0	65	53	3.99	4.43	1.33	605	888	3.9	7.3	1.9	60	12	42/21/37	26	77	47
Otero,Dan	29	R	14	8	1	87	45	2.28	3.50	1.10	698	539	1.6	4.7	3.0	69	7	56/24/20	28	80	76
	30	R	15	2	0	47	28	6.75	4.15	1.50	884	887	1.2	5.4	4.7	73	7	49/23/28	35	56	93
Parra,Manny	31	L	14	0	1	37	34	4.66	3.84	1.55	676	923	4.4	8.3	1.9	64	14	51/22/26	34	72	60
	32	L	15	1	0	32	23	3.90	3.77	1.18	742	610	1.7	6.4	3.8	48	11	46/23/31	31	67	94
Perez,Oliver	32	L	14	3	0	59	76	2.91	3.03	1.26	780	602	3.7	11.7	3.2	62	13	44/22/34	33	80	132
	33	L	15	2	0	41	51	4.17	3.61	1.32	533	867	3.3	11.2	3.4	66	13	36/24/40	35	70	127
Ramos,Cesar	30	L	14	2	0	83	66	3.70	4.39	1.35	650	689	4.2	7.2	1.7	58	8	44/19/37	28	75	37
	31	L	15	2	0	52	43	2.75	3.80	1.34	662	707	2.6	7.4	2.9	63	9	47/24/29	34	79	88
Richard,Clayton	31	L	15	4	0	42	22	3.83	3.75	1.28	534	820	1.5	4.7	3.1	61	7	59/26/15	31	71	81
Rodriguez,Fernando	30	R	14	1	0	9	4	1.00	4.55	0.67	413	300	2.0	4.0	2.0	58	7	33/11/56	16	83	29
	31	R	15	4	0	59	65	3.84	3.76	1.14	466	672	3.7	10.0	2.7	60	14	39/18/43	28	67	97
Russell,James	28	L	14	0	1	58	42	2.97	4.12	1.13	805	421	3.1	6.6	2.1	65	8	39/24/37	26	74	51
	29	L	15	0	1	34	20	5.29	4.70	1.50	688	974	2.4	5.3	2.2	61	8	40/27/33	34	65	49
Rzepczynski,Marc	28	L	14	0	1	46	46	2.74	3.12	1.33	441	944	3.7	9.0	2.4	53	16	60/19/22	33	78	100
	29	L	15	2	0	35	41	5.66	2.75	1.54	661	972	3.6	10.5	2.9	61	15	67/20/12	39	63	138
Sipp,Tony	30	L	14	4	4	51	63	3.38	3.06	0.89	503	531	3.0	11.2	3.7	62	14	31/21/47	22	65	129
	31	L	15	3	0	54	62	1.99	3.32	1.03	593	619	2.5	10.3	4.1	65	15	39/17/44	28	86	135
Stults,Eric	34	L	14	8	0	176	111	4.30	4.30	1.38	780	778	2.3	5.7	2.5	63	8	43/21/36	31	73	61
	35	L	15	1	0	48	31	5.85	4.57	1.28	711	879	2.5	5.9	2.4	66	7	38/21/42	27	59	55
Thayer,Dale	33	R	14	4	0	65	62	2.34	3.45	1.06	636	619	2.2	8.5	3.9	64	10	39/21/40	26	87	111
	34	R	15	2	0	38	25	4.06	4.88	1.38	786	743	3.6	6.0	1.7	57	8	38/21/41	28	74	27
Thornton,Matt	37	L	14	1	0	36	28	1.75	3.43	1.14	569	634	2.0	7.0	3.5	54	9	56/13/31	31	83	106
	38	L	15	2	0	41	23	2.18	4.50	1.06	484	690	2.4	5.0	2.1	58	9	44/23/34	25	81	47
Torres,Alexander	26	L	14	2	0	54	51	3.33	4.19	1.46	737	557	5.5	8.5	1.5	55	13	47/23/30	30	77	30
	27	L	15	0	1	34	35	3.15	4.76	1.51	799	655	6.8	9.2	1.3	50	10	48/18/34	24	87	7
Torres,Carlos	31	R	14	8	2	97	96	3.06	3.57	1.31	680	734	3.5	8.9	2.5	61	12	47/17/36	31	81	90
	32	R	15	5	0	58	48	4.68	3.88	1.37	750	739	2.8	7.5	2.7	61	10	48/23/29	33	66	85
Vargas,Jason	31	L	14	11	0	187	128	3.71	4.13	1.27	661	731	2.0	6.2	3.1	63	9	38/23/39	31	74	74
	32	L	15	5	0	43	27	3.98	4.71	1.35	809	712	2.5	5.7	2.3	65	8	41/19/40	30	74	53
Villanueva,Carlos	30	R	14	5	2	78	72	4.64	3.79	1.39	758	751	2.2	8.3	3.8	59	12	41/20/38	36	67	110
	31	R	15	4	2	61	55	2.95	3.94	1.16	661	689	3.1	8.1	2.6	62	13	42/19/39	27	78	82
Webb,Daniel	24	R	14	6	0	68	58	3.99	4.33	1.49	623	834	5.6	7.7	1.4	51	11	52/18/31	29	75	18
	25	R	15	1	0	30	22	6.30	5.82	2.10	965	841	6.6	6.6	1.0	57	11	50/22/28	38	70	-31
Webb,Ryan	28	R	14	3	0	49	37	3.83	3.64	1.26	613	649	2.2	6.8	3.1	64	8	49/23/29	32	68	89
	29	R	15	1	0	51	31	3.20	3.58	1.14	631	717	2.1	5.5	2.6	66	9	59/21/20	27	74	79

5-Year Injury Log

The following chart details the disabled list stints for all players during the past five years. Use this as a supplement to our health grades in the player profile boxes as well as the "Risk Management" charts that start on page 267. It's also where to turn when you want to check whether, say, Jed Lowrie's right hand soreness in spring training should be concerning (answer: very concerning).

For each injury, the number of days the player missed during the season is listed. A few DL stints are for fewer than 15 days; these are cases when a player was placed on the DL prior to Opening Day (only in-season time lost is listed).

Abbreviations:
Lt, L = left
Rt, R = right
fx = fractured
R/C = rotator cuff
str = strained
surg = surgery
TJS = Tommy John surgery (ulnar collateral ligament reconstruction)
x 2 = two occurrences of the same injury
x 3 = three occurrences of the same injury

Throughout the spring and all season long, BaseballHQ.com has comprehensive injury coverage.

FIVE-YEAR INJURY LOG — Batters

Batters	Yr	Days	Injury
Abreu,Jose	14	15	L ankle tendinitis
Abreu,Tony	13	103	Strained L knee + bursitis
Ackley,Dustin	15	28	R lumbar strain
Adams,Matt	13	15	R oblique strain
	14	14	Tightness in L calf
	15	105	Strained R quad
Adduci,James	14	118	Concussion; Fx Lt finger
Adrianza,Ehire	14	82	Strained R hamstring x 2
Almanzar,Michael	14	92	Patella tendinitis in L knee
Almonte,Zoilo	13	51	Sprained L ankle
Alonso,Yonder	13	41	R hand contusion
	14	55	Strained R forearm/R wrist tend
	15	46	Low back strain; bruised R shoulder
Alvarez,Pedro	11	66	R. quadriceps tightness
Andino,Robert	12	15	Subluxation of L. shoulder
Ankiel,Rick	11	37	R. wrist sprain
	12	10	Quad injury
Aoki,Norichika	14	20	Strained L groin
	15	40	Concussion; fx fibula
Arcia,Oswaldo	14	35	Strained R wrist
	15	30	R hip flexor strain
Arenado,Nolan	14	40	Fractured L middle finger
Arencibia,JP	12	43	Fractured R. hand
Arias,Joaquin	13	18	Appendicitis
Arruebarrena,Erisbel	14	21	Strained R hip flexor
Asche,Cody	14	26	Strained L hamstring
Avila,Alex	12	15	Strained R. hamstring
	13	31	L forearm bruise; Concussion
	14	5	Concussion
	15	55	Loose bodies in L knee
Aybar,Erick	11	17	Strained L. oblique muscle
	12	15	Fractured R. toe
	13	20	Bruised L heel
Baker,Jeff	11	14	L. groin strain
	13	35	Sprained R thumb
	15	21	L intercostal strain

FIVE-YEAR INJURY LOG — Batters

Batters	Yr	Days	Injury
Baker,John	11	158	Recovery from TJS
Barajas,Rod	11	25	Sprained R. ankle
Barmes,Clint	11	29	L. hand fracture
	14	50	Strained L groin
Barney,Darwin	11	15	L. knee sprain
	13	15	L knee laceration
Bartlett,Jason	12	140	Strained R. knee
	14	14	Sprained L ankle
Barton,Daric	11	27	Torn labrum in R. shoulder
	12	4	Sprained R. shoulder
Bautista,Jose	12	77	Inflam R. wrist/Surgery on R. wrist
	13	40	L hip bone bruise
Baxter,Mike	11	126	Torn ligament in L. thumb
	12	58	Displaced R. collarbone
Bay,Jason	11	21	Strained L. rib cage
	12	67	Non-displaced Rib+ Concussionx2
Beckham,Gordon	13	54	Fractured hamate bone, L wrist
	14	25	Strained L oblique
Beckham,Tim	14	133	Rec. from surgery R Knee- torn ACL
	15	25	R hamstring strain
Belt,Brandon	11	44	Hairline L. wrist fracture
	14	81	Concussion x 2/Fx L thumb
Beltran,Carlos	11	15	Strained R. hand
	14	29	Concussion; hyper ext. Rt elbow
	15	16	Strained L oblique
Beltre,Adrian	11	40	Strained L. hamstring
	14	12	Strained L quadriceps
	15	21	Sprained L thumb
Beltre,Engel	14	184	Fractured R tibia
Berkman,Lance	12	108	R. knee inflam x2 + L. calf str
	13	56	L hip inflammation
Betancourt,Yunies.	12	30	Sprained R. ankle
Betemit,Wilson	12	21	Injured R. wrist
	13	148	R PCL tear
Betts,Mookie	15	13	Concussion

FIVE-YEAR INJURY LOG — Batters

Batters	Yr	Days	Injury
Bianchi,Jeff	13	32	L hip bursitis
	14	74	Sprained R elbow
Blackmon,Charlie	11	83	Fractured L. foot
	12	135	Turf toe
Blanco,Gregor	15	9	Concussion
Blanco,Henry	12	59	Sprained L. thumb
Blanks,Kyle	11	26	Recovery from TJS
	12	173	Labrum tear L. shoulder
	13	80	L Achilles tendinitis
	14	109	Strnd L calf; L Achilles tendinitis
	15	129	Achilles tendinitis; cyst removal
Bloomquist,Willie	11	23	Strained R. hamstring
	12	23	Strained lower back
	13	122	Str. R Intercostal;L hand bruise
	14	67	Bruised R knee
Boesch,Brennan	11	20	Torn ligament in R. thumb
	15	8	R ankle contusion
Bogaerts,Xander	14	7	Concussion
Bogusevic,Brian	13	77	L hamstring strain
Bonifacio,Emilio	12	112	Sprained L. thumb x2; spr. R. knee
	14	39	Strained R ribcage
	15	16	Strained L oblique
Borbon,Julio	11	20	Inflam - L. hamstring
Bourgeois,Jason	11	50	Strained L. oblique
	15	84	Fractured L shoulder
Bourjos,Peter	11	15	Tight R. hamstring
	12	15	Sore R. wrist
	13	100	Fx Rt wrist; Strained Lt hammy
Bourn,Michael	13	25	R hand laceration
	14	56	Rec from surg: strained L hamstring
Brantley,Michael	11	34	Inflam in R. wrist
Brantly,Rob	15	45	Avulsion fracture, L thumb
Braun,Ryan	13	28	R thumb contusion
	14	10	strained R oblique muscle
Brett,Ryan	15	166	Subluxation of L shoulder
Brignac,Reid	14	31	Sprained L ankle
Brown,Domonic	13	13	Concussion
	15	28	L Achilles tendinitis
Bruce,Jay	14	16	Rec from meniscus repair on L knee
Buck,Travis	12	128	R. Achilles tendinitis
Buxton,Byron	15	45	Sprained L thumb
Byrd,Marlon	11	40	Facial fractures
	15	16	Fractured R wrist
Cabrera,Asdrubal	13	22	R quadriceps strain
	15	16	Strained R hamstring
Cabrera,Everth	13	18	Strained L hamstring
	14	75	Strained L hamstring x 2
	15	15	L foot contusion
Cabrera,Melky	13	82	Strained L knee; Tendinitis
	14	21	Fractured R pinky finger
Cabrera,Miguel	15	41	L calf strain
Cain,Lorenzo	12	89	Strained L. groin
	13	26	Strained L oblique
	14	18	Strained L groin
Cairo,Miguel	12	22	Strained L. hamstring
Calhoun,Kole	14	35	Sprained R ankle

FIVE-YEAR INJURY LOG — Batters

Batters	Yr	Days	Injury
Callaspo,Alberto	13	20	R calf tightness
	14	15	Strained R hamstring
Carp,Mike	12	91	Strained R. shoulder x2; R. groin
Carpenter,Matt	12	30	R. oblique strain
Casali,Curtis	14	5	Concussion
	15	40	Strained L hamstring
Casilla,Alexi	11	62	Strained R. hamstring
Castillo,Welington	12	71	MCL sprain in R. knee
	13	5	Surgery - R knee
	14	19	L ribcage inflammation
Castro,Jason	11	182	R. knee surgery
	12	36	R. knee swelling
	13	13	Cyst on R knee
	15	19	Strained R quad
Ceciliani,Darrell	15	27	Strained L hamstring
Cedeno,Ronny	11	20	Concussion
	12	46	L. intercostal strain+str R. calf
Cervelli,Francisco	11	50	Fractured L. foot; Concussion
	13	156	Fractured R hand
	14	64	Hamstring injury
Cespedes,Yoenis	12	25	Strained muscle in L. hand
	13	15	Strained muscle, L hand
Chavez,Endy	12	50	Strained intercostal muscle
Chirinos,Robinson	12	182	Concussion
	15	37	L shoulder strain
Chisenhall,Lonnie	12	71	Fractured R. ulna
Choice,Michael	14	14	Strained L hamstring
Choo,Shin-Soo	11	71	Fract. L. thumb; Strain L. oblique
	14	35	Bone spur in L elbow
Christian,Justin	12	15	Sprained L. wrist
Clevenger,Steve	12	33	Strained R. oblique
	13	169	L oblique strain
Coghlan,Chris	11	104	L. knee Inflam
	13	84	R calf irritation
Colon,Christian	14	12	fractured right middle finger
Cooper,David	12	42	Strained back
Corporan,Carlos	13	20	Concussion
	15	46	Sprained L thumb
Cousins,Scott	11	108	Lower back strain
Cowgill,Collin	12	24	Sprained L. ankle
	14	22	Fractured nose
	15	96	Sprained R wrist
Cozart,Zack	11	67	Hyperextended L. elbow
	15	116	R knee surgery
Craig,Allen	11	78	L. groin strain
	12	43	Surg recovery; L. hamstring strain
	14	16	Sprained L foot
Crawford,Carl	11	30	Strained L. hamstring
	12	148	Recovery from L. wrist surgery+ TJS
	13	33	Strained L hamstring
	14	43	Sprained L ankle
	15	84	Strained R oblique
Crisp,Coco	12	18	Infected ear/sinus
	13	15	Strained L hamstring
	15	104	Cervical strain; R elbow surg.
Crowe,Trevor	11	160	Recov. from surgery - R. shoulder
	13	51	Sprained AC joint in R shoulder

FIVE-YEAR INJURY LOG — Batters

Batters	Yr	Days	Injury
Cruz,Luis	13	24	Sprained R knee
Cruz,Nelson	11	34	Strained R. quad; Strained L. ham.
Cruz,Tony	13	17	Stress fracture, L forearm
Cuddyer,Michael	12	61	R. oblique strainx2
	13	15	Bulging disk in neck
	14	112	Strnd L hamstring x 2/strnd L should
	15	17	L knee pain
Culberson,Charlie	15	67	Lumbar disc inflammation
d Arnaud,Travis	14	14	Concussion
	15	88	Hyperextended L elbow; fx R hand
d'Arnaud,Chase	11	29	Fractured little finger on R. hand
	13	61	L thumb surgery
Darnell,James	12	139	R. shoulder subluxation
	13	34	Strained L oblique
Davis,Chris	11	22	Strained R. shoulder
	14	14	Strained L oblique
Davis,Ike	11	141	L. ankle sprain and bone bruise
	13	21	Strained R oblique
	15	80	Strained L hip; quad
Davis,Khristopher	15	37	Torn meniscus, R knee
Davis,Rajai	11	64	Sore R. ankle; Torn L. hamstring
	13	24	Strained oblique
De Aza,Alejandro	12	15	Bruised L. ribs
Decker,Jaff	15	13	L calf strain
DeJesus,David	13	39	R shoulder sprain
	14	74	Fractured L hand
Denorfia,Chris	11	35	Strained R. hamstring
	15	45	Strained L hamstring x2
DeRosa,Mark	11	91	Sore L. wrist
	12	85	L. abdominal strain+ oblique str
DeShields,Delino	15	20	Strained L hamstring
Desmond,Ian	12	26	Torn L. oblique
DeWitt,Blake	13	119	Lower back strain
Diaz,Jonathan	14	182	L hamstring injury
Diaz,Matt	12	75	R. thumb contusion
	13	134	L knee bone contusion
Dickerson,Corey	15	98	Non-displaced rib fx; fasciitis L ft x2
Dietrich,Derek	14	53	Strained R wrist
Dirks,Andy	12	61	Tendinitis in R. Achilles tendon
	14	184	Recovering from surgery on back
Donald,Jason	11	29	Fractured L. hand
Doumit,Ryan	11	135	L. ankle sprain
	13	8	Concussion
Drew,Stephen	12	83	Recovering from R. ankle surgery
	13	31	R Hamstring tight; Concussion
Duda,Lucas	13	46	Strained L intercostal
	15	16	Lower back strain
Dyson,Jarrod	13	37	R ankle sprain
Eaton,Adam	13	100	L elbow strain
	14	31	Rt oblique muscle; Rt hamstring
Ellis,A.J.	13	15	L oblique strain
	14	54	Sprained R ankle/L knee surgery
	15	15	R knee inflammation
Ellis,Mark	11	15	Strained R. hamstring
	12	46	Sprained L. leg
	13	22	Strained R quad
	14	29	Strained L oblique/L knee tend

FIVE-YEAR INJURY LOG — Batters

Batters	Yr	Days	Injury
Ellsbury,Jacoby	12	90	Subluxation of R. shoulder
	15	49	R knee sprain
Elmore,Jake	14	74	Strained L quadriceps
Encarnacion,Edwin	13	13	Surgery (cart) - L wrist
	14	39	Strained R quadriceps
Escobar,Alcides	15	7	Concussion & L cheek contusion
Escobar,Yunel	11	9	Inflam - L. elbow
	14	16	Sore R shoulder
Espinosa,Danny	13	15	Broken bone in R wrist
Ethier,Andre	12	15	Strained L. oblique
Featherston,Taylor	15	16	Uppen back strain
Federowicz,Tim	15	128	Torn meniscus, R knee
Fielder,Prince	14	129	Herniated disc in neck (surgery)
Fields,Josh	13	57	R forearm strain
	15	23	R groin strain
Figgins,Chone	11	33	Strained R. hip flexor
	14	52	Strained L quadriceps
Flaherty,Ryan	15	30	Strained R groin x2
Flowers,Tyler	13	28	R shoulder surgery
Forsythe,Logan	12	60	L. foot fracture
	13	71	Plantar fasciitis, R foot
Fowler,Dexter	11	40	L. abdominal strain
	13	15	R wrist soreness
	14	43	Strained R intercostal
Francisco,Ben	12	35	Strained L. hamstring
Francisco,Juan	11	31	L. calf strain
Franco,Maikel	15	48	Fractured L wrist
Franklin,Nick	15	42	Strained L oblique
Freeman,Freddie	13	15	Strained R oblique
	15	47	Strained R oblique; bruised R wrist
Freese,David	11	56	Broken hamate bone in L. hand
	13	8	Strained lower back
	14	17	Fractured R middle finger
	15	40	Fractured R index finger
Freiman,Nathan	15	35	Back strain
Fukudome,Kosuke	12	122	Strained R. oblique
Fuld,Sam	12	110	Surgery - R. wrist
	14	36	Concussion
Furcal,Rafael	11	70	Broken L. thumb
	12	34	R. elbow strain
	13	183	R elbow surgery
	14	174	Strained L hamstring x 2
Galvis,Freddy	12	119	Fracture of L4-5 veR.ebra
	14	15	Staph infection in L knee
Gamel,Mat	12	155	Torn R. ACL
	13	183	Torn R ACL
Garcia,Avisail	13	30	Bruised R heel
	14	128	Surgery on L shoulder torn labrum
Gardner,Brett	12	164	Sore R. elbow
Gattis,Evan	13	26	Oblique strain
	14	21	Bulging thoracic disc in back
Gennett,Scooter	15	14	L hand laceration
Gentry,Craig	11	14	Concussion
	13	27	Fractured L hand
	14	39	Fx R hand; lower back strain
Getz,Chris	12	89	Bruised ribs+str L. leg+fx L. thumb
	13	15	L knee sprain

FIVE-YEAR INJURY LOG — Batters

Batters	Yr	Days	Injury
Giambi,Jason	11	17	Strained L. quadriceps
	12	42	Viral syndrome
	13	11	Lower back strain
	14	118	L knee inflammation;RT calf;fx rib
Giavotella,Johnny	15	41	Personal medical condition
Gillaspie,Conor	14	11	Sore/bruised L hand
Gillespie,Cole	14	25	Strained oblique muscle
Gimenez,Chris	11	64	Strained L. oblique muscle
Gimenez,Hector	11	173	R. knee surgery
Goldschmidt,Paul	14	58	Fractured L hand
Gomes,Yan	14	7	Concussion
	15	42	R knee sprain
Gomez,Carlos	11	42	Fractured L. clavicle
	12	15	Strained L. hamstring
	15	15	R hamstring strain
Gomez,Hector	12	182	Groin strain
Gonzalez,Alex	12	151	R. knee injury
Gonzalez,Carlos	11	37	Strained R. wrist
	13	29	Sprained R middle finger
	14	51	L knee tendinitis/L finger inflam
Gonzalez,Marwin	12	38	Bruised R. heel
Gordon,Alex	15	54	Strained L groin
Gordon,Dee	11	22	Bruised R. shoulder
	12	68	Torn R. thumb ligament
	15	11	Dislocated L thumb
Gosewisch,Tuffy	15	129	Torn L ACL
Gosselin,Phil	15	105	Avulsion fracture, L thumb
Grandal,Yasmani	12	17	Strained R. oblique
	13	85	R knee sprain
	15	7	Concussion
Granderson,Curtis	13	113	Fx finger Lt hand; Fx Lt finger
Green,Grant	14	39	Lumbar strain
Green,Taylor	13	183	L hip labral injury
Gregorius,Didi	13	23	Concussion; R elbow strain
Grichuk,Randal	15	47	R elbow strain
Guillen,Carlos	11	127	Recov. fr L. knee surg; Sore L. wrist
Gutierrez,Franklin	11	71	Gastritis; Strained L. oblique
	12	128	Concussion + torn R. pec muscle
	13	123	Strained R hamstring x 2
Guyer,Brandon	12	144	Strained L. shoulder
	13	60	Fractured R middle finger
	14	24	Fractured L thumb
Guzman,Jesus	14	16	Back spasms
Gyorko,Jedd	13	32	Strained R groin
	14	52	Plantar fasciitis in L foot
Hafner,Travis	11	50	Strained R. oblique; Strain R. foot
	12	82	Inflamed lower back+sore R. knee
	13	60	Strained R rotator cuff
Hairston Jr.,Jerry	11	18	R. wrist fracture
	12	71	L. hip Inflam+ L. hammy str
	13	21	Strained L groin
Hairston,Scott	11	36	L. oblique strain
	14	29	Strained L oblique
Hamilton,Billy	15	38	Jammed & sprianed R Shoulder;
Hamilton,Josh	11	40	Fractured R. humerus
	14	55	Surgery on L thumb torn UCL
	15	89	L knee infl; L hammy; rec R shldr surg

FIVE-YEAR INJURY LOG — Batters

Batters	Yr	Days	Injury
Hanigan,Ryan	13	50	Sprained L wrist; L oblique
	14	54	Strained L oblique; Rt hamstring
	15	61	Fractured knuckle, R hand
Hannahan,Jack	12	19	Strained L. calf
	14	119	Rec from surgery on R shoulder
Hardy,J.J.	11	30	Strained L. oblique muscle
	15	47	Groin strain; L shoulder strain
Harper,Bryce	13	35	L knee bursitis
	14	64	Surgery on L thumb
Harrison,Josh	15	46	Torn L thumb ligaments
Hart,Corey	11	27	L. oblique strain
	13	183	Recovery from R knee surgery
	14	75	Bruised R knee; strained LT hammy
	15	103	L shoulder impingement
Hawpe,Brad	11	102	Strained R. middle finger
Headley,Chase	11	43	Fractured L. pinkie finger
	13	17	Broken L thumb
	14	15	Strained R calf
Heathcott,Zachary	15	62	Strained R quad
Hechavarria,Adeiny	13	15	Bruised L elbow
	14	11	Strained R triceps
Heisey,Chris	11	26	Strained L. oblique
	13	58	Strained R hamstring
Helton,Todd	12	77	R. hip labrum tear+ hip Inflam
	13	15	L forearm inflammation
Hermida,Jeremy	12	160	Strained R. hip flexor
Hernandez,Cesar	15	21	Dislocated L thumb
Hernandez,Enrique	15	35	L hamstring strain
Hernandez,Gorkys	15	11	L shoulder discomfort
Hernandez,Oscar	15	91	Fractured L hand
Hernandez,Ramon	12	50	L. hand strain
Herrera,Dilson	15	26	Fractured R middle finger
Herrera,Jonathan	11	23	R. index finger fracture
	12	45	Infection in L. wrist+ R. hammy str.
Heyward,Jason	11	23	Sore R. shoulder
	13	55	Fx R jaw; appendectomy
Hicks,Aaron	13	22	L hamstring strain
	14	22	Strained R shoulder;concussion
	15	34	Strained L ham; R forearm
Hill,Aaron	11	18	Sore R. hamstring
	13	71	Broken L hand
Holliday,Matt	11	15	L. quadriceps strain
	13	15	Strained R hamstring
	15	85	Strained R quad x 2
Holt,Brock	14	23	Concussion
Hosmer,Eric	14	31	Stress fracture in R hand
Howard,Ryan	12	93	Recov. Fr. L. Achilles tendon surg.
	13	86	L knee inflammation
Huff,Aubrey	12	94	Anxiety disorder+R. knee spr x 2
Hundley,Nick	11	71	R. oblique strain
	12	49	Torn meniscus in R. knee
	15	24	Cervical strain
Iannetta,Chris	12	80	Fractured R. wrist
Iglesias,Jose	14	184	Stress fracture in both shins
Inciarte,Ender David	14	7	Concussion
	15	31	Strained R hamstring

FIVE-YEAR INJURY LOG — Batters

Batters	Yr	Days	Injury
Infante,Omar	11	15	Fractured R. middle finger
	13	39	Sprained L ankle
	14	15	Disc irritation in lower back
Inge,Brandon	11	22	Mononucleosis
	12	68	Str. R. shouldx2+str groin x2
	13	23	R scapula soreness
Ishikawa,Travis T	15	65	Lower back strain x2
Izturis,Cesar	11	136	R. hand numbness; Strained groin
	12	27	Strained L. hamstring
Izturis,Maicer	13	40	Sprained L ankle
	14	169	Sprained L knee
	15	183	R groin strain
Jackson,Austin	12	15	Strained abdominal
	13	33	Strained R hamstring
	15	22	Sprained R ankle
Jackson,Ryan	14	27	Strained R wrist
Janish,Paul	13	40	Recovery from L shoulder surgery
Jaso,John	11	39	Stained R. oblique muscle
	13	67	Concussion
	14	15	Concussion
	15	88	L wrist contusion; L knee bursitis
Jay,Jon	12	38	Sprained R. shoulder
	15	79	Bone bruise, L wrist + tendon
Jennings,Desmond	12	24	Sprained L. knee
	13	39	Fractured L middle finger
	14	30	Bruised L Knee
	15	142	L knee bursitis
Jeter,Derek	11	20	Strained R. calf
	13	163	Lt ankle sorenesss; Rt calf; Rt quad
Johnson,Chris	15	40	Infection, L hand, Fx L hand
Johnson,Dan	14	33	Strained L hamstring
Johnson,Elliot	11	19	Sprained L. knee
Johnson,Kelly	15	26	R oblique strain
Johnson,Nick	12	98	Sprained R. wrist
Johnson,Reed	11	15	Lower back spasms
	13	43	L knee tendinitis
	15	159	Strained L calf
Johnson,Rob	12	50	Torn ligament in L. thumb
Joseph,Corban	13	24	Recovery from R shoulder surgery
Joyce,Matt	12	27	Tightness in lower back
	15	35	Concussion
Kalish,Ryan	11	4	Herniated cervical disc
	13	183	Recovery from R shoulder surgery
Kang,Jung-Ho	15	14	Torn L meniscus, fx L tibia
Kearns,Austin	12	15	R. hamstring strain
Kelly,Don	15	175	Fractured R ring finger
Kemp,Matt	12	58	Strained L. hamstring
	13	97	Str R ham; Sore A/c joint, L ankle
	14	16	Recovering from surgery on L ankle
Kendrick,Howie	11	15	Strained R. hamstring
	13	35	Sprained L knee
	15	56	Strained L hamstring
Kennedy,Adam	12	38	Strained R. groin
Keppinger,Jeff	11	57	L. foot surgery
	12	34	Broken R. big toe
	14	45	Rec from surgery on R shoulder
Kinsler,Ian	13	28	R intercostal strain

FIVE-YEAR INJURY LOG — Batters

Batters	Yr	Days	Injury
Kipnis,Jason	11	23	Strained R. hamstring
	14	26	Strained R oblique
	15	15	R shoulder inflammation
Kobernus,Jeff	14	74	Fractured L hand
Konerko,Paul	12	9	Concussion
	13	19	Strained lower back
Kotchman,Casey	13	138	Strained L oblique; hammy
Kotsay,Mark	12	33	Lower back strain+R. calf str
Kouzmanoff,Kevin	14	91	Herniated disc in back
Kratz,Erik	13	35	L knee surgery
	15	36	Plantar fasciitis, L foot
Kubel,Jason	11	52	Strained L. foot
	13	15	Strained L quad
La Stella,Tommy	15	119	Strained R oblique
Ladendorf,Tyler	15	91	Recovery from ankle surgery
Lagares,Juan	14	39	Strnd R intercostal/strnd R hamstring
Laird,Gerald	11	45	R. index finger fracture
	13	16	Kidney stone
	15	130	Lower back spasms
Lamb,Jacob	15	46	Stress reaction, L foot
Lambo,Andrew	15	152	Plantar fasciitis, L foot
LaRoche,Adam	11	130	Torn labrum in L. shoulder
	14	13	Strained R quadriceps
Lavarnway,Ryan	14	76	Strained L wrist
Lawrie,Brett	11	8	Fractured R. middle finger
	12	34	Strained R. oblique
	13	61	Sprained L ankle; L ribcage
	14	95	Strained L oblique; fx Rt finger
Lee,Carlos	12	15	Stained L. hamstring
Lee,Derrek	11	18	Strained L. oblique muscle
Lewis,Fred	11	35	Strained R. oblique
Lillibridge,Brent	11	20	Fract. metacarpal bone in R. hand
Lind,Adam	11	27	Soreness - lower back
	12	31	Strained mid-back
	14	52	Fx R foot; lower back tightness
Lobaton,Jose	11	46	Sprained L. knee
	12	45	Sore R. shoulder
Loney,James	15	55	Broken finger; R oblique
Longoria,Evan	11	30	Strained L. oblique muscle
	12	98	Torn L. hamstring
Lopez,Rafael	15	7	Fractured left hand
Lough,David	15	8	Strained L hamstring
Lowrie,Jed	11	52	Sore L. shoulder
	12	66	R. ankle + R. thumb sprains
	14	18	Fractured R index finger
	15	93	Torn ligament, R thumb
Lucas,Edward	14	30	Fractured L hand
Lucroy,Jonathan	11	12	Fractured R. pinkie finger
	12	58	R. hand fracture
	15	41	Broken L toe
Ludwick,Ryan	11	15	Mid-back muscle spasms
	13	132	Torn cartilage in R shoulder
Machado,Manny	13	5	Torn ligament - L knee
	14	79	Surgery L knee 10/13; R knee surgery
Mahoney,Joseph	13	59	Hammy strain; intercostal strain
Maldonado,Carlos	12	127	Strained lower back
Marisnick,Jake	15	16	Strained L hamstring

FIVE-YEAR INJURY LOG — Batters

Batters	Yr	Days	Injury
Markakis,Nick	12	40	Fractured R. hand
Marrero,Chris	12	184	Torn L. hamstring
Marson,Lou	13	173	Neck strain; Sore R shoulder
Marte,Starling	12	19	Strained R. oblique
	13	19	R hand contusion
	14	13	Concussion
Martin,Russell	14	26	Strained L hamstring
Martinez,Fernando	12	9	Concussion
	13	21	Strained L oblique
Martinez,J.D.	13	65	Sprnd R knee; Sprained L wrist
Martinez,Michael	12	65	R. foot fracture
Martinez,Victor	11	15	Strained R. groin
	12	183	Recovery from surgery - L. knee
	15	31	L knee inflammation
Mastroianni,Darin	13	121	Stress reaction in L ankle
Mathis,Jeff	13	44	Broken R collarbone
	15	53	Fractured R ring finger
Mauer,Joe	11	79	Bilateral leg weakness; Pneumonia
	13	41	Concussion
	14	40	Strained R oblique muscle
Maxwell,Justin	11	28	Recovery from TJS
	12	17	Loose bodies in L. ankle
	13	69	Fractured L hand; Concussion
Mayberry,John	14	40	L wrist inflammation
Maybin,Cameron	11	16	R. knee Inflam
	13	163	Strained L knee; Sore R wrist
	14	29	Ruptured L biceps tendon
McCann,Brian	11	19	Strained L. oblique
	13	36	Recovery from R shoulder surgery
	14	8	Concussion
McCutchen,Andrew	14	15	Fractured L rib
McDonald,Darnell	11	19	Strained L. quad muscle
	12	24	Strained R. oblique
McDonald,John	11	21	Strained R. hamstring
	12	29	Strained L. oblique
	13	26	Lower back discomfort
McKenry,Michael	13	64	L knee surgery
	15	47	Lateral meniscus tear, R knee
McLouth,Nate	11	89	L. oblique strain
	14	19	R shoulder inflammation
	15	183	R shoulder surgery
Mercer,Jordy	15	34	Lower leg contusion
Mesoraco,Devin	12	8	Concussion
	14	20	strnd L hamstring/strnd L oblique
	15	133	L hip strain
Middlebrooks,Will	12	54	Fractured R. wrist
	13	17	Low back strain
	14	94	Fx Rt index finger; strained Rt calf
Miller,Corky	13	25	R quad contusion
Molina,Yadier	13	15	Sprained R knee
	14	50	Torn ligament in R thumb
Montero,Miguel	13	28	Lower back strain
	15	21	Sprained L thumb
Moore,Adam	11	175	Surgery to repair R. meniscus
Moore,Jeremy	12	182	Recovering from L. hip surgery
Moore,Tyler	15	13	L ankle sprain
Morales,Kendrys	11	183	Recovery from surgeries - L. ankle

FIVE-YEAR INJURY LOG — Batters

Batters	Yr	Days	Injury
Morel,Brent	12	75	Strained back
Moreland,Mitch	12	40	Strained L. hamstring
	13	15	Strained R hamstring
	15	14	L elbow surgery
Morgan,Nyjer	11	36	Deep thigh bruise
	14	82	Sprained R knee
Morneau,Justin	11	80	Strain L. wrist; Post conc. synd.
	12	15	Sore R. wrist
	14	8	Strained neck
	15	111	Concussion
Morrison,Logan	11	22	L. foot strain
	12	67	R. knee Inflam
	13	70	Recovery from R knee surgery
	14	56	Strained R hamstring
Morse,Michael	12	58	Strained R. lat
	13	38	Strained R quad
	15	40	R ring finger strain
Murphy,Daniel	11	52	Torn ligament in L. knee
	14	11	Strained R calf
	15	25	Strained L quad
Murphy,David	14	26	Strained R abdominal
Murphy,Donnie	11	128	R. wrist Inflam
	12	15	L. hamstring strain
	14	15	Strained neck
Myers,Wil	14	80	Sprained R wrist
	15	104	Bone spurs, L wrist + tend
Nady,Xavier	11	47	Fractured L. hand
	12	69	R. wrist tendonitis
Nakajima,Hiroyuki	13	53	Strained L hamstring
Napoli,Mike	11	22	Strained L. oblique muscle
	12	35	Strained L. quadriceps
	14	14	Sprained L ring finger
Nava,Daniel	12	40	Sprained L. wristx2
	15	54	Strained L thumb
Navarro,Dioner	11	26	R. oblique strain
	15	40	Strained L hamstring
Neal,Thomas	13	53	Dislocated R shoulder
Negron,Kristopher	12	34	R. knee injury
	15	21	Torn labrum Lt shdlr
Nelson,Chris	12	37	Irreg. heaR.beat+ L. wrist Inflam
	13	19	Strained R hamstring
Nieuwenhuis,Kirk	15	30	Pinched nerve in back
Nieves,Wil	12	31	Turf toe in R. foot
	14	27	Strained R quadriceps
Nishioka,Tsuyoshi	11	85	Fract. L. fibula; Strain R. oblique
Nix,Jayson	11	23	Contusion - L. shin
	13	65	fX L hand; Strained Rt hammy
Nix,Laynce	12	73	Strained R. elbow
Norris,Derek	13	15	Fractured big toe, L foot
Nunez,Eduardo	13	61	L ribcage strain
	14	16	Strained R hamstring
	15	12	L oblique strain
Olivo,Miguel	12	23	Strained R. groin
Olt,Mike	15	84	Hairline fracture, R wrist
Ortiz,David	12	78	Strained R. achilles tendonx2
	13	20	R Achilles tendon soreness
Owings,Christopher	14	65	Strained L shoulder

FIVE-YEAR INJURY LOG — Batters

Batters	Yr	Days	Injury
Ozuna,Marcell	13	69	Torn L thumb ligament
Pacheco,Jordan	14	33	R shoulder tendinitis
Pagan,Angel	11	35	Pulled L. oblique
	13	125	Strained R hamstring
	14	43	Strained back
	15	21	R patella tendinitis
Panik,Joe	15	54	Lower back discomfort + inflam
Paredes,Jimmy	15	13	Lower back strain
Parrino,Andy	12	24	Injured R. hand
Pastornicky,Tyler	13	46	Torn L ACL
Paulino,Ronny	11	19	Anemia
Pearce,Steve	11	91	R. calf strain
	13	61	L wrist tendinitis x2
	15	33	L oblique strain
Pedroia,Dustin	12	15	Sprained R. thumb
	14	29	L thumb/wrist surgery
	15	67	R hamstring strain x2
Peguero,Francisco	14	85	Strained R wrist
Pena,Carlos	13	13	Appendectomy
Pena,Ramiro	11	50	Appendicitis
	13	105	R shoulder impingement
Pence,Hunter	15	112	L oblique; Fx L forearm; sore L wrist
Pennington,Cliff	12	18	Tendinitis in L. elbow
	14	64	Sprained ligament in L thumb
Perez,Eury	14	70	Fractured L toe
Perez,Juan C	15	12	Left oblique strain
Perez,Salvador	12	78	Surgery for torn L. meniscus
	13	7	Concussion
Petit,Gregorio	15	37	R hand contusion
Pham,Thomas	15	63	L quadriceps strain
Phelps,Cord	13	33	R wrist inflammation
Phillips,Brandon	14	38	Surgery for torn ligament on L thumb
Pierzynski,A.J.	11	20	Bruised L. wrist
	13	15	Strained R oblique
Pill,Brett	13	15	Recovery from minor knee surgery
Pina,Manuel	12	149	Surgery on R. knee
Pirela,Jose	15	32	Concussion
Plouffe,Trevor	12	23	Bruised R. thumb
	13	23	Concussion; Strained L calf
	14	15	Strained L oblique
Polanco,Placido	11	40	Lower back Inflam
	12	57	Lower back Inflamx2
	13	8	Concussion
Pollock IV,A.J.	14	93	Fractured R hand
Posey,Buster	11	126	Fract. L. fibula and torn ankle lig.
Prado,Martin	11	37	Staph infection in R. calf
	14	14	Appendectomy
	15	29	R shoulder sprain
Presley,Alex	11	33	L. hand contusion
	12	12	Concussion
	14	56	Strained R oblique muscle
Profar,Jurickson	14	183	Torn muscle in R shoulder
	15	183	Recovery from shoulder surgery
Puello,Cesar	15	182	Stress fracture in lower back
Puig,Yasiel	15	79	Strained R hamstring
Pujols,Albert	11	15	Fractured L. forearm
	13	65	Plantar fasciitis

FIVE-YEAR INJURY LOG — Batters

Batters	Yr	Days	Injury
Punto,Nick	11	99	SpoR.s hernia surgery
	14	37	Strained R hamstring
Quentin,Carlos	11	22	Sprained L. shoulder
	12	54	R. knee surgery
	13	61	R knee strain
	14	108	Sore L knee x 2
Quintero,Humberto	11	39	High R. ankle sprain
Raburn,Ryan	12	52	Sprain R. thumb; Strain R. quad
	13	15	Strained L Achilles
	14	14	Sore R wrist
Ramirez,Aramis	13	64	Sprained L knee x 2
	14	22	Strained L hamstring
Ramirez,Hanley	11	72	L. back strain
	13	60	Str L hamMY; R thumb ligament
	14	14	Strained R oblique
	15	30	R shoulder inflammation
Ramirez,Wilkin	13	109	Head Injury; Fractured L tibia
Ramos,Wilson	12	144	Torn R. knee ligament
	13	64	Strained L hamstring x 2
	14	50	Strained R hamstring/Fx L hand
Rasmus,Colby	11	23	Jammed R. wrist
	13	41	L oblique str; contusion - L eye
	14	33	Tightness in R hamstring
Reddick,Josh	13	39	Sprained R wrist x 2
	14	44	Strained R knee;hyper Rt knee
	15	8	Strained R oblique
Reimold,Nolan	12	156	Surgery for herniated disk
	13	129	Str Rt hammy; Nerve inflam neck
	14	108	Strnd L calf; cervical spine fusion
Rendon,Anthony	15	89	Strained L quad; Sprain L knee
Repko,Jason	11	36	Strain R. quad; Bursitis-L. should.
	12	62	Separation of R. shoulder
Revere,Ben	13	78	Broken R foot
Reyes,Jose	11	37	L. hamstring strain
	13	74	Sprained L ankle
	14	19	Tightness in L hamstring
	15	27	Cracked L rib
Reynolds,Mark	12	17	Strained L. oblique
Richardson,Antoan	15	89	Herniated disk in back
Rios,Alex	14	24	R thumb infection
	15	46	Fractured L hand
Rivera,Juan	12	148	Torn L. hamstring
Roberts,Brian	11	135	Concussion
	12	162	Surg.-torn R. hip labrum+concuss.
	13	86	Ruptured tendon, R knee
Robinson,Shane	13	15	Strained R shoulder
	14	34	Surgery on L shoulder
Rodriguez,Alex	11	44	Torn meniscus in R. knee
	12	40	Broken L. hand
	13	127	L hip surgery
Rodriguez,Sean	12	15	Fractured R. hand
Rollins,Jimmy	11	17	R. groin strain
Romine,Austin	12	182	Strained lower back
Rosales,Adam	11	67	Fractured R. foot
	13	25	Strained L intercostal
Rosario,Wilin	14	25	L wrist inflammation/viral infection

FIVE-YEAR INJURY LOG — Batters

Batters	Yr	Days	Injury
Ross,Cody	11	21	R. calf strain
	12	31	Fractured bone in L. foot
	13	62	L calf strain; Dislocated R hip
	14	71	Strained L calf/recovery R hip
Ross,David	13	77	Concussion x 2
	14	18	Plantar fasciitis in R foot
	15	8	Concussion
Rua,Ryan	15	69	Sprained R ankle
Ruf,Darin	14	49	Strained L oblique
Ruggiano,Justin	11	22	Bursitis in L. knee
	14	65	Surgery L ankle/strnd L hamstring
Ruiz,Carlos	11	15	Lower back Inflam
	12	35	Plantar fasciitis in L. foot
	13	29	Strained R hamstring
	14	26	Concussion
Rutledge,Josh	14	11	Viral infection
Ryan,Brendan	11	15	Sprained L. shoulder
	14	36	Pinched nerve in neck
	15	90	Upper back strain; strain R calf
Saltalamacchia,Jarrod	14	17	Concussion
	15	10	Strained neck
Sanchez,Angel	13	45	Lower back strain
Sanchez,Freddy	12	182	Recov. from surgery - R. shoulder
Sanchez,Hector	12	15	L. knee sprain
	13	15	Strained R shoulder
	14	37	Concussion
	15	27	Strained L hamstring
Sandoval,Pablo	11	45	Broken hamate bone in R. hand
	12	56	Strained L. hamstring+ Fx R. hand
	13	15	Strained L foot
Sands,Jerry	14	98	Strained L wrist
Santana,Carlos	12	10	Concussion
	14	10	Concussion
Santana,Daniel	14	21	Bone bruise in L knee
Saunders,Michael	13	18	Sprained R shoulder
	14	74	Strained Lt oblique; A/C joint inflam
	15	168	L knee inflam; rec L knee surg
Schafer,Jordan	11	26	Chip fracture in L. middle finger
	12	25	Shoulder
	13	37	R ankle contusion
	15	33	R knee MCL sprain
Schafer,Logan	14	13	Strained R hamstring
Schierholtz,Nate	11	38	Hairline fracture in R. foot
	12	19	Fractured R. great toe
Schneider,Brian	11	43	Straing L. hamstring
	12	77	Strain L. hamstring+ spr R. Ankle
Schoop,Jonathan	15	78	R knee sprain
Schumaker,Skip	11	37	R. triceps strain
	12	36	R. hammy strain+torn R. oblique
Scott,Luke	11	86	Bruise-R. knee; Strain R. should.
	12	50	Str R. oblique+back spasms
	13	46	Back spasms; Strained R calf
Scutaro,Marco	11	30	Strained L. oblique muscle
	14	170	Strained lower back x 2
	15	110	Recovery from back surgery
Segura,Jean	15	15	Fractured R pinky finger

FIVE-YEAR INJURY LOG — Batters

Batters	Yr	Days	Injury
Sellers,Justin	12	134	Bulging disc in lower back
	15	183	Sore L Achilles
Shuck,J.B. B	15	15	Strained L hamstring
Sierra,Moises	14	15	Strained L oblique
Silverio,Alfredo	13	183	Sprained R elbow
Simmons,Andrelton	12	63	Non-displaced fract. R. hand
Sizemore,Grady	11	77	Recv. L. knee surg.; Bruise R. Knee
	12	183	Recovery from back surgery
Sizemore,Scott	12	182	Recovery from torn ACL surgery
	13	173	Torn L ACL
Smith,Seth	12	18	Strained L. hamstring
Smoak,Justin	11	20	Fracture of the nose
	13	19	R oblique strain
	14	23	Strained L quadriceps
Smolinski,Jacob	14	53	Bone bruise in L foot
Snider,Travis	13	35	L big toe discomfort
Snyder,Brandon	13	24	Ulnar neuritis, R elbow
Snyder,Chris	11	126	Sore lower back
Sogard,Eric	12	58	Strained back/sprained ankle
Solano,Donovan	13	34	Strained L intercostal muscle
Solano,Jhonatan	12	78	L. oblique strain
Soler,Jorge	15	56	L oblique; Sprain L ankle
Soriano,Alfonso	11	15	L. quadriceps strain
Soto,Geovany	11	18	L. groin strain
	12	30	Torn L. meniscus
	14	126	Strained R groin; surg. Rt knee
Souza,Steven	14	22	Bruised L shoulder
	15	54	Fractured L hand; cut finger
Span,Denard	11	91	Concussion; Migraine headaches
	12	15	Strained R. sternoclavicular joint
	14	7	Concussion
	15	98	Core muscle surg; back; torn labr.
Spangenberg,Cory	15	45	L knee contusion
Spilborghs,Ryan	11	45	Plantar fascitis in R. foot
Springer,George	14	68	L quadriceps injury
	15	70	Fx R wrist; concussion
Stanton,Giancarlo	12	30	AR.hroscopic R. knee surgery
	13	41	Strained R hamstring
	15	100	L wrist hamate fracture
Stassi,Max	13	32	Concussion
Stewart,Chris	14	21	Surgery on R knee
	15	12	Strained R hamstring
Stewart,Ian	12	113	Sore L. wrist
	13	33	Strained L quad
	14	39	Bruised L hand
Stubbs,Drew	12	19	Strained L. oblique
Sucre,Jesus	13	72	L wrist sprain
Susac,Andrew	15	58	Sprained R wrist
Sweeney,Ryan	12	93	Concussion+toe+fx L. hand
	13	63	Fractured L rib
	14	74	Strnd L hamstring/strnd R hamstring
Swihart,Blake	15	17	Sprained L foot
Swisher,Nick	14	66	Hyperextend L knee; R knee soreness
	15	84	L knee inflam; rec knee surg (both)
Tabata,Jose	11	50	R. hand contusion
	13	39	Strained L oblique
Taylor,Chris	15	14	Fractured R wrist

FIVE-YEAR INJURY LOG — Batters

Batters	Yr	Days	Injury
Teagarden,Taylor	12	100	Strained back
	13	37	Dislocated L thumb
	14	37	Strained L hamstring
Teahen,Mark	11	24	Strained R. oblique muscle
Teixeira,Mark	13	167	Rt wrist surgery; Strained Rt wrist
	14	15	Strained R hamstring
	15	31	R shin bone bruise
Tejada,Miguel	11	28	Lower abdominal strain
	13	50	Strained R calf
Tejada,Ruben	12	48	Strained R. quadriceps
	13	37	R quad strain
Terdoslavich,Joseph	15	61	Sprained L wrist
Thames,Marcus	11	34	R. quad strain
Theriot,Ryan	12	15	R. elbow Inflam
Thole,Josh	12	24	Concussion
Thomas,Brad	11	141	R. elbow surgery
Thome,Jim	11	45	Strain L. oblique; Strain L. quad
	12	92	Strained lower back, Back spasms
Tolleson,Steve	15	31	Groin strain
Torrealba,Yorvit	13	8	Concussion
Torres,Andres	11	45	Strained L. Achilles Tendon
	12	24	L. calf strain
	13	39	Surgery, L Achilles
Tovar,Wilfredo	15	37	Concussion
Tracy,Chad	12	65	R. adductor strain
Travis,Devon	15	101	L shoulder strain; inflam
Treanor,Matt	11	32	Concussion
Trumbo,Mark	14	78	Stress fracture in L foot
Tuiasosopo,Matt	13	15	Strained L intercostal
Tulowitzki,Troy	12	126	Strained L. groin muscle
	13	27	Fractured rib, R ribcage
	14	69	Strained L hip flexor
Turner,Justin	12	18	Sprained R. ankle
	13	35	Intercostal strain
	14	19	Strained L hamstring
	15	13	R thigh skin infection
Uggla,Dan	13	15	Eye surgery
	15	24	Back spasms
Upton,B.J.	12	15	Soreness in lower back
	13	21	R adductor strain
Upton,Melvin	15	66	Sesamoiditis, L foot
Uribe,Juan	11	83	L. hip flexor muscle strain
	12	28	L. wrist injury
	14	51	Strained R hamstring x 2
Utley,Chase	11	53	R. knee tendinitis
	12	84	Worn caR.ilage behind L. kneecap
	13	31	Strained R oblique
	15	44	R ankle inflammation
Valaika,Chris	13	76	Fractured L wrist
Valbuena,Luis	13	29	R oblique strain
Valencia,Danny	14	21	Sprained L hand
Van Slyke,Scott	13	17	L shoulder bursitis
	15	15	L mid-back inflammation
Vazquez,Christian	15	189	R elbow sprain
Viciedo,Dayan	11	6	Fractured R. thumb
	13	21	Strained L oblique

FIVE-YEAR INJURY LOG — Batters

Batters	Yr	Days	Injury
Victorino,Shane	11	30	R. hamstring strain
	13	18	L hamstring strain
	14	139	Lower back; strained R Hammy x2
	15	56	L calf tightness; R ham strain
Votto,Joey	12	50	Torn medial meniscus in L. knee
	14	103	Strained L quadriceps x 2
Walker,Neil	13	32	Strained R oblique; R finger cut
	14	15	Appendectomy
Walters,Zachary	15	19	Strained R oblique
Weeks,Rickie	11	42	Sprained L. ankle
	13	53	L hamstring surgery
Wells,Casper	13	32	Vision complications
Wells,Vernon	11	28	Strained R. groin
	12	67	Torn ligament in R. thumb
Werth,Jayson	12	87	Broken L. wrist
	13	32	Strained R hamstring
	15	78	Rec. R shldr surg.; L wrist cont.
Whiteside,Eli	11	7	Concussion
Wieters,Matt	14	94	Strained R Elbow; TJS
	15	61	Recovery from R elbow surgery
Wigginton,Ty	11	16	L. oblique strain
Williams,Mason	15	106	R shoulder inflammation
Willingham,Josh	11	19	Strained L. achilles tendon
	13	39	Medial meniscus tear, L knee
	14	43	Fractured L wrist
Willits,Reggie	11	13	Strained L. calf
Wilson,Bobby	12	13	Concussion
Wilson,Jack	11	15	Bruised L. heel
	12	82	Dislocated R. pinky finger
Wise,DeWayne	13	65	Strained R hamstring
Wong,Kolten	14	15	Sore L shoulder
Worth,Danny	13	3	Dislocated L shoulder
Wright,David	11	67	Lower back stress fracture
	13	48	Strained R hamstring
	15	131	Strained R hamstring
Yelich,Christian	14	13	Strained lower back
	15	33	Rt knee contusion; lower back strain
Young Jr.,Eric	14	21	Strained R hamstring
Young,Chris	12	30	R. shoulder contusion
	14	15	Strained R quadriceps
Young,Delmon	11	39	Strain L. oblique; Sprain R. ankle
	13	30	Recovery from R ankle surgery
Young,Eric	12	45	L. intercostal muscle strain
Zimmerman,Ryan	11	65	L. abdominal strain
	12	17	Sore R. shoulder
	13	15	Strained L hamstring
	14	110	Fx R thumb/strained R hamstring
	15	47	Plantar fasciitis, L foot
Zobrist,Ben	14	15	Dislocated L thumb
	15	30	Medial meniscus tear, L knee
Zunino,Mike	13	38	Fractured L hamate bone

FIVE-YEAR INJURY LOG — Pitchers

Pitchers	Yr	Days	Injury
Aardsma,David	11	182	Recov. from surgery-L. hip; TJS
Abad,Fernando	11	88	L. shoulder tendinitis
	12	20	R. intercostal strain
Adams,Mike	13	117	Back Strain; R biceps tend.
	14	106	R rotator cuff inflammation
Adcock,Nathan	15	67	R elbow surgery
Affeldt,Jeremy	12	15	Sprained R. knee
	13	71	Strained L groin; R oblique
	14	18	Strained ligament in R knee
	15	40	L patella tendon; L shoulder strain
Albers,Matt	11	15	Sore R. lat muscle
	14	157	R shoulder tendinitis
	15	84	Broken finger, R hand
Alburquerque,Al	11	39	Inflam - R. elbow; Concussion
	12	141	Recov. fr. surg. - R. elbow
Alvarez,Henderson	13	95	Mild R shoulder inflammation
	14	14	R shoulder inflammation
	15	169	R shoulder inflammation x2
Anderson,Brett	11	115	Soreness in L. elbow
	12	137	Recovery from TJS
	13	119	R foot stress fracture
	14	144	Strained lower back/fx L finger
Anderson,Chase	15	19	R triceps inflammation
Anderson,Cody	15	18	L oblique strain
Araujo,Elvis	15	38	Strained L groin
Arredondo,Jose	11	60	R. shoulder Inflam
Arrieta,Jake	11	59	Bone spur in R. elbow
	14	34	Tightness in R shoulder
Arroyo,Bronson	14	105	R elbow tendinitis
	15	184	Recovery from R elbow surgery
Atchison,Scott	12	60	Tightness In R. forearm
	13	60	R groin strain; R elbow
	15	16	Sprained L ankle
Ayala,Luis	11	28	Strained lat muscle
	13	71	Anxiety disorder
Baez,Pedro	15	43	R pectoral strain
Bailey,Andrew	11	59	Strained R. forearm
	12	132	R. thumb surgery
	13	100	Rt biceps soreness; Rt shoulder str
Bailey,Homer	11	66	R. shoulder impingement
	14	16	Strained flexor tendon in R elbow
	15	174	Torn UCL, R elbow; TJS surgery
Baker,Scott	11	58	Strained R. flexor muscle
	12	182	TJS - R. elbow
	13	161	Strained R elbow
Balfour,Grant	11	15	Strained R. oblique muscle
Banuelos,Manuel	15	35	L elbow inflammation
Barnes,Scott	13	32	Sprained L wrist
Barrett,Aaron	15	86	R elbow sprain; R biceps
Bass,Anthony	12	72	R. shoulder Inflam
	14	49	Chest injury/strained R intercostal
Batista,Miguel	12	16	Lower back strain
Beachy,Brandon	11	39	L. oblique strain
	12	109	TJS
	13	160	R elbow inflam; R elbow surgery
	14	184	Recovering from TJS
	15	103	Recovery from R elbow surgery

FIVE-YEAR INJURY LOG — Pitchers

Pitchers	Yr	Days	Injury
Beato,Pedro	11	15	R. elbow tendinitis
	12	92	R. shoulder stiffness
	14	22	Sore R elbow
Beavan,Blake	14	98	R shoulder tendinitis
Beckett,Josh	12	18	Inflam in R. shoulder
	13	139	Neck & shoulder surgery
	14	87	L hip impinge x 2/sprained R thumb
Bedard,Erik	11	31	Sprained L. knee
Beeler,Dallas	15	43	R shoulder inflammation
Beimel,Joe	11	48	Sore L. elbow
	15	14	L shoulder inflammation
Belisle,Matt	15	74	R elbow inflammation
Beliveau,Jeff	15	171	L shoulder fatigue
Bell,Trevor	14	174	R elbow inflammation
Bellatti,Andrew	15	26	R shoulder tendinitis
Bergman,Christian	14	60	Fractured L hand/thumb
	15	32	R shoulder fatigue
Betances,Dellin	12	15	R. shoulder Inflam
Betancourt,Rafael	13	98	Strained R groin; R elbow; Appx
	15	18	Sinus infection & vertigo symptoms
Bettis,Chad	15	36	R elbow inflammation
Billings,Bruce	14	18	Strained R forearm
Billingsley,Chad	12	46	R. elbow pain
	13	177	R elbow surgery; finger bruise
	14	184	Recovering from TJS
	15	151	R flexor strain; R shlder; elbow surg
Black,Victor	14	11	Herniated disc in neck
	15	63	R shoulder weakness
Blackburn,Nick	11	38	Strained R. forearm
	12	18	Strained L. quad
Blackley,Travis	13	15	L shoulder strain
Blanton,Joe	11	127	Impingement in R. elbow
Blazek,Michael	15	52	Fractured R hand
Blevins,Jerry	15	167	Fractured L forearm
Bonilla,Lisalberto	15	183	R elbow impingement
Boyer,Blaine	15	12	R elbow inflammation
Braddock,Zach	11	32	Sleep disorder
Braden,Dallas	11	165	Surg. - torn capsule in L. shoulder
	12	182	Recov. fr. surg. - L. shoulder
Bradley,Archie	15	98	R shoulder tend; facial bruise
Brasier,Ryan	14	184	Strained R elbow
Bray,Bill	12	78	Lumbar strain+ L. groin str
Breslow,Craig	13	36	L shoulder tendinitis
	14	13	Strained L shoulder
Britton,Zach	11	17	Strained L. shoulder
	12	62	L. shoulder impingement
Brown,Brooks	15	74	R shoulder inflammation x2
Broxton,Jonathan	11	148	Sore R. elbow
	13	108	R flexor strain x 2
	14	9	Rec from surgery R elbow/forearm
Buchholz,Clay	11	103	Strained lower back
	12	24	Gastro-intestinal problem
	13	93	Neck strain
	14	28	Hyperextended L knee
	15	86	R flexor strain
Buchholz,Taylor	11	122	R. shoulder fatigue
Bueno,Francisley	14	55	Sprained L middle finger

FIVE-YEAR INJURY LOG — Pitchers

Pitchers	Yr	Days	Injury
Bundy,Dylan	15	11	Strained right shoulder
Burgos,Enrique	15	27	Sore R shoulder
Burgos,Hiram	13	37	R shoulder impingement
Burnett,A.J.	12	17	Fractured R. orbital bone
	13	28	Strained R calf
	15	41	R elbow inflammation
Burnett,Sean	13	150	Sore L forearm; L elbow surgery
	14	180	Torn UCL in L elbow; surgery recovery
Burton,Jared	11	135	AR.hroscopic surg-R. shoulder
Butler,Eddie	14	40	R rotator cuff inflammation
Byrdak,Tim	12	62	L. shoulder soreness
Cabral,Cesar	12	182	Fractured L. elbow
	13	75	L elbow pain
Cabrera,Edwar	13	183	L shoulder impingement
Cahill,Trevor	13	47	R hip contusion
Cain,Matt	13	15	R forearm contusion
	14	93	R elbow inflam/R ham/cut R finger
	15	100	R elbow nerve irrit.; flexor strain
Camp,Shawn	13	24	Sprained R big toe
Capps,Carter	14	97	Sprained R elbow
	15	63	R elbow strain
Capps,Matt	12	88	Irritation of R. rotator cuff
Capuano,Chris	13	39	L lat strain; Strained L calf
	15	43	Strained R quadriceps
Carignan,Andrew	12	120	TJS - R. elbow
Carlson,Jesse	11	182	Surgery - torn L. rotator cuff
Carlyle,Buddy	15	144	Lower back strain
Carp,Mike	14	36	Fractured R foot
Carpenter,Chris	12	171	Nerve irritation in R. shoulder
	12	182	Recov. fr. surg.-bone spur R. elbow
	13	183	Nerve irritation, R shoulder
Carpenter,David	14	15	Strained R biceps
	15	80	R shoulder inflammation
Carrasco,Carlos	11	16	Inflam - R. elbow
	12	183	Recovery from TJS
	15	13	R shoulder inflammation
Cashner,Andrew	11	150	R. rotator cuff strain
	12	59	Strained R. latissimus dorsi
	14	82	Sore R elbow/sore R shoulder
Casilla,Santiago	11	57	Sore R. elbow
	13	53	Cyst on R knee
	14	24	Strained R hamstring
Cassevah,Bobby	12	22	Inflam in R. shoulder
Castillo,Alberto	11	33	L. shoulder tendinitis
Castillo,Lendy	12	87	L. groin strain
Cecil,Brett	13	13	L elbow soreness
	14	16	Strained L groin
Ceda,Jose	12	184	TJS
	13	183	Recovery from R elbow surgery
Chacin,Jhoulys	12	111	R. shoulder Inflam
	13	15	L lower back strain
	14	128	R shoulder inflammation/strain
Chamberlain,Joba	11	115	TJS
	12	117	Dislocated R. ankle
	13	30	Strained R oblique
Chapman,Aroldis	11	39	L. shoulder Inflam
	14	41	Facial fractures, concussion

FIVE-YEAR INJURY LOG — Pitchers

Pitchers	Yr	Days	Injury
Chatwood,Tyler	13	31	R elbow inflammation
	14	168	Strnd R elbow/strnd L hamstring
Chavez,Jesse	15	19	Fractured rib
Chen,Bruce	11	49	Strained L. lat muscle
	14	64	Inflamed disc in lower back
Chen,Wei-Yin	13	58	Strained R oblique
Choate,Randy	11	44	L. elbow Inflam
Cingrani,Tony	13	15	Strained lower back
	14	17	L shoulder tendinitis
	15	37	Strained L shoulder
Cisnero,Jose	14	143	R elbow injury
Claudio,Alexander	15	34	L groin strain
Cobb,Alex	11	53	Surgery - rib cage
	13	60	Concussion
	14	38	Strained L oblique muscle
	15	183	R forearm tendinitis
Coello,Robert	12	101	Strained R. elbow
	13	98	R shoulder inflammation
Coffey,Todd	11	15	L. calf strain
	12	109	R. knee Inflam+TJS
Coke,Phil	11	15	Bone bruise in R. foot
	13	15	L groin strain
Cole,Gerrit	14	63	Tightness R lat/R shoulder fatigue
Coleman,Louis	14	14	Bone bruised/sprained R middle finger
Collins,Tim	14	27	Strained flexor in L elbow
	15	183	L elbow surgery
Collmenter,Josh	12	22	Ulcers
Colome,Alexander	13	94	Strained R elbow
	15	34	Pneumonia
Colon,Bartolo	11	20	Strained L. hamstring
	12	15	Strained R. oblique
	13	15	L groin strain
Contreras,Jose	11	135	R. elbow strain
	12	136	R. elbow strain
	13	16	Lower back inflammation
Cook,Aaron	11	69	Broken finger on R. hand
	12	49	Laceration of L. knee
Cook,Ryan	14	39	Strned R forearm; Rt shoulder inflam
Corbin,Patrick	14	184	Recovering from TJS
	15	91	Recovery from L elbow surgery
Cordero,Francisco	12	63	R. foot sesamoiditis
Cordier,Erik	15	42	R forearm strain
Cortes,Dan	11	15	Bruised L. ankle
Cosart,Jarred	15	37	Vertigo
Crain,Jesse	12	51	Strained R. shoulder+ L. oblique
	13	85	Sprained R shoulder
	14	183	Recovering from surgery on R biceps
Cravy,Tyler	15	17	R elbow impingement
Crotta,Michael	11	141	R. posterior elbow Inflam
Crow,Aaron	15	183	R elbow surgery
Cruz,Juan	11	15	Strained R. groin
	12	22	R. shoulder Inflam
Cruz,Rhiner	12	15	Sprained R. ankle
Cueto,Johnny	11	39	R. biceps/triceps irritation
	13	130	Strained R lat x 2; R shoulder
Cumpton,Brandon	15	106	R elbow surgery
Cunniff,Brandon	15	101	Strained R groin

FIVE-YEAR INJURY LOG — Pitchers

Pitchers	Yr	Days	Injury
Daley,Matt	11	120	R. shoulder Inflam
Danks,John	11	24	Strained R. oblique muscle
	12	137	Surgery - strained L. shoulder
	13	54	Recovery from L shoulder surgery
Darnell,Logan	15	15	Pneumonia
Darvish,Yu	13	15	Upper back strain
	14	61	Rt elbow inflam; stiff neck
	15	183	R elbow surgery
Davies,Kyle	11	111	Inflam R/C; Impingement R. should.
Davis,Erik	14	183	Sprained R elbow
	15	43	Recovery from R elbow surgery
Davis,Wade	11	15	Strained R. forearm
De Fratus,Justin	12	152	R. elbow sprain
De La Rosa,Dane	14	63	Rt shoulder irritation; Rt forearm
De La Rosa,Jorge	11	127	TJS
	12	168	TJS
	15	15	Strained L groin
De La Rosa,Rubby	11	59	TJS
De Vries,Cole	12	20	Fractured Rib
	13	48	R forearm strain
Deduno,Samuel	13	31	R shoulder soreness
	15	91	Lower back strain
deGrom,Jacob	14	12	Tendinitis in R rotator cuff
Del Rosario,Enerio	11	27	Strained R. shoulder
Delabar,Steve	13	29	R shoulder inflammation
Delgado,Randall	15	68	Sprained R ankle
Demel,Sam	11	38	R. shoulder tendinitis
Dempster,Ryan	12	37	R. quad strain, Tight R. lat.
Detwiler,Ross	13	116	Back strain; x 2
	15	18	L shoulder inflammation
Devine,Joey	11	2	Strained rhomboid- R. shoulder
	12	182	TJS - R. elbow
Diamond,Scott	13	13	Recovery from L elbow surgery
Dolis,Rafael	13	126	Strained R forearm
Dominguez,Jose	13	69	L quad strain
Doolittle,Sean	14	36	Strained R intercostal muscle
	15	136	L shoulder strain; torn rotator cuff
Dotel,Octavio	11	8	Sore L. hamstring
	12	16	Inflam in R. elbow
	13	163	R elbow inflammation
Doubront,Felix	11	8	Inflam - L. forearm
	12	15	Contusion in R. knee
	14	59	Strained L calf/strained L shoulder
Downs,Darin	13	28	L rotator cuff tendinitis
	14	14	Strained R oblique muscle
Downs,Scott	11	27	Fx L. big toe; Gastrointestinal virus
	12	21	Strained L. shoulder
	14	16	Sprained/stiff neck
Drabek,Kyle	12	112	TJS
	13	95	Recovery from R elbow surgery
Drake,Oliver	12	8	Tendinitis in R. shoulder
Duchscherer,Justin	11	182	Strained L. hip
Duensing,Brian	15	15	R intercostal strain
Duffy,Danny	12	143	TJS
	13	99	Recov Rt elbow surg; Rt flexor strain
	15	30	L biceps tendinitis
Duke,Zach	11	58	Broken L. hand

FIVE-YEAR INJURY LOG — Pitchers

Pitchers	Yr	Days	Injury
Edgin,Josh	13	62	Ribcage stress fracture
	15	183	L elbow surgery
Elbert,Scott	12	62	L. elbow Inflamx2
	13	183	Recovery from L elbow surgery
	14	132	TJS
Elias,Roenis	14	7	Strained flexor muscle in R elbow
Eovaldi,Nathan	13	79	Mild R shoulder inflammation
Erlin,Robert	14	88	Sore L elbow
Escalona,Edgmer	11	20	R. rotator cuff strain
	12	27	R. elbow Inflam
	13	22	R elbow inflammation
	14	84	R shoulder impingement
Escalona,Sergio	11	33	L. elbow tendinitis
	12	183	TJS
Escobar,Edwin	15	69	L elbow inflammation
Estrada,Marco	12	33	R. quadriceps strain
	13	64	Strained L hamstring
Familia,Jeurys	13	128	R elbow surgery
Farina,Alan	12	183	Recovery from TJS
Farnsworth,Kyle	12	86	Strained R. elbow
Feldman,Scott	11	105	Recov. fr. surg. - R. knee
	14	18	R biceps tendinitis
	15	83	R shoulder sprain; R knee surg
Feliciano,Pedro	11	183	Strained L. rotator cuff
	12	182	Recov. fr. surg. - R. shoulder
Feliz,Neftali	11	15	Inflam - R. shoulder
	12	136	TJS - R. elbow
	13	155	Recovery from R elbow surgery
	15	38	Axillary abscess on R side
Fernandez,Jose	14	140	Sprained R elbow
	15	120	R biceps strain; R elbow surg
Fields,Joshua	14	19	Sore R forearm
Fien,Casey M	15	29	R shoulder strain
Fife,Stephen	13	66	R shoulder bursitis x 2
	14	14	Recovery from TJS
Figaro,Alfredo	13	30	Strained R oblique
Figueroa,Pedro	14	159	L elbow inflammation
Fish,Robert	12	183	L. elbow tendinitis
Fister,Doug	12	47	Strained L. side
	14	41	Strained R lat
	15	34	R forearm tightness
Flores,Kendry	15	41	R shoulder tendinitis
Floyd,Gavin	12	31	Strain R. elbow flex+ tend R. Elbow
	13	155	R elbow surgery
	14	143	Recovery from TJS/fx R elbow
	15	149	R elbow surgery
Flynn,Brian	15	142	Torn L latissimus dorsi
Foltynewicz,Mike	15	13	Costochondritis
Francis,Jeff	13	24	L groin strain
Francisco,Frank	11	19	Sore R. pectoral
	12	42	L. oblique strain
	13	160	R elbow inflammation
Frasor,Jason	12	48	Tightness In R. forearm
	15	22	R shoulder strain
Frias,Carlos	15	61	R lower back tightness
Friedrich,Christian	12	67	Stress fract-R. side of lower spine
	13	53	Lower back inflammation

FIVE-YEAR INJURY LOG — Pitchers

Pitchers	Yr	Days	Injury
Frieri,Ernesto	11	15	Back problem
Fujikawa,Kyuji	13	153	R elbow strain; R forearm
	14	129	Recovering from TJS
	15	39	R groin strain
Furbush,Charlie	12	30	Strained L. triceps muscle
	15	88	L biceps tendinitis
Gallardo,Yovani	13	17	Strained L hamstring
Garcia,Christian	13	183	Strained R forearm tendon
Garcia,Freddy	11	20	Lacerated R. index finger
Garcia,Jaime	12	74	L. shoulder strain
	13	135	L shoulder strain
	14	69	L shoulder inflammation x 2
	15	75	L groin strain; recov L shldr surg
Garcia,Jason Emilio	15	85	R shoulder tendinitis
Garcia,Luis	14	13	Strained R forearm
Garcia,Onelki	14	184	Recovering from surgery on L elbow
Garland,Jon	11	133	L. oblique strain
Garza,Matt	11	13	R. elbow bone contusion
	12	68	R. elbow stress reaction
	13	51	Strained L lat
	14	27	Strained L oblique
	15	15	R shoulder tendinitis
Gast,John	13	127	L shoulder tightness
Gaudin,Chad	11	156	R. shoulder Inflam
	13	60	R elbow bruise; sore wrist
Gausman,Kevin	15	43	R shoulder tendinitis
Gearrin,Cory	14	184	Sprained R elbow
Gee,Dillon	12	88	Damaged aR.ery in R. shoulder
	14	55	Tightness in R lat
	15	25	Groin strain
Germen,Gonzalez	14	29	Illness/Flu
Goeddel,Erik	15	81	Strained R elbow
Gomes,Brandon	13	146	Strained R lat
Gomez,Jeanmar	13	23	R forearm tightness
Gonzalez,Edgar	13	104	Strained R shoulder
Gonzalez,Gio	14	30	L shoulder inflammation
Gonzalez,Miguel	13	17	R thumb blister
	14	11	Strained R oblique
	14	97	R arm fatigue
	15	45	R shoulder tend; R groin strain
Gorzelanny,Tom	11	26	L. elbow Inflam
	13	16	L shoulder tendinitis
	14	76	Rec from surgery on L shoulder
Graham,J.R.	15	16	R shoulder inflammation
Graveman,Kendall	15	100	Strained L oblique
Gregerson,Luke	11	28	L. oblique strain
Gregg,Kevin	14	45	R elbow inflammation
Greinke,Zack	11	35	Fractured L. rib
	13	33	Broken L collarbone
Griffin,A.J.	14	184	Strained flexor muscle in R elbow
	15	172	R shoulder strain
Griffin,AJ	12	27	Strained R. shoulder
Grilli,Jason	13	42	Strained R forearm
	14	28	Strained L oblique
	15	80	Torn L Achilles tendon
Grimm,Justin	15	26	R forearm inflammation
Guerra,Deolis	15	59	R knee inflammation

FIVE-YEAR INJURY LOG — Pitchers

Pitchers	Yr	Days	Injury
Guerra,Javy	12	63	Strained L. oblique+ R. knee Inflam
	15	16	R shoulder inflammation
Guerrier,Matt	12	133	R. elbow tendinitis
	13	53	R elbow soreness
Guthrie,Jeremy	12	22	R. shoulder sprain
Gutierrez,Juan	11	127	R. shoulder Inflam
Hagadone,Nick	15	89	Lower back strain
Hahn,Jesse	15	86	R forearm strain
Hale,David	15	61	Groin strain
Halladay,Roy	12	50	R. back strain
	13	111	R shoulder surgery
Hamels,Cole	11	16	L. shoulder Inflam
	14	27	L biceps tendinitis
Hammel,Jason	12	54	Injured R. knee
	13	38	R forearm tenderness
Hand,Brad	14	40	Sprained R ankle
Hanrahan,Joel	13	162	Rt elbow surgery; Sore Rt hamstring
	14	150	Recovering from TJS
Happ,J.A.	12	30	Fractured R. foot
	13	89	Head contusion
	14	18	Strained back
Harang,Aaron	11	29	Sore R. foot
	15	28	Plantar fasciitis
Harden,Rich	11	92	Strained R. shoulder
Haren,Dan	12	18	Stiff lower back
	13	15	R shoulder inflammation
Harris,Mitch	15	16	Groin strain
Harrison,Matt	13	177	Inflamed nerve in lower back
	14	55	Lower back inflam; back surg recovery
	15	156	Lower back inflam; back surg
Harvey,Matt	13	34	Torn R UCL
	14	183	Recovering from TJS
Hatcher,Chris	15	58	L oblique strain
Hawkins,LaTroy	11	22	R. shoulder surgery
	12	33	Fractured R. pinkie finger
	15	50	R biceps strain
Hawksworth,Blake	11	26	Strained R. groin
	12	183	R. elbow surgery
Hefner,Jeremy	13	51	Partially torn ligament, R elbow
Heilman,Aaron	11	20	R. shoulder tendinitis
Hellickson,Jeremy	12	15	Fatigued R. shoulder
	14	99	Recovering from surgery on R elbow
	15	22	Strained L hamstring
Hembree,Heath	15	37	R shoulder soreness
Henderson,Jim	13	15	Strained R hamstring
	14	150	R shoulder inflammation
	15	39	Recovery from R shoulder surgery
Hensley,Clay	11	62	L. rib contusion
	12	15	R. groin strain
Hernandez,David	14	184	Surgery on R elbow torn ligament
	15	64	Recovery from R elbow surgery
Hernandez,Roberto	11	15	Strained R. quad muscle
Herndon,David	12	157	TJS
Herrmann,Frank	13	182	R elbow surgery

FIVE-YEAR INJURY LOG — Pitchers

Pitchers	Yr	Days	Injury
Hill,Rich	11	119	Sprained L. elbow
	12	107	TJS recov.+Soreness in L. forearm
Hochevar,Luke	14	184	TJS
	15	32	Recovery from R elbow surgery
Holland,Derek	12	31	Fatigued L. shoulder
	14	164	Recovering from surgery on L knee
	15	130	Subscapular strain in R shoulder
Holland,Greg	12	21	Stress reaction in L. ribs
	15	18	R pectoral strain
Hollands,Mario	14	24	Strained flexor in L elbow
	15	183	Strained flexor tendon, L forearm
Horst,Jeremy	13	106	Strained L elbow
House,T.J.	15	20	L shoulder inflammation
Howell,J.P.	11	50	Recov. fr. surg. - L. labrum
Hudson,Daniel	12	137	R. shoulder impingement +TJS
	13	183	Recovery from R elbow surgery
	14	155	Recovering from TJS
Hudson,Tim	12	25	Recovering from back surgery
	13	67	Fractured R ankle
	15	49	R shoulder strain x 2
Huff,David	12	18	Strained R. hamstring
	14	20	Strained L quadriceps
Hughes,Jared	13	57	R shoulder inflammation
Hughes,Phil	11	82	Tired arm
	13	6	R upper back thoracic injury
	15	32	Lower back inflammation
Humber,Philip	11	15	Facial Contusion
	12	30	Strained R. elbow
Hunter,Tommy	11	92	Stained R. groin
	14	17	Strained L groin
Hutchison,Drew	12	110	TJS - R. elbow
	13	131	Recovery from R elbow surgery
Iglesias,Raisel	15	36	Strained L oblique
Irwin,Phillip	13	119	R arm fatigue
Iwakuma,Hisashi	14	35	Torn tendon in R middle finger
	15	73	R lat strain
Jackson,Edwin	14	29	Strained R lat
Jansen,Kenley	11	49	R. shoulder Inflam
	15	40	L foot surgery
Janssen,Casey	11	34	Sore R. forearm
	14	42	Strained lower back
	15	47	R rotator cuff tendinitis
Jenkins,Chad	14	24	Fractured R hand
Jenks,Bobby	11	132	Strain R. biceps; Tightness in back
	12	183	Recov. fr. surg. - back
Jennings,Dan	14	24	Concussion
	15	24	Neck inflammation
Jepsen,Kevin	13	82	Rt tricep tightness; Appendectomy
Jimenez,Ubaldo	11	17	Cuticle cut on R. thumb
	14	29	Sprained R ankle
Johnson,Josh	11	135	R. shoulder Inflam
	13	90	Strnd Rt forearm; Strnd Rt triceps
	14	184	Strained flexor in R forearm
	15	183	Strained R elbow
Johnson,Steve	13	86	Strained Rt oblique; Strained Rt lat
Jones,Nate	14	184	Strained L hip;TJS
	15	131	Recovery from R elbow surgery

FIVE-YEAR INJURY LOG — Pitchers

Pitchers	Yr	Days	Injury
Jordan,Taylor	13	44	Lower back strain
	14	55	Sore R elbow
Jurrjens,Jair	11	28	Sore R. torso
	12	64	Strained R. groin
Kahnle,Thomas	14	17	R shoulder inflammation
Karstens,Jeff	12	68	Sore R. shoulder
	13	183	R shoulder inflammation
Kazmir,Scott	11	178	Lower back stiffness
	13	18	Strained R rib cage
Kelley,Shawn	11	132	Recov. fr. surg. - R. elbow
	14	29	Strained lumbar spine
	15	14	Strained L calf
Kelly,Casey	13	183	R elbow surgery
	14	184	Recovering from TJS
Kelly,Joe	14	85	Strained L hamstring
	15	8	R biceps tightness
Kendrick,Kyle	13	8	Inflammation - R shoulder
	15	31	R shoulder inflammation
Kennedy,Ian	15	15	Strained L hamstring
Kershaw,Clayton	14	38	Back muscle inflam/strnd L shoulder
Kimball,Cole	11	111	R. shoulder Inflam
	12	184	Rehab from R. shoulder surgery
Kinney,Josh	13	89	Stress reaction, L shoulder
Kintzler,Brandon	11	147	R. triceps tendonitis
	12	151	Sore R. forearm
	14	15	Strained R rotator cuff
	15	75	L knee tendinitis
Kirkman,Michael	13	86	Cutaneous lymphoma in R triceps
Kluber,Corey	13	32	Sprained finger, R hand
Kohn,Michael	12	182	R. forearm strain
Krol,Ian	14	15	L shoulder inflammation
Kuo,Hong-Chih	11	56	L. low back strain
Lackey,John	11	24	Strained R. elbow
	12	182	TJS - R. elbow
	13	176	R biceps strain
Lannan,John	13	106	Strained L quad; L knee tend.
Latos,Mat	11	11	Strained R. shoulder
	14	76	Recovering from surgery on L knee
	15	21	L knee inflammation
League,Brandon P	15	88	Sore R shoulder
Leake,Mike	15	15	Strained L hamstring
Leathersich,John Victor	15	42	Recovery from L elbow surgery
LeCure,Sam	11	30	R. forearm strain
Lee,Cliff	12	20	L. oblique strain
	14	122	L flexor pronator strain x 2
Leroux,Chris	11	25	Strained L. calf
	12	151	Strained R. pectoral muscle
Lester,Jon	11	19	Strained lower L. lat muscle
Lewis,Colby	12	101	Surg. torn tendon R. elbow
	13	185	Recovery from R elbow surgery
Lidge,Brad	11	113	R. posterior rotator cuff strain
	12	46	Abdominal wall strain
Lilly,Ted	12	143	L. shoulder inflam.; str neck
	13	85	Neck sprain; R ribcage strain
Lincecum,Tim	15	95	R forearm contusion
Lincoln,Brad	11	11	Bruised R. arm
Lindgren,Jacob	15	28	L elbow surgery

FIVE-YEAR INJURY LOG — Pitchers

Pitchers	Yr	Days	Injury
Lindstrom,Matt	11	16	Nerve injury in upper R. arm
	12	47	Torn ligament in R. middle finger
	14	84	L ankle injury
Liriano,Francisco	11	36	Inflam L. should.; Strain L. should.
	13	41	Fractured R forearm
	14	32	Strained L oblique
Litsch,Jesse	11	60	Impingement in R. shoulder
	12	183	Surgery to repair R. biceps tendon
Lobstein,Kyle	15	102	L shoulder soreness
Locke,Jeff	14	12	Strained R oblique
Logan,Boone	14	86	Diverticulitis/L elbow inflam x 3
	15	18	L elbow inflammation
Lopez,Wilton	11	19	Irritation-ulnar nerve R. elbow
	12	28	Sprained R. elbow
Loux,Shane	12	62	Neck strain
Lowe,Mark	12	45	Strained R. intercostal muscle
	13	16	Neck stiffness
Luebke,Cory	12	159	TJS
	13	183	Recovery from L elbow surgery
	14	184	Recovering from TJS
	15	183	Strained L elbow
Lyles,Jordan	14	62	Fractured L hand
	15	126	Sprained L big toe
Lynn,Lance	11	50	L. oblique strain
	15	13	Strained R forearm
Lyon,Brandon	11	142	PaR.ially rotator cuff tear
Lyons,Tyler	14	36	Strained L shoulder
Machi,Jean M	15	18	Strained L groin
Madson,Ryan	11	26	R. hand contusion
	12	183	TJS
	13	127	Recovery from R elbow surgery
Maholm,Paul	11	42	L. shoulder strain
	13	32	Bruised L wrist
	14	58	Torn ACL in R knee
Maloney,Matt	11	87	L. oblique strain
Manship,Jeff	14	37	Strained R quadriceps
Marcum,Shaun	12	70	R. elbow tightness
	13	41	Neck Strain; TOS
Mariot,Michael	14	32	Strained R hamstring
Marmol,Carlos	12	16	Strained R. hamstring
Marquis,Jason	11	44	Fractured R. fibula
	12	43	Fractured L. wrist
	13	72	Strained R elbow
Marshall,Brett	14	82	Strained tendon in R middle finger
Marshall,Evan	15	27	Fractured skull
Marshall,Sean	13	131	Sprained L shoulder; Tendinitis
	14	127	Strnd L shoulder/L shoulder inflam
	15	183	Recovery from L shoulder surgery
Marte,Luis	12	51	Strained L. hamstring
	13	61	Recovery from R shoulder surgery
Martin,Christopher	15	22	R elbow tendinitis
Martin,Ethan	14	51	Strained R shoulder
Martinez,Carlos	15	9	Right shoulder strain
Martinez,Cristhian	13	176	R shoulder strain
Martinez,Nicholas	14	14	L side injury

FIVE-YEAR INJURY LOG — Pitchers

Pitchers	Yr	Days	Injury
Masset,Nick	12	182	Sore R. shoulder
	13	183	Recovery from R shoulder surgery
	14	15	Strained patellar tendon in L knee
Masterson,Justin	14	22	R knee inflammation
	15	40	R shoulder tendinitis
Mateo,Marcos	11	86	R. elbow soreness
	12	183	Sore R. elbow
	15	24	Strained neck
Matsuzaka,Daisuke	11	135	Sprained R. elbow
	12	121	TJS recovery+trained R. upper trap
	14	33	R elbow inflammation
Mattheus,Ryan	11	25	R. shoulder strain
	12	27	Plantar fascia strain in L. foot
	13	67	Fractured R hand
Matusz,Brian	11	59	Strained L. intecostal muscle
Matz,Steven	15	53	Partially torn L lat muscle
Maurer,Brandon	15	55	R shoulder inflammation
Mazzoni,Cory	15	31	Strained R shoulder
McAllister,Zach	13	50	Sprained R middle finger
	14	27	Strained lower back
McCarthy,Brandon	11	45	Stress reaction in R. scapula
	12	95	Strained R. shoulderx2 + skull Fx
	13	65	R shoulder inflammation
	15	161	Torn UCL, R elbow
McClellan,Kyle	11	15	L. hip flexor strain
	12	139	R. elbow strain
McCoy,Patrick	14	25	Strained R hamstring
McDonald,James	13	129	R shoulder discomfort
	14	183	R shoulder inflammation
McGee,Jake	15	86	Torn L knee menisc rec R elbow surg
McGowan,Dustin	11	158	Recov. fr. surg. - R. shoulder
	12	183	R. Plant. Fasciitis+R. should. surg.
	13	101	Strnd Rt oblique; Sore Rt shoulder
McHugh,Collin	14	15	R middle finger injury
McPherson,Kyle	13	34	Recovery from R elbow surgery
Medlen,Kris	11	178	Recovery from TJS
	14	184	Recovering from TJS
	15	112	Recovery from R elbow surgery
Meek,Evan	11	116	R. shoulder tendinitis
Mejia,Jenrry	13	160	R elbow inflamon; discomfort
	15	181	R elbow inflammation
Mijares,Jose	11	15	Strained L. elbow
Mikolas,Miles	14	30	Sore R shoulder
Miller,Andrew	12	32	Strained L. hamstring
	13	85	L foot surgery
	15	27	L flexor forearm muscle strain
Miller,Justin	13	62	Recovery from R elbow surgery
Milone,Tommy	14	23	Neck inflammation
	15	13	Strained L elbow
Minor,Mike	14	37	L shoulder tendinitis
	15	185	L rotator cuff inflammation
Mitchell,Bryan	15	10	Concussion, nasal fracture
Mitre,Sergio	11	75	Tendinitis in R. shoulder
Montero,Rafael	15	158	R rotator cuff inflammation
Moore,Matt	13	36	L elbow soreness
	14	174	L elbow injury
	15	88	Recovery from L elbow surgery

FIVE-YEAR INJURY LOG — Pitchers

Pitchers	Yr	Days	Injury
Morales,Franklin	11	33	Strained L. forearm
	12	41	Fatigue in L. shoulder
	13	106	Strained lower back; L pectoral
Moran,Brian	14	184	L elbow inflammation
Moreland,Mitch	14	111	Surgery on L ankle impingement
Moreno,Diego	15	64	R elbow inflammation
Morin,Michael	14	15	Lacerated L foot
	15	38	L oblique strain
Morris,Bryan	15	22	Lower back strain
Morrow,Brandon	11	21	Inflam - R. forearm
	12	74	Strained L. oblique
	13	121	R forearm strain
	14	122	Torn tendon sheath in R hand
	15	153	R shoulder inflammation
Mortensen,Clayton	13	15	R hip impingement
Morton,Charlie	12	137	Recovering from R. hip surgery+TJS
	13	74	Recovery from R elbow surgery
	14	35	R hip inflammation
	15	51	Hip injury
Moscot,Jon	15	111	L shoulder surgery
Moseley,Dustin	11	60	L. shoulder strain
	12	179	Strained R. shoulder
Motte,Jason	13	183	R elbow surgery
	14	77	Recovery TJS/strained lower back
	15	42	R shoulder strain
Moylan,Peter	11	143	Back surgery
Mujica,Edward	12	18	Fractured R. pinky toe
	15	28	Fractured R thumb
Myers,Brett	13	131	R elbow inflammation
Narveson,Chris	11	15	L. thumb laceration
	12	171	L. rotator cuff tear
	13	74	Sprained middle finger
Nathan,Joe	11	31	Strained R. flexor muscle
	15	179	R elbow flexor strain
Nelson,Jimmy	15	13	Head contusion
Nicasio,Juan	11	54	Neck surgery
	12	123	Strained L. knee
	15	11	L abdominal strain
Niemann,Jeff	11	45	Stiff back
	12	109	Fractured R. fibula
	13	183	R shoulder surgery
Niese,Jon	13	51	Partially torn L rotator cuff
	14	30	Strained L shoulder/L elbow inflam
Niese,Jonathon	11	36	Intercostal strain of the R. side
Nolasco,Ricky	14	38	Strained R elbow
	15	144	R ankle impinge.; R elbow inflam
Nolin,Sean	15	41	Recovery fr. bi-lateral core surgery
Norberto,Jordan	12	68	Str + tendinitis in L. shoulder
Norris,Bud	12	16	L. knee sprain
	14	11	Strained R groin
	15	20	Bronchitis
Norris,Daniel	15	27	R oblique strain
Nova,Ivan	12	17	Inflam in R. rotator cuff
	13	27	R triceps inflammation
	14	162	Torn UCL R elbow
	15	81	Recovery from R elbow surgery
Nuno,Vidal	13	23	Strained L groin

FIVE-YEAR INJURY LOG — Pitchers

Pitchers	Yr	Days	Injury
O Flaherty,Eric	14	95	Recovering from TJS
	15	31	L shoulder strain
O Sullivan,Sean	15	20	L knee tendinitis
Oberholtzer,Brett	15	60	Blisters on pitching hand x2
O'Day,Darren	11	85	Torn labrm R. hip+Inflam R. should.
Odorizzi,Jake	15	32	Strained L oblique
O'Flaherty,Eric	13	135	L elbow surgery
Ogando,Alexi	12	35	Strained R. groin
	13	87	R shoulder inflam x 2; R biceps
	14	117	R elbow inflammation
Ohlendorf,Ross	11	136	R. shoulder strain
	13	20	R shoulder inflammation
	14	184	Sprained R lumbar
	15	50	R groin strain
Oliver,Darren	13	22	L shoulder strain
Olmos,Edgar	15	47	L shoulder impingement
Olsen,Scott	11	182	L. shoulder Inflam
Olson,Tyler	15	24	R knee contusion
Ondrusek,Logan	11	18	Strained R. forearm
	14	27	Strained R shoulder
Ortiz,Joseph	14	128	Fractured L foot
Ortiz,Ramon	13	119	R elbow strain
Oswalt,Roy	11	63	Lower back Inflam
	13	60	Strained L hamstring
Ottavino,Adam	15	161	R triceps inflammation
Outman,Josh	12	37	Strained oblique
	15	120	L shoulder soreness
Oviedo,Juan	12	73	TJS
	13	183	Recovery from R elbow surgery
	14	22	Recovering from TJS
Owings,Micah	12	161	R. elbow surgery
Padilla,Vicente	11	161	R. elbow surgery
	12	15	Strained R. bicep
Parker,Blake	12	112	R. elbow stress react+bone bruise
Parker,Jarrod	14	184	Recovering from TJS
	15	184	Recovery from R elbow surgery
Parnell,Bobby	11	40	Circulatory issues R. middle finger
	13	61	Neck stiffness
	14	180	Torn MCL in R elbow
	15	81	R shoulder tend; rec R elbow surg
Parra,Manny	11	183	Facet joint injury in R. back
	13	30	Strained L pectoral muscle
	15	53	L Bicep tend., elbow strain; str. neck
Patton,Troy	12	39	Sprained R. ankle
	14	80	Sore L shoulder
Paulino,Felipe	12	149	TJS - L. elbow
	13	183	Recovery from R elbow surgery
	14	163	R rotator cuff inflammation
Paxton,James	14	115	Strained L lat in back
	15	107	Strained tendon in L middle finger
Peacock,Brad	15	184	L intercostal strain; rec R hip surg
Peavy,Jake	11	57	Recov.,R. should, Str adductor
	13	44	Fractured rib
	15	76	Back strain
Pelfrey,Mike	12	165	TJS
	13	15	Back strain
	14	149	Strained L groin

FIVE-YEAR INJURY LOG — Pitchers

Pitchers	Yr	Days	Injury
Pena,Tony	11	124	Tendinitis In R. elbow
Peralta,Joel	14	16	Illness
	15	78	Neck sprain; R shoulder soreness
Peralta,Wily	15	63	Strained L oblique
Perez,Chris	13	31	R shoulder soreness
	14	28	Bone spurs in R ankle
Perez,Juan	13	51	Torn UCL ligament, L elbow
Perez,Luis	12	87	TJS - L. elbow
	13	155	Recovery from L elbow surgery
Perez,Martin	13	43	Cracked ulna bone, L forearm
	14	141	L elbow inflammation
	15	109	Recovery from L elbow surgery
Perez,Rafael	12	161	Strained L. lat/ankle injury
Perez,Williams	15	34	L foot contusion
Perkins,Glen	11	26	Strained R. oblique muscle
	14	10	Strained L Forearm
Perry,Ryan	11	15	Infected eye
Pestano,Vinnie	13	16	R elbow tendinitis
Petricka,Jacob	15	15	Strained R forearm
Pettibone,Jonathan	13	63	Strained R shoulder
	15	183	Recovery from R shoulder surgery
Pettitte,Andy	12	83	Fractured fibula in L. ankle
	13	17	Strained L trapezius muscle
Phelps,David	13	71	R forearm strain
	14	56	R elbow inflammation/tendinitis
	15	49	Stress fracture, R forearm
Pimentel,Stolmy	14	56	Sprained R ankle/ R shoulder inflam
Pineda,Michael	12	182	Surgery torn labrum R. shoulder
	13	98	Recovery from R shoulder surgery
	14	99	Strained muscle in R shoulder
	15	27	Strained R forearm
Pomeranz,Drew	13	45	L bicep tendinitis
	14	26	Fractured R hand
	15	14	Sprained L AC joint
Pomeranz,Stuart	12	131	Strained L. oblique
Porcello,Rick	15	24	Strained R triceps
Pressly,Ryan	15	91	R lat strain
Price,David	13	47	L triceps strain
Pryor,Stephen	13	168	Torn R lat muscle
	14	19	Surgery torn lat muscle R shoulder
Purke,Matt	14	66	Recovering from TJS
Putkonen,Luke	14	161	R elbow inflammation
Putnam,Zach	13	110	R elbow soreness
	14	15	R shoulder inflammation
	15	15	R groin strain
Putz,J.J.	11	27	R. elbow tendinitis
	13	75	Strnd R elbow; dislocated finger
	14	35	Tightness in R forearm
Qualls,Chad	12	15	Irritation of L. toe
	15	14	Pinched nerve
Ramirez,Erasmo	12	62	Strained R. elbow flexor
Ramirez,Neil	14	12	Sore R triceps
	15	113	L ab soreness; R shoulder inflam
Ramirez,Ramon	12	24	Hamstring strain
Ramos,A.J.	14	17	R shoulder inflammation
Rasmus,Cory	15	106	R forearm strain; core muscle surg
Rauch,Jon	11	33	Appendicitis; Torn caR.ilge R. knee

FIVE-YEAR INJURY LOG — Pitchers

Pitchers	Yr	Days	Injury
Ravin,Joshua	15	34	L hernia
Ray,Chris	11	61	Strained R. shoulder
Reynolds,Matt	13	112	Strained L elbow
	14	184	Recovering from TJS
Rice,Scott	13	21	Sports hernia
Richard,Clayton	11	86	Strained L. shoulder
	13	122	L shoulder surgery; stomach virus
Richards,Garrett	11	21	R. adductor strain
	14	39	Torn patellar tendon in L knee
	15	15	Recovery from L knee surgery
Riefenhauser,Charles	15	36	L shoulder inflammation
Rienzo,Andre	15	20	L knee laceration
Rivera,Mariano	12	153	Torn ACL in R. knee
Rivero,Felipe Javier	15	29	Gastrointestinal bleeding
Roberts,Kenneth	15	26	L elbow inflammation
Robertson,David	12	33	Strained L. oblique
	14	14	Strained L groin
Robles,Maricio	11	74	Recov. fr. surg. - L. shoulder
Rodney,Fernando	11	39	Strained upper back
Rodriguez,Fernando	13	183	R elbow surgery
	14	31	Recovering from TJS
Rodriguez,Francisco	11	142	Inflam - R. shoulder
Rodriguez,Henry	11	28	R. arm injury
	12	91	Low back strain+ R. index finger
Rodriguez,Paco	14	55	Strained L shoulder
	15	127	Strained L elbow
Rodriguez,Wandy	11	21	Fluid in L. elbow
	13	116	L forearm tightness
	14	24	R knee inflammation
Roe,Chaz	15	22	R shoulder injury
Rogers,Esmil	11	84	R. lat strain
Rogers,Mark	13	152	R shoulder instability
Romero,J.C.	11	15	R. calf strain
Romo,Sergio	11	18	R. elbow Inflam
Rondon,Bruce	14	184	Surgery on R elbow
	15	71	R biceps tendinitis
Rosario,Sandy	12	110	R. quad strain
Ross,Robbie	12	20	Sore L. forearm
Ross,Tyson	11	66	Strained L. oblique muscle
	13	17	L shoulder subluxation
Rosscup,Zachary	14	31	Sore L shoulder
	15	58	L shoulder inflammation
Runzler,Dan	12	153	Strained lat muscle
Ryu,Hyun-Jin	14	35	Strained R hip/L shoulder inflam
Ryu,Hyun-jin	15	183	L shoulder inflammation
Sabathia,C.C.	12	15	Sore L. elbow+ strain abductor
	13	5	Strained L hamstring
	14	141	Fluid in R knee
	15	16	R knee inflammation
Sadler,Casey	15	34	R elbow discomfort
Saito,Takashi	11	88	L. hamstring strain
	12	126	Strained L. hamstring+ calf str
Salas,Fernando	13	36	R shoulder irritation
	14	21	R shoulder inflammation
Sale,Chris	14	30	Strained flexor muscle in R elbow
	15	7	Fractured R foot
Sanabia,Alex	13	126	R groin discomfort

FIVE-YEAR INJURY LOG — Pitchers

Pitchers	Yr	Days	Injury
Sanches,Brian	11	26	R. elbow strain
Sanchez,Aaron	15	40	R lat strain
Sanchez,Anibal	13	20	Strained R shoulder
	14	66	Strnd R pectoral muscle;cut Rt finger
	15	46	R rotator cuff inflammation
Sanchez,Eduardo	11	92	R. shoulder strain
Sanchez,Jonathan	11	80	L. biceps tendinitis
	12	61	L. bicep tendinitis
	12	36	Tendinitis in L. bicep
Sanit,Amauri	11	110	Inflam - R. elbow
Santana,Johan	11	182	L. sholder surgery
	12	70	Inflam of lower back+ spr R. ankle
	13	183	L shoulder surgery
	14	119	Rec from surgery on L shoulder
Santos,Sergio	12	166	Surgery torn labrum in R. shoulder
	13	109	R triceps strain
	14	34	Strained R elbow/forearm
	15	108	R elbow surgery
Saunders,Joe	12	15	L. shoulder strain
	14	51	Bruised L ankle
Savery,Joe	13	45	L elbow stiffness
Scahill,Rob	15	67	R forearm tightness
Scheppers,Tanner	14	158	R elbow inflammation x2
	15	29	L knee inflam; R ankle sprain
Schlereth,Daniel	12	166	Tendinitis in L. shoulder
Schlitter,Brian	14	14	R shoulder inflammation
Schugel,Andrew	14	111	R hamstring injury
Schumaker,Skip	14	43	Concussion/dislocated L shoulder
Schwimer,Michael	13	39	R shoulder strain
Scribner,Evan	11	27	R. shoulder strain
Septimo,Leyson	12	18	Inflam in L. biceps
	13	72	L shoulder strain
Sheets,Ben	12	25	R. shoulder Inflam
Sherrill,George	11	30	L. elbow Inflam
	12	177	TJS - L. elbow
Shoemaker,Matt	14	13	Strained Lt oblique
Siegrist,Kevin	14	60	Strained L forearm
Simmons,Shae	14	62	Strained R shoulder
Simon,Alfredo	11	16	Strained R. hamstring
Skaggs,Tyler	14	81	Strained L forearm; Rt hammy
	15	184	Recovery from L elbow surgery
Slaten,Doug	11	89	L. elbow ulnar neuritis
Slowey,Kevin	11	94	Sore R. biceps; Abdominal strain
	13	66	R forearm discomfort
Smith,Burch	15	180	R elbow surgery
Smith,Joe	11	15	Abdominal strain
Smith,Jordan	12	182	Sore R. elbow
Smyly,Drew	12	37	Strain R. intercostal+ fing. blister
	15	118	L shoulder soreness x2
Solis,Sammy Robert	15	20	L shoulder inflammation
Soria,Joakim	12	182	Recovering from TJS
	13	99	Recovery from R elbow surgery
	14	50	Strained L oblique
Soriano,Rafael	11	76	Inflam - R. elbow
	15	27	R shoulder inflammation
Stammen,Craig	15	173	Torn R flexor tendon
Stauffer,Tim	12	182	R. elbow sprain
	15	21	R intercostal strain
Stetter,Mitch	11	137	L. hip injury
Stites,Matthew	15	58	R elbow pain
Storen,Drew	12	106	Elbow injury
Strasburg,Stephen	11	160	Recovery from TJS
	13	15	Strained R latissimus dorsi
	15	58	L oblique; neck strain
Street,Huston	11	17	R. triceps strain
	12	72	Strained L. calf+ L. lat str
	13	15	Strained L calf
Stroman,Marcus	15	159	Torn ACL, L knee
Strop,Pedro	13	15	Lower back strain
	14	23	Strained L groin
Stults,Eric	12	48	Strained L. latissimus dorsi
Stutes,Michael	12	26	R. shoulder Inflam
	13	89	R biceps tendinitis
Surkamp,Eric	12	182	TJS
	13	88	Recovery from L elbow surgery
	15	6	Strained upper back
Swarzak,Anthony	12	33	Strained R. rotator cuff
	13	7	Fractured ribs
Talbot,Mitch	11	125	Strain R. elbow; Strain lower back
	11	56	Strained R. intercostal muscle
Tanaka,Masahiro	14	74	R elbow inflammation
	15	35	Strained R forearm
Taylor,Andrew	13	183	L labrum tear
Tazawa,Junichi	11	88	Recovery from TJS
Teaford,Everett	12	25	Strained lower abdominal
Tejeda,Robinson	11	36	Inflam - R. shoulder
Tepesch,Nicholas	13	57	R elbow inflammation
	15	166	Nerve inflammation, R arm
Thatcher,Joe	11	125	L. shoulder surgery
	12	37	Mid-back strain
	14	57	Sprained L ankle
Thayer,Dale	15	14	Strained R shoulder
Thompson,Taylor	15	132	Strained R shoulder
Thornburg,Tyler	14	114	Sore R elbow
Thornton,Matt	13	20	Strained R oblique
Tillman,Chris	13	5	Strained L abdominal
Tobin,Mason	11	162	TJS
Tolleson,Shawn	13	170	Strained lower back
Tomlin,Josh	11	35	Soreness in R. elbow
	12	72	Inflam in R. elbow+R. wrist
	13	146	Recovery from R elbow surgery
	15	117	R shoulder surgery
Troncoso,Ramon	13	21	Pericarditis
Turner,Jacob	14	24	Strained R shoulder
	15	183	Strained flexor tendon, R elbow
Uehara,Koji	12	77	Strained R. lat
	15	66	Fx R wrist; Strain L ham
Urena,Jose	15	28	L knee contusion
Valdes,Raul	12	62	Torn meniscus R. knee+Str R. hip
Vargas,Jason	13	56	Blood clot, L arm
	14	23	Appendectomy
	15	131	Torn lig., L elbow; L flexor strain x2
Varvaro,Anthony	15	133	Torn flexor tendon in R elbow

FIVE-YEAR INJURY LOG — Pitchers

Pitchers	Yr	Days	Injury
Venditte,Patrick	15	51	Strained R shoulder
Venters,Jonny	12	16	L. elbow impingement
	13	183	Sprained L elbow
	14	184	Recovering from TJS
Ventura,Yordano	15	20	Ulnar neuritis
Veras,Jose	14	18	Strained L oblique
VerHagen,Drew	14	28	Stress reaction in spine
Verlander,Justin B	15	66	Strained R triceps
Villanueva,Carlos	11	27	Strained R. forearm
Vincent,Nick	14	34	R shoulder fatigue
Vizcaino,Arodys	12	183	TJS
	13	183	Recovery from R elbow surgery
Vogelsong,Ryan	12	10	Strained lower back
	13	80	Fractured R hand
Wacha,Michael	14	74	Stress reaction in R shoulder
Wada,Tsuyoshi	12	182	TJS - R. elbow
	13	74	Recovery from L elbow surgery
	15	80	L deltoid inflam; L groin
Wainwright,Adam	11	182	TJS
	15	162	Torn L Achilles
Walden,Jordan	12	41	Strained R. bicep
	13	17	R shoulder inflammation
	14	30	Strained L hamstring
	15	155	R biceps inflammation
Walker,Taijuan	14	73	R shoulder impingement
Walters,PJ	12	79	Inflam in R. shoulder
Wang,Chien-Ming	11	121	Recovery from R. shoulder surgery
	12	113	Strained L. hamstring+R. hip str
Wang,Wei-Chung	14	53	Tightness in L shoulder
Weaver,Jered	12	22	Strained lower back
	13	51	Fractured L elbow
	15	49	L hip inflammation
Webb,Brandon	11	183	Recov. fr. surg. - R. shoulder
Webb,Daniel	15	24	Mid R back strain
Webb,Ryan	11	51	R. shoulder Inflam
Weiland,Kyle	12	162	R. shoulder bursitis
Wells,Randy	11	50	R. forearm strain
Westbrook,Jake	13	51	Sore back; R elbow inflammation
Wheeler,Dan	11	15	Strained L. calf
Wheeler,Zack	15	183	Torn ligament, R elbow
White,Alex	11	94	Soreness in R. middle finger
	13	184	R elbow strain
	14	63	Recovering from TJS
Whitley,Chase	15	143	Sprained R elbow
Wieland,Joe	12	150	TJS
	13	183	Recovery from R elbow surgery
	14	141	Recovering from TJS
Wilhelmsen,Tom	15	25	Hyperextended R elbow
Williams,Jerome	12	35	Respir. infection+str L. hamstring
	15	34	Strained L hamstring
Wilson,Alex	13	83	Sprained R thumb
Wilson,Brian	11	35	L. oblique strain
	12	174	TJS
	13	20	Recovery from R elbow surgery
	14	15	Nerve imflammation in R elbow
Wilson,C.J.	14	23	Sprained R ankle
	15	66	L elbow inflammation

FIVE-YEAR INJURY LOG — Pitchers

Pitchers	Yr	Days	Injury
Winkler,Daniel	15	158	Recovery from R elbow surgery
Withrow,Chris	12	32	R. shoulder strain
	14	127	TJS
Wojciechowski,Asher	14	87	Strained R lat muscle
Wolf,Randy	12	11	TJS 10/2012
Wood,Blake	12	182	TJS - R. elbow
	13	103	Recovery from R elbow surgery
Wood,Kerry	11	22	Blister on R. index finger
	12	19	R. shoulder fatigue
Wood,Tim	13	150	R rotator cuff strain
Workman,Brandon	15	175	R elbow soreness
Worley,Vance	12	54	Loose bodies in R. elbow+ Inflam
Wright,Mike	15	34	Strained L calf
Wright,Steven	14	70	Recovering from surgery sports hernia
	15	51	Concussion
Wright,Wesley	15	95	L shoulder inflammation
Wuertz,Michael	11	53	Strain L. hammy; Tndnts R. thumb
Yates,Kirby	15	41	R pectoral strain
Young,Chris	11	165	R. biceps tendinitis
	13	18	Strained L quad
Zambrano,Carlos	11	15	Lower back soreness
Zeid,Josh	14	64	Surgery L foot bilateral sesamoiditis
Zito,Barry	11	110	R. foot sprain
Zumaya,Joel	11	183	Recov. fr. surg. - R. elbow
	12	173	Recovery from TJS

Top 75 Impact Prospects for 2016

by Rob Gordon and Jeremy Deloney

Looking for a rookie infusion in 2016? Here's the place to start. The following is a list of 75 prospects most likely to contribute and have an impact in the 2016 season. These capsules provide a primer on the strengths and weaknesses of rookie-eligible players, attempting to balance raw skill, readiness for the majors and likelihood of 2016 playing time. Prospects are presented in alphabetical order; the chart on page 230 ranks the prospects and includes projected 2016 Mayberry scores.

For additional information, including profiles of over 1000 minor-leaguers, statistics, and our overall HQ100 top prospect list, see our sister publication, the *2016 Minor League Baseball Analyst*—as well as the weekly scouting reports and minor league information on BaseballHQ.com. Happy prospecting!

Miguel Almonte (RHP, KC) has spent the majority of his career as a starter, but was moved to the bullpen in Triple-A in mid-August in preparation for a call-up to the big leagues. Given his electric stuff, including a mid-90s fastball, he could serve a number of roles in the near-term. The Royals are particularly excited about his plus change-up.

Albert Almora (OF, CHC) turned things around after a sluggish start, hitting .301/.370/.464 in the second half, and continues to make slow, but steady progress. The former 6th overall pick is a solid offensive player with plus defensive tools that make him a fine real-world prospect, but could limit his fantasy appeal.

Tim Anderson (SS, CHW) spent the entire 2015 campaign in Double-A and showcased his plus-plus speed, stealing 49 bases while hitting .312 with 5 HR. He showed enough improvement with his defensive technique and should be able to stick at shortstop for the long-term. With more patience at the plate, some feel he could add more over-the-fence power.

Mark Appel (RHP, HOU) could conceivably be considered underrated despite being the number one overall selection in the 2013 draft. He hasn't been dominant as a pro, but his combination of quality offerings and moxie make him a viable mid-rotation starter. His command comes and goes and his fastball can be flat, but his secondary offerings are very good.

Orlando Arcia (SS, MIL) has quickly developed into one of the best young players in the game. He does everything well and had his best season, hitting .307/.347/.453 with 37 doubles, 8 home runs, and 25 SB as the youngest position player in the Double-A Southern League. He's a plus defender with good speed and a strong arm, which means he should be in the majors sooner rather than later.

Manny Banuelos (LHP, ATL) continues to be a somewhat perplexing. At times, the undersized hurler can be tantalizingly good, keeping hitters off-balance with a low-90s fastball, and a nasty breaking ball. But inconsistency is a problem. Banuelos had Tommy John surgery in 2013 and missed the end of the season with surgery to remove a bone spur from his pitching elbow.

Josh Bell (1B, PIT) is just starting to tap into his full potential. He has become a polished hitter with an advanced understanding of the strike zone and the ability to make consistent, hard contact. At 6'2", 235, Bell has shown surprisingly little power (7 HR in 489 AB in '15), but he should develop 15-20 HR power soon and walked as many times as he whiffed this year.

Aaron Blair (RHP, ARI) had an excellent season despite a decline in strikeouts. The 23-year-old went 13-5 with a 2.92 ERA, but saw his K/9 rate drop from 10.0 to 6.7. He does a good job of keeping hitters off-balance with his low-90s fastball, improved curve, and average change. He should get a chance to win a starting role in 2016 and has solid mid-rotation potential.

Archie Bradley (RHP, ARI) has an ideal power-pitching frame, but has struggled with injuries and ineffectiveness. Shoulder tendinitis limited him to 65 innings on the year and in eight starts in the majors, he walked almost as many as he struck out while posting a 5.80 ERA. Bradley still has premium, front-of-the-rotation stuff, but needs to prove he can stay healthy to have value in 2016.

Jose Berrios (RHP, MIN) was deserving of a late-season promotion to the majors, but the Twins admitted caution with his workload after he pitched 166.1 innings between Double-A and Triple-A in 2015. He is a very strong candidate to win a rotation spot in spring training. He exhibits above average command with all three offerings and can miss bats with any of them.

Lewis Brinson (OF, TEX) made strides in all aspects of his game in 2015, hitting 20 HR while making better contact and showing better selectivity at the plate. He has the potential to be a 20 HR / 20 SB player in the future while also hitting for a serviceable BA. If he continues to add polish and show improvement, he could be a key contributor in 2016.

Dylan Bundy (RHP, BAL) burst onto the big league scene as a 19-year-old, but has been beset by arm and shoulder issues since. He has only pitched 63 innings the last three seasons and was shut down after two innings in the Arizona Fall League due to elbow tightness. When healthy, his repertoire is magnificent and he exhibits above average command to boot, but he has had a very tough time staying out of the trainer's room.

Byron Buxton (OF, MIN) struggled in his time with the Twins in 2015, but he played the entire season as a 21-year-old. He's missed extensive action the past two seasons, though has as much athleticism and speed as any prospect in baseball. He could become a perennial All-Star as he doesn't have one obvious weakness in his game.

Gavin Cecchini (SS, NYM) had a breakout season, hitting .317/.377/.442 as a 21-year-old at Double-A. He has a good approach at the plate and made more consistent contact (89% ct%). He should add more power as he matures, but for now he's a contact-oriented player who should hit for average once he reaches the majors.

A.J. Cole (RHP, WAS) doesn't blow hitters away; instead he attacks the strike zone with a good low-90s fastball and a potentially plus change-up. In 19 Triple-A starts, Cole limited opposing hitters to a .227 oppBAA and walked just 34 in 105.2 IP. Strike throwers who keep the ball out of the middle of the plate can occasionally surprise once they reach the majors.

Wilson Contreras (C, CHC) has the look of a late bloomer. After hitting .248 and .242 the past two seasons, he slashed .333/.413/.478 to win the Southern League batting title. He always made consistent contact, but was more selective in 2015, and his solid bat speed results in average power. Moves well defensively with a strong arm that limits the running game, and has a chance to stick behind the dish.

J.P. Crawford (SS, PHI) has developed into one of the best all-around prospects in the majors. He tore the cover off the ball at High-A, hitting .392 over his first 21 games, which earned him a promotion to Double-A, where he held his own as one of the youngest players in the league. He isn't a burner on the bases and isn't likely to hit for a ton of power, but his plus glove and range will insure full-time AB and he is major league ready now.

David Dahl (OF, COL) suffered a ruptured spleen that cost him more than half of the season. Not surprisingly, he was rusty in his return, but should be 100% in 2016. Dahl is only 21 and is just tapping into his considerable potential. He doesn't have a clear path to playing time with the Rockies, but a quick start could force the issue.

Zach Davies (RHP, MIL) was acquired as part of the Gerardo Parra deal and was surprisingly successful in 6 late-season starts, going 3-2 with a 3.71 ERA. Despite his short, slight frame, he exhibits advanced command and a professional pitch mix, though without huge velcoity. Not a high upside, but a safe bet as a strike-thrower and groundballer.

Jose De Leon (RHP, LA) came out of nowhere to develop into one of the Dodgers best pitching prospects. The 24th round pick out of Puerto Rico dominated in the hitter-friendly CAL and then held his own when moved up to Double-A. For the year he was 6-7 with a 2.99 ERA, 163 K/37 BB in 114.1 IP.

Brandon Drury (3B, ARI) continues to be an intriguing prospect despite a troubling drop in power. The 23-year-old slugged 23 home runs in '14, but saw that number drop to just 4 in '15, though he did hit 40 doubles. Drury knows how to handle the bat and has a career slash line of .285/.334/.440. If the power of 2014 re-emerges he could be a bargain on draft day.

Michael Fulmer (RHP, DET) could be a benefactor with the Tigers rotation in flux. The 22-year-old was the primary target in the trade that sent Yoenis Cespedes to the Mets at the trade deadline. He had his best season to date and showed marked improvement with his change-up. He profiles as a durable, mid-rotation guy who can get groundball outs and strikeouts.

Joey Gallo (3B, TEX) may not have matched his 42 HR from 2014 between High-A and Double-A, but he reached the majors and showed off his immense pop at the big league level. His BA and strikeout rate won't impress, but he works counts to get on base and has tape measure power. He added to his versatility by playing both 3B and LF in 2015.

Lucas Giolito (RHP, WAS) continues to rocket his way to the majors after overcoming Tommy John surgery in 2012. He works in the 92-97 mph range, topping out at 100 mph and mixes in a plus 12-6 curve and a change-up that shows potential. A Top-10 overall prospect, his stuff is too good to keep him in the minors for long.

Tyler Glasnow (RHP, PIT) has plus raw stuff. He comes after hitters with a mid-90s heater and a plus hard curve that generates plenty of swings and misses. He does struggle with control at times, but over the course of four minor league seasons he has an 11.7 Dom rate and a miniscule .171 oppBAA. He's a long-shot to crack the Pirates rotation next spring, but has tremendous upside.

Marco Gonzales (LHP, STL) took a significant step back in 2015 and will need to make an adjustment. After going 9-5 with a 2.43 ERA in 2014, Gonzales was 1-5 with a 5.45 ERA and hitters in the PCL posted a .323 oppBAA in 69.1 IP. Gonzales throws plenty of strikes, but doesn't have overpowering stuff and needs to stay out of the middle of the zone. A prototypical command-and-control lefty.

Jon Gray (RHP, COL) continues to make steady progress, but has yet to have the kind of results expected from a player taken 3rd overall in the draft. Gray has good stuff, highlighted by his mid-90s heater and swing-and-miss slider, but he tends to find too much of the plate and NL hitters teed-off the tune of a .319 oppBAA in his 9 starts with the Rockies. The potential remains high, but comes with substantial risk in 2016.

Alen Hanson (2B, PIT) spent the entire year at Triple-A where he continued to put up solid if not spectacular numbers —.263/.313/.387 with 35 SB. Hanson is a solid all-around player whose primary fantasy asset is his plus speed. He's shown solid power in the past and should develop into an above-average fantasy 2B.

Jeff Hoffman (RHP, COL) came over to the Rockies as the key player in the Tulowitzki trade and gives the club yet another power arm. Hoffman had Tommy John surgery early in 2014 and looked 100% in his return to action, going 5-5 with a 3.03 ERA in 104 IP. Hoffman can hit 99 mph in short stints and mixes in a plus curve, but doesn't rack up tons of Ks and any young hurler pitching in Coors Field carries considerable risk.

Brian Johnson (LHP, BOS) was recalled to start one game for the Red Sox in July and later his season ended after elbow discomfort. Doctors found no structural damage, but he didn't pitch after August 3. His mature ability to mix pitches and change speeds give him a different dimension than most pitching prospects and he doesn't need to rely on velocity.

Micah Johnson (2B, CHW) began the season as the White Sox starting 2B before they sent him back to Triple-A in mid-May after a rough start. Then he hit .315 with 8 HR and 28 SB, and was elevated to Chicago in September. He's still not a sure thing to win the job in spring training, but he offers offensive ability and well above average speed.

Aaron Judge (OF, NYY) was not a September call-up as anticipated, but that doesn't mean the Yankees don't have him in their immediate plans. At 6'7", 275 pounds, he offers significant offensive upside with a solid approach at the plate and brute power. He'll need to curb his strikeouts, but he's a good hitter and an asset in RF where he possesses a strong arm.

Max Kepler (OF, MIN) took as big of a step forward as any prospect in baseball in 2015 and much will be expected of him going into 2016. With his assortment of tools, he can contribute in any number of ways. He owns a sweet left-handed swing, drives the gaps with hard hit balls, and can run well. Because he can play 1B and any outfield position, he has immediate value.

John Lamb (LHP, CIN) looks to be a bit of a late-bloomer. The 25-year-old had his best season as a pro going 10-2 with a 2.67 ERA. Improved command was the key to the breakout and a mid-season trade to the Reds opened the door for his MLB debut. Lamb held his own in 10 starts and should contend for a rotation spot.

Jorge Lopez (RHP, MIL) finally had a breakout after dealing adversity both on and off the field. When he's on, Lopez has plus stuff highlighted by a good 90-94 mph sinking fastball. Lopez looked dominant at Double-A, going 12-5 with an impressive 2.26 ERA in 24 starts and has as chance to be a part of a revamped Brewers rotation next year.

Mikie Mahtook (OF, TAM) performed better in the majors than he did at any level of the minors since he was a first round pick in 2011. His upside may not match that of other prospects, but he offers good tools with both the bat and glove. If he can improve his pitch selectivity and learn to use his speed more effectively, he could earn a full-time role.

Sean Manaea (LHP, OAK) was acquired from the Royals in late July and he gives the Athletics a high-ceiling pitcher in their organization. He was a supplemental first round pick in 2013 and was dominant at Double-A Midland upon the trade. The 23-year-old has high strikeout ability and could pay quick dividends. He just needs to avoid the minor injuries of his past.

Manuel Margot (OF, SD) has a unique skill set that could allow him to either hit at the top of the order or in the middle of the order depending on how much power he develops. Playing the entire season at age 20, the right-handed hitter ended the year in Double-A. His contact ability is exceptional and his power-speed combo is certainly intriguing.

Steven Matz (LHP, NYM) played a key role in the Mets second half run. His fastball sits at 92-96 with an average FB velocity of 94.7 mph. He also mixes in a plus curve and a change-up that shows decent potential. The key to his development has been improved command and the ability to stay healthy after missing more than two full seasons due to injury.

Nomar Mazara (OF, TEX) continues to blossom and added to his impressive resume with a solid stint in Triple-A to end the 2015 campaign. The 20-year-old already has a sound approach at the plate and offers power potential from the left side. He won't steal many bases, but is passable in right field with a very strong arm.

Billy McKinney (OF, CHC) started the season on fire, hitting .340 in his first 29 games at High-A, earning him a quick promotion to Double-A. The 21-year-old McKinney has a nice approach at the plate, a good understanding of the strike zone, and a nice line-drive swing. A fractured knee caused McKinney to miss the end of the season, but he should be 100% by spring.

Alex Meyer (RHP, MIN) seems to have lost some of his prospect status after a lackluster beginning of the season and horrific two games in the Twins bullpen in June. He ended the season on a high note and should compete for a prominent role in 2016. He still has a plus fastball and knockout breaking ball, but command and control still elude him.

Frankie Montas (RHP, CHW) made the leap from Double-A to the majors in September and was handled cautiously out of the bullpen. As a starter in Double-A, the 22-year-old consistently sat in the mid-to-high 90s with his fastball while adding more polish and bite to his slider. If his control continues to move in the right direction, he could be a dynamic #2-type starter.

Steven Moya (OF, DET) earned 8 AB with the Tigers in 2014 and didn't get back, as expected, until September 2015. There are some weaknesses in his game—strikeouts, plate discipline, speed—but the strengths he brings to the table are valuable. He has significant all-fields power and is a competent corner defender. There will be opportunities for him to contribute in 2016.

Tom Murphy (C, COL) isn't an elite-level prospect, but plays in the right organization and has the kind of power to make him a valuable fantasy asset. A shoulder injury cost him most of the 2014 season, but he had a solid rebound, hitting .256 with 26 doubles and 20 home runs. He played reasonably well in a brief stint with the Rockies and with the knee injury to Mike McKenry has a chance to see significant action in the majors in 2016.

Sean Newcomb (LHP, ATL) had a terrific season across three levels in the minors, ending in Double-A. He held hitters to a .199 oppBA in 2015 and his success can be attributed to his improved, plus curveball, and groundball tendencies. He can register strikeouts with multiple pitches and he could pitch meaningful innings with the Braves in 2016.

Pete O'Brien (C/OF, ARI) isn't the most glamorous prospect, but he has plus power and has been productive at every level. The Yankees and Diamondbacks both gave O'Brien an extended look behind the plate, but the jury is out whether he'll make it as a C or OF. O'Brien will need to play regularly to justify a roster spot, but his career line of 273/.323/.539 hints at the potential value.

Hector Olivera (2B, ATL) put up less than overwhelming numbers in his U.S. debut, hitting .272/.326/.376 in 125 AB. Still, he was a key piece of the three-team deal that sent Mat Latos and Jose Peraza to the Dodgers. Olivera has an enticing mix of power, bat speed, and the ability to barrel the ball consistently. His slow start was to be expected given his long layoff from game action and he should have a fulltime role with Braves starting in 2016.

Matt Olson (1B, OAK) is a big, hulking prospect with plenty of power and patience at the plate. He may not have much depth in his secondary skills, but he will get on base consistently and knock the ball out of the park. He hit 37 HR in 2014 at High-A and his output declined to 17 HR in 2015 in Double-A. However, he's walked at least 105 times in each of the past two years.

Jose Peraza (2B, LA) has some of the best speed in the minors. Peraza was traded from ATL and made his MLB debut before being sidelined with a hamstring injury. Starting the season as the youngest position player in the IL, Peraza racked up 37 SB in 118 games after swiping 60 bags in 2014. He doesn't walk much and is never going to hit for power, but he could steal 30-40 bases and should see plenty of action in 2016.

Brett Phillips (OF, MIL) was dealt to the Brewers along with Domingo Santana in the Carlos Gomez deal. Prior to the trade, Phillips was in the midst of a monster season and was hitting .320 with 27 doubles and 16 home runs. He cooled off following the trade, but has plus power and a track-record of hitting for average despite a fringy ct%. The Brewers have few advanced position prospects, so Phillips should be in the majors by mid-2016.

Jorge Polanco (SS, MIN) has been in the majors for each of the last two seasons, but he will likely compete for the starting shortstop job in spring training. In order for him to do so, he'll need to master his glovework. If necessary, he could slide over to 2B. The switch-hitter has good bat speed, makes easy contact, and uses his speed well.

Roman Quinn (OF, PHI) tends to fly under the prospect radar and will likely continue to do so after a hip flexor cost him the second half of the season. When healthy, which hasn't been often, Quinn has plus speed and managed to steal 29 bases while hitting .306/.56/.435 in 58 games. He continues to transition from SS to CF and has the kind of speed that makes him an excellent fantasy sleeper in 2016.

Colin Rea (RHP, SD) had a nice breakout season before being sidelined with a sore elbow. Rea isn't overpowering, but did a better job of coming after hitters with his low-90s sinker and hard breaking ball. He has easy velocity and repeats his delivery well. Should compete for a rotation spot this spring and is worth a flyer in NL-only formats.

A.J. Reed (1B, HOU) will likely never win a Gold Glove or a foot race, but he hit .340/.432/.612 with 30 doubles and 34 HR between High-A and Double-A. He is extremely selective at the plate, drawing 86 walks while also making good contact for a lefty slugger. He could be given a legitimate shot to win the starting 1B job in 2016.

Rob Refsnyder (2B, NYY) may not be a standout with any one particular skill, but he is a solid, consistent performer. He was promoted to the big leagues in mid-July before returning to Triple-A shortly thereafter. He'll need to work on his defense in order to compete for a starting job, but he can hit for a decent BA with some pop and SB ability.

Hunter Renfroe (OF, SD) has the tools to become a solid RF in the big leagues. He has plus bat speed that leads to above-average power and for the second straight year reached the 20 home run mark. On defense, he has a plus throwing arm and moves well, despite being only average runner. Can be overly aggressive at the plate, which will keep his BA in the .250 range unless he can make an adjustment.

Alex Reyes (RHP, STL) has legit front-of-the-rotation stuff and the club has proven both willing and able to utilize their young talent effectively. He overpowers hitters with a plus mid-90s fastball that tops out at 98 mph, a good hard curve, and a plus change-up. His 13.4 Dom rate in 2015 was tops among minor league starting pitchers. However, he will miss the first portion of the season due to a drug-related suspension.

Daniel Robertson (SS, TAM) broke his hand in early June and missed significant time before returning in August. He was a key piece of the trade between Oakland and Tampa Bay in January 2015 and he is expected to compete for time with the Rays in 2016 as a 22-year-old. The right-handed hitter doesn't profile as a star, but should become a solid, everyday player.

Gary Sanchez (C, NYY) has been a very good prospect for years and was rewarded with a September call-up by the Yankees. The jury is out on whether he'll be able to stick at catcher, but there are few questions about his ability to hit. He offers plus, raw power and above average hitting instincts. It is too early to move him off catcher and to 1B or DH.

Corey Seager (SS, LA) established himself as the top prospect heading into 2016. Seager is dynamic at the plate with a quick left-handed stroke that generates plus power. He squares the ball up consistently and hits the ball to all fields. Defensively he moves well with a strong arm, but could slide to 3B eventually. Seager should take over as the Dodgers starting SS in 2016 and is an early favorite for the NL Rookie of the Year award.

Richie Shaffer (3B, TAM) was a first round pick in the 2012 draft and some wrote him off after a lackluster 2014 campaign in Double-A. In 2015, he rebounded to hit 30 HR between three levels, including the majors. He split time between 1B and 3B and could be a candidate to win the starting 1B job in spring training. Expect a low BA with few SB, however.

Braden Shipley (RHP, ARI) had another solid season, going 9-11 with a 3.50 ERA in 27 Southern League starts. The 23-year-old has a good 92-94 mph sinking fastball and a potentially plus 12-6 curve. His Dom rate dipped from 9.1 to 6.8 as he pitched more to contact in 2015. Should settle in as a solid #3 starter and make his MLB debut by mid-2016.

Mallex Smith (OF, ATL) came over to the Braves as part of the Justin Upton deal and has some of the best speed in the minors. Smith draws a decent number of walks, barrels the ball consistently, and creates havoc on the bases. On the year, Smith hit .306/.373/.386 with 57 SB in 484 AB between Double and

Triple-A. He makes an excellent sleeper pick in deep NL-only formats.

Blake Snell (LHP, TAM) began the 2015 season with 46 consecutive scoreless innings and ended the year with a 1.41 ERA and 10.9 Dom in 134 innings across three levels. The 22-year-old exhibits three very good offerings in his arsenal and uses his height and arm slot to give hitters a difficult look. Given his ease of success in the high minors, he'll be given a legitimate opportunity.

Robert Stephenson (RHP, CIN) gets surprising velocity from his 6'2", 200 frame. His fastball sits at 93-96 mph and tops out at 99 and he mixes in a devastating power curve. His change-up and control lag behind for now and Stephenson walked 4.7 per nine in 2015. If everything comes together, Stephenson has the stuff to be a top-of-the-rotation starter and that could happen as soon as 2016—think Gerrit Cole back in 2012.

Trevor Story (SS, COL) is now able to see a path to full-time AB with the Troy Tulowitzki trade. The 22-year-old Story has some nice offensive tools and in 2015 he belted 40 doubles and 20 home runs to go along with a .279 average, though his year-to-year production has been inconsistent. If you are able to withstand some lean stretches, the hot streaks could be fantasy gold.

Jameson Taillon (RHP, PIT) missed the past two seasons, first with Tommy John surgery and then with a sports hernia. His fastball sits at 93-97 mph and tops out at 99 mph with a plus power curve. Below-average control was always an issue and it might take him time to regain his form after a long layoff.

Jake Thompson (RHP, PHI) came over to the Phillies as part of the Cole Hamels deal and becomes the top arm in the system. Thompson has a good 90-94 mph sinking fastball, a plus slider, and an inconsistent change-up. He has a similar profile to Rick Porcello (RHP, BOS) and needs to keep the ball down to have success.

Trayce Thompson (OF, CHW) was not considered a strong candidate to accumulate much major league time in 2015, but he held his own in a trial run with the big league club. He's always possessed good raw power, but his inability to make consistent contact hindered its usefulness. If he can continue to polish his stroke, he has a chance to be more than a reserve outfielder.

Trea Turner (SS, WAS) has a chance to win the starting job in 2016. The 22-year-old arrived in a trade with San Diego and has solid offensive potential. He can be overly aggressive at the plate and needs to make more consistent contact, but to date has been able to hit for average. His career minor league slash line is .322/.384/.454.

Julio Urias (LHP, LA) has been on the fast-track to the majors since coming to the U.S. in 2013. His dazzling arsenal—fronted by a mid-90s fastball, wicked curveball, and a developing change-up—and advanced pitchability give him star potential. Urias should make his MLB debut at some point in 2016 as a 19 year-old.

Nick Williams (OF, PHI) is a toolsy, athletic player who came over as a key part of the Cole Hamels deal. Williams has plus tools across the board and for the year hit .303/.354/.491 with 26 doubles, 17 home runs, and 13 SB. Williams is just 22, he is the Phillies CF of the future and should be ready to make his MLB debut by mid-2016.

Jesse Winker (OF, CIN) is a professional hitter with an advanced understanding of the strike zone. Winker posted a .390 OB% in 2015 and is just starting to tap into his long-term potential. The Reds will likely overhaul their OF in 2016 and Winker should be ready to make his big league debut by mid-season. The power might take a while to develop, but his ability to hit and get on base should give him value right away.

Bradley Zimmer (OF, CLE) has turned into one of the top prospects in baseball thanks his power, speed, defense, and instincts. Between High-A and Double-A, he surprisingly stole 44 bases while hitting 16 HR. At 6'4", 185 pounds, he covers a lot of ground in CF and he's expected to stay at that position for the long-term.

Top 75 Impact Prospects for 2016

The chart below lists projected Mayberry scores for the Top 75 Impact Prospects for 2016. Mayberry scores are explained in the Encyclopedia, and here reflect 2016 only, not a player's long-term impact. Batters are dark shaded; pitchers are lighter shaded.

RANK/BATTER/POS, TM	POWER	SPEED	BATAVG	PT '16
RANK/PITCHER/POS, TM	**ERA**	**DOM**	**SAVES**	**PT '16**
1 Corey Seager (SS, LA)	3	3	3	5
2 Byron Buxton (OF, MIN)	3	5	3	5
3 Steven Matz (LHP, NYM)	3	3	0	5
4 Trea Turner (SS, WAS)	1	5	3	3
5 Joey Gallo (3B, TEX)	4	1	2	3
6 Hector Olivera (2B, ATL)	3	2	2	3
7 J.P. Crawford (SS, PHI)	2	2	3	3
8 Jose Berrios (RHP, MIN)	2	3	0	3
9 Blake Snell (LHP, TAM)	2	4	0	1
10 Tyler Glasnow (RHP, PIT)	2	4	0	1
11 Orlando Arcia (SS, MIL)	1	3	2	1
12 Lucas Giolito (RHP, WAS)	3	3	0	1
13 Jose Peraza (2B, LA)	1	4	3	1
14 Alex Reyes (RHP, STL)	3	4	0	1
15 Robert Stephenson (RHP, CIN)	1	3	0	1
16 Nomar Mazara (OF, TEX)	2	1	3	3
17 Archie Bradley (RHP, ARI)	1	2	0	3
18 Tim Anderson (SS, CHW)	1	3	2	1
19 Trevor Story (SS, COL)	3	2	1	3
20 A.J. Reed (1B, HOU)	2	1	3	1
21 Nick Williams (OF, PHI)	2	2	3	1
22 Josh Bell (1B, PIT)	2	1	3	1
23 Julio Urias (LHP, LA)	2	3	0	1
24 Jake Thompson (RHP, PHI)	1	3	0	1
25 Lewis Brinson (OF, TEX)	3	3	1	1
26 Pete O'Brien (C/OF, ARI)	4	1	1	1
27 Aaron Judge (OF, NYY)	2	1	1	1
28 Brett Phillips (OF, MIL)	3	3	1	1
29 Brian Johnson (LHP, BOS)	3	1	0	1
30 Sean Newcomb (LHP, ATL)	1	2	0	1
31 Richie Shaffer (3B, TAM)	2	1	1	1
32 Mikie Mahtook (OF, TAM)	2	1	3	1
33 Dylan Bundy (RHP, BAL)	2	3	0	1
34 Jesse Winker (OF, CIN)	2	1	2	1
35 Mark Appel (RHP, HOU)	1	3	0	1
36 Hunter Renfroe (OF, SD)	3	1	1	1
37 Brandon Drury (3B, ARI)	3	1	2	1
38 Manuel Margot (OF, SD)	2	3	3	1

RANK/BATTER/POS, TM	POWER	SPEED	BATAVG	PT '16
RANK/PITCHER/POS, TM	**ERA**	**DOM**	**SAVES**	**PT '16**
39 Jameson Taillon (RHP, PIT)	1	3	0	1
40 Frankie Montas (RHP, CHW)	1	3	1	1
41 Jorge Polanco (SS, MIN)	1	1	3	1
42 Jon Gray (RHP, COL)	1	3	0	3
43 Marco Gonzales (RHP, STL)	2	1	0	1
44 David Dahl (OF, COL)	2	2	3	1
45 Alen Hanson (2B, PIT)	1	3	1	1
46 Bradley Zimmer (OF, CLE)	2	3	3	1
47 Tommy Murphy (C, COL)	3	1	2	1
48 Aaron Blair (RHP, ARI)	2	1	1	1
49 Miguel Almonte (RHP, KC)	2	2	0	1
50 Roman Quinn (OF, PHI)	1	4	2	1
51 Max Kepler (OF, MIN)	2	1	3	1
52 A.J. Cole (RHP, WAS)	1	1	0	3
53 Billy McKinney (OF, CHC)	1	1	3	1
54 Michael Fulmer (RHP, DET)	1	3	0	1
55 Micah Johnson (2B, CHW)	1	3	2	1
56 Braden Shipley (RHP, ARI)	1	1	1	1
57 Jose De Leon (RHP, LA)	2	3	0	1
58 Alex Meyer (RHP, MIN)	1	3	1	0
59 Colin Rea (RHP, SD)	2	1	0	3
60 Albert Almora (OF, CHC)	2	3	2	1
61 Manny Banuelos (LHP, ATL)	1	2	0	3
62 Daniel Robertson (SS, TAM)	1	2	3	1
63 Steven Moya (OF, DET)	4	1	1	3
64 Gary Sanchez (C, NYY)	3	1	2	1
65 Zach Davies (RHP, MIL)	3	1	0	3
66 Sean Manaea (LHP, OAK)	2	3	0	1
67 Matt Olson (1B, OAK)	3	1	2	1
68 Gavin Cecchini (SS, NYM)	1	2	3	1
69 John Lamb (LHP, CIN)	2	3	0	3
70 Jorge Lopez (RHP, MIL)	1	2	2	3
71 Trayce Thompson (OF, CHW)	2	3	1	1
72 Willson Contreras (C, CHC)	1	1	3	1
73 Mallex Smith (OF, ATL)	1	4	1	1
74 Jeff Hoffman (RHP, COL)	2	2	1	1
75 Rob Refsnyder (2B, NYY)	2	1	3	1

Top International Players for 2016 and Beyond

Since the 2008 edition, the *Baseball Forecaster* has profiled a handful of Japanese prospects who may make the jump to Major League Baseball in the coming years. This provides owners in deep keeper leagues to get the jump on talent before they arrive in the states. For example, that first column in 2008 included names like Koji Uehara (who made his MLB debut in 2009), Norichika Aoki (2012), and even a "hugely talented young pitcher" named Yu Darvish (also 2012).

As more MLB teams now draw regularly from the international player pool, we've expanded our coverage to include both Korean players as well as top Carribean talent—both high-upside teenagers of the past international signing period and Cuban players that could draw the interest of mutliple MLB teams. With each, we list a "possible" MLB ETA—but for most of these, you'll need to be patient.

Japanese and Korean Players *(by Tom Muhall)*

In 2015 the first effective offensive player from Asia since Aoki arrived in MLB, but he was from Korea and not Japan. Jung Ho Kang hit a very respectable 15 HR in 423 AB, with a solid BA. While as usual, there are more MLB-ready pitchers than hitters, there may be several interesting offensive players on the horizon.

Shogo Akiyama (OF, Seibu Lions) became just the sixth player with a 200-hit season in NPB history, a feat previously attained by Ichiro Suzuki and Norichika Aoki. What makes his accomplishment stand out is that he is the only player with 200 hits in a season since the "deader" ball was introduced in 2011. Akiyama was one of only eight .300 hitters in all of Japan this past season. He's a solid defender with decent five-category skills.
Possible ETA: 2017.

Takayuki Kajitani (OF, Yokohama DeNA Baystars) was an infielder who was moved to the outfield to improve his offense. He is similar to Aoki but with more power, and he could provide low double-digit HR and higher double-digit SB. Kajitani is getting close to posting time and could be a productive utility player in the majors.
Possible ETA: 2017.

Chihiro Kaneko (RHP, Orix Buffaloes) was poised to be an impact international free agent, but instead signed a four-year extension with the Buffaloes before the beginning of the 2015 season. As a result, Kaneko may not be bringing his sub-2.0 ERA to MLB anytime soon. Still, he indicated that becoming a MLB pitcher is something he would like to do "at some point." So hope springs eternal, but at age 32, it isn't springing as high anymore.
Possible ETA: 2017.

Yusei Kikuchi (LHP, Seibu Lions) drew interest from several MLB teams when it looked like he might pass up the Japanese draft and head to the majors in 2009. Instead, the lefty signed with a Japanese team. Just 24 years old and years away from international free agency, he would have to hope for the posting rules to loosen or a change of heart by his team.
Possible ETA: 2018.

Dae-ho Lee (1B, Fukuoka SoftBank Hawks) is a power hitting first baseman who plays solid defense. Lee dominated the Korean League, and set a world record for hitting a HR in nine straight games. He signed to play in Japan in 2012, where he promptly led his league in RBI and was voted best first baseman. Lee has played remarkably well in International games. His contract is up and he has announced his intent to test the MLB market in this offseason. At age 33, it's now or never.
Probable ETA: 2016.

Kenta Maeda (RHP, Hiroshima Toyo Carp) is a control pitcher (1.047 lifetime WHIP) with a solid fastball in the low 90s. The Gold Glover is nearing his peak years and won the Sawamura Award as the best starting pitcher for the second time this past season. Maeda has expressed a desire to pitch in MLB, but is under team control through 2016. His team owner has expressed reluctance to post him early, so we may have to wait until he attains international free agency. At just 160 pounds, some scouts feel he is "too slight" to pitch every fifth day in the majors. At worst, he projects to be a decent 3rd or 4th SP.
Possible ETA: 2016.

Nobuhiro Matsuda (3B, Fukuoka Softbank Hawks) has reached international free agency and announced his intent to test the MLB waters. He did hit 35 HR in 2015, but 23 were at home after his team moved in the fences. At age 32, and only once before in his career having exceeded 20 HR, someone may be buying high.
Probable ETA: 2016.

Seung-Hwan Oh (RHP, Hanshin Tigers) followed his sterling 2014 campaign (39 saves with a 1.76 ERA) with a solid 2015 season (41 saves and a 2.73 ERA) and now has the most saves in Japan for two seasons in a row. He previously dominated the Korean league before signing in Japan. His two-year contract with the Hanshin Tigers is up, so baring a surprise, he is ready to move up to MLB. Several teams have expressed an interest.
Probable ETA: 2016.

Shohei Otani (RHP and OF, Nippon Ham Fighters) is known as "The Fastball Prince" and would be a top MLB pitching prospect if he were not playing in Japan. Otani has an excellent fastball routinely touching 98 mph with the usual complement of supporting pitches including a splitter and curve. He finished the 2015 season with 196 strikeouts in 160⅔ innings. He has not looked overmatched when pitching against MLB players in exhibition or international games. Otani has the added attraction of being a pitcher who can also hit and play OF. Several MLB scouts are closely following his progress and any MLB team would love to sign the 21-year-old future star.
Possible ETA: 2018.

Byung-ho Park (1B, Nexen Heroes) looks like the next KBO player to follow Kang to the majors. Park is a two-time Korean League MVP who has hit 31, 37, 52 and 53 HR over the past four seasons. His defense is solid but he may project better as a DH. The Korean League ball parks are exceedingly offense-friendly, but 20 or even 25 HR is not out of reach for Park.
Probable ETA: 2016, with the Minnesota Twins.

Tetsuto Yamada (2B/SS, Tokyo Yakult Swallows) became only the ninth player in Japanese baseball history to hit for the "Triple 3" with a .329 BA, 38 HR and 34 SB. More impressively,

he is the first to lead a league in both HR and SB. Possibly the best all-round player in Japan, Yamada just turned 23 and despite being years away from the MLB, he is definitely a player to watch. Could this finally be the dominant middle infielder we've been waiting for?
Possible ETA: 2018.

Yuki Yanagita (OF, Softbank Hawks) became only the ninth player in Japanese baseball history to hit for the "Triple 3" with a…no, that's not a misprint. Two Japanese players achieved the elusive Triple 3 this season, with Yanagita joining Yamada by hitting .363 with 33 HR and 32 SB. This is another player to target if you have a long-term farm team.
Possible ETA: 2018.

Caveat about pitching stats in Japan: Japan instituted a new ball in 2011 which had lower-elasticity rubber surrounding the cork. The new design limited offense and inflated pitching stats. A more hitter-friendly ball was introduced in 2013 and HR increased to pre-2011 levels, but the slightly smaller and lighter ball still favors pitchers. Continue to be somewhat skeptical when analyzing pitching stats.

Caveat about hitting stats in Korea: Korean ball parks are notoriously hitter-friendly. Remember, Kang hit 40 HR in Korea the year before he joined the Pirates.

Carribean Players *(by Jeremy Deloney)*

Lazaro Armenteros (OF, Cuba) has yet to sign a contact with a major league club, but the 16-year-old has scouts abuzz based upon his five tools and sky-high ceiling. He already possesses a mature frame at 6'2", 205, but plays the game with passion and polish. Arementeros has present power that could grow to plus-plus and he runs well. He has the type of tools that could lead to .300+ seasons with 30+ HR and 20+ SB. The jury is out on his future defensive home— some project him in an outfield corner; others at 3B or 1B.
Possible ETA: 2021.

Vladimir Guerrero, Jr. (OF, TOR) signed out of the Dominican Republic for $3.9 million, and the 16-year-old shares some of the traits of his famous father of the same name. Guerrero has significant offensive upside based upon his brute raw power and sound hitting instincts. He makes easy contact with a quick stroke and exemplary hand-eye coordination. With his bat control and big frame, the right-handed hitter could prove to be a middle-of-the-order run producer, but he needs to be more selective at the plate.
Possible ETA: 2020.

Lucius Fox (SS, SF) is a multi-dimensional 18-year-old switch-hitter who brings a lot of intrigue with his $6 million price tag. Fox played high school baseball in the U.S. before returning to his birth country in the Bahamas. Fox has advanced skills for his age with both the bat and glove. His best current tool is his plus-plus speed, but he knows how to hit to all fields. His present gap power could evolve into above average pop and his defensive skills should allow him to play either SS, 2B, or CF.
Possible ETA: 2019.

Jhailyn Ortiz (OF, PHI) signed with the Phillies for a $4 million bonus. The 16-year-old Dominican has a very large frame—6'2", 260 pounds—that leads to well above average power. The right-handed hitter has a lot of kinks to work out on his overall game, but he can hit the ball a mile to all fields. His lack of athleticism and mobility will likely move him away from an outfield corner to 1B, but his bat is too good to ignore.
Possible ETA: 2022.

Yadier Alvarez (RHP, LA) is a 19-year-old who defected from Cuba and was granted free agency status by the Commissioner. The Dodgers signed Alvarez to a $16 million bonus. He is all about arm strength and therefore has a very high ceiling. With a fastball that ranges between 92-98 mph, he generates easy velocity with a lightning-quick arm. He also has two secondary offerings in a hard slider and change-up that both could develop into at least plus pitches. He'll take time to develop, but the payoff could be huge.
Possible ETA: 2018

Leodys Taveras (OF, TEX) received a $2.1 million bonus from the Rangers and they expect him to eventually grow into his immense tools. A thin and athletic 17-year-old, the switch-hitting Taveras is a solid defensive CF with a strong arm and plus speed. Once he rounds out his offensive game, he could become a spectacular player. He owns a clean swing from both sides and makes consistent contact. He'll need to clean up his pitch recognition and add strength to his lean frame, but he'll be worth the wait.
Possible ETA: 2020

Starling Heredia (OF, LA) is an aggressive player in all facets of the game. The 16-year-old was inked to a $2.6 million bonus and expectations are high. His raw power is his best current attribute and it is playable in games now. He struggles with breaking balls and selectivity, but he makes hard contact to all fields. Heredia also runs well despite his muscular build. He could become the prototypical RF with his power and very strong arm.
Possible ETA: 2021

MAJOR LEAGUE EQUIVALENTS

In his 1985 *Baseball Abstract*, Bill James introduced the concept of major league equivalencies. His assertion was that, with the proper adjustments, a minor leaguer's statistics could be converted to an equivalent major league level performance with a great deal of accuracy.

Because of wide variations in the level of play among different minor leagues, it is difficult to get a true reading on a player's potential. For instance, a .300 batting average achieved in the high-offense Pacific Coast League is not nearly as much of an accomplishment as a similar level in the Eastern League. MLEs normalize these types of variances, for all statistical categories.

The actual MLEs are not projections. They represent how a player's previous performance might look at the major league level. However, the MLE stat line can be used in forecasting future performance in just the same way as a major league stat line would.

The model we use contains a few variations to James' version and updates all of the minor league and ballpark factors. In addition, we designed a module to convert pitching statistics, which is something James did not originally do.

Players are listed if they spent at least part of 2014 or 2015 in Triple-A or Double-A and had at least 100 AB or 30 IP within those two levels (players who split a season at both levels are indicated as a/a). Major league and Single-A (and lower) stats are excluded. Each player is listed in the organization with which they finished the season. Some players over age 30 with major-league experience have been omitted for space.

These charts also provide the unique perspective of looking at two years' worth of data. These are only short-term trends, for sure. But even here we can find small indications of players improving their skills, or struggling, as they rise through more difficult levels of competition. Since players—especially those with any modicum of talent —are promoted rapidly through major league systems, a two-year scan is often all we get to spot any trends. Five-year trends do appear in the *Minor League Baseball Analyst.*

Used correctly, MLEs are excellent indicators of potential. But, just like we cannot take traditional major league statistics at face value, the same goes for MLEs. The underlying measures of base skill—contact rates, pitching command ratios, BPV, etc.—are far more accurate in evaluating future talent than raw home runs, batting averages or ERAs. This chart format focuses more on those underlying gauges.

Here are some things to look for as you scan these charts:

Target players who...

- had a full season's worth of playing time in AA and then another full year in AAA
- had consistent playing time from one year to the next
- improved their base skills as they were promoted

Raise the warning flag for players who...

- were stuck at the same level both years, or regressed
- displayed marked changes in playing time from one year to the next
- showed large drops in BPIs from one year to the next

BATTER	yr	b	age	pos	lvl	org	ab	hr	sb	ba	bb%	ct%	px	sx	bpv
Adames,Cristhian	14	B	23	SS	a/a	COL	475	2	8	258	6	82	54	77	8
	15	B	24	SS	aaa	COL	463	8	7	271	5	87	62	70	29
Adams,David	14	R	27	2B	a/a	BAL	376	7	3	203	5	78	78	75	9
	15	R	28	2B	aa	MIA	371	4	2	237	11	83	45	61	9
Adams,Lane	14	R	25	CF	aa	KC	405	8	29	232	8	76	97	131	40
	15	R	26	CF	a/a	KC	488	12	23	237	7	72	93	115	14
Adams,Trever	14	R	26	1B	aa	TEX	482	11	5	237	6	76	112	73	29
	15	R	27	1B	a/a	TEX	418	7	4	184	6	62	77	77	-55
Adrianza,Ehire	15	B	26	SS	aaa	SF	171	2	4	254	7	74	51	74	-27
Aguilar,Jesus	14	R	24	1B	aaa	CLE	427	14	0	260	10	74	131	24	29
	15	R	25	1B	aaa	CLE	510	16	0	235	7	73	107	25	3
Ahrens,Kevin	15	R	26	1B	aa	ATL	407	7	6	203	9	76	75	76	6
Alberto,Hanser	14	R	22	SS	aa	TEX	178	2	6	255	3	90	47	92	32
	15	R	23	SS	aaa	TEX	310	3	4	279	2	88	68	91	41
Alcantara,Arismendy	14	B	23	2B	aaa	CHC	335	8	16	272	5	72	143	154	62
	15	B	24	2B	aaa	CHC	454	9	12	198	6	68	94	145	5
Alfaro,Jorge	14	R	21	C	aa	TEX	88	4	0	245	5	73	123	24	9
	15	R	22	C	aa	TEX	190	4	2	225	4	65	126	89	-2
Aliotti,Anthony	14	L	27	1B	a/a	OAK	409	5	1	203	9	58	107	43	-50
	15	L	28	1B	a/a	OAK	402	3	0	209	6	69	52	21	-60
Allen,Brandon	14	L	28	1B	aaa	NYM	320	7	1	180	8	72	72	63	-19
	15	L	29	LF	aaa	NYM	406	10	3	195	7	70	102	58	-6
Allie,Stetson	14	R	23	1B	aa	PIT	407	14	7	204	11	67	110	52	-6
	15	R	24	RF	aa	PIT	409	11	5	172	8	64	96	55	-32
Almanzar,Michael	14	R	24	3B	a/a	BAL	183	5	1	223	5	73	94	39	-10
	15	R	25	3B	aaa	BAL	502	4	1	208	5	79	56	38	-15
Almonte,Abraham	14	B	25	CF	aaa	SEA	277	4	5	211	6	71	66	88	-23
	15	B	26	CF	aaa	CLE	252	3	9	239	10	77	88	118	36
Almora,Albert	14	R	20	CF	aa	CHC	142	2	0	212	1	84	72	94	24
	15	R	21	CF	aa	CHC	405	5	7	249	6	87	74	108	55
Altherr,Aaron	14	R	23	CF	aa	PHI	449	11	9	204	4	72	109	86	12
	15	R	24	CF	a/a	PHI	433	12	12	253	8	77	114	109	50
Alvarez,Dariel	14	R	26	CF	a/a	BAL	532	12	6	251	3	86	89	70	44
	15	R	27	RF	aaa	BAL	512	16	6	245	3	86	82	76	39
Amaral,Beau	14	L	23	CF	aa	CIN	30	0	1	142	11	81	55	103	23
	15	L	24	CF	aa	CIN	339	4	7	199	5	73	43	74	-38
Anderson,Bryan	14	L	28	C	a/a	OAK	253	6	0	242	8	75	110	57	22
	15	L	29	C	aaa	OAK	292	2	0	157	6	61	67	31	-79
Anderson,Lars	14	L	27	1B	a/a	CHC	211	4	0	244	8	78	101	31	21
	15	L	28	1B	a/a	LA	458	11	2	193	12	74	99	32	13
Anderson,Tim	14	R	21	SS	aa	CHW	44	1	0	326	0	77	99	50	3
	15	R	22	SS	aa	CHW	513	5	43	292	4	75	70	169	19
Andreoli,John	14	R	24	LF	aa	CHC	209	0	20	178	11	73	25	150	-18
	15	R	25	CF	aaa	CHC	379	4	24	234	10	70	77	148	6
Anna,Dean	14	L	28	SS	aaa	PIT	198	1	1	158	10	85	47	73	22
	15	L	29	2B	aaa	STL	445	2	3	207	10	83	44	68	9
Aplin,Andrew	14	L	23	CF	a/a	HOU	452	5	19	226	12	82	46	87	15
	15	L	24	CF	a/a	HOU	338	2	23	248	13	81	41	135	25
Arcia,Francisco	14	L	25	C	a/a	NYY	225	1	0	231	3	78	50	30	-30
	15	L	26	C	aa	NYY	238	3	3	216	6	83	43	55	-2
Arcia,Orlando	15	R	21	SS	aa	MIL	512	9	23	297	5	85	94	132	66
Arcia,Oswaldo	15	L	24	RF	aaa	MIN	282	10	0	179	5	69	109	34	-16
Arencibia,J.P.	14	R	28	C	aaa	TEX	190	9	1	215	3	66	141	37	-5
	15	R	29	1B	aaa	TAM	384	15	0	172	3	58	127	38	-47
Arruebarrena,Erisbel	14	R	24	SS	a/a	LA	180	1	1	209	5	63	64	67	-67
	15	R	25	SS	aa	LA	136	1	1	251	3	70	57	55	-50
Asencio,Yeison	14	R	25	RF	a/a	SD	536	10	5	226	3	84	67	65	20
	15	R	26	LF	aa	SD	482	10	5	245	2	90	59	53	29
Ashley,Nevin	14	R	30	C	aaa	PIT	203	1	0	182	6	75	60	32	-27
	15	R	31	C	aaa	MIL	337	6	0	228	6	72	68	54	-30
Asuaje,Carlos	15	L	24	2B	aa	BOS	495	6	7	226	8	80	71	92	24
Austin,Tyler	14	R	23	RF	aa	NYY	396	8	2	244	7	78	89	78	20
	15	R	24	RF	a/a	NYY	341	6	10	218	8	68	72	99	-24
Avery,Xavier	14	L	24	LF	aaa	SEA	400	6	21	223	6	73	82	109	4
	15	L	25	LF	aaa	MIN	476	5	16	253	7	72	68	111	-7
Baez,Javier	14	R	22	SS	aaa	CHC	388	18	12	231	6	63	174	99	37
	15	R	23	SS	aaa	CHC	281	10	13	285	6	69	118	118	19
Ballou,William	15	L	25	LF	a/a	WAS	178	4	8	268	8	79	95	124	47
Bandy,Jett	14	R	24	C	aa	LAA	312	11	2	219	8	77	95	36	13
	15	R	25	C	aaa	LAA	309	7	0	227	3	75	88	33	-11
Bantz,Brandon	14	R	27	C	aa	WAS	70	0	0	211	3	76	58	23	-33
	15	R	28	C	a/a	MIA	192	3	0	196	8	75	64	18	-24
Barfield,Jeremy	14	R	26	RF	aa	OAK	142	2	0	211	13	66	85	61	-23
	15	R	27	RF	a/a	COL	202	4	0	199	6	76	79	34	-11
Barnes,Austin	14	R	25	2B	aa	MIA	284	7	6	245	12	85	104	99	79
	15	R	26	C	aaa	LA	292	7	9	257	8	85	80	87	47
Barnes,Barrett	15	R	24	LF	aa	PIT	126	2	3	210	9	78	65	66	5
Barnes,Brandon	15	R	29	CF	aaa	COL	132	3	4	157	4	69	83	86	-22
Baron,Steven	14	R	24	C	aa	SEA	69	0	1	234	7	80	61	66	2
	15	R	25	C	a/a	SEA	291	2	5	215	7	73	62	88	-17
Bauers,Jake	15	L	20	1B	aa	TAM	257	4	5	249	6	83	78	70	29
Beck,Preston	15	L	25	RF	aa	TEX	343	4	6	189	8	80	51	96	7
Bell,Josh	14	B	22	RF	aa	PIT	94	0	3	249	6	87	17	71	-5
	15	B	23	1B	a/a	PIT	489	5	8	285	10	86	65	101	47
Belnome,Vince	14	L	26	1B	aaa	TAM	413	8	2	203	12	63	107	57	-20
	15	L	27	1B	a/a	NYM	279	1	1	156	9	57	61	65	-81
Beltre,Engel	14	L	25	RF	a/a	TEX	51	0	0	113	1	85	15	30	-36

BATTER	yr	b	age	pos	lvl	org	ab	hr	sb	ba	bb%	ct%	px	sx	bpv
Belza,Thomas	14	L	25	LF	aa	ARI	413	1	8	268	8	75	64	99	1
	15	L	26	3B	a/a	ARI	316	3	3	180	6	69	62	75	-39
Bemboom,Anthony	15	L	25	C	aa	LAA	257	4	2	220	7	73	53	63	-33
Benson,Joe	14	R	26	RF	a/a	MIA	424	6	10	208	9	72	82	101	4
	15	R	27	RF	a/a	NYM	302	3	8	191	8	74	65	107	-2
Berberet,Parker	15	R	26	C	aa	MIL	164	2	2	203	7	75	55	57	-23
Beresford,James	14	L	25	2B	aaa	MIN	507	1	6	240	5	83	54	75	11
	15	L	26	2B	aaa	MIN	498	1	2	269	5	87	35	46	1
Bernard,Wynton	15	R	25	CF	aa	DET	534	3	33	261	5	85	61	141	44
Bernier,Douglas	14	B	34	SS	aaa	MIN	404	4	4	219	7	76	73	64	-4
	15	B	35	3B	aaa	MIN	301	1	2	203	8	77	31	46	-36
Berry,Quintin	14	L	30	LF	aaa	BAL	365	2	16	213	9	70	56	85	-28
	15	L	31	RF	aaa	CHC	373	3	23	169	9	66	31	105	-59
Berset,Chris	14	B	26	C	a/a	CIN	142	0	0	145	8	75	12	29	-63
	15	B	27	C	a/a	CIN	182	0	0	162	5	74	44	31	-45
Berti,Jonathon	14	R	24	2B	aa	TOR	541	6	32	240	5	83	65	131	33
	15	R	25	2B	a/a	TOR	405	3	19	225	8	82	48	119	18
Bethancourt,Christian	14	R	23	C	aaa	ATL	343	6	5	241	3	79	74	67	4
	15	R	24	C	aaa	ATL	202	3	4	295	5	82	102	70	42
Bianucci,Michael	14	R	28	DH	aa	LAA	241	9	1	220	3	72	137	68	25
	15	R	29	DH	aa	KC	209	8	1	216	4	70	118	44	-3
Bichette,Dante	14	R	22	3B	aa	NYY	67	1	0	201	7	82	60	24	0
	15	R	23	1B	aa	NYY	254	2	0	210	4	79	56	44	-15
Bird,Gregory	14	L	22	1B	aa	NYY	95	6	0	231	13	69	217	17	85
	15	L	23	1B	a/a	NYY	318	12	1	257	9	80	120	47	50
Black,Daniel	14	B	27	DH	a/a	CHW	334	8	2	204	8	71	95	34	-10
	15	B	28	1B	aaa	CHW	111	5	0	266	16	73	125	59	43
Black,Daniel R.	14	L	26	2B	a/a	MIA	331	2	6	171	9	71	53	109	-23
Blair,Carson	14	R	25	C	aa	BOS	59	1	0	261	11	64	194	77	58
	15	R	28	C	a/a	OAK	286	6	1	197	10	59	118	77	-25
Blandino,Alex	15	R	23	SS	aa	CIN	115	3	2	214	12	79	92	50	30
Blash,Jabari	14	R	25	RF	a/a	SEA	289	12	4	177	9	62	148	74	8
	15	R	26	RF	a/a	SEA	406	22	6	216	9	63	169	88	32
Bond,Brock	15	B	30	2B	a/a	COL	120	0	2	184	7	79	6	48	-49
Bonifacio,Jorge	14	R	21	RF	aa	KC	505	3	7	213	7	74	59	87	-13
	15	R	22	RF	aa	KC	483	13	2	218	7	73	108	62	11
Bonilla,Leury	14	R	29	3B	aaa	SEA	278	1	3	169	4	70	60	62	-44
	15	R	30	3B	a/a	SEA	315	3	3	184	4	76	34	68	-39
Borbon,Julio	14	L	28	CF	aaa	BAL	466	4	22	223	5	81	33	108	-7
	15	L	29	CF	aaa	BAL	346	1	19	227	4	83	28	120	2
Borenstein,Zachary	14	L	24	LF	a/a	ARI	461	11	6	220	6	69	111	86	6
	15	L	25	LF	a/a	ARI	332	7	4	244	7	76	92	92	21
Bortnick,Tyler	14	R	27	2B	aaa	ARI	85	0	2	170	6	70	31	102	-50
	15	R	28	2B	aa	SEA	222	1	9	218	7	78	50	74	-8
Bostick,Christopher	15	R	22	2B	aa	WAS	296	6	14	229	3	80	78	131	31
Bowker,John	15	L	32	1B	aaa	PIT	338	6	1	185	3	76	63	29	-30
Boyd,Jayce	14	R	24	1B	aa	NYM	413	6	1	235	8	80	68	51	9
	15	R	25	LF	a/a	NYM	299	1	1	226	6	84	67	37	15
Bradley,Jackie	14	L	24	CF	aaa	BOS	66	1	0	189	3	70	40	41	-68
	15	L	25	CF	aaa	BOS	282	7	3	283	8	83	100	57	46
Brantly,Rob	14	L	25	C	aaa	MIA	364	2	0	203	4	80	47	39	-20
	15	L	26	C	a/a	CHW	203	7	0	267	3	82	90	40	19
Brentz,Bryce	14	R	26	LF	aaa	BOS	230	9	1	210	9	71	132	74	32
	15	R	26	RF	aaa	BOS	220	6	0	209	8	62	108	27	-40
Brett,Ryan	14	R	23	2B	aa	TAM	422	6	22	265	4	80	88	140	43
	15	R	24	2B	aaa	TAM	328	4	3	212	4	77	65	86	-3
Brignac,Reid	14	L	28	2B	aaa	PHI	128	4	2	207	8	69	118	88	16
	15	L	29	2B	aaa	MIA	347	3	2	214	8	78	61	55	-4
Brinson,Lewis	15	R	21	CF	a/a	TEX	140	6	4	295	7	74	133	95	46
Brito,Socrates	15	L	23	RF	aa	ARI	490	8	17	283	5	81	81	138	42
Britton,Buck	14	L	28	3B	a/a	BAL	457	11	2	226	5	85	82	57	34
	15	L	29	3B	aaa	LA	385	5	7	198	4	82	49	85	5
Brown,Corey	14	L	29	CF	aaa	BOS	325	11	4	186	6	60	142	70	-13
	15	L	30	CF	aaa	TAM	407	13	11	185	7	58	119	123	-18
Brown,Domonic	15	L	28	RF	aaa	PHI	210	2	7	203	5	77	59	95	-4
Brown,Gary	14	R	26	CF	aaa	SF	536	6	23	207	4	73	65	119	-10
	15	R	27	CF	aaa	LAA	397	4	9	180	3	78	52	112	-3
Brown,Trevor	14	R	23	C	aaa	SF	72	0	0	263	6	79	47	12	-28
	15	R	24	C	aaa	SF	283	1	1	216	5	78	54	45	-18
Broxton,Keon	14	R	24	CF	aa	PIT	407	10	18	227	9	67	119	133	24
	15	R	25	CF	a/a	PIT	491	7	31	234	9	65	101	158	8
Brugman,Jaycob	15	L	23	LF	aa	OAK	500	4	8	222	9	80	67	98	24
Bruno,Stephen	14	R	24	2B	aa	CHC	384	2	4	236	5	77	80	95	13
	15	R	25	2B	aa	CHC	342	1	7	224	6	78	50	84	-10
Buckley,Sean	15	R	26	LF	a/a	CIN	237	3	0	216	7	68	71	39	-43
Burg,Alex	14	R	27	3B	aa	MIA	227	4	1	209	9	65	82	59	-36
	15	R	28	DH	a/a	TEX	197	5	1	204	8	68	98	37	-22
Burns,Andrew	14	R	24	3B	aa	TOR	495	13	14	228	6	77	117	111	50
	15	R	25	3B	a/a	TOR	499	5	5	263	6	83	59	48	8
Burriss,Emmanuel	14	B	29	SS	aaa	WAS	444	4	15	231	6	89	51	113	44
	15	B	30	SS	aaa	WAS	377	2	9	225	6	85	44	99	17
Buss,Nicholas	14	L	28	RF	aaa	OAK	542	3	9	219	6	79	42	87	-9
	15	L	29	RF	aaa	ARI	284	2	6	216	5	84	51	93	16
Butler,Daniel	14	R	28	C	aaa	BOS	286	3	0	201	7	70	87	28	-26
	15	R	29	C	aaa	WAS	282	1	0	185	8	72	65	35	-31
Butler,Joey	14	R	28	LF	aaa	STL	86	2	0	274	13	76	88	21	9
	15	R	29	RF	aaa	TAM	120	4	0	260	8	66	136	61	10

BATTER	yr	b	age	pos	lvl	org	ab	hr	sb	ba	bb%	ct%	px	sx	bpv
Cabrera,Ramon	14	B	25	C	aa	PIT	440	4	1	221	5	89	50	30	18
	15	B	26	C	aaa	CIN	317	2	1	248	7	83	42	29	-11
Caldwell,Bruce	15	L	24	2B	aa	STL	294	6	3	225	10	67	106	64	-4
Calixte,Orlando	14	R	22	SS	aa	KC	374	8	7	216	6	74	83	74	-1
	15	R	23	SS	aaa	KC	354	6	18	206	6	75	62	118	-2
Campbell,Eric	14	R	27	1B	aaa	NYM	141	2	2	249	7	81	93	73	36
	15	R	28	3B	aaa	NYM	113	3	4	271	12	76	109	97	48
Candelario,Jeimer	15	B	22	3B	aa	CHC	158	4	0	264	10	85	92	40	49
Cantwell,Patrick	14	R	24	C	aa	TEX	276	1	1	238	5	77	59	66	-13
	15	R	25	C	a/a	TEX	242	2	0	151	5	74	35	78	-39
Canzler,Russ	14	R	28	DH	aaa	PHI	388	9	2	216	8	68	131	66	14
	15	R	29	1B	aaa	PHI	394	8	1	213	6	74	83	42	-11
Carbonell,Daniel	15	R	24	LF	aa	SF	206	1	8	134	2	71	31	163	-35
Carrera,Ezequiel	14	L	27	CF	aaa	DET	374	4	31	255	9	80	64	139	31
	15	L	28	CF	aaa	TOR	116	1	5	238	8	83	47	88	12
Carrillo,Xorge	14	R	25	C	a/a	NYM	207	1	0	213	4	80	42	36	-27
	15	R	26	C	aa	NYM	325	8	1	198	6	80	73	47	7
Casali,Curtis	14	R	26	C	a/a	TAM	226	3	0	213	13	65	95	8	-35
	15	R	27	C	aaa	TAM	112	3	1	164	11	68	77	44	-29
Casteel,Ryan	14	R	23	1B	aa	COL	436	14	2	261	6	78	107	49	27
	15	R	24	C	a/a	COL	145	2	1	279	1	72	88	68	-16
Castellanos,Alex	14	R	28	3B	aaa	SD	360	5	4	188	5	61	97	104	-36
	15	R	29	LF	aaa	NYM	280	10	3	227	5	65	168	97	34
Castillo,Ali	14	R	25	SS	aa	NYY	410	2	13	215	6	87	44	93	27
	15	R	26	SS	a/a	NYY	347	2	24	253	6	86	34	90	13
Castillo,Rusney	15	R	28	CF	aaa	BOS	156	2	8	244	7	79	64	79	5
Castro,Daniel	14	R	22	SS	aa	ATL	173	3	2	250	2	88	75	75	42
	15	R	23	SS	a/a	ATL	400	0	4	270	5	88	26	47	1
Castro,Harold	15	L	22	2B	aa	DET	336	1	14	234	3	81	38	117	-3
Cave,Jake	15	L	23	CF	a/a	NYY	529	2	15	256	7	78	53	117	4
Cecchini,Garin	14	L	23	3B	aaa	NYM	407	4	7	196	6	71	64	72	-31
	15	L	24	LF	aaa	BOS	422	6	8	201	8	74	58	69	-19
Cecchini,Gavin	15	R	22	SS	aa	NYM	439	6	3	286	8	86	72	65	38
Ceciliani,Darrell	14	L	24	CF	aa	NYM	395	5	11	231	4	73	68	106	-14
	15	L	25	CF	aaa	NYM	229	6	11	274	6	74	122	136	48
Cedeno,Ronny	14	R	31	2B	aaa	ARI	281	2	3	228	4	78	66	69	-5
	15	R	32	2B	aaa	SF	207	1	1	191	4	78	62	45	-16
Centeno,Juan	14	L	25	C	a/a	NYM	256	1	1	217	5	82	32	37	-24
	15	L	26	C	aaa	MIL	176	0	1	237	2	87	32	62	-3
Chambers,Adron	14	L	28	LF	aaa	TOR	180	4	1	233	7	78	79	38	2
	15	L	29	LF	aaa	CHC	261	1	6	216	7	74	63	92	-11
Chang,Ray	14	R	31	2B	a/a	CIN	150	0	0	171	5	80	48	40	-19
	15	R	32	1B	aa	CIN	240	1	1	222	9	79	56	56	-1
Charles,Arthur	15	L	25	DH	aa	PHI	289	7	1	177	9	58	111	58	-41
Chester,David	14	R	25	DH	aa	BOS	212	5	0	204	6	64	105	23	-40
	15	R	26	DH	aa	BOS	232	5	1	155	5	72	67	38	-35
Choice,Michael	14	R	25	LF	aaa	TEX	150	5	1	218	9	64	125	45	-10
	15	R	26	LF	aaa	CLE	460	11	2	206	6	65	113	66	-17
Ciriaco,Audy	14	R	27	1B	aaa	CLE	373	10	1	202	5	72	118	50	12
	15	R	28	3B	aaa	CLE	263	5	2	193	6	73	81	83	-6
Ciriaco,Juan	15	R	25	2B	aa	COL	297	0	14	246	1	85	28	127	4
Ciriaco,Juan A.	14	R	31	LF	aaa	SF	149	3	8	214	4	85	68	116	39
	15	R	32	2B	a/a	SF	242	1	9	180	2	78	50	92	-16
Clark,Matthew	14	L	28	1B	a/a	MIL	414	20	0	244	6	70	146	20	18
	15	L	29	1B	aaa	MIL	478	15	1	219	7	71	109	35	-2
Clevenger,Steve	14	L	28	C	aaa	BAL	226	1	1	237	6	83	52	35	0
	15	L	29	C	aaa	BAL	262	4	0	259	9	83	52	21	0
Coats,Jason	14	R	24	RF	aa	CHW	68	0	1	221	3	84	43	72	2
	15	R	25	LF	a/a	CHW	536	15	9	241	5	78	103	70	28
Cole,Hunter	15	R	23	RF	aa	SF	192	2	1	276	7	74	120	97	35
Coleman,Dusty	15	R	28	SS	a/a	KC	343	6	9	238	6	68	90	86	-18
Collins,Tyler	14	L	24	LF	aaa	DET	468	14	9	230	7	73	95	80	9
	15	L	25	LF	aaa	DET	190	2	7	207	8	77	54	74	-9
Colon,Christian	14	R	25	SS	a/a	KC	352	5	12	261	6	90	64	81	50
	15	R	26	SS	aaa	KC	192	1	6	239	8	89	38	65	25
Colvin,Tyler	14	L	29	RF	aaa	SF	163	1	1	161	4	66	70	81	-46
	15	L	30	RF	aaa	CHW	305	3	0	176	4	61	74	60	-70
Cone,Zach	15	R	26	RF	aa	TEX	144	2	0	210	3	62	102	10	-58
Conforto,Michael	15	L	22	LF	aa	NYM	173	5	1	282	10	77	113	75	44
Contreras,Willson	15	R	23	C	aa	CHC	454	6	3	298	9	84	86	69	48
Cordell,Ryan	15	R	23	CF	aa	TEX	221	4	8	191	4	64	69	134	-39
Cordero,Albert	15	R	25	C	aa	NYM	158	2	0	159	4	79	31	16	-45
Correa,Carlos	15	R	21	SS	a/a	HOU	215	8	14	298	9	79	148	142	98
Cowart,Kaleb	14	B	22	3B	aa	LAA	435	5	23	204	8	75	68	121	9
	15	B	23	3B	aaa	LAA	220	4	1	266	8	66	97	80	-18
Cox,Zack	14	L	25	3B	aaa	MIA	312	4	1	224	6	76	83	67	2
	15	L	26	3B	a/a	MIA	382	3	0	258	7	71	75	43	-28
Coyle,Sean	14	R	22	2B	aa	BOS	336	13	11	279	8	70	158	99	54
	15	R	23	2B	aaa	BOS	126	4	4	150	12	63	97	90	-18
Coyle,Tommy	15	L	25	2B	aa	TAM	354	4	15	188	11	63	79	116	-25
Craig,Allen	15	R	31	1B	aaa	BOS	343	3	0	229	10	75	52	12	-34
Crawford,J.P.	15	L	20	SS	aa	PHI	351	4	6	241	10	86	78	110	61
Cuevas,Noel	14	R	23	CF	aa	LA	425	5	4	189	5	75	57	94	-13
	15	R	24	LF	aa	COL	406	4	24	245	3	77	64	117	3
Culver,Cito	15	R	23	SS	a/a	NYY	387	3	7	189	5	72	56	108	-23
Cunningham,Jarek	14	R	25	3B	aa	PIT	309	5	2	198	6	75	83	85	6
	15	R	26	3B	aa	LA	209	6	2	180	9	57	140	99	-12
Cunningham,Todd	15	B	26	RF	aaa	ATL	329	2	7	226	5	87	44	104	29
Curley,Chris	14	R	27	3B	aa	CHW	504	4	5	225	4	82	64	75	10
	15	R	28	3B	a/a	CHW	126	3	0	168	4	74	75	39	-21
Curtis,Jermaine	14	R	27	3B	aaa	STL	225	0	3	194	11	88	25	58	14
	15	R	28	3B	aaa	CIN	227	2	4	223	7	86	42	68	13
Cuthbert,Cheslor	14	R	22	3B	a/a	KC	446	8	8	244	7	81	82	63	26
	15	R	23	3B	aaa	KC	397	9	4	250	7	84	79	69	36
Cutler,Charles	14	L	28	C	aa	CHC	284	3	1	243	10	85	56	39	18
	15	L	29	C	a/a	LAA	105	0	1	262	4	84	31	53	-16
D Arnaud,Chase	14	R	27	CF	aaa	PIT	376	1	21	196	5	75	58	151	2
	15	R	28	SS	aaa	PHI	497	4	20	211	4	83	44	132	18
Dahl,David	15	L	21	CF	aa	COL	288	6	18	274	3	75	96	152	29
Danks,Jordan	14	L	28	CF	aaa	CHW	348	11	1	202	8	62	120	35	-29
	15	L	29	LF	aaa	PHI	408	5	4	198	6	61	86	44	-62
Darvill,Wesley	14	L	23	SS	aa	CHC	121	1	1	200	5	79	46	73	-13
	15	L	24	1B	aa	CHC	191	2	2	148	8	75	26	70	-38
Davidson,Matthew	14	R	23	3B	aaa	CHW	478	15	0	164	7	61	112	21	-46
	15	R	24	3B	aaa	CHW	528	20	1	179	9	59	128	33	-32
Davis,Glynn	14	R	23	LF	aa	BAL	96	1	2	274	2	77	71	54	-15
	15	R	24	CF	aa	BAL	365	2	18	240	7	76	59	98	-3
Davis,Kentrail	14	L	26	RF	aa	MIL	359	2	10	203	11	75	70	86	4
	15	L	27	LF	aa	LAA	161	2	6	170	7	67	59	107	-38
Davis,Taylor	14	R	25	C	aa	CHC	138	3	0	268	6	88	99	42	58
	15	R	26	C	a/a	CHC	331	7	0	259	6	82	93	38	28
Dayleg,Terrence	14	R	27	3B	aa	MIA	199	1	1	191	3	71	80	54	-28
	15	R	28	2B	aa	MIA	275	2	1	180	4	74	54	63	-31
De la Cruz,Keury	14	L	23	LF	aa	BOS	258	5	2	273	4	77	99	45	10
	15	L	24	LF	aa	BOS	405	7	2	218	4	74	88	57	-5
Decker,Cody	14	R	27	1B	aaa	SD	449	15	0	182	6	56	144	46	-34
	15	R	28	1B	aaa	SD	373	12	1	178	6	62	118	43	-28
Decker,Jaff	14	L	24	LF	aaa	PIT	350	4	5	215	9	77	89	58	19
	15	L	25	LF	aaa	PIT	218	2	15	232	12	81	55	116	27
Delfino,Mitchell	15	R	24	3B	aa	SF	445	2	4	234	8	82	41	61	-4
Delmonico,Nick	15	L	23	3B	aa	CHW	223	3	2	215	9	74	117	51	25
DeMichele,Joey	14	L	23	2B	aa	CHW	91	0	1	128	5	73	45	108	-29
	15	L	24	2B	aa	CHW	488	2	13	219	7	72	56	111	-18
Den Dekker,Matthew	14	L	27	CF	aaa	NYM	335	5	5	234	6	74	104	100	23
	15	L	28	CF	aaa	WAS	269	6	6	207	6	72	79	99	-3
Dent,Ryan	14	R	25	SS	aa	BOS	122	1	0	213	4	70	92	71	-18
	15	R	26	SS	a/a	CHC	278	4	1	208	6	67	77	61	-39
DePew,Jake	14	R	22	C	aa	TAM	56	1	0	154	10	74	58	19	-28
	15	R	23	C	aa	TAM	197	2	0	196	5	63	77	59	-58
Diaz,Aledmys	14	R	24	SS	aa	STL	117	2	5	246	1	77	99	106	22
	15	R	25	SS	a/a	STL	425	9	4	230	5	82	87	67	30
Diaz,Argenis	14	R	27	SS	a/a	ARI	363	1	2	212	4	76	53	53	-25
	15	R	28	SS	aaa	MIN	302	0	3	216	6	79	34	79	-19
Diaz,Elias	14	R	24	C	a/a	PIT	359	4	2	261	6	83	66	38	8
	15	R	25	C	aaa	PIT	325	3	1	237	7	84	59	61	17
Diaz,Jonathan	14	B	29	SS	aaa	TOR	244	1	3	165	10	78	61	95	9
	15	B	30	SS	aaa	TOR	359	2	6	186	10	77	41	73	-15
Diaz,Juan	14	B	26	SS	aaa	MIA	464	6	3	215	3	70	82	56	-31
	15	B	27	3B	aaa	MIA	367	3	0	228	4	75	61	44	-26
Diaz,Yandy	15	R	24	3B	a/a	CLE	495	6	8	279	12	84	49	75	23
Dickerson,Alex	14	L	24	RF	aa	SD	137	2	0	273	5	75	113	79	27
	15	L	25	LF	aaa	SD	459	8	3	237	6	74	98	105	20
Dickson,O'Koyea	14	R	24	1B	aa	LA	461	12	3	218	5	83	106	66	49
	15	R	25	1B	aaa	LA	386	10	1	217	4	81	94	48	21
Diekroeger,Kenny	15	R	25	2B	a/a	KC	210	1	4	221	6	82	52	63	1
Dietrich,Derek	14	L	25	2B	aaa	MIA	82	4	1	248	3	74	122	50	16
	15	L	26	2B	aaa	MIA	192	5	0	222	6	73	112	73	17
Difo,Wilmer	15	R	23	SS	aa	WAS	359	2	22	256	3	77	69	157	16
Dixon,Brandon	15	R	23	2B	aa	LA	336	8	14	223	3	67	93	109	-16
Dominguez,Chris	14	R	28	RF	aaa	SF	496	11	13	199	3	63	97	92	-35
	15	R	29	1B	aaa	CIN	296	8	4	180	4	59	120	60	-39
Dominguez,Matt	15	R	26	3B	aaa	MIL	442	8	0	215	3	82	75	29	4
Domoromo,Luis	15	L	23	1B	aa	SD	408	3	6	227	4	74	49	105	-23
Dorn,Daniel	14	L	30	RF	aaa	ARI	247	7	1	223	7	70	119	83	15
	15	L	31	1B	aaa	TOR	289	9	2	316	7	77	140	83	60
Dosch,Drew	15	L	23	3B	aa	BAL	231	1	2	217	5	79	40	71	-19
Dozier,Hunter	14	R	23	3B	aa	KC	234	3	2	186	9	68	79	60	-24
	15	R	24	3B	aa	KC	475	9	5	182	7	66	94	81	-22
Drake,Yadir	15	R	25	RF	aa	LA	361	3	0	235	6	87	39	30	1
Drury,Brandon	14	R	22	3B	aa	ARI	105	3	0	274	5	81	118	16	33
	15	R	23	2B	a/a	ARI	524	4	3	265	4	84	73	42	16
Duffy,Matthew	14	R	25	1B	a/a	HOU	517	13	1	237	4	75	89	53	-3
	15	R	26	3B	aaa	HOU	490	14	3	231	6	77	93	76	20
Dugan,Kelly	14	L	24	RF	aa	PHI	253	4	1	253	8	74	98	57	9
	15	L	25	RF	a/a	PHI	299	2	2	228	5	70	56	59	-44
Dugas,Taylor	14	L	25	LF	a/a	NYY	351	1	5	251	9	80	51	82	7
	15	L	26	LF	a/a	NYY	251	0	7	202	10	82	33	77	-1
Duran,Edgar	14	B	23	SS	a/a	PHI	376	3	5	187	5	80	44	68	-14
	15	B	24	SS	aaa	PHI	135	0	0	138	7	80	35	33	-26
Duran,Juan	14	R	23	RF	aa	CIN	338	15	1	214	5	56	181	59	-1
	15	R	24	RF	aa	CIN	219	6	2	230	4	53	169	109	-10
Duvall,Adam	14	R	26	3B	aaa	SF	359	15	1	226	5	72	140	75	34
	15	R	27	1B	aaa	CIN	497	28	4	227	5	71	153	70	40
Dykstra,Allan	14	L	27	1B	aaa	NYM	343	9	0	194	12	63	121	41	-15

BATTER	yr	b	age	pos	lvl	org	ab	hr	sb	ba	bb%	ct%	px	sx	bpv
Dykstra,Cutter	14	R	25	2B	aa	WAS	358	4	7	223	7	74	71	77	-9
	15	R	26	2B	a/a	WAS	407	4	6	197	10	68	49	56	-53
Easley,Edward	14	R	29	C	aaa	STL	277	6	0	217	5	79	85	44	7
	15	R	30	C	aaa	STL	279	3	1	187	8	80	44	24	-19
Eibner,Brett	14	R	26	CF	aaa	KC	274	4	3	193	7	67	84	89	-21
	15	R	27	CF	aaa	KC	389	14	8	252	7	76	108	93	36
Elmore,Jake	14	R	27	2B	aaa	CIN	267	0	8	216	9	80	48	75	3
	15	R	28	3B	aaa	TAM	198	0	3	196	13	81	14	42	-25
Erickson,Gorman	14	B	26	C	aaa	LA	155	4	1	218	7	75	101	36	7
	15	B	27	C	aa	SD	198	2	1	178	8	77	58	34	-19
Esposito,Jason	15	R	25	3B	aa	BAL	174	3	1	166	5	62	61	56	-76
Espy,Richard	15	R	26	1B	aa	COL	209	4	3	183	4	76	66	55	-16
Evans,Nick	14	R	28	3B	aaa	ARI	198	7	0	270	6	82	133	53	65
	15	R	29	1B	aaa	ARI	520	10	0	226	6	72	89	23	-19
Evans,Zane	15	R	24	C	aa	KC	238	4	1	219	3	71	87	34	-30
Falu,Irving	14	B	31	2B	aaa	MIL	247	1	6	222	6	88	34	64	12
	15	B	32	2B	aaa	CIN	460	3	14	214	7	87	39	103	25
Farmer,Kyle	15	R	25	C	aa	LA	283	2	0	238	4	77	89	38	1
Farrell,Jeremy	14	R	28	3B	aa	CHW	243	2	1	189	6	64	77	67	-47
	15	R	29	3B	aa	CHW	190	2	1	180	3	60	72	76	-70
Farris,Eric	14	R	28	CF	aaa	MIN	483	3	12	227	4	86	47	78	14
	15	R	29	LF	aaa	MIN	297	1	4	212	5	84	31	74	-5
Fellhauer,Joshua	14	L	26	CF	a/a	MIL	262	0	1	218	9	69	68	76	-27
	15	L	27	RF	aa	MIL	200	2	6	205	11	74	49	66	-22
Ficociello,Dominic	15	B	23	1B	aa	DET	155	2	0	256	3	77	103	83	23
Field,Johnny	15	R	23	RF	aa	TAM	432	10	14	218	6	71	116	133	32
Field,Tommy	14	R	27	SS	aaa	PIT	339	4	3	225	6	76	78	96	11
	15	R	28	2B	aaa	TEX	369	10	4	197	9	73	102	81	18
Fields,Daniel	14	L	23	CF	a/a	DET	302	4	7	197	5	71	84	116	-3
	15	L	24	CF	aaa	DET	447	5	13	200	10	65	95	126	-3
Fields,Matthew	14	R	29	1B	aaa	KC	465	16	1	195	5	59	149	53	-19
	15	R	30	1B	a/a	ARI	197	3	1	180	5	49	125	62	-72
Fields,Roemon	15	L	25	CF	a/a	TOR	225	1	21	227	7	80	22	128	-7
Figueroa,Cole	14	L	27	3B	aaa	TAM	262	2	3	232	10	86	60	82	41
	15	L	28	3B	aaa	NYY	449	3	3	241	7	92	36	42	28
Fiorito,Dan	14	R	24	3B	a/a	NYY	378	3	1	198	5	78	65	58	-5
	15	R	25	1B	a/a	NYY	266	1	3	195	9	75	43	63	-29
Fletcher,Scott	14	R	26	DH	a/a	KC	183	5	3	233	5	64	87	69	-39
	15	R	27	DH	aa	CHW	252	6	3	197	8	65	100	99	-11
Flete,Bryant	15	L	22	SS	aa	CHC	123	1	0	175	11	76	38	58	-26
Flores,Jorge	14	R	23	SS	aa	TOR	205	0	4	265	4	85	39	66	2
	15	R	24	SS	aa	TOR	395	2	8	250	9	81	53	66	8
Flores,Ramon	14	L	22	RF	aaa	NYY	235	6	2	217	10	79	117	80	55
	15	L	23	LF	aaa	SEA	328	6	2	254	9	82	70	60	24
Flores,Rudy	15	L	25	1B	aa	ARI	440	12	1	212	5	64	109	36	-32
Florimon Jr.,Pedro	14	B	28	SS	aaa	MIN	280	3	9	210	7	65	96	124	-10
	15	B	29	SS	aaa	PIT	196	1	9	196	7	66	79	123	-18
Fontana,Nolan	14	L	23	2B	aa	HOU	229	1	4	225	17	62	113	57	-10
	15	L	24	SS	aaa	HOU	361	2	4	196	12	68	75	87	-17
Ford,Darren	14	R	29	LF	aaa	SF	321	2	21	205	5	69	41	106	-49
	15	R	30	CF	aaa	SF	380	6	22	191	6	73	60	122	-8
Franco,Angel	14	B	24	2B	aa	KC	338	1	6	206	6	84	34	82	2
	15	B	25	2B	a/a	KC	269	3	1	235	6	88	70	61	39
Franco,Maikel	14	R	22	3B	aaa	PHI	521	13	2	228	4	83	102	68	43
	15	R	23	3B	aaa	PHI	141	4	2	317	5	79	116	61	39
Franklin,Nick	14	B	23	2B	aaa	TAM	379	9	9	241	11	72	95	75	11
	15	B	24	2B	aaa	TAM	192	8	3	228	10	71	128	70	30
Frazier,Adam	15	L	24	SS	aa	PIT	377	1	9	282	6	88	52	97	36
Freeman,Michael	14	L	27	CF	aa	ARI	414	4	8	213	6	81	70	133	33
	15	L	28	RF	aaa	ARI	398	2	6	238	5	84	54	118	25
Freeman,Ronnie	15	R	24	C	aa	ARI	233	1	0	207	6	82	34	25	-22
Freiman,Nathan	14	R	27	1B	aaa	OAK	310	9	0	210	8	71	116	33	2
	15	R	28	DH	aaa	OAK	277	3	1	176	5	78	57	40	-18
Freitas,David	14	R	25	C	a/a	BAL	190	5	0	219	8	84	90	18	31
	15	R	26	C	a/a	BAL	261	7	1	213	5	84	83	41	26
Fryer,Eric	14	R	29	C	aaa	MIN	111	0	4	201	7	68	68	103	-27
	15	R	30	C	aaa	MIN	222	1	1	237	8	74	41	52	-38
Fuenmayor,Balbino	15	R	26	1B	a/a	KC	360	12	1	305	2	81	118	66	46
Fuentes,Reymond	14	L	23	CF	a/a	SD	327	4	18	239	7	76	68	137	16
	15	L	24	CF	aaa	KC	396	7	23	275	6	80	56	139	21
Gaedele,Kyle	14	R	25	LF	aa	SD	82	3	1	129	8	63	106	20	-39
	15	R	26	LF	aa	SD	100	1	2	176	9	51	73	49	-102
Gailen,Blake	15	L	30	RF	aa	LAA	267	7	5	184	12	77	90	72	28
Gale,Rocky	14	R	26	C	aaa	SD	228	0	1	216	2	81	35	31	-32
	15	R	27	C	aaa	SD	322	1	1	228	3	76	44	63	-33
Gallas,Anthony	14	R	27	LF	aa	CLE	280	11	0	235	5	68	141	41	11
	15	R	28	RF	a/a	CLE	444	14	2	207	5	68	117	58	-3
Gallo,Joey	14	L	21	3B	aa	TEX	250	18	2	218	11	52	252	46	47
	15	L	22	3B	a/a	TEX	321	19	2	215	11	53	210	47	20
Galloway,Isaac	14	R	25	CF	aa	MIA	314	2	6	181	3	60	77	132	-49
	15	R	26	CF	a/a	MIA	468	5	12	210	3	73	59	125	-16
Galvez,Jonathan	14	R	23	LF	aaa	SD	343	6	2	212	7	72	94	57	-3
	15	R	24	3B	a/a	NYM	269	2	3	198	7	69	63	79	-34
Gamache,Dan	14	L	24	2B	aa	PIT	138	4	0	226	5	75	123	42	22
	15	L	25	3B	a/a	PIT	346	3	3	269	5	81	59	55	-2
Gamel,Benjamin	14	L	22	LF	aa	NYY	544	2	11	235	5	82	57	84	13
	15	L	23	CF	aaa	NYY	500	10	11	276	8	76	99	130	38

BATTER	yr	b	age	pos	lvl	org	ab	hr	sb	ba	bb%	ct%	px	sx	bpv
Garcia,Adonis	15	R	30	3B	aaa	ATL	331	2	4	227	3	84	48	81	5
Garcia,Anthony	15	R	23	LF	a/a	STL	346	9	4	244	10	79	106	68	44
Garcia,Drew	14	B	28	SS	aaa	COL	304	3	3	182	4	62	84	67	-56
	15	B	29	SS	a/a	CHW	282	1	3	179	4	77	46	68	-25
Garcia,Eric	15	L	24	2B	aa	ATL	250	2	3	177	7	72	54	65	-32
Garcia,Greg	14	L	25	2B	a/a	STL	397	5	6	221	7	71	63	83	-25
	15	L	26	SS	aaa	STL	330	0	11	240	9	80	48	96	9
Garcia,Leury	15	B	24	SS	aaa	CHW	349	3	25	263	5	78	63	137	16
Garcia,Rene	14	R	24	C	aa	HOU	270	4	4	206	2	86	63	69	22
	15	R	25	C	a/a	PHI	192	0	0	266	2	90	29	32	-3
Garcia,Willy	14	R	22	RF	aa	PIT	439	12	6	232	4	65	133	93	5
	15	R	23	RF	a/a	PIT	480	11	3	245	4	73	83	86	-8
Garneau,Dustin	14	R	27	C	a/a	COL	263	5	3	197	6	83	86	62	34
	15	R	28	C	aaa	COL	303	10	1	217	5	83	88	36	24
Gaynor,Wade	14	R	26	3B	a/a	DET	381	9	8	193	6	61	148	118	12
	15	R	27	3B	a/a	DET	411	8	9	156	5	69	79	103	-17
Giansanti,Anthony	14	R	26	LF	aa	CHC	221	2	2	195	5	81	41	67	-11
	15	R	27	3B	a/a	CHC	186	0	2	182	6	78	29	67	-32
Gibson,Derrik	14	R	25	CF	a/a	BOS	369	3	8	259	8	79	70	100	19
	15	R	26	2B	a/a	BAL	226	1	3	210	12	76	31	76	-24
Gillespie,Cole	14	R	30	LF	aaa	TOR	140	5	4	288	11	79	133	104	75
	15	R	31	RF	aaa	MIA	247	0	5	232	7	84	46	81	16
Gillies,Tyson	14	L	26	CF	aaa	PHI	159	2	2	172	3	67	56	54	-65
	15	L	27	LF	aa	SD	162	1	2	205	1	66	48	59	-76
Gimenez,Chris	14	R	32	C	aaa	TEX	134	4	0	211	8	72	90	57	-7
	15	R	33	C	aaa	TEX	247	4	1	187	6	68	64	45	-47
Gindl,Caleb	14	L	26	RF	aaa	MIL	362	6	1	186	8	70	88	45	-17
	15	L	27	RF	aaa	TOR	307	4	2	202	6	79	59	62	-5
Glaesmann,Todd	14	R	24	RF	aa	ARI	166	1	4	186	4	66	70	80	-47
	15	R	25	CF	a/a	ARI	343	11	3	224	3	74	131	100	40
Glenn,Alex	15	L	24	LF	aa	ARI	172	3	3	221	6	77	112	122	49
Glenn,Brad	14	R	27	RF	a/a	TOR	403	12	2	228	7	68	125	62	4
	15	R	28	RF	aaa	TOR	226	4	0	208	6	67	100	41	-27
Godfrey,Sean	15	R	23	LF	aa	ATL	180	1	4	177	4	77	44	126	-9
Goebbert,Jake	14	L	27	LF	aaa	SD	280	8	1	209	10	75	110	71	29
	15	L	28	LF	aaa	SD	354	6	2	211	9	74	72	59	-9
Goeddel,Tyler	15	R	23	LF	aa	TAM	473	9	22	243	7	76	77	142	26
Gomez,Gilbert	15	R	23	CF	aa	NYM	161	1	2	112	11	66	38	91	-56
Gomez,Raywilly	14	B	24	C	aa	PHI	221	3	0	214	7	87	51	17	10
	15	B	25	DH	aa	LAA	244	1	2	254	11	87	29	36	4
Gonzales,Michael	14	L	26	1B	aa	MIN	106	2	0	219	6	72	100	28	-12
	15	L	27	DH	aa	MIN	229	3	0	173	7	69	64	25	-51
Gonzalez,Alfredo	15	R	23	C	aa	HOU	100	0	0	259	12	76	17	26	-51
Gonzalez,Benjamin	15	B	25	SS	a/a	SD	241	1	2	204	6	83	48	76	8
Gonzalez,Erik	14	R	23	SS	aa	CLE	129	1	5	315	4	79	68	127	20
	15	R	24	SS	a/a	CLE	549	8	16	231	4	79	69	123	16
Gonzalez,Miguel	14	R	24	C	a/a	CHW	146	2	0	202	4	84	74	42	18
	15	R	25	C	a/a	DET	219	2	2	203	4	79	74	58	2
Gonzalez,Yovan	14	R	25	C	aa	CIN	28	0	0	116	0	83	28	74	-21
	15	R	26	C	aa	CIN	112	5	0	194	9	83	91	19	29
Goodrum,Niko	15	B	23	SS	aa	MIN	209	4	13	216	9	74	75	152	21
Goodwin,Brian	14	L	24	CF	aaa	WAS	275	3	4	186	11	62	76	90	-39
	15	L	25	CF	aa	WAS	429	6	12	197	6	76	62	111	2
Gore,Terrance	14	R	23	LF	aaa	KC	20	0	8	213	7	78	0	233	-1
	15	R	24	LF	aa	KC	222	0	30	249	8	75	19	154	-18
Goris,Diego	14	R	24	SS	aa	SD	146	3	1	207	1	79	65	59	-8
	15	R	25	2B	a/a	SD	404	4	1	203	2	83	52	44	-9
Gragnani,Reed	15	B	25	2B	a/a	BOS	143	0	1	201	12	78	20	38	-34
Green,Austin	15	R	25	C	aa	DET	294	2	0	222	5	79	55	47	-13
Green,Dean	14	L	25	DH	aa	DET	409	7	0	255	4	78	85	33	0
	15	L	26	DH	a/a	DET	403	12	0	251	8	83	74	22	17
Green,Grant	14	R	27	SS	aaa	LAA	198	3	2	239	3	80	91	89	27
	15	R	28	LF	aaa	LAA	385	3	1	227	3	76	70	83	-7
Green,Taylor	14	L	28	3B	a/a	MIL	179	2	0	185	4	81	61	19	-13
	15	L	29	3B	aa	MIL	320	5	1	184	7	82	55	28	-4
Greene,Brodie	14	R	27	SS	aa	CIN	362	2	7	180	7	82	44	76	3
	15	R	28	2B	aa	PHI	299	0	1	184	8	83	37	49	-6
Gregor,Conrad	14	L	22	1B	aa	HOU	109	2	0	210	8	78	78	59	12
	15	L	23	1B	aa	HOU	435	8	4	206	10	73	92	71	10
Grossman,Robert	14	B	25	CF	aaa	HOU	175	3	7	275	8	73	111	69	21
	15	B	26	LF	aaa	HOU	347	3	9	197	10	70	57	80	-31
Guerrero,Emilio	15	R	23	3B	aa	TOR	183	2	1	213	4	68	81	70	-30
Guerrero,Gabriel	15	R	22	RF	aa	ARI	460	6	9	207	4	75	83	117	11
Guevara,Hector	14	R	23	2B	aa	TAM	102	1	0	183	6	89	79	15	37
	15	R	24	2B	aa	TAM	122	2	1	170	5	86	43	52	5
Guez,Ben	14	R	27	RF	aaa	DET	404	12	5	188	6	63	131	89	-1
	15	R	28	CF	aaa	MIL	115	5	5	222	11	64	128	86	10
Hagerty,Jason	14	B	27	1B	aa	SD	350	8	3	209	10	74	91	56	6
	15	B	28	C	a/a	SD	286	4	2	188	7	70	75	64	-25
Hague,Matt	14	R	29	3B	aaa	TOR	383	12	1	228	8	75	113	42	20
	15	R	30	1B	aaa	TOR	523	10	4	284	8	84	78	56	34
Hague,Rick	14	R	26	3B	aa	WAS	321	3	6	182	5	73	71	60	-20
	15	R	27	LF	a/a	WAS	342	1	4	198	4	73	64	83	-24
Halton,Sean	14	R	27	LF	aaa	MIL	416	6	0	238	5	73	96	54	-4
	15	R	28	DH	a/a	BAL	425	6	3	192	8	73	67	45	-25
Haniger,Mitch	14	R	24	RF	aa	ARI	267	8	3	233	6	81	88	88	35
	15	R	25	CF	aa	ARI	153	1	3	249	8	76	72	93	7

BATTER	yr	b	age	pos	lvl	org	ab	hr	sb	ba	bb%	ct%	px	sx	bpv
Hannemann,Jacob	15	L	24	CF	aa	CHC	434	5	13	202	5	70	77	150	0
Hanson,Alen	14	B	22	SS	aa	PIT	482	7	19	242	4	81	80	128	36
	15	B	23	2B	aaa	PIT	475	4	31	240	6	80	63	160	32
Harrell,Connor	15	R	24	CF	aa	DET	436	6	6	195	5	69	69	95	-27
Harris,Devin	14	R	26	LF	aa	SF	394	9	2	211	5	64	124	71	-12
	15	R	27	LF	aa	SF	404	10	3	202	7	67	114	77	-1
Harrison,Travis	15	R	23	RF	aa	MIN	396	4	2	210	11	72	77	75	-3
Hassan,Alexander	14	R	26	RF	aaa	BOS	408	6	2	251	10	69	114	52	5
	15	R	27	LF	aaa	TOR	351	2	0	263	6	78	73	46	1
Hawkins,Courtney	15	R	22	LF	aa	CHW	300	9	1	227	6	63	130	68	-8
Hayes,Danny	15	L	25	1B	aa	CHW	431	6	0	217	17	70	75	37	-12
Hazelbaker,Jeremy	14	L	27	RF	a/a	LA	361	5	13	177	5	66	72	121	-29
	15	L	28	RF	a/a	STL	403	8	16	247	7	68	112	152	23
Healy,Ryon	15	R	23	3B	aa	OAK	507	7	0	257	4	82	70	31	4
Heathcott,Zachary	14	L	24	RF	aa	NYY	33	0	0	155	7	56	72	68	-84
	15	L	25	CF	aaa	NYY	251	2	5	235	6	72	45	88	-38
Heineman,Tyler	14	B	23	C	aa	HOU	265	1	2	208	6	84	59	85	23
	15	B	24	C	a/a	HOU	277	2	1	236	5	91	52	55	34
Henry,Jabari	15	R	25	LF	aa	SEA	288	8	5	142	10	59	118	105	-14
Henson,Tyler	14	R	27	2B	aaa	PHI	426	7	13	217	6	62	109	103	-20
	15	R	28	2B	aaa	PHI	425	2	19	196	4	72	71	123	-10
Heras,Leonardo	14	L	24	LF	aa	HOU	313	4	14	201	11	78	71	125	32
	15	L	25	LF	a/a	HOU	293	4	9	194	8	75	68	126	10
Hernandez,Brian	14	R	26	1B	aa	LAA	458	5	4	261	6	78	68	43	-7
	15	R	27	3B	aa	LAA	516	6	1	208	6	77	60	40	-19
Hernandez,Gorkys	14	R	27	CF	aaa	CHW	189	0	5	174	5	69	45	73	-54
	15	R	28	CF	aaa	PIT	340	4	13	236	8	73	66	118	-2
Hernandez,Marco	15	L	23	SS	a/a	BOS	463	7	4	290	3	80	97	93	32
Hernandez,Teoscar	14	R	22	CF	aa	HOU	95	3	2	252	2	57	145	92	-23
	15	R	23	CF	aa	HOU	470	14	25	189	5	69	79	151	-2
Herrera,Dilson	14	R	20	2B	aa	NYM	241	8	7	296	8	75	132	106	57
	15	R	21	2B	aaa	NYM	327	8	9	278	6	79	99	97	39
Herrera,Elian	14	B	29	CF	aaa	MIL	115	0	3	236	5	78	74	123	20
	15	B	30	2B	aaa	MIL	210	2	2	267	6	81	68	74	16
Herrera,Javier	14	R	29	DH	aaa	SF	33	0	0	198	3	65	77	88	-44
	15	R	30	CF	aa	SF	109	1	0	171	10	56	45	79	-95
Hessman,Mike	14	R	36	3B	aaa	DET	420	19	3	191	8	66	139	67	14
	15	R	37	DH	aaa	DET	405	11	2	182	9	69	106	78	4
Hicks,Aaron	14	B	25	CF	a/a	MIN	220	4	2	250	11	79	96	66	39
	15	B	26	CF	aaa	MIN	149	2	2	299	8	77	123	109	59
Hicks,DJ	15	L	25	1B	aa	MIN	225	4	1	188	9	67	71	48	-40
Hicks,John	14	R	25	C	a/a	SEA	290	3	5	235	6	72	67	87	-17
	15	R	26	C	aaa	SEA	298	4	6	187	3	70	65	90	-31
Hinkle,Wade	15	L	26	1B	aa	LAA	347	6	2	210	9	68	80	37	-33
Hinshaw,Chad	15	R	25	CF	aa	LAA	263	1	23	252	10	66	68	119	-22
Hobson,KC	14	L	24	1B	aa	TOR	177	4	1	190	6	74	90	38	-8
	15	L	25	1B	aa	TOR	499	12	1	213	5	75	78	33	-16
Hoes,LJ	14	R	24	CF	aaa	HOU	128	1	4	246	8	72	64	65	-23
	15	R	25	RF	aaa	HOU	370	2	18	236	9	79	62	115	22
Holaday,Bryan	15	R	28	C	aaa	DET	161	1	1	175	4	75	52	50	-35
Holt,Tyler	14	R	25	CF	a/a	CLE	351	1	24	256	12	76	58	115	11
	15	R	26	CF	aaa	CLE	368	0	21	260	10	80	44	130	15
Hood,Destin	14	R	24	LF	a/a	WAS	382	8	7	255	4	76	99	81	17
	15	R	25	LF	a/a	PHI	366	8	5	228	4	67	120	100	6
Hoying,Jared	14	L	25	CF	aaa	TEX	509	18	13	223	5	68	145	113	35
	15	L	26	CF	aaa	TEX	485	17	15	179	4	74	112	133	35
Hunter,Cedric	14	L	26	LF	aa	ATL	399	10	11	246	10	84	108	93	72
	15	L	27	LF	aaa	ATL	474	10	9	239	5	82	70	85	23
Hyams,Levi	15	L	26	2B	aa	ATL	223	2	2	235	12	69	71	88	-15
Iribarren,Hernan	14	L	30	LF	aaa	CIN	249	1	1	169	6	76	37	60	-34
	15	L	31	3B	aaa	CIN	407	1	4	201	7	79	31	77	-20
Jackson,Brett	14	L	26	RF	aaa	ARI	240	4	3	163	6	49	105	95	-75
	15	L	27	RF	aaa	SF	159	2	4	168	10	61	64	73	-62
Jackson,Ryan	15	R	27	SS	aaa	LAA	373	1	1	222	7	73	48	44	-40
Jagielo,Eric	15	L	23	3B	aa	NYY	222	9	0	265	7	71	145	61	33
Jamieson,Sean	14	R	25	SS	aa	ARI	329	4	5	262	7	79	85	100	29
	15	R	26	3B	aa	ARI	294	5	8	235	9	69	77	82	-19
Jankowski,Travis	14	L	23	CF	aa	SD	100	0	8	206	6	84	39	138	21
	15	L	24	CF	a/a	SD	379	1	23	277	9	84	45	136	33
Jensen,Kyle	14	R	26	RF	aaa	MIA	497	15	1	197	6	64	120	34	-22
	15	R	27	RF	aaa	LA	417	15	0	206	5	67	130	43	-3
Jeroloman,Brian	14	L	29	C	aa	WAS	234	4	0	137	7	69	52	23	-59
	15	L	30	C	aa	WAS	130	0	0	171	16	77	23	33	-28
Jimenez,Antonio	14	R	24	C	a/a	TOR	313	3	2	223	5	81	78	55	14
	15	R	25	C	a/a	TOR	108	0	2	177	6	80	64	74	10
Johnson,Joshua	14	B	28	2B	aaa	WAS	258	0	4	185	10	80	26	69	-14
	15	B	29	2B	aaa	WAS	191	1	2	205	10	79	32	60	-18
Johnson,Micah	14	L	24	2B	a/a	CHW	419	4	15	242	6	80	61	94	13
	15	L	25	2B	aaa	CHW	311	7	22	274	8	76	89	129	32
Johnson,Sherman	15	L	25	2B	aa	LAA	490	5	17	176	13	76	71	115	21
Jones,Corey	14	L	27	3B	aa	DET	415	3	3	239	4	79	76	50	2
	15	L	28	2B	a/a	DET	343	1	2	225	6	80	48	54	-11
Jones,Duanel	15	R	22	3B	aa	SD	319	6	2	197	6	77	54	55	-19
Jones,JaCoby	15	R	23	SS	aa	DET	146	5	9	242	9	63	133	153	23
Jones,James	14	L	26	CF	aaa	SEA	156	1	5	219	5	75	58	111	-8
	15	L	27	CF	aaa	SEA	265	1	16	203	8	79	47	148	17
Jones,Mycal	14	R	27	CF	a/a	ATL	381	2	15	202	7	76	61	100	0
Joseph,Corban	14	L	26	DH	aaa	NYY	235	3	0	217	5	84	65	49	17
	15	L	27	2B	aa	BAL	369	5	2	233	5	88	55	46	23
Joseph,Tommy	14	R	23	C	aa	PHI	78	4	0	247	5	81	141	34	58
	15	R	24	1B	aaa	PHI	166	3	0	165	1	77	70	11	-29
Judge,Aaron	15	R	23	RF	a/a	NYY	478	20	6	237	9	66	137	81	20
Juengel,Matt	15	R	25	LF	aa	MIA	437	11	2	208	5	83	84	83	36
Ka aihue,Kila	15	L	31	1B	aaa	MIA	302	4	0	151	12	75	58	20	-22
Kang,Kyeong	14	L	26	DH	aa	BAL	376	9	1	232	6	73	103	56	5
	15	L	27	RF	aa	ATL	398	5	3	228	8	65	71	87	-39
Kazmar,Sean	14	R	30	3B	aaa	ATL	232	3	1	221	5	84	75	57	24
	15	R	31	3B	aaa	ATL	397	2	2	224	3	87	60	103	35
Kelly,Tyler	14	B	26	2B	aaa	SEA	456	9	7	203	10	74	76	75	1
	15	B	27	LF	aaa	TOR	371	3	3	200	11	83	40	69	6
Kemmer,Jon	15	L	25	RF	aa	HOU	364	14	7	275	8	70	144	109	48
Kemp,Anthony	14	L	23	2B	aa	HOU	233	3	10	254	8	84	73	125	51
	15	L	24	2B	a/a	HOU	464	2	25	258	8	83	43	116	20
Kennelly,Matt	14	R	25	C	aa	ATL	252	0	1	225	6	82	36	50	-15
	15	R	26	C	a/a	ATL	290	0	0	186	9	77	28	29	-39
Kepler,Max	15	L	22	1B	aa	MIN	407	7	14	294	11	84	112	135	88
Keyes,Kevin	14	R	25	RF	aa	WAS	402	13	1	190	6	71	100	36	-12
	15	R	26	1B	a/a	WAS	473	9	2	213	7	69	77	39	-35
Kieschnick,Roger	14	L	27	RF	aaa	ARI	369	9	3	199	4	71	112	78	7
	15	L	28	RF	aaa	LAA	399	8	2	191	4	65	90	63	-37
King,Jared	15	B	24	RF	aa	NYM	420	3	4	183	5	79	42	58	-21
Kirkland,Wade	15	R	26	SS	aa	OAK	229	3	3	204	2	62	66	94	-67
Kivlehan,Patrick	14	R	25	3B	aa	SEA	377	8	7	250	8	75	105	99	31
	15	R	26	LF	aaa	SEA	472	14	9	196	5	70	97	73	-9
Kleinknecht,Barrett	14	R	26	1B	aa	ATL	293	7	2	232	4	79	101	76	28
	15	R	27	1B	a/a	ATL	317	3	0	168	4	80	44	59	-18
Knapp,Andrew	15	B	24	C	aa	PHI	214	9	1	311	7	76	160	66	68
Kotchman,Casey	15	L	32	DH	aaa	KC	317	5	1	228	8	88	66	44	34
Krauss,Marc	14	L	27	1B	aaa	HOU	159	3	1	224	8	66	116	34	-16
	15	L	28	1B	aaa	DET	244	3	1	222	13	69	81	87	-3
Krist,Chadd	15	R	25	C	aa	MIA	153	2	0	162	7	69	55	71	-45
Krizan,Jason	14	L	25	LF	aa	DET	464	5	10	241	7	89	68	80	49
	15	L	26	RF	a/a	DET	485	6	10	209	8	87	54	79	32
Kubitza,Kyle	14	L	24	3B	aa	ATL	440	6	16	258	12	65	128	132	27
	15	L	25	3B	aaa	LAA	457	4	5	212	8	67	105	88	-5
Lake,Junior	14	R	24	LF	aaa	CHC	65	1	1	223	7	74	86	71	0
	15	R	25	LF	aaa	BAL	247	7	11	290	13	69	104	68	7
Lalli,Blake	14	L	31	C	aaa	ARI	284	2	0	198	5	74	62	32	-33
	15	L	32	C	aaa	ARI	246	2	0	185	4	85	37	15	-15
LaMarre,Ryan	14	R	26	CF	aaa	CIN	50	1	1	157	9	58	77	51	-68
	15	R	27	CF	aaa	CIN	300	8	9	217	5	63	107	89	-24
Landoni,Emerson	14	B	25	2B	aa	ATL	181	1	4	229	8	81	35	62	-12
	15	R	26	SS	aa	ATL	411	1	3	255	5	87	49	75	21
Landry,Leon	14	L	25	CF	aa	SEA	422	1	18	233	3	86	57	131	37
	15	L	26	CF	a/a	SEA	220	6	11	217	6	78	65	101	9
Langfels,Jayson	14	R	26	3B	aa	COL	307	3	11	243	9	64	63	106	-42
	15	R	27	3B	aa	COL	238	1	7	166	10	59	55	131	-58
Lara,Jordy	14	R	23	RF	aa	SEA	126	3	0	250	4	83	135	19	55
	15	R	24	3B	aa	SEA	443	6	0	207	6	78	78	58	4
Latimore,Quincy	14	R	25	LF	aa	WAS	303	7	10	225	7	72	81	92	-4
	15	R	26	RF	aa	BAL	442	18	5	237	7	72	140	101	47
Lavin,Peter	14	L	27	LF	aa	PHI	251	4	4	226	4	85	83	101	45
	15	L	28	CF	a/a	LA	447	7	5	200	6	79	73	80	13
Lavisky,Alex	14	R	23	C	aa	CLE	241	3	1	243	4	79	63	38	-12
	15	R	24	C	a/a	CLE	133	3	0	135	8	78	51	52	-14
Law,Adam	15	R	25	LF	aa	LA	229	0	8	205	6	82	34	103	-1
Lawley,Dustin	14	R	25	3B	aa	NYM	447	14	3	182	5	63	133	55	-12
	15	R	26	3B	aa	BOS	322	6	6	182	4	71	96	81	-6
Lee,Hak-Ju	14	L	24	SS	aaa	TAM	315	3	10	176	9	69	52	94	-36
	15	L	25	SS	aaa	TAM	313	2	16	185	8	61	66	111	-53
Lemon,Marcus	14	L	26	2B	a/a	DET	212	2	1	180	6	76	62	62	-13
	15	L	27	LF	a/a	CHW	265	3	2	225	5	72	60	79	-27
Lennerton,Jordan	14	L	28	1B	aaa	DET	410	7	0	199	11	67	100	43	-14
	15	L	29	1B	aaa	ATL	286	4	0	182	9	69	72	38	-36
Leonard,Patrick	15	R	23	3B	aa	TAM	446	7	9	219	9	67	103	108	2
Lerud,Steven	14	L	30	C	aaa	ATL	164	2	1	184	10	65	86	58	-32
	15	L	31	C	aaa	WAS	206	1	0	192	6	66	43	14	-84
Liddi,Alex	14	R	26	3B	a/a	LA	338	7	2	153	6	54	96	60	-74
	15	R	27	1B	aa	KC	481	9	6	237	4	69	116	102	9
Lin,Tzu-Wei	15	L	21	SS	aa	BOS	173	0	7	193	7	84	38	131	21
Lindor,Francisco	14	B	21	SS	a/a	CLE	507	9	23	247	7	79	66	104	15
	15	B	22	SS	aaa	CLE	229	2	8	264	9	82	67	109	33
Lindsey,Taylor	14	L	23	2B	aaa	SD	441	6	4	180	5	84	59	87	21
	15	L	24	2B	a/a	SD	291	3	3	150	9	77	56	63	-7
Lino,Gabriel	15	R	22	C	a/a	PHI	304	3	0	206	5	70	77	23	-41
Lipka,Matthew	14	R	22	CF	aa	ATL	106	0	8	168	6	84	48	112	24
	15	R	23	CF	aa	ATL	402	2	14	224	3	82	40	114	1
Liriano,Rymer	14	R	23	LF	a/a	SD	433	10	14	235	7	68	117	99	9
	15	R	24	RF	aaa	SD	472	9	12	229	8	66	96	96	-12
Lisson,Mario	14	R	30	3B	aa	SF	379	11	8	201	9	68	112	71	5
	15	R	31	3B	a/a	WAS	268	4	3	215	5	71	51	67	-42
Littlewood,Marcus	15	B	23	C	aa	SEA	195	6	1	203	8	76	91	34	6
Lollis,Ryan	14	L	28	LF	aa	SF	203	1	1	172	6	83	31	88	-3
	15	L	29	CF	a/a	SF	296	2	5	266	6	84	71	84	32

BATTER	yr	b	age	pos	lvl	org	ab	hr	sb	ba	bb%	ct%	px	sx	bpv
Loman,Seth	15	L	30	1B	aa	ATL	171	3	1	156	5	64	65	42	-65
Lombardozzi,Steve	14	B	26	2B	aaa	BAL	270	0	4	218	4	86	26	61	-7
	15	B	27	2B	aaa	PIT	355	0	11	237	6	87	30	69	8
Long,Matt	14	L	27	CF	a/a	LAA	416	6	16	185	8	65	75	126	-24
	15	L	28	LF	aaa	MIL	446	5	7	199	6	72	79	103	-3
Longley,Drew	14	R	26	C	aa	DET	25	0	0	199	3	46	56	100	-136
	15	R	27	C	aa	DET	104	3	0	174	4	54	141	55	-44
Lopez,Carlos	15	L	26	RF	aa	MIA	460	4	2	218	5	83	56	65	11
Lopez,Rafael	14	L	27	C	a/a	CHC	355	3	1	233	10	73	63	32	-25
	15	L	28	C	aaa	LAA	218	1	2	195	6	70	42	56	-54
Lowery,Jake	14	L	24	C	aa	CLE	219	4	1	169	10	63	83	77	-37
	15	L	25	C	aa	CLE	177	3	1	145	8	67	81	65	-28
Lozada,Jose	14	B	29	RF	a/a	WAS	165	1	3	211	5	74	27	56	-56
	15	B	30	3B	a/a	WAS	145	0	5	239	9	76	20	98	-28
Lucas,Edward	14	R	32	2B	aaa	MIA	46	0	0	187	8	72	18	19	-74
	15	R	33	3B	aaa	TEX	393	4	2	246	7	72	57	54	-31
Lucas,Jeremy	15	R	24	C	aa	CLE	238	2	0	217	8	80	51	32	-11
Machado,Dixon	14	R	22	SS	aa	DET	292	4	6	267	9	87	85	68	56
	15	R	23	SS	aaa	DET	509	3	12	230	5	82	44	91	4
Macias,Brandon	15	R	27	3B	a/a	MIL	158	2	2	202	6	83	59	92	21
Maggi,Andrew	14	R	25	3B	aa	PIT	347	2	26	227	9	81	37	95	3
	15	R	26	SS	aa	LAA	422	0	24	206	8	77	35	95	-19
Mahtook,Mikie	14	R	25	CF	aaa	TAM	489	9	15	251	7	67	121	113	14
	15	R	26	RF	aaa	TAM	385	3	8	206	4	69	81	102	-17
Maile,Luke	14	R	23	C	aa	TAM	351	4	2	232	7	75	77	69	0
	15	R	24	C	aaa	TAM	294	4	1	178	9	80	46	58	-4
Mancini,Trey	15	R	23	1B	aa	BAL	326	12	2	332	6	80	138	79	69
Margot,Manuel	15	R	21	CF	aa	BOS	258	2	16	263	6	85	98	137	76
Marlette,Tyler	14	R	21	C	aa	SEA	32	1	0	221	9	65	169	26	23
	15	R	22	C	aa	SEA	178	2	0	232	4	80	85	33	10
Marrero,Chris	14	R	26	1B	a/a	BAL	355	10	0	193	5	75	95	41	2
	15	R	27	1B	a/a	BOS	262	5	0	236	5	76	92	31	-2
Marrero,Christian	14	L	28	DH	aa	CHW	161	5	3	232	12	73	119	50	27
	15	L	29	RF	aa	CHW	450	11	2	226	12	78	77	56	17
Marrero,Deven	14	R	24	SS	a/a	BOS	454	5	13	235	7	77	89	92	24
	15	R	25	SS	aaa	BOS	375	5	10	236	7	74	59	88	-14
Marte,Alfredo	14	R	25	LF	aaa	ARI	270	7	4	257	8	74	108	88	26
	15	R	26	RF	aaa	LAA	343	4	5	245	6	70	86	83	-11
Marte,Jefry	14	R	23	3B	aa	OAK	405	7	7	219	8	81	66	62	13
	15	R	24	3B	aaa	DET	357	12	6	238	6	81	112	90	54
Marte,Ketel	14	B	21	SS	a/a	SEA	523	3	22	267	4	83	70	117	33
	15	B	22	SS	a/a	SEA	268	2	15	277	6	86	52	113	34
Marte,Luis	15	R	22	SS	aa	TEX	228	2	7	183	1	81	43	111	-5
Martinez,Alberth	15	R	24	CF	aa	SD	479	9	5	234	7	79	63	71	4
Martinez,Harold	15	R	25	3B	aa	PHI	260	3	1	242	5	78	58	67	-8
Martinez,Jose	14	R	28	3B	aaa	OAK	446	4	1	200	6	85	45	33	-1
	15	R	29	3B	aaa	MIN	337	4	2	207	4	87	48	51	13
Martinez,Jose A.	15	R	27	RF	aaa	KC	341	7	6	323	10	81	96	86	48
Martinez,Luis	14	R	29	C	aaa	OAK	231	2	0	170	5	76	68	24	-23
	15	R	30	C	a/a	BOS	274	1	1	172	8	75	47	22	-39
Martinez,Michael	14	B	32	2B	aaa	PIT	315	1	5	181	5	82	28	91	-9
	15	B	33	2B	aaa	CLE	363	4	9	230	6	79	75	108	21
Martinez,Osvaldo	14	R	26	SS	a/a	ATL	351	1	4	206	6	83	41	79	1
	15	R	27	SS	aa	BAL	433	2	7	211	6	82	31	70	-11
Martini,Nick	15	L	25	LF	a/a	STL	369	4	6	236	10	82	63	78	24
Martinson,Jason	14	R	26	SS	aa	WAS	466	6	15	187	6	68	69	113	-24
	15	R	27	3B	aaa	WAS	495	14	7	184	7	56	112	75	-47
Marzilli,Evan	14	L	23	CF	aa	ARI	285	2	6	225	7	74	79	112	12
	15	L	24	CF	aa	ARI	152	1	5	221	8	74	59	121	-2
Massey,Joseph	14	L	25	RF	aa	COL	469	7	21	234	5	79	71	126	24
	15	L	26	RF	aa	COL	260	1	9	204	7	80	58	118	19
Mastroianni,Darin	14	R	29	CF	aaa	TOR	364	4	15	223	7	75	71	98	3
	15	R	30	CF	aaa	WAS	443	2	19	208	5	77	55	101	-8
Mateo,Luis	14	R	24	SS	a/a	STL	302	2	2	206	3	80	57	51	-11
	15	R	25	SS	a/a	ATL	325	3	6	199	2	75	55	91	-22
Matthes,Kent	14	R	27	LF	a/a	OAK	396	10	5	175	5	64	117	84	-12
	15	R	28	RF	aaa	OAK	215	1	3	187	6	75	84	84	7
Maxwell III,Bruce	14	L	24	C	aa	OAK	85	0	0	116	7	58	40	49	-105
	15	L	25	C	aa	OAK	338	1	0	196	8	82	41	22	-16
May,Jacob	15	B	23	CF	aa	CHW	389	2	32	251	6	79	42	110	-3
Mayfield,David	15	R	25	2B	aa	HOU	173	5	2	216	8	75	80	74	3
Mayora,Daniel	14	R	29	3B	aa	LA	494	6	4	221	5	83	61	62	12
	15	R	30	3B	aa	LA	242	2	1	196	4	74	60	31	-38
Mazara,Nomar	14	L	19	RF	aa	TEX	85	3	0	300	8	74	158	49	55
	15	L	20	RF	a/a	TEX	490	12	2	276	8	78	87	59	18
Mazzilli,L.J.	15	R	25	2B	aa	NYM	335	0	4	220	8	80	49	87	1
McBride,Matt	14	R	29	RF	aaa	COL	187	4	0	231	3	88	81	42	38
	15	R	30	1B	aaa	COL	308	8	3	253	4	83	106	72	51
McCoy,Mike	14	R	33	SS	aaa	BOS	259	1	5	146	10	74	56	69	-19
	15	R	34	SS	aaa	SD	229	1	5	149	8	68	38	86	-54
McElroy,Casey	14	L	25	2B	aa	SD	347	7	1	204	10	82	62	52	16
	15	L	26	2B	a/a	SD	475	4	1	206	6	77	53	71	-13
McGuiness,Christoph	14	L	26	1B	aaa	PIT	420	6	0	211	9	80	86	36	22
	15	L	27	1B	aaa	PHI	327	2	1	176	11	76	48	33	-22
McKinney,Billy	15	L	21	RF	aa	CHC	274	2	0	262	8	81	97	30	28
McVaney,Jeff	15	R	25	RF	a/a	DET	453	2	13	223	7	77	54	111	2
Medica,Thomas	14	R	26	1B	aaa	SD	89	2	0	159	5	65	111	56	-20

BATTER	yr	b	age	pos	lvl	org	ab	hr	sb	ba	bb%	ct%	px	sx	bpv
Medina,Martin	14	R	24	C	aa	CHW	42	0	1	281	12	74	85	60	9
	15	R	25	C	aa	TOR	101	1	0	140	9	67	45	47	-60
Mejia,Alejandro	14	R	23	SS	aa	STL	163	2	2	233	6	86	40	48	6
	15	R	24	SS	a/a	STL	282	4	3	230	6	82	56	79	13
Mejias-Brean,Seth	14	R	23	3B	aa	CIN	226	3	1	204	10	75	56	52	-19
	15	R	24	3B	aa	CIN	405	6	7	221	12	72	75	91	1
Mendez,Luis	15	B	22	3B	aa	TEX	335	2	7	214	6	77	41	95	-16
Meneses,Heiker	14	R	23	SS	a/a	BOS	364	1	7	182	5	82	38	88	-5
	15	R	24	2B	aa	MIN	340	0	11	222	5	77	29	99	-29
Meredith,Brandon	14	R	25	DH	aa	HOU	127	6	3	195	12	67	151	58	33
	15	R	26	RF	aa	HOU	149	3	1	202	8	69	65	64	-36
Merrifield,Whit	14	R	25	LF	a/a	KC	483	5	12	271	6	82	96	95	45
	15	R	26	2B	aaa	KC	544	4	24	226	5	86	55	131	41
Mesa,Melky	14	R	27	CF	a/a	TOR	215	7	2	223	3	64	144	71	-1
	15	R	28	CF	a/a	TOR	420	7	2	214	3	58	123	83	-34
Michael,Levi	14	B	23	2B	aa	MIN	53	0	3	305	10	77	18	96	-27
	15	B	24	2B	aa	MIN	221	4	13	232	9	74	93	160	37
Mier,Jiovanni	14	R	24	SS	a/a	HOU	355	3	4	186	7	71	58	61	-37
	15	R	25	SS	aa	HOU	376	5	7	214	9	75	66	84	0
Miller,Ian	15	L	23	CF	aa	SEA	347	0	24	223	6	83	37	130	13
Miller,Michael	14	R	25	2B	aa	BOS	93	2	2	267	5	83	81	70	29
	15	R	26	2B	aa	BOS	412	3	9	214	5	85	55	94	22
Mitchell,Jared	14	L	26	LF	a/a	CHW	426	14	10	204	10	56	125	89	-26
	15	L	27	CF	a/a	LAA	311	3	10	163	8	52	76	120	-80
Moncrief,Carlos	14	L	26	RF	aaa	CLE	480	8	6	220	5	67	110	83	-6
	15	L	27	RF	a/a	CLE	365	9	9	191	13	71	79	90	2
Mondesi,Raul	15	B	20	SS	aa	KC	304	5	16	230	4	71	79	149	2
Monell,Johnny	14	L	28	C	aaa	LA	206	2	2	164	4	75	64	61	-20
	15	L	29	C	aaa	NYM	256	5	4	234	6	79	69	51	2
Montero,Jesus	14	R	25	DH	aaa	SEA	364	10	1	227	6	73	112	41	10
	15	R	26	1B	aaa	SEA	394	12	2	278	5	77	90	79	15
Montilla,Gerson	14	R	25	2B	aa	ARI	336	5	1	236	6	78	66	59	-4
	15	R	26	2B	aa	ARI	200	7	2	194	9	78	82	41	12
Moon,Chan	15	B	24	2B	a/a	HOU	254	2	12	212	9	77	45	106	-3
Moore,Adam	14	R	30	C	aaa	SD	312	7	1	197	5	64	96	34	-43
	15	R	31	C	aaa	CLE	330	5	0	225	5	60	89	18	-70
Moore,Logan	14	L	24	C	aa	PHI	190	3	0	187	7	71	97	22	-16
	15	L	25	C	a/a	PHI	229	3	0	211	6	75	61	40	-24
Mora,Angelo	15	B	22	2B	aa	PHI	113	3	0	293	10	72	114	96	32
Moran,Colin	14	L	22	3B	aa	HOU	112	2	0	268	6	77	75	25	-12
	15	L	23	3B	aa	HOU	366	7	1	266	8	75	95	53	10
Morban,Julio	14	L	22	RF	a/a	SEA	214	1	0	213	6	64	61	52	-64
	15	L	23	RF	a/a	SEA	160	1	1	172	8	60	66	96	-61
Morel,Brent	14	R	27	3B	aaa	PIT	336	2	5	213	6	77	64	86	-1
	15	R	28	3B	aaa	OAK	433	8	7	230	5	73	97	85	7
Moreno,Rando	15	B	23	SS	aa	SF	429	1	11	260	7	84	45	105	19
Morin,Parker	14	L	23	C	a/a	KC	192	2	0	175	5	67	60	20	-67
	15	L	24	C	aa	KC	178	3	1	275	5	78	96	92	28
Moroff,Max	15	B	22	2B	aa	PIT	523	5	14	264	10	78	69	99	17
Morris,Hunter	14	L	26	1B	a/a	MIL	356	9	0	231	4	73	103	38	-3
	15	L	27	1B	a/a	PIT	149	0	0	115	4	61	32	32	-111
Mota,Jonathan	14	R	27	1B	a/a	CHC	317	3	3	201	3	73	57	70	-33
	15	R	28	SS	a/a	CHC	306	3	1	199	4	78	46	60	-22
Motter,Taylor	14	R	25	RF	aa	TAM	452	12	11	230	5	81	83	90	31
	15	R	26	RF	aaa	TAM	486	10	21	241	9	76	106	100	39
Moya,Steven	14	L	23	RF	aa	DET	515	25	11	235	3	66	172	104	42
	15	L	24	RF	aaa	DET	500	16	4	205	4	65	116	44	-24
Muncy,Max	14	L	24	1B	aa	OAK	435	5	5	223	14	76	73	73	12
	15	L	25	3B	aaa	OAK	212	3	0	235	9	69	91	46	-17
Muno,Daniel	14	B	25	2B	aaa	NYM	359	8	5	187	9	71	75	69	-15
	15	B	26	3B	aaa	NYM	274	2	4	211	8	77	51	69	-13
Murphy,John	14	B	26	C	a/a	TOR	163	5	0	189	9	73	99	27	-2
	15	B	27	C	aa	TOR	286	3	0	187	9	75	63	53	-14
Murphy,Tom	14	R	23	C	aa	COL	94	4	0	198	10	71	134	30	22
	15	R	24	C	a/a	COL	394	16	4	231	5	66	150	80	21
Myers,D'Arby	14	R	26	LF	aa	OAK	213	1	7	249	6	79	73	105	17
	15	R	27	LF	a/a	LAA	189	1	6	187	4	82	26	107	-8
Myles,Bryson	14	R	25	LF	aa	CLE	300	4	9	220	6	66	90	102	-21
	15	R	26	LF	aa	CLE	365	8	21	233	9	72	103	126	30
Naquin,Tyler	14	L	23	CF	aa	CLE	304	3	11	274	7	73	69	127	2
	15	L	24	CF	a/a	CLE	327	6	11	272	9	74	104	96	31
Nash,Telvin	14	R	23	1B	aa	HOU	273	17	1	197	9	53	182	37	-12
	15	R	24	DH	aa	HOU	114	5	0	193	8	50	175	25	-36
Nathans,Tucker	15	L	27	LF	aa	BAL	115	3	2	198	4	74	72	93	-7
Navarro Jr,Efren	14	L	28	1B	aaa	LAA	273	2	1	228	8	77	68	59	-2
	15	L	29	1B	aaa	LAA	283	1	0	238	5	74	69	53	-21
Navarro,Raul	15	R	23	SS	a/a	ARI	263	0	4	213	8	74	33	41	-48
Navarro,Reynaldo	14	B	25	SS	a/a	CIN	485	10	4	235	6	86	87	48	41
	15	B	26	2B	aaa	BAL	360	6	4	236	6	85	69	72	31
Negron,Kristopher	14	R	28	SS	aaa	CIN	219	2	6	204	4	68	89	114	-13
	15	R	29	SS	aaa	CIN	204	4	2	174	5	70	56	53	-47
Nelson,Chris	14	R	29	3B	aaa	SD	319	3	0	186	6	70	56	33	-51
	15	R	30	3B	aaa	WAS	218	3	2	188	6	78	78	63	7
Newman,Matthew	14	L	26	RF	aa	TOR	298	5	1	208	4	68	123	69	-1
	15	L	27	RF	aa	TOR	336	8	0	177	6	64	89	43	-44
Ngoepe,Gift	14	B	24	2B	aa	PIT	437	6	9	196	7	66	82	111	-19
	15	R	25	SS	a/a	PIT	307	2	3	221	7	71	63	69	-30

BATTER	yr	b	age	pos	lvl	org	ab	hr	sb	ba	bb%	ct%	px	sx	bpv
Nicholas,Brett	15	L	27	C	aaa	TEX	403	9	1	219	5	77	78	39	-8
Nieto,Adrian	15	B	26	C	aa	CHW	256	4	0	177	15	64	74	42	-39
Nieuwenhuis,Kirk	14	L	27	LF	aaa	NYM	211	6	2	183	4	65	121	83	-9
	15	L	28	CF	aaa	NYM	105	5	1	241	6	74	143	103	53
Nimmo,Brandon	14	L	21	CF	aa	NYM	240	5	4	198	10	74	90	103	22
	15	L	22	CF	a/a	NYM	360	4	4	237	9	76	59	71	-7
Nina,Angelys	14	R	26	2B	aaa	COL	390	5	4	226	3	82	63	63	5
	15	R	27	2B	aaa	COL	420	3	11	245	3	87	51	102	29
Noel,Rico	14	B	25	CF	aaa	SD	333	1	19	187	7	69	35	106	-48
	15	R	26	CF	a/a	NYY	116	0	19	156	12	65	14	169	-52
Nola,Austin	14	R	25	SS	aa	MIA	499	1	6	217	10	78	47	83	-2
	15	R	26	SS	a/a	MIA	463	1	0	205	8	78	48	40	-22
Nolan,Kevin	14	R	27	SS	a/a	TOR	425	4	7	213	5	84	64	80	22
	15	R	28	SS	a/a	TOR	437	5	8	212	5	85	61	78	26
Noonan,Nick	14	L	25	SS	aaa	SF	379	2	4	184	3	69	47	51	-61
	15	L	26	SS	aaa	SF	308	2	1	209	5	67	50	44	-66
Noriega,Gabriel	14	R	24	3B	a/a	SEA	389	2	2	229	2	72	69	49	-36
	15	R	25	SS	a/a	KC	120	0	1	193	1	77	21	40	-59
Nunez,Gustavo	14	B	26	SS	aa	ATL	306	1	8	251	6	77	44	96	-14
	15	B	27	SS	aaa	PIT	340	1	15	232	5	82	30	101	-4
Nunez,Renato	15	R	21	3B	aa	OAK	381	13	1	242	5	81	100	47	32
O Brien,Peter	15	R	25	LF	aaa	ARI	490	17	1	229	4	70	138	77	23
O Conner,Justin	15	R	23	C	aa	TAM	429	7	8	197	2	66	94	115	-20
O Malley,Shawn	14	B	27	SS	a/a	LAA	350	2	9	243	8	81	65	123	31
	15	B	28	2B	aaa	SEA	310	3	13	219	4	80	47	118	2
O Neill,Mike	14	L	26	LF	a/a	STL	417	1	4	223	8	88	40	71	24
	15	L	27	LF	a/a	STL	263	0	3	229	11	89	20	35	9
Oberacker,Chad	14	L	25	LF	aa	OAK	291	1	6	179	6	79	53	108	5
	15	L	26	CF	aa	OAK	395	3	13	236	7	78	74	124	24
O'Brien,Christopher	14	B	25	C	aa	LA	354	5	2	210	7	78	103	59	28
	15	B	26	C	aa	BAL	115	4	0	210	5	83	102	36	37
Ochinko,Sean	14	R	27	C	a/a	TOR	80	2	0	177	3	88	77	16	25
	15	R	28	C	a/a	TOR	224	2	0	216	4	88	58	12	12
Odor,Rougned	14	L	20	2B	aa	TEX	129	5	5	268	4	82	91	104	45
	15	L	21	2B	aaa	TEX	108	4	2	327	9	90	149	127	136
Oh,Danny	15	L	26	LF	aa	NYY	242	1	8	255	5	84	58	111	27
Ohlman,Michael	14	R	24	C	aa	BAL	403	2	0	199	7	76	63	27	-21
	15	R	25	C	aa	STL	365	8	0	225	8	76	75	28	-9
Olson,Matt	15	L	21	1B	aa	OAK	466	12	4	216	15	68	123	57	20
Olt,Mike	14	R	26	1B	aaa	CHC	106	5	1	248	5	63	193	38	29
	15	R	27	3B	a/a	CHC	220	6	0	221	7	58	143	51	-23
Opitz,Shane	15	L	23	2B	aa	TOR	358	3	3	223	5	84	57	94	23
Orf,Nathan	15	R	25	3B	aa	MIL	424	2	4	245	12	81	63	84	24
Orlando,Paulo	14	R	29	CF	aaa	KC	501	3	21	230	5	79	58	119	9
	15	R	30	CF	aaa	KC	170	2	6	216	3	77	68	90	-2
Oropesa,Ricky	14	L	25	1B	aa	SF	349	3	0	202	7	70	63	19	-45
	15	L	26	1B	aa	SF	453	13	1	219	7	67	106	36	-22
Ortega,Rafael	14	L	23	CF	a/a	STL	379	5	13	210	9	82	46	102	14
	15	L	24	CF	aaa	STL	437	1	13	246	8	82	53	109	21
Ortiz,Danny	14	L	24	LF	a/a	MIN	424	9	2	252	2	78	110	93	34
	15	L	25	CF	aaa	MIN	484	14	3	221	5	76	108	85	29
Osborne,Zach	15	R	25	SS	a/a	COL	132	0	0	219	4	91	32	61	17
Osuna,Jose	15	R	23	LF	aa	PIT	323	6	5	253	4	80	82	86	20
Othman,Sharif	15	B	26	C	aa	MIA	282	2	0	198	5	72	43	35	-54
Ozuna,Marcell	15	R	25	CF	aaa	MIA	120	3	1	277	7	78	139	86	66
Paolini,Daniel	14	R	25	1B	aa	SEA	410	9	2	223	9	78	114	48	37
	15	R	26	1B	a/a	SEA	359	3	4	203	9	72	49	61	-36
Parker,Jarrett	14	L	25	RF	a/a	SF	442	9	8	224	8	66	111	98	2
	15	L	26	RF	aaa	SF	434	14	14	223	9	54	144	108	-16
Parker,Kyle	14	R	25	RF	aaa	COL	502	10	2	239	4	78	94	60	14
	15	R	26	1B	aaa	COL	357	7	4	234	4	67	91	90	-20
Parmelee,Chris	14	L	26	1B	aaa	MIN	118	5	0	257	8	76	130	8	31
	15	L	27	RF	aaa	BAL	239	6	3	279	10	75	88	51	6
Parmley,Ian	15	L	26	CF	aa	TOR	133	1	2	241	6	81	46	98	4
Parrino,Andy	14	B	29	SS	aaa	OAK	427	4	4	194	6	67	66	76	-43
	15	B	30	SS	aaa	OAK	287	3	0	211	7	65	60	60	-59
Pastornicky,Tyler	14	R	25	2B	aaa	ATL	176	1	5	238	4	84	32	69	-7
	15	R	26	3B	a/a	PHI	401	2	4	230	5	85	51	74	15
Patterson,Jordan	15	L	23	RF	aa	COL	185	6	7	271	5	76	149	81	60
Paulino,Carlos	14	R	25	C	a/a	PIT	100	1	0	220	3	69	51	31	-68
	15	R	26	C	a/a	MIN	172	0	0	223	7	90	45	63	31
Paulsen,Benjamin	14	L	27	1B	aaa	COL	435	13	2	235	7	69	140	71	25
	15	L	28	1B	aaa	COL	125	2	1	205	7	68	98	90	-8
Payton,Mark	15	L	24	RF	aa	NYY	264	5	4	228	7	74	64	66	-15
Peguero,Carlos	14	L	27	LF	aaa	KC	368	18	7	205	7	56	177	80	5
	15	L	28	RF	aaa	BOS	103	5	0	225	7	61	172	44	10
Pena,Francisco	14	R	25	C	aaa	KC	342	17	0	191	3	79	118	36	28
	15	R	26	C	aaa	KC	342	10	3	212	5	82	90	67	30
Pena,Ramiro	15	B	30	SS	aaa	SD	399	2	1	215	4	85	46	53	3
Pena,Roberto	15	R	23	C	aa	HOU	257	1	1	203	5	83	34	42	-15
Peraza,Jose	14	R	20	2B	aa	ATL	185	1	21	315	3	91	49	159	60
	15	R	21	2B	aaa	LA	481	3	26	260	3	90	37	136	36
Perez,Audry	14	R	26	C	aaa	STL	236	4	0	229	1	83	65	30	-4
	15	R	27	C	aaa	BAL	267	2	0	215	4	86	38	17	-9
Perez,Eury	14	R	24	RF	aaa	WAS	212	1	15	268	4	82	64	127	26
	15	R	25	CF	aaa	ATL	236	2	24	262	7	80	45	137	14
Perez,Juan	15	L	24	SS	a/a	CIN	387	3	17	203	7	77	64	133	13
Perez,Juan C.	15	R	29	RF	aaa	SF	321	4	11	197	3	75	82	123	11
Perez,Rossmel	14	L	25	C	a/a	CIN	280	3	1	267	6	90	66	47	39
	15	L	26	C	a/a	BAL	297	1	2	231	7	92	29	48	21
Perkins,Cameron	14	R	24	LF	a/a	PHI	451	4	6	230	5	80	75	66	11
	15	R	25	LF	aa	PHI	377	9	5	209	5	83	86	78	36
Peterson,D.J.	14	R	22	3B	aa	SEA	222	9	1	229	7	74	115	37	15
	15	R	23	1B	a/a	SEA	372	5	4	187	6	71	74	75	-20
Pham,Thomas	14	R	26	CF	aaa	STL	346	6	14	256	7	72	87	128	11
	15	R	27	CF	aaa	STL	171	4	6	262	8	75	91	98	19
Phelps,Cord	14	B	27	2B	aaa	BAL	343	5	1	205	9	79	64	73	9
	15	B	28	3B	aaa	PHI	397	2	4	180	9	74	35	63	-38
Phillips,Brett	15	L	21	CF	aa	MIL	214	1	8	285	9	72	105	143	33
Pierre,Gustavo	14	R	23	3B	aa	TOR	28	1	0	194	3	56	124	8	-67
	15	R	24	3B	aa	PHI	225	2	2	190	2	76	46	87	-25
Pina,Eudy	15	R	24	RF	aa	MIA	336	2	10	274	4	75	62	125	-4
Pina,Manny	14	R	27	C	a/a	DET	213	3	1	214	6	84	58	52	12
	15	R	28	C	aaa	DET	256	5	1	241	6	84	79	37	26
Pinder,Chad	15	R	23	SS	aa	OAK	477	10	5	270	4	76	96	71	12
Pinto,Josmil	14	R	25	C	aaa	MIN	208	4	0	241	10	80	112	36	43
	15	R	26	C	aaa	MIN	237	5	0	197	7	74	72	37	-18
Pirela,Jose	14	R	25	2B	aaa	NYY	535	8	11	254	5	84	67	108	33
	15	R	26	3B	a/a	NYY	241	3	4	274	8	88	63	81	43
Piscotty,Stephen	14	R	23	RF	aaa	STL	500	6	8	241	6	86	69	63	33
	15	R	24	RF	aaa	STL	320	8	4	231	9	78	115	75	48
Pizzano,Dario	14	L	23	LF	aa	SEA	272	6	1	195	11	84	89	66	51
	15	L	24	DH	aa	SEA	221	3	2	267	6	89	72	83	55
Pleffner,Shawn	15	L	26	1B	aa	WAS	394	2	2	232	7	81	53	43	-4
Pointer,Brian	15	L	23	LF	a/a	PHI	276	9	5	209	11	62	131	89	3
Polanco,Jorge	14	B	21	SS	aa	MIN	146	1	6	258	5	80	47	65	-12
	15	B	22	SS	a/a	MIN	482	5	16	266	6	84	59	96	27
Pompey,Dalton	14	B	22	CF	a/a	TOR	165	3	12	296	8	81	101	153	70
	15	B	23	CF	a/a	TOR	386	7	20	291	10	81	62	139	37
Powell,Boog	15	L	22	CF	a/a	TAM	444	2	15	266	10	80	53	121	22
Presley,Alex	15	L	30	CF	aaa	HOU	332	2	9	211	5	83	37	89	1
Pridie,Jason	14	L	31	CF	aaa	COL	418	7	15	209	5	79	72	114	19
	15	L	32	RF	aaa	OAK	478	13	14	242	8	73	100	130	29
Prince,Joshua	14	R	26	LF	aa	MIL	345	4	27	203	11	74	61	100	-1
	15	R	27	2B	aa	DET	117	2	6	166	9	75	55	81	-14
Querecuto,Juniel	15	B	23	SS	a/a	TAM	139	1	0	187	9	82	46	80	8
Quinn,Roman	15	B	22	CF	aa	PHI	232	4	23	272	6	79	63	171	32
Rademacher,Bijan	15	L	24	RF	aa	CHC	357	3	5	227	13	81	64	84	26
Ramirez,Jose	14	B	22	2B	aaa	CLE	245	4	15	268	7	86	82	107	59
	15	B	23	2B	aaa	CLE	174	1	13	269	8	94	67	139	90
Ramirez,Nick	14	L	25	1B	aa	MIL	490	16	1	197	8	63	126	62	-11
	15	L	26	1B	aa	MIL	432	14	2	215	11	69	104	47	-4
Ramos,Henry	14	B	22	RF	aa	BOS	181	2	2	310	5	78	78	77	7
	15	B	23	RF	aa	BOS	131	0	0	231	8	79	91	46	19
Ramsey,Caleb	14	L	26	RF	aa	WAS	473	1	13	194	5	82	31	81	-12
	15	L	27	RF	a/a	WAS	429	1	10	244	7	79	24	103	-16
Ramsey,James	14	L	25	CF	a/a	CLE	352	12	4	247	9	66	141	77	19
	15	L	26	LF	aaa	CLE	440	10	3	209	9	65	94	50	-29
Rankin,Pierce	14	R	25	C	aa	TOR	43	0	0	179	0	59	29	54	-122
	15	R	26	C	aa	TOR	105	3	0	214	6	72	75	24	-29
Rathjen,Jeremy	15	R	25	LF	aa	LA	203	6	2	172	6	69	101	63	-13
Ravelo,Rangel	14	R	22	1B	aa	CHW	476	10	8	272	9	82	105	75	53
	15	R	23	1B	a/a	OAK	189	2	0	260	6	77	76	60	3
Reed,A.J.	15	L	22	1B	aa	HOU	205	9	0	296	10	73	142	48	40
Reed,Michael	15	R	23	RF	a/a	MIL	439	5	20	239	12	71	97	126	27
Refsnyder,Rob	14	R	23	2B	a/a	NYY	515	12	7	279	8	77	115	76	41
	15	R	24	2B	aaa	NYY	450	9	10	244	10	81	81	91	39
Reginatto,Leonardo	14	R	24	2B	aa	TAM	54	0	0	107	8	81	0	9	-56
	15	R	25	SS	a/a	TAM	360	2	0	226	5	84	53	60	10
Reina,Adolfo	15	R	25	C	aa	SD	117	1	0	168	9	71	25	43	-62
Reinheimer,Jack	15	R	23	SS	aa	ARI	485	4	17	249	8	79	64	111	18
Renda,Tony	15	R	24	2B	aa	NYY	480	3	21	243	7	91	55	114	58
Renfroe,Hunter	14	R	22	LF	aa	SD	224	4	2	201	8	73	83	32	-14
	15	R	23	RF	a/a	SD	511	14	4	226	5	70	102	85	-1
Reyes,Elmer	14	R	24	SS	a/a	ATL	417	4	4	252	2	74	93	80	-1
	15	R	25	SS	aaa	ATL	111	1	0	189	4	82	40	56	-14
Reynolds,Matt	14	R	24	SS	a/a	NYM	478	4	13	267	6	74	60	105	-12
	15	R	25	SS	aaa	NYM	445	4	9	208	5	75	76	111	4
Rickard,Joey	14	R	23	CF	aa	TAM	206	1	7	208	10	78	40	84	-8
	15	R	24	LF	a/a	TAM	325	1	16	289	11	78	88	142	47
Riddle,J.T.	15	L	24	SS	a/a	MIA	176	3	0	260	4	85	61	61	17
Rieger,Ryan	14	L	24	1B	aa	MIA	100	1	0	214	4	76	101	47	11
	15	L	25	LF	aa	MIA	273	1	2	207	7	75	80	96	11
Rivera,Jose	14	R	24	2B	aa	COL	96	0	0	231	4	77	89	93	18
	15	R	25	2B	aaa	COL	132	1	0	216	3	70	63	36	-53
Rivera,T.J.	14	R	26	SS	aa	NYM	201	1	1	278	4	83	53	41	-5
	15	R	27	3B	a/a	NYM	403	5	1	254	3	85	65	51	16
Rivera,Yadiel	14	R	22	SS	aa	MIL	183	2	4	239	4	78	89	137	35
	15	R	23	SS	a/a	MIL	473	2	9	223	4	80	45	103	-2
Rivero,Carlos	14	R	26	3B	a/a	BOS	390	5	0	230	6	73	82	41	-16
	15	R	27	3B	aaa	BOS	453	7	2	224	5	75	64	54	-22
Roache,Victor	15	R	24	LF	aa	MIL	223	8	2	229	8	68	127	78	14
Robbins,James	15	L	25	1B	aa	DET	385	4	2	203	3	74	63	78	-23
Roberson,Tim	15	R	26	DH	aa	BOS	217	3	1	262	4	75	77	55	-9

BATTER	yr	b	age	pos	lvl	org	ab	hr	sb	ba	bb%	ct%	px	sx	bpv
Robertson,Daniel	15	R	30	CF	aaa	LAA	245	1	4	187	5	82	44	52	-7
Robertson,Daniel R.	15	R	21	SS	aa	TAM	299	3	2	245	8	78	84	100	30
Robinson,Derrick	15	B	28	CF	a/a	WAS	289	0	14	207	7	80	13	78	-29
Robinson,Drew	14	L	22	RF	a/a	TEX	354	10	7	177	8	61	132	107	-1
	15	L	23	2B	a/a	TEX	455	17	12	208	13	66	132	110	29
Robinson,Trayvon	14	B	27	LF	aaa	LA	400	3	6	166	5	65	70	72	-53
	15	B	28	CF	aaa	DET	239	2	8	185	9	82	51	100	18
Rodriguez,Aderlin	15	R	24	1B	aa	SEA	372	10	1	201	4	75	102	56	9
Rodriguez,Eddy	14	R	29	C	aaa	TAM	46	1	0	117	2	53	65	60	-113
	15	R	30	C	a/a	NYY	176	3	0	136	3	61	66	15	-90
Rodriguez,Jonathan	14	R	25	1B	aa	STL	406	8	7	220	9	73	82	71	-2
	15	R	26	1B	aa	STL	454	9	6	221	8	74	76	58	-8
Rodriguez,Josh	14	R	30	3B	aaa	MIA	424	5	4	185	6	66	75	68	-42
	15	R	31	3B	a/a	NYM	432	13	7	208	8	72	102	87	13
Rodriguez,Reynaldo	14	R	28	RF	a/a	MIN	493	15	4	223	6	79	117	76	46
	15	R	29	1B	aaa	MIN	502	12	10	210	6	80	99	129	52
Rodriguez,Ronny	14	R	22	2B	aa	CLE	413	4	3	202	5	75	75	60	-10
	15	R	23	1B	aa	CLE	269	10	4	265	3	75	121	94	33
Rodriguez,Steven	14	L	24	C	aa	ARI	105	0	0	237	10	72	87	44	-6
	15	L	25	C	aa	ATL	166	0	0	178	9	72	32	32	-57
Rodriguez,Yorman	14	R	22	CF	aa	CIN	450	8	9	234	8	71	88	103	1
	15	R	23	RF	aaa	CIN	308	10	3	249	5	70	108	94	6
Rogers,Jason	14	R	26	3B	a/a	MIL	493	15	4	248	7	77	113	84	39
	15	R	27	1B	aaa	MIL	122	6	0	276	12	76	132	20	42
Rohlfing,Danny	14	R	25	C	aaa	MIN	219	1	0	177	9	71	88	41	-12
	15	R	26	C	aaa	NYM	161	2	0	173	4	63	95	37	-52
Rohlinger,Ryan	14	R	31	2B	aaa	CLE	292	3	0	174	5	78	62	25	-17
	15	R	32	2B	a/a	CLE	275	4	0	147	11	83	40	30	-5
Rohm,David	14	R	24	RF	aa	ATL	364	0	2	221	4	71	63	76	-34
	15	R	25	RF	aa	ATL	321	1	4	223	8	81	36	72	-8
Rojas Jr.,Mel	14	B	24	CF	a/a	PIT	437	7	8	240	8	76	74	82	6
	15	B	25	CF	a/a	PIT	370	1	7	223	7	74	53	86	-21
Rojas,Miguel	14	R	25	SS	aaa	LA	159	2	4	227	3	84	65	74	18
	15	R	26	SS	aaa	MIA	249	2	2	261	4	88	68	88	43
Roller,Kyle	14	L	26	1B	a/a	NYY	456	21	1	250	9	62	176	54	24
	15	L	27	1B	aaa	NYY	426	13	0	197	10	61	109	38	-34
Romak,Jamie	14	R	29	3B	aaa	LA	418	13	2	191	4	66	127	61	-7
	15	R	30	3B	aaa	ARI	486	16	3	206	6	61	149	76	2
Romero,Deibinson	14	R	28	3B	aaa	MIN	419	5	0	215	9	75	93	38	5
	15	R	29	3B	aaa	PIT	126	4	0	239	11	80	127	47	59
Romero,Niuman	14	B	29	3B	aa	BAL	482	4	5	246	10	83	59	61	22
	15	B	30	SS	aaa	OAK	234	0	1	216	9	79	31	39	-27
Romero,Stefen	14	R	26	RF	aaa	SEA	151	7	1	280	3	76	135	61	40
	15	R	27	RF	aaa	SEA	476	11	6	220	4	77	96	94	22
Romine,Austin	14	R	26	C	aaa	NYY	285	5	1	196	6	77	77	38	-4
	15	R	27	C	aaa	NYY	338	6	0	220	5	81	70	29	0
Rondon,Jose	15	R	21	SS	aa	SD	100	0	1	168	3	83	22	74	-18
Roof,Jonathan	14	R	25	RF	aa	BOS	188	2	1	228	7	72	94	71	2
	15	R	26	RF	a/a	BOS	309	2	5	198	7	81	48	93	5
Rosa,Garabez	14	R	25	SS	aa	BAL	465	9	5	236	2	76	85	68	0
	15	R	26	2B	a/a	BAL	378	5	3	219	4	78	56	66	-14
Rosa,Viosergy	14	L	24	1B	aa	MIA	72	1	0	249	13	80	91	71	40
	15	L	25	1B	aa	MIA	387	7	0	183	13	73	68	26	-17
Rosario,Alberto	14	R	27	C	aa	LA	47	1	0	212	4	60	53	5	-106
	15	R	28	C	a/a	STL	165	1	0	148	3	84	47	33	-8
Rosario,Jose	15	R	24	2B	a/a	NYY	351	2	10	223	2	78	51	115	-5
Rottino,Vinny	15	R	35	1B	aaa	MIA	451	6	1	209	8	73	69	54	-18
Rua,Ryan	14	R	24	3B	a/a	TEX	471	14	4	265	7	77	108	59	28
	15	R	25	LF	aaa	TEX	142	5	2	167	9	64	97	61	-28
Ruiz,Rio	15	L	21	3B	aa	ATL	420	4	2	218	12	75	65	49	-8
Rutledge,Josh	14	R	25	SS	aaa	COL	54	1	2	276	7	75	73	53	-7
	15	R	26	SS	aaa	LAA	310	3	1	210	4	73	69	79	-19
Saladino,Tyler	14	R	25	SS	aaa	CHW	294	7	5	248	6	79	90	82	27
	15	R	26	SS	aaa	CHW	196	3	20	216	9	80	61	142	30
Salcedo,Edward	14	R	23	RF	aaa	ATL	364	7	9	178	7	69	97	90	-1
	15	R	24	3B	aa	KC	234	2	2	197	7	79	60	57	-3
Sanchez,Adrian	14	R	24	3B	aa	WAS	269	2	5	183	5	83	30	69	-12
	15	R	25	3B	aa	WAS	179	1	2	216	5	86	55	80	25
Sanchez,Carlos	14	B	22	2B	aaa	CHW	437	6	11	248	6	78	68	102	10
	15	B	23	2B	aaa	CHW	131	2	4	311	3	76	89	71	3
Sanchez,Gary	14	R	22	C	aa	NYY	429	12	1	246	8	77	89	26	4
	15	R	23	C	a/a	NYY	365	18	6	256	7	76	135	65	47
Sanchez,Jorge Tony	14	R	26	C	aaa	PIT	268	7	0	186	9	68	113	16	-14
	15	R	27	C	aaa	PIT	313	2	3	197	10	76	67	74	2
Sands,Jerry	14	R	27	RF	aaa	TAM	190	7	1	218	10	66	137	48	7
	15	R	28	DH	aaa	CLE	223	11	1	237	14	78	127	47	55
Sano,Miguel	15	R	22	3B	aa	MIN	241	11	4	243	11	70	157	99	58
Santana,Daniel	14	B	24	SS	aaa	MIN	97	0	3	240	5	68	96	140	3
	15	B	25	SS	aaa	MIN	152	2	5	293	4	82	101	135	58
Santana,Domingo	14	R	22	RF	aaa	HOU	443	12	4	256	10	61	134	62	-7
	15	R	23	RF	aaa	MIL	354	15	1	290	10	65	153	72	25
Sardinas,Luis	14	B	21	SS	a/a	TEX	349	1	8	254	2	84	59	104	23
	15	B	22	SS	aaa	MIL	390	1	12	245	4	84	43	115	16
Satin,Josh	14	R	30	3B	aaa	NYM	374	5	1	188	8	70	79	27	-30
	15	R	31	1B	aaa	CIN	235	4	1	196	10	75	67	42	-12
Schafer,Logan	14	L	28	CF	aaa	MIL	161	2	3	218	8	74	114	117	41
	15	L	29	CF	aaa	MIL	260	1	2	191	3	82	45	69	-5

BATTER	yr	b	age	pos	lvl	org	ab	hr	sb	ba	bb%	ct%	px	sx	bpv
Schebler,Scott	15	L	25	RF	aaa	LA	432	10	11	198	6	74	81	122	13
Schimpf,Ryan	14	L	26	2B	a/a	TOR	397	20	2	196	9	66	172	71	41
	15	L	27	DH	a/a	TOR	368	20	2	220	10	74	157	34	56
Schlehuber,Braeden	14	R	26	C	aa	ATL	239	2	1	190	7	85	50	49	10
	15	R	27	C	a/a	ATL	212	0	1	142	5	81	32	45	-27
Schoop,Sharlon	14	R	27	SS	aa	BAL	267	2	0	172	6	75	56	32	-32
	15	R	28	2B	a/a	BAL	251	1	1	184	7	76	31	36	-46
Schroder,Myles	14	B	27	3B	aa	SF	362	3	8	206	4	75	66	123	-2
	15	B	28	LF	aa	SF	369	5	12	212	5	72	48	107	-30
Schwarber,Kyle	15	L	22	C	a/a	CHC	257	13	1	292	13	69	162	59	50
Schwindel,Frank	15	R	23	1B	aa	KC	170	3	0	187	1	77	64	34	-27
Sclafani,Joe	14	B	24	2B	a/a	HOU	336	2	7	267	7	86	46	98	26
	15	B	25	2B	a/a	HOU	233	0	3	239	8	80	25	99	-14
Scruggs,Xavier	14	R	27	1B	aaa	STL	472	13	2	219	7	70	111	57	3
	15	R	28	1B	aaa	STL	383	9	3	183	9	67	96	57	-18
Seager,Corey	14	L	20	SS	aa	LA	148	2	1	304	5	71	140	96	35
	15	L	21	SS	a/a	LA	501	16	3	269	6	83	112	79	60
Segedin,Robert	14	R	26	3B	a/a	NYY	402	7	1	210	9	78	80	40	9
	15	R	27	1B	a/a	NYY	251	6	2	245	8	75	83	59	3
Seitzer,Cameron	14	L	24	1B	aa	TAM	450	10	2	203	8	77	93	46	15
	15	L	25	1B	a/a	TAM	413	9	0	262	8	74	95	34	0
Selsky,Steve	14	R	25	LF	a/a	CIN	287	2	1	226	11	63	69	42	-58
	15	R	26	RF	aaa	CIN	180	2	2	273	8	70	78	88	-14
Serna,Casey	14	R	25	SS	aa	PHI	165	2	1	227	2	83	54	64	-1
	15	R	26	SS	a/a	PHI	381	1	7	200	5	83	29	93	-3
Sever,Joe	15	R	25	1B	aa	CLE	105	2	0	194	5	72	55	18	-49
Severino,Pedro	15	R	22	C	aa	WAS	329	4	1	230	5	84	50	36	-3
Shaffer,Richie	14	R	23	3B	aa	TAM	427	14	3	191	9	68	142	88	34
	15	R	24	3B	a/a	TAM	393	19	3	226	10	63	166	65	28
Shank,Zach	15	R	24	2B	a/a	SEA	308	1	4	206	6	77	49	115	-7
Shaw,Nicholas	14	L	26	SS	aa	MIL	356	0	4	223	12	76	41	66	-19
	15	L	27	2B	aa	MIL	252	0	4	166	13	74	19	94	-34
Shaw,Travis	14	L	24	1B	a/a	BOS	490	16	6	252	8	78	121	74	48
	15	L	25	3B	aaa	BOS	289	4	0	231	7	79	67	45	0
Shoemaker,Brady	14	R	27	LF	aa	MIA	413	7	1	215	10	74	90	57	6
	15	R	28	LF	aaa	MIA	324	6	0	231	8	82	63	25	3
Sierra,Moises	15	R	27	RF	aaa	KC	235	2	10	240	6	75	43	70	-31
Silva,Juan	15	L	24	RF	a/a	CIN	260	2	6	188	12	76	61	104	8
Silva,Rubi	14	L	25	RF	aa	CHC	301	4	5	205	4	72	78	84	-16
	15	L	26	RF	aaa	CHC	298	8	4	233	1	66	115	117	-4
Singleton,Jonathan	14	L	23	1B	aaa	HOU	195	10	1	226	13	69	160	54	49
	15	L	24	1B	aaa	HOU	378	16	1	207	10	69	137	67	28
Sizemore,Scott	14	R	29	3B	aaa	NYY	289	5	0	202	6	62	108	53	-38
	15	R	30	3B	aaa	WAS	240	2	1	212	11	77	52	55	-12
Skipworth,Kyle	14	L	24	C	aaa	MIA	204	6	1	170	5	58	108	58	-52
	15	L	25	C	a/a	CIN	241	11	0	178	8	43	222	52	-19
Skole,Jake	14	L	22	CF	aa	TEX	342	5	5	200	9	68	87	86	-12
	15	L	23	CF	aa	NYY	211	6	9	216	10	66	100	97	-4
Skole,Matt	14	L	25	1B	aa	WAS	461	9	2	194	10	69	101	43	-10
	15	L	26	3B	a/a	WAS	465	15	2	200	11	69	104	41	-5
Slater,Austin	15	R	23	2B	aa	SF	199	0	1	278	6	73	57	62	-28
Smalling,Tim	14	R	27	LF	a/a	COL	265	3	5	218	6	78	93	95	27
	15	R	28	3B	aaa	COL	367	4	4	203	4	80	43	66	-15
Smith,Bryson	14	R	26	RF	aa	CIN	132	1	1	185	4	83	28	23	-27
	15	R	27	CF	a/a	CIN	168	3	2	230	5	74	77	81	-7
Smith,Dwight	15	L	23	LF	aa	TOR	460	6	3	246	8	84	73	76	35
Smith,Jordan	14	L	24	RF	aa	CLE	459	1	7	212	5	79	57	81	-1
	15	L	25	RF	aa	CLE	475	4	16	227	8	77	65	108	11
Smith,Kevan	14	R	26	C	aa	CHW	389	8	1	235	8	78	84	44	13
	15	R	27	C	aaa	CHW	319	5	0	215	7	75	63	52	-20
Smith,Mallex	15	L	22	CF	a/a	ATL	484	2	51	288	9	80	49	163	28
Smith,Marquez	14	R	29	1B	aa	CIN	32	1	0	119	4	52	134	44	-63
	15	R	30	1B	aa	CIN	408	7	6	212	10	68	86	84	-10
Smith,Tyler	14	R	23	SS	aa	SEA	70	1	1	235	14	79	66	78	21
	15	R	24	SS	aa	SEA	443	2	8	234	10	78	56	64	-4
Snyder,Brandon	14	R	28	1B	aaa	BOS	126	6	1	169	6	52	182	30	-23
	15	R	29	DH	aa	BAL	334	9	1	227	8	61	134	72	-10
Snyder,Michael	14	R	24	1B	aa	LAA	166	2	1	184	6	63	91	43	-49
	15	R	25	DH	aa	LAA	167	4	2	202	8	59	101	53	-52
Solis,Ali	14	R	27	C	aaa	TAM	251	2	0	166	2	63	56	65	-76
	15	R	28	C	a/a	LA	234	1	0	114	3	65	40	16	-96
Sosa,Ruben	14	B	24	LF	a/a	HOU	236	3	18	225	8	67	99	160	11
	15	B	25	LF	aa	LAA	119	1	9	243	10	78	70	163	40
Soto,Elliot	14	R	25	SS	a/a	CHC	242	1	3	202	8	80	47	56	-8
	15	R	26	SS	aa	MIA	414	0	5	215	11	77	26	76	-23
Soto,Neftali	14	R	25	3B	aaa	CIN	278	2	0	244	5	82	74	15	3
	15	R	26	1B	aaa	CHW	199	2	0	208	11	76	38	26	-34
Spring,Matthew	14	R	30	C	a/a	BOS	137	5	0	194	6	57	201	38	15
	15	R	31	C	aaa	BOS	199	4	0	160	8	56	110	15	-65
Stallings,Jacob	15	R	26	C	aa	PIT	265	2	3	228	4	72	60	64	-35
Stamets,Eric	14	R	23	SS	aa	LAA	344	3	10	211	6	80	52	107	7
	15	R	24	SS	aa	CLE	331	4	6	207	6	87	52	81	27
Stanley,Cody	14	L	26	C	aa	STL	385	8	10	230	6	79	74	86	16
	15	L	27	C	aaa	STL	271	5	1	189	6	78	59	51	-12
Starling,Bubba	15	R	23	CF	aa	KC	331	8	3	227	7	71	105	100	13
Stassi,Brock	14	L	25	1B	aa	PHI	440	6	2	192	6	87	47	61	17
	15	L	26	1B	aa	PHI	466	12	2	245	11	83	90	46	41

BATTER	yr	b	age	pos	lvl	org	ab	hr	sb	ba	bb%	ct%	px	sx	bpv
Stassi,Max	15	R	24	C	aaa	HOU	294	9	1	171	6	63	94	63	-41
Story,Trevor	14	R	22	SS	aa	COL	205	8	2	191	10	60	144	79	2
	15	R	23	SS	a/a	COL	512	17	16	260	7	71	149	140	61
Strausborger,Ryan	14	R	26	LF	a/a	TEX	361	4	15	227	5	80	74	142	36
	15	R	27	RF	aaa	TEX	345	7	20	228	5	77	85	129	27
Sturgeon,Cole	15	L	24	RF	aa	BOS	133	0	3	187	3	75	64	101	-10
Suarez,Eugenio	14	R	23	SS	a/a	DET	198	6	7	251	7	74	145	100	60
	15	R	24	SS	aaa	CIN	203	8	3	233	10	77	110	80	41
Swanner,William	14	R	23	1B	aa	COL	104	3	1	260	3	66	125	40	-17
	15	R	24	1B	aa	COL	358	15	5	242	9	63	142	38	-5
Sweeney,Darnell	14	B	23	2B	aa	LA	490	10	11	239	10	73	108	81	22
	15	B	24	2B	aaa	LA	472	7	24	229	6	71	87	117	4
Szczur,Matthew	14	R	25	CF	aaa	CHC	414	1	22	218	5	78	38	100	-15
	15	R	26	CF	aaa	CHC	267	6	14	241	6	77	76	113	15
Tabata,Jose	14	R	26	RF	aaa	PIT	146	0	1	226	4	89	50	47	21
	15	R	27	RF	aaa	LA	237	2	2	210	6	85	40	56	3
Taijeron,Travis	14	R	25	RF	aa	NYM	330	11	1	193	9	60	165	40	4
	15	R	26	RF	aaa	NYM	394	17	1	211	10	53	166	60	-14
Tartamella,Travis	14	R	27	C	a/a	STL	224	1	0	133	4	70	29	14	-83
	15	R	28	C	aaa	STL	118	0	0	156	3	61	40	25	-108
Tauchman,Michael	15	L	25	LF	aa	COL	507	3	19	270	7	85	53	108	31
Tavarez,Aneury	15	L	23	RF	a/a	BOS	252	5	5	226	4	71	101	89	1
Taylor,Chris	14	R	24	SS	aaa	SEA	302	3	9	269	7	70	106	123	19
	15	R	25	SS	aaa	SEA	343	3	11	237	9	78	64	104	14
Taylor,Tyrone	15	R	21	CF	aa	MIL	454	3	9	250	6	87	50	86	28
Teagarden,Taylor	14	R	31	C	aaa	NYM	178	8	0	202	8	53	149	16	-45
	15	R	32	C	aaa	CHC	197	3	0	232	7	53	110	42	-70
Tejeda,Oscar	14	R	25	3B	aa	WAS	54	1	0	164	1	73	36	99	-46
	15	R	26	3B	aa	BOS	392	3	3	216	5	77	62	64	-10
Telis,Tomas	14	B	23	C	a/a	TEX	406	4	6	281	4	89	67	83	44
	15	B	24	C	aaa	MIA	330	4	3	265	5	88	53	67	24
Thomas,Anthony	14	R	28	2B	aa	MIN	453	8	10	192	5	62	117	130	-5
	15	R	29	2B	aa	CHW	329	7	5	200	6	60	116	95	-25
Thomas,Mark	14	R	26	C	aa	ARI	204	7	0	163	5	63	127	65	-14
	15	R	27	C	aa	ARI	195	4	2	148	7	62	115	73	-21
Thompson,Trayce	14	R	23	CF	aa	CHW	518	13	15	203	9	66	128	116	24
	15	R	24	CF	aaa	CHW	388	12	9	231	5	77	105	103	33
Tilson,Charlie	14	L	22	CF	aa	STL	139	1	2	208	3	78	49	89	-13
	15	L	23	CF	aa	STL	539	3	34	255	6	85	46	135	32
Tomlinson,Kelby	14	R	24	2B	aa	SF	433	1	39	233	7	79	33	146	1
	15	R	25	2B	a/a	SF	389	2	17	277	6	82	54	121	23
Toole,Justin	14	R	28	3B	a/a	CLE	236	0	2	216	4	83	45	59	-5
	15	R	29	2B	a/a	CLE	207	0	1	194	4	77	29	68	-38
Torres,Ramon	15	B	22	SS	aa	KC	189	3	3	251	7	87	69	67	40
Torreyes,Ronald	14	R	22	2B	aaa	HOU	460	2	9	258	4	94	43	90	45
	15	R	23	SS	a/a	LA	418	4	4	230	5	90	46	83	32
Tovar,Wilfredo	14	R	23	SS	aa	NYM	255	2	6	230	6	90	33	70	20
	15	R	24	SS	aaa	NYM	357	2	21	225	4	86	38	101	17
Towey,Cal	15	L	25	RF	aa	LAA	316	2	9	187	12	59	73	109	-45
Travis,Sam	15	R	22	1B	aa	BOS	243	3	7	287	10	85	88	85	59
Trinkwon,Brandon	15	L	23	2B	aa	LA	190	2	4	210	11	85	33	100	18
Triunfel,Carlos	14	R	24	SS	aaa	LA	300	2	1	167	2	78	50	62	-21
	15	R	25	SS	aaa	SF	314	3	2	217	2	78	69	90	-1
Tucker,Preston	14	L	24	LF	a/a	HOU	536	18	4	236	7	73	122	45	21
	15	L	25	LF	aaa	HOU	129	8	1	238	6	76	123	30	27
Tuiasosopo,Matt	14	R	28	LF	aaa	CHW	409	9	1	178	10	62	89	28	-50
	15	R	29	RF	aaa	CHW	356	14	2	183	11	56	153	56	-13
Turner,Stuart	15	R	24	C	aa	MIN	327	3	4	190	9	77	49	66	-14
Turner,Trea	15	R	22	SS	a/a	WAS	454	6	25	304	7	78	80	134	30
Urrutia,Henry	14	L	27	RF	aaa	BAL	204	0	1	212	2	70	55	52	-54
	15	L	28	DH	aaa	BAL	460	10	1	253	7	79	72	37	1
Valaika,Chris	14	R	29	1B	aaa	CHC	352	7	1	213	6	72	87	36	-17
	15	R	30	SS	aaa	CHC	334	5	1	202	5	70	80	39	-32
Valaika,Patrick	15	R	23	SS	aa	COL	468	7	15	225	5	74	87	126	15
Valdespin,Jordany	14	L	27	2B	aaa	MIA	222	4	10	204	9	84	67	97	39
	15	L	28	LF	aaa	MIA	256	1	5	242	5	85	50	107	26
Valera,Breyvic	14	B	22	2B	aa	STL	227	0	3	254	5	89	33	79	20
	15	B	23	2B	aa	STL	360	2	1	201	6	92	29	51	20
Valle,Sebastian	14	R	24	C	a/a	PHI	240	4	0	201	3	75	72	19	-30
	15	R	25	C	aa	PIT	247	3	1	236	6	75	90	35	-5
Vargas,Kennys	14	B	24	1B	aa	MIN	356	12	0	243	9	79	103	22	23
	15	B	25	1B	a/a	MIN	244	10	0	244	14	67	117	52	9
Varona,Dayron	15	R	27	CF	aa	TAM	277	7	3	211	4	77	85	108	17
Vasquez,Andy	14	L	27	LF	aa	PIT	272	7	11	207	3	74	104	100	17
	15	L	28	CF	a/a	PIT	143	2	1	190	2	72	69	84	-26
Vasquez,Danry	15	L	21	LF	aa	HOU	277	0	2	217	4	83	39	61	-7
Vaughn,Cory	14	R	25	RF	a/a	NYM	371	7	7	155	6	65	79	86	-37
	15	R	26	CF	aaa	NYM	195	3	3	158	7	61	92	86	-40
Vazquez,Jan	15	B	24	C	aa	COL	211	3	2	209	9	69	70	80	-23
Velez,Eugenio	14	B	32	LF	aaa	MIL	404	5	18	237	5	78	77	103	15
	15	B	33	LF	aaa	TAM	213	1	11	209	6	73	57	111	-14
Vettleson,Drew	14	L	23	RF	aa	WAS	248	6	2	207	3	67	112	72	-13
	15	L	24	RF	aa	WAS	289	4	9	178	7	66	63	114	-37
Viciedo,Dayan	15	R	26	1B	aaa	CHW	251	7	0	244	6	79	89	41	14
Villanueva,Christian	14	R	23	3B	a/a	CHC	457	8	1	199	6	74	108	40	10
	15	R	24	3B	a/a	CHC	479	15	2	221	6	79	92	50	20
Villar,Jonathan	14	B	23	SS	aaa	HOU	190	2	17	219	11	63	51	149	-40
Vincej,Zachary	15	R	24	SS	aa	CIN	286	5	6	215	12	80	55	57	7
Vogelbach,Daniel	15	L	23	1B	aa	CHC	254	5	1	241	15	73	98	50	17
Wade,Tyler	15	L	21	SS	aa	NYY	113	1	2	194	2	77	46	50	-35
Waldrop,Kyle	14	L	23	RF	aa	CIN	232	7	2	278	5	78	127	66	46
	15	L	24	RF	a/a	CIN	447	7	2	210	3	70	73	51	-38
Walker,Adam	15	R	24	LF	aa	MIN	502	22	9	203	7	57	171	99	11
Walker,Christian	14	R	23	1B	a/a	BAL	532	21	1	252	7	72	123	41	17
	15	R	24	1B	aaa	BAL	534	19	1	243	8	72	120	38	14
Walker,Keenyn	14	B	24	CF	aa	CHW	110	2	8	128	7	42	72	151	-112
	15	B	25	CF	aa	CHW	203	2	10	163	8	69	25	85	-62
Wallace,Brett	14	L	28	1B	aaa	TOR	472	14	0	232	6	65	99	23	-38
	15	L	29	3B	aaa	SD	239	5	1	215	6	68	76	36	-42
Walsh,Colin	14	B	25	2B	a/a	OAK	249	2	1	221	8	70	49	38	-53
	15	B	26	2B	aa	OAK	487	8	12	242	15	68	105	82	14
Walters,Zachary	14	B	25	2B	aaa	CLE	268	12	0	258	5	70	184	69	60
	15	B	26	LF	aaa	CLE	341	8	3	214	7	72	103	75	10
Washington,David	15	L	25	RF	aa	STL	340	11	3	224	6	59	123	45	-37
Wates,Austin	14	R	26	CF	aaa	MIA	392	1	24	224	8	80	49	123	12
	15	R	27	RF	aaa	MIA	305	1	3	197	5	78	51	63	-16
Weber,Garrett	14	R	25	2B	a/a	ARI	396	6	0	267	4	76	88	61	4
	15	R	26	2B	a/a	ARI	404	7	1	249	7	76	89	72	12
Weeks,Jemile	14	B	27	2B	aaa	BAL	207	1	5	221	11	82	60	95	30
	15	B	28	2B	aaa	BOS	235	1	6	179	9	73	57	104	-10
Weems,Beamer	15	B	28	SS	a/a	TEX	212	1	0	182	6	80	60	40	-7
Weisenburger,Adam	14	R	26	C	a/a	MIL	239	2	1	211	10	78	64	48	-2
	15	R	27	C	aa	MIL	273	2	2	197	12	77	55	62	-4
Weiss,Erich	15	L	24	2B	aa	PIT	112	0	3	216	5	79	35	102	-15
Wendle,Joe	15	L	25	2B	aaa	OAK	577	7	10	250	3	78	92	127	30
Wheeler,Ryan	14	L	26	3B	aaa	LAA	302	3	0	193	4	74	45	20	-50
	15	L	27	DH	aaa	MIN	128	2	0	221	1	75	61	45	-34
Wheeler,Timothy	14	L	26	LF	aaa	COL	416	7	5	188	5	71	95	69	-7
	15	L	27	RF	aaa	COL	384	7	10	198	8	63	75	93	-41
Whitaker,Josh	14	R	25	RF	a/a	OAK	281	8	3	236	5	73	105	55	4
	15	R	26	RF	aa	OAK	355	8	5	203	5	72	101	86	6
White,Tyler	15	R	25	3B	a/a	HOU	403	10	1	267	13	78	91	40	24
Wickens,Stephen	14	R	25	3B	aa	MIN	161	0	4	184	4	80	32	81	-20
	15	R	26	3B	aa	MIN	264	1	11	209	9	80	50	124	18
Wilkerson,Shannon	14	R	26	CF	a/a	BOS	461	1	9	228	5	78	65	100	4
	15	R	27	CF	aa	MIN	185	1	8	238	6	84	40	140	24
Wilkins,Andrew	14	L	26	1B	aaa	CHW	491	22	0	231	5	77	142	29	41
	15	L	27	1B	aaa	LA	434	14	0	199	7	73	108	33	4
Williams,Jackson	14	R	28	C	aaa	COL	242	3	2	196	8	73	73	31	-24
	15	R	29	C	aa	SF	276	1	1	187	8	77	33	51	-31
Williams,Mason	14	L	23	CF	aa	NYY	507	4	17	196	7	85	47	108	27
	15	L	24	CF	a/a	NYY	201	0	11	288	11	87	54	87	40
Williams,Matthew	14	R	25	SS	aa	STL	304	1	10	207	10	76	37	85	-18
	15	R	26	SS	a/a	STL	206	2	5	187	11	79	41	77	-6
Williams,Nick	14	L	21	LF	aa	TEX	62	0	1	211	3	65	54	92	-63
	15	L	22	CF	aa	PHI	475	15	10	270	6	77	107	101	35
Williamson,Johnathar	15	R	25	RF	a/a	SF	448	9	3	232	9	72	93	87	7
Wilson,Jacob	14	R	24	2B	aa	STL	131	4	2	259	6	80	131	50	54
	15	R	25	3B	a/a	STL	427	12	1	188	6	75	88	48	0
Wilson,Josh	14	R	33	SS	aaa	TEX	305	3	1	181	3	64	58	48	-76
	15	R	34	2B	aaa	DET	262	2	7	192	5	67	61	91	-41
Wilson,Kenneth	14	R	24	CF	a/a	OAK	447	1	22	202	5	71	55	133	-19
	15	R	25	CF	aa	MIA	497	5	29	233	8	75	72	145	22
Winker,Jesse	14	L	21	LF	aa	CIN	77	2	0	186	12	68	113	43	4
	15	L	22	LF	aa	CIN	443	14	7	264	13	79	99	73	43
Wisdom,Patrick	14	R	23	3B	aa	STL	452	10	4	183	6	64	100	82	-26
	15	R	24	3B	aa	STL	414	10	8	198	6	71	91	97	0
Wise,Jeremy	14	R	28	DH	a/a	TEX	142	8	0	252	6	66	205	24	47
	15	R	29	1B	a/a	TEX	263	6	1	175	7	65	87	28	-45
Witherspoon,Travis	15	R	26	CF	aa	LA	147	3	3	186	6	64	68	68	-53
Witte,Jantzen	15	R	25	1B	aa	BOS	314	3	2	255	8	83	88	55	38
Wolters,Tony	14	L	22	C	aa	CLE	341	1	2	221	8	76	50	61	-21
	15	L	23	C	aa	CLE	239	2	3	192	7	71	48	83	-38
Wong,Joey	14	L	26	3B	aa	COL	257	1	4	194	6	77	59	90	-2
	15	L	27	3B	a/a	COL	225	0	3	221	5	80	54	84	0
Wood,Eric	15	R	23	3B	aa	PIT	334	1	2	208	7	72	43	72	-41
Worth,Danny	14	R	29	2B	aaa	DET	223	1	6	164	8	53	92	94	-69
	15	R	30	SS	aaa	ARI	350	4	3	228	7	63	102	76	-29
Wren,Kyle	14	L	23	CF	aa	ATL	205	0	10	252	6	78	64	135	16
	15	L	24	CF	a/a	MIL	518	1	28	235	6	83	31	103	4
Wright,Ryan	14	R	25	2B	aa	CIN	219	2	1	170	3	72	63	58	-35
	15	R	26	2B	aa	CIN	304	1	2	210	7	85	49	78	18
Wright,Zachary	15	R	25	C	aa	WAS	102	1	2	118	10	64	57	63	-55
Yarbrough,Alex	14	B	23	2B	aa	LAA	544	4	5	256	5	74	86	75	1
	15	B	24	2B	aaa	LAA	500	2	1	187	3	68	60	57	-55
Yastrzemski,Mike	14	L	24	CF	aa	BAL	184	2	1	213	5	79	96	85	32
	15	L	25	LF	aa	BAL	476	5	7	215	7	76	79	95	12
Ynoa,Rafael	14	B	27	SS	aaa	COL	427	3	4	236	5	79	77	67	10
	15	B	28	2B	aaa	COL	224	1	3	229	4	81	56	100	9
Young Jr.,Eric	15	B	30	LF	aaa	NYM	257	1	16	174	8	76	30	123	-16
Zambrano,Eliezer	14	B	28	C	aa	SF	194	1	0	212	4	83	21	31	-31
	15	B	29	C	aa	SF	184	1	0	154	3	86	30	26	-14
Zarraga,Shawn	14	B	25	C	a/a	MIL	262	1	1	261	12	86	60	26	27
	15	B	26	C	a/a	LA	185	1	0	238	7	80	52	18	-16

PITCHER	yr	t	age	lvl	org	ip	era	whip	bf/g	ctl	dom	cmd	hr/9	h%	s%	bpv
Acevedo,Andury	15	R	25	a/a	NYY	40	4.41	1.81	6.6	5.1	5.4	1.1	1.0	34	78	20
Achter,A.J.	14	R	26	a/a	MIN	79	2.79	1.07	7.1	3.0	7.1	2.3	0.5	25	75	91
	15	R	27	aaa	MIN	48	3.87	1.09	4.4	2.8	6.6	2.4	1.2	24	69	65
Adams,Austin	15	R	24	a/a	LAA	40	3.90	1.54	6.1	8.2	9.4	1.1	0.0	26	72	99
Additon,Nicholas	14	L	27	a/a	BAL	119	4.74	1.66	16.7	3.9	5.4	1.4	0.6	34	71	38
	15	L	28	a/a	BAL	111	7.16	1.82	19.0	3.5	4.7	1.3	0.8	37	59	21
Adleman,Timothy	14	R	27	aa	CIN	79	3.57	1.36	11.0	2.4	6.4	2.6	1.0	31	77	61
	15	R	28	aa	CIN	150	3.77	1.57	24.4	3.5	5.4	1.6	0.7	33	77	41
Alaniz,Ruben	14	R	23	aa	HOU	29	7.10	1.88	9.8	7.8	4.0	0.5	0.6	28	60	18
	15	R	24	aa	HOU	57	5.30	1.78	18.8	3.7	3.4	0.9	0.3	35	68	18
Albers,Andrew	15	L	25	aaa	TOR	84	8.61	2.09	20.5	3.2	4.8	1.5	1.1	41	58	6
Alexander,Scott	15	L	26	aaa	KC	63	3.39	1.23	6.3	2.6	5.4	2.1	0.8	28	75	56
Alger,Brandon	15	L	24	aa	SD	60	4.28	1.60	5.5	5.9	7.0	1.2	0.8	30	74	50
Almonte,Miguel	15	R	22	a/a	KC	104	5.42	1.48	15.9	3.6	6.9	1.9	0.6	33	62	62
Alvarez,Dario	15	L	26	a/a	NYM	42	3.38	1.24	3.6	4.5	10.9	2.4	0.5	30	73	115
Alvarez,R.J.	14	R	23	aa	SD	43	1.37	1.03	4.4	2.6	11.3	4.3	0.0	32	85	172
	15	R	24	aaa	OAK	35	5.04	1.72	5.1	4.6	8.6	1.9	0.5	38	70	70
Anderson,Chris	15	R	23	a/a	LA	133	5.46	1.64	22.8	4.3	5.8	1.4	1.1	32	68	28
Anderson,Cody	15	R	25	a/a	CLE	71	2.59	1.28	22.5	1.9	5.6	3.0	0.3	32	80	87
Anderson,John	14	L	26	aa	TOR	69	6.12	1.54	11.1	4.5	7.6	1.7	1.2	31	61	47
	15	L	27	a/a	TOR	124	7.06	1.95	19.7	3.6	4.4	1.2	1.0	38	63	7
Anderson,Matthew	14	R	23	aa	SEA	66	5.77	1.54	22.2	1.8	5.3	3.0	0.6	36	61	66
	15	R	24	a/a	SEA	71	4.65	1.38	6.3	3.0	7.3	2.4	0.7	33	67	73
Andriese,Matt	15	R	26	aaa	TAM	65	3.02	1.39	21.1	1.5	7.7	5.2	0.3	38	78	140
Antigua,Jeffry	14	L	24	a/a	CHC	55	4.60	1.56	11.0	3.4	4.6	1.4	0.7	32	71	31
	15	L	25	a/a	CHC	133	4.66	1.49	19.2	3.3	4.3	1.3	0.9	30	70	25
Antolin,Dustin	14	R	25	aa	TOR	43	4.41	1.58	5.1	3.4	9.1	2.7	0.0	40	69	106
	15	R	26	aa	TOR	56	4.25	1.71	6.8	3.2	7.3	2.3	0.4	39	74	69
Appel,Mark	14	R	23	aa	HOU	39	4.07	1.31	23.0	2.9	7.6	2.6	0.5	32	68	89
	15	R	24	a/a	HOU	132	4.84	1.52	22.9	3.4	6.4	1.9	0.9	33	69	47
Arias,Gabriel	14	R	25	a/a	CLE	149	4.29	1.43	23.5	2.5	4.5	1.8	0.8	32	71	38
	15	R	26	a/a	ARI	129	5.37	1.56	23.5	2.6	4.7	1.8	1.1	33	67	25
Armstrong,Shawn	15	R	25	aaa	CLE	50	3.18	1.48	4.6	5.0	12.0	2.4	0.0	38	76	128
Aro,Jonathan	15	R	25	a/a	BOS	74	4.21	1.26	8.9	2.4	7.0	2.9	0.3	32	65	97
Arrowood,Ryan	14	R	24	aa	COL	88	5.31	1.61	9.7	3.8	3.6	1.0	0.9	31	67	11
	15	R	25	a/a	COL	59	8.30	1.99	10.2	4.7	4.7	1.0	2.0	35	60	-24
Asher,Alec	15	R	24	a/a	PHI	134	4.72	1.49	24.0	2.8	6.3	2.3	1.8	32	75	28
Astin,Barrett	15	R	24	aa	CIN	77	7.38	1.90	25.8	5.0	6.2	1.3	1.5	36	62	8
Atherton,Tim	15	R	26	aa	OAK	78	5.53	1.67	23.3	3.7	5.2	1.4	0.5	35	66	38
Augliera,Mike	14	R	24	aa	BOS	148	5.94	1.54	25.8	1.3	3.8	3.0	0.8	35	61	50
	15	R	25	aa	BOS	114	6.83	1.94	19.4	2.9	4.9	1.7	0.9	40	64	20
Aumont,Phillippe	14	R	25	aaa	PHI	55	4.62	1.74	7.2	6.6	8.8	1.3	0.4	35	72	72
	15	R	26	aaa	TOR	83	4.85	1.87	20.5	8.0	7.3	0.9	0.8	31	75	41
Avila,Andres	15	R	25	aa	OAK	48	4.47	1.54	6.6	2.6	6.2	2.4	0.9	35	72	55
Axelrod,Dylan	14	R	29	aaa	CIN	130	4.80	1.55	23.7	3.2	5.7	1.8	1.0	33	71	36
	15	R	30	aaa	CIN	106	7.01	1.94	22.9	2.9	4.5	1.5	1.8	38	67	-13
Bacus,Dakota	15	R	24	a/a	WAS	95	4.77	1.53	17.1	3.2	4.2	1.3	0.8	31	70	24
Baker,Corey	15	R	26	aa	STL	97	4.40	1.44	10.9	3.6	6.4	1.8	0.5	32	69	60
Baker,Scott	14	R	33	aaa	TEX	38	4.10	1.48	27.2	2.9	5.1	1.8	1.5	31	78	21
	15	R	34	aaa	LA	77	4.18	1.13	23.4	0.9	4.5	5.2	0.8	29	64	113
Balester,Collin	15	R	29	a/a	CIN	57	3.25	1.30	5.6	2.7	4.3	1.6	0.8	28	77	39
Ballew,Travis	14	R	23	aa	HOU	51	6.77	1.91	6.6	5.6	6.3	1.1	0.9	36	64	26
	15	R	24	a/a	HOU	67	4.43	1.58	5.9	3.2	6.5	2.1	0.3	36	70	68
Banuelos,Manuel	14	L	23	a/a	NYY	64	5.16	1.43	12.9	4.2	6.8	1.6	1.7	27	69	28
	15	L	24	aaa	ATL	85	2.97	1.43	22.5	4.6	6.4	1.4	0.3	30	78	66
Barbato,John	14	R	22	aa	SD	31	3.10	1.20	4.7	2.7	8.6	3.2	0.9	30	77	99
	15	R	23	a/a	NYY	67	3.56	1.39	7.1	3.6	8.1	2.2	0.9	32	77	71
Barbosa,Andrew	15	L	28	aa	ATL	47	4.86	1.54	10.9	4.8	8.5	1.8	0.2	34	66	83
Barnes,Daniel	15	R	26	aa	TOR	61	4.11	1.69	6.8	3.1	9.1	2.9	1.0	40	78	76
Barnes,Jacob	14	R	24	aa	MIL	106	5.10	1.41	19.4	3.4	5.5	1.6	0.9	30	65	40
	15	R	25	aa	MIL	75	4.90	1.75	8.8	4.2	8.3	2.0	0.4	39	71	73
Barnes,Matt	14	R	24	aaa	BOS	128	5.10	1.50	24.0	3.4	6.0	1.8	0.6	33	65	52
	15	R	25	aaa	BOS	38	5.95	1.91	10.5	6.0	7.9	1.3	0.9	37	69	42
Barnes,Scott	14	L	27	aaa	CLE	32	4.46	1.36	5.3	4.7	7.9	1.7	0.9	27	69	65
	15	L	28	a/a	TOR	62	7.93	1.89	8.9	2.6	5.9	2.3	1.7	39	59	14
Barnette,Tyler	15	R	23	aa	CHW	76	3.22	1.54	11.4	3.4	5.2	1.5	0.5	33	80	46
Barreda,Manuel	14	R	26	aa	MIL	73	3.70	1.66	7.0	5.4	7.9	1.5	1.3	32	82	41
	15	R	27	aa	MIL	45	4.53	1.81	6.6	6.3	8.0	1.3	2.0	31	82	15
Barrett,Jake	14	R	23	a/a	ARI	55	3.38	1.39	4.2	4.1	6.4	1.5	0.5	29	76	61
	15	R	24	a/a	ARI	53	5.27	1.73	5.1	3.8	7.2	1.9	0.6	38	69	57
Barrios,Yhonathan	15	R	24	a/a	MIL	60	3.54	1.53	5.4	3.5	4.7	1.3	0.4	32	77	41
Bassitt,Chris	14	R	25	aa	CHW	35	1.85	1.33	24.0	4.1	7.8	1.9	0.6	29	89	75
	15	R	26	aaa	OAK	69	4.67	1.35	22.1	2.7	7.1	2.6	0.1	34	62	94
Bates,Colin	14	R	26	aa	WAS	87	4.20	1.50	9.68	1.5	4.0	2.7	0.4	35	71	59
	15	R	27	aa	WAS	111	5.91	1.73	18.1	2.6	3.8	1.4	1.0	36	66	10
Batista,Frank	14	R	25	a/a	CHC	46	2.37	1.28	4.68	2.7	5.4	2.0	1.1	28	88	45
	15	R	26	a/a	CHC	118	3.59	1.52	19	3.1	4.5	1.4	0.8	32	78	30
Batista,Lay	15	R	26	a/a	MIA	53	6.37	1.65	6.4	6.5	6.0	0.9	0.7	28	60	40
Baumann,George	14	L	27	aaa	KC	90	3.69	1.46	9.67	3.2	5.1	1.6	0.6	32	75	45
	15	L	28	aaa	KC	77	4.21	1.47	9.71	3.3	7.2	2.2	0.7	34	72	66
Bawcom,Logan	14	R	26	aaa	SEA	46	5.20	1.69	5.15	4.7	5.2	1.1	1.1	32	71	19
	15	R	27	aaa	SEA	76	4.86	1.65	7.51	3.5	5.9	1.7	0.7	35	70	44
Baxendale,D.J.	14	R	24	aa	MIN	25	6.96	1.69	16.1	1.8	4.1	2.3	0.7	37	57	36
	15	R	25	aa	MIN	118	4.51	1.58	22.7	3.1	5.5	1.8	0.6	35	72	46
Beachy,Brandon	15	R	29	aaa	LA	47	4.44	1.51	20.4	4.1	5.2	1.3	0.9	30	72	31
Beato,Pedro	14	R	28	aaa	ATL	48	4.87	1.45	4.91	3.4	6.6	1.9	1.4	31	70	39
	15	R	29	aaa	BAL	75	4.59	1.74	5.4	3.9	5.4	1.4	1.0	35	76	22
Beck,Chris	15	R	25	aaa	CHW	54	4.28	1.45	23.2	2.7	5.5	2.0	0.7	33	71	52

PITCHER	yr	t	age	lvl	org	ip	era	whip	bf/g	ctl	dom	cmd	hr/9	h%	s%	bpv
Bedrosian,Cam	14	R	23	a/a	LAA	39	2.25	0.76	3.7	3.2	13.1	4.0	0.2	22	69	188
	15	R	24	aaa	LAA	36	2.65	1.27	6.1	3.0	9.0	2.9	0.0	34	77	121
Beede,Tyler	15	R	22	aa	SF	72	6.67	1.52	24.1	4.6	5.3	1.2	0.5	30	53	44
Beeler,Dallas	14	R	25	aaa	CHC	124	4.12	1.34	25.8	2.5	4.9	2.0	0.6	30	69	52
	15	R	26	aaa	CHC	111	4.95	1.59	23.2	3.2	5.5	1.7	0.4	35	68	49
Belfiore,Michael	14	L	26	aaa	DET	91	4.22	1.66	11.7	3.8	4.5	1.2	1.2	32	78	11
	15	L	27	aaa	BAL	135	8.79	2.08	26.5	4.4	4.2	1.0	1.7	37	58	-22
Belisario,Ronald	15	R	32	aaa	BOS	37	4.37	1.67	5.1	3.7	3.6	1.0	0.7	33	74	15
Bell,Chadwick	15	L	26	aa	TEX	141	5.75	1.64	23.3	2.9	5.9	2.1	0.8	36	65	46
Bellatti,Andrew	15	R	24	aaa	TAM	46	6.46	1.61	10.3	3.0	7.2	2.4	1.0	36	59	56
Below,Duane	14	L	29	aaa	DET	117	5.14	1.80	24.5	3.6	3.4	0.9	1.1	34	73	-3
	15	L	30	aaa	NYM	49	2.42	1.27	18.4	1.5	3.9	2.6	0.8	30	85	52
Benedict,Matt	14	R	25	aa	PIT	53	6.23	1.75	8.1	4.0	4.6	1.1	0.3	35	62	34
	15	R	26	a/a	PIT	106	7.42	1.75	20.2	1.9	3.4	1.8	0.7	37	55	20
Berken,Jason	14	R	31	aaa	SF	132	4.85	1.72	25.0	3.0	4.5	1.5	0.7	36	72	25
	15	R	32	aaa	PHI	113	6.37	1.90	19.1	3.1	4.7	1.5	1.2	38	68	8
Berrios,Jose	15	R	21	a/a	MIN	166	3.44	1.15	24.5	2.0	8.0	4.0	0.7	31	71	117
Berry,Timothy	14	L	23	aa	BAL	133	4.02	1.36	24.2	3.0	6.1	2.0	0.9	30	73	53
	15	L	24	aa	BAL	82	9.87	2.05	17.4	4.0	5.1	1.3	1.2	39	50	4
Bettis,Chad	14	R	25	aaa	COL	55	3.54	1.31	11.4	3.4	6.8	2.0	0.2	31	71	82
	15	R	26	a/a	COL	42	4.57	1.64	23.6	2.9	6.0	2.1	1.6	35	77	24
Biagini,Joseph	15	R	25	aa	SF	130	3.28	1.37	23.7	2.6	4.8	1.8	0.4	31	75	56
Bibens-Dirkx,Aust	14	R	29	a/a	TOR	113	4.93	1.51	14.4	2.1	5.5	2.6	1.7	33	73	30
	15	R	30	a/a	TOR	114	6.59	1.83	21.3	3.1	6.3	2.0	1.5	38	66	22
Biddle,Jesse	14	L	23	aa	PHI	82	5.82	1.58	22.7	4.7	7.5	1.6	1.3	32	65	40
	15	L	24	a/a	PHI	125	5.88	1.86	24.4	4.5	5.5	1.2	1.0	36	69	20
Billings,Bruce	14	R	29	a/a	LA	96	5.40	1.73	20.7	3.2	4.9	1.6	1.0	36	70	23
	15	R	30	aaa	WAS	121	5.53	1.71	20.4	2.5	4.8	1.9	0.6	37	67	39
Binford,Christian	15	R	23	a/a	KC	119	6.39	1.78	24.9	2.9	4.2	1.5	0.8	37	63	19
Blach,Ty	14	L	24	aa	SF	141	3.56	1.41	23.9	2.5	4.8	2.0	0.5	32	75	53
	15	L	25	aaa	SF	165	4.72	1.45	26.1	1.7	4.2	2.5	0.7	33	67	49
Black,Corey	14	R	23	aa	CHC	124	3.99	1.48	20.6	5.2	7.3	1.4	1.0	28	76	50
	15	R	24	aa	CHC	86	5.94	1.58	10.2	5.2	8.9	1.7	0.8	33	62	68
Black,Victor	14	R	26	aaa	NYM	19	1.22	1.43	4.7	7.1	7.2	1.0	0.0	24	91	82
	15	R	27	a/a	NYM	33	6.66	2.14	4.4	7.6	7.1	0.9	0.9	37	69	27
Blackburn,Clayton	15	R	22	aaa	SF	123	2.69	1.30	22.1	2.2	6.3	2.9	0.3	33	79	88
Blackley,Travis	15	L	33	aaa	MIA	87	8.12	1.95	18.1	3.0	4.9	1.6	1.7	39	59	-4
Blackmar,Mark	15	R	23	aa	CHW	151	4.91	1.55	25.5	3.7	3.3	0.9	0.6	31	68	19
Blair,Aaron	14	R	22	aa	ARI	46	2.36	1.08	22.6	3.0	7.6	2.5	0.9	25	83	85
	15	R	23	a/a	ARI	160	3.29	1.25	25.1	2.7	5.7	2.1	0.8	28	76	59
Blanton,Joe	15	R	35	aaa	KC	39	5.58	1.46	24.1	2.7	4.8	1.8	2.0	29	68	3
Bleich,Jeremy	14	L	27	a/a	NYY	111	5.56	1.72	19.3	4.4	5.8	1.3	1.1	34	69	25
	15	L	28	a/a	PIT	53	3.98	1.51	6.1	2.5	4.8	1.9	0.3	34	73	53
Bleier,Richard	14	L	27	a/a	TOR	87	5.45	1.67	11.1	1.3	3.7	2.9	2.0	35	73	9
	15	L	28	a/a	WAS	172	3.70	1.42	26.0	1.0	2.5	2.6	0.4	33	73	50
Bochy,Brett	14	R	27	aaa	SF	54	3.79	1.54	6.7	4.3	6.1	1.4	1.0	31	79	35
	15	R	28	aaa	SF	58	3.33	1.46	5.8	3.6	5.1	1.4	0.4	31	77	49
Bolsinger,Michael	14	R	26	aaa	ARI	92	4.10	1.44	23.0	3.0	6.8	2.3	0.6	34	72	70
	15	R	27	aaa	LA	47	2.70	1.14	18.5	3.4	9.3	2.7	0.4	29	77	113
Boscan,Wilfredo	15	R	26	aaa	PIT	126	4.04	1.65	22.5	3.3	4.7	1.4	0.2	35	74	44
Bowden,Michael	15	R	29	aaa	MIN	123	4.06	1.55	16.8	2.7	5.2	1.9	0.6	34	74	47
Bowman,Matthew	14	R	23	a/a	NYM	135	2.82	1.25	22.8	2.1	7.3	3.5	0.5	33	78	106
	15	R	24	aaa	NYM	140	5.41	1.71	22.7	3.0	4.2	1.4	0.9	35	69	17
Boyd,Matt	15	L	24	a/a	DET	115	2.05	0.98	22.9	2.2	6.7	3.0	0.7	24	84	95
Bracho,Silvino	15	R	23	aa	ARI	45	2.38	1.12	4.8	1.9	10.1	5.4	0.8	33	83	156
Bradford,Chase	15	R	26	aaa	NYM	64	4.18	1.69	5.4	1.9	5.3	2.8	0.4	39	74	65
Bradford,Chasen	14	R	25	a/a	NYM	73	2.72	1.25	5.2	1.1	6.9	6.2	0.7	34	81	150
Bradley,Jed	14	L	24	aa	MIL	87	5.45	1.85	23.9	3.9	6.3	1.6	1.0	38	72	29
	15	L	25	a/a	MIL	59	7.44	1.90	6.4	3.4	5.8	1.7	0.4	41	58	43
Brady,Michael	14	R	27	a/a	LAA	68	4.83	1.51	6.5	2.9	6.5	2.2	0.5	35	67	67
	15	R	28	aa	LAA	119	5.24	1.47	16.0	1.0	6.6	6.7	0.9	38	65	145
Brault,Steven	15	L	23	aa	PIT	90	2.25	1.08	23.4	1.8	6.5	3.7	0.1	30	78	121
Brice,Austin	15	R	23	aa	MIA	125	5.72	1.62	22.2	5.0	7.6	1.5	0.7	33	64	55
Bridwell,Parker	15	R	24	aa	BAL	97	5.38	1.64	24.1	3.8	7.1	1.8	0.9	36	68	50
Brigham,Jacob	14	R	26	aaa	PIT	92	4.88	1.45	21.9	2.7	5.2	1.9	1.1	31	68	36
	15	R	27	a/a	ATL	91	4.86	1.49	19.6	2.4	5.6	2.4	0.2	35	65	70
Britton,Drake	14	L	25	aaa	BOS	58	7.74	2.31	6.7	6.2	4.6	0.7	1.4	39	67	-18
	15	L	26	aaa	CHC	83	6.18	1.57	13.1	3.8	3.9	1.0	0.8	31	60	17
Broadway,Michae	15	R	28	aaa	SF	48	1.05	0.78	4.4	1.6	9.1	5.8	0.0	25	85	196
Broderick,Brian	15	R	29	aaa	KC	62	4.12	1.59	6.5	2.7	3.9	1.5	0.7	34	75	25
Brooks,Aaron	14	R	24	aaa	KC	139	4.21	1.37	23.3	1.6	5.0	3.2	0.8	33	71	68
	15	R	25	aaa	OAK	119	4.46	1.47	25.5	1.7	6.2	3.6	0.8	36	71	82
Brothers,Rex	15	L	28	aaa	COL	42	6.09	1.99	4.52	10.5	9.5	0.9	0.3	31	67	76
Brown,Dennis	15	R	25	aa	CLE	30	4.53	1.51	26.3	1.3	5.4	4.3	1.5	35	75	66
Broyles,Shane	15	R	24	a/a	COL	47	5.30	1.59	6.43	5.2	7.4	1.4	1.1	31	68	43
Bucciferro,Tony	14	R	25	aa	CHW	36	5.94	1.65	26.8	1.7	4.4	2.6	0.9	37	64	40
	15	R	26	aa	CHW	83	6.86	2.07	19.4	2.8	2.7	1.0	1.7	38	70	-36
Buchanan,David	14	R	25	aaa	PHI	57	4.64	1.74	21.7	3.4	6.0	1.8	0.5	38	73	47
	15	R	26	aaa	PHI	55	3.58	1.70	24.7	3.6	4.1	1.1	0.4	35	79	27
Buchanan,Jake	14	R	25	aaa	HOU	88	4.18	1.37	23.2	1.6	3.9	2.4	0.7	32	70	48
	15	R	26	aaa	HOU	81	5.23	1.68	12.2	2.4	4.2	1.7	0.6	36	68	32
Buchter,Ryan	14	L	27	aaa	ATL	63	3.82	1.62	5.71	6.0	7.2	1.2	0.7	30	78	51
	15	L	28	aaa	CHC	51	2.26	1.44	5.02	5.0	8.5	1.7	0.0	32	83	94
Burawa,Daniel	15	R	26	a/a	ATL	65	3.63	1.45	7.08	4.9	6.6	1.3	0.7	28	76	54
Burdi,Nick	15	R	22	aa	MIN	44	5.06	1.70	6.58	6.3	9.3	1.5	0.6	34	70	72
Burgos,Hiram	14	R	27	aaa	MIL	18	8.15	2.11	22.2	5.5	8.0	1.4	1.3	41	61	26
	15	R	28	a/a	MIL	110	4.68	1.47	23.6	3.9	6.4	1.7	0.7	31	68	53

PITCHER	yr	t	age	lvl	org	ip	era	whip	bf/g	ctl	dom	cmd	hr/9	h%	s%	bpv
Burke,Greg	15	R	33	a/a	TOR	62	4.15	1.39	5.41	3.2	7.4	2.3	1.4	31	75	52
Burns,Cory	14	R	27	a/a	TAM	64	6.17	1.82	6.87	2.4	6.5	2.7	1.2	40	67	43
	15	R	28	aa	TOR	55	8.34	2.13	8.45	3.8	5.9	1.5	0.7	43	59	26
Buschmann,Matth	15	R	31	aaa	BAL	135	7.14	1.81	27.1	4.1	5.3	1.3	1.5	35	62	3
Busenitz,Alan	15	R	25	aa	LAA	53	8.78	2.14	16.5	2.7	5.3	1.9	1.3	43	58	10
Butler,Eddie	14	R	23	a/a	COL	113	4.65	1.45	25.4	2.8	4.2	1.5	1.0	30	70	24
	15	R	24	aaa	COL	63	6.76	1.73	26.2	3.7	4.2	1.1	1.1	34	61	7
Butler,Keith	15	R	26	aaa	STL	32	7.08	1.80	5.15	5.8	5.0	0.9	1.1	31	61	11
Cabral,Cesar	14	L	25	a/a	NYY	39	7.76	2.04	5.88	8.4	8.3	1.0	0.9	35	61	43
	15	L	26	a/a	BAL	44	6.77	1.83	4.35	5.0	7.7	1.5	0.0	39	59	71
Cabrera,Alberto	14	R	26	aaa	CHC	66	4.07	1.34	6.83	4.5	6.6	1.5	1.4	25	75	38
	15	R	27	aaa	DET	56	8.57	2.00	5.75	5.2	5.6	1.1	1.9	35	59	-15
Cabrera,Edwar	14	L	27	a/a	TEX	146	4.29	1.63	21.7	2.9	5.4	1.9	0.8	35	75	40
	15	L	28	a/a	TEX	78	5.24	1.56	10.4	2.2	5.3	2.4	0.9	35	67	48
Cahill,Trevor	14	R	26	aaa	ARI	28	3.65	1.49	20.4	6.0	6.7	1.1	1.2	25	80	37
	15	R	27	aaa	CHC	36	6.16	1.76	15.1	4.6	4.7	1.0	0.8	33	64	18
Campos,Leonel	14	R	27	a/a	SD	82	6.40	1.78	9.03	5.4	9.6	1.8	0.8	39	63	67
	15	R	28	aaa	SD	50	2.92	1.09	5.11	3.8	9.6	2.6	0.3	27	73	119
Carle,Shane	15	R	24	a/a	COL	166	5.06	1.52	26.7	1.9	4.4	2.4	1.0	34	68	38
Carpenter,David	14	R	27	a/a	LAA	62	2.32	1.37	5.8	3.5	6.6	1.9	0.1	32	82	78
	15	R	28	aaa	ATL	51	2.58	1.40	5.35	4.6	6.9	1.5	0.2	30	81	73
Carpenter,Ryan	15	L	25	aa	COL	167	6.29	1.58	26.2	2.3	5.5	2.4	1.7	34	63	25
Carroll,Scott	14	R	30	aaa	CHW	23	1.86	1.43	24.4	4.2	3.8	0.9	0.0	29	85	47
	15	R	31	aaa	CHW	83	5.22	1.87	24.3	4.1	3.7	0.9	1.3	34	75	-10
Casey,Jarrett	14	L	27	a/a	CHW	59	2.86	1.46	7.94	4.7	3.9	0.8	0.7	26	83	23
	15	L	28	aaa	CHW	57	6.24	1.90	7.43	4.6	5.4	1.2	1.6	35	70	-2
Cash,Ralston	15	R	24	a/a	LA	58	4.01	1.33	4.82	4.2	7.6	1.8	1.2	27	74	55
Casilla,Jose	14	R	25	aa	SF	66	4.63	1.34	6.67	3.0	4.3	1.4	0.6	29	65	39
	15	R	26	aa	SF	56	1.99	1.59	5.29	3.3	4.1	1.2	0.0	34	86	45
Castillo,Lendy	14	R	25	aa	CHC	41	4.73	1.92	5.4	9.1	7.3	0.8	1.0	29	77	38
	15	R	26	aa	TOR	32	6.55	2.12	8.41	7.1	5.3	0.7	1.5	34	71	-8
Castro,Angel	14	R	32	aaa	OAK	114	5.08	1.64	16.9	2.7	4.2	1.6	1.0	34	70	19
	15	R	33	aaa	OAK	60	4.33	1.56	6.96	3.4	4.8	1.4	1.0	32	75	24
Castro,Miguel A.	15	R	21	aaa	COL	33	3.85	1.64	6.19	5.0	7.0	1.4	1.3	31	81	31
Castro,Simon	15	R	27	aaa	COL	57	5.06	1.56	6.94	3.5	8.7	2.5	1.3	36	71	62
Celestino,Miguel	14	R	25	a/a	BOS	52	5.28	1.45	5.69	3.7	8.3	2.3	1.6	31	68	51
	15	R	26	a/a	CIN	71	4.73	1.81	7.6	4.6	5.6	1.2	1.4	34	77	11
Cervenka,Hunter	14	L	24	aa	CHC	62	4.45	1.34	5.34	4.7	7.9	1.7	0.2	29	64	88
	15	L	25	a/a	ATL	38	5.42	2.05	5.78	7.0	11.1	1.6	0.6	43	73	76
Cessa,Luis	15	R	23	a/a	DET	139	5.51	1.62	24.8	2.4	6.2	2.6	0.5	38	65	66
Chacin,Jhoulys	15	R	27	aaa	ARI	129	3.46	1.38	27	3.1	4.8	1.6	0.4	30	75	49
Chalas,Miguel	15	R	23	a/a	CHW	70	6.13	1.46	8.13	2.8	6.0	2.2	0.9	33	57	53
Chapman,Jaye	15	R	28	a/a	MIL	65	3.22	1.44	4.67	3.6	7.2	2.0	0.8	32	80	62
Chapman,Kevin	14	L	26	aaa	HOU	44	1.35	1.55	4.47	5.1	10.7	2.1	0.0	38	90	111
	15	L	27	aaa	HOU	53	5.34	1.82	5.01	4.5	8.3	1.8	0.5	40	70	63
Chargois,J.T.	15	R	25	aa	MIN	33	3.24	1.53	4.49	5.5	7.3	1.3	0.3	31	78	69
Chen,Bruce	14	L	37	a/a	KC	15	10.71	2.65	21	2.0	6.6	3.3	1.9	52	60	15
	15	L	38	aaa	CLE	31	2.60	0.96	23.4	1.0	5.0	4.9	1.6	23	86	95
Christiani,Nick	14	R	27	aaa	CIN	28	7.73	2.54	6.26	5.9	3.6	0.6	0.8	43	69	-14
	15	R	28	a/a	CIN	36	8.62	2.91	7.94	8.3	4.4	0.5	0.4	45	68	-2
Church,John	14	R	28	a/a	NYM	57	3.86	1.46	5.54	2.4	7.0	2.9	0.7	35	75	76
	15	R	29	aaa	NYM	71	4.29	1.37	4.87	2.1	4.3	2.1	0.8	31	70	42
Cimber,Adam	15	R	25	a/a	SD	59	3.18	1.38	5.38	2.2	5.9	2.6	0.7	33	79	67
Claudio,Alexande	14	L	22	a/a	TEX	43	2.65	1.06	16.5	0.8	5.0	6.0	0.2	29	74	153
	15	L	23	aaa	TEX	40	3.61	1.43	5.87	1.6	6.6	4.1	0.5	36	75	103
Clay,Caleb	14	R	26	aaa	LAA	76	4.44	1.35	26.4	1.7	4.3	2.5	1.2	30	71	37
	15	R	27	a/a	ARI	115	6.51	1.88	23.6	2.8	3.4	1.2	1.2	37	66	-7
Clemens,Paul	14	R	26	aaa	HOU	46	4.50	1.41	10.3	4.5	6.5	1.5	0.8	28	69	51
	15	R	27	aaa	KC	47	7.97	2.01	14.1	5.9	5.0	0.9	1.3	35	60	-2
Cleto,Maikel	14	R	25	aaa	CHW	35	6.37	1.63	7.09	4.1	10.8	2.6	2.0	37	66	55
	15	R	26	aaa	CHW	51	4.17	1.34	6.84	5.1	8.7	1.7	1.5	25	74	56
Clevinger,Michael	15	R	25	aa	CLE	158	3.79	1.29	24	2.4	6.8	2.8	0.6	32	71	85
Cochran-Gill,Trey	15	R	23	a/a	SEA	56	5.46	1.76	7.28	5.0	4.7	0.9	0.0	34	66	43
Coello,Robert	14	R	30	aaa	BAL	56	2.27	1.50	5.23	6.5	8.1	1.2	0.6	27	87	68
	15	R	31	aaa	TEX	95	5.95	1.81	25.8	4.6	4.3	0.9	1.0	33	68	7
Cole,A.J.	14	R	22	a/a	WAS	134	3.32	1.39	22.6	1.9	6.2	3.2	0.6	34	77	83
	15	R	23	aaa	WAS	106	4.16	1.37	21.1	3.0	5.3	1.8	0.8	30	71	45
Cole,Taylor	15	R	26	aa	TOR	164	5.62	1.72	26.6	3.3	5.8	1.7	1.4	36	70	21
Coleman,Casey	14	R	27	aaa	KC	68	3.06	1.38	8.15	3.8	5.3	1.4	0.5	29	79	50
	15	R	28	aaa	KC	82	6.81	2.18	12.5	5.1	4.3	0.9	0.8	39	68	2
Coleman,Louis	14	R	28	aaa	KC	40	4.56	1.37	5.94	3.6	8.8	2.4	1.3	31	71	67
	15	R	29	aaa	KC	64	2.39	1.42	7.13	3.7	6.3	1.7	0.7	30	86	55
Collier,Tommy	14	R	25	aa	DET	86	6.63	1.59	22.2	4.0	3.9	1.0	1.5	29	60	-4
	15	R	26	aa	DET	108	5.82	1.56	26.4	2.6	4.8	1.8	0.6	35	61	42
Colon,Joseph	14	R	24	aa	CLE	138	3.91	1.48	23.7	3.5	5.3	1.5	0.5	32	74	47
	15	R	25	a/a	CLE	49	4.30	1.52	6.39	2.8	7.2	2.6	0.7	36	72	72
Concepcion,Gera	15	L	23	aa	CHC	32	9.76	2.56	5.5	8.5	6.1	0.7	1.2	41	61	-3
Conley,Adam	14	L	24	aaa	MIA	60	6.12	1.57	22	3.7	5.9	1.6	0.4	34	58	55
	15	L	25	aaa	MIA	107	3.39	1.39	23.7	3.7	5.4	1.5	0.3	30	75	56
Contreras,Carlos	14	R	23	aa	CIN	20	3.11	1.39	9.35	4.9	10.6	2.2	0.0	34	75	118
	15	R	24	aaa	CIN	40	3.91	1.81	5.92	7.4	10.9	1.5	1.0	35	81	69
Cook,Ryan	15	R	28	aaa	BOS	43	4.95	1.56	5.05	4.1	5.7	1.4	0.8	32	69	37
Cooney,Tim	14	L	24	aaa	STL	158	3.57	1.36	25.4	2.5	5.6	2.2	1.0	30	77	48
	15	L	25	aaa	STL	89	3.10	0.96	23.9	1.6	5.1	3.2	0.9	23	72	82
Cooper,Jordan	14	R	25	a/a	CLE	85	5.78	1.48	9.91	3.8	5.6	1.5	1.3	29	63	27
	15	R	26	a/a	CLE	106	6.07	1.95	22.9	4.3	3.5	0.8	1.2	36	70	-11
Cooper,Matthew	14	R	26	a/a	CHC	68	3.89	1.46	5.97	4.3	7.1	1.7	0.4	32	73	67
	15	R	27	aaa	CHC	68	3.28	1.51	5.91	4.1	6.6	1.6	0.6	32	79	56

PITCHER	yr	t	age	lvl	org	ip	era	whip	bf/g	ctl	dom	cmd	hr/9	h%	s%	bpv
Copeland,Scott	15	R	28	aaa	TOR	125	4.76	1.70	26.9	3.2	3.8	1.2	0.9	34	73	10
Cordero,Jimmy	15	R	24	aa	PHI	42	2.99	1.18	5.55	4.0	7.4	1.9	0.5	25	75	83
Cordier,Erik	14	R	28	aaa	SF	53	3.63	1.42	4.75	5.2	8.8	1.7	0.5	30	75	81
	15	R	29	aaa	MIA	40	1.98	1.69	5.15	7.0	8.2	1.2	0.0	32	87	80
Cornely,John	14	R	25	aa	ATL	69	3.05	1.30	6.14	4.7	7.8	1.7	0.3	28	76	85
	15	R	26	a/a	BOS	62	6.39	1.72	6.22	6.5	7.6	1.2	1.1	31	63	41
Correia,Kevin	15	R	35	aaa	SF	38	4.19	1.42	26.6	2.9	4.4	1.5	0.8	30	72	32
Coshow,Cale	15	R	23	aa	NYY	33	4.73	1.48	23.9	3.8	4.9	1.3	0.4	31	66	46
Cotham,Caleb	15	R	28	a/a	NYY	57	3.27	1.34	6.77	2.5	7.5	3.0	0.5	34	76	94
Cotton,Chris	15	L	25	a/a	HOU	44	3.72	1.32	5.16	2.5	6.0	2.4	0.9	31	74	61
Cotton,Jharel	15	R	23	a/a	LA	70	2.96	1.24	17.8	2.8	8.9	3.2	0.6	32	77	109
Couch,Keith	14	R	25	aa	BOS	100	3.94	1.53	24.2	2.1	5.2	2.5	0.3	36	73	66
	15	R	26	aaa	BOS	125	9.18	2.08	23.5	4.2	3.5	0.8	1.0	38	54	-10
Coulombe,Daniel	14	L	25	aa	LA	21	2.64	1.37	4.89	3.9	10.9	2.8	0.4	35	81	117
	15	L	26	aaa	LA	41	3.72	1.54	4.74	5.0	7.2	1.4	0.2	32	74	70
Crabbe,Timothy	14	R	26	aaa	CIN	94	4.63	1.67	14	3.6	4.7	1.3	0.9	34	74	22
	15	R	27	a/a	CHW	82	5.27	1.77	10.1	4.9	7.2	1.5	1.1	35	72	35
Cravy,Tyler	15	R	26	aaa	MIL	95	4.59	1.47	24.1	3.1	5.7	1.8	0.7	32	69	50
Creasy,Jason	15	R	23	aa	PIT	147	4.95	1.56	23.8	2.9	3.5	1.2	0.6	32	68	21
Crick,Kyle	14	R	22	aa	SF	90	4.14	1.58	17.3	5.8	9.6	1.7	0.6	33	74	79
	15	R	23	aa	SF	63	4.28	2.02	8.48	10.2	8.9	0.9	0.3	32	78	70
Cruz,Fernando	15	R	25	a/a	CHC	35	8.96	2.03	10.1	6.0	7.0	1.2	2.0	36	57	-3
Cruz,Luis	14	L	24	a/a	HOU	125	4.01	1.34	19.9	2.7	7.3	2.7	1.2	31	74	66
	15	L	25	aaa	HOU	116	4.59	1.58	18.2	4.0	6.0	1.5	1.4	31	75	23
Cuevas,William	15	R	25	a/a	BOS	136	4.38	1.49	22.6	4.0	6.8	1.7	0.5	32	70	61
Culver,Malcom	14	R	24	a/a	KC	65	5.27	1.72	6.71	4.0	6.6	1.7	0.5	37	68	51
	15	R	25	aa	KC	58	5.27	1.74	6.15	4.8	7.1	1.5	0.3	36	68	59
Danish,Tyler	15	R	21	aa	CHW	142	5.91	1.93	25.9	4.2	5.1	1.2	1.1	37	70	10
Darnell,Logan	14	L	25	aaa	MIN	115	4.61	1.59	22	4.0	5.6	1.4	1.3	31	75	20
	15	L	26	aaa	MIN	78	4.01	1.65	9.92	3.3	5.9	1.8	0.4	36	75	52
Davies,Kyle	14	R	31	a/a	CLE	154	5.04	1.59	26.2	2.6	4.3	1.7	1.1	34	70	19
	15	R	32	aaa	NYY	153	5.00	1.71	25.6	2.7	4.4	1.6	0.7	36	71	27
Davies,Zachary	15	R	22	aaa	MIL	128	3.51	1.42	22.7	3.1	6.3	2.0	0.5	33	75	66
Davis,Erik	15	R	29	a/a	WAS	46	6.10	2.21	6.57	6.3	6.4	1.0	0.5	41	71	30
Davis,Rookie	15	R	22	aa	NYY	33	5.71	1.62	24.6	2.3	5.7	2.5	0.4	38	62	65
Dayton,Grant	14	L	27	a/a	MIA	72	3.61	1.52	6.26	3.4	7.6	2.2	1.1	34	80	56
	15	L	28	a/a	LA	57	5.24	1.37	5.71	2.5	7.9	3.2	0.4	35	59	102
De La Cruz,Joel	15	R	26	aa	NYY	84	4.69	1.57	16.1	2.7	3.6	1.3	0.9	33	71	15
De la Rosa,Eury	14	L	24	aaa	ARI	39	2.52	1.35	4.56	4.2	6.8	1.6	0.6	28	84	62
	15	L	25	a/a	SD	60	3.46	1.66	5.45	5.0	6.8	1.4	0.8	33	81	43
De La Torre,Jose	14	R	29	a/a	MIL	43	6.14	1.93	6.75	5.4	8.4	1.6	1.1	39	69	40
	15	R	30	aaa	CIN	65	4.98	1.83	5.92	6.1	4.9	0.8	0.9	31	74	16
De Leon,Jorge	14	R	27	a/a	HOU	69	3.50	1.45	6.37	3.1	6.4	2.0	0.7	33	77	58
	15	R	28	a/a	MIA	55	6.64	1.92	6.21	5.1	4.4	0.9	1.4	34	67	-8
De Leon,Jose	15	R	23	aa	LA	77	4.54	1.30	19.7	3.3	10.6	3.2	1.6	32	71	90
De Los Santos,At	15	R	23	aa	WAS	58	4.35	1.30	6.09	1.9	7.0	3.7	1.0	32	69	89
Dean,Pat	14	L	25	aa	MIN	144	5.94	1.81	25.6	2.0	4.1	2.1	1.3	38	69	12
	15	L	26	aaa	MIN	179	4.06	1.46	28.4	2.0	3.8	1.9	0.6	33	73	37
DeCecco,Scott	15	L	24	aa	SEA	63	8.04	2.07	15.4	4.9	6.5	1.3	0.6	41	59	33
DeLoach,Tyler	14	L	23	aa	LAA	35	2.84	1.04	22.7	4.3	8.5	2.0	0.8	20	76	90
	15	L	24	a/a	LAA	139	5.43	1.53	24.2	3.4	7.3	2.1	0.8	35	64	61
Demny,Paul	14	R	25	aa	WAS	41	3.10	1.55	8.08	4.3	6.3	1.4	0.6	32	82	49
	15	R	26	a/a	WAS	59	3.13	1.50	5.83	6.0	8.5	1.4	0.5	29	80	75
Dennick,Ryan	14	L	27	a/a	CIN	50	2.80	1.43	3.66	3.4	5.8	1.7	0.0	33	78	71
	15	L	28	a/a	LA	57	6.52	1.69	5.01	2.6	5.5	2.1	0.6	38	59	48
Devenski,Christop	14	R	24	aa	HOU	41	4.41	1.33	17.2	3.9	6.9	1.8	1.6	26	73	36
	15	R	25	aa	HOU	120	3.58	1.43	21.2	2.6	6.5	2.6	1.0	33	78	59
Diamond,Scott	14	L	28	aaa	CIN	123	7.69	1.96	22.7	2.4	3.8	1.5	1.3	39	61	-5
	15	L	29	aaa	TAM	150	5.10	1.77	24.7	1.8	4.1	2.3	0.9	38	72	28
Diaz,Dayan	14	R	25	aa	BOS	16	3.67	1.66	6.66	4.1	7.1	1.7	0.0	37	76	74
	15	R	26	aaa	BOS	73	2.45	1.43	8.34	4.2	6.4	1.5	0.4	30	84	61
Diaz,Edwin	15	R	21	aa	SEA	104	5.20	1.41	22.1	3.0	8.0	2.7	0.4	35	61	91
Diaz,Jairo	14	R	23	aa	LAA	33	2.73	1.37	5.08	2.7	11.3	4.1	0.6	39	82	137
	15	R	24	aaa	COL	55	5.73	1.79	5.4	6.2	6.5	1.0	1.3	31	70	22
Diaz,Luis	14	R	22	aa	BOS	77	4.66	1.40	25.1	3.0	6.3	2.1	0.9	31	68	55
	15	R	23	aa	BOS	137	6.87	1.79	23.3	4.0	4.7	1.2	0.8	35	60	20
Dillard,Tim	14	R	31	a/a	MIL	65	5.22	1.42	5.83	2.8	5.9	2.1	0.9	32	64	50
	15	R	32	aaa	MIL	54	6.90	1.90	9.43	4.0	5.5	1.4	0.7	38	62	28
Dimock,Michael	14	R	25	aa	SD	57	3.99	1.41	6.18	2.7	8.2	3.0	1.0	34	74	82
	15	R	26	a/a	SD	60	2.23	1.03	4.71	0.9	8.6	9.6	0.8	31	84	233
Dodson,Zackry	14	L	24	aa	PIT	123	4.88	1.58	22.5	3.1	4.4	1.4	0.7	33	69	29
	15	L	25	aa	PIT	162	4.29	1.38	24.3	1.9	3.9	2.0	0.6	32	69	45
Dolis,Rafael	15	R	27	aaa	DET	66	6.00	1.89	7.27	6.4	5.4	0.9	0.3	34	66	36
Donatello,Sean	15	R	25	aa	MIA	33	5.18	1.51	5.16	3.1	5.6	1.8	0.5	33	64	51
Donofrio,Joseph	14	R	25	a/a	STL	60	1.64	1.16	4.54	3.1	8.5	2.7	0.4	29	88	106
	15	R	26	a/a	STL	73	4.93	1.58	7.65	4.5	4.7	1.0	0.7	30	69	28
Doolittle,Ryan	14	R	26	aa	OAK	47	3.84	1.59	6.97	3.8	7.1	1.9	0.8	35	77	56
	15	R	27	aa	OAK	57	3.78	1.57	6.25	2.7	5.5	2.1	0.8	35	77	47
Doubront,Felix	14	L	27	a/a	CHC	28	5.26	1.62	20.7	3.9	7.7	2.0	0.0	38	64	84
	15	L	28	aaa	TOR	48	3.93	1.51	23.1	4.1	6.4	1.5	0.3	33	73	62
Doyle,John	14	R	29	a/a	ATL	109	5.16	1.66	13.6	3.3	5.0	1.5	0.7	35	69	31
	15	R	30	a/a	BAL	159	3.51	1.42	25.9	1.6	4.5	2.9	0.9	33	78	53
Drabek,Kyle	14	R	27	aaa	TOR	99	5.85	1.86	14.5	3.1	4.9	1.6	1.5	37	71	4
	15	R	28	aaa	CHW	137	5.05	1.70	25.9	4.3	4.3	1.0	0.8	33	70	18
Drake,Oliver	14	R	27	aa	BAL	53	3.84	1.30	4.34	3.1	9.3	3.0	0.4	34	70	111
	15	R	28	aaa	BAL	44	1.38	1.22	4.23	4.2	10.2	2.4	0.3	30	90	115
Duffey,Tyler	15	R	25	a/a	MIN	138	3.28	1.28	25.7	2.1	6.3	3.0	0.1	33	72	100

PITCHER	yr	t	age	lvl	org	ip	era	whip	bf/g	ctl	dom	cmd	hr/9	h%	s%	bpv
Dull,Ryan	15	R	26	a/a	OAK	61	0.88	1.03	5	2.5	8.4	3.3	0.3	28	94	124
Dunning,Jake	14	R	26	aaa	SF	65	4.42	1.44	7.28	3.4	5.6	1.7	0.5	31	69	53
	15	R	27	aaa	SF	46	7.56	2.15	17.6	4.3	5.4	1.3	1.5	40	66	-5
Duran,Omar	15	L	25	aa	OAK	35	8.13	2.16	5.81	6.2	6.5	1.1	0.5	40	60	34
Dwyer,Christophe	14	L	26	aaa	KC	66	6.32	1.71	10.7	5.4	6.8	1.3	1.0	33	63	34
	15	L	27	aaa	KC	92	5.43	2.03	13.5	5.9	4.6	0.8	0.5	36	72	20
Dziedzic,Jonathar	15	L	24	a/a	KC	142	4.45	1.51	22.7	2.4	4.9	2.0	0.8	33	72	41
Edwards,Carl	15	R	24	a/a	CHC	55	3.28	1.31	6.35	6.9	10.3	1.5	0.2	24	73	111
Edwards,Jonathar	14	R	26	a/a	TEX	49	5.47	1.74	6.57	6.3	8.9	1.4	0.9	34	69	57
	15	R	27	aaa	SD	37	1.21	0.91	3.7	2.6	10.0	3.8	0.2	26	88	153
Eflin,Zach	15	R	21	aa	PHI	132	4.04	1.29	23.5	1.5	4.2	2.8	0.9	30	71	55
Ege,Cody	15	L	24	a/a	MIA	52	1.11	1.30	5.49	4.2	8.6	2.1	0.5	29	95	89
Eickhoff,Jerad	15	R	25	a/a	PHI	133	4.67	1.36	24.2	2.8	7.2	2.6	1.2	31	69	61
Elias,Roenis	15	L	27	aaa	SEA	61	7.68	1.74	23.3	2.5	5.5	2.2	1.2	37	55	29
Ellington,Brian	15	R	25	a/a	MIA	44	3.19	1.09	6.67	2.8	7.8	2.7	0.0	28	67	116
Ellis,Chris	15	R	23	aa	LAA	78	4.89	1.69	23.5	4.8	6.2	1.3	1.1	33	73	28
Erlin,Robert	14	L	24	a/a	SD	21	6.08	1.88	19.7	2.3	6.7	2.9	1.1	42	69	49
	15	L	25	aaa	SD	125	5.27	1.53	22.7	2.5	6.3	2.6	1.3	34	68	46
Escat,Gene	15	R	26	a/a	BAL	70	6.02	2.07	10.3	7.0	5.8	0.8	1.0	35	71	15
Esch,Jacob	15	R	25	a/a	MIA	115	5.22	1.56	24.1	3.5	5.5	1.6	0.6	33	66	43
Escobar,Edwin	14	L	22	aaa	BOS	138	6.14	1.67	24.8	2.9	6.5	2.2	1.3	36	65	36
	15	L	23	aaa	BOS	50	7.13	1.86	12.2	5.0	3.6	0.7	1.7	31	64	-23
Espino,Paolo	14	R	27	a/a	WAS	120	4.49	1.19	19.2	1.8	6.6	3.7	0.9	30	64	91
	15	R	28	a/a	WAS	156	4.99	1.51	24.1	2.0	5.1	2.6	1.1	34	69	43
Estevez,Carlos	15	R	23	aa	COL	36	6.72	1.67	4.75	2.5	8.7	3.5	0.8	41	58	91
Evans,Bryan	14	R	27	aaa	MIA	112	4.81	1.44	13.3	3.7	6.5	1.8	1.0	30	68	47
	15	R	28	aa	COL	73	5.54	1.48	26.2	2.6	5.9	2.3	1.9	31	68	22
Eveland,Dana	14	L	31	aaa	NYM	46	3.58	1.54	16.7	2.2	8.7	3.9	0.9	39	79	101
	15	L	32	aaa	BAL	55	3.42	1.46	7.18	3.0	5.3	1.8	0.0	34	74	67
Faria,Jake	15	R	22	aa	TAM	75	2.77	1.14	22.9	3.5	10.1	2.9	0.6	29	77	118
Farmer,Buck	14	R	23	a/a	DET	19	6.40	1.62	21.5	3.6	4.9	1.4	1.0	33	60	24
	15	R	24	aaa	DET	87	5.07	1.45	23.1	2.7	6.2	2.3	0.7	33	65	61
Farquhar,Daniel	15	R	28	aaa	SEA	38	3.30	1.46	6.03	2.3	7.6	3.3	0.7	36	79	90
Farrell,Luke	15	R	24	aa	KC	93	3.80	1.44	20.9	2.9	5.0	1.7	0.7	31	75	43
Faulkner,Andrew	15	L	23	a/a	TEX	100	4.65	1.47	12.7	4.4	7.7	1.8	0.9	31	70	60
Feliz,Michael	15	R	22	aa	HOU	79	2.43	0.97	19.9	2.2	7.1	3.2	0.6	24	78	106
Ferguson,Andrew	14	R	26	a/a	KC	160	3.80	1.34	24.6	2.6	5.3	2.1	1.0	30	75	45
	15	R	27	a/a	KC	105	3.33	1.27	19.4	2.3	6.9	3.1	1.3	30	80	69
Fernandez,Raul	15	R	25	aa	CHW	61	6.01	1.61	7.55	3.8	5.5	1.4	0.8	33	62	34
Ferrell,Jeff	15	R	25	a/a	DET	38	3.28	1.17	5.46	2.3	8.1	3.6	1.9	27	84	72
Finnegan,Brando	15	L	22	a/a	CIN	57	7.15	1.84	14.1	5.9	8.8	1.5	1.1	37	61	47
Fisher,Carlos	14	R	31	aaa	ATL	33	3.70	1.45	6.13	4.2	8.5	2.0	0.3	34	73	87
	15	R	32	aaa	ATL	56	2.42	1.49	5.62	5.4	7.2	1.3	0.6	29	86	58
Flande,Yohan	14	L	28	aaa	COL	88	6.86	1.95	23.4	3.6	4.8	1.4	1.2	38	65	7
	15	L	29	a/a	COL	71	6.00	1.78	27.3	1.7	3.7	2.2	1.8	37	71	-3
Fleck,Kaleb	14	R	25	aa	ARI	63	3.30	1.52	4.91	4.2	9.0	2.2	0.7	35	80	80
	15	R	26	aaa	ARI	52	3.64	1.44	5.28	4.0	9.1	2.3	0.4	35	74	95
Fleet,Austin	14	R	27	a/a	SF	140	3.43	1.37	17.8	3.1	5.5	1.7	0.5	30	75	56
	15	R	28	aaa	SF	32	7.62	1.84	21.3	3.3	4.3	1.3	1.0	37	57	11
Flemer,Matthew	15	R	25	aa	COL	170	6.03	1.68	27.2	2.4	3.4	1.4	1.0	35	64	8
Flores,Kendry	15	R	24	a/a	MIA	115	3.00	1.12	23.9	2.4	5.3	2.2	0.5	26	74	74
Floro,Dylan	14	R	24	aa	TAM	179	3.91	1.45	27.2	1.2	4.8	4.1	0.2	36	71	99
	15	R	25	aaa	TAM	133	6.31	1.62	23.5	1.5	4.6	3.0	0.7	37	60	56
Foltynewicz,Mike	14	R	23	aaa	HOU	103	5.26	1.50	21.1	4.3	7.8	1.8	0.9	32	65	61
	15	R	24	aaa	ATL	57	4.65	1.61	25.1	4.4	8.7	2.0	1.3	34	75	52
Fontanez,Randy	14	R	25	aa	NYM	33	4.97	1.60	6.7	3.6	7.5	2.1	0.8	36	69	61
	15	R	26	a/a	LA	58	6.63	1.72	14.7	4.0	5.3	1.3	1.1	34	62	19
Fornataro,Eric	14	R	26	aaa	STL	56	2.76	1.27	5.21	3.2	4.4	1.4	0.4	27	79	49
	15	R	27	aaa	WAS	50	7.96	1.91	6.62	5.5	4.4	0.8	0.4	35	55	23
Francescon,P.J.	14	R	25	aa	CHC	69	4.22	1.56	7.03	4.3	5.1	1.2	0.6	31	73	37
	15	R	26	a/a	CHC	61	1.82	1.20	5.48	3.3	6.8	2.0	0.8	26	90	68
Francis,Jeff	14	L	33	aaa	CIN	49	4.04	1.59	26.8	2.4	6.3	2.6	0.7	37	76	63
	15	L	34	aaa	TOR	92	3.92	1.51	21	1.6	5.9	3.7	0.5	37	74	89
Frankoff,Seth	14	R	26	a/a	OAK	64	3.66	1.37	5.5	3.0	7.7	2.6	0.8	33	75	79
	15	R	27	a/a	OAK	61	4.51	1.49	5.56	3.7	6.4	1.7	1.1	31	72	43
Frazier,Parker	14	R	26	a/a	CHW	70	5.22	1.72	7.53	3.3	4.7	1.4	1.1	35	71	15
	15	R	27	a/a	OAK	87	4.89	2.01	26.4	4.3	3.4	0.8	0.4	38	75	9
Frias,Edison	15	R	25	aa	HOU	34	6.36	1.83	19.6	2.8	9.4	3.4	0.9	45	65	85
Fuller,James	14	L	27	aa	MIN	56	3.11	1.64	6.58	5.2	8.3	1.6	0.3	35	81	73
	15	L	28	a/a	OAK	43	5.47	1.70	6.08	4.0	6.2	1.6	0.7	36	67	44
Fulmer,Michael J.	15	R	22	aa	DET	118	2.61	1.23	22.7	2.3	7.3	3.1	0.6	31	81	94
Gage,Matt	15	L	22	aa	SF	39	5.94	1.46	18.4	2.5	6.1	2.5	0.5	35	57	71
Gagnon,Drew	14	R	24	aa	MIL	155	4.74	1.43	23.5	3.8	5.9	1.6	1.3	29	70	32
	15	R	25	a/a	MIL	111	8.51	2.03	20.6	5.6	4.6	0.8	1.6	35	58	-13
Gamboa,Eduardo	15	R	31	aaa	BAL	113	8.06	2.21	21.9	8.8	4.6	0.5	0.8	33	62	7
Gant,John	15	R	23	aa	ATL	100	4.36	1.54	24.2	3.7	6.9	1.8	0.3	35	70	69
Garcia,Edgar	15	R	28	a/a	ARI	104	5.63	1.61	18.5	3.8	4.1	1.1	1.5	30	68	-1
Garcia,Jarlin	15	L	22	aa	MIA	37	5.90	1.64	23.4	4.2	7.3	1.7	0.9	35	64	49
Garcia,Onelki	15	L	26	a/a	CHW	56	6.83	2.10	7.25	5.6	9.4	1.7	0.7	44	66	57
Garrison,Taylor	14	R	24	aa	NYY	39	4.33	1.38	6.82	3.7	5.0	1.4	0.6	29	68	44
	15	R	25	aa	NYY	39	6.75	2.09	13.8	3.1	5.3	1.7	2.3	40	73	-23
Garton,Ryan	15	R	26	aa	TAM	61	3.55	1.41	6.29	5.0	8.4	1.7	0.3	30	74	85
Gast,John	14	L	25	aaa	STL	59	5.09	1.38	20.8	3.2	4.4	1.4	1.1	28	64	25
	15	L	26	aaa	STL	122	5.82	1.82	23.5	3.2	5.2	1.6	0.9	38	68	25
Gaviglio,Sam	15	R	25	aaa	SEA	102	5.15	1.40	20.4	2.9	5.8	2.0	1.3	30	66	39
Gearrin,Cory	15	R	29	aaa	SF	43	3.14	1.42	5.52	3.2	7.2	2.3	0.7	33	80	69
Gee,Dillon	15	R	29	a/a	NYM	95	5.38	1.66	28.2	2.0	4.9	2.4	0.8	37	67	44

PITCHER	yr	t	age	lvl	org	ip	era	whip	bf/g	ctl	dom	cmd	hr/9	h%	s%	bpv
Germano,Justin	15	R	33	aaa	SEA	89	3.14	1.05	19.1	1.4	5.0	3.5	1.1	25	76	78
Germen,Gonzalez	14	R	27	aaa	NYM	23	2.06	1.29	5.18	3.5	6.7	1.9	0.7	28	87	67
	15	R	28	aaa	COL	37	5.03	1.68	6.11	5.0	5.6	1.1	1.0	31	72	23
Gillheeney,James	14	L	27	a/a	SEA	120	5.86	1.65	19.8	3.5	7.0	2.0	1.2	36	66	42
	15	L	28	a/a	SEA	129	4.99	1.52	20.1	2.9	5.2	1.8	0.6	34	66	47
Giolito,Lucas	15	R	21	aa	WAS	47	4.68	1.52	25.7	3.2	7.2	2.3	0.4	36	68	76
Girodo,Chad	15	L	24	a/a	TOR	33	1.91	1.28	5.41	0.6	6.1	10.3	0.0	36	83	248
Givens,Mychal	15	R	25	aa	BAL	57	2.38	1.14	6.49	2.8	10.0	3.6	0.2	32	79	138
Glasnow,Tyler	15	R	22	a/a	PIT	104	2.69	1.16	20.7	3.3	9.3	2.8	0.2	30	76	120
Goforth,David	15	R	27	aaa	MIL	47	3.18	1.54	5.39	5.6	5.2	0.9	0.5	28	80	42
Gonzales,Marco	14	L	22	a/a	STL	84	2.97	1.16	22.4	1.9	7.8	4.1	0.8	30	78	112
	15	L	23	a/a	STL	76	5.34	1.68	21.4	2.6	5.6	2.1	1.1	37	70	34
Gonzalez,Alex	14	R	22	aa	TEX	73	3.37	1.41	20.7	3.2	6.6	2.1	0.5	33	76	70
	15	R	23	aaa	TEX	88	4.40	1.61	24.5	3.3	4.8	1.5	0.3	35	71	43
Gonzalez,Juan	14	R	24	aa	LA	70	3.23	1.58	5.7	5.5	5.2	0.9	0.2	30	79	48
	15	R	25	a/a	LA	50	1.95	1.11	4.47	2.8	7.6	2.7	0.2	28	82	107
Gonzalez,Nelson	14	R	24	aa	COL	67	5.79	1.59	6.32	3.8	5.6	1.5	0.6	33	62	43
	15	R	25	a/a	COL	69	4.21	1.42	6.97	2.9	6.3	2.2	1.0	32	72	54
Gonzalez,Severin	15	R	23	aaa	PHI	88	6.13	1.59	24.3	1.9	4.1	2.1	1.0	35	62	29
Goody,Nicholas	15	R	24	a/a	NYY	62	2.16	1.22	5.86	3.3	10.3	3.1	0.4	32	83	123
Gorski,Darin	14	L	27	a/a	NYM	100	3.18	1.34	21.9	2.6	7.6	2.9	1.3	31	83	68
	15	L	28	aaa	NYM	137	5.89	1.82	22.7	4.5	5.6	1.2	1.3	35	70	12
Grace,Matt	15	L	27	aaa	WAS	49	3.45	1.53	5.57	3.4	4.3	1.3	0.2	33	76	43
Gray,Jonathan	14	R	23	aa	COL	124	5.35	1.41	21.9	3.2	6.4	2.0	1.0	31	63	51
	15	R	24	aaa	COL	114	5.42	1.71	24.6	3.3	6.9	2.1	0.9	38	69	48
Green,Chad	15	R	24	aa	DET	149	4.99	1.67	24.7	2.8	6.5	2.4	0.6	38	70	59
Greene,Shane	14	R	26	aaa	NYY	66	5.64	1.84	20.6	3.8	6.1	1.6	0.5	39	68	44
	15	R	27	aaa	DET	35	5.02	1.67	22.5	3.2	4.0	1.3	0.6	34	70	23
Greenwood,Nick	14	L	27	aaa	STL	51	3.31	1.15	7.45	1.8	5.1	2.8	0.7	28	73	74
	15	L	28	aaa	STL	129	7.00	1.77	18.5	1.8	3.1	1.7	1.2	37	60	3
Gregorio,Joan	15	R	23	aa	SF	79	4.02	1.41	9	4.0	7.0	1.8	0.7	31	72	63
Grube,Jarrett	14	R	33	aaa	LAA	147	5.25	1.48	23.4	2.3	5.5	2.4	1.3	33	67	38
	15	R	34	aaa	CLE	80	3.37	1.47	22.8	2.5	5.8	2.3	1.5	32	84	32
Grullon,Juan	15	L	25	aa	TEX	40	6.68	1.68	7.13	4.0	6.0	1.5	2.3	31	66	-8
Gsellman,Robert	15	R	22	aa	NYM	92	4.05	1.35	24.1	2.5	4.2	1.7	0.4	30	69	48
Guaipe,Mayckol	15	R	25	aaa	SEA	47	2.88	1.31	5.11	1.7	5.8	3.3	0.5	33	79	87
Guerra,Deolis	14	R	25	aaa	MIN	52	5.54	1.55	6.32	3.3	7.4	2.3	0.9	35	65	60
	15	R	26	aaa	PIT	37	1.61	0.94	5.51	2.0	6.9	3.4	0.3	25	83	120
Guerra,Junior	15	R	30	a/a	CHW	83	4.80	1.50	11.6	4.7	8.5	1.8	1.2	31	71	58
Guerrero,Tayron	15	R	24	a/a	SD	56	3.11	1.31	4.82	4.8	8.4	1.8	0.4	28	76	86
Guerrieri,Taylor	15	R	23	aa	TAM	36	1.69	1.09	17.6	2.0	6.0	3.1	0.5	27	87	94
Guilmet,Preston	14	R	27	aaa	BAL	48	4.72	1.26	4.93	2.0	7.7	3.9	1.4	31	66	89
	15	R	28	aaa	MIL	50	2.60	1.20	5.19	2.8	6.4	2.3	0.2	29	78	86
Gunkel,Joe	15	R	24	aa	BAL	123	3.76	1.32	24.2	1.8	5.5	3.0	0.8	32	73	70
Gurka,Jason	15	L	27	aaa	COL	63	4.19	1.57	7.9	3.0	5.6	1.9	0.7	35	74	48
Gustave,Jandel	15	R	23	aa	HOU	59	2.45	1.40	5.38	3.8	6.6	1.7	0.3	31	83	69
Gutierrez,Juan	15	R	32	aaa	WAS	61	6.06	2.25	7.54	4.3	5.3	1.2	0.6	43	72	18
Hader,Joshua	14	L	20	aa	HOU	20	6.61	1.58	17.6	6.7	9.9	1.5	0.9	30	57	73
	15	L	21	aa	MIL	104	4.11	1.38	18.2	3.3	9.2	2.8	1.0	33	73	85
Hagens,Bradin	14	R	25	aa	ARI	135	4.40	1.51	20.9	3.8	3.7	1.0	0.6	30	71	25
	15	R	26	a/a	TAM	134	4.01	1.47	19.1	3.7	5.2	1.4	0.4	31	72	49
Hald,Kyle	14	L	25	aa	STL	137	4.31	1.52	24.8	3.0	5.5	1.8	1.1	32	75	34
	15	L	26	a/a	STL	124	5.81	1.63	21.2	2.7	4.6	1.7	0.9	35	65	26
Hale,David	15	R	28	aaa	COL	50	9.09	2.23	23	4.2	4.9	1.1	1.0	42	58	1
Haley,Justin	14	R	23	aa	BOS	38	1.52	1.38	26.3	3.9	6.6	1.7	0.5	30	92	64
	15	R	24	aa	BOS	124	6.61	1.80	21.2	3.9	5.7	1.5	0.6	37	61	38
Haley,Trey	14	R	24	aa	CLE	17	8.09	2.06	5.42	6.9	6.8	1.0	2.2	34	64	-11
	15	R	25	aaa	CLE	55	3.36	1.69	5.77	5.6	8.1	1.5	0.0	36	78	79
Hall,Brooks	14	R	24	aa	MIL	26	3.32	1.35	21.7	2.5	4.7	1.9	0.4	31	75	55
	15	R	25	aa	MIL	106	6.43	1.60	18.8	2.8	5.6	2.0	1.3	34	61	27
Hall,Cody	15	R	27	aaa	SF	68	3.82	1.54	6.86	3.6	5.7	1.6	0.3	34	74	56
Hall,Kris	15	R	24	a/a	OAK	74	3.05	1.72	8.61	7.1	7.6	1.1	0.6	31	83	56
Hamburger,Mark	14	R	27	a/a	MIN	71	4.85	1.60	14.2	3.7	5.2	1.4	0.4	34	68	44
	15	R	28	aaa	MIN	68	4.98	1.86	7.07	3.4	6.1	1.8	0.5	40	72	45
Hancock,Justin	14	R	24	aa	SD	59	4.63	1.70	20.5	3.5	5.4	1.6	0.8	36	74	33
	15	R	25	a/a	SD	131	3.66	1.58	24	3.6	5.6	1.6	0.6	34	77	45
Hand,Donovan	14	R	28	aaa	MIL	80	6.66	1.89	7.98	2.8	6.3	2.2	1.3	40	66	28
	15	R	29	aaa	CIN	97	7.28	1.81	13.6	2.0	3.8	1.9	1.7	37	62	-6
Hankins,Derek	14	R	31	aaa	DET	152	7.23	1.95	25.9	2.6	3.0	1.1	1.2	38	63	-14
	15	R	32	a/a	DET	99	7.89	2.01	24	3.5	4.2	1.2	1.8	38	63	-20
Hansen,Kyle	15	R	24	aa	CHW	67	5.18	1.67	7.03	4.7	5.3	1.1	0.6	33	68	36
Hanson,Tommy	14	R	28	aaa	CHW	50	7.09	1.82	23	5.8	4.5	0.8	2.0	29	64	-19
	15	R	29	aaa	SF	53	6.48	1.96	23	4.8	5.1	1.1	1.3	36	69	0
Harlan,Thomas	14	L	24	aa	PIT	61	3.92	1.34	22.9	2.3	3.0	1.3	0.8	29	72	22
	15	L	25	aa	PIT	87	4.26	1.48	9.82	2.4	5.4	2.3	0.6	34	71	58
Harper,Bryan	14	L	25	aa	WAS	15	5.06	1.94	6.08	4.4	5.1	1.2	0.6	38	73	25
	15	L	26	aa	WAS	46	4.07	1.46	5.14	4.1	5.2	1.3	1.1	28	76	26
Harper,Ryne	14	R	25	aa	ATL	77	3.16	1.39	6.73	3.0	9.1	3.1	0.6	36	79	101
	15	R	26	aa	ATL	34	2.54	1.19	5.86	3.2	8.9	2.7	0.3	30	79	111
Harrison,Matt	14	L	29	aa	TEX	16	2.45	1.31	22	2.7	4.1	1.5	0.0	30	79	58
	15	L	30	a/a	TEX	35	8.65	2.15	28.7	4.6	4.0	0.9	0.0	41	55	23
Hatley,Marcus	15	R	27	aaa	STL	49	3.72	1.67	6.07	3.6	4.4	1.2	0.6	34	78	27
Hauschild,Michae	14	R	24	aa	HOU	99	4.83	1.33	20.5	2.3	6.8	3.0	0.5	33	62	88
	15	R	25	a/a	HOU	138	3.82	1.40	23.3	2.3	6.3	2.8	0.6	34	73	76
Haviland,Shawn	14	R	29	aa	OAK	146	4.92	1.57	25.7	3.5	4.3	1.2	0.9	32	70	20
	15	R	30	aaa	BOS	114	6.78	1.87	21.4	2.8	4.7	1.7	1.2	38	64	11
Hayes,Drew	14	R	27	aa	CIN	71	5.06	1.67	6.16	5.3	7.7	1.5	0.7	34	69	56
	15	R	28	a/a	CIN	64	3.86	1.87	6.35	5.2	6.8	1.3	0.4	38	79	47

PITCHER	yr	t	age	lvl	org	ip	era	whip	bf/g	ctl	dom	cmd	hr/9	h%	s%	bpv
Haynes,Kyle	15	R	24	a/a	NYY	116	4.94	1.70	15.5	4.1	5.7	1.4	0.8	35	71	35
Head,Louis	14	R	24	aa	CLE	36	3.43	1.53	5.45	3.9	8.2	2.1	0.7	35	79	70
	15	R	25	aa	CLE	60	5.59	1.71	5.82	5.3	7.3	1.4	0.4	35	65	59
Healy,Tucker	15	R	25	aa	OAK	55	2.13	1.12	4.85	4.1	6.9	1.7	0.0	24	79	93
Heaney,Andrew	14	L	23	a/a	MIA	137	3.48	1.20	23	2.3	7.9	3.4	0.6	31	72	107
	15	L	24	aaa	LAA	78	4.50	1.53	24.3	2.5	7.2	2.9	0.2	38	68	92
Hembree,Heath	14	R	25	aaa	BOS	46	4.91	1.62	4.25	3.7	8.6	2.3	1.1	37	72	62
	15	R	26	aaa	BOS	32	3.40	1.33	4.53	3.3	7.2	2.1	0.4	31	74	81
Henderson,Jim	15	R	33	a/a	MIL	34	5.66	2.00	4.92	6.2	6.0	1.0	1.6	34	75	-1
Hensley,Steven	14	R	28	aa	BAL	60	2.67	1.44	6.95	4.4	6.4	1.5	0.8	29	85	50
	15	R	29	aaa	LAA	45	7.30	2.09	8.43	3.9	6.4	1.7	1.6	41	67	6
Hernandez,Carlos	14	L	27	aa	COL	124	3.99	1.59	19.6	1.8	4.9	2.8	0.7	37	76	57
	15	L	28	a/a	COL	41	7.30	1.97	24.3	1.8	3.9	2.1	2.8	38	70	-37
Hernandez,Jefri	15	R	24	aa	TEX	32	5.02	1.85	6.04	4.0	6.9	1.7	0.3	40	71	56
Hernandez,Moise	14	R	30	aa	SEA	61	7.66	2.02	9.46	3.7	4.0	1.1	1.0	39	61	0
	15	R	31	aa	SEA	98	7.72	2.08	16	3.8	4.1	1.1	0.8	40	61	5
Herrera,Ronald	15	R	20	aa	SD	44	4.82	1.46	23.4	2.7	6.6	2.4	0.8	34	67	64
Herrmann,Frank	14	R	30	aaa	CLE	30	8.14	2.07	5.18	6.3	6.8	1.1	2.0	36	63	-8
	15	R	31	aaa	PIT	53	5.35	1.87	5.62	1.9	6.4	3.3	0.8	43	71	67
Hessler,Keith	15	L	26	a/a	ARI	44	3.41	1.13	4.27	2.7	7.3	2.7	0.9	26	73	81
Heyer,Kurt	14	R	23	a/a	STL	152	5.10	1.43	23.1	2.6	5.4	2.1	1.1	31	66	41
	15	R	24	a/a	STL	84	4.48	1.55	8.91	2.4	5.0	2.1	0.6	35	71	48
Hill,Rich	14	L	34	aaa	NYY	43	3.87	1.42	6.28	4.4	8.5	1.9	0.0	33	70	97
	15	L	35	aaa	BOS	54	4.59	1.74	8.21	6.3	7.4	1.2	0.9	32	75	42
Hill,Taylor	14	R	25	aaa	WAS	144	3.28	1.26	23.5	1.5	4.2	2.8	1.0	30	78	54
	15	R	26	aaa	WAS	119	7.35	2.03	26.2	2.4	4.1	1.7	0.8	41	63	14
Hinojosa,Dalier	15	R	29	aaa	PHI	55	5.14	1.73	8.63	4.2	6.6	1.6	0.7	36	70	45
Hively,RJ	14	R	26	aa	ARI	62	3.64	1.62	5.01	4.5	6.2	1.4	0.2	34	76	58
	15	R	27	a/a	ARI	55	5.82	1.91	9.63	4.3	6.0	1.4	0.6	39	68	35
Hoffman,Jeff	15	R	22	aa	COL	48	4.12	1.21	21.5	2.5	5.8	2.3	0.9	28	68	63
Holmberg,David	14	L	23	aaa	CIN	93	4.90	1.72	23.4	3.0	4.7	1.6	0.4	37	70	38
	15	L	24	aaa	CIN	120	5.75	1.81	26.5	3.3	4.6	1.4	1.5	36	71	-2
Holmes,Brian	15	L	24	aa	HOU	71	5.91	1.76	20.3	4.0	7.6	1.9	1.6	37	70	30
Horst,Jeremy	14	L	29	aaa	PHI	63	5.12	1.63	6.27	4.9	6.1	1.2	0.7	32	68	41
	15	L	30	a/a	MIL	60	3.37	1.89	5.57	5.8	6.8	1.2	1.1	35	86	25
House,Austin	15	R	24	aa	COL	52	6.29	2.22	5.07	3.5	5.3	1.5	0.3	45	69	32
Houser,Adrian	15	R	22	aa	MIL	70	6.14	1.57	22.1	3.0	6.2	2.1	1.9	33	65	18
Hoyt,James	14	R	28	a/a	ATL	60	3.95	1.62	5.09	4.0	9.1	2.3	0.8	38	77	74
	15	R	29	aaa	HOU	49	4.10	1.43	4.43	2.2	9.3	4.3	0.2	39	69	135
Huchingson,Chas	14	L	25	aa	NYM	29	3.17	1.31	4.79	4.7	6.8	1.4	0.6	26	77	65
	15	L	26	a/a	NYM	56	4.68	1.77	5.07	6.4	6.7	1.0	0.3	33	72	52
Huff,David	15	L	31	aaa	LA	57	2.71	1.21	10.1	1.3	5.1	3.9	0.8	30	81	89
Hunter,Kyle	14	L	25	aa	SEA	75	3.80	1.50	8.49	2.5	4.6	1.9	1.0	33	77	33
	15	L	26	aa	SEA	44	3.55	1.42	7.84	4.0	4.7	1.2	0.5	29	75	42
Huntzinger,Brock	14	R	26	aaa	BAL	81	3.55	1.34	7.16	2.9	6.6	2.3	1.1	30	77	59
	15	R	27	aaa	OAK	56	6.05	1.90	6.18	6.5	6.6	1.0	1.6	32	71	9
Hurlbut,David	15	L	26	a/a	MIN	107	4.65	1.69	26.8	3.2	4.0	1.2	0.4	35	71	29
Hursh,Jason	15	R	24	a/a	ATL	97	6.82	1.99	13.8	3.6	5.2	1.4	0.5	41	64	28
Hyatt,Nate	15	R	25	aa	LAA	43	6.59	2.16	5.91	8.1	7.3	0.9	0.7	37	69	36
Hynes,Colt	14	L	29	aaa	TOR	62	5.34	1.53	5.47	1.9	5.9	3.1	1.5	35	68	48
	15	L	30	a/a	TOR	48	5.37	1.77	4.66	4.2	5.6	1.3	0.6	36	69	36
Ibarra,Edgar	15	L	26	aaa	LAA	61	5.41	1.72	5.68	4.4	7.8	1.8	0.6	37	68	61
Infante,Gregory	14	R	27	a/a	TOR	46	2.68	1.27	4.62	3.9	6.8	1.7	0.0	29	76	87
	15	R	28	a/a	TOR	57	4.85	2.14	5.51	7.3	6.3	0.9	0.7	37	78	25
Inman,Jeffrey	14	R	27	aa	PIT	25	1.23	1.29	5.63	4.0	4.8	1.2	0.0	27	89	64
	15	R	28	a/a	PIT	38	3.76	1.56	5.33	2.3	5.8	2.5	0.0	38	73	79
Irwin,Phillip	14	R	27	aaa	TEX	73	5.91	1.77	16	4.6	6.9	1.5	0.6	37	65	50
	15	R	28	a/a	TEX	32	8.01	2.01	19.1	3.5	6.6	1.9	1.4	41	61	19
Isler,Zach	15	R	25	a/a	CHW	36	5.89	1.49	6.21	2.1	3.3	1.6	1.7	30	64	-5
Jackson,Jay	15	R	28	a/a	SD	74	2.69	1.24	5.59	2.3	8.2	3.6	0.2	33	78	120
Jackson,Luke	14	R	23	a/a	TEX	123	6.29	1.47	20.4	3.8	7.6	2.0	1.2	32	58	53
	15	R	24	aaa	TEX	66	5.47	1.67	7.63	5.0	8.8	1.8	0.5	37	66	74
Janas,Stephen	15	R	23	aa	ATL	68	6.22	1.74	24	2.7	3.9	1.4	0.2	37	61	36
Jankowski,Jordan	14	R	25	aa	HOU	108	4.12	1.20	14.5	2.2	8.4	3.8	1.1	31	69	102
	15	R	26	aaa	HOU	62	3.49	1.55	4.95	4.9	9.1	1.8	0.0	36	75	96
Jaye,Myles	14	R	23	aa	CHW	132	6.06	1.67	24.7	3.9	4.3	1.1	0.8	33	63	19
	15	R	24	aa	CHW	148	4.55	1.51	24.6	3.3	5.4	1.6	0.7	32	70	43
Jenkins,Chad	14	R	27	aaa	TOR	44	6.58	1.55	9.16	2.1	4.4	2.1	1.4	33	59	20
	15	R	28	aaa	TOR	94	4.81	1.81	10.6	3.0	4.6	1.5	0.8	37	74	22
Jenkins,Tyrell	15	R	23	a/a	ATL	138	4.11	1.55	24.2	4.1	5.1	1.2	0.5	31	73	40
Jensen,Chris	14	R	24	aa	OAK	160	3.58	1.43	26.2	3.5	4.4	1.2	0.2	30	73	49
	15	R	25	aa	OAK	166	5.31	1.61	26.3	3.4	3.9	1.1	0.9	32	68	15
Jensen,Michael	15	R	25	aa	CHC	32	2.75	1.60	6.49	4.8	6.7	1.4	0.0	34	81	70
Jerez,Williams	15	L	23	aa	BOS	37	4.59	1.56	7.36	4.3	6.3	1.5	0.5	33	70	53
Jimenez,Cesar	14	L	30	aaa	PHI	50	1.89	1.22	5.28	3.1	6.2	2.0	0.0	29	83	87
	15	L	31	aaa	PHI	57	4.99	1.78	6.43	3.3	4.8	1.4	0.9	36	73	21
Johnson,Brian	15	L	25	aaa	BOS	96	3.71	1.38	22.4	3.4	6.8	2.0	0.7	31	74	64
Johnson,Cole	14	R	26	aa	MIN	73	4.84	1.49	6.39	2.7	7.9	2.9	0.8	36	68	80
	15	R	27	a/a	MIN	52	4.43	1.72	6.74	3.8	6.3	1.6	0.6	37	74	46
Johnson,DJ	15	R	26	aa	MIN	50	5.89	1.82	6.11	4.8	5.7	1.2	0.4	36	66	40
Johnson,Erik	14	R	25	aaa	CHW	106	7.25	1.98	25.3	4.9	4.5	0.9	1.1	36	63	2
	15	R	26	aaa	CHW	133	3.30	1.41	24.4	3.3	7.5	2.2	0.5	33	77	79
Johnson,Hobbs	15	L	24	aa	MIL	117	5.47	1.73	21.3	6.8	6.1	0.9	0.6	30	67	41
Johnson,Jacob	15	R	25	a/a	CIN	80	6.99	1.90	10.7	3.8	4.7	1.3	1.3	37	64	0
Johnson,Jeff	15	R	25	aa	CLE	51	1.46	1.06	3.91	3.6	8.1	2.3	0.0	26	85	114
Johnson,Pierce	14	R	23	aa	CHC	92	2.93	1.33	21.2	5.4	7.6	1.4	0.8	25	81	64
	15	R	24	aa	CHC	95	2.52	1.29	24.4	3.2	5.8	1.8	0.4	29	81	66
Johnson,Stephen	15	R	24	aa	CIN	67	3.89	1.39	5.62	4.5	9.3	2.0	0.4	32	71	94
Johnson,Steve	14	R	27	aaa	BAL	38	8.58	2.32	15	7.5	5.8	0.8	2.6	36	67	-41
	15	R	28	aaa	BAL	55	3.90	1.50	7.39	3.4	8.3	2.5	0.6	36	74	83
Jokisch,Eric	14	L	25	aaa	CHC	158	4.33	1.36	25.5	1.9	6.6	3.5	0.8	34	69	88
	15	L	26	aaa	CHC	70	5.32	1.74	22.8	3.2	4.1	1.3	0.8	35	70	15
Jones,Chris	14	L	26	aaa	BAL	120	4.27	1.53	14.9	2.8	5.0	1.8	0.4	34	71	52
	15	L	27	aaa	BAL	150	4.86	1.71	22.7	2.2	4.8	2.2	1.5	36	76	18
Jones,Tyler	15	R	26	aa	ATL	44	4.17	1.69	5.08	4.1	8.4	2.1	0.0	39	73	87
Jordan,Taylor	14	R	25	aaa	WAS	31	4.74	1.41	21.8	2.3	6.4	2.8	0.9	33	67	67
	15	R	26	aaa	WAS	104	4.15	1.43	23.2	2.6	4.1	1.6	0.4	32	70	43
Joseph,Jonathan	15	R	27	aa	OAK	91	4.60	1.54	12.4	3.0	5.6	1.9	1.1	33	73	34
Jungmann,Taylor	15	R	26	aaa	MIL	59	7.38	1.72	24.5	4.7	6.6	1.4	0.4	36	54	54
Jurrjens,Jair	14	R	28	aaa	COL	81	5.56	1.79	26.8	3.4	4.0	1.2	1.0	35	70	7
	15	R	29	aaa	COL	71	9.61	2.34	21.4	3.4	3.5	1.1	1.7	42	59	-34
Kasparek,Kenn	14	R	29	a/a	PIT	49	3.06	1.29	5.63	1.5	5.4	3.6	0.4	33	76	95
	15	R	30	a/a	BAL	52	9.02	2.14	6.79	3.1	5.8	1.9	1.7	42	58	0
Kehrt,Jeremy	14	R	29	a/a	LA	78	4.71	1.69	14.1	3.0	3.7	1.2	0.5	35	72	22
	15	R	30	aa	LA	120	4.87	1.60	24	2.3	5.3	2.3	0.7	36	70	49
Kelly,Casey	15	R	26	a/a	SD	96	5.61	1.71	14.5	3.7	5.5	1.5	0.6	36	66	38
Kelly,Ryan	14	R	27	aa	ATL	28	4.11	1.19	5.1	3.5	9.0	2.6	1.1	27	69	86
	15	R	28	a/a	ATL	47	1.10	1.03	4.41	2.9	7.3	2.5	0.0	26	88	112
Kensing,Logan	14	R	32	aaa	SEA	88	4.09	1.55	7.84	3.5	6.1	1.8	0.5	34	73	56
	15	R	33	aaa	SEA	32	2.47	1.37	7.14	2.8	5.3	1.9	0.3	32	82	63
Kiekhefer,Dean	14	L	25	a/a	STL	71	3.19	1.12	5.11	0.8	6.3	8.4	1.0	30	76	183
	15	L	26	aaa	STL	60	2.79	1.44	5.09	1.1	4.3	4.1	0.8	35	83	81
Kingham,Nick	14	R	23	a/a	PIT	159	3.51	1.25	24.9	2.7	5.4	2.0	0.4	29	72	66
	15	R	24	aaa	PIT	31	5.43	1.51	22.6	2.0	7.3	3.7	0.8	37	64	88
Kirkman,Michael	14	L	28	aaa	TEX	54	5.35	1.69	6.81	5.2	7.6	1.5	1.2	33	70	40
	15	L	29	aaa	MIL	32	3.49	1.73	4.42	8.9	7.2	0.8	0.4	26	80	63
Kirsch,Chris	15	L	24	aa	TAM	55	6.56	1.73	22.9	3.9	6.2	1.6	0.5	37	60	48
Kittredge,Andrew	15	R	25	a/a	SEA	75	4.76	1.49	8.99	3.3	6.0	1.8	0.7	33	68	51
Klein,Phil	14	R	25	a/a	TEX	52	0.63	0.91	5.84	3.7	9.7	2.6	0.0	22	92	138
	15	R	26	aaa	TEX	64	3.90	1.42	15	4.2	6.4	1.5	0.3	30	71	65
Klimesh,Bennett	14	R	24	aa	CIN	16	7.26	1.66	4.78	4.0	11.5	2.9	0.7	43	54	104
	15	R	25	a/a	CIN	31	6.96	2.17	5.58	9.9	6.6	0.7	0.9	32	67	28
Kline,Branden	14	R	23	aa	BAL	17	6.81	1.86	26	5.8	4.1	0.7	0.6	33	62	15
	15	R	24	aa	BAL	39	4.93	1.62	21.8	4.7	5.1	1.1	1.2	30	72	15
Knigge,Tyler	14	R	26	a/a	PHI	76	4.14	1.41	7.15	2.7	4.5	1.6	0.3	32	69	52
	15	R	27	a/a	SEA	62	5.37	1.77	6.44	3.8	5.1	1.4	0.5	37	68	36
Knudson,Guido	15	R	26	a/a	DET	60	3.33	1.44	6.36	4.8	6.8	1.4	0.5	29	78	61
Koch,Matt	15	R	25	aa	ARI	96	4.38	1.48	11.4	1.9	4.7	2.4	0.6	34	71	53
Kohlscheen,Steph	14	R	26	a/a	SD	70	2.40	1.17	5.5	1.4	7.3	5.0	0.7	32	83	130
	15	R	27	a/a	SD	77	4.07	1.55	7.64	3.1	5.9	1.9	0.6	34	74	54
Kolarek,Adam	14	L	25	a/a	NYM	56	6.20	1.83	5.46	3.2	5.8	1.8	0.3	40	64	50
	15	L	26	aa	NYM	67	5.56	1.51	5.69	4.0	6.7	1.7	0.6	32	62	56
Korecky,Bobby	14	R	35	aaa	TOR	64	2.91	1.34	4.84	3.0	6.3	2.1	0.6	31	80	66
	15	R	36	aaa	TOR	48	6.22	2.17	5.48	3.3	5.0	1.5	0.9	43	72	11
Kraus,Kyle	15	R	25	a/a	BOS	52	6.02	1.53	14.1	1.9	3.8	1.9	1.4	33	63	12
Krol,Ian	15	L	24	aaa	DET	31	2.80	1.22	4.52	3.9	7.7	2.0	0.0	29	74	99
Kubitza,Austin	15	R	24	aa	DET	134	7.34	2.09	24.3	3.4	5.1	1.5	0.5	42	63	27
Kuchno,John	15	R	24	aa	PIT	68	3.96	1.39	7.13	2.9	3.4	1.2	0.9	28	74	16
Kuhl,Chad	15	R	23	aa	PIT	153	2.78	1.22	23.7	2.2	4.8	2.2	0.5	29	78	63
Kurcz,Aaron	15	R	25	aaa	OAK	59	4.58	1.84	5.61	5.9	8.4	1.4	0.6	37	75	57
Laffey,Aaron	14	L	29	aaa	WAS	147	4.69	1.64	26.2	2.4	4.0	1.7	0.6	35	71	32
	15	L	30	aaa	COL	90	5.51	2.07	16.3	4.9	4.4	0.9	1.0	38	75	-1
LaFromboise,Rob	14	L	28	aaa	PIT	57	5.26	1.86	4.23	3.4	5.6	1.6	0.6	39	71	36
	15	L	29	aaa	PIT	54	4.20	1.43	4.28	3.8	6.1	1.6	0.9	30	72	46
Lail,Brady	15	R	22	a/a	NYY	143	3.93	1.45	22.7	2.9	4.2	1.5	0.5	31	73	39
Lamb,Christopher	15	L	25	aa	OAK	34	11.66	2.40	12.6	7.3	5.7	0.8	1.7	39	50	-18
Lamb,John	14	L	24	aaa	KC	138	4.30	1.57	22.5	4.3	6.8	1.6	1.1	32	76	40
	15	L	25	aaa	CIN	111	3.61	1.41	23.6	3.2	8.1	2.5	0.8	33	77	76
Lamb,Will	14	L	24	aa	TEX	33	1.42	1.51	5.5	7.7	7.5	1.0	0.4	24	92	72
	15	L	25	aa	TEX	57	5.55	1.73	5.51	4.4	6.5	1.5	0.5	36	67	47
Lambson,Mitchell	14	L	24	aa	HOU	33	1.53	1.00	5.48	1.4	8.2	6.0	1.2	27	95	149
	15	L	25	a/a	ATL	57	3.17	1.38	6.01	3.4	7.0	2.0	0.4	32	77	76
Lamm,Mark	14	R	26	aaa	ATL	27	6.74	2.15	8.49	6.1	6.5	1.1	0.7	40	67	28
	15	R	27	aa	ATL	43	4.07	1.76	6.79	4.7	3.9	0.8	0.3	34	75	27
Landazuri,Stephe	14	R	22	aa	SEA	96	4.75	1.26	20.6	3.4	6.6	2.0	1.1	27	65	54
	15	R	23	a/a	SEA	127	6.53	1.72	22.1	4.0	5.1	1.3	0.4	35	59	38
Lane,Jason	14	L	38	aaa	SD	150	4.16	1.49	26.9	1.5	3.6	2.4	0.8	34	73	39
	15	L	39	aaa	SD	164	5.94	1.78	26.9	2.6	2.9	1.1	1.4	35	69	-14
Lannan,John	14	L	30	aaa	NYM	35	6.18	1.97	20.7	3.4	3.8	1.1	1.4	37	71	-12
	15	L	31	aaa	COL	152	7.61	2.15	29	2.7	3.5	1.3	1.0	42	64	-5
Lara,Braulio A.	14	L	26	a/a	TAM	58	7.04	1.72	5.82	5.0	7.2	1.4	0.7	35	57	50
	15	L	27	a/a	SF	50	7.33	1.99	7.56	3.9	6.5	1.6	0.7	41	61	37
Lara,Confesor	15	R	25	aa	DET	42	6.05	1.75	7.44	2.5	3.8	1.5	0.8	37	65	17
Lara,Rainy	14	R	23	aa	NYM	109	4.22	1.39	22.9	2.0	5.2	2.6	0.9	32	72	55
	15	R	24	aa	NYM	134	4.42	1.44	23.8	2.5	5.5	2.2	1.0	32	71	47
Lawrence,Casey	14	R	27	aa	TOR	151	5.03	1.57	25.6	1.9	4.4	2.3	0.7	35	68	43
	15	R	28	a/a	TOR	168	6.96	2.00	29.9	2.0	4.1	2.0	0.8	42	64	21
Leclerc,Jose	15	R	22	aa	TEX	103	6.65	1.75	18.1	6.3	7.3	1.2	0.7	33	61	47
Lecure,Sam	15	R	31	aaa	CIN	60	7.86	1.94	6.97	4.4	5.1	1.1	1.7	36	61	-10
Lee,Brett	15	L	25	aa	MIN	96	3.68	1.34	24.9	2.8	3.3	1.2	0.4	29	72	35
Lee,Chen	14	R	28	aaa	CLE	30	4.07	1.51	5.19	2.8	8.6	3.0	0.3	38	72	101
	15	R	29	aaa	CLE	58	5.01	1.55	5.31	2.9	7.6	2.7	0.6	37	67	77
Lee,Chris	15	L	23	aa	BAL	38	4.06	1.58	23.9	5.0	5.2	1.0	0.0	31	71	54
Lee,Jacob	15	R	26	aa	CLE	62	5.93	1.84	7.86	3.0	5.6	1.9	0.4	40	66	47
Lee,Michael	14	R	28	a/a	TOR	147	5.54	1.58	24.8	2.7	4.5	1.7	0.9	34	65	27
	15	R	29	aa	TOR	36	7.40	2.18	25.7	3.0	3.5	1.2	1.1	42	66	-12

PITCHER	yr	t	age	lvl	org	ip	era	whip	bf/g	ctl	dom	cmd	hr/9	h%	s%	bpv
Lee,Thomas	15	R	26	a/a	STL	142	3.92	1.35	21.1	2.0	4.2	2.1	0.9	31	73	40
Lee,Zach	14	R	23	aaa	LA	151	4.45	1.41	22.8	2.6	5.0	1.9	0.8	31	69	43
	15	R	24	aaa	LA	113	2.95	1.20	24	1.4	5.4	3.9	0.4	31	76	103
Leiter,Mark	15	R	24	aa	PHI	47	5.52	1.59	25.9	2.1	6.3	2.9	0.7	38	65	69
Leon,Arnold	14	R	26	aaa	OAK	145	5.00	1.62	23.8	3.1	6.3	2.1	0.6	36	69	55
	15	R	27	aaa	OAK	58	3.85	1.49	12.5	3.3	6.5	2.0	1.2	32	78	42
Leone,Dominic	15	R	24	a/a	ARI	37	5.60	1.43	5.83	4.0	7.3	1.8	0.5	31	59	68
Leroux,Chris	14	R	30	aaa	NYY	58	6.53	1.70	22	3.7	5.5	1.5	1.3	34	63	19
	15	R	31	a/a	PHI	85	5.23	1.59	12.5	3.4	5.0	1.5	0.9	33	67	30
Leyer,Robinson	15	R	22	aa	CHW	38	6.55	1.81	14.8	4.5	6.2	1.4	0.9	36	63	30
Light,Pat	15	R	24	a/a	BOS	63	5.25	1.61	5.9	5.8	7.9	1.4	0.8	31	68	55
Lincoln,Brad	14	R	29	aaa	PHI	123	6.57	1.79	21.1	4.8	6.2	1.3	1.2	35	64	22
	15	R	30	aaa	PIT	60	5.95	2.10	7.61	6.8	6.0	0.9	0.5	37	70	30
Lively,Ben	15	R	23	aa	PHI	144	4.67	1.55	25.1	2.8	6.1	2.2	1.0	35	72	46
Lively,Mitchell	15	R	30	aaa	WAS	35	3.52	1.28	7.97	4.0	5.3	1.3	0.3	26	71	59
Liz,Radhames	14	R	31	a/a	TOR	61	4.31	1.65	22.7	4.2	4.9	1.2	0.6	33	74	31
	15	R	32	aaa	PIT	64	1.99	1.34	16.7	3.8	7.3	1.9	0.0	31	83	90
Locante,William	15	L	25	aa	ARI	42	7.93	2.12	4.72	7.8	6.6	0.8	0.9	36	61	25
Loewen,Adam	14	L	30	aa	PHI	103	4.32	1.63	27	5.3	4.9	0.9	0.8	30	74	27
	15	L	31	a/a	PHI	58	2.69	1.61	6.46	6.6	8.6	1.3	0.4	31	84	74
Logan,Blake	15	R	23	a/a	MIA	75	4.98	1.53	10.2	3.3	7.6	2.3	1.2	34	70	55
Lollis,Matthew	14	R	24	aa	TAM	74	4.54	1.58	6.62	3.8	7.2	1.9	1.0	34	73	51
	15	R	25	aa	TAM	64	4.16	1.36	5.66	4.5	7.3	1.6	0.8	28	71	61
Long,Jaron	14	R	23	aa	NYY	69	2.87	1.21	25.3	1.5	5.5	3.7	0.3	31	76	102
	15	R	24	a/a	NYY	155	5.77	1.80	24.6	1.9	5.1	2.6	0.8	40	68	45
Long,Nathan	14	R	28	aa	OAK	150	3.95	1.57	23.5	3.2	5.7	1.8	1.1	33	78	35
	15	R	29	a/a	OAK	151	5.46	1.73	24.5	4.5	5.0	1.1	0.9	33	69	21
Lopez,Frank	15	L	21	aa	TEX	75	5.62	1.72	21.3	4.0	6.0	1.5	1.1	35	69	26
Lopez,Jorge	15	R	22	aa	MIL	143	3.10	1.29	24.6	3.6	7.6	2.1	0.8	29	79	71
Lopez,Yoan	15	R	22	aa	ARI	48	6.04	1.63	21.4	4.5	5.2	1.1	0.9	31	63	25
Lorenzen,Michael	15	R	23	aaa	CIN	43	2.45	1.14	28.4	1.8	3.5	2.0	0.9	26	84	40
Luetge,Lucas	14	L	27	aaa	SEA	62	3.58	1.48	6.38	3.8	8.1	2.1	0.8	34	78	70
	15	L	28	aaa	SEA	49	5.70	1.79	7.79	4.1	5.3	1.3	1.4	35	71	8
Lugo,Seth	15	R	26	a/a	NYM	136	4.32	1.40	23.9	2.3	6.9	3.0	0.8	34	70	77
Lujan,Matthew	15	L	27	aa	SF	108	4.50	1.81	24.9	4.1	5.8	1.4	0.5	37	75	38
Lyman,Scott	15	R	25	aa	MIA	79	7.87	2.05	25.7	4.8	4.7	1.0	0.6	39	59	17
Lyons,Tyler	14	L	26	a/a	STL	83	4.97	1.55	24.3	2.0	6.6	3.4	0.9	37	69	74
	15	L	27	aaa	STL	95	3.71	1.45	25.3	1.3	7.0	5.5	1.2	37	79	114
Magnifico,Damien	15	R	24	aa	MIL	54	1.68	1.44	5.44	4.3	5.4	1.3	0.8	28	93	40
Mahle,Greg	15	L	22	aa	LAA	35	3.74	1.40	4.81	2.7	8.1	3.0	0.3	36	72	103
Manaea,Sean	15	L	23	aa	OAK	50	2.46	1.34	22.9	3.7	9.3	2.5	0.6	32	84	95
Manship,Jeff	14	R	29	aaa	PHI	25	5.94	2.25	16.1	7.2	5.7	0.8	0.4	39	72	24
	15	R	30	aaa	CLE	32	2.97	1.42	5.84	3.0	6.6	2.2	1.2	31	84	50
Mantiply,Joe	15	L	24	a/a	DET	63	2.83	1.24	6.6	1.9	5.7	2.9	0.7	30	79	78
Marban,Jorge	15	R	27	a/a	BOS	46	1.70	1.54	6.69	5.9	5.9	1.0	0.0	29	88	63
Marcum,Shaun	14	R	33	aaa	CLE	15	3.00	1.26	7.82	3.8	4.4	1.1	0.7	25	78	40
	15	R	34	aaa	CLE	88	4.87	1.60	24.4	2.5	5.1	2.0	1.0	35	71	35
Marimon,Sugar	15	R	27	aaa	ATL	82	4.70	1.56	21	3.3	4.4	1.3	0.6	33	69	33
Marin,Terance	15	R	26	aaa	CHW	77	4.08	1.48	17.4	2.4	4.1	1.7	0.7	33	73	36
Marinez,Jhan	14	R	26	a/a	LA	40	6.41	1.82	5.67	6.4	8.2	1.3	1.0	34	65	46
	15	R	27	a/a	TAM	67	2.88	1.33	5.6	3.9	7.5	1.9	0.7	29	81	71
Mariot,Michael	14	R	26	aaa	KC	20	5.60	1.45	6.1	3.2	8.6	2.7	0.9	35	61	82
	15	R	27	aaa	KC	62	3.15	1.35	6.16	2.6	7.8	3.0	0.5	34	77	95
Markel,Parker	14	R	24	aa	TAM	17	4.25	1.67	4.68	4.7	6.4	1.4	0.0	35	72	64
	15	R	25	a/a	TAM	60	4.17	1.71	5.82	4.8	5.7	1.2	0.8	33	77	32
Marks,Justin	14	L	26	aaa	TEX	39	5.76	1.72	8.11	3.8	6.6	1.7	1.0	36	67	37
	15	L	27	aaa	ARI	109	6.05	1.71	17.6	4.0	5.4	1.3	1.0	34	65	23
Marmol,Carlos	15	R	33	aaa	CLE	31	3.03	1.86	5.18	9.2	10.4	1.1	0.4	33	84	84
Maronde,Nick	14	L	25	a/a	CLE	30	10.84	2.56	8.49	9.8	9.7	1.0	1.8	42	57	11
	15	L	26	a/a	CLE	92	6.57	1.95	12.5	3.5	7.4	2.1	1.2	42	67	35
Marshall,Brett	14	R	24	aaa	CIN	70	7.01	1.90	20.7	6.3	6.4	1.0	1.3	33	64	17
	15	R	25	aa	COL	42	8.41	1.77	27.3	3.5	5.2	1.5	1.1	36	51	20
Marshall,Evan	14	R	24	aaa	ARI	17	0.54	0.91	4.44	2.5	8.4	3.4	0.0	25	93	141
	15	R	25	aaa	ARI	32	6.58	1.95	4.98	3.4	5.6	1.7	0.3	41	64	44
Marte,Kelvin	14	L	27	a/a	SF	123	4.69	1.47	22	2.3	4.3	1.9	0.9	32	69	34
	15	L	28	aa	SF	130	3.82	1.58	22	3.3	4.1	1.2	0.4	33	75	34
Martin,Cody	14	R	25	aaa	ATL	156	3.92	1.45	24.7	3.2	6.9	2.1	1.0	32	76	56
	15	R	26	aaa	OAK	94	5.12	1.54	22.9	4.2	6.8	1.6	0.8	32	67	49
Martin,Ethan	14	R	25	aaa	PHI	48	4.89	1.57	7.22	4.1	7.0	1.7	0.4	34	68	64
	15	R	26	aa	PHI	52	3.77	1.37	10.3	2.8	4.5	1.6	0.6	30	73	42
Martin,Josh	15	R	26	aa	CLE	67	3.22	1.21	6.16	2.8	8.7	3.1	0.7	31	75	103
Martin,Kyle	15	R	24	aa	BOS	42	5.77	1.63	6.93	3.6	8.4	2.3	0.7	38	64	73
Martin,Rafael	14	R	30	a/a	WAS	54	1.87	1.05	5.77	2.1	7.4	3.5	0.2	29	82	122
	15	R	31	aaa	WAS	56	4.89	1.36	5.09	3.1	7.8	2.5	0.8	32	64	77
Martinez,David	14	R	27	aaa	HOU	83	6.35	1.69	17	3.3	5.4	1.6	0.6	36	60	40
	15	R	28	a/a	TEX	67	4.30	1.66	6.15	3.9	4.9	1.3	0.8	33	75	26
Martinez,Juancito	15	R	26	aa	MIA	39	6.99	1.93	5.74	7.6	3.3	0.4	0.7	29	62	7
Martinez,Nicholas	15	R	25	aaa	TEX	31	3.73	1.50	22.3	2.2	4.2	1.9	0.3	34	74	49
Mateo,Marcos	14	R	30	aaa	CHC	37	5.16	1.72	5.14	4.8	7.6	1.6	0.9	36	71	48
	15	R	31	aaa	SD	32	1.76	1.10	5.02	3.5	8.5	2.5	0.3	27	85	109
Mateo,Victor	14	R	25	aa	TAM	166	4.49	1.52	25.7	3.0	4.4	1.5	0.7	32	71	34
	15	R	26	a/a	ATL	148	4.69	1.63	24.3	3.7	4.0	1.1	0.6	33	71	23
Matz,Steven	14	L	23	aa	NYM	71	2.23	1.14	23.5	1.6	7.7	4.8	0.4	32	81	140
	15	L	24	a/a	NYM	102	2.10	1.08	23.3	2.8	7.9	2.8	0.5	27	83	102
Mayberry,Whit	15	R	25	aa	DET	36	3.85	1.82	9.37	1.9	5.9	3.1	0.9	41	81	57
Mayers,Mike	14	R	23	a/a	STL	81	3.26	1.47	24.9	2.5	5.2	2.1	0.4	34	78	58
	15	R	24	aa	STL	47	7.10	1.68	21	3.8	5.6	1.5	1.5	33	59	15
Mazzaro,Vin	15	R	29	aaa	ATL	47	4.01	1.72	7.57	3.9	6.0	1.5	0.0	37	74	61
Mazzoni,Cory	14	R	25	a/a	NYM	64	4.25	1.25	23.7	2.0	7.0	3.5	0.7	32	67	94
	15	R	26	aaa	SD	34	3.82	1.12	5.15	3.0	10.0	3.3	0.0	31	62	141
McBryde,Jeremy	15	R	28	aaa	LAA	64	4.86	1.58	4.52	3.1	7.5	2.4	0.4	38	68	79
McCarthy,Michael	14	R	27	a/a	BOS	101	6.56	1.55	15.7	2.2	4.9	2.2	1.4	34	59	26
	15	R	28	a/a	BOS	122	7.10	1.83	18.9	3.9	3.4	0.9	1.1	34	61	-6
McCormick,Phil	14	L	26	aa	SF	65	4.42	1.56	5.72	4.1	6.8	1.6	0.5	34	71	58
	15	L	27	aa	SF	57	2.89	1.75	4.52	3.9	4.7	1.2	0.0	36	82	45
McCoy,Patrick	14	L	26	a/a	DET	45	3.66	1.30	6.18	1.9	5.2	2.8	0.7	31	73	69
	15	L	27	a/a	BAL	69	6.19	1.98	8.12	3.6	5.1	1.4	1.0	40	69	13
McCullers,Lance	15	R	22	aa	HOU	32	0.63	0.97	17.3	3.8	12.0	3.1	0.3	26	96	151
McCutchen,Danie	14	R	32	aaa	CHW	86	9.68	2.02	19	2.8	5.7	2.0	3.7	37	59	-57
	15	R	33	aaa	SD	132	3.75	1.33	17.2	2.0	4.4	2.3	0.9	30	74	44
McFarland,Blake	14	R	26	aa	TOR	35	2.72	1.34	7.75	4.1	7.6	1.8	0.3	30	80	82
	15	R	27	a/a	TOR	58	3.03	1.17	5.01	1.8	9.1	5.0	0.9	32	78	136
McFarland,T.J.	14	L	25	aaa	BAL	24	4.34	1.34	20	3.0	7.5	2.5	0.0	34	64	100
	15	L	26	aaa	BAL	53	4.70	1.42	14	2.9	4.2	1.4	0.0	32	63	54
McGough,Scott	15	R	26	a/a	MIA	30	3.18	1.49	5.69	4.9	3.7	0.8	0.6	27	80	24
McGowan,Dustin	15	R	33	aaa	PHI	40	5.65	2.08	6.28	6.4	4.9	0.8	0.6	36	72	15
McGowin,Kyle	15	R	24	aa	LAA	154	5.58	1.46	24.4	2.9	6.2	2.1	1.0	33	62	49
McGregor,Scott	15	R	29	aaa	WAS	107	6.07	1.90	18.7	3.5	3.8	1.1	1.3	36	70	-7
McGuire,Deck	14	R	25	a/a	OAK	150	5.44	1.58	24.4	3.3	4.9	1.5	1.1	32	67	24
	15	R	26	a/a	LA	137	4.53	1.39	19.2	2.4	6.4	2.7	0.9	33	68	67
McKinney,Brett	15	R	25	aa	PIT	30	8.78	2.07	6.12	4.0	7.2	1.8	1.4	42	57	22
McMyne,Kyle	15	R	26	aa	CIN	62	3.79	1.79	5.47	5.4	3.7	0.7	0.4	32	79	18
Medina,Jhondanie	15	R	22	aa	PIT	62	3.04	1.28	5.65	4.9	5.3	1.1	0.2	24	75	61
Medina,Yoervis	15	R	27	aaa	CHC	40	7.00	1.86	5.85	5.4	7.0	1.3	1.0	36	62	32
Medlen,Kris	15	R	30	a/a	KC	30	5.03	1.47	21.7	1.7	4.2	2.4	2.9	29	80	-19
Meek,Evan	14	R	31	aaa	BAL	42	2.49	1.12	4.21	1.0	5.8	6.0	0.6	30	80	147
	15	R	32	aaa	WAS	38	3.27	1.71	5.69	5.5	5.6	1.0	0.3	33	80	45
Mejia,Adalberto	14	L	21	aa	SF	108	5.05	1.46	21	2.4	6.0	2.5	0.6	34	65	64
	15	L	22	aa	SF	51	3.13	1.24	17.4	3.3	5.8	1.7	0.3	28	74	69
Melville,Timothy	14	R	25	aa	KC	129	6.93	1.89	23.4	5.0	5.7	1.1	1.0	36	63	18
	15	R	26	aaa	DET	152	5.89	1.62	25	4.4	4.6	1.0	1.0	31	64	17
Mendez,Gilberto	15	R	23	aa	WAS	61	4.86	1.58	6.1	2.6	6.3	2.5	0.8	36	70	58
Mendez,Roman	14	R	24	aaa	TEX	31	4.41	1.76	5.74	3.4	7.0	2.1	1.2	38	78	37
	15	R	25	aaa	TEX	36	3.57	1.36	4.97	2.4	6.7	2.7	1.5	31	81	52
Mendoza,Francis	14	R	27	aa	TEX	65	3.65	1.52	6.27	4.8	7.0	1.5	1.1	30	80	41
	15	R	28	a/a	TEX	67	2.90	1.70	6.85	4.7	5.5	1.2	0.0	35	81	53
Mercedes,Melvin	14	R	24	aaa	DET	60	6.12	1.62	5.83	2.4	3.7	1.5	1.3	33	64	4
	15	R	25	a/a	DET	60	6.28	1.92	7.49	3.7	6.0	1.6	0.5	40	66	39
Mercedes,Simon	15	R	23	aa	BOS	79	6.13	1.76	9.82	4.5	6.0	1.3	1.0	35	65	28
Merritt,Ryan	15	L	23	a/a	CLE	171	4.77	1.42	26.8	1.2	4.8	4.0	0.6	35	66	89
Meyer,Alex	14	R	24	aaa	MIN	130	4.42	1.56	21.2	4.5	8.6	1.9	0.7	34	72	70
	15	R	25	aaa	MIN	92	6.76	1.97	11.6	5.2	7.7	1.5	0.5	41	64	52
Miller,Adam	15	R	26	aa	ARI	56	4.02	1.91	5.33	4.9	8.0	1.6	0.0	41	77	72
Miller,Jim	14	R	32	aaa	NYY	57	4.36	1.67	7.15	3.6	6.9	1.9	0.6	37	74	55
	15	R	33	aaa	TAM	74	4.04	1.44	7.2	1.7	5.9	3.5	1.4	34	77	59
Miller,Justin	14	R	27	aaa	DET	45	2.41	1.14	4.66	2.6	5.9	2.2	0.5	27	80	76
	15	R	28	a/a	COL	38	2.84	1.33	5.09	3.3	7.4	2.2	0.7	31	81	73
Miller,Trevor	14	R	23	a/a	SEA	114	4.64	1.39	14.6	3.2	6.2	1.9	0.4	32	65	67
	15	R	24	aa	SEA	46	6.51	1.84	8.3	3.3	4.6	1.4	1.2	37	66	7
Mills,Brad	14	L	29	aaa	TOR	107	2.94	1.22	21.7	2.3	6.5	2.9	0.8	30	79	79
	15	L	30	aaa	OAK	137	6.25	1.77	26.3	4.3	4.5	1.0	0.9	34	64	13
Milner,Hoby	14	L	23	aa	PHI	143	4.76	1.52	24.9	3.5	4.7	1.3	1.7	29	75	2
	15	L	24	aa	PHI	61	4.25	1.42	8.92	2.5	5.1	2.0	1.0	31	73	39
Milone,Tommy	14	L	27	aaa	MIN	28	6.88	1.97	26.8	3.9	4.9	1.3	1.8	37	68	-14
	15	L	28	aaa	MIN	39	1.05	0.97	29.3	0.8	8.1	9.8	0.6	30	95	244
Minaya,Juan	15	R	25	a/a	HOU	55	3.16	1.41	6.6	3.5	8.1	2.3	0.4	34	77	89
Miranda,Ariel	15	L	26	aa	BAL	45	5.06	1.60	24.8	4.1	6.5	1.6	0.3	35	66	61
Misch,Pat	15	L	34	aaa	MIA	72	4.83	1.62	20	3.5	3.6	1.0	0.6	33	70	20
Mitchell,Bryan	14	R	23	a/a	NYY	103	5.17	1.65	20	4.0	7.0	1.7	1.2	35	71	38
	15	R	24	aaa	NYY	75	4.18	1.57	22	4.9	6.2	1.3	0.2	32	71	60
Mizenko,Tyler	15	R	25	aa	SF	50	2.69	1.57	5.93	2.6	4.1	1.6	0.4	34	83	39
Molleken,Dustin	14	R	30	aaa	MIL	74	6.43	1.79	6.35	5.0	8.1	1.6	1.1	37	65	43
	15	R	31	aaa	CLE	53	4.85	1.78	6.05	5.4	6.7	1.2	0.9	34	74	34
Montas,Frankie	15	R	22	aa	CHW	112	3.95	1.43	20.7	4.3	7.6	1.8	0.3	32	71	78
Montgomery,Mark	14	R	24	a/a	NYY	51	2.54	1.30	5.42	4.7	7.4	1.6	0.7	26	83	70
	15	R	25	a/a	NYY	51	3.70	1.20	4.43	3.4	7.8	2.3	0.5	28	69	90
Montgomery,Mich	14	L	25	aaa	TAM	126	5.32	1.50	21.8	3.5	5.8	1.6	0.7	32	64	47
	15	L	26	aaa	SEA	65	4.23	1.26	24.2	2.4	6.5	2.7	0.4	31	65	87
Moore,Matt	15	L	26	aaa	TAM	40	4.59	1.39	24.2	2.9	10.5	3.6	1.4	35	72	96
Morales,Andrew	15	R	22	aa	STL	130	5.19	1.70	22.6	2.9	5.0	1.7	1.1	36	71	23
Moran,Brian	15	L	27	aa	SEA	30	4.54	1.77	5.57	5.3	6.9	1.3	0.7	35	75	44
Moreno,Diego	15	R	29	aaa	NYY	54	3.26	1.36	8.63	3.3	5.3	1.6	0.3	30	75	61
Morey,Robert	14	R	26	a/a	MIA	57	5.72	2.02	18.4	4.4	4.3	1.0	0.5	39	71	15
	15	R	27	aaa	MIA	87	6.39	1.91	18.7	3.8	4.2	1.1	0.8	37	66	11
Morgan,Adam	15	L	25	aaa	PHI	68	5.93	1.84	24.5	3.8	3.7	1.0	1.2	35	69	-5
Morimando,Shaw	14	L	22	aa	CLE	56	4.24	1.50	24.4	2.5	5.3	2.1	0.3	35	70	61
	15	L	23	aa	CLE	159	4.23	1.48	24.4	3.8	6.3	1.7	0.6	32	72	54
Morris,AJ	14	R	28	a/a	PIT	97	3.49	1.47	19.7	2.7	4.6	1.7	0.5	32	77	43
	15	R	29	aaa	PIT	85	3.44	1.48	8.27	2.6	5.5	2.1	0.3	34	76	62
Morris,Elliot	15	R	23	aa	SD	102	5.44	1.66	21.7	3.9	5.6	1.4	0.5	35	66	42
Morrow,Bryce	14	R	26	aa	SD	89	3.68	1.33	23.1	2.0	5.7	2.9	0.7	32	73	73
	15	R	27	a/a	SD	75	5.07	1.61	17.6	2.9	4.9	1.7	0.7	35	68	36
Mortensen,Clayto	14	R	29	aaa	KC	76	5.73	1.71	21.5	2.8	5.2	1.9	1.3	36	69	20
	15	R	30	aaa	KC	107	7.74	1.96	21.3	5.8	4.8	0.8	1.0	35	59	9

PITCHER	yr	t	age	lvl	org	ip	era	whip	bf/g	ctl	dom	cmd	hr/9	h%	s%	bpv
Mortensen,Jared	15	R	27	a/a	TAM	127	4.67	1.47	21	2.9	6.1	2.1	1.1	32	70	45
Moscot,Jon	15	R	24	aaa	CIN	54	4.17	1.50	26.1	3.4	4.9	1.4	1.2	30	76	21
Mullee,Conor	15	R	27	a/a	NYY	46	4.53	1.56	7.75	3.2	7.0	2.2	0.9	35	72	56
Munson,Kevin	14	R	25	aaa	ARI	62	2.65	1.18	4.45	2.9	9.5	3.2	0.7	31	80	113
	15	R	26	a/a	ARI	35	4.89	1.56	4.84	6.5	6.9	1.1	1.2	26	71	37
Murata,Toru	15	R	30	aaa	CLE	164	4.33	1.56	26.7	2.9	4.1	1.4	1.2	32	76	13
Murray,Colton	15	R	25	a/a	PHI	78	3.23	1.26	6.09	3.8	7.5	2.0	0.4	28	74	83
Murray,Matt	14	R	25	aa	KC	76	5.40	1.56	11.8	2.9	5.7	2.0	0.5	35	64	54
	15	R	26	a/a	KC	93	5.20	1.71	13.1	3.7	4.7	1.3	1.0	34	71	17
Musgrave,Harriso	15	L	23	aa	COL	57	4.75	1.50	22.3	2.3	6.8	3.0	1.7	34	74	46
Musgrove,Joe	15	R	23	aa	HOU	45	2.51	1.00	21.5	1.2	5.8	4.8	1.5	24	87	98
Nappo,Gregory	14	L	26	a/a	MIA	52	2.74	1.04	5.14	2.0	6.0	3.1	0.7	25	77	88
	15	L	27	a/a	MIA	65	3.41	1.28	6.19	2.8	7.2	2.6	0.7	30	75	79
Nazario,Iden	15	L	26	aa	STL	38	3.24	1.38	5.66	4.5	6.3	1.4	0.5	28	77	61
Neal,Zachary	14	R	26	a/a	OAK	150	3.65	1.35	25.1	1.2	5.0	4.1	0.8	33	75	87
	15	R	27	a/a	OAK	168	5.68	1.62	26.6	2.0	4.1	2.0	0.9	35	65	27
Needy,James	14	R	23	aa	SD	146	3.20	1.34	23.3	3.0	6.2	2.1	0.4	31	76	72
	15	R	24	a/a	SD	130	5.70	1.56	23.8	3.0	5.6	1.8	0.9	34	63	41
Negrin,Yoannis	14	R	30	aaa	CHC	59	7.15	2.15	11.7	6.3	5.3	0.8	0.9	38	66	8
	15	R	31	aaa	CHC	30	3.91	1.33	9.68	2.8	6.7	2.4	1.4	29	76	50
Neris,Hector	14	R	25	a/a	PHI	77	4.25	1.32	6.67	3.5	6.7	1.9	1.1	28	70	55
	15	R	26	aaa	PHI	37	4.62	1.95	6.59	6.3	7.0	1.1	0.3	37	75	49
Nesbitt,Angel	15	R	25	aaa	DET	40	7.78	2.16	7.43	5.0	5.2	1.0	0.8	40	62	12
Newcomb,Sean	15	L	22	aa	LAA	36	3.36	1.34	21.4	5.7	8.6	1.5	0.5	26	75	83
Nicolino,Justin	14	L	23	aa	MIA	170	3.29	1.19	24.4	1.1	3.6	3.4	0.5	30	72	79
	15	L	24	aaa	MIA	115	4.64	1.69	25.9	2.4	4.0	1.7	0.9	36	74	21
Nina,Aroni	15	R	25	aa	KC	51	6.48	2.06	5.75	8.5	6.9	0.8	0.4	34	66	45
Noesi,Hector	15	R	28	aaa	CHW	65	4.83	1.25	24.1	2.8	6.0	2.2	1.4	27	65	44
Nola,Aaron	14	R	21	aa	PHI	24	2.88	1.33	19.9	1.8	5.0	2.8	1.6	30	88	39
	15	R	22	a/a	PHI	109	2.72	1.15	24.1	1.5	6.8	4.6	0.7	31	79	121
Nolin,Sean	14	L	25	aaa	TOR	87	4.69	1.48	22.1	3.9	6.3	1.6	0.8	31	69	49
	15	L	26	aaa	OAK	47	3.40	1.48	14.5	4.0	5.6	1.4	1.0	30	81	34
Norberto,Jordan	15	L	29	aaa	TAM	45	6.82	2.07	6.72	6.9	6.0	0.9	0.7	36	66	25
Norris,Daniel	14	L	21	a/a	TOR	58	4.93	1.33	18.6	3.8	11.9	3.1	1.3	34	66	105
	15	L	22	aaa	TOR	91	6.06	1.80	26.2	4.4	7.0	1.6	0.7	38	65	46
Northcraft,Aaron	14	R	24	a/a	ATL	130	5.36	1.67	22.5	3.8	6.7	1.8	0.6	36	67	54
	15	R	25	a/a	SD	83	4.39	1.54	9.33	4.2	5.3	1.3	0.6	31	71	40
Nuding,Zachary	14	R	24	a/a	NYY	154	4.59	1.49	23.7	2.6	5.5	2.1	1.1	33	71	40
	15	R	25	aa	CLE	41	4.60	1.44	7.22	4.0	4.8	1.2	0.8	28	69	31
Nuno,Vidal	15	L	28	aaa	SEA	57	3.91	1.33	26.1	1.4	5.8	4.2	1.2	32	75	83
O Sullivan,Sean	14	R	27	aaa	PHI	149	5.28	1.62	26.4	3.2	4.5	1.4	1.2	33	70	13
	15	R	28	aaa	PHI	56	4.27	1.48	26.9	3.5	5.2	1.5	0.6	31	71	42
Oberholtzer,Brett	14	L	25	aaa	HOU	31	5.01	1.35	25.9	0.9	7.5	8.8	2.7	33	75	143
	15	L	26	aaa	HOU	70	4.24	1.32	24.2	1.5	5.5	3.5	1.2	31	72	68
Obispo,Wirfin	14	R	30	aaa	PIT	48	5.08	1.69	4.81	5.4	6.5	1.2	0.4	33	68	53
	15	R	31	a/a	MIL	33	10.28	1.94	5.67	5.9	6.7	1.1	1.6	35	45	7
O'Brien,Michael	14	R	24	a/a	CIN	97	4.56	1.43	15.9	3.5	6.0	1.7	1.0	30	70	43
	15	R	25	aa	BAL	49	7.28	1.82	14.3	2.8	5.0	1.8	0.5	39	57	37
Ogando,Nefi	15	R	26	a/a	PHI	63	3.54	1.52	6.08	4.8	6.5	1.4	0.5	31	77	54
O'Grady,Chris	15	L	25	a/a	LAA	58	3.65	1.15	5.09	2.1	7.4	3.6	0.9	29	71	99
O'Grady,Dennis	14	R	25	a/a	SD	69	4.14	1.63	5.41	3.7	6.4	1.7	0.8	35	76	45
	15	R	26	a/a	SD	96	6.16	1.80	13.1	4.2	5.5	1.3	1.0	36	66	22
Ohlendorf,Ross	15	R	33	aaa	TEX	35	6.22	1.90	6.35	4.0	7.7	1.9	0.7	41	66	53
Okert,Steven	14	L	23	aa	SF	33	3.04	1.13	5.43	2.9	8.8	3.0	0.7	28	75	105
	15	L	24	aaa	SF	61	3.95	1.55	5.15	4.1	8.5	2.0	0.8	35	76	69
Oliver,Andrew	14	L	27	aaa	PIT	64	2.94	1.38	5.6	6.6	8.8	1.3	0.4	25	79	87
	15	L	28	aaa	BAL	57	6.41	1.98	6.67	8.0	7.8	1.0	1.1	33	68	35
Oliveros,Lester	14	R	26	a/a	MIN	66	2.11	1.26	5.36	3.9	9.4	2.4	0.0	32	81	116
	15	R	27	aaa	MIN	36	5.57	1.87	6.97	3.8	8.8	2.3	1.0	42	71	59
Olmos,Edgar	14	L	24	a/a	MIA	78	4.40	1.39	6.41	3.4	5.7	1.7	0.9	29	70	46
	15	L	25	aaa	SEA	33	3.55	1.40	6.96	3.2	7.8	2.4	0.0	35	72	98
Olson,Tyler	15	L	26	aaa	SEA	54	4.58	1.52	9.43	2.6	7.2	2.7	1.1	35	72	63
Omahen,John	15	R	26	aa	ARI	78	3.89	1.64	26.6	3.4	4.3	1.3	0.0	35	74	46
Ortega,Jose	14	R	26	aaa	DET	58	4.63	1.73	6.13	6.0	5.7	1.0	0.7	31	74	32
	15	R	27	aaa	COL	54	6.82	1.92	5.65	6.3	5.0	0.8	0.9	33	64	16
Ortiz,Joseph	14	L	24	aa	TEX	16	5.85	1.95	5.87	1.2	3.7	3.0	1.5	41	73	18
	15	L	25	aaa	CHC	55	6.24	1.60	6.4	2.8	3.4	1.2	0.7	33	60	17
Osich,Josh	15	L	27	a/a	SF	41	1.64	1.10	4.34	2.9	7.8	2.7	0.2	28	85	108
O'Sullivan,Ryan	14	R	24	aa	PHI	113	4.52	1.51	13.2	3.4	4.7	1.4	0.9	31	71	29
	15	R	25	aa	PHI	53	2.82	1.35	6.1	3.2	4.3	1.4	0.6	28	81	39
Overton,Dillon	15	L	24	aa	OAK	65	3.27	1.33	20.6	2.1	5.3	2.6	0.5	32	76	70
Owens,Henry	14	L	22	a/a	BOS	159	3.67	1.25	24.9	3.3	8.2	2.5	0.6	30	71	90
	15	L	23	aaa	BOS	122	4.44	1.36	24.3	4.5	6.3	1.4	0.6	27	67	58
Owens,Rudy	14	L	27	aaa	HOU	135	4.88	1.42	22.9	2.3	5.6	2.5	0.7	33	65	60
	15	L	28	a/a	COL	68	7.50	1.98	19.3	3.6	4.6	1.3	1.4	38	63	-5
Partch,Curtis	14	R	27	aaa	CIN	47	5.44	1.68	5.2	4.9	8.2	1.7	0.7	36	67	62
	15	R	28	aaa	SF	64	4.15	1.54	5.79	3.9	8.8	2.3	0.4	37	72	88
Patton,Troy	15	L	30	aaa	KC	30	3.40	1.46	6.49	3.1	5.2	1.7	0.7	31	79	43
Paulino,Felipe	14	R	31	aaa	CHW	20	11.45	2.78	22	8.7	5.5	0.6	2.8	40	61	-62
	15	R	32	aaa	CHC	104	6.50	1.93	24.7	5.2	5.4	1.0	0.9	36	66	16
Payano,Victor	15	L	23	aa	TEX	93	5.95	1.81	14.8	6.3	6.3	1.0	1.4	31	69	16
Pazos,James	15	L	24	a/a	NYY	43	1.72	1.23	6.4	3.5	8.7	2.5	0.3	30	87	105
Peavey,Greg	14	R	26	a/a	NYM	144	4.33	1.31	24.7	2.5	6.4	2.6	0.8	31	68	70
	15	R	27	a/a	MIN	147	6.76	1.67	24.5	2.6	4.0	1.5	1.2	35	60	10
Peavy,Jake	15	R	34	aaa	SF	32	7.16	1.77	24.8	2.8	5.8	2.1	1.2	38	60	28
Pena,Ariel	15	R	26	aaa	MIL	83	4.79	1.50	8.3	3.7	7.3	2.0	1.0	33	69	56
Pena,Felix	14	R	24	aa	CHC	28	8.78	1.88	21.7	5.7	7.0	1.2	1.8	34	54	9
	15	R	25	aa	CHC	130	4.63	1.42	22	3.6	8.0	2.2	0.8	33	68	73

PITCHER	yr	t	age	lvl	org	ip	era	whip	bf/g	ctl	dom	cmd	hr/9	h%	s%	bpv
Penny,Brad	14	R	36	aaa	MIA	28	2.62	1.49	23.8	3.2	6.1	1.9	0.0	35	80	75
	15	R	37	aaa	CHW	135	6.71	2.08	27.6	2.8	4.0	1.4	1.1	41	68	-1
Peralta,Starling	15	R	25	aa	CHC	54	2.45	1.23	5.64	3.2	3.6	1.1	0.9	24	85	25
Peralta,Wandy	15	L	24	aa	CIN	117	6.67	1.90	19	5.0	5.4	1.1	0.8	36	64	22
Perez,Clario	15	R	23	aa	PIT	35	4.37	1.43	7.36	3.6	4.4	1.2	0.5	30	68	40
Perez,Luis	15	L	30	a/a	TOR	66	6.68	1.98	8.57	5.7	5.6	1.0	0.6	37	65	25
Perez,Tyson	14	R	25	aa	HOU	39	2.41	1.11	5.07	3.3	5.6	1.7	0.8	23	82	60
	15	R	26	a/a	HOU	48	2.83	1.11	4.46	2.5	5.3	2.1	0.6	25	76	66
Perez,Williams	15	R	24	aaa	ATL	39	1.55	1.29	19.9	2.5	7.3	2.9	0.3	33	89	99
Pestano,Vinnie	14	R	29	aaa	LAA	38	1.75	1.23	4.09	3.5	8.6	2.5	0.2	31	86	107
	15	R	30	aaa	LAA	34	2.26	0.84	3.59	2.0	8.2	4.0	0.2	24	72	147
Peterson,Mark	14	R	24	aa	KC	16	2.13	1.60	5.77	3.6	6.4	1.8	0.6	35	89	54
	15	R	25	aa	KC	73	3.55	1.56	8.24	3.4	4.2	1.2	0.9	31	80	19
Petree,Nick	15	R	25	aa	STL	54	5.13	1.74	24.8	2.4	4.6	1.9	0.5	38	69	40
Petrick,Zachary	14	R	25	a/a	STL	134	4.44	1.38	20.8	2.7	5.2	1.9	1.0	30	70	42
	15	R	26	aaa	STL	157	5.23	1.52	24.4	1.7	5.0	3.0	0.8	36	66	60
Phillips,Zach	15	L	29	aaa	CHW	55	4.65	1.64	5.3	4.2	8.0	1.9	0.2	37	70	77
Pill,Tyler	14	R	24	a/a	NYM	129	3.55	1.16	22.4	2.0	7.4	3.8	0.7	30	70	110
	15	R	25	a/a	NYM	118	6.47	1.69	22.2	3.5	4.7	1.3	1.2	34	62	12
Pimentel,Carlos	14	R	25	aaa	CHC	101	6.47	1.82	16.2	4.9	6.9	1.4	1.7	35	67	13
	15	R	26	aaa	CHC	143	3.59	1.52	23	4.6	6.0	1.3	0.8	30	78	41
Pimentel,Stolmy	15	R	25	aaa	TEX	72	6.94	1.95	20.1	4.5	6.1	1.4	1.3	38	65	12
Pinder,Branden	15	R	26	aaa	NYY	35	3.92	1.45	6.56	2.9	7.4	2.6	1.1	33	76	63
Pineiro,Joel	14	R	36	a/a	LAA	44	6.74	2.03	26.7	2.3	3.2	1.4	1.6	39	69	-22
	15	R	37	a/a	TOR	77	6.67	1.80	27.2	1.9	3.1	1.7	0.7	38	62	15
Pineyro,Ivan	14	R	23	aa	CHC	49	6.38	1.82	20.5	4.3	6.4	1.5	1.4	36	67	19
	15	R	24	a/a	MIA	146	4.59	1.43	23.9	2.7	5.9	2.2	0.5	33	67	65
Pino,Yohan	14	R	31	aaa	MIN	73	3.49	1.25	18.5	3.4	6.4	1.9	1.3	25	78	46
	15	R	32	aaa	KC	79	6.73	1.72	22.3	2.7	5.6	2.1	1.7	36	64	13
Pirela,Jesus	15	L	26	a/a	TEX	60	4.04	1.51	6.18	4.7	8.5	1.8	0.7	32	74	71
Pivetta,Nick	15	R	22	aa	PHI	43	8.05	1.92	20.5	5.7	5.8	1.0	1.9	33	60	-7
Plutko,Adam	15	R	24	aa	CLE	116	3.89	1.23	24.8	1.9	5.9	3.2	0.9	30	70	78
Pounders,Brooks	15	R	25	aa	KC	49	2.75	1.35	25.7	3.6	4.5	1.3	0.6	28	81	40
Prado,Marcel	14	R	27	aa	BAL	75	5.67	1.54	8.01	4.2	5.4	1.3	0.6	31	62	41
	15	R	28	aa	BAL	42	6.67	2.25	7.28	7.2	5.2	0.7	0.6	38	69	14
Pries,Jordan	14	R	24	a/a	SEA	154	4.14	1.31	23.5	2.9	6.0	2.1	0.9	29	70	57
	15	R	25	aaa	SEA	88	5.21	1.44	23.5	2.5	5.1	2.0	0.9	32	64	43
Pruitt,Austin	15	R	26	aa	TAM	160	3.72	1.44	26.2	2.2	5.6	2.5	0.2	35	72	76
Pruneda,Benino	15	R	27	aa	KC	38	4.94	1.72	5.61	4.9	6.0	1.2	0.3	35	69	50
Quevedo,Heri	15	R	25	aa	BOS	57	7.08	2.10	14.7	6.2	5.7	0.9	1.1	37	66	10
Quirarte,Edwin	14	R	28	aa	SF	84	4.01	1.47	7.03	3.3	4.2	1.3	0.4	31	72	38
	15	R	29	a/a	SF	63	4.67	1.62	11.6	2.6	5.7	2.2	0.4	37	70	58
Ramirez,J.C.	14	R	26	a/a	CLE	44	3.63	1.45	5.41	3.9	4.8	1.2	1.3	28	80	18
	15	R	27	aaa	SEA	43	2.85	1.39	4.89	3.4	6.0	1.8	0.4	31	80	64
Ramirez,Jose	15	R	25	aaa	SEA	63	4.17	1.39	6.44	3.9	7.9	2.0	0.8	31	71	71
Ramirez,Noe	15	R	26	aaa	BOS	43	3.47	1.52	6.17	4.4	6.3	1.4	0.3	32	76	61
Ranaudo,Anthony	14	R	25	aaa	BOS	138	3.44	1.41	24.3	3.7	5.8	1.6	0.7	30	77	50
	15	R	26	aaa	TEX	118	6.01	1.72	25.5	3.8	5.4	1.4	1.3	34	67	15
Rapada,Clay	14	L	33	aaa	BAL	38	7.21	1.90	5.66	3.7	4.8	1.3	2.1	35	66	-22
	15	L	34	aaa	SF	44	3.32	1.66	4.32	3.3	4.8	1.4	0.5	35	81	35
Rasmussen,Robe	14	L	25	aaa	TOR	43	3.64	1.35	5.12	3.8	7.6	2.0	0.0	32	70	93
	15	L	26	aaa	SEA	42	2.41	1.12	4.87	4.0	6.8	1.7	0.2	24	78	87
Rauh,Brian	15	R	24	aa	WAS	41	6.25	1.67	23	2.3	5.1	2.2	1.7	35	66	16
Ray,Robbie	14	L	23	aaa	DET	100	5.14	1.66	22.5	4.0	5.5	1.4	0.6	34	68	38
	15	L	24	aaa	ARI	42	3.70	1.71	21	5.3	10.2	1.9	0.2	39	77	93
Rea,Colin	15	R	25	a/a	SD	102	1.94	1.07	22	2.0	5.9	3.0	0.2	28	82	99
Rearick,Christoph	15	R	28	a/a	SD	49	5.11	1.92	5.53	5.9	5.3	0.9	0.9	34	74	17
Redmond,Todd	15	R	30	aaa	TOR	79	6.69	1.99	16.5	3.6	5.0	1.4	0.9	40	66	13
Reed,Chris	14	L	24	a/a	LA	158	3.91	1.33	23.5	3.2	6.4	2.0	0.7	30	72	62
	15	L	25	a/a	MIA	55	6.82	1.81	6.74	6.1	5.7	0.9	0.8	32	61	27
Reed,Cody	15	L	22	aa	CIN	78	3.32	1.28	24.7	2.9	8.2	2.9	0.6	32	75	95
Reed,Jake	15	R	23	aa	MIN	47	7.19	1.74	6.13	3.9	6.1	1.6	0.6	37	56	44
Reed,Jimmy	15	L	25	a/a	STL	91	5.89	1.66	22.6	1.9	5.0	2.6	1.3	37	66	33
Reyes,Alexander	15	R	21	aa	STL	35	3.21	1.10	17	4.2	11.5	2.7	0.2	28	69	138
Reyes,Arturo	15	R	23	aa	STL	124	3.96	1.50	24.4	3.0	5.8	2.0	0.3	34	72	64
Reyes,James	14	L	25	a/a	TEX	56	8.15	1.78	6.48	3.0	6.2	2.1	1.5	37	54	22
	15	L	26	aaa	TEX	62	3.03	1.57	6.68	2.7	4.5	1.7	0.2	35	80	50
Reyes,Jo-Jo	14	L	30	aaa	PHI	21	13.60	2.99	24	4.0	2.9	0.7	1.1	49	52	-40
	15	L	31	aaa	LAA	68	5.14	1.76	20.7	3.0	4.5	1.5	0.9	36	72	18
Reyes,Jorge	14	R	27	a/a	ATL	76	4.04	1.38	6.26	4.7	6.7	1.4	0.8	27	72	56
	15	R	28	a/a	ATL	85	6.41	1.76	11.8	3.5	5.9	1.7	1.4	36	65	19
Reynolds,Daniel	14	R	23	a/a	LAA	42	3.38	1.40	5.72	3.0	8.1	2.7	0.2	35	74	99
	15	R	24	aa	LAA	43	5.82	1.58	4.44	5.8	8.8	1.5	0.2	33	60	83
Reynolds,Matt	15	L	31	aaa	ARI	50	6.35	1.67	4.99	3.3	5.7	1.7	1.0	35	62	32
Rhame,Jacob	15	R	22	aa	LA	50	3.74	1.14	5.08	3.3	9.0	2.8	1.1	27	71	92
Rice,Scott	15	L	34	aaa	NYM	40	2.00	1.51	3.07	6.6	7.4	1.1	0.2	27	87	72
Richard,Clayton	14	L	31	a/a	ARI	21	7.45	2.27	27.1	2.3	2.5	1.1	1.5	42	69	-36
	15	L	32	aaa	CHC	63	2.45	1.39	26.5	2.2	3.1	1.4	0.5	31	84	30
Riefenhauser,Cha	14	L	24	aaa	TAM	58	1.71	1.25	6.02	3.8	7.0	1.8	0.5	28	89	75
	15	L	25	aaa	TAM	35	3.59	1.08	4.66	1.9	7.3	3.8	0.3	29	65	123
Rienzo,Andre	14	R	26	aaa	CHW	47	4.46	1.63	20.8	5.1	6.8	1.3	0.9	32	74	42
	15	R	27	aaa	MIA	78	4.23	1.57	22.7	4.2	4.9	1.2	0.6	31	73	34
Rivero,Armando	14	R	26	a/a	CHC	65	2.73	1.26	5.41	4.2	11.0	2.6	0.9	30	83	104
	15	R	27	aaa	CHC	57	3.93	1.58	5.23	5.6	6.6	1.2	0.7	30	76	48
Roach,Donn	14	R	25	aaa	SD	77	4.37	1.67	18.3	4.0	4.4	1.1	0.2	34	72	38
	15	R	26	aaa	TOR	143	5.15	1.62	25.4	1.9	2.8	1.4	0.8	35	68	12
Roberts,Kenneth	15	L	27	aaa	PHI	35	6.10	2.04	6.48	1.2	6.3	5.4	1.0	46	71	95

PITCHER	yr	t	age	lvl	org	ip	era	whip	bf/g	ctl	dom	cmd	hr/9	h%	s%	bpv
Roberts,Will	15	R	25	a/a	CLE	157	4.72	1.36	25.2	1.4	4.0	2.8	1.3	31	69	40
Robertson,Montre	15	R	25	aa	DET	31	4.51	1.90	9.76	4.7	6.7	1.4	1.1	38	78	28
Robinson,James	14	R	26	a/a	ATL	70	2.92	1.35	6.75	1.9	7.2	3.8	0.3	35	78	112
	15	R	27	aa	BAL	62	4.57	1.31	5.36	2.7	5.9	2.2	1.3	29	69	46
Robowski,Ryan	14	L	26	aa	DET	78	4.67	1.50	8.61	4.0	6.8	1.7	1.1	31	71	45
	15	L	27	a/a	DET	33	9.13	2.32	9.87	2.8	6.1	2.2	1.7	46	61	3
Rodgers,Brady	14	R	24	a/a	HOU	127	4.96	1.35	19.6	1.4	5.5	4.0	1.1	33	65	79
	15	R	25	aaa	HOU	116	4.85	1.52	23.9	1.9	5.8	3.0	1.0	35	70	59
Rodriguez,Bryan	15	R	24	a/a	SD	146	4.98	1.66	24.2	2.4	4.6	1.9	0.4	37	69	43
Rodriguez,Eduarc	14	L	21	aa	BOS	120	4.46	1.45	23.3	2.7	7.0	2.6	0.5	35	68	78
	15	L	22	aaa	BOS	48	4.10	1.32	25	1.4	7.0	5.0	0.4	35	68	130
Rodriguez,Joely	15	L	24	a/a	PHI	129	7.27	1.90	19.1	4.1	4.4	1.1	0.9	37	61	9
Rodriguez,Pedro	15	R	28	aa	SF	61	3.21	1.38	6.92	2.0	5.7	2.9	0.5	34	77	77
Rodriguez,Richar	14	R	24	a/a	HOU	49	3.60	1.06	7.05	1.4	8.0	5.6	0.8	30	68	149
	15	R	25	a/a	BAL	84	3.64	1.27	7.43	2.7	6.4	2.4	1.3	28	77	54
Roenicke,Josh	14	R	32	aaa	COL	90	7.64	2.23	15.6	3.9	3.1	0.8	1.6	40	67	-35
	15	R	33	aaa	MIL	123	7.71	2.14	24.4	3.3	3.9	1.2	1.5	40	65	-18
Rogers,Esmil	14	R	29	aaa	TOR	49	4.60	1.60	17.9	3.9	5.7	1.5	0.5	34	71	46
	15	R	30	aaa	NYY	35	5.11	1.91	23.4	3.9	5.4	1.4	0.0	40	70	48
Rogers,Taylor	14	L	24	aa	MIN	145	3.97	1.46	25.9	2.3	5.7	2.5	0.3	35	71	73
	15	L	25	aaa	MIN	174	5.62	1.67	27.9	2.5	5.1	2.0	0.6	37	65	46
Roibal,Reinier	15	R	26	aa	PHI	49	2.00	1.10	7.62	2.0	7.2	3.7	0.7	28	86	107
Romero,Enny Mai	14	L	23	aaa	TAM	126	5.36	1.57	22.1	3.7	7.2	2.0	1.0	34	67	52
	15	L	24	aaa	TAM	46	5.98	1.60	12	3.4	7.4	2.2	1.0	36	63	54
Rondon,Jorge	14	R	26	aaa	STL	62	3.25	1.38	5.13	2.9	5.8	2.0	0.4	32	76	66
	15	R	27	aaa	BAL	61	3.68	1.32	7.17	3.5	5.7	1.6	0.0	30	69	74
Rosenbaum,Danie	14	L	27	aaa	WAS	20	5.49	1.58	22	2.3	3.1	1.3	0.5	34	64	23
	15	L	28	aa	BOS	40	8.43	2.40	19.1	7.2	4.4	0.6	1.3	38	65	-18
Rosin,Seth	14	R	26	a/a	PHI	58	4.64	1.65	6.06	3.1	5.5	1.8	1.1	35	74	30
	15	R	27	aaa	PHI	68	4.30	1.73	6.62	3.1	5.2	1.7	0.7	37	76	35
Ross,Austin	14	R	26	aa	MIL	26	3.89	1.78	23.9	3.0	7.9	2.6	0.9	41	80	64
	15	R	27	a/a	MIL	70	6.14	1.87	6.73	3.4	7.9	2.3	0.7	42	66	60
Ross,Greg	14	R	25	aa	ATL	78	2.54	1.23	24.3	2.4	4.2	1.8	0.5	28	81	52
	15	R	26	aa	ATL	138	5.42	1.72	25	3.4	4.4	1.3	0.5	36	67	29
Ross,Joe	15	R	22	a/a	WAS	76	3.30	1.19	21.8	2.3	6.8	3.0	0.6	30	74	90
Roth,Michael	14	L	24	aa	LAA	141	3.31	1.41	27	3.4	4.2	1.2	0.6	29	78	34
	15	L	25	aaa	CLE	124	6.55	1.79	18.5	3.3	4.5	1.4	1.8	35	67	-10
Rowen,Benjamin	14	R	26	aaa	TEX	47	3.94	1.36	5.77	1.8	4.6	2.6	0.4	32	70	66
	15	R	27	a/a	TOR	65	2.91	1.20	5.41	1.5	4.7	3.3	0.2	31	74	92
Rucinski,Drew	14	R	26	aa	LAA	149	4.15	1.48	24.6	2.6	6.8	2.6	0.5	35	71	77
	15	R	26	aaa	LAA	112	5.67	1.71	23.1	3.2	5.6	1.8	1.4	35	69	20
Rumbelow,Nick	15	R	24	aaa	NYY	53	5.73	1.37	5.96	2.4	8.2	3.4	0.9	34	58	91
Runion,Sam	14	R	26	a/a	WAS	38	5.47	1.43	6.96	2.1	6.6	3.2	0.7	35	61	80
	15	R	27	a/a	WAS	65	4.09	1.66	6.07	3.4	6.3	1.8	0.5	37	75	54
Runzler,Dan	14	L	29	aaa	SF	46	3.42	1.71	5.38	7.0	7.6	1.1	0.3	31	79	65
	15	L	30	aaa	ARI	38	5.98	2.30	4.94	6.9	7.0	1.0	0.5	42	73	32
Rusin,Chris	14	L	28	aaa	CHC	146	5.57	1.70	28.7	2.7	4.5	1.7	1.1	36	68	19
	15	L	29	aaa	COL	34	8.79	2.18	24.5	3.3	3.4	1.0	2.3	39	62	-50
Ruth,Eric	14	R	24	a/a	NYY	18	5.44	1.43	19.1	4.7	4.1	0.9	0.6	26	61	31
	15	R	25	a/a	NYY	124	4.72	1.56	24.8	3.3	4.8	1.5	0.8	33	71	30
Ryan,Kyle	14	L	23	a/a	DET	160	4.52	1.36	25.7	2.0	4.5	2.2	0.9	31	68	45
	15	L	24	aaa	DET	103	5.12	1.66	27.2	3.0	4.3	1.4	0.3	36	67	38
Sadler,Casey	14	R	24	aaa	PIT	125	3.31	1.28	24.4	1.6	4.4	2.7	0.7	30	76	60
	15	R	25	aaa	PIT	81	5.44	1.39	26.2	2.8	4.2	1.5	1.0	29	62	26
Sampson,Adrian	14	R	23	a/a	PIT	167	3.12	1.19	23.9	1.8	4.7	2.6	0.5	29	75	70
	15	R	24	aaa	SEA	163	4.67	1.47	24.9	1.8	5.8	3.2	0.6	36	68	76
Sampson,Keyvius	14	R	23	aaa	SD	92	5.34	1.54	10.5	5.5	8.2	1.5	1.4	29	68	44
	15	R	24	a/a	CIN	83	4.45	1.71	23.4	5.4	7.0	1.3	0.5	34	73	54
Sanabia,Alex	14	R	26	aaa	MIA	134	5.01	1.62	21.3	2.7	5.5	2.1	1.0	36	70	38
	15	R	27	aaa	LAA	87	6.92	1.94	16	3.0	4.5	1.5	0.8	40	63	17
Sanburn,Nolan	15	R	24	aa	CHW	30	9.13	1.98	6.54	8.1	7.6	0.9	0.4	34	50	53
Sanchez,Angel	14	R	25	aa	PIT	110	6.64	1.74	21.8	2.7	4.2	1.5	0.8	36	61	21
	15	R	26	a/a	PIT	137	3.37	1.32	24.7	2.2	4.9	2.2	0.6	31	76	57
Sanchez,Jake	15	R	26	a/a	OAK	151	5.60	1.76	25.6	2.9	4.9	1.7	0.7	38	68	31
Santiago,Andres	14	R	25	aa	LA	129	4.58	1.48	21.3	3.4	5.6	1.6	1.0	31	71	36
	15	R	26	a/a	CHC	79	4.82	1.68	13.6	4.5	5.1	1.1	0.3	34	69	43
Santos,Eduard	15	R	26	aa	LAA	58	3.08	1.28	6.13	5.1	9.8	1.9	0.5	27	77	98
Sappington,Mark	15	R	25	aa	TAM	68	4.49	1.75	6.5	6.1	7.7	1.3	0.4	34	73	61
Satterwhite,Cody	14	R	27	aa	NYM	58	2.48	1.19	4.85	3.4	7.9	2.3	0.5	28	80	92
	15	R	28	aaa	NYM	72	4.67	1.58	5.56	3.6	6.9	1.9	0.8	35	71	55
Saupold,Warwick	15	R	25	a/a	DET	124	5.17	1.50	18.4	3.3	5.3	1.6	0.5	32	64	48
Schlitter,Brian	15	R	30	aaa	CHC	45	2.12	1.87	4.65	6.1	5.3	0.9	0.2	34	89	38
Schlosser,Gus	14	R	26	aaa	ATL	99	4.74	1.57	17.5	4.4	5.2	1.2	0.6	31	70	36
	15	R	27	aa	COL	47	7.84	2.13	8.25	4.9	4.5	0.9	1.3	38	63	-10
Schugel,Andrew	14	R	25	aa	ARI	148	4.48	1.52	24.7	3.2	5.7	1.8	0.2	34	68	62
	15	R	26	a/a	ARI	115	5.81	1.71	24.9	2.5	4.9	1.9	0.8	37	66	33
Schultz,Jaime	15	R	24	aa	TAM	135	4.22	1.56	21.9	6.0	9.5	1.6	0.7	31	74	76
Schuster,Patrick	14	L	24	a/a	ARI	45	3.37	1.37	3.28	4.8	6.5	1.3	0.8	26	78	51
	15	L	25	aa	CIN	54	4.46	1.68	4.67	4.8	6.4	1.3	0.2	35	72	56
Scott,Robby	14	L	25	aa	BOS	60	2.61	1.41	7.2	2.4	6.2	2.6	0.5	34	83	73
	15	L	26	a/a	BOS	75	6.25	1.68	8.93	3.0	6.4	2.1	1.2	37	64	39
Scott,Tayler	15	R	23	aa	CHC	31	6.19	1.84	9.64	6.0	5.3	0.9	0.9	32	66	18
Segovia,Zack	15	R	32	a/a	SD	48	7.77	1.77	20	3.4	5.5	1.6	1.1	36	55	22
Selman,Sam	14	L	24	a/a	KC	97	4.93	1.61	13	5.2	6.9	1.3	0.6	32	69	52
	15	L	25	aa	KC	56	6.63	1.97	6.58	7.0	8.6	1.2	0.5	38	65	57
Severino,Luis	15	R	21	a/a	NYY	99	3.16	1.14	20.7	2.6	7.9	3.1	0.2	30	71	114
Sewald,Paul	15	R	25	aa	NYM	51	2.15	0.99	4.44	1.8	8.2	4.5	0.6	27	81	137

PITCHER	yr	t	age	lvl	org	ip	era	whip	bf/g	ctl	dom	cmd	hr/9	h%	s%	bpv
Shaban,Ronald	15	R	25	aa	STL	49	3.05	1.24	4.62	2.7	6.7	2.5	0.5	30	76	82
Shackelford,Kevir	14	R	25	aa	MIL	50	5.94	1.78	5.76	3.3	3.8	1.2	0.7	36	66	15
	15	R	26	aa	CIN	39	5.09	1.97	5.29	4.5	4.9	1.1	0.4	39	73	28
Shackleford,Stepl	14	R	25	aa	SEA	64	3.63	1.50	6.25	4.2	8.3	2.0	0.4	34	75	80
	15	R	26	aa	PHI	55	5.35	1.57	4.53	4.2	7.6	1.8	0.6	35	65	64
Sherfy,Jimmie	14	R	23	aa	ARI	38	6.16	1.52	4.46	4.3	8.9	2.1	1.1	34	60	65
	15	R	24	aa	ARI	50	8.75	1.83	5.25	5.3	7.5	1.4	0.7	37	49	47
Sherriff,Ryan	14	L	24	a/a	STL	69	3.10	1.44	6.64	2.5	5.6	2.2	0.5	33	79	63
	15	L	25	a/a	STL	40	3.30	1.48	5.69	3.3	6.0	1.8	1.1	31	82	39
Shibuya,Tim	15	R	26	a/a	MIN	49	5.76	1.65	8.17	2.0	3.4	1.7	0.6	36	64	25
Shipers,Jordan	14	L	23	aa	SEA	22	7.33	2.03	8.9	6.9	3.9	0.6	0.8	33	63	5
	15	L	24	aa	SEA	37	10.10	2.47	8.24	5.2	7.0	1.3	1.3	46	58	6
Shipley,Braden	15	R	23	aa	ARI	157	4.60	1.49	24.1	3.3	5.7	1.7	0.5	33	68	53
Shirley,Thomas	14	L	26	a/a	HOU	117	2.88	1.23	15.9	2.5	6.3	2.5	0.7	29	79	75
	15	L	27	aaa	HOU	41	3.45	1.18	14.9	2.5	6.5	2.6	0.7	28	72	79
Simmons,James	14	R	28	a/a	WAS	106	6.60	1.60	18.7	2.9	4.8	1.7	1.4	33	60	16
	15	R	29	a/a	WAS	40	5.59	1.46	9.58	1.6	5.3	3.4	0.8	35	61	70
Simmons,Seth	14	R	26	aa	ARI	48	1.99	1.13	5.38	3.6	8.9	2.5	0.2	28	82	112
	15	R	27	a/a	ARI	75	3.66	1.32	5.88	3.6	8.1	2.2	0.6	31	73	84
Simms,John	14	R	22	aa	WAS	59	5.10	1.52	23.3	2.0	5.4	2.7	0.8	35	67	56
	15	R	23	aa	WAS	45	5.58	1.63	25	3.1	5.6	1.8	0.6	36	65	45
Sims,Lucas	15	R	21	aa	ATL	48	3.97	1.31	21.9	5.5	9.7	1.8	0.2	28	68	104
Sinnery,Brandon	15	R	25	aa	ARI	90	6.71	1.87	24.8	3.4	4.4	1.3	1.3	37	65	-1
Sitton,Kraig	14	L	26	aa	COL	66	5.37	1.66	6.16	3.7	4.3	1.2	1.6	31	72	-5
	15	L	27	aa	COL	58	4.82	1.84	5.85	2.6	4.3	1.6	0.0	40	71	44
Siverio,Misael	15	L	26	aa	SEA	122	5.44	1.73	21.3	3.9	6.6	1.7	0.5	37	67	53
Slegers,Aaron	15	R	23	aa	MIN	37	5.59	1.54	26.6	2.9	4.8	1.7	0.7	33	63	37
Smith,Alex	15	R	26	aa	NYY	39	3.61	1.54	6.86	3.2	5.7	1.8	0.0	35	74	68
Smith,Blake	14	R	27	aa	LA	33	4.34	1.65	5.73	4.2	7.0	1.7	0.5	36	73	57
	15	R	28	a/a	CHW	53	4.28	1.79	5.55	5.8	8.4	1.5	0.8	36	77	56
Smith,Caleb	15	L	24	a/a	NYY	135	4.71	1.58	22.9	4.1	5.4	1.3	0.7	32	71	36
Smith,Chipper	14	L	24	aa	MIA	65	4.94	1.39	19.6	4.3	6.4	1.5	1.3	27	68	36
	15	L	25	aa	MIA	89	5.54	1.68	19.1	3.6	6.1	1.7	0.6	36	66	47
Smith,Chris	14	R	33	aaa	SD	43	5.17	1.51	13.4	3.7	7.4	2.0	0.9	33	66	58
	15	R	34	a/a	SD	138	3.92	1.45	24.5	3.1	6.5	2.1	0.7	33	74	60
Smith,Greg	14	L	31	aaa	PHI	157	5.73	1.70	26.3	2.4	3.9	1.6	1.2	35	68	9
	15	L	32	aaa	ATL	120	4.07	1.63	17.2	2.3	3.9	1.7	0.5	36	75	33
Smith,Josh	15	R	28	a/a	CIN	142	5.00	1.53	25.8	2.5	6.2	2.5	0.7	36	67	61
Smith,Joshua	15	L	26	aa	PIT	48	6.32	1.75	6.4	6.3	4.5	0.7	0.5	30	62	27
Smith,Nate	14	L	23	aa	LAA	62	3.57	1.38	23.8	4.3	8.3	1.9	0.5	31	74	83
	15	L	24	a/a	LAA	138	4.21	1.33	23.8	2.6	5.7	2.2	1.0	30	71	52
Smith,Slade	14	R	24	aa	DET	52	6.53	1.89	7.37	1.8	3.5	1.9	0.7	40	64	20
	15	R	25	aa	DET	41	8.59	1.93	7.15	3.9	4.8	1.2	1.3	37	55	0
Smith,Steve	14	R	28	a/a	LA	108	5.41	1.53	16.2	3.0	4.1	1.4	1.3	31	67	11
	15	R	29	a/a	LA	48	6.84	2.26	13.7	4.4	4.8	1.1	1.4	41	71	-13
Snell,Blake	15	L	23	a/a	TAM	113	1.95	1.11	21.2	3.4	9.4	2.8	0.5	28	85	112
Snodgrass,Jack	14	L	27	aa	SF	131	4.33	1.52	23.8	3.0	4.6	1.5	0.1	34	69	53
	15	L	28	a/a	SF	72	5.53	1.70	19.3	4.5	4.5	1.0	0.7	33	67	21
Snodgress,Scott	14	L	25	a/a	CHW	139	4.54	1.56	21	4.0	5.1	1.3	1.0	31	73	27
	15	L	26	a/a	LAA	34	10.96	2.40	5.33	4.6	6.3	1.4	0.5	46	50	26
Snow,Forrest	14	R	26	a/a	SEA	76	4.49	1.38	16	2.9	7.2	2.5	1.1	32	70	63
	15	R	26	aaa	SEA	121	4.26	1.38	17.5	2.8	5.8	2.1	1.5	29	75	33
Socolovich,Migue	14	R	28	aaa	NYM	59	3.22	1.49	5.01	2.6	8.2	3.1	0.6	37	80	90
	15	R	29	aaa	STL	33	3.07	1.08	6.07	3.5	7.2	2.0	0.3	24	71	93
Somsen,Layne	15	R	26	a/a	CIN	62	3.77	1.50	9.98	4.9	7.2	1.5	0.7	30	76	59
Soto,Giovanni	15	L	24	aaa	CLE	54	3.55	1.35	4.87	5.0	7.2	1.4	0.2	28	72	79
Spann,Matthew	15	L	24	a/a	WAS	62	5.55	1.78	25.9	4.1	4.6	1.1	0.2	36	66	37
Spomer,Kurt	14	R	25	a/a	LAA	34	2.69	1.41	7.25	4.1	3.0	0.7	0.2	27	80	31
	15	R	26	a/a	LAA	64	4.46	1.55	6.11	3.1	4.1	1.3	1.3	31	75	8
Spruill,Ezekiel	14	R	25	aaa	ARI	79	6.17	1.47	12.1	2.2	6.5	2.9	1.1	34	58	62
	15	R	26	aaa	BOS	114	5.89	1.88	15.3	3.1	4.1	1.3	0.8	38	68	13
Stanek,Ryne	15	R	24	aa	TAM	62	4.71	1.46	16.5	4.5	5.1	1.1	1.0	27	70	28
Stauffer,Tim	15	R	33	aaa	NYM	59	3.02	1.25	20.1	1.9	4.2	2.2	0.6	29	78	55
Stem,Craig	14	R	24	aa	LA	26	8.10	2.16	6.72	6.0	5.6	0.9	0.0	40	58	39
	15	R	25	a/a	MIA	58	7.53	1.92	7.06	4.0	5.3	1.3	1.3	38	61	8
Stephenson,Robe	15	R	22	a/a	CIN	134	4.84	1.45	22.9	4.9	8.5	1.7	0.9	30	68	66
Stewart,Zach	14	R	28	aaa	ATL	106	5.45	1.87	24.9	3.1	3.9	1.3	0.5	38	70	19
	15	R	29	aaa	LAA	39	3.66	1.58	14.4	2.9	4.7	1.6	0.8	34	79	31
Stoffel,Jason	14	R	26	aaa	HOU	65	3.53	1.63	5.33	3.9	7.7	2.0	0.4	37	78	70
	15	R	27	a/a	BAL	57	6.35	1.47	5.29	4.2	7.3	1.7	1.0	31	56	54
Stowell,Bryce	14	R	28	a/a	TAM	52	2.44	1.43	5.63	4.0	7.4	1.9	0.2	33	82	81
	15	R	29	a/a	TAM	32	6.73	2.34	5.5	8.3	7.5	0.9	0.9	40	71	24
Straily,Dan	14	R	26	aaa	CHC	118	5.47	1.58	25.9	3.8	7.5	2.0	1.4	33	68	41
	15	R	27	aaa	HOU	123	5.35	1.60	24.6	1.9	7.3	3.9	1.0	39	68	83
Stratton,Chris	15	R	25	a/a	SF	148	4.70	1.45	24.3	4.0	5.5	1.4	0.5	30	67	50
Stripling,Ross	15	R	26	aa	LA	67	5.15	1.42	22	2.6	6.0	2.3	1.2	32	66	45
Strong,Michael	15	L	27	a/a	MIL	66	4.91	1.40	5.57	4.9	6.6	1.4	1.0	27	66	47
Stults,Eric	15	L	36	a/a	LA	90	4.38	1.42	23.9	2.3	4.6	2.0	0.6	32	69	47
Stumpf,Daniel	15	L	24	aa	KC	71	4.39	1.36	7.04	4.0	7.7	1.9	0.8	30	69	68
Sturdevant,Tyler	14	R	29	a/a	CLE	58	3.38	1.31	5.17	2.9	6.4	2.2	0.7	30	76	67
	15	R	30	aaa	CLE	31	4.72	1.43	5.12	3.4	6.5	1.9	2.0	28	75	21
Suarez,Albert	14	R	25	aa	TAM	56	4.99	1.71	23.1	3.0	4.3	1.4	0.6	36	71	25
	15	R	26	aa	LAA	163	3.96	1.34	25.1	2.3	5.4	2.4	0.9	31	72	56
Suero,Wander	15	R	24	aa	WAS	34	8.22	1.92	9.48	3.9	6.2	1.6	1.1	39	56	22
Sulbaran,Juan	14	R	25	aa	KC	127	4.19	1.66	22.8	4.0	6.4	1.6	0.8	35	76	42
	15	R	26	a/a	KC	132	6.83	1.79	21.8	3.6	5.1	1.4	2.0	34	66	-11
Sulbaran,Miguel	15	L	21	a/a	NYY	71	5.73	1.72	21.5	3.9	5.4	1.4	0.3	36	64	44

PITCHER	yr	t	age	lvl	org	ip	era	whip	bf/g	ctl	dom	cmd	hr/9	h%	s%	bpv
Sullivan,Gerald	15	R	27	aaa	SD	46	5.23	1.41	5.69	2.7	6.8	2.5	0.5	34	61	77
Surkamp,Eric	14	L	27	aaa	CHW	79	5.28	1.69	19.7	2.6	7.9	3.1	1.1	40	70	68
	15	L	28	aaa	LA	114	4.05	1.51	18.3	2.5	6.1	2.4	1.0	34	76	51
Suter,Brent	14	L	25	aa	MIL	152	4.84	1.49	23.5	3.3	5.8	1.7	1.0	32	69	39
	15	L	26	a/a	MIL	118	3.07	1.48	19.6	3.3	5.1	1.5	0.6	32	81	42
Teaford,Everett	15	L	31	aaa	TAM	103	7.44	1.96	18.9	3.4	4.7	1.4	1.2	39	62	4
Tejeda,Enosil	14	R	25	a/a	CLE	57	3.70	1.25	5.12	2.2	8.0	3.6	0.8	32	72	103
	15	R	26	a/a	CLE	43	1.74	1.26	4.91	3.6	6.2	1.7	0.0	29	85	82
Tepera,Ryan	15	R	28	aaa	TOR	34	1.71	1.13	6.39	4.2	7.7	1.8	0.4	24	87	90
Texeira,Kanekoa	14	R	28	aaa	ATL	70	5.79	1.87	25.4	4.9	3.3	0.7	0.9	33	70	-3
	15	R	29	aaa	ATL	101	5.28	1.82	18.1	5.2	4.9	0.9	0.7	34	71	22
Thielbar,Caleb	15	L	28	aaa	SD	44	2.25	1.49	5.03	4.6	4.1	0.9	0.4	28	86	36
Thomas,Christopl	14	R	26	aa	STL	28	1.53	0.95	5.49	2.0	6.1	3.0	0.3	24	85	105
	15	R	27	a/a	STL	74	3.68	1.27	6.08	2.1	6.0	2.9	0.7	31	72	75
Thomas,Ian	14	L	27	a/a	ATL	17	5.16	1.58	7.47	4.0	8.5	2.1	1.1	35	69	59
	15	L	28	a/a	LA	58	5.37	1.58	11.1	2.6	7.0	2.7	1.0	37	67	61
Thomas,Michael	14	L	25	aa	LA	59	2.80	1.57	5.43	5.7	9.5	1.7	0.4	33	83	84
	15	L	26	a/a	LA	34	5.52	1.49	5.24	4.2	6.9	1.6	0.9	31	63	49
Thompson,Jake	14	R	20	aa	TEX	47	3.74	1.39	21.8	4.3	8.6	2.0	0.7	31	74	79
	15	R	21	aa	PHI	133	4.09	1.34	23	2.8	6.9	2.5	0.8	32	71	73
Thornburg,Tyler	15	R	27	aaa	MIL	89	6.25	1.86	24.4	4.0	4.6	1.2	2.1	34	72	-22
Thornton,Zachary	14	R	26	aaa	NYM	67	3.30	1.30	5.11	2.6	8.1	3.1	0.5	33	75	101
	15	R	27	aaa	NYM	62	4.11	1.45	4.18	3.4	6.4	1.9	0.3	33	70	69
Todd,Jess	14	R	28	aaa	ARI	72	3.94	1.46	5.84	3.3	6.2	1.9	0.6	32	74	56
	15	R	29	aaa	BOS	82	8.12	2.07	18.2	4.1	3.6	0.9	0.9	39	59	-5
Tolliver,Ashur	14	L	26	aa	BAL	23	3.88	1.66	5.64	2.1	7.8	3.8	0.5	41	76	99
	15	L	27	aa	BAL	59	4.19	1.71	6.82	5.2	7.2	1.4	0.4	35	75	57
Tomshaw,Matthev	15	L	27	a/a	MIA	124	6.97	1.80	18.4	2.4	5.2	2.2	0.8	39	60	37
Tonkin,Michael	14	R	25	aaa	MIN	45	3.59	1.38	4.85	2.5	7.3	2.9	0.4	34	74	91
	15	R	26	aaa	MIN	41	1.58	0.93	4.66	1.2	7.8	6.3	0.6	27	87	173
Tracy,Matthew	15	L	27	a/a	NYY	90	5.48	1.77	14.3	4.1	5.2	1.3	0.7	35	69	27
Trepagnier,Brytor	15	R	24	aa	ATL	57	5.73	1.99	6.57	7.3	4.2	0.6	0.4	33	70	23
Triggs,Andrew	14	R	25	a/a	KC	62	3.42	1.29	5.8	2.4	4.3	1.8	0.6	29	74	48
	15	R	26	aa	BAL	61	1.45	1.09	5.54	1.8	8.1	4.4	0.0	32	85	149
Troncoso,Ramon	14	R	31	aaa	KC	44	5.26	1.58	8.06	2.5	4.8	1.9	0.6	35	66	42
	15	R	32	a/a	LA	39	3.04	1.48	5.46	3.0	3.8	1.3	0.3	32	79	37
Tropeano,Nichola	14	R	24	aaa	HOU	125	3.20	1.04	20.9	2.3	7.4	3.2	0.8	26	72	100
	15	R	25	aaa	LAA	88	4.69	1.53	23.9	3.2	8.1	2.5	0.7	36	70	76
Tsao,Chin-hui	15	R	34	a/a	LA	44	4.35	1.34	5.39	3.3	7.7	2.3	1.1	30	70	66
Tuivailala,Sam	14	R	22	a/a	STL	22	2.50	1.27	4.81	3.4	11.4	3.4	0.0	37	78	146
	15	R	23	aaa	STL	45	1.74	1.22	4.23	4.9	7.1	1.5	0.4	24	87	78
Turley,Josh	14	L	24	aa	DET	50	4.17	1.49	23.9	2.8	4.0	1.4	1.4	30	77	7
	15	L	25	aa	DET	153	4.26	1.45	26.1	2.2	4.7	2.1	1.1	32	73	35
Turley,Nikolas	14	L	25	aaa	NYY	60	5.53	1.81	21.5	6.7	5.3	0.8	1.5	29	73	5
	15	L	26	aaa	SF	103	4.92	1.49	23.3	4.3	6.0	1.4	1.1	29	69	35
Unsworth,Dylan	15	R	23	aa	SEA	66	5.09	1.52	22.2	1.7	6.0	3.5	0.9	37	67	76
Urckfitz,Patrick	15	L	27	aaa	MIA	53	6.16	1.95	6.87	4.4	5.3	1.2	1.1	37	69	11
Urena,Jose	15	R	24	aaa	MIA	68	3.50	1.47	26.4	2.7	4.4	1.6	0.5	32	77	41
Urias,Julio	15	L	19	a/a	LA	73	3.99	1.19	19.4	2.3	9.1	4.0	0.5	33	66	127
Valdez,Jose	15	R	25	a/a	DET	57	4.13	1.74	6.04	6.4	5.2	0.8	0.5	30	76	34
Vargas,Cesar	15	R	24	a/a	NYY	73	4.19	1.53	6.91	3.0	7.9	2.6	0.3	37	71	88
Vasquez,Anthony	14	L	28	a/a	BAL	124	6.21	1.84	21.3	3.2	5.0	1.6	1.7	37	69	0
	15	L	29	a/a	PHI	134	5.43	1.64	21.3	3.9	3.9	1.0	0.6	32	66	21
Velasquez,Jonath	14	R	29	aa	NYM	55	4.05	1.22	5.02	2.2	6.2	2.8	0.4	31	65	89
	15	R	30	a/a	NYM	55	3.77	1.16	4.24	1.8	5.5	3.1	0.9	28	70	74
Velasquez,Vincer	15	R	23	aa	HOU	33	2.18	1.07	14.3	3.5	10.7	3.0	0.6	27	82	127
Venditte,Patrick	15	L	30	aaa	OAK	41	2.14	1.32	7.32	4.0	6.4	1.6	0.5	28	86	64
Verdugo,Ryan	14	L	27	aaa	BOS	75	5.44	1.46	17	3.3	7.5	2.3	1.2	33	64	58
	15	L	28	aaa	LAA	71	4.49	1.40	7.14	4.0	6.7	1.7	0.4	30	67	66
Verhagen,Drew	14	R	24	aaa	DET	110	4.56	1.49	25	2.1	4.1	2.0	0.5	34	68	45
	15	R	25	a/a	DET	34	4.33	1.53	7.47	3.7	5.3	1.4	0.3	33	70	50
Verrett,Logan	15	R	25	aaa	NYM	65	4.59	1.42	15.2	2.5	6.2	2.5	0.8	33	68	63
Villanueva,Elih	14	R	28	aaa	MIA	137	4.97	1.62	22.5	3.2	5.1	1.6	1.0	34	71	27
	15	R	29	a/a	BAL	168	5.69	1.61	26.6	2.4	3.6	1.5	1.0	34	65	13
Vincent,Nick	15	R	29	aaa	SD	50	3.13	1.39	5.29	2.7	9.3	3.4	0.8	36	80	103
Viramontes,Martir	15	R	26	aa	MIL	49	9.51	2.33	6.87	7.0	4.7	0.7	1.2	38	58	-9
Volstad,Chris	14	R	28	aaa	LAA	39	5.63	1.56	24.6	2.5	4.2	1.7	1.3	33	66	16
	15	R	29	aaa	PIT	156	4.48	1.66	25.8	2.7	4.0	1.5	0.2	36	71	39
Voth,Austin	14	R	22	aa	WAS	19	6.60	1.60	17.1	3.7	7.4	2.0	1.7	33	61	32
	15	R	23	aa	WAS	157	3.70	1.27	23	2.3	7.0	3.0	0.6	31	71	88
Wada,Tsuyoshi	14	L	33	aaa	CHC	114	3.71	1.48	25.7	2.6	7.0	2.7	1.3	34	80	55
	15	L	34	a/a	CHC	91	5.59	1.79	24.6	3.0	5.0	1.6	0.7	38	68	30
Wagner,Tyler	15	R	24	aa	MIL	152	3.20	1.42	25.8	3.1	6.0	2.0	0.6	32	79	58
Wahl,Bobby	15	R	23	aa	OAK	32	4.37	1.61	5.97	3.8	8.3	2.2	0.5	38	72	77
Waldron,Tyler	14	R	25	a/a	PIT	41	4.06	1.39	10.2	2.5	6.0	2.4	0.6	33	71	68
	15	R	26	aaa	STL	76	5.48	1.46	7.07	1.4	3.7	2.6	1.7	32	67	18
Wall,Josh	14	R	27	aaa	PIT	45	3.75	1.64	5.54	3.8	6.8	1.8	0.4	36	77	62
	15	R	28	aaa	PIT	37	3.38	1.25	5.15	2.7	6.6	2.5	0.3	31	72	89
Walters,P.J.	14	R	29	a/a	TOR	142	7.05	1.83	24.4	3.4	6.0	1.8	1.6	37	63	12
	15	R	30	a/a	WAS	88	7.62	2.04	16.5	3.9	5.2	1.3	1.3	40	63	4
Wang,Chien-Minç	14	R	34	aaa	CHW	173	4.90	1.81	28.6	3.5	2.9	0.8	0.4	36	72	11
	15	R	35	aaa	SEA	130	6.52	1.96	28.2	2.4	2.7	1.1	0.8	39	66	-4
Webb,Tyler	14	L	24	a/a	NYY	56	4.89	1.48	5.99	3.5	10.3	2.9	1.0	37	68	93
	15	L	25	aaa	NYY	38	3.89	1.64	6.78	2.9	8.0	2.8	1.3	38	81	58
Weber,Ryan	15	R	25	a/a	ATL	100	3.16	1.14	10.4	1.0	4.5	4.6	0.9	29	76	100
Weber,Thad	15	R	31	aaa	DET	161	5.77	1.68	26.8	2.7	4.1	1.5	1.4	34	68	5
Webster,Allen	14	R	24	aaa	BOS	122	3.91	1.42	24.6	3.4	6.1	1.8	0.7	31	74	53
	15	R	25	aaa	ARI	77	8.41	1.97	24.6	2.8	5.9	2.1	0.9	42	55	32
Weiss,Zack	15	R	23	aa	CIN	52	3.11	1.20	4.64	2.6	10.5	4.1	1.2	32	80	117
Weller,Blayne	15	R	25	a/a	ARI	62	6.48	1.55	20.8	3.3	4.8	1.5	0.8	32	57	31
Wendelken,Jeffre	15	R	22	a/a	CHW	59	4.17	1.31	6.24	2.7	9.3	3.4	1.2	33	72	94
West,Aaron	14	R	24	aa	HOU	24	6.24	1.43	14.8	3.7	4.1	1.1	1.6	26	59	3
	15	R	25	aa	HOU	84	3.30	1.30	11.6	1.2	6.1	5.0	0.6	34	76	120
West,Matthew	14	R	26	a/a	TEX	57	4.14	1.62	6.14	3.1	7.9	2.6	1.0	38	77	65
	15	R	27	a/a	LA	51	4.62	1.48	6.7	3.0	7.1	2.3	0.6	35	69	69
Westwood,Kyle	15	R	24	aa	HOU	132	4.92	1.59	22.4	1.8	4.1	2.3	0.9	35	70	35
Wheeler,Beck	15	R	27	aa	NYM	59	4.33	1.45	5.83	4.3	6.9	1.6	0.4	31	69	67
Wheeler,Jason	14	L	24	a/a	MIN	79	3.49	1.33	25.3	2.1	5.3	2.6	1.1	31	78	54
	15	L	25	a/a	MIN	138	6.99	1.74	25.1	2.8	4.6	1.7	1.3	36	60	11
White,Alex	14	R	26	aaa	HOU	64	7.17	1.88	12	4.4	6.1	1.4	1.0	37	61	24
	15	R	27	aaa	HOU	83	5.58	1.71	22.2	4.8	3.8	0.8	0.9	31	68	8
Whiting,Boone	14	R	25	aaa	STL	97	4.40	1.53	20	4.0	7.4	1.9	0.7	34	72	61
	15	R	26	aaa	COL	95	8.41	2.29	20.2	6.2	4.3	0.7	1.5	38	64	-24
Wieland,Joe	14	R	24	a/a	SD	33	2.87	1.08	21.3	1.2	6.2	5.0	0.5	30	74	133
	15	R	25	aaa	LA	114	5.13	1.55	22.6	1.9	6.0	3.2	0.6	37	66	77
Wilk,Adam	14	L	27	aaa	PIT	147	5.50	1.64	23.3	2.7	4.8	1.8	1.1	35	68	25
	15	L	28	aaa	LAA	145	5.82	1.73	24.4	2.3	5.1	2.2	0.9	38	66	36
Wilkerson,Aaron	15	R	26	aa	BOS	41	3.56	1.22	23.5	3.2	6.1	1.9	0.0	29	68	85
Williams,Ryan	15	R	24	aa	CHC	88	3.34	1.16	20.6	1.7	5.3	3.1	0.2	30	69	93
Williams,Trevor	14	R	22	aa	MIA	15	6.66	2.00	24.1	3.5	7.2	2.0	0.0	44	63	68
	15	R	23	a/a	MIA	131	4.84	1.60	23.2	3.0	5.8	1.9	0.6	35	69	49
Williamson,Fabiai	14	L	26	a/a	CIN	60	4.74	1.61	5.21	4.6	8.3	1.8	0.9	34	72	60
	15	L	27	a/a	MIA	47	7.29	2.09	5.81	8.1	6.8	0.8	1.0	34	65	24
Wilson,Tyler	15	R	26	aaa	BAL	94	5.25	1.60	24.6	2.1	4.7	2.3	1.2	35	70	28
Wimmers,Alex	14	R	26	aa	MIN	22	4.71	1.36	6.96	2.6	8.7	3.3	1.3	33	69	83
	15	R	27	aa	MIN	115	5.61	1.63	17.1	3.5	5.9	1.7	0.6	35	64	46
Windle,Tom	15	L	23	aa	PHI	97	4.91	1.64	12.8	4.7	5.2	1.1	0.6	32	70	34
Winkler,Kyle	14	R	24	aa	ARI	29	5.49	1.94	6.9	6.3	8.9	1.4	1.5	37	75	33
	15	R	25	a/a	LAA	42	4.50	1.32	5.66	3.0	6.5	2.2	0.4	31	64	76
Wisler,Matthew	14	R	22	a/a	SD	147	4.01	1.31	21.6	2.2	7.6	3.4	1.1	32	73	84
	15	R	23	aaa	ATL	65	5.60	1.46	23.2	1.9	6.0	3.2	0.8	35	61	72
Wittgren,Nick	14	R	23	aa	MIA	66	4.02	1.45	5.42	1.9	6.4	3.4	0.7	35	73	82
	15	R	24	aa	MIA	64	3.79	1.22	4.88	1.2	7.7	6.5	0.8	34	71	156
Wojciechowski,As	14	R	26	aaa	HOU	76	5.22	1.61	22.4	2.5	5.7	2.3	1.2	35	70	36
	15	R	27	aaa	HOU	115	5.52	1.66	25.8	3.3	5.4	1.7	1.1	35	68	27
Wolf,Randy	14	L	38	aaa	LAA	87	4.31	1.68	20.5	3.4	6.0	1.8	0.6	36	74	47
	15	L	39	aaa	TOR	140	4.30	1.81	28.1	3.3	5.2	1.6	0.4	38	76	39
Wolf,Ross	15	R	33	aaa	TEX	106	8.09	2.08	20	2.6	2.7	1.0	0.3	41	58	5
Wood,Austin	15	R	25	a/a	LAA	80	5.14	1.64	11.5	4.7	4.8	1.0	0.6	31	68	30
Wood,Blake	14	R	29	a/a	KC	33	7.03	2.36	5.9	8.8	8.0	0.9	0.9	40	70	29
	15	R	30	aaa	PIT	59	5.02	1.67	4.62	4.3	7.6	1.8	0.3	37	68	68
Wood,Grady	15	R	25	aa	SEA	60	5.32	1.68	7.5	5.0	5.1	1.0	0.7	32	68	31
Wooten,Eric	14	L	24	aa	NYY	40	5.10	1.49	24.4	2.6	4.0	1.5	0.9	32	66	24
	15	L	25	a/a	NYY	85	6.61	1.87	22.1	3.7	5.3	1.4	1.2	37	65	13
Wooten,Robert	14	R	29	aaa	MIL	22	7.63	1.69	4.65	2.4	6.7	2.8	0.6	40	52	70
	15	R	30	aaa	MIL	52	5.86	1.67	5.3	2.8	6.5	2.3	2.1	35	71	15
Worley,Vance	14	R	27	aaa	PIT	46	5.01	1.29	27	0.8	6.2	7.9	0.6	35	60	182
	15	R	28	aaa	PIT	34	3.28	1.30	28	1.4	4.1	2.8	1.1	30	80	47
Wright,Daniel	15	R	24	aa	CIN	155	5.93	1.53	25	3.0	6.6	2.2	0.5	35	59	66
Wright,Justin	14	L	25	a/a	STL	58	3.77	1.30	5.05	3.1	6.5	2.1	0.3	31	69	79
	15	L	26	a/a	STL	57	3.45	1.36	4.94	2.7	6.9	2.6	0.0	34	72	96
Wright,Mike	15	R	25	aaa	BAL	81	3.52	1.35	22.5	3.3	5.6	1.7	0.7	29	75	52
Wright,Steven	14	R	30	a/a	BOS	100	5.01	1.51	27.1	2.4	4.7	1.9	1.2	33	69	28
	15	R	31	aaa	BOS	52	6.17	1.88	30.6	3.3	5.3	1.6	0.5	40	65	36
Wyatt,Heath	14	R	26	aaa	STL	66	4.65	1.34	6.13	2.3	3.8	1.7	0.6	30	65	40
	15	R	27	a/a	STL	74	2.71	1.18	6.14	3.0	4.7	1.6	0.5	26	78	54
Ybarra,Tyler	14	L	25	aa	TOR	53	5.76	1.57	6.12	5.4	6.0	1.1	1.7	27	67	12
	15	L	26	aa	COL	44	7.75	2.20	5.86	6.5	6.8	1.1	0.3	41	62	39
Ynoa,Gabriel	14	R	21	aa	NYM	66	4.00	1.28	24.7	1.4	5.2	3.6	1.1	31	72	71
	15	R	22	aa	NYM	152	4.50	1.35	25.4	1.8	4.3	2.4	0.9	31	68	46
Younginer,Madisc	15	R	25	a/a	BOS	77	4.19	1.44	8.03	3.2	5.3	1.6	0.6	31	71	50
Zarate,Robert	15	L	28	aaa	TAM	40	3.90	1.34	9.88	3.8	8.5	2.2	0.5	32	71	88
Zastryzny,Rob	15	L	23	aa	CHC	61	7.38	1.92	20.6	4.3	6.1	1.4	1.4	38	63	11
Zeid,Joshua	14	R	27	aaa	HOU	19	2.72	1.37	4.6	4.5	8.1	1.8	1.0	28	85	64
	15	R	28	aaa	DET	71	5.93	1.86	7.87	5.7	5.4	1.0	0.6	34	67	28
Zimmer,Kyle	15	R	24	aa	KC	48	3.46	1.33	13.3	2.7	7.6	2.8	0.8	32	76	83
Zito,Barry	15	L	37	aaa	OAK	138	4.78	1.68	25.9	4.7	4.3	0.9	0.8	31	72	19
Zokan,Jacob	15	L	24	aa	SEA	59	5.11	1.80	21	4.2	5.5	1.3	1.3	35	75	12

The Transition to DFS

by Todd Zola

Daily Fantasy Sports (DFS) is an offshoot of traditional fantasy sports. While there are major differences between the formats, many of the same analytic methods that are integral to seasonal fantasy baseball are just as relevant for DFS. What follows is a general overview of DFS for those fantasy baseball traditionalists looking to make the transition to DFS.

General Format

1. While there are contests that can be played for free, the overwhelming majority of DFS contests are pay-for-play where the winners are compensated a percentage of their entry fee, in accordance with the rules of that game. The average overall payout for the various sites is 90 percent.

2. DFS baseball contests are generally based on a single day's slate of games, with a few encompassing multiple days. Depending on the number of games and start-time of a day's schedule, sites will offer contests within varying time frames. For example, only day games or only night games might be available for some contests.

3. The vast majority of DFS formats are points-based salary cap games, though a few utilize snake drafts to construct rosters.

Most Popular Contests

1. **Cash Games:** There are three primary styles of cash games; the common element is that all winners are compensated equally regardless of where they finish in the standings.

   A. 50/50: Those that finish in the top half of the standings wins almost twice their entry fee.

   B. Multipliers: A portion of the field earns 2x, 3x, 4x etc. their entry fee. The most common multiplier is a double-up, where a little less than half the field doubles their entry.

   C. Head-to-Head: Two combatants play each other; the winner earns almost twice their entry fee.

2. **GPP Tournaments:** Guaranteed prize pool, or GPP tournaments, state prizes for winners upfront, and are required to fulfill the advertised payout structure regardless of the number of entries. On the average, between 10 and 20 percent of the field cashes, with the overall winner earning the largest prize and everything else scaled downward.

3. **Survivor:** A survivor contest is a multiple-slate format where a portion of the entries survives to play the following day. The last day of a survivor contest is basically a tournament, with the winner earning the largest prize and the others scaled down.

4. **Qualifiers:** Most sites run contests with a very large prize pool. In most cases, entry into these tournaments emanates from winning a qualifier tournament.

5. **Satellites:** The entry point of many qualifiers is beyond what many casual players can afford. To accommodate this populace, many sites run satellite contests with the prize being a free entry into a qualifier.

DFS Analysis

1. **Projected performance:** Seasonal fantasy and DFS share a common theme. Both start with a baseline performance expectation with the objective to construct a roster with maximum point-scoring potential. The one-day time frame, though, entails adjusting the baseline performance based on that days' match-up. For both hitters and pitchers, there are analytic tools to help gauge if the player is likely to perform better or worse than their baseline expectation. This adjusted expectation is then considered in context with the player's salary to determine his potential contributions relative to the other players.

2. **wOBA:** While it has its shortcomings, weighted on base average, or wOBA, has evolved as a favorite metric to help evaluate both hitters and pitchers. In theory, wOBA correlates pretty well with DFS points. It's not perfect but among the readily available metrics, it's the best. In a nutshell, wOBA is a souped up version of on-base percentage (OBP) where the components of OBP are multiplied by a coefficient derived from the run-scoring matrix. Something to keep in mind is wOBA is not park-corrected, so the number from a hitter playing half his games in a pitcher's park is more impressive than the same number with a hitter's venue for his home park. A park-corrected version of wOBA is wRC+, but the latter is not as readily attainable.

3. **Pitching:** In seasonal fantasy, especially rotisserie formats, limiting baserunners and run prevention are as important as strikeouts. In DFS, those are secondary to innings and strikeouts, the two chief means of accruing points. Limiting hits and runs are helpful—but mass quantities of whiffs and innings are crucial.

Tips for Players New to DFS

1. **Start slow and be prepared to lose:** While cogent analysis can increase your chances of winning, the variance associated with a single day's worth of outcomes doesn't assure success. In theory, if you play ample volume you'll win more than you lose. However, even for the most seasoned DFS players, short-term losing streaks are inevitable. A such, when you're first entering the space, be conservative with your bankroll so you don't deplete it before you really get the hang of the format. It's probably best to start with low cost cash games before embarking on tournament play.

2. **Minimize the number of sites you play:** The DFS space is dominated by two sites but there are other options. Playing on too many sites simultaneously can be overwhelming since there are nuances among each game. At the beginning, stick to one or two then once you're comfortable, consider expanding to others.

3. **Bankroll management:** While there is no one-size-fits-all process, the recommended means to manage your bankroll is to risk no more than 10% on a given day. Within that portion, the suggested ratio is 80% cash games to 20% GPP tournament action. The principle behind this is two-fold. First, playing just ten percent should allow you to withstand most unlucky stretches without having to redeposit. Second, if things play out properly, you'll be funding your GPP entries with cash game winnings.

Once you get the knack of DFS, you can adjust these percentages to match your strengths and weaknesses, as well as your agenda.

4. General Strategies

A. Cash Games: Conventional wisdom preaches to be conservative in cash games since you don't need to be the high scorer; most of the time you just need to be in the top 45 to 50 percent since double-ups and 50/50s are the most popular cash games. Upper level starting pitchers, the most reliable subset of players, thus make excellent cash game options. With respect to hitting, it's best to spread your choices among several teams and not overload on one team. In general, you're looking for players with a high floor and aren't concerned about their ceiling.

B: GPP Tournaments: In tournaments with a larger number of overall entrants, the more contrary your lineup needs to be to differentiate yourself from the pack. In cash, focus on what's probable. Here, it's more a matter of what's plausible. You're paying for a player's ceiling. A common ploy is to look to select a lesser priced, though risky pitcher with a favorable match-up who has an opportunity to have an ace-like game. It's also very common to overload—or stack—several players from the same team, hoping that squad scores a bunch of runs. Then, your lineup benefits from a cascade effect (where more than one of your hitters gets points on the same event).

5. Miscellaneous Tips

A. Pay extra attention to games threatened by weather, as well as players who are not a lock to be in the lineup that day. The latter is especially true on Sundays, when managers will often give reserves a chance to play, and on day games after night games when regular catchers often sit. There will inevitably be entries with players not active which helps tip the advantage in your favor, especially in cash games.

B. Unless you're challenging a friend or family member, avoid playing head-to-head until you're comfortable playing and have enjoyed some success. One avenue professional DFS players utilize to build their own bankroll is to take advantage of new players by picking up their posted head-to head games as well as posting their own in hopes that an inexperienced player picks up their challenge. On the other hand, playing heads-up against people you know for low stakes is a great way to learn how to play DFS.

C. Stay disciplined. The worst thing you can do is eat up your bankroll quickly by entering into tournaments, trying to chase that big cardboard check that won't fit into your ATM machine. If you take it slow, your baseball knowledge will carry you until you learn the nuances of DFS play in general and tournament play specifically.

D. Most importantly, have fun. For most players, DFS is a way to embellish their enjoyment of baseball. Sure, there are some professionals, but if you play smart, the entry fee can be the equivalent of paying for entertainment the same way others pay for a movie, good meal, round of golf or day at the slopes. Obviously, you want to win, but hopefully you're also in it for the challenge of mastering the unique skills intrinsic to DFS.

Using BaseballHQ Tools in DFS

by Vlad Sedler

Daily Fantasy Baseball (DFS) can be an arduous and challenging venture. Prognosticating production is tough; results on a given day are often unpredictable and sometimes counterintuitive. Professional DFS players spend several hours a day slicing data and have spent every day since the inception of DFS perfecting their systems, looking to find edges and advantages.

One of the advantages that BaseballHQ.com provides is a full arsenal of base performance indicators—BPIs—that your competition may not be paying attention to. Some of these BPIs were crafted 20 years ago or more, and have a long-standing history of helping us win season-long leagues. These classic indicators, as well as some of our newer tools, can be utilized to help us in DFS.

Upon review of a typical day's slate, most DFS players consider lefty / righty splits, home / road splits, park factors and to some degree, batter vs pitcher history. Gut and intuition should also factor into the equation. If a player sticks out in a team's lineup, and a few researched factors support the play, it usually isn't a good idea to talk oneself out of it or continue to tweak lineups. Some sites have more aggressive pricing than others, making it tougher to build lineups filled with studs. Salaries adjust daily based on recent performance on all DFS sites, and some inflate pricing for hitters playing in power havens like Coors Field. Adding BHQ's BPIs into the equation can provide us with an even more granular view to make confident decisions.

In cash games (double-ups or 50/50s), payouts go to approximately 45 to 50 percent of the field, simply look to build lineups using players with high floors. Look for consistent, steady production from hitters with high contact rates, upper tier walk rates and overall solid on-base skills in advantageous matchups against weaker pitchers.

Tournaments and GPPs (guaranteed prize pools) typically pay 10 to 20 percent of entrants. These contests require more of a swing-for-the-fences approach—choosing sluggers who are more prone to streaks and whose day-over-day performances may be more volatile. These players typically have higher strikeout rates than average, but with above average PX and xPX indicators. Several members of the Houston Astros come to mind—players like Chris Carter, Evan Gattis and Luis Valbuena. Stacking several of these types of hitters against weaker fly ball pitchers on the right day can lead to a very fruitful outcome.

Here are some of the different base performance indicators to consider for cash games and tournaments:

Cash Game BPIs

bb%: Walks per plate appearance. This simple indicator may receive only a quick glance when building lineups, but it is imperative in providing insight on a batter's underlying approach and plate discipline. Walks also equal points in all DFS scoring structures. A walk rate over 8 percent is considered above average in this current pitching-dominated era, and above 12 percent, excellent. As an example, one reasonably priced player typically known as a batting average drain happened to be among the league's elite in BB% in 2015—Carlos Santana at 16%. Walk rate is an especially great BPI to consider when selecting catchers for cash games and 50/50s. Any hitters with a great eye at the plate are typically solid options for cash games because they are less likely to give you a low or negative point total, because they are receiving points for the free passes.

ct%: Contact rate ((AB-K)/AB) is another byproduct of good plate discipline, reflecting the percentage of balls put in play. Eighty-five percent or higher is considered strong, and approaching 90% is where you will find several consistent .300-plus batting average guys like Jose Altuve, Buster Posey and Michael Brantley. Similar to bb%, players with great or elite contact rates tend to provide those lineup slots with a higher floor, and less chance of a negative score as you would have from a free swinger with a high strikeout rate. Leadoff and two-hole hitters with good OBPs and elite contact rates like Daniel Murphy (92%) and Yangervis Solarte (89%) are underrated in DFS due to lack of power, but are well suited for cash games where you don't want to take a zero or negative points at any position.

xBA: Expected Batting Average measures a hitter's BA by multiplying his contact rate by the chance that a ball in play falls for a hit. Though batting average and xBA tend to correlate with one another, hitters whose BA is far below their xBA are the ones to keep an eye out as they may be due for some good luck with hard-hit balls falling in for hits. The xBA leaderboard is also a good place to find affordable, extreme LHP-killers like Chris Young (.327 BA vs LHP).

Tournament / GPP BPIs

PX / xPX: In contests with hundreds or thousands of players and a smaller threshold of payout, projecting home runs are imperative. Home runs are the single greatest multi-point event in DFS formats. Using PX (power index) and xPX (expected power index) together can help identify underperformers who are due in the power category. PX measures power and extra base hits and xPX takes into account the quality of contact. Forty-plus home runs hitters in 2015, Bryce Harper and Nolan Arenado were among the major league PX leaders - but with lower xPX scores—signifying that they may have overachieved power-wise. Ditto, outfielders Colby Rasmus and Randal Grichuk, whose xPX scores were significantly lower than their PX scores. On the opposite end of the spectrum, Matt Kemp's 30-point variance (120 PX, 150 xPX) sticks out. It could be a sign of things to come as Kemp trades in contact for power over the final few years of his career.

There are several other BPIs that are helpful for targeting hitters in larger tournaments where we are looking to swing for the fences with stacks of the night. These include HR/F (home run per fly ball rate) and BPV (base performance value) which describes a hitter's overall raw skill level and takes into account batting eye, contact rate, power and speed.

Subscribers using BaseballHQ.com's unique BPIs have a true edge over non-subscribers, and the data can be utilized to one's advantage when building DFS lineups. Digging deeper into some of the universal indicators (LHP/RHP splits, bb%, ct%) as well as proprietary ones (BPV, xPX) is a fun exercise if you love working with spreadsheets, numbers and are dedicated to improving and competing in daily fantasy baseball.

Choosing Pitchers in DFS

by Brandon Kruse

The criteria for choosing a pitcher(s) for DFS may be more narrow and specific than for a full-season league, but the focus on underlying skills should remain. While it's simple to pay up for a Kershaw or Scherzer, using skill and playing the percentages can help you find a suitable lower-priced option—or at least help you avoid riskier targets. Here are some criteria that we recommend when picking a pitcher:

Major Considerations

- How are his overall skills? Look for the following minimums: 2.9 Ctl (bb/9), 7.7 Dom (k/9), 2.6 Cmd (k/bb), and 1.0 HR/9.
- Is he home or away? In 2015, MLB pitchers had the following splits: 3.76 ERA, 7.9 Dom, 2.8 Cmd at home, 4.16 ERA, 7.7 Dom, and 2.5 Cmd on the road.
- Is he pitching at Coors Field? (Even the best pitchers are a risky start there.)

Moderate Considerations

- What has his recent performance been like? Most pitchers go through ups and downs—even Kershaw had a 3.97 ERA in May. Examine walks and strikeouts over his last 4-5 starts. A sudden drop in dominance or loss of command can be a sign of fatigue or injury. BaseballHQ.com's Playerlink, provides each pitcher's skill stats over the last 31 days, including their xERA, which can be a quick-glance way to determine who has been pitching well.
- How good or bad is his opponent? What is the opposing team's OPS for the season? Have they been hot or cold over the last 7-10 days?

Minor Considerations

- Are there any L/R issues in play? Does the pitcher have wide platoon splits? What about the opposing team?
- Is the park the game will be played in a hitter's park, a pitcher's park, or is it mostly neutral? (With the aforementioned exception of Coors Field.)
- Has the pitcher faced this team already this season? If so, how did he fare? (Look at the underlying skills rather than just his ERA.) Again, on BaseballHQ.com's Playerlink, you can see a pitcher's in-season skill stats against every team he has faced that year.

You will hopefully be left with a tiered list of pitching options, ripe for comparing individual risk/reward level against their price point. On sites that allow you to use two pitchers, you may be willing to take on more risk with a cheap second pitcher if he affords you the ability to pair an ace with a respectable hitting lineup.

Following these criteria won't guarantee you'll pick the highest-scoring pitcher on a given day (no system can reliably do that), nor will it ensure you'll avoid every disaster, but it should help lower your overall risk level, and consistently steer you toward the options that will give you the best shot at success.

BaseballHQ.com also offers a Daily Dashboard page where we rate each day's starters based on a number of criteria, and also offer more in-depth analysis of a handful of them, including our Best SP choices, Worst SP choices, and Risk/Reward options.

PITCHING: HRAKing Mass

by Patrick Davitt

To simplify the mechanics of choosing starting pitchers for "streaming" and for DFS, BaseballHQ.com invented a new metric: HRAK, which is short for HR Average per 6 K.

For a pitcher, the home run is an unqualified disaster. In 2014, starters had a 2.63 cumulative ERA in games where they allowed no HR—and a 5.34 ERA when they did. Numbers In 2015 were very similar.

At the same time, though, strikeouts reduce the effects of HR on ERAs:

HR Games			No-HR Games		
ALL	6+K	6-K	ALL	6+K	6-K
5.34	2.36	6.24	2.63	1.69	3.34

This is an idea we can use—in daily leagues, but also in seasonal leagues where streaming starters is an option. The HRAK metric is a quick way to assess whether a pitcher's opponents are prone to whiffing and not so prone to hitting homers.

We first found out how many home runs each team hit and struck out per-game basis, at home and on the road. Then we calculated the ratio of how many HRs the team hit, home and road, per every six strikeouts.

Overall per-game averages are 1 HR, 7.6 Ks and 0.8 HRAK. We thought that teams that scored under the 0.8 mark would hit fewer HRs, strike out more, or, ideally, both. These are the ideal opponents, against whom we want to send our starters.

It turned out that the truism that pitchers get better results at home is accurate. HR/G, K/G and HRAK are all more favorable to pitchers working at home. The exception is the Mariners, who on the road hit slightly more HR and struck out slightly less than they did at home.

For home pitching starts, we wanted to see our pitchers up against the visiting Padres, Braves, Pirates, Twins, Mets and Phillies. The Phils' HRAK was actually under 0.50 on the road. Teams to avoid for home pitching starts are the Mariners, Yankees and Giants, all right around or slightly over 1.0 HRAK.

For pitching road starts—hitters at home—we should send our guys up against the Marlins, D'Backs, Indians, Giants, Cubs and Braves (yes, the Braves are on both lists).

And we almost surely should not pitch our guys on the road against the Orioles, Yankees and maybe the Astros. The Astros lead baseball in HRAK at their home park, but they also whiff a ton, generating a 1.1 HRAK. And we surely would not start a pitcher on the road at Rogers Centre in Toronto. The Blue Jays had a remarkable 1.5 HRAK, partly because they bashed the heck out of the ball and partly because they cut their Ks from 8.0/game on the road to well under 6.0 at home.

Now we should close by saying that if we had Clayton Kershaw, Zack Greinke or Max Scherzer, or an ace of similar ilk, we would probably just start him everywhere.

A Hitter's Potential in a One-Game Sample

by Todd Zola

One of the keys to building a DFS lineup is identifying players in a favorable spot. That is, searching for players whose situation in one game portends outcomes better than baseline expectations. Here are seven factors to consider:

1. Home versus away

2015	BB%	K%	ISO	wOBA	wRC+	HR	R	SB	PA
Full	7.7%	20.4%	0.150	0.313	96	4909	20647	2505	183627
Home	8.0%	19.9%	0.155	0.321	101	2473	10556	1235	90121
Away	7.4%	20.9%	0.145	0.306	92	2436	10091	1270	93506
2014	**BB%**	**K%**	**ISO**	**wOBA**	**wRC+**	**HR**	**R**	**SB**	**PA**
Full	7.6%	20.4%	0.135	0.310	96	4186	19761	2764	183928
Home	7.9%	19.9%	0.138	0.316	100	2094	9967	1406	90221
Away	7.3%	20.8%	0.132	0.304	93	2092	9794	1358	93707

Hitters' skills are better at home—but note this doesn't result in more HR or SB steals, two big contributors to DFS scoring. The main reason: the home team doesn't always bat in the ninth inning.

Action Item: Top-of-the-order hitters are likely to get the extra at bat at home or on the road, so maximize points potential by using those hitters at home. However, if you're using a bottom-of-the-order guy without any teammates, best to use him in away games.

2. Handedness

2015	BB%	K%	wOBA	wRC+
LHB vs. RHP	8.8%	19.1%	0.324	104
RHB vs. LHP	8.2%	20.1%	0.320	101
RHB vs. RHP	6.5%	21.3%	0.304	90
LHB vs. LHP	7.2%	22.3%	0.295	84
2014	**BB%**	**K%**	**wOBA**	**wRC+**
LHB vs. RHP	8.6%	19.0%	0.315	100
RHB vs. LHP	8.1%	19.8%	0.322	105
RHB vs. RHP	6.5%	21.5%	0.303	91
LHB vs. LHP	7.2%	22.3%	0.290	83

As expected, on the average hitters perform better when they enjoy the platoon advantage over the opposing pitcher. The left-on-right and right-on-left splits should be considered equal, followed by right-on-right and left-on-left.

However, realize that an individual hitter doesn't own his career splits until he's been in the league 10 seasons. Many analysts will employ reverse splits to identify strong DFS plays, but more often than not the sample size of that data is too small and needs to be regressed to league average.

Action Item: Unless a hitter is a seasoned veteran, assume his platoon splits tend towards league average. Thus, focusing on players that enjoy the platoon advantage can add potential to your lineup.

3. Batting order spot

The number of points a player generates is a function of how many plate appearances he gets along with the opportunity he has to produce runs. Some MLB teams will use speedy hitters without much power at the top, while others will deploy high on-base hitters with a bit more pop, so the following league average data needs to be used in conjuction with a player's specific context. On the average, the top points producer hits third. The leadoff batter and cleanup man are next, with the second and fifth hitter sharing the third spot. There's a drop off after that, more so in the NL since the pitcher doesn't drive in many runs.

Action Item: In cash games, concentrate on hitters fifth or higher, with the sole exception a base-stealing threat hitting ninth in the AL. If stacking, it's viable to use hitters from lower in the order.

4. Park factors

Beware, not all favorable home run parks also boost run scoring. In addition, home run factors for right-handed hitters can differ significantly than lefty swingers and vice versa.

Action Item: If you're stacking several hitters from one team, focus on venues that favor run scoring since you're looking to get multiple-credit for runs and RBI. If you're using a stand-alone power hitter, then hone in on sluggers in venues that boost homers for his handedness.

5. Quality of opposing pitcher

It stands to reason that you want to target batters facing inferior pitchers—preferably those that don't strike out many hitters. Keep in mind that even though you may feel it's safe to use a strong hitter against a strong pitcher, the rest of the lineup isn't likely to generate much offense. So while the hitter in a vacuum may do fine, his RBI and run-scoring potential is tempered.

Action Item: The most crucial match-up consideration is quality of opposing pitcher. The other factors are important, but they don't supersede your hitter facing a lesser pitcher. In fact, a stealth means to differentiate your lineup is not to prioritize an inferior player with a platoon or park factor edge over a superior player lacking the platoon boost. Too many filter out right-on-right match-ups without even considering the quality of pitcher.

6. Historical batter versus pitcher data

One of the more polarizing analytical processes is the proper way to frame batter versus pitcher data, or BvP. Certain hitters very likely enjoy a tangible edge over certain pitchers, but there's no way of delineating the scenarios that are real from those that are random. Some will set an arbitrary number of plate appearances as their filter to consider BvP "real," but statistically, it takes hundreds of plate appearances for the outcomes to stabilize.

Action Item: The best use of BvP data is to fade a hitter in tournament play that has had well-publicized success against the opposing pitcher as a means to differentiate your lineup. Otherwise, there's nothing wrong with using a hitter with history of success against the opposing pitcher so long as he has some of the other factors in his favor.

7. Hot and cold streaks

Much like BvP data, hitters can go on genuine hot and cold streaks, but there is no definitive means of determining when that will end. However, if during a cold streak a hitter is whiffing at a clip above his average, it is defensible to avoid using him until he starts to make better contact.

Action Item: Similar to BvP, fading a hot player is a way to deploy a contrarian lineup. Further, depending on how quickly the DFS site adjusts its pricing, a hot player's cost may increase to the point his potential return on investment is minimal or negative—whereas cold players may see their price tag drop to the point their return on investment is elevated.

HITTERS: Benefits of Stacking

by Dave Potts

Stacking, which is taking several hitters from the same team, is a common strategy in DFS tournaments. The reasoning is twofold: First, when a team matches up against a bad pitcher, you want as many hitters as possible facing that pitcher. Second, DFS points can piggyback on each other for each singular outcome. For example, if you roster Andrew McCutchen, and he hits an RBI double that scores Starling Marte and Gregory Polanco, you get credit for a double and 2 RBI. But if you also have Marte and Polanco on your roster, you receive not only McCutchen's points, but points for the runs scored by the other two players.

Stacking increases both the potential upside and downside for your team. Thus, stacking is not recommended in cash games, where your goal is a solid base of points, but it is a very viable strategy in tournaments. If you can identify a high-scoring team, particularly one that is not obvious to the masses, it makes sense to get a lot of exposure to that team.

However, be aware of a few things about stacking:

1) Stacking is a very common strategy; obvious MLB teams will be stacked by a lot of contestants. You cannot simply load up the 1-4 hitters from COL or TOR at home and expect to win a DFS tournament. If those players are affordable, then other contestants will roster them, and you will not be gaining an edge. If you feel strongly about a stack, use it even at high ownership—but know the rest of your roster will need to come through in order to win.

2) Understand the scoring and roster rules of the site. There is a big difference in stacking between FanDuel and DraftKings. On FanDuel, you can only roster four players from the same team, while on DraftKings, you can use as many as six. Essentially, you need to be more certain of which hitters from the stack you are using on FanDuel. If a team's scoring is spread out, you won't be able to get access to a majority of the runs. On DraftKings, by using a full six-player stack, you have a better chance getting the right players on your team. But it also increases the likelihood of your competition having those players.

3) Home runs are crucial to DFS scoring. Regardless of stacking, you almost always need some home runs to win. If you pick the right team to stack, but miss out on the guy who hits a three-run homer, then your stack will not win. Always pay attention to individual matchups when choosing players for your stack. While you are counting on the whole team to be involved in the scoring, you should have a reason behind every player you put on your roster.

4) It can be advantageous to use bottom-of-the-order hitters, or to leave the team's top hitter out of your stack. On high scoring teams, you will find that big days come from all parts of the batting order; it's not always the heart of the order that scores the most runs. You can separate yourself by either using a stack that others won't have, or by using less obvious players in your stack.

There are endless ways to build DFS lineups, and you shouldn't get locked into one way of thinking. Stacking has proven to be a winning tournament strategy, but it is not the only winning strategy. Never use it as a shortcut, because it is much more difficult than it appears to be on the surface.

DAILY FANTASY INDICATORS

Top OPS v LHP, 2014-2015

Hitter	OPS
Tulowitzki, Troy	1133
Stanton, Giancarlo	1108
Goldschmidt, Paul	1095
Cruz, Nelson	1047
Martinez, Victor	1026
Donaldson, Josh	1014
Votto, Joey	999
Altuve, Jose	990
Trout, Mike	971
Bautista, Jose	960
Beltre, Adrian	958
Martinez, J.D.	957
Zimmerman, Ryan	955
Wright, David	946
Cabrera, Miguel	943
Napoli, Mike	940
Holliday, Matt	938
Rodriguez, Alex	926
Prado, Martin	916
McCutchen, Andrew	915
Harper, Bryce	906
Cain, Lorenzo	904
Rizzo, Anthony	903
Cuddyer, Michael	901
Pollock, A.J.	901
Zobrist, Ben	899
Longoria, Evan	891
Jones, Adam	888
Braun, Ryan	888
Johnson, Chris	882
Rosario, Wilin	881
Abreu, Jose	879
Springer, George	875
Fowler, Dexter	875
Werth, Jayson	875
Arenado, Nolan	866
Posey, Buster	866
Ramirez, Aramis	856
Forsythe, Logan	854
Pearce, Steve	853
Encarnacion, Edwin	853

Top OPS v RHP, 2014-2015

Hitter	OPS
Harper, Bryce	1010
Dickerson, Corey	970
Trout, Mike	963
Goldschmidt, Paul	947
Ortiz, David	937
Encarnacion, Edwin	931
Gonzalez, Carlos	927
Cabrera, Miguel	925
McCutchen, Andrew	921
Votto, Joey	919
Brantley, Michael	916
Abreu, Jose	913
Stanton, Giancarlo	911
Bautista, Jose	910
Rizzo, Anthony	906
Lind, Adam	905
Peralta, David	902
Turner, Justin	898
Morneau, Justin	898
Freeman, Freddie	896
Fielder, Prince	882
Gonzalez, Adrian	876
Bryant, Kris	875
Martinez, J.D.	874
Duda, Lucas	872
Arenado, Nolan	869
Davis, Chris	866
Machado, Manny	864
Cano, Robinson	852
Pollock, A.J.	850
Posey, Buster	846
Cespedes, Yoenis	845
Cruz, Nelson	843
Carpenter, Matt	841
Puig, Yasiel	837
Reddick, Josh	835
Coghlan, Chris	831
Choo, Shin-Soo	829
Teixeira, Mark	829
Donaldson, Josh	828
Heyward, Jason	827

Top L-R Splits, 2014-2015

Hitter	OPS vL-vR
Tulowitzki, Troy	321
Johnson, Chris	317
Wright, David	287
Napoli, Mike	262
Ruiz, Carlos	249
Martinez, Victor	240
Zimmerman, Ryan	236
Prado, Martin	235
Altuve, Jose	230
Hicks, Aaron	226
Rosario, Wilin	220
Cruz, Nelson	204
Longoria, Evan	198
Stanton, Giancarlo	197
Iannetta, Chris	197
Cozart, Zack	190
Suzuki, Ichiro	188
Donaldson, Josh	186
Davis, Rajai	186

Top R-L Splits, 2014-2015

Hitter	OPS vR-vL
Gennett, Scooter	483
Lind, Adam	418
Gonzalez, Carlos	360
De Aza, Alejandro	356
Davis, Ike	351
Joyce, Matt	349
Peralta, David	300
Ethier, Andre	292
Adams, Matt	285
Dickerson, Corey	269
LaRoche, Adam	268
Sandoval, Pablo	267
Polanco, Gregory	238
Coghlan, Chris	237
Reddick, Josh	232
Miller, Bradley	227
Heyward, Jason	227
Venable, Will	217
Valbuena, Luis	217

600+ PA, 2014-2015

DAILY FANTASY INDICATORS

Most Consistent SP

Pitcher	QC*
Greinke,Zack	176
Arrieta,Jake	170
Kershaw,Clayton	164
Price,David	150
Scherzer,Max	140
Keuchel,Dallas	140
Tanaka,Masahiro	134
Ross,Tyson	134
Cole,Gerrit	132
Kluber,Corey	132
Bumgarner,Madison	132
Harvey,Matt	124
Verlander,Justin	120
Archer,Chris	118
Gray,Sonny	118
Sale,Chris	118
Shields,James	116
Hamels,Cole	108
Quintana,Jose	108
Burnett,A.J.	108
deGrom,Jacob	102
Hernandez,Felix	102
Garcia,Jaime	100
Martinez,Carlos	96
Cueto,Johnny	94
Lester,Jon	92
Bettis,Chad	90
Liriano,Francisco	90
Richards,Garrett	90
Wacha,Michael	88
Lackey,John	86
Miller,Shelby	86
Wilson,C.J.	84
Iwakuma,Hisashi	80
Zimmermann,Jordan	80
Hahn,Jesse	76
McHugh,Collin	74
Syndergaard,Noah	74
Porcello,Rick	72
Gausman,Kevin	70

15+ Games Started, 2015
**Quality-Consistency score*

Most DOMinant SP

Pitcher	DOM%
Greinke,Zack	88%
Kershaw,Clayton	88%
Arrieta,Jake	85%
Scherzer,Max	82%
Price,David	81%
Cole,Gerrit	78%
Kluber,Corey	78%
deGrom,Jacob	77%
Hernandez,Felix	77%
Keuchel,Dallas	76%
Harvey,Matt	76%
Tanaka,Masahiro	75%
Ross,Tyson	73%
Bumgarner,Madison	72%
Lester,Jon	72%
Buchholz,Clay	72%
Archer,Chris	71%
Gray,Sonny	71%
Sale,Chris	71%

Most DISastrous SP

Pitcher	DIS%
Greene,Shane	56%
Buchanan,David	47%
Kendrick,Kyle	44%
Butler,Eddie	44%
Vogelsong,Ryan	41%
Lincecum,Tim	40%
Peralta,Wily	40%
Hutchison,Drew	39%
Williams,Jerome	38%
Bolsinger,Michael	38%
Gonzalez,Miguel	38%
Wisler,Matthew	37%
Pelfrey,Mike	37%
Rodriguez,Wandy	33%
Latos,Mat	33%
Foltynewicz,Mike	33%
Graveman,Kendall	33%
Lorenzen,Michael	33%
Kazmir,Scott	32%

Best Parks - LH HR

Ballpark	Factor
BAL	37%
MIL	33%
CIN	31%
NYY	29%
NYM	24%
HOU	22%
COL	15%
LA	15%
TOR	14%

Worst Parks - LH HR

Ballpark	Factor
SF	-41%
MIA	-36%
BOS	-30%
OAK	-25%
WAS	-20%
LAA	-15%
ATL	-14%
STL	-13%
KC	-12%
MIN	-10%

Best Parks - Runs

Ballpark	Factor
COL	40%
BOS	7%
BAL	7%

Worst Parks - Runs

Ballpark	Factor
NYM	-13%
SF	-12%
SEA	-10%
LA	-10%
LAA	-8%
SD	-7%

Note: for Runs, the best parks for hitters are also the worst for pitchers

Best Parks - RH HR

Ballpark	Factor
PHI	40%
NYY	26%
CHC	24%
MIL	23%
COL	21%
TOR	21%
CIN	17%
CHW	13%
HOU	12%

Worst Parks - RH HR

Ballpark	Factor
PIT	-27%
SF	-24%
MIA	-22%
KC	-18%
NYM	-18%
TB	-17%
WAS	-12%

Best Parks - Ks

Ballpark	Factor
CIN	11%
ATL	10%

Worst Parks - Ks

Ballpark	Factor
COL	-18%
DET	-10%
MIN	-9%

Best Parks - BB

Ballpark	Factor
CHW	14%

Worst Parks - BB

Ballpark	Factor
LA	-17%

This section provides rankings of projected skills indicators for 2016. Rather than take shots in the dark predicting league leaders in the exact number of home runs, or stolen bases, or strikeouts, the Forecaster's Leaderboards focus on the component elements of each skill.

For batters, we've ranked the top players in terms of pure power, speed, and batting average skill, breaking each down in a number of different ways to provide more insight. For pitchers, we rank some of the key base skills, differentiating between starters and relievers, and provide a few interesting cuts that might uncover some late round sleepers. Plus, some potential gainers/faders lists in several categories.

These are clearly not exhaustive lists of sorts and filters. If there is another cut you'd like to see, drop us a note and we'll consider it for next year's book. Also note that the database at BaseballHQ.com allows you to construct your own custom sorts and filters. Finally, remember that these are just tools. Some players will appear on multiple lists—even mutually exclusive lists—so you have to assess what makes most sense and make decisions for your specific application.

Power

Top PX, 400+ AB: Top power skills among projected full-time players.

Top PX, -300 AB: Top power skills among projected part-time players. Possible end-game options are here.

Position Scarcity: A quick scan to see which positions have deeper power options than others.

Top PX, ct% over 80%: Top power skills among the top contact hitters. Best pure power options here.

Top PX, ct% under 70%: Top power skills among the worst contact hitters. These are free-swingers who might be prone to streakiness or lower batting averages.

Top PX, FB% over 40%: Top power skills among the most extreme fly ball hitters. Most likely to convert their power into home runs.

Top PX, FB% under 35%: Top power skills among those with lesser fly ball tendencies. There may be more downside to their home run potential.

Speed

Top Spd, 400+ AB: Top speed skills among projected full-time players.

Top Spd, -300 AB: Top speed skills among projected part-time players. Possible end-game options here.

Position Scarcity: A quick scan to see which positions have deeper speed options than others.

Top Spd, OB% .330 and above: Top speed skills among those who get on base most often. Best opportunities for stolen bases here.

Top Spd, OB% under .300: Top speed skills among those who have trouble getting on base. These names may bear watching if they can improve their on base ability.

Top Spd, SBO% over 20%: Top speed skills among those who get the green light most often. Most likely to convert their speed into stolen bases.

Top Spd, SBO% under 15%: Top speed skills among those who are currently not getting the green light. There may be sleeper SBs here if given more opportunities to run.

Batting Average

Top ct%, 400+ AB: Top contact skills among projected full-time players. Contact does not always convert to higher BAs, but is still strongly correlated.

Top ct%, -300 AB: Top contact skills among projected part-time players. Possible end-gamers here.

Low ct%, 400+ AB: The poorest contact skills among projected full-time players. Potential BA killers.

Top ct%, bb% over 9%: Top contact skills among the most patient hitters. Best batting average upside here.

Top ct%, bb% under 6%: Top contact skills among the least patient hitters. These are free-swingers who might be prone to streakiness or lower batting averages.

Top ct%, GB% over 50%: Top contact skills among the most extreme ground ball hitters. A ground ball has a higher chance of becoming a hit than a non-HR fly ball so there may be some batting average upside here.

Top ct%, GB% under 40%: Top contact skills from those with lesser ground ball tendencies. These players make contact but hit more fly balls, which tend to convert to hits at a lower rate than GB.

Pitching Skills

Top Command: Leaders in projected K/BB rates.

Top Control: Leaders in fewest projected walks allowed.

Top Dominance: Leaders in projected strikeout rate.

Top Ground Ball Rate: GB pitchers tend to have lower ERAs (and higher WHIP) than fly ball pitchers.

Top Fly Ball Rate: FB pitchers tend to have higher ERAs (and lower WHIP) than ground ball pitchers.

High GB, Low Dom: GB pitchers tend to have lower K rates, but these are the most extreme examples.

High GB, High Dom: The best at dominating hitters and keeping the ball down. These are the pitchers who keep runners off the bases and batted balls in the park, a skills combination that is the most valuable a pitcher can own.

Lowest xERA: Leaders in projected skills-based ERA.

Top BPV: Two lists of top skilled pitchers. For starters, those projected to be rotation regulars (180+ IP) and fringe starters with skill (<150 IP). For relievers, those projected to be frontline closers (10+ saves) and high-skilled bullpen fillers (<9 saves).

Potential Gainers and Faders

These charts look to identify upcoming changes in performance by highlighting 2015 results that were in conflict with their corresponding skill indicators.

PX Gainers/Faders: Compares PX to xPX.

BA Gainers/Faders: Compares batter hit rate (h%) to HctX.

Dom Gainers/Faders: Compares K/9 to SwK%.

Ctl Gainers/Faders: Compares BB/9 to FpK%.

Additional details are provided on the page in which the charts appear.

Risk Management

These lists include players who've accumulated the most days on the disabled list over the past five years (Grade "F" in Health) and whose performance was the most consistent over the past three years. Also listed are the most reliable batters and pitchers overall, with a focus on positional and skills reliability. As a reminder, reliability in this context is not tied to skill level; it is a gauge of which players manage to accumulate playing time and post consistent output from year to year, whether that output is good or bad.

Mayberry Portfolio3 Plan

Players are sorted and ranked based on how they fit into the three draft tiers of the Portfolio3 Plan used in conjunction with the Mayberry Method, as detailed on page 54.

BATTER SKILLS RANKING - POWER

TOP PX, 400+ AB

NAME	POS	PX
Sano,Miguel	0	214
Davis,Chris	0 3 9	206
Stanton,Giancarlo	9	206
Carter,Chris	3	188
Harper,Bryce	9	179
Trout,Mike	8	175
Goldschmidt,Paul	3	171
Davis,Khristopher	7	169
Duda,Lucas	3	169
Encarnacion,Edwin	0 3	160
Schwarber,Kyle	2 7	160
Arenado,Nolan	5	159
Grichuk,Randal	7 8	159
Martinez,J.D.	9	159
Bryant,Kris	5	159
Dickerson,Corey	7	157
Teixeira,Mark	3	157
Bautista,Jose	0 9	156
Gonzalez,Carlos	9	153
Donaldson,Josh	5	153
Ortiz,David	0	153
Cruz,Nelson	0 9	150
Upton,Justin	7	150
Rizzo,Anthony	3	148
Conforto,Michael	7	148
Moss,Brandon	3 9	146
Bruce,Jay	9	145
Howard,Ryan	3	145
Alvarez,Pedro	3	144
Abreu,Jose	0 3	144
Votto,Joey	3	143
Zimmerman,Ryan	3	143
Pederson,Joc	8	143
Soler,Jorge	9	143
Santana,Domingo	8 9	140
Springer,George	9	140
Gattis,Evan	0	139
Cespedes,Yoenis	7 8	139
Cabrera,Miguel	3	139
Belt,Brandon	3	138

TOP PX, 300 or fewer AB

NAME	POS	PX
Gallo,Joey	7	189
Shaffer,Richie	3	162
Bird,Gregory	3	157
Olt,Mike	5	153
O'Brien,Peter	7	153
Gutierrez,Franklin	7	152
Arencibia,J.P.	2	151
Duvall,Adam	7	151
Raburn,Ryan	0	148
Story,Trevor	6	145
Van Slyke,Scott	3 7 9	138
Reed,A.J.	0	138
Ruggiano,Justin	7	137
Pearce,Steve	3 7	134
Wallace,Brett	3	134
Chirinos,Robinson	2	133
Singleton,Jonathan	3	132
Soto,Geovany	2	130
Blanks,Kyle	3	130
Colabello,Chris	3 7	128
Marte,Jefry	3	128
McKenry,Michael	2	126
Susac,Andrew	2	126

POSITIONAL SCARCITY

NAME	POS	PX
Sano,Miguel	**DH**	214
Davis,Chris	2	206
Encarnacion,Edwin	3	160
Bautista,Jose	4	156
Ortiz,David	5	153
Cruz,Nelson	6	150
Schwarber,Kyle	**CA**	160
Arencibia,J.P.	2	151
Saltalamacchia,Jarrod	3	151
Chirinos,Robinson	4	133
Soto,Geovany	5	130
McKenry,Michael	6	126
Susac,Andrew	7	126
Phegley,Joshua	8	126
Davis,Chris	**1B**	206
Carter,Chris	2	188
Goldschmidt,Paul	3	171
Duda,Lucas	4	169
Shaffer,Richie	5	162
Encarnacion,Edwin	6	160
Bird,Gregory	7	157
Teixeira,Mark	8	157
Rizzo,Anthony	9	148
Moss,Brandon	10	146
Dozier,Brian	**2B**	124
Espinosa,Danny	2	120
Schoop,Jonathan	3	119
Franklin,Nick	4	114
Herrera,Dilson	5	112
Odor,Rougned	6	112
Rendon,Anthony	7	110
Russell,Addison	8	110
Arenado,Nolan	**3B**	159
Bryant,Kris	2	159
Olt,Mike	3	153
Donaldson,Josh	4	153
Frazier,Todd	5	135
Valbuena,Luis	6	132
Valencia,Danny	7	129
Reynolds,Mark	8	128
Carpenter,Matt	9	126
Kang,Jung-ho	10	123
Story,Trevor	**SS**	145
Seager,Corey	2	134
Correa,Carlos	3	129
Tulowitzki,Troy	4	126
Crawford,Brandon	5	125
Kang,Jung-ho	6	123
Desmond,Ian	7	120
Russell,Addison	8	110
Davis,Chris	**OF**	206
Stanton,Giancarlo	2	206
Gallo,Joey	3	189
Harper,Bryce	4	179
Trout,Mike	5	175
Davis,Khristopher	6	169
Rasmus,Colby	7	168
Schwarber,Kyle	8	160
Grichuk,Randal	9	159
Martinez,J.D.	10	159
Dickerson,Corey	11	157
Bautista,Jose	12	156
Gonzalez,Carlos	13	153
O'Brien,Peter	14	153
Gutierrez,Franklin	15	152
Duvall,Adam	16	151

TOP PX, ct% over 80%

NAME	Ct%	PX
Encarnacion,Edwin	83	160
Arenado,Nolan	84	159
Bautista,Jose	81	156
Ortiz,David	82	153
Cabrera,Miguel	82	139
Ramirez,Hanley	81	124
Jones,Adam	80	124
Machado,Manny	82	123
Lind,Adam	80	123
Gonzalez,Adrian	81	122
Betts,Mookie	86	119
D Arnaud,Travis	80	119
Beltran,Carlos	82	116
Franco,Maikel	83	116
Moustakas,Mike	84	115
Turner,Justin	82	114
Morales,Kendrys	81	114
Holliday,Matt	80	114
McCann,Brian	81	112
Odor,Rougned	82	112
Seager,Kyle	82	112
Pujols,Albert	88	111
Rendon,Anthony	80	110
Travis,Devon	81	110
Lowrie,Jed	82	110
Pollock,A.J.	85	109
Piscotty,Stephen	82	109
Ackley,Dustin	82	108
Drury,Brandon	83	108
Cano,Robinson	85	108
Blanco,Andres	80	107
Cuddyer,Michael	81	107
Walker,Neil	81	106
Blackmon,Charlie	83	106
Jaso,John	80	106
Hosmer,Eric	82	105
Ramirez,Aramis	85	105
Brantley,Michael	90	105
Reddick,Josh	84	105
Hernandez,Enrique	81	103

TOP PX, ct% under 70%

NAME	Ct%	PX
Sano,Miguel	63	214
Davis,Chris	64	206
Stanton,Giancarlo	67	206
Gallo,Joey	51	189
Carter,Chris	63	188
Rasmus,Colby	66	168
Shaffer,Richie	65	162
Schwarber,Kyle	67	160
Bryant,Kris	64	159
Bird,Gregory	70	157
Olt,Mike	60	153
O'Brien,Peter	69	153
Gutierrez,Franklin	70	152
Arencibia,J.P.	64	151
Saltalamacchia,Jarrod	64	151
Moss,Brandon	68	146
Story,Trevor	66	145
Howard,Ryan	69	145
Alvarez,Pedro	69	144
Pederson,Joc	65	143
Soler,Jorge	70	143
Santana,Domingo	62	140
Springer,George	69	140

Top PX, FB% over 40%

NAME	FB%	PX
Sano,Miguel	43	214
Davis,Chris	43	206
Stanton,Giancarlo	42	206
Carter,Chris	50	188
Duda,Lucas	51	169
Rasmus,Colby	48	168
Shaffer,Richie	44	162
Encarnacion,Edwin	45	160
Schwarber,Kyle	42	160
Arenado,Nolan	42	159
Grichuk,Randal	43	159
Bryant,Kris	45	159
Bird,Gregory	45	157
Teixeira,Mark	42	157
Bautista,Jose	46	156
Olt,Mike	40	153
O'Brien,Peter	42	153
Ortiz,David	42	153
Arencibia,J.P.	45	151
Duvall,Adam	45	151
Saltalamacchia,Jarrod	44	151
Upton,Justin	42	150
Rizzo,Anthony	42	148
Moss,Brandon	48	146
Bruce,Jay	41	145
Story,Trevor	45	145
Pederson,Joc	43	143
Gattis,Evan	41	139
Cespedes,Yoenis	41	139
Van Slyke,Scott	43	138
Reed,A.J.	42	138
Belt,Brandon	41	138
Ruggiano,Justin	40	137
Frazier,Todd	43	135
Granderson,Curtis	44	134
Pearce,Steve	47	134
Chirinos,Robinson	42	133
Singleton,Jonathan	53	132
Napoli,Mike	40	132
Valbuena,Luis	45	132

Top PX, FB% under 35%

NAME	FB%	PX
Goldschmidt,Paul	34	171
Dickerson,Corey	35	157
Alvarez,Pedro	32	144
Abreu,Jose	32	144
Votto,Joey	33	143
Soler,Jorge	32	143
Santana,Domingo	29	140
Springer,George	34	140
Cabrera,Miguel	33	139
Hamilton,Josh	34	137
Paulsen,Benjamin	32	135
Braun,Ryan	32	134
Seager,Corey	32	134
Wallace,Brett	32	134
Valencia,Danny	33	129
Correa,Carlos	30	129
Colabello,Chris	29	128
Ozuna,Marcell	33	126
Ramirez,Hanley	33	124
Martin,Russell	33	124
Choo,Shin-Soo	29	124
Thompson,Trayce	32	124
Kang,Jung-ho	28	123

BATTER SKILLS RANKING - SPEED

TOP Spd, 400+ AB

NAME	POS	Spd
Buxton,Byron	8	183
Gordon,Dee	4	173
Hamilton,Billy	8	164
Deshields Jr.,Delino	7 8	161
Hechavarria,Adeiny	6	161
Burns,Billy	8	157
Revere,Ben	7 8	156
Herrera,Odubel	8	156
Kiermaier,Kevin	8	155
Fowler,Dexter	8	154
Marte,Starling	7	151
Gose,Anthony	8	151
Betts,Mookie	8	150
Segura,Jean	6	149
Pollock,A.J.	8	148
Rosario,Eddie	7 9	147
LeMahieu,DJ	4	147
Spangenberg,Cory	4	146
Ahmed,Nick	6	145
Escobar,Alcides	6	145
Marte,Ketel	6	143
Trout,Mike	8	143
Piscotty,Stephen	7	141
Semien,Marcus	6	141
Springer,George	9	140
Inciarte,Ender	7 8 9	140
Grichuk,Randal	7 8	140
Eaton,Adam	8	140
Duffy,Matt	5	139
Cain,Lorenzo	8	138
Lindor,Francisco	6	137
Iglesias,Jose	6	137
Owings,Christopher	4 6	135
Jackson,Austin	8 9	135
Olivera,Hector	5	134
Odor,Rougned	4	133
Hicks,Aaron	8	131
Puig,Yasiel	9	131
Bryant,Kris	5	130
Blackmon,Charlie	8	130

TOP Spd, 300 or fewer AB

NAME	POS	Spd
Anderson,Tim	0	172
Jankowski,Travis	8	165
Dyson,Jarrod	7 8	165
Davis,Rajai	7 8	156
Bourjos,Peter	8	152
Tomlinson,Kelby	4	149
Suzuki,Ichiro	7 9	143
Alberto,Hanser	4	140
Taylor,Chris	6	139
Crawford,J.P.	0	138
Herrera,Dilson	4	137
Story,Trevor	6	136
Rutledge,Josh	4	135
Marisnick,Jake	8	135
Arcia,Orlando	6	135
Turner,Trea	4	135
Santana,Daniel	6	134
Pham,Thomas	8	132
Sardinas,Luis	4	131
Orlando,Paulo	7 9	128
Rodriguez,Yorman		127
Featherston,Taylor	4 5 6	127
De Aza,Alejandro	7 9	126

POSITIONAL SCARCITY

NAME	POS	Spd
Anderson,Tim	**DH**	172
Crawford,J.P.	2	138
Sano,Miguel	3	124
Profar,Jurickson	4	118
Mazara,Nomar	5	109
Bell,Josh	6	108
Realmuto,Jacob	**CA**	127
Hundley,Nick	2	125
Swihart,Blake	3	120
Cervelli,Francisco	4	119
Perez,Carlos	5	108
Norris,Derek	6	107
Murphy,John Ryan	7	106
Plawecki,Kevin	8	104
Morneau,Justin	**1B**	119
Canha,Mark	2	118
Forsythe,Logan	3	112
Rogers,Jason	4	107
Paulsen,Benjamin	5	105
Belt,Brandon	6	104
Myers,Wil	7	102
Muncy,Max	8	101
Bird,Gregory	9	101
Trumbo,Mark	10	99.4
Gordon,Dee	**2B**	173
Peraza,Jose	2	169
Tomlinson,Kelby	3	149
LeMahieu,DJ	4	147
Spangenberg,Cory	5	146
Hernandez,Cesar	6	143
Hernandez,Enrique	7	141
Alberto,Hanser	8	140
Duffy,Matt	**3B**	139
Olivera,Hector	2	134
Bryant,Kris	3	130
Featherston,Taylor	4	127
Perez,Hernan	5	125
Holt,Brock	6	119
Saladino,Tyler	7	118
Harrison,Josh	8	117
Romine,Andrew	9	117
Machado,Manny	10	116
Hechavarria,Adeiny	**SS**	161
Segura,Jean	2	149
Ahmed,Nick	3	145
Escobar,Alcides	4	145
Marte,Ketel	5	143
Semien,Marcus	6	141
Taylor,Chris	7	139
Lindor,Francisco	8	137
Buxton,Byron	**OF**	183
Jankowski,Travis	2	165
Dyson,Jarrod	3	165
Hamilton,Billy	4	164
Deshields Jr.,Delino	5	161
Burns,Billy	6	157
Davis,Rajai	7	156
Revere,Ben	8	156
Herrera,Odubel	9	156
Kiermaier,Kevin	10	155
Fowler,Dexter	11	154
Bourjos,Peter	12	152
Marte,Starling	13	151
Gose,Anthony	14	151
Betts,Mookie	15	150
Pollock,A.J.	16	148

TOP Spd, .330+ OBP

NAME	OBP	Spd
Gordon,Dee	334	173
Revere,Ben	336	156
Herrera,Odubel	340	156
Fowler,Dexter	363	154
Marte,Starling	338	151
Betts,Mookie	364	150
Pollock,A.J.	344	148
LeMahieu,DJ	331	147
Trout,Mike	398	143
Springer,George	359	140
Eaton,Adam	357	140
Duffy,Matt	335	139
Blanco,Gregor	348	138
Cain,Lorenzo	345	138
Pompey,Dalton	335	136
Turner,Trea	332	135
Olivera,Hector	348	134
Puig,Yasiel	349	131
Bryant,Kris	356	130
Gardner,Brett	335	129
Aoki,Norichika	346	129
Altuve,Jose	352	128
Guyer,Brandon	345	127
Yelich,Christian	366	126
De Aza,Alejandro	331	126
Kinsler,Ian	333	125
Sano,Miguel	340	124
Span,Denard	349	122
Ellsbury,Jacoby	333	122
Travis,Devon	345	121
Pedroia,Dustin	348	121
McCutchen,Andrew	402	121
Dickerson,Corey	337	120
Braun,Ryan	358	120
Peralta,David	349	119
Cervelli,Francisco	340	119
Morneau,Justin	356	119
Profar,Jurickson	336	118
Coghlan,Chris	339	118
Miller,Bradley	331	118

TOP Spd, OBP under .300

NAME	OBP	Spd
Peraza,Jose	278	169
Hamilton,Billy	292	164
Hechavarria,Adeiny	299	161
Segura,Jean	290	149
Rosario,Eddie	280	147
Ahmed,Nick	279	145
Escobar,Alcides	294	145
Suzuki,Ichiro	297	143
Grichuk,Randal	300	140
Alberto,Hanser	266	140
Story,Trevor	289	136
Owings,Christopher	278	135
Marisnick,Jake	278	135
Santana,Daniel	287	134
Sardinas,Luis	272	131
Altherr,Aaron	300	130
Orlando,Paulo	264	128
Infante,Omar	272	128
Rodriguez,Yorman	287	127
Featherston,Taylor	258	127
Perez,Hernan	274	125
Sweeney,Darnell	290	124
Lagares,Juan	300	123

Top Spd, SBO% over 20%

NAME	SBO%	Spd
Gordon,Dee	44%	173
Anderson,Tim	27%	172
Peraza,Jose	32%	169
Jankowski,Travis	35%	165
Dyson,Jarrod	55%	165
Hamilton,Billy	59%	164
Deshields Jr.,Delino	28%	161
Burns,Billy	29%	157
Davis,Rajai	37%	156
Revere,Ben	27%	156
Herrera,Odubel	21%	156
Marte,Starling	33%	151
Gose,Anthony	32%	151
Betts,Mookie	20%	150
Tomlinson,Kelby	23%	149
Segura,Jean	23%	149
Pollock,A.J.	23%	148
Marte,Ketel	24%	143
Inciarte,Ender	23%	140
Taylor,Chris	25%	139
Cain,Lorenzo	22%	138
Pompey,Dalton	27%	136
Marisnick,Jake	30%	135
Arcia,Orlando	26%	135
Turner,Trea	26%	135
Santana,Daniel	26%	134
Bourn,Michael	20%	132
Altherr,Aaron	21%	130
Jennings,Desmond	20%	130
Blackmon,Charlie	34%	130
Orlando,Paulo	22%	128
Altuve,Jose	26%	128
Castillo,Rusney	23%	127
Sweeney,Darnell	25%	124
Ellsbury,Jacoby	27%	122
Martin,Leonys	27%	122
Shuck,J.B.	25%	119
Villar,Jonathan	43%	119
Saladino,Tyler	25%	118
Nunez,Eduardo	22%	117

Top Spd, SBO% under 15%

NAME	SBO%	Spd
Hechavarria,Adeiny	10%	161
Fowler,Dexter	14%	154
Ahmed,Nick	10%	145
Trout,Mike	10%	143
Piscotty,Stephen	12%	141
Semien,Marcus	11%	141
Hernandez,Enrique	6%	141
Grichuk,Randal	12%	140
Duffy,Matt	9%	139
Crawford,J.P.	9%	138
Iglesias,Jose	13%	137
Story,Trevor	13%	136
Rutledge,Josh	8%	135
Olivera,Hector	0%	134
Odor,Rougned	15%	133
Pham,Thomas	12%	132
Puig,Yasiel	13%	131
Bryant,Kris	11%	130
Aoki,Norichika	15%	129
Infante,Omar	7%	128
Rodriguez,Yorman	8%	127
Suarez,Eugenio	11%	125
Hundley,Nick	7%	125

BATTER SKILLS RANKING - BATTING AVERAGE

TOP ct%, 400+ AB

NAME	Ct%	BA
Aoki,Norichika	92	282
Revere,Ben	90	305
Altuve,Jose	90	315
Simmons,Andrelton	90	269
Martinez,Victor	90	275
Brantley,Michael	90	307
Panik,Joe	89	295
Murphy,Daniel	89	286
Aybar,Erick	89	267
Loney,James	89	284
Posey,Buster	88	313
Solarte,Yangervis	88	272
Span,Denard	88	293
Molina,Yadier	88	277
Kinsler,Ian	88	287
Ramirez,Alexei	88	265
Reyes,Jose	88	285
Pujols,Albert	88	266
Beltre,Adrian	88	296
Inciarte,Ender	88	288
Suzuki,Kurt	87	239
Pedroia,Dustin	87	281
Markakis,Nick	87	283
Prado,Martin	87	286
Escobar,Yunel	87	267
Escobar,Alcides	87	261
Iglesias,Jose	86	272
Cabrera,Melky	86	283
Phillips,Brandon	86	277
Olivera,Hector	86	276
Zobrist,Ben	86	274
Andrus,Elvis	86	267
Betts,Mookie	86	303
Perez,Salvador	85	267
Flores,Wilmer	85	260
Cano,Robinson	85	304
Sandoval,Pablo	85	257
Pollock,A.J.	85	294
Pillar,Kevin	85	277
Lucroy,Jonathan	84	279
Segura,Jean	84	260
Castillo,Rusney	84	267
Fielder,Prince	84	275
Arenado,Nolan	84	294
Moustakas,Mike	84	263
Reddick,Josh	84	265
Rollins,Jimmy	83	245
Gregorius,Didi	83	256
Encarnacion,Edwin	83	284
Marte,Ketel	83	271
Gordon,Dee	83	297
Harrison,Josh	83	292
Wong,Kolten	83	261
Hechavarria,Adeiny	83	266
Cozart,Zack	83	252
Ahmed,Nick	83	239
Gennett,Scooter	83	273
Ellsbury,Jacoby	83	274
Realmuto,Jacob	83	260
Parra,Gerardo	83	278
Blackmon,Charlie	83	277
Franco,Maikel	83	267
Rios,Alex	82	264
Castro,Starlin	82	273
Heyward,Jason	82	278
Odor,Rougned	82	274

LOW ct%, 400+ AB

NAME	Ct%	BA
Santana,Domingo	62	233
Carter,Chris	63	214
Sano,Miguel	63	247
Bryant,Kris	64	261
Davis,Chris	64	254
Pederson,Joc	65	230
Taylor,Michael	65	232
Baez,Javier	65	247
Schwarber,Kyle	67	241
Stanton,Giancarlo	67	275
Souza,Steven	68	261
Moss,Brandon	68	233
Gose,Anthony	68	239
Howard,Ryan	69	237
Springer,George	69	267
Alvarez,Pedro	69	236
Soler,Jorge	70	261
Grichuk,Randal	70	253
Desmond,Ian	70	252
Belt,Brandon	71	271
Duda,Lucas	71	256
Martinez,J.D.	71	276
Upton,Justin	71	261
Davis,Khristopher	72	251
Lamb,Jacob	72	267
Byrd,Marlon	72	258
Myers,Wil	72	246
Rodriguez,Alex	73	240
Trout,Mike	73	300
Buxton,Byron	73	268
Bruce,Jay	73	243
Granderson,Curtis	73	247
Gomes,Yan	73	260
Castillo,Welington	73	242
Goldschmidt,Paul	73	305
Trumbo,Mark	73	251

TOP ct%, 300 or fewer AB

NAME	Ct%	BA
Toscano,Dian	91	240
La Stella,Tommy	89	278
Shuck,J.B.	89	253
Pena,Brayan	89	263
Ramirez,Jose	89	260
Colon,Christian	88	254
Telis,Tomas	88	259
Castro,Daniel	88	254
Sogard,Eric	87	239
Aviles,Mike	86	236
Suzuki,Ichiro	86	252
Murphy,David	86	266
Bell,Josh	86	270
Ruiz,Carlos	85	235
Ramirez,Aramis	85	268
Pirela,Jose	85	257
Alberto,Hanser	84	245
Crisp,Coco	84	235
Arcia,Orlando	84	294
Nunez,Eduardo	84	266
Crawford,J.P.	84	244
Amarista,Alexi	84	218
Clevenger,Steve	84	251
Adames,Cristhian	83	260
Hill,Aaron	83	249
Sardinas,Luis	83	245
Jankowski,Travis	83	249

TOP ct%, bb% over 9%

NAME	bb%	Ct%
Toscano,Dian	14	91
Posey,Buster	9	88
Pedroia,Dustin	9	87
Markakis,Nick	9	87
Zobrist,Ben	12	86
Crisp,Coco	11	84
Crawford,J.P.	9	84
Fielder,Prince	11	84
Rollins,Jimmy	9	83
Encarnacion,Edwin	12	83
Heyward,Jason	10	82
Ortiz,David	13	82
Lowrie,Jed	10	82
Cabrera,Miguel	13	82
Fuld,Sam	9	82
Tejada,Ruben	9	82
Morrison,Logan	9	82
Hanigan,Ryan	11	81
Gonzalez,Adrian	9	81
Profar,Jurickson	9	81
Bautista,Jose	16	81
McCann,Brian	9	81
Elmore,Jake	10	81
Mauer,Joe	11	81
Pompey,Dalton	9	81
Lind,Adam	10	80
Blanco,Gregor	11	80
Jaso,John	13	80
Rendon,Anthony	10	80
Holliday,Matt	12	80
Correa,Carlos	9	80
Ethier,Andre	9	80
Rizzo,Anthony	11	79
Ellis,A.J.	14	79
Robinson,Clint	9	79
Tulowitzki,Troy	10	79
Kipnis,Jason	9	79
Donaldson,Josh	11	79
Coghlan,Chris	10	78
Wright,David	12	78

TOP ct%, bb% under 6%

NAME	bb%	Ct%
Revere,Ben	4	90
Altuve,Jose	5	90
Murphy,Daniel	6	89
Aybar,Erick	4	89
Pierzynski,A.J.	4	88
Ramirez,Alexei	5	88
Peraza,Jose	3	88
Inciarte,Ender	5	88
Telis,Tomas	4	88
Castro,Daniel	4	88
Escobar,Alcides	4	87
Aviles,Mike	5	86
Infante,Omar	4	86
Iglesias,Jose	5	86
Phillips,Brandon	5	86
Perez,Salvador	3	85
Flores,Wilmer	4	85
Pillar,Kevin	4	85
Alberto,Hanser	3	84
Segura,Jean	3	84
Arcia,Orlando	5	84
Nunez,Eduardo	5	84
Arenado,Nolan	5	84

Top ct%, GB% over 50%

NAME	GB%	Ct%
Aoki,Norichika	59.6	92
Revere,Ben	59.2	90
Simmons,Andrelton	53.9	90
Shuck,J.B.	56.1	89
Aybar,Erick	51	89
Span,Denard	50.9	88
Inciarte,Ender	51.8	88
Telis,Tomas	64	88
Castro,Daniel	61.3	88
Pedroia,Dustin	50.1	87
Escobar,Yunel	52.9	87
Iglesias,Jose	56.3	86
Andrus,Elvis	52.2	86
Suzuki,Ichiro	57	86
Pirela,Jose	58	85
Pollock,A.J.	50.1	85
Segura,Jean	59.6	84
Castillo,Rusney	59.8	84
Nunez,Eduardo	53	84
Adames,Cristhian	57.5	83
Marte,Ketel	52.3	83
Gordon,Dee	58.1	83
Hechavarria,Adeiny	52	83
Sardinas,Luis	62.5	83
Jankowski,Travis	63.5	83
Jay,Jon	58.9	83
Garcia,Adonis	50.4	83
Drury,Brandon	56.3	83
Parra,Gerardo	50.3	83
Castro,Starlin	50.3	82
Heyward,Jason	51.6	82
Hosmer,Eric	52	82
Burns,Billy	50.5	82
Kendrick,Howie	58.1	82
Barnhart,Tucker	51.9	82
Fuld,Sam	55.2	82
LeMahieu,DJ	55.8	82
Vazquez,Christian	50.2	82
Perez,Eury	61.1	81
Gosselin,Phil	57	81

Top ct%, GB% under 40%

NAME	GB%	Ct%
Kinsler,Ian	35.3	88
Beltre,Adrian	39.7	88
Betts,Mookie	39.4	86
Ramirez,Aramis	38.6	85
Arenado,Nolan	35.5	84
Moustakas,Mike	38	84
Reddick,Josh	35.9	84
Rollins,Jimmy	38	83
Encarnacion,Edwin	35.5	83
Navarro,Dioner	38.1	83
Hill,Aaron	38.4	83
Blackmon,Charlie	39.3	83
Seager,Kyle	34.9	82
Ortiz,David	36.4	82
Beltran,Carlos	38	82
Lowrie,Jed	33.7	82
Gonzalez,Adrian	38.6	81
Bautista,Jose	38.7	81
McCann,Brian	35.3	81
Vogt,Stephen	35.1	81
Pompey,Dalton	39.3	81
Cabrera,Asdrubal	37	80
Rizzo,Anthony	37.2	79

POTENTIAL SKILLS GAINERS AND FADERS - BATTERS

Power Gainers

Batters whose 2015 Power Index (PX) fell significantly short of their underlying power skill (xPX). If they show the same xPX skill in 2016, they are good candidates for more power output.

Power Faders

Batters whose 2015 Power Index (PX) noticeably outpaced their underlying power skill (xPX). If they show the same xPX skill in 2016, they are good candidates for less power output.

PX GAINERS

NAME	PX	xPX
Middlebrooks,Will	92	139
Gyorko,Jedd	99	130
Ross,David	80	129
Rogers,Jason	92	129
Wright,David	99	129
Avila,Alex	78	124
Navarro,Dioner	81	123
Morneau,Justin	93	122
Morrison,Logan	92	121
Hill,Aaron	80	121
Adams,Matt	96	119
Rivera,Rene	78	118
Semien,Marcus	96	117
Taylor,Michael	96	115
Posey,Buster	88	113
Lamb,Jacob	88	113
Martinez,Victor	73	111
Robinson,Clint	95	111
Maxwell,Justin	93	111
Campbell,Eric	71	111
Beltre,Adrian	98	110
Rodriguez,Sean	90	109
Crawford,Carl	93	108
Fielder,Prince	94	107
Ozuna,Marcell	93	107
Johnson,Chris	70	107
Rollins,Jimmy	84	106
Realmuto,Jacob	89	106
Utley,Chase	87	106
Butler,Billy	92	105
Rendon,Anthony	75	105
Davis,Ike	95	105
Lucroy,Jonathan	83	104
Denorfia,Chris	80	104
Peralta,Jhonny	88	103
Tejada,Ruben	71	101
Cervelli,Francisco	70	100

PX FADERS

NAME	PX	xPX
Butler,Joey	108	63
Nunez,Eduardo	101	67
Almonte,Abraham	104	73
Rosario,Wilin	106	74
Lindor,Francisco	106	75
Davis,Rajai	112	78
Francoeur,Jeff	116	82
Ramirez,Hanley	102	84
Zobrist,Ben	109	86
Brantley,Michael	108	88
Beckham,Tim	145	88
Puig,Yasiel	115	89
Desmond,Ian	114	92
Colabello,Chris	142	94
Souza,Steven	140	99
Hernandez,Enrique	122	99
Blanco,Andres	143	102
Correa,Carlos	145	104
D Arnaud,Travis	138	107
Conger,Hank	159	110
Bour,Justin	142	111
Valencia,Danny	152	111
Alvarez,Pedro	155	115
Gonzalez,Carlos	167	127
Bradley,Jackie	184	134
Teixeira,Mark	180	136
Cruz,Nelson	171	138
Donaldson,Josh	171	139
Grichuk,Randal	204	140
Rasmus,Colby	180	149
Trout,Mike	191	154
Gutierrez,Franklin	231	160
Harper,Bryce	210	161
Sano,Miguel	225	174

BA Gainers

Batters who had strong Hard Contact Index levels in 2015, but lower hit rates (h%). Since base hits come most often on hard contact, if these batters can make hard contact at the same strong rate again in 2016, they may get better results in terms of hit rate, resulting in a batting average improvement.

BA Faders

Batters who had weak Hard Contact Index levels in 2015, but higher hit rates (h%). Since base hits come most often on hard contact, if these batters only make hard contact at the same weak rate again in 2016, they may get worse results in terms of hit rate, resulting in a batting average decline.

BA GAINERS

NAME	h%	HctX
Ortiz,David	27	150
Lowrie,Jed	24	131
Pujols,Albert	22	128
Zimmerman,Ryan	28	128
Encarnacion,Edwin	27	127
Frazier,Todd	28	127
Murphy,Daniel	28	126
Bautista,Jose	24	124
Middlebrooks,Will	24	124
Seager,Kyle	28	123
Teixeira,Mark	25	122
Castillo,Welington	27	121
Ackley,Dustin	25	120
Solarte,Yangervis	28	120
Bruce,Jay	26	117
Martinez,Victor	26	117
Alvarez,Pedro	28	116
Ramirez,Aramis	26	116
Plouffe,Trevor	28	116
Howard,Ryan	27	116
Ruf,Darin	27	115
Hill,Aaron	26	115
Coghlan,Chris	28	114
Smoak,Justin	26	114
Ramirez,Hanley	26	113
Rodriguez,Alex	28	113
Utley,Chase	24	113
Morrison,Logan	24	111
McCann,Brian	24	110
Werth,Jayson	26	110
Valbuena,Luis	24	110
Navarro,Dioner	27	110
Gattis,Evan	27	109
Guerrero,Alexander	26	109
Flores,Wilmer	27	109
Butler,Billy	28	108
Pederson,Joc	26	106

BA FADERS

NAME	h%	HctX
Tomlinson,Kelby	38	52
Stewart,Chris	35	64
Gordon,Dee	39	66
Butler,Joey	38	67
Carrera,Ezequiel	35	75
Gose,Anthony	35	77
Spangenberg,Cory	35	83
Swihart,Blake	36	86
Herrera,Odubel	39	86
Eaton,Adam	35	89
Lindor,Francisco	36	91
Holt,Brock	35	91
LeMahieu,DJ	36	94
Johnson,Chris	36	94
Peterson,Shane	35	96
Hundley,Nick	36	97
Colabello,Chris	41	98
Travis,Devon	35	98
Paulsen,Benjamin	36	100
Upton,Melvin	35	100
Bogaerts,Xander	37	100
Tomas,Yasmany	36	100
Paredes,Jimmy	37	104
Murphy,John	37	104
Springer,George	35	105
Soler,Jorge	37	106
Escobar,Yunel	35	106
Denorfia,Chris	35	106
Grichuk,Randal	37	107
Kipnis,Jason	36	107
Bryant,Kris	38	107
Cervelli,Francisco	36	107
Sano,Miguel	40	109
Hernandez,Enrique	37	111
Cruz,Nelson	35	113
Wright,David	35	113
Lamb,Jacob	35	114

PITCHER SKILLS RANKINGS - Starting Pitchers

Top Command (k/bb)

NAME	Cmd
Kershaw,Clayton	6.6
Hughes,Phil	6.3
Sale,Chris	5.5
Strasburg,Stephen	5.4
Tanaka,Masahiro	5.3
Scherzer,Max	5.3
Bumgarner,Madison	5.2
Price,David	5.1
Kluber,Corey	5.0
Pineda,Michael	4.9
Iwakuma,Hisashi	4.8
Zimmermann,Jordan	4.7
Harvey,Matt	4.7
Syndergaard,Noah	4.7
Tomlin,Josh	4.5
Greinke,Zack	4.5
Carrasco,Carlos	4.5
Fernandez,Jose	4.3
deGrom,Jacob	4.2
Lyons,Tyler	4.1
McCarthy,Brandon	4.1
Hernandez,Felix	3.9
Lester,Jon	3.9
Colon,Bartolo	3.9
Keuchel,Dallas	3.9
Cole,Gerrit	3.8
Nola,Aaron	3.7
Stroman,Marcus	3.6
Porcello,Rick	3.6
Hamels,Cole	3.6
Arrieta,Jake	3.5

Top Control (bb/9)

NAME	Ctl
Hughes,Phil	1.1
Tanaka,Masahiro	1.5
Iwakuma,Hisashi	1.5
Colon,Bartolo	1.5
Tomlin,Josh	1.5
Pineda,Michael	1.6
Zimmermann,Jordan	1.6
Kershaw,Clayton	1.6
Buehrle,Mark	1.8
Price,David	1.8
Bumgarner,Madison	1.8
Lyons,Tyler	1.9
Fister,Doug	1.9
Kluber,Corey	1.9
Greinke,Zack	1.9
Nicolino,Justin	1.9
McCarthy,Brandon	1.9
Nola,Aaron	1.9
Harvey,Matt	1.9
Scherzer,Max	2.0
Porcello,Rick	2.0
Sale,Chris	2.0
Lewis,Colby	2.0
Strasburg,Stephen	2.0
Chen,Wei-Yin	2.0
Wainwright,Adam	2.0
Syndergaard,Noah	2.1
Keuchel,Dallas	2.1
Hendricks,Kyle	2.1
Oberholtzer,Brett	2.1
Corbin,Patrick	2.1

Top Dominance (k/9)

NAME	Dom
Darvish,Yu	10.9
Sale,Chris	10.9
Fernandez,Jose	10.9
Kershaw,Clayton	10.8
Strasburg,Stephen	10.7
Scherzer,Max	10.5
Carrasco,Carlos	9.9
Syndergaard,Noah	9.6
Liriano,Francisco	9.6
Hill,Rich	9.5
Bumgarner,Madison	9.4
Kluber,Corey	9.4
McCullers,Lance	9.4
Salazar,Danny	9.2
Archer,Chris	9.2
Arrieta,Jake	9.2
Price,David	9.2
Snell,Blake	9.2
Harvey,Matt	9.1
deGrom,Jacob	9.1
Rodon,Carlos	9.1
Kennedy,Ian	9.1
Ross,Tyson	9.0
Finnegan,Brandon	9.0
Gonzalez,Gio	8.9
Iglesias,Raisel	8.9
Hernandez,Felix	8.9
Moore,Matt	8.8
Hamels,Cole	8.8
Martinez,Carlos	8.8
Glasnow,Tyler	8.8

Top Ground Ball Rate

NAME	GB
Anderson,Brett	64
House,T.J.	61
Keuchel,Dallas	60
Garcia,Jaime	59
Ross,Tyson	58
Bradley,Archie	58
Morton,Charlie	58
Stroman,Marcus	57
Perez,Martin	56
Alvarez,Henderson	55
Cosart,Jarred	55
Hernandez,Felix	55
Finnegan,Brandon	54
Davies,Zachary	54
Gray,Sonny	54
Cobb,Alex	54
Richards,Garrett	53
Arrieta,Jake	53
Chatwood,Tyler	53
Gibson,Kyle	53
Martinez,Carlos	53
Montgomery,Michael	53
Wilson,Tyler	52
Hernandez,Roberto	52
Despaigne,Odrisamer	52
Peralta,Wily	52
Niese,Jon	52
Bolsinger,Michael	52
Graveman,Kendall	52
Hahn,Jesse	52
Carrasco,Carlos	52

Top Fly Ball Rate

NAME	FB
Young,Chris	59
Boyd,Matt	54
Johnson,Erik	52
Santiago,Hector	50
Estrada,Marco	50
Morgan,Adam	49
Owens,Henry	49
Weaver,Jered	47
Asher,Alec	45
Griffin,A.J.	45
Wright,Mike	45
Lewis,Colby	45
Montero,Rafael	44
Odorizzi,Jake	44
Peavy,Jake	44
Fiers,Mike	44
Scherzer,Max	44
Wright,Steven	43
Foltynewicz,Mike	43
Norris,Daniel	43
Peacock,Brad	43
Beachy,Brandon	43
Verlander,Justin	42
Wisler,Matthew	42
Hughes,Phil	42
Harang,Aaron	42
Moore,Matt	41
Nolin,Sean	41
Conley,Adam	41
Gonzales,Marco	41
Shoemaker,Matthew	41

High GB, Low Dom

NAME	GB	Dom
Anderson,Brett	64	6.3
House,T.J.	61	6.3
Bradley,Archie	58	6.9
Morton,Charlie	58	6.6
Perez,Martin	56	5.7
Alvarez,Henderson	55	4.6
Cosart,Jarred	55	6.1
Davies,Zachary	54	6.6
Chatwood,Tyler	53	5.4
Gibson,Kyle	53	6.4
Montgomery,Michae	53	6.4
Wilson,Tyler	52	5.5
Hernandez,Roberto	52	5.6
Despaigne,Odrisamer	52	5.4
Peralta,Wily	52	6.2
Niese,Jon	52	6.2
Graveman,Kendall	52	5.8
Hahn,Jesse	52	6.7
Leake,Mike	51	5.9
Heston,Chris	51	6.5
Perez,Williams	51	5.8
Locke,Jeff	51	6.6
Rusin,Chris	50	5.0
Medlen,Kris	50	6.4
Duffey,Tyler	50	6.9
Nova,Ivan	50	6.5
Lyles,Jordan	50	5.9
Butler,Eddie	49	4.9
Wainwright,Adam	49	7.0
Gallardo,Yovani	49	6.6
Kelly,Joe	49	6.7

High GB, High Dom

NAME	GB	Dom
Ross,Tyson	58	9.0
Hernandez,Felix	55	8.9
Finnegan,Brandon	54	9.0
Arrieta,Jake	53	9.2
Martinez,Carlos	53	8.8
Carrasco,Carlos	52	9.9
Liriano,Francisco	51	9.6
Kershaw,Clayton	49	10.8
Gonzalez,Gio	49	8.9
Ryu,Hyun-Jin	49	8.6
Cole,Gerrit	48	8.7
Lester,Jon	47	8.7
Rodon,Carlos	47	9.1
Hamels,Cole	47	8.8
Syndergaard,Noah	46	9.6
McCullers,Lance	46	9.4
Archer,Chris	46	9.2
Snell,Blake	46	9.2
Harvey,Matt	46	9.1
Hill,Rich	46	9.5
Iglesias,Raisel	45	8.9
deGrom,Jacob	45	9.1
Glasnow,Tyler	45	8.8
Kluber,Corey	45	9.4
Strasburg,Stephen	44	10.7
Bundy,Dylan	44	8.6
Bumgarner,Madison	44	9.4
Fernandez,Jose	44	10.9
Sale,Chris	43	10.9
Price,David	43	9.2
Darvish,Yu	40	10.9

Lowest xERA

NAME	xERA
Kershaw,Clayton	2.41
Sale,Chris	2.78
Strasburg,Stephen	2.79
Fernandez,Jose	2.80
Carrasco,Carlos	2.81
Arrieta,Jake	2.91
Keuchel,Dallas	2.95
Hernandez,Felix	3.00
Bumgarner,Madison	3.01
Kluber,Corey	3.02
Syndergaard,Noah	3.04
Scherzer,Max	3.05
Harvey,Matt	3.07
Greinke,Zack	3.12
Stroman,Marcus	3.12
Price,David	3.12
deGrom,Jacob	3.15
Tanaka,Masahiro	3.15
Darvish,Yu	3.20
Ross,Tyson	3.21
Cole,Gerrit	3.21
Lester,Jon	3.25
Garcia,Jaime	3.27
Martinez,Carlos	3.29
Ryu,Hyun-Jin	3.30
Hamels,Cole	3.31
McCullers,Lance	3.32
Iwakuma,Hisashi	3.33
Liriano,Francisco	3.34
Archer,Chris	3.35
Matz,Steven	3.37

Top BPV, 180+ IP

NAME	BPV
Kershaw,Clayton	177
Sale,Chris	164
Strasburg,Stephen	160
Scherzer,Max	151
Carrasco,Carlos	148
Bumgarner,Madison	142
Syndergaard,Noah	142
Kluber,Corey	142
Price,David	137
Harvey,Matt	135
Hernandez,Felix	132
deGrom,Jacob	129
Greinke,Zack	128
Arrieta,Jake	126
Keuchel,Dallas	126
Lester,Jon	122
Cole,Gerrit	122
Hamels,Cole	116
Zimmermann,Jordan	115
Iglesias,Raisel	112
Archer,Chris	111
Salazar,Danny	111
Martinez,Carlos	105
McCullers,Lance	105
Hughes,Phil	105
Nola,Aaron	103
Ross,Tyson	103
Porcello,Rick	102
Quintana,Jose	101
Cueto,Johnny	101
Kennedy,Ian	100

Top BPV, <150 IP

NAME	BPV
Ryu,Hyun-Jin	116
McCarthy,Brandon	111
Bundy,Dylan	108
Lyons,Tyler	107
Garcia,Jaime	105
Tomlin,Josh	101
Berrios,Jose	98
Cobb,Alex	95
Snell,Blake	94
Gausman,Kevin	94
Ross,Joe	92
Latos,Mat	89
Hutchison,Drew	89
Shoemaker,Matthew	86
Andriese,Matt	86
Fister,Doug	84
Glasnow,Tyler	84
Skaggs,Tyler	83
Hill,Rich	83
Bailey,Homer	83
Chavez,Jesse	83
Tropeano,Nicholas	81
Medlen,Kris	81
Minor,Mike	80
Floyd,Gavin	80
Erlin,Robert	80
Cooney,Tim	77
Anderson,Chase	77
House,T.J.	75
Roark,Tanner	75
Bolsinger,Michael	74

PITCHER SKILLS RANKINGS - Relief Pitchers

Top Command (k/bb)

NAME	Cmd
Scribner,Evan	7.5
Jansen,Kenley	6.9
Romo,Sergio	6.4
Hendriks,Liam	5.9
Uehara,Koji	5.8
Garcia,Yimi	5.8
Strickland,Hunter	5.4
McGee,Jake	5.3
Melancon,Mark	5.2
Perkins,Glen	5.1
Capps,Carter	5.0
Petit,Yusmeiro	5.0
Robertson,David	4.9
Salas,Fernando	4.9
O Day,Darren	4.9
Qualls,Chad	4.8
Fien,Casey	4.8
Baez,Pedro	4.7
Miller,Andrew	4.7
Rodriguez,Francisco	4.7
Gregerson,Luke	4.5
Papelbon,Jonathan	4.4
Kimbrel,Craig	4.3
Osuna,Roberto	4.2
Givens,Mychal	4.2
Soria,Joakim	4.2
Mujica,Edward	4.2
Rondon,Hector	4.1
Madson,Ryan	4.1
Watson,Tony	4.1
Doolittle,Sean	4.0

Top Control (bb/9)

NAME	Ctl
Scribner,Evan	1.2
Mujica,Edward	1.4
Fien,Casey	1.5
Hendriks,Liam	1.5
Melancon,Mark	1.6
Strickland,Hunter	1.6
Qualls,Chad	1.6
Garcia,Yimi	1.6
Romo,Sergio	1.6
Petit,Yusmeiro	1.7
Maness,Seth	1.7
Uehara,Koji	1.8
Gregerson,Luke	1.8
Perkins,Glen	1.8
Papelbon,Jonathan	1.9
Motte,Jason	1.9
Bergman,Christian	1.9
Salas,Fernando	2.0
Jansen,Kenley	2.0
Hunter,Tommy	2.0
Baez,Pedro	2.0
Kontos,George	2.1
Blanton,Joe	2.1
Janssen,Casey	2.1
Watson,Tony	2.1
Madson,Ryan	2.1
Rodriguez,Francisco	2.1
O Day,Darren	2.1
Loup,Aaron	2.1
McGee,Jake	2.1
Nuno,Vidal	2.1

Top Dominance (k/9)

NAME	Dom
Chapman,Aroldis	15.9
Miller,Andrew	14.0
Jansen,Kenley	13.9
Kimbrel,Craig	13.7
Capps,Carter	13.1
Betances,Dellin	12.6
Robertson,David	12.2
Allen,Cody	11.7
Smith,Will	11.4
Cecil,Brett	11.3
Kelley,Shawn	11.3
Rosenthal,Trevor	11.1
McGee,Jake	11.1
Burgos,Enrique	11.1
Giles,Ken	11.1
Fields,Joshua	11.0
Armstrong,Shawn	11.0
Grimm,Justin	10.9
Boxberger,Brad	10.9
Knebel,Corey	10.8
Grilli,Jason	10.8
Walden,Jordan	10.8
Kela,Keone	10.7
Givens,Mychal	10.7
Ramos,A.J.	10.6
Davis,Wade	10.6
Dunn,Mike	10.6
Smith,Carson	10.6
Siegrist,Kevin	10.5
Uehara,Koji	10.4
Jones,Nate	10.4

Top Ground Ball Rate

NAME	GB
Britton,Zach	74
Ziegler,Brad	70
Dyson,Sam	67
Smith,Carson	65
Sanchez,Aaron	65
Petricka,Jacob	64
Hughes,Jared	62
Gott,Trevor	61
Treinen,Blake	61
Garcia,Luis	61
Johnson,Jim	61
Morris,Bryan	60
Qualls,Chad	59
Jeffress,Jeremy	58
Chafin,Andrew	58
Maness,Seth	58
Familia,Jeurys	58
Duke,Zach	57
Parnell,Bobby	57
Melancon,Mark	56
Loup,Aaron	56
Cahill,Trevor	56
Gregerson,Luke	55
Smith,Joe	54
Frias,Carlos	54
Oberg,Scott	54
Cedeno,Xavier	53
Axford,John	53
Masterson,Justin	53
Strop,Pedro	53
Madson,Ryan	53

Top Fly Ball Rate

NAME	FB
Clippard,Tyler	57
Garcia,Yimi	53
Geltz,Steve	52
Robles,Hansel	50
Uehara,Koji	50
Neshek,Pat	49
Fields,Joshua	48
Neris,Hector	47
Jansen,Kenley	47
Hoover,J.J.	47
Siegrist,Kevin	47
Velasquez,Vincent	46
Osuna,Roberto	46
Doolittle,Sean	45
Fien,Casey	45
Matusz,Brian	45
Allen,Cody	44
Street,Huston	44
Baez,Pedro	44
Grilli,Jason	43
Petit,Yusmeiro	43
McGee,Jake	43
Smyly,Drew	43
Feliz,Neftali	43
Wood,Travis	43
Salas,Fernando	43
O Day,Darren	42
Boxberger,Brad	42
Reed,Addison	42
Nuno,Vidal	42
Motte,Jason	42

High GB, Low Dom

NAME	GB	Dom
Ziegler,Brad	70	5.6
Sanchez,Aaron	65	6.5
Petricka,Jacob	64	5.9
Hughes,Jared	62	4.9
Gott,Trevor	61	6.1
Treinen,Blake	61	6.8
Johnson,Jim	61	6.8
Morris,Bryan	60	6.5
Maness,Seth	58	6.0
Parnell,Bobby	57	7.0
Frias,Carlos	54	5.7
Hale,David	50	5.7
Gomez,Jeanmar	50	5.8
Wilson,Alex	49	5.7
Schultz,Bo	49	5.8
Williams,Jerome	48	5.9
Bettis,Chad	48	7.0
Rivero,Felipe	48	6.8
Farmer,Buck	46	5.4
Godley,Zachary	46	6.9
Mujica,Edward	45	6.0
Hand,Brad	45	6.4
Hunter,Tommy	45	6.8
Morales,Franklin	44	6.5
Villarreal,Pedro	42	6.0
Kontos,George	42	6.9
Jackson,Edwin	42	7.0
Phelps,David	41	7.0
Banuelos,Manny	39	6.9
Bergman,Christian	37	4.6
Collmenter,Josh	37	5.9

High GB, High Dom

NAME	GB	Dom
Britton,Zach	74	8.6
Smith,Carson	65	10.6
Jeffress,Jeremy	58	8.6
Familia,Jeurys	58	9.8
Duke,Zach	57	9.3
Cedeno,Xavier	53	9.2
Axford,John	53	10.1
Strop,Pedro	53	10.4
Madson,Ryan	53	8.6
Kela,Keone	52	10.7
Kahnle,Thomas	52	8.6
Freeman,Sam	51	8.5
Araujo,Elvis	51	8.5
Rodney,Fernando	51	8.5
Cecil,Brett	50	11.3
Rondon,Hector	50	9.5
Knebel,Corey	49	10.8
Caminero,Arquimedes	49	8.7
Miller,Andrew	49	14.0
Alburquerque,Al	48	9.9
Shreve,Chasen	47	9.6
Putnam,Zach	47	9.0
Wilson,Justin	47	9.0
Betances,Dellin	47	12.6
Jones,Nate	47	10.4
Ottavino,Adam	47	8.8
Cishek,Steve	47	8.8
Grimm,Justin	47	10.9
Kimbrel,Craig	46	13.7
Watson,Tony	46	8.5
Giles,Ken	45	11.1

Lowest xERA

NAME	xERA
Miller,Andrew	2.09
Chapman,Aroldis	2.17
Kimbrel,Craig	2.25
Jansen,Kenley	2.30
Britton,Zach	2.41
Smith,Carson	2.42
Capps,Carter	2.43
Robertson,David	2.54
Cecil,Brett	2.64
Kela,Keone	2.72
Melancon,Mark	2.73
Betances,Dellin	2.74
Familia,Jeurys	2.80
Romo,Sergio	2.81
Armstrong,Shawn	2.83
McGee,Jake	2.84
Rodriguez,Francisco	2.90
Rondon,Hector	2.90
Giles,Ken	2.93
Givens,Mychal	2.94
Gregerson,Luke	2.95
Strop,Pedro	2.96
Dyson,Sam	2.97
Davis,Wade	2.98
Jones,Nate	3.04
Qualls,Chad	3.05
Knebel,Corey	3.06
Smith,Will	3.06
Allen,Cody	3.06
O Day,Darren	3.07
Uehara,Koji	3.07

Top BPV, 10+ Saves

NAME	BPV
Jansen,Kenley	208
Miller,Andrew	198
Chapman,Aroldis	188
Kimbrel,Craig	183
Robertson,David	173
Smith,Carson	156
Uehara,Koji	151
Britton,Zach	142
Rodriguez,Francisco	141
Melancon,Mark	139
Familia,Jeurys	139
Giles,Ken	139
Rondon,Hector	138
Allen,Cody	137
Perkins,Glen	132
Gregerson,Luke	131
Davis,Wade	131
Strickland,Hunter	129
Doolittle,Sean	126
Osuna,Roberto	124
Grilli,Jason	121
Papelbon,Jonathan	121
Rosenthal,Trevor	121
Tolleson,Shawn	114
Boxberger,Brad	106
Ottavino,Adam	105
Vizcaino,Arodys	99
Ramos,A.J.	94
Street,Huston	91
Rondon,Bruce	90
Casilla,Santiago	88

Top BPV, <10 Saves

NAME	BPV
Capps,Carter	185
Romo,Sergio	161
McGee,Jake	161
Cecil,Brett	155
Scribner,Evan	150
Smith,Will	145
Kela,Keone	143
O Day,Darren	142
Hendriks,Liam	141
Givens,Mychal	139
Betances,Dellin	139
Baez,Pedro	135
Kelley,Shawn	134
Garcia,Yimi	133
Salas,Fernando	132
Qualls,Chad	131
Madson,Ryan	129
Soria,Joakim	125
Knebel,Corey	125
Hatcher,Chris	124
Storen,Drew	124
Smyly,Drew	123
Watson,Tony	121
Cedeno,Xavier	119
Loup,Aaron	118
Fields,Joshua	117
Petit,Yusmeiro	117
Morin,Michael	116
Grimm,Justin	114
Strop,Pedro	112
Dyson,Sam	112

POTENTIAL SKILLS GAINERS AND FADERS - PITCHERS

Dom Gainers

From a pitcher's swinging-strike rate (SwK%) , we can establish a typical range in which we would expect to find their Dom (k/9). The pitchers on this list posted a 2015 Dom that was in the bottom of that expected range based on their SwK%. The names above the break line are in the bottom 10% of that range, and are the strongest candidates for Dom gains. The names below the break line are in the bottom 25%, and are also good candidates for strikeout gains.

Dom Faders

From a pitcher's swinging-strike rate (SwK%) , we can establish a typical range in which we would expect to find their Dom (k/9). The pitchers on this list posted a 2015 Dom that was in the top of that expected range based on their SwK%. The names above the break line are in the top 10% of that range, and are the strongest candidates for a Dom fade. The names below the break line are in the top 25%, and are also good candidates for a Dom fade.

DOM GAINERS

NAME	SwK	K/9
Richards,Garrett	12	7.6
De La Rosa,Rubby	12	7.2
McHugh,Collin	11	7.6
Teheran,Julio	11	7.7
Kazmir,Scott	11	7.6
Ramirez,Erasmo	11	6.9
Hellickson,Jeremy	11	7.5
Iwakuma,Hisashi	11	7.7
Latos,Mat	11	7.7
Colome,Alexander	11	7.2
Gibson,Kyle	10	6.7
Estrada,Marco	10	6.5
Lohse,Kyle	10	6.4
Young,Chris	10	6.1
Santana,Ervin	10	6.8
Greinke,Zack	13	8.1
Harvey,Matt	12	8.9
Pineda,Michael	12	8.7
Tanaka,Masahiro	12	8.1
de la Rosa,Jorge	12	8.1
Gausman,Kevin	12	8.3
Keuchel,Dallas	11	8.4
Walker,Taijuan	11	8.3
Odorizzi,Jake	11	8.0
Lackey,John	10	7.2
Samardzija,Jeff	10	6.9
Cueto,Johnny	10	7.5
Gray,Sonny	10	7.3
Miller,Shelby	10	7.5
Volquez,Edinson	10	7.0
DeSclafani,Anthony	10	7.4
Wacha,Michael	10	7.6
Nelson,Jimmy	10	7.5
Hutchison,Drew	10	7.7
Shoemaker,Matthew	10	7.7
Verlander,Justin	10	7.6
Elias,Roenis	10	7.6
Bettis,Chad	10	7.7

DOM FADERS

NAME	SwK	K/9
Phelps,David	5	6.2
Colon,Bartolo	7	6.3
Haren,Dan	7	6.3
Vogelsong,Ryan	7	7.2
Jimenez,Ubaldo	8	8.2
Hendricks,Kyle	9	8.4
Lynn,Lance	9	8.6
Ray,Robbie	9	8.4
Fiers,Mike	10	9.0
Karns,Nathan	10	8.9
McCullers,Lance	10	9.2
Wood,Travis	11	10.5
Strasburg,Stephen	12	11.0
Archer,Chris	13	10.7
Kelly,Joe	8	7.4
Cashner,Andrew	9	8.0
Santiago,Hector	9	8.1
Happ,J.A.	9	7.9
Porcello,Rick	9	7.8
Chavez,Jesse	9	7.8
Jungmann,Taylor	9	8.1
Bolsinger,Michael	9	8.1
Bauer,Trevor	10	8.7
Gonzalez,Gio	10	8.7
Arrieta,Jake	11	9.3
Lester,Jon	11	9.1
Martinez,Carlos	11	9.2
Hammel,Jason	11	9.1
Kennedy,Ian	11	9.3
Rodon,Carlos	11	9.0
Salazar,Danny	12	9.5
Kluber,Corey	13	9.9
Bumgarner,Madison	13	9.6
Shields,James	13	9.6
Ross,Tyson	13	9.7
deGrom,Jacob	13	9.7
Syndergaard,Noah	13	10.0

Ctl Gainers

From a pitcher's first-pitch strike rate (FpK%), we can establish a typical range in which we would expect to find their Ctl (bb/9). These pitchers posted a 2015 Ctl that was in the bottom of that expected range based on their FpK%. The names above the break line are in the bottom 10% of that range, and are the strongest candidates for Ctl gains. The names below the break line are in the bottom 25%, and are also good candidates for Ctl gains.

Ctl Faders

From a pitcher's first-pitch strike rate (FpK%) , we can establish a typical range in which we would expect to find their Ctl (bb/9). These pitchers posted a 2015 Ctl that was in the top 10% of that expected range based on their FpK%, making them the strongest candidates for a Ctl fade.

CTL GAINERS

NAME	FpK	BB/9
Rusin,Chris	67	2.8
Wood,Travis	62	3.5
Vogelsong,Ryan	60	3.9
Bauer,Trevor	59	4.0
Lorenzen,Michael	57	4.5
Phelps,David	65	2.7
Sanchez,Anibal	65	2.8
Martinez,Carlos	63	3.2
Kelly,Joe	62	3.3
Cashner,Andrew	62	3.2
Locke,Jeff	62	3.2
Gonzalez,Miguel	62	3.2
Ray,Robbie	61	3.5
Garza,Matt	61	3.5
Gonzalez,Gio	60	3.5
Shields,James	60	3.6
Elias,Roenis	60	3.4
Ross,Tyson	58	3.9
Koehler,Tom	58	3.7
de la Rosa,Jorge	58	3.9
Perez,Williams	57	3.9

CTL FADERS

NAME	FpK	BB/9
Kluber,Corey	63	1.8
May,Trevor	63	2.0
Cueto,Johnny	63	2.0
Tanaka,Masahiro	63	1.6
Lewis,Colby	63	1.8
Peavy,Jake	63	2.0
Cole,Gerrit	62	1.9
Samardzija,Jeff	62	2.1
Fister,Doug	62	2.1
Lester,Jon	61	2.1
Hammel,Jason	61	2.1
Keuchel,Dallas	61	2.0
Leake,Mike	61	2.3
Buehrle,Mark	61	1.5
Feldman,Scott	61	2.2
Weaver,Jered	61	1.9
Happ,J.A.	60	2.4
Porcello,Rick	60	2.0
Arrieta,Jake	60	1.9
Shoemaker,Matthew	60	2.3
Odorizzi,Jake	60	2.4
Roark,Tanner	60	2.1
Salazar,Danny	59	2.6
Garcia,Jaime	59	2.1
Gray,Sonny	59	2.6
Collmenter,Josh	59	1.8
Dickey,R.A.	59	2.6
Despaigne,Odrisamer	58	2.3
Pelfrey,Mike	58	2.5
Anderson,Brett	58	2.3
Rodriguez,Eduardo	57	2.7
Estrada,Marco	57	2.7
Gausman,Kevin	55	2.3

RISK MANAGEMENT

GRADE "F" in HEALTH

Pitchers
Alvarez,Henderson
Anderson,Brett
Bailey,Homer
Barrett,Aaron
Beachy,Brandon
Bradley,Archie
Buchholz,Clay
Bundy,Dylan
Cain,Matt
Capps,Carter
Cashner,Andrew
Chacin,Jhoulys
Chatwood,Tyler
Cobb,Alex
Colome,Alexander
Corbin,Patrick
Danks,John
Darvish,Yu
de la Rosa,Jorge
Doolittle,Sean
Duffy,Danny
Feldman,Scott
Feliz,Neftali
Fernandez,Jose
Fister,Doug
Floyd,Gavin
Garcia,Jaime
Garza,Matt
Gee,Dillon
Graveman,Kendall
Griffin,A.J.
Grilli,Jason
Harrison,Matt
Hellickson,Jeremy
Hochevar,Luke
Holland,Derek
Hudson,Daniel
Hutchison,Drew
Iwakuma,Hisashi
Janssen,Casey
Jones,Nate
Lackey,John
Lee,Cliff
Lewis,Colby
Lincecum,Tim
Lobstein,Kyle
Lyles,Jordan
Madson,Ryan
McCarthy,Brandon
Medlen,Kris
Mejia,Jenrry
Minor,Mike
Montero,Rafael
Moore,Matt
Morton,Charlie
Motte,Jason
Nolasco,Ricky
Nova,Ivan
Ottavino,Adam
Parker,Jarrod
Parnell,Bobby
Paxton,James
Peacock,Brad
Peavy,Jake
Pelfrey,Mike
Perez,Martin
Phelps,David
Pineda,Michael

Pitchers
Putnam,Zach
Rodriguez,Wandy
Rondon,Bruce
Ryu,Hyun-Jin
Sabathia,CC
Sanchez,Anibal
Scheppers,Tanner
Skaggs,Tyler
Smyly,Drew
Soria,Joakim
Strasburg,Stephen
Stroman,Marcus
Tanaka,Masahiro
Thornburg,Tyler
Tolleson,Shawn
Tomlin,Josh
Uehara,Koji
Vizcaino,Arodys
Wainwright,Adam
Walden,Jordan
Weaver,Jered
Wheeler,Zack
Wilson,C.J.
Wright,Steven

Batters
Adams,Matt
Beckham,Tim
Blanks,Kyle
Cervelli,Francisco
Cozart,Zack
Crawford,Carl
Crisp,Coco
Cuddyer,Michael
Davis,Ike
Garcia,Avisail
Gutierrez,Franklin
Hamilton,Josh
Hanigan,Ryan
Hart,Corey
Iglesias,Jose
Jaso,John
Jennings,Desmond
Lawrie,Brett
Lowrie,Jed
Mesoraco,Devin
Moreland,Mitch
Morneau,Justin
Myers,Wil
Pagan,Angel
Pence,Hunter
Profar,Jurickson
Ramos,Wilson
Reimold,Nolan
Saunders,Michael
Soto,Geovany
Span,Denard
Springer,George
Stanton,Giancarlo
Swisher,Nick
Teixeira,Mark
Tulowitzki,Troy
Vazquez,Christian
Victorino,Shane
Werth,Jayson
Wieters,Matt
Wright,David
Zimmerman,Ryan

Highest Reliability Grades - Health / Experience / Consistency (Min. Grade = BBB)

CA	POS	Rel
Posey,Buster	23	AAA
Perez,Salvador	2	BAB
Montero,Miguel	2	BBB

1B/DH	POS	Rel
Posey,Buster	23	AAA
Gonzalez,Adrian	3	AAA
Cruz,Nelson	09	AAB
Butler,Billy	0	AAB
Santana,Carlos	03	AAB
Encarnacion,Edwin	03	BAA
Pujols,Albert	03	BAA
Canha,Mark	37	ABB
Moss,Brandon	39	ABB
Smith,Seth	079	ABB
Solarte,Yangervis	35	ABB
Valbuena,Luis	35	ABB
Alvarez,Pedro	3	ABB
Carter,Chris	3	ABB
Shaw,Travis	3	ABB
Freeman,Freddie	3	BAB
Goldschmidt,Paul	3	BAB
Duda,Lucas	3	BBB
Napoli,Mike	3	BBB

2B	POS	Rel
Dozier,Brian	4	AAA
Kinsler,Ian	4	AAA
Zobrist,Ben	47	BAA
Murphy,Daniel	45	BAA
Phillips,Brandon	4	BAB
Walker,Neil	4	BBB

SS	POS	Rel
Andrus,Elvis	6	AAA
Aybar,Erick	6	AAA
Cabrera,Asdrubal	6	AAA
Desmond,Ian	6	AAB
Peralta,Jhonny	6	AAB
Ramirez,Alexei	6	AAB
Rollins,Jimmy	6	AAB
Segura,Jean	6	AAB
Simmons,Andrelton	6	AAB
Crawford,Brandon	6	ABB
Hechavarria,Adeiny	6	ABB
Semien,Marcus	6	ABB

3B	POS	Rel
Seager,Kyle	5	AAA
Frazier,Todd	5	AAB
Castellanos,Nick	5	ABA
Murphy,Daniel	45	BAA
Headley,Chase	5	BAA
Plouffe,Trevor	5	BAA
Prado,Martin	5	BAA
Solarte,Yangervis	35	ABB
Valbuena,Luis	35	ABB
Beltre,Adrian	5	BAB
Sandoval,Pablo	5	BAB
Arenado,Nolan	5	BBB

OF	POS	Rel
Jones,Adam	8	AAA
Markakis,Nick	9	AAA
Marte,Starling	7	AAA
Upton,Justin	7	AAA
Cruz,Nelson	09	AAB
Hunter,Torii	9	AAB
Calhoun,Kole	9	ABA
Polanco,Gregory	9	ABA
Zobrist,Ben	47	BAA
Fowler,Dexter	8	BAA
Canha,Mark	37	ABB
Moss,Brandon	39	ABB
Smith,Seth	079	ABB
De Aza,Alejandro	79	ABB
Pederson,Joc	8	ABB
Pillar,Kevin	8	ABB
Suzuki,Ichiro	79	ABB
Thompson,Trayce	9	ABB
Byrd,Marlon	79	BAB
Gomez,Carlos	8	BAB
Heyward,Jason	9	BAB
Jackson,Austin	89	BAB
Hamilton,Billy	8	BBA
Revere,Ben	78	BBA
Yelich,Christian	78	BBA
Inciarte,Ender	789	BBB

RP	Rel
Kimbrel,Craig	AAA
Melancon,Mark	AAA
Rosenthal,Trevor	AAB
Wood,Travis	AAB
Allen,Cody	ABA
Collmenter,Josh	ABA
Papelbon,Jonathan	ABA
Reed,Addison	ABA
Rodriguez,Francisco	ABA
Romo,Sergio	ABA
Ziegler,Brad	ABA
Rodney,Fernando	BAA
Cishek,Steve	ABB
Rondon,Hector	ABB
Holland,Greg	BAB
Perkins,Glen	BAB

SP	Rel
Archer,Chris	AAA
Buehrle,Mark	AAA
Bumgarner,Madison	AAA
Gallardo,Yovani	AAA
Gibson,Kyle	AAA
Gray,Sonny	AAA
Hernandez,Felix	AAA
Keuchel,Dallas	AAA
Koehler,Tom	AAA
Lester,Jon	AAA
Lohse,Kyle	AAA
Miley,Wade	AAA
Quintana,Jose	AAA
Santana,Ervin	AAA
Santiago,Hector	AAA
Scherzer,Max	AAA
Shields,James	AAA
Teheran,Julio	AAA
Tillman,Chris	AAA
Volquez,Edinson	AAA
Zimmermann,Jordan	AAA
Miller,Shelby	AAB
Samardzija,Jeff	AAB
Locke,Jeff	ABA
Martinez,Carlos	ABA
Dickey,R.A.	BAA
Gonzalez,Gio	BAA
Kennedy,Ian	BAA
Kluber,Corey	BAA
Leake,Mike	BAA
Lynn,Lance	BAA
Porcello,Rick	BAA
Price,David	BAA
Ross,Tyson	BAA
Simon,Alfredo	BAA
Bauer,Trevor	ABB
Hernandez,Roberto	ABB
Nelson,Jimmy	ABB
Roark,Tanner	ABB
Wood,Alex	ABB
Guthrie,Jeremy	BAB
Chavez,Jesse	BBA
Ventura,Yordano	BBA

RISK MANAGEMENT

GRADE "A" in CONSISTENCY*

Pitchers (min 120 IP)
Archer,Chris
Buehrle,Mark
Bumgarner,Madison
Gallardo,Yovani
Gibson,Kyle
Gray,Sonny
Hernandez,Felix
Keuchel,Dallas
Koehler,Tom
Lester,Jon
Miley,Wade
Quintana,Jose
Santana,Ervin
Santiago,Hector
Scherzer,Max
Shields,James
Teheran,Julio
Tillman,Chris
Volquez,Edinson
Zimmermann,Jordan
Locke,Jeff
Martinez,Carlos
Dickey,R.A.
Gonzalez,Gio
Kennedy,Ian
Kluber,Corey
Leake,Mike
Lynn,Lance
Porcello,Rick
Price,David
Ross,Tyson
Simon,Alfredo
Chavez,Jesse
Ventura,Yordano
Smyly,Drew
Bettis,Chad
Anderson,Brett
Cashner,Andrew
Danks,John
Darvish,Yu
de la Rosa,Jorge
Duffy,Danny
Feldman,Scott
Garcia,Jaime
Garza,Matt
Holland,Derek
Iwakuma,Hisashi
Lackey,John
Moore,Matt
Morton,Charlie
Nolasco,Ricky
Nova,Ivan
Peavy,Jake
Ryu,Hyun-Jin
Strasburg,Stephen
Stroman,Marcus
Tanaka,Masahiro
Wainwright,Adam
Weaver,Jered
Wilson,C.J.
Cole,Gerrit
Cueto,Johnny
Eovaldi,Nathan
Gonzalez,Miguel
Harang,Aaron
Kazmir,Scott
Kelly,Joe
Latos,Mat
Liriano,Francisco
Matz,Steven

Pitchers (min 120 IP)
Niese,Jon
Verlander,Justin
Walker,Taijuan
Chen,Wei-Yin
Colon,Bartolo
Gausman,Kevin
Greinke,Zack
Hamels,Cole
Kershaw,Clayton
Odorizzi,Jake
Sale,Chris
De La Rosa,Rubby
DeSclafani,Anthony
Heaney,Andrew
Hendricks,Kyle
Jungmann,Taylor
Rodriguez,Eduardo
Severino,Luis

Batters (min 400 AB)
Seager,Kyle
Andrus,Elvis
Aybar,Erick
Cabrera,Asdrubal
Dozier,Brian
Kinsler,Ian
Posey,Buster
Gonzalez,Adrian
Jones,Adam
Markakis,Nick
Marte,Starling
Upton,Justin
Castellanos,Nick
Calhoun,Kole
Polanco,Gregory
Murphy,Daniel
Headley,Chase
Plouffe,Trevor
Prado,Martin
Zobrist,Ben
Encarnacion,Edwin
Pujols,Albert
Fowler,Dexter
Hamilton,Billy
Revere,Ben
Yelich,Christian
Lawrie,Brett
Duffy,Matt
Freese,David
Flores,Wilmer
Escobar,Eduardo
Ahmed,Nick
Gregorius,Didi
Seager,Corey
Sanchez,Carlos
Wong,Kolten
Peterson,Jace
Kendrick,Howie
Zimmerman,Ryan
McCann,James
Gardner,Brett
Aoki,Norichika
Gordon,Alex

*Ranked by Reliability score: AAA, AAB, etc. Equal scores ranked by Health, Experience.

TOP COMBINATION OF SKILLS AND RELIABILITY

Maximum of one "C" in Reliability Grade

BATTING POWER (Min. 400 AB)

PX >100	PX	Rel
Carter,Chris	188	ABB
Trout,Mike	175	AAC
Goldschmidt,Paul	171	BAB
Davis,Khristopher	169	BCB
Duda,Lucas	169	BBB
Encarnacion,Edwin	160	BAA
Arenado,Nolan	159	BBB
Bautista,Jose	156	CAB
Ortiz,David	153	BAC
Cruz,Nelson	150	AAB
Upton,Justin	150	AAA
Rizzo,Anthony	148	AAC
Moss,Brandon	146	ABB
Bruce,Jay	145	AAC
Alvarez,Pedro	144	ABB
Pederson,Joc	143	ABB
Santana,Domingo	140	ACB
Gattis,Evan	139	BCB
Cespedes,Yoenis	139	AAC
McCutchen,Andrew	135	AAC
Frazier,Todd	135	AAB
Braun,Ryan	134	BBC
Granderson,Curtis	134	CBB
Smith,Seth	133	ABB
Valbuena,Luis	132	ABB
Trumbo,Mark	130	CBB
Gomez,Carlos	129	BAB
Byrd,Marlon	128	BAB
Ozuna,Marcell	126	BCB
Crawford,Brandon	125	ABB
Martin,Russell	124	ABC
Dozier,Brian	124	AAA
Jones,Adam	124	AAA
Cron,C.J.	124	ACB
Machado,Manny	123	CAB
Lind,Adam	123	CBB
Gonzalez,Adrian	122	AAA
Castellanos,Nick	121	ABA
Castillo,Welington	120	BCB
Freeman,Freddie	120	BAB
Desmond,Ian	120	AAB
Plouffe,Trevor	118	BAA
Longoria,Evan	117	BAC
Santana,Carlos	117	AAB
Marte,Starling	116	AAA
Moustakas,Mike	115	ABC
Calhoun,Kole	114	ABA
Canha,Mark	114	ABB
McCann,Brian	112	BBC
Gordon,Alex	112	CBA
Seager,Kyle	112	AAA
Pujols,Albert	111	BAA
Cabrera,Asdrubal	109	AAA
Cano,Robinson	108	AAC
Norris,Derek	108	ACB
Walker,Neil	106	BBB
Escobar,Eduardo	106	ACA
Blackmon,Charlie	106	CAB
Hosmer,Eric	105	AAC
Reddick,Josh	105	CBB
Fowler,Dexter	104	BAA
Freese,David	104	CBA
Montero,Miguel	104	BBB
Vogt,Stephen	102	BCB
Beltre,Adrian	101	BAB
Suarez,Eugenio	101	ACB
Semien,Marcus	101	ABB

RUNNER SPEED (Min. 400 AB)

Spd 100+	SX	Rel
Gordon,Dee	173	BAC
Hamilton,Billy	164	BBA
Hechavarria,Adeiny	161	ABB
Revere,Ben	156	BBA
Herrera,Odubel	156	ACB
Kiermaier,Kevin	155	ACB
Fowler,Dexter	154	BAA
Marte,Starling	151	AAA
Gose,Anthony	151	ACB
Segura,Jean	149	AAB
LeMahieu,DJ	147	ABC
Ahmed,Nick	145	ACA
Escobar,Alcides	145	AAC
Trout,Mike	143	AAC
Semien,Marcus	141	ABB
Inciarte,Ender	140	BBB
Owings,Christopher	135	BCB
Jackson,Austin	135	BAB
Blackmon,Charlie	130	CAB
Gardner,Brett	129	CAA
Aoki,Norichika	129	CBA
Realmuto,Jacob	127	ACB
Yelich,Christian	126	BBA
Suarez,Eugenio	125	ACB
Kinsler,Ian	125	AAA
Reddick,Josh	124	CBB
McCutchen,Andrew	121	AAC
Simmons,Andrelton	120	AAB
Braun,Ryan	120	BBC
Rios,Alex	119	CBB
Canha,Mark	118	ABB
Galvis,Freddy	117	BCB
Machado,Manny	116	CAB
Upton,Justin	116	AAA
Santana,Domingo	116	ACB
Gregorius,Didi	116	ACA
Dozier,Brian	115	AAA
Desmond,Ian	115	AAB
Reyes,Jose	115	CBB
Andrus,Elvis	112	AAA
Escobar,Eduardo	111	ACA
Cespedes,Yoenis	110	AAC
Wong,Kolten	110	ACA
Parra,Gerardo	110	AAC
Heyward,Jason	109	BAB
Rollins,Jimmy	109	AAB
Gomez,Carlos	109	BAB
Polanco,Gregory	109	ABA
Ramirez,Alexei	108	AAB
Norris,Derek	107	ACB
Pillar,Kevin	107	ABB
Kendrick,Howie	106	CAA
Granderson,Curtis	106	CBB
Markakis,Nick	105	AAA
Prado,Martin	105	BAA
Aybar,Erick	105	AAA
Zobrist,Ben	105	BAA
Gattis,Evan	104	BCB
Pederson,Joc	101	ABB
Ozuna,Marcell	101	BCB

OVERALL PITCHING SKILL

BPV over 85	BPV	Rel
Chapman,Aroldis	188	CAB
Kimbrel,Craig	183	AAA
Kershaw,Clayton	177	CAA
Robertson,David	173	CBA
Sale,Chris	164	CAA
Romo,Sergio	161	ABA
Cecil,Brett	155	BCA
Scherzer,Max	151	AAA
Smith,Will	145	ACA
Bumgarner,Madison	142	AAA
O Day,Darren	142	BCA
Kluber,Corey	142	BAA
Rodriguez,Francisco	141	ABA
Melancon,Mark	139	AAA
Betances,Dellin	139	ACB
Rondon,Hector	138	ABB
Price,David	137	BAA
Allen,Cody	137	ABA
Harvey,Matt	135	CBB
Perkins,Glen	132	BAB
Hernandez,Felix	132	AAA
Gregerson,Luke	131	ACA
deGrom,Jacob	129	ABC
Greinke,Zack	128	CAA
Arrieta,Jake	126	CAB
Keuchel,Dallas	126	AAA
Lester,Jon	122	AAA
Papelbon,Jonathan	121	ABA
Rosenthal,Trevor	121	AAB
Watson,Tony	121	ACB
Holland,Greg	119	BAB
Loup,Aaron	118	ACB
Hamels,Cole	116	CAA
Zimmermann,Jordan	115	AAA
Tazawa,Junichi	114	BCA
Archer,Chris	111	AAA
Salazar,Danny	111	ABC
Martinez,Carlos	105	ABA
Reed,Addison	105	ABA
Hendricks,Kyle	104	ACA
Ross,Tyson	103	BAA
Porcello,Rick	102	BAA
Quintana,Jose	101	AAA
Smith,Joe	101	ACB
Kennedy,Ian	100	BAA
Maness,Seth	99	ACB
DeSclafani,Anthony	98	ACA
Shields,James	96	AAA
Gonzalez,Gio	94	BAA
Samardzija,Jeff	94	AAB
May,Trevor	94	ACA
Ramos,A.J.	94	ACA
Wilson,Justin	93	ACA
Wood,Alex	92	ABB
Benoit,Joaquin	92	ACA
Gray,Sonny	92	AAA
Warren,Adam	89	ACB
Ventura,Yordano	88	BBA
Dunn,Mike	88	ACA
Chen,Wei-Yin	87	CAA
Shaw,Bryan	86	ACA
Shoemaker,Matthew	86	ACB
Wood,Travis	86	AAB
Colon,Bartolo	85	CAA

PORTFOLIO 3 PLAN - HITTERS

TIER 1 Hitters

Rel BBB+; xBA score 3+; Power OR Speed score 3+

BATTERS	Age	Bats	Pos	MM	REL	MAY	R$
Goldschmidt,Paul	28	R	3	5245	BAB	97	$39
Revere,Ben	28	L	79	0555	BBA	91	$34
Arenado,Nolan	25	R	5	4155	BBB	87	$33
Marte,Starling	27	R	7	3545	AAA	113	$33
Encarnacion,Edwin	33	R	03	5055	BAA	95	$28
Kinsler,Ian	34	R	4	2335	AAA	87	$28
Jones,Adam	30	R	9	4335	AAA	100	$27
Gonzalez,Adrian	34	L	3	4045	AAA	87	$27
Cruz,Nelson	36	R	80	4135	AAB	83	$27
Heyward,Jason	26	L	8	2435	BAB	85	$26
Beltre,Adrian	37	R	5	3245	BAB	85	$25
Yelich,Christian	24	L	79	2445	BBA	91	$25
Pujols,Albert	36	R	30	3145	BAA	83	$25
Seager,Kyle	28	L	5	3135	AAA	80	$25
Andrus,Elvis	27	R	6	1435	AAA	87	$24
Freeman,Freddie	26	L	3	4135	BAB	79	$24
Inciarte,Ender	25	L	879	1545	BBB	87	$20
Ramirez,Alexei	34	R	6	1345	AAB	83	$20
Pillar,Kevin	27	R	9	2435	ABB	85	$19
Crawford,Brandon	29	L	6	4135	ABB	79	$18
Walker,Neil	30	B	4	3235	BBB	75	$18
Zobrist,Ben	35	B	47	3245	BAA	89	$18
Aybar,Erick	32	B	6	1345	AAA	87	$17
Simmons,Andrelton	26	R	6	1335	AAB	76	$15
Smith,Seth	33	L	780	4235	ABB	85	$12
Thompson,Trayce	25	R	8	4431	ABB	15	$7

TIER 2 Hitters

Rel BCC+; 5 PT; xBA, Power, or Speed score 3+ <$20

BATTERS	Age	Bats	Pos	MM	REL	MAY	R$
Murphy,Daniel*	31	L	45	2255	BAA	89	$23
Desmond,Ian*	30	R	6	3415	AAB	83	$22
Duda,Lucas*	30	L	3	5025	BBB	69	$22
Polanco,Gregory*	24	L	8	2425	ABA	83	$22
Phillips,Brandon*	35	R	4	1235	BAB	67	$22
Dozier,Brian*	29	R	4	4325	AAA	93	$21
Fowler,Dexter*	30	B	9	3515	BAA	89	$20
Davis,Khristopher	28	R	7	5235	BCB	83	$20
Segura,Jean	26	R	6	1525	AAB	83	$19
Wong,Kolten	25	L	4	1425	ACA	73	$19
Calhoun,Kole	28	L	8	3225	ABA	76	$19
Parra,Gerardo	29	L	879	2345	AAC	85	$19
Escobar,Alcides	29	R	6	0525	AAC	73	$18
Gattis,Evan	29	R	0	4035	BCB	66	$18
Moustakas,Mike	27	L	5	3035	ABC	64	$18
Kiermaier,Kevin	26	L	9	2535	ACB	87	$18
Jackson,Austin	29	R	98	2425	BAB	79	$17
Cabrera,Asdrubal	30	B	6	3325	AAA	87	$17
Markakis,Nick	32	L	8	1235	AAA	73	$17
Ozuna,Marcell	25	R	9	4235	BCB	77	$17
Castellanos,Nick	24	R	5	4025	ABA	70	$17
Santana,Carlos	30	B	30	3125	AAB	70	$17
Gomes,Yan	28	R	2	4325	BCC	74	$17
Solarte,Yangervis	28	B	53	2145	ABB	73	$16
Semien,Marcus	25	R	6	3415	ABB	79	$16
Realmuto,Jacob	25	R	2	2435	ACB	81	$16
Prado,Martin	32	R	5	1235	BAA	70	$16

* Tier 2 players should generally be less than $20. If you pay more than $20, you should be aware of the extra risk.

TIER 2 Hitters (Cont.)

Rel BCC+; 5 PT; xBA, Power, or Speed score 3+ <$20

BATTERS	Age	Bats	Pos	MM	REL	MAY	R$
Miller,Bradley	26	L	69	3325	ACC	72	$16
Molina,Yadier	33	R	2	1135	BBC	55	$16
Perez,Salvador	26	R	2	2235	BAB	73	$16
Rosario,Eddie	24	L	78	3425	ACC	77	$15
Martin,Russell	33	R	2	4125	ABC	69	$15
Plouffe,Trevor	30	R	5	3225	BAA	76	$15
Byrd,Marlon	38	R	78	4125	BAB	73	$15
Cron,C.J.	26	R	30	4135	ACB	75	$15
McCann,Brian	32	L	2	3025	BBC	55	$14
Piscotty,Stephen	25	R	7	3345	ACC	83	$14
Flores,Wilmer	24	R	64	2035	ACA	61	$14
Alvarez,Pedro	29	L	3	4125	ABB	73	$14
Hechavarria,Adeiny	27	R	6	1525	ABB	79	$13
Rollins,Jimmy	37	B	6	2425	AAB	83	$13
Gose,Anthony	25	L	9	1505	ACB	64	$13
Suarez,Eugenio	24	R	6	3315	ACB	69	$13
Chisenhall,Lonnie	27	L	85	3315	ACB	69	$13
Norris,Derek	27	R	2	3315	ACB	69	$13
Canha,Mark	27	R	37	3315	ABB	73	$13
Owings,Christopher	24	R	46	2515	BCB	72	$12
Castillo,Welington	29	R	2	4215	BCB	66	$12
Escobar,Eduardo	27	B	67	3225	ACA	73	$12
Montero,Miguel	32	L	2	3015	BBB	52	$12
Valbuena,Luis	30	L	53	4025	ABB	67	$12
Carter,Chris	29	R	3	5015	ABB	67	$12
Escobar,Yunel	33	R	5	1135	AAC	61	$12
Bour,Justin	28	L	3	3015	ACC	50	$12
Moss,Brandon	32	L	83	4005	ABB	55	$11
Santana,Domingo	23	R	89	4205	ACB	64	$11
Vogt,Stephen	31	L	23	3025	BCB	55	$11
Pederson,Joc	24	L	9	4105	ABB	61	$10
Galvis,Freddy	26	B	6	1405	BCB	55	$8

TIER 3 Hitters

Health>"F"; xBA score 3+; Power or Speed score 3+ <$15

BATTERS	Age	Bats	Pos	MM	REL	MAY	R$
Marte,Ketel	22	B	6	1533	ADC	38	$15
Coghlan,Chris	31	L	78	3435	CCB	79	$15
Ethier,Andre	34	L	87	3145	ABD	71	$14
Travis,Devon	25	R	4	3453	DFC	36	$14
D Arnaud,Travis	27	R	2	3235	DFB	55	$13
Valencia,Danny	31	R	57	4133	ADD	33	$12
Swihart,Blake	24	B	2	2433	AFB	37	$11
Hernandez,Enrique	24	R	4OF	3133	BCB	33	$10
Drury,Brandon	23	R	5	3043	AFC	30	$9
Ackley,Dustin	28	L	79	3333	ACA	44	$9
Nunez,Eduardo	29	R	6	2431	CFB	9	$9
Ramirez,Jose	23	B	64	1431	ACF	9	$9
Utley,Chase	37	L	4	2333	DBC	31	$9
Marte,Jefry	25	R	3	4231	ACB	12	$7
Raburn,Ryan	35	R	0	4131	BFF	8	$7
Giavotella,Johnny	28	R	4	1333	BCB	33	$7
Rosario,Wilin	27	R	3	3131	ACB	9	$5
Tomlinson,Kelby	26	R	4	1531	ADC	10	$5
Colon,Christian	27	R	6	0351	ACB	10	$5
Smolinski,Jacob	27	R	7	3231	BDB	9	$4
Perez,Eury	26	R	7	0431	BDA	9	$4
Shuck,J.B.	29	L	8	1431	ADD	9	$4
Refsnyder,Rob	25	R	4	2331	ADB	10	$3
Blanco,Andres	32	B	54	3031	AFF	6	$3
Ramirez,Aramis	38	R	5	3230	CBB	0	$0

PORTFOLIO 3 PLAN

TIER 1 Pitchers

Rel BBB+; xERA score 3+ and K/9 score 3+

PITCHERS	Age	Th	MM	REL	MAY	R$
Bumgarner,Madison	26	L	5405	AAA	126	$29
Price,David	30	L	4405	BAA	108	$27
Scherzer,Max	31	R	5505	AAA	133	$27
Kimbrel,Craig	28	R	5530	AAA	72	$26
Kluber,Corey	30	R	5405	BAA	121	$25
Melancon,Mark	31	R	5331	AAA	91	$25
Keuchel,Dallas	28	L	5305	AAA	120	$23
Rodriguez,Francisco	34	R	5530	ABA	69	$22
Allen,Cody	27	R	4530	ABA	61	$21
Lester,Jon	32	L	4305	AAA	106	$21
Hernandez,Felix	30	R	5405	AAA	126	$20
Rondon,Hector	28	R	5430	ABB	62	$20
Archer,Chris	27	R	3405	AAA	100	$19
Rosenthal,Trevor	26	R	4531	AAB	86	$19
Papelbon,Jonathan	35	R	3331	ABA	66	$19
Perkins,Glen	33	L	3430	BAB	47	$15
Ross,Tyson	29	R	4405	BAA	108	$13
Martinez,Carlos	24	R	4405	ABA	108	$13
Shields,James	34	R	3305	AAA	93	$13
Kennedy,Ian	31	R	3405	BAA	95	$10
Ventura,Yordano	25	R	3305	BBA	85	$10
Gonzalez,Gio	30	L	3405	BAA	95	$9
Romo,Sergio	33	R	5510	ABA	20	$8

TIER 2 Pitchers

Rel BCC+; PT score 3+; xERA or K/9 score 3+ <$20

PITCHERS	Age	Th	MM	REL	MAY	R$
deGrom,Jacob*	28	R	4405	ABC	98	$25
Gray,Sonny*	26	R	3205	AAA	87	$20
Zimmermann,Jordan	30	R	3205	AAA	87	$16
Salazar,Danny	26	R	3405	ABC	87	$15
Wood,Alex	25	L	3205	ABB	79	$12
Quintana,Jose	27	L	3205	AAA	87	$11
Hendricks,Kyle	26	R	3203	ACA	40	$11
Lynn,Lance	29	R	2305	BAA	76	$9
Porcello,Rick	27	R	3205	BAA	83	$8
Karns,Nathan	28	R	2303	ACC	33	$5
Chavez,Jesse	32	R	2303	BBA	36	$1
Bauer,Trevor	25	R	1305	ABB	61	$1
Santiago,Hector	28	L	1303	AAA	32	$1

* Tier 2 players should generally be less than $20. If you pay more than $20, you should be aware of the extra risk.

TIER 3 Pitchers

Health > "F"; xERA score 3+ <$15

PITCHERS	Age	Th	MM	REL	MAY	R$
Smith,Carson	26	R	5520	ADB	37	$14
Betances,Dellin	28	R	5511	ACB	39	$13
McCullers,Lance	22	R	4405	ADF	80	$13
Iglesias,Raisel	26	R	3405	CFF	61	$12
Strickland,Hunter	27	R	4321	AFA	46	$12
Watson,Tony	31	L	4311	ACB	30	$11
Severino,Luis	22	R	3303	ADA	41	$11
Liriano,Francisco	32	L	3403	DAA	42	$11
Walker,Taijuan	23	R	3305	DCA	69	$11
O Day,Darren	33	R	4510	BCA	16	$10
Casilla,Santiago	35	R	3320	DBB	22	$10
Hammel,Jason	33	R	3303	DAB	37	$10
McGee,Jake	29	L	5510	DCA	16	$8
Kela,Keone	23	R	5510	ADB	18	$8
Harris,Will	31	R	4311	ADA	30	$8
Cecil,Brett	29	L	5510	BCA	18	$6
Siegrist,Kevin	26	L	3510	DDD	10	$6
Herrera,Kelvin	26	R	3311	ADA	25	$6
Hendriks,Liam	27	R	4410	ACC	14	$6
Jeffress,Jeremy	28	R	4310	ADA	14	$5
Garcia,Yimi	25	R	3410	ADA	13	$5
Smith,Will	26	L	4510	ACA	17	$5
Givens,Mychal	26	R	5500	AFD	0	$5
Benoit,Joaquin	38	R	3410	ACA	13	$5
Kelley,Shawn	32	R	4510	DDA	13	$5
Strop,Pedro	31	R	5510	CCA	18	$4
Pomeranz,Drew	27	L	3411	DCC	22	$4
Storen,Drew	28	R	4410	CCA	14	$4
Grimm,Justin	27	R	4510	BCC	15	$4
Cedeno,Xavier	29	L	4400	ADB	0	$4
Dyson,Sam	28	R	5310	ADB	15	$4
McAllister,Zach	28	R	3411	DCB	23	$3
Salas,Fernando	31	R	4400	CDA	0	$3
Berrios,Jose	22	R	3301	AFB	10	$3
Baez,Pedro	28	R	4400	CDD	0	$2
Armstrong,Shawn	25	R	5500	AFB	0	$2
Wilson,Justin	28	L	3400	ACA	0	$2
Knebel,Corey	24	R	4510	AFD	13	$2
Petit,Yusmeiro	31	R	3301	ACC	11	$2
Tazawa,Junichi	30	R	3310	BCA	12	$1
Snell,Blake	23	L	3400	AFF	0	$1
Quackenbush,Kevin	27	R	3400	ADB	0	$1
Hatcher,Chris	31	R	3500	DDD	0	$1

Universal Draft Grid

Most publications and websites provide cheat sheets with ranked player lists for different fantasy draft formats. The biggest problem with these tools is that they perpetrate the myth that players can be ranked in a linear fashion.

Since rankings are based on highly variable projections, it is foolhardy to draw conclusions that a $24 player is better than a $23 player is better than a $22 player. Yes, a first round pick is better than a 10th round pick, but within most rounds, all players are pretty much interchangeable commodities.

But typical cheat sheets don't reflect that reality. Auction sheets rank players by dollar value. Snake draft sheets rank players within round, accounting for position and categorical scarcity. But just as ADPs have a ridiculously low success rate, these cheat sheets are similarly flawed.

We have a tool at BaseballHQ.com called the Rotisserie Grid. It is a chart—that can be customized to your league parameters—which organizes players into pockets of skill, by position. It is one of the most popular tools on the site. One of the best features of this grid is that its design provides immediate insight into position scarcity.

So in the *Forecaster*, we have transitioned to this format as a sort of Universal Draft Grid.

How to use the chart

Across the top of the grid, players are sorted by position. First and third base, and second and shortstop are presented side-by-side for easy reference when considering corner and middle infielders, respectively.

The vertical axis separates each group of players into tiers based on potential fantasy impact. At the top are the Elite players; at the bottom are the Fringe players.

Auction leagues: The tiers in the grid represent rough break-points for dollar values. Elite players could be considered those that are purchased for $30 and up. Each subsequent tier is a step down of approximately $5.

Snake drafters: Tiers can be used to rank players similarly, though most tiers will encompass more than one round. Any focus on position scarcity will bump some players up a bit. For instance, with the dearth of Elite catchers and the wealth of Elite outfielders, one might opt to draft Buster Posey (from the Gold tier) before the Elite level A.J. Pollock. The reason we target scarce positions early is that there will be plenty of solid outfielders and starting pitchers later on.

To build the best foundation, you should come out of the first 10 rounds with all your middle infielders, all your corner infielders, one outfielder, at least one catcher and two pitchers (at least one closer).

The players are listed at the position where they both qualify and provide the most fantasy value. Additional position eligibility (20 games) is listed in parentheses. Listings in bold are players with high reliability grades (minimum "B" across the board).

Each player is presented with his 7-character Mayberry score. The first four digits (all on a 0-5 scale) represent skill: power, speed, batting average and playing time for batters; ERA, dominance, saves potential and playing time for pitchers. The last three alpha characters are the reliability grade (A-F): health, experience and consistency.

Within each tier, players are sorted by the first character of their Mayberry score. This means that batters are sorted by power; pitchers by ERA potential. If you need to prospect for the best skill sets among players in a given tier, target those with 4s and 5s in whatever skill you need.

CAVEATS and DISCLAIMERS

The placement of players in tiers does not represent average draft positions (ADP) or average auction values (AAV). It represents where each player's true value may lie. It is the variance between this true value and the ADP/AAV market values—or better, the value that your league-mates place on each player—where you will find your potential for profit or loss.

That means ***you cannot take this chart right into your draft with you***. You have to compare these rankings with your ADPs and AAVs, and build your draft list from there. In other words, if we project Mookie Betts as a "Elite" level pick but you know the other owners (or your ADPs) see him as a third-rounder, you can probably wait to pick him up in round two. If you are in an auction league with owners who overvalue Cubs, and Kris Bryant (projected at $27) gets bid past $30, you will likely take a loss should you decide to chase the bidding.

Finally, this chart is intended as a preliminary look based on current factors. For Draft Day, you will need to make your own adjustments based upon many different criteria that will impact the world between now and then. Daily updates appear online at BaseballHQ.com. A free projections update is available in March at **http://www.baseballhq.com/content/ron-shandlers-2016-baseball-forecaster**

Simulation League Cheat Sheet

Using Runs Above Replacement creates a more real-world ranking of player value, which serves simulation gamers well. Batters and pitchers are integrated, and value break-points are delineated.

Universal Draft Grid

TIER	FIRST BASE		THIRD BASE		SECOND BASE		SHORTSTOP	
Elite	**Goldschmidt,Paul**	**(5245 BAB)**	**Arenado,Nolan**	**(4155 BBB)**	Altuve,Jose	(2545 AAD)		
	Cabrera,Miguel	(4155 BAF)	Donaldson,Josh	(4345 AAD)	Gordon,Dee	(1535 BAC)		
	Rizzo,Anthony	(4145 AAC)	Machado,Manny	(4345 CAB)				
Gold	**Encarnacion,Edwin**	**(5055 BAA)**	Bryant,Kris	(4405 ACC)	Cano,Robinson	(3155 AAC)	Correa,Carlos	(4255 AFF)
	Davis,Chris (O)	(5035 AAF)			**Kinsler,Ian**	**(2335 AAA)**		
	Abreu,Jose	(4145 ABD)						
	Votto,Joey	(4245 DAF)						
	Gonzalez,Adrian	**(4045 AAA)**						
	Hosmer,Eric							
Stars	**Duda,Lucas**	**(5025 BBB)**	**Frazier,Todd**	**(4225 AAB)**	**Dozier,Brian**	**(4325 AAA)**	Seager,Corey	(4245 AFA)
	Freeman,Freddie	**(4135 BAB)**	Carpenter,Matt	(4235 AAD)	Odor,Rougned	(3335 ADF)	Kang,Jung-ho (3)	(4145 AFF)
	Belt,Brandon	(4325 CCC)	**Beltre,Adrian**	**(3245 BAB)**	**Murphy,Daniel (3)**	**(2255 BAA)**	Tulowitzki,Troy	(4235 FBF)
	Pujols,Albert	**(3145 BAA)**	**Seager,Kyle**	**(3135 AAA)**	Kipnis,Jason	(2335 BAF)	**Desmond,Ian**	**(3415 AAB)**
			Longoria,Evan	(3225 BAC)	Panik,Joe	(2245 BBD)	Lindor,Francisco	(2435 ACC)
					Kendrick,Howie	(1345 CAA)	Reyes,Jose	(1435 CBB)
					LeMahieu,DJ	(1535 ABC)	**Andrus,Elvis**	**(1435 AAA)**
					Phillips,Brandon	**(1235 BAB)**	Bogaerts,Xander	(1425 ABD)
Regulars	Lind,Adam	(4235 CBB)	**Castellanos,Nick**	**(4025 ABA)**	Rendon,Anthony (3)	(3335 CBC)	**Crawford,Brandon**	**(4135 ABB)**
	Teixeira,Mark	(4145 FDD)	Franco,Maikel	(3235 BCF)	Baez,Javier	(3305 ADF)	Russell,Addison (2)	(3215 AFB)
	Zimmerman,Ryan	(4245 FCA)	Turner,Justin	(3245 CDF)	**Walker,Neil**	**(3235 BBB)**	**Cabrera,Asdrubal**	**(3325 AAA)**
	Trumbo,Mark (O)	(4115 CBB)	Moustakas,Mike	(3035 ABC)	**Zobrist,Ben (O)**	**(3245 BAA)**	**Semien,Marcus**	**(3415 ABB)**
	Moreland,Mitch	(4125 FCC)	Tomas,Yasmany (O)	(3225 ADB)	Schoop,Jonathan	(3115 CDD)	Miller,Bradley (O)	(3325 ACC)
	Santana,Carlos	**(3125 AAB)**	Olivera,Hector	(2035 AFF)	Pedroia,Dustin	(2335 DAC)	**Peralta,Jhonny**	**(2025 AAB)**
	Mauer,Joe	(2245 CAC)	**Solarte,Yangervis (1)**	**(2145 ABB)**	Harrison,Josh (3)	(2335 BCF)	**Ramirez,Alexei**	**(1345 AAB)**
			Duffy,Matt	(1535 ADA)	Wong,Kolten	(1425 ACA)	**Segura,Jean**	**(1525 AAB)**
			Prado,Martin	**(1235 BAA)**			**Aybar,Erick**	**(1345 AAA)**
							Simmons,Andrelton	**(1335 AAB)**
							Escobar,Alcides	(0525 AAC)
Mid-Level	**Carter,Chris**	**(5015 ABB)**	Valencia,Danny (O)	(4133 ADD)	Lawrie,Brett (3)	(3325 FCA)	Suarez,Eugenio	(3315 ACB)
	Adams,Matt	(4023 FCC)	**Valbuena,Luis (1)**	**(4025 ABB)**	Travis,Devon	(3453 DFC)	Escobar,Eduardo (O)	(3225 ACA)
	Cron,C.J.	(4135 ACB)	**Plouffe,Trevor**	**(3225 BAA)**	Hernandez,Enrique (O)	(3133 BCB)	Castro,Starlin (2)	(2225 AAD)
	Alvarez,Pedro	**(4125 ABB)**	Wright,David	(3225 FCF)	Forsythe,Logan (1)	(2315 CCC)	Flores,Wilmer (2)	(2035 ACA)
	Howard,Ryan	(4023 DBB)	Chisenhall,Lonnie (O)	(3315 ACB)	Spangenberg,Cory	(2525 BDB)	**Rollins,Jimmy**	**(2425 AAB)**
	Moss,Brandon (O)	**(4005 ABB)**	Lamb,Jacob	(3215 BDB)	Gennett,Scooter	(2233 ACC)	Cozart,Zack	(2325 FCD)
	Smoak,Justin	(4023 BCC)	Freese,David	(3025 CBA)	Johnson,Micah	(1313 ADC)	Owings,Christopher (2)	(2515 BCB)
	Colabello,Chris (O)	(4113 ACF)	Lowrie,Jed	(3333 FBB)	Hernandez,Cesar	(1523 ACC)	Gyorko,Jedd (2)	(2015 CCC)
	Napoli,Mike	**(4103 BBB)**	**Headley,Chase**	**(2125 BAA)**			Mercer,Jordy	(2125 BCB)
	Myers,Wil (O)	(3315 FDD)	**Sandoval,Pablo**	**(2025 BAB)**			Gonzalez,Marwin (31)	(2133 ADC)
	Canha,Mark (O)	**(3315 ABB)**	Escobar,Yunel	(1135 AAC)			Marte,Ketel	(1533 ADC)
	Bour,Justin	(3015 ACC)					**Hechavarria,Adeiny**	**(1525 ABB)**
	Morneau,Justin	(2033 FCC)					Gregorius,Didi	(1225 ACA)
	Loney,James	(1035 CBB)					Iglesias,Jose	(0425 FDB)
Bench	**Shaw,Travis**	**(4123 ABB)**	Dietrich,Derek (O)	(4113 BDA)	Espinosa,Danny	(4303 ACC)	Beckham,Tim (2)	(3413 FFD)
	Paulsen,Benjamin	(4123 ACA)	Reynolds,Mark (1)	(4103 ACA)	Johnson,Kelly (1O)	(3213 BDC)	Nunez,Eduardo	(2431 CFB)
	Ruf,Darin (O)	(4123 BDB)	Asche,Cody (O)	(3113 ACA)	Drew,Stephen	(3113 CCF)	Arcia,Orlando	(2521 AFF)
	Pearce,Steve (O)	(4223 DDF)	Drury,Brandon	(3043 AFC)	Herrera,Dilson	(3411 AFC)	Ramirez,Jose (2)	(1431 ACF)
	Bird,Gregory	(4123 AFA)	Uribe,Juan	(3113 CCB)	Turner,Trea	(2521 AFF)	Villar,Jonathan	(1501 ACB)
	Marte,Jefry	(4231 ACB)	Garcia,Adonis	(2133 ADB)	Utley,Chase	(2333 DBC)	Galvis,Freddy	(1405 BCB)
	Van Slyke,Scott (O)	(4213 BDF)	Guerrero,Alexander (O)	(2201 AFB)	Sanchez,Carlos	(1225 ACA)	Hardy,J.J.	(1205 CBB)
	LaRoche,Adam	(3205 BBD)	Saladino,Tyler	(1523 ACB)	Peterson,Jace	(1215 ADA)	Ahmed,Nick	(1215 ACA)
	Davis,Ike	(3013 FDB)			Giavotella,Johnny	(1333 BCB)	Goins,Ryan (2)	(1213 ACB)
	Montero,Jesus	(3123 ADB)			Infante,Omar	(1323 BBD)	Santana,Daniel	(1521 ACF)
	Rosario,Wilin	(3131 ACB)			Holt,Brock (3O)	(1423 ACC)	Tejada,Ruben	(1125 BCB)
	Morrison,Logan	(2123 DCB)			La Stella,Tommy	(1241 DDD)		
	Alonso,Yonder	(2133 DDB)			Herrera,Elian (3)	(1313 ADB)		
	Rogers,Jason	(2323 ACB)			Peraza,Jose	(0513 AFC)		
					Sogard,Eric	(0313 ACB)		
Fringe	Shaffer,Richie	(5201 ADC)	Olt,Mike	(4001 CDA)	Flaherty,Ryan	(3201 BDA)	Story,Trevor	(4501 ADF)
	Wallace,Brett	(4111 ACB)	Ramirez,Aramis	(3230 CBB)	Franklin,Nick	(3301 BCB)	Taylor,Chris	(2501 ADC)
	Singleton,Jonathan	(4003 ACA)	Urshela,Giovanny	(2033 ACB)	Blanco,Andres (3)	(3031 AFF)	Adames,Cristhian	(1221 ACB)
	Moore,Tyler (O)	(4111 ADB)	Cowart,Kaleb	(2301 ACB)	Hill,Aaron (3)	(2221 BCB)	Pennington,Cliff (2)	(1301 CFC)
	Morse,Michael	(4011 DDF)	Middlebrooks,Will	(2103 DDB)	De Jesus,Ivan	(2111 ACA)	Garcia,Greg	(1211 ACB)
	Blanks,Kyle	(4201 FFB)	Beckham,Gordon	(2211 BDB)	Refsnyder,Rob	(2331 ADB)	Amarista,Alexi	(1411 ACA)
	Muncy,Max	(3101 ADA)	Gillaspie,Conor	(2020 ACC)	Rutledge,Josh	(2311 ADB)	Aviles,Mike (3O)	(1211 ADA)
	Robinson,Clint (O)	(2031 ACC)	Cuthbert,Cheslor	(1321 ACB)	Tomlinson,Kelby	(1531 ADC)	Featherston,Taylor (23)	(1401 AFF)
	Hart,Corey	(2201 FFB)	Perez,Hernan	(1411 ACA)	Pirela,Jose	(1321 BCA)	Colon,Christian	(0351 ACB)
	Elmore,Jake	(0201 BDB)	Johnson,Chris (1)	(1103 BBC)	Castro,Daniel	(1221 AFA)	Romine,Andrew (3)	(0401 ADA)
					Alberto,Hanser	(1411 ADB)	Cabrera,Everth	(0411 CDD)
					Gosselin,Phil	(1221 DDD)		
					Sardinas,Luis	(0413 ADA)		

Universal Draft Grid

TIER	CATCHER		DH		OUTFIELD			
Elite					Trout,Mike	(5445 AAC)	Pollock,A.J.	(3555 CBC)
					Harper,Bryce	(5255 CBF)	**Marte,Starling**	**(3545 AAA)**
					McCutchen,Andrew	(4435 AAC)	Brantley,Michael	(3355 AAD)
					Braun,Ryan	(4445 BBC)	**Revere,Ben**	**(0555 BBA)**
					Betts,Mookie	(3545 ACC)		
Gold	**Posey,Buster (1)**	**(2145 AAA)**			Stanton,Giancarlo	(5235 FBC)	**Gomez,Carlos**	**(4425 BAB)**
					Cespedes,Yoenis	(4235 AAC)	Dickerson,Corey	(4255 DCD)
					Jones,Adam	**(4335 AAA)**	Pence,Hunter	(4435 FBB)
					Peralta,David	(4345 ADF)	Blackmon,Charlie	(3535 CAB)
					Springer,George	(4525 FCB)	Cain,Lorenzo	(2535 CBC)
					Cruz,Nelson	**(4135 AAB)**	**Heyward,Jason**	**(2435 BAB)**
					Bautista,Jose	(4245 CAB)	**Hamilton,Billy**	**(1505 BBA)**
					Upton,Justin	**(4325 AAA)**	Ellsbury,Jacoby	(1525 DAC)
					Kemp,Matt	(4335 DBC)		
Stars	Lucroy,Jonathan	(2245 CBC)	Ortiz,David	(4055 BAC)	Gonzalez,Carlos	(4235 CCF)	Herrera,Odubel	(2525 ACB)
			Morales,Kendrys	(3035 BAF)	Martinez,J.D.	(4235 BBF)	Gardner,Brett	(2525 CAA)
					Choo,Shin-Soo	(4135 BAF)	**Polanco,Gregory**	**(2425 ABA)**
					Puig,Yasiel	(4425 CBC)	Span,Denard	(1455 FBB)
					Bruce,Jay	(4225 AAC)	Deshields Jr.,Delino	(1505 ADD)
					Fowler,Dexter	**(3515 BAA)**	**Inciarte,Ender**	**(1545 BBB)**
					Yelich,Christian	**(2445 BBA)**	Castillo,Rusney	(1435 AFF)
					Eaton,Adam	(2435 CBC)		
Regulars	Gomes,Yan	(4325 BCC)	Sano,Miguel	(5325 AFC)	Davis,Khristopher	(5235 BCB)	Holliday,Matt	(3135 DBB)
	Martin,Russell	(4125 ABC)	Gattis,Evan	(4035 BCB)	Granderson,Curtis	(4325 CBB)	Beltran,Carlos	(3035 BBD)
	Wieters,Matt	(3025 FDD)	Rodriguez,Alex	(4125 DDB)	Grichuk,Randal	(4325 BCD)	Rosario,Eddie	(3425 ACC)
	Hundley,Nick	(3215 CDC)	Fielder,Prince	(2025 DBD)	Conforto,Michael	(4145 AFF)	**Pillar,Kevin**	**(2435 ABB)**
	Realmuto,Jacob	(2435 ACB)	Martinez,Victor	(2045 DAF)	Souza,Steven	(4305 CDC)	Parra,Gerardo	(2345 AAC)
	Perez,Salvador	**(2235 BAB)**	**Butler,Billy**	**(2025 AAB)**	Soler,Jorge	(4225 BFF)	Cabrera,Melky	(2245 CBD)
	Molina,Yadier	(1135 BBC)			Ozuna,Marcell	(4235 BCB)	Hicks,Aaron	(2425 CCC)
					Ramirez,Hanley	(4245 DCF)	Kiermaier,Kevin	(2535 ACB)
					Werth,Jayson	(3225 FBF)	Garcia,Avisail	(2215 FCB)
					Buxton,Byron	(3505 BFF)	**Jackson,Austin**	**(2425 BAB)**
					Gordon,Alex	(3125 CBA)	Pompey,Dalton	(2513 AFB)
					Calhoun,Kole	**(3225 ABA)**	Burns,Billy	(1525 ADF)
					Reddick,Josh	(3425 CBB)	Markakis,Nick	(1235 AAA)
					Taylor,Michael	(3405 ADB)	Aoki,Norichika	(1455 CBA)
Mid-Level	Schwarber,Kyle (O)	(4115 AFF)	Jaso,John	(3133 FDB)	Rasmus,Colby	(5213 BCD)	Almonte,Abraham	(2325 ACD)
	Castillo,Welington	(4215 BCB)			Bradley,Jackie	(4225 ACF)	Crawford,Carl	(2433 FDB)
	McCann,Brian	(3025 BBC)			**Byrd,Marlon**	**(4125 BAB)**	Dyson,Jarrod	(1521 AFA)
	D Arnaud,Travis	(3235 DFB)			Hamilton,Josh	(4123 FCA)	Gose,Anthony	(1505 ACB)
	Norris,Derek	(3315 ACB)			**Smith,Seth**	**(4235 ABB)**	Maybin,Cameron	(1425 DDB)
	Montero,Miguel	**(3015 BBB)**			Santana,Domingo	(4205 ACB)	Martin,Leonys	(1403 ACB)
	Mesoraco,Devin	(3223 FDF)			Altherr,Aaron	(4423 ADF)	Blanco,Gregor	(1523 ACB)
	Vogt,Stephen (1)	(3025 BCB)			**Pederson,Joc**	**(4105 ABB)**	Rios,Alex	(1423 CBB)
	Swihart,Blake	(2433 AFB)			Young,Chris	(4313 BDB)	Pagan,Angel	(1423 FCB)
	Ramos,Wilson	(2025 FCB)			Coghlan,Chris	(3435 CCB)	Lagares,Juan	(1413 BCB)
					Ethier,Andre	(3145 ABD)	Jankowski,Travis	(1523 AFC)
					Piscotty,Stephen	(3345 ACC)		
					Cuddyer,Michael	(3343 FCF)		
					Davis,Rajai	(2523 BCA)		
Bench	Chirinos,Robinson	(4123 DDB)	Raburn,Ryan	(4131 BFF)	Gallo,Joey	(5303 AFA)	Guyer,Brandon	(2423 DDA)
	Saltalamacchia,Jarrod	(4003 ACB)	Vargas,Kennys	(3011 ADA)	Mahtook,Mikie	(4413 ABC)	Murphy,David	(2023 ACB)
	Phegley,Joshua	(4123 ADB)	Profar,Jurickson	(2321 FFF)	Arcia,Oswaldo	(4003 BDC)	**De Aza,Alejandro**	**(2411 ABB)**
	Grandal,Yasmani	(3005 CDB)	Paredes,Jimmy	(2301 ACB)	Gutierrez,Franklin	(4223 FFF)	Brown,Domonic	(2213 BBC)
	Joseph,Caleb	(3113 ACC)	Anderson,Tim	(1501 AFA)	**Thompson,Trayce**	**(4431 ABB)**	Collins,Tyler	(2213 ACA)
	Flowers,Tyler	(3003 ACB)			Tucker,Preston	(4021 ACA)	Butler,Joey	(2101 AFA)
	Navarro,Dioner	(2123 BDC)			Duvall,Adam	(4221 ACB)	Orlando,Paulo	(2421 ACA)
	McCann,James	(2225 ACA)			Ruggiano,Justin	(4201 CDB)	Pham,Thomas	(2421 CDB)
	Cervelli,Francisco	(1213 FFC)			Ackley,Dustin	(3333 ACA)	Venable,Will	(1513 ACD)
	Pierzynski,A.J.	(1033 ACC)			Sweeney,Darnell	(3303 ADB)	Bourn,Michael	(1503 CBA)
	Bethancourt,Christian	(1213 ADB)			Upton,Melvin	(3503 DCB)	Crisp,Coco	(1313 FCD)
	Perez,Carlos	(1413 ADB)			Marisnick,Jake	(3503 ACB)	Young,Delmon	(1221 AFD)
					Jennings,Desmond	(2423 FCB)	Gillespie,Cole	(1311 AFF)
					Hunter,Torii	**(2123 AAB)**	**Suzuki,Ichiro**	**(0521 ABB)**
					Saunders,Michael	(2303 FFD)		
Fringe	Castro,Jason	(4203 CBC)	Reed,A.J.	(4021 AFF)	O Brien,Peter	(4011 AFA)	Swisher,Nick	(2101 FCB)
	Soto,Geovany	(4003 FFC)	Crawford,J.P.	(2421 AFF)	Reimold,Nolan	(3301 FFC)	Joyce,Matt	(2101 BCC)
	McKenry,Michael	(4111 DFF)	Mazara,Nomar	(2421 AFC)	Smolinski,Jacob	(3231 BDB)	Snider,Travis	(2111 ADD)
	Zunino,Mike	(4003 ACA)	Toscano,Dian	(1231 AFF)	Weeks,Rickie	(3201 BDF)	Fuld,Sam	(1421 CDC)
	Susac,Andrew	(4301 BFA)	Vazquez,Christian	(1011 FFA)	Moya,Steven	(3201 ADC)	Urrutia,Henry	(1131 ADF)
	Arencibia,J.P.	(4101 ACA)	Bell,Josh	(1311 AFF)	Rua,Ryan	(3201 CFC)	Shuck,J.B.	(1431 ADD)
	Perez,Roberto	(3103 ADC)	Clevenger,Steve	(1011 DFC)	Parker,Kyle	(3111 ACB)	Victorino,Shane	(1411 FDC)
	Conger,Hank	(3001 AFC)			Sizemore,Grady	(2211 DFA)	Peterson,Shane	(1211 ACB)
	Casali,Curtis	(3203 BFF)			Rodriguez,Yorman	(2401 ADB)	Carrera,Ezequiel	(1410 ADB)
	Iannetta,Chris	(3001 BCC)			Bourjos,Peter	(2401 CFB)	Jay,Jon	(0231 DCC)
	Avila,Alex (1)	(3001 CDA)			Francoeur,Jeff	(2113 ADC)	Perez,Eury	(0431 BDA)
	Ellis,A.J.	(2011 CDD)			Den Dekker,Matthew	(2211 ADA)		
	Rupp,Cameron	(2003 ADD)						
	Maldonado,Martin	(2001 AFD)						
	Rivera,Rene	(2003 ADF)						
	Murphy,John Ryan	(2111 AFC)						
	Hanigan,Ryan	(1111 FFB)						
	Suzuki,Kurt	(1115 ACC)						
	Pena,Brayan	(1021 ADB)						
	Ruiz,Carlos	(1221 CCB)						

Universal Draft Grid

TIER	STARTING PITCHERS				RELIEF PITCHERS			
Elite	Arrieta,Jake	(5405 CAB)						
	Kershaw,Clayton	(5505 CAA)						
Gold	**Bumgarner,Madison**	**(5405 AAA)**	Greinke,Zack	(4305 CAA)	Chapman,Aroldis	(5530 CAB)	Jansen,Kenley	(5530 DAA)
	Kluber,Corey	**(5405 BAA)**	Harvey,Matt	(4405 CBB)	Davis,Wade	(5531 ABD)	**Kimbrel,Craig**	**(5530 AAA)**
	Sale,Chris	(5505 CAA)	**Price,David**	**(4405 BAA)**	Giles,Ken	(5531 ADF)		
	Scherzer,Max	**(5505 AAA)**						
Stars	Carrasco,Carlos	(5505 DBC)	Cole,Gerrit	(4305 DBA)	Britton,Zach	(5330 BBF)	Robertson,David	(5530 CBA)
	Fernandez,Jose	(5503 FCB)	deGrom,Jacob	(4405 ABC)	Familia,Jeurys	(5531 DCD)	**Rodriguez,Francisco**	**(5530 ABA)**
	Hernandez,Felix	**(5405 AAA)**	**Lester,Jon**	**(4305 AAA)**	Gregerson,Luke	(5330 ACA)	**Rondon,Hector**	**(5430 ABB)**
	Keuchel,Dallas	**(5305 AAA)**	Cueto,Johnny	(3205 DAA)	**Melancon,Mark**	**(5331 AAA)**	**Allen,Cody**	**(4530 ABA)**
	Strasburg,Stephen	(5505 FAA)	**Gray,Sonny**	**(3205 AAA)**	Miller,Andrew	(5530 DCB)		
	Syndergaard,Noah	(5405 ADB)						
Regulars	Hamels,Cole	(4405 CAA)	Salazar,Danny	(3405 ABC)	Osuna,Roberto	(4430 ADF)	**Papelbon,Jonathan**	**(3331 ABA)**
	Stroman,Marcus	(4203 FDA)	Wainwright,Adam	(3205 FAA)	**Rosenthal,Trevor**	**(4531 AAB)**	Ramos,A.J.	(3531 ACA)
	Tanaka,Masahiro	(4303 FAA)	**Zimmermann,Jordan**	**(3205 AAA)**	Uehara,Koji	(4530 FBB)	Tolleson,Shawn	(3430 FCF)
	Archer,Chris	**(3405 AAA)**			Boxberger,Brad	(3530 ACD)	Street,Huston	(2330 DAB)
Mid-Level	Darvish,Yu	(4503 FBA)	Ross,Joe	(3203 ADC)	Betances,Dellin	(5511 ACB)		
	Garcia,Jaime	(4203 FCA)	Severino,Luis	(3303 ADA)	Smith,Carson	(5520 ADB)		
	Iwakuma,Hisashi	(4203 FAA)	**Shields,James**	**(3305 AAA)**	Doolittle,Sean	(4530 FCC)		
	Martinez,Carlos	**(4405 ABA)**	Walker,Taijuan	(3305 DCA)	O Day,Darren	(4510 BCA)		
	McCullers,Lance	(4405 ADF)	**Wood,Alex**	**(3205 ABB)**	Strickland,Hunter	(4321 AFA)		
	Ross,Tyson	**(4405 BAA)**	Fiers,Mike	(2303 ACD)	Watson,Tony	(4311 ACB)		
	Hendricks,Kyle	(3203 ACA)	Lackey,John	(2205 FAA)	**Ziegler,Brad**	**(4030 ABA)**		
	Iglesias,Raisel	(3405 CFF)	McHugh,Collin	(2205 ABF)	Casilla,Santiago	(3320 DBB)		
	Liriano,Francisco	(3403 DAA)	Nola,Aaron	(2205 ADD)	**Perkins,Glen**	**(3430 BAB)**		
	Matz,Steven	(3203 DDA)	Odorizzi,Jake	(2305 CBA)	Smyly,Drew	(3403 FBA)		
	Pineda,Michael	(3303 FCB)	**Teheran,Julio**	**(2205 AAA)**				
	Quintana,Jose	**(3205 AAA)**	Wacha,Michael	(2205 CBB)				
	Richards,Garrett	(3205 DAB)						
Bench	Ryu,Hyun-Jin	(4303 FBA)	Kazmir,Scott	(2203 DAA)	Cecil,Brett	(5510 BCA)		
	Cashner,Andrew	(3205 FAA)	**Leake,Mike**	**(2005 BAA)**	Jones,Nate	(5510 FDF)		
	Corbin,Patrick	(3203 FCB)	**Lynn,Lance**	**(2305 BAA)**	Kela,Keone	(5510 ADB)		
	Gonzalez,Gio	**(3405 BAA)**	**Miller,Shelby**	**(2205 AAB)**	McGee,Jake	(5510 DCA)		
	Hammel,Jason	(3303 DAB)	Moore,Matt	(2403 FCA)	**Romo,Sergio**	**(5510 ABA)**		
	Kennedy,Ian	**(3405 BAA)**	**Nelson,Jimmy**	**(2203 ABB)**	Harris,Will	(4311 ADA)		
	Porcello,Rick	**(3205 BAA)**	Rodon,Carlos	(2403 ADF)	Hendriks,Liam	(4410 ACC)		
	Ventura,Yordano	**(3305 BBA)**	**Samardzija,Jeff**	**(2205 AAB)**	Jeffress,Jeremy	(4310 ADA)		
	Buchholz,Clay	(2203 FBB)	**Santana,Ervin**	**(2105 AAA)**	Smith,Joe	(4210 ACB)		
	Chen,Wei-Yin	(2105 CAA)	Tomlin,Josh	(2203 FDD)	Smith,Will	(4510 ACA)		
	de la Rosa,Jorge	(2203 FAA)	Verlander,Justin	(2205 DAA)	Soria,Joakim	(4410 FCB)		
	DeSclafani,Anthony	(2205 ACA)	**Buehrle,Mark**	**(1005 AAA)**	Garcia,Yimi	(3410 ADA)		
	Duffey,Tyler	(2103 ADC)	**Dickey,R.A.**	**(1005 BAA)**	Grilli,Jason	(3520 FBB)		
	Hahn,Jesse	(2101 DDB)	Estrada,Marco	(1203 DAB)	Herrera,Kelvin	(3311 ADA)		
	Holland,Derek	(2203 FCA)	Heaney,Andrew	(1105 ADA)	Siegrist,Kevin	(3510 DDD)		
	Hughes,Phil	(2105 DAC)	Weaver,Jered	(1103 FAA)	May,Trevor	(2311 ACA)		
	Karns,Nathan	(2303 ACC)			Vizcaino,Arodys	(2520 FDC)		
					Wilhelmsen,Tom	(2320 CCB)		
					Clippard,Tyler	(1311 ACC)		
Fringe	Anderson,Brett	(3103 FCA)	Rea,Colin	(2101 BFF)	Armstrong,Shawn	(5500 AFB)	Warren,Adam	(3201 ACB)
	Berrios,Jose	(3301 AFB)	**Roark,Tanner**	**(2101 ABB)**	Capps,Carter	(5510 FDB)	Wilson,Justin	(3400 ACA)
	Bundy,Dylan	(3301 FFF)	Rodriguez,Eduardo	(2203 ADA)	Dyson,Sam	(5310 ADB)	Axford,John	(2510 ACA)
	McCarthy,Brandon	(3201 FBA)	Sanchez,Anibal	(2303 FAB)	Givens,Mychal	(5500 AFD)	Brach,Brad	(2401 ADB)
	Snell,Blake	(3400 AFF)	Shoemaker,Matthew	(2203 ACB)	Qualls,Chad	(5210 CCA)	Chafin,Andrew	(2201 ADC)
	Anderson,Chase	(2203 BCC)	Skaggs,Tyler	(2203 FDB)	Strop,Pedro	(5510 CCA)	**Cishek,Steve**	**(2410 ABB)**
	Bailey,Homer	(2201 FBC)	Wheeler,Zack	(2301 FCA)	Baez,Pedro	(4400 CDD)	Colome,Alexander	(2301 FCA)
	Chavez,Jesse	**(2303 BBA)**	**Bauer,Trevor**	**(1305 ABB)**	Cedeno,Xavier	(4400 ADB)	Delgado,Randall	(2401 DCB)
	Davies,Zachary	(2101 ADA)	Colon,Bartolo	(1005 CAA)	Duke,Zach	(4400 BDD)	Dunn,Mike	(2510 ACA)
	Eovaldi,Nathan	(2103 DAA)	Conley,Adam	(1203 ADB)	Grimm,Justin	(4510 BCC)	Fien,Casey	(2210 CCB)
	Fister,Doug	(2101 FAB)	Cooney,Tim	(1201 ADC)	Kelley,Shawn	(4510 DDA)	Gott,Trevor	(2100 AFA)
	Floyd,Gavin	(2201 FDA)	De La Rosa,Rubby	(1203 ACA)	Knebel,Corey	(4510 AFD)	Hardy,Blaine	(2200 ADB)
	Gausman,Kevin	(2303 CDA)	Duffy,Danny	(1203 FBA)	Madson,Ryan	(4300 FDF)	Hochevar,Luke	(2310 FDC)
	Gibson,Kyle	**(2105 AAA)**	Eickhoff,Jerad	(1205 ADF)	Salas,Fernando	(4400 CDA)	Hunter,Tommy	(2110 CCA)
	Glasnow,Tyler	(2300 AFF)	Feldman,Scott	(1003 FAA)	Scribner,Evan	(4400 BDB)	Janssen,Casey	(2210 FCB)
	Gray,Jonathan	(2201 ADC)	**Gallardo,Yovani**	**(1105 AAA)**	Storen,Drew	(4410 CCA)	Jepsen,Kevin	(2310 DCC)
	Happ,J.A.	(2303 DAB)	Hellickson,Jeremy	(1203 FBD)	Benoit,Joaquin	(3410 ACA)	Kontos,George	(2100 ADC)
	Hill,Rich	(2400 DDA)	Heston,Chris	(1103 ACC)	Fields,Joshua	(3500 BDA)	Matusz,Brian	(2400 ADA)
	Hutchison,Drew	(2303 FBC)	Lewis,Colby	(1105 FBF)	Hatcher,Chris	(3500 DDD)	Maurer,Brandon	(2200 DDB)
	Kelly,Joe	(2103 DCA)	Milone,Tommy	(1103 CCC)	Hudson,Daniel	(3310 FDA)	Morris,Bryan	(2101 BCB)
	Latos,Mat	(2203 DBA)	Montero,Rafael	(1201 FDB)	McAllister,Zach	(3411 DCB)	Neshek,Pat	(2300 ADC)
	Lyons,Tyler	(2201 BDB)	Nova,Ivan	(1103 FDA)	Morin,Michael	(3400 DDB)	Nuno,Vidal	(2201 ACC)
	Medlen,Kris	(2103 FCC)	Owens,Henry	(1301 ADB)	Ottavino,Adam	(3320 FDB)	**Reed,Addison**	**(2411 ABA)**
	Miley,Wade	**(2205 AAA)**	Peavy,Jake	(1103 FBA)	Petit,Yusmeiro	(3301 ACC)	Robles,Hansel	(2400 ADB)
	Minor,Mike	(2201 FCD)	Ray,Robbie	(1203 ADD)	Pomeranz,Drew	(3411 DCC)	Sanchez,Aaron	(2111 CDB)
	Morton,Charlie	(2103 FCA)	**Santiago,Hector**	**(1303 AAA)**	Quackenbush,Kevin	(3400 ADB)	Velasquez,Vincent	(2501 AFF)
	Niese,Jon	(2103 DAA)	**Tillman,Chris**	**(1103 AAA)**	Rondon,Bruce	(3520 FDD)	**Wood,Travis**	**(2400 AAB)**
	Paxton,James	(2201 FCB)	Tropeano,Nicholas	(1201 ADF)	Shaw,Bryan	(3210 ACA)	Geltz,Steve	(1311 ADB)
	Perez,Martin	(2003 FDB)	**Volquez,Edinson**	**(1205 AAA)**	Tazawa,Junichi	(3310 BCA)	Hoover,J.J.	(1310 ACA)
	Ramirez,Erasmo	(2103 BCB)	Wilson,C.J.	(1203 FAA)	Walden,Jordan	(3500 FDA)	Wilson,Alex	(1010 DDB)

Universal Draft Grid

TIER	STARTING PITCHERS				RELIEF PITCHERS			
Below Fringe	Lee,Cliff	(4300 FBA)	Montgomery,Michael	(1101 ADA)	**Holland,Greg**	**(4500 BAB)**	**Rodney,Fernando**	**(2310 BAA)**
	Cobb,Alex	(3200 FBA)	Norris,Daniel	(1303 BDB)	Loup,Aaron	(4300 ACB)	Ross,Robbie	(2210 ACF)
	House,T.J.	(3100 BDF)	Oberholtzer,Brett	(1001 DDB)	Barrett,Aaron	(3300 FDA)	Shreve,Chasen	(2400 ADD)
	Andriese,Matt	(2101 ADC)	Parker,Jarrod	(1100 FCF)	Blanton,Joe	(3300 CDA)	Bettis,Chad	(1203 CDA)
	Bolsinger,Michael	(2201 ADB)	Peacock,Brad	(1300 FCA)	Cahill,Trevor	(3310 BDA)	Blazek,Michael	(1200 DDF)
	Erlin,Robert	(2101 DDA)	Pelfrey,Mike	(1003 FBF)	Caminero,Arquimedes	(3300 ADF)	Burgos,Enrique	(1510 BFF)
	Feliz,Michael	(2200 AFF)	Peralta,Wily	(1103 DAB)	Diaz,Jose	(3500 ADB)	Cingrani,Tony	(1501 DDC)
	Finnegan,Brandon	(2401 AFF)	Perez,Williams	(1003 CDC)	Farquhar,Daniel	(3400 ADC)	**Collmenter,Josh**	**(1001 ABA)**
	Giolito,Lucas	(2300 AFF)	Rodriguez,Wandy	(1101 FDA)	Johnson,Jim	(3110 ABC)	De Fratus,Justin	(1210 DDB)
	Graveman,Kendall	(2001 FDB)	Simon,Alfredo	**(1003 BAA)**	Lowe,Mark	(3400 CDF)	Feliz,Neftali	(1210 FDD)
	Jimenez,Ubaldo	(2305 CAB)	Vogelsong,Ryan	(1201 DAB)	Maness,Seth	(3100 ACB)	Gomez,Jeanmar	(1000 ACA)
	Lincecum,Tim	(2300 FAB)	Wilson,Tyler	(1000 ADA)	Treinen,Blake	(3110 ADB)	Hand,Brad	(1101 CCA)
	Nolasco,Ricky	(2205 FBA)	Wisler,Matthew	(1103 ADC)	Alburquerque,Al	(2500 DDB)	Jackson,Edwin	(1200 CBA)
	Sabathia,CC	(2303 FAB)	Worley,Vance	(1001 BDD)	Alvarez,Jose	(2200 ADD)	Kahnle,Thomas	(1300 ADA)
	Alvarez,Henderson	(1001 FBB)	Asher,Alec	(0001 ADD)	Araujo,Elvis	(2300 CFC)	Morales,Franklin	(1100 DCB)
	Anderson,Cody	(1001 BDF)	Banuelos,Manny	(0101 CDB)	Avilan,Luis	(2200 ADB)	Motte,Jason	(1100 FDA)
	Bassitt,Chris	(2203 AFF)	Boyd,Matt	(1200 FFF)	Bedrosian,Cam	(2400 AFF)	Neris,Hector	(1201 ADB)
	Beachy,Brandon	(2201 DDB)	Buchanan,David	(1101 ADB)	Freeman,Sam	(2300 ADB)	Oberg,Scott	(1210 ADB)
	Bradley,Archie	(2203 AFF)	Butler,Eddie	(1200 FFF)	Frias,Carlos	(2000 DDB)	Parnell,Bobby	(1210 FDF)
	Brooks,Aaron	(2201 DDB)	Cravy,Tyler	(1101 ADB)	Garcia,Luis	(2300 ADA)	Phelps,David	(1201 FBA)
	Cain,Matt	(1103 FBB)	Gonzales,Marco	(0100 ADF)	Gilmartin,Sean	(2300 ADC)	Scheppers,Tanner	(1200 FDB)
	Chacin,Jhoulys	(1000 FBB)	Gonzalez,Alex	(0001 ADA)	Graham,J.R.	(2200 BDB)	Schultz,Bo	(1000 ADF)
	Chatwood,Tyler	(1001 FDA)	Guthrie,Jeremy	**(0001 BAB)**	Hughes,Jared	(2000 CDB)	Tepera,Ryan	(1200 ADD)
	Cole,A.J.	(1101 ADC)	Harang,Aaron	(0103 DAA)	Masterson,Justin	(2201 DBC)	Thornburg,Tyler	(1200 FDC)
	Cosart,Jarred	(1103 CCB)	Harrison,Matt	(0000 FFC)	Mejia,Jenrry	(2300 FCB)	Villarreal,Pedro	(1000 ADC)
	Danks,John	(1105 FAA)	Holmberg,David	(0000 ADC)	Mujica,Edward	(2110 CCA)	Williams,Jerome	(1000 DBA)
	Despaigne,Odrisamer	(1001 ADA)	Johnson,Erik	(0101 ACF)	Nicasio,Juan	(2300 DCD)	Barraclough,Kyle	(0510 AFF)
	Doubront,Felix	(1101 DCB)	Kendrick,Kyle	(0001 CAA)	Norris,Bud	(2301 CAB)	Bergman,Christian	(0000 DDB)
	Elias,Roenis	(1203 ACB)	Lobstein,Kyle	(0001 FDB)	Petricka,Jacob	(2010 BCA)	Farmer,Buck	(0001 ADB)
	Foltynewicz,Mike	(1213 ADC)	Martinez,Nicholas	(0001 ACF)	Putnam,Zach	(2410 FDC)	Godley,Zachary	(0101 AFF)
	Garza,Matt	(1203 FBA)	Matzek,Tyler	(0000 ADD)	Rivero,Felipe	(2100 BDC)	Hale,David	(0001 DCC)
	Gee,Dillon	(1000 FBB)	Morgan,Adam	(0001 ADB)				
	Gonzalez,Miguel	(1103 DAA)	Moscot,Jon	(0101 FDC)				
	Greene,Shane	(1101 CDB)	Nicolino,Justin	(0003 ADF)				
	Griffin,A.J.	(1100 FCF)	Nolin,Sean	(0101 CDA)				
	Hernandez,Roberto	**(1000 ABB)**	Rusin,Chris	(0000 ACC)				
	Jungmann,Taylor	(1205 ADA)	Sampson,Keyvius	(0201 ADC)				
	Koehler,Tom	**(1105 AAA)**	Urena,Jose	(0001 BDB)				
	Lamb,John	(1203 ADB)	Webster,Allen	(0100 ADD)				
	Locke,Jeff	**(1103 ABA)**	Wright,Mike	(0001 CDA)				
	Lohse,Kyle	**(1101 AAA)**	Wright,Steven	(0001 FDA)				
	Lorenzen,Michael	(1003 ADB)	Young,Chris	(0001 DCF)				
	Lyles,Jordan	(1003 FCB)						

SIMULATION LEAGUE DRAFT TOP 500+

NAME	POS	RAR
Trout,Mike	8	59.0
Kershaw,Clayton	P	56.1
Harper,Bryce	9	55.2
Goldschmidt,Paul	3	49.5
Votto,Joey	3	46.5
McCutchen,Andrew	8	45.9
Cabrera,Miguel	3	45.7
Posey,Buster	23	44.3
Betts,Mookie	8	36.4
Donaldson,Josh	5	34.7
Stanton,Giancarlo	9	34.4
Correa,Carlos	6	34.3
Arenado,Nolan	5	33.3
Cano,Robinson	4	32.9
Brantley,Michael	78	31.9
Arrieta,Jake	P	31.9
Price,David	P	30.4
Greinke,Zack	P	30.1
Fernandez,Jose	P	29.7
Harvey,Matt	P	28.6
Bumgarner,Madison	P	28.4
Encarnacion,Edwin	3	28.0
Dickerson,Corey	7	27.3
Bautista,Jose	9	27.3
Altuve,Jose	4	27.0
deGrom,Jacob	P	26.8
Seager,Corey	6	26.1
Tulowitzki,Troy	6	26.0
Gray,Sonny	P	25.9
Pollock,A.J.	8	25.3
Keuchel,Dallas	P	24.7
Kluber,Corey	P	24.6
Rizzo,Anthony	3	23.9
Peralta,David	7	23.4
Lucroy,Jonathan	2	23.2
Cole,Gerrit	P	22.9
Sale,Chris	P	22.9
Abreu,Jose	3	22.6
Wainwright,Adam	P	22.2
Syndergaard,Noah	P	21.9
Braun,Ryan	9	21.7
Cueto,Johnny	P	21.5
Scherzer,Max	P	21.1
Archer,Chris	P	20.9
Carpenter,Matt	5	20.2
Lester,Jon	P	19.5
Beltre,Adrian	5	19.4
Hernandez,Felix	P	19.4
Conforto,Michael	7	19.2
Machado,Manny	5	19.1
Strasburg,Stephen	P	18.8
Choo,Shin-Soo	9	18.1
Davis,Wade	P	17.9
Carrasco,Carlos	P	17.7
Ross,Tyson	P	17.6
Watson,Tony	P	17.2
Cruz,Nelson	9	17.1
Giles,Ken	P	17.0
Betances,Dellin	P	17.0
Upton,Justin	7	16.7
Tanaka,Masahiro	P	16.6
Chapman,Aroldis	P	16.4
Kimbrel,Craig	P	16.2

NAME	POS	RAR
Zobrist,Ben	47	16.2
Bryant,Kris	5	16.0
Cain,Lorenzo	8	15.9
Wieters,Matt	2	15.8
Gonzalez,Adrian	3	15.6
Davis,Chris	39	15.5
Panik,Joe	4	15.4
Cespedes,Yoenis	78	15.4
Stroman,Marcus	P	15.4
Martinez,J.D.	9	15.4
Melancon,Mark	P	15.3
Hamels,Cole	P	15.1
Gonzalez,Carlos	9	15.1
Quintana,Jose	P	14.8
Wood,Alex	P	14.7
O Day,Darren	P	14.6
Smyly,Drew	P	14.6
Garcia,Jaime	P	14.6
Wacha,Michael	P	14.3
Murphy,Daniel	45	14.2
Rendon,Anthony	45	14.2
Kinsler,Ian	4	14.1
Freeman,Freddie	3	13.9
Kipnis,Jason	4	13.9
D Arnaud,Travis	2	13.8
Martinez,Carlos	P	13.8
Ortiz,David	0	13.8
Zimmermann,Jordan	P	13.6
Matz,Steven	P	13.6
Britton,Zach	P	13.4
Yelich,Christian	78	13.4
Severino,Luis	P	13.4
Martin,Russell	2	13.1
Kemp,Matt	9	13.0
Familia,Jeurys	P	13.0
Crawford,Brandon	6	12.5
Smith,Carson	P	12.5
Jansen,Kenley	P	12.4
Springer,George	9	12.4
Turner,Justin	5	12.4
Harris,Will	P	12.3
Teixeira,Mark	3	12.3
Kang,Jung-ho	56	12.2
Miller,Andrew	P	12.1
Salazar,Danny	P	12.0
Richards,Garrett	P	12.0
Davis,Khristopher	7	11.9
Liriano,Francisco	P	11.8
Pedroia,Dustin	4	11.6
Lind,Adam	3	11.6
Shields,James	P	11.4
Duda,Lucas	3	11.4
Travis,Devon	4	11.3
Fowler,Dexter	8	11.1
Jones,Adam	8	11.1
Werth,Jayson	7	11.1
McHugh,Collin	P	10.9
Kendrick,Howie	4	10.8
Kela,Keone	P	10.8
Allen,Cody	P	10.6
McCullers,Lance	P	10.6
Span,Denard	8	10.6
Grandal,Yasmani	2	10.4

NAME	POS	RAR
Nola,Aaron	P	10.3
Holliday,Matt	7	10.2
Papelbon,Jonathan	P	10.1
Blackmon,Charlie	8	10.1
Cecil,Brett	P	10.0
Jeffress,Jeremy	P	10.0
Pence,Hunter	9	9.9
Reyes,Jose	6	9.9
Puig,Yasiel	9	9.9
Montero,Miguel	2	9.9
Walker,Neil	4	9.8
Rodriguez,Francisco	P	9.8
Gordon,Alex	7	9.7
Dyson,Sam	P	9.7
Strickland,Hunter	P	9.6
McGee,Jake	P	9.6
Gomez,Carlos	8	9.6
Peralta,Jhonny	6	9.5
Odor,Rougned	4	9.4
Eaton,Adam	8	9.4
Schwarber,Kyle	27	9.4
Gomes,Yan	2	9.3
Zimmerman,Ryan	3	9.3
Iwakuma,Hisashi	P	9.3
Ryu,Hyun-Jin	P	9.3
Mesoraco,Devin	2	9.2
Gonzalez,Gio	P	9.1
Norris,Derek	2	9.1
Darvish,Yu	P	9.0
Seager,Kyle	5	9.0
Heyward,Jason	9	8.9
Buchholz,Clay	P	8.7
Smith,Seth	79	8.7
Marte,Starling	7	8.7
Sano,Miguel	0	8.7
Hundley,Nick	2	8.7
Miller,Bradley	68	8.7
Hendricks,Kyle	P	8.6
Teheran,Julio	P	8.5
Ramos,A.J.	P	8.4
Fiers,Mike	P	8.4
Molina,Yadier	2	8.4
Ross,Joe	P	8.3
Bogaerts,Xander	6	8.3
Rosenthal,Trevor	P	8.2
Lindor,Francisco	6	8.1
Capps,Carter	P	8.1
Givens,Mychal	P	8.1
Hosmer,Eric	3	8.0
Chirinos,Robinson	2	7.9
Lackey,John	P	7.9
McCann,Brian	2	7.9
Gregerson,Luke	P	7.9
Cedeno,Xavier	P	7.8
Uehara,Koji	P	7.6
Corbin,Patrick	P	7.6
Madson,Ryan	P	7.5
Smith,Will	P	7.5
Romo,Sergio	P	7.4
Rodon,Carlos	P	7.4
Lynn,Lance	P	7.4
Kelley,Shawn	P	7.3
Hendriks,Liam	P	7.3

NAME	POS	RAR
Vogt,Stephen	23	7.1
Olivera,Hector	5	7.0
Rondon,Hector	P	7.0
Smith,Joe	P	7.0
Jones,Nate	P	7.0
Robertson,David	P	6.9
Warren,Adam	P	6.9
Iglesias,Raisel	P	6.9
Vizcaino,Arodys	P	6.9
Perez,Salvador	2	6.9
Wright,David	5	6.9
Soria,Joakim	P	6.8
Strop,Pedro	P	6.8
Hahn,Jesse	P	6.8
Armstrong,Shawn	P	6.8
Herrera,Kelvin	P	6.8
Ozuna,Marcell	8	6.8
Longoria,Evan	5	6.7
Chen,Wei-Yin	P	6.7
Garcia,Yimi	P	6.6
Osuna,Roberto	P	6.6
Realmuto,Jacob	2	6.5
Cooney,Tim	P	6.4
Grimm,Justin	P	6.4
Ziegler,Brad	P	6.4
Benoit,Joaquin	P	6.4
Street,Huston	P	6.3
Cashner,Andrew	P	6.3
Kennedy,Ian	P	6.1
Ventura,Yordano	P	6.1
Clippard,Tyler	P	6.0
Tolleson,Shawn	P	6.0
Cabrera,Asdrubal	6	6.0
Hughes,Jared	P	6.0
May,Trevor	P	6.0
Ethier,Andre	79	6.0
Belt,Brandon	3	5.9
Beltran,Carlos	9	5.9
McAllister,Zach	P	5.9
Brach,Brad	P	5.9
Shaw,Bryan	P	5.8
Gordon,Dee	4	5.8
Hammel,Jason	P	5.7
Hardy,Blaine	P	5.7
Navarro,Dioner	2	5.7
Swihart,Blake	2	5.6
Frazier,Todd	5	5.5
Coghlan,Chris	79	5.4
Desmond,Ian	6	5.4
Casilla,Santiago	P	5.3
Castillo,Welington	2	5.3
Odorizzi,Jake	P	5.3
Morris,Bryan	P	5.3
Cervelli,Francisco	2	5.2
Wilhelmsen,Tom	P	5.2
Santana,Ervin	P	5.2
Walden,Jordan	P	5.1
Miller,Shelby	P	5.1
Storen,Drew	P	5.1
Morneau,Justin	3	5.0
Jepsen,Kevin	P	4.8
Pomeranz,Drew	P	4.8
Cuddyer,Michael	7	4.8

SIMULATION LEAGUE DRAFT — TOP 500+

NAME	POS	RAR
Granderson,Curtis	9	4.8
Baez,Pedro	P	4.7
Cabrera,Melky	7	4.6
Latos,Mat	P	4.6
Boxberger,Brad	P	4.6
Dozier,Brian	4	4.6
Gott,Trevor	P	4.6
Bundy,Dylan	P	4.6
Siegrist,Kevin	P	4.4
Duffey,Tyler	P	4.3
Montero,Rafael	P	4.3
Hatcher,Chris	P	4.3
Verlander,Justin	P	4.3
Nelson,Jimmy	P	4.3
DeSclafani,Anthony	P	4.2
Ramirez,Hanley	7	4.2
Knebel,Corey	P	4.2
Chafin,Andrew	P	4.2
Petit,Yusmeiro	P	4.1
Wilson,Justin	P	4.1
Arcia,Orlando	6	4.1
Duke,Zach	P	4.0
Saltalamacchia,Jarrod	2	4.0
Moustakas,Mike	5	4.0
Moore,Matt	P	3.9
Herrera,Odubel	8	3.9
Paxton,James	P	3.9
Grilli,Jason	P	3.9
Maness,Seth	P	3.8
Valbuena,Luis	35	3.8
Valencia,Danny	57	3.7
Freeman,Sam	P	3.7
Davies,Zachary	P	3.7
Sanchez,Aaron	P	3.6
Soler,Jorge	9	3.6
Reed,Addison	P	3.6
Porcello,Rick	P	3.6
Geltz,Steve	P	3.6
Franco,Maikel	5	3.6
Van Slyke,Scott	379	3.6
Doolittle,Sean	P	3.5
Perez,Roberto	2	3.5
Wood,Travis	P	3.4
Cishek,Steve	P	3.3
Delgado,Randall	P	3.3
La Stella,Tommy	4	3.3
Turner,Trea	4	3.3
Hernandez,Enrique	48	3.3
Reddick,Josh	9	3.2
Ellis,A.J.	2	3.2
Wheeler,Zack	P	3.2
Gallardo,Yovani	P	3.2
Maurer,Brandon	P	3.1
Gilmartin,Sean	P	3.0
Walker,Taijuan	P	3.0
Kontos,George	P	3.0
Lee,Cliff	P	3.0
Farquhar,Daniel	P	3.0
Forsythe,Logan	34	2.9
Medlen,Kris	P	2.8
Bailey,Homer	P	2.8
Rivero,Felipe	P	2.8
Pineda,Michael	P	2.8

NAME	POS	RAR
Solarte,Yangervis	35	2.8
Matusz,Brian	P	2.8
Prado,Martin	5	2.8
Tazawa,Junichi	P	2.7
Garcia,Luis	P	2.7
Kazmir,Scott	P	2.6
Neshek,Pat	P	2.6
Avilan,Luis	P	2.6
Shreve,Chasen	P	2.6
Gomez,Jeanmar	P	2.6
Hochevar,Luke	P	2.6
McKenry,Michael	2	2.5
LeMahieu,DJ	4	2.5
Loup,Aaron	P	2.4
Buehrle,Mark	P	2.4
Qualls,Chad	P	2.4
Escobar,Eduardo	67	2.4
Nuno,Vidal	P	2.3
Ottavino,Adam	P	2.3
Lowe,Mark	P	2.3
Quackenbush,Kevin	P	2.2
Heaney,Andrew	P	2.2
Hamilton,Josh	7	2.2
Colome,Alexander	P	2.2
Leake,Mike	P	2.2
Frias,Carlos	P	2.1
Perkins,Glen	P	2.0
Holland,Greg	P	2.0
Myers,Wil	38	2.0
Ellsbury,Jacoby	8	1.9
Pierzynski,A.J.	2	1.9
Velasquez,Vincent	P	1.9
Graveman,Kendall	P	1.9
Hudson,Daniel	P	1.9
Glasnow,Tyler	P	1.8
Rasmus,Colby	789	1.8
Semien,Marcus	6	1.8
Petricka,Jacob	P	1.8
Putnam,Zach	P	1.8
Lamb,Jacob	5	1.7
Motte,Jason	P	1.7
Buxton,Byron	8	1.7
Grichuk,Randal	78	1.6
Susac,Andrew	2	1.5
Salas,Fernando	P	1.5
Niese,Jon	P	1.5
Lowrie,Jed	5	1.5
Blanco,Gregor	789	1.5
Cobb,Alex	P	1.5
Hill,Rich	P	1.3
Revere,Ben	78	1.3
Castro,Jason	2	1.3
Russell,Addison	46	1.3
Gardner,Brett	78	1.3
Fister,Doug	P	1.2
Snell,Blake	P	1.2
Mejia,Jenrry	P	1.2
Tepera,Ryan	P	1.2
Castro,Starlin	46	1.1
Alburquerque,Al	P	1.1
Lyons,Tyler	P	1.1
Hunter,Tommy	P	1.1
Phillips,Brandon	4	1.1

NAME	POS	RAR
Treinen,Blake	P	1.0
Pillar,Kevin	8	1.0
Phegley,Joshua	2	0.9
Bassitt,Chris	P	0.9
Castellanos,Nick	5	0.9
Iannetta,Chris	2	0.9
Rea,Colin	P	0.9
Nunez,Eduardo	6	0.8
Pearce,Steve	37	0.7
Pederson,Joc	8	0.7
Hicks,Aaron	8	0.7
Dunn,Mike	P	0.7
Refsnyder,Rob	4	0.6
Spangenberg,Cory	4	0.6
Harrison,Josh	45	0.6
Berrios,Jose	P	0.6
Martinez,Nicholas	P	0.6
Gonzalez,Alex	P	0.6
Murphy,John Ryan	2	0.6
Wilson,Alex	P	0.5
Gausman,Kevin	P	0.5
Caminero,Arquimedes	P	0.5
Samardzija,Jeff	P	0.4
Parker,Jarrod	P	0.4
Anderson,Brett	P	0.4
Diaz,Jose	P	0.4
Estrada,Marco	P	0.4
Roark,Tanner	P	0.3
Reed,A.J.	0	0.2
Herrera,Dilson	4	0.2
Aoki,Norichika	7	0.2
Soto,Geovany	2	0.2
Cahill,Trevor	P	0.2
Pujols,Albert	3	0.2
Conger,Hank	2	0.2
Alvarez,Jose	P	0.2
Skaggs,Tyler	P	0.1
Nicasio,Juan	P	0.1
Conley,Adam	P	0.1
Tomlin,Josh	P	0.1
Utley,Chase	4	0.1
Kiermaier,Kevin	8	0.1
Robles,Hansel	P	0.1
Ramirez,Aramis	5	0.0
Fien,Casey	P	0.0
de la Rosa,Jorge	P	0.0
Araujo,Elvis	P	0.0
Collmenter,Josh	P	-0.1
Souza,Steven	9	-0.1
Holland,Derek	P	-0.1
Giolito,Lucas	P	-0.2
Bird,Gregory	3	-0.2
Barrett,Aaron	P	-0.3
Volquez,Edinson	P	-0.3
Ross,Robbie	P	-0.3
Joseph,Caleb	2	-0.3
Pham,Thomas	8	-0.3
Karns,Nathan	P	-0.4
Rondon,Bruce	P	-0.4
Ray,Robbie	P	-0.4
Feliz,Michael	P	-0.4
Rollins,Jimmy	6	-0.4
Raburn,Ryan	0	-0.4

NAME	POS	RAR
Worley,Vance	P	-0.4
Flores,Wilmer	46	-0.5
Eovaldi,Nathan	P	-0.5
Morales,Franklin	P	-0.6
Bolsinger,Michael	P	-0.6
Wilson,C.J.	P	-0.6
Suarez,Eugenio	6	-0.6
Happ,J.A.	P	-0.6
McCarthy,Brandon	P	-0.6
Gibson,Kyle	P	-0.6
Barraclough,Kyle	P	-0.6
Cole,A.J.	P	-0.7
Floyd,Gavin	P	-0.7
Hoover,J.J.	P	-0.7
Gennett,Scooter	4	-0.7
Axford,John	P	-0.7
Ackley,Dustin	78	-0.8
Thornburg,Tyler	P	-0.8
Markakis,Nick	9	-0.8
Duffy,Matt	5	-0.8
Blazek,Michael	P	-0.9
Ramirez,Erasmo	P	-0.9
Santana,Carlos	3	-0.9
Pena,Brayan	2	-0.9
Morin,Michael	P	-0.9
Rodriguez,Eduardo	P	-0.9
Perez,Martin	P	-1.0
Johnson,Jim	P	-1.0
De Aza,Alejandro	79	-1.0
Fields,Joshua	P	-1.1
Piscotty,Stephen	7	-1.1
Hutchison,Drew	P	-1.1
Ramirez,Jose	46	-1.1
Uribe,Juan	5	-1.1
Jaso,John	0	-1.1
Schoop,Jonathan	4	-1.2
Bedrosian,Cam	P	-1.2
Rutledge,Josh	4	-1.3
Rodney,Fernando	P	-1.3
Shoemaker,Matthew	P	-1.3
Fielder,Prince	0	-1.3
Holt,Brock	459	-1.3
Feldman,Scott	P	-1.4
House,T.J.	P	-1.4
Napoli,Mike	3	-1.4
Griffin,A.J.	P	-1.4
Chavez,Jesse	P	-1.4
Duffy,Danny	P	-1.4
Casali,Curtis	2	-1.5
Avila,Alex	23	-1.5
Hill,Aaron	45	-1.5
Scheppers,Tanner	P	-1.5
Marte,Ketel	6	-1.6
Tucker,Preston	7	-1.6
Graham,J.R.	P	-1.6
Mujica,Edward	P	-1.6
Andriese,Matt	P	-1.6
Tropeano,Nicholas	P	-1.7
Moscot,Jon	P	-1.7
Byrd,Marlon	79	-1.8
Miley,Wade	P	-1.8
Cingrani,Tony	P	-1.8
Mauer,Joe	3	-1.8

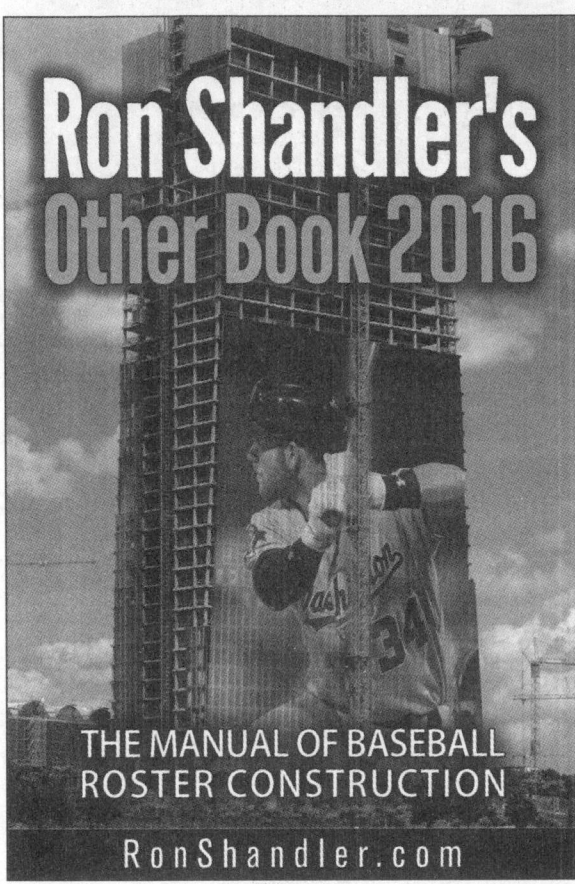

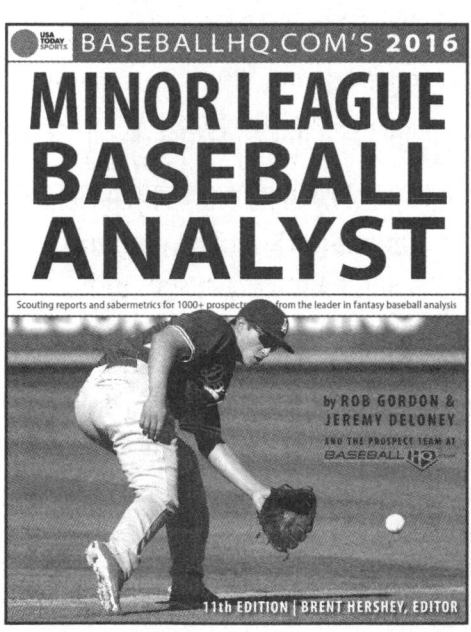

2016 CHEATER'S BOOKMARK

Abbrv	Term	Formula / Desc.	BAD UNDER	'15 LG AVG AL	'15 LG AVG NL	BEST OVER
BATTING STATISTICS			**BENCHMARKS**			
Avg	Batting Average	h/ab	235	256	260	280
xBA	Expected Batting Average	*See glossary*		267	270	
OB	On Base Average	(h+bb)/(ab+bb)	290	314	320	340
Slg	Slugging Average	total bases/ab	350	413	410	450
OPS	On Base plus Slugging	OB+Slg	650	728	730	780
bb%	Walk Rate	bb/(ab+bb)	6%	8%	8%	10%
ct%	Contact Rate	(ab-k) / ab	73%	78%	78%	83%
Eye	Batting Eye	bb/k	0.30	0.39	0.40	0.50
PX	Power Index	Normalized power skills	80	100	100	120
Spd	Speed Score	Normalized speed skills	80	100	100	120
SBO	Stolen Base Opportunity %	(sb+cs)/(singles+bb)		8%	9%	
G/F	Groundball/Flyball Ratio	gb / fb		1.3	1.4	
G	Ground Ball Per Cent	gb / balls in play		44%	46%	
L	Line Drive Per Cent	ld / balls in play		21%	21%	
F	Fly Ball Per Cent	fb / balls in play		35%	33%	
BPV	Base Performance Value	*See glossary*	20	40	40	55
RC/G	Runs Created per Game	*See glossary*	3.00	4.41	4.49	5.00
RAR	Runs Above Replacement	*See glossary*	0.0			10.0

Batting statistics do not include pitchers' batting statistics

Abbrv	Term	Formula / Desc.	BAD OVER	'15 LG AVG AL	'15 LG AVG NL	BEST UNDER
PITCHING STATISTICS			**BENCHMARKS**			
ERA	Earned Run Average	er*9/ip	4.50	4.01	3.91	3.00
xERA	Expected ERA	*See glossary*		3.76	3.64	
WHIP	Baserunners per Inning	(h+bb)/ip	1.50	1.29	1.30	1.15
BF/G	Batters Faced per Game	((ip*2.82)+h+bb)/g	28.0			
PC	Pitch Counts per Start		120	94	92	
OBA	Opposition Batting Avg	Opp. h/ab	280	254	255	235
OOB	Opposition On Base Avg	Opp. (h+bb)/(ab+bb)	350	312	314	290
BABIP	BatAvg on balls in play	(h-hr)/((ip*2.82)+h-k-hr)		293	299	
Ctl	Control Rate	bb*9/ip		2.9	2.9	2.5
hr/9	Homerun Rate	hr*9/ip		1.1	1.0	1.0
hr/f	Homerun per Fly ball	hr/fb		11%	11%	
S%	Strand Rate	(h+bb-er)/(h+bb-hr)		72%	73%	
DIS%	PQS Disaster Rate	% GS that are PQS 0/1		22%	22%	15%
			BAD UNDER	**'15 LG AVG AL**	**'15 LG AVG NL**	**BEST OVER**
RAR	Runs Above Replacement	*See glossary*	0.0			+10
Dom	Dominance Rate	k*9/ip		7.6	7.9	9.0
Cmd	Command Ratio	k/bb		2.6	2.7	3.3
G/F	Groundball/Flyball Ratio	gb / fb		1.27	1.42	
SwK	Swinging Strike Percentage	swinging strikes/pitches		61%	61%	63%
FpK	First Pitch Strike Percentage	first pitch strikes/batters		10%	10%	11.5%
BPV	Base Performance Value	*See glossary*	75	82	87	100
DOM%	PQS Dominance Rate	% GS that are PQS 4/5		47%	49%	60%
Sv%	Saves Conversion Rate	(saves / save opps)		69%	69%	80%
REff%	Relief Effectiveness Rate	*See glossary*		67%	67%	80%

NOTES